MANAGEMENT FOR PRODUCTIVITY

[Handwritten annotations:]

VISION Mgmt Process

PLAN
3 w's
HOW

DIRECT
sell plan
convience

Communication

Objective

ORGANIZE
1. task
2. people
3. Materials
4. Motivation

Decision making

Control

Coordination

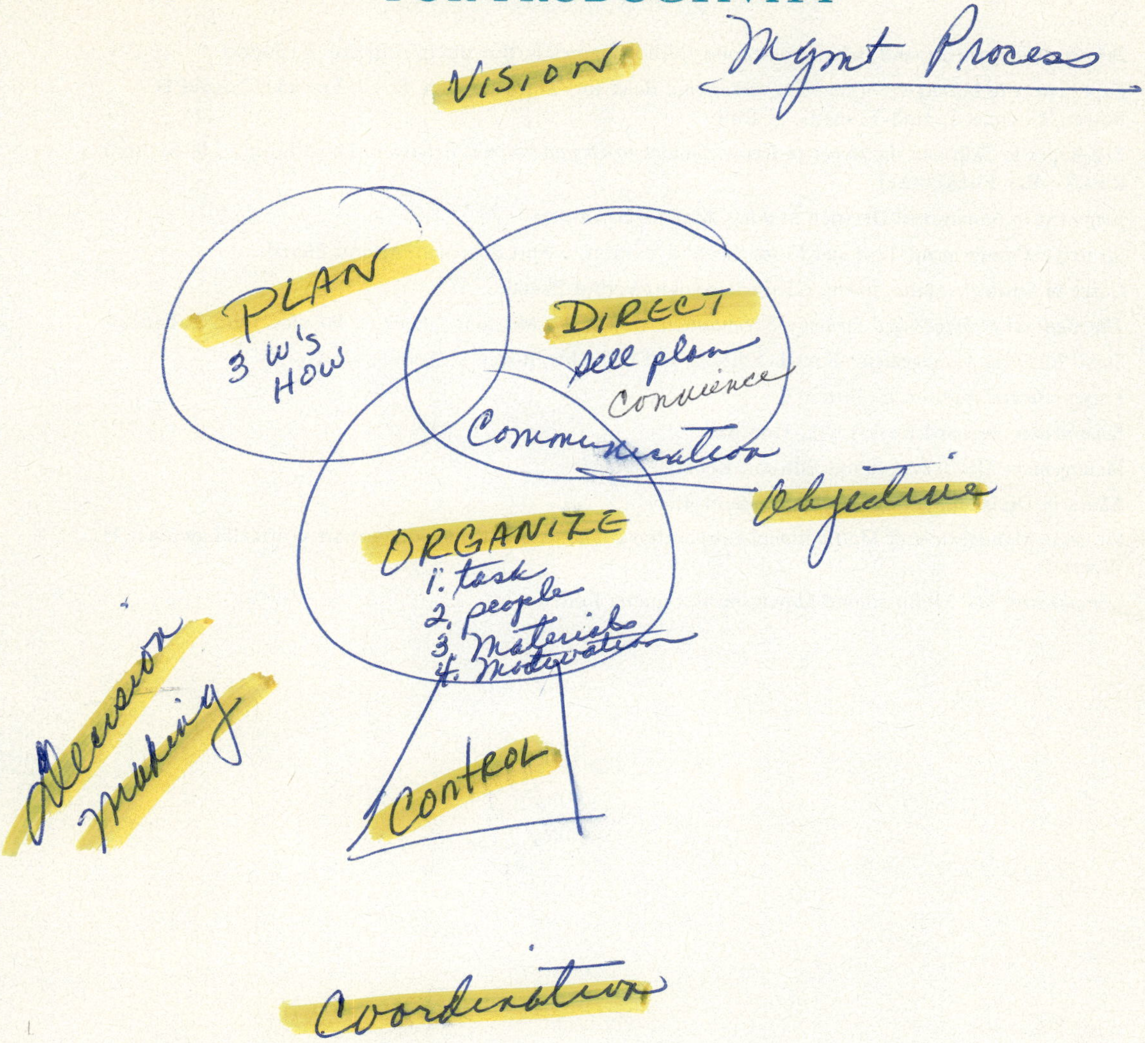

To the Student: A Study Guide for the textbook is available through your college bookstore under the title Study Guide to Accompany *Management for Productivity,* 3rd edition by John R. Schermerhorn, Jr. The Study Guide can help you with course material by acting as a tutorial, review, and study aid. If the Study Guide is not in stock, ask the bookstore manager to order a copy for you.

WILEY SERIES IN MANAGEMENT

WILEY

The Wiley Series in Management

MANAGEMENT FOR PRODUCTIVITY

THIRD EDITION

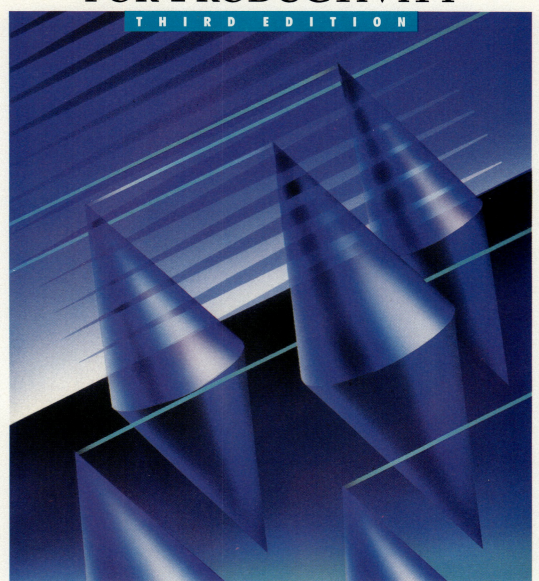

John R. Schermerhorn, Jr.

SOUTHERN ILLINOIS UNIVERSITY AT CARBONDALE

JOHN WILEY & SONS

New York—Chichester—Brisbane—Toronto
Singapore

Cover and Text Design: Jerry Wilke
Cover Art: Roy Wiemann
Production Supervisor: Katharine Rubin
Photo Editor: Stella Kupfcrberg
Photo Research: Anne Manning
                 Charles Hamilton
Editorial Supervisor: Gilda Stahl
Copyeditor: Glenn Petry

Library of Congress Cataloging in Publication Data:

Schermerhorn, John R.
   Management for productivity.

Includes bibliographies and indexes.
   1. Management.   I. Title.
HD31.S3326   1989   658   88-27879
ISBN 0-471-63115-9

Printed in the United States of America

10 9 8 7 6 5 4 3

To my sons John Christian and Charles Porter

While you played
I wrote.
But always,
I was listening
and loving
you.

1984

It's later now.
Don't worry.
Time
means love shared,
by you
and me.

1986

Think
of all the fun
we have.
Here, there, everywhere,
doing things
together.

1989

About the Author

JOHN R. SCHERMERHORN, JR., is Professor of Management in the College of Business and Administration at Southern Illinois University at Carbondale. Dr. Schermerhorn teaches graduate and undergraduate courses in management, and previously served as Head of the Department of Management and Associate Dean of the college. He earned a Ph.D. in Organizational Behavior from Northwestern University and has taught at Tulane University, the University of Vermont, and the Chinese University of Hong Kong. Highly concerned with helping the discipline of management serve the needs of practicing managers, he has written *Management for Productivity* to help others bridge the gap between the theory and practice of management.

Dr. Schermerhorn has prior work experience in business and hospital administration, and remains professionally active in management training and consultation with a variety of organizations in the United States. He is committed to the international dimensions of our world, and has professional experience in China, Egypt, Indonesia, the Philippines, Poland, and Tanzania, among other countries. With special interests in higher education for business and management, he is a popular guest speaker at colleges and universities on curriculum issues, instructional methods and development, academic administration, and related matters.

A member of the Academy of Management, where he is past chairperson of the Management Education and Development Division, Dr. Schermerhorn is known to educators and students alike as senior co-author of *Managing Organizational Behavior,* third edition (John Wiley & Sons, 1988). His published research appears in the *Academy of Management Journal, Academy of Management Review, Academy of Management Executive, Journal of Management, Journal of Management Development* and *Group and Organization Studies,* among other scholarly journals.

Preface

There is no room for error in educating the students who are to lead our organizations in the 1990s and beyond. The managers of tomorrow, in particular, must be prepared to respond to the challenges of continued change and complexity if our society is to prosper and we along with it. *Management for Productivity,* third edition, while retaining its original focus on achieving productivity through good management, has been thoroughly revised and updated with this reality in mind. As a responsible author of an introductory management textbook, I could no more be content with past successes, than can the executives in any of today's organizations. Like them, my time for reaching ahead and striking a new benchmark for excellence was today—not tomorrow. This book has been revised and rewritten to set that standard anew.

As you explore this latest edition of *Management for Productivity,* you will find the essentials of management presented in a systematic and thorough way. The discussion is substantive at all times, but also seeks reader involvement through interesting examples and a lively writing style. It strives for complete coverage of the basic functions of management, but with special attention to managerial decision making and problem-solving in a dynamic environment. From a curriculum standpoint, the book is thorough in covering AACSB guidelines. Special chapters on ethics and social responsibility, innovation, change and conflict, the international arena, information systems, labor-management relations, and operations management add depth to the traditional functional coverage. Fully integrated treatments of management in diverse settings, and a special emphasis throughout on information and human resource issues further strengthen its curriculum base and career significance.

Yet, *Management for Productivity,* third edition, has a character of its own. It is not just an inventory or summary of current management theory. Many, perhaps too many, of these catalogs and compendia already exist in the textbook guise. This book is a statement—personal and professional. It is the embodiment of my feel for the challenges of the future, the wealth of knowledge available to deal with these challenges, and the great energy and intellect our students have ready to apply to the task at hand—given ample reasons and a decent chance.

Against this backdrop, the subject matter in *Management for Productivity* has been carefully chosen to meet accreditation guidelines while still serving students' needs for a realistic and useful introduction to the field of management. The book blends a healthy respect for past traditions of the discipline with new research and theoretical developments. It is written on the assumption that the *basics,* the *fundamentals,* the *foundations* of management, must be understood before the latest developments and trends can be addressed in an informed manner. It also includes frequent illustrations and examples in response to my belief that the material presented in a management book should serve the real needs of everyday managers.

All management educators face common challenges as we labor at a difficult but compelling task—preparing tomorrow's managers. This book was created in the pursuit of instructional excellence through these constructive balances.

■ *The balance of research insights with introductory education*—We must understand which of the theories and concepts of our discipline are appropriate for the introductory student, and we must be willing to forego attention to others that serve only more advanced scholarly interests.

■ *The balance of management theory and managerial practice* — We must understand the needs of student readers to sense the applications of relevant material, and we must be able to bring to their attention appropriate, interesting, and understandable examples.

■ *The balance of present understandings and future possibilities* — We must recognize where the real world of management is heading in dynamic times, and we must select and present materials that lead students in those directions with confidence and self-respect.

■ *The balance of what "can" be done and what is, purely and simply, the "right" thing to do* — We must be willing to take stands on issues — equal employment opportunity, quality of work life, ethics, and social responsibility, to name but a few; and, we must not let the importance of "contingency" in management theory betray the ultimate need for "action" in management practice.

There are risks as well as opportunities in the preceding statements — risks for me, for you, and for our students. Yet, we live in a world when humankind itself is at risk in the ever-faster race to the future. In the field of management, as in any discipline, responsible educators must stand forth with what they know and with what they believe. Yes — "of course, yes" — these are times of great challenge in management. But our successes or failures in responding to them will be told in the lives and careers of our students. We cannot afford to be timid or aloof in helping them prepare for the uncertainties of tomorrow. More than ever before, students require more than pure exposure to the ideas and possibilities of a discipline. They have pressing needs for direction as well as suggestion, for application as well as information, and for integration as well as presentation. Our instructional approaches and materials must deliver on all these dimensions and perhaps more. Part of my opportunity is to put into your hands and those of your students a textbook that can meet these needs. Whether your classroom is small or large, and whether your institution is college or university, the opportunities for progress through education are equally great. *Management for Productivity,* third edition, is my contribution to these challenges and our students' futures.

JOHN R. SCHERMERHORN, JR., *Professor*
Department of Management
Southern Illinois University at Carbondale
Carbondale, Illinois 62901   USA

Book At-a-Glance

The first goal of *Management for Productivity,* third edition, is to cover the right topics in sufficient depth and breadth that the student gains a solid exposure to the fundamentals of management theory as they apply in the contemporary environment. The second goal—which is necessary for the first to succeed—is for the book to attract and hold the reader's interest.

Very positive feedback from faculty and students alike reports our past success on both these dimensions. In this new and thoroughly updated third edition, we have further extended our efforts to accomplish these goals with even higher standards of excellence. The many aspects of the book—including its organization, design features, and support package—combine to offer a professional and engaging learning experience for the reader, as well as a timely and complete instructional foundation for the instructor. We are proud to offer this introductory textbook for those who are concerned about management in the 1990s.

Organization of Material

Management for Productivity, third edition, is organized in a part and chapter sequence consistent with the traditional treatment of management principles. However, this traditional coverage is firmly grounded in the complex and dynamic environment characteristic of the advent of the 1990s. It also clearly focuses attention on productivity as a basic criterion of managerial and organizational success. The book thus develops the fundamentals of management with sensitivity for the contemporary real world settings in which readers will be asked to function as managers. Although covering all the basics in a thorough and substantive manner, the third edition of *Management for Productivity* rises to the challenges ahead as

a most timely introduction to the fundamentals of management.

Part One of the book, *Introduction,* sets the stage for a directed study of management. It contains three chapters introducing management as a scientific discipline, the history of management thought, and the basic challenges of managerial decision making and problem solving. The next four parts of the book follow a traditional sequence, but with a special emphasis on productivity. These parts are:

■ Part Two, *Planning for Productivity*
■ Part Three, *Organizing for Productivity*
■ Part Four, *Leading for Productivity*
■ Part Five, *Controlling for Productivity.*

Within each part, the chapters are arranged in a logical and developmental order. The initial chapter presents fundamentals of the management function under study. Subsequent chapters develop and extend aspects of the function in greater depth. Of course, and out of respect for the preferences of individual instructors, the chapters within each part can be used in any order or combination at the instructor's discretion.

Part Six, *Productivity in the Contemporary Environment,* examines the fundamentals of management in the context of major issues representing the demanding environment of the 1990s within which modern managers will function. Separate chapters address the application of management theories in an environment that challenges the modern manager to achieve success in—

■ Managing innovation, change and conflict
■ Managing labor-management relations
■ Managing in an international arena
■ Managing with ethics and social responsibility

For the instructor's convenience, the prior chapters are written for use in any sequence or combination. They may also be separately assigned in conjunction with chapters from other parts of the book.

Part Seven of the book, *Conclusion,* provides a futuristic look at management. It highlights a fast-changing modern world of complex social trends, advanced technology, high stress, and dynamic career opportunities. The final chapter encourages students to look ahead into the exciting world of the mid and late 1990s, and move into this world with the desire and confidence to successfully master great challenges and opportunities.

A special Management Applications Module provides additional material on basic quantitative decision techniques. Use of this module will round out the introduction to the field of management science presented in chapter discussions. It also complements the material on operations management in Chapter 16.

Special Design Features

Management for Productivity, third edition, is designed to both captivate the reader's attention and present essential subject matter in a logical and developmental fashion. Design features throughout the book help bridge the gap between management theory and practice by engaging the reader in subject matter presentations supported by frequent examples and applications. Written with a guiding sensitivity to learning theory as well as the needs of today's college and university student, this book uses the following design features to support the reader's pursuit of knowledge and understanding.

■ *State-of-the-art layout* The format of the book communicates a professional character most appropriate to the practice of management. The format creates a stimulating visual orientation to the subject matter that is not only attractive in design, but also mature and professional in its approach. The intent throughout is to absorb the reader within the visual context common to the journals, magazines, and newspapers representing the important professional, business, and management literature of today.

■ *Creative and custom-designed illustrations* Incorporated in the book are over 300 illustrations, charts, photographs, and tables that highlight major topics, concepts, and issues in a way that further communicates the substance of the book to the reader. These illustrations complement text explanations to facilitate student understanding of key points. All figure illustrations have been redone in the third edition to communicate a professional tone consistent with training materials found in the corporate classroom. Many figures contain case illustrations that further direct the reader's attention to real-world applications of the concepts being presented.

■ *Lively and conversational writing style* The text is written by an experienced and successful author who gives careful attention to making the material meaningful for the reader. Instructors and students using the second edition enthusiastically report that the author transforms the substance of an academic discipline into an interesting and applied perspective of great appeal to the career-oriented student.

■ *Numerous real-world examples* The frequent examples used to communicate how theories and concepts apply to the real world of management have been completely updated to bring in the latest and most relevant current events. All examples are closely integrated with text discussion to extend the reader's thinking in a structured and developmental fashion. Beyond this, however, we have tried to establish a new industry standard for the frequency and quality of examples for the reader. In addition to standard in-text examples, the third edition offers expanded opportunities for learning and applications in the form of

Part Opening Perspectives—editorial-style features that introduce part content through examples and themes representing the current management environment, complemented by the author's editorial viewpoints.

Chapter Openers—an always interesting and compelling selection of examples that support chapter content and involve the reader in an ever-changing sampling of real-world issues and situations.

Illustrative Cases—this added feature found in every chapter gives extended attention to a management application in one organization or situation.

Newslines—updates and reports summarized from the recent press that communicate the relevance of chapter material, and use a photo-enhanced design format to stimulate interest in current events.

"At" . . . Reports—these reports bring specific and dedicated examples of how progressive organizations are handling the concept or issue under discussion.

■ *Thorough coverage of management in all types of organizations operating in domestic and international settings* Throughout the book, examples, apply the practice of management to organizations of all types and sizes operating in a wide variety of environments. The features just reported provide the reader with continuing exposure to management in small businesses, large businesses, not-for-profit organizations, and international businesses. Frequent in-text examples combine with a selection of end-of-chapter features—including a *Career Perspective, Case Application,* and *Class Exercise*—to further illustrate how text material applies in the various organizational settings within which a student's career orientation may lie.

■ *Fully integrated emphasis on careers* The book requires students to think seriously about how the field of management relates to their future careers. Examples in each chapter present management applications in a full spectrum of occupational choices. In addition, each chapter concludes with a *Career Perspective,* a special illustration that helps the reader to think seriously about his or her career aspirations, and consider how chapter topics relate to career opportunities and success. All new for the third edition, these perspectives are fully integrated with chapter material. In addition, they build a consistent self and career discovery theme from "Stephen Shaw's Interview" in Chapter 1, through "Climbing the Ladder of Success" in Chapter 8, to "Balance Drives the Young Execs" in Chapter 21.

A Professional Learning Instrument

Management for Productivity, third edition, is a professional learning instrument that offers an integrated and effective educational opportunity for the student. It has been created with a respect for the student reader and an understanding of learning theory. The book is designed to engage the reader in a self-instructional experience supported by the following carefully selected pedagogical elements. The overall learning potential of the book is enhanced by the following instructional

■ *Part and Chapter Openers* Highlight provocative real-world experiences or situations that attract reader interest and clearly place text topics in the setting of day-to-day management practice.

■ *Planning Ahead* Introduces the major topics to

be covered in the chapter and establishes a framework for targeted reading.

■ *Chapter Summary* Immediately follows the last section of a chapter and overviews major chapter themes.

■ *Thinking Through the Issues* Ten questions that stimulate the reader to review major issues relating to chapter content.

■ *The Manager's Vocabulary* Lists key terms of the chapter as a reminder, reading check, and test study guide.

■ *Career Perspective* A short vignette that helps the reader consider a personal career application or opportunity relevant to chapter material.

■ *Case Application* A real-world experience or situation that requires the student to analyze and solve a managerial problem or explore a managerial opportunity.

■ *Class Exercise* A quick-hitting exercise, easy to use in both large and small classes, that engages students in a learning situation requiring personal reflection, sharing with others, and focused class discussion.

■ *References* Notes directing the reader's attention to sources used by the author in developing chapter topics.

■ *Part Integrating Cases* Two comprehensive cases at the conclusion of each book part that require students to apply in an integrated fashion their learning from all chapters in the part.

■ *Glossary* A list at the end of the book that contains definitions of key terms and cross references them with the chapters in which they are presented.

As you can see, the new edition of *Management for Productivity* offers a comprehensive blend of design features that create a truly enriching learning experience for the reader. The book is a self-contained learning instrument for student and instructor alike. It stands as a complete instructional resource that does not require the separate purchase of costly supplements such as case and exercise books.

Complete Instructional Support Package

Management for Productivity, third edition, is supported by a comprehensive learning package that further assists the instructor in creating a motivating and enthusiastic educational environment. This package of supplementary resources has been carefully changed, revised, and updated with an emphasis on the instructor's needs for quality and consistency in all supplementary materials. Like others, we have suffered some past inadequacies in the attempt to offer a great diversity of materials. We have now decided that quality and usability of materials count more than sheer size of the support package. We believe you can use the supplements with the assurance that they can meet the scrutiny of students and pass the test of your instructional standards. They have been developed, tested, and carefully refined by a number of experienced educators. The result offers a variety of easy and creative ways for the instructor to provide students with an innovative and complete learning experience. The specially designed and expanded instructional support package for the new edition of *Management for Productivity* groups the supplements in an easy to use fashion. The first group contains the *core* instructional support items; the second group contains *enhancement* instructional support materials.

Core Instructional Support
- Active Learning Guide
- Triviability Game
- Instructor's Resource Manual
- Transparency Acetates and Masters
- Test Bank (print and computerized)
- Gradebook PC Software
- ***Active Learning Guide*** Developed by Marilyn Gardner and William Gardner, of Southern Illinois University at Carbondale, the active learning guide is a comprehensive student resource that complements the substance and pedagogical style of the textbook.

It helps students assimilate the subject matter, identify its practical implications, and pinpoint the areas they need to review. Included for each text chapter are a set of learning objectives, a chapter overview, a programmed learning drill, and a self-test procedure. All questions, developed from major text headings and key terms, are arranged in a checklist format, allowing students to study efficiently by helping them identify what topics they need to review. Special sections include tips on how to study and how to manage time.
- ***Triviability Game*** Packaged with the study guide, this software program allows students to study and review management terms and concepts while working individually or as a team. From one to five students can match their management wits through a spin-the-wheel model of chance. Questions are weighted with points based on difficulty level. After each question, students can call up and print out a screen that explains why their answer is correct or incorrect. Triviability is a captivating study alternative with many possible applications for classroom exercises and individual/group projects.

- ***Instructor's Resource Manual*** Prepared by William Gardner of Southern Illinois University at Carbondale, this manual is a unique, comprehensive, integrating guide to building a *system of customized instruction*. The manual begins with helpful sections on the philosophy and design of the text, sample course outlines, a matrix that guides you in the best use of the text and supplements, and an overall guide to the supplements. Next, lecture outlines for each chapter are clearly presented, along with an inventory of all available supplements that correspond directly with that chapter. Each outline assists the instructor in organizing lecture contents, choosing material from other text supplements, bringing in outside examples, and otherwise taking full advantage of text discussion. Special emphasis is placed on how major chapter points can be reinforced—through transparencies, discussion questions, newslines, and videos. Answers to questions in Thinking Through the Issues, responses to Career Perspective and Case Application questions, procedures for utilizing Class Exercises to full advantage, analyses of Part Integrating Cases, plus many other instructional support opportunities are also available on a chapter-by-chapter and part-by-part basis. The manual has been developed in conjunction with an instructional design expert and with the author to ensure maximum usefulness for the instructor.

- ***Transparency Acetates and Masters*** Over 150 transparency acetates are available to adopters for immediate use in class and in management training programs. Professionally prepared, they follow an easy-to-read style and format common to the instructional materials found in corporate classrooms. In addition to a wide selection of key figures presented in the text, these acetates include many supplementary lists which summarize key concepts and managerial guidelines covered in text discussion. With the added support of a companion set of numerous ready-to-copy transparency masters, this package provides a versatile opportunity to add high quality visual support to the instructor's classroom presentations and training programs.

Test Bank Over 3000 all-new multiple-choice, true/false, and essay questions have been prepared by educational psychologists in conjunction with the author and other management experts. The test bank has been reviewed and class-tested at schools across the country. It identifies questions both by learning type (application or recall) and level of difficulty, and identifies the text page on which the answer can be found. The test bank is available both in a printed test bank and in microcomputer formats. A write-in and phone-in service is provided for adoptors who do not have computer facilities. Simply fill out a request form, or call the number we provide, and within 48 hours from receipt, you will receive a printed exam, ready for duplication.

■ **Gradebook PC Software** A computerized grading program, GRADISK, simplifies course record keeping by allowing student's grades to be maintained and processed on a personal computer.

Enhancement Instructional Support
■ AIM Lecture Supplement
■ Management Development Video Program
■ MICROTRONICS Management Simulation
■ Writing to Learn Manual

■ **AIM Lecture Supplement** AIM provides the interested instructor with one week of hands-on teaching materials allowing extended study in areas of special management application. AIM authors are subject matter experts who have prepared for each topic two supplementary lectures, individual and group student project assignments, additional readings, and test items. For the third edition of *Management for Productivity,* this innovative and useful supplement allows the instructor to accent the following topics in a manner complementary to text coverage: INTERNATIONAL MANAGEMENT, PRODUCTIVITY IMPROVEMENT IN MANAGEMENT, ETHICAL ISSUES IN MANAGEMENT, and MICROCOMPUTERS IN THE WORKPLACE.

■ **MANAGEMENT DEVELOPMENT VIDEO PROGRAM** Produced by Wilson Learning Corporation, an acknowledged leader in the field of management and sales training, this creative video program presents several dramatized case scenarios of managers facing motivation and leadership challenges in the contemporary workplace. These programs comprise a genuine hands-on teaching and training tool as used by practicing professionals in many Fortune 500 companies. A highly integrative Teacher's Manual provides step-by-step instructions for exciting multi-media class sessions that will enhance student participation and learning in both large-lecture and small class settings. This manual, prepared by Sid Nachman of Drexel University and William Gardner of Southern Illinois University at Carbondale, describes how the video can be stopped at any point, enabling instructors to elicit comments, criticisms, and alternative approaches from students so that they can develop appropriate responses to a remarkable variety of situations. It also fully describes the video segments and offers a wide variety of options for using them in class and as focal points for lectures, discussions, or role plays. With a special capability to further build essential managerial skills and competencies in dealing with human behavior in organizations, the video addresses such topics as Establishing Performance Objectives and Expectations, Coaching for Improved Performance, Reviewing Performance Accomplishments, and Managing High- Marginal- and Low-Performers in the Workplace.

■ **MICROTRONICS** A very simple-to-use business simulation, Microtronics allows students to gain stimulating experience in management decision-making and team management, while learning experientially. In addition to making many managerial decisions, the game also includes behavioral and judgmental type incidents that print out after each decision. These incidents deal with issues such as turnover, absenteeism, and productivity. A unique benefit of these incidents is that they provide ''bottom-line'' feedback in costs of hiring and training employees and production issues. Students can work together as teams while solving management problems with computer support.

■ **Writing to Learn** The ability of students to communicate effectively in writing is a skill highlighted over and over again for its importance in managerial work. For those instructors who want to sharpen their students' communication skills, this exciting new manual offers guidelines and exercises to help students both learn and write better in applications common to managerial situations.

Management for Productivity, third edition, with its package of instructional supplements clearly offers the instructor a way to create an exciting, interesting, and in-depth learning experience for students. A truly comprehensive and self-contained learning instrument, this book was written for the 1990s, and for both instructor and student. Use it with enthusiasm and great success!

Acknowledgments

Management for Productivity, third edition, was made possible through the extraordinary support provided me by many fine people. To begin, this book and the entire learning package are the results of the efforts of my editor Cheryl Mehalik and her excellent support group at John Wiley & Sons. The commitment of Cheryl, publisher Rick Leyh, and all the Wiley staff to excellence and discipline receive my highest personal respect. Special thanks go to the following superb group of Wiley personnel who worked tirelessly on the project: John Balbalis (illustration), Stella Kupferberg and Anne Manning (photo research), Jerry Wilke, Ann Renzi and Sheila Granda (design), Gilda Stahl and Glenn Petry (editing), Katharine Rubin (production), Rita Kerrigan (supplements), Barbara Heaney (developmental editor) and Martha Cooley (freelance feature writer).

As always, a very special acknowledgment goes to my wife, Ann, for being willing to put up with the demands, absences, and peculiarities of a husband who continues to enjoy writing books. Although she and our sons, Christian and Porter, have learned how to cope, it's still not easy. Only they know what it's like to have a husband and father who sometimes has difficulty finding time for the lawn, the house, the car, evenings, mornings, weekends . . . and just plain fun. Only I know how much their support and sacrifices mean in my quest to help others make a difference in tomorrow's terribly challenging world.

Finally, I am proud to recognize and publicly thank the many colleagues from colleges and universities around the country whose thorough reviews and suggestions helped develop my thinking and create this finished product. My greatest appreciation goes to the following management educators.

Raymond Alie
WESTERN MICHIGAN UNIVERSITY

Ken Aupperle
KENT STATE UNIVERSITY

Hrach Bedrosian
NEW YORK UNIVERSITY

Douglas A. Benton
COLORADO STATE UNIVERSITY

Robert Bjorkland
RIDER COLLEGE

Allen Bluedorn
UNIVERSITY OF MISSOURI

Peggy Brewer
EASTERN KENTUCKY UNIVERSITY

Dale Brown
SOUTHERN ILLINOIS UNIVERSITY AT CARBONDALE

Edward Brown
SINCLAIR COMMUNITY COLLEGE

Aaron A. Buchko
MICHIGAN STATE UNIVERSITY

Bob Bulls
J.S. REYNOLDS COMMUNITY COLLEGE

Joe Byrnes
BENTLEY COLLEGE

James J. Carroll
WILLIAM PETERSON COLLEGE (NJ)

William C. Childress
LANSING COMMUNITY COLLEGE

Charles Cole
UNIVERSITY OF OREGON

Joseph Cox
BAYLOR UNIVERSITY

Martha Crumpacker
WASHBURN UNIVERSITY

Jagdish Danak
EASTERN MICHIGAN UNIVERSITY

Lincoln Deihl
KANSAS STATE UNIVERSITY

Robert Dennehy
PACE UNIVERSITY

C.S. Pete Everett
DES MOINES AREA COMMUNITY COLLEGE

Dan Farrell
WESTERN MICHIGAN UNIVERSITY

Ellen J. Frank
SOUTHERN CONNECTICUT STATE UNIVERSITY

Joel Fuerst
RHODE ISLAND COLLEGE

John Gelles
VENTURA COLLEGE

James Genseal
JOLIET JUNIOR COLLEGE

Edward Giermak
COLLEGE OF DUPAGE

Michael Gurdon
UNIVERSITY OF VERMONT

Theodore Hansen
SALEM STATE COLLEGE

Alan Hollander
SUFFOLK COUNTY COMMUNITY COLLEGE

David Holt
JAMES MADISON UNIVERSITY

John H. Jackson
THE UNIVERSITY OF WYOMING

Ronald A. Klocke
MANKATO STATE UNIVERSITY (MN)

Ed Knod
WESTERN ILLINOIS UNIVERSITY

Reuben Krolick
CALIFORNIA STATE UNIVERSITY

Patrick Kroll
UNIVERSITY OF MINNESOTA

Janina C. Latack
OHIO STATE UNIVERSITY

Howard Ludlow
SETON HALL UNIVERSITY

James McElroy
IOWA STATE UNIVERSITY

Curtis McLaughlin
UNIVERSITY OF NORTH CAROLINA

Joe Michlitsch
SOUTHERN ILLINOIS UNIVERSITY AT EDWARDSVILLE

Solon D. Morgan
DREXEL UNIVERSITY

Donald Nelson
MERRIMACK COLLEGE

Joseph Paolillo
UNIVERSITY OF WYOMING

Tim Peterson
TEXAS A & M UNIVERSITY

John Pierce
UNIVERSITY OF MINNESOTA AT DELUTH

Phil Quaglieri
NORTHERN ILLINOIS UNIVERSITY

James Rago
CLEVELAND STATE UNIVERSITY

V. Jean Ramsey
WESTERN MICHIGAN UNIVERSITY

Richard Randall
NASSAU COMMUNITY COLLEGE

Elizabeth Redstone
CUYAHOGA COMMUNITY COLLEGE

M. J. Riley
KANSAS STATE UNIVERSITY

Maurice Sampson
COMMUNITY COLLEGE OF PHILADELPHIA

Klaus Schmidt
SAN FRANCISCO UNIVERSITY

Richard Schoning
CALIFORNIA POLYTECHNIC UNIVERSITY

Charles Strain
OCEAN COUNTY COLLEGE

Charles Stubbart
UNIVERSITY OF MASSACHUSETTS-AMHERST

Laurence Stybel
BABSON COLLEGE

Jim Swenson
MOOREHEAD STATE UNIVERSITY

Gail E. Sype
GRAND VALLEY STATE COLLEGE

Shiela Teitelbaum
KINGSBOROUGH COMMUNITY COLLEGE

James B. Thomas
PENNSYLVANIA STATE UNIVERSITY

Kenneth G. Van Tine
BOWLING GREEN STATE UNIVERSITY

Trudy G. Verser
WESTERN MICHIGAN UNIVERSITY

Donald Warrick
UNIVERSITY OF COLORADO

Mark Wellman
BOWLING GREEN STATE UNIVERSITY

Harold K. Wilson
SOUTHERN ILLINOIS UNIVERSITY AT CARBONDALE

Charles Yauger
ARKANSAS STATE UNIVERSITY

Frank Yeandel
ST. MARY'S COLLEGE

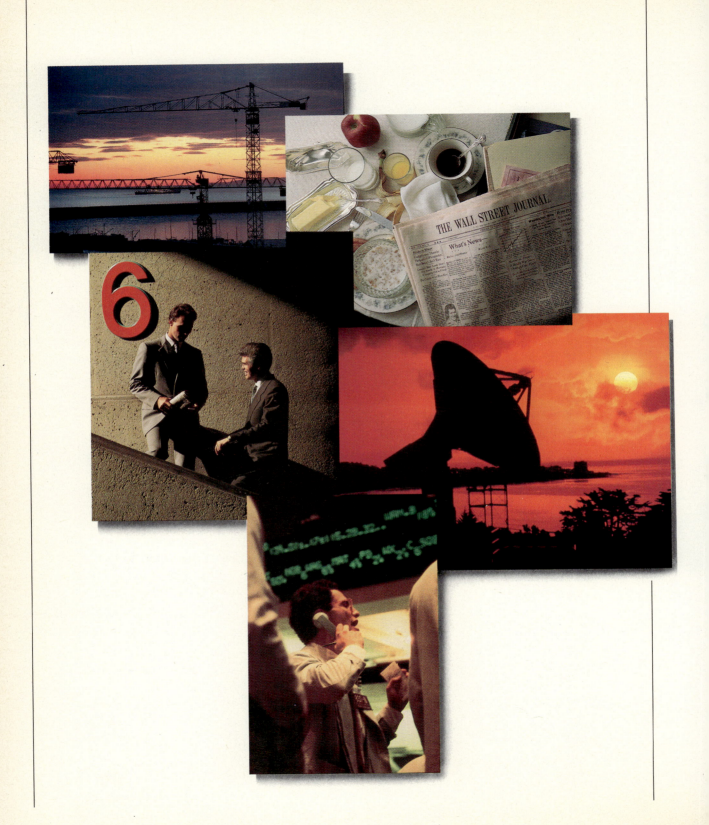

Contents

Managerial Decision Making and Problem Solving

PLANNING FOR PRODUCTIVITY

CONTENTS

CONTENTS

CHAPTER 12

Leading Through Motivation

CHAPTER 13

Leading Through Group Dynamics

CONTENTS

CONTENTS

CHAPTER 16

Operations Management and Control

PART 6

PRODUCTIVITY IN THE CONTEMPORARY ENVIRONMENT

CHAPTER 17

Managing Innovation, Change and Conflict

CONTENTS

Managing Labor-Management Relations

Managing In an International Arena

Managing With Ethics and Social Responsibility

P A R T

7

CONTENTS

CONTENTS

Memorandum to the Reader

TO: The Reader
FROM: John Schermerhorn
SUBJECT: *Management for Productivity,*
Third Edition

This book is written for you, someone who will contribute to management and the success of organizations in the complicated world of the 1990s. Being a manager is a special type of challenge because it involves working in a position of supervisory responsibility. The field of management offers a body of scientific knowledge that can help you fulfill this responsibility successfully and in a way that benefits you, the persons with whom you work, the organization for which you work, and society as a whole. The many learning opportunities contained in this book should help prepare you to be an effective manager in each of these respects.

The Book In Perspective

Two points about the book and my goals in writing it for you are especially important. First, managers exist in all types of organizations. The issues, concepts, theories, and insights of this book are useful no matter where you plan to work—in small or large business, education, government, health services, or social services. Second, my personal commitment has been to provide an active learning opportunity filled with practical insights and truly useful knowledge. Although there is a lot of theory in this book, the theory is explained, illustrated, and applied in ways that should help you perform more effectively in the workplace.

To take full advantage of the book, however, you must read carefully and stay involved each step of the way. Keep in mind that *Management for Productivity,* third edition, is written:

1. To present management theory as it applies to actual practice in all types of organizations and occupational settings.
2. To emphasize the practical applications of theory and concepts, and help you perform more effectively as a manager.
3. To involve you as an active participant in a self-contained experience as a way of increasing your learning.

Key Features of the Book

Special features make this a reader-oriented book. They are briefly introduced here so you can use them as they appear throughout the text. The features are of two types: (1) practical reference points and (2) study aids.

Practical Reference Points

It is important for you to know what is happening in the real world of management. My task is to acquaint you with a knowledge base that you can use to analyze work situations and systematically choose and implement good responses. This decision-making and problem-solving capability requires you to be familiar with many management concepts and theories that most textbooks simply present to the reader. *Management for Productivity,* third edition, does more. It explains and applies them with the assistance of the following features.

Part-Opening Perspectives My editorial commentary, reflecting the major themes addressed by each part of the book, and using examples and viewpoints from the professional literature.

Chapter Openers Short vignettes at the beginning of each chapter, which use timely examples to provoke your interest in topics to be presented.

Newslines Summaries from newspaper and news-magazine articles that show how text material is reflected in the day-to-day "problems" and "opportunities" of practicing managers.

Illustrative Cases, At . . . Examples, and In-Text Activities Special cases, practical examples, and in-text learning activities which can help you consider the meaning of key terms and concepts.

Career Perspectives End-of-chapter career situations for you to think about and respond to as part of your self-assessment and discovery of career opportunities in management fields.

Case Applications End-of-chapter short cases that ask you to step into management situations and take and defend appropriate managerial actions based on an application of chapter content.

Class Exercises End-of-chapter exercises designed to examine your perspectives on chapter content and relate them to the perspectives held by others in the class.

Part Integrating Cases Comprehensive cases at the end of each major part of the book that offer an opportunity to apply the theories and concepts to actual management situations in an integrated way.

Study Aids

This book has an important academic side. You must read about and study the field of management in order to someday use it when facing problems and opportunities in the workplace. To help you achieve this understanding, the third edition of *Management for Productivity* provides these additional study aids.

Planning Ahead Specific statements at the beginning of each chapter that highlight the key topics to be discussed.

Summary An overview at the end of each chapter that briefly outlines the major themes introduced in the reading.

Thinking Through the Issues Ten end-of-chapter questions that stimulate your thinking on major issues relating to chapter content.

The Manager's Vocabulary An end-of-chapter list of key terms introduced in the chapter, useful as a study check and for test reviews.

Glossary A list at the end of the book that defines all key terms referenced in each Manager's Vocabulary and notes the chapter in which each was originally introduced.

These features were chosen to help you learn more when reading this book. Planning Ahead, for example, should be especially useful when you read a chapter for the first time. The Summary, Thinking Through the Issues, and the Manager's Vocabulary are additional chances to review chapter material and consider whether or not you have covered it sufficiently. Finally, the Glossary of key terms and definitions combines with the other features to help you study for exams and maximize your learning.

A Final Comment Before You Begin

Management for Productivity, Third Edition, will involve you in a learning process. Think seriously as you read. Think about yourself, the work experiences you have had, and your career aspirations. Think about other people, their feelings, and how their work experiences compare with your own. Think about how important the field of management is to your education and your career. Think about the demanding and exciting world of work in the 1990s and your role in it. And finally, read these pages enthusiastically and enjoy this introduction to management as you learn!

INTRODUCTION

Productivity and the New Era for Management

Productivity has been one of the great buzzwords of recent years, but it is clearly much more than a trendy concept. As a measure of success in producing necessary goods and services, productivity is a crucial social and economic issue. And for organizations seeking to prosper in a world of great complexity, the goal of "productivity improvement" is one that simply must be attained.[1]

Indeed, current productivity challenges focus more and more on the manager, a person whose efforts can result in definite performance gains or losses for the organization. But what do these challenges really mean? We'll take a brief look in this "Perspective" at some of the implications of a new era for management—one in which productivity is the watchword.

"MANAGING . . . NOW IT MEANS GETTING VALUE ADDED, AND THAT'S A REVOLUTION."

must meet the challenges of an unpredictable world by using, "a judicious combination of old principles and new ways of applying them."[2]

Sometimes, though, conflicts with established ways of doing things are unavoidable. Sara F. Rolfes, a young manager of General Motor Corporation's Corvette air-bag program, discovered this firsthand. Rolfes decided to trust her observations and instincts in tackling production problems of the company's Camaro launch. She was advised by "more tenured" managers not to deal with assembly workers. Of her seniors, she said that "they had never gotten anywhere with hourly workers in the past because they probably had been dealing in a confrontational environment with them for 20 years." Rolfes chose to ignore past practice. Working together, she and the assembly employees got the Camaro moving.[3]

ARE THE OLD WAYS STILL GOOD ENOUGH?

As most of us know from what we've experienced and read, organizational life is changing fast and furiously. Managers are scrambling to keep up.

As the accompanying chart shows, the time demands on senior executives are especially great. However, managers at all levels of responsibility must keep on their toes in today's ever-shifting environment. Harvard Business School Professor D. Quinn Mills believes that the style of up-and-coming managers is becoming very different from that of their predecessors; it will by necessity be looser, less formal. In his book *The New Competitors,* Mills characterizes the modern manager as a generalist, not a specialist—a person with wide-ranging interests and ideas. But Mills cautions that the successful manager

PRODUCTIVITY AND THE VALUE-ADDED MANAGER

The quest for productivity improvement will undoubtedly dominate the 1990s and beyond. Many economists and most workers agree that better performance is the only way to go. But this doesn't just happen, even when everyone wants it—and that's where the link between productivity and sound management comes in. Fluctuations in the economy may be an unpleasant fact of life, but they aren't the only element determining organizational health. As one economist puts it, beyond the swings of the

NOTES
1. "The Productivity Paradox," *Business Week* (June 6, 1988), pp. 100–114.
2. D. Quinn Mills, *The New Competitors* (New York: Wiley, 1985), p. 4.
3. "Fast-Track Kids," *Business Week* (November 10, 1986), p. 91.
4. "Can America Compete?" *Business Week* (April 20, 1987), p. 47.
5. Peter Nulty, "How Managers Will Manage," *Fortune* (February 2, 1987), p. 48.
6. Herbert Blanchett, "Debunking Management Myths," *Stanford GSB,* vol. 51 (Summer 1983), pp. 9–10.

economic pendulum, "it comes down to management."[4] The manager's job is to ensure that funds are deployed effectively—or, in the words of Boston University Professor George Labovitz, "to identify and remove obstacles to productivity." More and more, competitive firms are ousting managers who can't enhance the bottom line. And managers who survive downsizing—the corporate staff contractions so common in our time—are expected to make tangible contributions to profits. "Managing," Mark Bieler, senior vice-president of human resources at Bankers Trust, explains, ". . . now means getting value added, and that's a revolution."[5]

SUCCESS IN AN UNCERTAIN WORLD— WHAT DOES IT TAKE?

Having heard about some of the demands on today's managers, you are probably asking yourself these questions: What do those demands boil down to? In such an uncertain world, what does it take to make it? Interestingly, despite their divergent experiences, old-school CEOs and young newcomers to management are often able to see eye to eye on the ingredients for success. Consider the criteria offered by H. B. (Bruce) Atwater Jr., chairman and CEO of General Mills, Inc., during a speech at Stanford University.

■ **Intelligence** "You don't have to be a genius, but . . . the problems we deal with are tremendously complex, and it does take a reasonable amount of mental horsepower to deal effectively with them."

■ **Decisiveness** "There are a number of people who see 67 sides to a question and can never reach a conclusion. You have to know what kind of facts to get, when to stop getting

them, and how and when to make a decision."

■ **Ability to handle conflict well** "What we are talking about here is the ability to get an issue out in the open and up for useful discussion even under difficult circumstances . . . the person who shies away from disagreement and who takes criticism personally will not be a good manager."

■ **Mental agility and conceptual thinking** "Can you take a very complex situation, sort it out, put it back together, and make the necessary—and correct—decision? You've got to be able to develop and see clearly a single broad picture that's made up of a whole series of ambiguous and divergent facts."

■ **High tolerance for stress** The day deals almost entirely with the dif-

ficult, the troublesome, and with conflict . . . the successful business executive has to know how to handle them all. A high energy level and good physical well-being are essential."[6]

Management for Productivity is written to help you achieve success in this new era for management. One thing *is* certain: you are likely to succeed in direct proportion to your enthusiasm and preparation for the demands of managerial work. So read and study this book with excitement, and with Bruce Atwater's final words of advice in mind: "It's very important to have a commitment to whatever it is you choose to do . . . a commitment to the job and to doing it as well as you possibly can." ■

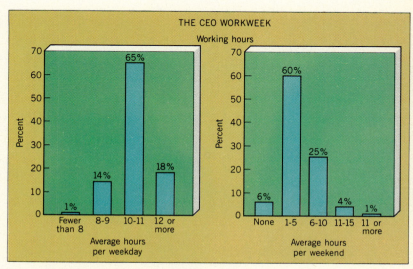

Source: *The Wall Street Journal* survey on executive style.

THE CEO WORKWEEK
Working hours

Average hours per weekday: Fewer than 8 — 1%; 8-9 — 14%; 10-11 — 65%; 12 or more — 18%

Average hours per weekend: None — 6%; 1-5 — 60%; 6-10 — 25%; 11-15 — 4%; 11 or more — 1%

Managers, Management, and Productivity

Management for the 1990s and Beyond

The rules of the game are changing. *New managers* have their sights set on an exciting, unpredictable future—one in which both opportunities and risks will be plentiful.

What distinguishes the up-and-coming managers, men and women under 35 years old, from their (typically) white male predecessors? Generalizations are dangerous, but "fast-trackers" do seem to share certain traits—for instance, flexibility and a willingness to job-hop—that were not common in corporate culture several years ago. The new managers are bright, ethnically diverse, very hard-working people. They are neither as risk-averse nor as patient as their 40-and-over counterparts. In the words of industrial psychologist Paul Leinberger, "they want to control their own destiny"—and seeking job security is not the only way to go, in their view.

While the new managers are by nature independent and confident, many are aware of the occasionally disturbing effects of their attitudes and behavior on those who've paved the way before them. Roger Ballou, a young vice-president at American Express, noted that while he likes having time on his side, he needs to be sensitive to the feelings of older colleagues. Accusations of arrogance or precociousness are sometimes leveled at managers such as Ballou. "It's kind of like the best of times and the worst of times," he says.

Yet, faced with the major challenge of improving productivity, the new managers realize that new approaches are needed. A "bunker mentality" is useless in a fast-changing environment. Managers for the 1990s and beyond are being encouraged in their thinking by academics and experts who see this new breed as the bright hope of management's future. As one professor at USC puts it, "a manager had better have more meaningful plans now than slashing budgets." Imaginative fast-trackers are quite likely to agree. They are willing to experiment with solutions, and they are prepared to learn from their mistakes.

Armed with optimism, advanced degrees, and computer literacy, the new managers have every intention of going far without taking a lifetime to do so. Call them idealistic if you will. The facts remain. New managers are already part of the managerial revolution, and they are changing the way things get done in organizations everywhere. ■

Source: Information from John McCormick and Bill Powell, "Management for the 1990s," *Newsweek* (April 25, 1988), pp. 47–48, and "Fast-Track Kids," *Business Week* (November 10, 1986), pp. 90–96.

All managers play impor-
tant roles in helping or-
ganizations contribute to
modern society. Chapter 1
introduces you to the challenges of being a good manager. Key topics in the
chapter include:

Managers
Organizations
Managers in Organizations
Productivity and the
**   Manager**
The Management Process
The Nature of Managerial
**   Work**
Managerial Skills and
**   Competencies**
The Study of Management

Work is an activity that produces value for other people.[1] The
subject of work and the need for it
to be done well enough that indi-
viduals and society as a whole may prosper and grow
makes the material covered in the following pages
meaningful. *Management for Productivity* is about
managers and other people at work in organizations.
Reading and learning from this book should help you
understand the many events that will give meaning
to your future work experiences and career. As suggested in the chapter opener, the *new managers* of the
1990s and beyond face a demanding future. Chapter
1 sets the foundations for you to join their ranks and
achieve your full managerial potential.

MANAGERS

A **manager** is a person in an organization who is
responsible for the work performance of one or
more other persons. People are a basic resource of
organizations. As **human resources**, they use **material resources** such as information, technology,
raw materials, facilities and money to produce
goods and services. If the people perform well, the
organization performs well; if the people don't, the
organization can't. The *manager's job* is to help
the organization achieve a high level of performance

through the utilization of its human
and material resources. More simply,
a manager's job is to get things done
through other people.

Managers are therefore universal. They are essential to organizations of all types and sizes.
Schools, hospitals, government agencies, small retail businesses, hotels, and large corporate enterprises all have managers working toward the same
general goal of improved performance for the organization. As the noted management theorist and
consultant Peter Drucker says in his book *The
Changing World of the Executive,*[2]

> Society in this century has become a society of organi-
> zations. Social tasks—from providing goods and
> services to education and care of the sick and the
> elderly . . . are now increasingly performed in and
> through large organizations. These organizations . . .
> are designed for continuity and are run by professional
> managers. . . . Careers in organizations—that is, ca-
> reers as managers and other professionals—are the
> principal career opportunities for educated people.

You should agree with Drucker's statement.
Organizations are essential to society and managers
are essential to the success of all organizations regardless of their size or type. The basic task of any
manager, furthermore, is to help the organization
perform. Keep this goal in mind as you proceed now
with the study of management. Consider too, these
additional thoughts of Henry Mintzberg, another
well-known theorist. They nicely set the stage for

what follows in this chapter and the rest of the book.[3]

> No job is more vital to our society than that of the manager. It is the manager who determines whether our social institutions serve us well or whether they squander our talents and resources. It is time to strip away the folklore about managerial work, and time to study it realistically so that we can begin the difficult task of making significant improvement in its performance.

ORGANIZATIONS

Formally defined, an **organization** is a collection of people working together in a division of labor to achieve a common purpose. Because organizations accomplish tasks that are beyond individual capabilities alone, they are important elements in society. One of the most significant new products of recent times—the personal computer—helps to illustrate this fact.

ILLUSTRATIVE CASE: APPLE COMPUTER, INC.

Some time ago Stephen Wozniak and Steven Jobs, working at home and in their spare time, created a computer of compact size and considerable power. The two men were **entrepreneurs**, persons willing to take risks to pursue innovation and opportunities in an uncertain environment. Their revolutionary machine became the foundation of what is now a billion-dollar multinational company—Apple Computer, Inc.[4]

In the Beginning It all began in 1976 when Jobs and Wozniak raised $1300 by selling a VW microbus and a scientific calculator to build a typewriter-sized computer. Jobs, who had worked one summer in the orchards of Oregon, christened the computer "Apple." They produced the first Apple Computers in a makeshift production facility located in a garage. Their organization most likely resembled the entrepreneurial start-up shown in Figure 1.1. Before long, the two entrepreneurs probably hired a few part-time workers to help assemble the computers

and do other odd jobs. Most likely, though, Jobs and Wozniak still helped do everything from purchasing needed parts and materials, to helping in the production process, to selling the finished computers.

Some Time Later As the demand for computers increased, Jobs and Wozniak needed to increase their production capabilities and turn their personal attention to more managerial concerns. They sought professional assistance to obtain much-needed venture capital in an effort to rapidly expand the new company's production capabilities. They needed to hire full-time assembly workers, salespersons, and purchasing agents, among others, and they needed to hire other people to help manage them. As the company grew, the two had to rely more and more on the other people to do work they had previously done themselves. This reallocation of work to other people, and the need to coordinate their individual efforts, created a slightly more complex "organization." As owner-managers of the fledgling small business, Jobs and Wozniak became more than computer builders. They had to make sure that the performance potential of Apple Computer, Inc., was realized through the collective efforts of many other people.

Even Later What began as a small two-person operation grew at one point in the mid-1980s to employ over 6000 employees. But as the organization itself became more and more complex, as depicted in Figure 1.2, a new professional management group led by former Pepsico executive John Sculley took control. After considerable internal conflict and well-publicized turmoil, both Jobs and Wozniak left to pursue other business interests. They had become very wealthy from their entrepreneurial venture, but their company had changed dramatically from a small firm run by its owner-managers, into a large business run by professional managers. Still, the company's success in a dynamic marketplace has been the envy of its competitors.

Organizations as Employers

There are many types of organizations in which people find employment. For our purposes, it is helpful to recognize the distinctive opportunities of large businesses, small businesses, international businesses, and nonprofit organizations. Each is a work setting for managers, and each will be fre-

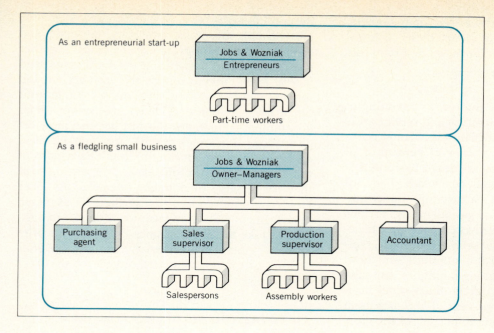

FIGURE 1.1 *The evolution of Apple Computer, Inc.: A transition from entrepreneurial start-up to small business enterprise.*

quently used as the basis for examples and illustrative cases throughout this book. Wherever your career goals might lie, the importance of developing and successfully applying the requisite managerial capabilities remains high.

Large Businesses IBM, American Express, Sears, and Procter & Gamble join Apple Computer as large businesses with which you are surely familiar. Such large for-profit employers include manufacturing concerns, providing both consumer and industrial products. They also include service firms such as banks and investment houses in financial services, hotel and restaurant chains in the hospitality services, airlines and rental car companies in transportation services, and major accounting and adver-

FIGURE 1.2 *The evolution of Apple Computer, Inc.: A view of its top management structure as a multinational business.*

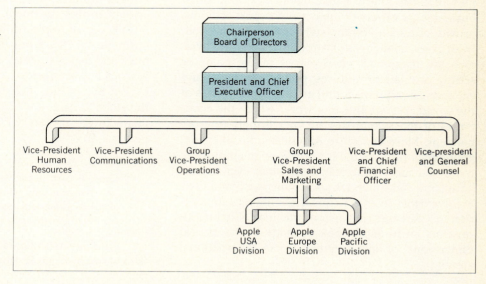

tising firms in professional services, among others. Taken individually or as a group, these "colossal giants" of the business world play an important role in society.

Small Businesses Smaller enterprises operating in many of the same manufacturing and service areas as large businesses, are also mainstays of most economies. In the United States over 97 percent of all businesses are classified by the Small Business Administration (SBA) as small businesses. They include sole proprietorships, partnerships, franchises, the activities of individual professionals, various part-time operations, as well as corporations. Especially common in retail and service industries, typical examples in your local community are travel agencies, restaurants, clothing boutiques, specialty shops, and many, many others. Such small businesses employ about 50 percent of U.S. non-farm workers, account for about 40 percent of the gross national product, and offer more than 80 percent of all new jobs created in the private sector. *Newsline 1.1,* the first of many reports we will introduce from the recent press, comments further on the economic significance of small businesses in the American economy.

International Businesses Many large and small enterprises operate on a global scale, doing business in more than one country. Exxon, Ford, Sony, and even McDonald's are but a few well-known examples of large international businesses. For small businesses, a variety of import and export activities provide attractive commercial opportunities as well. In all cases, challenges of running a successful business are magnified when placed in the complex setting of different cultures, political systems, and economic conditions found among the countries of the world. Yet, we live in a world where the economies of most countries are increasingly interdependent. More and more Americans, for example, are now working in the U.S. for foreign employers; more and more American firms than ever before, both large and small, are also trying to expand their involvements in international commerce. In addition to references throughout the book, Chapter 19 presents an in-depth look at many of the critical dimensions of management in an international arena.

Nonprofit Organizations The chances are that your local schools, hospitals, university, museums and civic centers are non-profit organizations. Together with government agencies at the local, state, and federal levels, they comprise the very diverse and important public sector of the economy. A nonprofit organization is one considered tax-exempt under government regulations. But just because these organizations don't seek profits like their business counterparts doesn't mean they don't have many of the same managerial problems and opportunities as they try to serve their public clientele.[5] As Peter Drucker says, "Today, surely, there is as much 'management' outside of business as there is in business."[6] Like the small businesses, nonprofits offer attractive employment alternatives to those persons seeking career opportunities outside of the large corporate setting.

Three Ingredients of Organizations

All organizations begin with people. Beyond that, they involve three ingredients: a common purpose, a division of labor, and a hierarchy of authority. Let's take a detailed look at each of these ingredients as a special characteristic of organizations as the settings in which managers work.

Purpose

The **purpose of an organization** is to produce a good or service that satisfies the needs of its customers or clients. This emphasis on production is evident in the Apple Computer example. It is also evident in this statement of corporate purpose for AT&T, one of Apple's competitors in the computer business: "AT&T's business is information movement and management: providing quality products, systems and services to a diversity of markets in the United States and, increasingly, to nations around the globe."[7] And, it is further evident in these comments by John Akers, CEO of Apple's biggest competitor—IBM:[8]

> How do we change our capability as a nation to play a vigorous part on the world scene? . . . In the end we can change it only with production—the production of quality goods and quality services that we and others around the world want to buy.

One way to understand this concept of purpose is to view any organization as an **open system.** This

SMALL BUSINESSES
FUEL BIG GROWTH IN JOBS

N E W S L I N E 1.1

There's a revival of sorts in Allentown, PA, and scores of other communities around the United States these days. While large, Fortune 500-type employers are cutting payrolls by slashing jobs, thousands of smaller companies with less-familiar names are creating tens of thousands of new jobs. The small business sector is "a hidden economy, and it's booming," says David L. Birch, management professor at Massachusetts Institute of Technology and consultant on job creation. Most of the new jobs in smaller enterprises come from fast-moving start-ups and older firms that are reinventing themselves to take advantage of new attractive opportunities.

Bortz Chocolate Novelties, Inc., has been in the same old brick building on a downtown Reading, PA, street since 1916. But its business today is much different than it was then—for it, success has meant being able to change with the times. "Before you had just the same old hollow mold every year," says Frances Bortz, "You'd sell it every year and they'd buy it every year." Even though the old designs still sell, Bortz is working hard inventing new treats. "The name of the game is new products," says the company's chief financial officer.

One major force in the small business environment appears to come from women. They comprise the "fastest growing segment of the small business community," says Carol Crockett, director of the U.S. Small Business Association's Office of Women's Business Ownership. Women are now starting small businesses at twice the rate men are, and by the year 2000 there are likely to be as many businesses owned by women as men.

Source: Information from David L. Birch, "Down, But Not Out," *Inc.* (May 1988), pp. 20–21; William Glaberson, "In Allentown and Elsewhere, Small Companies are Fueling a Big Growth in Jobs," *The New York Times* (May 1, 1988) pp. F-1, F-5; and David E. Gumpert, "Each Year a Million New Businesses," *The New York Times,* (April 17, 1988), p. F-17.

is a system that interacts with its environment and transforms resource inputs into finished goods and/or services as product outputs. Figure 1.3 depicts Apple Computer, Inc. as an open system. Apple's employees are human resource inputs that combine in the transformation process with various material resource inputs to create microcomputers and related software as finished products. The resources are obtained from Apple's external environment, which also consumes the company's products and thereby justifies it's existence. In this way, consumer feedback completes the linkage between organization and environment in this open-systems model. Today, the best organizations are recognized for their willingness to solicit and respond to consumer feedback. For example,[9]

at Western Digital a specialized electronics company, production manager Kathy Braun learned that a major customer was concerned about the $150 price of the computer disk-drive controller boards. Kathy redesigned the board to get the price down to $100. Not only was the original customer happy, but a flood of orders for the board came in from new markets. About the experience, Digital's chief executive Roger Johnson says: "A company has to be more customer-oriented now."

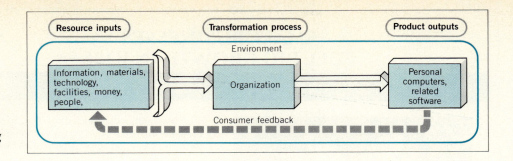

FIGURE 1.3 *An open-systems view of a computer manufacturing firm.*

Division of Labor

All organizations require the performance contributions of many people. The founders of Apple realized at a certain point in the growth of their firm that they could not do all the required work by themselves. Other people had to be hired to assist in accomplishing essential tasks. The final result was a collection of many people performing jobs that, when added together, resulted in the production of computers and software. This process of breaking work into smaller components and assigning them as tasks to be performed by individuals and groups is called the **division of labor.**

A division of labor is indicated by the different job titles shown earlier in Figure 1.2. It is apparent in all organizations, including colleges and universities. The work of your instructor, for example, differs from that of others teaching accounting, marketing, history, or biology. Their work, in turn, differs from that performed by the director of university housing, the dean of students, and the manager of the student bookstore. The effort of each person is necessary, however, if the university is to achieve its educational purpose.

Hierarchy of Authority

After work is divided into many parts, something must be done to make sure that the separate work efforts combine to achieve desired results. That is, the division of labor must be coordinated if organizations are to achieve performance success. Managers are responsible for seeing to it that this occurs.

One way in which a manager coordinates the division of labor is through **formal authority.** For now, you may think of this as the right to assign tasks and direct other persons to perform work relevant to the organization's purpose. When a manager uses authority, accountability is created in his or her relationships with subordinates. This is the requirement that they answer back to the manager for their performance accomplishments. We say in this regard that a manager holds subordinates accountable for performance.

When many managerial positions exist in one organization, the result is a **hierarchy of authority.** This arranges positions in order of increasing authority, and clarifies the performance accountability of each person to a higher-level manager. Looking back at Figure 1.2, the chairperson of the board is the highest level of formal authority for Apple Computer, Inc. A hierarchy of authority has been created, though, to include the president, vice-presidents, and the managers and other personnel who work for them.

MANAGERS IN ORGANIZATIONS

Now that we share an appreciation of the organization as a manager's work setting, let's speak more precisely about various levels and types of managers, as well as the basic challenge that all managers share.

Managerial Levels

It is common to differentiate managers according to level or relative standing in an organization's hierarchy of authority. This distinction is shown in Figure 1.4.

Top-Level Managers

Job titles common to the highest levels of management include chief executive officer, chief operating officer, president, and vice-president. Persons at this level ensure that objectives are set and accomplished in accord with the organization's purpose. They are often called **executives** because they are senior managers having broad responsibility for a significant part of the organization or for the organization as a whole.[10] In particular, top managers monitor the environment to identify potential problems and opportunities, and develop appropriate strategies and long-range objectives. They must be future oriented, and frequently make decisions under highly competitive and uncertain conditions.

Going back to the example of Apple Computer, Inc., it is the task of President John Sculley to stay abreast of trends in the personal computer markets and formulate ways for the company to stay ahead of its competition. By the mid 1990s, for example, Apple's success will depend on how well the top management team does in mobilizing the organization to meet the continuing challenges of IBM, AT&T, Zenith and other major computer manufacturers. Here is a sampler of things on the minds of chief executives of other firms in the computer industry.[11]

Our goal is to create a lean organization that encourages people to work effectively across organizational boundaries. . . . We want to encourage teamwork, not empire building.

John Young, *Hewlett-Packard*

Creating wealth—developing products or services of value to customers—is neither quick nor easy. Often it requires persistence, even stubbornness, and the willingness to keep one's eye fixed on long-term objectives.

Robert Price, *Control Data*

Typically, American businessmen and women not only do not think globally, they don't yet understand the importance of doing so, or what is involved in doing so effectively.

Joe Henson, *Prime Computer*

Middle-Level Managers

Middle managers constitute the intermediate level in an organization's hierarchy of authority. They report to managers at the top level, while lower-level managers report to them. In so doing, they interpret directions set by higher managers into plans and action guidelines for lower-level personnel; and they pass information upward in the hierarchy to keep top managers informed about lower-level concerns. Examples of middle managers include clinic directors in a hospital, deans in a university, and division managers, plant managers, branch sales managers, or personnel directors in a business.

Much recent publicity about middle managers has related to corporate "downsizing" and "restructuring." In the attempt to cut costs, some organizations have reduced the number of middle managers in their employ. These trends will be discussed later in the book, but they shouldn't be misinterpreted.

FIGURE 1.4 *Levels of management in an organization's hierarchy of authority.*

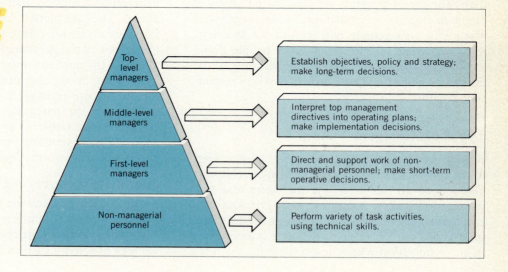

The middle managers who guide the affairs of major subunits, such as departments or divisions, are crucial to organizations. They set short-range objectives, make operating decisions, and more generally initiate the wide variety of actions needed to implement organizational strategies. They also work with peers to help coordinate the affairs of multiple subunits with one another. Furthermore, this middle level of responsibility is a testing ground from which many organizations fill top management appointments.

First-Level Managers

Job titles such as supervisor, section head, team leader, and foreman are common to persons at the first-line or supervisory level of management. These are the people to whom operating employees report. First-level managers implement the plans and directives of middle and upper management levels on a daily basis. This task can be very demanding. Supervisors, for example, can experience a lot of stress when the expectations of workers and higher managers come into conflict. Think of the supervisor whose boss clamors for overtime work to meet a special order at the same time that subordinates complain they are overworked and need time for their families. Such situations demand considerable judgment and interpersonal skill on the manager's part.

Most persons enter the workforce as a technical specialist—for example, in sales, personnel, finance, or accounting—and report to a first-line supervisor. Sooner or later, however, the likelihood is that their career progress will lead to positions of direct managerial responsibility. Like them, your first job in management will typically be as a first-level supervisor in charge of other people doing technical work. Table 1.1 summarizes some of the things you will be expected to do in this very responsible position.[12]

Types of Managers

It is convenient to classify the types of managers found in organizations. Three of the more common distinctions are between line managers and staff managers, between functional managers and general managers, and between administrators and managers. First, recall that a manager is any person in an organization who is responsible for the work

TABLE 1.1 *Typical Responsibilities of a First-Level Supervisor*

- Plan work to be done each day and monitor results.
- Assign specific tasks to individual subordinates.
- Prepare daily, weekly, and monthly work schedules..
- Counsel subordinates about their work.
- Recommend subordinates for new assignments.
- Select and train new employees to fill job vacancies.
- Assist higher managers to prepare budgets.
- Complete performance appraisals of subordinates.
- Recommend pay increases for subordinates.
- Maintain production and personnel records.
- Advise higher levels on work needs and improvements.
- Keep subordinates motivated in their work.

performance of one or more other people. This definition holds equally well for each of the following managerial types.

Line Managers and Staff Managers

Line managers have responsibility for work activities that make a direct contribution to production of the organization's basic product or service. Their efforts clearly influence the process whereby resource inputs are transformed into product or service outputs. The president, retail manager, and department supervisors in Figure 1.5 all have line responsibilities. Their jobs, in one way or another, are all directly involved in the sales operation of this small retail store.

Staff managers, by contrast, use their special technical expertise to support the efforts of line personnel. In this retailing example, the personnel manager and finance manager have staff responsibilities. They are there to help the line manager and salespersons by providing special support services. In the case of the personnel manager this is to help maintain the needed human resources, for example by advising on the recruitment of new employees; for the finance manager it is to help make sound decisions on the investment of the company's financial resources. Other titles common to staff managers are senior auditor, strategic planning analyst, and public relations manager.

Functional Managers and General Managers

Another useful distinction in business firms is between functional managers and general managers. **Functional managers** have responsibility for a single area of activity such as finance, marketing, pro-

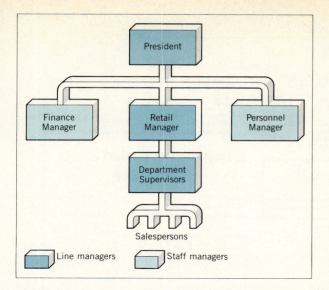

FIGURE 1.5 *Line and staff managers in a small retail store.*

business policy. This course typically offers a general manager's view of the corporate enterprise.

The forthcoming collage presents a sample of help-wanted ads from a newspaper. Note the job opportunities for functional managers in various fields of specialization, as well as for the general management trainees. Although these jobs require qualifications that may lie beyond your present capabilities, they represent the types of career opportunities that will surely come your way in the future.

Administrators and Managers

A third distinction in the vocabulary of management is between people called administrators and those called managers. In fact, the terms are basically equivalent. The main distinction is that **administrators** are managers who work in public or nonprofit organizations as opposed to business concerns. They hold job titles such as hospital administrator, public administrator, city administrator, and human-service administrator.

duction, personnel, accounting, or sales. Note that these functional areas directly correspond to course titles found in college and university programs of study in business and administration.

General managers are responsible for more complex organizational subunits that include many functional areas of activity. A good example is a plant manager who oversees many separate functions, including purchasing, warehousing, sales, personnel, and accounting. As you progress through your academic program of study, courses in the various functional areas may well be integrated in a final capstone course on strategic planning and

The Manager's Challenge

Most managers are subordinates and superiors simultaneously. Think about what this statement means. As subordinates, managers are held accountable by their superiors (or "bosses") for the performance of their work units. Herein lies every **manager's challenge:** to fulfill an accountability to superiors for work-unit performance, while depending on the efforts of subordinates to make this performance possible.

Assume you are the supervisor of a work group assembling components for Apple Computer, Inc.

FIGURE 1.6 *The "manager's challenge" as viewed by a production supervisor.*

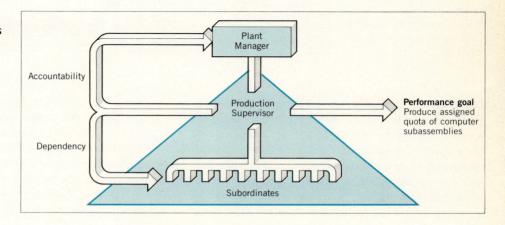

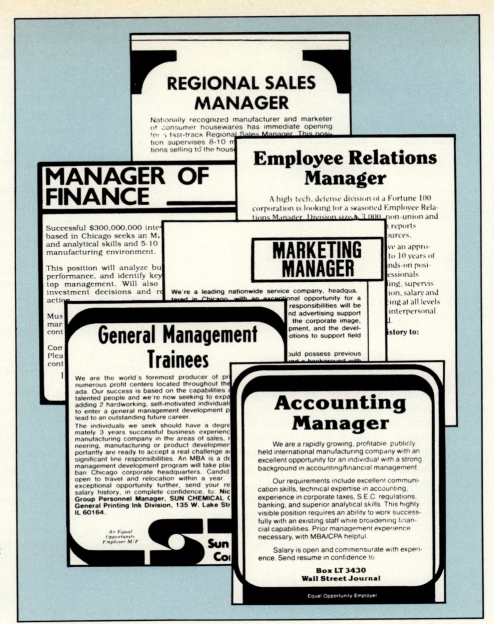

REGIONAL SALES MANAGER

Nationally recognized manufacturer and marketer of consumer housewares has immediate opening for a fast-track Regional Sales Manager. This position supervises 8-10 m
tions selling to the house

MANAGER OF FINANCE

Successful $300,000,000 inte
based in Chicago seeks an M
and analytical skills and 5-10
manufacturing environment.

This position will analyze bu
performance, and identify key
top management. Will also
investment decisions and re
action

Mus
mar
cont

Com
Plea
cont

Employee Relations Manager

A high-tech, defense division of a Fortune 100 corporation is looking for a seasoned Employee Relations Manager. Division size 3,000 non-union and
reports
urces.

ve an appro-
to 10 years of
nds-on posi-
essionals
ing, supervis
ion, salary and
ng at all levels
interpersonal
d.

istory to:

MARKETING MANAGER

We're a leading nationwide service company, headqua
tered in Chicago, with an exceptional opportunity for a
responsibilities will be
nd advertising support
the corporate image,
pment, and the devel-
otions to support field

ould possess previous
nd a background with

General Management Trainees

We are the world's foremost producer of pr
numerous profit centers located throughout the
ada. Our success is based on the capabilities
talented people and we're now seeking to expa
adding 2 hardworking, self-motivated individuals
to enter a general management development p
lead to an outstanding future career.
The individuals we seek should have a degre
mately 3 years successful business experienc
manufacturing company in the areas of sales,
neering, manufacturing or product developmen
portantly are ready to accept a real challenge a
significant line responsibilities. An MBA is a de
management development program will take plac
ban Chicago corporate headquarters. Candid
open to travel and relocation within a year.
exceptional opportunity further, send your re
salary history, in complete confidence, to: **Nic**
Group Personnel Manager, SUN CHEMICAL (
General Printing Ink Division, 135 W. Lake Str
IL 60164.

*An Equal
Opportunity
Employer M/F*

Accounting Manager

We are a rapidly growing, profitable, publicly held international manufacturing company with an excellent opportunity for an individual with a strong background in accounting/financial management.

Our requirements include excellent communication skills, technical expertise in accounting, experience in corporate taxes, S.E.C. regulations, banking, and superior analytical skills. This highly visible position requires an ability to work successfully with an existing staff while broadening financial capabilities. Prior management experience necessary, with MBA/CPA helpful.

Salary is open and commensurate with experience. Send resume in confidence to

**Box LT 3430
Wall Street Journal**

Equal Opportunity Employer

Career advancement in a wide variety of fields frequently requires the ability to achieve success working in a managerial capacity.

The diagram in Figure 1.6 depicts the basic manager's challenge: At the same time you are held accountable by the plant manager for a daily quota of computer subassemblies, you depend on the contributions of ten subordinates to make this performance possible. In the final result, you are responsible for work that is in large part produced by someone else. This reality will be most evident on those days when the work unit fails to meet its quota. When this happens, the plant manager won't ask your subordinates what went wrong; she or he will come direclty to you and ask that question! You can't avoid responsibility by saying, in return, "My subordinates are the ones who didn't do the work."

It is the manager's job to ensure high performance of the work unit. This book is designed to help you master this basic manager's challenge, regardless of the level or type of managerial position you hold and in whatever type of organization you might work.

PRODUCTIVITY AND THE MANAGER

Somewhere near a Ford Motor Company plant in Dearborn, Michigan, a tavern once displayed the following sign.

> I Spend Forty Hours a Week
> Here—Am I Supposed
> to Work, Too?

Somewhere in California, a person was seen in a t-shirt with the following words printed boldly on its front.

> I Work 90 Hours
> a Week and Love It

The contrast between the sign and the t-shirt epitomizes the manager's challenge about which we just spoke. It is one thing for people to join organizations as employees; it is quite another for them to make useful performance contributions as well. The ultimate criterion of managerial success is the performance accomplishment—or "productivity"—of the group of people reporting to the manager. That is, the manager's bottom line is work-unit productivity.

What Is Productivity?

Productivity is a summary measure of the quantity and quality of work performance with resource utilization considered. The traditional economic definition of productivity focuses on the ratio of product or service outputs to resource inputs. Sample productivity indices are output per person-hour (business), clients served per staff member (social agency), and student credit hours taught per full-time equivalent faculty member (university).

From a manager's perspective, productivity reflects a broader performance measure. It identifies success or failure in producing goods and services in quantity, of quality, and with a good use of resources. Other things being equal, productivity rises

in a work situation when the quantity of outputs increases, the quality of outputs increases, and/or the cost of resources utilized decreases. For example,[13]

at Rockwell International Corporation productivity increased through improved *quantity* when an investment in shop-floor personal computers and robots increased by 79 percent the speed with which products moved through one plant and helped to more than double sales.

at Xerox Corporation productivity increased through improved *quality* when a corporate-wide commitment to total quality helped the company reduce its component defect rates from 8,000 per million to 1,300 and improve customer services.

at National Steel Corporation productivity increased through improved *resource utilization* when labor-management cooperation resulted in a reduction in the number of person-hours required to make a ton of steel from more than five to about four.

Figure 1.7 shows productivity as a criterion of work achievement that applies to individuals, groups and organizations. A major part of every manager's job, accordingly, is to establish and maintain the conditions for productivity. Managers are in a position to directly influence the productivity of individuals and groups under their supervision. They are also in a position to help integrate these performance contributions to facilitate high productivity for the organization as a whole.

Productivity involves doing a job or task in the best possible way all of the time. Achieving productivity requires the creative combination of appropriate technology and skilled people into a well-functioning total performance system. As *Newsline 1.2* points out, the human resource is an essential component of this system. Indeed, the ultimate test of any manager's competence may well be his or her ability to establish conditions in which the work ethic can prosper and all of an organization's resources—human and material—are best utilized to produce goods and services.

Performance Effectiveness and Performance Efficiency

Two criteria measure a manager's success in the quest for productivity and personal accomplish-

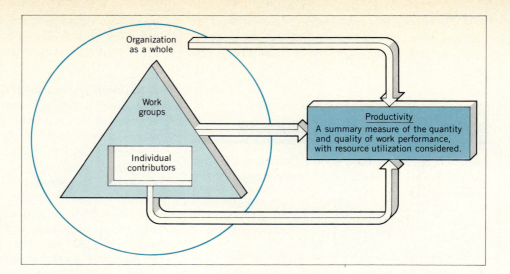

FIGURE 1.7 *Three levels of productivity accomplishments in organizations.*

ment: performance effectiveness and performance efficiency. **Performance effectiveness** is a measure of task output or goal accomplishment. If you are the production supervisor depicted earlier in Figure 1.6, performance effectiveness means meeting the daily production targets, *both* quantity and quality, for your work unit. True productivity, however, requires more comprehensive performance accomplishment. After all, you might meet production targets, but waste resources in the process. Thus, a second criterion of productivity—efficiency—is also used as an indicator of managerial success.

Performance efficiency is a measure of the resource cost associated with goal accomplishment—that is, outputs realized compared to inputs

consumed. This is most obvious in the cost of labor (e.g., in terms of employee wages), but it also includes the cost of all resources used in the production process. Measures of equipment utilization, facilities maintenance, and returns on capital investment are all efficiency criteria. Going back to the example of the production supervisor, the most efficient manager is the one who meets the daily production quota at minimum cost with respect to resource utilization.

Figure 1.8 shows various combinations of performance effectiveness and efficiency. A manager can be effective but inefficient, efficient but ineffective, ineffective and inefficient, or both effective and efficient. The latter case is optimum from a produc-

FIGURE 1.8 *Performance effectiveness, performance efficiency— and managerial success.*

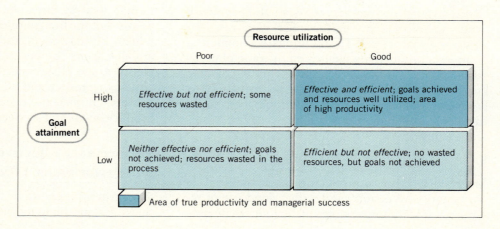

THE WORK ETHIC LIVES!

Popular opinion may have it that the Japanese are the hardest-working people in the world, but Americans have no cause for concern about the work ethic in the United States. The Department of Labor recently reported that 107 million U.S. workers were putting in long hours at full-time jobs, and that over 5 million, or 5.4 percent of all those employed, held more than one job—the highest proportion in over 20 years. IBM recently calculated that Americans work an average of 1873 hours annually (a total topped only by Japan). And absenteeism in U.S. offices and factories, according to the Bureau of Labor Statistics, has dropped to 4.7 percent a week—the lowest level since the BLS began recording such data, and well below levels reported in England, France, and Canada.

Labor Department surveys indicate that fewer than 1 worker in 10 would prefer more leisure time and a lower wage; many would actually prefer longer hours and more pay. In their book *Starting with the People,* pollster Daniel Yankelovich and executive Sidney Harman contend that Americans are willing to do more at work, but they also want more in return. Concerns for job security are also high in light of corporate cost-cutting measures and a fast-changing economy. AFL-CIO economist John Zalusky maintains that most workers would rather lose a paid holiday than face a health-benefit loss or a pay cut. Yet other factors—such as incentive and job-enrichment schemes—affect the quality and quantity of work performed. Increasingly, employers recognize that output is not simply a function of wages; people work hard for many complex and interacting reasons.

Columbia University Professor David Lewin foresees an easing of workers' job-security fears. Lewin expects that demographic changes—especially the decreased birth rates of the 1960s and early 1970s—will bring about a reduction in the entry of young workers into the marketplace, thereby tilting the wage-bargaining scales in labor's favor. While there's no telling what the future of the work ethic will be, today's worker is a hard worker—and wants it that way.

Source: Information from *The Wall Street Journal* (July 5, 1988), p. 1. "The Work Ethic Lives," *Time* (September 7, 1987), pp. 40–42.

---

tivity standpoint. True managerial success entails both effectiveness in goal attainment and efficiency in resource utilization.

Productivity and Quality of Working Life

The issue of resource utilization highlights another facet of productivity that is of great significance in today's world of strong social and humanistic val-

ues. This deals with human-resource utilization in the performance process. Productivity is ideally achieved through high performance (effectiveness and efficiency) *and* with a sense of personal satisfaction by the people doing the work. Both performance and satisfaction should result when managers work with individuals and groups to achieve high productivity.

This concept of personal satisfaction is reflected in the **quality of working life, (QWL)** a term that has gained deserving prominence as an indicator of the overall quality of human experiences in the workplace.[14] The QWL concept expresses an important respect for people in their work environments. Just as machines that are poorly maintained break down and eventually wear out altogether, so too do the human resources suffer from neglect and adverse working conditions. Over the long term, the human resources of organizations must be well maintained if their continued performance contributions are to be ensured. Managers are increasingly expected, and rightfully so, to facilitate productivity for the organization while maintaining the quality of working life for its members.

The potential benefits of this approach are illustrated[15]

at General Electric where jobs in one plant were redesigned to give workers the opportunity to set their own production schedules. They set them 50 percent higher than the ones previously set by management.

at Ford where assembly workers at one overseas plant were switched into one job classification and allowed to do their own quality control—even to the point of stopping the assembly line when necessary. They achieved a substantially lower defect rate in the first year of operations.

at Aetna Life where jobs were redesigned into 12-person teams that plan their own workflow, work schedules, and staffing needs. The teams now handle all claims functions previously done in several different departments.

This expanded view of productivity is a consistent theme throughout the book. We will address many managerial innovations designed to improve both productivity and the quality of working life. These include such practices as job enrichment, autonomous work groups, alternative work schedules, quality control circles, and profit-sharing pay plans, among many others. As you read on, keep in mind that a high quality of working life is one that offers the individual such things as

- Adequate and fair pay for a job well done.
- Safe and healthy working conditions.
- Opportunity to learn and use new skills.
- Room to grow and progress in a career.
- Social integration into the organization.
- Protection of individual rights.

- A balance of work and nonwork demands.
- Pride in the work itself and the organization.

THE MANAGEMENT PROCESS

If productivity is the ultimate measure of managerial success, the management process is the means employed to achieve it. In this respect, "management" is something managers do in their quest for productivity. Accordingly, the **management process** is defined as the process of planning, organizing, leading, and controlling the utilization of resources to accomplish the organization's purpose. Success in implementing the management process requires a capability to make decisions, solve problems, and take action to use resources effectively and efficiently.

This book is devoted to the study of management as a body of knowledge that offers insight into this process. Thus **management** is also a field of academic inquiry based on scientific foundations and that is an important action foundation for any manager.

Four Functions of Management

Planning, organizing, leading, and controlling are the four basic **management functions.** Although Parts 2, 3, 4, and 5 of this book are devoted to each of these functions respectively, consider for the moment their basic definitions with examples from a new product development effort set in a computer firm.

Planning Determining what is to be achieved, setting goals, and identifying appropriate action steps. Planning centers on determining goals and the means to achieve them.

> *Example* The company president anticipates a technological breakthrough in microcomputers. He determines that a new version of the current product line needs to be developed within two years.

Organizing Allocating and arranging human and material resources in appropriate combinations to implement plans. Organizing turns plans into action potential by defining tasks, assigning personnel, and supporting them with resources.

> *Example* A special task force on new product development is established. People are assigned, meeting facilities made available, and necessary technical support established. The designated task force head will report directly to the president.

Leading Guiding the work efforts of other people in directions appropriate to action plans. Leading involves building commitments and encouraging work efforts that support goal attainment.

> *Example* At the first task-force meeting the president clarifies the need for a new computer, helps the group to establish a reasonable timetable for action, and identifies the rewards that can be expected from goal accomplishment.

Controlling Monitoring performance, comparing results to goals, and taking corrective action. Controlling is a process of gathering and interpreting performance feedback as a basis for constructive action and change.

> *Example* The president stays in touch with the task force to monitor its progress over time; a special meeting is called to discuss problems when it appears the timetable may be slipping; appropriate adjustments in the timetable and task-force activities are made.

Another way to describe the four functions of management is as a series of task-related decisions made by managers. These decisions are:

- *Planning* Deciding what work is to be done.
- *Organizing* Deciding how the work is to be done and who is to do it.
- *Leading* Deciding how to make sure the work gets done.
- *Controlling* Deciding if the work is or is not getting done, and what to do if it isn't.

Management Functions at Different Managerial Levels

Responsibility for the four management functions rests with all managers working in all types of organizations. Research does indicate, however, that

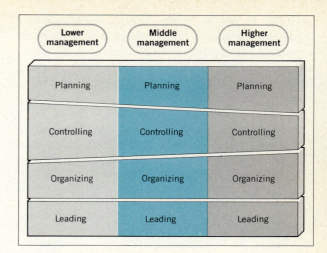

FIGURE 1.9 *Relative time spent on the management functions at each managerial level.*

the relative emphasis on each function varies across managerial levels.[16] As shown in Figure 1.9, time allocated to planning and organizing tends to increase at higher management levels; time spent on controlling is proportionately greater at lower management levels; time spent on leading is relatively similar at each management level.

In summary, managers implement the four management functions in the process of utilizing resources to support the organization's purpose. As we look further into the nature of managerial work, remember that planning, organizing, leading, and controlling are basic activities through which managers achieve productivity.

THE NATURE OF MANAGERIAL WORK

The likelihood is that your career will sooner or later include the responsibility of being a manager. Have you ever thought seriously about what this means? That is, have you specifically considered what managers actually do on a day-to-day basis, and then considered the implications in terms of the required personal skills and competencies?[17]

A Day in the Life of a Manager

Henry Mintzberg is a management researcher who has thought seriously about what a manager does each day. In fact, his book, *The Nature of Managerial Work,* has become a classic in the field. The book reports his in-depth examination of the daily activities of corporate chief executives. One interesting excerpt from his observations regarding an executive's workday follows.[18]

> There was no break in the pace of activity during office hours. The mail (average of 36 pieces per day), telephone calls (average of five per day), and meetings (average of eight) accounted for almost every minute from the moment these executives entered their offices in the morning until they departed in the evenings. A true break seldom occurred. Coffee was taken during meetings, and lunchtime was almost always devoted to formal or informal meetings. When free time appeared, ever-present subordinates quickly usurped it. If these managers wished to have a change of pace, they had two means at their disposal—the observational tour and the light discussions that generally preceded scheduled meetings. But these were not regularly scheduled breaks, and they were seldom totally unrelated to the issue at hand: managing the organization.

> . . . As a result, the manager is a person with a perpetual preoccupation. The manager can never be free to forget the job, and never has the pleasure of knowing, even temporarily, that there is nothing else to do. No matter what kind of managerial job, managers always carry the nagging suspicion that they might be able to contribute just a little bit more. Hence they assume an unrelenting pace in their work.

Clearly, a manager's job in any organizational setting will be busy and demanding. You should read and think about the prior description of executive work as it relates to your personal goals and aspirations. It no doubt reflects some of the reasons there is increasing concern for "job stress" and "job burnout" in managerial ranks. These topics will be discussed in more detail in later chapters. For now, though, recognize that to be a manager means to face considerable pressure. This book contains many insights that should help you to handle this pressure successfully and to achieve satisfaction in your work.

Overall, daily managerial work is well characterized as involving:[19]

1. *Long hours* A workweek of at least 50 hours is typical, and up to 90 hours is not unheard of. Length of workweek tends to increase as one advances to higher managerial levels.

2. *Intense activity* The busy day of a manager includes many (even hundreds of) separate incidents. The number of such incidents is usually greater at lower management levels.

3. *Fragmentation and variation* Interruptions are frequent in managerial work. Tasks are completed quickly and involve many different types of activities.

4. *Many media* Managers rely on many communication media. The use of media includes telephone conversations, in-person conversations during scheduled and unscheduled meetings, as well as reading and writing memos, letters, and reports.

5. *Interpersonal contacts* Interaction with other people consumes the majority of a manager's day. Little time is spent working alone; most time is spent in contact with subordinates, peers, superiors, and other persons inside and outside of the organization.

Managerial Roles

Other research findings shed additional light on the nature of managerial work. Henry Mintzberg, whose study of chief executives has served as a landmark in studies of managerial behavior, views managerial work as characterized by:[20]

1. *Interpersonal relationships* Most of a manager's time is spent interacting through oral and written communications with persons inside and outside of the work unit.

2. *Information processing* A major part of any manager's job is information processing, that is, giving, receiving and analyzing information.

3. *Decision making* Managers ultimately use information to make decisions that solve problems and/or take advantage of opportunities.

Mintzberg associates these characteristics with a set of 10 action roles that managers must be prepared to play. As described in Table 1.2, each role falls into one of the three categories just listed and derives from the formal authority underlying a manager's position in the organization. Essentially, a manager's formal authority creates interpersonal roles, informational roles, and decisional roles.

Each of these roles represents a set of behaviors

TABLE 1.2 *The Ten Managerial Roles Identified by Henry Mintzberg*

Role	Description	Example
Interpersonal Roles		
Figurehead	Symbolic head; performs routine duties of a legal or social nature	Greeting visitors; signing legal documents
Leader	Responsible for motivation of subordinates and for staffing and training	Most activities involving subordinates
Liaison	Maintains network of outside contacts	Processing mail; making phone calls; going to meetings
Informational Roles		
Monitor	Seeks and receives information to understand organization and environment	Processing mail; maintaining personal contacts; reading periodicals and reports
Disseminator	Transmits information to other organization members	Forwarding reports and memos; making phone calls; holding meetings
Spokesperson	Transmits information to outsiders	Forwarding reports and memos; making phone calls; holding meetings
Decisional Roles		
Entrepreneur	Initiates organizational improvement projects	Holding strategy sessions; identifying new responsibilities and new product ideas
Disturbance handler	Responsible for corrective action when organization faces unexpected crises	Resolving subordinate conflicts; adjusting to environmental crises
Resource allocator	Responsible for allocation of human and other resources	Scheduling; budgeting; giving rewards
Negotiator	Responsible for representing the organization in negotiations	Negotiating union contracts; making sales

Source: Abridged and adapted from pp. 92–93 in *The Nature of Managerial Work* by Henry Mintzberg. Copyright © 1973 by Henry Mintzberg. Adapted by permission of Harper & Row, Publishers, Inc.

and activities which you should be prepared to perform as a manager. Recent findings, however, indicate that managers at all hierarchical levels perform similar roles but with a different emphasis.[21] The roles of disseminator, figurehead, negotiator, liaison, and spokesperson, for example, appear more important for higher-level management than lower-level ones. In addition, the type of job a manager holds may also influence the relative importance of various roles. As might be expected, managers working in sales seem to emphasize the interpersonal roles while those working in accounting and finance emphasize the informational ones.

Managerial Agendas and Networks

Another useful approach to managerial work is found in John Kotter's observational studies of general managers. You should recall that a general manager is someone who has responsibility for multiple activities and components within an organization. In his book *The General Managers,* Kotter refers to this as among the most intellectually and interpersonally demanding of all management jobs. He identifies these two critical activities as fundamental to a general manager's success in mastering daily challenges.[22]

1. *Agenda setting* Effective general managers figure out what to do despite uncertainty, great diversity, and an enormous amount of potentially relevant information. They develop agendas for their jobs that include goals and plans spanning long and short time frames. These agendas are usually incomplete and loosely connected in the beginning, but become more specific as the manager utilizes information continually gleaned from many different sources.

2. *Networking* Effective general managers get things done through a large and diverse set of people despite having little direct control over most of them. They devote considerable time and effort to developing relationships among the people whose cooperation is needed to satisfy their emerging agendas. These networks become important resources for both implementing and updating the agendas over time.

In all daily events and activities, therefore, managers must be continually alert to opportunities for advancing their agendas through interpersonal relationships with other persons. Consider this short example of effective behavior by a general manager (GM).[23]

> On his way to a meeting, a GM bumped into a staff member who did not report to him. Using this opportunity, in a two-minute conversation he: (a) asked two questions and received the information he needed; (b) reinforced their good relationship by sincerely complimenting the staff member on something he had recently done; and (c) got the staff member to agree to do something that the GM needed done.

Figure 1.10 portrays the complexity of the interpersonal networks or "trade-routes" in which general managers can engage to fulfill their task responsibilities. You can see why the interpersonal side of management gets so much attention from scholars and consultants alike. This is particularly true since many of the relationships in the figure must be maintained without the manager having formal authority over the other persons.

MANAGERIAL SKILLS AND COMPETENCIES

A **skill** is an ability to translate knowledge into action that results in the desired performance. Truly important skills for managers are those that help them to help others become productive in their work. The field of management offers a knowledge base for the initial development of these managerial skills.

The Essential Skills

Robert L. Katz classified the essential skills of managers into three categories—technical, human, and conceptual.[24] **A technical skill** is an ability to use a special proficiency or expertise relating to a method, process, or procedure. Accountants, engineers, market researchers, and computer scientists for example, possess technical skills acquired through formal education. Most jobs have technical skill components. Some require preparatory education (e.g., the staff accountant), while others allow skills to be learned through appropriate training and job experience (e.g., a technical salesperson).

Human skill is the ability to work well in cooperation with other persons. It emerges as a spirit of trust, enthusiasm, and genuine involvement in interpersonal relationships. A person with good human skills will have a high degree of self-awareness and a capacity to understand or empathize with the feelings of others. Given the highly interpersonal nature of managerial work, human skills are critical for all managers.

All good managers ultimately have the ability to view the organization or situation as a whole and solve problems to the benefit of everyone concerned. This is a **conceptual skill** that draws heavily on one's analytical and diagnostic capacities to identify problems and opportunities, gather and interpret relevant information, and make good problem-solving decisions that serve the organization's purpose. It involves the ability to break problems down into smaller parts, to see the relations among the parts, and to recognize the implications of any one problem for others. Such a capacity for *multidimensional thinking* is increasingly recognized as important to managerial success.[25]

Although all three skills are essential for all managers, their relative importance tends to vary across levels. Figure 1.11 shows that technical skills are somewhat more important at lower management levels where supervisors are dealing with concrete problems. Broader and more ambiguous problems along with longer-term decisions dominate the

4. Communication skills

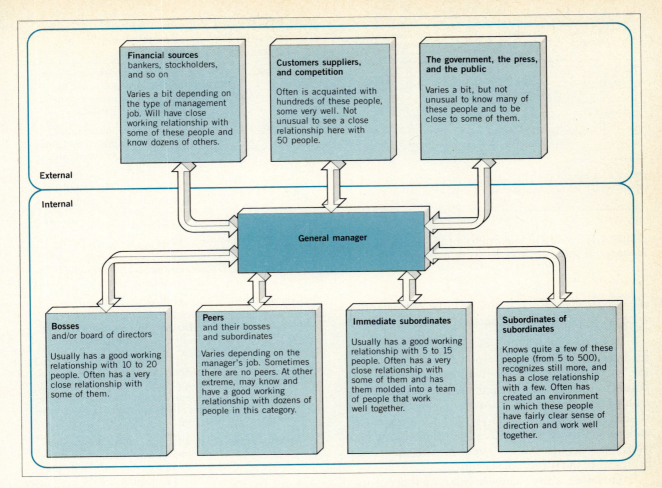

FIGURE 1.10 *A typical interpersonal network maintained by a general manager.*

manager's concerns at higher levels, where conceptual skills gain in relative importance. As the figure shows, human skills remain fairly consistent in their importance across the managerial levels.

Developing Managerial Competencies

Management educators are now trying to identify the broad set of competencies needed to achieve success in management. A **managerial competency,** is a skill or personal characteristic that contributes to high performance in a management job.[26] Table 1.3 reviews a number of competencies that are being highlighted for their relevance to managerial effectiveness. Some other personal characteristics worth considering are:[27]

- *Resistance to stress* The ability to accomplish work even under stressful conditions.
- *Tolerance for uncertainty* The ability to accomplish work in uncertain or unstructured situations.
- *Social objectivity* The ability to act free of racial, ethnic, gender, and other prejudices or biases.
- *Inner work standards* The ability and desire to set high performance standards and always do a good job.
- *Stamina and adaptability* The ability to sustain long work hours and the flexibility to adapt to changes.

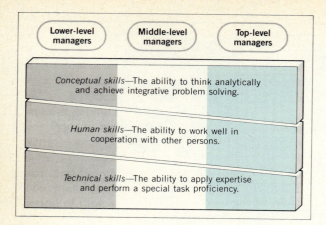

FIGURE 1.11 *Relative importance of the essential managerial skills at three levels of management.*

■ *Self-confidence* The ability to be consistently decisive and display one's personal presence.

Now is a good time to assess your current readiness for managerial responsibilities. You can use Table 1.3 and the above listing as initial checkpoints to review your strengths and weaknesses on managerial competencies. At the same time, you should be asking just what you can do to develop and refine these competencies over time as foundations for long-run career success. This question brings us to the subject of learning.

Learning is any change in behavior that occurs as a result of experience. In effect, learning is also a skill—one that reflects your capability to take advantage of work and other experiences, and to grow and develop personally as a result.

Perhaps the most critical part of your learning about management will, in the long run, come from "learning by doing"—that is, continuing to learn about managing while you are working. To begin this requires a willingness to always think actively about what is happening, try and explain why things are happening the way they are, and examine alternative responses with the potential to improve things in the future. In addition, many organizations offer a variety of formal management training and career development programs for their employees. Participating seriously in them is another important opportunity for continuing your education and mastering the necessary managerial skills and competencies. For example,[28]

TABLE 1.3 *Selected Skills and Personal Characteristics Considered Highly Valuable to Managers*

Planning and organizing	The ability to establish a course of action, to achieve goals, and to allocate resources and personnel to accomplish necessary tasks.
Leadership	The ability to use interpersonal relationships to stimulate and guide people toward the accomplishment of important tasks.
Delegation and control	The ability to define tasks and assign work to others, and to monitor performance to ensure task accomplishment.
Information gathering	The ability to analyze problems, to identify key issues, interpret and integrate themes, and search for relevant information.
Decision making	The ability to use logic and information to choose among alternative courses, and to commit oneself to a resulting course of action.
Written and oral communication	The ability to express one's ideas or viewpoints in writing, to make oral presentations, and to communicate with others both individually and in groups.
Self-objectivity	The ability to realistically evaluate personal strengths and weaknesses, and to understand one's skills and motives in relation to a job.

Source: Developed from the American Assembly of Collegiate Schools of Business, *Outcome Measurement Project*, Phase II and Phase III Reports (St. Louis: AACSB, 1986 & 1987).

at Mobile Corporation the career development emphasis is on nurturing the growth of "multitalented" managers who have more than technical skills. Corporate research has identified that Mobil's *best* managers are good communicators who listen, encourage initiative and risk taking by others, and help them feel empowered by giving them the authority needed to do what needs to be done. The company trys to develop such capabilities among all levels of management by offering a world-wide program of workshops and seminars on these and related topics. The expected benefits extend to the managers involved, the people who work for them, and the firm as a whole.

THE STUDY OF MANAGEMENT

With the prior points in mind, let's overview the way *Management for Productivity,* Third Edition, is organized for you as a learning instrument. The book contains seven major parts. Part 1 introduces the field of management and its significance to the practicing manager. It consists of the present chapter plus two others—"Historical Perspectives on Management" (Chapter 2) and "Managerial Decision Making and Problem Solving" (Chapter 3).

The next four parts cover each of the managerial functions: Part 2, Planning for Productivity; Part 3, Organizing for Productivity; Part 4, Leading for Productivity; and Part 5, Controlling for Productivity. Note that each of the part titles includes "productivity" as the ultimate focus of a manager's efforts. The individual chapters are written, accordingly, to help you develop an action capability with each function. Although you will study theories and concepts throughout, the emphasis of every chapter will include applications toward real managerial problems.

Part 6, Productivity in the Contemporary Environment, introduces the dynamic setting within which managerial decision making and problem solving occurs in today's world. Separate chapters in this part of the book introduce you to the challenges of implementing the management functions in respect to innovation, change and conflict (Chapter 17), labor management relations (Chapter 18), the international arena (Chapter 19), and managerial ethics and social responsibility (Chapter 20).

When the book concludes in Part 7 with Chapter 21, titled "Management for Productivity: A Career Perspective," these various components of management should be clear in your mind. By that time also, you will have learned many things to help you achieve success in those phases of your career that entail managerial responsibilities. A special Management Applications Module at the end of the book allow you to pursue in further depth a number of quantitative decision techniques.

Summary

A manager is a person in an organization who is responsible for the work performance of one or more other persons. An organization is a collection of people working together in a division of labor to achieve a common purpose. Managers are the very heart of organizations; they are the "glue" that

FIGURE 1.12 *A comprehensive view of "management for productivity."*

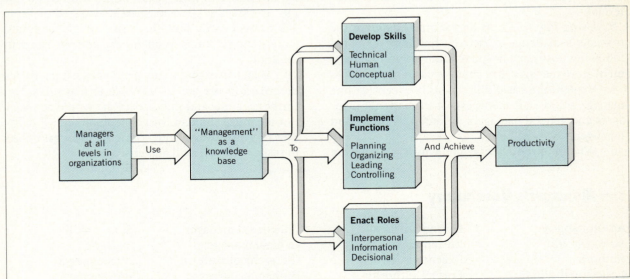

holds the components of organizations together. Through the efforts of managers, organizations fulfill their purposes by producing useful goals and services. Every manager's goal is to ensure high performance in that part of the organization for which he or she is responsible. A manager's basic challenge, therefore, is to fulfill this performance accountability while depending on subordinates to do the required work.

Figure 1.12 summarizes the central theme of Chapter 1. Managers at all levels in organizations draw on "management" as a knowledge base to develop the essential skills (technical, human, conceptual) that allow them to successfully implement the management functions (planning, organizing, leading, and controlling) while fulfilling various roles (interpersonal, informational, and decisional). The desired end result is high productivity for indi-viduals, groups, and the organization as a whole. Productivity, in turn, is a measure of the quality and quantity of work performance with resource utilization considered.

As we move further into the study of management, remember that the goal of this book is to help you
- Understand the essence of managerial work.
- Learn a basic vocabulary shared and used by managers.
- Establish proper knowledge foundations for developing the essential managerial skills and competencies.
- Become familiar with each of the four basic management functions.
- Anticipate some of the major challenges faced by managers who must fulfill their responsibilities in today's dynamic environment.

Thinking Through the Issues

1. What is a manager? What is an organization? Why do organizations need managers?
2. Diagram each of the following organizations as open systems according to Figure 1.3: a local hospital, a department store, the fire department, a franchise restaurant.
3. Explain the distinction between top-level, middle-level, and first-level managers. What are some job titles common to each level? In what basic ways does managerial work differ among these three levels?
5. Using Figure 1.6 as an example, diagram the manager's challenge for persons holding each of the following positions: hospital administrator, department store manager, fire chief, restaurant owner.
4. Explain the basic differences between (a) line managers and staff managers, (b) functional managers and general managers, (c) administrators and managers.
6. What is "productivity" and why is it a criterion of managerial success? How does productivity relate to the concepts of performance effectiveness and performance efficiency?
7. What does the term "quality of working life" mean? Is it consistent with the concept of productivity? Explain your answer using examples where appropriate.
8. List and define the four management functions. Give examples of how they would be used by two of the persons listed in question 5.
9. Review the 10 managerial roles listed in Table 1.2. Show exactly how these roles might be found among the activities of one of the persons listed in question 5.
10. Select five skills and personal characteristics described in the text as valuable to managers. Describe each one and indicate if Katz would consider it a technical, human, or conceptual skill. Finally, how do you evaluate your strengths and weaknesses in respect to each skill and characteristic?

The Manager's Vocabulary

Accountability	Division of labor	Functional manager	Human skill
Administrator	Entrepreneur	General manager	Learning
Authority	Executive	Hierarchy of authority	Line manager
Conceptual skill	Formal authority	Human resources	Management

Management functions
Management process
Manager
Manager's challenge
Managerial competency

Material resources
Open system
Organization
Performance
  effectiveness

Performance efficiency
Productivity
Purpose of an
  organization
Quality of working life

Skill
Staff manager
Technical skill
Work

STEPHEN SHAW'S INTERVIEW

This really happened.

Stephen Shaw was elated when he read the letter inviting him for an on-site visit with the company that was his top choice for full-time employment after graduation. A college senior, he had interviewed with company representatives on campus just a few weeks earlier. The letter, signed by the Senior Employment & Staffing Representative, read in part:

Dear Stephen:
We would like you to gain additional information about the [company name] Management Training Program and allow us an opportunity to further review your abilities and interests. A visit has been scheduled for Wednesday . . . Once you have checked into the hotel, please report to the hospitality suite by 2:00 pm. After a brief meeting we'll take a tour of the city. Dinner will follow, offering you an opportunity to mingle informally with members of the employment staff, some current management trainees, and senior company management . . . Thursday will consist of a series of interviews, activities, and information sessions . . . If you have any questions, please contact me . . . We at [company name] look forward to sharing information about our Company, our City, and our mutual career interests . . . Sincerely.

Stephen prepared for the visit by reviewing notes from his on-campus interview, reading all the company literature he could find, and thinking about the Management Training Program as it had been described to him. He was impressed by this statement in one brochure: "Our Management Training Program has been designed to nurture the talent of high potential people, providing concentrated experiences that assist them to become effective middle/upper level managers."

On the appointed day, Stephen arrived to find himself part of a group of six candidates who had been invited to interview at the same time for openings in the training program. The afternoon and evening group sessions with company representatives were informative. Everyone was friendly and helpful.

When the evening ended, about 9:00 pm, the Employment Representative took Stephen aside and handed him a paper with three problems written on it. "Think about them," she said, "and be prepared to discuss your responses during tomorrow's interviews. I'll pick you up at 7:00 am and we'll have breakfast together. Goodnight."

These were the problems Stephen Shaw had to respond to the next day.
A) You are a supervisor. In front of a number of other people, you ask an employee to do something. The employee refuses. *What do you do?*
B) It is Friday. You are asked by your supervisor to submit a report by next Monday. You feel there is not enough time to include the detail necessary for a good report. No extension can be granted. *What do you do?*
C) You have a subordinate who has a lot of seniority. He is at a point where you can't promote him or increase his salary. But you feel the need to bring his performance back up to par. *What do you do?*

Questions
1.   How would you respond to each of the problems posed to Stephen by the company recruiter? How would you justify these responses from a managerial perspective?

Case Application

THROUGH THE LOOKING GLASS

The Center for Creative Leadership runs a simulation called Looking Glass, Inc. It is designed to reflect the demanding, fast-paced, and complex nature of managerial work. Many organizations send people to the center to participate in the simulation and develop their managerial skills and competencies. This is the report of one participant who was given the role of Plant Manager, Commercial Glass Division, in the simulation.[29]

I got to my desk at Looking Glass on Monday morning. It was 8:00, fully one hour before the day would begin and the switchboard would open. The morning mail had yet to be delivered. Still, my in-basket was already overloaded with memos. I began to read quickly, voraciously, knowing these few moments were precious. Once the day actually began, interruption would follow interruption. The incessant ringing of the phone and the inevitable meetings would preclude reflection and concentrated reading.

As usual, my in-basket was a potpourri of problems and issues that required my attention. Some were serious—a possible shortage of soda ash, an ingredient critical to my glass manufacturing operation; a letter from the EPA threatening to shut down my plant if the emissions from the stacks could not be cleaned up; other problems with equipment and personnel. There were also the seemingly less consequential issues—the invitation to a brunch at the V.P.'s home; the request from the local Rotary Club for a speaker at their next meeting, which had been routed to me by my boss, the Director of Manufacturing for the Commercial Glass Division. Since I am ambitious and eager to get ahead, I knew that my responses to these invitations were almost as important to my career as my decisions on the soda ash and emission problems.

I was beginning to feel a little less overwhelmed by 8:45. I had at least glanced at all the memos. I had begun to establish priorities and to think about how to attack the most pressing problems. Then the quiet ended.

I heard the voices of my boss and the other Plant Manager in Commercial Glass. The voices grew louder as they came down the hall. "Damnit," I thought, as I realized they were discussing the possible conversion of Mike's plant to a new float process of making glass, "it's just like Mike to get in his bid for capital at the end of a conversation about next week's golf game." I had to do something. If he got the dollars to convert to the float process, I wouldn't get the money I needed to replace my decrepit smelter. Without a new smelter there was no way to increase my production figures and reduce the number of light bulb shipments coming back because the glass casings were too thick.

I decided to get a cup of coffee and get into the conversation.

"Just the person I wanted to see," my boss said to me as I approached the coffee machine. "We're having a division meeting at 9:30. I'll want to discuss union, EPA, sales figures for the quarter, and the production problems in your plant."

I groaned inwardly. Another meeting, and I really needed to get on the soda ash thing. I smiled, "Of course, Bill." He started back to his office with Mike in tow. I had missed a chance to bring up the smelter issue. Maybe at the next meeting.

I poured coffee, thinking that perhaps I could get the soda ash question resolved—or at least delegated—by the time for the meeting. My stomach began the familiar tightening. Sales figures, I thought anxiously. They were pretty grim last quarter. Of course, if you're running at 105 percent of capacity, how are you going to sell more? I knew this was a bottom-line oriented company. And the bottom-line sales figures on the flat glass products we were producing had been at bottom for some time. . . .

I looked at my watch: 9:05. I mumbled an excuse and walked away from the kaffeeklatsch. Rude maybe, but I wasn't prepared for the 9:30 meeting, and the soda ash question and all the other in-basket problems still needed to be resolved. I got on the phone and called my purchasing man. Yes, he knew about the impending soda ash problem. What did I want him to do? I resisted the urge to tell him irritably that I was paying *him* to be on top of these things and to give *me* suggestions. He was new in the job, and although I prefer to manage people who need virtually no training or supervision, you sometimes have to suit your management style to the situation. I explained what I felt should be done: assess our reserves; contact all suppliers about supply over the next six months; contact all other Looking Glass plants to learn about corporate-wide stores of soda ash and determine whether we could share supplies.

9:20. The meeting was 10 minutes away and I wasn't prepared. But the phone was ringing insistently and my secretary was away. . . . I grabbed my notes and memos and dashed to the meeting, my phone jangling behind me.

The meeting seemed interminable. Lots of talk. Not many decisions. My mind kept wandering back to the soda ash problem, the emission problem, the smelter problem. Then we were talking about sales. I winced when my plant's dismal record was paraded. There were good reasons why we couldn't sell more, although it would take too long to explain them. Fighting back my frustration, I promised to do better.

Then came the issue of capital allocation. Mike made his presentation first, but I was ready when he finished. I had spent time rehearsing my pitch. I articulated my needs; a new smelter and a new line to feed it. With the new line I could increase production and supply new products. The new line would also help reduce energy consumption and emissions. After I finished, Cheryl, Manager of R&D, made her presentation, asking for money to explore a new Japanese glassmaking process. In light of my immediate needs, it was hard for me to think corporately. I wanted the resources for my plant. I couldn't really look at the long-term impact of a new process.

We left the meeting with decisions on the union problems and a game plan to ward off the EPA threat. There was no action on capital allocation. Still, it was a better-than-average meeting.

I returned to my desk. There were four phone messages and five more memos. The phone rang. A plant manager in the Advanced Products Division was requesting a meeting at 1:00 to discuss tactics for a performance appraisal task force we'd been appointed to. Since I was supposed to chair the committee, I agreed reluctantly to a meeting over lunch. . . .

Fatigued with the pressures, I pushed aside the bigger problems, hoping to get a sense of accomplishment by dealing with some smaller ones. I dashed off memos saying "yes" to the brunch and the Rotary Club appearance, approved a raise for my Plant Engineer, and dictated a note to legal about the EPA predicament.

Then I concentrated on my notes for the luncheon meeting. I made two calls to get information. One source couldn't give me what I needed, and the other's line was busy.

Before I was ready, it was time to meet and eat. My stomach had registered the full shock of a frenetic, demanding, often frustrating Monday morning in the Looking Glass. Maybe for lunch I'd have a large bowl of lettuce.

Questions

1. What is the "manager's challenge" as faced by the plant manager in this case? In what specific ways is "productivity" an important issue for her?
2. Is the plant manager fulfilling all responsibilities in the management process—that is, planning, organizing, leading and controlling? Why or why not?
3. To what extent is the plant manager doing a good job of a) enacting the interpersonal, decisional and informational roles described by Henry Mintzberg . . . and b) setting agendas and networking as described by John Kotter? Justify your analysis using facts in the case.
4. Overall, how would you assess the performance of the plant manager in this case? What are her apparent strengths and weaknesses in terms of technical, human and conceptual skills? Which skills and competencies seem to need further development to enhance her managerial performance and career potential? Explain and justify your answers.

Class Exercise: What Managers Do

Managers maintain a complex set of relationships with other persons in the work setting. These interpersonal relationships involve, at a minimum, contacts with subordinates, peers elsewhere in the organization, and superiors. They may also include contacts with outsiders such as clients and resource suppliers.

1. Think about the questions that follow. Record your answers in the spaces provided.

    a. What percent of a typical manager's time in interpersonal relationships would be spent with her or his

_____ subordinates?

_____ boss?

_____ peers and outsiders?

100 percent = total time

    b. How many hours do managers work per week?

    c. What percent of a manager's time is spent in the following activities?

_____ scheduled meetings?

_____ unscheduled meetings?

_____ desk work?

_____ telephone calls?

_____ walking around the organization?

100 percent = total time

2. Talk over your responses with a nearby classmate. Explore similarities and differences in your answers. Try to understand each other's reasoning.

3. Be prepared to participate in class discussion led by your instructor.

References

[1] *Work in America: Report of a Special Task Force to the Secretary of Health, Education and Welfare* (Cambridge: MIT Press, 1973), p. 3.

[2] Peter F. Drucker, *The Changing World of the Executive* (New York: T. T. Times Books, 1982), p. xi. See also Peter F. Drucker, "Management: The Problems of Success," *Academy of Management Executive,* Vol. 1 (1987), pp. 13–20.

[3] Henry Mintzberg, "The Manager's Job: Folklore and Fact" *Harvard Business Review,* Vol. 53 (July–August 1975), p. 61.

[4] For a history of Apple Computer, Inc. see Michael Moritz, *The Little Kingdom* (New York: Morrow, 1984). For reports on the restructuring of Apple's top management see Bro Uttal, "After the Fall," *Fortune* (August 5, 1985), pp. 20–24 and, John Sculley, *Odyssey: Pepsi to Apple* (New York: Harper & Row, 1987).

[5] For a discussion of the research issues see James L. Perry and Hal G. Rainey, "The Public-Private Distinction in Organization Theory: A Critique and Research Strategy," *Academy of Management Review,* Vol. 13 (1988), pp. 182–201.

[6] Drucker, op. cit.

[7] Information from *AT&T Annual Report 1987.*

[8] Reported in the *Harvard Business Review,* Vol. 66 (May–June 1988), p. 178.

[9] Reported in John McCormick and Bill Powell, "Management for the 1990s," *Business Week* (April 25, 1988), pp. 47–48.

[10] See Eli Ginzberg (ed./Executive Talent (New York: Wiley, 1988) p. 2.

[11] Reported in the *Harvard Business Review,* Vol. 66 (May–June 1988), p. 178.

[12] For a perspective on the first-level manager's job see Steven Kerr, Kenneth D. Hill, and Laurie Broedling, "The First-Level Supervisor: Phasing Out or Here to Stay?" *Academy of Management Review,* Vol. 11(1986), pp. 103–117; and Leonard A. Schlesinger and Janice A. Klein, "The First-Line Supervisor: Past, Present and Future," pp. 370–382 in Jay W. Lorsch (ed.), *Handbook of Organizational Behavior* (Englewood Cliffs, N.J.: Prentice-Hall, 1987).

[13] Examples reported in "Business Day," *The New York Times* (December 29, 1987), pp. D1, D5; and, "The Productivity Paradox," *Business Week* (June 6, 1988), pp. 100–114.

[14] See David A. Nadler and Edward E. Lawler III, "Quality of Work Life: Perspectives and Directions," *Organizational Dynamics,* Vol. 11 (1983), pp. 22–36.

[15] Information from John J. Sherwood, "Creating Work Cultures with Competitive Advantage," *Organizational Dynamics,* Vol. 16 (1988), pp. 5–26.

[16] Thomas A. Mahoney, Thomas H. Jerdee, and Stephen J. Carroll, "The Job(s) of Management," *Industrial Rela*

tions, Vol. 4 (February 1965), pp. 97–110. For a related study see Luis Gomez-Mejia, Joseph McCann, and Ronald C. Page, "The Structure of Managerial Behaviors and Rewards," *Industrial Relations,* vol. 24 (1985), pp. 147–154.

[17]For a review and update on research into what managers "really" do see Fred Luthans, "Successful vs. Effective Real Managers," *Academy of Management Executive,* Vol. II (1988), pp. 127–132.

[18]Abridged and adapted from p. 30 in *The Nature of Managerial Work* by Henry Mintzberg. (New York: Harper & Row, 1973), p. 30. Copyright © 1973 by Henry Mintzberg. Reprinted by permission of Harper & Row, Publishers, Inc.

[19]Summarized from Morgan W. McCall, Jr., Ann M. Morrison, and Robert L. Hannan, *Studies of Managerial Work: Results and Methods,* Technical Report #9 (Greensboro, N.C.: Center for Creative Leadership, 1978) pp. 7–9. See also, John P. Kotter, "What Effective General Managers Really Do," *Harvard Business Review* Vol. 60 (November–December 1982a), pp. 156–167.

[20]Mintzberg (1973), op. cit., p. 46.

[21]Cynthia M. Pavett and Alan W. Lau, "Managerial Work: The Influence of Hierarchical Level and Functional Specialty," *Academy of Management Journal,* Vol. 26 (1983), pp. 170–177.

[22]See Kotter, op. cit., and also his book *The General Managers* (New York: The Free Press, 1982).

[23]Kotter, op. cit. (1982), p. 164.

[24]Robert L. Katz, "Skills of an Effective Administrator," *Harvard Business Review,* Vol. 52 (September–October 1974), p. 94.

[25]Daniel J. Isenberg, "How Senior Managers Think," *Harvard Business Review,* Vol. 62 ((November–December 1984), pp. 81–90.

[26]Richard E. Boyatzis, *The Competent Manager: A Model for Effective Performance* (New York: Wiley, 1982).

[27]This is a sample of additional factors from both the AACSB and American Management Association approaches. For more information see *Outcome Measurement Project,* Phase I and Phase II Reports (St. Louis: American Assembly of Collegiate Schools of Business, 1986 & 1987); and, Edward A. Powers, "Enhancing Managerial Competence: The American Management Association Competency Program," *Journal of Management Development,* Vol. 6 (1987), pp. 7–18.

[28]See Allen E. Murray, "Do You Have What it Takes to Succeed?" *Management Digest Quarterly,* Vol. 2 (1988).

[29]This case is from Diana Hawes, "Through the Looking Glass — A Manager in Action," reprinted by permission from *Across the Board* (New York: The Conference Board, Inc., October 1980), pp. 57–59.

Historical
Perspectives on
Management

A Lesson from 431 B.C.

If an idea is really good, it's likely to have a solid history. Take the concept of "corporate culture." The oration delivered by Pericles at the funeral of Athenian soldiers in 431 B.C. "is one of history's most powerful statements of the shared values and beliefs of an organization—its culture." At least so says John K. Clemens, coauthor of the recent book, *Classic Touch: Leadership Lessons from Homer to Hemingway.*

Pericles, the father of Athen's Golden Age, knew the power of a good idea in unifying and motivating people. He also understood a leader's responsibility to identify what is unique about an organization and then communicate these differences to its members. Facing the perils of war with Sparta, he used the occasion of the funeral speech to clearly define "corporate culture"—the Athenian state.

Among the specific things on Pericles' mind that day were:

Individual dignity and merit: ". . . When it is a question of putting one person before another in positions of public responsibility," he said, "what counts is not membership of a particular class, but the actual ability . . ."

Organizational uniqueness and innovation: Athens, he said, ". . . does not copy the institutions of our neighbors. It is more a case of our being a model to others than our imitating anyone else."

Commitment to the organization: "Here each individual is interested not only in his own affairs, but in the affairs of the state as well," he said.

Balance in work and nonwork activities: He reminded listeners that "when work is over we are in a position to enjoy all kinds of recreation for our spirits."

Pericles raised democracy to new heights in Athens and helped make it one of the strongest city–states of his time. He had his finger on "corporate culture" long before management theorists coined the term. But like many other historical events, the management lessons are quite durable—their implications transcend time. After all, just as Pericles had to, leaders of modern organizations must stand forth and communicate to all concerned what their organizations stand for and what gives them special meaning in the eyes of members and outsiders alike. We can only wonder how many can do the job as well. ■

Source: Information and quotations from John K. Clemens, "A Lesson from 431 B.C.," *Fortune* (October 13, 1986), pp. 161–162. See also John K. Clemens and Douglas Mayer, *Classic Touch: Leadership Lessons from Homer to Hemmingway* (New York: Dow Jones, 1987).

Today's managers benefit from the organized body of knowledge we call "management." It is a source of theories which offer insight and guidance for managerial thinking and action. A **theory** is a set of concepts and ideas that explains and predicts physical and social phenomena. A **management theory** explains and predicts the behavior of organizations and their members. Managers use management theories to make good decisions in their daily efforts to plan, organize, lead, and control for productivity.

Although Pericles—in the chapter opening example—didn't have access to the same body of knowledge we do today, his experience and wisdom still led him to develop a workable theory of management—one that apparently contributed to the "golden age" of Athens. Fortunately for us, people throughout history have thought systematically about management and organization practices. The result of their accumulated efforts is found in the pages of this book. To best understand the many ideas, insights, and concepts that follow, however, it is helpful to recognize the historical "roots" of current thinking. This chapter discusses several important historical perspectives on management, and introduces the modern approach which integrates them for direct application by present day managers.

PERSPECTIVES ON MANAGEMENT

J. Paul Getty was a successful businessman and also one of the richest men in the world. Some time ago

Getty was asked about his views on the "fine art of being the boss." He began with the following story.[1]

I had occasion to choose one person from a list of five candidates for promotion to a top executive position. Accompanying the mass of reports and documents concerning the five was a covering roster that listed them according to the length of their experience. The first on the list was far and away the most experienced, in the sense that he'd held executive positions nearly five years longer than his closest rival. Had I been content to use amount of experience as the sole yardstick, he would have been my choice.

According to legend, the Roman emperor Hadrian once found himself in an analogous position. One of his generals, the story goes, felt overdue for promotion. He took his case to the emperor and cited his long service as justification. "I am entitled to a more important command," he declared. "After all, I'm very experienced—I've been in ten battles."

Hadrian, a shrewd judge of men and their abilities, did not consider the man qualified for higher rank. He waved a casual hand at some army donkeys tethered nearby. "My dear general," Hadrian said dryly, "take a good look at those donkeys. Each of them has been in at least *twenty* battles—yet all of them are still donkeys."

Getty's point is that experience alone is not a good indicator of managerial ability. He further implies that formal education alone, such as reflected in a college degree, may not be a good predictor of eventual managerial success either. Getty states that management is something that "cannot be systematized, learned by rote nor practiced according to formula. It . . . is an art—even a creative art." Think about this statement. Is management an art? Or is it something more—perhaps a science as well?

Management as an Art

An **art** is something a person practices based on skills applied to achieve a desired result. We admire, for example, painters, writers, actors, and dancers. When good, they are "artists" in the true sense of the word. Can we say, as J. Paul Getty would, that the successful manager is every bit the "artist," too?

History is replete with examples of persons who achieved managerial success without formal training. J. Paul Getty was one of these people. Another is Katherine Graham, former owner of the *Washington Post.* She assumed leadership of the company after the untimely death of her husband, and after previously devoting herself to marriage and her family. At the time of her retirement years later, Graham's managerial successes were legendary. She lacked the benefit of formal training but had developed her managerial expertise to the point of excellence.

Persons like Katherine Graham take full advantage of any and all opportunities to learn through experience, something pointed out in Chapter 1 as an important commitment for you to make. In fact, all successful managers probably have a special abil-

ity to learn quickly from experience. They not only participate in events of the day, they look hard at the important situations, formulate personal theories to explain them, and use these theories when making decisions to take appropriate action. They arrive at the capacity to manage well through a combination of experience, practice, judgment and intuition. These are things we should all take advantage of to the extent of our capabilities. And, in this sense, we should be willing to accept the challenge of mastering the "art" of management.

Management as a Science

Good management, however, has sure and strong scientific foundations as well. A **science** is a body of knowledge systematically created via the scientific method. Table 2.1 lists the steps in the scientific method and shows how managers in one company applied them to solve a particular problem. The scientific approach to problem solving is further discussed in Chapter 3.

Science is an action foundation available to help each of us in our everyday lives. You study the sciences of mathematics, psychology, economics, and others to learn basic principles that help you to deal with events, decisions, and people. Management also has the characteristics of a science. It can

TABLE 2.1 *The Scientific Method Applied to Management: The Case of Improved Manufacturing Productivity*

Steps in Scientific Method	Case Application in Management
1. Observations are made regarding real-world events and occurrences.	*Example* Company officials become convinced that productivity in a manufacturing plant could be higher.
2. An explanation for the events and occurrences is formulated.	*Example* The officials agree that productivity improvement could result from increased worker involvement in quality control.
3. Statements are made that use the explanation to predict future events and occurrences.	*Example* Company officials and a team of researchers predict that holding periodic group meetings to discuss quality control will increase worker commitment to quality and that productivity gains will result.
4. Predictions are verified by an examination made under systematic and controlled conditions.	*Example* Two groups of workers are selected for study and their existing levels of productivity are measured. For three months one group holds meetings once a week to discuss quality; in the other, no such meetings are held. Productivity is measured again for both groups. The prediction that regular work-group meetings to discuss quality control will improve productivity is verified by the data.

be studied, learned, and then practiced with an increased probability of success.

The management discipline applies learning from other sciences to establish insights for managerial practice. Figure 2.1 shows several major roots of management as a scientific field of inquiry. These include the behavioral and social sciences, as well as engineering and mathematics. Generally, we can say that management as a science does the following.

1. *Provides managers with a way of thinking systematically about the behavior of people at work in organizational settings* Researchers use the scientific method to examine experiences and to establish cause–effect relationships among various work outcomes and the conditions that give rise to them. The field of management doesn't have all the answers. But, it does offer a logical approach that will help you solve real problems in your work situations.

2. *Provides managers with a "vocabulary" of terms and concepts that allow work experiences to be clearly analyzed, shared, and discussed* Although you may not like to learn new terms and their definitions, it is important to your managerial future. With concepts specified, managers can verbalize their impressions of work situations, share them with one another, and better understand their experiences. All organzied activities depend on a vocabulary. Sports are a good example. It is far easier to play and learn to play a game such as soccer when you can converse with other players about critical issues in a common vocabulary. Managers need to converse with one another for similar purposes. The field of management provides the vocabulary.

3. *Provides managers with "techniques" for dealing with many of the problems that commonly occur in the work setting* There is good theory behind the present state of management knowledge. The theories discussed in this book have been carefully selected for their practical applications. There is no "theory for theory's sake." Without an ability to turn "theory" into "practice," the study of management would not have much personal value. Keep this in mind and carefully consider the applications as we discuss them along the way.

Management as a Profession

There is continuing debate whether or not management is a "profession" and managers are "profes-

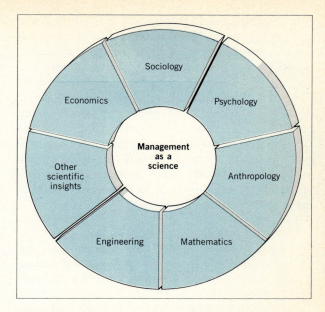

FIGURE 2.1 *Elements in the scientific roots of management as an academic discipline.*

sionals" in the true sense of these words. On the one hand, scholars believe that the traditional professions of medicine, law, accounting and the like share a number of characteristics which the management occupations, in general, do not possess. For example, the scholar Edgar Schein states that:[2]

■ There are no formal educational requirements for entry into management.

■ There is no system of accreditation or licensing for managers.

■ Managers do not have specific clients. They serve a broad group of organizational "stakeholders."

■ There is no clear code of managerial ethics that is universally enforced by peer review.

■ There is no common body of knowledge that is required understanding for someone to be a manager.

Yet, we can say that management is coming closer than ever before to satisfying these criteria. For example, as the science of management advances, the knowledge base is becoming clearer, more extensive, and better defined. The American Assembly of Collegiate Schools of Business (the AACSB) plays an important role in the accreditation of undergraduate and graduate curricula in business and management. The AACSB is also considering ways of measuring the degree to which academic programs actually help their students acquire the managerial skills and competencies described in Chapter 1. Finally, there is more and more attention being given to managerial ethics and related codes of conduct in management education and practice.

Thus, even though management may not be a true profession, it is an occupation with a very *professional character*. And as Peter Drucker reminds us, it will continue to be a career path of major social importance.[3]

> . . . management pertains to every single social institution. In the last hundred years every major social function — caring for the sick, education, and defense, for example — have become lodged in a large and *managed* organization. . . . Management has become the pervasive, the universal organ of modern society.

THE EVOLUTION OF MANAGEMENT THOUGHT

One of the delightful aspects of contemporary society is a reawakening of interest in our past. People everywhere are investigating their "roots" and trying to learn as much as possible about the experiences of their ancestors. Some people, myself included, feel that understanding our roots helps to understand better who we are at present. There is growing recognition of this point in respect to business history (see *Newsline 2.1*). More and more academic programs include business history among their courses of study, and individual firms are finding that corporate histories can be the source of valuable insights into problems and opportunities of the present.[4] The same logic can be applied to the body of knowledge we now refer to as management. To understand better what management is today, it is useful to identify its roots from the past.

Early Management Thinking

Table 2.2 presents several of the earliest sources of systematic management thinking.[5] The list begins with 5000 B.C. and the ancient Sumerian civilization. It includes the efforts of early Egyptians to construct the great pyramids, and the list goes on through the Babylonians, Romans, and Machiavelli to more familiar times.

The Industrial Revolution and Beyond

Perhaps the most significant transition in the evolution of management thought began during the

TABLE 2.2 *Early Examples in the Evolution of Management Thought*

Approximate Dates	Source	Major Contribution
5000 B.C.	Sumerians	Used written records to assist operation of governments and commerce
4000–2000 B.C.	Egyptians	Organized efforts of 100,000 people for constructing pyramids
2000–1700 B.C.	Babylonians	Code of Hammurabi set standards for wages, obligations of contracting parties, and penalties
300 B.C.–300 A.D.	Romans	Ran empire using effective communication and centralized control
1300	Venetians	Established legal framework for commerce
1500	Machiavelli	Developed guidelines for use of personal power
1776	Adam Smith	Used division of labor as a key to private enterprise
1800	Eli Whitney	Used interchangeability of parts as basis of mass production
19th century	Many	Employed various management techniques in the formation of productive large-scale corporate enterprises

STUDYING
BUSINESS HISTORY

Corporate archives—often dusty collections of memos, minutes, drawings, and other evidence of things past—are the subject of ongoing debate among managers and historians. Some scorn nostalgia and urge that such collections be tossed; others argue for regular maintenance and archiving of documents that may have much to teach contemporary managers. Says George Smith, president of Winthrop Group, which consults on corporate history: "You don't need archives for sentimental reasons, but because in business, turnover is swift and memory is short."

Businesses have traditionally used corporate histories to advance marketing campaigns; Wells Fargo, for example, has a history department whose archives are used for the bank's ads. But some companies have found another use

for their archives: as repositories of the wisdom—and folly—of previous managers, these collections can be helpful in a variety of planning efforts. One midwestern manufacturer hired Winthrop Group to document regularly the progress of an experimental project so that no valuable insights would be lost. And an Alcoa Corp. manager discovered, during the course of a study of the organization's history, that losses from a 60-year-old anti-trust suit were responsible for Alcoa's longstanding reluctance to pursue international business opportunities.

Corporate restructuring may threaten to bury company histories, and space shortages or inadequate maintenance have caused the demise of a number of collections. Yet advocates of corporate histories continue with their preservation efforts, in some cases shipping endangered materials to university basements. Winthrop Group has written ten full-length histories in six years, and business students are showing interest in the subject of business history—a sign that bodes well for those dust-covered boxes.

Source: As reported in Amanda Bennet, "For Those Who Write Business History, It Helps to Have the Skills of a Detective," *Wall Street Journal* (May 27, 1988), p. 15; Elizabeth M. Fowler, "Studying Business History," *New York Times* (July 14, 1987), p. D-5; Frederick Rose, "In Wake of Cost Cuts, Many Firms Sweep Their History Out the Door," *Wall Street Journal* (December 21, 1987), p. 21.

---

days of the industrial revolution. Picture the world of the 1700s. It was a time of social change when 13 colonies separated from England to become the United States of America. It was a time when the growth in population necessitated a tremendous leap forward in the manufacture of basic staples and consumer goods. It was also the time of industrial revolution, and when Adam Smith established the management principles we now know as specialization and the division of labor. These principles which revolutionized the world of work are clarified

in a timeless example, about the making of common pins, taken from Smith's treatise *Wealth of Nations*.[6]

> One man draws out the wire, another straights it, a third cuts it, a fourth points it, a fifth grinds it at the top for receiving a head; to make the head requires two or three distinct operations! To put it on, is a peculiar business, to whiten the pins is another; it is even a trade by itself to put them into the paper; and the important business of making a pin is in this manner divided into about eighteen distinct operations, which in some manufactories are all performed by distinct

hands, though in others the same man will sometimes perform two or three of them. . . . Ten persons, therefore, could make among them upward of forty-eight thousand pins a day. Each person, therefore . . . might be considered as making four thousand eight hundred pins in a day. But if they had all wrought separately and independent . . . they certainly could not each of them have made twenty; perhaps not one pin in a day; that is . . . perhaps not the four thousand eight hundredth part of what they are at present capable of performing, in consequence of a proper division and combination of their different operations.

You perhaps know Adam Smith's legacy best through the achievements of Henry Ford, whose efforts in the mass production of automobiles also reflect these basic principles. Fortunately, while Ford and other industrial pioneers of the late 1800s and early 1900s were employing specialization and division of labor with great success, other persons were thinking further about the world of work and its managerial implications. Their legacy in the continued development of management thinking is now represented in the following schools of thought: the classical, behavioral, quantitative and modern approach to management.[7]

CLASSICAL APPROACHES TO MANAGEMENT

There are three branches of the classical approach to management: (1) scientific management, (2) administrative principles, and (3) bureaucratic organization. Figure 2.2 associates each of these branches with a prominent person in the history of manage-ment thought. The classical approaches generally share the assumption that people are rational and economically oriented in their approach toward work.

Assumption: People Are Rational

Every manager makes assumptions about the people with whom he or she works—be they subordinates, superiors, peers, customers, or suppliers. One assumption is that people are most responsive to economic incentives; that is, they will rationally consider opportunities made available to them and do whatever is necessary to achieve the greatest economic gain. Classical management theory reflects this assumption to some extent.

Scientific Management

In 1911 Frederick W. Taylor published *The Principles of Scientific Management*. This interesting book became a cornerstone of the scientific management approach and is still provocative reading today.[8]

Taylor's Contributions

Early in his book, Taylor makes the following statement: "The principal object of management should be to secure maximum prosperity for the employer, coupled with the maximum prosperity for the employee." He goes on to offer managers four principles of **scientific management** to meet this responsibility.

1. Develop a "science" for every job; this includes rules of motion, standardized work implements, and proper working conditions.

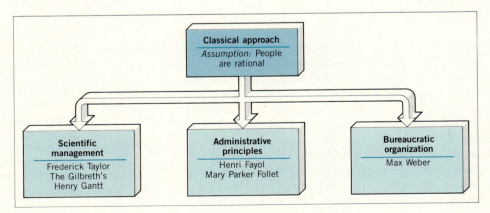

FIGURE 2.2 *Major branches in the classical approach to management.*

2. Carefully select workers with the right abilities for the job.

3. Carefully train these workers to do the job; offer them proper incentives to cooperate with the job science.

4. Support these workers by planning their work and by smoothing the way as they go about their jobs.

Taylor viewed these principles as a stark contrast to the ordinary management practices of his day. In this world of work:

■ Jobs were done by rule-of-thumb methods, with no standard times, methods, or motions.

■ Training was not emphasized and, at best, was an apprentice system.

■ Almost all of the work and most of the responsibility rested with workers.

■ The idea of management as a group performing unique duties was not widespread.

As a result of the prior conditions, Taylor felt that most workers of his time performed below their true capacities. He also felt that a scientific approach to management resulting in proper direction and monetary incentives could correct the problem. Instead of relying on tradition, hearsay, guesswork, or rules of thumb, he advised managers to apply his four principles and act on the basis of facts proved through research and experimentation.

Contributions of the Gilbreths

While Taylor is often called "the father of scientific management," Frank Gilbreth and Lillian Gilbreth are the acclaimed pioneers of motion study in industry.[9] **Motion study** is the science of reducing a job or task to its basic physical motions.

The Gilbreths' work with motion study established the foundations for later advances in the areas of job simplification, work standards, and incentive wage plans. Their most popularized study dealt with bricklaying. In at least one case, motion study reduced the number of motions used by bricklayers and tripled their productivity at the task.

As they are still used today, motion studies analyze how a person performs a task. Performance improvement is sought by such means as eliminating wasted movements and smoothing workflows. Consider two examples of work improvements based on these concepts.[10]

One of the Gilbreth's contributions to management theory was an emphasis on the study and improvement of motions as a way of increasing job performance.

In the jewelry industry. Skilled assemblers at one company were using up to 30 percent of their time moving things to and from inventory. An industrial engineering consultant reassigned this work to unskilled laborers, and used stopwatches to complete time-and-motion studies and establish production standards for piece-rate pay. Under the new system, average individual earnings increased 60 cents per hour, and company productivity increased.

At United Parcel Service. Workers in this most profitable of U.S. transportation companies perform under carefully calibrated productivity standards. At regional sorting centers they are timed according to strict task requirements, with sorters being expected to load vans at the rate of 500–600 packages per hour. Stops on the regular routes of van drivers

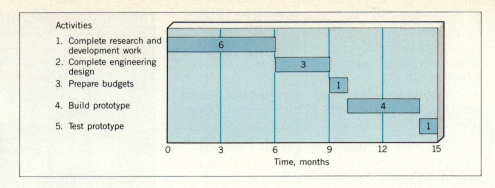

FIGURE 2.3 *A simplified Gantt Chart: The case of the new computer prototype.*

are studied with a stopwatch, and supervisors generally know within six minutes how long a driver's pickups and deliveries will take.

Henry Gantt's Contributions

Other related and lasting contributions to management practice came from the work of Henry Gantt, a colleague of Taylor. He extended Taylor's work with piece-rate pay to create an innovative task and *bonus* wage scheme. Under this system, each worker meeting daily production goals would receive the standard wage plus a bonus, and the worker's supervisor would also receive a bonus. In this way Gantt tried to build performance incentives for both the worker and manager.

Henry Gantt is perhaps better known for his *Gantt Chart* which graphically depicts the scheduling of tasks required to complete a production operation or project. An example is shown in Figure 2.3. In the figure, the left column lists activities required to complete a new computer prototype. To the right, bars are extended to indicate the time needed to perform each activity. This chart provides a visual measure of both what needs to be done on the computer project and the progress that has been made to date.

The Gantt Chart method for task analysis and scheduling facilitates the planning and controlling of complex projects involving multiple tasks. Modern managers still use this basic Gantt Chart, which is also the precursor to PERT (Program Evaluation Review Technique), CPM (Critical Path Method), and other operations management techniques to be discussed in Chapter 16.

Lessons from Scientific Management

Taylor, the Gilbreths, Gantt, and their contemporaries used scientific techniques to try to improve the productivity of people at work. Their early efforts remain influential in modern approaches to management and will be reflected throughout this book. In particular, the significant lessons of scientific management relate to:

■ The use of compensation as an incentive for increased production.

■ The design of jobs, specification of work methods, and identification of needed forms of supervisory support.

■ The proper selection of individuals to work in these jobs once they are designed.

■ The training of individuals to perform according to task requirements and to the best of their abilities.

■ The use of rational and systematic approaches to solve management problems and improve performance.

Administrative Principles

Another classical approach to management evolved from systematic attempts to document and understand the experiences of successful managers. Among the contributors to this administrative-principles school of thought, Henri Fayol stands out as a successful manager as well as a scholar and writer.

Fayol's Principles of Management

Henri Fayol was a high executive in French industry. In 1916 he published *Administration Industrielle et Generale* outlining his views on the proper management of organizations and the people within them.[13] His book offered the five "rules" of management that follow. As you can see, these rules closely resemble the four basic functions of management defined in Chapter 1.

1. *Foresight*   To complete a plan of action; to prepare a scheme for the future.
2. *Organization*   To provide resources needed to implement the plan; to mobilize effort in support of the plan.
3. *Command*   To get the best out of people working toward the plan; to lead; to select and evaluate workers properly.
4. *Coordination*   To ensure that the efforts of subunits fit together properly; to ensure that information is shared and any problems solved.
5. *Control*   To verify progress; to make sure things happen according to plan; to take any necessary corrective action.

Listed in Table 2.3 are 14 principles of management that Fayol specified as particular ways of implementing the prior rules. You will find many of these principles underlying our review of contemporary management concepts and theories throughout this book.

Mary Parker Follett: Dynamic Administration

Another major contributor in this school of thought was Mary Parker Follett.[14] An energetic and idealistic woman, Follett was eulogized upon her death in 1933 as "one of the most important women America has yet produced in the fields of civics and sociology."

With an early career in social work and community service, Follett brought an understanding of groups and a deep commitment to human cooperation to her writings about businessnes and other organizations. She believed that groups were mechanisms through which diverse individuals could combine their talents for a greater good. She viewed an organization as a "community" in which managers and workers should labor in harmony, without one party dominating the other, and with the ability to talk over and truly reconcile conflicts and differences. In this sense, Follett believed managers should play key roles in helping people in organizations to cooperate with one another and achieve the needed *integration* of interests.

Even though written in the 1920s and 1930s, Follett's words of wisdom sustain their impact on the field of management yet today. Indeed, her progressive ideas about people and their role in the workplace anticipated in many ways the attention to the human factor which dominated management thinking in later years. Consider the following sample of insights found in *Dynamic Administration: The Collected Papers of Mary Parker Follett.*

■   Follett felt that making everyone employed by a company an owner in the business would create feelings of collective responsibility. Today we ad-

TABLE 2.3   *Fayol's General Principles of Management*

1. **Division of work**   The object of division of work is to produce more and better work with the same effort. It is accomplished through reduction in the number of tasks to which attention and effort must be directed.
2. **Authority and responsibility**   Authority is the right to give orders, and responsibility is its essential counterpart. Whenever authority is exercised responsibility arises.
3. **Discipline**   Discipline implies obedience and respect for the agreements between the firm and its employees. Establishment of these agreements binding a firm and its employees from which disciplinary formalities emanate should remain one of the chief preoccupations of industrial heads. Discipline also involves sanctions judiciously applied.
4. **Unity of command**   An employee should receive orders from one superior only.
5. **Unity of direction**   Each group of activities having one objective should be unified by having one plan and one head.
6. **Subordination of individual interest to general interest**   The interest of one employee or group of employees should not prevail over that of the company or broader organization.
7. **Remuneration of personnel**   To maintain the loyalty and support of workers, they must receive a fair wage for services rendered.
8. **Centralization**   Like division of work, centralization belongs to the natural order of things. However, the appropriate degree of centralization will vary with a particular concern, so it becomes a question of the proper proportion. It is a problem of finding the measure that will give the best overall yield.
9. **Scalar chain**   The scalar chain is the chain of superiors ranging from the ultimate authority to the lowest ranks. It is an error to depart needlessly from the line of authority, but it is an even greater one to keep it when detriment to the business ensues.
10. **Order**   A place for everything and everything in its place.
11. **Equity**   Equity is a combination of kindliness and justice.
12. **Stability of tenure of personnel**   High turnover increases inefficiency. A mediocre manager who stays is infinitely preferable to an outstanding manager who comes and goes.
13. **Initiative**   Initiative involves thinking out a plan and ensuring its success. This gives zeal and energy to an organization.
14. **Esprit de corps**   Union is strength, and it comes from the harmony of the personnel.

Source: Abridged from Henri Fayol, *General and Industrial Administration* (New York: Pitman, 1949), pp. 20–41.

dress the same issues under such labels as employee-ownership, profit sharing, and gain-sharing plans.

■ Follett argued that business problems typically involve a wide variety of factors that must be considered not in isolation, but in relationship to one another. Today the label "systems theory" describes the same phenomenon.

■ Follett expressed the idea that businesses should be considered as services, and that private profits should always be considered vis-a-vis the public good. Today we pursue the same issues under the labels of managerial ethics and corporate social responsibility.

Lessons of the Administrative-Principles Approach

It is from the works of Fayol, Follett and their contemporaries that management theory derives its present emphasis on the process of planning, organizing, leading, and controlling. Proponents of the administrative-principles approach believe that managers following general principles of management will achieve productivity. They are often criticized, however, for being too willing to generate management principles from case histories and individual experiences without subjecting them to rigorous scientific scrutiny. In addition, they are criticized because the principles sometimes break down when scientific scrutiny is applied. Indeed, part of the richness of modern management theory lies in its ability and willingness to use scientific research to establish precisely when and under what conditions various principles operate to best advantage—and what to do when they don't.

Bureaucratic Organization

Max Weber was a German intellectual whose life and work paralleled those of Taylor and Fayol. Weber's contribution to management can be summed up as follows: managers using proper organizational structures will achieve productivity. At the heart of Weber's thinking lies his concept of "bureaucracy."

Bureaucracy

Perhaps your image of a bureaucracy is of long registration lines, red tape, and the like. For Max Weber, by contrast, a **bureaucracy** could be an ideal, intentionally rational, and very efficient form of organization founded on principles of logic, order, and legitimate authority. Weber described it as follows[15]

> The purely bureaucratic type of administrative organization . . . is, from a purely technical point of view, capable of attaining the highest degree of efficiency. . . . It is superior to any other form in precision, in stability, in the stringency of its discipline, and in its reliability. It thus makes possible a particularly high degree of calculability of results for the heads of the organization and for those acting in relation to it. It is finally superior both in intensive efficiency and in the scope of its operations and is formally capable of application to all kinds of administrative tasks.

Several special characteristics identify the Weberian notion of bureaucracy.

1. *A division of labor* in which authority and responsibility are clearly defined.
2. Every employee's work *duties and responsibilities explicitly defined.*
3. Standard *rules and procedures.*
4. Offices or positions organized in a *hierarchy of authority.*
5. Organizational members selected for their *technical competence.*
6. *Career managers* working for fixed salaries.

Lessons from Weber

The anticipated advantages of bureaucracy, are efficiency in the utilization of resources and fairness or equity in the treatment of employees and clients. The possible disadvantages of bureaucracy include a preponderance of red tape, rigidity in handling problems, resistance to change, and employee apathy. Surely your experience includes examples of both the advantages and disadvantages of bureaucratic features of organizations.

Weber's work has a major impact on management as a scientific field of inquiry today. Researchers still examine the characteristics of bureaucracy to determine for what size organizations and under what environmental conditions they work best. As indicated in *Newsline 2.2,* such structural issues are the concern of managers worldwide.

BEHAVIORAL APPROACHES TO MANAGEMENT

Classical theorists like Taylor, Fayol, Follett, Weber, and others, assumed that a rational person

Anxious to upgrade China's high-tech and manufacturing industries, the Chinese political leadership is encouraging managers of various enterprises to take a fresh look at how they run their operations. Direct foreign investment in China is growing steadily; even once-reluctant Japan now invests in Chinese manufacturing ventures. Aware of the important opportunities that this influx of money creates, some Chinese managers are starting to address the problems in their plants.

Most state-owned factories have poor reputations for quality control, cost-effectiveness, and marketing. As a step toward rectifying this situation, China's State Economic Commission has begun to administer, in conjunction with the European Economic Community, a program to place teams of business students in state-owned factories, where they diagnose managerial problems and recommend solutions. These teams

have found that most managers are impeded by very bureaucratic organizational structures that discourage initiative and creativity. Top-heaviness is a particular burden, as one student explained: "In the factory we studied there [were] . . . maybe five levels [of management] before you go to the workers. We think that isn't so good."

This student's team drew up an organizational chart for the factory it studied, whereas another team performed a marketing survey for a grateful pharmaceutical factory. Still another set of students encouraged a transformer plant to shift to standardized products—something the engineer-managers hadn't thought of, as they lacked training in sales and profit management.

The state's backing of such hands-on training indicates China's desire to improve management by borrowing techniques from foreigners, even nonsocialist ones. It may take some time to win over most managers, but already a core of open-minded Chinese business-people are touting the benefits of Western-style management—and China's politicians are listening. One Japanese executive familiar with China reports that it will not take long for "this very smart elite [to] show up in active management of the government."

Source: As reported in "The Next 'Asian Miracle' May Be Underway—in China," *Business Week* (November 2, 1987), pp. 144–145; James R. Schiffman, "Using Western Management Techniques, Chinese Students Find Factories' Faults," *Wall Street Journal* (August 3, 1987), p. 11; and James R. Schiffman, "Pressured, Japan Sinks Money into China," *Wall Street Journal* (February 18, 1988), p. 14.

---

would respond to proper economic incentives, job designs, management practices, and organizational structures. In the 1930s, an alternative approach to management emerged to place greater emphasis on the human factor. Major branches in this behavioral approach to management are shown in Figure 2.4. They include the famous Hawthorne studies and Maslow's theory of human needs, as well as theories generated from these foundations by Douglas McGregor and Chris Argyris.

Assumption: People Are Social and Self-Actualizing

The various branches of the behavioral approach generally reflect a shared belief in the social and self-actualizing nature of people. People at work are assumed to act on the basis of (1) desires for satisfying social relationships, (2) responsiveness to group pressures, and (3) the search for personal fulfillment. This basic assumption has its roots in

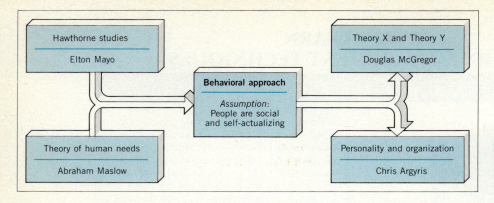

FIGURE 2.4 *Major branches in the behavioral approach to management.*

the Hawthorne studies and the seminal theory of human needs developed by Abraham Maslow.

The Hawthorne Studies

In 1924 the Western Electric Company initiated a study of individual productivity in the company's Chicago plant known as the Hawthorne Works.[16] The company was interested in examining Taylor's first principle of scientific management by studying the effects of physical working conditions on individual work outputs.

The Illumination Studies

Between 1924 and 1927, a series of studies was conducted to determine how various levels of illumination affected output. The intensity of light for different work groups was varied, changes in output measured, and the results analyzed. The researchers were disappointed, however. They failed to find any relationship between level of illumination and production. In some groups, output "bobbed" up and down at random; in others it increased steadily; in one group it increased even though illumination was reduced to the level of moonlight! Perplexed by these results, the researchers concluded that unforeseen "psychological factors" somehow interfered with the experiments.

The Relay-Assembly Test-Room Studies

In 1927, researchers, led by Elton Mayo, from Harvard University began a new series of studies to examine the effect of worker fatigue on output. Care was taken to design a scientific test that would be free of the "psychological effects" thought to have confounded the earlier illumination studies.

Six workers who assembled relays were isolated for intensive study in a special test room. They were subjected to various rest pauses, lengths of workday, and lengths of workweek, while their production was regularly measured. Once again, researchers were unable to find any direct relationship between changes in physical working conditions and output. Productivity increased regardless of the changes made.

This time Mayo and his colleagues concluded that the new "social setting" created in the test room accounted for the increased productivity. Two factors were singled out as having special importance. First was the group atmosphere in the test room. The workers shared pleasant social relations with one another and the desire to do a good job. Second, supervision was more participatory. Test-room workers were made to feel important, were given a lot of information, and were frequently asked for their opinions. This was not the case in their normal work situations.

Later Studies

Until worsening economic conditions forced termination in 1932, Mayo's studies continued at Hawthorne. During this time, interest focused on such things as employee attitudes, interpersonal relations, and group relations. In one study, an almost unbelievable 21,126 employees were interviewed to learn what they liked and disliked about their work environment. "Complex" and "baffling" results led the researchers to conclude that the same things (e.g., work conditions, wages) can be sources of satisfaction for some workers and dissatisfaction for others. In other words, people are different!

The final Hawthorne study was conducted in

the bank wiring room and centered on the work group. One of its "surprises" was the finding that people would restrict their output in order to avoid the displeasure of the group, even if it meant sacrificing pay that could otherwise be earned by increasing output. This pointed out that the work group can have strong negative as well as positive influences on individual productivity.

Lessons of the Hawthorne Studies

Conclusions of the Hawthorne studies highlighted the social aspects of work and their potential impact on individual productivity. From them we learned that people's feelings, attitudes, and relationships with co-workers should be important to management. We learned that the nature of the work group should be important. And we also learned about what is now known among researchers as the **Hawthorne effect.** This is the tendency of persons who are singled out for special attention to perform as anticipated merely because of the expectations created by the situation. In the case of the relay test operators, for example, productivity may have improved simply because the workers thought higher output was what the researchers wanted.

The Hawthorne studies were an important turning point in the history of management thought. They helped shift the attention of managers and management researchers away from the technical and structural aspects of work as emphasized by the classical approach, and toward social and human factors as keys to productivity. Indeed, they prompted the viewpoint that managers using good human relations would achieve productivity. This change in focus contributed to the emergence of the "human relations movement" during the 1950s and 1960s. It also set the stage for what evolved further into what is now known as the modern field of **organizational behavior,** the study of individuals and groups in organizations.[17]

Scholars now look back and criticize the Hawthorne studies for poor research design, weak empirical support for conclusions drawn, and for the tendency of researchers to over-generalize findings.[18] Yet, their significance as a turning point in the evolution of management thought remains intact. From this point in time on, the human dimension was firmly established as an essential concern of management. Thus, the ultimate significance of the Hawthorne studies may not be for what the researchers directly produced, but what they indirectly created. That is, the emergence of new management thinking in which the individual employee was no longer viewed as just a worker, but also a human being. The work of Abraham Maslow, an eminent psychologist was also very influential in this regard.

Abraham Maslow: A Theory of Human Needs

A **need** is a physiological or psychological deficiency a person feels the compulsion to satisfy. This is a significant concept for managers because needs create tensions that affect a person's work attitudes and behaviors. Abraham Maslow identified five levels of human needs: physiological, safety, social, esteem, and self-actualization. Maslow's **hierarchy of needs** is shown in Figure 2.5.

The Theory

Maslow's theory of human needs is based on two fundamental principles.[18]

1. *The deficit principle*   A satisfied need is not a motivator of behavior; people act to satisfy "de-

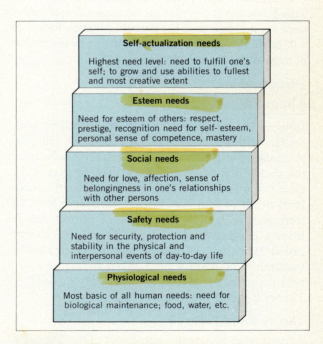

FIGURE 2.5   *Maslow's hierarchy of human needs.*

prived" needs—that is, needs for which a satisfaction "deficit" exists.

2. *The progression principle* The five needs exist in a hierarchy of prepotency; a need at any level only becomes activated once the next lower-level need has been satisfied.

These two principles view people as seeking to satisfy the five needs in sequence. A deprived need dominates individual attention and determines behavior. Once this deficit is satisfied, the next higher-level need is activated and progression up the hierarchy occurs. At the level of self-actualization, the deficit and progression principles cease to operate. The more this need is satisfied, the stronger it grows.

Lessons from Maslow's Theory

Maslow's theory sensitizes us to the basic human needs that people bring with them to their work. It suggests that a manager's job is (1) to provide avenues for individual need satisfaction that also support essential organization and work-unit goals, and (2) to remove any obstacles blocking need satisfaction and causing frustration, negative attitudes, or dysfunctional behavior. In general, the managerial implication of Maslow's theory has much in common with the Hawthorne studies—that is, managers who satisfy human needs will achieve productivity. This humanistic orientation remains a major influence on management theory and practice today. It will be discussed more critically in our examination of motivation theories in Chapter 12.

Douglas McGregor: Theory X and Theory Y

Douglas McGregor was heavily influenced by both the Hawthorne studies and Maslow's work. His classic book, *The Human Side of Enterprise,* advanced the thesis that managers could benefit greatly by giving more attention to the social and self-actualizing needs of people at work.[20] McGregor felt that managers must shift their view of human nature from a perspective he called "Theory X" to one called "Theory Y." These are common terms in the vocabulary of management. Even today, you will hear people referred to as either Theory X (bad!) or Theory Y (good!) managers.

Theory X and Theory Y

According to McGregor, a manager of the **Theory X** model views his or her subordinates as by nature

- Disliking work.
- Lacking in ambition.
- Irresponsible.
- Resistant to change.
- Preferring to be led rather than to lead.

Theory Y, by contrast, involves an alternative set of assumptions. A manager operating under a **Theory Y** perspective views subordinates as

- Willing to work.
- Willing to accept responsibility.
- Capable of self-direction.
- Capable of self-control.
- Capable of imagination, ingenuity, creativity.

Lessons from Theory X and Theory Y

Theory X assumptions can cause managers to be overly directive, very narrow, and control-oriented in their approach to people at work. These supervisory behaviors, McGregor pointed out, tend to foster passive, dependent, and reluctant subordinates.

A Theory Y perspective encourages managers to allow subordinates more participation, freedom, and responsibility in their work. Theory Y managers delegate authority, allow subordinates to participate in decisions, and offer them greater job autonomy and task variety. This creates more opportunities for the satisfaction of esteem and self-actualization needs through work. McGregor felt people would respond to such treatment with initiative and high productivity. It is easy to see the humanistic appeal of his work.

Chris Argyris: Personality and Organization

Chris Argyris is a productive scholar who continues to make significant contributions to management thinking.[21] His early work on personality and organization is consistent with the belief in a higher order of human nature advanced by Maslow and McGregor.

The Theory

Argyris believes that certain management principles found among the classical management approaches are inconsistent with the mature adult personality. The resulting incongruence between individual personality and the organization causes conflict, frustration, and failure for people at work. Consider the following examples of classical management principles and the unfortunate results predicted by Argyris.

Task specialization Assumes people will behave more efficiently as tasks become specialized.

> *Result* Inhibits self-actualization.

Chain of command Assumes efficiency is increased by a strict hierarchy where top directs and controls bottom.

> *Result* Creates dependent and passive workers with little control over their work environments.

Unity of direction Assumes efficiency will increase when work is planned and directed by one supervisor.

> *Result* Creates ideal conditions for psychological failure; psychological success requires that individuals define their own goals.

Span of control Assumes efficiency will increase when a supervisor's responsibility is limited to five or six immediate subordinates.

> *Result* Creates dependent and passive workers with little control over their work environments.

Lessons from the Theory

Argyris predicts that a mismatch between workers' mature personalities and management practices will create absenteeism, turnover, aggression toward higher levels of authority, apathy, alienation, and a focus on compensation as the ever-increasing trade-off for their unhappiness. One current example related to the concerns of Argyris is called the **glass ceiling effect.**[22] As noted in *Newsline 2.3,* this term describes an unfortunate situation still encountered by too many women managers. For them, hard work and success means that they are able to rise in the hierarchy of large organizations—but only up to a point. Then "glass ceilings" imposed by parochial attitudes of top-level managers create invisible barriers that prevent them from progressing further into senior executive positions. The net result of such frustration is that many of these women eventually leave their corporate jobs to become entrepreneurs and/or run smaller businesses.

In sum, Argyris, suggests that managers who treat people positively and as responsible adults will achieve productivity. His advice is for managers to accommodate the mature personality by expanding job requirements to allow more task variety and responsibility, and by adjusting supervisory styles to include more participation and better human relations.

QUANTITATIVE APPROACHES TO MANAGEMENT

About the same time that the Hawthorne studies were prompting some theorists to develop behavioral approaches to management, other scholars were creating quantitative techniques to facilitate managerial decision making.

Assumption: Applied Mathematics Can Help Solve Management Problems

The foundation of the quantitative approaches rests in the shared assumption that mathematical techniques can be applied to help solve management problems. This thrust developed into a discipline we now know as **management science** or **operations research.** These interchangeable terms describe a scientific approach to management that uses mathematical techniques to analyze and solve problems.

Foundations, Techniques, and Applications

The quantitative approach to management generally proceeds as follows: a problem is encountered, it is systematically analyzed, appropriate mathematical computations are made, and an optimum solution is selected as a result. This is a truly scientific approach to managerial decision making and problem solving.

Foundations

The essence of any quantitative management approach includes these characteristics:

1.   *Primary focus on decision making* The end result of problem analysis will include direct implications for managerial action.

2.   *Based on economic decision criteria* Final actions are chosen on such criteria as costs, revenues, and rates of return on investment.

BREAKING THE GLASS CEILING

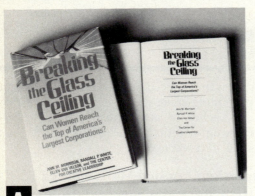

Although women account for a clear majority of the white-collar workforce, they remain a minority in managerial ranks. The authors of one recent study, *Breaking the Glass Ceiling,* argue that as women ascend the corporate ladder, they confront a series of "glass ceilings"—invisible but real barriers to the acquisition of upper-management responsibilities and rewards. Among these ceilings are poor or nonexistent daycare, flextime, or job-sharing benefits, without which women who are also mothers are hindered professionally.

Other observers disagree that such ceilings are present, although they admit that the path of female managers is not without its bumps. Regina Herzlinger, a Harvard Business School professor, contends that women are now in the middle-management pipeline and will begin, from here on, to realize the rewads of their labor. By 1997, she says, "there will be 20 to 30 female big-company CEOs [and] by 2011, we will see the deluge."

As the numbers of women in management increase, corporate culture will need to adjust to a new reality. Herzlinger maintains that U.S. companies are learning to accept "all kinds of people, as long as they are talented and productive"—and that if female managers are dissatisfied with their progress up the ladder, the cause is likely to be "a low organizational level that makes men unhappy as well." The issue of child care is undeniably thorny, as is the lack of "a set of comfortable, acceptable images of the new male—female work relationship." Yet significant changes are in the making and women face exciting professional prospects as well as challenges in their work lives.

Source: As reported in Amanda Bennett, "The CEO's World: Sexism and Salary," *Wall Street Journal* (November 29, 1987), p. 9; Regina Herzlinger, "Dancing on the Glass Ceiling," *Wall Street Journal* (February 17, 1988), p. 22; and Robert B. Tucker, "The Company She Keeps," *United* magazine (November 1986), pp. 43–146.

---

3. *Use of formal mathematical models* Possible solutions to problems are specified as mathematical equations and then analyzed according to mathematical rules and formulas.

4. *Frequent use of computers* Heavy reliance is placed on computers and their advanced processing capabilities.

Techniques

Several basic quantitative techniques are listed here. Linear programming, simulation, and queuing theory are but a few of the more common names you might recognize. The list also gives a brief example of each technique as it applies to actual management practice. These techniques are discussed in greater detail in the Management Applications Module, "Quantitative Decision Techniques: An Introduction to Management Science," found at the end of the book.

Forecasting Making projections into the future through mathematical calculations.

Inventory modeling Controlling inventories by mathematically establishing how much to order and when.

Linear programming Calculating how best to allocate scarce resources among competing uses.

Queuing theory Computing the number of service personnel or work stations that will minimize customer waiting time and service cost.

Network models   Breaking large and complex tasks into smaller components for analysis, planning and control (e.g. PERT and CPM).

Simulation   Making a model of a problem and using a computer to solve the problem many times under various decision circumstances.

Regression analysis   Predicting relationships among two or more variables to show how changes in one affects others.

Applications

One way to view applications of quantitative approaches to management is in a career perspective. The collage of "help-wanted" ads shows a sample of job titles for persons specializing in applied quantitative analysis. Perhaps you aspire to one of these or similar positions that depend on expertise in applied mathematics, computer science and related decision techniques.

The wide variety of careers involving quantitative analysis and computer skills offers many attractive opportunities in current job markets.

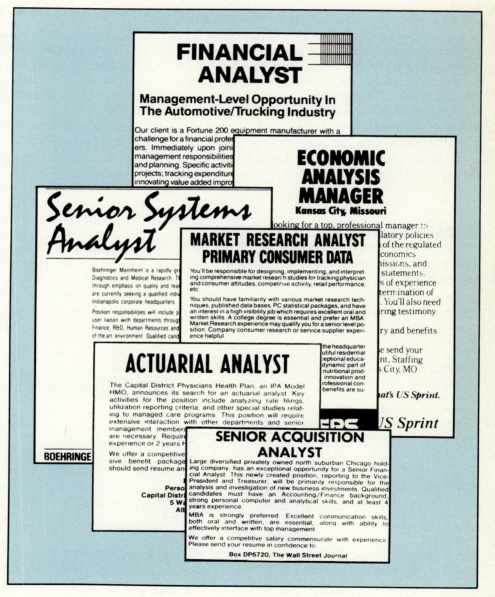

Quantitative Analysis Today

The methods of quantitative analysis offer special value in addressing the technical problems faced by organizations. The perspective shared by these approaches is that managers using quantitative decision techniques will achieve productivity. Software developments now make many of these techniques available to the manager through desktop personal computers. This greatly expands their potential application throughout the managerial ranks. It is important, however, to keep the quantitative management approaches in perspective. Most mathematical solutions to managerial problems must still be supported by good judgment and an appreciation for the human factors involved. Success in the application of quantitative techniques depends on both the technical expertise of the management scientist and the willingness of other persons to implement the recommended problem solutions. A well-rounded and truly comprehensive view of problems, including both technical and human-resource considerations, is the ideal direction advocated by modern management approaches.

MODERN APPROACHES TO MANAGEMENT

Today there is a convergence of management thinking. Modern approaches to management recognize that the prescriptions of the classical, behavioral, and quantitative schools do not apply universally in every situation, or to the exclusion of one another.

Instead, they try to identify the best and most useful insights of the other approaches, and to creatively extend them using new ideas and concepts developed in the dynamic context of the contemporary environment. Figure 2.6 summarizes this logic. Because modern management approaches are what this entire book is all about, they are only generally introduced here. Beginning with Chapter 3, we will investigate them systematically, in detail, and with an emphasis on their situational or contingency applications.

Assumption: People Are Complex

An alternative to the assumptions that people are basically rational/economically-oriented or social/self-actualizing is the following viewpoint—people are complex and variable. In particular:

■ They attend to multiple and varied needs.

■ They change these patterns of needs, action tendencies, and desires over time.

■ They respond to a wide variety of organizational demands and managerial strategies.

This is the guiding assumption of modern management approaches. It recognizes that people are different and change over time. Managers must be able to understand these individual differences and respect them when making decisions and taking action. Two important concepts in this regard are systems and contingency. As you read on, keep this summary perspective of the modern management approaches in mind: managers using systems and contingency thinking will achieve productivity.

FIGURE 2.6 *Modern management theory in relationship to its historical roots: The classical, behavioral, and quantitative approaches.*

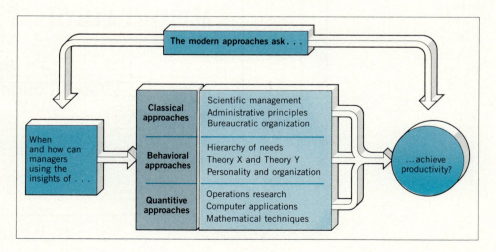

The Systems View of Organizations

The term *organization* was defined in Chapter 1. It was further described as an open system that receives resource inputs from the environment and transforms them into product or service outputs, which are returned to the environment for consumption. Formally speaking, a **system** is a collection of interrelated parts that function together to achieve a common purpose. An **open system,** as you should recall, is one that interacts with its environment; a **closed system** does not. Within the vocabulary of management, these systems terms are frequently used.[23]

Subsystem   A smaller component that exists within a larger system.

System boundary   The point of separation between a system and its external environment.

Feedback   Information about system performance that can be used for purposes of adaptation, control, and constructive change.

Equifinality   The ability of a system to achieve the same end state from a variety of paths.

Entropy   A universal tendency of all living systems to move toward discontinuity and death.

Negative entropy   The tendency toward system continuity and survival; a reversal of the entropic process.

Homeostasis   A dynamic state of equilibrium or balance in the relationship between a system and its environment.

The significance of managerial contributions to the organization as a well-functioning system traces, in part, to the insights of Chester Barnard. He served for many years as chief executive officer of the New Jersey Bell Telephone Company. His book *The Functions of the Executive* views the essence of any organizaton as "cooperation"—that is, a willingness of people to communicate and interact with one another to serve a common purpose.[24] Something larger than the individual—a "system"—results from this willingness to cooperate. The "system" allows people to accomplish far more together than they could acting as individuals alone.

It is the function of the executive or manager to make this cooperation possible. In so doing, the vitality of the organization as a total system can be ensured. Among the executive functions are the formulation of organizational purpose, managing subsystem relationships and dealing with the conflicts inevitable to a complex system.

Illustrative Case: Midwest Power and Light Company

Figure 2.7 introduces the complexity of organizational systems in the example of a small electric utility company. Using just a sample of the actual number of subsystems that compose the utility, the figure shows many different subunits must work together—or "cooperate"—in order to produce and sell electric power to the utility's customers. It is the job of the president, vice-president for operations, and the respective subunit managers to make this cooperation possible. They must make sure not only that the necessary tasks get done (such as purchasing, power generation, distribution, and accounting), but also that they get done in an integrated way that facilitates high productivity for the enterprise as a whole—that is, the "total system."

When looking at the organization as a collection of subsystems, it is helpful to recognize five special functions that the multiple but differentiated components perform.[25]

1.   *Production subsystems*   are directly involved in the manufacture of products or delivery of services. Like the power generation unit in the electric utility, these production, manufacturing, and service subunits largely accomplish the transformation of resource inputs into organizational outputs.

2.   *Boundary-spanning subsystems*   interact directly with representatives of the external environment. These include both "input" boundary-spanners like the purchasing department in the utility which acquires needed resources, and "output" boundary-spanners like the sales and distribution department which sells and delivers electricity to its customers.

3.   *Adaptive subsystems*   provide the stimulus for innovation and change within the organization. This requires monitoring the external environment for new ideas, changes in technology, and new problems and opportunities. The engineering and design department serves an adaptive function for the electric utility; other common examples include planning, market research, and research and development units.

4.   *Maintenance subsystems*   help keep things running in a smooth and orderly fashion throughout

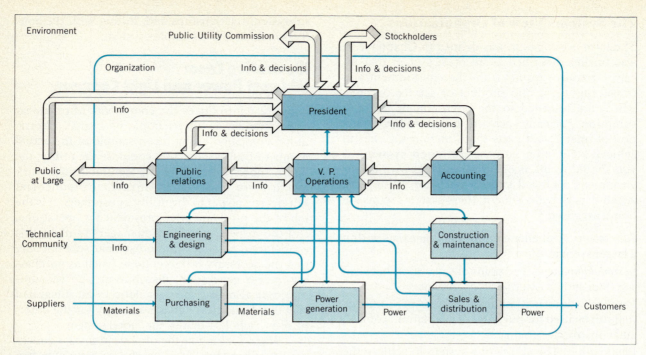

FIGURE 2.7 *Midwest Power and Light Company as a complex organizational system.*

Source: Developed from H. Randolph Bobbitt, Jr., Robert H. Breinholt, Robert H. Doktor, and James P. McNaul, *Organizational Behavior: Understanding and Prediction* (Englewood Cliffs, NJ: Prentice-Hall, 1974), p. 219.

the organization. The accounting department serves the electric utility by maintaining important cost and financial records; the construction and maintenance department fulfills a similar role by helping maintain equipment, buildings, and other aspects of the physical plant. Personnel departments are also maintenance subsystems. They are devoted to the acquisition and continuation of the organization's human resources.

5. *Managerial subsystems* direct, monitor, and integrate the work of the other subsystems of organizations. As we noted earlier, this subsystem represents the essential managerial task as performed at all levels throughout an enterprise. That is, to make sure the required work gets done in an integrated fashion. In the electric utility, the president and vice-president are top-level managers within this subsystem. Their job, as with all top-level managers, is to formulate objectives and strategy for the organizaton as a whole, and set the stage for action. Middle and lower-level managers are supposed to follow-through by implementing them in a cooperative way.

Open Systems and the Environment

The environment is a critical element in the open-systems perspective. Because it is a source of resources and feedback, it has a significant impact on organizations. As the environment changes over time, for example, it is the manager's job to stay informed and help the organization respond in a productive way. The crisis of the U.S. auto industry during the late 1970s and early 1980s illustrates what can happen when managers fail to remain in contact with dynamic environments and help their organizations respond to them. In this particular case, foreign auto makers did a better job of recognizing the significance of petroleum shortages and changing consumer tastes. They also responded to them with appropriate products.

Feedback is also central to an open system. It reflects the environment's evaluation of an organization or a subsystem. Through feedback, managers learn how well the organization's or subsystem's products or services are being received. This is reflected in the willingness of the environment to continue providing important resource inputs in exchange for them. Based on feedback, constructive action can be taken by managers to maintain or improve organizational productivity. When properly used, feedback helps ensure the survival and longer-term prosperity of the enterprise.

Contingency Thinking

Contingency approaches to management theory emphasize environmental differences and the need for managers to respond appropriately to them. **Contingency thinking** tries to match managerial responses with the unique problems and opportunities posed by different situations. This strong foundation of the modern management approaches emerged during the 1950s and 1960s in the tradition of the "classics" introduced in Table 2.4. Indeed, part of the strength of the contingency perspective traces to its systematic development over time and in a number of diverse research contexts. The net result has been very significant to our present study of management. No longer is there an attempt to find "the one best way to manage in all circumstances." Rather, the essence of the contingency perspective is to help managers analyze and understand situational differences and choose responses that best facilitate productivity in each circumstance.

Recent advances in management theory draw heavily on this contingency viewpoint. You will encounter them at key points throughout the chapters to come. For now it is sufficient to introduce the logic of contingency thinking based on the general insights of several of the works highlighted in the table. Consider the contingency issues of organizational structure as just one example. Generally speaking the choice of a "best" structure will depend on situational factors. These include the rate of change in the organization's environment, the nature of its primary technology, and the strategy which it pursues. Furthermore, we also know that what is an effective structure for one organization may not work well for the same organization at another point in time. And what is effective structure for one organization may not work well for another organization facing different circumstances. The critical issue in all cases is achieving a correct "match" between the demands and challenges of the situation and the organization's structural responses. This is the type of contingency

TABLE 2.4 *A Reader's Guide to Some 1950s and 1960s "Classics" Contributing to the Contingency Tradition of Management Theory*

1958   *James G. March and Herbert A. Simon* systematically inventory in *Organizations* (New York: Wiley) an extensive set of research propositions based on the organization as a decision making system.

1958   *Fred Fiedler* presents research on contingency leadership in *Leadership Attitudes and Group Effectiveness* (New York: Wiley).

1961   *Rensis Likert's New Patterns of Management* (New York: McGraw-Hill) presents views on participative management based on an extensive research program at the University of Michigan.

1961   *Tom Burns and George Stalker* present their research on the contingency relationship between environment and organization structure in *Organization for Innovation* (London: Tavistock).

1962   *Alfred D. Chandler, Jr.* establishes in *Strategy and Structure* (Cambridge, MA: MIT Press) the contingency relationship between organizational strategy and structure.

1963   *Eric L. Trist* and colleagues present research on the importance of "socio-technical systems" in *Organizational Choice* (London: Tavistock).

1964   *Michel Crozier* in *The Bureaucratic Phenomenon* (Chicago: University of Chicago Press) establishes a contingency relationship between organization structure and culture.

1965   *Joan Woodward* presents her research on the relationship between technology and organizaton structure in *Industrial Organization: Theory and Practice* (London: Oxford University Press).

1966   *Daniel Katz and Robert L. Kahn* integrate an open systems perspective on organizations in *The Social Psychology of Organizations* (New York: Wiley).

1967   *James D. Thompson* in *Organizations in Action* (New York: McGraw-Hill) presents an integrated model of organizations in relationship to their external environments.

1967   *Paul R. Lawrence and Jay W. Lorsch* summarize their research on contingency relationships between organization structures and environments in *Organization and Environment* (Cambridge, MA: Harvard University Press).

thinking that we will develop throughout the book and in respect to a wide variety of management issues.

The Approach of This Book

One of the strengths of contingency thinking is the attempt to deal with the inherent complexity and variability of work situations. As management theory continues to develop from this vantage point, however, it must also rise to the challenge of a number of emerging forces. We live in a dynamic world in which the rate of change that affects our lives seems to further accelerate with time. A number of environmental trends of special significance to the future of modern management are highlighted in concept and by example throughout the book. They include:

■ *The Internationalization of Management.* Prompted in part by popularization of Japanese management practices through such books as *Theory Z* by William Ouchi,[26] management scholars now stress the importance of an international and comparative perspective. They recognize that management is not just a "western" discipline, but one whose future development will include contributions from all parts of the world. Chapter 19 on management in an international arena treats these issues in depth.

■ *Continuing Advances in Technology and Information.* Everyone is aware of the dramatic advances in microprocessors and electronic information processing technologies in the past decade. Their impact is felt throughout an organization from the many applications of computer-based information

systems, discussed in Chapter 15, to computer-aided manufacturing and service delivery, discussed in Chapter 16. Management theory will continue to seek better understanding of not just the technologies themselves, but also their integration with the human factor in work environments that may be best described as "socio-technical systems."

■ *Increasing Emphasis on Strategy and Competition.* One offshoot of both the prior trends is more intense competition among organizations for resources and markets on a worldwide basis. News reports are replete with examples of business successes, failures, hostile take-overs, mergers, acquisitions and the like. In Chapter 5 we will examine the work of Michael Porter and others who feel that achievement of a truly competitive edge depends on managers who can think and act strategically in the midst of environmental change and uncertainty.[27]

■ *Renewed Attention to Managerial Ethics and Social Responsibility.* What issue is more in the news and at the forefront of our concerns than this? We have been shocked with so many reports of "white collar crimes" and unethical behavior in the managerial ranks that they are losing their sensational character. But they haven't lost impact on those who study and think seriously about the practice of management. In Chapter 20 on managerial ethics and

FIGURE 2.8 *A practical framework for studying the field of management.*

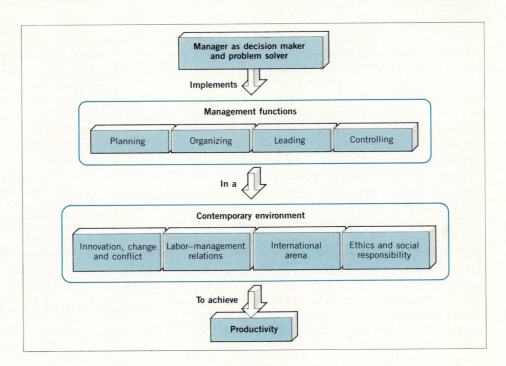

social responsibility we will examine these issues in depth, offer some informed advice, and hopefully cause you to think positively about your future managerial responsibilities.

This book uses the framework presented in Figure 2.8 to help you understand the theories and concepts of management, as well as their application and utilization in the workplace. As shown in the figure, managers make decisions and solve problems while implementing the basic management functions—planning, organizing, leading, and controlling—to achieve productivity in a dynamic environment. Among the important considerations in this action setting of the modern manager are the challenges of innovation, change and conflict, labor–management relations, the international arena, and ethics and social responsibility.

Summary

This chapter examined the historical foundations of management as a scientific discipline. Four major schools of thought were introduced—the classical, behavioral, quantitative, and modern.

Classical management approaches emphasize the rational side of people. The works of Taylor, Fayol, Follett, and Weber suggested ways of structuring tasks, organizations, and managerial actions with this in mind. The behavioral approaches, in contrast, focus on the social and self-actualizing tendencies of people at work. The Hawthorne studies and a subsequent generation of theorists, including Maslow, McGregor, and Argyris, emphasize the importance of good human relations, group dynamics, and supervisory styles in the workplace.

The quantitative approaches specify mathematical techniques for solving management problems. Given that an optimum problem solution can be found and implemented, these approaches offer managers ways to solve problems subject to quantitative measurements.

Today, a comprehensive approach to management offers an expanded view of people at work. It recognizes the complex and variable nature of every human being. It also views organizations as complex open systems operating in dynamic and ever-changing environments. This modern management approach seeks to define situational contingencies under which various managerial responses are most appropriate. The importance of systems and contingency thinking underlies the manager's basic responsibility to act as a decision maker and problem solver. Chapter 3 addresses these topics in detail. It is an important prelude to your study of the four management functions and the contemporary environment within which they must be implemented to achieve productivity.

Thinking Through the Issues

1. Is management an "art" and/or a "science"? Is it a "profession"? Why or why not?

2. What were Taylor's four principles of scientific management? How did they differ from the prevailing wisdom of his day?

3. Explain which major parts of this book relate most closely to the work of Fayol.

4. What are the major characteristics of Weber's bureaucracy? Why did he consider it an *ideal* form of organization?

5. What is the managerial significance of Maslow's theory of human needs? How did it influence McGregor's notions of Theory X and Theory Y?

6. Explain Argyris's theory of personality and organization. In what specific ways is it critical of certain classical management principles?

7. What are the foundations of the quantitative management approach? What are some of the quantitative techniques which may be useful to the modern manager?

8. Choose an organization with which you are familiar. Explain its characteristics as an "open system."

9. What does "contingency thinking" mean in the context of modern management theory?

10. Compare and contrast the assumptions underlying each of the major management approaches—classical, behavioral, quantitative, and modern.

The Manager's Vocabulary

Bureaucracy
Closed system
Contingency thinking
Entropy
Equifinality
Feedback
Gantt chart
Glass ceiling effect

Hawthorne effect
Hierarchy of needs
Homeostasis
Management science
Management theory
Motion study
Need
Negative entropy

Open system
Operations research
Organizational behavior
Profession
Quantitative analysis
Science
Scientific management
Subsystem

System
System boundary
Theory
Theory X
Theory Y

NICE GRADUATION PRESENT

CAREER PERSPECTIVE

How many graduates with a brand new MBA get to take over the top job in an organization right from the start? The answer, of course, is "not many." But then Linda Rice isn't just *any* recent MBA graduate. Her father, John Johnson, is the founder of Johnson Publishing Company. With diverse interests in publishing, broadcasting, cosmetics, and insurance, it is the largest black-owned company in the U.S. Johnson promoted Linda, at the age of 29, to be president and chief operating officer of the company as soon as she graduated with her master's degree from Northwestern University. At 69 himself, he intends to continue to set policy and strategy for the company, but will otherwise give Linda responsibility for day-to-day operations.

Linda Rice takes over the job with some definite actions in mind. She wants to introduce a new contemporary look to the company's national magazines. She wants to sell two of the company's ailing radio stations and invest the proceeds in its TV operations. And she intends to spend some time working behind cosmetic counters at stores around the country to develop ideas for boosting sales.

Some business experts wonder how well the company will do under Rice's leadership. One of her former marketing professors says, "There aren't many 29-year-olds capable of running a $175 million company." But others seem confident that she will rise to the occasion, and perform well. The editor of *Black Enterprise* magazine puts it this way: "She certainly has the sophistication and training to do the job."

Questions
1. If Linda Rice is to succeed in her new job, how much will she need to depend on (a) the "art" and (b) the "science" of management? Explain your answer.
2. Are there any disadvantages to "starting at the top" like this? In what ways, if any, would more experience in the company—say several years working in various capacities—benefit Linda in taking over the top job?
3. Try to put yourself in Linda's shoes, but with your own experience and education to date. Could *you* succeed in this job? Would you want to start right "at the top" like she did? Why or why not?

Source: Information from "A Nice Graduation Present: Johnson Publishing," *Business Week* (July 13, 1987), p. 40.

CASE APPLICATION
THE NEW BRANCH MANAGER

David Bertini was an outstanding salesman.[28] He was promoted to branch manager of his sales branch when the former manager left the company. As branch manager, David was responsible for planning, organizing, leading, and controlling his salespeople.

He was pleased with the promotion, although he was not sure how a manager should behave. He assumed that because he received the promotion for being such a good salesman, being a model salesman was the key to being a good branch manager.

He started officially as branch manager on Monday morning. Tuesday, one of his salespeople, Sally Chapin, told him that one of his old accounts was considering going to the competition. David told Sally not to worry. "I'll find out what's going on." He leaned over his desk and began dialing the customer's number before Sally had a chance to finish her explanation as to why she thought the customer was considering the competition. Within 15 minutes, David discovered that price was the problem and made a special deal with the customer. He confirmed the sale. After he finished the telephone call, David smiled at Sally and said, "Any time you need help, come right in and ask!"

Two months later, David was talking to Bill Rinehart, the regional sales manager, and asked him, "How do I get my salespeople to come and ask me for help? They seem to stay away, and I know that some of them are having problems." Bill offered to visit David's branch and help him find out what the problem was.

After spending several hours at the branch office, Bill sat down with David. Bill had been surprised to find out that David was making his salespeople feel incompetent because he always interfered with their sales efforts. At least, that's how they saw it. Bill knew that David had sound coaching skills; that was why he had received the promotion. The conversation was enlightening to David. He discovered that he got the promotion because of skills he had shown in helping some new salespeople from another branch a year earlier, not because of his own sales record. As he and Bill discussed the situation, David began to see that the branch manager is supposed to guide, coach, and help his salespeople. He should be helping each of them figure

out why a customer was backing down or why a customer ordered less than the month earlier.

David had many of the appropriate skills to be branch manager. Bill had known that good sales managers have some different skills than good salespeople and had considered this in making the promotion. David's problem had been that his self-image and social role had not changed when his job demands changed. Bill felt that the talk, reviewing his image of the branch manager's repsonsibilities with David, and giving David several books on sales management would take care of the problem. David called Bill several weeks later and said, "Being a manager is tough, but I like it. Thanks for the talk, Bill."

Bill thought the problem had been solved until eight months later when he noted that sales at David's branch had dropped continuously for three months. Bill was concerned because this represented the first quarter that the branch had been operating under sales goals and plans that were developed while David was branch manager. Bill called David and said, "I noticed that sales are down. What's going on?"

"Well, Bill, this damn recession has people cautious. They're afraid of getting caught with too much inventory," replied David. Bill was not satisfied with that answer. "But you have been down each of the past three months. Are you sure that's all due to inventory concerns?" David added, "Actually, it's a combination of things. One of them I could use your help with. Some of my salespeople don't seem to be working as hard as they have before. It's like they never came back from vacation."

Bill decided it was time for another trip to David's branch. What Bill discovered was complicated. At first it seemed that several of David's key salespeople were still angry at David for having fired Sally Chapin a number of months previously. He asked David if he had considered discussing why he had fired Sally at one of his staff meetings. David did not like the idea because it meant that he would have to hold a staff meeting. Bill was again surprised that David did not have regular staff meetings. He asked David, "How do you know what's going on with your people?" David told him that he met with each person individually and discussed various issues at least once a month. David tried to explain to Bill that it allowed him to develop a more personal relationship with each one. The story unfolded like an onion. Soon Bill learned that David had never met with his staff to discuss the branch's sales goal and plan of action. Some of the salespeople did not even know what the branch's overall goal was.

"David, how can you get people to pull together if they don't even know their shared sales goal?" Bill was feeling frustrated with David and began pushing his questions at David faster. David attempted to explain. "I have always felt that individual sales goals are important. The branch goal is only meaningful for me."

Questions

1. What suggestions for improving David Bertini's performance as a manager can be found among the ideas set forth by the major branches of the classical approach to management?
2. What suggestions for improving David Bertini's performance as a manager can be found among the ideas set forth by (a) Abraham Maslow, (b) Douglas McGregor, and (c) Chris Argyris?
3. What suggestions for improving David Bertini's performance as a manager can be found in the concept of *contingency thinking* and the *open-systems perspective* which are fundamental to the modern management approach?
4. What does the experience of David Bertini imply about a) the "art," and b) the "science" of management? Explain and justify your answer using the facts of the case.

The Nature of Human Nature

Everyone makes assumptions about people and human nature. This class exercise is designed to help you explore your assumptions, and consider their implications for management.

1. Read each of the following 10 pairs of statements.[29] Choose *the* statement in each pair that you must agree with. Circle the letter associated with that statement in the right-hand column. Put a "1" in the space beside that letter. Do this for all 10 pairs of statements.

1. It's only human nature for people to do as little work as they can get away with.   a. _____

When people avoid work, it's usually because their work has been deprived of meaning.   b. _____

2. If employees have access to any information they want, they tend to have better attitudes and behave more responsibly.   c. _____

If employees have access to more information than they need to do their immediate tasks, they will usually misuse it.   d. _____

3. One problem in asking for the ideas of employees is that their perspective is too limited for their suggestions to be of much practical value.   e. _____

Asking employees for their ideas broadens their perspective and results in the development of useful suggestions.   f. _____

4. If people don't use much imagination and ingenuity on the job, it's probably because relatively few people have much of either.   g. _____

Most people are imaginative and creative but may not show it because of limitations imposed by supervision and the job.   h. _____

5. People tend to raise their standards if they are accountable for their own behavior and for correcting their own mistakes.   i. _____

People tend to lower their standards if they are not punished for their misbehavior and mistakes.   j. _____

6. It's better to give people both good and bad news because most employees want the whole story, no matter how painful.   k. _____

It's better to withhold unfavorable news about business because most employees really want to hear only the good news.   l. _____

7. Because a supervisor is entitled to more respect than those below him in the organization, it weakens his prestige to admit that a subordinate was right and he was wrong.   m. _____

Because people at all levels are entitled to equal respect, a supervisor's prestige is increased when he supports this principle by admitting that a subordinate was right and he was wrong.   n. _____

8. If you give people enough money, they are less likely to be concerned with such intangibles as responsibility and recognition.   o. _____

If you give people interesting and challenging work, they are less likely to complain about such things as pay and supplemental benefits.   p. _____

9. If people are allowed to set their own goals and standards of performance, they tend to set them higher than the boss would.   q. _____

If people are allowed to set their own goals and standards of performance, they tend to set them lower than the boss would.   r. _____

10. The more knowledge and freedom a person has regarding his job, the more controls are needed to keep him in line.   s. _____

The more knowledge and freedom a person has regarding his job, the fewer controls are needed to ensure satisfactory job performance.   t. _____

2. *Score* your responses by adding up the points you assigned as follows:

SCORE I _____ = a + d + e + g + j + l + m + o + r + s

SCORE II _____ = b + c + f + h + i + k + n + p + q + t

3. Read back through the statements used to create each score. Think about what it may mean that you are higher on one score than the other. Is there a pattern here that might reflect the assumptions you make when dealing with other people? In what ways might these assumptions influence your approach to management?

4. Share your scores with a nearby classmate. Discuss the questions raised above as they relate to the scores obtained by each of you. Await further class discussion led by your instructor.

References

[1]Excerpted from J. Paul Getty, "The Fine Art of Being the Boss, *Playboy* (June 1972), p. 143.

[2]Schein's views on the status of management as a profession are presented in "Management Education: Some Troublesome Realities and Possible Remedies," *Journal of Management Development,* vol. 7 (1988), pp. 5–15.

[3]These comments are found in Peter F. Drucker's article "management: The Problems of Success," *Academy of Management Executive,* Vol. 1 (1987), pp. 13–19.

[4]Alfred Sloan's book, *My Years with General Motors* (New York: Doubleday, 1964), is a good example. For an extensive discussion on the value of studying business history, see Alan M. Kantrow (ed), "Why History Matters to Managers," *Harvard Business Review,* Vol. 64 (January–February 1986), pp. 81–88.

[5]A thorough review and critique of the history of management thought, including management in ancient civilizations, is provided by Daniel Wren, *The Evolution of Management Thought,* Third Edition (New York: Wiley, 1987).

[6]Adam Smith, *An Inquiry into the Nature and Causes of the Wealth of Nations,* Fifth Edition (Edinburgh: Adam and Charles Black, 1859), p. 3.

[7]For a research perspective on the historical development of the management discipline see Daniel A. Wren and John A. Pearce II (editors), *Papers Dedicated to the Development of Modern Management: Celebrating 100 Years of Modern Management.* (Mississippi State, MS: Academy of Management, 1986); and, Wren, op cit., 1987.

[8]References to Taylor's work are from Frederick W. Tay-

lor, *The Principles of Scientific Management* (New York: W.W. Norton, 1967), originally published by Harper & Brothers in 1911. See Charles W. Wrege and Amedeo G. Perroni, "Taylor's Pig-Tale: A Historical Analysis of Frederick W. Taylor's Pig-Iron Experiments," *Academy of Management Journal,* Vol. 17 (March 1974), pp. 6–27, for a stinging criticism; see Edwin A. Locke, "The Ideas of Frederick W. Taylor: An Evaluation," *Academy of Management Review,* Vol. 7 (1982), p. 14, for an excellent treatment of the contemporary signficance of Taylor's work.

[9]See Frank B. Gilbreth, *Motion Study* (New York: Van Nostrand, 1911).

[10]Information from Steven P. Galante, "Costume-Jewelry Makers Aim to Sparkle at Manufacturing," *The Wall Street Journal* (December 22, 1984), p. 21; and, Kenneth Labich, "Big Changes at Big Brown," *Fortune* (January 18, 1988), pp. 56–64.

[11]See Henry L. Gantt, *Industrial Leadership.* (Easton, Md.: Hive, 1921; Hive edition published in 1974).

[12]See also, Henry C. Metcalfe and Lyndall Urwick (eds), *Dynamic Administration: The Collected Papers of Mary Parker Follett* (New York: Harper & Brothers, 1940); James D. Mooney, *The Principles of Administration,* Revised Edition (New York: Harper & Brothers, 1947); Lyndall Urwick, *The Elements of Administration* (New York: Harper & Brothers, 1943) and *The Golden Book of Management* (London: N. Neame, 1956).

[13]Available in the English language as Henri Fayol, *General and Industrial Administration* (London: Pitman, 1949); subsequent discussion is based on M. B. Brodie, *Fayol on Administration* (London: Pitman, 1949).

[14]See Metcalfe and Urwick, op. cit.; and M. P. Follett, *Freedom and Coordination* (London: Management Publications Trust, 1949). Discussion developed in part from Judith Garwood, "A Review of *Dynamic Administration: The Collected Papers of Mary Parker Follett,*" *New Management,* Vol. 2 (1984), pp. 61–62. Eulogy from Richard C. Cabot, *Encyclopedia of Social Work,* Vol. 15, s.v., "Follett, Mary Parker," p. 351.

[15]A.M. Henderson and Talcott Parsons (editors and translators), *Max Weber: The Theory of Social Economic Organization* (New York: The Free Press, 1947), p. 337.

[16]The Hawthorne studies are described in detail in F. J. Roethlisberger and William J. Dickson, *Management and the Worker* (Cambridge, Harvard University Press, 1966); and G. Homans, *Fatigue of Workers* (New York: Reinhold, 1941). For an interview with three of the women participants in the relay-assembly test-room studies see R. G. Greenwood, A. A. Bolton, and R. A. Greenwood, "Hawthorne a Half Century Later: Relay Assembly Participants Remember," *Journal of Management,* Vol 9 (1983), pp. 217–231.

[17]A good review of the emergence of organizational behavior as a scientific discipline is provided by Paul R. Lawrence, "Historical Development of Organizational Behavior," pp. 1–9 in Jay W. Lorsch (ed.), *Handbook of Organizational Behavior* (Englewood Cliffs, N.J.: Prentice-Hall, 1987).

[18]The criticisms of the Hawthorne studies are detailed in Alex Carey, "The Hawthorne Studies: A Radical Criticism," *American Sociological Review,* Vol. 32 (1967), pp. 403–416; H.M. Parsons, "What Happened at Hawthorne?," *Science* (Vol. 183 (1974), pp. 922–932; and, B. Rice, "The Hawthorne Defect: Persistence of a Flawed Theory," *Psychology Today,* Vol. 16 (1982), pp. 70–74. See also Wren, op. cit., 1987.

[19]This discussion on Maslow's theory is based on Abraham H. Maslow, *Eupsychian Management* (Homewood Ill.: Richard D. Irwin, 1965) and Abraham H. Maslow, *Motivation and Personality,* Second Edition (New York: Harper & Row, 1970).

[20]Douglas McGregor, *The Human Side of Enterprise* (New York: McGraw-Hill, 1960).

[21]This section is based on Chris Argyris, *Personality and Organization* (New York: Harper & Row, 1957).

[22]See Ann M. Morrison, Randall P. White and Ellen Van Velsor, *Breaking the Glass Ceiling.* (Reading, MA: Addison-Wesley, 1987).

[23]The ideas of Ludwig von Bertalanffy contributed to the emergence of this systems perspective on organizations. See his article, "The History and Status of General Systems Theory," *Academy of Management Journal,* Vol. 15 (1972), pp. 407–426. This viewpoint is further developed by Daniel Katz and Robert L. Kahn in their classic book, *The Social Psychology of Organizations* (New York: Wiley, 1978).

[24]Chester I. Barnard, *The Functions of the Executive* (Cambridge. Harvard University Press, 1938), p. 65.

[25]Katz & Kahn, op cit.

[26]See William G. Ouchi, *Theory Z: How American Business Can Meet the Japanese Challenge.* (Reading, MA: Addison-Wesley, 1981).

[27]See Michael E. Porter, *Competitive Strategy: Techniques for Analyzing Industries and Competitors.* (New York: The Free Press, 1980). See also J. Quinn Mills, *The New Competitors.* (New York: Wiley, 1986).

[28]This case is adapted from Richard E. Boyatzis, *The Competent Manager* (New York: Wiley, 1982), pp. 36–39. Used by permission.

[29]David A. Whetten and Kim S. Cameron, *Developing Management Skills* (Glenview, Il: Scott, Foresman, 1984), pp. 351–352. Used by permission.

Managerial
Decision Making
and Problem Solving

A Brave New World of Decision Making

Decisions—big and small, momentous and routine—are the stuff of a manager's daily work life. Yet most managers' decision-making skills, according to the Center for Decision Research at the University of Chicago's Graduate School of Business, are underdeveloped. A decade of study has convinced the Center that managers suffer from many decision flaws—glitches in the way they sort and assess information—which often have negative consequences for their work. Among the flaws identified by the Center are poor framing (allowing a problem to be defined by the language or context it's presented in, rather than exploring every perspective), and availability bias (seizing on the most available evidence even if it goes against the larger picture).

It might be said that the only thing worse than a bad decision is no decision at all—and managers are constantly pressured to make fast, accurate choices among options. However, one of the most serious problems in decision making is overconfidence. Too many managers, according to the Center, are not aware of their own assumptions and prejudices—and the quality of their decisions suffers for this. Managers reluctant to challenge and question themselves have trouble bringing the needed flexibility to bear on complex decisions.

However, this and other decision-related problems *can* be turned around. In fact, millions of managers are being trained to become better decision makers. Paul Shoemaker, the Center's director, points out that managers must improve decision making to keep up with competitors. He cites the example of Japanese managers who have been taught not to view complaining customers as annoyances, but as valued informants on product value.

Research on Artificial Intelligence (computer-based reasoning systems) points to an increased understanding of how humans make decisions—and how they can make better ones. In the near future, powerful AI systems will be enrolled to help make strategic judgments, and computerized simulators will allow managers to practice making decisions under diverse scenarios. The successful manager will develop multiple methods—intuitive, rational, and computerized—for arriving at final judgments, and will learn how to balance and synthesize these methods in routine as well as unexpected decision-making situations. The researchers anticipate a new generation of "decision architects"—managers who frame problems and oversee judgments made by human and electronic subordinates. ∎

Source: Information from John McCormick, "The Wisdom of Solomon," *Newsweek* (August 17, 1987), pp. 62–63.

Imagine how Lee Iacocca, the CEO of Chrysler Corporation must have felt. His company was charged in a widely publicized federal suit with selling "as new" autos that had been driven up to 400 miles by employees. It all began when a few Chrysler executives were caught speeding by Missouri troopers, who later discovered the cars' odometers were disconnected. Iacocca's first inclination was to fight the suit and defend the practice as normal quality control testing. After reconsidering, he changed his mind. The company pleaded "no contest" to federal charges on the matter and agreed to pay more than $16 million to owners of the suspect vehicles.[1] "Did we screw up? You bet we did," Iacocca told a group of reporters, going on to say the company practice "went beyond dumb and reached all the way to stupid." To back up the admission, Chrysler ran full page ads in major newspapers. One said, in part, "Disconnecting odometers is a lousy idea. That's a mistake we won't make again at Chrysler. Period." It was signed, *Lee Iacocca*.

Not all managerial problems are as sensational as the one just described. But the responsibility to make good decisions and solve a multitude of problems extends to all managers working in all situations. And just as Lee Iacocca had to work through the problem, even to the point of changing his mind, most managerial problems involve complications that severely challenge a manager's decision-making and problem-solving capabilities. The chapter opener highlights this point. Effective managers locate problems to be solved, make good problem-solving decisions, and then take the action necessary to implement these decisions in day-to-day practice. This chapter introduces the key elements of managerial decision making and problem solving. It will help you further develop the requisite managerial skills and competencies.

MANAGERIAL PROBLEM SOLVING

A **problem** exists whenever there is a difference between an *actual* situation and a *desired* situation, that is, when there is a difference between what *is* and what *should be*. For example, a manager faces a possible problem when turnover or absenteeism increases in the work unit, when performance falls for a particular subordinate, or when an executive communicates dissatisfaction with something that has been said or done. The challenge in each of the prior cases is to proceed with effective **problem solving**. This is the process of identifying a discrepancy between actual and desired state of affairs and then taking action to resolve the discrepancy.

Notice the emphasis on action in the prior definition. The problem solving process is not complete until action has been taken to resolve what has been identified as a problem. For managers, however, the nature of the organization as a work setting makes this process especially challenging. Our discussion of managerial problem solving, accordingly, recognizes the unique action demands created by the following "facts of managerial life."[2]

■ *Managers make decisions within the organization's hierarchy of authority.* The types of problems to be solved and decisions to be made will vary by managerial level. Relevant and necessary information must often be obtained from subordinates and other persons. Managers must be sensitive to alternative viewpoints while depending on these people to help make and implement decisions. This requires an understanding of both the human dynamics and total systems implications of any problem situation.

■ *Managers make decisions dealing with interrelated "networks" of problems.* Managers usually face more than one problem at the same time and these problems are often interrelated. Action taken in respect to one problem can easily have implications for another. Broad and integrative thinking is required to solve problems singly and in relationship with one another.

■ *Managers make decisions in a shifting field of problem priorities.* Selecting the *right* problem to work on at any given moment is important. Managers must determine if a particular problem is truly *solvable* given available resources. They must also be adept at sorting through competing demands to identify the most significant problems of the moment.

■ *Managers make decisions in many unexpected problem situations.* Many of the problems managers encounter occur unexpectedly. They can't always be planned for in advance, and they may demand creative solutions. Managers must be able to solve these spontaneous problems while still focusing on a general long-term sense of direction.

■ *Manager's make decisions in many situations that are ambiguous and ill-defined.* Many of the problems managers face will be open-ended and ill-structured. It may be unclear where the information exists to solve certain problems and the resulting solutions may be imperfect, incomplete, or temporary. This requires a tolerance for ambiguity and inconsistency.

Problem Solving and the Managerial Functions

Table 3.1 gives examples of problem-solving decisions you should be prepared to make in the man-

TABLE 3.1 *Some Problem-Solving Decisions which Arise in the Process of Planning, Organizing, Leading, and Controlling for Productivity*

Planning for Productivity

What is the mission of my organization and work unit?
What should our objectives be?
What strategies should be pursued?
How big a budget is required?
When should staff meetings be held?

Organizing for Productivity

How should the division of labor be accomplished?
How can coordination be achieved?
Who should have decision-making authority?
What staffing needs exist for the various jobs?
How can we train people to best use new technologies?

Leading for Productivity

What can be done to increase individual work efforts?
What can be done to reduce turnover and absenteeism?
What information should my subordinates have?
Why has morale dropped in my work unit?
Should our reward system be changed?

Controlling for Productivity

How can performance be measured?
Can new technology streamline operations?
What information systems are needed?
Why haven't we achieved our objectives?
What can be done to increase performance in the future?

agement process. The quality of managerial problem solving in the context of planning, organizing, leading, and controlling directly influences organizational productivity. Indeed, the very concept of the "manager's challenge" as introduced in Chapter 1 involves managerial accountability for results. This accountability extends all the way to the top of the pyramid, where even the senior executives must account for their decisions and actions. These two headlines portray the "downside" of this issue:

> ## THE BOSS OF ALLEGIS CORP. LOST HIS JOB
> *(Fortune Magazine)*
>
> ## PORSCHE CHIEF QUITS ABRUPTLY AS STRATEGY FAILS
> *(The Wall Street Journal)*

NEW IDEAS
ARE HARD TO FIND

Faced with diminishing Sugar-Free Kool-Aid sales, General Foods hit on the idea of inviting six teams of business-school students to participate in a contest to develop a marketing plan for its ailing product. For a full day, students from Stanford, Michigan, Northwestern, Pennsylvania, Columbia, and Chicago universities poured over GF-supplied data. They worked up strategies that they then presented, in 20-minute pitches, to a panel of judges from GF, one of its consultants, and its ad agencies.

The student teams were divided on which segment of the consumer market GF should target. Several said that parents should be the focus of ads; one team proposed new packaging. The Michigan team (which eventually won the contest) suggested that all adults be targeted and that GF make use of the phrase "low-calorie" as part of the product's description.

The contest judges expressed disappointment in the lack of originality of the students' proposals. None of the ideas were new. GF's Douglas Smith wondered if the students had been given too much data, which may have encouraged them to be overly concerned with numbers and less with broader strategic issues. Business schools, Smith averred, "deal with . . . analysis and facts. But they don't help people much to use the other side, which is judging and intuitive."

Smith and many other businesspeople fear that the "number-crunching" skills of recent graduates may work against them in settings where human relations skills are prized. There is general agreement among students as well as professionals, however, that on-the-job experience is the best place to acquire "right-brain" skills. One participant in GF's competition was enthusiastic about the experience, despite losing, because it taught her something new in a nonacademic, hands-on setting: "It's the best opportunity to apply what we've learned," she said.

Source: As reported in Trish Hall, "When Budding MBAs Try to Save Kool-Aid, Original Ideas Are Scarce," *Wall Street Journal* (December 25, 1986), p. 31.

On the more positive side, here are some examples of "decisions that made a difference" for two of America's fasting growing companies.[3]

At Compaq Computer the firm was just another start-up in a crowded market for IBM compatible products. But its founders made two key decisions that solved the problem of differentiating Compaq from its competitors. One was the decision to produce their now-famous portable computer—which became an instant success. The other was to develop strong relationships with retailers—and they won the distribution battle.

At Liz Claiborne the once-fledgling firm needed a market niche and a way to beat the problems of large overhead. The founders decided to clothe women in the workforce—and they rode the crest of the wave as women entered the labor market in record numbers. They also decided to break with garment industry tradition by *not* building their own manufacturing plants—this gave them a substantial competitive edge in production flexibility.

Problem-Solving Styles

Generally speaking, managers approach problems in three different ways. Managers may be

1. *Problem avoiders* Those who ignore informa-

tion that would otherwise signal the presence of a problem.

2. *Problem solvers* Those who act to solve problems when they arise—that is, who are good at *reacting* to a defined problem.

3. *Problem seekers* Those who actively look for problems to solve or opportunities to explore as a matter of routine—that is, who are *proactive* in anticipating problems before they occur.

Although there will be times when problem avoidance is an appropriate managerial response, managers must be able to react well and solve problems when they arise. Ultimately, though, success at problem seeking may well distinguish the exceptional managers from the merely good ones. Problem seekers are forward-thinking managers who anticipate problems and opportunities and take appropriate action to gain the advantage. They don't just wait for problems to develop and suddenly present themselves for immediate, and perhaps "knee-jerk" responses.

Newsline 3.1 highlights another prominent issue in respect to managerial problem-solving styles—the difference between systematic and intuitive thinking. And as the newsline indicates, some employers criticize today's college graduates as being too systematic in approaching problems. The result, they say, is a loss of creativity in the process. How about you? Are you more systematic or intuitive in problem solving?

A **systematic thinker** approaches problems in a rational and analytical fashion. This person is able to break a complex problem into smaller components and then address them in a logical and integrated fashion. A systematic thinker can be expected to make a plan before taking action, search in an orderly fashion for information to facilitate problem-solving, and consider this information in a step-by-step fashion often in consultation with others. An **intuitive thinker**, by contrast, is more flexible and spontaneous. This person is likely to respond imaginatively to a problem based on a quick and broad overview of the situation and possible alternative courses of action. An intuitive thinker can be expected to deal with many aspects of a problem at once, jump from one issue to another quickly, and consider "hunches" based on experience or spontaneous ideas.

The subject of intuition will come up again

later in this chapter. For now, it is sufficient to recognize that effective problem solving often depends on the ability to mix systematic and intuitive thinking well. Remember:

1. *Systematic problem solving* tends to be thorough and more balanced as a variety of information and the ideas of many persons are taken into account. But, it can be time consuming and lack creativity.

2. *Intuitive problem solving* tends to be quick and less complex in terms of the amount of information and number of people involved in decision making. But, it may fail to consider all aspects of the problem, and runs the risk of good solutions being ignored.

THE PROBLEM-SOLVING PROCESS

Figure 3.1 describes the problem solving process as a series of five steps, beginning with problem identification and ending with the evaluation of implemented solutions. The logic of this figure is especially important because it also underlies the models of planning and strategic planning presented in Chapters 4 and 5. In a moment we will review the step-by-step process in detail. First, let's refer back to the figure to distinguish between three action terms—choice making, decision making and problem solving.[4]

1. **Choice making** is the narrowest activity depicted in Figure 3.1. It involves the selection of a preferred course of action from a set of alternatives. Managers make choices in various ways. The economic/rational and "satisficing" models of choice making, as well as the use of judmental heuristics will be discussed in some detail in this chapter.

2. **Decision making** is the process of identifying a problem and choosing among alternative possible solutions. It is a more encompassing concept than choice making. Explored later in this chapter are the differences between making decisions by individual, consultative, and group approaches.

3. **Problem solving** is the broadest activity in the figure. As already defined, it is the process of identifying a problem and then taking action to resolve it. Creativity is a major element in problem solving. It takes creativity to find the right problems; it takes creativity to choose good solutions; and it takes

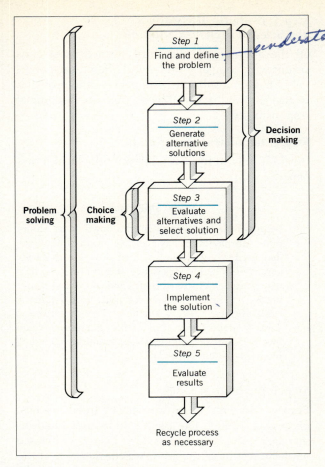

understand

FIGURE 3.1 *Major steps in the problem-solving process.*

creativity to implement these solutions in a productive way.

study

Steps in the Problem-Solving Process

The problem-solving process includes specific responsibility for

- Finding and defining the problem.
- Generating alternative solutions.
- Evaluating alternatives to select a solution.
- Implementing the preferred solution.
- Evaluating results.

Step 1: Find and Define the Problem *problem analysis*

In the first stage of the problem-solving process, the manager is concerned with finding and defining the problem. Questions to be asked include: "What is the *actual* situation?" "What is the *desired* situation?" "What is the *cause* of the difference?" This is a stage of information gathering, information processing, and deliberation. It often begins with the appearance of *symptoms* indicating the presence of a problem. The manager's goal is to assess a situation properly and look beyond symptoms to find out what is wrong. In so doing, special care must be taken not to confuse symptom and problem. A crucial mistake is to address a symptom while ignoring the true problem. Merely reprimanding a subordinate for absenteeism, for example, might never solve the real problem of dissatisfaction with a new job assignment.

Step 2: Generate Alternative Solutions

Once the problem is defined, it is possible to formulate one or several potential solutions. More information is gathered, data analyzed, and the pros and cons of possible alternative courses of action established. This effort to identify, clarify, and evaluate alternative solutions is critical to any problem-solving effort. Creativity is extremely important. The end result can only be as good as the quality of the alternative solutions generated in this step.

Step 3: Evaluate Alternatives and Select a Preferred Solution

This is the point of choice. Given the alternatives, along with the pros and cons of each, a manager can choose a preferred course of action. The questions of how and by whom this final choice is made must be successfully resolved in each problem situation. In some cases the manager alone should make the choice; in others a group approach might be best. In some cases, the best alternative may be selected on a cost–benefit criterion; in others, additional criteria may enter into play. In all cases, the ethical aspects of a manager's choices are increasingly emphasized in today's society. The end-of-chapter exercise gives you an initial chance to address this issue. Later in the book, Chapter 20 is devoted to managerial ethics social responsibility.

Step 4: Implement the Solution

Given the preferred solution, appropriate action plans can be established for its implementation. This is a point where action is initiated and directions set. It is also a time when the manager must have the support of other key persons whose efforts will actually implement the solution as chosen. People will be more diligent and thorough in helping to implement decisions they accept—and therefore to which they are committed. Thus the degree to which these persons have or have not been involved in the prior steps may substantially affect the success of the total problem-solving process. A good alternative that is arrived at improperly may end up poorly implemented.

Step 5: Evaluate Results

The problem-solving process remains incomplete until the manager checks to ensure that, after the intended actions are taken, the desired and actual situations are finally one and the same. That is, true problem solving includes establishing an information system to gather feedback on actions taken, evaluate results and allow for the process to be recycled as necessary.

Illustrative Case:
Small Firm Makes Tough Decision

On December 31, the Indal Aluminum Company decided to close down its Murphysboro, Illinois, plant. There were 172 employees six months prior to the closing, but by December market conditions were forcing layoffs and the company could not find a buyer for the local plant. Some employees had been with the company 18 years, others as little as six months. All were to get severance pay equal to one week per year's service. Indal officials, though, worried about a new problem. Let's try and recreate the steps they followed in problem solving.

Step 1: Find and Define the Problem

Closing the plant will put many people, some with long tenure at Indal, out of work. The negative impact on them, their families, and the local community, would be great.

Step 2: Generate Alternative Solutions

Many things could be done, including:

1. Simply close the plant on schedule.
2. Offer some workers transfers to new jobs at other Indal plants.
3. Offer some transfers, and actively help everyone find new jobs in the local area.

Step 3: Evaluate Alternatives and Select a Preferred Solution

Of the alternatives, the third seemed most consistent with company values and offered the potential of having a substantial impact on the problem. It also showed a good sense of corporate social responsibility.

Step 4: Implement the Solution

Indal ran this ad for several days in the local newspaper.

Indal Skill Bank

Because of an imminent plant shutdown, Indal Aluminum, Murphysboro, has a sizable group of qualified, dedicated, and well-motivated employees with a wide variety of skills and experience. It is our intent to help match our demonstrated talents and abilities with your needs. . . . These employees commute from within the circle of Chester, Percy, DuQuoin, Benton, Pittsburg, Anna & Grand Tower. If an interested employer would like to explore possibilities & opportunities, including frank evaluation, please call.

Step 5: Evaluate Results

For over 15 days the ad was run by Indal at a cost exceeding $2600. The plant's industrial relations manager, John Hogan, said, "I've been very pleased with the results of the ad. It was designed to try to relocate laid-off Indal employees in new jobs in the southern Illinois area."

FINDING AND DEFINING PROBLEMS

Problem finding involves identifying gaps between actual and desired states and determining their causes. These gaps may represent performance deficiencies or unexplored opportunities. The manager who is good at finding problems to be solved is continually searching and scanning the work environment for indicators of potential problems or opportunities. In his book *Innovation and Entrepreneurship,* Peter Drucker notes that many managers fail to do this.[5] As a result they lose important opportunities for innovation. The *entrepreneurial manager,* by contrast, is alert to the situation and environment and quick to identify problems to be solved and opportunities to be explored.

The Role of Information

Finding and defining problems is an ongoing information-gathering and information-processing responsibility of managers. In Chapter 15 which is devoted to "management information systems," **information** is defined as data made relevant for decision making. That is, information is knowledge that a manager can use for problem solving. Knowing where and how to get the right information is an important capability that affects the entire problem solving process. At least five sources of information can be very useful in helping managers identify actual or potential problems. They are:[6]

1. *Information obtained by examining deviations from past experience.* When a previous and satisfactory pattern of performance is interrupted, the manager has a good signal that a problem might exist.

2. *Information obtained by examining deviations from plans.* When results are falling short of projections, the chances are that one or more problems might exist.

3. *Information obtained by speaking with other people.* Peers, subordinates, or higher-level managers within the organization, as well as outsiders such as customers and resource suppliers, can be the source of problem-identifying information.

4. *Information obtained by watching the performance of other organizations or work units.* The performance of other comparable organizations, especially competitors, can be a good indicator of how well the organization is doing. By the same token, the performance of other subunits within an organization can provide similar insight to the manager regarding his or her workunit's achievements.

5. *Information obtained from personal or institutional memory.* Effective managers "remember" what has happened in the past—to themselves and to others. Through memory, forged by personal intellectual discipline and/or diligent record keeping, managers can continue to benefit from past successes and failures by applying that learning to events taking place in the present.

These information aids to managerial problem finding are further illustrated in Table 3.2. The example is based on the failure of Laker Airways, the

---

TABLE 3.2 *Information Aids to Managerial Problem-Finding: A Case of failure for Laker Airways*

Sir Freddie Laker began a no-frills transatlantic Skytrain air service. His cheap fares revolutionized air travel and made both him and Laker Airways widely heralded success stories. But after rapid expansion, the airline collapsed. The failure was based in part on Freddie Laker's decision to purchase new planes in a declining world economy. Laker might have been able to anticipate critical problems before they occurred by acting as follows.

1. *He could have examined deviations from past experience.*	Laker Airways surely maintained historical data on costs, passenger usage, and revenues. Trends could well have been detected in these data that showed increasing costs, decreasing revenues, and declining transatlantic customers.
2. *He could have examined deviations from plans.*	If Laker Airways had specific objectives for such things as passenger loads and revenues, actual performance could have regularly been compared to these objectives. As soon as a gap between objectives and actual performance appeared, steps could have been taken to answer the question "Why?"
3. *He could have listened to other people.*	When deciding whether or not to make a major investment in new planes, Laker could have been extra diligent in gathering reactions to his proposals. A special task force could have been established to act as devil's advocate arguing against the investment; customer surveys of future travel plans could have been taken.
4. *He could have better analyzed the competition.*	Other airlines surely faced similar economic pressures. By carefully watching their behavior, Laker might have realized that he should move more cautiously with capital investments in new planes—or not at all.
5. *He could have remembered past problems with this strategy.*	If Sir Freddie had expanded rapidly once before, only to experience later financial pressures, or known of another airline that did so, this memory might have led him to expect problems to arise. He might have been more alert to leading indicators of their occurrence and/or he might have moved more slowly in the first place.

---

pioneer cut-rate air service between the United States and England.

Types of Managerial Problems

Managers face many problems in their day-to-day work. They can be classified as routine or nonroutine, expected or unexpected, and crisis.

Routine and Nonroutine Problems

Routine problems arise on a regular basis and can be addressed through standard responses. Called **programmed decisions,** these responses select solutions determined by past experience as appropriate for the problem at hand. Good examples of programmed decisions are to reorder inventory automatically when on-hand stock falls below a predetermined level, to place students on probation when they fall below a certain grade-point average, or to initiate an IRS audit when charitable contributions reported on an income tax return exceed a certain limit.

    Nonroutine problems are unique and new. Because they have not been encountered before, standard responses are not available. They call for **nonprogrammed decisions** which create solutions tailored to fit the specific situation at hand. The information requirements for defining and resolving nonroutine problems are typically high. As Figure 3.2 shows, these types of problems predominate among those faced by higher-level managers. This

FIGURE 3.2 *Time spent on routine and nonroutine problems by various levels of managers.*

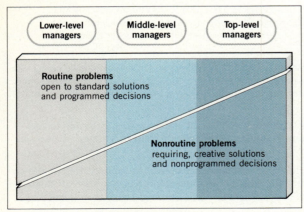

Time on problems

is one reason why the demands on a manager's conceptual skills, as discussed in Chapter 1, increase as one moves up the hierarchy of authority. Lower-level managers spend a greater proportion of their time dealing with more routine problems.

Expected and Unexpected Problems

Another way to view managerial problems is as expected or unexpected. **Expected problems** are anticipated situations that will require decisions sometime in the future. The manager can plan ahead for these problems and develop specific ways of dealing with them. For example, a typical manager may expect to encounter problems when making decisions on periodic staff pay raises and promotions, vacation requests, and committee assignments.

    Unexpected problems, rightly or wrongly, catch the manager by surprise. They are not anticipated and are addressed by reaction after their occurrence. Astute and "proactive" managers—ones we earlier called problem-seekers—are prepared to handle a variety of "unexpected" problems. Consider the surprise employee absence. Although it can't be predicted that a specific employee will be absent on any given day, it can be anticipated that absences will sometimes occur. Rather than waiting for this to happen, and then trying to decide what to do, a more proactive approach can be taken. A procedure or rule could be established to handle these "unexpected" but now "anticipated" absences when they occur. In the example, a standby list of temporary substitute workers might be maintained for use as needed.

Crisis Problems

A **crisis problem** is an unexpected problem that can lead to disaster if not resolved quickly and in an acceptable manner. No one can avoid crises, and the public-at-large is well aware of the immensity of corporate crises in the modern world. The Tylenol poisonings and related product tampering incidents that periodically occur, the Union Carbide disaster in India, the Chernoybl nuclear power plant explosion in the Soviet Union, the Ashland oil spill in the Monongahela River, and airline hijackings by terrorists, are but a few sensational examples. *Newsline 3.2* indicates that more and more firms now anticipate that crises will occur. They are installing "early

HOW TO PREPARE FOR THE WORST

In the days after the nuclear cooling-system breakdown at Three Mile Island, Governor Richard Thornburgh assembled a crisis management team that he referred to as an "ad-hocrasy"—a group of trusted associates and specialists, none of whom had ever operated under such extreme pressure. The group's role was to contain error and rumor in the face of a terrifying possibility—a reactor meltdown. In Thornburgh's view the team did as well as could be expected, but hysteria still resulted. Union Carbide's CEO, Warren Anderson, also had to manage a grave crisis—the death of over 2000 people in Bhopal, India, after a toxic leak in one of the company's plants. Surprising other CEOs, Anderson flew to India in response to the crisis, stating that his presence on the scene was necessary to facilitate fast action.

These and other incidents offer dramatic proof of the perils corporations face by being unprepared for crises. As potential disasters range from financial scandal to a physically endangered populace, many businesses are confessing to an urgent need for well-devised plans and trained personnel to implement them. Yet only 50 percent of all businesses possess them, claims author and consultant Stephen Fink; often, public relations departments bear the burden of crisis management.

Companies often have advanced warnings of a crisis but tend to ignore or minimize them. Once a crisis erupts, it may prompt a "quick-fix" approach with entirely negative consequences. Experts caution that a company must first take stock of its vulnerabilities and then figure out a way to deal with the most serious threats it might face. Simulations and training are useful, say some consultants, so that organizations will be better equipped to deal with the authorities and the media—two big players in any crisis.

"Facing the music" is a strategy that proved successful for one company—Procter & Gamble—which pulled Rely tampons off the market after their linkage with toxic shock syndrome. P&G's fast action actually boosted its image; its new product, Always, claimed 17 percent of the market.

Source: As reported in Nancy Jeffrey, "Preparing for the Worst: Firms Set Up Plans to Help Deal with Corporate Crises," *Wall Street Journal* (December 7, 1987), p. 25; Caryn A. Wiener, "Crisis Control: Handling Major Industrial Accidents," *NYU Business* (Fall 1986/Winter 1987), pp. 42–44.

---

warning" crisis information systems and developing crisis-management plans.

At any level of management, crises may catch a manager completely by surprise. They will require quick action under very stressful conditions. Research indicates that managers may erroneously react to crisis by isolating themselves and trying to solve the problem alone.[7] This is an unfortunate tendency which denies the manager crucial information and assistance at the very time when they are most needed. It can also create even more problems since the manager may end up making critical decisions with poor or inadequate information, and from a limited personal perspective. Here's an example of one manager who learned this lesson, to the benefit of his small firm and its employees.[8]

At Springfield Remanufacturing, Corporation the CEO Jack Stack faced a crisis. A GM representative gave him 90 days notice that 5,000 engines were being cut from their standing order with his firm. This would mean the loss of about 100 jobs. Stack spent two months agonizing on how to deal with the problem, and his frustrations only grew. Then he realized that the employees should participate in the decisions to be made. He held a series of meetings to share and discuss the facts. Everyone agreed that before people were laid off, every effort should be made to take on new jobs—even ones they were unfamiliar with. They wanted to try *anything* in order to survive. And survive they did. Employees worked extra hours to learn new products and satisfy new customers. Within a year revenues were up and the foundations were set for an actual *increase* in the workforce by 100.

The ability to handle crises may be the ultimate test of a manager's problem-solving capabilities. The process begins with taking care to isolate and identify the real problem(s) underlying the crisis. This is where information and the involvement of others is crucial. Further guidelines on taking "quick action" in response to crisis situations follow.[8]

■ Prepare for action by knowing as much as possible about all phases of the operation you are responsible for.

■ Build a network of reliable sources of information and advice, and be willing to use them when needed.

■ Don't accept the problem as delivered; acquire information quickly to confirm and define it for yourself.

■ Take quick action only on absolutely urgent aspects of the problem.

■ Test your responses before acting whenever possible, even if just with one or more key people.

■ Don't shirk your responsibility—address the problem, even in face of risk and incomplete information.

■ Remember to learn from the situation; think about what can be done to keep it from happening the next time.

Barriers to Good Problem Definition

The way a problem is originally defined can effect the success of problem-solving. What follows are three common barriers to accurate problem definition. Each has special potential to interfere with the initial stage of the problem-solving process.

Defining the Problem Too Broadly or Too Narrowly

It is easy to jump into a situation and define the problem too broadly or too narrowly. To take a classic example, the problem stated as "build a better mousetrap," might better be defined as "get rid of the mice." The latter definition opens up the situation to a much wider range of problem-solving options than does the former. Consider this additional example of attempts to improve the quality of work life in automobile assembly operations.[10]

At Volvo the Kalmar plant's innovative production facility is now famous world-wide. Its beginnings trace to a task force set up by President Pehr Gyllenhammar to redesign operations so that "people should rule the machine," and not vice-versa. After he rejected several of their proposals to modify Volvo's traditional assembly-line, the design group took a fresh approach. The problem which was first defined as "redesign the assembly line," was redefined as "create more flexibility for workers in the assembly process." Out of this new thinking came the idea of a mobile assembly platform around which groups of people could work, and which could carry a car from place to place around the plant. And given this concept, the project group was able to design a totally new assembly process that satisfied Gyllenhammar.

Another reason why problems are sometimes misdefined is **selective perception,** the tendency of people to define problems from their own points of view. It often occurs when persons of different technical or functional backgrounds tackle the same problem. The likelihood in a business setting, for example, is that marketing, production, and finance specialists will define a problem in terms of their respective areas of expertise. This is why good managers explore alternative points of view to ensure that the best problem definition is achieved.

Focusing on Symptoms Instead of Causes

Symptoms alert managers to the presence of potential problems. They serve as indicators that problems may exist, but they shouldn't be mistaken for the problems themselves or for their causes. Common symptoms of management problems in organizations include the appearance of employee absenteeism, turnover, tardiness, negative attitudes, poor quality work and declining work quantity, among other possibilities. Such observed changes in behavior or performance are problem *symptoms;* the underlying reasons for their occurrence are the problem *causes.*

Informed managers understand this distinction when dealing with daily problems. They know how to spot problem symptoms (e.g., an increase in absenteeism) and then determine their root causes (e.g., the introduction of a new complex computer system into job routines). In this example, a manager who simply disciplines an employee for being absent, that is, who treats the symptoms, is avoiding the true problem—employee discomfort and even fear of working with the new computer. As a result, loss of productivity through failure to utilize the computer to its full potential is likely to continue; occasional employee absenteeism may continue as well.

Choosing the Wrong Problem

Finally, another key aspect of finding and defining problems is knowing which ones to focus on at any given point in time. Managers should give priority to problems that offer the most significant benefits in terms of correcting performance deficiencies or taking advantage of opportunities for new performance gains. They should also give priority to problems that are truly solvable, given a realistic investment of time and other resources. "No action"—at least "no action for the time being"—can be a legitimate response to some problem situations. In the midst of a hectic work pace and sometimes confusing array of simultaneous demands, good managerial judgment in selecting problems to define and address is essential. As one manager comments:[11]

> I have to sort through so many issues at once. There are ten times too many. . . . One of the frustrations is that I don't want to tell my people that their number one problems have lower priorities than they think they should get.

GENERATING AND EVALUATING ALTERNATIVE SOLUTIONS

Once a problem is identified and defined, problem solving proceeds with the formulation and analysis of alternative potential solutions. This is a time when information is needed to discover alternative courses of action and learn the possible consequences of each. The manager's responsibilities here include both the search for and evaluation of information pertinent to the problem at hand. A common mistake in this phase of problem solving is being too quick in selecting a particular solution for implementation. Managers sometimes fail because they chose a convenient alternative that has damaging side effects, one that won't work fast enough, or one that simply isn't as good as others that might have been discovered with a little extra effort in the first place.

As a manager, you will be especially challenged in this step by nonroutine problems—those that appear unexpectedly and with unique characteristics. Finding a good solution to them will always require something extra on your part. That something extra is **creativity,** an application of ingenuity and imagination that results in a novel approach or unique solution to a problem.

Take a moment to test your creativity. Each of the following puzzles actually symbolizes a familiar word or phrase. Solving each requires you to be creative in looking at things with a fresh and unrestrained eye. See how well you do—the answers will come later.

1	2	3	4
SAND	MIND / MATTER	O / M.D. / PH.D. / D.D.D.	DICE / DICE

Creativity in Problem Solving

The greater the creativity that can be brought to bear on a problem, the more alternative solutions of potential value that are likely to be considered and the greater the likelihood that they will be rigorously evaluated. A lack of creativity constrains problem solving and can compromise the quality of any solutions achieved.

Individual Creativity

Let's look back to your earlier problem-solving efforts with the word and symbol puzzles. The correct answers are (1) "sandbox," (2) "mind over matter," (3) "three degrees below zero," and (4) "paradise." Just as the puzzles now look easier in retrospect, creativity is something that can be enhanced through discipline and good managerial judgment. To stimulate individual creativity one must overcome[12]

1. *Perceptual blocks* Confusion of important and insignificant data; an inability to "see the forest through the trees."

2. *Cultural blocks* Taboos and traditions that guide thinking in habitual ways.
3. *Emotional blocks* Internalized fears of making a mistake or being criticized if "wrong."
4. *Intellectual blocks* Language or symbolic inadequacies that confine thinking.

Blocks such as these can impair individual creativity in the problem-solving process. Good alternatives may fail to be discovered or considered, and poor ones may be selected for implementation merely because they are readily available. Table 3.3 reviews a number of techniques which can help you avoid such blocks and improve individual creativity. A willingness to take advantage of groups as problem-solving resources can help as well.

Group Techniques to Improve Creativity in Problem Solving

Groups can be of great help to managers in the alternative-generation phase of the problem-solving process. Two useful approaches are the brainstorming and nominal group techniques.

In **brainstorming,** groups of five to ten members meet to generate ideas. Four rules typically govern the process.

1. *All criticism is ruled out* Judgment or evaluation of ideas must be withheld until the idea-generation process has been completed.
2. *"Freewheeling" is welcomed* The wilder or more radical the idea, the better.

TABLE 3.3 *Ten Techniques for Enhancing Creative Thinking*

1. *Look for multiple "right answers."* Most of us have been trained to seek *the* right answer. By following this trend, we often fail to find other equally good (or sometimes better) ways to do things.
2. *Avoid excessive logic at first.* In order to germinate ideas, we can benefit from the kind of thinking that uses metaphors, fantasy, and diffuse and divergent viewpoints. Later, logic is most helpful when we get practical and evaluate ideas in terms of putting them into action or practice.
3. *Challenge rules.* What this means is that flexibility enhances creativity. Inspect ideas, challenge the way things have always been, ask *why?* each time you are tempted to accept an idea *because . . .*
4. *Be practical.* Ask *what if?* questions, seeking to think of the practical results that would be obtained *if* things were different. To do this, however, we each need to allow our imaginations to have free rein.
5. *Use ambiguity.* When communicating, we all want to be as clear as possible. When looking for new ideas, however, a little ambiguity can be helpful. It makes us stop and look at things differently as we seek to "de-fuzz" the situation. Often, that is when we discover a new way to look at the problem.
6. *Foster the creative side of errors.* While many people have been trained to avoid error (and seek one *right* answer), creativity comes from errors. Playing it safe often keeps us from trial-and-error behavior, from seeking a new (and better) way to do something, and finally, from using our failures to stimulate a new path to success. Don't be afraid of being wrong. Use the experience to look at your goal afresh.
7. *Use play to fertilize your thinking.* When we play, we put aside many of the blocks to creative thinking that have already been discussed. When we play, we tinker, we experiment, we are spontaneous, we just have fun. In the process, we may discover a new way to do something, a way we would not have discovered if we had approached the problem with a serious search for the quick right answer.
8. *Go outside your area of specialization.* Hunt for new ideas, new information, new models, and so forth. Use analogs and models from other disciplines.
9. *Use foolish thinking and nonconformist behavior to generate new ideas.* Most people are afraid to look foolish, so they act like everyone else, staying within established norms. Like the right-answer seekers they may miss the opportunity to try things in a new, different, or even innovative way.
10. *Believe you are creative and you will be.* Creative behavior *can* be your self-fulfilling prophecy. If you perceive yourself as capable of creative thinking you can become a creative problem solver. If you assume you are not, then you will act accordingly—and you won't be.

Source: These techniques are described by Roger Van Oech in his book *A Whack on the Side of the Head* (New York: Warner Books, 1983). This presentation is from Roy J. Lewicki, Donald D. Bowen, Douglas T. Hall, and Francine S. Hall, *Experiences in Management and Organizational Behavior,* Third Edition (New York: Wiley, 1988), pp. 96–97. Used by permission.

3. *Quantity is important* The greater the number of ideas, the greater the likelihood of obtaining a superior idea.

4. *Building on one another's ideas is encouraged* Participants should suggest how ideas of others can be turned into better ideas, or how two or more ideas can be joined into still another idea.

By prohibiting criticism, brainstorming reduces fears of ridicule or failure on the part of individuals. Typical results include more enthusiasm, involvement, and a freer flow of ideas. Because of this, brainstorming often proves superior to open group discussions as a basis for creative thinking and the generation of possible solutions to problems.

There will be times when the persons whose help is needed in problem solving have quite different opinions and goals. The differences may even be so extreme that antagonistic argument can be predicted for a group meeting. In such cases, a nominal group technique could be more appropriate than brainstorming. A **nominal group** works like this:[13]

1. Participants work alone and respond in writing with possible solutions to a stated problem.
2. These ideas are then read aloud in round-robin fashion *without* any criticism or discussion.
3. The ideas are recorded on large newsprint as they are read aloud.
4. The ideas are then discussed and clarified in round-robin sequence. Evaluative comments are not allowed.
5. A written voting procedure ranks the alternatives in terms of priority.
6. Steps 4 and 5 are repeated as desired to add further clarification to the process.

Nominal grouping can aid problem solving and improve creativity in the process. It allows alternatives to be generated and evaluated without risking the inhibitions, hostilities, and distorted outcomes that may accompany more unstructured meeting formats.

Two other group approaches that you might become involved with are synectics and the Delphi technique. **Synectics,** the joining together of apparently unrelated elements, is used to break existing patterns of thinking. Participants in a synectics group are asked to generate verbal and visual analogies with seemingly irrelevant things in order to open new avenues of thought and bring more creativity to problem solving. The **Delphi technique,** by contrast, is a written survey method for gathering expert opinions from a group of persons without having to bring them together for a group meeting. Usually, an initial survey is distributed and the results tallied. The results are sent back to the original respondents along with additional questions. This process is repeated until the desired pool of information and viewpoints is attained. One benefit of the Delphi technique is getting people to speak their minds frankly because their anonymity is protected.

Problem Conditions or Environments

Figure 3.3 describes three different conditions or environments under which problem-solving decisions are made—certainty, risk, and uncertainty. The degree of certainty has a definite impact on problem-solving, and managers must make problem-solving decisions under each of these environmental conditions. In particular the degree of uncer-

FIGURE 3.3 *Three environmental conditions for managerial problem solving and decision making.*

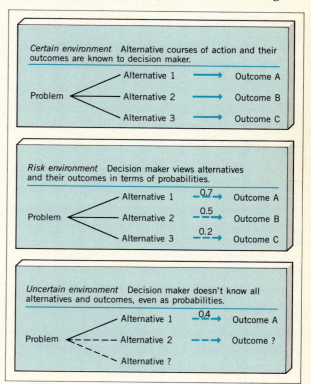

CERTAIN ENVIRONMENT Alternative courses of action and their outcomes are known to decision maker.

RISK ENVIRONMENT Decision maker views alternatives and their outcomes in terms of probabilities.

UNCERTAIN ENVIRONMENT Decision maker doesn't know all alternatives and outcomes, even as probabilities.

tainty increases for the more complex and nonroutine problems characteristic of top management responsibility.

Certain Environments

Certainty exists in the problem environment when information is sufficient to know what the alternatives are and predict the results of each. When one invests money in a savings account, certainty exists as to the interest that will be earned over a given period of time. Certainty is an ideal condition for managerial problem solving. The challenge is simply to study the alternatives and choose the one offering a satisfactory or even ideal solution. Unfortunately, certainty is the exception instead of the rule in managerial problem environments.

Risk Environments

Risk involves a lack of complete information regarding action alternatives and their consequences, but it includes some sense of the "probabilities" associated with their possible occurrence. A **probability,** in turn, is the degree of likelihood that an event will occur. Probabilities are usually expressed as percentages, or as a number of chances out of ten. It is common, for example, to hear students estimating the probability of getting an A on their exams. One student might refer to an 80 percent probability of an A; another calls the same likelihood an eight-out-of-ten chance.

Risk is a fairly common decision environment faced by managers. It is especially typical for entrepreneurs and organizations depending on ideas and continued innovation for their success. For example,[14]

At Cray Research the one-product firm has this mission statement: Cray Research designs, manufactures, markets and supports the most powerful computer systems available. CEO John Rollwagen says, "If somebody else makes the world's most powerful computer, we're in deep weeds." He adds, "If nobody wants to buy the world's most powerful computer, we're also in deep weeds. So those are two very clear risks." But as a participant in the dizzying race to develop and sell new technology, Rollwagen also states: "I believe by taking those risks we absolutely maximize the odds that we will make the world's most powerful computer and that we'll figure out how to sell it."

At General Motors CEO Roger Smith also takes risks. The decision to build an entire new plant to manufacture a new car by the name of "Saturn" is certainly a big one. The last time GM introduced a totally new car was 1926 when the Pontiac first appeared. Although Smith considers Saturn critical to GM's long-term competitiveness, industry analysts feel only time will tell if the marketplace is ready and willing to buy this new GM car.

Uncertain Environments

When information is so poor that managers are unable to even assign probabilities to the likely outcomes of those alternatives that are known, **uncertainty** exists. This is the most difficult of the three environments. Uncertainty forces managers to rely heavily on individual and group creativity to succeed in problem solving. It requires unique, novel, and often totally innovative alternatives to existing patterns of behavior. Responses to uncertainty are based on intuition, educated guess, and hunch. The best continuing example of uncertainty in today's managerial environment is expressed in this headline. It reflects the highly volatile and difficult economic situation that planners and decision makers have had to contend with ever since the stock market crash of 1987.

> THE ECONOMY: UNCERTAINTY
> ISN'T ABOUT TO GO AWAY.
> (*Business Week*)

Techniques for Analyzing Alternatives

The analysis of alternatives examines how well each possible course of action can solve the problem at hand. Typical evaluation criteria are the cost, timeliness, and overall quality of an alternative, as well as its ethical soundness. The challenge in this stage of problem solving rests largely with the difficulty of concluding exactly how well each alternative will actually solve the problem. Of course, this challenge varies with the type of environment in which the problem exists. The quantitative decision techniques described in the Management Applications Module at the end of the book are relevant here, as are the spreadsheet and related applications software now available for desk-top computers. In addition, managers should be able to use and understand inventories of alternatives, decision matrices, and payoff tables.

Inventory of Alternatives

Problem solving under certain conditions is the best of all possible worlds. An **inventory of alternatives** works well in such circumstances. It lists each alternative and summarizes favorable and unfavorable points of each. This facilitates making a final choice through **cost–benefit analysis** which compares the costs and benefits of all alternative courses of action with one another.

Let's work with a case example. Assume you are the accounting manager for a small company. You rely greatly on the support of a personal computer in your work. Today, the four-year-old computer has broken down. You know you need a computer, but you face a dilemma in choosing among these possible courses of action.

1. Repair the computer.
2. Replace it with a used one.
3. Replace it with a new but identical one.
4. Replace it with a more advanced one.

This is a problem for which you can gather information and analyze alternatives with considerable certainty. The major challenge is to make sure that all possible issues are considered and that the facts are accurate. The inventory of alternatives shown in Table 3.4 does this in the present case. With the information displayed in such form, your choice among the alternatives can be made with greater confidence that all relevant things have been considered.

Decision Trees

A **decision tree** graphically illustrates the alternatives available to a manager attempting to solve a problem. It assists in the careful analysis of multiple courses of action in more risky conditions. Consider another example. The president of World Systems Corporation has a problem. The firm is experiencing increased sales. The director of marketing wants to add additional production equipment to keep pace with demand; the plant manager is more cautious and wants to meet demand for the short term by increased overtime. Neither one of the alternatives offers entirely certain outcomes. What should the president do?

The decision tree shown in Figure 3.4 helps in the analysis of this problem. It focuses attention on potential outcomes associated with the alternative courses of action. The relevant managerial questions become: "What can happen if we (1) add equipment and sales rise, (2) add equipment and sales fall, (3) add overtime and sales rise, (4) add overtime and sales fall?" The cash flows noted at the end of each branch of the decision tree are the plant manager's estimates of what would result in each situation.

Looking at the information presented in the figure, you might be tempted to conclude that adding equipment is the best bet. It offers the highest

TABLE 3.4 *Inventory of Alternatives: The Case of the Computer Repair-Replacement Decision*

	Alternative	Time Delay	Estimated Costs	Favorable Points	Unfavorable Points
A	Repair computer.	14 days	$2000	You are familiar with the computer; it has worked well in the past.	Might break down again soon; not as powerful as some new computers; takes longer to fix.
B	Buy used computer.	8 days	$4000	Same as old computer; no new training necessary.	May not last as long as new one; not as powerful as some new computers; will take time to find.
C	Buy new but identical computer.	5 days	$6000	Same as old computer; no training necessary; likely to last a long time.	Relatively expensive; not as powerful as some new computers.
D	Buy new more advanced computer.	5 days	$8000	Most powerful computer available; likely to last a long time.	Most expensive; new training necessary; will take time to learn all capabilities.

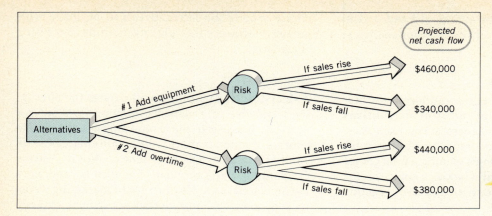

FIGURE 3.4 *Decision-tree analysis: The World Systems Corporation Case*

potential net cash flow—$460,000 . . . if sales rise. The *if* in the last statement, though, is the trick. You don't know with complete *certainty* that sales will rise.

In actual fact, the President called the plant manager and marketing director to a meeting. They discussed the recent rise in sales and discussed what might happen in the future. They agreed that while there was a 60 percent likelihood sales would rise, there was a 40 percent chance they would stabilize or even drop. This allowed for a more extended analysis to be accomplished.

Decision Matrices or Payoff Tables

A **decision matrix** or **payoff table** extends decision-tree analysis by displaying the various outcomes for each alternative course of action while taking the probabilities of their occurrence into account. It typically involves calculation of an **expected value** for each alternative course of action—that is, the dollar value of the predicted outcomes for an alternative multiplied by the probability of its occurrence.

After analyzing the decision tree, the president of World Systems constructed the decision matrix shown in Table 3.5. Cells in the table show the expected values *(EV)* of each outcome as income produced times the probability of its occurrence. Total expected values are also calculated for each alternative—adding equipment or adding overtime—by summing the expected values for each if sales rise or fall. In the example, the total expected value of adding equipment is $412,000; for adding overtime it is $416,000.

At this point the president and her advisors are better prepared to make a decision under the risk conditions associated with this problem. They would most likely choose to add overtime since it has a higher expected value.

CHOOSING AMONG ALTERNATIVES: MAKING THE DECISION

Once alternatives are generated and evaluated, a final choice among them must be made. At this point

TABLE 3.5 *Decision Matrix or Payoff Table: The World Systems Corporation Case*

Possible Future Conditions	Decision Alternatives	
	Add Equipment	Add Overtime
Sales rise (P = 0.6)	EV = $276,000 ($460,000 × 0.6)	EV = $264,000 ($440,000 × 0.6)
Sales fall (P = 0.4)	EV = $136,000 ($340,000 × 0.4)	EV = $152,000 ($380,000 × 0.4)
Total expected value	$412,000	$416,000

P = Probability.
EV = Expected value.

in the problem-solving process, a manager must answer three questions.

1. Is a decision really required?
2. How should the decision be made?
3. Who should be involved in the decision?

Deciding *to* Decide

Managers are too busy and have too many valuable things to do with their time to respond personally to every problem situation that comes their way. The effective manager knows when to delegate decisions to others, how to set priorities, and when not to act at all. When presented with a problem, it is recommended that a manager ask the following questions.

1. *Is the problem significant?* A significant problem is one whose solution can make a real difference by improving operations. Small and less significant problems should not get as much time and attention as bigger ones. Even if a mistake is made, the cost of error on small problems is also small.

2. *Is the problem solvable?* Some problems are unsolvable. No matter how hard you try and no matter how many resources you invest, they can't be solved—at least to the point where they would make a significant and timely difference in operations.

3. *Might the problem resolve itself?* Putting problems in rank order leaves the less significant for last . . . if any time remains. Surprisingly, many of these will resolve themselves or be solved by others before the manager gets to them. One less problem to solve leaves time for other uses.

4. *Is this my decision to make?* Many decisions can be made by persons at other levels. Some should be delegated. Others can and should be referred to higher levels. This is especially true for decisions that have consequences for a larger part of the organization than that under a manager's immediate control.

Asking and answering the prior questions adds discipline to managerial decision making. In particular, it can help managers avoid a potentially damaging tendency called **escalating commitment.** This is the tendency to continue to pursue a course of action that is not working, in the vain hope that more effort and perhaps more resources will reverse the trend.[15] In such cases, managers let the momen-

tum of the situation overwhelm them and sacrifice good judgment for continuity of decision making. They are unable to "call it quits," even when the facts deem this action appropriate. Avoiding such escalation requires objectivity in decision making based on a willingness to (1) deal with "negative" information rather than disregard or downplay it, and (2) depersonalize the situation to avoid the "hero's fallacy" of being blind to one's own mistakes. This recently happened.[16]

at Gap, Incorporated when the decision was made to discontinue Banana Republic's *Trips* magazine after just one issue. Gap chairman Donald Fisher pulled the second issue just as it was going to press. He said the cancellation was made "to allow the company to concentrate on the new positioning of its clothing business."

at Volkswagen when the company's only U.S. assembly plant was closed down after ten years of operations. Some 2,500 blue- and white-collar workers were dismissed. The company said the workers did nothing wrong. Slumping sales and increased small car competition were cited in justification of the controversial move.

Deciding *How* to Decide

Decisions made by managers can be initially divided into those made under the assumptions of classical decision theory and those made under more behavioral assumptions. The use of judgmental heuristics offers yet another approach to managerial decision making.

Classical Decision Theory

Classical decision theory views the manager as acting in a world of complete certainty. The manager faces a clearly defined problem, knows all possible action alternatives and their consequences, and then chooses the alternative giving the best or "optimum" resolution of the problem. Classical theory is often used as model for how managers ideally should make decisions. The techniques for analyzing alternatives just discussed, establish the foundations for optimizing decisions to be made from this classical perspective. A wide variety of computer software support and quantitative decision techniques also assist managers in such rational approaches to problem solving.

Behavioral Decision Theory

Behavioral scientists question the assumptions underlying classical decision theory. Perhaps best represented by the work of Herbert Simon,[17] they recognize cognitive limitations, or limits to our human information-processing capabilities. These limitations compromise the ability of managers to make perfectly rational decisions according to the classical model. They create a **bounded rationality** in which managerial decisions are rational only within the boundaries defined by the available information.

Behavioral decision theory assumes that people act only in terms of what they perceive about a given situation. Because such perceptions are frequently imperfect, the behavioral decision maker acts with limited information. This is especially applicable to managers making decisions about ambiguous problems in risky and uncertain conditions. They have only partial knowledge about the available action alternatives and their consequences. Consequently, they are likely to choose the first alternative that appears to give a satisfactory resolution of the problem. Herbert Simon, who won a Nobel Prize for his work, calls this a **"satisficing"** style of decision-making—choosing the first satisfactory alternative that comes to your attention.

Judgmental Heuristics

Faced with complex environments, limited information, and cognitive limitations, people adopt various means to make problem-solving and decision-making easier. These simplifying strategies for decision making are called **heuristics.** The use of heuristics can simplify problem solving, but they may also create difficulties. This possibility was first introduced in the chapter opener—as systematic errors to which most people are prone in decision situations. An awareness of the following judgmental heuristics and their potential biases can help you to improve managerial decision making.[18]

1. *The availability heuristic.* Using information "readily available" from memory as a basis for assessing a current event or situation. An example is deciding whether or not to invest in a new product based upon your recollection of how well similar new products have performed in the recent past.

> *Potential bias* Readily available information may be fallible and affected by irrelevant factors. In the example, the new products which

recently failed may have been good ideas that were released to market at the wrong time of year.

2. *The representativeness heuristic.* Assessing the likelihood of something occurring based upon its similarity to a stereotyped set of occurrences. An example is deciding to hire someone for a job vacancy simply because they graduated from the same school attended by your last and most successful new hire.

> *Potential bias* The representative stereotype may fail to discriminate important and unique factors relevant to the decision. In the example, the new hire may have career expectations inappropriate to the requirements of the job.

3. *The anchoring and adjustment heuristic.* Making decisions based on adjustments to a previously existing value or starting point. An example is deciding on a new salary level for an employee by simply adjusting upward their prior year's salary by a reasonable increment.

> *Potential bias* Anchoring and adjustment may inappropriately bias a decision toward the starting point. In the example, the individual's market value may be substantially higher than what they were earning; a simple adjustment won't keep them from looking for another job.

An effective manager understands judgmental heuristics and their potential biases. When used in an informed and disciplined manner, heuristics become valuable decision aids which can save time and in many cases, result in very adequate decisions. Figure 3.5 thus includes them along with the classical and behavioral approaches as important resources for managerial problem solving and decision making.

Deciding *Who* Should Decide

The actual choice of a particular problem solution can be arrived at through individual, consultative, or group methods. In practice, these methods result in decisions of the following types.

1. *Individual decisions* The manager makes the choice alone, based on information he or she possesses, and without the participation of other per-

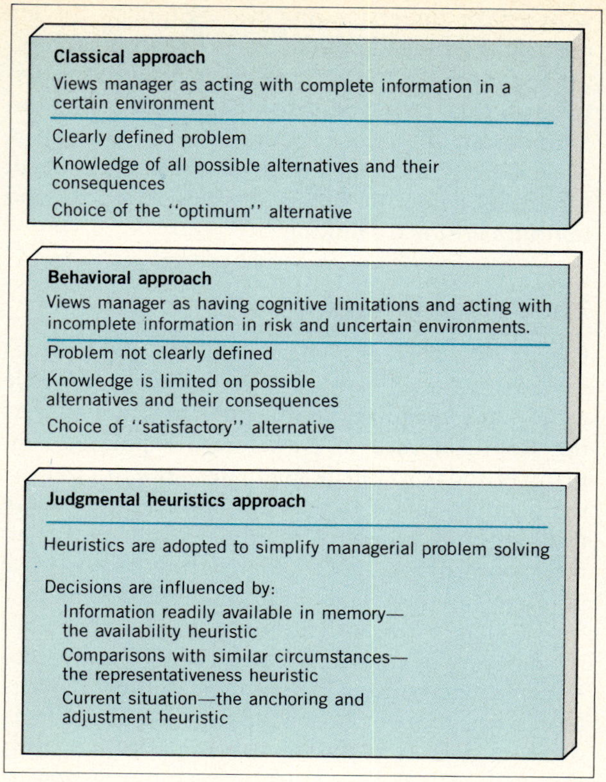

Classical approach

Views manager as acting with complete information in a certain environment

Clearly defined problem

Knowledge of all possible alternatives and their consequences

Choice of the "optimum" alternative

Behavioral approach

Views manager as having cognitive limitations and acting with incomplete information in risk and uncertain environments.

Problem not clearly defined

Knowledge is limited on possible alternatives and their consequences

Choice of "satisfactory" alternative

Judgmental heuristics approach

Heuristics are adopted to simplify managerial problem solving

Decisions are influenced by:

Information readily available in memory— the availability heuristic

Comparisons with similar circumstances— the representativeness heuristic

Current situation—the anchoring and adjustment heuristic

FIGURE 3.5 *The classical, behavioral and judgmental heuristics approaches to managerial problem solving and decision making.*

sons. This method reflects the manager's position of formal authority in the organization. It also presumes he or she has sufficient expertise to make a good decision regarding the matter at hand.

2. *Decision via consultation* The manager seeks information and advice on the problem from other persons. This consultation may be done individually, one-on-one, or in a group setting. Based on this information received and its interpretation, the manager then makes a final choice.

3. *Group decisions* The manager not only consults with other persons for information inputs, but also asks them to participate in problem-solving discussions and in making the actual choice. This is the most participative of the three methods. As noted earlier, it can also add creativity to the problem-solving process.

Good managers use each of these approaches to make a final choice in the problem-solving

process. The key is to know *when* to use each method. Chapter 10 examines these options in detail as part of a manager's approach to leadership. For now it is sufficient for you to recognize that there are both assets and liabilities to the use of group as opposed to individual problem-solving approaches.[19] The assets of group problem solving include:

1. *Greater sum total of knowledge and information* The involvement of more than one person increases the information that can be brought to bear on the problem.

2. *Better understanding of final decision* Because participants in group problem solving are involved in all stages of discussion, comprehension of the decision is high.

3. *Increased acceptance of final decision* Participants in group problem-solving are more inclined to accept both the final decision and the responsibility for making it work.

Overall, these assets suggest that use of more group-oriented methods of problem solving can increase acceptance, understanding, and quality of the final decision. However, there are potential liabilities to group problem solving as well. They include:

1. *Social pressure to conform* The desire to be a good member and go along with the group can lead people to conform prematurely to poor decisions.

2. *Individual domination* A dominant individual may emerge and control the group's choice.

3. *Time requirements* Groups are frequently slower to reach decisions than individuals acting alone.

IMPLEMENTING THE SOLUTION AND EVALUATING RESULTS

The final challenges in the problem-solving process are to implement the chosen solution and evaluate results. Implementation is a managerial responsibility that speaks for itself. Nothing new can or will happen unless action is taken. Managers not only need the courage and creativity to arrive at a decision, they also need the ability and willingness to take action to implement the decision and actually solve the problem. For example,[20]

at United Parcel Service a few days before one Christmas a regional manager learned that the railroad had left a flatcar carrying two UPS trailers on a siding in central Illinois. The manager paid for a high-speed diesel to get the flatcar into Chicago ahead of an Amtrak passenger train. He had two UPS Boeing 727s diverted to Chicago to get the contents of the trailers to their destinations in Florida and Louisiana in time for Christmas. The manager didn't ask permission, but took quick and decisive action to solve the problem. He received high praise from his superiors as a result.

A common implementation error is failure to involve in the earlier stages of problem solving those persons whose support is necessary to insure effective implementation. Managers who understand this get the people who have to do the job involved in the process from the beginning. Implementation typically follows—quickly, smoothly, and to everyone's satisfaction. Here's an example.[21]

At Ford Motor Company when it was decided to build the Taurus, management showed the tentative designs to workers and asked their help in designing a new car that would be easy to build. No less than 1401 ideas were suggested. By allowing others to participate in the early stages, Ford gained their creativity and commitment to follow through with necessary actions. The result was a quicker design cycle and a highly successful new product.

Evaluation is an often neglected but still essential component in problem solving. It is necessary to compare actual results to the desired outcomes to see if the problem really has been resolved. Evaluation can also reveal where modifications can be made in the original solution to improve its results over time. Both the positive and negative consequences of the chosen course of action should be evaluated. If the original solution appears inadequate, it may require a return to earlier steps in the problem-solving process to generate a modified or new solution. In this way problem solving becomes a dynamic and ongoing activity within the management process.

IMPROVING MANAGERIAL PROBLEM SOLVING

Many ideas for improving managerial problem solving have been advanced in this chapter. They begin with a basic understanding of the problem-solving process as it extends all the way from problem finding to the evaluation of implemented solutions. Beyond all this, however, three major areas stand out as important directions for the development of personal skills and competencies. These are the role of intuition, computer-based decision support and multidimensional thinking.

The Role of Intuition

Earlier, we described the "intuitive thinker" as someone who is flexible and spontaneous and able to respond imaginatively to problem situations. As the Kool-Aid case in Newsline 3.1 pointed out, many of today's college graduates are criticized by their employers for an over-emphasis on systematic thinking and a lack of ability when it comes to intuitive thinking. Indeed, there is now a resurgence of interest in the role of intuition in management.

To begin, research indicates that intuitive ability may vary by managerial level. In one study, top-level managers scored higher than middle- or lower-level managers on their ability to use intuition in decision making.[22] As one executive in this study reported: "I do believe in using my intuitive powers on most of my decisions, large or small." In addition, it appears that the use of intuition varies. Sometimes intuition is used in an exploratory sense to gain a novel perspective or sense of direction; in others it is used in an integrative sense to double-check the results of a systematic process. Problem situations in which managers report using their intuitive abilities to best advantage include:

- When several alternatives exist.
- When each alternative has good support.
- When a high level of uncertainty exists.
- When little precedent exists.
- When the "facts" are limited.
- When time is limited.

There are two important points to remember, though, as you think about this subject of intuition. First, intuitive thinking should complement systematic thinking, not completely replace it. What the new reports are really doing is giving managers more confidence in using their intuition when it feels right. Second, intuition is not pure "guesswork." It is more and more viewed as something that requires hard work and which depends, in part, on experience and knowledge. To the extent that intuition is based on "hunches," they should be "educated and informed" ones. *Judgment* is a good word to use here. John Gardner defines this as the ability to combine insights of hard data, questionable data, and intuition to arrive at decisions that future events prove to be correct.[23] *Newsline 3.3* documents Honda's success with good managerial judgments on a variety of fronts, and in a highly competitive environment.

Computer-Based Decision Support

While interest in the intuitive side of problem solving grows, it is important to recognize continuing advancements on the systematic side of the process as well. Very significant among these is the ever-more powerful computer-based support for decision making. Chapter 15 on "Control and Management Information Systems" addresses this topic in detail. For now, however, we must once again point out that any manager in today's technology and information-rich work environment should be able to use the personal computer to full advantage. Two examples are data-base management and spreadsheet/graphics software. Spreadsheet programs, in particular, help managers analyze multiple alternatives under various assumptions and risk conditions using powerful "if–then" analyses. They substantially extend the reach of analytical techniques such as the decision matrix or payoff table discussed earlier.

In addition, structured **decision support systems** can provide quick and informed responses to recurring problems. They allow users to interact with computer data bases and process information to help solve semistructured and unstructured problems. Sample applications include the analysis of new products, examining trends and making forecasts, and managing inventories. Finally, **expert systems** are even more advanced programs which simulate the judgment of human experts in a problem situation. They assist managerial decision making by first requiring that a logical sequence of issues be considered, and then performing sophisticated analyses based on information provided in response to them. Among other applications, expert systems are now used in industry to help diagnose operating problems with complex equipment, and to determine what combinations of people and machines should be used to manufacture a specialty product.

Multidimensional Thinking

Multidimensional thinking is the capacity to view many problems at once, in relationship to one another, and across long and short time horizons.[24] The importance of this type of thinking grows the higher one goes in the managerial ranks and the more general one's managerial responsibilities become. Senior managers, in particular, are described as dealing with "portfolios" of problems and opportunities consisting of multiple and interrelated issues. Good problem solving requires that these problems be "mapped" into a network that can be managed actively over time as priorities, events, and demands continuously change. Consider this example of how complex and tangled the issues facing a general manager can get.[25]

> I decided not to build a manufacturing plant in Japan. It is a low-price market with little chance to make money. Yet it is important to maintain a presence so we have credibility with Japanese contractors. . . . Because of their culture, Japanese companies don't change suppliers unless there are major problems. I made the decision not to expand manufacturing into Japan despite the fact that our sales people wanted us to do it. The sales director in the North Pacific argued that it could help the relationship with contractors. He is probably right, but I've got undercapacity elsewhere. . . . It's a balancing act.

Not only are issues intertwined in problem situations like the one just described, but time frames are too. A manager must be able to make decisions and take action in the short run, in ways that benefit longer run objectives. And through all the daily challenges of problem solving, there is still a need to retain a sense of direction. The ability to do so is called **strategic opportunism,** remaining focused on long-term objectives while being flexible enough to solve short-term problems and take advantage of new opportunities.[26] This concept conveys the positive approach a modern manager needs to apply these many ideas on decision making and problem solving to the topic covered in the next part of this book—*Planning for Productivity.*

HONDA
LOOKS TO THE WEST

The Japanese president of Honda, Tadashi Kume, admits that on home turf Honda has never done as well as its larger rivals, Toyota and Nissan, whose outlets far outnumber Honda's. Having faced reality, the company's management has made a decision to pursue a risky but thus far profitable alternative to the thriving Japanese car market—the U.S. market. "In the future, I expect America to take on a more important position in our total business," says Kume.

Developing a foreign market has its pitfalls, but Honda's management has deliberately chosen to focus on American customers, who right from the start became big fans of Honda's reliable,

high-performance cars. Lacking official support for its efforts to establish an export network in Japan, Honda set up a factory in 1982 in Ohio, just before voluntary import quotas came into play. The plant's profits have been rising continuously since then.

Speedy product development is a necessity in a competitive environment that pits imports and domestic cars against one another. Honda brings cars to market in under four years—at least a year faster than most of its American rivals. Moreover, Honda employs crest-of-the-wave developmental techniques that involve close cooperation among marketers, engineers, and designers. Manufacturing employees, too, are encouraged to use their own initiative to increase efficiency. The result is an impressive quality and productivity record—and loyal buyers of U.S.-made Honda products. Kume recognizes that his company is a latecomer to the industry, but he is pleased with the outcome of his decision to push for a bright spot in the American market. Not surprisingly, the American competition has taken note. "Honda is fierce," concedes GM's President Robert Stempel—a judgment with which Kume surely agrees.

Source: As reported in "The Americanization of Honda," *Business Week* (April 25, 1988), pp. 90–96.

Summary

Managers spend enormous amounts of time attempting to solve problems and explore opportunities that occur in the day-to-day process of planning, organizing, leading, and controlling. Problem solving is a process of identifying discrepancies between actual and desired states of affairs and taking action to resolve those discrepancies. The five general steps in this process are to (1) find and define the problem, (2) generate alternative solutions, (3) evaluate alternatives and select a preferred solution, (4) implement the solution, and (5) evaluate results and take corrective action when necessary.

All managers must be good at looking for and finding problems toward which to direct attention. This is a major test of the manager as a problem solver. True managerial success will depend on your ability to identify performance gaps and opportunities in sufficient time to resolve them to the benefit of the individuals involved and the productivity of the organization. As part of our review, we examined

■ Types of problems faced by managers and how they vary by managerial level.

- Creativity as a necessary element in problem solving.
- Decision aids for problem solving in certain, risk and uncertain environments.
- The need to know when to, how to, and who should make the decisions required in problem solving.

The chapter also addressed a host of additional issues spanning escalating commitments, economic versus behavioral decision models, the use of judgmental heuristics, the assets and liabilities of group decision making, the role of intuition, computer-based support systems, and multidimensional thinking.

Thinking Through the Issues

1. What is the difference between "systematic" and "intuitive" thinking? How would a manager's problem-solving style differ under each of these approaches?

2. Explain the difference between choice making, decision making, and problem solving.

3. Identify the five steps in the problem-solving process. Give examples of each step as they might be followed by a manager in an organization with which you are familiar.

4. Explain how the types of problems faced by managers may vary among top, middle, and lower management levels.

5. Identify three barriers to accurate problem identification. Explain steps that can be taken by managers to avoid each barrier.

6. What are the differences between brainstorming and nominal grouping as ways to increase creativity through the use of groups?

7. Show how a decision matrix or payoff table is a more advanced way of analyzing alternatives than the decision tree.

8. What is a) an inventory of alternatives, and b) a decision matrix or payoff table? How can each help a manager in the problem solving process?

9. Explain the difference between classical and behavioral decision theory. How does "optimizing" differ from "satisficing" when a manager chooses among alternative courses of action?

10. What is a "heuristic" as applied to problem solving? Identify three judgmental heuristics commonly used by people in decision situations. What are the potential biases that might result from the use of each heuristic?

The Manager's Vocabulary

Behavioral decision theory	Decision matrix	Inventory of alternatives	Problem solving
Bounded rationality	Decision support systems	Multidimensional thinking	Programmed decisions
Brainstorming	Decision tree	Nominal group	Risk
Certainty	Delphi technique	Nonprogrammed decisions	Routine problems
Choice making	Escalating commitment	Nonroutine problems	Satisficing
Classical decision theory	Expert systems	Payoff table	Selective perception
Cost–benefit analysis	Expected problems	Probability	Strategic opportunism
Creativity	Expected value	Problem	Synectics
Crisis problem	Heuristics	Problem finding	Systematic thinker
Decision making	Intuitive thinker		Uncertainty
			Unexpected problems

Everyone is talking about creativity these days and it is a good time to inquire into your creative capacities. There is no magical list of traits that describe all creative thinkers. But, here are some of the factors which might make a difference.[27]

Personality   Creative people tend to be independent, persistent, and highly motivated. They are willing to take risks, are somewhat skeptical, and can be a bit hard to get along with at times. They don't mind disorder and have a good sense of humor.

Social habits   The stereotype of the creative "loner" is out. The creative types tend to be gregarious people who spend a lot of time exchanging ideas with others—often those who are equally stimulating.

Education   Schooling doesn't necessarily make a difference. Many experts are even concerned that the "logical" approach of most curricula may hurt rather than help. It has been reported that a child's creativity may decline 90 percent between the ages of five and seven, and that adult creativity at the age of 40 is less than 2 percent what it was when the same person was only two years old.

Intelligence   The stereotype of the creative "genius" is also out. Creative people don't necessarily have exceptionally high IQ scores. Given good basic intelligence, nonintellectual traits like personality and background become more important.

Hard work   Above all, creative people seem to work hard and apply their intelligence to master things. Thus it isn't "genius" that counts as much as it is "inspiration" and a willingness to work hard at things.

Questions

1.   Evaluate yourself on each of the prior traits of the creative person. How creative are you?
2.   What can you do to further improve upon your creative capabilities?
3.   To what extent will success in your anticipated career depend on your ability to achieve creativity on the job? What are the implications of this answer for your personal career planning?

Case Application

CRISIS MANAGEMENT AT ASHLAND OIL

When John R. Hall, chief executive of Ashland Oil, Inc., answered an early morning phone call, trouble was on its way.[28] A million or more gallons of diesel fuel from one of Ashland's storage tanks was flowing down the Monongahela River. Water supplies in river towns of Pennsylvania, Ohio, and West Virginia were threatened. The riverside storage tank had ruptured while being filled and the effects of the accident were spreading as rapidly as the oil spill itself headed for the Ohio River. Not only were the health of the communities threatened and the environmental impact potentially disastrous, Ashland faced the prospect of huge liability claims.

The crisis developed quickly. Mr. Hall had to make equally quick and risky decisions. At first he decided the disaster was under control and didn't need all of his attention. He felt his job was to keep tabs on the cleanup and preserve his company's reputation. Eventually he flew to Pittsburgh to publicly apologize and admit the company had made mistakes. He also pledged to pay any "reasonable expenses" for cleaning up the mess.

This is a brief chronology of how Mr. Hall and his staff responded to the oil spill crisis.

SUNDAY: As soon as the president of Ashland Petroleum Co. told Mr. Hall that one million gallons of diesel fuel had spilled into the Monongahela River, Mr. Hall knew he had a serious problem. "But

I didn't know how serious," says the chemical engineer. He spent much of Sunday trying to answer that. Rushing to his office, he and president Charles J. Luellen sat in front of a speaker phone talking with colleagues at the accident site and elsewhere.

Almost immediately, Mr. Hall believed that although this was a massive environmental problem, it could be controlled. He also quickly discarded the idea of going to the disaster site himself. His emergency-management team there could handle the logistical decisions, and it was still unclear what had caused the spill. "He didn't want to make an official appearance until he could provide some answers," says vice president and media chief J. Dan Lacy.

He also isolated himself from distractions, allowing subordinates to handle all outside queries. And he didn't issue a press release under his name. Says Mr. Lacy: "I didn't recommend a press release. When a situation is evolving so rapidly, a release isn't good enough." About the only non-company contact Mr. Hall made was to a concerned Pennsylvania Gov. Robert Casey late Sunday. "I told him we intended to clear up the mess as fast as we could," Mr. Hall recalls.

MONDAY: Mr. Hall arrived at work at 6:30 a.m., about a half-hour earlier than usual. He decided against devoting his regular three-hour Monday morning meeting with top executives solely to the spill. He believed the crisis was being handled well and didn't demand all his attention—although he dashed in and out of the meeting for periodic updates.

He was wrong. By mid-morning, things were unraveling. "Phones were ringing off the wall," says one company executive, with calls coming from public officials, reporters and local water companies, as well as members of Ashland's own emergency management team. Emerging were several troublesome discrepancies about the spill. Reporters initially had been told that the storage tank was new and the company held a permit to construct it. But, Mr. Hall learned, his spokesmen had spoken too soon; in fact, the tank was reconstructed from 40-year-old steel without a written permit. (Mr. Lacy says new information Monday "from several sources" made Ashland aware "that what we said previously wasn't exactly right.") In addition, Mr. Hall discovered less-complete-than-usual testing had been conducted on the tank.

A cautious executive, Mr. Hall pondered each

of these new facts and became more quiet than usual—a clear sign to colleagues that he was angry at them. "It was obvious that he was frustrated, upset and eager to get the right information," an Ashland vice president says.

The situation soon worsened when the crisis turned from just an environmental mess to a public-health-and-safety concern. With river currents unusually fast, crews couldn't trap all the spill and, consequently, 750,000 Pennsylvania residents faced having no water—a scenario Mr. Hall hadn't anticipated. "That changed the situation completely," says Mr. Lacy. "It was no longer a situation in which we could simply do everything to clean up the river. All of a sudden people were involved very directly, and they needed answers."

For Mr. Hall, that sparked the feeling that he ought to make a public statement at the accident site. By late Monday, he was debating that with his staff. His lawyers advised against it, arguing Mr. Hall shouldn't admit any mistakes. The liability issue was a worry. But Mr. Hall felt he had to be candid. "Our company had inconvenienced the lives of a lot of people, and I felt it was only right to apologize," he says.

TUESDAY: On his corporate jet, en route to Pittsburgh, Mr. Hall rehearsed for his press conference ("How long will it take to clean up the spill?" a press relations manager tested him; "How much will it cost?").

The first stop was the spill site at Jefferson Borough, outside Pittsburgh, where he surveyed the collapsed tank and commended tired workers on their "good job." Then he traveled to downtown Pittsburgh to confront dozens of reporters, who barraged him with questions about whether Ashland met government regulations. Ignoring his lawyers' advice to sidestep questions about permits and testing procedures, Mr. Hall admitted Ashland didn't have a written permit for the tank and had conducted tests that met federal standards, but that were less extensive than is typical for the company.

He was troubled about flaws in the company's operating procedure, and felt the only way to clear the slate was to divulge everything he knew. "If we made mistakes, we have to stand up and admit them," he says. "I would have preferred that we had done some things differently—like (not) using 40-year-old steel." During the oft-hostile press conference, he perspired heavily, and laughed nervously when asked if he would forgo a shower to help conserve water supplies.

WEDNESDAY & THURSDAY: Mr. Hall canceled business trips to Lexington, Ky. and Washington, D.C., to stay in Pittsburgh for a whirlwind public relations campaign. He met with the city's political leaders, the editorial boards of local papers and telephoned the governors of Ohio and West Virginia, where the spill was making its way. Mr. Hall, says a colleague, "wanted to reinforce the view that even though mistakes may have been made, we want to do what's right." With water supplies restored for most Pittsburgh-area residents and the crisis eased, Mr. Hall planned to fly back to Ashland last night, where he must now face the legal aftermath.

In retrospect, what would Mr. Hall have done differently? "He would have wanted more accurate information faster," says Mr. Lacy. Says Mr. Hall: "I suppose you always should be prepared for the unexpected—and are never as prepared as you'd like to be."

Questions

1. How well did John Hall do in responding to this problem? Why? Was his approach to the problem more systematic or intuitive? Explain your answer.

2. Assume you are a consultant hired to help Hall and his staff analyze their performance in this crisis situation. What exactly was done right and wrong in the case from a crisis management perspective, and why?

3. Present your own approach to the case in respect to the five steps in the problem solving process described in Figure 3.1. In particular, (a) how you feel the problem should have been defined, (b) what action alternatives should have been considered, and (c) what could Hall have done to insure effective and speedy implementation of all problem-solving responses? Explain and justify your answers.

Class Exercise: Kate Simpson's Dilemma

1. Read and think about the following situation. Not too long ago, 18 men and women sat around a table at the Fort Worth, Texas, division of General Dynamics Corporation. They were trying to resolve a dilemma in which Kate Simpson had become involved.[29]

> Kate, is a new employee at a small firm which helps nonprofit hospitals get financing. One of the firm's clients wants to hire a consultant. Kate is asked to analyze the competitive proposals received from outside firms. She finds that Roberts & Co.'s proposal is the best of three received so far. Her boss's deputy puts a copy of the Roberts's proposal in an envelope and asks her to deliver it to a friend of his at the firm whose proposal has not yet been received. He says, "I told him we'd let him glance at the Roberts's version." Kate's boss is out of the office and won't return for several hours. She wonders what to do.

2. What is at issue here is a special aspect of problem solving—the ethics of decision making—that we will address at considerable length in Chapter 20 on "Managing with Ethics and Social Responsibility." The episode is used in an ethics workshop designed to make participating managers more aware about the ethical aspects of decision making. The managers in the workshop at General Dynamics debated Kate's situation at some length.

3. What do you think Kate should do, and why? Be specific in (a) defining the problem Kate faces, (b) identifying possible action alternatives, and (c) evaluating these alternatives to select a preferred response.

4. After coming to your own conclusion about how Kate should resolve this problem, share your views with a classmate sitting nearby. Find out what his or her views are. Discuss the case situation further and try to understand one another's viewpoints.

5. Be prepared to share your thoughts on the case in general class discussion led by the instructor.

References

[1] Information from articles in *Newsweek* (July 6, 1987), p. 37 and (July 13, 1987), p. 51; and an Associated Press release "Chrysler Pleads No Contest to Suit," appearing in the *Southern Illinoisan* (December 15, 1987).

[2] These points were developed from David A. Kolb, Irwin M. Rubin, and James M. McIntyre, *Organizational Psychology: An Experimental Approach,* Second Edition (Englewood Cliffs, NJ: Prentice-Hall, 1974), pp. 42–43; and, Daniel J. Isenberg, "How Senior Managers Think," *Harvard Business Review,* Vol. 62 (November–December 1984), pp. 81–90.

[3] Information from Stuart Gannes, "America's Fastest-Growing Companies," *Fortune* (May 23, 1988), pp. 28–40.

[4] See George P. Huber, *Managerial Decision Making* (Glenview, Ill.: Scott, Foresman, 1975), p. 11; Ralph Kilmann, *Beyond the Quick Fix: Managing Five Tracks to Organizational Success* (San Francisco: Jossey-Bass, 1984).

[5] Peter F. Drucker, *Innovation and Entrepreneurship: Practice and Principles* (New York: Harper & Row, 1985).

[6] Developed in part from William F. Pounds, "The Process of Problem Finding," *Industrial Management Review,* Vol. 11 (Fall 1969), pp. 1–19. See also Walter Kiechel III, "Unlocking the Managerial Memory," *Fortune* (December 21, 1987), pp. 183–184.

[7] For scholarly reivews see Dean Tjosvold, "Effects of Crisis Orientation on Managers' Approach to Controversy in Decision Making," *Academy of Management Journal,* Vol. 27 (1984), pp. 130–138; and, Ian I. Mitroff, Paul Shrivastava, and Firdaus E. Udwadia, "Effective Crisis Management," *Academy of Management Executive,* Vol. 1 (1987), pp.283–292.

[8] Information from Jack Stack, "Crisis Management by Committee," *Inc.* (May 1988), p. 26.

[9] For a comprehensive discussion see the special section on "Crisis Management: Curing Our Corporate Myopia," *New Management,* Vol. 5 (1987), pp. 19–37. This list is developed from Morgan W. McCall, Jr. and Robert Kaplan, *Whatever it Takes: Decision Makers at Work* (Englewood Cliffs, NJ: Prentice-Hall, 1985).

[10] "Kalmar: Ten Years Later," *Via Volvo,* Vol. IV (Spring/Summer 1984), pp. 14–19; and, Steve Lohr, "Making Cars the Volvo Way," *The New York Times* (June 23, 1987), pp. D1, D5.

[11] Quoted in Isenberg, op. cit., 1984, p. 87.

[12] Tom Taliaferro, *Instructor's Film Guide for Creative Problem Solving: "How to Get Better Ideas"* (Del Mar, Cal.: CRM McGraw-Hill Films).

[13] See Andre L. Delbecq, Andrew H. Van de Ven, and David H. Gustafson, *Group Techniques for Program Planning* (Glenview, Ill.: Scott, Foresman, 1975).

[14] Information from George Melloan, "Staying Ahead of the Pack at Cray Research," *The Wall Street Journal* (February 23, 1988), p. 31; and, Alex Taylor III, "Back to the Future at Saturn," *Fortune* (August 1, 1988), pp. 66–72.

[15] See Barry M. Staw, "The Escalation of Commitment to a Course of Action," *Academy of Management Review,* Vol. 6 (1981), pp. 577–587; and, Barry M. Staw and Jerry Ross, "Knowing When to Pull the Plug," *Harvard Business Review,* Vol. 65 (March–April 1987), pp. 68–74. Information reported in Marilyn Chase, "Banana Republic Founders Quit; Magazine Closes," *The Wall Street Journal* (April 21, 1988), p. 36; and an Associated Press news release, Volkswagen's U.S. Plant Closing (July 14, 1988).

[17] For a sample of Simon's work, see Herbert A. Simon, *Administrative Behavior* (New York: The Free Press, 1947); James G. March and Herbert A. Simon, *Organizations* (New York: Wiley, 1958); and, Herbert A. Simon, "Making Management Decisions: The Role of Intuition and Emotion," *Academy of Management Executive,* Vol. 1 (1987), pp. 57–64.

[18] This presentation is based on the work of R. H. Hogarth, D. Kahneman & A. Tversky, and others as discussed in Max H. Bazerman, *Judgement in Managerial Decision Making* (New York: Wiley, 1986).

[19] The classic work on this topic is Norman R. F. Maier, "Assets and Liabilities in Group Problem Solving: The Need for an Integrative Function," *Psychological Review,* Vol. 4 (1967), pp. 239–249.

[20] "Behind the UPS Mystique: Puritanism and Productivity," *Business Week* (June 6, 1983), p. 66.

[21] Information from "How the Best Get Better," *Business Week* (September 14, 1987), pp. 98–120, as excerpted from Robert H. Waterman's book, *The Renewal Factor* (New York: Bantam, 1987).

[22] This research is reported in Weston H. Agor, "The Logic of Intuition: How Top Executives Make Decisions," *Organizational Dynamics,* Vol. 14 (1986), pp. 5–18. See also, Weston H. Agor, "How Top Executives Use Their Intuition to Make Important Decisions," *Business Horizons,* Vol. 29 (1986), pp. 49–53. John W. Gardner, "The Context and Attributes of Leadership," *New Management,* Vol. 5 (Spring 1988), pp. 18–22.

[24] Isenberg op. cit., 1984.

[25] This example is from Robert E. Kaplan, *The Warp and Woof of the General Manager's Job,* Technical Report 27

(Greensboro, NC: Center for Creative Leadership, 1986).

[26]Daniel J. Isenberg, "The Tactics of Strategic Opportunism," *Harvard Business Review,* Vol. 65 (March–April 1987), pp. 92–97.

[27]Information from "Are You Creative," *Business Week* (September 30, 1985), pp. 80–84. For further ideas on building your creative capacities see two books by Roger von Oech: *A Whack on the Side of the Head* (New York: Warner Books, 1983), and *A Kick in the Seat of the Pants* (New York: Harper & Row, 1986).

[28]Information from Clare Ansberry, "Case Study in Crisis Management," *The Wall Street Journal* (January 6, 1988), p. 17; and "A Million Gallons of Trouble for Ashland," *Business Week* (January 18, 1988), p. 23. Quotes excerpted from Ansberry, op cit. Reprinted by permission of *The Wall Street Journal,* © Dow Jones & Company, Inc. 1988.

[29]This incident is reported in Alan L. Otten, "Ethics on the Job: Companies Alert Employees to Potential Dilemmas," *The Wall Street Journal* (July 14, 1986), p. 17.

PART 1

Marshall Field's Store Manager

Linda Koslow is the general manager of the Marshall Field's department store in Chicago's Oak Brook, Illinois, suburb. The 37-year-old Koslow is nervous as Christmas season approaches, a five-week period of high pressure for retailers. At Marshall Field's Oak Brook store—the third largest in Field's 25 store chain—Christmas shopping accounts for about $22.5 million of annual $90 million sales. More than 25 percent of the store's profits are also made during this season. Koslow, who works six days a week and 10 hours per day, says: "The first 10 months of the year are dress rehearsal for the last two."

This is Koslow's 17th season in retailing. She began as a jewelry sales clerk at a Famous-Barr store in St. Louis. After getting a chance to manage in the candy department, she decided to make her career in stores. Soon after moving to Chicago as a buyer for Field's, she switched to store management. Three years ago she was promoted to her present position. One of the managers who reports to her comments, "She brings an enthusiasm and a very positive attitude to the job."

Koslow manages a staff of more than 1200 people, 400 of whom are hired temporarily for the Christmas rush. She is accountable for keeping expenses in line with sales trends.

Source: Information from Francine Schwadel, "Season's Tidings: Christmas Sales' Lack of Momentum Tests Store Manager's Mettle," *The Wall Street Journal* (December 16, 1987), pp. 1, 14. [a] The excerpts are from the Schwadel article. Reprinted by permission of *The Wall Street Journal*, © Dow Jones & Company, Inc., 1987.

Since she can't set prices, she adjusts staff to keep expenses on target. She also tries to increase sales by keeping staff morale high, and by moving "hot selling" items into prominent display locations. What follows is a description of Linda Koslow's approach to her job during the all-important Christmas period.[a]

SOBER APPRAISAL

Koslow had drawn up her holiday staffing plans on the assumption that her store's sales would rise 7 percent above last year's. But in early November she cut her forecast to a meager 3 percent gain—not even enough to cover the increase in prices—and she decided to hire about 50 fewer seasonal sales clerks than she had planned. . . .

> Koslow manages
> a staff of more than
> 1200 people,
> 400 of whom are hired
> temporarily for the
> Christmas rush.

The same week, the store's consumer electronics department was dismantled when Field's ended its leasing agreement with an electronics supplier. That left Koslow scrambling to fill the old electronics area with stuffed animals from her stockrooms. It also made year-to-year sales comparisons more difficult, as last year's numbers included higher-priced electronic goods.

Koslow, who views cheerleading as a big part of her job, was crestfallen. She had planned to lead a Christmas pep rally that weekend, but she postponed it. "I didn't want to send the wrong message," she says. "I didn't want the managers focusing on a party when we were getting them to have fewer [sales] people on the floor."

She finally held the party on the Saturday before Thanksgiving. The store's managers performed a goofy skit about a new Field's store opening in Andy Griffith's fictional hometown of Mayberry. Then, clutching white Mistletoe teddy bears that Field's sells for Christmas, they led more than 200 of the store's employees in a musical wish list. To the tune of "White Christmas," they sang about their hopes for a holiday "just like the one we had last year."

"It's going to be a great season," Koslow shouted at the end of the program. "Let's do it." Later, she privately was less effusive: "Nobody knows if people are going to start shopping again and when," she conceded.

UPS AND DOWNS

To her relief, sales perked up at Koslow's store on the Friday after Thanksgiving. A special two-hour sale—featuring discounts as deep as 50 percent on down comforters, sweaters, dresses, toys, gold chains and pearl strands, table linens and boxed Christmas cards—drew early-morning crowds that make Koslow squeal with delight. . . .

By late afternoon, when her secretary started tallying each department's 3 P.M. sales total, Miss Koslow gushed: "I haven't had a good day like this to brag about in a long time."

So that is exactly what she did. She called the manager at the chain's flagship store in Chicago. She called her boss. . . .

The next morning, the printer in the store's basement computer office spit out a detailed report of Friday's sales volume. The total was 26 percent higher than last year's.

> She brings an enthusiasm and a very positive attitude to the job.

Later, over coffee, she perused the printouts, looking for hot spots. One was contemporary men's clothing—an area that had gotten a lot of her attention lately. In anticipation of the opening of a new Bigsby&Kruthers men's store in the mall in early November, she had worked with her staff to beef up her selection and presentation of European-cut clothing. When the new store opened, she liked its looks and predicted that it might make business tougher for Field's. Looking over her post-Thanksgiving numbers, she concluded happily that the new shop hadn't hurt her store.

But Friday's bonanza was short-lived. On Saturday, the crowds were thin, despite discounts of 20 to 50 percent on certain items. Koslow fretted about the steady rain, which she said might be keeping shoppers away.

The 3 P.M. readings confirmed her fears. She glanced at the figures, then started flipping through a Field's Christmas catalog. Pressed for an assessment, she finally said: "It doesn't look like we'll make our plan."

She didn't. Sales on Saturday fell 6.5 percent from last year's level. On Sunday, the store rang up a 4.4 percent gain. The result was a respectable 9.5 percent increase for the three-day weekend, and Koslow seemed pleased.

During the next two weeks, the pattern was steadier, but the sales gains were more modest. Nevertheless, the totals exceeded Koslow's conservative expectations. "She's upbeat because we're still holding our own," explained Candy Greener, an assistant general manager. "We're doing better than a lot of other stores."

A GENERAL MANAGER'S PERSPECTIVE

The key to Koslow's strategy this Christmas has been flexibility. She trained more seasonal employees than usual as "flyers" who can move around the store and work in any department. "I'm funding anybody that's cooking," she has told her managers repeatedly.

Miss Koslow has also tried to pump up sales by making some last-minute floor moves. In the men's sweater department, she had two islands of display cases ripped out to make room for display cubes that hold more merchandise. She also created a department for a new women's

> The key to Koslow's strategy this Christmas has been flexibility.

> She has cruised the store's four floors several times a day to check staffing levels and displays.

sportswear label called Multiples, replacing Coca-Cola clothing, which had fizzled.

As general manager, Miss Koslow doesn't have complete control over her store's profits because she doesn't control prices. Those are dictated by the company's buyers, who also adjust their plans as the season progresses. The day after Thanksgiving, for instance, the buyers ordered an emergency markdown of 40 percent on a line of women's sportswear. The following week, they slashed 33 percent from the price of slow-moving Mistletoe Bears.

Miss Koslow, meanwhile, has concentrated on the details of running a big store. She has cruised the store's four floors several times a day to check staffing levels and displays, stopping along the way to pick up candy wrappers and empty hangers and to give shoppers directions.

On busy days, she has spent a few hours in the store's administrative office, collecting surplus cash, making change for her department managers and getting a feel for the day's results. On a Saturday in early December, for instance, she learned that Louis Vuitton handbags, priced between $175 and $285 were selling briskly. "There's no recession, not at Oak Brook anyway," she concluded.

But despite such momentary triumphs, the Christmas season is a grind. At one point, Miss Koslow complained about not having been to the grocery store in so long that "my cat and I are sharing Meow Mix."

QUESTIONS

1. Describe Linda Koslow's "manager's challenge" in respect to her position as general manager of the Marshall Field's store. What type of problem environment does she most frequently deal with in this case? What are the implications of this environment for her abilities to master the "manager's challenge?"

2. Is Linda Koslow (a) using the essential managerial skills, (b) enacting the key managerial roles, and (c) implementing the four management functions? Use examples from the case to support your answers.

3. Analyze Linda Koslow's overall success as a general manager. What are the things she seems to be doing *right* in helping her store achieve per-

formance "effectiveness" and performance "efficiency"? What do you think she could do better to make her store achieve even higher "productivity" in the future? Why? ■

Turmoil and Transformation at Apple Computer, Inc.

It's been a rocky road for Apple Computer, Inc. over the last several years. The mid-1980s saw the company in the midst of sales declines and internal turmoil that eventually led to the departure of the company's founders Steve Jobs and Steve Wozniak. By 1988 Apple's chief executive John Sculley was selected by *Fortune* magazine as one of the "top business people of the year." The reason for the award was stated as "his success in . . . turning the company, once widely dismissed as a glorified toymaker, into a highly profitable producer of serious computers for the

desktops of corporate America." Part I of this case presents a chronology of newspaper reports on the major events underlying Apple's time of turmoil. Part II describes how Sculley directed its transformation into a major player in the computer industry.

■

Jobs loses direct control over the manufacturing and marketing of the Macintosh. . .

■

PART I

DATELINE—MARCH 1, 1985 (CUPERTINO, CALIF)—Apple Computer Inc., the precocious adolescent of the personal-computer industry, is suffering new growing pains because of management departures, new-product disappointments and growing tension between its major divisions.

In the past three months, the company has witnessed a stream of defections by senior and middle managers.

Among those who have quit or announced plans to quit are Steve Wozniak, Apple's co-founder, and Joseph Graziano, chief financial officer. . . .

The talent drain, particularly from the middle management ranks, has led to some internal upheaval at Apple. "The organizational chart is filled with TBH's, which stands for 'to be hired,' " said one mid-level marketing manager. "It's tough to get things done. . . ."

John Sculley, president and chief executive officer, insists the wave of departures hasn't disrupted operations, adding that "Apple's management team is alive and well and continuing to work."

This winter, he said, Apple has been going through another phase in a difficult transition from a small freewheeling venture to a large corporation, and some of the "old guard" are finding themselves at odds with the new organization.

"Apple is a big business now," said Mr. Sculley.

"That's a fact of life. Some people can't adjust and, as a result, we've lost some good people. But Apple can't stay in the garage forever. The company has to adjust to a changing

Source: Part I excerpted from Patricia A. Bellew, "Apple Computer Attempts to Deal With Unrest Caused by Defections and New-Product Problems," *Wall Street Journal* (March 1, 1985), p. 4, and, "Apple Realigns Operations to Cut Costs, Bolster Stability; Job's Duties Reduced," *Wall Street Journal* (June 3, 1985), p. 2. Reprinted by permission of the Wall Street Journal. Copyright © 1985 Dow Jones and Company, Inc. All rights reserved. Additional information from USA Today (September 19, 1985), p. 1. Part II information from Brenton R. Schlender, "Calculated Move: Apple Computer Tries to Achieve Stability but Remain Creative," *The Wall Street Journal* (July 16, 1987), pp. 1, 10; "Corporate Antihero John Sculley," *Inc.* (October 1987), pp. 49–58; "Growing Apple Anew for the Business Market," *Fortune* (January 4, 1988), pp. 36–37; and, Janet Guyon, "An Ex-Pepsi Man Takes the Apple Challenge," *The Wall Street Journal* (January 22, 1988), p. 16.

industry. I'm trying to bring in the strongest successors I can find."

Among former employees and insiders, complaints about the internal turmoil in the wake of managers' departures and an encroaching bureaucracy are common. And tension between the two divisions that make the Macintosh and the Apple II personal computers—always strong—has intensified.

Workers say morale at the Apple II division, the company's primary money-maker, is at its lowest ebb in years. They blame what they call lack of support from management. "The Apple II always is a loser" in the company's framework, said Mr. Wozniak, the quirky genius who developed the computers responsible for Apple's instant success in the late 1970s.

Mr. Wozniak said technical improvements to the Apple II were delayed for years by top management in favor of developing such ill-fated personal computers as the Apple III and the Lisa. The Apple II line accounted for about 70% of Apple's $698.3 million in revenue for the first quarter ended Dec. 28.

In response to questions, Mr. Sculley conceded that the Apple II division had suffered from "second-class citizen status" in earlier years but "is getting more internal attention and more corporate resources now."

Still, morale among Apple II workers, already hurt by the marketing and engineering defections, eroded still further as word began trickling out that Mr. Wozniak sold all but a "nominal amount" of his Apple stock.

. . . analysts expressed concern over an apparent slowing in the sales momentum of the Macintosh personal computer, which was introduced a year ago. The Macintosh is the lynchpin in Apple's as-yet unsuccessful effort to gain a firm foothold in the office market.

Apple's new automated "Macfactory" is being expanded to be capable of manufacturing about one million computers a year. Last year, according to outside market research reports, the company sold about 275,000 of the machines.

While analysts say the company must put substantial resources behind its latest-generation machine to remain a first-string competitor, some are concerned about the company's high-risk strategy. . . .

DATELINE—JUNE 3, 1985 (CUPERTINO, CALIF.)—Apple Computer Inc. said its chairman and co-founder, Steven P. Jobs, relinquished day-to-day operating responsibilities as part of a major reorganization aimed at lowering costs and restoring some stability to the company.

> . . . changes were made to heighten the company's efficiency and to make Apple a highly focused, unified and flexible company.

Officials of the nation's second-largest personal-computer maker also indicated that the company is considering another round of cost reductions, which could include more layoffs, plant closings and advertising cutbacks. . . .

The restructuring, which was announced Friday, splits Apple into two functional groups and dissolves its two product-oriented divisions. The company's new operations group will oversee the manufacturing and distribution of the Apple II and Macintosh personal computer lines, along with

product development. Marketing and sales will be overseen by the second group; the product divisions previously had greater independence in marketing and sales. The changes are expected to lessen the intense rivalry between the product divisions and help trim costs.

Under the restructuring, Mr. Jobs loses direct control over the manufacturing and marketing of the Macintosh personal computer, the cornerstone product in Apple's risky plan to penetrate the office market. Mr. Jobs led the development team that designed and last year introduced the machine.

The 30-year-old Mr. Jobs, who held the post of general manager of Apple's Macintosh division, will retain the title of chairman.

Of Mr. Jobs's new responsibilities, Apple would say only that its mercurial co-founder "will take on a more global role in new product innovations" and "will continue to be a creator of powerful ideas and the champion of Apple's spirit. . . ."

Mr. Jobs declined to comment on the change in his duties. But a former Apple senior manager and associate of Mr. Jobs said it was unlikely that the chairman had voluntarily agreed to give up his involvement in day-to-day operations.

The restructuring centralizes control and places greater power in the hands of two top executives, one an Apple veteran and the other a seasoned marketing executive brought in by Mr. Sculley shortly after he joined the company. . . .

One problem the reorganization is expected to resolve is the morale-sapping rivalry between the product divisions. Some insiders had complained that the Apple II division suffered from "second-class citizenship" within the company as Apple officials and the news media lavished attention on the Macintosh computer, Apple's showcase product. The popular, eight-year-old Apple II computer is Apple's prime money-maker.

Morale hit a new low during the company's annual meeting in January, when Macintosh division employees got front row seats to hear the zealous Mr. Jobs describe future Macintosh products. The Apple II division watched via closed-circuit television from a nearby auditorium.

In a prepared statement, Mr. Sculley said the organizational and managerial changes were made to heighten the company's efficiency and to make Apple "a highly focused, unified and flexible company." Through a spokeswoman, Mr. Sculley declined to comment further.

DATELINE—SEPTEMBER 19, 1985 (CUPERTINO, CALIF.)—Steve Jobs resigned as chairman of Apple Computer, Inc. His announced plans are to start a new venture to develop powerful computers for higher education.

PART II

Stripping Steve Jobs of the company he had helped cofound was one of the hardest things John Sculley said he had ever had to do. But that wasn't all, he also had to lay off 20 percent of the workforce and reorient the firm's single-minded focus from products to markets. By doing this, Sculley pursued a singular vision—to prove that creativity and controls could coexist at the company.

Sculley came to Apple in 1983 from his previous position as president of Pepsico, and with an educational background that included an undergraduate degree in architecture and an MBA. He had no prior experience in the computer industry, and at Apple he made some major blunders at first. He spent heavily on advertis-

ing, as he had done at Pepsico, and he didn't spend enough on research and development. When the Macintosh was first introduced, it came out with too-little power and software support. The forecasted sales of 60,000+ per month turned out to total a little over 20,000.

> **Sculley faced the task of holding the company together and preserving the innovative spirit that Jobs had personified.**

When Jobs left, Sculley faced the task of holding the company together and preserving the innovative spirit that Jobs had personified. He acted quickly to maintain order by promoting Delbert Yocam from within to be chief operating officer. He installed the "spirited" Jean-Louis Gasse as head of new product development. Gasse came to Cupertino from France where he had headed up Apple's Paris operations. His job was to put the Mac back on track; Yocam was supposed to smooth the feathers left ruffled by Jobs departure. On top of it all, Sculley embarked on a plan to install Apple as a mainstay supplier of personal computers to the business market—a domain previously held sacrosanct by IBM and makers of IBM-compatibles.

In March 1988 Apple introduced two new computers for the business user—the Macintosh SE and the Macintosh II. Under Sculley's leadership and in a clear departure from Jobs' preferences, they are "open Macs" which accommodate microprocessors from other companies. Business buyers quickly responded and Apple's sales jumped with over half of

the sales and most of the profits now coming from sales of computers and laser printers to business users. Before Sculley joined the firm, Apple was virtually nonexistent in this marketplace.

Sculley appears dedicated to pushing the right new products through the company's bureaucracy. He's a person who at least one co-worker describes as poor at smalltalk. "Sometimes I think he's more comfortable in front of a thousand people than he is mingling at a cocktail party," she says. An industry analyst comments on his influence on the firm: "People at Apple appreciate that he saved the company from ruin . . . but nobody really knows what to make of [him]." For now, at least, Sculley's formula for success seems to be working.

QUESTIONS

1. What type of problem environment did CEO John Sculley operate in during Part I of the case? What were the major "problems" which created difficulties for Apple Computer, Inc. in Part I of the case? Make a list of these problems and show how each specifically relates to one of the four management functions—planning, organizing, leading, and controlling?

2. What do you feel Sculley did *right* in his attempt to restore Apple's productivity and overall reputation as a leader in the computer industry, and why? What do you feel he did *wrong* and why? Do you feel confident that Apple will maintain its current record of success in the future? Explain your answer.

3. Based on the information provided here, do you feel John Sculley is an "effective manager?" Justify your answer by reference to his apparent abilities in respect to Katz's three essential managerial skills. ∎

PLANNING FOR PRODUCTIVITY

4 Fundamentals of Planning

5 Strategic Planning

Creating a Twenty-First-Century Organization

In organizations small and large, young and established, planning is a topic much on managers' minds. Everyone agrees that some plan is better than none—yet inflexible or overly ambitious plans can be severely restricting, if not ultimately damaging, to organizations operating in an era of rapid and profound change. Planning, as we will see in Chapters 4 and 5, is a delicate balancing act in which short- and long-term interests, prospects and problems are weighed against one another. The process requires healthy doses of hard-nosed realism as well as a solid grounding in planning theory. Now more than ever, planners must look at present and anticipated conditions with clear, open eyes.

What are the major challenges facing managers charged with planning? Broadly put, those challenges spring from the extraordinary burgeoning of high technology and the powerful influence of the "information age." Somewhat more narrowly stated, the challenges include developing labor shortages, economic uncertainties,

"FLEXIBILITY AND INGENUITY . . . ARE IMPORTANT "TOOLS" FOR PLANNING."

shifting values, and ongoing social transformations of the workforce—to name just a few. As managers confront a variety of challenges, they are increasingly aware of the need for planning on two fronts—the long and the short—and for strategies that further incorporate goals in specific, measurable ways.

The story of how two of the American automobile industry's chief players, Ford and GM, are negotiating their way through the maze of planning options is an instructive one. In this Perspective we'll compare their paths to the future and, in so doing, uncover some of the hows and whys of planning.

FORD: THE GLOBAL CAR COMPANY

How does Ford Motor Company think about the twenty-first century? In a word—"internationally." Ford's CEO, Donald Petersen, intends to lead the company into the number-one spot of what he sees as a global industry. His approach to planning begins with the premise that an American automobile manufacturer has to be prepared for a glut of cars in this country by the end of the century. The only route to long-term success, argues Petersen, is short-term economizing and careful strategizing for the future.

At the center of Petersen's vision for Ford's future is what he calls "centers of excellence." They will be located around the world. On the basis of local expertise and market requirements, these centers will be chosen to develop a particular component (such as the suspension system) for all Ford cars. The idea is to avoid wasteful duplication of R&D efforts and to make the most of Ford's specialists in various areas.[1]

How will Ford attain this vision? Petersen has begun by radically trim-

NOTES
1. "Can Ford Stay on Top?" *Business Week* (September 28, 1987), p. 80.
2. "Can Ford Stay on Top?" pp. 85–86.
3. "General Motors: What Went Wrong," *Business Week* (March 16, 1987), pp. 104–106.
4. Roger B. Smith, "Creating a 21st Century Corporation," *The Futurist* (November–December, 1986), pp. 20–23.
5. Alex Taylor III, "Back to the Future at Saturn," *Fortune* (August 1, 1988), pp. 62–72.

ming costs, laying off thousands and closing unprofitable plants to save several billion dollars. Accompanying the cuts are aggressive strategies that deal in the short term but address the long haul as well. Quality improvements are a major focus; assembly workers have authority to stop the line if they believe quality is being compromised. Moreover, the old top-down organization structure is being replaced by a team-oriented one, and

> **Now more than ever, planners must look at present and anticipated conditions with clear, open eyes.**

promotions and bonuses are tied to teamwork and company-wide quality enhancements. To facilitate the development of a global company, Petersen encourages top managers to serve abroad, and Ford has launched a global technology database network to keep its divisions in close touch.[2]

Ford is banking on buyers' tastes and governmental regulations remaining sufficiently homogeneous that its global efforts will pay off. In any case, the steps already taken have altered the face of Ford: teamwork and participative management are increasingly the name of the game at Ford Motor Company.

GM: STAGING A COMEBACK

The GM chapter of our story begins with trouble. Once the car industry's leader in the United States, General Motors Corporation now struggles to revamp its image and revitalize flagging sales. Recently, Ford's profits had topped the combined total earn-

ings of both GM and Chrysler—a humbling experience for gigantic GM. The corporation now finds itself at a tricky pass; how it plans for the future will have a critical effect on its potential for restored leadership in the industry.

Before we look at GM's path to the twenty-first century, however, we need to take a brief detour into the past, to discover the reasons for GM's current plight. At the start of the 1980s, GM's dominance was undisputed and its profits huge. What went wrong? Several things, all exacerbated by the size of the corporation.

Having assumed continued increases in gas prices and consumer demand for smaller cars, GM spent over $5 billion on capital improvements in 1980 to gear up for a generation of foreign-sized cars. But gas prices fell—and foreign cars themselves grew popular. In the meantime, GM's management had lost sight of costs other than those for labor. The corporation invested heavily in robotics, a technology with kinks GM had difficulty troubleshooting. In the process managers fell out of touch with workers on the

> **. . . inflexible or overly ambitious plans can be severely restricting . . .**

floor—people with real experience with the technology. Moreover, GM's rigid organizational hierarchy (14 management layers) did not handle gracefully the needed restructuring efforts initiated by CEO Roger Smith, and workers' and managers' morale suffered. Finally, GM's lackluster car designs had a major dampening effect on sales, not to mention esprit de corps.[3]

Smith, aware of his corporation's reduced standing, was not going to take all this sitting down. He illuminated his vision for GM's future.[4] Stressing that a successful business must lead, not follow, change—and that change is the only constant—Smith declared that GM had developed a financial recovery plan and set firm goals for the future (including international market penetration,

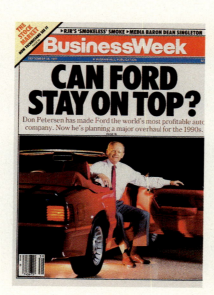

highest-quality products, and innovation). Smith then claimed that GM had embarked on a three-pronged strategy involving reorganization, diversification, and acquisition. This ongoing strategy had already generated salutory results. Reorganization had moved decision making closer to the marketplace and encouraged

---

... both short- and long-term planning involve enlightened risk-taking.

---

teamwork. Diversification had created a more broadly based business, and new acquisitions had helped fill in technological gaps such as data processing and systems engineering.

The three-pronged strategy continues, albeit slowly, and GM's costs have been cut by at least $3 billion. What may be the biggest venture of all, GM's new state-of-the-art Saturn plant, is also the biggest question mark.[5] How well the firm does in this project is critical to the strategy. Smith remains confident that GM will enter the next century a stronger, better corporation as a consequence of the planning process initiated by top management. The stakes are high—and the outcome lies, of course, in the future.

THE PLANNER'S TOOLBOX

As the Ford-GM story indicates, a company's plans begin in its view of itself and grow out of its view of where it can go and what it can become. The possible paths to the future *are* bewildering: GM's short-term plans for the 1980s—along with their long-term implications—went awry, and Ford's ambitious plans for the year 2000 may be no more foolproof than its competitors'. What then, you may well ask, are the elements of managerial planning trade, and are they reliable? Theories and methods abound, but seasoned managers tend to agree that the best plans are those which start and end in a realistic view of the organization and its environment. Flexibility and ingenuity—traits we encountered in the Part 1 Perspective—are "tools" as important for planning as for any other managerial function.

Ultimately, both short- and long-term planning involve enlightened risk-taking. To quote CEO Smith, arguably an expert on long shots, you select a course of action "for a plausible, possible, and desirable future—and you go with it." ■

Fundamentals of Planning

Taking the Long View

Managers are playing high-tech catch-up—a game with high stakes. Not so long ago it was possible for a company to go about its business without planning for advances in technology that weren't directly related to its products or services. Those days are gone. Anticipating technological developments has become a high priority even for nontechnology companies—the most far-sighted of which recognize that refined computer hardware and software can supply a needed competitive edge. And high-tech organizations are scrambling faster than ever to keep one step ahead of new developments in their fields.

The pace of technological change quickens each year, and even organizations with technology units have trouble predicting the future. Harvard Business School Professor Oscar Hauptmann maintains that in effect, today's organizations are "aiming at a moving target." To keep within range, some companies are decentralizing as a means of improving their long-range planning. National Cash Register, after suffering through the overnight obsolescence of its mechanical cash registers when competitors' electronic machines hit the market, decided that it had to guard against future surprises. "We didn't react quickly enough," says Elton White, the company's executive vice-president for product marketing and strategic planning. "We didn't pay enough attention to trends."

NCR now has 21 product development centers that operate autonomously and undertake most of the company's technology research. Similarly, 3M Company has split itself into term research, one investigates products on a 5- to 10-year development schedule, and the third looks at technological developments even further in the future.

NCR and 3M have obvious cause for concern about obsolescence; their products ride the crests of high-tech waves. Yet even service industries such as banking are jumping on the technology bandwagon and preparing to take advantage of new developments. One unit of Fidelity Investments, a mutual fund, is composed of a dozen scientists who undertake advanced R&D projects such as computer voice-recognition systems and home-computer systems for tracking and managing funds. While not all of these explorations will bear fruit (indeed, flawed software approaches have cost the company millions of dollars), Fidelity Systems' President Michael Simmons believes that the risks must be taken. Other companies, fearing the losses that can result from failed R&D or overly hasty responses to technological trends that end up going nowhere, hire long-range planning consultants or engage in joint ventures to spread the risk.

The cost of keeping up with change is high no matter what route is chosen, and careful analysis and planning are more essential than ever. A good dose of realism is healthy, too. The experience of Fidelity's Simmons has taught him that "the situation changes long before you get the job done." NCR's White undoubtedly knows just what he means. ∎

Source: Information from Paul Duke Jr., "Taking the Long View," *Wall Street Journal* (June 12, 1987), pp. 33–34D.

Managers must look ahead, make good judgments about future conditions, and then plan and act accordingly on a daily basis. Key topics in this chapter include

Planning as a Management
  Function
Benefits of Planning
Types of Plans Used by
  Managers
The Planning Process
Forecasting as a Planning
  Aid
Making Planning Effective

The process of management involves looking ahead. Good managers are able to assess the future and make provision for it. **Planning,** the first of the four basic managerial functions, is how this responsibility is carried out. It is formally defined as a process of setting objectives and determining what should be done to accomplish them. Planning is an applied problem-solving and decision-making effort through which managers act to ensure the future success of their organizations and work units, as well as themselves. Consider this definition as presented in the Eaton Corporation's Annual Report.[1]

> *Planning* at Eaton means taking the hard decisions before events force them upon you, and anticipating the future needs of the market before the demand asserts itself.

To achieve effectiveness at any level of responsibility, a manager must be a good planner. Henri Fayol, who you should remember as an important figure in the history of management thought, went so far as to consider planning the most important management function. As such, it has three action characteristics that present special challenges to the manager. Planning is:

1. *Forward thinking* Through planning managers decide what to do and how before it must actually be done.
2. *Decision making* Planning involves making decisions that identify desired future states of affairs, and define the actions required to achieve them.

3. *Goal oriented* Planning targets efforts on activities needed to accomplish objectives and arrive at a desired end result.

PLANNING AS A MANAGEMENT FUNCTION

Figure 4.1 depicts the relationship of planning to the other management functions in the ultimate quest for productivity. What is sometimes called the primacy principle of planning recognizes that planning is the first and most basic of all the functions. As a foundation of the management process, planning identifies what needs to be done and sets the stage for further managerial efforts at

Organizing Allocating and combining resources to allow task accomplishment.

Leading Guiding the efforts of human resources toward task accomplishment.

Controlling Monitoring task accomplishments and taking necessary corrective action.

ILLUSTRATIVE CASE: THE HOSPITAL ADMINISTRATOR

The importance of planning among the management functions and the demands that it can make on a manager's time are well evidenced in this case of a hospital administrator.[2] The hospital was undertaking a three-year building-expansion program that would result in a 25 percent increase in the size

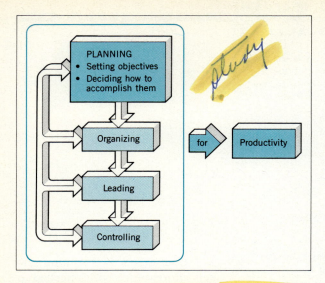

FIGURE 4.1 *Planning for productivity—viewed in relationship with the other management functions.*

of the hospital. A great deal of the administrator's time was spent dealing with physicians, staff members, architects, the hospital board, and other concerned persons in planning how to construct the addition. During the period observed by the researchers, about 14 percent of the administrator's telephone conversations related specifically to planning the best way to meet the needs of the hospital. Scheduled and unscheduled meetings were also frequently used for planning the expansion program. During these meetings, various people sat down and studied each alternative and their potential impact on the entire hospital. Overall, approximately 37 percent of the administrator's available time was devoted to the identification of alternatives and a determination of their feasibility. This and uncounted additional time was spent on planning for this one single event.

This example shows how someone planned to meet the challenges of a special situation. As you might have expected, it shows the hospital administrator planning in an intense and systematic fashion. But, it also shows that the planning was accomplished in a work setting quite characteristic of the nature of managerial work as first described in Chapter 1. That is, the administrator planned while facing the demands of busy and complex work days. Planning was done not just once, but was quite continuous over the time period. And, the planning

was accomplished through a network of important interpersonal relationships maintained by the administrator.

Current thinking on planning recognizes that managers don't always plan alone, in a quiet room, and only once or twice a week. For truly effective managers planning is an ongoing activity. It provides a foundation for both getting specific and major projects like the hospital building expansion done on time and within budget, and for maintaining an overall sense of direction in day-to-day work. Planning, simply stated, is an essential managerial responsibility.

Some managers, of course, plan more than others, some do it better than others, and some neglect planning on occasion. Their reasons for neglecting planning can be any or all of the following:

- They just don't think about the future.
- They are impatient and act before thinking.
- They feel others should do the planning.
- They let daily pressures drive out planning.

BENEFITS OF PLANNING

This chapter will pose and answer several questions regarding the fundamentals of planning. These questions include, "What is a plan?" "What is planning?" and "How do managers plan?" For now the question is, "Why should managers plan?" Four important answers to this question follow.

Stability, Adaptability, and Contingency

Managers plan for various circumstances. They may plan for stability—that is, to ensure continuation of existing success in a fairly stable environment. They may plan for adaptability to ensure successful reaction to frequent changes in a more dynamic and uncertain environment. They may also plan for contingency in the sense that they anticipate events that may occur in the future and identify appropriate actions that may be taken should they do so. Effective planning benefits organizations by helping them achieve results through an action-oriented and forward-thinking posture.

Clarified Means–End Chains

A **means–end chain** links the work efforts of individuals and groups at various levels of the organization to a common purpose. Planning helps clarify higher-level objectives as the ends toward which lower-level objectives are directed as means. In Figure 4.2, for example, a marketing vice-president's objective of increasing sales is the *end* toward which a middle-level marketing manager's objective of adding new customers becomes a *means*. By clarifying means–end chains, planning facilitates unity of purpose and helps managers coordinate the organization as a complex system of people, tasks, structures, and resources.

Performance Improvement

Organizations in modern society are facing increasing challenges from many sources. These include greater government regulation, ever more complex technologies, more environmental uncertainties, and the sheer cost of investments in labor, capital, and other supporting resources. As you would expect, planning offers important advantages to organizations and their managers in such circumstances. Research, for example, indicates that both large and small firms with formal planning systems achieve better financial performance than those that do not.[3] The performance benefits of planning relate to these major points.

1.   *Planning focuses managers' attention on objectives that can generate results*; it creates a performance-oriented sense of direction.

FIGURE 4.2   *A sample means-end chain in a consumer products company: marketing's contribution to improved profits.*

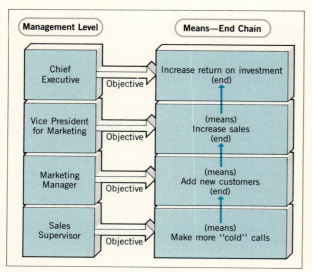

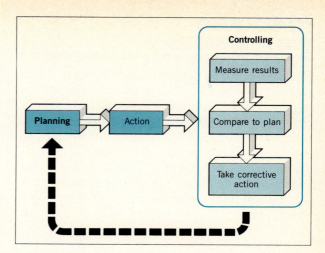

FIGURE 4.3   *The important relationship between planning and controlling as management functions.*

2.   *Planning helps managers set priorities*; it helps focus energies on the most important problems and opportunities.

3.   *Planning helps managers emphasize organizational strengths*; it helps in allocating resources to best overall advantage.

4.   *Planning helps managers cope with ever-changing external environments*; it helps to anticipate problems and opportunities so they can best be dealt with.

5.   *Planning facilitates control*; it clarifies initial expectations and provides a basis for evaluating actual results.

Better Control

Figure 4.3 highlights the special connection between planning and controlling. Control involves responsibility for the measurement and evaluation of action results, and the reformulation of plans where appropriate. Planning helps make this all possible by defining objectives and specifying appropriate actions in the first place. Planning and controlling, therefore, are forever interrelated in the process of management. Without control, planning lacks follow-through; without plans, controlling lacks a guiding frame of reference. Simply put, planning leads to controlling, which leads to further planning. This essential relationship of planning and controlling in the management process will be discussed again in Part 5 on "Controlling for Productivity."

TYPES OF PLANS
USED BY MANAGERS

Planning, a process of thinking before taking action, creates plans which are then used to guide actions as they are taken over time. A **plan** is a statement of the intended means for accomplishing a desired result. Because a plan describes an intended course of action, it should answer the questions of "what?" "how?" "when?" "where?" and "who?" The "what" and the "how" are clearly in evidence in this excerpt from one of the Evans Products Company's plans.[4]

> We will strive to maintain our strong consumer image as the "building materials specialist" by stocking ranges of merchandise which allow the customer to choose quality products at a variety of price levels.

Every good plan is also an action statement that includes a clear-cut objective. This **planning objective,** in turn, is the desired future state or end result to be accomplished through implementation of the plan. For example,[5]

At IBM these planning objectives were set by top management in response to tough competition in the computer industry:

■ *Reduce costs* to cut costs by as much as $2.25 billion, or 7 percent from current levels.

■ *Add new products* to add new products including a more powerful personal computer, a new mainframe series, and new high-performance software to link computer systems.

■ *Streamline management* to reduce the managerial workforce by 40,000 persons worldwide.

■ *Become more aggressive in marketing* to create 5000 new marketing and sales jobs, an increase of 22 percent, and listen more closely to customer needs.

There are many different types of plans with which you will become involved as a manager. These plans may be differentiated in terms of the time frames covered (short-range and long-range), scope of activities represented (strategic and operational), and the specific uses to which they are put (standing-use and single-use). As Figure 4.4 shows, responsibilities for making and implementing the various types of plans vary across managerial levels. In general, there is a cascade effect of means–end

chains. Plans created by managers at one level establish the action framework within which plans at the next lower level become defined. When it comes to the planning function,

1. *Top-level managers* spend greater proportions of their time creating long range, strategic, and standing-use plans applicable to the organization as a whole.

2. *Middle-level managers* focus their planning efforts on creating operational and standing use plans that implement the planning objectives of top managers and set action guidelines for lower-level managers.

3. *Lower-level managers* are more concerned with creating and using short-range and single-use plans that implement the operational plans of middle management on a day-to-day basis.

Short-Range and Long-Range Plans

It is common to differentiate plans according to the time horizons they represent—short, intermediate, or long term. A rule of thumb is that **short-range plans** cover one year or less, **medium-range plans** cover one to two years, and **long-range plans** cover up to five years or more. Naturally the planning objectives in a manager's action agenda will be more specific in the short run and less clear-cut over the longer term. Take for instance, these financial objectives as they guide the thinking of one general manager.[6]

FIGURE 4.4 *How planning varies by management level in organizations.*

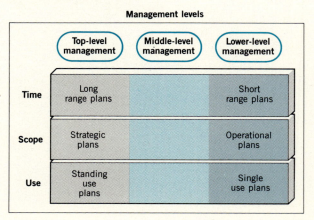

Long range objective   A general notion of the desired return on investment (ROI) expected in 10 years.
Medium range objective   A more specific set of sales and income targets covering the next five years.
Short range objective   A detailed list of sales, income, expense, and ROI objectives for the next three months.

Organizations need plans covering all of these time frames. And even though top-level managers are more directly responsible for setting long-range plans, all managers should still have a sense of direction that extends beyond the immediate future. Otherwise, the pressures of daily events may create confusion and detract from the continuity of one's actions.

As you consider the prior point, you should be aware of some research by Elliot Jaques on the "time frames" of individuals. He suggests that people vary in their capability to think out, organize, and work through events of different time horizons.[7] In fact, Jaques feels that most of us work most comfortably with three-month time spans, a smaller group of people work well with a one-year span, while only about one person in several million can handle a 20-year time frame. This is a provocative point when you consider the fact that the responsibilities of managers working at various levels in organizations require a capability to plan over quite different periods of time. Although a supervisor may face planning challenges that rest mainly in the three-month range, the next higher manager may deal with a one-year range, while a vice-president deals with five years, and the chief executive must have a vision extending 10 years or more. Career progress and success at higher management levels, therefore, clearly requires the conceptual skills to work well with longer range time frames.

long range plan

Strategic and Operational Plans

Another useful perspective on plans is the scope or breadth of activities they represent. **Strategic plans** are comprehensive in scope and reflect longer term needs and directions of the organization or subunit. Top management planning of this scope involves determining where the organization should go in terms of overall objectives, and then deciding what strategies and resources are required to enable this to happen. Think back to the example of IBM for a moment. At the same time that management was planning to cut costs, streamline management, add new products, and improve marketing over the short run, they also redirected the firm's long-term strategy toward *more diversification*. Specifically, they chose to accelerate IBM's move into high-margin software and services. Here's another case of a company that pursued just the reverse strategy— *less diversification.*[8]

At Borden, Inc.   over $2 billion in revenue growth was accomplished when management decided to sell businesses unrelated to its traditional dairy industries. These ranged from interests as diverse as women's apparel and fertilizer. They continued to pursue growth, however, by acquiring new dairy-related businesses.

Operational plans, sometimes called **tactical plans,** are more limited in scope and address those activities and resources required to implement strategic plans. Tactical or operational planning, accordingly, deals more with the allocation of resources and scheduling of actual work activities than with the selection of strategies. Operational plans typical to a business firm include:

Production plans   Dealing with the methods and tools needed by people in their work.
Financial plans   Dealing with the money required to support various operations.
Facilities plans   Dealing with facilities and layouts required to support task activities.
Marketing plans   Dealing with the requirements of selling and distributing goods or services.
Personnel plans   Dealing with personnel recruiting, selection, and placement to staff jobs.

Strategic plans establish an action framework through which an organization intends to survive and prosper in its environment. They allow operational plans to be specified and implemented to the benefit of the organization as a whole. As Figure 4.5 suggests, using the Borden's case, a hierarchy of strategic and operational plans can be a significant coordinating force. It helps to ensure that task activities on the part of each individual and group within the organization interrelate to accomplish overall objectives. As the foundations on which operational plans are based, strategic plans constitute an important interface between operational plans and organizational objectives. Strategic plans and the process

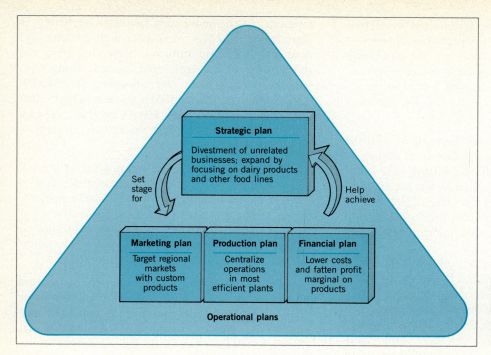

FIGURE 4.5
Relationships among strategic and operational plans: the Case of Borden, Inc.

of strategic planning are so important that the next chapter is devoted to these topics.

Standing-Use and Single-Use Plans

Plans also differ according to frequency or repetitiveness of use. A **single-use plan** is used once. It is designed to meet the needs of a unique situation and will probably not be used again in its exact form. Budgets and schedules are good examples. They are designed to fit a specific project or time period, and are discontinued when the project is completed or the time has expired.

Standing-use plans, on the other hand, are designed to be used again and again. They exist in the form of organizational policies, procedures, and rules. Once put in place, they guide activities in various situations to ensure consistency over time. Both standing-use and single-use plans are very important to managers.

Policies

A **policy** is a standing-use plan that communicates *broad* guidelines for making decisions and taking action. Policies are found in all aspects of an organization. In general, they tend to focus a manager's thinking on important issues and provide guidance on appropriate and/or inappropriate activities in relationship to them. A good policy, in turn, is one that is

- *Communicated to all concerned.* A policy cannot guide anyone's actions if people don't know of its existence.
- *Clear and understandable.* A policy cannot guide anyone's actions if people don't understand its intentions.
- *Stable but flexible.* A policy that changes too frequently will cause confusion; however, policies do need modification over time as circumstances change.

One area in which organizations are being more sensitive to the need for clear-cut policy, for example, is in respect to sexual harassment in the workplace. The response of one major corporation to this issue is clearly communicated in this policy statement.[9]

Sexual harassment related to one's job is a violation of the sex discrimination coverage of Title VII of the Civil Rights Act of 1964. It's also a violation of [the company's policy] . . . sexual harassment will not be tolerated in any form, whether committed by supervisors, other employees or non-employees. Any individual found violating this policy can be subject to disciplinary action up to and including termination, and possibly prosecution by the victim.

Policies such as this are essential to organizations. They help to ensure that day-to-day actions and decisions are consistent with values, strategies and objectives. Some common examples of topics addressed by organizational policies are shown in Table 4.1. Policies should help organizations to

1. *Coordinate activities*   The broad guidelines established by policies help to interrelate various people and work groups around common action themes.
2. *Achieve efficiency*   The action guidelines provided by policies can reduce the time spent by managers in answering questions and/or giving directions about various issues; policies contain standing answers to such questions.
3. *Develop human resources*   By setting "broad" guidelines, policies allow people to experience personal responsibility for their actions, exercise some discretion in decision making, and further develop themselves as individual contributors.
4. *Communicate a desired image*   Formal policy statements are easily communicated to external publics and organization members to clarify an image of what the organizaton is and/or intends to be.

Procedures and Rules

Procedures and rules are more specific in their action implications than organizational policies. **Pro-** cedures and **rules** are standing-use plans that precisely describe what actions are to be taken in specific situations. They emphasize details in specifying things people are expected to do and not to do in the course of their work. Whereas policies are broad guidelines for action, procedures and rules communicate *precise* guidelines that permit little or no individual discretion. They are often found in employee handbooks or manuals that outline what are commonly called SOPs—standard operating procedures.

Let's return to the prior example of a sexual harassment policy. Under such a policy, top management will want to ensure that everyone receives fair, equal, and nondiscriminatory treatment should an alleged violation occur. One way to do so, is to identify a series of procedures that specify what actions are to be taken and how, in order to process a complaint. This is the essence of any rule or procedure—the communication of a precise and relatively strict plan of action for handling certain recurring situations.

Budgets

Managers develop single-use plans for a specific circumstance or time frame. They include both budgets and schedules. **Budgets** are plans that commit resources to activities, projects, or programs. Managers typically become involved with three basic types of budgets—fixed, flexible, and zero-based. A **fixed budget** allocates resources on the basis of a single estimate of costs. The estimate establishes a fixed pool of resources that can be used, but not exceeded, in support of the specified purpose. A **flexible budget,** by contrast, allows the allocation of resources to vary in proportion with various levels of activity. Managers operating under flexible budgets can expect increments in resource allocations when activity increases from one estimated level to the next.

The intent of zero-based budgeting is for managers to totally reconsider their priorities, objectives, and activities at the start of each new budget cycle. Under a **zero-based budget,** a project or activity is budgeted as if it were brand new. Managers cannot assume that resources previously allocated to a project or activity will simply be continued in the future. Instead, all projects compete anew for available funds. Zero-based budgeting is used by businesses, government agencies, and other types of

TABLE 4.1 *Examples of Areas Typically Addressed by Organizational Policies*

Ethics	To conduct organizational affairs by high human and moral standards, with an ultimate sense of social responsibility.
Conditions of work	To maintain clean, safe, and technically superior working conditions for all employees.
Compensation	To provide the best compensation for contributions made, while remaining fair in relation to the labor market and general economic conditions.
Employment opportunity	To employ people without regard to race, sex, religion, or national origin.

HOW CEOS
MANAGE THEIR TIME

NEWSLINE 4.1

For senior managers and chief executives, devising a strategy for managing time efficiently is one of the great challenges of professional life. Most CEOs work at least 60 hours a week, and many find that their schedules are jammed far in advance with a wide range of demands. To make the most of each 24 hours, busy executives know that the first order of business is establishing a set of guiding principles for how to spend their time. They then must delegate effectively so they can concentrate on priorities.

Author and management professor John Kotter argues against overly rigid time-manage-ment tactics. Executives with a clear long-term vision of where their organizations are going, he stresses, are able to make quick adjustments in their schedules when unforeseen opportunities or problems arise. Having cultivated an ability "to be highly efficient in choosing what to react to and what to ignore," such executives can maximize their time without sacrificing flexibility and creativity.

Weekly "free-think" time is crucial, most executives agree—but like everything else, it must be plotted into a schedule. Many CEOs report that their best ruminating occurs on airplanes, tennis courts, or walks with the dog. Harvard Business School's Abraham Zaleznik characterizes many American managers as too structured and organized. "Life is a combination of action and reflection," he states, and time taken away from the latter may hurt the former.

Source: As reported in Ford S. Worthy, "How CEOs Manage Their Time," *Fortune* (January 18, 1988), pp. 88–97.

---

organizations to help ensure that only the most desirable programs receive funding. It is especially useful in dynamic environments where a need exists to avoid budgeting on the basis of historical precedent instead of present-day realities.

Budgets are powerful management tools. They allocate and commit resources across multiple and often competing uses. In so doing, budgets help clarify and reinforce action priorities, maintain coordination, and facilitate evaluation and control of results. Good managers anticipate the future well enough to bargain for and obtain an adequate budget. They are also able to achieve performance objectives while remaining within the budget. Poor managers may fail to anticipate the future properly, commit to objectives for which budgets are inadequate, and/or act irresponsibly in expending resources and overrunning budgets. Because of their managerial significance, we will deal more extensively with budgets in Chapter 15 as part of our review of controlling as a managerial function.

Schedules

Schedules are single-use plans that tie activities to specific time frames or targets. Most typically they commit time and labor to an organizational project or activity. We use schedules every day in the form of calendars, appointment books, and simple reminders or "do lists" of things to be done and when. An important part of any schedule is the assignment of priorities to activities. Good schedules not only denote what needs to be done, they also identify what needs to be done first. The Gantt Chart, introduced in Chapter 2, is technique for accomplishing this. You should recall that such charts specify and keep track of the sequence of activities that must be completed to finish the many parts of a complex project on time and in correct sequence.

Newsline 4.1 shows how some corporate CEOs try to carefully manage their time schedules. But don't neglect the fact that this challenge is important at all levels of managerial responsibility. All managers are bombarded each day by a multitude of tasks and demands that can be hard to balance in the face of frequent interruptions, crises, and unexpected events. The result is that managers sometimes lose track of their personal schedules and fall prey to what time management consultants identify as "time wasters." Their advice often includes the following "do's" and "don'ts."[10]

■ Do hire a good secretary who can screen your mail and phone calls.
■ Don't face your desk toward an open door because it invites interruptions.
■ Do learn how to say no to people who want to divert you from work you should be doing.
■ Don't be overcome by telephone interruptions or visitors without appointments.
■ Do prioritize tasks to be done according to importance and urgency.
■ Don't become involved in routines and details that should be delegated to others.

Figure 4.6 describes three different categories of managerial time—boss-imposed time, system-imposed time, and self-imposed time.[11] The first two are often more difficult to change, while self-imposed time is more open to personal scheduling. However, too many managers allow too much of their self-imposed time to be dominated by other persons. They give up "discretionary" time in the process.

One important issue in the prior list is learning how to manage the willingness of subordinates to take initiative and solve problems on their own. Consider this conversation held in an office hallway.[12]

Scene A manager sees her subordinate coming down the hall. As they near one another the subordinate says—"Good morning. By the way *we've* got a problem. You see . . ." and he goes on to describe a situation. Eventually the manager replies—"So glad you brought this up. I'm in a rush right now. Let *me* think about it and *I'll let you know.*"

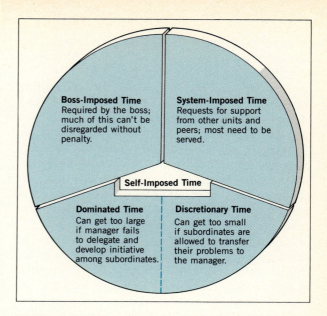

FIGURE 4.6 *Three categories of management time.*

At this point, the subordinate has transferred the problem to the manager. The manager, in turn, has committed some of her self-imposed time to solve the *subordinate's* problem. An alternative approach would have had the manager query the subordinate on some of the details, assist him to think it through, and then offer encouragement while clarifying the expectation that *he* would shortly have the situation resolved. This safeguards the manager's valuable discretionary time for other uses. It also helps develop an independent and capable subordinate who is more willing to think and act on his own.

THE PLANNING PROCESS

We have been talking about the various types of plans with which managers become involved. Plans, though, are outcomes; they are the results of planning—the process of deciding what needs to be done to accomplish objectives. Earlier in this chapter we reviewed the case of a hospital administrator to show that managers do in fact plan. Whether or not managers plan well, of course, is quite another matter. Have you ever heard of the Edsel automobile? In 1952 the Ford Motor Company introduced the first prototype of the Edsel. It was heralded as the car of the future. By the time Edsels came off the assembly line in the late 1950s, however, they were a $350 million flop. They just didn't sell.

The failure of the Edsel could reflect a planning breakdown at the highest executive level in Ford Motor Company. Why, for example, didn't top-level managers recognize the changes in consumer tastes that were occurring at the time and plan accordingly? Or did they recognize the changes, but fail to assess them properly and incorporate their implications into decision making? Perhaps the Ford managers could have benefited from more systematic attention to the steps in a formal planning process.

Now it's General Motors' turn. Surely you have heard a bit about GM's loss of market share in the United States and how CEO Roger Smith invested heavily in new manufacturing technologies to restore the company's competitive position. The company is also planning to build a new car called "Saturn." Like the Edsel was to Ford, Saturn is supposed to be GM's "car of the future." Whether it will be or not, only time will tell. Keep this situation in mind as you consider the steps in formal planning now described.

Steps in Formal Planning

Like problem solving, planning can formally be thought of as a series of steps. As shown in Figure 4.7, these steps are as follows.

Step 1: Define your objectives

This establishes where you want to go. Ideally, objectives are specific enough that you will know you have arrived when you get there or how far off the mark you are at various points along the way.

Step 2: Determine where you stand vis-à-vis objectives

This step evaluates current status vis-à-vis the desired future state. It includes an analysis of current strengths and weaknesses in terms of being able to accomplish your objectives in the future.

Step 3: Develop your premises regarding future conditions

This step involves analyzing the situation for external factors that may inhibit goal accomplishment, and forecasting future trends as they relate to these same factors. Sometimes this is called the *generation of future scenarios*.

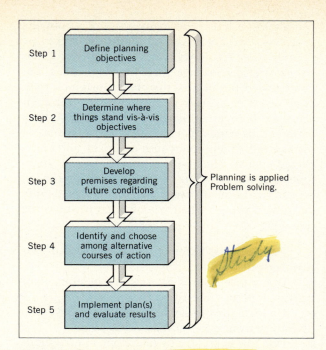

FIGURE 4.7 *Five steps in the formal planning process: an example of applied problem solving.*

Step 4: Identify and choose among alternative courses of action

This step is the point of actual decision. Here you list and evaluate action alternatives for resolving any discrepancy between where you are and where you want to be. Then you choose one or more alternatives to formulate a course of action appropriate to the achievement of your objectives. This course of action becomes the plan.

Step 5: Implement the plan and evaluate results

This is the action stage where actual results are determined. To achieve your objectives you must both establish a plan and implement it well. True implementation also involves evaluation of results to ensure accomplishment of objectives. When actual results are less than planned objectives, corrective action should be taken to modify the original plan and/or the actions through which it is implemented.

Thus, the planning process is really a special application of the more general problem-solving process examined in Chapter 3. This relationship between problem solving and planning is also highlighted in Figure 4.6.

SQUIBB'S PRESCRIPTION FOR SUCCESS

I n the competitive world of pharmaceuticals, Squibb Corporation is noteworthy for its constant product innovation—and for a combined "inside-out/outside-in" approach to planning that has paid off handsomely. Since the 1960s Squibb has sunk profits from its consumer businesses (including baby food and perfume) into drug R&D efforts. As new products are developed and successfully marketed, Squibb has been selling off its less profitable consumer units, thus garnering even more money for its lucrative drug innovations—a cycle that has bred big profits.

The inside-out side of Squibb's planning strategy has entailed careful, realistic choices of product targets. Its R&D staff focus on areas in which they have scientific expertise and are fairly sure to achieve a major breakthrough, thereby minimizing wasted effort and false starts. The outside-in side has entailed constant communication between Squibb's savvy marketers and the R&D staff. "Our commercial colleagues often see niches where there are no good products," explains Zola Horovitz, vice-president for research planning.

In this way Squibb concentrates on what it does best while simultaneously looking for new niches—openings where it can use its research prowess to beat out the competition. With sales of $60 million for one drug alone, the anti-infective aztreonam, Squibb's approach is a clear success.

Source: As reported in "Squibb's Rx for Success: Find a Need and Fill It," *Business Week* (October 5, 1987), p. 80.

Different Approaches to Planning

The planning process can be approached in different ways. The more common approaches are compared and contrasted here.[13]

Inside-Out versus Outside-In Planning

Inside-out planning involves focusing your efforts and energies on doing what you already do, but trying to do it as best as you can. Planning from the inside out is not going to make dramatic changes in an organization's product outputs, but it can result in maximum effectiveness and good resource utilization. Dick Levin, a specialist on long-range planning, tells of a friend who uses this approach.[14]

My good friend Jim is president of a very successful miniconglomerate in the communications industry in Chapel Hill. Jim says the measure of an organization's success is its "humpability factor." (And I've never seen an organization the size of his—250 persons—in my experience with more humpability than Jim's.) Humpability is Jim's term for sheer work, output, effort, push, drive—Jim says once he established absolute, unflagging humpability in his organization, the firm found that it could be anything better than the competition. (It's a fact. His company is in eight separate businesses, and all do well.) Jim's focus is on the inside—keeping up the humpability of the troops. "Whatever comes through the door, we can probably make money at it," he says. He probably can; the financial health of his diverse holdings attests to it.

Levin has another friend, Sid, who uses **outside-in planning.** That is, he analyzes the external environment and makes the internal adjustments necessary to exploit the opportunities and minimize the problems it offers. Sid operates in the highly competitive corrugated box business. He once made boxes used in department stores for dresses, hosiery, and the like. But the demand slipped as stores stopped including boxes with material purchases. Sid looked around at his options in the corrugated box industry. He saw large and established firms waging wars with one another for this market. Instead of competing with them, Sid decided to serve the market niche they were avoiding—the small special-order business.

Newsline 4.2 shows how the benefits of both inside-out and outside-in planning work well for Squibb, a major pharmaceuticals company. Planning in most settings should have similar capabilities to combine inside and outside perspectives to best advantage. In general, the managerial implications of these two planning approaches are:

1. *Use inside-out planning* when you want to do what you and/or other people are already doing, but want to do it better. The planning objective in this case is to determine "how" to do it better. Jim did this well.
2. *Use outside-in planning* when you want to find a unique niche for your activities—that is, to do something no one else is ding. The planning objective here is to find the available niches and select the one(s) you are likely to exploit to best advantage. Sid was superb at this approach to planning.

Top-Down versus Bottom-Up Planning

Another important dilemma in planning relates to the choice of where in an organization the process should begin. **Top-down planning** is where top management sets the broad objectives and then allows lower management levels to make plans within these constraints. **Bottom-up planning** begins with plans that are developed at lower levels without such constraints. They are then sequentially passed up the hierarchy to top-management levels.

The inevitable managerial question becomes: should planning start at the very top of the organization and then filter down, or should it begin at the bottom and build up to the top? We can explore this question with the help of another of Dick Levin's classic examples.[15]

My university sets a terrible example of bottom-up long-range planning. At Chapel Hill we're comprised of 14 colleges and schools, enrolling 21,000 students. Periodically, the chancellor puts out a memo to the vice-chancellors and provost calling for a long-range plan, and the vice-chancellors and provost put out a memo to all the schools and colleges calling for a long-range plan, and the deans of the schools and colleges put out a memo to all the department heads calling for a long-range plan, and the department heads put out a memo to their faculties calling for a long-range plan. Then the faculty members send their long-range plan to their department heads, and the department heads edit, condense, and retype the plans, put them into a common binder, and send them to their deans who edit, condense, and retype all the department plans, put them into a common binder, and send them to the vice-chancellors or provost, who edit, condense, and retype them, put them into a common binder, and send them to the chancellor's planning assistant who edits, retypes, and condenses them and adds a bit of editorial glue before putting them in a common binder and giving them to the chancellor. End of tale. End of plan too.

A person of never-ending experiences, Levin goes on to speak of another case taken from his university. This one involved a new dean who decided to make a plan and then unveil it to his faculty, an extreme top-down approach. This didn't work either; Levin reports that "the dean got *stomped* (Southern expression for 'after serious reflection, returns to full-time teaching and research')."

Both bottom-up and top-down planning approaches have disadvantages. When followed to the extreme, bottom-up planning may fail to result in an integrated overall direction for the organization as a whole. This occurs when multiple plans from various subsystems reflect uncoordinated or even conflicting action directions. But a major advantage of this approach is a strong sense of commitment and ownership among those involved in the planning at lower levels. Pure top-down planning, on the other hand, sometimes fails on just this latter point. It may not satisfy the needs of lower levels to influence the planning process through which future directions guiding their actions become set.

Levin ultimately suggests that the best planning begins at the top, but then proceeds in a way that allows serious inputs from all levels. *Newsline 4.3* illustrates this in the demanding international business setting. Managers are thus advised to combine the best elements of both the top-down and bottom-up planning approaches. That is, managers should

■ Communicate to all concerned the basic planning assumptions (who we are, what we want to be, and what the future is expected to hold).

THE WORLDWIDE
ARM OF TEXAS INSTRUMENTS

N E W S L I N E 4.3

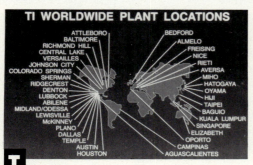

TI WORLDWIDE PLANT LOCATIONS

ATTLEBORO
BALTIMORE
RICHMOND HILL
CENTRAL LAKE
VERSAILLES
JOHNSON CITY
COLORADO SPRINGS
SHERMAN
RIDGECREST
DENTON
LUBBOCK
ABILENE
MIDLAND/ODESSA
LEWISVILLE
McKINNEY
PLANO
DALLAS
TEMPLE
AUSTIN
HOUSTON

BEDFORD
ALMELO
FREISING
NICE
RIETI
AVERSA
MIHO
HATOGAYA
OYAMA
HIJI
TAIPEI
BAGUIO
KUALA LUMPUR
SINGAPORE
ELIZABETH
OPORTO
CAMPINAS
AGUASCALIENTES

Texas Instruments has spread out to 50 countries—but its CEO, Jerry Junkins, is determined that the corporation, a leader in the microchip industry, won't be spread thin. His goal is global efficiency: keeping on top of diverse foreign markets and synchronizing product development and manufacturing so that the largest number of customers will be served.

In Junkins's view, planning and communicating are the keys to a successful global campaign. When he took over, Texas Instruments had problems with excess capacity in some plants and low stock in others—the result of insufficient coordination among regional managers. Now these managers meet quarterly to develop a worldwide strategy, balancing conflicts of interest and committing to firm product development plans that benefit the corporation as a whole. In TI's Japanese plants, for instance, plant expansion is discouraged even though demand is high because other regions, such as the United States, may have spare capacity that is hurting them. In return, U.S.-based plants must agree to supply inventory-hungry Japanese plants even if demand escalates at home.

Every day, TI personnel communicate over a 40,000-computer network to ensure that the corporation stays a step ahead of technological advances, the competition, and new markets. Junkins has turned around a company that suffered severe losses when he first came aboard— and he is determined to keep planning for leadership in the international marketplace.

Source: As reported in "The Long Arm of Jerry Junkins," *Fortune* (March 14, 1988), p. 48.

■ Seek inputs on these and related planning issues from all levels in the organization.

■ Lay out various action alternatives, but let all levels comment on their relative merits and demerits.

■ Work hard all along the way to get commitment from all levels on the final choice of action direction.

Contingency Planning

Contingency planning involves the identification of alternative courses of action that can be used to modify an original plan if and when circumstances change with time. Planning, by definition, involves thinking ahead. The more uncertain the future, however, the more likely that one's original assumptions, predictions and intentions may prove to be in error. Unexpected problems and events frequently occur. When they do, plans may have to be changed to take new developments into account. It is better to anticipate that things might not go as expected and be prepared with alternative action plans than to be caught by surprise. Such contingency planning thus supplements or extends the formal planning process. It involves these basic steps.[16]

1. Identification of the things that *might* go wrong and interfere with the success of original plans.
2. Estimation of the likelihood that each of these things actually *will* go wrong.
3. Examination of the cost and inconvenience of preparing plans to deal with each of these things.
4. Selection of those things that are most significant *and* most reasonable to address.
5. Preparation of plans for dealing with those things.

The key in contingency planning is to identify early in the planning process what possible shifts or changes in future events could affect current plans. Sometimes this is accomplished by simply good forward thinking; other times it is assisted by the use of "devil's advocate" positions where people develop "worst case" scenarios of future events. Given the identification of such future "contingencies," alternative plans can be created for implementation if and when they actually occur. Contingency planning, by looking ahead in this fashion, allows for quick action when preselected "trigger points" occur and indicate that an existing plan is no longer desirable. For example,[17]

at Chrysler Corporation company planners watched closely as U.S. government officials debated whether or not to end import quotas on foreign cars. The decision was made with considerable debate and conjecture. No one was able to predict beforehand just which way the decision would go. But the company was prepared with a contingency plan. As soon as the government announced the end of import quotas, Chairman Lee Iacocca unveiled Chrysler's plan to import 200,000 more cars a year from its Japanese affiliate, Mitsubishi Motors. If the import quotas had been maintained, Chrysler would have followed its original plan to open new domestic assembly and production facilities. As it turned out, Iacocca said—"we had plan B and we went to it."

FORECASTING AS A PLANNING AID
Study

Forecasting is an attempt to predict outcomes that will happen in the future. All good plans involve forecasts. But forecasting, in itself, is not planning. Planning is a more comprehensive activity that involves deciding what to do about the implications of forecasts once they are made.

A forecast is a vision of the future that creates premises which managers can use as a basis for planning.[18] Forecasts thereby involve assumptions about what will happen in the future. When properly performed, they are a major resource to the manager in the planning process. Unfortunately, this task is not as easy as it may seem. Could you, for example, have predicted the advent of the digital watch and the personal computer? Do you believe

that by the mid 1990s powerful computers will be available in a size just slightly larger than the pocket calculators of today? Indeed, the inability of forecasting to provide perfect predictions of the future is what makes contingency planning so useful to managers.

Types of Forecasts

As a manager you will encounter various types of forecasts. Some of the more obvious ones are economic, technological, competitive, and consumer forecasts. Less obvious but still very important are forecasts of new laws and government regulations, resource availabilities, labor supplies, and political events. In each of these cases, the forecast addresses a critical factor with the potential to seriously impact the planning process.

Forecasting Techniques

A number of forecasts used by managers are exemplified in the accompanying "tear sheets" from major business publications. Periodicals such as *Business Week, Fortune,* and others, regularly report a variety of such forecasts as a service to their readers. They are based on both qualitative and quantitative forecasting techniques.

Qualitative Forecasting Techniques

Qualitative forecasting techniques use expert opinions to predict the future. In some cases a single person of special expertise or reputation may be consulted. For example, it is common for former secretaries of State of the United States to consult for large corporations on international affairs. Their job is to analyze political and economic events and forecast the risks associated with various operating strategies. Panels of experts are also a common source of qualitative forecasts. Their opinions may be gathered and refined to a consensus through the Delphi technique, introduced in Chapter 3 as a group approach to creative problem-solving. They may also be gathered through more open-ended forums. For example,[19]

at Bell South Corporation when senior executives wanted to glimpse what the information age might bring by the year 2000, they weren't interested in consensus. They just wanted good "imaginative" thinking. To get it they asked a panel of five persons, with distinguished records in areas as disparate as

HOW CHEAPER OIL MAY LEAD TO A NEW WAVE OF IMPORTS

as much of a surprise are using more ener-

HOW LONG CAN THE TRADE DEFICIT KEEP SHRINKING?

Many economists are hopir

WILL U. S. FACTORIES NEED ANOTHER EXCHANGE-RATE FIX?

Everyone knows that the comeback of is largely the re- depreciation of

SLOWER DELIVERIES MAY SIGNAL FASTER INFLATION

With a humming factory sector propell- ing the economic expansion toward

Forecasts are not plans. They are visions of the future that managers can use as inputs to the formal planning process.

economics and poetry, to share their insights on one question: "What will the future hold?"

Quantitative Forecasting Techniques

Quantitative forecasting techniques use mathematical and statistical analyses of data banks to predict future events. Because such techniques require more sophisticated training, managers often rely on staff experts or outside consultants to prepare and even interpret quantitative forecasts for them. Typical forecasts relate to interest rates, growth in Gross National Product (GNP), unemployment, and inflation, among others.

Among the more popular quantitative forecasting techniques are time-series analysis, econometric modeling, and statistical surveys.

Time-series analysis This forecasting method makes predictions by projecting trends of the past and present into the future. Through statistical routines such as regression analysis, historical comparisons are made and trends are extrapolated into the future.

Econometric modeling This forecasting technique builds complex computer models to simulate future events based on probabilities and multiple assumptions. Predictions are statistically made based on the relationships discovered to exist among variables included in the models. General economic trends are typically forecasted via econometric models.

Statistical surveys Opinion polls and attitude surveys such as those reported in newspapers and on television are examples of statistical surveys used to forecast events. They are often used to predict consumer tastes, employee preferences, and political choices for the future. The forecast itself is based on statistical analysis of the answers respondents provide to survey questions. Such surveys vary greatly in their confidence factors according to the rigor underlying the survey and research designs, as well as the strength of the statistics used to analyze results.

Forecasting Errors

In the final analysis, forecasting always relies on human judgment. Even the most sophisticated quantitative approaches still require interpretation. Forecasting is thus a good example of where "art" and intuition enter into management practice. As such, it is subject to error and should always be treated cautiously. Some classic examples of historical forecasting errors follow, along with a more recent forecast whose accuracy remains to be determined.[20] Read and enjoy them, but don't neglect the potential for error when you use forecasts to help make plans.

<u>On the Automobile</u>
"The ordinary 'horseless carriage' is at present a luxury for the wealthy; and although its price

will probably fall in the future, it will never, of course, come into as common use as the bicycle."

The Literary Digest (1899)

On the Atomic Bomb

"That is the biggest fool thing we have ever done. . . . The bomb will never go off, and I speak as an expert in explosives."

Admiral William D. Leahy (1945)

On Lifestyles

"A typical worker in the year 2019 will need to earn $165,000 a year to maintain an average life style, and an average home will cost $630,000."

Relocation Consultant (1984)

MAKING PLANNING EFFECTIVE

Planning isn't all that managers can and should do, but it is extremely important. Good planning can go far in helping managers organize, lead, and control organizations to achieve productivity. Bad planning can also have just as dramatic, but negative, effects on productivity. Before leaving this chapter, it is appropriate to review some helpful planning guidelines. Let's preface this review with a short case.[21]

ILLUSTRATIVE CASE: ENTO INTERNATIONAL

After many years of success as a supplier to basic processing industries, top managers at Ento International began to see that its future profitability was being threatened. New steel-industry processes were slowing the growth of demand for Ento's products, and it was widely believed that present developments in the aluminum industry would soon have a similar effect.

Ento's top managers watched these developments with growing concern and finally concluded that the company could no longer afford the luxury of concentrating only on production improvements. They decided that what Ento needed in order to prepare for a less certain future was a formal strategic planning program.

Ento's management made what it considered a good start on the program. They created a central planning department to develop the planning system and put the executive vice-president in charge. The vice-president hired a prestigious consulting firm, and with its help the planning department staff was soon hard at work on Ento's first strategic plan. Planning procedures recommended by the consultants were adopted, and guidelines were issued to the company's divisional managers for gathering planning data. The department also developed sophisticated mathematical techniques to help in analyzing and evaluating alternatives and instructed the divisional managers in their use. Each manager was also given a planning manual with step-by-step instructions for producing a long-range plan for his or her division.

All this activity kept a lot of people busy, and top management was at first very impressed. However, after two years it became clear that strategic planning was not succeeding in clearing up some of Ento's major problems. Sales and profits had not improved, and the implementation of the long-range plan had not been effective. Furthermore, people throughout the organization were frustrated about having to complete complex forms and carry out elaborate procedures as part of the planning activities each year.

What went wrong at Ento International? The answer to this question involves both the limits of planning and the proper organization of the planning process itself. With the case as background, an examination of these issues can help you to put the fundamentals of planning into a final managerial perspective.

Limits of Planning

Planning has its limits as well as potential benefits. Among the many factors that may cause planning to fail are the following pitfalls. They deserve your attention as things which can be avoided by the informed manager. Plans may fail because

■ Top management fails to incorporate formal planning into the organization's routines.
■ Those who plan are not knowledgeable or skilled in each step of the planning process.
■ Poor information is used for planning, and actions are misdirected from the start.

- There is a lack of necessary support for plans, and action follow-through suffers.
- Unforeseen events occur and disrupt plans that were otherwise quite adequate.
- There is an unwillingness to modify or cancel poor plans.
- Managers overemphasize the details as opposed to the purpose of planning.
- Managers are unwilling to give up established objectives and replace them with new ones.
- Resistance to change by organizational members inhibits the implementation of plans.

Organizing for Planning

Although planning is a responsibility of every manager, organizations benefit from well-planned and well-coordinated planning systems. **Participative planning** is a key phrase here. The planning *process* should actively include as many as possible of the people who will be affected by the resulting plans and/or who will be asked to help implement them. Participation can increase the creativity and information available for planning, and increase the understanding, acceptance, and commitment of people to final plans. This is a major asset of the group approaches to problem-solving discussed in Chapter 3. And the same point holds here in respect to planning. For the most part, planning should not be an individual activity. It should be organized and accomplished in a participative manner that builds commitment along the way among all those whose support and efforts may be needed to actually implement the final plans.[22]

Figure 4.8 highlights the importance of participation to the formal planning process. To gain the commitments needed to facilitate implementation, the figure shows that proper attention must be given to involving others during all prior steps in the planning process. Even though the process may initially take more time, the actual implementation may go more quickly and be more effective in the final result.

Another important issue in developing good planning systems relates to the frame of reference used as a starting point. All too often, planning is done in a setting where the participants are "inward" thinking and limited in their awareness of things outside the immediate work setting. Successful planning doesn't accept things the way they are,

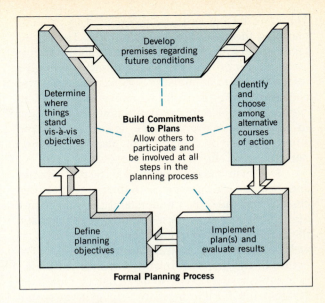

FIGURE 4.8 *Building commitment to implementation: an essential requirement for effective planning.*

it challenges the status quo. One way to organize for this is through a technique known as **benchmarking.** This refers to the use of external comparisons to gain an added perspective on current performance and help initiate the planning process.[23] Here's a case in point.

At Xerox management uses its Japanese competitors to benchmark production cost comparisons for developing manufacturing plans. They also find benchmarks from noncompetitors who are known for special expertise. In the customer service area, for example, they use the outdoor sporting goods retailer and mail-order house L.L. Bean, Inc. A planning team visited Bean's operations, prepared an extensive report, and helped create a plan which modernized Xerox's warehouse and distribution systems.

As the planning needs of organizations grow, there is a corresponding need to increase the sophistication of the overall planning system itself. This can be done by designating or hiring **staff planners,** persons who take responsibility for leading and coordinating the planning function for the total organization or one of its major subsystems. Organizations may invest even more heavily in the planning function by forming staff planning groups.

These are formal work units assigned to promote planning throughout the organization. They bring together persons of special expertise, allow them to focus efforts on specific planning tasks, and go a long way toward helping the organization as a whole coordinate multiple planning efforts. The sophistication of staff planning activities tends to be greater in larger and more complex organizations, and where executives deemphasize planning in their personal work efforts.

Staff planners must be good at the participative and benchmarking aspects of planning just discussed, and they must understand the *staff* nature of their roles. Both of these responsibilities demand the ability to handle interpersonal relationships, as well as to perform technical planning functions. The nature of the line-staff relationships, in particular, is a subject covered in some detail in Part 3 on "Organizing for Productivity." In general a staff planner is usually expected to

- Assist line managers in preparing plans.
- Develop special plans upon request.
- Gather and maintain planning information.
- Assist in communicating plans to others.
- Monitor in-use plans and suggest changes.

Management Levels and Planning

Table 4.2 contrasts the differences in planning at the three basic levels of management. It helps clarify the planning responsibilities you will encounter at various career stages.

Supervisory Planning

Planning at the first or supervisory level of management is short run in nature and based on guidelines established by higher-level plans. It is usually tied to monthly, quarterly and annual budgets, and deals with the immediate use of resources to satisfy performance targets. Supervisors, department heads, group leaders, and others at this management level spend considerable time developing work schedules that assign personnel to various shifts or projects. They also apply rules and procedures to maintain consistency of actions over time in respect to important organizational policies. They should also participate in the planning activities of the middle-management ranks.[24]

Planning by Middle Managers

Middle managers are the interface between higher-level planning and the supervisory planning just described. The efforts of middle managers greatly assist in creating the integrated means-end chains of plans described earlier in the chapter. Middle managers are key links between what goes on at the top and lower levels of managerial responsibility. To the extent middle managers do their jobs well, planning and action at both the top and bottom of the managerial pyramid will be better coordinated. Middle-management planning is designed to implement higher-level strategic plans to accomplish performance targets on an intermediate and long-term basis. In addition, middle managers are concerned with establishing policies, procedures, budgets, and

TABLE 4.2 *Typical Planning Responsibilities at Three Levels of Management*

Level	Planning Focus	Time Horizon	Planning Activities
Top management	Total organization	Long range	Establish long-run directions, set guiding strategies, allocate resources
Middle management	Division or major subsystem	Long range and medium range	Set supporting policies, procedures, budgets; allocate and utilize resources
Supervisory management	Work unit or department	Short range	Set supporting schedules; implement policies, procedures, budgets; utilize resources

schedules to guide supervisors in decision making and in the allocation of resources within their work units.

Top Management Planning

Managers at the top or executive level center their attention on longer-range strategic issues. These responsibilities center on establishing overall organizational objectives and identifying the strategies capable of ensuring their achievement. The desired result is a strategic focus that provides a sense of identity and integration for planning activities at the other management levels. Top management planning is the pinnacle of an organization's means-end chain. It is supposed to target the planning of middle-level and lower-level managers to achieve integration around a common purpose.

The next chapter investigates in greater detail the process of strategic planning. Before moving on, however, consider the following exchange of quotations. They nicely conclude this look at the fundamentals of planning.[25]

I am the master of my fate,
I am the captain of my soul.

W. E. Henly

Not without a plan, you're not.

R. I. Levin

Summary

A plan is a statement of the intended means for accomplishing a desired objective. Planning is the process through which managers select objectives and then decide what must be done in order to attain them. The potential benefits of planning are numerous. They include opportunities for greater integration of means-end chains and improved performance, as well as establishing action foundations for stability, adaptability, and contingency in day-to-day operations. As such, planning is one of the basic management functions. It is an essential responsibility of any manager, but it demands a capability to plan well in a complex and often dynamic environment.

Managers become involved with plans that vary in terms of time horizon (short and long term), scope (strategic and operational), use (single use and standing use), and level of attention (top, middle, and lower management). Important types of operational plans include policies, procedures or rules, budgets, and schedules.

Planning is an extension of the problem-solving process you studied in Chapter 3. It involves the five steps of (1) defining objectives, (2) determining where things stand relative to the objectives, (3) developing premises regarding future conditions, (4) identifying and choosing among alternative courses of action, and (5) implementing the plan and evaluating results. Forecasting is a planning aid that can be accomplished through both qualitative and quantitative techniques. Planning is done by managers at all levels in the organizational hierarchy. It can also be done by persons or groups specially designated to act as staff planners for the organization as a whole.

Thinking Through the Issues

1. What is planning? Why is it critical for successful accomplishment of the other management functions?

2. What is the difference between a "plan" and a "planning objective"? Use examples to explain.

3. List three benefits of planning. Explain the important relationship between planning and controlling.

4. What are the major differences between a) short- and long-range plans, and b) strategic and operational plans?

5. What are policies, and why are they useful in organizations? What are procedures, and why are they useful in organizations?

6. List the five steps in the formal planning process and give examples of each. Explain how this process relates to "problem solving" as described in Chapter 3.

7. How do "inside-out" and "outside-in" planning differ from one another? How do "top-down" and "bottom-up" planning differ from one another?

8. What role does forecasting play in the planning process? Explain the forecasting techniques available to managers.

9. How do planning responsibilities vary among top-, middle- and lower-level managers?

10. Explain what can be done to try and make planning more effective in an organization.

The Manager's Vocabulary

Benchmarking
Bottom-up planning
Budget
Contingency planning
Fixed budget
Flexible budget
Forecasting
Inside-out planning

Long-range plans
Means–end chain
Medium-range plans
Operational plan
Outside-in planning
Participative planning
Plan
Planning

Planning objective
Policy
Procedures
Qualitative forecasting
Quantitative
  forecasting
Rules
Schedule

Short-range plan
Single-use plan
Staff planner
Standing-use plan
Strategic plan
Tactical plans
Top-down planning
Zero-based budget

INTERNSHIPS MAKE A DIFFERENCE

CAREER PERSPECTIVES

Learning by doing is big now on college campuses, as it should be. More and more students are taking advantage of internship opportunities to sample possible career choices before their academic programs are completed. Internships are great for career planning, and they often give the interns a fast track to job opportunities in their occupations of personal choice.[26]

Jeff Marx was a journalism major at Northwestern University. But he wasn't sure he really *wanted* to be a journalist. For three months he interned at the Lexington *Herald-Leader* newspaper. After the experience he knew he wanted to be a reporter; after he graduated Marx was hired back full-time by the *Herald-Leader*. Another Northwestern business student, Dan Lambert, interned with a pharmaceutical firm where he put in 11-hour days. But he worked on major accounts and an executive took him under his wing to offer useful advice and business involvements. Lambert commented, "You don't get that in school."

More and more colleges are now formalizing internship contacts for their students. These programs can be done during the summer months or during the regular academic year. In most cases, the activity helps students develop and refine their career plans. Spending some time in the actual work environment helps remove the textbook "glamor" and introduce students to more of the daily realities of what they'll eventually be doing.

Of course not all internships are successful. In some cases the organizational sponsors don't give the intern "real" work to do, but limit their participation to observation. In other cases the employer is really looking for "free labor" and confines the intern to such duties as answering the telephone and making photocopies. As a prospective intern, it is incumbent upon you to make known to the potential employer that you want to learn through substantive involvement in the job, not just observation or clerical support. If you succeed in getting a good internship though, the chances are that you'll also be gaining an important advantage over your competitors in the job market. Not only will you have a firsthand look at the career and its opportunities, you're gaining valuable industry contacts and at least one potential employer is getting an early look at you. In addition, you've got great material to add more depth and polish to your resume.

Questions
1. What opportunities to pursue an internship exist in your college or university program? Have you explored the opportunity? If not, why not?

2. If you were to pursue an internship, with what type of organization would you most like to work? Even more specifically, name three possible employers you could contact to request an internship appointment.

3. Apply the planning process as described in Figure 4.7 to the specific case of your personal career planning? In what phase of this process could an internship facilitate planning? Explain your answer.

Case Application

SMALL BUSINESS DILEMMA AT GAIN SOFTWARE

GAIN Software was founded three years ago by Gerald Mandel, Alice Barber, Ignacio de Santos, and Norma Zimmer. During their senior year in college, the four worked on the idea of forming a business based on developing and selling computer software specifically oriented to the needs of small retail businesses. These establishments typically deal with service bureaus or companies that handle their payroll, billings, accounts payable, and other standard services. Few grow large enough to afford to do their own computer or data processing work internally.

"We felt," said Gerry, "that with the development of the PC [personal computer] and breakthroughs in telecommunications, we could offer something to even small retailers that they couldn't buy anywhere else. We developed software to help them with their purchasing, inventory control, pricing, and promotions. Our software isn't designed to handle big, basic operations like payroll, billing, etc. It is supposed to give small-to-medium-sized retail stores a means of making better decisions on what to buy in what quantity, where, and for what terms. Then it helps them with inventory control, pricing, and special promotions."

"Using basic hardware, owners or managers of such businesses can have daily—in some cases, hourly—access to information they need to make key decisions," said Norma. "At reasonable prices, we can hook them up to regional data sources and through low-cost telecommunications give them access to information and sources that only large stores or chains could tap into before."

"We tested our ideas," Ignacio said, "as a project in a new ventures course and created a business plan. We wrote some of our own software—Alice is a real genius in that area—and then designed systems using readily available equipment for several small stores. We offered to *give* them the software and our services in selecting equipment and show them how to use it if they paid for the equipment and paid telephone access charges and so on. We did three stores for under $8,000 each and all three are convinced they got their money back in months."

After graduation, Gerald, Ignacio, and Norma created a partnership and launched their venture. Alice decided to accept an attractive offer from a large company, but agreed to let them use software she had written and to develop new software for the company. "We agreed to pay her a relatively small sum for each package she puts together," said Gerry, "and to pay her a royalty for every system we sell that incorporates it. Alice is still our biggest software developer, but we have three or four others we can contract with if she is too busy."

The three partners have done extremely well since graduation. While the first year was difficult, they believe they now have a winning formula and team. "For the last two years," Norma said, "We have each earned six-figure salaries and bonuses. While we have been putting in incredible hours, we are making more money than we ever dreamed of at this stage. In addition, we have paid off our original loans and have money in the bank. We have access to a sizable line of credit if we choose to expand; I know we could attract equity money."

Expansion—how, and how fast—has created the first serious disagreement among the three partners. Each has a quite different view on how to capitalize further on their current success. The plans are outlined as follows.

Gerry's Plan "I want us to keep doing what we are doing now. We have thousands of good-sized communities and cities to target. What we have been doing is picking one and spending a few days to a week researching it. We get data on retail establishments, analyze it, and select a small target group of three to six businesses. Then we really study these businesses and design, in rough form, systems for them. We all work on these systems jointly. When we are ready, we each take one or two stores and go in for the sale. We often haven't even been in the store before and the owners are amazed at what we know about their businesses.

"Every time, if we have done our homework, we sell 75 to 100 percent of our initial target group. We 'low ball' the cost and really custom-tailor the product for them. With them as our base, we then blitz the rest of the town. The companies we sell initially become our strongest support team, as long as we stay away from their major competitors. "We do much more standard packages and charge full price as we move through town. When we have covered the biggest and best stores, we head for home, pick our next target, and start our research and plans again.

"We have an answering service and a twelve-hour-a-day hot line to handle any questions or problems that crop up. Finally, we *charge* them a small fee to receive our 'newsletter' and our special reports on new equipment and software. We now have a big enough customer base to use the newsletter and reports to set up a good mail-order operation, if we could find someone to run it for us.

"My plan is to keep right on doing what we are doing. . . . Later, if we want, we could add one, two, or three new partners, teach them a piece at a time until we know we can trust them, and grow slowly without risk.

Norma's Plan "I find a lot of what Gerry says appealing," said Norma, "but his approach has a

number of flaws. While I'm not nuts about trying to keep up this pace, I can handle it. What I can't handle is the realization that we may be giving up millions. We have a winning formula but we must leverage our time and capitalize on it. Second, if we don't build a bigger, stronger organization *fast*, we may lose not only opportunities but the whole program. A few 'copycats' have already tried to imitate our approach and are using it with some success. They haven't hit us head-on in the same town, and probably won't for a while, but this thing may pyramid and we may have fifty carbon copies to deal with in the near future.

"My plan is to get big as fast as possible. We must set up an organization—not a big one, but one that can do what we do now on a regional or even national basis. We can hire specialists in software, hardware, and telecommunication to design systems. Them, through either our own sales group or by franchising, we can sell, install, and maintain the systems. "I want us to borrow what we can, incorporate, and sell up to 40 percent of our stock to either a venture capitalist or to the public. I am sure we can raise enough money to operate not only on a larger scale, but a lot more professionally and not have to kill ourselves in the process. . . . I want us all to just take a month off, rest up, and then spend the next several months getting the money, designing our structure, building systems, and hiring people."

Ignacio's Plan "My recommendation is that we sell out and sell out fast while we have something to sell. Sooner than later, a big computer or telecommunications company is going to either buy out one of our imitators or set up their own operation. Once they realize just how much there is to make, they will go for it. I believe we should spend our month off studying possible buyers. Then we should show them our books—not our 'tricks,' but our books. If we get a good lawyer or 'finder' to help us, I'll bet we could get a big chunk of money up front and either royalties or stock.

"I would be willing to work for the big company to help them get started and Norma might, if she had no choice, do the same. In fact, she might parlay this into a big executive job with the acquiring company running this operation for them. Gerry might help during the transition but if he wants out, that's okay. There should be enough money for him to start up something new on his own. Who knows—maybe I'll join him. Out of respect for Norma, both Gerry and I have agreed to take a month away from the business and relax. Then we will get together and try to resolve this."

Questions

1. Given the ideas presented in the case, whose plans appear to be based on the "inside-out" and "outside-in" approaches? Is one approach more appropriate than the other in these circumstances? Explain and justify your answers.

2. Overall, do you believe GAIN is well-positioned for the future? Why or why not? As a planning consultant, what specific planning objectives do you think the three partners should set for both the short-range and long-range? Why?

3. As a planning consultant, how would you address these planning objectives using the steps of the formal planning process described in Figure 4.7? Be specific in documenting what you would do in each step and why.

4. What would you do to get the commitment of all three partners to the final plan? Can any plan absolutely satisfy all three of them, or is this an unrealistic expectation? Explain your answers.

Class Exercise: Beating the Time Wasters

1. Scheduling one's personal time is an important daily planning activity. This is especially true for persons serving in managerial jobs. Alex MacKenzie, author of the book, *The Time Trap,* includes the following as among the top "time wasters" people encounter in their work.[28]
- Telephone interruptions
- Unannounced drop-in visitors
- Meetings, scheduled and unscheduled
- Lack of objectives
- Failure to delegate routine matters
- Indecision and procrastination
- Inability to say "no"
- Fatigue

2. Choose five of these time wasters which you feel currently cause you problems in managing your personal time. Make a list of three things you could do to eliminate each of these time wasters—effective immediately.

3. Share your choices of time wasters with a nearby classmate. Ask for additional suggestions for how to deal with each one. Do the same for your classmate in return.

4. Be prepared to participate in additional classroom discussion on personal time management as led by your instructor.

References

[1]*Eaton Corporation Annual Report 1985,* Eaton Corporation, Cleveland, Ohio.

[2]This case is developed from William F. Glueck, *Management,* Second Edition (Hinsdale, Ill.: The Dryden Press, 1980), pp. 242–243.

[3]For a classic study see Stanley Thune and Robert House, "Where Long Range Planning Pays Off," *Business Horizons,* Vol. 13 (1970), pp. 81–87. For a critical review of the literature see Milton Leontiades and Ahmet Tezel, "Planning Perceptions and Planning Results," *Strategic Management Journal,* Vol. 1 (1980), pp. 65–75; and, J. Scott Armstrong, "The Value of Formal Planning for Strategic Decisions," *Strategic Management Journal,* Vol. 3 (1982), pp. 197–211. For special attention to the small business setting, see Richard B. Robinson, Jr., John A. Pearce II, George S. Vozikis and Timothy S. Mescon, "The Relationship between Stage of Development and Small Firm Planning and Performance," *Journal of Small Business Management,* Vol. 22 (1984), pp. 45–52; and, Christopher Orphen, "The Effects of Long-Range Planning on Small Business Performance: A Further Examination," *Journal of Small Business Management,* Vol. 23 (1985), pp. 16–23. For a recent empirical study of large corporations see Vasudevan Ramanujam and N. Venkatraman, "Planning and Performance: A New Look at an Old Question," *Business Horizons,* Vol. 30 (1987), pp. 19–25.

[4]From Evans Products Company's *1980 Annual Report.*

[5]Information from "How IBM is Fighting Back," *Business Week* (November 17, 1986), pp. 152–157.

[6]A related discussion and the basis for this example is found in Jay A. Conger and John P. Kotter, "General

Managers," pp. 392–403 in Jay W. Lorsch (ed.), *Handbook of Organizational Behavior* (Englewood Cliffs, NJ: Prentice-Hall, 1987).

[7] See Eliott Jaques, *The Form of Time* (New York: Russak & Co., 1982). For a report on this research see Walter Kiechel III, "How Executives Think," *Fortune* (February 4, 1985), p. 127.

[8] Information from *Business Week,* op cit.; and Bill Saporito, "How Borden Milks Packaged Goods," *Fortune* (December 21, 1987), pp. 139–144.

[9] Corporate policy statement used with anonymity.

[10] See R. Alex MacKenzie, *The Time Trap* (New York: AMACOM, American Management Associations, 1972), and John A. Prestbo, "Don't Waste Time," *Wall Street Journal* (December 11, 1978), p. 28.

[11] See William Oncken, Jr. and Donald L. Wass, "Management Time: Who's got the Monkey?", *Harvard Business Review,* Vol. 52 (September–October 1974), pp. 75–80, and featured in a *HBR* Retrospect, *Harvard Business Review,* Vol. 65 (March–April 1987), p 19.

[12] This conversation is from Ibid.

[13] This and the subsequent section are developed from a discussion by Dick Levin, *The Executive's Illustrated Primer of Long Range Planning* (Englewood Cliffs, N.J.: Prentice-Hall, Inc., 1981), pp. 80–88 and 93–97.

[14] Levin, op. cit., p. 81. Reprinted by permission of Prentice-Hall, Inc. Englewood Cliffs, New Jersey.

[15] Levin, op. cit., pp. 93–94. Reprinted by permission of Prentice-Hall, Inc. Englewood Cliffs, New Jersey.

[16] Based on Russel L. Ackoff, *Management in Small Doses* (New York: Wiley, 1986).

[17] Example from Damon Darlin, "Chrysler Cancels Plans for a New Plant in U.S.," *The Wall Street Journal* (March 8, 1985), p. 7.

[18] For a thorough review of forecasting see J. Scott Armstrong, *Long-Range Forecasting,* Second Edition (New York: Wiley, 1985).

[19] Information contained in "Toward the Year 2000: Perspectives on the Information Age," *Bell South Corporation Annual Report,* 1986.

[20] Forecasts from Christofer Cerf and Victor S. Navasky, *The Experts Speak* (New York: Pantheon, 1984); "It'll Never Fly, Orville: Two Centuries of Embarrassing Predictions," *Saturday Review* (December 1979), p. 36; *Wall Street Journal* (September 4, 1984), p. 1.

[21] Adapted from Kjell A. Ringbakk, "Why Planning Fails," *European Business* (Spring 1971), pp. 15–27.

[22] This perspective is discussed by Armstrong, op. cit.

[23] Reported in Frances Gaither Tucker, Seymour M. Zivan and Robert C. Camp, "How to Measure Yourself Against the Best," *Harvard Business Review,* Vol. 65 (January–February 1987), pp. 8–10.

[24] For more thoughts on the nature of supervisory management responsibilities see Leonard A. Schlesinger and Janice A. Klein, "The First-Line Supervisor: Past, Present, and Future," pp. 358–369, in Lorsch, op. cit., 1987.

[25] Quotes from Levin, op. cit., p. 14.

[26] Selected information from "Interns Take Flight," *Newsweek on Campus* (October, 1986), pp. 50–52.

[27] This case is abridged from William H. Newman, E. Kirby Warren, and Andrew R. McGill, *The Process of Management: Strategy, Action, Results* (New York: Prentice-Hall, 1987), pp. 303–307. Used by permission.

[28] See MacKenzie, op. cit.

Strategic Planning

A
Flexible High-Flyer

Coke and Pepsi, the chief combatants in the "cola wars," have been going at it in a seemingly endless series of market-share skirmishes—and lately, Coke's future has been looking quite promising. Coke's share of the U.S. soft-drink market now outstrips its rival's and Coke is aggressively pursuing markets abroad. By staking claims in such diverse industries as bottling, entertainment, and clothing, Coke's management has displayed a knack for innovation and entrepreneurial risk-taking that mark a real strategic departure from the company's laid-back (some say sleepy) approach of years past.

CEO Roberto Goizueta, who took the reins in the early 1980s, wasted little time in overturning some longstanding Coke traditions and developing a new strategy. Without resorting to layoffs, salary cuts, or perk-stripping, Goizueta forced his managers to focus on declining returns—and to allocate capital to their areas according to the rigorous financial standards he applied to the soft-drink side of Coke's business. Dropping various no-go ventures and opening Coke's PR department (and his own office) to reporters, Goizueta launched a multi-front campaign to put Coke at the top.

First, the company's label went on diet cola and five other soft drinks—a move that proved brilliant, despite "New" Coke's failure and the just-in-time reintroduction of "classic" Coke. The new products definitely swelled Coke's market share. Then, with some artful financial restructuring—taking on debt and acquiring several bottling businesses as well as Columbia Pictures (a brash move that threw Wall Street)—Coke found itself making out well as an investor. Spinning off its bottling holdings for public trading while keeping 49 percent of the stock, Coke retained a large measure of control and reaped hefty profits. Goizueta envisions using this strategy for the entertainment unit, too.

Coke's approach has changed the company's image considerably. Gone is the stereotype of the smug soft-drink giant; Coke is now seen as a good example of what twenty-first-century conglomerates will look like. Goizueta has his eye on international growth, but he is a careful planner, and he understands that vast quantities of capital will be needed to realize his vision. He has given Coke's new acquisitions the freedom to tap equity markets on their own in order to provide each business under the Coke roof with "the best capital structure with which to grow."

The company's turnaround formula, a mix of diversification, flexible financial retooling, and ever-new advertising, seems highly effective thus far. One Coke manager, Bryan Dyson, spoke to the bottom line—and implicitly to Pepsi—when he stated: "With all the speeding up, you need to be agile and quick. Otherwise you miss out." Will the 1990s be any different? ■

Source: Information from Thomas Moore, "He Put the Kick Back into Coke," *Fortune* (October 26, 1987), pp. 46–56, and Betsy Morris, "Coca-Cola's Corporate Strategy Is Divide and Conquer," *Wall Street Journal* (October 8, 1987), p. 6.

Question What do the following headlines, as reported in *The Wall Street Journal, Business Week,* and others, share in common?

Answer Each conveys the strategy employed by an organization in its attempt to ensure operating success in a challenging environment.

SONY BUYS CBS RECORDS

USAIR NURTURES CRUCIAL MERGER

GENERAL MILLS STARTS CHAIN OF ITALIAN RESTAURANTS

MONTGOMERY WARD SOLD BY MOBIL

The articles that accompany these headlines report on organizations taking or about to take risks to achieve continued success in a challenging environment. Sony is diversifying and expanding internationally by buying into a new side of the consumer-electronics business; USAir is pursuing competitive growth through acquisition of another major airline; General Mills is diversifying in the attempt to improve the fortunes of its restaurant division; and, Mobil is retrenching to refocus on its oil and chemical operations. The people employed by these companies will be affected by the decisions, and the managers who made the decisions are taking risks— both organizational and personal. Many careers, at all levels in these companies, are on the line as the quality of "strategic" decisions is put to the test of actually achieving performance success.

An important key to the long term prosperity of any organization, not just the corporate giants like Coca-Cola, Sony, USAir, Mobil and others, is high quality strategic thinking on the part of its managers. This chapter is designed to help you better understand the strategic issues challenging organizations for which you work, as well as the strategies being pursued in response to them. It focuses on strategy and objectives, strategic planning approaches, and timely strategic planning issues to help develop your capabilities in this regard. The importance of these topics cannot be overemphasized. As the following example shows, even the most famous of U.S. entrepreneurs—Henry Ford— was deficient in this respect.[1]

Surely you have heard—
■ That Henry Ford, starting with nothing in 1905, had 15 years later built the world's largest and most profitable manufacturing enterprise.
■ That the Ford Motor Company, in the early 1920s, dominated and almost monopolized the American automobile market and held a leadership position in most of the other important automobile markets of the world.

But did you also know—

■ That, only a few years later, by 1927, this seemingly impregnable business empire was in shambles? Having lost its leadership position and barely able to stay a poor third in the market, it lost money almost every year for 20 years or so.

■ That in 1944 the founder's grandson Henry Ford III, then only 26 years old and without training or experience, took over. He ousted his grandfather's cronies two years later in a palace coup, brought in a totally new management team and saved the company.

STRATEGY AND STRATEGIC MANAGEMENT

A **strategy** is a comprehensive plan of action that sets critical direction and guides the allocation of resources for an organization. It is a focus for action that represents a "best guess" regarding what must be done to ensure longer-run prosperity for the organization or one of its subsystems. In essence, strategy defines the direction in which an organization intends to move in a competitive environment. It is a choice made by decision makers that specifies how they plan to match the organization's strengths and weaknesses with opportunities and threats in the external environment. Strategy in other words, is the means through which an organization intends to come to terms with its environment.

Strategic management is the managerial responsibility for formulating and implementing strategies that will lead to long-term success for an organization and its component parts.[2] Any manager, at any level in the hierarchy of authority, is responsible for strategic management. For supervisory and middle-level managers, this relates to the long-term needs and interests of many individual work units and groups within the total organization. For top-level managers, as suggested in the prior headlines and *Newsline 5.1,* this responsibility extends to the organization as a whole and its major divisions.

ILLUSTRATIVE CASE:
THE MAKING OF A COMEBACK AT AT&T

The outlook for AT&T was grim on that Labor Day when CEO Jim Olson gathered his 27 top executives together at a Cape Cod resort.[3] Since being forced to divest itself of $150 billion in assets by a federal antitrust ruling, the company had experienced one problem after another. The company that had once been the largest private employer in the world, had been fiercely loyal to its employees and expected them to be loyal in return, and had built without competition the largest and best telephone system in the world, was in shock. While its offspring the "baby bells" were prospering as independent companies, "Ma bell" was hurting.

Olson unveiled a broad plan of action. Called the "single enterprise strategy," it was designed to create a new AT&T. The expressed vision was of a new, slimmer, more flexible company whose components operated as one integrated organization. Olson's strategy was for AT&T to: protect and expand its core businesses of long distance telephone service and equipment manufacturing, get its computer business profitable, and increase the share of company revenues coming from overseas business. Implementing the strategy would require trade-offs, commitments and concessions from the senior executives whose operations would be affected by restructuring and changes.

They met and discussed the issues for five days, eventually reaching agreement. But Olson wanted more—he wanted *commitment* to the strategy and to its implementation. One by one he faced those present and asked them to stand before the entire group. "Are you with me?" Olson asked. "Yes," came the replies. One of those present remarked: "It was pretty dramatic . . . a powerful moment . . . a catharsis." — *purge, cleanse*

At last reports, the company has made big gains over its situation at the time of this conference. It has consolidated and streamlined many operations to cut overall costs, invested over $6 billion in equipment for its long distance business, restructured its international division, and changed product marketing approaches in its computer division. Olson's single-enterprise strategy seems to have added order and direction to what was once a chaotic situation. As AT&T president Robert E. Allen said, "We didn't wake up until . . . the business began to play out . . . Now, we're paying much more attention to outside forces, we're totally market driven."

Yet the strategic issues facing AT&T still continue. When Jim Olson died unexpectedly of cancer,

CORPORATE
STRATEGY FOR THE 1990s

N E W S L I N E 5.1

Most managers and experts agree that restructuring became the most significant organizational event of our times—and that it is here to stay. Indeed, for many organizations, restructuring is necessarily an ongoing process; it is the logical response to such pressures as the threat of takeover, active foreign rivals, and the ever-soaring costs of doing business. But restructuring aside, what will the 1990s bring in the way of new challenges, and what corporate strategies are likeliest to meet those challenges effectively?

One clear challenge is the need for solid corporate control over businesses that are attractive to raiders. Because even well-defended industries such as banking are the objects of takeovers, the CEOs of large companies are reconsidering ways and means of retaining control over diverse operations. Flexible modes of manufacturing and ready access to capital and information have democratized the playing field; no longer do big companies automatically have the edge in terms of corporate control. Moreover, the "cost of complexity," as some call it—the cost of creating and marketing multiple products or services—often minimizes any saving from size.

Recognizing this, far-sighted CEOs are concentrating on cash flows and return on equity and assets—on tangible measures of value that will enable sound decisions to be made concerning acquisitions and divestments. And as organizations approach the twenty-first century, managers are being called upon to pick up the pace of innovation—what Harvard Business School Professor Michael Porter calls "the final portion of the restructuring mandate."

Union Carbide's CEO, Robert D. Kennedy, sums up the big picture: "You have to keep looking at the boundary conditions, thinking the unthinkable: Should I sell this business? Should I buy another?"

Source: Walter Keichel III, "Corporate Strategy for the 1990s," *Fortune* (February 29, 1988), pp. 34–42.

---

the firm's board elected Robert Allen at the age of 53 to be his replacement. His challenge is to keep AT&T's comeback on track. Shortly after his appointment, Allen himself said that his greatest challenge is to continue executing Olson's strategy for the company.

Levels of Strategy

The concept of strategy can and should be applied at different levels in organizations.[4] Figure 5.1 shows three well recognized levels of strategy as they might apply to the AT&T case. They are cor-

porate strategy, business strategy and functional strategy. A fourth, less recognized, but still very important level of strategy overlays or encompasses all of them. It is called institutional strategy.

Corporate Strategy

Corporate strategy is strategy for the organization as a whole. It answers the question "what business or businesses should we be in" in order to set direction and guide resource allocations for the total enterprise. In **M-form organizations,** that is those having multiple product and/or service divisions, corporate strategy identifies the major areas of busi-

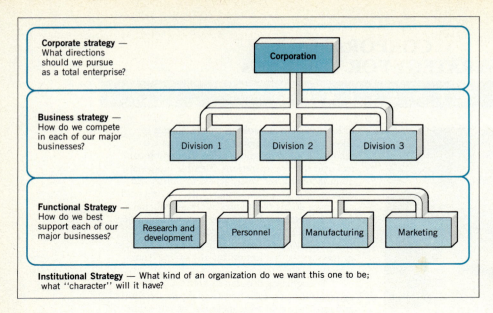

Corporate strategy — What directions should we pursue as a total enterprise?

Corporation

Business strategy — How do we compete in each of our major businesses?

Division 1   Division 2   Division 3

Functional Strategy — How do we best support each of our major businesses?

Research and development   Personnel   Manufacturing   Marketing

Institutional Strategy — What kind of an organization do we want this one to be; what "character" will it have?

FIGURE 5.1 *Four levels of organizational strategy in a business conglomerate.*

ness in which a company intends to compete. Typical decisions made at this level of strategy will relate to the use of resources for acquisitions, new business development, divestitures, joint ventures and the like. An important corporate strategy decision in the AT&T case was to continue in the computer business, even though it was still unprofitable at the time strategy was being set.

Business Strategy

Business strategy is the strategy for a single division or *strategic business unit* (SBU) that operates with some autonomy vis-a-vis others. The selection of a business strategy involves answering the question, "how are we going to compete in this particular business area?" Typical business strategy decisions include choices about product/service mix, facilities locations, manufacturing technologies, and the like. In single-business enterprises, business strategy is the corporate strategy; in M-form organizations, there will be many separate business strategies. At AT&T, for example, there are at least three major business strategies subsumed under CEO Olson's single-enterprise strategy. They are strategies for the firm's long-distance services, computer, and international divisions.

Functional Strategy

Functional strategy is strategy which guides activities within a specific functional area of operations.

In Figure 5.1 the standard business functions of marketing, manufacturing, finance, and research and development illustrate this level of strategy. The question to be answered in selecting functional strategies becomes, "how can we best apply functional expertise to serve the needs of the business?" AT&T's manufacturing strategy, for example, now includes producing more of its telephone equipment overseas in countries with low labor costs.

Institutional Strategy

Finally, there is another level of strategy that encompasses and affects all of those talked about so far. **Institutional strategy** identifies core values and beliefs that give the organization as a whole a distinctive character or identity. It answers, for insiders and outsiders alike, the question: "What kind of organization do we intend this to be?" In the case of AT&T, the answer to this question is not quite clear, although CEO Olson indicated that he wanted all of AT&T's many units to operate as one organization and with a sense of team spirit.

Selecting institutional strategy involves making decisions and commitments that define the human and social standards by which the organization intends to operate in pursuit of corporate, business, and functional strategies. Obviously, not all organizations have clear institutional strategies. Indeed, a compelling message of the best selling book *In Search of Excellence* and its offspring, is that much more attention should be given to this level of strategy.[5] The common appeal is for more leadership and "vision" to establish a respected personality for an organization that distinguishes it in a competitive field. This includes organization-wide dedication to such principles as the popular attributes of excellence listed in Table 5.1. Perhaps the best continuing example is,[6]

at IBM where the institutional strategy is expressed in these undeniable words. "The character of the company is shaped by its three basic beliefs . . ."

■ *Respect for the individual.* Caring about the dignity and rights of each person in the organization.

■ *Customer service.* Giving the best service of any company in the world.

■ *Excellence.* Believing that all jobs and projects should be performed in a superior way.

This strong and clear institutional strategy communicates the *way* in which IBM intends to operate as a corporate competitor with AT&T and others in the markets of the world. As stated, the beliefs establish the *character* of the company—that is, a personality or identity that sets IBM apart from other corporations. Institutional strategies can build "character" for organizations and create for them a respected image in the eyes of their employees, customers and external public-at-large.

TYPES OF STRATEGIES

There are many alternatives available to organizations as they pursue strategies at each of the prior levels. One useful way of classifying them is in respect to the four "grand" strategies of growth, retrenchment, stability, and combination.[7] These strategies are introduced here along with examples from companies that will be the source of illustrations at various points in the book.

Growth Strategies

Growth strategies seek the expansion of current operations. They are popular strategies because growth is necessary for long-run survival in some industries, and many managers still equate growth with effectiveness. There are several different ways to pursue growth strategies, but they fall into two general categories. In the first category are four strategies which pursue growth without changing the underlying nature of the organization.

■ *Concentration* Focusing on a single product, service, technology and/or market. Trying to do the one thing very well, and growing through concentrated expertise and solid reputation. McDonald's continued growth as a fast-food restaurant is a good example.

■ *Market development* Seeking to sell existing products or services in new markets. Growing by

TABLE 5.1 *Lessons from America's Best Run Companies: The Eight Attributes of Excellence*

1. *Bias for action.* A desire for doing something—anything—rather than sending a question through cycles and cycles of analyses and committee reports.
2. *Close to the customer.* Learning the preferences of people served; catering to them by providing unparalleled quality, service, and reliability.
3. *Autonomy and entrepreneurship.* Fostering many leaders and many innovators throughout the organization; encouraging practical risk taking; supporting "good tries."
4. *Productivity through people.* Treating all employees as the source of quality and productivity gains; making everyone feel their work counts toward organziational success.
5. *Hands-on, value driven.* Keeping in touch with operations by having managers who regularly visit the "front line" and talking to people at work.
6. *Stick to the knitting.* Staying reasonably close to businesses the organization knows best; staying away from operations beyond existing expertise.
7. *Simple form, lean staff.* Keeping structural forms and systems elegantly simple with few administrative levels and lean top-level staffs.
8. *Simultaneous loose-tight properties.* Pushing autonomy down to the lowest levels for product development, but remaining fanatic in creating devotion to core values held dear.

Source: Developed from pp. 13–15 in *Search for Excellence: Lessons from America's Best-Run Companies* by Thomas J. Peters and Robert H. Waterman, Jr. Copyright © 1982 by Thomas J. Peters and Robert H. Waterman, Jr. Reprinted by permission of Harper & Row, Publishers, Inc.

expanding the market through the attraction of new customer groups and/or by adding new sales territories such as overseas markets. Apple's new penetration of the business market for personal computers is an example.

■ *Product development* Using research and development to create new products or services in related areas, or to modify existing ones. Growing through increased sales to old customers and through the attraction of new customers. Coke's new strategy of coming up with Diet Coke, Cherry Coke, and other "versions" of its traditional Coca-Cola exemplifies product development.

■ *Innovation* Creating an entirely new product, service or technology that makes old ones obsolete. Growing through continued improvements that encourage old customers to "upgrade" to the new offerings, and attract new customers because of their innovative qualities. IBM's continued introduction of new computer models illustrates the innovation strategy.

Among these strategies, concentration, market development, and product development can provide opportunities for growth while still keeping the organization close to its "distinctive competencies." They try to utilize existing strengths in new and productive ways, but without taking the risks of great shifts in direction. Innovation is a decidedly more risky strategy.

In the second category of growth strategies are ones which tend to change the nature of an organization by adding to its complexity through acquisitions or the creation of new operating units. In general the following five strategies offer ways of dealing with environments that are troublesome because of the strength of competition, restricted access to markets, or uncertainties in supply and distribution channels.

■ *Horizontal integration* Expanding through acquisition of other organizations operating in the same industry. This typically involves mergers and the purchasing of competitors. The merger of USAir and Piedmont, introduced in the opening headlines, illustrates growth by horizontal integration.

■ *Vertical integration* Expanding through acquisition or creation of operations which supply resources to the organization and/or distribute its products. Movie studios that also own movie theaters are vertically integrated companies; steel firms

which own mines from which they get coal for power generation are also vertically integrated.

■ *Joint venturing* Expanding through cooperation with one or more other organizations. This allows an organization to combine efforts with others to accomplish things otherwise beyond its own capabilities. Joint ventures are common in the international arena. *Newsline 5.2* presents an interesting look at this strategy and some of its international complications.

■ *Concentric diversification* Expanding through the acquisition or creation of new operations that deal in related products or services. Going back to Coke again, the company's acquisition of Minute Maid involved growth through concentric diversification. While staying in the beverage business, fruit juices were a departure from the company's product line.

■ *Conglomerate diversification* Expanding through the acquisition or creation of new operations that deal in entirely unrelated products or services. This strategy creates the classic M-form organization like GE which buys and sells businesses in such diverse areas as household appliances, aircraft engines, and military weaponry.

Retrenchment Strategies

Retrenchment strategies involve decisions to slow down and cut back in order to improve performance through greater operating efficiencies. Although frequent in American industry of late, retrenchment strategies are less popular than growth strategies. To pursue retrenchment, on the surface at least, can be an admission of past failures. Thus, until recently retrenchment has been viewed as a strategy of "last resort" by most managers. Today, however, it has achieved a new legitimacy in the corporate world. There are three basic retrenchment strategies.

■ *Turnaround* Cutting back on personnel and other costs, and "restructuring" or streamlining operations in order to correct problems and improve operating efficiency. AT&T is pursuing, in part at least, a turnaround strategy. The firm has eliminated over 75,000 jobs in a four-year period.

■ *Divestiture* Selling parts of the organization to cut costs, improve operating efficiency, and/or return to more integrated activities in line with the organization's distinctive competency. Good examples of the latter type of divestiture by oil companies

BATTLE
OF THE KOREAN GIANTS

The CEOs of Samsung, Hyundai, and Daewoo, three of Korea's biggest *chaebols* or family-run conglomerates, take seriously their companies' roles in shaping the future of Korea's economy. But Samsung's Lee, Hyundai's Chung, and Daewoo's Kim have very different views of how to compete with their opponents in Japan for profitable markets in the West—especially in America.

Samsung Group is Korea's largest conglomerate and leads a high technology push among the nation's firms. CEO B. C. Lee expects export prices to keep rising, and feels the company must focus on increased R&D and streamlined manufacturing to prosper in the future. He looks to both Japan and the United States for ideas and markets. Samsung has joint ventures with a number of leading American firms, but is now investing heavily to gain direct name recognition for its products. Lee wants to broaden Samsung's image, but also worries about growing "protectionist" feelings in America.

Hyundai's Chung believes that reliance on foreigners is risky. His corporation maintains tight control over all aspects of its business at home and abroad. The company's Excel subcompact car is aggressively marketed in the United States under the Hyundai name—as are Hyundai computers, although they are distributed by an American company.

Daewoo's Kim has several dozen technical-cooperation agreements and several joint ventures with American companies that have put up around $400 million. Daewoo's products appear under such labels as GM, Caterpillar, and Carrier. Kim values the partnerships he has formed, and he has not focused on advertising Daewoo's name. In his view, the future of Korean business lies in collaboration with other nations' enterprises; such ventures allow technology to be obtained more quickly.

Samsung, Hyundai, and Daewoo continue to compete philosophically as well as economically, while simultaneously sharing in the responsibility for Korea's economic future. As Lee says, "Are our multinationals up to the challenge? That remains to be seen."

Source: As reported in "Daewoo vs. Hyundai: Battle of the Korean Giants," *BusinessWeek* (December 15, 1986), pp. 72–73; and Andrew Tanzer, "South Korea Marches to Its Own Drummer," *Forbes* (May 16, 1988), pp. 84–89.

---

which had become too diversified are Exxon's sale of its office equipment division and Mobil's sale of Montgomery Ward.

■ *Liquidation* Closing down operations through outright sale of assets or declaration of bankruptcy. This "last resort" retrenchment strategy is perhaps best illustrated by two "near misses" in the corporate world. One is Chrysler, saved from bankruptcy by U.S. government investment; the other is Texaco, which managed to negotiate a survival settlement with Pennzoil after losing a massive lawsuit to the rival company.

Stability and Combination Strategies

The two other grand strategies are stability and combination. A **stability strategy** maintains the present course of action. It is typically used when an organization is already doing very well in a receptive environment, when "low risk" is important to decision makers, and/or when time is needed to adjust after a period of involvement with one or more other strategies. Pursuit of stability is not a "do nothing" approach however. It is a useful and important strategy that simply seeks to continue an existing pattern of operations.

A **combination strategy** simultaneously employs more than one of the other strategies. This combination of strategies can involve the organization as a whole, or it can reflect different strategic approaches among subsystems. For example, an M-form conglomerate like GE might seek growth overall, but do so by pursuing growth in some divisions, stability in others, and retrenchment in still others. Combination strategies are common, especially for complex organizations operating in dynamic and highly competitive environments.

Strategy Formulation and Strategy Implementation

In order to achieve a positive impact on organizational and/or subsystem performance, strategy must both be well formulated and implemented. **Strategy formulation** is the process of choosing among the various strategies just discussed, and tailoring them to fit the organization's actual circumstances. In general, strategies may be formulated through the entrepreneurial insight of one person, as the by-product of management reactions to organizational problems, or through systematic planning and analysis.[8] The latter approach will dominate our attention in this chapter. It most probably helped create the single-enterprise strategy now pursued by AT&T. As with most strategy formulation, the process involved a number of persons from different parts and levels of the company, even though it was developed in the final form by CEO Olson and his closest associates.

Once strategies are developed, they must be successfully acted upon to achieve the desired results. This is the process of **strategy implementation.** It involves the many elements of management that constitute subsequent chapters of this book. More will be said on this topic a bit later in the chapter. For now, the critical point is that successful strategy implementation depends on the achievement of good "fits" between the strategies and their means of implementation. Operating plans and policies within the many areas of an enterprise must

support and reinforce strategies. Likewise, the other management functions of organizing, leading, and controlling must be well applied to support and reinforce the strategy. All of this, in turn, requires a strong commitment on the part of organization members to what the strategy represents. Getting this commitment through participative planning, as discussed in Chapter 4, is part of the strategic challenge.

In the AT&T case, CEO Olson wisely recognized the importance of this last point. The *process* through which the single-enterprise strategy was formulated created a high level of involvement among key members of the firm's top management team. When he asked everyone to stand to publicly affirm their personal commitments after the group consensus was reached, the implementation phase of the company's single-enterprise strategy had already begun.

STRATEGY AND ORGANIZATIONAL OBJECTIVES

Organizational objectives are the specific ends or goals which an organization seeks to achieve. Any strategy should have a clear and complementary relationship with organizational objectives. Objectives identify desired accomplishments and symbolize the reason for an organization's existence. Strategies, in turn, represent the "means" through which these objectives are pursued as "ends" at any given point in time.

Types of Organizational Objectives

As shown in Figure 5.2, it helps to distinguish between the official and operating objectives of organizations. **Official objectives** reflect the organization's basic purpose in society. They represent the overall desired direction for an organization in respect to its environment. Found stated in writing in such documents as annual reports, charters and information brochures, they identify to employees and external publics alike the **domains**—product markets for goods and/or services—in which organizations intend to operate. They also provide anchor points for the eventual development of strategies and action plans dedicated to their fulfillment. For example,

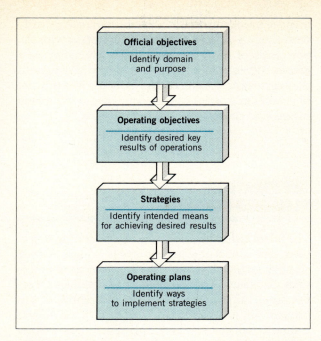

FIGURE 5.2 *The relationship among organizational objectives, strategies, and operating plans.*

at AT&T the firm expresses its official objective as being a leader in "the electronic movement and management of information—in the United States and around the world." From this statement the company's employees as well as outside observers expect the company to be involved worldwide in a variety of information related businesses. They would not expect the company to pursue business opportunities in unrelated areas such as financial services (the domain of American Express) or fast-food restaurants (the domain of McDonald's).

at GE the firm views itself as a broad-based conglomerate whose official objective is "to become the most competitive enterprise in the world—not only in the 1980s, but in the 1990s and beyond." By definition, GE's domain is much broader than AT&T's, and the firm can be expected to operate in such diverse areas as aerospace, consumer electronics, transportation systems, and financial services.

Operating objectives, by contrast, are specific ends toward which organizational resources are actually allocated. They are more tangible than official objectives and represent key results that organiza-

tions pursue in their day-to-day activities. Operating objectives are "key result areas" to be met in the pursuit of official objectives. As such they become the basis for establishing concrete performance targets to be pursued through the various levels and types of strategies, as well as the short and long-run operating plans which implement them. Peter Drucker identifies the following important operating objectives of organizations.[9]

- *Profitability* Producing goods or services at a net profit in the business sector or within budget allowances in the public sector.
- *Market standing* Gaining a share of the market for the organization's goods or services.
- *Human resources* Recruiting and maintaining a high-quality workforce.
- *Financial resources* Acquiring and retaining the financial capital needed to conduct operations.
- *Physical resources* Acquiring and maintaining the physical assets—plant, equipment and technology—needed to conduct operations.
- *Efficiency* Using all types of resources well to operate the organization at low cost.
- *Quality* Maintaining high quality of goods and/or services produced by the organization.
- *Innovation* Achieving the level of new product or process development required to keep the organization competitive over time.
- *Social responsibility* Serving the public good by making a positive contribution to the environment and overall quality of life.

Hierarchies of Objectives

A **hierarchy of objectives** is a series of objectives linked to one another at the various levels of management such that each higher-level objective is supported by one or more lower-level ones. Any and all of the operating objectives just identified should be pursued in well-integrated means-end chains that link relevant decisions and activities throughout the organization. Figure 5.3 presents a hierarchy of quality objectives for a large manufacturing firm. The corporate-level quality objective to "deliver error-free products that meet customer requirements 100 percent of the time," cascades down the hierarchy level-by-level to the job of shift supervisor in one of the company's plants. At this level the corporate quality objective is served by the supervisor's commitment to "assess capabilities of ma-

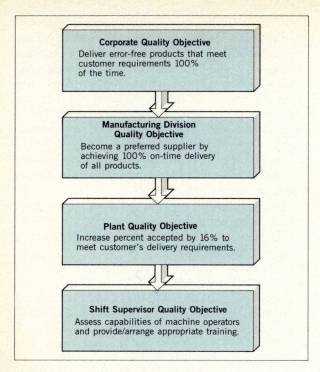

FIGURE 5.3 *A sample hierarchy of objectives: striving for high quality at the manufacturing plant.*

chine operators and provide/arrange appropriate training."

The existence of such integrated hierarchies of objectives is important at any organization for several reasons.

1. They help coordinate activities and decisions at all levels with the organization's overall objectives.
2. They provide a basis for performance measurement at all management levels.
3. They help avoid **suboptimization**—that is, having some subunits accomplish their objectives at the expense of others in the organization.
4. They help prevent **displacement of objectives** wherein means become more important than the ends they were originally intended to serve.

In Chapter 14 we will discuss **management by objectives,** usually referred to as MBO, as a management technique that assists in clarifying and implementing an organization's hierarchy of objectives.[10] MBO is a process of joint objective setting between a superior and subordinate. It involves

managers working with their subordinates to clarify performance objectives that are consistent with the objectives of the work unit and organization as a whole. When this process is followed throughout the organization, MBO helps clarify the hierarchy of objectives as a series of well-defined and integrated means-end chains.

THE STRATEGIC PLANNING PROCESS

The relationship between strategy, operating objectives, and official objectives is linear in logic. A good strategy facilitates achievement of operating objectives. Satisfaction of the operating objectives serves the official objectives, which should represent fulfillment of the organization's basic purpose. Now it is time to talk about strategic planning in the following sense of the term: strategic planning creates strategy to serve organizational objectives.

Strategic Planning Defined

Chapter 4 defined a strategic plan as one that is comprehensive in scope and reflects the overall direction of the total organization or one of its subunits. **Strategic planning,** accordingly, is the process of formulating and implementing strategic plans. Viewed as a systematic process, strategic planning includes determining the major objectives of the organization, choosing the strategies needed to achieve them, and identifying the resources and plans necessary to implement these strategies and achieve the desired results.

Strategy and objectives are an organization's way of maintaining a positive relationship with its external environment. Strategic planning at the enterprise level helps make this happen. Figure 5.4 portrays both strategy formulation and strategy implementation as key phases of the strategic planning process. The essence of the systematic approach shown in the figure rests with the problem-solving process introduced in Chapter 3 (see Figure 3.1) and the formal planning process described in Chapter 4 (see Figure 4.7). Strategic planning is a special approach to problem-solving and planning that involves these steps.

1. Identify organizational purpose and key objectives.
2. Assess current performance vis-à-vis purpose and objectives.
3. Create strategic plans to accomplish purpose and objectives.
4. Implement the strategic plans.
5. Evaluate results and renew the strategic planning process as necessary.

Although strategic planning for the organization as a whole is largely a top management responsibility, managers at all levels must be prepared to participate in the steps just described. It is also true that every manager should lead the strategic planning process for his or her area of immediate work responsibility. Indeed, you should reread each of the five prior steps after replacing the word "organizational" in Step 1 with "work unit." This exercise brings into clearer perspective the importance of strategic planning at the work unit level. It also highlights once again an important part of what we earlier called every manager's "strategic management" responsibility.

Finally, it is helpful to put strategic planning in a managerial perspective by thinking of it as a process of answering a series of questions about an organization and its environment. Thinking strategically about your organization or one of its subunits, for example, would mean seeking answers to at least five basic questions.

1. Where are we now?
2. Where do we want to be in the future?
3. How can we get there?
4. What route is best for us?
5. How and when can we implement it?

The reason for doing all this is made quite clear by Peter Drucker.[11]

> The future will not just happen if one wishes hard enough. It requires decision—now. It imposes risk—now. It requires action—now. It demands allocation of resources, and above all, of human resources—now. It requires work—now.

A major element of the "work" with which Drucker is so concerned is strategic planning.

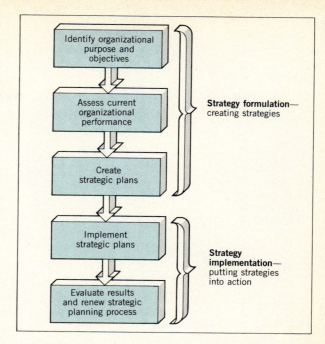

FIGURE 5.4 *Major components in a systematic approach to the strategic planning process: strategy formulation and strategy implementation.*

MAJOR ELEMENTS OF STRATEGY FORMULATION

Strategy formulation, the first phase of the strategic planning process, depends for its success on the ability of managers to conduct the appraisal described in Figure 5.5. The four major elements in this appraisal are the analysis of (1) the organization's mission and purpose, (2) the organization's values and corporate culture, (3) the organization's internal strengths and weaknesses, and (4) opportunities and threats in the organization's environment. Our discussion of all the elements will include the identification of strategic planning principles useful to managers at all organizational levels—regardless of whether their responsibilities are to lead, participate in, or merely implement the results of strategic planning.

Analysis of Mission:
What Is the Organization's Purpose?

Very early in this book we singled out *purpose* as one of the basic ingredients of organizations. Earlier

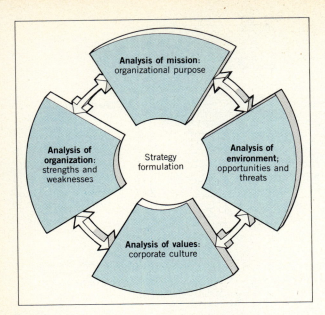

FIGURE 5.5 *The major elements in strategy formulation: analysis of mission, values, organization, and environment.*

in this chapter we tied organizational purpose to the concept of official objectives. In practice, organizations often express their official objectives or purposes in the form of written **mission statements** that define for all concerned the organization's chosen role in society and the ways it intends to fulfill this role. Here are two examples.[12]

At Nynex Corporation   the annual report states: "*Our mission is clear:* To be a leader in the information industry. To know and capture the full potential of our many markets. To anticipate communications requirements with quality services at competitive prices. To be a profitable company with steady earnings growth."

At Kraft, Inc.   the annual report states: "*The new Kraft has a new mission:* To become the leading food company in the world with respect to quality people, quality products, quality business plans, growth, returns and innovation."

The strategic planning process begins with an analysis of mission. This often involves either the writing of a mission statement for the first time, or the rewriting of a mission statement that is no longer quite relevant. Both the NYNEX and Kraft mission

statements are relatively recent. They are designed to provide a sense of common direction to organization members by defining what business each organization wants to be in and setting each clearly apart from other companies, particularly competitors. A good mission statement helps strategy formulation by targeting plans on directions consistent with an overriding sense of organizational purpose.[13]

Mission statements should create a clear sense of identity for the organization in the eyes of its major "stakeholders," ideally indicating how each can expect to be served. **Stakeholders** are members of the external environment, stockholders, suppliers, creditors, community groups, and others, who are directly involved with the organization and/or affected by its operations. Through a **strategic constituencies analysis** the interests of external stakeholders are reviewed along with the organization's record in responding to their interests. An important test of any strategy is how well it serves the strategic constituencies or stakeholder groups of the organization. Figure 5.6 shows how NCR, Inc. has explicitly included stakeholders in its mission statement which reads in part[14]

At NCR: We believe in building mutually beneficial and enduring relationships with all of our stakeholders, based on conducting business activities with integrity and respect.

Management researchers have placed increasing emphasis on how a clear sense of mission and purpose can help create high performing organizations. Our first strategic planning principle recognizes the importance of the analysis of mission and purpose in any strategic planning process.

STRATEGIC PLANNING PRINCIPLE NO. 1

Strategy and objectives should direct effort toward accomplishment of the organization's basic mission and overall purpose.

Analysis of Values:
What Is the Corporate Culture?

A person's decisions and actions will always be affected in part by **values**—broad beliefs about what is or is not appropriate. **Corporate culture** is the

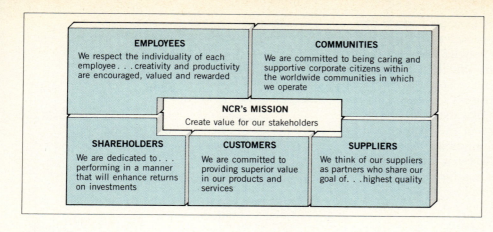

FIGURE 5.6 *External stakeholders and the corporate mission statement: an example of NCR, Inc.*

Source: Information for this example is from *The Wall Street Journal* (November 23, 1987), pp. 9–12.

predominant value system for the organization as a whole. Through corporate cultures, the values of managers and other individuals are shaped and pointed in common directions. The resulting benefits are two-fold. First, the presence of clear and strong values gives *character* to an organization in the eyes of employees and external stakeholders. It helps to back up the organizational mission statement with an added depth of identity. Second, the shared values help guide and direct behavior within an organization in meaningful ways.

In their book *Corporate Cultures: The Rites and Rituals of Corporate Life,* Terrence Deal and Allen Kennedy say this about the importance of shared values and a strong corporate culture.[15]

> If employees know what their company stands for, if they know what standards they are to uphold, then they are much more likely to make decisions that will support those standards. They are also more likely to feel as if they are an important part of the organization. They are motivated because life in the company has meaning for them.

Deal and Kennedy also point out that corporate culture is subject to considerable influence by initial founders, such as Thomas J. Watson, Sr., of IBM, or the chief executives of the moment. It is also supported by rituals, ceremonies, stories, myths, symbols, and heroes which embody and reinforce core values.

An examination of organizational values and corporate culture is an essential early step in strategy formulation. Corporate culture complements the sense of mission and purpose just discussed to set a performance tone for the organization in general and the strategic planning process in particular. A good example of the relationship between mission, values, and strategy is found—[16]

at Corning Glass Works where senior management of the Technical Products Division embarked on a major strategic review that resulted in agreement on the following statements. They were later expressed in a formal document introducing the division to its stakeholders.

Mission To grow profitably through the worldwide marketing of Corning's glass and glass-ceramic technologies, as well as extensions thereof, and to actively support the exploration and development of new technologies.

Values
- Excellence as the standard of performance.
- Leadership and professionalism in marketing.
- Effective communication with each other and our customers.
- Teamwork through a participative style of management.
- A working environment that fosters innovation, enhances growth, and maximizes individual development.

Strategy Growth by emphasizing market opportunities . . . leveraging our technology with outside partners . . . managing our base business to maximize return on equity . . . striving for leadership and professionalism in marketing . . . striving for product and cost leadership in manufacturing . . . becoming world class in Total Quality.

Another aspect of this example further illustrates a truly progressive approach to strategic planning. The last page of the booklet from which the prior information came contains the signatures of the many Corning personnel who participated in the Technical Products Division's strategic planning process. These signatures, like the verbal testimonies asked by CEO Olson in the earlier case of AT&T, evidence their commitments to work hard and follow-through to effectively implement the strategy. This adds further significance to the second strategic planning principle.

STRATEGIC PLANNING PRINCIPLE NO. 2

Strategy and objectives should be consistent with prevailing values and the corporate culture.

Analysis of the Organization: What Are Its Strengths and Weaknesses?

Elements 3 and 4 in the strategic planning process together constitute what is commonly called a **SWOT analysis,** that is an analysis of organizational **s**trengths, **w**eaknesses, as well as environmental **o**pportunities and **t**hreats.[17] Conducting a SWOT analysis should result in a realistic understanding of the organization in relationship to its environment. It should also assist in the creation of strategies which take maximum advantage of strengths and opportunities while minimizing weaknesses and threats. The two elements already covered add important context to the SWOT analysis by initially focusing the planning process on basic "institutional" factors relating to organizational purpose and values.

A SWOT analysis, now illustrated in Figure 5.7, begins with an internal appraisal of the organization's strengths and weaknesses. When done well, such an analysis helps establish a realistic basis for the formulation of strategies—corporate, business, and/or functional. A large number of internal factors should be considered. They include the functional capabilities of the organization in respect to such things as its sales, marketing, manufacturing, finance, human resources, and research and development activities. In addition, an assessment should be made of the organization's resources and operations in terms of:

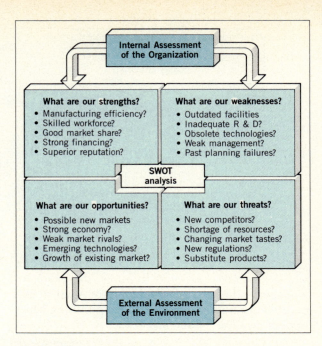

FIGURE 5.7 *A sample SWOT analysis: assessing organizational strengths and weaknesses, and environmental opportunities and threats.*

1. *Human resources* To what extent are the right numbers of high quality technical and managerial personnel available?
2. *Physical and financial resources* To what extent does the organization have access to other essential resources, such as facilities, equipment, supplies, and money?
3. *Technology.* To what extent does the organization have access to advanced technologies, technical improvements and/or have the capability to develop or access them in the future?
4. *Information* To what extent does the organization possess information offering a strategic advantage, including special product expertise and knowledge not presently available to others?
5. *Systems* To what extent is the organization supported by appropriate systems for processing information, ensuring quality control, maintaining resource flows, developing new products, distributing final goods or services, and the like?

A major goal at this stage of the strategic planning process is to identify special strengths or "distinctive competencies" which give the organization an advantage over its competitors. Of the many possible sources of such advantage, Figure 5.7 highlights questions which might be directed toward the available technology, expertise of human resources, manufacturing efficiencies, management talent, and financial strength, among many other possibilities. Weaknesses, of course, are the other side of the picture. They represent things like inadequate technologies, deficient expertise, poor market position, lack of research and development, insufficient financing, and other deficiencies which detract from an organization's ability to be competitive and achieve high performance.

In order for any strategy to succeed, the organization must be internally capable of implementing it well. With this point in mind, consider the third strategic planning principle.

STRATEGIC PLANNING PRINCIPLE NO. 3

Strategy and objectives should build upon the internal strengths and minimize any weaknesses of the organization.

Analysis of Environment:
What Are the Opportunities and Threats?

The second part of the SWOT analysis depicted in Figure 5.7 involves the analysis of environmental opportunities and threats. The external environment is a dynamic and complex force with which organizations and their managers must contend. We will have more to say about the environment at

many times throughout the book. To begin here, note that varying environmental conditions have different implications for strategy formulation and implementation. In particular,

1. *Stable environments lend themselves to more programmed strategies.* When there is little change in the environment, strategies can be specified in great detail because the organziation's needs are likely to remain fairly constant over time. Such programmed strategies are implemented with precision and under strict control over time.

2. *Dynamic environments require more flexible strategies.* When the environment is changing, programmed strategies can inhibit the organization's adaptation to new circumstances. Flexibility is necessary to allow for variation of strategic emphasis to keep abreast of changing environmental conditions over time.

3. *Uncertain environments call for contingency strategies.* When the environment is highly unpredictable, the strategic challenge moves beyond even the advantage that flexibility provides. Uncertainty requires contingency planning in the sense that a set of alternative strategies exist, each ready for implementation when a specific change of circumstances makes it appropriate.

Given the intended direction for the enterprise as clarified in the mission statement, it is necessary to assess how actual and projected future environmental conditions may affect its accomplishment. Major factors to consider include a variety of economic, political, social, technological, and competitive forces. Figure 5.8 depicts these factors as com-

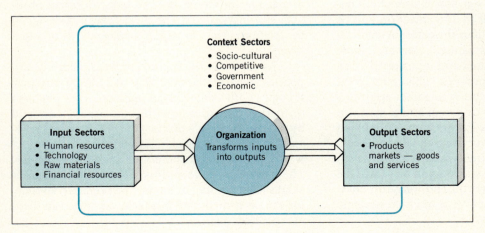

Context Sectors
- Socio-cultural
- Competitive
- Government
- Economic

Input Sectors
- Human resources
- Technology
- Raw materials
- Financial resources

Organization
Transforms inputs into outputs

Output Sectors
- Products markets — goods and services

FIGURE 5.8 *Major sectors in an organization's planning environment: an open-systems model.*

prising key sectors in an organization's planning environment. It shows how they come into play as important influences on the input–output relationships essential to daily affairs of the organization as an open system. Developments in each sector of the environment can be a source of opportunities and/or threats which must be considered for their strategic planning implications. Broadly speaking, strategic planning requires a good understanding of an organization's:

1. *Economic environment* Consists of background economic conditions with the potential to affect demand for goods or services and the supplies of essential resources.

2. *Political environment* Includes governmental units at regional, state, national, and international levels; special-interest groups and other political entities; and the legal-judicial framework of society.

3. *Social environment* Consists of the value systems, social and demographic patterns, and other basic characteristics of persons comprising the society.

4. *Technological environment* Includes the available technologies and the related capability of society to develop or acquire appropriate technologies in the future.

5. *Competitive environment* Consists of the current and future competition, their strategies and domains, and their operating strengths and weaknesses.

Other things being equal, the richer the environment in terms of support provided to the organization on economic, political, social, or technological grounds, the better off the organization will be in operational terms. Whether the external environment is richer or poorer in nature, however, it must always be properly identified and interpreted as an input to the planning process. This puts great weight on the manager's ability to gather appropriate information on the environment and to spot and interpret important trends. Forecasting as discussed in Chapter 4 is an important managerial tool in this regard. Indeed, all planning, whether done for an entire organization or a subcomponent, must be consistent with both short-run and long-run environmental challenges. Our fourth and final strategic planning principle follows.

STRATEGIC PLANNING PRINCIPLE NO. 4

Strategy and objectives should be consistent with the opportunities and threats contained in the organization's external environment.

STRATEGIC PLANNING MODELS

A number of models are available to assist in the strategic planning process, particularly in respect to the formulation of corporate and business strategies. An understanding of the major alternatives will give you a good introduction to the planning directions now pursued by managers, staff planners, and consultants. These are the Boston Consulting Group's (BCG) portfolio model, Porter's competitive model, Miles and Snow's adaptation model, and the incremental-emergent model found in the work of Quinn and Mintzberg.

The Portfolio Model

Figure 5.9 summarizes the portfolio planning model offered by the Boston Consulting Group. Known as the **BCG matrix** this is an approach to strategy formulation based on market growth rate and market share.[18] It is most useful in multi-business or multi-product situations. Here, management must decide how to allocate resources among a "portfolio" of opportunities in order to best achieve overall objectives. As the former CEO of Norton Company said, "Portfolio planning became relevant to me as soon as I became CEO. I was finding it very difficult to manage and understand so many different products and markets."[19] The BCG matrix is designed to facilitate the strategic management of such diversity.

As shown in the figure, portfolio planning emphasizes a particular approach to a SWOT analysis. It begins with a detailed comparison of the business or market growth rate with the market share held by an organization's products. This comparison results in the following classifications.

■ *Stars* are high share/high growth businesses. They produce large profits through high market shares in expanding markets. The preferred strategy for stars is growth and further investments in them are recommended.

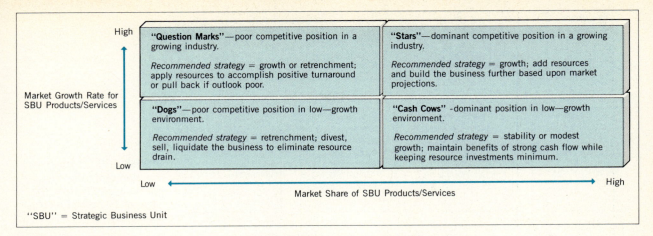

FIGURE 5.9 *Alternative strategies within the* BCG Matrix: *a portfolio model for strategic planning.*

■ *Cash Cows* are high-share/low-growth businesses. They produce large profits and a strong cash flow through high market shares in stable or slowly growing markets. The preferred strategy is stability or modest growth to maximize cash flows for use in other businesses.

■ *Question Marks* are low share/high growth businesses. They do not produce much profit, but compete in rapidly growing markets. The preferred strategy is growth, but the risk is that further investments will not result in improved market shares. Only the most promising question marks should be targeted for growth; others become retrenchment candidates.

■ *Dogs* are low-share/low-growth businesses. They do not produce much profit and offer little future potential for improvement. The preferred strategy is to retrench by divestiture of dogs.

Although it can oversimplify a complex decision situation, the portfolio model is a useful strategic planning tool. Its major appeal rests largely on the ability of managers using the BCG matrix to clearly focus attention on the comparative strengths and weaknesses of multiple businesses and/or products. For example

at General Electric management historically used portfolio planning to good advantage. The company's mission is simply stated: "to become the most competitive enterprise in the world—not only in the 1980s, but in the 1990s and beyond." But the means for achieving this end is quite complicated. As shown in Figure 5.10, GE is a diverse conglomerate whose complexity must be well managed to create the right portfolio of businesses at any point in time. GE's senior executives seek to do this by:

■ Defining key businesses to be No. 1 or No. 2 in their industries.

■ Concentrating resources on key businesses.

■ Shifting the mix of businesses toward technology and services.

The Competitive Model

Another popular strategic planning approach is the competitive model developed by Michael Porter.[20] It gives specific planning attention to the organization's competitors, current and potential, in the external environment. The basic forces in this competitive environment are described in Figure 5.11. They are the threat of new entrants, bargaining power of suppliers, bargaining power of buyers, threat of substitute products or services, and rivalry or jockeying for position among industry firms. Porter believes these forces govern the state of industry competition which, in turn, must be properly addressed to formulate effective strategy. Critical of the portfolio model for leading corporate strategists into unwarranted diversification, Porter further believes that his competitive model can lead to the selection of better strategies.

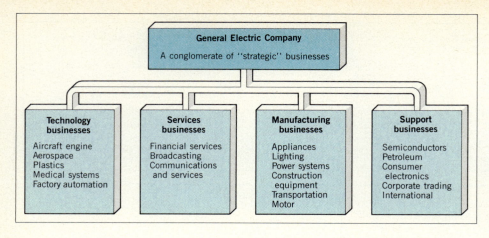

FIGURE 5.10 *A diverse conglomerate or "M-form" organization: the case of General Electric Company.*

A good SWOT analysis, from this perspective, would begin by examining the competitive forces in an organization's environment. This provides a frame of reference for further assessment of organizational strengths and weaknesses. Then strategies can be chosen which give the organization a "strategic advantage" relative to the competition. Based on his empirical research, Porter identifies three *generic strategies* organizations may pursue to gain such a strategic advantage in their competitive environments. They are:

1.   *Differentiation*   creating uniqueness such that the organization's goods and services are clearly distinguished from those of its competitors. The

FIGURE 5.11 *Michael Porter's model of the strategic forces affecting industry competition.*

Source: Adapted with permission of The Free Press, a Division of Macmillan, Inc. from *Competitive Strategy,* by Michael E. Porter. Copyright © 1980 by The Free Press.

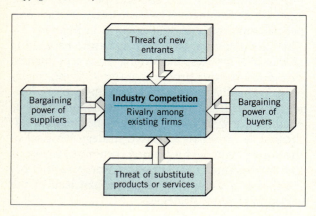

objective is to develop a customer group that is loyal to the organization's products, and uninterested in those of competitors.

2.   *Cost leadership*   achieving lower costs than competitors by improving on the efficiency of production, distribution, and other organizational systems. The objective is to create a basis for profits that are above the industry averages.

3.   *Focus*   concentrating on a special market niche in terms of customer group, geographical region, and/or product or service line. The objective is to be able to better serve the targeted market through concentration of organizational resources and expertise.

The Adaptive Model

An approach that gives special attention to environmental factors in the strategic planning process is the adaptive model of Miles and Snow.[21] The major premise of this model is that organizations should pursue product/market strategies that are congruent with the nature of their external environments. A well-chosen strategy, in this sense, allows an organization to successfully adapt to environmental challenges. The four strategies in the adaptive model follow along with examples of organizations that have used each to good advantage.

1.   *Defender strategy*   emphasizing existing products and current market share without seeking growth. This strategy is suited only for a stable environment and perhaps in declining industries. *Defenders,* like many small local retailers in our communities, try to maintain their operating do-

mains with only slight modifications over time. Many suffer long-term decline in the face of competition from national chains as a result.

2. *Prospector strategy* pursuing innovation and new opportunities, in the face of risk and with prospects for growth. This is the opposite of the defender strategy and it is best suited for dynamic and high-growth environments. A *prospector* like Apple Computer, Inc., "leads" and challenges its industry by using existing technology to new advantage, and creating new products to which competitors must respond.

3. *Reactor strategy* responding to competitive pressures in order to survive. This is the exact opposite of the prospector strategy—it is a "follow-as-last resort" approach. *Reactors* don't have real strategies in the long-term and coherent sense of the concept. Some public utilities and other organizations operating in restricted environments under government regulation may use this strategy to some extent.

4. *Analyzer strategy* maintaining stability while very selectively responding to opportunities for innovation and change. This lies between the prospector and reactor strategies—it is a "follow-the-leader-when-things-look-good" approach, and then always with the security of having a stable core business. Many of the "clone" makers in the personal computer industry are *analyzers*. That is, they wait and see what the industry leaders do and how well it works out, before modifying their own operations.

The Incremental-Emergent Model

Throughout this chapter and in particular reference to the three prior models, we have emphasized rational and formal approaches to the strategic planning process. But as important as it is to understand and utilize this systematic side of planning, there is another side that can't be neglected—the incremental-emergent side.[22] This alternative model recognizes that not all strategies are formulated at one point in time and then implemented at another. Rather, they are often created and applied in an incremental and emergent fashion.

To begin, consider this quote which James Brian Quinn uses to begin one of his articles on this subject.[23]

> When I was younger I always conceived of a room where all these [strategic] concepts were worked out

for the whole company. Later I didn't find any such room. . . . The strategy [of the company] may not even exist in the mind of one person. I certainly don't know where it is written down. It is simply transmitted in the series of decisions made.

Quinn's article goes on to argue that strategic shifts in organizations rarely occur in the singular and clear-cut fashion that the emphasis on formal strategic planning suggests. Instead, his ideas on **logical incrementalism** view strategies emerging over time as a series of incremental changes to existing patterns of behavior. These incremental changes, in turn, presumably occur as managers learn from their experiences and engage in intuitive as well as systematic thinking.

The incrementalism Quinn describes has much in common with Henry Mintzberg's and John Kotter's pragmatic views of managerial behavior introduced earlier in this book. As you should recall, they view managers as developing and implementing action agendas, or plans, through interpersonal relationships in a hectic day-to-day work setting. For example, Mintzberg points out[24]

1. *Managers favor verbal communications* This suggests relational or interactive means of gathering planning data, rather than ordered and sequential ones.

2. *Managers frequently deal with impressions, speculations and feelings* This suggests they are more likely to "synthesize" than "analyze" data in their search for the "big picture."

3. *Managers work at a fast pace, perform a wide variety of duties, and are subject to frequent interruptions* This suggests they may be denied quiet time alone to think and plan in a systematic fashion.

In the face of these basic challenges, Daniel Isenberg says effective managers must have the capacity for *strategic opportunism*. This was defined in the last chapter as the ability to stay focused on long-term objectives while still being flexible enough to master short-run challenges—both as problems to be resolved and opportunities to be explored. In his book *The Renewal Factor,* Robert H. Waterman, Jr. uses a similar concept he calls *informed opportunism.*[25] He points out that highly successful companies "treat information as their main competitive advantage and flexibility as their main strategic weapon." They plot strategy as a general sense of direction but recognize that the future is

THE RICHES
IN MARKET NICHES

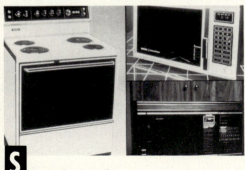

Some of today's fast-growing medium-sized organizations are extremely good at discovering and exploiting corners of the market that their larger competitors overlook—or simply fail to grab quickly enough. By choosing narrowly focused niches and developing specialized and/or high-performance products, these companies are outstripping the giants in some areas. They pick their targets carefully, move fast, and consolidate their positions well.

Valspar Corporation is a fast-growing mid-size company that specializes in a low-tech commonplace: paint. Its management's strategy is to keep the product lines of all acquired companies focused on paint, and this approach has worked well—Valspar's earnings grew 22

percent in one year. Valspar also offers decision-making freedom, performance bonuses, and stock ownership to its managers—an incentive formula that inspires loyalty. Many other mid-size companies also make stock offerings to their managers so as to spur serious commitment and hard work.

AFG Industries, which makes unique lines of tempered and colored glass, stands out as a prime example of a mid-size company that has moved quickly to control a special corner of the glass marketplace. Having positioned itself as the main supplier of specialty products such as microwave oven doors, AFG now earns better profit margins than any of its larger competitors manufacturing commodity glass.

Like other profitable mid-size firms, AFG invests heavily in its production capacity. But these successful organizations also take care that customer relations do not slide as profits rise. R. D. Hubbard, the chief executive of AFG, boasts that his company makes quick deliveries even on small requests—so that customers remain faithful when it comes time for big orders.

Source: As reported in Peter Nulty, "What a Difference Owner-Bosses Make," *Fortune* (April 25, 1988), pp. 97–104, and Stuart Gannes, "The Riches in Market Niches," *Fortune* (April 27, 1987), pp. 227–230.

---

uncertain. As a result they are willing to respond to appropriate opportunities as they arise. Waterman goes on to note that top managers at the best organizations "sense opportunity where others can't . . . act while others hesitate, and demur when others plunge." *Newsline 5.3* reports on some who have done just that.

Such reasoning has led Mintzberg to identify what he calls *emergent strategies*. They develop progressively over time as "streams" of decisions made by managers as they learn from as well as respond to their situations. There is an important element of "craftsmanship" here that Mintzberg worries may be overlooked by managers who choose and discard strategies in rapid succession while using the formal

planning models. Like Quinn, he feels strategies can and do emerge incrementally over time and in building-block fashion. Indeed, one of the benefits Mintzberg associates with the incremental-emergent model of strategic planning is that it allows managers and organizations to become really good at *implementing* strategies, not just formulating them. He says[26]

> . . . most of the time senior managers should not be formulating strategy at all; they should be getting on with making their organizations as effective as possible in pursuing the strategies they already have.

These comments nicely introduce the final section in this chapter.

STRATEGY IMPLEMENTATION

Early in this chapter we identified strategic management as the managerial responsibility for formulating *and implementing* strategies that lead to the longer-term success of an organization or one of its subunits. No strategy, no matter how well it is formulated, can achieve the desired results if it isn't properly implemented. Effective strategy implementation, in turn, depends on good direction from top management, the comprehensiveness of the original strategic planning process, and the strength of the management systems put in place to support and reinforce the strategy.

Top Management Responsibilities

Any manager, at any level in an organization, is responsible for strategic management as it pertains to his or her immediate work unit. Within this work unit, the manager is "top management" and must be willing to accept responsibility for all aspects of the strategic planning process. Of course, the best illustration is the CEO or chief executive officer who is responsible for the strategic direction of the organization as a whole. The CEO must initiate and direct strategic planning, see to it that good strategic choices are made, and ensure that these choices are implemented, evaluated, and revised as necessary over time. Like other top managers, CEOs surely have access to help in this task. Other managers can and should help, staff planners often help, and even outside consultants may be hired to help as well. Still, as the one ultimately in charge, the CEO is accountable for results. Perhaps the most notable recent example of top management accountability occurred—[27]

at United Airlines where CEO had almost single-handedly developed a strategy for the company to diversify and become a travel-services conglomerate. This involved changing the company's name to Allegis Corporation and investing heavily in the hotel and rental car businesses. But Ferris had difficulty implementing the strategy. He ran into trouble with employees, most notably United pilots who went on strike and later tried to buy the airline with investor support. A group of dissident shareholders was vocal in opposing the strategy, and financial performance under the plan was lackluster. Finally,

the Allegis board announced that Richard Ferris had resigned—both he and his failed strategy were being replaced.

Some common reasons for top manager failures in strategic management include[28]

1. *A power-hoarding manager creates overambitious, incautious strategies that ignore environmental signals.* These managers have not developed adequate strategic planning systems.
2. *A power-hoarding manager refuses to change an existing unsuccessful strategy.* These managers do not accept advice from subordinates and don't search the environment themselves for relevant developments.
3. *The manager creates no strategy at all.* These managers expect the organization to run itself without a strategy.
4. *The manager creates a strategy that is overambitious given the resource base of the organization.* These managers have not adequately analyzed the organization's strengths and weaknesses.

Multilevel or Comprehensive Strategic Planning

Even though top managers are usually the strategists, and even though strategic management and operating management have their fundamental differences, each level of management needs the other in order to do its own job well. Strategic management sets the guidelines or action framework for operating management. It provides the sense of direction and cohesion that helps the many diverse parts of the organization work together. Operating management, in turn, uses resources to do the things necessary to implement strategy and realize its impact on organization objectives. Without the applied efforts of operating managers, strategies would remain well-intentioned ideas that never achieve their desired results.

Thus, good strategy implementation requires an integrated and comprehensive organization-wide approach to planning, action, and evaluation, just as we discussed in the last chapter. Figure 5.12 shows how such multilevel-strategic planning involves all layers of management in a major company. This figure is a good one to think about. It shows how your task responsibilities might fit into

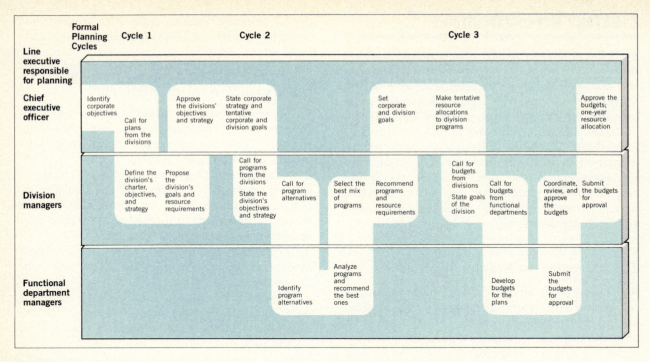

FIGURE 5.12 *Multilevel or comprehensive strategic planning in a large diversified company.*

Source: Permission of the *Harvard Business Review*. Exhibit from "Strategic Planning in Diversified Companies" by Richard F. Vancil and Peter Lorange (January–February 1975), pp. 84–85. Copyright © 1975 by the President and Fellows of Harvard College. All rights reserved.

the strategic planning process throughout a managerial career. Early in this career you will typically work at a lower management level where operational concerns stress strategy implementation. Later on, when you assume middle and upper management responsibilities, these concerns will shift to reflect greater emphasis on strategy formulation.

Making Strategic Planning Effective

There are pitfalls to be avoided and guidelines to be followed by managers trying to succeed at strategic planning. Let's look first at pitfalls.

Pitfalls to Avoid

Strategic planning failures fall into two general categories. *Failures of substance* reflect inadequate attention to the major planning elements previously discussed—analysis of purpose and mission, managerial values and corporate culture, organizational strengths and weaknesses, and, environmental opportunities and threats. Either these elements were neglected or improper conclusions were drawn. Prior discussion should give you a sensitivity to the issues and help you attend them more systematically in actual planning situations.

Failures of process, on the other hand, reflect poor handling of the ways in which the elements of strategic planning were addressed. These include process errors during both the strategy formulation and implementation stages. One sample of corporate executives, for example, identified the following six *pre*implementation factors as the cause of some of their strategic planning problems.[29]

- Poor preparation of line managers.
- Faulty definition of business units.
- Vaguely formulated objectives.
- Inadequate information.
- Badly handled reviews of business unit plans.
- Poor link of planning with control systems.

At the top of the prior list, and central to many planning errors, is the failure to include key persons in the planning effort. As a result their commitments—something pointed out several times so far as essential to action follow-through on plans—may be insufficient to achieve the desired results. This may be due to over-centralization of planning in top management, or from too much delegation of planning activities to staff planners or separate planning departments. Another process failure to guard against is getting so bogged down in details that the planning process becomes an end in itself, instead of a means to an end. Finally, strategy implementation will always be compromised if management systems are not mobilized in support of strategy. Indeed, the entire management process is at issue here—from the development of complementary operating plans, design of appropriate organization structures, and staffing of the human resources, on to providing leadership and reinforcement, and controlling results.

Guidelines to follow

Research on the strategic planning approaches of both large and small U.S. businesses isolates significant differences between high performers and low performers.[30] In comparison with their low-performing counterparts, high performing organizations

■ Emphasize planning, maintain planning departments, and allocate significant resources to planning processes;
■ Have more structured planning processes that involve a wide range of people—both line and staff;
■ Carefully check their planning assumptions and have a strong external orientation;
■ Emphasize retrospection, that is on analyzing past performance and identifying reasons for past failures;
■ Achieve better integration among all functional areas, and emphasize the strategic importance of multiple functions;
■ Have top managers who devote considerable time to planning.

The management literature also offers a basic set of guidelines for making strategic planning effective. Think about this final advice on how to best fulfill your managerial responsibility of *planning for productivity*.

1. *Become a "strategic actor" as opposed to a "trapped executive."* The trapped executive is reactive, focuses on solving daily problems, acts aloof and critical of others, and pays attention to weaknesses.[31] The strategic actor, by contrast, is proactive and accepts responsibility for truly strategic thinking. This involves staying in contact with employees at all levels, communicating organizational philosophy, acting warm, supportive and expressive, paying attention to strengths, and talking frequently about future goals.
2. *Get the right people involved.* Avoid process pitfalls. Make sure the right people from all levels are involved in strategic planning. This is the key to gaining needed commitments and follow-through.
3. *Use a checklist for minimizing errors of substance.* Here are seven ways to know when you've got the right strategic plan.[32]

> *Check One:* Is the strategy responsive to the external environment?
>
> *Check Two:* Does the strategy have a sustainable competitive advantage?
>
> *Check Three:* Is the strategy consistent with organizational purpose and mission?
>
> *Check Four:* Is the risk in the strategy a reasonable risk?
>
> *Check Five:* Does the strategy have an appropriate time horizon?
>
> *Check Six:* Does the strategy provide adequate flexibility for the organization?
>
> *Check Seven:* Is the strategy feasible?

4. *Don't be afraid to conclude that an existing strategy is good or even the best one.* It's easy to assume that change is always for the better. Remember, there is benefit in doing strategic planning even if the final decision is to stay with an existing strategy. The benefit lies in making a renewed commitment based on rigorous analysis and informed judgment.
5. *Approach strategic planning with responsibility for the total process in mind.* Look back to Figure 5.4, which identifies the strategic planning process. Remember that true strategic management, however, doesn't stop with appraisal or even with the choice of a strategy. It includes responsibility for

implementation and follow-through evaluation as well.

6. *Use strategic planning as a stepping-stone for success in all the management functions.* When done well, strategic planning helps managers fulfill their planning, organizing, leading, and controlling responsibilities. When these are done well in return, they help in the implementation and evaluation of strategic plans.

7. *Remember that a good strategy alone will not ensure organizational success.* A strategy merely sets the stage for action. The action, in turn, will only be as good as the ability of the rest of the organization and its members to implement strategy in a coordinated manner. Effective management requires both planning and "follow through." This observation by Harold Geneen, past CEO of IT&T and author of the best-seller *Managing,* captures the point.[33]

> You decide what it is that you want to do, and then you start doing it. It never ceases to amaze me how many people can give this lip servce and then not follow through. It is the *follow-through* that is all-important.

Summary

Strategy is a comprehensive plan that sets critical direction and guides the allocation of resources for an organization or subunit. Through a variety of strategies organizations can pursue stability, growth, retrenchment, and combination to prosper in the face of environmental challenges. The process through which strategies are formulated and implemented is strategic management.

Strategic planning identifies organizational objectives and determines the strategies that govern the use of resources to achieve these objectives. It can be viewed as a formal planning approach involving both strategy formulation and implementation. The major elements to be addressed in strategy formulation are:

1. *Analysis of mission.* What is the organization's purpose?
2. *Analysis of values.* What is the corportate culture?

3. *Analysis of the organization.* What are its strengths and weaknesses?
4. *Analysis of the environment.* What opportunities and threats does it hold?

A number of strategic planning models were introduced in respect to this process. They were the portfolio model using the BCG matrix, Porter's competitive model, the adaptive model of Miles and Snow, and the incremental-emergent model represented by the work of Quinn and Mintzberg. Strategy implementation became the final focus of this review of strategic planning. Top managers were singled out as the major enterprise strategists, but managers at all levels were shown to have responsibility for strategic management. All managers are also responsible for helping the organization benefit from truly comprehensive, multilevel strategic planning. Finally, we recognized pitfalls to be avoided and several guidelines to be followed for doing effective strategic planning in organizations.

Thinking Through the Issues

1. What is "strategy," what are three different levels at which strategy is applied in organizations, and what is "strategic management"?
2. Growth is one of the most popular "grand" strategies pursued by organizations. Explain several ways an organization can pursue growth. Contrast them with other ways an organization can retrench during difficult times.
3. Explain the difference between the official and operating objectives of an organization. Why is it important for organizations to operate with clear and well-integrated "hierarchies of objectives"?
4. What is a "mission statement" and how does it differ from the "corporate culture"? Why are both of these factors considered important elements in the strategy formulation process?
5. List the major questions that a manager or staff planner would ask when conducting a "SWOT"

analysis. Explain how such an analysis contributes to the strategic planning process.

6. Explain the Boston Consulting Group's portfolio model of strategic planning. What is the "BCG matrix? What are the recommended strategies for dealing with "stars," "question marks," "dogs," and "cash cows"?

7. Compare and contrast Porter's "competitive model" and Miles and Snow's "adaptive model" for their respective insights to a manager engaged in strategic planning for an organization.

8. How does the "incremental-emergent model" differ from the strategic planning approaches addressed in questions #6 and 7? Is this model something that can be used in conjunction with the other approaches? Explain your answer.

9. Prepare a summary of the major considerations a top manager should address in respect to "implementing" strategies. What can be done, in particular, to ensure that middle-level and lower-level managers feel included in the planning process?

10. List the four strategic planning principles identified in this chapter. Explain the managerial significance of each.

The Manager's Vocabulary

BCG matrix
Business strategy
Combination strategy
Competitive
 environment
Corporate culture
Corporate strategy
Displacement of
 objectives
Domain
Economic
 environment

Functional strategy
Growth strategy
Hierarchy of
 objectives
Institutional Strategy
Logical
 incrementalism
M-form organization
Management by
 objectives (MBO)
Mission statement
Official objective

Operating objective
Organizational
 objective
Political environment
Retrenchment strategy
Social environment
Stability strategy
Stakeholders
Strategic business unit
Strategic
 constituencies
 analysis

Strategic management
Strategic planning
Strategy
Strategy formulation
Strategy
 implementation
Suboptimization
SWOT analysis
Technological
 environment
Values

SHAPING ONE COMPANY'S FUTURE

CAREER PERSPETIVES

At 34, Michael White became vice-president for strategic planning at Avon Product's Inc. $1.1 billion beauty division.[34] A Phi Beta Kappa graduate of Boston College, with a master's degree in International Economics from Johns Hopkins University, Michael's business career began in management consulting. But after ten years of consulting with Arthur Andersen & Co. and Baine & Co, he had tired of too many airline trips and too many unused studies. About his decision to make a career change he says, "I wanted to be part of building an organization as opposed to constantly whispering in someone's ear." The

strategic planning position at Avon was especially attractive to him because, "It was a chance to be a small part of a team to shape the future of a major corporation. That's more than what a consultant can ever hope to do."

Michael also feels the new job at Avon will allow him to adopt a different life-style, in particular one that better accomodates his family life. While traveling two or three days a week for 52 weeks a year on consulting assignments, he says,"I was missing too many birthdays, soccer games, and school plays." But the new job is also a big challenge. Working with a group of 12 professionals,

Michael must manage the development of strategic plans to chart a new course and improve the profitability of Avon's fragrance and cosmetics business. Meeting the challenge is central to his ambition to run a major business someday. But Michael says he's just one of many young people who want to feel they make a difference. "American industry is changing," he says, "and it has to change. There aren't any easy businesses anymore. You've got to fight for what you've got."

Questions

1. As a vice-president for strategic planning at Avon, which of the strategic planning models addressed in this chapter might be of special value in helping Michael White to do his new job well? . . . and why?

2. In what specific ways to you feel it would be different to be a "consultant" on strategic planning versus a line or staff manager "in charge of" strategic planning?

3. Has Michael White's career developed in ways you might like to pursue someday? Why or why not?

Case Application

TV NETWORKS PURSUE DIFFERENT STRATEGIES

When NBC announced its intention to purchase a cable television channel from Telecommunications, Inc., it was an aggressive first move by the company into this side of the TV business.[35] Thomas S. Rogers, a vice-president, negotiated the purchase for NBC. He said, it "will certainly be a major step" into the cable business and that other similar acquisitions may follow. Until now, ABC with a big investment in ESPN and others has been the only network involved in the cable business. CBS stands resolutely aside with no professed interest in such investments.

As NBC, ABC, and CBS continue to battle for market share and success in a competitive industry, they do so with different strategies. Times have changed markedly from the days when the presidents of each network faced the common challenge of trimming bloated staffs and inefficient operations. Now that the major cost-cutting stands complete, each is proceeding a bit differently to address the current challenge—business expansion in a highly competitive environment. Industry analysts are carefully watching new developments as they try to determine which company is in the best shape for the long haul.

Robert C. Wright, president of NBC, works with a specific vision of the future. He foresees a major shrinkage in the audience for network TV. Among the trends he notes are continued use of home VCRs, the emerging role of independent stations and the growing influence of cable services.

To counteract the impact of these trends, Wright wants to get NBC directly involved not only with cable TV but also with producing programs directly for cable services. The new acquisition of a cable TV channel gives him a chance to expand NBC's business while remaining in a TV-related area.

ABC is already a more broad-based enterprise than NBC. It is involved in publishing operations and cable TV interests, as well as network TV. Thomas C. Murphy runs the company with a special concern for upgrading its prime time television programming from its current last-place ranking. He feels that if ABC shows can gain in TV ratings, the network can add major advertising revenues in the years ahead. Like Wright at NBC, Murphy also believes the traditional network audience will decline in the future. But he intends to increase ABC's share of that market and the revenues that go along with it. Thus, Murphy's strategic emphasis is on network programming. He says, "we're willing to pay for quality."

Lawrence A. Tisch operates CBS with a different vision of the future and a different strategy. He thinks the audience decline has probably fallen about as low as it's going to fall. In the short run, therefore, he's content to run CBS as a cost-conscious and trimmed-down enterprise. Having sold CBS interests in records, magazines, and textbook publishing, he now sits on a large cash hoard of over $3 billion. His main goal is pushing CBS—now a broadcast network and station owner—up in the ratings and regaining the coveted Number 1 slot. On the issue of long-term strategy he simply says, "I'm flexible." Some outside directors are concerned that the company faces an uninspiring future in its present state. "We're not happy," says one, "we've asked for a plan or a strategy. But it's not in his [Tisch's] nature to lay out a strategy." Another comments, "We say let's do something with the money to help the business. He doesn't want to buy cable because it's too expensive."

Questions

1. What are the "grand" strategies at NBC, ABC, and CBS? Exactly how is each network pursuing its grand strategy?

2. Apply the "portfolio model" to analyze the strategies being pursued by each of the TV networks. Is each company currently operating in a manner consistent with the strategic recommendations of this model? Why or why not? Do the same with Porter's competitive model.

3. Based on the facts of the case and your own impressions of the television industry, which of these companies do you feel will be "Number 1" in the TV industry in 1995? Why do you make this prediction?

Class Exercise: The Best Mission Statements

1. Mission statements, as pointed out in this chapter, can be very important sources of direction for organizations and their members. A well-conceived and widely-shared sense of mission, furthermore, can help in the formulation and implementation of appropriate organizational strategies. Unfortunately, not all organizations have mission statements *and* not all mission statements are good ones.

2. Consider these *criteria of an effective mission statement:*[36]

    a. It sets forth organizational directions for which progress can be measured.

    b. It clearly differentiates the organization from others.

    c. It clearly defines the business or operating domain the organization intends to function within.

    d. It is relevant to all of the organization's key stakeholders.

    e. It is exciting and inspiring.

3. Turn back to the section of the text where descriptions are provided of the corporate mission statements for NYNEX Corporation and Kraft, Inc. Evaluate how well each of these statements fulfills each of the prior criteria. Be specific in identifying where a given mission is strong or weak, and why.

4. Now turn back to the section of the text where the mission statement for Corning Glass Works' Technical Products Division is described. Evaluate how well this statement fulfills each of the prior criteria. Be specific in identifying where it is strong or weak, and why.

5. Consider the differences in your evaluations of the three mission statements, and think about which of these organizations you might most like to work for. Share the results of your evaluations with a near-by classmate. Be prepared to participate in further class discussion led by your instructor.

References

[1]From Peter F. Drucker, *Management: Tasks, Responsibilities, Practices* (New York: Harper & Row, 1973), pp. 380, 381.

[2]A selection of books on strategic management includes: Arthur A. Thompson and A. J. Strickland III, *Strategic Management: Concepts and Cases* (Plano, TX: Business Publications, 1984); J.A. Pearce and R.B. Robinson, Jr., *Strategic Management: Strategy Formulation and Imple-* mentation (Homewood, IL.: Richard D. Irwin, 1985); James H. Higgins and Julian W. Vincze, *Strategic Management and Organizational Policy,* Third Edition (Hinsdale, IL: Dryden Press, 1986); Samuel C. Certo and J. Paul Peter, *Strategic Management: Concepts and Applications* (New York: Random House, 1988).

[3]Information for this case is reported in "Can Jim Olson's Grand Design Get AT&T Going?" *Business Week* (De-

cember 22, 1986), pp. 48–49; "AT&T: The Making of a Comeback," *Business Week* (January 18, 1988), pp. 56–62; Janet Guyon, "AT&T Names Robert Allen New Chairman," *The Wall Street Journal* (April 21, 1988), p. 4.

[4]This discussion is based on Richard G. Hammermesh, *Making Strategy Work: How Senior Managers Produce Results* (New York: Wiley, 1986).

[5]Thomas N. Peters and Robert H. Waterman, Jr., *In Search of Excellence: Lessons from America's Best-run Companies* (New York: Harper & Row, 1982).

[6]From *IBM . . . Yesterday and Today* (Armonk, NY: IBM Corporation, undated).

[7]The four grand strategies were originally described by William F. Glueck, *Business Policy: Strategy Formulation and Management Action,* Second Edition (New York: McGraw-Hill, 1976). The strategy alternatives are described by Thompson and Strickland, op. cit., 1984, and, Pearce and Robinson, op. cit., 1985.

[8]Hammermesh, op. cit.

[9]Peter F. Drucker's views on organizational objectives are expressed in his classic books, *The Practice of Management* (New York: Harper & Row, 1954); and, *Management: Tasks, Responsibilities, Practices* (New York: Harper & Row, 1973). For a more recent commentary see his article, "Management: The Problems of Success," *Academy of Management Executive,* Vol. 1 (1987), pp. 13–19.

[10]For a good overview of MBO, see Anthony P. Raia, *Managing by Objectives* (Glenview, Il.: Scott, Foresman, 1974.

[11]Drucker, op. cit., p. 122.

[12]Statements from NYNEX and Kraft, Inc. *Annual Reports.*

[13]See the end-of-chapter exercise "The Best Mission Statements;" and, Russel L. Ackoff, *Management in Small Doses* (New York: Wiley, 1986), pp. 38–42, for additional thoughts on the purposes to be served by corporate mission statements.

[14]See a series of advertisements appearing in *The Wall Street Journal* (November 23, 1987), pp. 9–12.

[15]Terrence E. Deal and Allen A. Kennedy, *Corporate Cultures: The Rites and Rituals of Corporate Life* (Reading, MA: Addison-Wesley, 1982), p. 22. For a good additional review of corporate culture see also Ralph H. Killmann, M. J. Saxon and R. Serpa (eds), *Managing Corporate Cultures* (San Francisco: Jossey-Bass, 1985).

[16]This information is found in the brochure, *Technical Products Division,* Corning Glass Works, Inc., 1987. Used by permission.

[17]See Thompson and Strickland, op. cit.

[18]See Gerald B. Allan, "A Note on the Boston Consulting Group Concept of Competitive Analysis and Corporate Strategy," Harvard Business School, Intercollegiate Case Clearing House, ICCH9-175-175 (June 1976). For a discussion of the approach's weaknesses see Richard A. Bettis and William K. Hall, "The Business Portfolio Approach—Where It Falls Down in Practice," *Long Range Planning,* Vol. 16 (1983), pp. 95–104. The portfolio approach is extensively described in Hammermesh, op. cit., 1986.

[19]This quote is from Richard G. Hamermesh, "Making Planning Strategic," *Harvard Business Review,* Vol. 64 (July–August 1986), pp. 115–120.

[20]For a discussion of Michael Porter's approach to strategic planning see his books *Competitive Strategy: Techniques for Analyzing Industries and Competitors* (New York: The Free Press, 1980) and *Competitive Advantage* (New York: The Free Press, 1986); and, his *Harvard Business Review* article, op. cit., 1987.

[21]The adaptive model is described in Raymond E. Miles and Charles C. Snow's book, *Organizational Strategy, Structure, and Process* (New York: McGraw-Hill, 1978); and, their articles "Designing Strategic Human Resources Systems," *Organizational Dynamics,* Vol. 13 (Summer 1984), pp. 36–52, and "Fit, Failure, and the Hall of Fame," *California Management Review,* Vol. XXVI (Spring 1984), pp. 10–28.

[22]The incremental-emergent approach to strategic planning is introduced in: James Brian Quinn, "Strategic Change: Logical Incrementalism," *Sloan Management Review,* Vol. 20 (Fall 1978), pp. 7-21; Daniel J. Isenberg, "The Tactics of Strategic Opportunism," *Harvard Business Review,* Vol. 65 (March–April 1987), pp. 92–97; Henry Mintzberg "Planning on the Left Side and Managing on the Right," *Harvard Business Review,* Vol. 54 (July–August 1976), pp. 46–55; Henry Mintzberg and James A. Waters, "Of Strategies, Deliberate and Emergent," *Strategic Management Journal,* Vol. 6 (1985) pp. 257–272; and, Henry Mintzberg, "Crafting Strategy," *Harvard Business Review,* Vol. 65 (July–August 1987), pp. 66–75.

[23]James Brian Quinn, op cit., p. 7.

[24]Mintzberg, op. cit., 1976.

[25]Information from "How the Best Get Better," *Business Week* (September 4, 1987), pp. 98–120. See also Robert H. Waterman, Jr., *The Renewal Factor* (New York: Bantam Books, 1987).

[26]Mintzberg, op. cit., 1987, p. 73.

[27]For information on this case see Amanda Bennett, "What Went Wrong: Experts Look at the Sudden Upheaval at Allegis," *The Wall Street Journal* (June 24,

1987), p. 25; and, Kenneth Labich, "How Dick Ferris Blew It," *Fortune* (July 6, 1987), pp. 42–45.

[28]Developed from Glueck, op. cit., p. 57.

[29]This study is reported in Daniel H. Gray, "Uses and Misuses of Strategic Planning," *Harvard Business Review,* Vol. 64 (January–February 1986), pp. 89–97.

[30]See Christopher Orphen, "The Effects of Long-Range Planning on Small Business Performance: A Further Examination," *Journal of Small Business Management,* Vol. 23 (1985), pp. 16–23, for a study of small businesses; see Vasudevan Ramanujam and N. Venkatraman, "Planning and Performance: A New Look at an Old Question," *Business Horizons,* Vol. 30 (May–June 1987), pp. 19–25 for a study of formal planning by large corporations.

[31]Larry E. Greiner, "Senior Executives as Strategic Actors," *New Management,* Vol. 1 (1983), pp. 11–15.

[32]Developed from Dick Levin, *The Executive's Illustrated Primer of Long Range Planning* (Englewood Cliffs, N.J.: Prentice-Hall, 1981), pp. 98–100; and David A. Aaker, "How to Select a Business Strategy," *California Management Review,* Vol. XXVI (Spring 1984), pp. 167–175.

[33]Harold Geneen with Alvin Moscow, *Managing* (Garden City, N.Y.: Doubleday, 1984), p. 47.

[34]Information from "Fast-Track Kids," *Business Week* (November 10, 1986), pp. 90–104.

[35]Information from Patricia Sellers, "Lessons from TV's New Bosses," *Fortune* (March 14, 1988), pp. 115–130; Dennis Kneale, "NBC Plans to Buy Cable-TV Channel in Aggressive First Step into Business," *The Wall Street Journal* (May 3, 1988), p. 2; and, "Has Larry Tisch Sold Too Much of CBS's Future?" *Business Week* (July 25, 1988), pp. 52–54.

[36]These criteria for effective mission statements are based on Ackoff, op. cit.

The Case of the Missing Time

It was 7:30 Tuesday morning when Chet Craig, general manager of the Norris Company's Central Plant, swung his car out of the driveway of his suburban home and headed to the plant in Midvale, six miles away. The trip to the plant took about 20 minutes and gave Chet an opportunity to think about plant problems without interruption.

The Norris Company operated three printing plants and did a nationwide business in quality color work. It had about 350 employees, nearly half of whom were employed at the Central Plant. The company's headquarters offices were also located in the Central Plant building.

Chet had started with the Norris Company as an expeditor in its Eastern Plant 10 years ago, after his graduation from Ohio State. After three years he was promoted to production supervisor, and two years later was made assistant to the manager of the Eastern Plant. A year and a half ago he had been transferred to the Central Plant as assistant to the plant manager; one month later, when the manager retired, Chet was promoted to general plant manager.

Chet was in good spirits this morning. Various thoughts occurred to him as he said to himself, "This is going to be the day to really get things done." He thought of the day's work, first one project, then another, trying to establish priorities. He decided

that the open-end unit scheduling was probably the most important— certainly the most urgent. He recalled that on Friday the vice-president had casually asked him if he had given the project any further thought. Chet realized that he had not been giving it any attention lately. He had been meaning to get to work on his idea for over three months, but something else always seemed to crop up.

"I haven't had time to really work

He thought of the day's work, first one project then another, trying to establish priorities.

---

it out," he said to himself. "I'd better get going and finish it off one of these days." He then began to break down the objectives, procedures, and installation steps in the project. It gave him a feeling of satisfaction as he calculated the anticipated cost savings. "It's high time," he told himself. "This idea should have been completed a long time ago."

Chet had first conceived the open-end unit scheduling idea almost two years ago, just prior to leaving the Eastern Plant. He had talked it over with the general manager of the Eastern Plant, and both agreed that it was a good idea and worth developing. The idea was temporarily shelved

when Chet had been transferred to the Central Plant a month later.

His thoughts returned to other plant projects he was determined to get under way. He started to think through a procedure for the simpler transport of dies to and from the Eastern Plant. He thought of the notes on his desk: the inventory analysis he needed to identify and eliminate some of the slow-moving stock items, the packing controls that needed revision, and the need to settle on a job printer to do the outside printing of simple office forms. There were a few other projects he could not recall offhand, but he felt sure that he could tend to them sometime during the day. Again, he said to himself, "This is the day to really get rolling."

When he entered the plant, Chet was met by Al Noren, the stockroom foreman, who appeared troubled. "A great morning, Al," said Chet, cheerfully.

"Well, I don't know, Chet; my new man isn't in this morning," said Noren morosely.

"Have you heard from him?" asked Chet.

"No, I haven't."

"These stock handlers take it for granted that if they're not here, they don't have to call in and report. Better ask Personnel to call him."

Al hesitated a moment. "Okay, Chet," he said, "but can you find me a man? I have two cars to unload today."

Making a note of the incident, Chet headed for his office. He greeted some workers discussing the day's work with Marilyn Benton, the office manager. As the meeting broke up,

Source: Copyright © 1971, Northwestern University. All names and organizational designations have been disguised. Northwestern University cases are reports of concrete events and behavior prepared for class discussion. They are not intended as examples of good or bad administrative or technical practices.

Marilyn took some samples from a clasper and showed them to Chet and asked if they should be shipped that way, or if it would be necessary to inspect them. Before he could answer, Marilyn went on to ask if he could suggest another clerical operator for the sealing machine to replace the regular operator, who was home ill. She also told him that Gene, the industrial engineer, had called and was waiting to hear from Chet.

> **Chet had first conceived the open-end unit scheduling idea almost two years ago . . .**

Chet told Marilyn to ship the samples and made a note of the need for a sealer operator and then called Gene. He agreed to stop by Gene's office before lunch and started on his routine morning tour of the plant. He asked each supervisor the volumes and types of orders they were running, the number of people present, how the schedules were coming along, and the orders to be run next; he helped the folding room supervisor find temporary storage space for consolidating a carload shipment; discussed quality control with a pressman who had been running poor work; arranged to transfer four people temporarily to different departments, including two for Al in the stockroom; talked to the shipping supervisor about pickups and special orders to be delivered that day. As he continued through the plant, he saw to it that reserve stock was moved out of the forward stock area; talked to another pressman about his re-

quested change of vacation schedule; had a "heart-to-heart" talk with a press helper who seemed to need frequent assurance; approved two type and one color okays for different pressmen.

Returning to his office, Chet reviewed the production reports on the larger orders against his initial projections and found that the plant was running slightly behind schedule. He called in the folding room supervisor and together they went over the lineup of machines and made several changes.

During this discussion, the composing room supervisor stopped in to cover several type changes, and the routing supervisor telephoned for approval of a revised printing schedule. The stockroom supervisor called twice—first to inform Chet that two standard, fast-moving stock items were dangerously low; later to advise him that the paper stock for the urgent Dillon job had finally arrived. Chet telephoned this information to the people concerned.

He then began to put delivery dates on important inquiries received from customers and salespersons. (The routine inquiries were handled by Marilyn.) While he was doing this he was interrupted twice—once by a sales correspondent calling from the West Coast to ask for a better delivery date than originally scheduled; once by the vice-president of Personnel, asking Chet to set a time when she could hold an initial induction interview with a new employee.

After dating the customer and sales inquiries, Chet headed for his morning conference in the executive office. At this meeting he answered the vice-president of Sales' questions in connection with "hot" orders, complaints, the status of large-volume orders, and potential new orders. Then he met with the vice-president and general production manager to an-

swer questions on several production and personnel problems. Before leaving the executive offices, he stopped at the office of the purchasing agent to inquire about the delivery of some cartons, paper, and boxes, and to place an order for some new paper.

On the way back to his own office, Chet conferred with Gene about two current engineering projects. When he reached his desk and looked at his watch. It was 10 minutes before lunch—just time enough to make a few notes of the details he needed to check in order to answer knotty questions raised by the vice-president of Sales that morning.

After lunch Chet started again. He began by checking the previous day's production reports; did some rescheduling to get out urgent orders; placed delivery dates on new orders and inquiries received that morning; consulted with a foreman on a personal problem. He spent about 20 minutes going over mutual problems with the Eastern Plant.

> **. . . one of the greatest returns a company gets from a manager is innovative thinking and accomplishments.**

By midafternoon Chet had made another tour of the plant, after which he met with the vice-president of Personnel to review a touchy personal problem raised by one of the clerical employees, the vacation schedules submitted by his supervisor, and the pending job evaluation program. Following this conference, Chet hurried back to his office to complete the special statistical report for Universal Waxing Corporation, one of Norris's biggest customers. When he finished the report he discovered that it was 6:10, and he was the only one left in the office. Chet was tired. He put on his coat and headed for the parking lot. On the way out he was stopped by the night supervisor and the night layout supervisor for approval of type and layout changes.

As he drove home, Chet reviewed the day he had just completed. "Busy?" he asked himself. "Too much so—but did I accomplish anything?" The answer seemed to be "Yes, and no—there was the usual routine, the same as any other day. The plant kept going and it was a good production day. Any creative or special work done?" Chet winced. "I guess not."

With a feeling of guilt Chet asked himself, "Am I an executive? I'm paid like one, and I have a responsible assignment and the authority to carry it out. My supervisors at headquarters think I'm a good manager. Yet one of the greatest returns a company gets from an executive is innovative thinking and accomplishments. What have I done about that? Today was just like other days, and I didn't do any creative work. The projects I was so eager to work on this morning are no further ahead than they were yesterday. What's more, I can't say that tomorrow night or the next night they'll be any closer to completion. This is a real problem, and there must be some answer to it.

"Night work? Yes, sometimes. This is understood. But I've been doing too much night work lately. My wife and family deserve some of my time. After all, they are the people for whom I'm really working. If I spend much more time away from them, I'm not meeting my own per-

sonal objectives. I spend a lot of time on church work. Should I eliminate that? I feel I owe that as an obligation. Besides, I feel I'm making a worthwhile contribution in this work. Maybe I can squeeze a little time from my fraternal activities. But where does recreation fit in?"

Chet groped for the solution. "Maybe I'm just rationalizing because I schedule my own work poorly. But I don't think so. I've studied my work habits and I think I plan intelligently and delegate authority. Do I need an assistant? Possibly, but that's a long-time project and I don't believe I could justify the additional overhead expense. Anyway, I doubt whether it would solve the problem."

"Today was just like other days, and I didn't do any creative work. The projects . . . are no further ahead . . ."

By this time Chet had turned off the highway into the side street leading to his home. "I guess I really don't know the answer," he said to himself as he pulled into his driveway. "This morning everything seemed so simple, but now. . . ."

Questions

1. Why can't Chet get his job done? Or, is he really doing fine and just doesn't realize it? What is it, exactly, that a general manager like Chet should be expected to do in a situation like this? Explain your answers.
2. Specifically, is Chet fulfilling his responsibilities under the manage-

ment function of planning? Is he fulfilling his responsibilities for strategic planning and strategic management? Why or why not?
3. As an external consultant, what concerns do you have about the situation described in this case? What recommendations would you make to Chet as possible ways of improving upon the situation—both in the plant overall, and in respect to his own work performance? Why? ■

Strategic Changes at United Parcel Service

"Our goal is not to chase *them,* our job is to leapfrog *them.*" These fighting words are spoken by Robert Hughes, strategic planning manager at United Parcel Service. *Them* is Federal Express, and the object of contention between the two companies is future domination in the overnight express business—a market in which Federal's market share is 58 percent, while UPS's is 15 percent and growing—mostly at the expense of smaller competitors in the market like Airborne Express, Emery/Purolator, DHL Worldwide, and the U.S. Postal Service.

Industry leader Federal Express is well established and operates with the support of advanced computer technology and carefully planned operations. It has built a reputation by being consistent in picking up packages on the same day orders are placed, delivering the next morning, and knowing at all times where the package is enroute to its final destination.

For both UPS and Federal Express the stakes are high in this profitable market. And like UPS, Federal's management doesn't take the competition lightly. Theodore L. Weise, senior vice-president at Federal Express, sums it up this way: "We feel our God-given right is 100 percent of the overnight express business."

UPS has earned its reputation as tops in its industry in the *Fortune* magazine corporate reputations survey. It is the most profitable U.S. transportation company, and is highly regarded for reliable service and steady prices—its air rates have not changed since the company initiated overnight express service in 1983, and they are lower than those charged by Federal Express.

Federal's market share is 58 percent, while UPS's is 15 percent and growing.

This admirable company which began in 1908 as a Seattle, Washington, messenger service, still adheres to a basic principle established by the late founder James E. Casey. He felt the company should be "owned by its managers and managed by its owners." As a result, UPS is today a closely held corporation whose 15,000 managers and supervisors own most of the stock, which they earn through a generous bonus plan. This stock must be sold back to the company when an employee leaves or retires. One result of employee stock ownership is that company executives can make long-run strategic decisions without having to worry about how they will be received by investors on Wall Street.

Most employees have so far worked their ways up the hierarchy. Usually they start as parcel sorting clerks and drivers of the more than 47,000 brown delivery vans which frequent the streets of America's 50 states as well as Canada, Puerto Rico, and West Germany.

Tight operations and controls also characterize the company. Rules and procedures abound at UPS, with everything from safe-driving to worker dress codes to facilities cleanliness specified in detail. All tasks relating to the pick-up, sorting, transport and delivery of parcels is carefully programmed following strict productivity standards. Workers and their supervisors know exactly what is supposed to be done and how fast. To date, most of this has been handled manually, and UPS has avoided the high technology approach to delivery services chosen by its competitor Federal Express.

But now computer technology is coming to UPS also. The company was spurred into action by customer response to Federal's capabilities. They responded by first buying two small computer firms. Two years of work with these subsidiaries resulted in field testing of new computerized tracking devices—central dispatchers can follow progress of field vans by computer, drivers can record all their customer transactions by computer, drivers have access to computerized routing directions, and computer scanning can now speed parcels to delivery through more efficient sorting. Still, UPS which has previously done things "the old way" must adapt its ways and successfully integrate the new technology into its culture and operations.

UPS has more to integrate than technology alone, however, in its

Source: Information from Kenneth Labich, "Big Changes at Big Brown," *Fortune* (January 18, 1988), pp. 56–64; and, Larry Reibstein, "Turbulence Ahead: Federal Express Faces Challenges to its grip on Overnight Delivery," *The Wall Street Journal* (January 8, 1988), pp. 1, 8.

quest for dominance in the overnight express market. Air express is growing at a 30 percent rate at the company, whereas its ground business is growing at only about 7 percent. In response, UPS is expanding its plane fleet and building new air hubs on each coast.

UPS is expanding its plane fleet and building new air hubs on each coast.

All this requires hiring new personnel, many of whom will come into professional and even managerial positions without the UPS tradition of having "worked their way up." It also requires bringing the outsiders into the UPS corporate culture without adverse affects for those who are already a part of it.

Harvard Professor Jeffrey Sonnenfeld believes this will be accomplished without too much difficulty, since "people will make things work out because they want their company to succeed." However, there are signs of unrest beginning to appear in the company's unionized labor force, where union leaders are complaining that tough productivity standards are starting to "harrass" workers as management continually pushes for productivity increases. The company also experienced difficulty in its new overseas operations trying to get its West German employees to adapt. By hiring some German managers and learning how to respond to local tastes, it finally was able to work through some of the cultural and language differences which almost caused the new venture to fail.

UPS thus blends a strong dose of tradition guided by the continuing influence of principles established by founder Casey, with a new sense of drive in a highly competitive environment. New technology, expanded size, and a larger workforce are part of an aggressive market posture. UPS is spending heavily to establish many of the same services as its arch-rival Federal Express—continuous tracking of packages, letter-drop boxes, and store counters. The company which prides itself on washing each and every one of its vehicles everyday, is also pursuing an extensive campaign to broaden its image with the public. A $35 million advertising program promotes the message— "We run the tightest ship in the shipping business." While doing so, UPS executives are also busy planning for the future where they believe electronic data transfer will have a major effect on the transportation industry.

Federal Express CEO Frederick Smith, had the same vision some five years ago. He invested heavily in a new product called Zapmail, a document transmission service, and failed. Federal Express pulled out of

---

. . . union leaders are complaining that tough productivity standards are starting to "harrass" workers . . .

---

this market after taking a tax write-off of $190 million. Yet, UPS plans to forge ahead in this risky market. Strategic planning manager Wesley Hughes says, "In ten years we will be a big player in the field."

Federal Express, of course isn't just sitting by while UPS steps up the pressure. Federal is expanding into UPS's mainstay "loading dock" market for big parcels, where it faces risks too. But Federal has already started a major advertising campaign depicting itself as a major player in this part of the market that UPS has totally dominated in the past.

How will it all turn out in this high stakes confrontation between two industry giants? Harvard Professor Sonnenfeld speaks confidently about UPS's ability to make the necessary changes. He feels the company is inspiring to its employees who "feel their mission is pure, and they seem to find that exhilarating." Other experts see continuing strength on the part of Federal Express. They bet that if Federal can cut costs enough to keep prices within reach of those charged by UPS, its established reputation and momentum will meet the test of added competition.

QUESTIONS

1. Complete a "SWOT" analysis of the strategic planning challenges confronting UPS. What are the major strengths from which the company should try to formulate its future strategies? What are the primary weaknesses it must overcome to do so successfully?

2. Use Porter's competitive model to analyze the position of UPS in its industry. Based upon this analysis, do you feel the current strategy of UPS as presented in the case is a good one? Explain your answer along with any strategy changes which you might recommend.

3. To what extent does "corporate culture" play a role in the ability of UPS to successfully implement its chosen strategy? Is the UPS strategy consistent with this culture or not. What are the overall implications of this match/mismatch for effective strategy implementation? ■

ORGANIZING FOR PRODUCTIVITY

The Future of Workplace Alternatives

The question of how to get organized for success is a pressing one, and it has many possible answers. Modern managers are discovering that they must explore and become familiar with a wide array of organizational forms. The most appropriate structure is not necessarily an inherited one, or even one that works for a competitor; rather, it is the structure most likely to enhance productivity and the prospects for long-term success.

In this Perspective we'll look at some nontraditional ways to organize workplaces. Many thoughtful observers argue that organizationally, the keys to success are flexibility and streamlining. Tom Peters, co-author of *A Passion for Excellence,* refers to the desirability of "lean-form" organizations—ones capable of creative as well as efficient responses to a competitive environment. Let's look at how this translates in practice.

NOTES
1. Tom Peters and Nancy Austin, "A Passion for Excellence," *Fortune* (May 13, 1985), p. 23; and Rosabeth Moss Kanter, David V. Summers, and Barry A. Stein, "The Future of Workplace Alternatives," *Management Review* (July 1986), p. 30.
2. "Getting Man and Machine to Live Happily Ever After," *Business Week* (April 20, 1987), p. 61.
3. "Detroit vs. the UAW: At Odds Over Teamwork," *Business Week* (August 24, 1987), pp. 54–55.
4. Rosabeth Moss Kanter, *The Change Masters* (New York: Simon & Schuster, 1974). The example is from Kanter, "All That Glitters Is Not Gold," *Wall Street Journal* (July 22, 1985), p. 14.
5. Quotes from John McCormick and Bill Powell, "Management for the 1990s," *Newsweek* (April 25, 1988), pp. 47–48.
6. John W. Gardner, "The Moral Aspect of Leadership," *New Management,* Vol. 5 (1988), p. 12.

"THE WORKER OF THE 1990S HAS TO BE CAPABLE OF AUTONOMOUS ACTION."

SEEKING PRODUCTIVITY

American workplaces have been evolving in fundamental ways for several decades. Alternative work practices—"flex-time," quality circles, teams—are increasingly accepted as the norm in some industries, and most organizations have at least entertained the idea of experimenting with workplace alternatives.

One important and accelerating trend in both new and mature organizations is the trimming and decentralizing of managerial staffs. Along with this goes delegation of increased responsibility to smaller divisional groups—a trend far past the tinkering stage; large businesses such as Campbell Soup and Hewlett-Packard are making major structural changes along decentralized lines.[1] According to several management experts, flatter alternatives to hierarchical top-down structures "are becoming permanent fixtures rather than passing, fads," although the benefits of such alternatives are not always adequately understood or publicized.

REDESIGNING JOBS

Some observers, pointing to shop-floor practices that are now "moving into the ranks of professionals and managers," maintain that job design itself is undergoing a revolution. At Westinghouse, for instance, workers have considerable decision-making authority; using computer-aided design techniques, they can "switch rapidly from one special order to another"—a situation that has brought about a major productivity increase.[2] Teamwork, an approach to job design that is gaining in popularity, has contributed significantly to rises in both productivity and profits in some sectors. At New United Motor Manufacturing Inc., GM–Toyota's joint venture, teams allow the plant to make roughly the same number of cars with half the workers. Teams at NUMMI have also reduced the need for relief workers, minimized boredom, and maximized worker flexibility.[3] For such innovations as work-

> ... workplace redesign is
> the wave of the future ...

place alternatives and redesigned jobs to be viable, managers must be willing to give up power—and all workers must be prepared to perform in a less hierarchical and more cooperative environment.

Peters argues that in the future, every employee must be an "owner," which he defines as "part of the strategic information stream of the business." Moreover, as employees gain more control and acquire more responsibility, the distribution of rewards will also have to change—a fact that is sure to meet with resistance in some corporate cultures.

CHOOSING STRUCTURES

If the goal is to increase operational efficiency as well as encourage creativity and innovation, what is the best organizational structure for success? The answer depends, naturally, on the organization—and finding it requires imagination and a willingness to stay open to possibilities and change.

Rosabeth Moss Kanter, author of *The Change Masters,* cautions that some companies may be "in danger of going overboard" in the "unorganized and unintegrated" direction. Kanter cites the misfortunes of an instrument manufacturer that decentralized to the extreme and assigned all long-range planning responsibility to division managers. Flaws became apparent as each division planned for itself and found reasons not to cooperate with other divisions; as a result, the company missed major opportunities.[4]

Yet for every organization there is an appropriate structure, and man-

agement's job is to identify it. Much is made of the need for looser structures—and often success does lie in decentralizing. But jumping on the bandwagon of a particular structure, no matter how exciting it sounds in theory, is no guarantee of a good fit. Hewlett-Packard is an interesting instance of a company searching for a way through the many structural possibilities open to it. Facing ebbs in earnings, Hewlett-Packard took the controversial step of centralizing all purchasing for manufacturing—an action that cut against the organization's historically decentralized way of operating. CEO John Young was certain that this move was needed to further the goal of standardizing the Spectrum computer line's design. Hewlett-Packard kept its focus on R&D for the Spectrum line, despite concerns about earnings and structure. The corporation achieved the desired design standardization—and reaped dramatic profits from it.[5]

MAKING COMMITMENTS

Structural change, even when it's for the clear good of the organization, is

> ... managers must be
> willing to give up power.

often wrenching. Morale may suffer as employees and managers alike question the direction of change and worry about the shape of the future. Ongoing and honest communication is essential so that everyone is aware of the possibilities. Another key ingredient is articulation by management of a broad goal to which cost cutting is logically connected. At Cummins Engine, for example, CEO Henry Schacht made quality improvement the main corporate

> CHARACTERISTICS OF
> THE NEW WORKPLACE
>
> - Flatter organization structures
> - Self-contained work units
> - Decentralized decision making
> - Enriched individual jobs
> - More "teamwork"
> - Emphasis on participation and worker involvement

goal—and when personnel reductions were needed, Schacht took, in his words, "a slice off the pyramid" at every level, not just at the bottom. The layoffs made sense, in light of the stated goal, and they were done fairly in the eyes of remaining employees.

Richard Foster of McKinsey & Company, a leading management consulting firm, maintains that the 1990s will be a showdown between "attackers—those who try to make money by changing the order of things—[and] defenders, those who protect the status quo." He and others argue that in this battle, positive employee morale becomes a crucial weapon. The innovator, says Foster, "is often more powerful than he appears, because he is more motivated." And Daniel Greenberg, CEO of Electro Rent Corporation, stresses that being open to options for organizational structure implies a very different relationship between employee and manager. "The more you want people to have creative ideas and solve difficult problems," says Greenberg, "the less you can afford to manage them with terror."

Of course, a new relationship brings with it a large responsibility for management: that of ensuring that the right people are hired. The

> Structural change ... is
> often wrenching.

worker of the 1990s and beyond has to be tolerant of flexible ways of operating and capable of a fair degree of autonomous action. He or she must also be comfortable with constant advances in technology—which often translate into ongoing training. Clearly, employees who are unenthusiastic about such conditions will not deal well with jobs in which they must actively help management handle the task of learning about, adapting to, and integrating new technologies.

Job security has much to do with workers' willingness to share such responsibility, of course. But along with guaranteeing that wherever possible employees will be retrained for new work rather than losing old jobs, managers must also consider the util-

---

. . . in the future, every employee must be an "owner."

---

ity of "gain-sharing" and "pay-for-knowledge" compensation programs—and then find workers who are excited about them. Simply demanding allegiance is not enough; the incentives must be genuine and powerful. What this boils down to, in the eyes of some experts, is the need for organizations run according to solid "sociotechnical" guidelines—that is, principles for balancing employees' psychological needs with the requirements of technology. Author

John Gardner eloquently describes the kind of attitude that characterizes the balanced organization: "an attitude that is fiercely impatient with impediments to healthy growth and that never ceases to seek out the undiscovered possibilities in each of us."[6]

A growing number of observers believe that the momentum for change already exists, and workplace redesign is the wave of the future. Organizations that do not at least consider changing their structures will risk appearing old-fashioned. The greatest challenge lies in achieving the correct fit between situational demands and the supporting structures necessary to meet them. Chapters 6 through 9 contain information and insights to help you meet that challenge. ■

Fundamentals of Organizing

Smashing the Corporate Pyramid

Nucor Corporation proves beyond a doubt that streamlining can make for strength in the domestic "minimill" steel industry. Over the past several years, Nucor's CEO, F. Kenneth Iverson, has steered the once-failing company on an impressive course of steady growth and rising profits. Iverson is convinced that Nucor's managerial philosophy is the mainstay of its success. He sums up the core of this philosophy in no uncertain terms: "The most important thing American industry needs to do is to reduce the number of management layers." Iverson has definitely followed his own advice. Nucor is a prime example of a lean-form organization—anti-bureaucratic, decentralized, and highly responsive to the marketplace as well as to its employees' need for job security.

When Nucor first began making steel, Iverson bet on the company's ability to outflank large steel mills by surpassing their productivity levels. He put together a trim management structure with only four layers, and he pushed decentralized decision making. Each of Nucor's divisions has operational autonomy, and all of its workers are rewarded with bonuses on the basis of their productivity. If Nucor gains, so do they; if it suffers, everyone—including Iverson—feels the pinch, in what the CEO calls his "share-the-pain" program. Moreover, workers and managers wear the same color hardhats, have the same number of vacation days, and everyone shares a strong sense of job security. That sense is bolstered by the fact that Nucor almost never lays off employees for lack of work. Nucor's top managers believe that all employees have a right to feel that "if they are doing their job properly, they will have a job tomorow." And Iverson is convinced that a streamlined organizational structure works best when manages are given plenty of latitude to make decisions on their own. "Everyone who works lives in some kind of cage," he once explained. "You can't have anarchy, so I want to set the bars of the cage as far out as possible so every manager has the opportunity to rattle around in his own style."

With sales now over $750 million, Nucor's profits increased over one 10-year period by a whopping 1250 percent. An extraordinary success story, Nucor is also an illuminating example of the benefits of a trim organizational structure. Ken Iverson picks up his own phone. He also heads one of the most productive and best-paid teams in the world. ■

Source: Information from David L. Fortney, "The Little Steel Mill That Could," Reader's Digest (August 1985), pp. 110–114; "Iverson: Smashing the Corporate Pyramid," *Business Week* (January 21, 1985), p. 71; and Tom Peters, "There Are No Excellent Companies," *Fortune* (April 27, 1987), p. 348.

Organizing, the process of dividing and coordinating work among many people, is the second management function. This chapter contributes to your understanding of management by introducing the following topics.

Organizing as a
    Management Function
Organization Structure
Structure from a Manager's
    Perspective
Departmentation
Vertical Coordination
Horizontal Coordination

The overwhelming majority of all people in developed societies are employees of an organization; they derive their livelihood from the collected income of an organization, see their opportunities for career and success primarily as opportunities within an organization, and define their social status largely through their position within the ranks of an organization.

Peter F. Drucker

With these words Peter Drucker quite clearly identifies the importance of organizations in modern society and to our individual lives. This point has been implicit to our thinking throughout the prior chapters. Indeed, as Drucker also says—"In a society of organizations, *managing* becomes a social function and *management* the constitutive, the determining, the differential organ of society."[1] Organizations must be well managed, in other words, to best serve their social purposes. The chapter opening example of the Nucor Corporation shows how the management insights and leadership of Ken Iverson helped one company organize itself to achieve high productivity. Such progressive thinking can improve operations in organizations of all types and sizes. With this point in mind, it is now time to develop a more fundamental understanding of organizations as (1) instruments of work that produce essential goods and services for society, and (2) work settings within which managers and other persons apply their efforts.

Our study begins by revisiting the concept of organization itself. In Chapter 1, an **organization** was defined as a collection of people in a division of labor working together to achieve a common purpose. The four basic elements in this definition are the foundation for this and the next three chapters in Part 3. These elements are:

1. *Collection of people* The very reason for organizations to exist at all is to combine the efforts of many people to accomplish more than they are otherwise capable of doing. This is called **synergy,** the creation of a whole that is greater than the sum of its individual parts.

2. *Division of labor* The work of the organization must be subdivided and allocated as specific tasks to be performed by individuals and groups. This process of dividing up the labor is called **specialization.** It allows people to develop skills and expertise appropriate to their assigned tasks, and thereby gain in performance effectiveness.

3. *Working together* The separate and specialized activities of many people must be *coordinated* if synergy is to be achieved. Unless people work together, their accomplishments will fail to benefit the organization's overall performance objectives.

4. *Common purpose* This is the mission of the organization. It offers a common sense of direction to all concerned. This is a point of unity around which the division of labor is implemented and coordinated.

ORGANIZING AS A MANAGEMENT FUNCTION

Organizing is the second management function. Once plans are created, the manager's task is to "organize" the human and physical resources properly to carry them out. There is an important difference, though, between the thing we call "organization" and the management function called "organizing." *Organization* (the noun) results from or is created by the efforts of managers to *"organize"* (the verb). **Organizing,** therefore, is a process of dividing work into manageable components and coordinating results to serve a specific purpose.

Figure 6.1 depicts this critical role of organizing as one of the managerial functions. Organizing helps turn plans into performance results. It is the basis for defining tasks, allocating resources to them, and arranging resources and tasks in productive combinations. The benefits of good organizing efforts by managers are many. When done well, organizing—

- Clarifies who is supposed to do what.
- Clarifies who is in charge of whom.
- Clarifies channels for communication.
- Focuses resources on objectives.

As indicated in the figure, planning sets the stage for organizing activities by managers. Given the existence of plans that identify what needs to be done, a manager's responsibilities for organizing include deciding how to

- Divide required work into smaller tasks.
- Assign tasks to capable people.
- Allocate necessary supporting resources.
- Coordinate work to achieve desired results.

In the vocabulary of management, this decision making must address two fundamental questions.

1. *How should work efforts and workers be specialized in a division of labor?* That is, how should the multiple components of the organization be *differentiated* from one another?
2. *How should work efforts and workers be coordinated in return?* That is, how should the multiple components of the organization be *integrated* to ensure a common result?

Underlying these two seemingly straightforward questions lies a perplexing dynamic. The differentiation of work tasks creates a corresponding

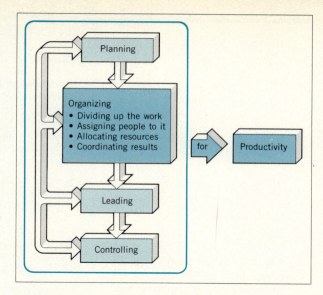

FIGURE 6.1 *Organizing for productivity—viewed in relationship with the other management functions.*

need for integration if a common purpose is to be served. As differentiation increases, however, integration becomes ever more difficult. Thus, managers are continually challenged to achieve the right amounts of both differentiation and integration when organizing the resources under their control. This challenge is highlighted in the international business arena in *Newsline 6.1.*

ORGANIZATION STRUCTURE

The **structure** of an organization is the formal system of working relationships that divide up and coordinate both the tasks to be done, and the resources—human and material—needed to do them. High productivity depends on both resources and structures being appropriate to the tasks at hand. One without the other will be insufficient to ensure performance success. Structure helps arrange the resources of organizations in productive task combinations.

Selecting and implementing the "best" structure for an organization or one of its subunits, accordingly, is an important and continuing managerial concern. As a PepsiCo vice-president says, "We

CITICORP♦VICKERS DA COSTA

Foreseeing an increasingly global market, the advertising firm of Young & Rubicam recently combined two joint ventures to create HDM, a multinational agency with offices in over 20 countries. Its worldwide chairperson is a Frenchman, Alain de Pouzilhac, and its president and CEO is an American, Tim Pollak; a third senior executive is Japanese. Pollak and de Pouzilhac were strangers before the merger, but both relish the creative side of advertising—and both are enthusiastic about HDM's prospects. Having recently opened an office in Beijing, where HDM is the only full-service international ad agency, Pollak describes China as "a new kind of adventure." Says his colleague de Pouzilhac: "China is so big a market you can't be important in that area without an office there."

Europe, too, is big—and it will get bigger when tariff barriers are lifted, thereby turning the continent into a truly common market. Faced with over 330 million potential customers in a borderless market, European and foreign businesses are likely to invest vast sums in media advertising—and HDM is getting set to assist them.

Source: As reported in Philip H. Dougherty, "HDM Takes a Global Approach," *New York Times* (April 13, 1988), p. D17.

---

are always looking at ways to improve our organizational structure."[2] **Restructuring** is a word you frequently read and hear about in this context. It refers to managerial efforts to *reorganize* or change an organization's structure in the attempt to increase productivity and otherwise improve performance. This is a complex issue that will be addressed throughout this chapter and the next. For now, let's use a short case to introduce the challenges of choosing organization structures.

ILLUSTRATIVE CASE:
THE RESTRUCTURING OF GENERAL FOODS

It was a Monday morning in August when Philip L. Smith, General Food's Chairperson, confirmed the rumors.[3] The company would be reorganized in the attempt to streamline operations and increase profits at the lagging food producer. Under pressure from its parent company Philip Morris, GF's top management are trying to transform the company into a lean and efficient marketing machine by changing its structure.

Under Smith's plan, the firm will be split into three operating divisions, each to be headed by a president and run as separate companies. Each president will be accountable to Smith for the division's performance, but will have the autonomy to run their operations as they see fit. The three new divisions group similar product lines together. They are General Foods USA—which handles such products as Jello and Kool-Aid, General Foods Coffee; International—responsible for Maxwell House, Sanka and related brands—and Oscar Mayer Foods; with its meat packaging products.

A large percentage of GF's corporate staff personnel will also be eliminated. Smith believes the company was carrying far too many staff people, and that the "top-heavy" structure was delaying critical decisions. Under the old system, eight levels of managerial approval were needed before a product manager could proceed with an annual business plan. These procedures not only slowed things down, but reduced individual initiative in the firm. "Under the new approach, each manager will be freer to make important decisions—and will be held accountable for them," Smith says. If he is right, the restructuring should get GF's products more quickly to the marketplace, reduce costs, and increase productivity.

For his part, Smith is concerned that the change in structure may result in morale problems. He admits that, "this plan may require some fine tuning." And he recognizes that building appropriate organization structures is a continuing task. "Breaking the company up into small components has to be leading in the right direction," he says, while going on to note: "If it doesn't take us all the way to where we need to go, we will do something else."

Organization Charts and the Formal Structure

You know the concept of structure best in the form of an **organization chart,** that is, a diagram describing the basic arrangement of work positions within an organization. Charts such as the one in Figure 6.2 convey useful information about an organization's basic structure. From an organization chart, one can typically determine

1. *The division of work.* Each box on an organization chart represents a position to which work is assigned along with someone to do it.
2. *Type of work performed.* The position titles convey the nature of the work assigned to the position holder.
3. *Supervisor–subordinate relationships.* The lines between positions show who reports to whom in the hierarchy of authority.
4. *Communication channels.* The lines on the chart show formal channels for the transfer of information throughout the organization.
5. *Subunit groups or components.* A complete organization chart shows how various positions are grouped together under common managers to form subunits, often called divisions or departments.
6. *The levels of management.* A complete organization chart shows management levels in the entire hierarchy of authority.

A typical organization chart, in summary, shows the various components in an organization's basic division of labor and the lines of formal authority and communciation linking them to one another. Because of this, these charts are said to

FIGURE 6.2 *Organization chart: a partial look at the top-management structure of a community college.*

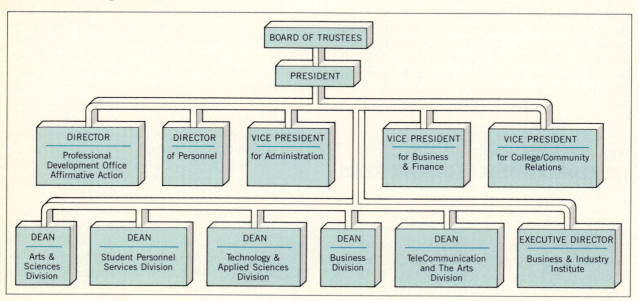

represent the **formal structure** of the organization. This is the structure of the organization in its ideal state—it depicts the way the organization is intended to function.

The Informal Structure

There is often a difference between what is described in the organization chart and the ways things really get done day to day in an organization. Behind every formal structure typically lies a shadow organization. This "structure behind the structure"—this set of unofficial but critical working relationships, this pattern of actual daily work activity—is the **informal structure.**

No manager can succeed without understanding both the formal and informal structures of his or her work setting. For example[4]

> When Bill Smith graduated from engineering school and joined the laboratory of a large manufacturing company, he was assigned the task of supervising four laboratory technicians who checked production samples. In some ways he did supervise them, but in other ways he was restricted by the group itself, which was quite frustrating. He soon found that each technician protected the others so that it was difficult to fix responsibility for sloppy work. The group appeared to restrict its work in such a way that about the same number of tests were made every day regardless of his urging to speed up the work. Although Bill was the designated supervisor, he observed that many times the technicians, instead of coming to him, took problems to an older technician across the aisle in another

section. Bill soon realized that these situations were evidence of an informal organization and that he had to work with it as well as the formal organization.

Figure 6.3 contrasts the formal and informal structures present in this case. Note that although the technicians formally report to Bill, they informally defer to an older technician in another unit for guidance. Bill must learn to work with the informal structure that includes this external person, as well as the formal structure that does not.

Potential Benefits of Informal Structures

Informal structures can be helpful in organizations. In particular, they can help supplement formal structures to better deal with changing times, new or unusual situations, and diverse human needs. The potential benefits of informal structures include helping organizational members to:

- Accomplish their work
- Overcome limits of the formal structure.
- Communicate with one another.
- Support and protect one another.
- Satisfy social needs.
- Gain a sense of identification and status.

Potential Costs of Informal Structures

Potential costs or disadvantages are also associated with informal structures. Because they exist outside the formal authority system, informal structures can be independent and at times prone to act contrary to the best interests of the organization as a whole.

FIGURE 6.3 *Contrasts between formal and informal structures: the case of an engineering laboratory.*

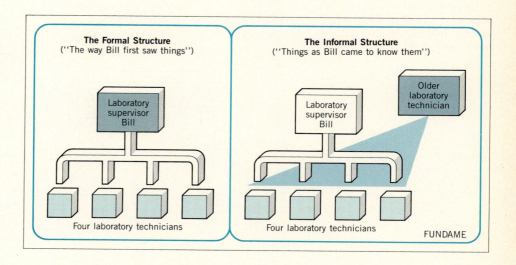

The Formal Structure
("The way Bill first saw things")

Laboratory supervisor Bill

Four laboratory technicians

The Informal Structure
("Things as Bill came to know them")

Laboratory supervisor Bill

Older laboratory technician

Four laboratory technicians

FUNDAME

Among the liabilities that may result are:

- Resistance to change.
- Diversion of managerial attention.
- Diversion of efforts from objectives.
- Susceptibility to rumor.

STRUCTURE FROM A MANAGER'S PERSPECTIVE

As shown in Figure 6.4, structure represents two things to a manager. First, structure is a characteristic of the setting within which a manager must work. It is the surrounding organization of which the manager and his or her work unit are smaller parts. A basic responsibility of every manager is to properly link the work unit with other components in the total organizational system. This requires an ability to understand the surrounding structures, and to be able to work well within them. "To work well" in this case means to obtain the support necessary to maintain work-unit productivity over time.

Second, structure is something managers create. In this case the manager's task is to ensure that the structures under his or her control do the best possible jobs of facilitating high performance. Middle-level or lower-level managers are responsible for properly structuring work units to accomplish their tasks and thereby contribute to organizational objectives; top managers are responsible for creating comprehensive structures for the organization as a whole. In both these cases, structuring is synonymous with organizing. "To structure" or "to organize" is to create an organization for accomplishing intended results through work.

Influences on Structure

Modern management theory addresses structure from a contingency perspective. The goal is to help managers identify and implement structures that best fit the demands of various situations. When structure "fits" or matches well with situational challenges, the organization is best prepared to achieve its performance objectives. From a contingency viewpoint, there are at least five major influences on structure: environment strategy, technology, people, and size. Chapter 7 is devoted to a review of these influences and their managerial implications. It addresses how, why, and with what implications such factors should and do impact managerial decisions that create structure for an organization or one of its subunits. In the meantime, several basic propositions can be stated.

1. *Structure should be appropriate to the external environment.* Environments pose different challenges to organizations depending on the complexity, variability, and uncertainty of their major components. Structures appropriate to one type of

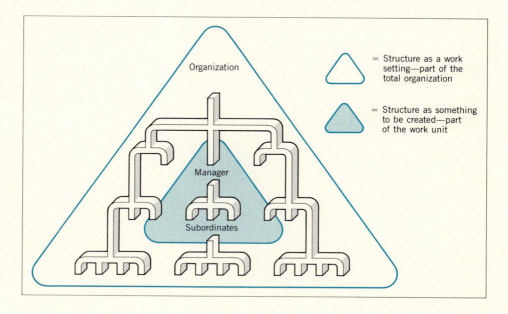

FIGURE 6.4 *Two managerial perspectives on organization structure: (1) as a work setting, and (2) as something to be created.*

Organization

Manager

Subordinates

= Structure as a work setting—part of the total organization

= Structure as something to be created—part of the work unit

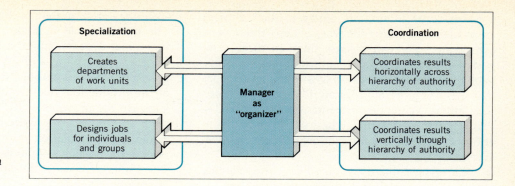

FIGURE 6.5 *Major elements in the specialization and coordination of work in organizations.*

environment may not work well in alternative ones.

2. *Structure should follow strategy.* An organization's structure should be consistent with and support the overall objectives of the organization and its strategy for achieving them.

3. *Structure should be appropriate to the basic technology of the organization.* Mass production of automobiles requires a different type of structural support than the process of refining oil. Likewise, the service intensity of a hospital emergency room requires a different strucure than the service routines of a bank.

4. *Structure should be appropriate to the people within the system.* People vary in their skills, interests, needs, and personalities. These individual differences must be accommodated by organization structures to maximize support for individual work efforts.

5. *Structure should accommodate organizational size.* As organizations grow they tend to become more complex in terms of people, technologies, functions, and even environments. These complexities, along with pressures of size, create additional need for structural accommodations.

Components of Structure

When it comes to creating effective organization structures, managers must do a good job of achieving both proper specialization and coordination. Figure 6.5 depicts these two action responsibilities in relationship to one another.

Specialization

Specialization is the process through which multiple work tasks are defined in a division of labor. Managers are concerned with specialization (1) by job design and (2) by departmentation.

Specialization by **job design** is the allocation of specific work tasks to individuals and groups. Chapter 8 is devoted exclusively to this topic. It is essential for a manager to know what choices are available when designing jobs for individuals and groups in the organization. Specialization by **departmentation** is the creation of work units or groups by placing several jobs under the authority of a common manager. Several alternative forms of departmentation will be discussed shortly.

Coordination

Once specialization has been accomplished, steps must be taken to integrate the resulting division of labor to accomplish overall organizational objectives. **Coordination** is the process of linking the specialized activities of individuals and groups to one another and ensuring that a common purpose is served. It provides for proper communication among organizational components, enables them to understand one another's activities, and helps them to work well together in the general work flow.

There are two dimensions of coordination to be accomplished: (1) vertical and (2) horizontal. **Vertical coordination** coordinates the activities of individuals and groups up and down the hierarchy of authority. **Horizontal coordination,** in contrast, cuts across the organization to coordinate the activities of individuals and groups working at or close to the same level in the hierarchy. Both dimensions of coordination will be discussed in this chapter.

DEPARTMENTATION

Departmentation, as noted earlier, is a process of grouping people and activities together under the supervision of a common manager. Many choices are available regarding the types of departments one can create.[5] We will discuss them in three categories—functional, divisional, and matrix forms. Each form has special advantages and disadvantages that make it more appropriate for some situations than others. When departmentation is done well— that is, when a good match between form and situation is achieved—it contributes to organizational success by[6]

■ *Clarifying authority relationships* by specifying who does what work and who reports to whom.

■ *Facilitating communication and control* by grouping together people with the same or related job responsibilities.

■ *Increasing decision quality* by helping to ensure decisions are made at points where appropriate information and competence are located.

Functional Departmentation

Functional departmentation groups together in the same organizational unit people performing similar or closely related activities. Functional structures are common in business organizations. The first example in Figure 6.6 shows the basic functional departments of a business—marketing, finance, production, and personnel. In this structure, all production problems are the responsibility of the production vice-president, marketing problems are the province of the marketing vice-president, and so on. The figure also shows how functional departmentation is done in other types of organizations such as schools and hospitals.

Functional structures are best suited for stable environments and strategies. They also work well in smaller and less complex organizations dealing with only one or a few products or services. Their major advantages and disadvantages are summarized in Table 6.1. The advantages derive from having people of similar technical expertise, interests, and responsibilities grouped together in one unit. Because these people tend to have similar training and professional development needs, functional departments provide good opportunities for specialized interests to be developed to the maximum. This creates economies of scale and helps form collegial work groups good at solving technical problems.

FIGURE 6.6 *Functional departmentation in a business firm, hospital, and school.*

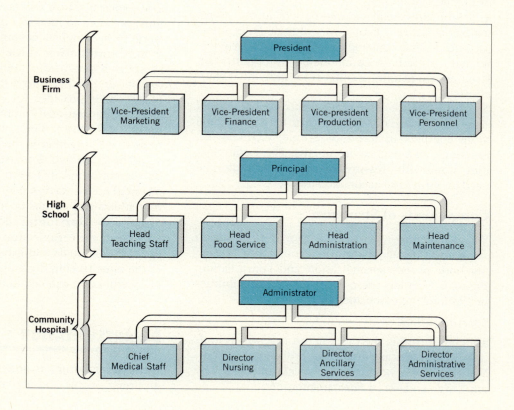

TABLE 6.1 *Potential Advantages and Disadvantages of Functional Departmentation*

Advantages of Functional Departmentation

Allows task assignments consistent with technical training	Allows economies of scale within functions
Supports in-depth training and skill development	Promotes high-quality technical problem solving
Reduces technical demands on the supervisor	Provides technical career paths

Disadvantages of Functional Departmentation

Reduced accountability for total product or service delivery	Overspecialization and restricted view of organizational objectives
Communication breakdowns across functions	Too many problems referred upward in hierarchy
Narrow, self-centered perspectives within functions	Slow response to environmental changes

Functional departmentation has potential disadvantages as well. Because the same good or service passes through the hands of many separate departments in the production process, it is sometimes hard to pinpoint responsibilities for error. Personnel in functional departments can also develop overly narrow and technical viewpoints that lose the total system perspective. Failures to communicate across department lines often lead to the referral of interdepartmental problems up the hierarchy for resolution. Response time to environmental changes becomes quite slow. Functional department heads, as a result, may spend too much time working on problems that should actually be resolved at lower levels.

Divisional Departmentation

Divisional departmentation is the formation of departments based on product, customer, territory, or time differences. Divisional structures are useful in organizations pursuing strategies of rapid and diversified growth, with differences among major product areas. They can help address the challenges of dynamic environments with changing problems and opportunities, that functional structures have difficulty dealing with. For example,[7]

at AT&T the company encountered difficulty coordinating activities in its new computer business. The solution was to reorganize from functional to divisional lines. Previously, AT&T's separate marketing, sales, development, and manufacturing activities made it difficult to translate customer needs into products. Their new computer-oriented division, based on product lines, was created to solve such problems and streamline operations.

Figure 6.7 shows divisional departmentation in various types of organizations. In each case attention is directed toward the special focus of the division, be it product, territory, client, or time. Some aspects of these different forms of divisional departmentation follow.[8]

■ *Product departmentation* groups together jobs and activities relating to a single product or service. Product divisions are common in large organizations. At IBM, for example, the Information Products Division has worldwide responsibility for typewriters, printers, copiers and associated supplies and programming. Product structures clearly identify managerial responsibilities for product lines. Costs, profits, problems, and successes can be traced to one central point of managerial responsibility. This not only creates product accountability, it also encourages managers to be responsive to changing market demands and customer tastes.

■ *Territory departmentation* groups together jobs and activities located in the same place or geographical region. IBM uses this form of departmentation both domestically and worldwide. It divides the United States into two marketing divisions—North-Central and South-West; in its World Trade Corporation it divides up the world into two groups—Asia-Pacific and Europe-Middle–East-Africa. Territorial or geographic structures like this are also quite common, especially among multinational corporations. They allow organizations to focus attention on the unique characteristics and requirements of particular regions and thereby achieve an appropriate differentiation of products/services.

■ *Customer departmentation* groups together jobs and activities that serve specific customers or clients. American Hospital Supply Corporation uses customer structures to give separate attention to its hospital and laboratory customers; many business firms use them to give separate customer attention to industrial firms and consumers; banks use them

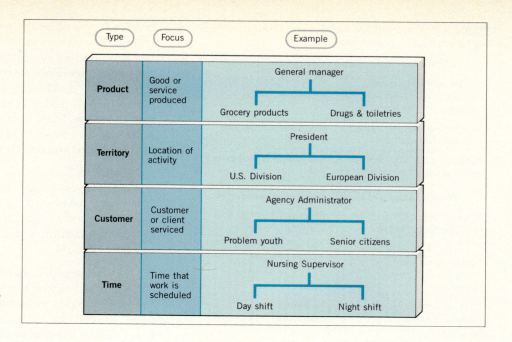

Type	Focus	Example
Product	Good or service produced	General manager — Grocery products / Drugs & toiletries
Territory	Location of activity	President — U.S. Division / European Division
Customer	Customer or client serviced	Agency Administrator — Problem youth / Senior citizens
Time	Time that work is scheduled	Nursing Supervisor — Day shift / Night shift

FIGURE 6.7 *Divisional departmentation accomplished by product, territory, customer, and time.*

to give separate attention to consumer and comercial customers for loans. The major appeal of these structures is the ability to develop special expertise in serving the special needs of separate customer groups.

■ *Time departmentation* groups together jobs and activities that are performed on the same work shift or time schedule. This is very common in organizations where certain operations extend across more than the standard eight-hour per day and five-day per week work schedules. Take the case of hospitals, most of which operate 24 hours per day seven days

TABLE 6.2 *Potential Advantages and Disadvantages of the Divisional Forms of Departmentation*

Advantages of Divisional Departmentation

Flexible in response to environmental changes	Concentrates functional attention on common tasks
Improves coordination across functions	Facilitates growth by adding new divisions

Disadvantages of Divisional Departmentation

May not allow for sufficient depth of technical expertise	Duplication of efforts across divisions
May overemphasize division versus organizational objectives	May result in unhealthy competition among divisions

a week. Organizing nurses by shifts—day, evening, and night—allows for management control across all hours of operation. Hotels, restaurants, airlines and many other service businesses also make use of time departmentation.

Organizations using the various forms of divisional departmentation hope to gain the advantages listed in Table 6.2. These include having departments that are more responsive to change, more sensitive to total system problems and opportunities, and more accommodating of the special needs or requirements of the persons, projects, or products represented in the divisional focus. As a result, the divisional form of departmentation is popular among large organizations with diverse operations cutting across many products, territories, and customers.

There are also potential disadvantages to departmentation by division. The table indicates that a divisional focus may reduce economies of scale as personnel and activities become duplicated across divisions. It can also result in less depth of technical competency and expertise in the functional areas and create situations where divisional objectives may be overemphasized to the detriment of the organization as a whole.

Finally, it is important to recognize that divisional and functional structures can be used in different parts of the same organization, and thereby allow different needs to be served.[9] Called the **hybrid structure,** this approach is depicted in Figure 6.8. In this case we see a large urban bank with branches in several sections of the city. The separate branch operations represent territorial divisions. Within each branch, functional departments such as personnel, marketing, and legal affairs give specialized support for bank operations. The branch operations in turn, are divided into three major product departments—loans, savings accounts and checking accounts. And within the loan departments, separate customer groups handle commercial and consumer loans.

Matrix Departmentation

A third basic form of departmentation is known as **matrix departmentation** or **matrix organization.** This approach combines functional and divisional structures in the *same* part of an organization to create a matrix of permanent cross-functional teams. It is an attempt to merge the technical advantages of functional structures with the integrating potential of divisional structures in situations requiring dedicated efforts to achieve specific product or project goals.

The example shown in Figure 6.9 is of a small manufacturing firm where several projects operate at any given time. These projects require expertise from each of the functions, but are different enough from one another to require special managerial attention. In the matrix, personnel are still employed in a standard functional hierarchy and report up this hierarchy to a functional department head. In addition, however, they are assigned to cross-functional teams focusing on specific projects or programs. These personnel represent the technical function on the team, but with a special focus on project objectives as well. Members of the project teams thus have a dual allegiance to higher authority: (1) to their respective functional managers, and (2) to the project manager. A design engineer, for example, would report to the engineering manager on functional matters as well as to a project manager on matters applying functional expertise to a project.

FIGURE 6.8 *Hybrid structure: the use of functional and divisional departmentation in a large urban bank.*

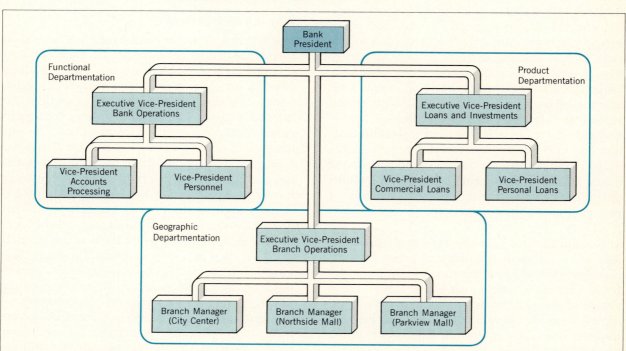

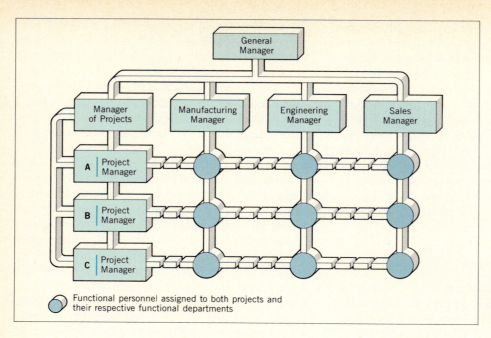

FIGURE 6.9 *Matrix departmentation in a small multi-project business firm.*

This "two-boss" system exemplifies the matrix concept.

Who Uses a Matrix?

The matrix form grew out of developments during the late 1950s and early 1960s in the U.S. aerospace industry.[10] It has now gained a strong foothold in industry, with promising applications in diverse settings such as manufacturing (e.g., aerospace, electronics, pharmaceuticals), service (e.g., banking, brokerage, retailing), professional (e.g., accounting, advertising, law), and nonprofit (e.g., city, state, and federal agencies, hospitals, universities). There is also growing awareness that matrix departmentation can help manage the complexity of multinational corporations. The flexibility offered by the matrix structure helps accommodate cross-national differences as well as multiple product, program, or project orientations. For example,

at General Electric a matrix structure helps organize work on various military projects. Program managers dedicted to weapons applications for different customers—Army, Air Force, Navy—are in charge of program teams consisting of persons assigned from all relevant functions. The program manager is available at any time to answer inquiries on the status of the weapons application; a common

focus on the program helps team members work together to solve problems; functional identities anchor team members in technical career paths, while giving the function special representation in program deliberations.

Why is a Matrix Used?

The advantages of the matrix form are several. It creates permanent cross-functional teams for decision making and problem solving. This stimulates interfunctional cooperation and provides a mechanism for handling diverse products or services in a balanced manner. It also makes it easy to change or grow in new product or service directions. The customer or client of a matrix organization always has a program manager available to respond to questions, provide status reports, address problems, or serve as a consultant. By the same token, chief executives such as the general manager in the last figure have similar access to both program and functional managers. This helps them know what is going on, right or wrong, and why. The matrix also forces decision making down to the lowest operating level where the necessary information exists. This frees top managers from many routine day-to-day problem-solving chores. As more decisions are made at the program level, these managers have more time to devote to strategic planning and the many external factors of organizational significance. Thus, the matrix is suited for organizations pursuing growth strategies in dynamic and complex environments.

The matrix also has limits. Some disadvantages of the matrix structure include:

1. *Power struggles*   The "two-boss" system can set up power struggles as functional and program managers each strive to attain maximum advantage for personal perspectives.
2. *Anarchy*   Unless great care is taken to clarify the workings of the "two-boss" system, employees may become confused when unable to identify appropriate higher authority.
3. *"Groupitis"*   Program teams may become too focused on themselves and the group process, and lose sight of production goals.
4. *Excessive cost*   The matrix adds overhead in extra salaries for program managers; this creates problems when the need for a matrix is not well established and/or a matrix operation is made more complex than necessary.

VERTICAL COORDINATION

Dividing up the labor by grouping people together into various types of departments is only one part of the manager's organizing responsibility. It is also necessary to properly coordinate results if the organization's purpose is to be adequately served. The multiple and differentiated parts of an organization must somehow be combined into a well functioning whole. The foundation for this coordination is authority.

Authority, you should recall from earlier chapters, is the right of command. It represents a right to take action and a right to expend resources. The upward and downward flow of authority from one managerial level to the next constitutes the organization's hierarchy of authority. **Vertical coordination** is the process of using the hierarchy of authority to help integrate the separate and specialized components of an organization.

What follows is an introduction to four fundamental elements in vertical coordination: (1) chain of command, (2) span of control, (3) delegation, and (4) centralization-decentralization. Each of these elements has received considerable attention throughout the history of management thought. The result is a series of classic principles of organization that are defined and critiqued in coming discussion.

Chain of Command

Let's use Figure 6.10 as a point of reference. It depicts four levels of management in the organization chart at Nucor Corporation, the innovative steel company highlighted in the chapter opener. The solid line in the figure shows the **chain of command,** or formal and unbroken line of authority that vertically links all persons with successively higher levels of management. The following principle from the classical school of management indicates how the chain of command should operate.

SCALAR PRINCIPLE

There should be a clear and unbroken chain of command linking every person in the organization with successively higher levels of authority up to and including the top manager.

One tendency in many organizations is for the chain of command to get very "long" and include many levels of management. This is one reason

FIGURE 6.10   *Four levels of management in the chain of command at Nucor Corporation.*

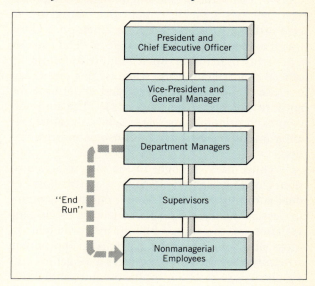

frequently cited for lingering inefficiencies and low productivity in some of America's industries—steel for one. In contrast to the complex chain of command at many of the large mills, however, some innovative structures are appearing in their smaller competitors. For example,[11]

at Nucor Corporation the firm has become well known as a very successful "mini-mill" company that operates with a very short chain of command. There are only three hierarchical levels standing between the nonmanagerial employees and CEO Ken Iverson. In most organizations of Nucor's size, there would be more levels of management. The firm's short chain of command is given as one of the reasons why it has been innovative and profitable in an industry beset by productivity problems.

A second classical management principle relates to how the chain of command is implemented in daily managerial practice. At issue is something called "unity of command."

UNITY-OF-COMMAND PRINCIPLE

Each person in an organization should report to one and only one supervisor.

By recommending that each subordinate report to only one supervisor, this principle's intention is to ensure clarity in the transmission of orders through the chain of command and continuity in the completion of work assignments. Violation of unity-of-command occurs when a higher-level manager bypasses someone's immediate supervisor to give orders to that person. This situation is illustrated in Figure 6.10 as a hypothetical "end run" by a department manager. Such a failure to follow the official chain of command when issuing orders can confuse the individual worker and undermine the authority of his or her supervisor. The unity-of-command principle, therefore, advises against creating multiple reporting relationships in organizations.

Think back, though, to the matrix organization. One of its central elements is a "two-boss" or dual-authority system. Although this runs contrary to classical advice, the matrix concept is a legitimate violation of the unity-of-command principle. In those situations where the matrix is an appropriate structure, the potential advantages to be gained outweigh such risks as the confusion and conflict just

mentioned. Furthermore, knowing full well that the matrix violates unity of command, matrix managers can take special precautions to avoid such problems. Working to ensure good communication between program managers, functional managers, and program team members is but one example of what can be done in this regard.

Span of Control

Span of control is the number of subordinates reporting directly to a manager. There was a time in the history of management thought when people searched for the ideal span of control. Although the magic number was never found, the following principle evolved.

SPAN-OF-CONTROL PRINCIPLE

There is a limit to the number of persons one manager can effectively supervise; care should be exercised to keep the span of control within manageable limits.

Factors Influencing Spans of Control

Even though an exact or ideal span of control can't be calculated, there are certain factors which set limits on how large or small spans of control should be in various situations. They include:[12]

1. *Similarity of tasks.* A supervisor can take on a broader span of control when subordinates are doing similar jobs. As the diversity of subordinates' tasks increases, closer supervision and a narrower span of control may be necessary.
2. *Complexity of tasks.* A supervisor can take on a broader span of control when the tasks performed by subordinates are routine and not very complex. Subordinates performing more complex tasks may need more frequent and direct assistance from the supervisor. This may require a narrower span of control.
3. *Competency of subordinates.* A supervisor can take on a broader span of control when subordinates are highly trained and possess strong technical skills. When subordinates are less competent in their jobs, a narrower span of control may be needed to allow more frequent and direct involvement of the supervisor.
4. *Physical proximity of subordinates.* A supervisor can take on a broader span of control when subordinates are working near one another. The

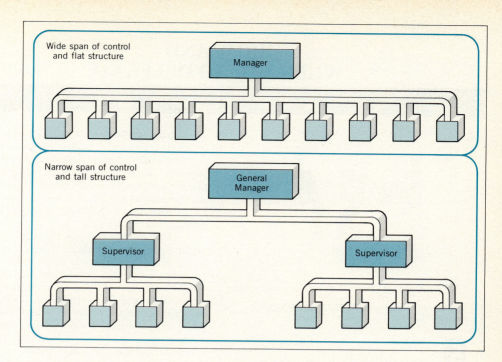

FIGURE 6.11 *Span of control: differences between "flat" and "tall" structures.*

farther apart subordinates are located, the more time required to maintain contact with them. This may require a narrower span of control.

5. *Required coordination in task performance.* A supervisor can take on a broader span of control when subordinates are independent of one another in performing their jobs. When the work of subordinates is highly interrelated and/or they must work closely with the supervisor in performing assigned tasks, a narrower span of control may be appropriate.

Span of Control and Levels in the Hierarchy

Span of control and the number of levels in an organization's heirarchy of authority are interrelated. Organizations with generally wider spans of control tend to be *flat*—they have few levels of management. Organizations with generally narrower spans of control tend to be *tall*—they have many levels of management. These differences are illustrated in Figure 6.11.

Whenever spans of control are reduced, the likelihood is that new management personnel will be added. Moving from the "flat" to the "tall" organization in the figure, for example, introduces an extra management level. Before making such a change, therefore, serious thought should always be

given to both the cost of the added supervision and the potential consequences of having more levels in the chain of command. As noted earlier, the number of management levels is a popular target for organizational cost-cutting or "downsizing" efforts. The removal of management levels—typically middle managers in particular—shortens the chain of command and can increase the autonomy of persons working for supervisors with wider spans of control. As Nucor Corporation demonstrates, many organizations function very well with relatively flat organization structures.

Delegation

All managers must decide how much work they should do themselves and what should be assigned to others. At issue is **delegation,** the process of distributing and entrusting work to other persons. Delegation involves "empowering" others so that they can exercise initiative and apply their skills in task performance. There are three steps in this process.

1. *The manager assigns responsibility.* The person who is delegating indicates what work or duties the subordinate is expected to do.
2. *The manager grants authority to act.* Along with the assigned work, the authority to take nec-

HOW AND
WHEN *NOT* TO DELEGATE

N E W S L I N E   6.2

"All I need is a chair, I delegate everything."

Drawing by Joseph Farris; © 1983 The New Yorker Magazine, Inc.

Several recent events in American corporate and political history point up some basic rules of management related to delegation. Peter Drucker has suggested that the Reagan administration violated a cardinal rule of management in the Iran-Contra scandal: "it confused delegation of authority with abdication of responsibility." Delegation, Drucker insists, "requires greater accountability and tighter control. . . . Above all it requires that the subordinate to whom a task is delegated keep the boss fully informed." The chaos that resulted from the administration's failure to obey this rule stands in contrast to the situation following Union Carbide's Bhopal toxic-leak disaster, when the company's CEO, Warren Anderson, accepted full responsibility and refused to delegate his duty to a subordinate.

These two instances are the extremes, one might argue—yet most executives regularly face situations in which they must decide how and when to delegate. James Jenks and John Kelly, two authors of a book on the subject, suggest that there are certain points at which delegation of responsibility or duties is inappropriate. When sudden changes occur, when power and prestige must be made visible, when policy is at issue, and when personnel must be praised, reprimanded, or discharged, it is important that managers do the job themselves. As these authors put it, "no matter how distasteful, disruptive, or dangerous some duties may be, certain ones should never be delegated."

Source: As reported in James Jenks and John Kelly, "When a Manager is Duty-Bound Not to Pass the Buck," *Wall Street Journal* (July 1, 1985), p. 10, and Peter Drucker, "Drucker on Management," *Wall Street Journal* (March 24, 1987), p. 32.

essary actions (such as to spend money, direct the work of others, use raw materials, or represent the organization to outsiders) is granted to the subordinate.

3. *The manager creates accountability.* In accepting an assignment, a subordinate takes on a direct obligation to the supervisor to complete the job as designed.

Responsibility, authority, and accountability are the foundation of vertical coordination through delegation. **Responsibility** is the obligation to perform that results when a subordinate accepts assigned tasks. **Authority** is delegated by the superior to provide the subordinate with sufficient rights of command to carry out the assigned tasks. **Accountability** is the requirement for a subordinate to an-swer to the supervisor for results accomplished in the performance of any assigned duties. It is a commitment by the subordinate to the supervisor to fulfill the obligation and carry out duties as agreed.

Another classical principle of organization warns managers not to delegate things to subordinates without giving them sufficient authority to perform. When the authority delegated is not equal to the responsibility created, the risk is reduced subordinate performance, confusion, and conflict—or all three.

AUTHORITY-AND-RESPONSIBILITY PRINCIPLE

Authority should equal responsibility when work is delegated from supervisor to subordinate.

A common managerial mistake is the failure to

delegate. Sometimes this is due to a lack of trust in others, or it may trace to personal inflexibility and insecurities in getting things accomplished. Whatever the reasons, however, failure to delegate can be damaging. It not only overloads the manager with work that could be done by others, it also robs others of many opportunities to fully utilize their talents and experience the satisfactions of responsibility. A good example of what can happen when a manager is willing to empower others through delegation occurred—[13]

at Stew Leonard's   where good management and a commitment to customers has built "the world's largest dairy store." One Sunday night just before closing a customer was checking out. She had just finished telling the cashier that her family had just returned from vacation and she was buying food for the children's school lunches, when she discovered that she had left her purse at home. "Don't worry," said the cashier Betsy, "the next time you're in the store you can pay for your groceries." The customer asked: "Do you have the authority to let me walk out without paying . . . ?" Betsy said yes, but the customer double-checked with the manager. He said, "When it comes to keeping our customers happy . . . each of us has the authority to use our own best judgment and treat every customer the way we'd like to be treated ourselves." Needless to say, the happy customer told this story over and over again in the community—to Stew Leonard's great pleasure.

Another managerial mistake is the failure to do delegation right. *Newsline 6.2* provides some advice on this issue. Additional "ground rules" for delegating include:[14]

- Carefully choose who you delegate to.
- Make the assignment clear.
- Agree on standards of performance.
- Agree on a timetable of performance.
- Encourage and allow independent action.
- Show trust in the other person.
- Give feedback on performance.
- Recognize performance progress.
- Help out when things go wrong.
- Don't forget *your* accountability.

Centralization–Decentralization

A question frequently asked by managers is: "Should authority for most decisions be concen-

trated at the top levels of an organization, or should it be dispersed by extensive delegation throughout all levels of management?" The former approach is referred to as **centralization;** the latter is called **decentralization.**

No classical principle governs centralization–decentralization, but there is debate over which approach is "best." There are those who feel that only decentralization is consistent with the values found in free and democratic societies. Others feel that with knowledgeable people at the top of organizations there is no need to take important decisions out of their hands.

Centralization–decentralization does not have to be an "either/or" choice. Both approaches have legitimate roles to play. It is a matter for the effective manager to decide when each is most appropriate to maintain desired coordination, and then to be able to implement the decision well. In many ways, the real managerial issue is finding the proper blend of both for the organization or situation at hand. Two examples make this point.

At IBM   the firm's basic organizing philosophy, for example, involves "the centralization of control and decentralization of operations." This essentially means that lower levels have some discretion in selecting and implementing various means to accomplish objectives set by higher management.

At Nucor Corporation   a similar approach appears to work. The general manager of each division is responsible for the division as if it were a business by itself. CEO Iverson says, "The general managers are the ones who make the decisions. All I do is make sure everyone understands that's what we agreed on."

HORIZONTAL COORDINATION

The final topic for this chapter is **horizontal coordination**, the process through which activities are laterally integrated across levels instead of up and down the chain of command. The matrix form of departmentation is one example of how organizations can be structured to distribute authority in a way that improves lateral coordination among people and subunits. Other ways will be examined in Chapter 7. These include the formation of cross-functional teams, task forces, and liaison personnel.

When it comes to horizontal coordination in organizations, though, our attention must first go to line-staff relationships and the concept of functional authority.

Line and Staff Relations

Chapter 1 described the role of staff managers as supporting the activities of line managers by providing advice and technical assistance in their areas of expertise. When this staff role is effectively done throughout an organization, it helps ensure uniform and coordinated action with respect to relevant technical matters. In a large retail chain such as K-Mart or J. C. Penney, for example, line managers in each store make day-to-day operating decisions directly connected with the sale of merchandise. Staff specialists at the corporate or regional levels, though, provide direction and support so that all stores operate with the same credit, purchasing, employment, and advertising procedures. In this way, staff activities facilitate horizontal coordination across the many geographically dispersed stores.

Personal Staff versus Specialized Staff

Staff assignments can be made on either a personal or specialized basis. **Personal staff** appointments are "assistant-to" positions that provide special administrative support to higher-level positions. They help the higher managers extend time by assuming administrative details and other more routine matters. At IBM, several hundred managers are selected annually to serve for a year in such "administrative assistant" posts. The choicest assignments are to be in the half dozen or so persons chosen to assist on the CEO's personal staff.[15] In Figure 6.12, the assistant to the president is acting in a personal staff capacity.

    Specialized staff performs a technical service or provides special problem-solving expertise for other parts of the organization. Specialized staff can be a single person such as the corporate attorney shown in the figure, or a complete unit such as the personnel department also shown in the figure. Note that line relationships will still exist within staff units. For example, the figure shows that those persons assigned to the personnel staff unit are under the personnel director's formal line of authority.

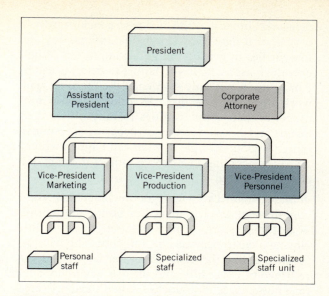

FIGURE 6.12 *Personal and specialized staff elements in an organization.*

Other specialized staff assignments you can expect to find in organizations include those concerning legal matters, public relations, advertising, planning, accounting, and labor relations.

Staff Authority vis-à-vis the Line Manager

The distinction between line and staff is not always clear-cut, and conflict in the working relations between line and staff personnel sometimes causes problems. It helps in this regard to clarify a continuum of staff authority in relationship to line personnel. At the one extreme, staff is purely *advisory* in its authority. A staff person can be consulted at a line manager's discretion and staff advice can be accepted or rejected at the line manager's discretion. At the other extreme is **functional authority**. This is the authority to direct the activities of other persons or units lying outside the formal chain of command. Here, staff managers and personnel are able to *require* that others do as requested—as long as those requests fall within the bounds of the staff's technical expertise. Functional authority, therefore, rests on special knowledge and extends only over matters to which this knowledge directly applies. For example, a personnel department may *advise* line managers on desired qualifications for hiring new workers (advisory authority); the personnel

CUTTING BACK
THE HEADQUARTERS STAFF

N E W S L I N E 6.3

Large corporate staffs used to be an accepted fact of organizational life, but no longer: lean-thinking CEOs are paring down corporate staffs to increase efficiency and reduce costs. Large size, it appears, is no reason for overstaffed headquarters—as Hanson Industries N.A. illustrates. Although Hanson has quadrupled in size in just a few years, its corporate staff numbers below 100—far less than the staffs of either USI or SCM, two of the companies Hanson has acquired. Hanson's corporate expenses are also impressively low—about 20 percent of the combined expenses of Hanson, SCM, and USI at the time of the merger. Hanson's corporate streamlining efforts extended to SCM's data services center, an $8 million drain on the budget. David Clarke, Hanson's CEO, justified these cuts by claiming that his executives were overloaded with data.

A growing number of CEOs, concerned about bloated corporate staffs, believe that operating managers should decide what corporate services they need and can pay for. At General Foods, for example, line managers allocate their divisions' resources to their own business interests. Not all companies are this radical, however. AT&T has decentralized some corporate services such as marketing but does not allow its operating managers to do without all staff services. Nonetheless, the trend is toward downsizing. Hanson's Clarke pondered the necessity of 30 outside consultants and asked himself: "Why should the company spend another $2 million a year to help me do my job?" Increasingly, other CEOs are wondering the same thing.

Source: As reported in Thomas Moore, "Goodbye, Corporate Staff," *Fortune* (December 21, 1987), pp. 65–76.

---

department may *require* the managers to follow equal-employment-opportunity hiring guidelines (functional authority).

Guidelines on the Use of Staff

The staff components of organizations support line managers with both administrative assistance and specialized technical expertise. *Newsline 6.3,* however, indicates that staff assignments can be overdone. At times they, too, become prime targets for cost-cutting and "downsizing" efforts.

There is really no one best way of dividing the work between line and staff in an organization. What is best for any given organization is a cost effective staff component that satisfies needs for specialized technical assistance.

At TRW Systems like other companies in the newsline, the approach that works best is "don't let them ever get too large." At one time TRW had fewer than 500 people on its corporate staff out of a total employment of nearly 100,000 employees.

At IBM on the other hand, things seems to work well on the principle of "don't let them ever stay too long in one place." The company rotates its managers between line and staff positions, trying to make sure no staff person is away from a line-management job for more than 18 months.

Summary

This chapter introduces organizing as a management function. Organizing is a process of dividing work into manageable components and coordinating results to serve the organization's purpose. Underlying this process is authority, the manager's right to command, the right to act, the right to allocate resources. Authority sets the stage for managerial decisions that initially create an appropriate division of labor and then coordinate results.

Two basic elements in specialization, the process through which the organizational division of labor is established, are: (1) forming work units or departments, and (2) designing specific jobs for individuals and groups. The latter topic is the subject of Chapter 8. The former involves departmentation, which can be accomplished through functional, divisional, and matrix forms.

The need for coordination among the multiple and specialized components of organizations can also be viewed as a two-dimensional managerial responsibility. In respect to vertical coordination, the goal is to establish appropriate authority relationships through the chain of command, span of control, delegation, and centralization-decentralization. Each issue is the subject of a classic principle of organization that still merits consideration by the modern manager.

Horizontal coordination, on the other hand, cuts across levels of authority. At issue here are good line-staff relations as well as more general lateral relations to be discussed in Chapter 7. As you put the present chapter in perspective, remember that managers must divide and then coordinate work to accomplish organizational objectives. This is what "organizing" is all about.

Thinking Through the Issues

1. Explain the importance of organizing relative to the other management functions.
2. Draw an organization chart for an organization with which you are familiar. Explain the hierarchy of authority as it applies to this organization.
3. What is the difference between the formal and informal structure of an organization? Give examples of each in a work situation with which you are familiar.
4. What does it mean to say that, for a manager, structure is (a) a characteristic of the work setting, and (b) something to be created?
5. How does specialization by job design differ from specialization by departmentation?
6. State four different ways an organization can use a divisional form of departmentation. Give examples of each.
7. How does a matrix organization combine the advantages of both the functional and divisional forms of departmentation?
8. State four classic principles of organization. Give a reason why each may be valid for the modern manager.
9. What is "functional authority" in line–staff relationships? Give an example.
10. Clarify the difference between personal and specialized staff in an organization.

The Manager's Vocabulary

Accountability
Authority
Centralization
Chain of command
Coordination
Customer
  departmentation
Decentralization
Delegation
Departmentation

Divisional
  departmentation
Formal structure
Functional authority
Functional
  departmentation
Horizontal
  coordination
Hybrid structure
Informal structure

Job design
Matrix
  departmentation
Organization
Organization chart
Organizing
Personal staff
Product
  departmentation
Responsibility

Restructuring
Span of control
Specialization
Specialized staff
Structure
Synergy
Territory
  departmentation
Time departmentation
Vertical coordination

Case Application

TECHNOLOGY SYSTEMS, INC.

Technology Systems, Inc. was founded by Carol King, an engineer. Initially the firm had about a dozen employees engaged in the manufacturing and assembly of a full line of high quality digital thermostats that Carol designed and patented. As sales expanded, Carol kept adding facilities and employees to handle the increased business. Originally the thermostats were sold to industrial customers, who were the mainstays of the business. Recently a "high-tech" version was developed to control the energy environments of fast-food restaurants. Considerably different from the industrial model, it requires special manufacturing attention. This thermostat has many potential buyers, and Carol feels it represents the possible "wave of the future" for the company.

Two years ago the company was purchased by a small conglomerate, Diversified Industries. Technology Systems was reorganized and Carol became president of the new company. At the time, Diversified's chief executive also recommended that the organization structure of Technology Systems be clearly defined.

Carol had never felt an organization chart was necessary, feeling "I've always done the thinking here." Even though accustomed to managing things on an informal basis, Carol set up the organization chart in Figure 6.13. This was done without consulting Diversified's management.

This organizational structure was put into effect. Carol proceeded to work frantically 12 to 14 hours each day. Much of the time was spent in the

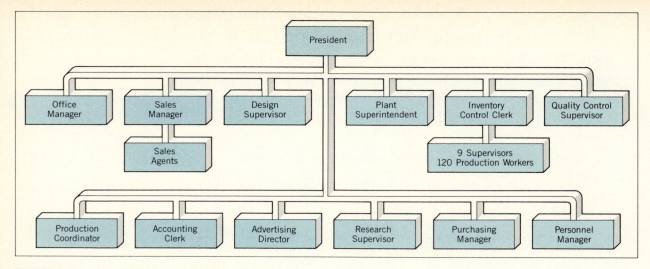

FIGURE 6.13 *Organization chart: Technology Systems, Inc.*

plant supervising the production line. When not supervising the manufacturing process, Carol would move from department to department solving one problem after another.

On one typical work day, Carol:

1. Told purchasing to change suppliers of the basic electric wiring.
2. Hired a new accounts receivable clerk and production worker.
3. Reviewed and made corrections on advertising copy for a national trade journal.
4. Expedited a shipment of thermostats for a long-time account.

After a year of this kind of activity, Carol began to feel that the structure was not functioning properly. There were continual machine breakdowns, sales were down, and profits were off. The new high-

tech thermostat was languishing, with some production difficulties and poor marketing. The problem, Carol felt, was friction between the department heads. They were just not cooperating. The only solution appeared to be—dismiss the "troublemakers" in charge of several of the departments and hire new and more cooperative ones. To complicate things further, a family physician told Carol to slow down.

Questions

1. Would dismissing the "troublemakers" remedy the situation for Carol? Why or why not?
2. What *is* the problem in this case?
3. Would a restructuring of the organization be appropriate? If so, what would you recommend and why?

Class Exercise: Corporation Profile

1. Southwestern Bell Corporation is headquartered in St. Louis.[17] With assets of about $20.3 billion, revenues of more than $7.9 billion, more than 8.8 million customers, and 67,490 employees, it ranks as one of the largest corporations in the world. The Southwestern Bell parent company provides overall financial management and strategic planning for four principal subsidiaries: Southwestern Bell Telephone Company (61,770 employees), Southwestern Bell Publications (4170) employees),

Southwesern Bell Telecom (840 employees), and Southwestern Bell Mobile Systems (250 employees).

2. Listed below are a number of position titles held by members of top management at the various companies. Read and think about the titles from a "structural" perspective. Arrange these job titles in an organization structure that you feel makes good sense. Draw this structure as a formal organization chart.

Corporation Officers

Chairperson and Chief Executive Officer
Vice-Chairperson Human Resources
Vice-Chairperson and Chief Financial Officer
Vice-Chairperson Strategic Planning

Telephone Company
Officers

President and Chief Executive Officer
Executive Vice-President Marketing and
 Operations
Executive Vice-President Finance and External
 Affairs
President Arkansas Division
President Missouri Division
President Texas Division
Vice-President Public Relations (Texas)
Vice-President Operations Staff (Texas)

Officers of Other Subsidiaries

President and Chief Executive Officer,
 Southwestern Bell Telecom
President and Chief Executive Officer,
 Southwestern Bell Mobile Systems

3. Identify on your organization chart *corporate staff positions* and *division staff positions*. Identify where your structure shows *functional* and *divisional departmentation*. Make sure your chart is logical and consistent.

4. Share your organization chart with a nearby classmate and discuss points raised in #3. Do the same in respect to your classmate's choice of structure. Does one structure seem more preferable than the other? Why or why not?

5. Be prepared to participate in class discussion led by your instructor.

References

[1]The two quotes are from Peter F. Drucker, "Management: The Problems of Success," *Academy of Management Executive,* Vol. 1 (1987), pp. 13–19.

[2]"PepsiCo Expected to Reorganize its Soft-Drink Line," *The Wall Street Journal* (February 1, 1988), p. 35.

[3]Information for this case is from Aimee L. Stern, "GF Tries the Old Restructure Ploy," *Business Month* (November 1987), pp. 37–39.

[4]This example is found in Keith Davis, *Human Relations at Work* (New York: McGraw-Hill, 1967), p. 212.

[5]For a discussion of departmentation, see H. I. Ansoff and R. G. Bradenburg, "A Language for Organization Design," *Management Science,* Vol. 17 (August 1971), pp. B705–731; Mariann Jelinek, "Organization Structure: The Basic Conformations," in Mariann Jelinek, Joseph A. Litterer, and Raymond E. Miles (eds.), *Organizations by Design: Theory and Practice* (Plano, Texas: Business Publications, 1981), pp. 293–302; Henry Mintzberg, "The Structuring of Organizations," pp. 276–304 in James Brian Quinn, Henry Mintzberg, and Robert M. James (eds.), *The Strategy Process: Concepts, Contexts, & Cases* (Englewood Cliffs, NJ: Prentice-Hall, 1988).

[6]David R. Hampton, *Contemporary Management,* Second Edition (New York: McGraw-Hill, 1981), p. 260.

[7]See "Bob Kavner Likes Hard Jobs. He'll Love This One," *Business Week* (July 25, 1988), pp. 64–66.

[8]These alternatives are well described by Mintzberg, op. cit.

[9]For a review of more complex structures see Robert B. Duncan, "What is the Right Structure?" *Organizational Dynamics,* Vol. 7 (979), pp. 59–80.

[10]Excellent reviews of matrix concepts are found in Stanley M. Davis and Paul R. Lawrence, *Matrix* (Reading, MA: Addison-Wesley, 1977); Paul R. Lawrence, Harvey F. Kolodny, and Stanley M. Davis, "The Human Side of the Matrix," *Organizational Dynamics,* Vol. 6 (1977), pp. 43–61; and, Harvey F. Kolodny, "Evolution to a Matrix Organization," *Academy of Management Review,* Vol. 4 (1979), pp. 543–553.

[11]Information on Nucor is found in *33 Metal Producing,* Vol. 24 (1986), and *Nucor Corporation 1986 Annual Report.* See also Richard E. Hattwick, "Business Leadership: Kenneth Iverson of NUCOR," *Journal of Behavioral Economics,* Vol. XVI (Fall 1987), pp. 97–104.

[12]See for example, David Van Fleet, "Span of Management Research and Issues," *Academy of Management Journal* Vol. 26 (1983), pp. 546–552.

[13]Information from Stew Leonard, "Love Your Customer," *Management Digest Quarterly,* Vol. 2 (1988), published by the American Management Associations.

[14]Developed from Roger Fritz, *Rate Your Executive Potential* (New York: John Wiley & Sons, 1988), pp. 185–186.

[15]See "Cultivating Tomorrow's Execs," *Industry Week* (July 27, 1987), pp. 33–38.

[16]Information from Carol Hymowitz, "Small-Business Owners Discover Giving Up Authority Isn't Easy," *The Wall Street Journal* (May 23, 1985), p. 29.

[17]Information from *Southwestern Bell Corporation Annual Report,* 1987.

Organizational Design

New Products: Picking Up the Pace

A tiger team, as Honeywell defines it, is a group of marketers, designers, and engineers on the prowl for new products—a team that collaborates closely in order to speed up the product development cycle. Honeywell's team recently came up with a new thermostat in a quarter of the time usually required to design and build one. "We told them to break all the rules," says vice-president John Bailey—"but get it done in 12 months."

Honeywell is not alone in its concern over the time it takes to bring products from conception to market. To be competitive, manufacturers are learning that they have to shorten development cycles—and that means rethinking the way things are usually done. At Xerox, Ford, Kodak, and Allen-Bradley (among many other companies), teams of employees from production, engineering, marketing, and design stick with a product from start to finish. They are discovering the benefits: faster responsiveness to potential niches in the market and more effective incorporation of new technologies in their businesses. At Allen-Bradley, for instance, the old methods of developing industrial controls, in which each department acted like a runner in a relay race, has been replaced by a team approach. All departments work together to develop products that meet customer needs and manufacturing requirements at the same time. Among the results is a new electrical contactor produced in a third of the time normally required.

Management authority Peter Drucker argues that R&D strategy for new product development needs to be "business-driven," not technology-driven. He cites as an example the Japanese development of VCRs: "They started out with a business goal and a business strategy and then put very small teams of highly competent people to work on the new science and technology needed. The Americans who had first put pictures on tape were technology-driven; they ended up with industrial applications for small, not-very-profitable niche markets." A strong advocate of teamwork, Drucker praises organizations that use "cross-functional" groups from marketing, finance, and manufacturing to guide R&D efforts from the beginning.

The Japanese are, of course, famous for their teamwork in the auto industry—and their approach is being heavily copied here. Honda calls its group discussions of new products *wai-gaya*—in essence, pow-wows with a business purpose. James Rucker, in charge of a GM group looking for new means of cutting lead-time, puts it another way. "We're not talking about rocket science here," he says. "We're talking about business discipline." ■

Source: Information from John Bussey and Douglas R. Sease, "Speeding Up," Wall Street Journal (February 23, 1988), p. 19; "U.S. Industry's Unfinished Struggle," New York Times (February 21, 1988), pp. 31–37; and Peter Drucker, "Best R&D Is Business-Driven," Wall Street Journal (February 10, 1988), p. 17.

The chapter opener illustrates how some organizations are changing their structures to improve teamwork, gain creativity, and shorten new product development cycles. Consider, too, the following set of newspaper headlines selected from the business press. Each headline introduces an article explaining how management in the subject firm is also modifying organization structures. While the exact responses vary, the firms are being reorganized in the attempt to improve their performance.[1]

LUFTHANSA JETTISONS BUREAUCRATIC BAGGAGE

MONSANTO RECOMBINES

At Lufthansa management is struggling to come to terms with rapid growth. A consulting firm recommended, among other things, changes in the firm's "duplicative and bureaucratic" ways. "From time to time, you must ask the question of what can be done better than before. A company with 40,000 employees is different from a company with 10,000," a senior consultant said.

At Monsanto the firm has restructured in response to the recommendations of an extensive high-level task force report. The objectives were to eliminate duplication of efforts, improve vertical coordination, and facilitate more growth. They recognized that the new structure alone couldn't guarantee future success. But as the president said, "While organization by itself doesn't get anything done, at the very least we ought to improve the odds and remove the impediments to success."

ORGANIZATIONAL DESIGN IN CONCEPT AND PRACTICE

What happened at each of these companies is an example of **organizational design,** the process of choosing and implementing an appropriate structural configuration for an organization and/or subunit. The purpose of organizational design activities like those just illustrated is twofold: (1) to better facilitate the flow of information people need to make decisions and successfully implement plans, and (2) to better coordinate diverse activities so that multiple components of an organization serve a common purpose. When done well, organizational design achieves a proper match between internal structures and such situational factors as environment, technology, strategy, size, and people.

As you read on, recall that structure is significant to any manager from two perspectives. As described in the last chapter:

1. *Managers must understand the structure of the total organization as a work setting.* Managers are

responsible for serving as good linkages between their subunits and other components of the organization. This task is made easier when a manager understands how the rest of the system is structured.

2. *Managers must make good choices to create structures in those portions of organizations under their direct control.* The president of a company, for example, must be sure the total organization is structured properly; a department manager is concerned about work-unit structure. Both must lead the process of organizational design in their areas of managerial responsibility.

This chapter builds upon the foundations of Chapter 6 to examine how managers can use contingency thinking to design organizations and subunits for productivity. To begin, it is important to admit that every organization is different. Rarely, if ever, will you find one organization or subunit whose needs and situational demands are exactly the same as another's. This means that any organization requires special attention from a design standpoint. The structures used at any given point in time should "fit" the organization's unique circumstances. In true contingency fashion, this is what top managements at Lufthansa and Monsanto were trying to achieve. They were trying to adjust existing structures in response to changing situations, and do so in such a way that organizational performance was enhanced.

ILLUSTRATIVE CASE:
IBM's CORPORATE OVERHAUL

When IBM Chairman John Akers addressed the gathering of stock analysts and reporters, they already knew what to expect. News had leaked the day before that the world's biggest computer maker, facing its third straight year of disappointing earnings, was reorganizing. A *Wall Street Journal* headline introduced the rest of the story—"IBM Unveils Sweeping Restructuring in Bid to Decentralize Decision-Making."[2]

At the heart of IBM's restructuring was Mr. Aker's belief that the company was too big and unwieldy to spot market niches and bring new products quickly to market. Old customers were switching their allegiance to other computer companies and complained that IBM was just taking too long to make new products available. As a result, the company's share of the personal computer market was declining at the same time that business was improving for other companies. Inside the firm, groups marketing rival products often competed against one another for the same customers. Akers was reported as believing too much of his time was spent resolving internal squabbles over "turf" and trying to unlock "logjams" delaying progress.

The announced changes in IBM's corporate structure were intended to correct these problems. The essentials of the reorganization involved:

■ Creation of IBM United States, a new organization with total responsibility to oversee all IBM operations in America. Named to head the new unit was Terry Lautenback, described as one of IBM's "toughest trouble shooters," and recognized as a possible future successor to Akers as the corporation's chief executive.

■ Creation of six main product and marketing groups within IBM United States. Each group is headed by a general manager with wide latitude in decision making. The goal is to speed up product development and respond more swiftly to changing technologies and consumer needs.

"This is a major delegation of authority," said Mr. Akers in describing the reorganization. "In many ways, we now have several IBM companies." He reemphasized his goal of making IBM faster at bringing out new products. And he noted that in coming years many corporate staff personnel would be reassigned to posts which bring them into closer contact with customers. When asked to comment on the changes, one of the company's directors said, "John [Akers] found everything was coming onto his desk, and he had more than he could cope with." Another director said, "he [Akers] wanted an organization which resolved more problems before they got to him."

Organizational Design:
A Problem-Solving Perspective

Organizational design is best viewed from a problem-solving perspective. John Akers reorganized IBM with the objective of speeding up product development and customer responsiveness. He was trying to achieve it through decentralization and the creation of new product divisions. Figure 7.1 depicts how such efforts at organizational design can serve problem-solving purposes. Note, of course,

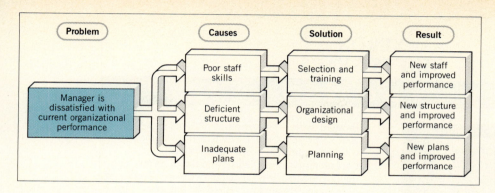

Problem	Causes	Solution	Result
Manager is dissatisfied with current organizational performance	Poor staff skills	Selection and training	New staff and improved performance
	Deficient structure	Organizational design	New structure and improved performance
	Inadequate plans	Planning	New plans and improved performance

FIGURE 7.1 *A problem-solving approach to organizational design.*

that the causes of poor performance may be something other than a deficient structure. In such cases managerial responses discussed elsewhere in the book may be needed. At the very least, though, structure should always be considered as a possible cause of performance problems.

Whenever a manager observes a difference between what the organization or subunit is capable of achieving and what is actually happening, efforts to redesign the organization may be called for. IBM had suffered declining performance for over three years before Akers took action to reorganize. When he finally did so, the increasing difficulty of top management to make responsive and timely decisions was a major stimulus to action. Indeed, observed breakdowns in managerial decision making are major symptoms or indicators that structural changes may be needed. These breakdowns include:

■ *Slow decision making.* By the time decisions get made, opportunities are missed or problems become magnified beyond reasonable solution. Decision makers may be *reacting* to situations, rather than being *proactive* in anticipating them. They may be bogged down in never-ending conflicts. They may also be overloaded with decisions that should be delegated, or they may not know it is their job to make decisions.

■ *Poor quality decision making.* The decisions which are being made do little to help achieve desired performance levels. Decision makers may be using poor, outdated, or limited information. They may be protecting self-interests or acting with narrow and incomplete viewpoints. And the wrong people may be making the decisions in the first place.

■ *Lack of innovation in decision making.* The decisions which are being made reveal little or no crea-

tivity in responding to problems or taking advantage of opportunities. Decision makers may be overly constrained by rules and procedures, too allegiant to traditional ways of doing things, and/or unaware of important information and developments elsewhere in the organization or in its environment.

What's at issue in these decision breakdowns is both information and people. Organizational design, accordingly, is an attempt to create structures which bring the right information to the right people in time to make and implement good decisions.

A CONTINGENCY APPROACH TO ORGANIZATIONAL DESIGN

Any discussion of organizational design necessarily begins with a thorough look at bureaucracy. A **bureaucracy,** as described in Chapter 2, is a form of organization described by the German sociologist Max Weber.[2] Many people, perhaps even yourself, view bureaucracy in a negative sense. For Weber, though, a bureaucracy was a desirable form of organization—and bureaucrats were the people who made it work.

Bureaucratic Features of Organizations

As first introduced in Chapter 2, the characteristics of an ideal bureaucracy include:

1. *A clear-cut division of labor.* Each position has well-defined authority and responsibility.
2. *Positions arranged in a hierarchy of authority.* Each lower-level position is supervised by a higher-level one.
3. *Positions staffed on the basis of technical compe-*

XEROX
SHIFTS GEARS

When Peter McColough became CEO of Xerox in 1966, he initiated much-needed managerial changes. Under Xerox's founder, Joseph Wilson, the corporation had become the leader of the copier market, but it suffered from lack of financial controls and a very loose organizational structure. McColough, a Harvard MBA, stressed professional management. He brought order—but too much of it, believes Xerox's present CEO, David Kearns, who took over from him. The corporation's stuffy, bureaucratic culture had slowed the decision-making process, introduced unnecessary layers of management, and prevented the business from responding quickly in a fast-paced market.

Kearns cut 15,000 employees, created small product-delivery teams, and urged diversification as a means of regaining a solid competitive posture. Xerox's new financial-services acquisitions now provide for half of the corporation's profits. In addition, Kearns, a quality fanatic, instructed his managers to reduce the number of vendors they used in order to tighten quality control. The quality drive in Xerox's $10 billion reprographics and information systems business resulted in savings of over $2 billion. Kearns believes that Wilson would be pleased to see his company now—bigger and stronger.

Source: As reported in "Culture Shock at Xerox," *Business Week* (Jun 22, 1987), pp. 106–110, and "Remaking the American CEO," *New York Times* (January 25, 1987), p. C-8.

---

tence. Appointments and promotions are based on expertise and competence.

4. *A formal system of impersonal rules and standards.* Uniformity and coordination are ensured by consistent application of written rules and standards.

You can see that the ideal bureaucracy is based on logic, order, and the legitimate use of formal authority. Organizations adopting these bureaucratic features are supposed to be orderly, fair, and highly efficient as a result. Notwithstanding these intentions, bureaucracies don't always function in the intended fashion.[4] As suggested in *Newsline 7.1*, the classic bureaucratic form of organization is prone to the following limitations in practice.

1. *Bureaucratic structures can be too rigid and formal.* Because they rely heavily on rules and procedures, bureaucracies are not well suited for rapidly changing and uncertain environments. It is difficult to change formal procedures to adapt to new conditions as they arise.

2. *Bureaucratic structures can become unwieldy as organizations grow in size.* As the number of levels in the hierarchy of authority increases, persons at higher management levels can grow increasingly out of touch with lower-level operations. Top management decisions may fail to reflect operational realities as a result.

3. *Overspecialization in bureaucratic structures can reduce employee initiative.* As jobs become more highly specialized and defined by procedures, individuals sacrifice autonomy and independence. Creativity and problem solving may be lost as people conform to rules instead of reaching out in new directions.

Beyond Bureaucracy

Modern management theory, instead of viewing all bureaucratic structures as inevitably flawed and dysfunctional whatever the circumstance, takes a "contingency" perspective on the issue. This approach to organizational design asks the questions:

1. When is a bureaucratic form the appropriate structural design for an organization?
2. What alternatives to bureaucracy can be used when it is not a good choice?

The contingency direction represented in the research conducted in England during the early 1960s by Tom Burns and George Stalker.[5] Their pioneering study helps us to think about what lies "beyond bureaucracy" and introduces a useful view of organizational design.

MECHANISTIC AND ORGANIC ORGANIZATIONS

The research of Burns and Stalker had roots in the open-systems view of organizations depicted in Figure 7.2. The external environment is an important variable in this perspective. It is the source of resource inputs, the consumer of product outputs, and the source of performance feedback. When theorists first recognized this input–output interdependency between the organization and its environment, they introduced a dynamic element into thinking about organization structures. Attention shifted away from seeking universal principles of organization and toward seeking the best fit between structure and a wide variety of environmental conditions that might exist.

Burns and Stalker investigated 20 manufacturing firms in England and Scotland. They concluded that two quite different organizational structures could be successful, depending on the nature of a firm's environment. The bureaucratic form of organization thrived when the environment was stable, but experienced difficulty when the environment was rapidly changing and uncertain. In the latter environments, successful organizations were less formal and more decentralized. They used a different type of structure that emphasized horizontal relations, flexibility, and managerial discretion. Each of these factors seemed to help the organizations solve problems and explore opportunities as their environments changed over time. Burns and Stalker called the two different but equally successful structures "mechanistic" and "organic" organizations, respectively. Figure 7.3 portrays them as opposite extremes on a continuum of organizational design strategies.

Later studies in the United States and elsewhere confirmed these results. Today, the literature of modern management theory recognizes there are many ways to run an organization, not just one. For any organization or subunit to survive and prosper over time, informed managers must choose and implement structures appropriate to the opportunities and problems that emerge in the environment.

Mechanistic Structures

Mechanistic structures are highly bureaucratic in form. As shown in Figure 7.3, they involve more

FIGURE 7.2

Organization–environment interdependencies in the open-systems view of organizations.

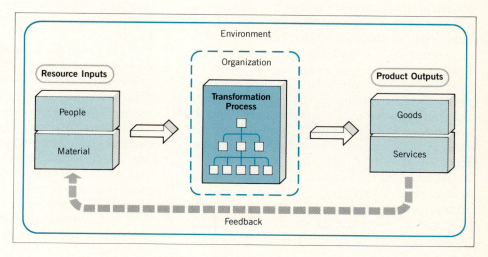

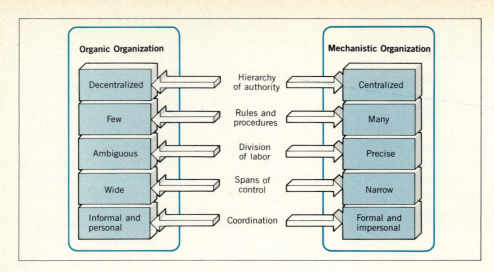

FIGURE 7.3 *A continuum of organizational design strategies: organic and mechanistic organizations.*

centralized authority, many rules and procedures, a precise division of labor, narrow spans of control, and formal and impersonal means of coordination. Decision making in mechanistic structures adheres to the chain of command. A good example of a successful organization designed on a mechanistic configuration is found—[6]

at McDonald's where your local restaurant is a relatively small operation that focuses on quality, and thrives on consistency of both product and service. Each store operates just like every other and under the close guidance of corporate management. Local personnel work in orderly and disciplined ways guided by the many rules and procedures found in a 300+ page operations manual. A clear division of labor is in effect as crew leaders in special uniforms work along side counter personnel and cooks, each of whom knows exactly what to do— but, always does it under the watchful eye of a supervisor. The latest in technology facilitates not only "fast" food preparation, but the creation of exactly the same products each and every time in each and every store. Once again, the rules and procedures specify just how the human factor is to work with the machine to achieve desired performance.

As based on the bureaucratic model, this type of mechanistic design tends to work best for organizations operating under certain conditions in relatively stable environments. In the case of McDonald's, in fact, the company is so strong in the

fast-food business that it tends to create the environment to which its competitors must then respond.

Henry Mintzberg identifies three distinct bureaucratic forms of the mechanistic organization.[7] They vary in the size of middle management, administrative support staff, and technical/professional staff. As shown in Figure 7.4, these forms are:

1. *The machine bureaucracy.* This structure is common to mass-production organizations performing highly specialized and standardized work. It consists of a clear hierarchy of authority with a large middle management group. Line personnel are arranged in functional groupings and are assisted by large technical and supporting staffs. Authority for major decisions is concentrated at the top; there is relatively little decentralization. The machine bureaucracy works best in simple and stable environments.

2. *The professional bureaucracy.* Highly trained professional workers, such as those in hospitals and universities, are the mainstays of this structure. Standardization of skills allows for highly trained professionals to work with considerable autonomy. The structure becomes decentralized as professional workers make decisions within their areas of expertise. A large support staff backs up the professionals and handles administrative affairs. Middle management is relatively small. This structure works well in stable but complex environments.

3. *The divisionalized bureaucracy.* The divisionalized form operates with a number of separate in-

ternal units found under a common organizational umbrella. Divisions, formed according to product, client, or geographic differences, individually operate as machine bureaucracies. They are coordinated by top management working with a large technical support staff at the corporate level. This allows for considerable division autonomy while still providing necessary headquarters control. Divisionalized structures work best in diversified markets and stable environments.

Organic Structures

Criticisms of mechanistic structures are largely based on their lack of adaptability during times of change. In her book, *The Change Masters,* Rosabeth Moss Kanter picks up on this theme. She notes that the ability to respond quickly to today's rapidly changing environment distinguishes successful organizations from less successful ones. Specifically, Kanter states[8]

> The organizations now emerging as successful will be, above all, flexible; they will need to be able to bring particular resources together quickly, on the basis of

short-term recognition of new requirements and the necessary capacities to deal with them. They will be organizations . . . with a whole host of sensing mechanisms for recognizing emerging changes and their implications. . . . The balance between static plans—which appear to reduce the need for effective reaction—and structural flexibility needs to shift toward the latter.

The organic organization identified by Burns and Stalker has much in common with the adaptive and flexible systems envisioned by Kanter. Figure 7.3 summarizes the basic characteristics of **organic structures** as decentralized authority, fewer rules and procedures, less precise division of labor, wider spans of control, and informal and personal means of coordination. Whereas mechanistic structures tend to work best under stable conditions, organic structures do better when dynamic environments require flexibility in responding to changing conditions. For example,[9]

at Anchor Brewing Company the small San Francisco-based firm uses an organic design to good advantage. Founded and still run by Fritz Maytag,

FIGURE 7.4 *Structural profiles for mechanistic organizations: three different configurations.*

Source: Developed from Henry Mintzberg, "The Structuring of Organizations," pp. 300–303 in James Brian Quinn, Henry Mintzberg, and Robert M. James (eds.) *The Strategy Process: Concepts, Contexts, & Cases* (Englewood Cliffs, NJ: Prentice-Hall, 1988).

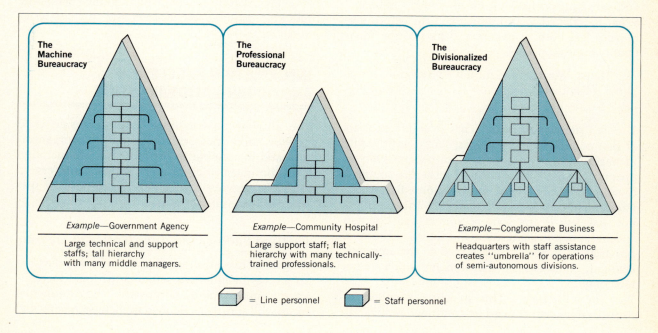

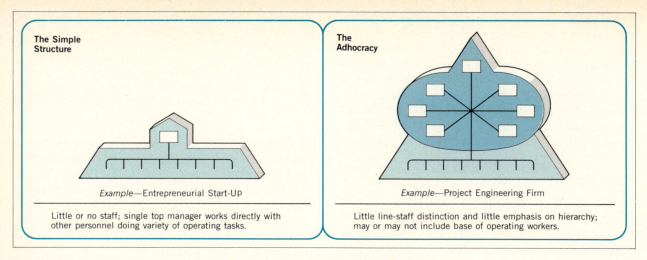

The Simple Structure	The Adhocracy
Example—Entrepreneurial Start-Up	*Example*—Project Engineering Firm
Little or no staff; single top manager works directly with other personnel doing variety of operating tasks.	Little line-staff distinction and little emphasis on hierarchy; may or may not include base of operating workers.

FIGURE 7.5 *Structural profiles for organic organizations: two different configurations.*

Source: Developed from Henry Mintzberg, "The Structuring of Organizations," pp. 300–303 in James Brian Quinn, Henry Mintzberg, and Robert M. James (eds.) *The Strategy Process: Concepts, Contexts, & Cases* (Englewood Cliffs, NJ: Prentice-Hall, 1988).

the company is a unique, flexible and innovative competitor that keeps the pressure on many larger firms in its industry. Maytag says, "We can brew wheat beer on Monday, barley wine on Tuesday, ale on Wednesday, steam beer on Thursday, Anchor Porter on Fridays." He notes that he delegates heavily, saying "I've always thought that it was more fun and satisfying to have all chiefs and no indians." What he created is an innovative firm whose employees feel both in charge and part of the high-quality brewing process.

Henry Mintzberg identifies two distinct forms of the organic organization.[10] As also shown in Figure 7.5, they are:

1. *The simple structure.* This structure consists of one or a few top managers, few if any middle managers, and the nonmanagerial persons who do operating work. This is a "lean" structure common to small entrepreneurial organizations. Because of its simplicity and centralized control, this organization has few if any staff personnel and operates without much formalization and standardization of activities. It is able to adapt well to dynamic and changing conditions in environments which are not too complex.

2. *The adhocracy.* This structure is suited for organizations that depend on continued innovation for success in dynamic and complex environments. In such settings, the mechanistic forms are too rigid and the simple structure is too centralized. Line-staff distinctions largely disappear as the adhocracy builds close lateral working relationships based on knowledge and expertise rather than authority. Highly decentralized, this organizational form creates networks within which highly skilled personnel can work together on projects and in cross-functional teams.

INFORMATION PROCESSING AND ORGANIZATIONAL DESIGN

The ultimate goal in organizational design is to provide supportive structures that help organizations and their subunits achieve high productivity. The contingency approach advises managers to choose structures that are appropriate to their specific operating circumstances.

Critical Factors in Organizational Design

Critical factors affecting the choice of organization structures include two sets of situational forces—environmental and contextual. Environmental forces will shortly be defined to include general and

TABLE 7.1 *Management Questions Regarding the Critical Factors in Organizational Design*

Critical Factors	Strategic Questions
External Environmental forces	
General & specific	What are the significant elements in the external environment, and what do we know about them?
Internal Contextual forces	
Strategy	What are the purpose, objectives, and basic strategy of the organization? What does management really want to achieve?
Technology	What are the basic tasks of the organization? How are equipment, tools, methods and knowledge used to accomplish these tasks?
Size	How many people does the organization employ, and what changes in workforce size are expected?
People	What types of people work in the organization, and what needs and expertise do they have?

specific factors in the external environment of the organization. Contextual forces include strategy, technology, size, and people.

Table 7.1 summarizes basic questions that can be asked relative to these critical factors. Answering the questions for a given organization provides a useful description of the environmental and contextual contingencies that bear important implications for organizational design. Although the answers will describe the situation facing an organization, they won't specify the preferred choice of organizational structure. To help managers get to this point, existing theory must be pushed one step further into the realm of information processing.

Information Processing as an Integrating Concept

Organizations are information-processing systems.[11] In order for plans to be set, actions taken, results evaluated, and corrective measures instituted, people must (1) have access to pertinent information and (2) process and interpret it properly as a basis for problem solving, decision making, and action. Information processing, in turn, becomes more difficult as the situation gets more uncertain.

A brief review of research on communication networks will help you clarify this developing argument. Figure 7.6 depicts two basic communication networks, the wheel and the all-channel. The center column in the figure summarizes research concluding that the all-channel network does a better job on complex tasks—that is, on diverse tasks with a large number of component elements. This success results when high interaction among members makes it easier to process the greater amounts of information required to solve complex problems. The wheel network, with more restricted information-processing capabilities, performs better at simple tasks.[12]

Look now at the right column in the figure. It equates the wheel network to a mechanistic structure that emphasizes the vertical hierarchy of authority as a basis for communication and problem solving. The all-channel network, by contrast, emphasizes lateral as well as vertical communication and interaction. This open flow of information is more characteristic of an organic structure.

The two ends on the continuum of organizational design strategies therefore offer different information-processing capabilities. Generally stated, organic structures better satisfy the information-processing requirements of complex problems common to more uncertain situations; mechanistic structures better satisfy the information-processing requirements of simpler problems found in more certain situations.

Figure 7.7 extends this point further. Those environmental and contextual forces considered critical factors in organizational design are so identified *because* they infuence situational uncertainty. We can now summarize the underlying argument of the contingency approach to organizational design as follows.

1. Structures should be consistent with the information-processing requirements of major problems facing decision makers.

2. Information processing required for successful problem solving increases as uncertainty in the situation increases.

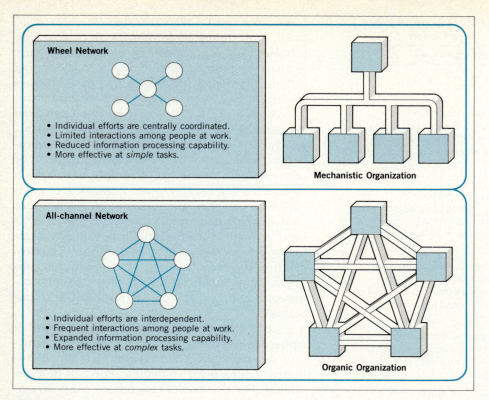

FIGURE 7.6 *Two group communication networks and their organizational design implications.*

FIGURE 7.7 *An information-processing view of organizational design.*

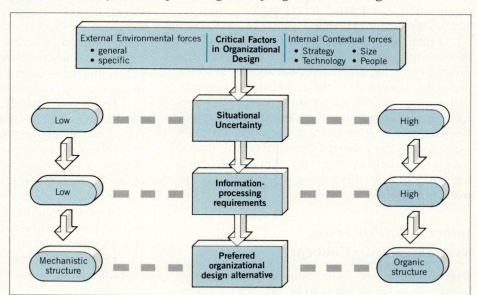

3. The degree of situational uncertainty is determined by critical factors in the external environment and internal context of the organization.

Our attention now shifts toward providing you with a means for analyzing environment and context to determine their organizational design implications.

EXTERNAL ENVIRONMENT

The external environment is an important factor in organizational design. Its influence is summarized in the following design guideline.

ORGANIZATIONAL DESIGN GUIDELINE NO. 1

When environmental uncertainty is high, a more organic structure is best; when environmental uncertainty is low, a more mechanistic structure is best.

Two questions logically follow from this guideline: (1) What determines environmental uncertainty? (2) What are the key elements in the external environment of organizations? Let's take first things first.

Environmental uncertainty is the rate and predictability of change associated with important environmental elements. A *certain environment* is composed of relatively stable and predictable elements. As a result, few changes in the goods or services produced, or in the manner of production, are necessary over time. Mechanistic structures, therefore, are quite adequate under such conditions. An *uncertain environment* will have more dynamic and less predictable elements. Changes occur frequently and may catch decision makers by surprise. As a result, organizational responses must be flexible and adaptive over relatively short time horizons. This requires more organic structures.

To create good structure/situation fits, however, managers must know what to look for when scanning environments to establish their organizational design implications. This requires awareness of both the general and specific components of the external environment.

The General Environment

The **general environment** consists of the socio-cultural, economic, technological, legal-political, and other background conditions which can substantially influence the operations of an organization. This portion of the environment forms a general context for managerial decision making as depicted in Figure 7.8, using the example of Pillsbury Company. Since we will refer to them on occasion throughout the remainder of this book, several general environmental components are highlighted here.

Socio-Cultural Conditions

Organizations are influenced by the general nature of the societies within which they operate. Social factors such as population demographics, family structures, educational opportunities and attainments, and value systems influence the nature of the available workforce as well as the tastes and expectations of customers. Cutural values indicate what actions are important, right, proper, and desirable from a societal perspective. They change slowly over time, vary widely across national and ethnic boundaries, and represent background social influences of significance to organizations. Organizations that operate in more than one country are particularly influenced by variations in cultural values. This issue is thoroughly reviewed in Chapter 19, "Managing in an International Arena."

Economic Conditions

The economic prosperity in a region substantially influences the amount of resources available to help organizations grow and develop, and the capability of consumers to buy goods and services produced. Economic prosperity encourages the growth of organizations, and changes in the economic health of a country or region can have a dramatic impact on their performance. In the early 1980s, for example, the American economy was sluggish and interest rates were exceptionally high. Chrysler came close to failure; Braniff Airways went out of business in 1982. The economy grew more favorable through the mid-1980s. Chrysler became a great success story and Braniff was back in business—albeit on a more limited scale than before. Then came "black Monday" and the great around-the-world stock market crashes of October 1987 . . . everyone won-

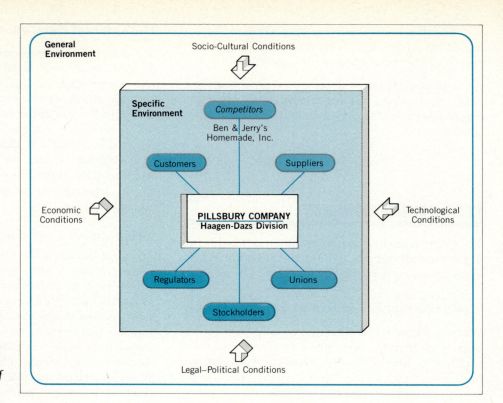

FIGURE 7.8 *General and specific environments of organizations: the case of Pillsbury Company.*

In the figure:

General Environment

Socio-Cultural Conditions

Specific Environment

Competitors
Ben & Jerry's Homemade, Inc.

Customers

Suppliers

PILLSBURY COMPANY
Haagen-Dazs Division

Economic Conditions

Technological Conditions

Regulators

Unions

Stockholders

Legal–Political Conditions

---

dered what would come next in an increasingly unpredictable and *global* economy!

Technological Conditions

The nature of technological opportunities is also important within the general environments of organizations. When you think of this issue, a number of dramatic examples come to mind. They include knowledge development in such areas as biotechnology, superconductivity, and advanced telecommunications, as well as continued advances in computers and electronic information processing. We live in an age where sophisticated microprocessors play ever more important roles in our daily lives. The nature of work is increasingly characterized by electronic word processing, electronic mail, desktop computing, computer-assisted design and manufacturing (CAD-CAM), robotics, and many other related capabilities. Many industries—automobile manufacturing for one—are changing as a result of these developments, and many others—such as biotechnology—are appearing entirely new to the scene. Yet it is not only the availability of technologies that counts in this dynamic environment; the

ability of organizations to access and effectively "manage" them is essential as well. The significance of technological conditions in the environment of organizations is well communicated in this headline from a series of ads once placed in *The Wall Street Journal* by the Motorola Company. The series was entitled—"Meeting the Japanese Challenge."

> Give American Workers
> the Right Tools
> and They Can
> Outperform Anybody
> in the World

Legal–Political Conditions

Governments influence organizations through the services they provide, and by laws and regulations that restrict certain actions while protecting other freedoms. The relative stability of this underlying legal–political framework is an important issue. Business firms within the United States must not only understand today's regulations on environmental pollution, they must also anticipate how these will change in the future. As we will discuss in

BEN & JERRY'S
TAKES PILLSBURY TO COURT

N E W S L I N E 7.2

Ben & Jerry's Homemade Inc., the small Vermont ice-cream maker, may be small—but it knows how to defend its turf in battles for market share. "What's the Doughboy afraid of?" was one of its taunts to Pillsbury Company, when Ben & Jerry's sued its big competitor, Pillsbury-owned Haagen-Dazs, for forcing its distributors to push Haagen-Dazs exclusively. At that time the two companies signed an out-of-court agreement, but recently they locked horns again in a legal battle. Ben & Jerry's accused Haagen-Dazs of violating the settlement's terms, and Haagen-Dazs appealed to annul a court-ordered extension of the original agreement.

Ben & Jerry's acknowledges that Haagen-Dazs was the first company to open up the premium ice-cream market, but its executives argue that Pillsbury has no right to "coerce" distributors. Now Ben & Jerry's is considering a new anti-Haagen-Dazs media blitz to keep the battle—and thus the B&J name—in the limelight. Anticipating expansion, the profitable little ice-cream company isn't going to pull its punches, as can be seen in its prospectus for an issue of debt for a new factory in Vermont. The prospectus contains examples of the lawsuit-publicity campaign—to illustrate, in its words, B&J's "innovative marketing techniques."

Source: As reported in "Is Haagen-Dazs Trying to Freeze Out Ben & Jerry's?" *Business Week* (December 7, 1987), p. 65.

Chapter 20, "Managing with Ethics and Social Responsibility," the legal–political system of a country is a major constraint within which both individuals and organizations must operate.

The Specific Environment

The **specific environment** consists of the actual organizations, groups, and persons with whom an organization must interact in order to survive and prosper. Depicted also in Figure 7.8, it represents the resource suppliers, regulators, clients, consumers and others, upon whom an organization depends for its existence. Sometimes called the *task environment,* the specific environment is different for each organization. For the typical business it consists of people and organizations of immediate consequence. Notice in the figure, for example, that

at Pillsbury Company an important element in the firm's specific environment is Ben & Jerry's Homemade, Inc. *Newsline 7.2* further introduces you to the issues involved here. Of particular interest is the importance of tiny Ben & Jerry's as a competitor to Pillsbury's much larger Haagen-Dazs division—so important, in fact, that some of the tactics used by Pillsbury are being questioned in court.

Thus, we have a two-fold illustration here. On the one hand, Ben & Jerry's and Pillsbury are part of each other's specific environments. On the other hand, the relationship between the two competitors calls into play the background significance of the U.S. legal environment and its regulations guiding business competition. This represents part of the general environment in which the two competitors operate.

INTERNAL ORGANIZATIONAL CONTEXT

In addition to the external environment, a manager must be prepared to analyze the internal **organizational context** for action. This includes its technology, size, strategy, and people. Each of these internal elements is another critical factor that may influence an organization's structure and performance.

Technology

Earlier we addressed the importance of background technological conditions in an organization's external environment. Now we refer to **technology**, in the more immediate and applied sense, as the combination of knowledge, equipment, and work methods used in the organization to transform resource inputs into product outputs. This is technology *as employed* in the organization to create goods and/or services. It represents the way tasks are accomplished using tools, techniques, and know-how. The availability of proper technology is a major element in efforts to increase productivity. It is a necessary form of support for the efforts of people in their jobs. And the nature of the technologies in use must be considered by managers when selecting and changing organizational structures.

Thompson's View of Technology

James D. Thompson classifies technologies as intensive, mediating, or long-linked.[13] In **intensive technology** there is uncertainty as to how to produce desired outcomes, and there is high interdependence among the members of the work force. People must be brought together to combine a variety of techniques and information creatively to solve problems. Examples include a hospital emergency-room team and members of a research and development laboratory. Standard operating procedures are difficult to define for an intensive technology. Coordination is achieved by mutual adjustments among people as they work together on a task.

Mediating technology links together parties seeking a mutually beneficial exchange of values. It is common in service industries. Banks, for example, link creditors and depositors in a way that pools their reliance on one another. If one creditor defaults on a loan, no one depositor is injured. Stockbrokers, real estate firms, employment agencies, retailers, and insurance companies are further examples of organizations using a mediating technology.

An automobile assembly line is a classic example of **long-linked technology.** This is a mass-production process relying on highly specialized jobs performed in a closely controlled sequence to create a final product. The long-linked technology is relatively inflexible and is most appropriate for very standardized tasks.

Woodward's View of Technology

Joan Woodward classifies manufacturing technology into three categories: small batch, mass production, and continuous process.[14] Each of these is illustrated in the accompanying photographs. In **small-batch production,** such as the bicycle shop, a variety of custom products are tailormade to fit customer specifications. The machinery and equipment used are generally not elaborate, and considerable individual craftsmanship is often needed. In **mass production** the organization produces a large number of one or a few products with an assembly-line type of system. The work of one person or group is highly dependent on others. Equipment is often mechanically sophisticated and accompanied by detailed instructions for workers. Mass production is the equivalent to Thompson's long-linked technology, and is well illustrated by the toy manufacturing assembly line. Organizations using **continuous-process technology** produce a few products through the continuous feeding of raw materials into a highly automated production system. Classic examples are automated chemical plants and oil refineries.

The Technological Imperative

In the early 1960s Joan Woodward conducted a study of technologies and structures in English manufacturing firms. Among some 100 manufacturing plants, she observed that structure varied systematically as technology changed from small-batch to mass production to continuous process. Even more significantly, she concluded that having the right combination of structure and technology was critical. Successful small-batch and continuous-process plants had flexible structures, while their more rigidly structured counterparts were less successful. Successful mass-production operations, by contrast, were rigidly structured. Their counterparts with flexible structures were less successful.

*Woodward's classification of manufacturing technologies is illustrated by this **small-batch specialty** bicycle shop, **continuous process** oil refinery, **and** mass production **toy factory.***

The summary implications of Woodward's research have become known as the **technological imperative;** that is, that technology is a major influence on organizational structure. Woodward's work thus contained the contingency theme that structure should vary in accordance with the nature of the prevailing technology. The more complex the technology in terms of its problem-solving requirements, the more organic the appropriate structure; the less complex the technology, the more mechanistic the appropriate structure. This general relationship can now be stated as another organizational design guideline.

ORGANIZATIONAL DESIGN GUIDELINE NO. 2

When technological complexity is high, such as in small-batch, continuous-process, and intensive technologies, a more organic structure is best; when technological complexity is low, as in long-linked, mass-production, and some mediating technologies, a more mechanistic structure is best.

Size

Size, typically measured by number of employees, is also an important factor in organizational design. Growth in size creates pressure to increase specialization and differentiation by adding departments, management levels, and even personnel with new types of expertise. The added complexity caused by this increased diversity among people and components can also cause coordination problems.

Research has sought to determine precisely how the problems and pressures of increased size relate to organizational structures. Although it is clear that larger organizations tend to have more mechanistic structures than smaller ones, it is not clear that this *should* be the case.[15] In fact one of the concerns about large organizations is that the tendency to become more bureaucratic limits their adaptability and responsiveness in changing environmental conditions. *Newsline 7.3,* however, indicates that many large firms manage to stay successful and innovative even while growing in size.

What may be most significant in this respect is that the more successful large firms find unique ways to overcome the disadvantages of increased size. They do this by organizing around many small subunits which are allowed to operate with consid-

CAN BIG STILL BE BEAUTIFUL?

The large corporation is a vanishing breed in the United States, say some experts; restructuring has changed forever its place in the business landscape. Indeed, the transformations are abundant—yet restructuring has not brought on doom for all large companies. Some, having made needed organizational refinements, are now flourishing. And in general, Fortune 500 companies are reaping about two-thirds of all profits in the United States.

The most successful of the giants manage their "core business"—those in which they are strongest—effectively, and they have gained experience in the whens and wheres of diversification. Economies of scale have helped, too. Borden, for example, makes both regional and national brands of pasta. Because it buys a huge volume of wheat to produce the pasta, Borden is able to get the wheat at a discount. Thus, it can now readily meet local tastes with its regional brands while enjoying a large national market share, both at low production costs—the ideal combination for a large organization. And Gulf & Western, once an unwieldy conglomerate, pared itself down to three areas of business on the basis of what its CEO, Martin Davis, perceived as its mainstays of managerial strength: publishing, entertainment, and financial services. Its net earnings rose almost $200 million in one five-year period as a result of this restructuring.

Deciding on the appropriate core businesses and making use of a restructuring strategy as "a permanent part of a company's response to shifting economic forces," in the words of GAF chief executive Samuel Heyman, are big challenges. And because restructuring has entailed heavy job losses in some cases, large corporations may face a renewed push for regulation—a fact that has some managers worrying about inadequate representation in Washington. Yet the big corporation still has its place in the sun, as the profit-share figures show.

Source: As reported in Walter Guzzardi, "Big Can Still Be Beautiful," *Fortune* (April 25, 1988), pp. 50–64.

---

erable autonomy within the total organizational framework. This approach is notably found[16]

at Campbell Soup which reorganized its traditional functional firm into more than 50 independent units—and experienced a five-fold increase in new product introductions.

at 3M Corporation whose top management believes that 200–300 persons is the upper limit for plant size—and has achieved a reputation for innovativeness that is the envy of other businesses.

Another structural way of managing large organizational size and still retaining the creative edge is through **intrapreneurship**, the pursuit of entrepreneurial behavior by individuals and subunits within large organizations.[17] This concept was popularized by the book *In Search of Excellence* when such subunits were given the name "skunkworks."[18] It has been used to good advantage[19]

at Apple Computer where a small group of highly creative and motivated persons created the MacIntosh computer. Under the direction of Steve Jobs, they worked together in a separate facility and free from the requirements governing Apple's more routine operations. The result was a highly innovative and successful product.

at Honeywell where a customer threatened to take

a request for a new thermostat to a competitor after being told Honeywell would need four years to develop it. The company swung into action and a special "tiger team"—highlighted in the chapter opener—was set up to do the job. Consisting of marketing, design, and engineering employees, the team was given total freedom. "We told them to break all the rules but get it done in 12 months," said John Biley, Honeywell's vice-president and general manager. The team did.

What is most significant about the prior two examples from an organization design perspective, is that the new products were developed by small "organic" structures which operated *inside* larger and more "mechanistic" corporate settings. More and more organizations are now making use of these **simultaneous structures**. In them, mechanistic and organic structures co-exist to accomplish organizational needs for both production efficiency and continued innovation. Of course the presence of simultaneous structures further complicates the management of multiple subunits in an already complex organization—a point addressed in a coming section on subsystems design.

Overall, new developments in organziation design show how larger firms are increasingly able to adopt many of the advantages commonly associated with smaller-sized operations. And the smaller organizations, in turn, appear to operate well with either mechanistic or organic structures, depending on other factors of environment and context. It is precisely this latter point—the apparent overshadowing of size-structure relationships by the influence of other factors—that makes it difficult for researchers to be more definitive in their conclusions. Thus, our third organizational design guideline is stated as follows.

ORGANIZATIONAL DESIGN GUIDELINE NO. 3

Organizations tend to adopt more mechanistic structures as they increase in size; however, organizations of any size may find the advantages of organic or mechanistic structures desirable, depending on the influence of other critical factors of environment and context.

Strategy

Chapter 6 made the point that strategy influences structure. Research on strategy–structure relationships largely originates with the pioneering work of Alfred Chandler, Jr.[20] He analyzed the histories of Du Pont, General Motors, Sears, and Standard Oil of New Jersey in depth and concluded that "structure follows strategy." That is, structure must support strategy if desired results are to be achieved. In this way, Chandler introduced contingency thinking in respect to strategy–structure relationships.

Chandler's work and the research that has followed can be interpreted in this fashion. When an organization pursues a stability strategy, this choice should be based on the premise that little change will be occurring in the external environment. Accordingly, the organization's structure should provide for great certainty in the relationship between operations and plans. This requires a more functional and mechanistic structure. When strategy is growth oriented, however, the situation as a whole becomes more complex and uncertain. Operations and plans are likely to require considerable change and adaptation over time. The appropriate structure is one that can facilitate and support the inevitable modifications. This structure will require decentralization and should be more organic.

This logic of matching strategy and structure is summarized as a fourth organizational design guideline.

ORGANIZATIONAL DESIGN GUIDELINE NO. 4

Stability strategies will be more successful when supported by mechanistic structures; growth strategies will be more successful when supported by organic structures.

Consider the situation—[21]

at Saatchi & Saatchi where ambition and rapid growth propelled a basement operation to the largest advertising-agency holding company in the world. Saatchi reached the top via frenzied acquisition, and now has offices in 80 countries with billings in excess of $8.3 billion. The founding brothers, Charles and Maurice, want to offer customers one-stop service on everything from advertising and public relations to management consulting to financial advice. But fast growth has created a need for more integration in this empire of many separate firms. Attempts are underway to build a structure that allows for "organic growth" and encourages client referrals among units. To fulfill their global strategy for becoming a premier business services company, the Saatchi brothers must now find a way to foster a degree of cooperation not yet seen among its many business units.

Thus, structure should help organizations implement strategy. When necessary, managers should adjust structure to be congruent with any changes in strategy.

People

The fourth critical factor in organizational context is people, the human resources that staff the organization for action. The characteristics of individuals staffing the organization are important to organizational design. But an initial word of caution is appropriate as you first consider the relationship between people and organizational structure. People are different, and they vary greatly in their reactions to organizational situations. What we refer to here about the *general* tendencies of people may or may not prove true for any one *individual*. Still, it is helpful to have a basis for thinking about appropriate people–structure relationships in a general sense.

Research on this subject involves a search for congruency. That is, it is recognized that organizational design should provide the human resources of organizations with the supporting structures they need to achieve both high performance and satisfaction. Chapter 2, for example, introduced Chris Argyris as a contributor to the behavioral school of management thought. He feels that the needs of a healthy and mature person are inconsistent with the constraints imposed on them by mechanistic structures. This "incongruency" thesis implicitly argues for organization structures to be more organic and less mechanistic in nature.

Modern theory moves beyond Argyris's viewpoint to address people–structure relationships in a contingency fashion. The prevailing argument is that there should be a good "fit" between structures and the people who staff them.[22] From the individual's perspective, this fit is influenced by those enduring aspects of personality and ability that predispose certain patterns of behavior. Because mechanistic structures are stable and well defined, they appeal to people who like task direction and more routine in their work. Because organic structures are flexible and less defined, they appeal to people wanting autonomy and more variety in their

work. Good examples are scientists and other professionals who often prefer to work with more freedom at complex and uncertain tasks. Given their advanced educations and expertise, the discipline and routine of a mechanistic structure most probably would *not* support these people well in their work.

As we move into later chapters of this book, the human resource, in both its individual and group forms, will become more and more a focus of attention. The "fit" between the person and organization will be addressed from many perspectives— including motivation and needs, group dynamics, leadership, and job designs. For now, we simply recognize that people do represent another critical factor in organizational design.

ORGANIZATIONAL DESIGN GUIDELINE NO. 5

Mechanistic structures will appeal more to persons prefering routine tasks and greater direction in their work; organic structures will appeal more to persons desiring autonomy and greater variety in their work.

SUBSYSTEM DESIGN

Use of the word *contingency* in the vocabulary of organizational design highlights the fact that there is no one best way for organizations to structure themselves. As we have said several times, organization structure must match key factors in environment and context. This point holds both for the organization as a whole, and for its subsystems.

A **subsystem** was defined in Chapter 2 as a single department or work unit headed by a manager and operating as a smaller part of a larger organization. A comprehensive approach to organizational design provides appropriate structures for each subsystem in an organization as well as proper coordination among them.

The Lawrence and Lorsch Study

A key study of organizational designs was reported in 1967 by Paul Lawrence and Jay Lorsch of Harvard University. They studied ten firms in three different industries—plastics, consumer foods, and containers.[23] The firms were chosen because they varied in their performance success; the industries were chosen because they represented different levels of environmental uncertainty. The plastics industry faced a highly uncertain environment composed of many diverse, changing, and unpredictable elements. The container industry operated at the other extreme in a very certain environment. In between was the consumer-goods industry in an environment of moderate uncertainty.

This research was unique in that it examined both the relationship between external environment and total system structure, and the relationship between the structures of subsystems and specific subcomponents of the firm's external environment. The results can be summarized as follows:

1. *The overall structures of successful firms in each industry matched their respective environmental challenges.* Successful plastics firms in uncertain environments had more organic structures; successful container firms in certain environments had more mechanistic structures.

2. *Subsystems in the successful firms had structures that matched the challenges of their respective subenvironments.* Different subsystems within a firm had to assume different structures to accommodate the special problems and opportunities of their respective subenvironments.

3. *Subsystems in the successful firms were well integrated with one another.* Subsystems in successful firms were well integrated, even when they maintained different structures.

Thus, Lawrence and Lorsch sensitize us to the fact that even within an organization, differences among subsystems will emerge. This occurs as each tries to position itself best to meet the special demands of its respective subenvironment. Indeed, the five organizational design guidelines already discussed apply equally well to the choice of subsystem structures. A given subsystem may be more mechanistic or organic in orientation, depending on the strategic factors in *its* environment and context.

Differentiation and Integration

Figure 7.9 depicts some basic operating differences between three divisions in one of the firms studied by Lawrence and Lorsch. The illustration shows how R&D, manufacturing and sales subunits adopt different perspectives and structures in response to their unique needs. This creates a special organiza-

FIGURE 7.9 *Key differences in perspective among the R&D and manufacturing and sales divisions in a consumer products firm.*

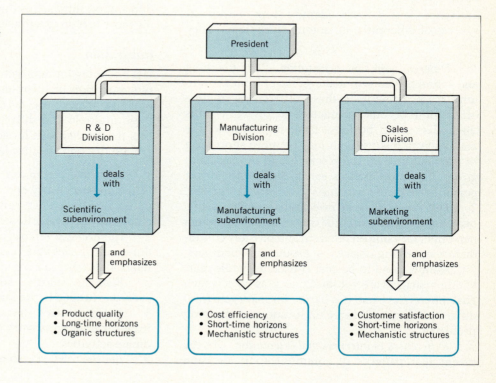

tional design problem—to allow for subsystems to develop unique characteristics, while still ensuring that resulting activities are properly coordinated to accomplish overall organizational objectives. Lawrence and Lorsch address this problem from the standpoint of differentiation and integration.

Differentiation is the degree of difference that exists among the internal elements of the organization. **Integration** is the level of coordination achieved among these elements. As subunits in organizations adopt different structures in response to their unique needs, they will and should become differentiated from one another. This differentiation, in turn, creates a need for management responses that ensure proper integration of the subunits into a well-functioning whole. Organizational design at the subsystem level involves selection of both differentiated structures and appropriate integrating mechanisms. A basic paradox makes this a particularly challenging managerial task.

> *Paradox.* Increased differentiation creates the need for greater integration. However, integration becomes more difficult to achieve as differentiation increases.

Differentiation

Lawrence and Lorsch identify four important sources of differentiation among subsystems. They are:

1. *Differences in time orientation.* The planning and action horizons of managers vary from short to long term. Sometimes these differences in time orientation become characteristic of work units themselves. In a business firm, for example, the manufacturing subsystem may be more short term in orientation than the research and development group. These differences can make it difficult for personnel from the two units to work well together.
2. *Differences in goal orientation.* The specific tasks assigned to a subunit can result in subsystem personnel focusing on different and possibly contradictory operating objectives. Production managers, for example, tend to be cost conscious, while marketing managers are volume conscious. When such goal differences exist, it is harder for managers from different subunits to agree on solutions to common problems.
3. *Differences in interpersonal orientation.* To the extent that patterns of communication, decision

making, and social interaction vary from one unit to the next, it may be harder for personnel from different subsystems to work together. The interpersonal "style" of the unit manager may also vary on such broad dimensions as strong "task" orientation to strong "people" orientation.
4. *Differences in structure.* The structure of subsystems will vary in the specialization of labor as well as in their overall tendencies toward a mechanistic or organic configuration. Structure affects the behavior and expectations of unit personnel. It may inhibit working relationships between units as a result. A manager from a mechanistic unit may well be bound by strict rules and procedures that limit his or her discretion in interunit negotiations. This could be quite frustrating for someone from a more organic unit who is used to flexible problem solving and is willing to make an on-the-spot decision.

In general, the Lawrence and Lorsch study suggests an organizational design guideline regarding levels of subsystem differentiation.

ORGANIZATIONAL DESIGN GUIDELINE NO. 6

Organizations facing more uncertain external environments will require greater internal differentiation among subsystems than will organizations facing more certain external environments.

Integration

It is one thing for managers to allow for appropriate differentiation in subsystem design; it is quite another to achieve the needed coordination among these multiple and differentiated units. Table 7.3 lists the mechanisms for achieving subsystem integration through effective lateral relations as:[24]

1. *Rules and procedures* Required activities and behaviors are clearly specified. People in different units know that when certain situations arise, specific rules are to be followed.
2. *Hierarchical referral* When rules and procedures are inadequate, coordination problems are referred upward to a common superior.
3. *Planning* Goals and targets are set to keep everyone headed in the same direction.
4. *Direct contact among managers* Managers from separate units work directly together to coordinate activities.
5. *Liaison roles* Persons are specially assigned to

TABLE 7.3 *Mechanisms for Creating Effective Lateral Relations among Subsystems in Organizations*

Mechanism for Lateral Relations	Complexity	Information-Processing Capacity	Organizational Design
Rules and procedures	Low	Low	Mechanistic
Hierarchical referral	↑	↑	↑
Planning			
Direct contacts			
Liaison roles			
Task forces			
Teams	↓	↓	↓
Matrix organizations	High	High	Organic

Source: Developed from Jay Galbraith, *Organizational Design* (Reading, Mass.: Addison-Wesley, 1977).

provide communication and coordination between units.

6. *Task forces* People from separate units are placed on a task force to coordinate activities for a specific period of time.

7. *Teams* Teams are similar to task forces, but are more permanent and have more decision-making authority.

8. *Matrix organizations* Permanent interunit coordination is fostered through the matrix form of departmentation.

The goal in subsystem design is to use the mechanism for lateral relations that accomplishes the required level of integration. When subsystem differentiation is low, an organization can rely on integrating mechanisms more common to mechanistic structures—rules and procedures and hierarchical referral. High differentiation requires more elaborate means for achieving integration. The trend toward the use of cross-functional teams for new product design and development, as discussed in the chapter opener, is one of the ways in which organizations are responding to this type of problem. As shown in the table, appropriate choices for integrating highly differentiated subsystems range from such teams or task forces to the use of a matrix approach. Each of these mechanisms for creating lateral relations is consistent with more organic structures. Our seventh and final organizational design guidelines follows accordingly.

ORGANIZATIONAL DESIGN GUIDELINE NO. 7

The greater the need for and difficulty of achieving integration among highly differentiated subsystems, the more an organization's mechanisms for creating lateral relations must shift toward task forces, teams, and the matrix, and away from rules, procedures, and hierarchical referral.

Managing Subsystem Design

A basic responsibility of every manager is to ensure that the work unit he or she supervises is properly structured to achieve high productivity. Action steps a manager can use to double-check the desirability of a given structure at any point in time include:

1. Analyze the external environment for elements most important to the affairs of the subsystem.
2. Configure subsystem structure to match these environmental demands and opportunities, as well as the size, technologies, strategies, and people that form the operating context of the subsystem itself.
3. Examine the degree of differentiation between the subsystem and others in the organization.
4. Choose a mechanism for achieving integration through effective lateral relations that is consistent with the degree of differentiation.
5. Repeat each step at regular intervals to make constructive modifications over time.

Summary

This chapter on organizational design introduces the critical factors important to managers striving to

solve problems arising from inadequate or inappropriate organizational structures. The basic goal of organizational design is to match structure with the general environment and internal operating context in a way that facilitates high productivity. The environment includes both general and specific elements; context includes size, technology, strategy, and people. Two primary alternatives constitute the basic continuum of organizational design strategies. At one extreme are mechanistic structures adhering to the bureaucratic model of organization described by Max Weber. At the other extreme are organic structures that are more flexible and less hierarchical in nature.

A contingency model of organizational design includes situational uncertainty and information processing as core elements. Factors that increase or decrease situational uncertainty affect an organization's information-processing requirements. Any organization must maintain a structural configuration capable of handling its information-processing needs over time. When the match between structure and information processing needs is a good one, the organization's chance for performance success is increased; when a mismatch occurs, it will be harder for the organization to succeed.

The contingency approach to organizational design includes a series of guidelines that take meaning at two levels of management responsibility—the total organization and the subsystem. Top managers are responsible for ensuring that the structural configuration of the organization as a whole is compatible with its environment and context, and that subsystem relationships are properly differentiated and integrated. At the subsystem level, middle and lower managers must ensure that work-unit structures meet the needs of their special situations and circumstances. By analyzing work-unit environment and context, and by being aware of a subsystem's relationships with other units, any manager will be better prepared to master this ongoing challenge.

Thinking Through the Issues

1. What is "organizational design"? What types of problems in organizations may indicate that an organizational design response is needed?
2. Identify five characteristics of an ideal bureaucracy. Give examples of two organizations that satisfy these characteristics.
3. Describe three basic differences between mechanistic and organic structures.
4. What roles do situational uncertainty and information processing play in organizational design?
5. Distinguish between the general and specific environments as factors of importance in organizational design.
6. State and defend an organizational design proposition summarizing the basic contingency relationship between environment and organizational structure.
7. What is the "technological imperative"? What is its organzational design implication?
8. Why is strategy an important factor to consider in organizational design?
9. Explain how the concepts of differentiation and integration apply to subsystem design in organizations. How does this relate to the concept of "simultaneous structures"?
10. Among the mechanisms for creating lateral relations among subsystems, which are more appropriate in mechanistic organizations? Organic organizations? Why?

The Manager's Vocabulary

Bureaucracy	Integration	Organic structures	Small-batch
Continuous-process	Intensive technology	Organizational	production
technology	Intrapreneurship	context	Specific environment
Differentiation	Long-linked technology	Organizational design	Subsystem
Environmental	Mass production	Simultaneous	Technological
uncertainty	Mechanistic structures	structures	imperative
General environment	Mediating technology	Size (of organization)	Technology

Case Application

BRAND MANAGEMENT CHANGES AT PROCTOR & GAMBLE

Classic brand management isn't *in* anymore at Proctor & Gamble.[26] What had become an institution in the consumer products business, and a mainstay at P&G, is giving way as the marketplace changes and new classes of consumers change along with it.

Bruce Miller used to spend most of his time thinking only about "Crisco." As brand manager he was supposed to know everything about the cooking fat market and how to keep his brand on top of the sales heap. He essentially ran the Crisco brand as his own competitive business, crafting marketing and advertising strategies, and planning product designs—all while his ideas and plans were kept secret from P&G's other brand managers. After all,

they were his competitors too. Many conflicts and inefficiencies crept into this system as brand managers fought over resources, and cooperation was restricted.

About his former role, Miller says, "We thought of ourselves as the hub of the wheel." But then he also adds, "We didn't have much contact with manufacturing or with purchasing. We'd go to research and ask for something and they'd say, 'that's impossible.' We'd say, 'Do it anyway.'" In a rigid structure, marketing tended to dominate the company and research had trouble getting attention for even major breakthroughs. Olestra, a cholesterol and calorie-free fat substitute languished for more than 20 years without a sponsor. When the subject was raised, a former P&G engineer claims the marketers kept insisting that P&G's purpose was selling "products" not "ingredients."

P&G was also famous for slow and centralized decision making. Bruce Miller complained that he had to get approval from layers of superiors for all decisions. Another former brand manager says it took 12 months and a $50,000 market research study just to get a "flip-top" cap approved for Prell shampoo. Once a week, the 40-member administrative committee used to meet at the firm. As the highest-ranking body, it would make decisions on all major promotions and spending plans.

Now P&G executives recognize they are mainly competing in slow-growth markets. They are dealing with consumers with highly specialized and changing tastes. They are dealing in markets where new products proliferate at a fast pace. As a result, they have also recognized the need to develop new management strategies. Classic brand management has thus given way to more emphasis on what P&G calls "business teams" and a new level of "category managers."

A business team is described by CEO John Smale as a concept that says, "When you're going to address a problem, get the people who have something to contribute in the way of creativity, if not direct responsibility. Get them together." Brand managers still exist at P&G, but they are now part of such teams where people from manufacturing, sales, and research participate with equal rank. They are also linked closely with other category brand managers who oversee an entire set of related products, and who emphasize "cooperation" not "competition" among P&G's in-house brands. In effect,

the brand managers of related lines will now report to them. Yet the new category managers sometimes invite friction on the teams as they learn to work in the new framework, and "team spirit" isn't always easy to come by. One former brand manager left the company. He said: "With teams, it's difficult to make you own mark and see how good you really are, I wanted the opportunity to dig my own grave or build my own pedestal."

Even the administrative committee has lost some of its power. Now, a 20-member executive panel is supposed to meet weekly and address the most important issues. Other decisions, including some of the spending decisions, are to be delegated to lower levels including the new category managers. Through it all P&G hopes to become more agile and responsive in today's dynamic consumer products environment. Not everyone is confident what the results will be. One critic feels the category managers will further complicate and slow decision making. A former P&G executive says: "It's lunatic. Every other company is reducing management levels. Proctor is going in the opposite direction."

Questions

1. Summarize the major disadvantages of P&G's traditional brand manager approach. Why was this approach especially troublesome for the company as it tried to compete in slow-growth markets?
2. What organizational design issues are evident in this case—(a) at the level of the total organization, and (b) at the subsystem level?
3. Is the "business team" concept a good solution to P&G's apparent problems with brand management? Why or why not? What other organizational design alternatives would you suggest, if any? Why?

Class Exercise: Organizational Design Alternatives

1. Think about the local organizations with which you are familiar. Good examples are a sporting goods store, small clothing boutique, popular restaurant, college or university registrar's office, student organization, health clinic or hospital, bank, and post office.
2. Working with a nearby classmate, choose two of these organizations which you feel should have quite different organizational designs.
3. Describe the ideal designs for these organiza-

tions using the mechanistic and organic alternatives presented in Figures 7.4 and 7.5.
4. Justify your choices in Step #3 by analyzing the design implications of key features in each organization's environment (general and specific) and context (technology, size, strategy, people). That is, for each organization you should be able to answer the question—"Why is this the best design?"
5. Double-check your analysis by determining whether or not your recommendations are con-

sistent with the organizational design guidelines presented in the textbook.

6. Be prepared to share your examples and participate in class discussion led by the instructor.

References

[1]Information on these cases is from David Nicklaus, "Monsanto Recombines," *St. Louis Post Dispatch* (July 4, 1982), p. 5E; and, Susan Carey, "Lufthansa Jettisons Bureaucratic Baggage," *The Wall Street Journal* (September 30, 1986), p. 37.

[2]Information for this case is reported in Michael W. Miller and Paul B. Carroll, "IBM Unveils a Sweeping Restructuring in Bid to Decentralize Decision-Making," *The Wall Street Journal* (January 29, 1988), p.3; Paul B. Carroll, "IBM Turns to Two Who Get the Job Done," *The Wall Street Journal* (February 1, 1988), p. 27; and, "Can This Elephant Dance?" *Time* (February 8, 1988), p. 52.

[3]Max Weber, *The Theory of Social and Economic Organization,* translated by A. M. Henderson and H. T. Parsons (New York: Free Press, 1947).

[4]For classic treatments of bureaucracy see Alvin Gouldner, *Patterns of Industrial Bureaucracy* (New York: Free Press, 1954); and Robert K. Merton, *Social Theory and Social Structure* (New York: Free Press, 1957).

[5]Tom Burns and George M. Stalker, *The Management of Innovation* (London: Tavistock, 1961).

[6]For a consumer's critique of McDonald's see Penny Moser, "The McDonald's Mystique," *Fortune* (July 4, 1988), pp. 112–116.

[7]This discussion is based on Henry Mintzberg, "The Structuring of Organizations," pp. 276–304 in James Brian Quinn, Henry Mintzberg, and Robert M. James (eds.) *The Strategy Process: Concepts, Contexts, & Cases* (Englewood Cliffs, NJ: Prentice-Hall, 1988).

[8]See Rosabeth Moss Kanter, *The Change Masters* (New York: Simon & Schuster, 1983). Quote from Rosabeth Moss Kanter and John D. Buck, "Reorganizing Part of Honeywell: From Strategy to Structure," *Organizational Dynamics,* Vol. 13 (Winter 1985), p. 6.

[9]This example is reported in David E. Gumpert, "The Joys of Keeping the Company Small," *Harvard Business Review,* Vol. 64 (July–August 1986), pp. 6–8, 12–14.

[10]Mintzberg, op. cit.

[11]This perspective is well described in Jay Galbraith, *Organizational Design* (Reading, Mass.: Addison-Wesley, 1977); Michael L. Tushman and David A. Nadler, "Information Processing as an Integrating Concept in Organizational Design," *Academy of Management Review,* Vol. 3 (July 1978), pp. 613–624.

[12]See the research summary in Marvin E. Shaw, *Group Dynamics* (New York: McGraw-Hill, 1971), pp. 137–153.

[13]James D. Thompson, *Organizations in Action* (New York: McGraw-Hill, 1967).

[14]Joan Woodward, *Industrial Organization: Theory and Practice* (London: Oxford University Press, 1965).

[15]See Peter M. Blau and Richard A. Schoennerr, *The Structure of Organizations* (New York: Basic Books, 1971).

[16]See Tom Peters, "There are No Excellent Companies," *Fortune* (April 27, 1987), pp. 341–352.

[17]See Gifford Pinchot, III, *Intrapreneuring: Or Why You Don't Have to Leave the Corporation to Become an Entrepreneur* (New York: Harper & Row, 1985).

[18]Thomas J. Peters and Robert H. Waterman, Jr., *In Search of Excellence* (New York: Harper & Row, 1982).

[19]See John Bussy and Douglas R. Sease, "Speeding Up: Manufacturers Strive to Slice Time Needed to Develop Products," *The Wall Street Journal* (February 23, 1988), pp. 1, 24.

[20]Alfred D. Chandler, Jr., *Strategy and Structure: Chapters in the History of American Industrial Enterprise* (Cambridge, Mass.: MIT Press, 1962).

[21]Information from "Is the New, Improved, Giant Economy-Size Saatchi Really Better?" *Business Week* (December 21, 1987), pp. 60–62.

[22]See Jay Lorsch and John Morse, "Organizations and Their Members: A Contingency Approach (New York: Harper & Row, 1974).

[23]Paul R. Lawrence and Jay W. Lorsch, *Organization and Environment* (Boston: The Division of Research, Graduate School of Business Administration, Harvard University, 1967).

[24]These integration mechanisms are explained in Galbraith, op. cit.

[25]Information from Paul B. Carroll and Janet Guyon, "IBM Turns to Two Who Get the Job Done," *The Wall Street Journal* (February 1, 1988), p. 34.

[26]Information from Jolie Solomon and Carol Hymowitz, "Team Strategy: P&G Makes Changes in the Way it Develops and Sells Its Products," *The Wall Street Journal* (August 11, 1987), pp. 1, 10; and, "The Marketing Revolution at Proctor & Gamble," *Business Week* (July 25, 1988), pp. 72–77.

*Designing Jobs
for Individuals
and Groups*

THE JOY
OF WORKING

It's really satisfying to work for the *Inc. 500*—the fastest growing small and midsize companies in America. At least that's what a recent survey of 2800 workers by *Inc.* magazine and the Hay Group, a management consulting firm, shows. Many employees in smaller organizations tend to find their jobs more challenging and rewarding, personally if not financially, than do employees in larger organizations. These differences in satisfaction are attributed to greater opportunities in the smaller firms for work that offers a sense of accomplishment, a culture that values initiative and ideas, and a willingness to treat employees with respect.

What other factors affect job satisfaction? Job security, good pension plans, and profit sharing are among the typical offerings of the large employer—but to many workers these benefits do not outweigh negatives such as the lack of a strong commitment to quality or the presence of a restrictive hierarchy. Increasingly, it seems that a sense of partnership is attractive to employees—and even a higher salary may not make up for its lack. As Michael Cooper, a Hay Group consultant, puts it, "the trick is to find systems that will allow a company to replicate the commitment and excitement that was so important during the start-up phase."

Cooper maintains that the smaller company can sustain its employees' enthusiasm by empowering them and giving them a sense of shared purpose. In particular, managers of smaller fast-growing companies indicated in the survey that they feel they have more challenges and opportunities than they would in a big company—and that their creativity is more likely to be recognized. The small and midsize companies surveyed ". . . are not successful simply because they have a good product or a brilliant founder," reports Cooper. "They are also successful because they have managed their people in ways that keep their involvement and sense of partnership high."

Of course, the picture isn't completely rosy; small companies have their frustrations—especially the fastest growing ones. Here employees report concerns that favorites are being played, plans kept secret, and worker interests and suggestions ignored. Another Hay consultant, Harold Glass, calls these "warning signals" that "shouldn't just be dismissed as predictable grousing. They are extremely accurate predictors of future problems. . ." Yet although some employees complained of being left out of small companies' communication loops, few had major criticisms of the commitment to quality, innovation, and competitiveness displayed by their CEOs.

Overall the survey results are positive and impressive. "If I were a *FORTUNE 500* CEO, I'd be worried," says Cooper, "The positive attitudes of their employees give small companies a great competitive advantage." ■

Source: Information from Curtis Harman and Steven Perlstein, "The Joy of Working," *Inc.* (November 1987), pp. 61–71.

T he organizing process was described in Chapter 6 as involving managerial decisions to divide up the work to be accomplished and then coordinate results to serve a specific purpose. In the past two chapters we emphasized the broader issues of creating supportive organization structures, both at the level of the total system and in respect to subsystems. Now our attention is directed toward a manager's responsibilities to design the *jobs* which individuals and groups perform within these structures. Ideally, these jobs will allow people to experience the "joy of working" as described in the chapter opener.

This chapter is about people at work and the jobs they perform. Specifically, the goal is to acquaint you with various ways for designing jobs that facilitate high productivity and provide high levels of satisfaction for the people who do them. Let's begin with the meaning of work itself.

Working 9 to 5; what a way to make a living,
Barely getting by; it's all taking and no giving.
They just use your mind, and they never give you credit,
It's enough to drive you crazy if you let it.

"9 to 5" by Dolly Parton

Is this what "work" means to you—"9 to 5 . . . all taking and no giving . . . never give you credit . . . drive you crazy if you let it"? Or is there something more that one can get from work? Some sense of accomplishment and satisfaction, if you will?

Let's take another example, with a similar play on words. Karen Nussbaum is a labor activist.[2] Several years ago she founded an organization called "9 to 5." It is devoted to improving women's salaries and promotion opportunities in the workplace. Nussbaum, however, got into this business indirectly through a former job as a secretary at Harvard University. Describing what she calls the "incident that put her over the edge," Nussbaum says:

> one day . . . I was sitting at my desk at lunchtime, when most of the professors were out. A student walked into the office and looked me dead in the eye and said, "isn't *anyone* here?"

From that beginning has sprung Nussbaum's organization and her personal commitment to "remake the system so that it doesn't produce these individuals."

Although in different ways and through different mediums, both Parton and Nussbaum are expressing concerns for the lack of individual respect and satisfaction sometimes experienced by people in the workplace. It doesn't have to be this way.

THE MEANING OF WORK

Work was defined in Chapter 1 as an activity that produces value for other people. What, though, do you think about when you see or hear the word "work"? A hit song by Dolly Parton for example, describes it as follows.[1]

THE LURE
OF TEAMWORK

Teamwork, a word traditionally linked with sports, brings to mind games in which small groups of people swap roles and responsibilities quickly and effectively to win a play. In a manufacturing setting teamwork is increasingly seen as a big plus—indeed, as a virtual necessity in some cases. The usual mass-production approach to manufacturing, in which one worker does only one job, has been criticized by labor experts and workers alike as inefficient; it dampens worker initiative and discourages quality-control efforts. When organized in small teams, assembly workers can do several different tasks and shift easily from one to another. This variety makes work more interesting, and it also allows employees to exercise control over the work process itself—to make suggestions about increasing its efficiency, to organize the process in ways that ensure high quality, and to troubleshoot on the spot. In fact, a key element of teamwork is an increase in autonomy. Unlike mass production, where management dictates the rules, teamwork encourages workers to take responsibility for all aspects of their jobs.

Fewer job classifications are one result of teamwork; higher productivity (20 to 40 percent, according to some sources) is another. Workers on teams are usually guaranteed job security if they find more efficient ways of working—a promise that is a major boost for team cooperation and creativity. In a growing number of industries, teamwork is the name of the game.

Source: As reported in "Detroit vs. the UAW: At Odds Over Teamwork," *Business Week* (August 24, 1987), pp. 54–55.

Fortunately, more and more managers in today's organizations are taking enlightened and mature viewpoints toward other people at work and the tasks they ask them to perform. Expanded individual responsibility and "teamwork"—highlighted in *Newsline 8.1*—are both important. Here are two other examples which help to introduce some of the ideas we will address throughout this chapter.[3]

■ *At Applied Energy Services* the founder and CEO Roger Sant claims the six-year-old company has succeeded by applying the philosophy—"Management has no monopoly on intellect." In the plants, workers participate in *autonomous work groups* called "families." Each one organizes itself, does its work, makes improvements in operations, and works directly with other families to achieve the needed integration of workflows. Sant says, "I am continually amazed at the way our workers take the initiative for improving the company." He adds,

"Companies that don't allow their workers to think and act on their own initiative are only benefiting from an eighth of their people's capacity."

■ *At Chaparral Steel* one of America's innovative mini-mills, success is based on a number of innovative work practices. Gordon Forward, president and CEO says, "It's really amazing what people can do when you let them." He gives the example of plant security guards. Not content to let them sit idle, Forward allows them to take on expanded responsibilities. On the night shift they enter data into computers on such things as purchase orders and the day's quality results. They also learn to be paramedics, run the ambulance, fill the fire extinguishers, and some are even training to perform accounting functions. The same breadth of responsibility holds true for all employees. When someone has a problem with the firm's products, Forward sends a team of people who actually do the work out to talk to the customer and come back with new ideas for work improvements. About Chaparral's employees Forward says, "We expect them to act like owners."

As the prior examples show, work can and should be more than a source of economic livelihood for people. It should involve a give-and-take, a positive and mutually beneficial exchange of values between the individual and the organization.

The Psychological Contract

You are probably familiar with the word *contract* as it is used to describe a formal written agreement between labor unions and organizations on such matters as employee pay, work hours, vacation privileges, and seniority rights. But there is another "contract" that links individuals to their work organizations. This **psychological contract** is the shared set of expectations held by the individual and the organization, specifying what each expects to give to and receive from the other in the course of their working relationship.[4]

A psychological contract represents the exchange of values expected to result from an individual's decision to work for the organization and the organization's decision to employ the individual in return. Figure 8.1 depicts this exchange in terms of inducements and contributions. An individual offers **contributions** or work activities of value to the organization. These contributions, such as effort, time, creativity, and loyalty, make the individual a productive resource for the organization. **Induce-**

ments are things of value that the organization gives to the individual in return for such contributions. They include pay, fringe benefits, training, and other opportunities.

When the exchange of values between the individual and the organization is fair, a state of inducements–contributions balance exists. This represents a positive or healthy psychological contract. In a sense, the rest of this chapter deals with managing psychological contracts. Both the organization and the individual can benefit when the "fit" between the individual and the job is a good one. A high quality of work life for the individual and productivity for the organization are the ideal results.

Work and the Quality of Life

The quality of life is everyone's concern, and the quality of work is an important component in the quality of life for most of us. This reality makes the manager's responsibility a most important one from a social as well as organizational perspective. This point is evident in the prior examples of Dolly Parton's hit song and Karen Nussbaum's organization "9 to 5." It is even more dramatically illustrated in these compelling words of a steelworker.[5]

> When I come home, know what I do for the first twenty minutes? Fake it. I put on a smile. I got a kid three years old. Sometimes she says, "Daddy, where've you been?" I say, "Work." I could have told her I'd been in Disneyland. What's work to a three-year-old kid? If I feel bad, I can't take it out on the kid. Kids are born innocent of everything but birth. You can't take it out on your wife either. That is why you go to a tavern. You want to release it there rather than do it at home. What does an actor do when he's got a bad movie? I got a bad movie every day.

Clearly, the experiences people have at work can spill over to affect their nonwork activities, just as nonwork experiences can affect their working lives. Every employee of every organization, including yourself, clearly pursues two overlapping lives—a work life and a nonwork life. The way managers treat people at work may have consequences extending far beyond the confines of the actual work setting. Poor management practices can decrease someone's quality of life, not just the quality of work life. Good management has the opportunity to increase both.

FIGURE 8.1 *The exchange of inducements and contributions in a psychological contract.*

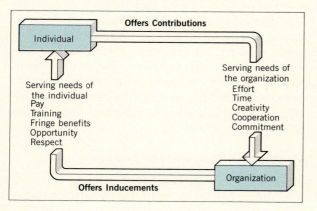

TABLE 8.1 *Trends in the Changing Nature of the Workplace*

Issue	Old Ways	New Ways
Organization structures	Taller with many management levels	Flater with fewer management levels
Authority	Centralized with power concentrated in top management	Decentralized with greater "empowerment" of workers at all levels
Role of staff	Large and diversified	Small and concentrated
Job designs	Work is simplified and narrow; managers "think," workers "do"	Work is multiskilled and broad; workers "think" and "do"
Work group	None; a formal unit with an ad hoc social aspects	Central; a focus for integrated socio-technical systems
Compensation	Pay set by the job classification and individual performance	Pay linked to skills acquired and individual and group performance
Training	Worker is replaceable; gets little training limited to one job	Worker is valuable; encouraged to learn new skills and many jobs

Table 8.1 highlights some of the emerging management and organizational practices that are helping to change the nature of work, and positively contribute to high-quality work lives for the people involved. Modern managers must be aware of these changes and the opportunities they represent for creating well-balanced and healthy psychological contracts. Indeed, managers are increasingly being expected to focus their attention on creating "work environments" within which people can perform on their own initiative and with a minimum of outside control.[6] The goal, of course, remains two-fold—to organize work in such a way that high levels of *both* job performance *and* job satisfaction are achieved.

JOBS, JOB SATISFACTION AND JOB PERFORMANCE

A **job** is a collection of tasks performed in support of organizational objectives. In practice most jobs are backed by a formal **job description,** a written statement that details the duties and responsibilities of any person holding the job. A good job description specifies the tasks the person staffing the job is expected to perform and thus helps ensure that individual efforts serve organizational objectives. Figure 8.2 shows how each job or position in a typical organization chart is associated with a writ-

ten job description. These positions are staffed by people, the human resources of organizations, who are expected to fulfill the responsibilities detailed in the formal job descriptions.

Job satisfaction is the degree to which an individual feels positively or negatively about various aspects of the job, including assigned tasks, the work setting, and relationships with co-workers. It represents the personal meaning or perceived "quality" of one's job and associated work experiences. **Performance** is the quantity and quality of task contributions made by an individual or group at work. Job or task performance is the reason for creating a particular job in the first place. It is a cornerstone of overall organizational productivity. Performance, as is commonly said, is the "bottom line" for people at work.

A manager's concerns with both job satisfaction and performance are quite immediate and specific. Some workers achieve a sense of personal satisfaction from their jobs, while others do not. Some workers achieve high levels of task performance, while others do not. The test of a manager's skill is to discover what work means to individual subordinates and then create work environments that help them achieve high levels of satisfaction *and* performance.

Herzberg's Two-Factor Theory

Frederick Herzberg is a psychologist who has studied job satisfaction in detail. His two-factor theory

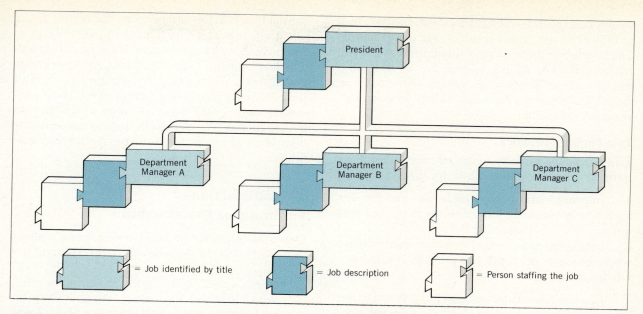

FIGURE 8.2 *Jobs, job descriptions, and people—the building blocks of organizations.*

is one of the most frequently praised and criticized of all management theories.[7] After examining almost 4000 responses of people to questions about their work, Herzberg and his associates noticed that different things were identified as sources of job satisfaction and job dissatisfaction. A summary of the results is presented in Table 8.2. More recently, Herzberg reports similar findings in several countries located in Europe, Africa, the Middle East and Asia.[8]

Hygiene Factors

Items causing feelings of *job dissatisfaction* are most often associated with *job context;* that is, they relate more to the work setting than the nature of the work itself. Sources of job dissatisfaction are called **hygiene factors** and include such things as working conditions, interpersonal relations, organizational policies and administration, supervision, and salary.

Hygiene factors in Herzberg's theory only affect job *dis*satisfaction. Improving them, such as adding piped-in music or changing rules on smoking in the workplace, can make people less dissatisfied. It will not, however, contribute to improved job satisfaction. Remember, hygiene factors exist in a job context and affect job dissatisfaction.

Satisfier Factors

To improve *job satisfaction,* Herzberg argues that a manager's attention must shift away from hygiene and toward **satisfier factors.** As shown on the right side of Table 8.2, satisfiers are part of *job content* and relate to what people actually do in their work. They include such things as a sense of achievement, rec-

TABLE 8.2 *Sources of Job Satisfaction and Job Dissatisfaction in Herzberg's Two-Factor Theory*

Factors that Led to Extreme Dissatisfaction	Factors that Led to Extreme Satisfaction
Company policy and administration	Achievement
Supervision	Recognition
Relationship with supervisor	
Work conditions	Work itself
Salary	Responsibility
Relationship with peers	
Relationship with subordinates	Advancement
Status	Growth
Security	

Source: Developed from Frederick Herzberg, "One More Time, How Do You Motivate Employees?" an HBR Classic, *Harvard Business Review,* Vol. 65 (September–October 1987), p. 109–120.

ognition, responsibility, advancement, and personal growth experienced as a result of task performance. The two-factor theory argues that improvements in job content (i.e., adding satisfier factors to a job), can increase satisfaction. In contrast to the hygiene factors, satisfier factors exist in job content and affect job satisfaction.

Two-Factor Dynamics

Two principles summarize the managerial implications associated with the two-factor theory.

1. Improvements in hygiene factors can prevent and/or help eliminate job dissatisfaction; they will not improve job satisfaction.
2. Improvements in satisfier factors can increase job satisfaction; they will not prevent or eliminate job dissatisfaction.

Because job satisfaction and job dissatisfaction are separate dimensions in Herzberg's theory, people at work may fall into any of the combinations shown in Table 8.3. The most positive result is the shaded combination of low dissatisfaction and high satisfaction. Faced with any of the other cases, the manager's goal should be to correct poor hygiene to eliminate any sources of job dissatisfaction and to build satisfier factors into job content to maximize opportunities for job satisfaction.

Implications

Even though management scholars debate the merits and faults of the two-factor theory,[9] it is still useful. Most managers allocate considerable time, attention, and other resources to improving things that Herzberg would consider hygiene factors. Special office fixtures, attractive lounges for breaks, and even high base salaries are examples. The two-factor theory cautions against expecting too much from these investments alone. It suggests that true job

satisfaction requires attention to the nature of the job itself, especially in respect to such things as responsibility and opportunity for personal growth and development. Thus, Herzberg's theory reminds managers that there are two important aspects of all jobs: (1) what people do in terms of job tasks—*job content*, and (2) the work setting in which they do it—*job context*. We will use both dimensions in our discussion of job design as a managerial responsibility.

The Satisfaction–Performance Relationship

One offshoot of the two-factor theory is a controversy illustrated by the following conversation.[10]

> As Ben walked by smiling on the way to his office, Ben's boss remarked to a friend: "Ben really enjoys his job and that's why he's the best damn worker I ever had. And that's reason enough for me to keep Ben happy." The friend replied: "No, you're wrong! Ben likes his job because he does it so well. If you want to make Ben happy you ought to do whatever you can to help him further improve his performance."

The central question in the conversation is whether or not a satisfied worker will automatically be a high performer.[11] Can a manager increase a person's job performance by doing things to increase his or her job satisfaction? Will a decline in job satisfaction cause a corresponding decrease in performance? The possible answers to these questions involve three alternative points of view, each with different managerial implications.

1. Satisfaction causes performance (S → P).
2. Performance causes satisfaction (P → S).
3. Rewards cause both performance and satisfaction (R → P, R → S).

Argument: Satisfaction Causes Performance (S → P)

If this argument is true, managers should strive to improve the job satisfaction of subordinates as a means of increasing their work performance. Researchers, however, generally advise that job satisfaction alone is not a good predictor of individual work performance.[12] Seeking to increase performance simply by increasing job satisfaction is not a good managerial decision.

TABLE 8.3 *Combinations of Job Satisfaction and Job Dissatisfaction in Herzberg's Two-Factor Theory*

Job Dissatisfaction	Job Satisfaction
High	Low
Low	Low
High	High
Low	High

  = manager's goal

Argument: Performance Causes Satisfaction (P → S)

If this second argument is true, managers are advised to focus their attention directly on performance. When high performance is achieved, the reasoning goes, job satisfaction will naturally follow. The key to this relationship is that the performance must be properly rewarded. Researchers believe that when performance is followed by valued rewards job satisfaction results.

Argument: Rewards Cause Both Performance and Satisfaction (R → P, R → S)

The third argument suggests that when rewards are properly allocated, both job satisfaction and high performance will result. The managerial implications of this perspective are straightforward. If you are only interested in creating high job satisfaction, pass out high rewards. If you are interested in high work performance as well, allocate **performance contingent rewards**—that is, give larger rewards to high performers and smaller rewards to low performers.

Modern management theory builds from this third approach to the satisfaction–performance relationship. It emphasizes both performance *and* satisfaction as the desired key results of people's efforts at work. Since managers are held accountable for the work performance of their subordinates, their concern for performance speaks for itself. But, let's not forget that job satisfaction is a significant object of the manager's attention in its own right. A person's satisfaction with their pay, co-workers, supervisor, tasks, and the work itself can and does affect a variety of job-relevant behaviors.[12] These include such things as absenteeism, tardiness, turnover, and receptivity to ideas and directions. In addition, and

as we have already agreed, job satisfaction is of clear psychological importance to the person as an essential component in the quality of their work life.

Thus, it is understandable why managers must be concerned about creating work environments within which their subordinates can accomplish high levels of task performance *and* experience job satisfaction in the process. A major step forward in this regard is the creation of proper job designs.

JOB DESIGN IN CONCEPT AND PRACTICE

Job design was defined in Chapter 6 as the process through which specific work tasks are allocated to individuals and groups. As shown in Figure 8.3, a manager's efforts in job design should address job content and job context. That is, job design encompasses the specification of task attributes (job content) and the creation of a supportive work setting (job context).

ILLUSTRATIVE CASE: DATAPOINT CORPORATION

Datapoint Corporation manufactures desktop computers.[14] Jackson White has just been employed by Datapoint. He is a competent person who enjoys interpersonal relationships. He also likes to participate in interesting conversations, and he feels good when being helpful or stimulating to others. How do you think he will react to each of the following job designs?

The Assembly-Line Job Jackson reports to a work station on the computer assembly line. A partially

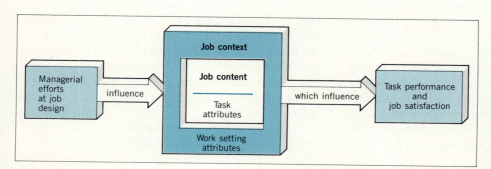

FIGURE 8.3 *Two managerial responsibilities in job design: designing job content and job context.*

assembled circuit board passes in front of him on a conveyor belt every 1½ minutes. He adds two pieces to each board and lets the conveyor take the unit to the next work station. Everyone gets a 10-minute break in the morning and afternoon. There is a ½-hour lunch period. Jackson works by himself in a quiet setting.

PREDICTION NO. 1

Note your predictions for Jackson White's job satisfaction and performance.

Job satisfaction:	Low	Moderate	High
Job performance:	Low	Moderate	High

The Modified Assembly Line Job Jackson works on the same assembly line. Now, however, a circuit board comes to his station every 12 minutes, and he performs a greater number of tasks. He adds several pieces to the board, adds a frame, and installs an electric switch. Periodically, Jackson changes stations with one of the other workers and does a different set of tasks with the same circuit board. In all other respects, the work setting is the same as in the first job described.

PREDICTION NO. 2

Note your predictions for Jackson White's job satisfaction and performance.

Job satisfaction:	Low	Moderate	High
Job performance:	Low	Moderate	High

The Team-Assembly Job Jackson is part of a team responsible for completely assembling circuit boards for the computers. The team has a weekly production quota, but makes its own plans for the speed and arrangement of the required assembly processes. The team is also responsible for inspecting the quality of the finished boards and for correcting any defective units. These duties are shared among the members and are discussed at team meetings. Jackson has been selected by the team as its plant liaison. In addition to his other duties, he works with people elsewhere in the plant to resolve any production problems and achieve plant-wide quality objectives.

PREDICTION NO. 3

Make a final set of predictions for Jackson White's job satisfaction and performance.

Job satisfaction:	Low	Moderate	High
Job performance:	Low	Moderate	High

A Continuum of Job Design Strategies

A continuum of the job design strategies implied in the case as shown in Figure 8.4. The strategies are job simplification, job enlargement and rotation, and job enrichment. Each strategy varies in the degree of specialization involved in the division of labor. The contingency orientation of modern management theory recognizes that there are situations in which highly specialized jobs are best and others in which less specialization is appropriate. Managers must learn to employ each of the strategies to proper advantage. For the moment, you should be able to associate each job design strategy with its application in the Datapoint case. Go back and note which job design strategy—simplification, enlargement and rotation, enrichment—best describes each of Jackson White's jobs. Read on to verify your answers.

Job Simplification

Job simplification involves standardizing work procedures and employing people in clearly defined and highly specialized tasks. Simplified jobs are very narrow in **job scope,** the number and combination of different tasks a person performs. Jackson White's first job in the case was of this type. Another classic example is found in this statement, attributed to Henry Ford, about jobs on the automobile assembly—"The man who puts in the bolt doesn't put on the nut. And the man who puts on the nut doesn't tighten it." The most extreme form of job simplification is, of course, complete **automation**—the total mechanization of a job. While our concern here is with forms of job simplification that still involve the human element, we will deal with automation and its growing contemporary significance at other points in the book.

Job simplification is often done with the expectation of increased productivity through lower skill requirements for workers, easier and quicker train-

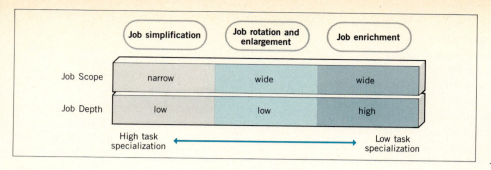

FIGURE 8.4 *A continuum of job design strategies: variations in job scope and job depth.*

ing, and less difficult supervision. On the other hand, it can sometimes reduce productivity because of the cost of related absenteeism and turnover, and poor performance due to boredom and dissatisfaction. Although jobs narrow in scope appeal to some people, disadvantages emerge when they prove inconsistent with what people really desire from their work. This issue can be analyzed from the perspective of Maslow's hierarchy of human needs introduced in Chapter 2. In the case of Jackson White, for example, an important social need is thwarted in his assembly line job, which prevents interaction with co-workers. Thus we would predict that his job satisfaction would be low. He might be frequently absent from work, and boredom may lead to a high error rate. His overall performance could be just adequate to prevent him from being fired.

Job Rotation and Job Enlargement

Job rotation and job enlargement are strategies of job design that increase the number and variety of tasks performed by a worker. They both expand *job scope*. This is assumed to offset some of the disadvantages of job simplification, and increase job performance and satisfaction.

Job rotation increases task variety by periodically shifting workers among jobs involving different sets of task assignments. While no one job is changed in design, the workers gain variety in their tasks by switching jobs on a regular basis. Job rotation can be done on almost any time schedule, such as an hourly, daily, or weekly basis.

Job enlargement increases task variety by combining into one job two or more tasks that were previously assigned to separate workers. Figure 8.5 shows that this can be accomplished through *horizontal loading* which pulls prework and/or later work stages into the job. In this strategy, the old job

design is permanently changed through the added variety of component tasks.

Jackson White's second job on the modified assembly line is an example of job enlargement with occasional job rotation. Instead of doing only one task in circuit board assembly, he now does three. Furthermore, he occasionally changes jobs with another worker to complete a different phase of the assembly process. Because job enlargement and rotation can reduce some of the monotony of highly simplified jobs, we would expect an increase in White's satisfaction and performance. Satisfaction should remain only moderate, however, since the job still doesn't respond completely to White's social needs. Although his work quality should increase as boredom is reduced, some absenteeism associated with the incomplete satisfaction is likely to keep job performance at a moderate level.

FIGURE 8.5 *Steps in improving a job through horizontal and vertical loading.*

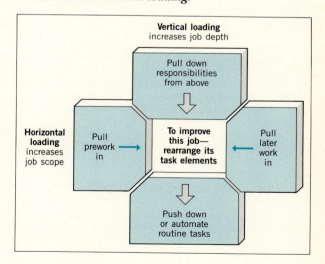

Job Enrichment

Frederick Herzberg, as reflected in his two-factor theory, considers it illogical to expect high levels of satisfaction and performance from persons whose jobs are designed according to the rules of simplification, enlargement, or rotation. "Why," he asks, "should a worker become motivated when one or more 'meaningless' tasks are added to previously existing ones, or when work assignments are rotated among equally 'meaningless' tasks?" Thus he recommends **job enrichment** as the practice of building satisfier factors into job content. In Herzberg's words again, "If you want people to do a good job, give them a good job to do."[15] Job enrichment is the means through which he believes this end is achieved.

Job enrichment differs from other job design strategies in that it seeks to expand not just job scope, but also **job depth**—the extent of planning and evaluating duties performed by the individual worker rather than the supervisor. As depicted in Figure 8.5, changes designed to increase job depth are sometimes referred to as *vertical loading*. Remember that job enlargement and rotation expand only job scope, while job enrichment also increases job depth.

Jackson White's team-assembly job contains elements of job enrichment. The team is responsible for doing some planning and evaluation duties, as well as actual product assembly. White should respond well to the challenges of this arrangement. It also provides the opportunity to satisfy his strong social needs. He should get added satisfaction from acting as the team's plant liaison. High performance and satisfaction are the predicted results.

Seven principles guiding Herzberg's approach to job enrichment are listed in Table 8.4. Note that each principle is an action guideline designed to increase the presence of satisfier factors in job content. Note, too, that the job-enrichment principles reflect increased job depth, or vertical loading, by allowing subordinates to share in work planning and evaluating responsibilities as well as in direct task accomplishment. Some additional objectives in Herzberg's approach to job enrichment are:

■ *Providing greater task feedback on product quality from client and supervisor*. This adds recognition and achievement to job content.

■ *Allowing self-scheduling, authority to communicate, control of resources, and accountability*. This adds responsibility to job content.

■ *Stimulating new learning and the development of unique expertise*. This adds advancement and growth to job content.

A DIAGNOSTIC APPROACH TO JOB ENRICHMENT

Modern management theory takes job enrichment a step beyond the work of Frederick Herzberg. Most

TABLE 8.4 *Herzberg's Principles of Job Enrichment: Ways of Building Satisfier Factors into Job Content*

Principle	Job Content Factors Involved
1. Remove some controls while retaining accountability	Responsibility and achievement
2. Increase the accountability of individuals for own work	Responsibility and recognition
3. Give a person a complete natural unit of work (module, division, area, and so on)	Responsibility, achievement, and recognition
4. Grant additional authority to an employee, provide job freedom	Responsibility, achievement, and recognition
5. Make periodic reports directly available to worker instead of to supervisor	Recognition
6. Introduce new and more difficult tasks not previously handled	Growth and learning
7. Assign individuals specific or specialized tasks, enable them to become experts	Responsibility, growth, and advancement

Source: Reprinted by permission of the *Harvard Business Review.* Excerpt from "One More Time: How Do You Motivate Employees?" by Frederick Herzberg, Vol. 46 (January–February, 1968). p. 53. Copyright © 1968 by the President and Fellows of Harvard College, all rights reserved. See also the reprint of this article as an HBR Classic in *Harvard Business Review,* Vol. 65 (September–October 1987), pp. 109–120.

important it recognizes in true contingency fashion that job enrichment is not for everyone. Among the present directions in job design, the job characteristics model developed by Richard Hackman and his associates offers a useful diagnostic approach for managers.[16]

The Job Characteristics Model

The model described in Figure 8.6 offers a diagnostic approach to job enrichment. Five core job characteristics represent the task attributes of special importance. A job that is high in the core characteristics is considered enriched. These characteristics are:

Skill variety   The degree to which a job requires a variety of different activities in carrying out the work and involves the use of a number of different skills and talents of the individual.

Task identity   The degree to which the job requires completion of a "whole" and identifiable piece of work—that is, one that involves doing a job from beginning to end with a visible outcome.

Task significance   The degree to which the job has a substantial impact on the lives or work of other people elsewhere in the organization or in the external environment.

Autonomy   The degree to which the job gives the individual substantial freedom, independence, and discretion in scheduling the work and in determining the procedures to be used in carrying it out.

Feedback (from the job itself)   The degree to which carrying out the work activities required by the job results in the individual obtaining direct and clear information on the results of his or her performance.

Hackman and his colleagues developed a Job Diagnostic Survey to measure the degree to which these core characteristics are present in a job.[17] You have an opportunity in the end-of-chapter exercise to use portions of this survey to analyze the "motivating potential" of several jobs. For now, simply recognize that the more poorly a job scores on each of the prior core characteristics, the less motivational it is expected to be. Accordingly, the more

FIGURE 8.6   *Core job characteristics and individual work outcomes in a diagnostic model of job enrichment.*

Source: J. Richard Hackman and Greg R. Oldham, "Development of the Job Diagnostic Survey," *Journal of Applied Psychology*, Vol. 60, 1975, p. 161. Copyright by the American Psychological Association. Adapted by permission of the publisher and author.

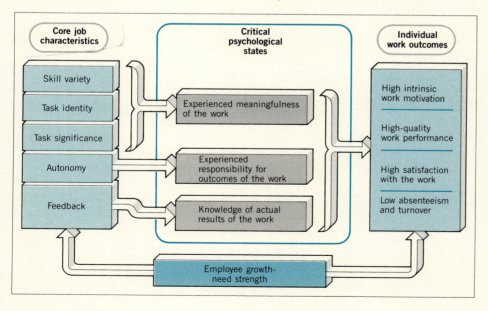

attractive it becomes as a candidate for job enrichment.

Looking again at Figure 8.6, note that the diagnostic model views job satisfaction and performance as influenced by three critical psychological states of the individual: (1) experienced meaningfulness of the work, (2) experienced responsibility for the outcomes of the work, and (3) knowledge of actual results of work activities. These psychological states, in turn, are affected by the presence or absence of the five core job characteristics.

The model recognizes, however, that the core characteristics will not affect all people in the same way. The key contingency variable in this respect is **growth-need strength**—that is, the individual's desire to achieve a sense of psychological growth in his or her work. A person high in growth-need strength seeks higher-order need satisfaction at work. In Maslow's hierarchy-of-needs theory this includes needs for ego fulfillment and self-actualization. The expectation is that people with strong growth needs will respond positively to enriched jobs, while people low in growth-need strength may have negative reactions and find enriched jobs a source of anxiety.

Finally, Hackman and his colleagues recommend five ways to enrich jobs which are low in the core characteristics. These implementation concepts are:

1. *Forming natural units of work.* Making sure that the tasks people perform are logically related to one another and provide a clear and meaningful task identity.
2. *Combining tasks.* Expanding job responsibilities by pulling together into one larger job a number of smaller tasks previously done by others.
3. *Establishing client relationships.* Allowing people to maintain contact with other persons who, as clients inside and/or outside the organization, use the results of his or her work.
4. *Opening feedback channels.* Providing opportunities for people to receive performance feedback as they work, and to learn how this performance is changing over time.
5. *Vertical loading.* Giving people more control over their work by increasing authority for planning and controlling activities previously done by supervisors.

One way to keep these concepts in perspective is to parallel them with the job satisfactions experienced by persons who own and run their own businesses, as reported in Table 8.5. Notice that such things as "pride," "control," "freedom," "self-reliance," and "customer contact" are prominent right at the top of the list. In many ways, the prior implementation concepts are attempts to increase the sense of *ownership* people feel in their work and clarify the *significance* of their jobs to other people—both things that are already built into the owner-manager's work.

TABLE 8.5 *Important Sources of Satisfaction for Small Business Owners*

A survey of 198 small business owners resulted in this ranking of the most important sources of job satisfaction.

1. Pride in product/service
2. Control
3. Freedom
4. Flexibility
5. Self-reliance
6. Customer contact
7. Income
8. Employee contact
9. Recognition
10. Privacy
11. Security
12. Status

Source: Data collected by Cicco & Associates, Inc., and reported in "Are Money and Status Losing Their Allure?" *The Wall Street Journal* (January 12, 1988), p. 31.

ILLUSTRATIVE CASE:
TRAVELERS INSURANCE COMPANY

To help you apply the diagnostic approach as a practicing manager, let's work through an example.[18] Travelers Insurance Company depends heavily on computerized information processing. This information is generated from keypunched cards that serve as input to the computer. The keypunch operator's job is to transfer data onto punched cards from printed or written documents supplied by user departments.

Requests for keypunching come from many departments within the company. These requests are received in the keypunch unit by assignment clerks who review the requests for accuracy, legibility, etc. Rejected requests are sent to the unit supervisor, who corrects the problems through direct contact with the user departments. Accepted requests are parceled out to keypunch operators in batches requiring approximately one hour of punching time.

The operators are supposed to punch exactly the information on the input documents, even when obvious coding mistakes exist. A verifier then checks all punching for accuracy as measured against the supporting documents. Any punching errors are randomly assigned back to the operators for correction.

PREDICTION

1. Use the scale below to assess the keypunch operator's job on the five core job characteristics.

Skill variety:	Low	High
Task identity:	Low	High
Task significance:	Low	High
Autonomy:	Low	High
Feedback:	Low	High

2. Based on your analysis of the job, what do you predict in terms of an operator's job performance and satisfaction?

Job performance:	Low	Moderate	High
Job satisfaction:	Low	Moderate	High

If you predicted low performance and satisfaction, you were right. Top managers in the company became concerned because the keypunch operators were apathetic and sometimes hostile toward their jobs. Error rates were high and absenteeism was frequent. Professional consultants were hired to look into the situation. They identified the following weaknesses in the core characteristics of the keypunch operator's job.

Skill variety There was none. Only a single skill was involved, the ability to accurately punch the data recorded on input documents.

Task identity It was virtually nonexistent. Keypunch batches were assembled to provide an even work load in the unit, but did not create whole and identifiable jobs for the operators.

Task significance None was apparent. The keypunching operation was a necessary step in providing service to the company's customers. The individual operator, however, was isolated by an assignment clerk and a supervisor from any knowledge of what the operation meant to the user department, let alone its meaning to the ultimate customer of the company.

Autonomy There was none. The operators had no freedom to arrange their daily tasks to meet production schedules, or to resolve problems with the user departments, or even to correct, while punching, information that was obviously wrong.

Feedback There was none. Once a punching batch left the operator's hands, he or she was not guaranteed feedback on its quality, since punching errors were randomly assigned back to the operators for correction.

The consultants decided to enrich the keypunch job design for some of the operators. They made these changes using the five implementation concepts just discussed.

1. *Forming natural work units.* The random assignment of work batches was discontinued. Instead, each operator was assigned continuing responsibility for certain accounts—either user departments or specific recurring jobs. Now all work for a given account always goes to the same operator.

2. *Combining tasks.* Some planning and evaluating duties were included along with the central tasks of keypunching. These changes are elaborated upon as we discuss additional changes later.

3. *Establishing client relationships.* Each operator was allowed direct contact with keypunch clients. The operator, not the assignment clerks, now inspects input documents for correctness and legibility. When problems arise, the operator, not the supervisor, takes them up with the client.

4. *Opening feedback channels.* The operators are provided with a number of additional sources of data about their performance. The computer department now returns incorrect cards to the operators who punched them; operators correct their own errors. Each operator also keeps a personal file of punching errors. These can be reviewed to deter-

mine trends in the frequency and types of errors being made. Each operator receives a weekly computer printout summarizing errors and productivity. This report is sent directly to the operator not to the supervisor.

5. *Vertical loading.* Operators now have the authority to correct obvious coding errors on input documents. They also set their own punching schedules and plan their daily work, as long as they meet deadlines. Some competent operators have been given the option of not having their work verified.

A number of positive results were realized under the newly enriched job design. These included decreased absenteeism, reduced error rate, and increased job satisfaction. Overall, a 39.6 percent productivity gain occurred.

Questions and Answers on Job Enrichment

There are a number of other questions you should be asking in regard to job enrichment. Answering these questions gives us a way of summarizing previous discussion.

Question: "Is It Expensive to Do Job Enrichment?"

Job enrichment can be costly. It is unlikely that the enrichment of the keypunch operator's job cost very much. But the cost of job enrichment will grow as the required changes in the work flow technology and physical characteristics of the work setting become more complex.

Question: "Will People Demand More Pay for Doing Enriched Jobs?"

Herzberg argues that if employees are being paid truly competitive wages (i.e., if pay dissatisfaction does not already exist), the satisfactions of performing enriched tasks will be adequate compensation for the increased work involved. But one study reports that 79 percent of the people whose jobs were enriched in one company felt that they should have been paid more.[19] A manager must be cautious on this issue. Any job-enrichment program should be approached with due recognition that pay may be an important issue for the people involved.

Question: "What Do the Unions Say About Job Enrichment?"

It's hard to speak for all unions. Suffice it to say that the following comments of one union official sound a note of caution.[20]

> Better wages, shorter hours, vested pensions, a right to have a say in their working conditions, the right to be promoted on the basis of seniority, and all the rest. That's the kind of job enrichment that unions believe in. And I assure you that that's the kind of job enrichment that we will continue to fight for.

Question: "Should Everyone's Job Be Enriched?"

No, not everyone's job should be enriched. The informed manager will make careful decisions when considering job enrichment as a way of promoting satisfaction and performance among individuals in the work unit. Cost, technological constraints, and union opposition among other factors, may make it difficult to enrich some jobs. The people most likely to respond favorably to job enrichment are those seeking higher-order or growth-need satisfactions at work, who are not dissatisfied with hygiene factors in the job context, and who have the levels of training, education, and intelligence required to do the enriched job.

CREATIVE WORK-GROUP DESIGNS

Job design principles can be applied at the group as well as individual level of attention. Thus it is appropriate to shift our attention to examine emerging ideas for creative work-group designs.

Autonomous Work Groups

Let's start by comparing and contrasting the accompanying photographs taken in three different automobile manufacturing plants. Given a choice, in which setting would you prefer to work?

The first photo shows a traditional assembly line at one of General Motor's older plants. It has been said that such a setting "epitomizes the conditions that contribute to employee dissatisfaction: fractionation of work into meaningless activities, with each activity repeated several hundred times

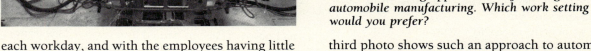

Three contrasting approaches to job design in automobile manufacturing. Which work setting would you prefer?

each workday, and with the employees having little or no control over work pace or any other aspect of working conditions."[21]

But, what are the alternatives? What can we do to protect workers from the alienation and frustration that often accompany work in such settings? One answer to this question is suggested in the second photo showing a glimpse of another GM plant. It involves increasing automation as far as possible, and trying to minimize the role of the human actor in highly routine aspects of the production process. The growing use of robots and other computer technologies in manufacturing is a good example of this approach.

Yet another answer to the question moves in the opposite direction—that is, it involves applying job enrichment at the group level. This is done by creating **autonomous work groups,** self-managed work teams responsible for accomplishing defined performance objectives. They have the discretion to decide how tasks will be distributed among individuals and at what pace work will progress in order to meet these objectives. Members of autonomous work groups may even establish pay grades, and train and certify members in required job skills. The

third photo shows such an approach to automobile assembly at Volvo's Kalmar plant in Sweden.

ILLUSTRATIVE CASE: VIA VOLVO

In the early 1970s Pehr G. Gyllenhammer, managing director of the Volvo Group's executive committee, was frustrated with the traditional assembly line where each worker did one task—over, and over again.[22] He wanted a radical change in the firm's production methods. He said: "We want to produce a plant that, without sacrificing efficiency and financial result, provides the possibility for employees to work in groups, communicate freely, exchange jobs with each other, vary the rate of work, feel product identification . . . Gyllenhammer wanted a system which created the atmosphere of a small workshop, while still being fully automated, and which allowed for decentralization and delegation. The design of a radical new production facility was the foundation for this. What seemed like a "noble dream" for Gyllenhammer at the time, has since resulted in the Kalmar plant depicted in the bottom photograph.

Take another look at that photo. This innovative plant was specially built to accommodate autonomous work-group principles in automobile manufacturing. What makes the Volvo approach so different is an emphasis on self-managing teams responsible for performing sets of tasks. Workers exchange jobs within teams, and are each capable of doing several different jobs. This reduces the monotony of the work, and makes it easier to fill in for workers who are out sick or on vacation. Team members also monitor their own progress against production targets, and even vary the pace of work. An innovative technology—mobile assembly platforms—carry car assemblies from one place to another and replace the traditional assembly line. Even the building is different. Assembly workers operate in areas filled with natural light from large exterior windows, and comfortable lounges are easily accessible. All this is designed to encourage high-quality production by persons who find their work challenging and satisfying.

The benefits of Volvo's experience with autonomous work groups at Kalmar are reported as

- Improved worker attitudes.
- Improved quality of output.
- Lower absenteeism and turnover.
- Ease of covering absent workers.
- Reduced numbers of supervisory personnel.

Now Volvo is ready for the next phase in its attack on the traditional assembly line. A $315 million new plant is being constructed at Uddevalla, where work teams will complete an even greater variety of tasks. Plans call for a *standstill production system* in which teams cluster in teams around a car that may stay at their work station for hours. Gyllenhammar says, "I want the people in a team to be able to go home at night and really say, 'I built that car.' That's my dream."

The dream is shared by Volvo workers, who strongly endorse the ideas in the Uddevalla plant. They look forward to building further upon the autonomy provided in the Kalmar facility. If the successes achieved so far are any indication, the next phase in Volvo's workplace revolution should be another benchmark for workplace design and manufacturing productivity.

Socio-Technical Systems

At the heart of Volvo's innovations and most progressive developments in work group designs is an attempt to successfully integrate the needs and capabilities of people with the advantages of new technology. More and more progressive managers are viewing job design from the perspective of **socio-technical systems.** The goal is to create social systems that allow technology to be used to best advantage, while still providing opportunities for individual satisfaction and personal growth.

The socio-technical systems approach has its origins in research conducted in British coal mines in the late 1940s by a group of scientists led by Eric Trist from the Tavistock Institute.[23] In the job design traditions of the time, technical systems were chosen first and the human factor then "forced to fit." Trist's group emphasized the mutual adaptation of the human factor and technology into a smoothly functioning socio-technical "system."

Newsline 8.2 is a reminder of how technological developments are changing the nature of work in many settings. Fortunately, the emergence of new technology is accompanied by a renewed awareness of the importance of creating integrated socio-technical systems job designs. In particular, autonomous work groups can be used to enhance the social and human dimensions of work in a growing variety of ways. Consider these examples.[24]

At Shenandoah Life Insurance Co. it once took 27 working days and the separate attention of 32 clerks working in three different departments to process a typical policy conversion. Now the clerks are organized in teams of five to seven members who work with a computerized processing system. Each team performs all functions previously distributed over the three departments and team members share required functions. Typical case-handling time has dropped to two days; clerks have learned new skills, are more satisfied, and earn higher pay; the company processes 50 percent more applications with 10 percent fewer employees.

At Tektronix Inc. assembly-line manufacturing in the metals division was converted to teams several years ago. Six to 12 workers in each "cell" now turn out a product that can be manufactured in relatively few steps. One of the cells now produces as many defect-free pieces in three days as it once took an

entire assembly line to do in 14 days with twice as many people.

New developments in socio-technical systems design now often combine autonomous work groups with some form of computer technology. A good example is *advanced manufacturing technology* or AMT, which includes a variety of computer assisted design and computer integrated manufacturing options. For example,[25]

at General Motors the new Saturn Plant being built in Tennessee, is supposed to use AMT as part of its attempt to become the "factory of the future." But the company also plans an important role for autonomous work group concepts as well. The traditional lock-step assembly line is being designed "out" and a team assembly approach is being designed "in." Some intended features of the Saturn Plant include:

■ Workers formed into self-directing teams of 6 to 15 persons.

■ Each team working on a major component of the car—engine, transmission, dashboard, front-end, etc.

■ Job rotation within teams whose members are paid "salaries" rather than hourly wages.

■ Computer-controlled delivery vehicles that move the various sub-assemblies to a final modular assembly line.

GM's objective at the Saturn plant is to combine people and technology in ways that will allow the company to be at the forefront of its industry well into the twenty-first century. More broadly stated, what we are seeing in the Saturn project and others like it are illustrations of how modern managers are responding to changing times by modifying organizations and job designs in new and promising ways. The new-form organizations emphasize high technology, enriched jobs and autonomous work groups designed with the logic of integrated socio-technical systems in mind. Table 8.6 summarizes important contrasts between traditional and socio-technical systems approaches to job design.

ALTERNATIVE WORK SCHEDULES

The author Robert Schrank has 60-plus years working as a laborer, farmhand, machinist, union organizer, business executive, and city official. He is aptly described as "one of the few experts on manual labor who has actually done very much of it." He says at one point in his book *Ten Thousand Working Days*—[26]

> I am skeptical of people who tell factory workers their jobs can become creative, autonomous, challenging and self-actualizing. . . . A production worker simply cannot decide on his own that the engine coming down the line should have four cylinders instead of eight or that a car body should be red instead of blue.

TABLE 8.6 *Contrasts between the Traditional and Socio-Technical Systems Approaches to Job Design*

Traditional job design emphasizes . . .	Socio-technical systems job design emphasizes . . .
Specialized, simple jobs	Whole, complex jobs
Hierarchical control	Worker autonomy
Centralized authority	Delegated authority
Individual rewards	Group/systems rewards
Segmentation of activities	Elimination of barriers
Faith in technical solutions	Human and technical focus
People undervalued	Human resources valued
Ignorance of environment	Attention to environment

Source: Excerpted from William A. Pasmore, *Designing Effective Organizations: A Sociotechnical Systems Perspective* (New York: Wiley, 1988), p. 102. Used by permission.

Schrank is not very enthusiastic about job enrichment and autonomous work groups. After observing one European experiment where people worked in pairs to assemble entire engines, he commented, "I was wondering, if I assembled 100 to 200, maybe 400 engines, what would the challenge be?" His suggested alternative is to provide workers with some of the amenities usually reserved only for managers and professional workers. One example is letting more workers have flexibility in setting their work schedules. In effect, Schrank is redirecting our attention back to the job context or work setting as an important, even if sometimes neglected, component of job design. Let's pursue the issue further in respect to several alternatives to the traditional eight hours per day, five days per workweek schedule.

The Compressed Workweek

A **compressed workweek** is any work schedule that allows a full-time job to be completed in less than the standard five days of eight-hour shifts.[27] Its most common form is the "4-40"—that is, 40 hours of work accomplished in four 10-hour days.

A 4-40 schedule for a work unit of three employees is presented in Figure 8.7. As the figure shows, one advantage of the 4-40 schedule is three consecutive days off from work each week. This benefits the individual in the form of more leisure time and lower commuting costs. The organization should benefit from lower absenteeism and any higher performance that may result. Disadvantages include such things as the possibility of increased

FIGURE 8.7 *A sample compressed work week or "4-40" work schedule.*

Employee	Mon.	Tues.	Wed.	Thurs.	Fri.	Sat.	Sun.
Guyon	On	On	On	On	Off	Off	Off
White	Off	On	On	On	On	Off	Off
Vicars	Off	Off	On	On	On	On	Off

The "4-40" Schedule

On = Employee works 10-hour shifts on four consecutive days.
Off = Employee is off on three consecutive days.

fatigue and family adjustment problems for the individual, as well as increased scheduling problems, possible customer complaints, and union-opposition problems for the organization.

Flexible Working Hours

Flexible working hours (also called "flexitime" and "flextime") is a term used to describe any work schedule that gives employees some choice in the pattern of daily work hours.[28] A sample flexible working-hour schedule is depicted in Figure 8.8. Employees in this example work four hours of "core" time—that is, time they *must* be present at work. In this case core time falls between 9–11 am and 1–3 pm. They are then free to choose another four hours of work from "flextime" blocks.

Flexible working hours gives people greater autonomy in work scheduling. Early risers may choose to come in earlier and leave earlier, while still completing an eight-hour day; late sleepers may choose to start later in the morning and leave later. In between these extremes are opportunities to attend to personal affairs such as dental appointments, home emergencies, and bank visits. Such flexibility can help organizations attract and hold employees with special outside responsibilities, such as working parents with young children. The added personal discretion flex-time allows may also encourage workers to develop positive attitudes and increased commitment to the organization. Among the reports from the field are comments that the approach—"treats people as adults" *(Prime Computer),* is "a big success" *(Smith Kline Beckman),* and results in "productivity increases and tardiness goes down" *(Wells Fargo Bank).*[29]

Job Sharing

Job sharing is a work schedule wherein one full-time job is split between two persons. Job sharing often occurs where each person works one-half day, although it can also be done on such bases as weekly or monthly sharing arrangements. When it is feasible for jobs to be split and then shared, organizations may benefit by being able to employ talented people otherwise unable to work. The qualified specialist who is also a parent may feel unable to stay

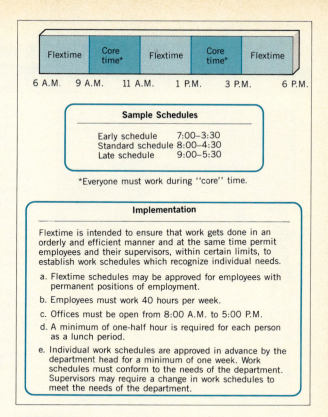

FIGURE 8.8 *A sample flexible working hours or "flex-time" work schedule: the case of university civil-service employees.*

away from home for a full workday, but be able to work a half-day. Job sharing allows two such persons to be employed as one.

A related, but more controversial, approach is **work-sharing** wherein employees in an organization agree to work fewer hours in order that staff cutbacks can be avoided. Rather than losing 20 percent of a firm's workforce to temporary layoffs in an unexpected business downturn, for example, a work-sharing program would cut everyone's hours by 20 percent but still keep them all employed. Work-sharing allows employers to retain trained and loyal workers, even when forced to temporarily economize by reducing labor costs. For very senior employees whose lengths of service might otherwise protect them from layoff, the disadvantage is lost earnings. From the point of view of someone who would otherwise be terminated,

DISPOSABLE EMPLOYEES

About 25 percent of all American workers, mostly women, are part of a "contingent" workforce—a group composed of part-timers, people who work at home, and employees of contractors. Contingent work is particularly on the rise in the low-skill end of the service sector. Airlines, retailers, and hospitals are among the industries making use of such workers, some of whom "telecommute" to work via computer links.

Full-time temporary workers are another growing segment—nearly a third—of the national workforce. Professional and technical temporaries are in high demand by companies that opt to save money by using temps and minimizing expensive full-time staff. Although some tempo-

rary workers think of "temping" as a career, others complain about low pay and nonexistent benefits. The issue of discrimination against temporary and contingent workers is a serious one, labor analysts agree. Without an adequate "social safety net," the income and benefits of these employees are endangered. Unions and some political leaders are pushing for legally mandated benefit levels, but large numbers of part-timers currently work without health insurance. The flip side of labor cost savings may be a second-class status for workers who have no option but contingent employment.

Finally, some experts fear that cultivating a large pool of low-skilled workers may seem convenient for employers but is ultimately damaging to American competitiveness. Integrating these workers into the permanent staff of an organization isn't always easy. Says Richard Belous of the Conference Board, a business research group: "If corporate executives think using contingent workers is going to be a free lunch, they are going to be surprised."

Source: As reported in David Kirkpatrick, "Smart New Ways to Use Temps," *Fortune* (February 15, 1988), pp. 110–116; "Part-Time Workers: Rising Numbers, Rising Discord," *Business Week* (April 1, 1985), pp. 62–63; "The Disposable Employee Is Becoming a Fact of Corporate Life," *Business Week* (December 15, 1986), pp. 52–56.

however, it allows continued work—albeit with reduced earnings—and with a preferred employer. Work-sharing has the endorsement of some labor unions and is now legal in more than a dozen states. It is prohibited in many others because of complications relating to unemployment compensation and benefits laws.

Work-at-Home

Another significant development in work scheduling is the growing popularity of **work-at-home.** This includes a variety of alternatives ranging from self-employment and entrepreneurship, to the freedom granted by corporate employers to spend all or part of one's work time in the home environment.

The latter approach has been greatly facilitated by the advent of the home computer and convenient telephone linkages back to central computers and offices. **Telecommuting** describes work done at home using a computer terminal with linkages to the office or other places of work. Working at home frees the job-holder from the constraints of commuting, fixed hours, special work attire, and even direct contact with supervisors. It is especially popular among computer programmers, although it is also found in such diverse areas as marketing, financial analysis, and secretarial support.

Work-at-home and telecommuting have advantages and disadvantages. When asked what they liked about them, a survey of "homeworkers" conducted by *The Wall Street Journal* reported increased productivity, fewer distractions, being your own boss and having more time for yourself. On the negative side they identified working too much, having less time to yourself, difficulty of separating work and personal life, and having less time for family.[30] Other considerations for the individual are possible feelings of isolation and loss of visibility for promotion. Managers, in turn, may be required to change routines and procedures to accomodate the difficulties of supervising people from a distance.

Part-Time Work

Newsline 8.3 introduces a final trend in work scheduling that also has its controversial side. **Part-time work** is done on a schedule that classifies the employee as "temporary" and requires less than the standard 40-hour work week. Many employers are turning to part-timers or "temps" to meet a very broad range of work needs. No longer is the work of part-timers confined to the traditional areas of clerical services, sales personnel, and unskilled labor. It is now possible to hire on a part-time basis every-thing from executive support, such as a chief financial officer, to such special expertise as engineering, computer programming, and market research, to regular clerical help. Projections are that some 18 million people will soon be working as temporaries, with many doing so indefinitely and as many as 70 percent being female.[31]

Because temporary workers can be easily hired and/or terminated in response to changing needs, employers like the flexibility they offer in controlling labor costs. On the other hand, concerns are that "temps" may lack specific job capabilities and the commitment of permanent workers. The result may be lower productivity. Perhaps the most controversial issue relates to the different treatment "temps" often receive from employers. They may be paid less than full-time counterparts, and they often fail to qualify for important fringe benefits such as health care, life insurance, pension plans, and paid vacations. As we look to the future, at least one fact is clear. Part-time work will continue to grow in importance and will require the special attention of managers and researchers.

Summary

This chapter has examined job design—the process of arranging work tasks for individuals and groups as part of the manager's organizing responsibility. Jobs are the basic interface between people and their work organization. A psychological contract forms around the exchange work contributions by individuals for inducements offered by the organization. True balance of inducements and contributions is ideal. It is a balance you should always strive to maintain for yourself in future jobs and for subordinates.

Jobs have the potential to produce two key work results: task performance and job satisfaction. Although we cannot say that a satisfied worker will always be a high performer, we can say that both high performance and high satisfaction are important goals to strive for in any job situation.

Major job design strategies are simplification, enlargement rotation, and enrichment. We reviewed a diagnostic approach to job enrichment that carefully analyzes task attributes as part of any job-design process. It was pointed out, too, that job enrichment is most appropriate for persons actively seeking higher-order or growth-need satisfactions in their work. Autonomous work grouping is a related technique for enriching job content at the group level. The Volvo experience exemplifies one application of this approach. The role of technology is a critical aspect of job design. Socio-technical systems designs seek to integrate people and technology in creative arrangements, often team oriented, that serve both individual needs and technical demands.

The work setting is another important job-design element. Work schedules are a good example of attributes in the job context that are important background components in any job design. Compressed workweeks, flexible working hours, job sharing, work-at-home, telecommuting, and part-time work were presented as alternative ways of arranging work schedules to accommodate individual and organizational preferences.

Thinking Through the Issues

1. What is a psychological contract? Describe the psychological contract for a job you have recently held. Why is this concept important to managers?

2. Define the concept of job satisfaction. Which is more important for managers to emphasize for persons under their supervision—high task performance or high job satisfaction? Why?

3. Describe the difference between hygiene factors and satisfier factors in Herzberg's two-factor theory. Give examples of each.

4. How does job enlargement differ from job rotation? Give an example of how each might operate in practice.

5. How does job simplification differ from job enrichment? Give an example of how each might operate in practice.

6. Describe the diagnostic approach to job enrichment advocated by Hackman. What role does growth-need strength play in the Hackman approach?

7. Define the term "autonomous work group." Would it be correct to call this job enrichment for groups? Why or why not?

8. Explain the concept of "socio-technical systems" as it relates to job design. Give an example of how an organization might design jobs based on this concept. In what ways is this different from the more traditional approach to job design?

9. Is flextime something you would advocate as a policy in your organization? Why or why not? How do you feel about the compressed work week, and job sharing? Please explain.

10. What are the implications of work-at-home and part-time work for a) the people who do them, b) managers, and c) society as a whole? Are there any things you are especially concerned about? Why?

The Manager's Vocabulary

Automation
Autonomous work groups
Autonomy
Compressed workweek
Contributions
Feedback (from job)
Flexible working hours
Growth-need strength
Hygiene factors
Inducements
Job
Job depth
Job description
Job design
Job enlargement
Job enrichment
Job rotation
Job satisfaction
Job scope
Job sharing
Job simplification
Part-time work
Performance
Performance contingent rewards
Psychological contract
Satisfier factors
Skill variety
Socio-technical systems
Task identity
Task significance
Telecommuting
Work-at-home
Work-sharing

CLIMBING THE LADDER OF SUCCESS

CAREER PERSPECTIVE

". . . don't let your babies grow up to flip burgers. And for heaven's sake, don't let them deliver pizza, wait tables, serve beverages or clean kitchens." Or, at least so opens a commentary published in *The Wall Street Journal* by Pizza Hut's senior vice-president for personnel, David Zemelman.[32] He goes on to complain that many people have the wrong impression of opportunities for employment in the service industries in general. And he disputes critics who say that the fast-food restaurant business in particular fails to provide young people with marketable skills and career ladders.

Zemelman goes on to say that workers in fast-food restaurants learn interpersonal and teamwork skills that will serve them well in future jobs in any industry. They also learn how to deal with co-workers, interact with the general public, to become comfortable taking *and* giving directions, and they learn what it's like to have responsibility. At least one survey reports that job satisfaction among teenage workers in the industry is quite high. Reasons cited for liking their jobs include: gaining job experience, learning responsibility, and "having a good time."

When Pizza Hut surveyed its staff to find out what attracted them to the company, furthermore, two reasons were most commonly given—they had friends working there who encouraged them, or they had been a customer and liked the atmosphere. When asked what they liked most about their work, two answers again predominated—they liked the "flexible" hours, and they liked the

"teamwork" that made it "fun" to spend time on the job.

Finally, Zemelman points out that more than 1100 of the company's 2700 restaurant managers began as drivers, cooks, or service personnel. The majority of higher-level executives, furthermore, come from the ranks of restaurant managers who have been promoted for high performance.

Questions

1. Think of a local fast-food restaurant with which you are familiar. Based on your observations, do you agree with the opening quotation, or Zemelman's point of view? Why?
2. In what ways exactly are *you* learning and developing the interpersonal and teamwork skills Zemelman says are important to any job? What else could you be doing?
3. Would it be appealing to you to spend some time working in this type of setting? Is there a possible career opportunity represented here for you? Explain your answers.

Case Application

JOB DESIGN AT MOT SURGICAL CORPORATION

Mot Surgical Corporation is a subsidiary of a large pharmaceutical company producing drugs and related medical products.[33] Mot specializes in surgical sutures and has three manufacturing plants. At the time of the case, Mot's parent corporation had supported employee quality of work life for several years. It had encouraged its subsidiaries to increase employee involvement and to design meaningful jobs. The newest plant in the southwestern United States was seen as a potential site to enrich jobs, which at Mot's older plants had been routinized for years.

Traditionally, the jobs involved in producing surgical sutures were divided according to the three main stages of production. First, the job of *swager* involved attaching a surgical needle to a filament made of a catgut or synthetic fiber. The needle and filament were placed in a press, and the press joined the two together. The swaging activities were of a short time cycle, highly standardized, and repetitive; workers sat at individual presses turning out

dozens of finished products per hour. Second, the job of *inspector* involved examining the finished swaging product for defects. Product quality was especially important because the condition of sutures can affect the outcome of surgery. Inspectors took samples of swaging product and visibly examined them. The job took extreme concentration for defects were difficult to detect. Inspectors passed poor quality work back to relevant swagers and passed good product on to the next production stage. Third, the job of *handwinder* involved taking acceptable swaging product and winding it by hand into a figure-eight for packaging. Like swaging, handwinding activities were highly routinized and repetitive; handwinders sat at individual work stations and wound literally thousands of figure-eights per hour.

The activities surrounding the suture jobs were also highly programmed and scheduled. The market for surgical sutures was relatively stable. Production runs were long and scheduled well in advance of actual production. Changes in schedule were rare. Similarly, the production methods associated with swaging, inspection, and handwinding were highly programmed, and technical changes in production were infrequent. The primary goal of management was for workers to produce large quantities of acceptable product.

Prior to hiring in the new plant, the three suture jobs were placed into discrete groups according to the specific type of suture produced. People in each product group were to be trained in all three jobs. Members would stay on a job for a specified period of time and then rotate to another job. Performance of the swaging and handwinding jobs also included some minor set-up, inspection, and scheduling activities. Weekly meetings were also planned so employees could share information, solve common problems, and make work-related decisions. The new, more enriched jobs were expected to result in high productivity and quality of work life.

Mot made great efforts to recruit people who were likely to respond favorably to enriched jobs. Newspaper advertisements and job interviews explicitly mentioned the enriched nature of the new jobs and the promise that employees would be involved in decision making. Potential recruits were shown the new plant setup, and asked about their desire to learn new things and to be involved in decision making. About thirty people were hired and trained in the new job initially; additional employees were assimilated into the new plant over the next few months. The training program was oriented to learning the swaging, inspection, and handwinding jobs and to gaining problem-solving skills.

As training progressed and the plant gradually started production, several unexpected problems emerged. First, employees found it difficult to rotate among the different jobs without a considerable loss of production. The swaging, inspection, and handwinding tasks involved entirely different kinds of manual dexterity and mental concentration. Each time people switched from one job to another, much relearning and practice was necessary to achieve a normal level of production. The net results of this rotation was lower-than-expected productivity. When this problem persisted, workers were urged to stay on one particular job.

A second problem concerned employee involvement in decision making. During the early stages of the plant start up, workers had ample opportunities for decision making. They were involved in solving certain break-in problems and deciding on housekeeping, personnel, and operating issues. They were undergoing training and had time to devote to problem solving without heavy pressures for production. Over time, however, plant operations became more routine and predictable, and there was less need for employee decision making. Moreover, increased pressures for production cut into the limited time devoted to decision making.

A third problem involved employee behaviors and attitudes. After six months of operation, employee absenteeism and turnover were higher than the local industry average. People complained that the job was more routine and boring than they had expected. They felt that management had sold them a bill of goods about opportunities for decision making. These behaviors and attitudes were especially prevalent among those who were hired first and had participated in the initial recruiting and start-up.

Questions

1. Analyze the individual jobs in the new plant as they were initially designed. Use the five core characteristics in Hackman's diagnostic model of job enrichment for this analysis. To what extent were these jobs enriched? What happened to this level of enrichment over time?
2. How could the new plant have utilized autonomous work groups and some of the ideas of sociotechnical systems design? Explain your answer and give specific illustrations.
3. Why did Mot experience problems with employee withdrawal and lowered performance in this case? What can be done now to restore the situation to one of high performance and high satisfaction?

Class Exercise: A Job's Motivating Potential

1. Listed below are five questions based on Hackman and Oldham's Job Diagnostic Survey.[34]
   a. To what extent does this job require a person to do a variety of different things at work, and to use a variety of skills and talents?
   b. To what extent does this job allow a per-

son to do "a whole and identifiable piece of work," that is to do something from beginning to end and with a visible outcome?

c. To what extent is this job significant or important, in the sense that it has a substantial impact on the lives or work of other people?

d. To what extent does this job provide a person with autonomy, the ability to decide on their own how to do the required work?

e. To what extent does the person receive direct feedback on performance simply as a result of doing the job, and not from co-workers or supervisors?

2. Choose two jobs with which you are familiar— e.g., bank teller or bookstore manager. Use the following scale to rate the jobs on each of the above characteristics.

1.... 2.... 3.... 4.... 5.... 6.... 7

Very little   Moderately   Very much

Record your scores for each dimension below.

		Job #1	Job #2
a.	variety	_____	_____
b.	identity	_____	_____
c.	significance	_____	_____
d.	autonomy	_____	_____
e.	feedback	_____	_____

3. Use the following formula to compute the *Motivating Potential Score* (MPS) for each of the jobs.

$$MPS = \left[\frac{(\text{variety [a]} + \text{identity [b]} + \text{significance [c]})}{3} \right] \times \text{autonomy [d]} \times \text{feedback [e]}$$

4. Share your computations, and the reasons for them, with a nearby classmate. Discuss the jobs each of you rated. Do you consider them enriched, or not? Why?

5. Examine ways that the MPS of each job might be improved. Be prepared to share your results and participate in general class discussion led by the instructor.

References

[1]Lyrics from "9 to 5" by Dolly Parton. Published by Velvet Apple/Fox Fanfare Music, Inc. © 1980 Velvet Apple Music & Warner-Tamerlane Publishing Corp. All rights reserved. Used by permission.

[2]This example is reported in *Esquire* (December 1986), p. 243. Emphasis is added to the quotation.

[3]Information from Alan Kantrow, "Wide Open Management at Chaparral Steel," *Harvard Business Review*, Vol. 64 (May-June 1986), pp. 96–102; and, Roger Sant, "Play By Your Own Rules," *Success* (May 1988), p. 10.

[4]John P. Kotter, "The Psychological Contract: Managing the Joining Up Process," *California Management Review*, Vol. 15 (Spring 1973), pp. 91–99.

[5]Studs Terkel, *Working* (New York: Avon Books, 1975), p. 7.

[6]This point is nicely made by John J. Sherwood, "Creating Work Cultures With Competitive Advantage," *Organizational Dynamics*, Vol. 16 (Spring 1988), pp. 4–27.

[7]The complete two-factor theory is in Frederick Herzberg, Bernard Mausner, and Barbara Bloch Synderman, *The Motivation to Work*, Second Edition (New York: Wiley, 1967); Frederick Herzberg, "One More Time: How do You Motivate Employees?" *Harvard Business Review*, Vol. 47 (January–February 1968), pp. 53–62 and re-

printed as an HBR classic in Vol. 65 (September–October 1987), pp. 109–120.

[8]Frederick Herzberg, "Worker's Needs: The Same Around the World," *Industry Week* (September 21, 1987), pp. 29–32.

[9]Critical reviews are provided by Robert J. House and Lawrence A. Wigdor, "Herzberg's Dual-Factor Theory of Job Satisfaction and Motivation: A Review of the Evidence and a Criticism," *Personnel Psychology,* Vol. 20 (Winter 1967), pp. 369–389; and Steven Kerr, Anne Harlan, and Ralph Stogdill, "Preference for Motivator and Hygiene Factors in a Hypothetical Interview Situation," *Personnel Psychology,* Vol. 27 (Winter 1974), pp. 109–124.

[10]For a complete discussion of this controversy see Charles N. Greene, "The Satisfaction–Performance Controversy," *Business Horizons,* Vol. 15 (October 1972), pp. 31–41; Charles N. Greene and Robert E. Craft, Jr., "The Satisfaction–Performance Revisited," in Kirk Downey, Don Hellriegel, and John Slocum (eds.), *Organizational Behavior: A Reader* (St. Paul, Minn.: West Publishing, 1977), pp. 187–201. The quote is from Greene, p. 31.

[11]For a classic work see A. H. Brayfield and W. H. Crockett, "Employee Attitudes and Employee Performance,"

Psychological Bulletin, Vol. 51 (1955), pp. 396–424. For a good recent discussion of job satisfaction and performance issues see Barry M. Staw, "Organizational Psychology and the Pursuit of the Happy/Productive Worker," *California Management Review,* Vol. XXVIII (Summer 1986), pp. 40–53.

[12] Michelle T. Iaffaldano and Paul M. Muchinsky, "Job Satisfaction and Job Performance: A Meta-Analysis," *Psychological Bulletin,* Vol. 97 (1985), pp. 251–273.

[13] See Edwin A. Locke, "The Nature and Causes of Job Satisfaction," pp. 1267–1349 in Marvin D. Dunnette (ed.), *Handbook of Industrial and Organizational Psychology* (Chicago: Rand McNally, 1976).

[14] Developed from an example in Edward E. Lawler III, *Motivation in Work Organizations* (Monterey, CA: Brooks-Cole, 1973), pp. 154–155.

[15] These quotes are from Herzberg, op. cit., *Harvard Business Review* (1968 and 1987).

[16] For a complete description of the job characteristics model, see J. Richard Hackman and Greg R. Oldham, *Work Redesign* (Reading, MA: Addison-Wesley, 1980); additional descriptions of directions in job design research and practice are available in Ramon J. Aldag and Arthur P. Brief, *Task Design and Employee Motivation* (Glenview, IL: Scott, Foresman, 1979), and Ricky W. Griffin, *Task Design: an Integrative Approach* (Glenview, IL: Scott, Foresman, 1982).

[17] The Job Diagnostic Survey is described in J. Richard Hackman and Greg Oldham, "Development of the Job Diagnostic Survey," *Journal of Applied Psychology,* Vol 60. (1975), pp. 159–170; and, in Hackman and Oldham, op. cit. (1980).

[18] Developed from J. Richard Hackman, Greg Oldham, Robert Janson, and Kenneth Purdy, "A New Strategy for Job Enrichment," *California Management Review,* Vol. XVII (1975), pp. 51–71. See also Karlene H. Roberts and W. Glick, "The Job Characteristics Approach to Task Design: A Critical Review," *Journal of Applied Psychology,* Vol. 66 (1981), pp. 193–217.

[19] Paul J. Champagne and Curt Tausky, "When Job Enrichment Doesn't Pay," *Personnel,* Vol. III (January–February 1978), pp. 30–40.

[20] William W. Winipsinger, "Job Enrichment: A Union View," in Karl O. Magnusen (ed.), *Organizational Design, Development and Behavior: A Situational View* (Glenview, Ill.: Scott, Foresman, 1977), p. 22.

[21] William F. Dowling, "Job Redesign on the Assembly Line: Farewell to Blue-Collar Blues," *Organizational Dynamics* (Autumn 1973), p. 51.

[22] Information on the Volvo experience is from Berth Jönsson, "The Myths of Volvo," *New Management,* Vol.

1 (1983), pp. 30–33; "Kalmar: Ten Years Later," *Via Volvo,* Vol. II (Spring/Summer 1984), pp. 14–19; *Via Volvo,* Vol. V (No. 2 1987), p. 16; and, Steve Lohr, "Making Cars the Volvo Way," *The New York Times* (June 23, 1987), pp. D1, D5.

[23] See the classic article by Fred Emery and Eric Trist, "Sociotechnical systems," in C. W. Churchman and M. Verhurst (eds.), *Management Science, Models and Techniques* (New York: Pergamon, 1960). Recent developments are described in Richard Walton, "From Control to Commitment in the Workplace," *Harvard Business Review,* Vol. 64 (March–April 1985), pp. 77–94. A comprehensive review is provided by William A. Pasmore, *Designing Effective Organizations: A Sociotechnical Systems Perspective* (New York: Wiley, 1988).

[24] These examples are reported in "Management Discovers the Human Side of Automation," *Business Week* (September 29, 1986), pp. 70–75; David Buchanan, "Job Enrichment is Dead: Long Live High Performance Work Design," *Personnel Management,* (May 1987), pp. 40–43; and Sherwood, op. cit., 1988.

[25] Information from Noel M. Tichy and May Anne Devanna, *The Transformational Leader* (New York: Wiley, 1986); Thomas Moore, "Make or Break Time," *Fortune* (February 15, 1988), pp. 32–49; and, Alex Taylor III, "Back to the Future at Saturn," *Fortune* (August 1, 1988), pp. 66–72.

[26] Robert Schrank, *Ten Thousand Working Days* (Cambridge: MIT Press, 1978); this review adapted from Roger Ricklefs, "The World of Work as Seen by a Worker," *The Wall Street Journal* (May 26, 1978), p. 19.

[27] See Allan R. Cohen and Herman Gadon, *Alternative Work Schedules: Integrating Individual and Organizational Needs* (Reading, Mass.: Addison-Wesley, 1978), p. 125; Simcha Ronen and Sophia B. Primps, "The Compressed Work Week as Organizational Change: Behavioral and Attitudinal Outcomes," *Academy of Management Review,* Vol. 6 (1981), pp. 61–74.

[28] Ibid., pp. 54–64.

[29] Information from *The Wall Street Journal* (March 15, 1988), p. 1.

[30] This survey is reported in *The Wall Street Journal* (January 20, 1988), p. 31.

[31] See David Kirkpatrick, "Smart New Ways to Use Temps," *Fortune* (February 15, 1988), pp. 110–116.

[32] Information from David Zemelman, "Climbing the Ladder of Success with a Spatula," *The Wall Street Journal* (February 4, 1988), p. 18.

[33] Edgar F. Huse and Thomas G. Cummings, *Organizational Development and Change,* Third Edition (St. Paul, MN: West, 1985), pp. 55–56. Used by permission.

[34] Developed from Hackman and Oldham, op. cit. (1975).

Staffing
The Human
Resources

The Art of Hiring "10s"

Hiring smart is not simply desirable; it's a crucial part of organizational success. Indeed, hiring the best people available—those who will keep costs down, display ingenuity as well as diligence, and generally add value to the organization—is one of a manager's most important tasks. Because mistakes in this area can be expensive and demoralizing, many organizations are stressing the need for sound decisions about new personnel.

How does a manager locate exceptional employees? There is no sure-fire formula, but experienced managers develop rigorous interviewing skills, know how to check references, and keep their eyes open for prospective employees. The first step in hiring an employee for a specific job, of course, is to identify all the requirements of the job; then the position must be advertised in appropriate places. Many managers start by asking their current employees for referrals: often the best people are found through in-house networking. Once candidates are located, they must be interviewed, preferably by several people—and here's where preparation counts, say human resource experts. Sweeping questions tend to be met with sweeping answers. The idea is to ask questions that will elicit useful and clear information about the candidate's skills, experience, and personality. Checking references is another important aspect of hiring. While the right candidate should receive praise from several quarters, the hiring organization may need to do a little digging to get a full report on the individual's weaknesses as well as strengths.

Martin Jacknis, president of Results Marketing Company, believes that an organization is in danger of hiring increasingly less competent people unless each manager doing the hiring maintains standards at all times. In his firm, Jacknis insists on universal employee education on company policy and product information, clearly communicated standards of excellence, open critiques of staff failures (including his own), and hiring "as high as reality goes." Jacknis admits that what he calls the "law of diminishing expertise" may be ubiquitous, but he adds that "once you're aware of it, you can come up with specific ways to combat it—and even reverse its effects."

It is important, says management authority Jack Falvey, for managers to maintain their skills in hunting for and interviewing prospective employees; getting rusty in this area is not a good idea. Falvey urges managers to keep up good contacts in academic and professional communities; they come in handy in times of need. "If you manage in isolation," he warns, "with no outside contacts and no meetings with potential employees until you have a vacancy, is it any wonder that you lack selection skills or make bad hiring choices?" And when the right person *is* located and brought on board, follow-up interviews after several months are always smart—to double-check that employer and employee are both pleased with the outcome of the hiring decision. ■

Source: Information from Brian Dumaine, "The New Art of Hiring Smart," *Fortune* (October 17, 1987), pp. 78–81, and I. Martin Jacknis, "The Art of Hiring '10s,' " *Inc.* (October, 1987), pp. 145–146.

All organizations must be staffed with high-quality talent in order to achieve key performance objectives. Chapter 9 examines the full range of staffing responsibilities you will face as a manager. Specific topics of study include

The Staffing Process
Human Resource Planning
Recruitment
Selection
Orientation
Training and Development
Replacement

These slogans say it all. "*People are our most important asset.*" "*It's people who make the difference.*" "It's the *people* who work for us who . . . determine whether our company thrives or languishes."[1] Such testimonials are found in newspaper and television ads, in annual reports, in corporate recruiting literature, in speeches and in organizational newsletters. What they all add up to is recognition that once plans have been made and structures and jobs designed to implement them, the organization must be properly staffed with human resources if it is to achieve high productivity. **Staffing** is the process of filling jobs with appropriate persons. It is an integral part of every manager's organizing responsibilities. Fortunately, the field of managmeent offers considerable insight into what the chapter opener referred to as the "art of hiring '10s'."

THE STAFFING PROCESS

Finding, hiring, and then maintaining a competent and dedicated workforce is the crux of the staffing challenge. Without proper human resources, even the best-designed organization guided by well-made plans can't achieve it's true performance potential. The ultimate aim of all managers, accordingly, is to make sure that the jobs under their responsibility are filled with talented persons *capable* of achieving high performance.

Staffing and Performance

To succeed with the staffing process, a manager must first understand three factors with the potential to significantly influence the performance potential of individuals at work—ability, support, and effort. The relationships among these factors are summarized in this *individual performance equation*.

$$\text{Performance} = \text{ability} \times \text{support} \times \text{effort}$$

The logic of the equation follows. High performance is possible only when the organization's human resources have the *ability* to do the work, are willing to exert the necessary *effort,* and have proper *support.* Take away any one or more of these elements and performance will suffer. A hard-working person with great support can't perform without the required abilities. A capable person willing to work hard can't perform without good support. The capable person who is well supported but unwilling to exert the necessary effort won't be a high performer either.

Figure 9.1 indicates that each element in the individual performance equation is addressed through different managerial initiatives. Support is achieved, in large measure, through proper design of organization structures and jobs. Effort is influenced via leadership, the subject of the next four chapters. Ability is a staffing issue. As such, proper staffing is an essential ingredient in the total management process. This excerpt from an advertisement once run by the Motorola Corporation sums the point up well.

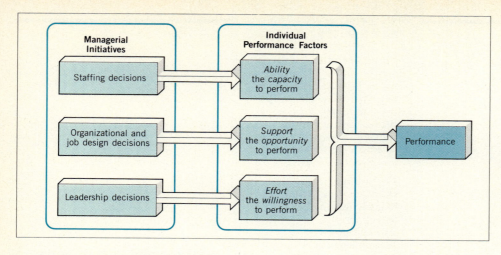

FIGURE 9.1
Managerial decisions and the three individual performance factors— ability, support, and effort.

PRODUCTIVITY IS:
LEARNING HOW TO HIRE THE
PERSON WHO IS *RIGHT* FOR THE JOB

As the following example shows, a new automobile plant in the midwestern United States is taking this advice most seriously.

ILLUSTRATIVE CASE:
DIAMOND STAR MOTORS

Bob Warner lost his job of 12 years with a coal mining equipment company located in West Virginia.[2] He moved back to his native Illinois and became one of 550 applicants for about 100 group leader positions at Diamond Star Motor Corporation. The new firm is a joint venture between Chrysler Corporation and Mitsubishi Motors Corporation of Japan. The assembly plant is planned to produce 240,000 cars annually and employ almost 3000 workers.

But getting a job at Diamond isn't easy. It's much more complicated than just filling out an application and sitting for a brief interview. It all adds up to a very sophisticated approach to hiring and training based largely on the Japanese traditions of Mitsubishi.

Prospective employees are carefully screened on a variety of matters. They take aptitude tests, drug tests, and other written exams. Potential assembly workers perform in simulated assembly-line situations to demonstrate their capabilities. Poten-

tial group leaders perform in assessment centers where they are asked in simulated conditions to counsel troubled workers, teach workers how to handle equipment, and show organizational abilities by processing an in-basket full of paperwork. And that's not all. All applicants also undergo in-depth counseling and personal interviews which address their potential loyalty to the company, team spirit, and individual versatility. The whole process takes up to three days for applicants who want to become group leaders, and one and one-half days for those seeking to work on the assembly line. A company spokesperson says the approach "allows us to make sure our assessments are as unbiased as possible . . . and it also shows us the individuals we hire are very interested in working for Diamond Star."

Once he was hired, Bob Warner found that Diamond's concern and commitment to human resource development didn't stop with the assessment process. He was sent to Japan for six weeks of initial training. While there he went step-by-step through all required operations, from the most simple to the most complex. He says, "It's so much different from American plants where they just throw you on the job and say 'here it is.' The Japanese believe in very thorough training."

About his experience to date, Warner expects that Diamond's attention to staffing will pay off in the form of a highly qualified and motivated workforce that can outperform traditional American plants. "I think we can blend some of the Japanese ideas with American ways of doing things. I think their philosophy of team spirit and company commitment will sell over here.''

Elements in the Staffing Process

The prior case clearly illustrates the basic objective of staffing—to match people and jobs in a manner that facilitates continuing high performance. The staffing process itself involves developing an appropriate work force by planning for and implementing effective recruitment, selection, orientation, training and development, and replacement activities. Briefly, the managerial significance of the major elements in the staffing process includes:

1. *Human resource planning*   Good planning identifies staffing needs and ensures they are met by ongoing analysis of performance objectives, job requirements, and available personnel.
2. *Recruitment*   Once staffing needs are identified, effective recruiting is needed to establish a pool of qualified candidates for open jobs.
3. *Selection*   Candidates in the recruiting pool must be carefully evaluated relative to requirements; capable and interested people must be matched with appropriate jobs.
4. *Orientation*   New personnel must be properly introduced to their jobs, work setting, co-workers, organizational policies and procedures, and supervisory expectations.
5. *Training and development*   Opportunities for continued training and development should maintain job skills and enhance individual capabilities for assuming increasing responsibilities over time.
6. *Replacement*   Persons must sometimes be removed or reassigned from their jobs; replacement includes promotions, transfers, and retirements that are voluntary, as well as involuntary terminations.

Figure 9.2 summarizes these six elements in the staffing process. Taken together they focus managerial attention on both the acquisition and maintenance of the human resources necessary to staff organizations for productivity.

Staffing and Human Resource Management

Human resource management is a term used to describe the wide variety of activities involved in staffing organizations and ensuring that the per-

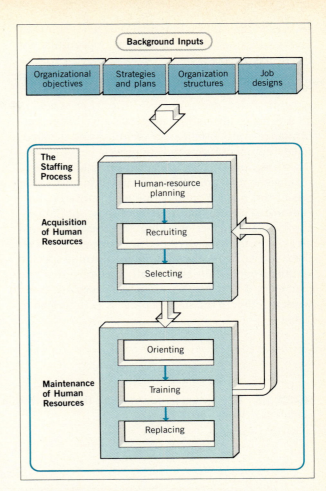

FIGURE 9.2 *Major elements in the staffing process as a key managerial responsibility.*

formance potential of every employee is fully realized. Because of the increasing complexity and importance of human resource issues in organizations, a human resource department or personnel department appears on most organization charts. Increasingly, this department is headed by a senior manager reporting directly to the chief executive officer and managing a team of staff specialists. In a dynamic environment complicated by legal issues, labor shortages, economic turmoil, changing corporate strategies, new organization and job designs, high technology, and changing personal values and expectations, such specialists are often needed to assist the rest of an organization manage its human resources to their fullest potential. The net result is an emerging career area full of great opportunity for interested persons.

A typical human resource department is shown in Figure 9.3. Note that the department employs persons with a wide variety of special expertise in all aspects of the staffing process, as well as in performance evaluation, career planning and development, compensation and employee benefits, and labor relations—areas of broader human resource management responsibility discussed in later chapters of this book. You may pursue advanced education and a career in one or more of these specialities. Even as a manager working in other functional areas, you must be prepared to work closely with these specialists. As we move on to examine specific staffing responsibilities in detail, remember that line managers and human resource specialists often work together in the staffing process as suggested in Table 9.1.

HUMAN RESOURCE PLANNING

Human resource planning, sometimes called **personnel planning,** is the process of analyzing staffing needs and identifying actions to satisfy these needs over time.[3] The purpose of human resource planning is to make sure the organization always has the right people available to do the required work. For the manager, this involves identifying staffing needs, examining the availability of personnel, and determining what additions and/or replacements are required to maintain a staff of the desired size and quality.

Why Human Resource Planning Is Important

These newspaper headlines from *The Wall Street Journal* help introduce the importance of human resource planning to organizations.

FIGURE 9.3 *Key personnel functions in the organization chart for a human resources department.*

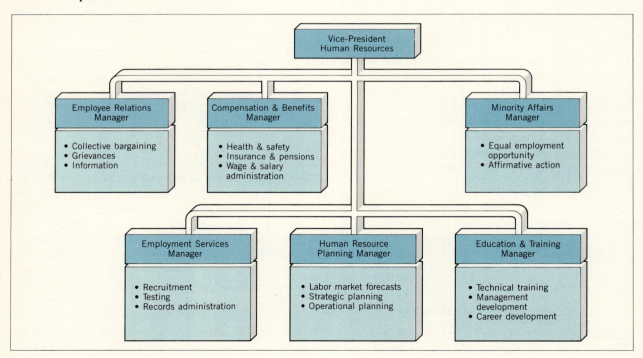

TABLE 9.1 *Possible Division of Labor in the Staffing Process Between Line Managers and Staff Human Resource Specialists*

In Respect to . . .	The Line Manager . . .	While the Staff Human Resource Specialist . . .
Recruiting	Requests filling a vacancy according to certain job specifications	Advertises the vacancy; develops candidate pool; ensures advertising meets government regulations
Selection	Interviews candidates and chooses most qualified	Screens applicants; ensures hiring is consistent with organizational policies and government regulations
Orientation	Orients new employee to job, performance expectations, and co-workers	Processes paperwork for new employee; orients employee to organization as a whole
Training and development	Monitors training needs; advises on training options; does on-job training	Arranges off-job training programs; designs and conducts some programs
Replacement	Recommends promotions, transfers, separations	Reviews such decisions for consistency with policies and regulations; processes related paperwork

A SHALLOW LABOR POOL . . .

GROWING SHORTAGE OF SKILLED CRAFTSPEOPLE TROUBLES SOME FIRMS

YOUNG PEOPLE SHUN FACTORIES

To begin, effective human resource planning can help organizations to anticipate personnel shortages—like those indicated in the headlines—and determine how best to deal with them. Planning helps to identify future staffing needs, anticipate shortages and surpluses in labor supplies, and target personnel recruitment and replacement efforts. In particular, we can identify these timely reasons why human resource planning is important to organizations and their managers.

1. *Human resource planning helps relate the staffing process to the corporate purpose and culture.* Special human resource plans must often be set to properly match newly hired personnel with the corporate purpose and culture. The activities at Diamond Star Motors, as described earlier, are indicative of the how complex this challenge is for a truly concerned employer. The responsible staff at Diamond Star were not just hiring people, they were implementing personnel plans with the specific objective of finding, hiring, and retaining the best available people who fit the new firm's intended culture.

2. *Human resource planning helps relate the staffing process to the requirements of organizational strategies.* Human resource plans are among the key operational plans needed to support and implement strategies. Two good examples are the special needs of growth and retrenchment strategies in today's demanding environment. In the former instance the problem is to increase staff, sometimes in difficult labor markets, without sacrificing quality and in order to meet expanding needs. In the latter it is to decrease staff when *downsizing* operations—and to do so in a humane and responsible manner consistent with societal as well as organizational needs. The role of good plans and the support of knowledgeable human resources specialists are crucial to enterprise success in such situations.

3. *Human resource planning helps relate the staffing process to the requirements of new computer-based technologies.* Among the many other human resources challenges facing organizations today stands the need to achieve a good fit between the

human resources and new technologies. The emergence of computerized work stations in the office, in the warehouse, on the factory floor, and at the service counter is changing not only the nature of work but the skills needed by the workers themselves. Human resource planning helps managers stay abreast of such changes and develop the "people policies" and staffing strategies needed to best integrate the human factor with the new machines.[4]

What Human Resource Planning Involves

A basic approach to human resource planning is shown in Figure 9.4. The process begins with a review of organizational strategies and objectives. This establishes the practical frame of reference against which human resource requirements and the internal supply of personnel can be forecast. Human resource planning must complement strategic planning to ensure that organizations have the right number of people with the right skills available to do the required jobs. It makes quite a difference, for example, if the organization is pursuing a growth or retrenchment strategy. Ultimately, the process should produce action plans capable of correcting

FIGURE 9.4 *Major elements in the human resource planning process.*

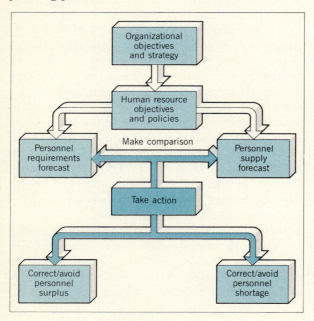

any actual or projected staffing surplus or shortage. At its very core, human resource planning involves establishing staffing needs, and auditing and forecasting human resource availabilities. All this must be done, of course, in due consideration for any requirements in the governing legal and regulatory environment.

Establishing Staffing Needs

Job analysis is the orderly study of job requirements and facets that can influence performance results. It is the beginning point in any systematic effort to identify staffing needs. A job analysis is conducted to determine just *what* is done, *when, where, how, why,* and by *whom.* It will typically examine:[5]

■ *Work activities* Exactly what tasks need to be accomplished.
■ *Performance standards* Expected output in quantity and quality.
■ *Work technologies* Machines, tools, other job technologies.
■ *Job-related tangibles and intangibles* Knowledge applied, materials processed, products or services performed during work.
■ *Job context* Work schedules, physical conditions, social relations, compensation.
■ *Personal requirements* Requisite education, training, skills, experience, and other attributes required for the job.

The information gained through job analysis is the basis for written job descriptions and specifications. These, in turn, provide a point of departure for the rest of the staffing process. Chapter 8 introduced the **job description** as a written statement detailing the duties and responsibilities of a job. A **job specification** is a list of the qualifications required of any job occupant. Such specifications usually include education, experience, and skill requirements for the job. With a good job description and job specification in hand, a manager can begin the search for people with the right qualifications to do the job well.

Many organizations employ persons with specialized skills as job analysts. The job description and job specification for a job analyst working in the human resource department of one company are shown in Figure 9.5. Whether job analysis is done by a line manager or job analyst, the informa-

JOB TITLE: Job Analyst DEPARTMENT: Human Resources
IMMEDIATE SUPERVISOR: Manager, Compensation and Benefits

Summary:

Under the guidance of the compensation and benefits manager: collects, analyzes and develops occupational data concerning jobs, job qualifications, and job requirements. Prepares job descriptions, job specifications, and job classification systems.

Duties:

1. Interviews workers and supervisory personnel to analyze tasks performed, and identify skill requirements.
2. Analyzes conditions of work, including the physical environment, travel requirements, etc.
3. Analyzes the amount of supervision received and the amount of supervision given as part of the job.
4. Develops task statements describing all duties and tasks performed.
5. Prepares written job descriptions and job specifications.
6. Evaluates the comparative difficulty of jobs and establishes job classifications.
7. Recommends the redesign of jobs as appropriate.
8. Performs additional duties as assigned.

Job Specification:

Experience: Three years of employment in personnel work, preferred with at least one year relating to activities associated with duties 1 through 7 above. Entry level appointment possible with exceptional educational record.

Education: College degree required, preferably in business administration or psychology with coursework in human resources or personnel management..

Skills: Must be effective in oral and written communication, have strong interpersonal skills, be capable of working effectively in a team setting, and have a high degree of individual initiative.

FIGURE 9.5 *Job description and job specification for the position of job analyst in a human resources department.*

tion on which it is based can be collected by a variety of methods. These include direct observation, interviews, and questionnaire surveys of the job holder and/or supervisor, job diaries kept by the job holder, and recordings of job activities on videotape or film.

Forecasting and the Human Resource Audit

Forecasting the supply of human resources involves projecting future staffing needs and the anticipated supply of appropriate personnel, including external labor market conditions. It is important to know, for example, how many people of what qualifications will be required by the organization, how many currently are in place, and how gaps between the two will be handled. A forecast that future needs will be greater than the present supply calls for an active recruiting strategy; a forecast that future needs will be less than present supply may require a strategy of planned terminations and/or nonreplacement.

An important step in human resource forecasting is the examination of the skills and performance of current employees. This involves a **human resource audit** or systematic inventory of the strengths and weaknesses of existing personnel. A good audit helps managers plan promotions and career enhancement activities for personnel in their areas of responsibility, and plan for appropriate training, development, or replacement where weaknesses exist.

One special application is in regards to what are referred to in many organizations as *high potentials*. Consider the situation[6]

at IBM where executives in charge of all units are asked to identify "high potential" people, that is those who it is believed can reach the senior executive level during their careers. IBM then tries to develop these people by carefully planning their progress through various jobs. They are given a broadening set of experiences within the first ten years. They are expected to move from job to job to test their potential every 18 to 24 months, and they are routinely rotated between line and staff duties. The job assignments are associated with additional training, offered both inside and outside of the company.

Another application of the human resource audit involves formal **succession planning,** that is planning for the replacement of key personnel over time. A case in point is the choice of new chief executives.[7] This is a very significant decision for small and large organizations alike. It has the capacity to greatly influence the future direction and prosperity of the enterprise, and it can be controversial. For example,[8]

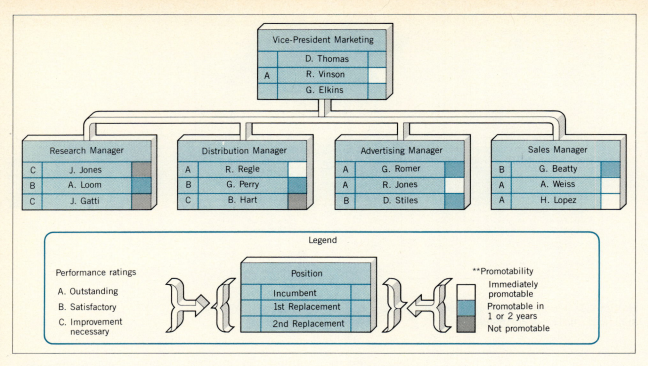

FIGURE 9.6 *A human resource inventory chart: the case of the marketing department.*

at Wal-Mart investors and company insiders wondered, for years who would replace the legendary Sam Walton as head of the firm. There appeared to be two competitors—David Glass, the president, and Jack Shewmaker, chief financial officer. When Glass was ultimately given the job, Shewmaker's retirement was also announced and *The Wall Street Journal* commented "it was unlikely that either one would have been content working for the other."

Succession planning in general is facilitated by the maintenance of a comprehensive **human resource inventory chart** such as the one shown in Figure 9.6. Sometimes called a **replacement chart,** it records the substitutability, transferability, or promotability of persons in key positions. Such charts are useful in planning future staff actions. In the figure, for example, the poor-performing head of research should probably be replaced. Some persons on the chart are ready to move into higher responsibilities immediately; others could do so given more time in their present jobs and/or proper training. Let's look again—[9]

at IBM where the executive in charge of IBM's succession planning maintains a replacement chart for each person in about 1600 executive positions. This chart shows the present job incumbent and several likely replacements spanning a four-year period. The chart also rates each person's potential to eventually reach the top. With this and other information available, the executive tracks their progress to plan for everyone's continued development . . . and for their effective replacement.

The Legal Environment of the Staffing Process

Human resource planning, like all planning, must be sensitive to government regulations and the legal environment within which the organization operates. In the United States, the issues grow increasingly complex as old laws become modified, new ones are added, and changes occur among the state and federal agencies which monitor them. Some highlights of the legal and regulatory environment affecting the staffing process are presented in Table

TABLE 9.2 *Legal Implications for the Staffing Process of Selected Pieces of Federal Legislation Passed Since 1960*

Major Legislation	Legal Impact
Equal Pay Act (1963)	Prohibits wage discrimination on the basis of gender; requires equal pay for equal work regardless of gender
Title VII, Civil Rights Act (1964) and Equal Employment Opportunity Act (1972)	Prohibits employment discrimination based on race, color, religion, gender, or national origin
Occupational Safety and Health Act (1970)	Protects workers from safety and health hazards in the workplace, under the supervision of the Occupational Safety and Health Administration (OSHA)
Age Discrimination in Employment Act (1967; amended in 1978 and 1981)	Prohibits employment discrimination based on age; specifically protects persons 40–70 years of age
Vocational Rehabilitation Act (1973)	Mandates affirmative action programs for hiring, placing, and advancing handicapped persons
Mandatory Retirement Act; Employee Retirement Income Security Act (1974)	Prohibits mandatory retirement before age 70; provides certain pension vesting rights for employees
Privacy Act (1974)	Gives employees the legal right to examine letters of reference about them
Pregnancy Discrimination Act (1978)	Requires pregnancy-maternity to be treated as any other disability
Veteran's Readjustment Act (1973)	Prohibits employment discrimination against disabled veterans and Vietnam-era war veterans
Immigration Reform and Control Act (1986)	Prohibits the employment of anyone who is not an American citizen or an alien authorized to work in the United States

9.2. In addition, most American managers are affected by a collection of federal and state laws relating to employment discrimination and organized labor among other employment situations. Selected examples are briefly highlighted here.

Employment Discrimination

In the U.S. legal environment, laws protecting individual rights against discrimination in employment are of special significance. Among these, the *Civil Rights Act of 1964* and the *Equal Employment Opportunity Act of 1972* stand out for their guarantees of individual liberties in the form of **equal employment opportunity.** This is the right of people to employment without regard to race, color, national origin, religion or gender. The *Vocational Rehabilitation Act of 1973* extended such protection to the handicapped; the *Age Discrimination Act of 1981* extended it to persons between the ages of 40 and 70.

EEO, as it is commonly known, is federally enforced by the Equal Employment Opportunity Commission (EEOC) and generally applies to all public and private organizations employing 15 or more people. Virtually everyone is accorded this legal protection. When discrimination is encountered, legal charges can be filed and court action taken to resolve complaints. *Newsline 9.1* introduces some of the issues in specific respect to age discrimination.

As a general rule, the statutes on employment dicrimination do not restrict the employer's right to establish **bona fide occupational qualifications.** These are criteria for employment—including age

AGE DISCRIMINATION:
A NEW CORPORATE BIAS?

"How I envy you, Tompkins, with that great big wonderful world out there waiting for you to retire into!"

Drawing by Whitney Darrow, Jr.: © 1974 The New Yorker Magazine, Inc.

In 1967 Congress passed the Age Discrimination in Employment Act. This law, subsequently revised, prevents employers from making decisions about hiring or firing workers over 40 years old on the basis of their age. Jury trials are allowed under the law, and litigants who prove willful discrimination have collected double damages in some cases.

A growing number of over-40 workers, particularly white males who believe they have been dismissed from their jobs without good cause, are filing lawsuits under the age act. They argue that their performance records are flawless and that their employers have laid them off solely because of their age, in order to bring in younger workers. In one instance a 63-year-old man claimed that he was told his position would be terminated even as a young man was being hired to assume his responsibilities; in another case a 62-year-old trainee in a police program was terminated for "medical reasons" despite having passed several earlier physical exams.

Just a few years ago, a fourth of all court actions filed by the Equal Employment Opportunity Commission were related to age discrimination. As the number of older workers rises—in the year 2010 more than half of the nation's workforce is expected to be over 40—more people are likely to take advantage of the legal protection afforded by the age act. Employers are recognizing the need to tread carefully where older workers are involved; inappropriate remarks or unwarranted dismissals could be countered with a lawsuit.

Source: As reported in Sydney P. Freedburg, "Forced Exits? Companies Confront Wave of Age-Discrimination Suits," *Wall Street Journal* (October 13, 1987), p. 37, and "Sample of U.S. Worker Complaints About Age Discrimination," *Christian Science Monitor* (January 5, 1988), p. 6.

or gender—which can be clearly justified as being related to someone's capacity to perform a job. In order to prevent a man from becoming an airline flight attendant or a woman from becoming a pilot, for example, an airline recruiter would have to prove that a person of that gender could not do the job in question. Obviously, it is very difficult to establish such qualifications in most jobs.

Equal employment opportunity legislation helps guarantee people's rights as employees. It protects you as well as others. But as a manager, it also requires you to act consistent with EEO guidelines. Failure to comply with antidiscrimination laws is not only disrespectful and unjustified in a free society, it can also be a very expensive mistake. It cost United Airlines as much as $38 million in back pay for flight attendants who were forced out of their jobs by the company's former "no marriage policy"; a jury awarded a GM worker $1.25 million in back pay, damages, and accrued interest to a female General Motors employee who filed a lawsuit alleging racial and sex discrimination at work.

Whereas equal employment opportunity laws prohibit discrimination in recruitment, hiring, and promotion, **affirmative-action programs** are designed to increase employment opportunities for women and other minorities including veterans, the aged, and the handicapped. Based on two Executive Orders originaly issued by President Lyndon B. Johnson, affirmative-action requirements apply to all organizations doing business with the federal government. The intent of the program is to ensure that women and other minorities are represented in the work force in proportion to their actual availability in the area labor market. Organizations that fail to meet these proportions must pursue assigned affirmative-action goals to increase the hiring and/or advancement of minorities. Failure to comply with affirmative-action guidelines can result in loss of federal funding and contracts.

Organized Labor

Another important legal consideration in human resource planning and the staffing process relates to organized labor. You may be employed by an organization whose work force is represented in whole or part by a labor union. The unions act as bargaining agents which negotiate *legal* contracts that affect many aspects of human resource management. Typical provisions, for example, relate to job specifications, seniority rules, compensation practices and benefits, grievance mechanisms, and procedures for hiring, promoting, transferring and dismissing workers, among other related matters. In all such respects, the managers, workers and union representatives are subject to the provisions of governing legislation. Major examples include the *Wagner Act of 1935* — protects employees by recognizing their rights to join unions and engage in union activities; the *Taft–Hartley Act of 1947* — protects employers from unfair labor practices by unions and allows workers to decertify unions; and, the *Civil Service Reform Act, Title VII of 1978* — clarifies the rights of government employees to join and be represented by labor unions.

Chapter 18 discusses the legal environment and other issues in labor–management relations in detail. For now, the U.S. automobile industry illustrates how organized labor influences human resource management practices in business. For years representatives of Ford, General Motors, and Chrysler have bargained with the strong, demanding leadership of the United Auto Workers (UAW). The contracts negotiated are complex in terms of work rules, and expensive in compensation and benefit packages. Any human resource planning in this industry has to take the UAW and its desires into account. Lately, however, the automakers and the UAW have tried to work more closely together to reduce production costs while still maintaining basic worker rights and benefits. Each side seems more willing to recognize that the productivity and future survival of the industry depends on cooperation and mutual adjustment to new and challenging times. As a case-in-point,[10]

at General Motors the union was involved very early in planning for the new Saturn plant. This included participation by union representatives and management personnel in a series of brainstorming sessions that included field trips to unique manufacturing plants in Japan, West Germany, and Sweden.

RECRUITMENT

Recruitment is a set of activities designed to attract a qualified pool of job applicants to an organization. Emphasis on the word *qualified* is important. Effective recruiting brings employment opportunities to the attention of persons with abilities and skills appropriate to job specifications. In the staffing process, human resource planning leads to recruiting, which sets the stage for selection.

The Recruitment Process

The three steps in the recruitment process are: (1) advertisement of a job vacancy, (2) preliminary contact with potential job candidates, and (3) initial screening to create a pool of qualified applicants. Figure 9.7 shows separate events in the collegiate recruiting process as they involve line managers and staff recruiters from the organization, and the student as potential job applicant. Project yourself into this situation. You are near graduation and want a full-time job that relates to your major field of study. What will the three steps in the recruiting process look like from your side of things? Probably the following.

1. *Job advertisement* The organization advertises its job vacancies by posting short job descriptions at

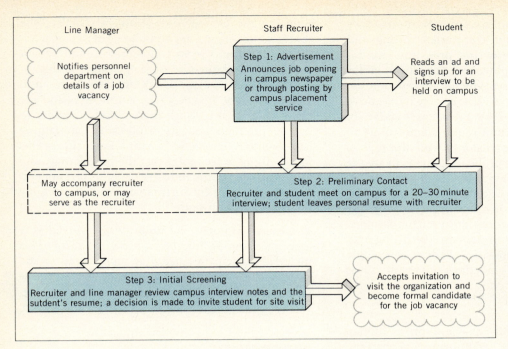

Line Manager	Staff Recruiter	Student

Notifies personnel department on details of a job vacancy

Step 1: Advertisement Announces job opening in campus newspaper or through posting by campus placement service

Reads an ad and signs up for an interview to be held on campus

May accompany recruiter to campus, or may serve as the recruiter

Step 2: Preliminary Contact Recruiter and student meet on campus for a 20–30 minute interview; student leaves personal resume with recruiter

Step 3: Initial Screening Recruiter and line manager review campus interview notes and the sutdent's resume; a decision is made to invite student for site visit

Accepts invitation to visit the organization and become formal candidate for the job vacancy

FIGURE 9.7 *Line manager and staff recruiter roles in the on-campus recruitment of college students for job vacancies.*

the campus placement center and/or in the campus newspaper.

2. *Preliminary contact* You sign up for an interview with a recruiter on campus; during a short (20–30 minute) interview you present a written résumé of your background and explain your job qualifications.

3. *Initial screening* The recruiter discusses interview results and your résumé with appropriate line managers; based on their knowledge of job specifications, you are among the candidates selected for a formal visit to the organization.

External and Internal Recruitment

There are two basic categories of job candidates toward whom recruiting efforts can be directed— qualified employees ready for promotion or transfer from within the organization, and persons from the outside. **Internal recruitment** involves making employees aware of job vacancies through job posting and personal recommendations. Most organizations have a procedure for announcing vacancies through newsletters, bulletin boards, and the like. They also rely on managers to recommend subordinates who are good candidates for advancement. **External recruitment** involves the attraction of job candidates

from sources outside of the organization. Newspapers, employment agencies, colleges, technical training centers, personal contacts, walk-ins, employee referrals, and even persons in competing organizations are among the sources of external recruits.

Each of these recruitment strategies offers potential advantages and disadvantages to the organization. Internal recruitment is usually the least expensive, deals with persons of known performance records, and leads to a pool of candidates who are already familiar with the internal workings of the organization. A history of serious internal recruitment can be very encouraging to employees. It demonstrates opportunities to advance in one's career by working hard and achieving high performance at each point of responsibility. For example,[11]

at Proctor & Gamble the company is known for an emphasis on internal recruiting. Persons writing to inquire about job opportunities are sent a brochure that states:

> We're looking for achievers . . . we seek exceptionally able college graduates who have already demonstrated a superior ability to achieve, and who possess the potential for rapid personal growth after they join us. . . . We hire at the beginning level and *promote from*

within, strictly on the basis of performance. [Emphasis added.]

External recruiting, on the other hand, brings in outsiders with fresh perspectives. It also provides a source of specialized expertise or work experience that is not otherwise available from insiders. Overall, a mixture of external and internal recruiting allows the manager and organization to gain the best advantage of each as circumstances allow.

Realistic Recruitment

Two contrasts can be found in prevailing recruitment philosophies.[12] *Traditional recruitment* often seeks to "sell" the organization to outsiders. During the recruitment process only the most positive features of the job and organization are communicated to potential candidates. At the extreme, bias may even be introduced as these features are exaggerated while negative features are concealed. This form of recruitment is designed to attract as many candidates as possible. The problem is that it tends to create unrealistic expectations by the newly hired person. In terms used in Chapter 8, the individual's psychological contract then becomes distorted when these expectations are left unfulfilled once on the job. Premature turnover, the early resignation of new hires, often occurs in these circumstances.

Consider what happened to Lynda McDermott who left her job at an accounting firm to become executive vice-president of a new management consulting company.[13] The new job sounded ideal—it offered what her boss said would be a major role in bringing in new business. She says, "I *perceived* that I was brought in as a partner to help the business grow." Eleven months later Lynda quit, claiming her boss was "a wonderful salesperson." Unfortunately, and contrary to what she thought they had agreed upon, he only allowed her to become involved in routine administrative duties.

Realistic job previews try to provide the candidate with all pertinent information about the job and organization without distortion and *before* the job is accepted. Instead of "selling" the organization by communicating only positive features, this approach tries to be realistic and balanced in the information provided. It tries to be fair in depicting actual job and organizational features. While positive aspects are not ignored, the candidate is also told about potential negative ones. As a result of this more complete view of the job and organization, new employees should have more realistic job expectations at the time of initial entry. A healthy psychological contract, higher levels of early job satisfaction and less premature turnover are the anticipated benefits.

SELECTION

Selection is the process of choosing from a pool of applicants the person or persons best meeting job specifications. It involves identifying those applicants who offer the greatest performance potential as employees. Increasingly, the emphasis in selection is on someone's demonstrated capacity to achieve and excel in a responsible job. This was first evident in the illustrative case on Diamond Star Motors early in the chapter. It was also well expressed in the prior quote from Proctor & Gamble's recruiting brochure which said, in part—"we seek exceptionally able college graduates who have already demonstrated a superior ability to achieve, and who possess the potential for rapid personal growth after they join us." And, it is found[14]

at Stew Leonard's where the dairy store's focus on customer service begins with the selection of new employees. The moment an applicant sits down for an interview, the "spirit" of customer service is put to the test. Jill Travello, the director of personnel, looks above all else for a good attitude. This is emphasized over experience and education, among other things. Stew says, "If applicants have a good attitude, we can do the rest . . . but if they have a bad attitude to start with, everything we do seems to fail." Jill interviews 15 to 25 applicants per position before selecting the one who is just exactly what she is looking for.

Steps in the Selection Process

Steps in a typical selection process are (1) completion of a formal application form, (2) further interviewing, (3) testing, (4) reference checks, (5) physical examination, and (6) final analysis and decision to hire or reject. Briefly highlighted here, these steps are also shown in Figure 9.8, along with sample reasons why applicants might be rejected in each stage.

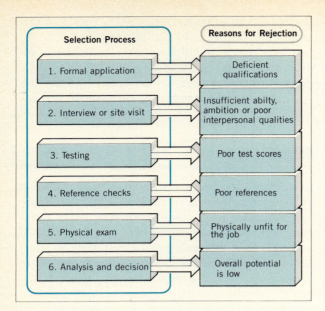

Selection Process	Reasons for Rejection
1. Formal application	Deficient qualifications
2. Interview or site visit	Insufficient abilty, ambition or poor interpersonal qualities
3. Testing	Poor test scores
4. Reference checks	Poor references
5. Physical exam	Physically unfit for the job
6. Analysis and decision	Overall potential is low

FIGURE 9.8 *Steps in the typical selection process: the case of the rejected job applicant.*

Job-Application Forms

Among the elements in the selection process, the job-application form declares the individual a formal candidate for the job vacancy. It summarizes the applicant's personal history and qualifications. The personal résumé is often included with the job application. This important document should accurately summarize an applicant's special qualifications. You, for example, should exercise great care in preparing your résumé for job searches. As a manager, you should also learn how to screen the applications and résumés of other persons for facts that can help you make a good selection decision.

Interviews

Formal interviews allow job candidates and key persons from within the organization to learn more about one another than the application form and résumé make possible. Usually more than one interview is involved. An initial screening interview often leads to a series of more intense on-site interviews with one's potential supervisor and co-workers, as well as with representatives of the human resource department.

Any interview is an extremely important part of the selection process because of the information exchange it allows. Thus it is important for both the

job candidate and the persons serving as interviewers to fulfill the interviewing task well. Four things to remember when you are the one *taking* job interviews are:

1. *Preparation is essential* Get ready for the interview by finding out all you can about the potential employer, including key products or services, size, history, and even the names and backgrounds of key executives; finding out all you can about the position being filled, including the required skills and qualifications, as well as specific job responsibilities; thinking about what you have to offer as a prospective employee, including careful analysis of your educational background, skills, and experience as they relate to the vacant position.

2. *First impressions count* Create a desirable image for yourself by wearing conservative, neat, and business-like clothing; being very carefully groomed; being early, rather than late; acting courteous, calm, and professional; and projecting a sense of enthusiasm.

3. *Think before answering questions* Show confidence in your work potential by being patient and carefully answering all questions; using words and grammer well; giving organized and focused answers; and remembering to show poise and self-confidence.

4. *Ask, don't just answer, questions* Take advantage of the opportunity to ask questions of the interviewer. Don't forget that obtaining a realistic job preview is in part your responsibility. Many applicants are so concerned about getting the job that they gloss over important issues, or fail to ask probing questions. Be polite, but get the information you need to make a good job choice.

Now, let's view interviewing from the other side of the process. When you are the one *doing* the interviewing, remember:[15]

■ *Plan ahead and create a good climate for the interview* Review the job specifications and job description, as well as the candidate's application. Allow sufficient time for an uninterrupted interview. Choose a quiet place, hold all phone calls, and give the candidate your sincere and undivided attention. Be the perfect host or hostess. Try to establish a friendly, open rapport with the applicant.

■ *Conduct a goal-oriented interview* Be sure to get the information needed to make a good employment decision. Ask questions about the candidate's education, experience, knowledge and skills, work habits, and career interests. Some things to look for include: creativity and the ability to be innovative in one's work; independence and the ability to work without close supervision; initiative and the ability to be a self-starter; and a high energy level and the ability to work under pressure.

■ *Avoid any questions that may imply discrimination* Ask only for information that directly relates to a candidate's abilities to do the job.[16] All questioning should be limited to the job applied for, and the candidate's *bona fide* qualifications for it. Table 9.3 presents guidelines on interviewing do's and don'ts distributed to all supervisors in one organization.

■ *Answer the questions asked of you . . . and even some that may not be asked* Remember that ensuring a realistic job preview is an important part of your interviewing responsibility. While your task certainly involves "selling" the candidate on the job and organization, it also involves being as complete and realistic as possible in presenting valid information to the candidate.

■ *Write notes on the interview immediately upon completion* Don't risk forgetting the details or your impressions; make good notes that can be reviewed later for deliberation and decision making.

Employment Tests

Testing, as illustrated in the Diamond Star Motors case at the beginning of the chapter, is frequently used in the screening of job applicants. It offers the opportunity to gather additional information about a person, outside of the limitations of application forms and interview settings. Some of the common employment tests are:

1. *Intelligence tests* designed to assess a person's general mental capacity in respect to memory, verbal comprehension, and quantitative skills.
2. *Aptitude tests* designed to assess a person's specific job skills and abilities, and the potential for acquiring such competencies.
3. *Personality tests* designed to assess a variety of personal traits and characteristics, including attitudes, values, and beliefs.
4. *Interest tests* designed to assess a person's occupational interests in terms of likes and dislikes for different job opportunities.

Each of these tests is often given in a written form, but new developments in testing extend the process into actual demonstrations of job-relevant skills and personal characteristics. **Work-sampling** is a testing approach that assesses a person's performance on a set of tasks which directly replicate those required in the job under consideration. In the Diamond Star Motors case, work sampling was used when applicants for assembly-line jobs were asked to work on a small assembly line while being graded by observers on their performance.

TABLE 9.3 *Employment Interviewing Guidelines for Supervisors: Acceptable and Unacceptable Questions*

Subject	Do Not Ask	Okay to Ask
Age	Questions showing preference for a specific age group	If person is 18 years of age or not
Family	About family planning, family size, children's ages, child-care plans, spouse's employment, or salary	About freedom to travel if job requires, meeting work schedule requirements if all applicants asked the same questions
Handicaps	General questions that bring out information that is not job related	Whether person has mental, physical or medical impairments that would prevent them from doing the job applied for
Marital status	Whether person is married, single, separated, divorced, engaged	Nothing
National origin	About ancestry; birthplace of applicant, parents, or spouse; native language	Ability to speak, read, or write english or foreign language if the job requires
Religion	About religious affiliation	Anticipated absences from the job

An **assessment center** is a testing approach that evaluates a person's potential by observing his or her performance in experiential activities designed to simulate the day-to-day nature of managerial work. A typical assessment center engages job candidates in a series of activities over a one-three day period. These require participation in role playing, simulations, case analyses, and the like. A panel of experts evaluates the individual's performance during the exercise. As was the case with Bob Warner in the Diamond Star Motors example, this evaluation then becomes used for selection purposes. Assesment centers are also used to help design appropriate training and development programs for high-potential employees.

The goal of any employment test, written or experiential, is to gather information that will help predict the applicant's eventual performance success on the job. To do so, a test must be both valid and reliable. A **valid test** measures exactly what it intends to relative to the job specification—for example, intelligence or manual dexterity. A **reliable test** yields approximately the same results over time if taken by the same person.

Because invalid and/or unreliable tests can create bias in selection decisions, the testing process is often controversial. It is also subject to legal constraints. Under Equal Employment Opportunity legislation, any employment test used as a criterion of selection must be defensible on the grounds that it actually measures an ability required to perform the job. Thus testing is an aspect of the selection process that should be carefully administered by persons with special training in testing theory and practice. This expertise is often found with the personnel or human resource staff specialists of an organization.

Reference Checks

Reference or background checks are inquiries to prior employers, academic advisors, family members, and/or friends regarding the qualifications, experience, and past work records of a job applicant. Although they may also be biased, such as when friends are prearranged "to say the right things if called," reference checks can be helpful to both the potential employer and the applicant. They may reveal important information on the applicant that was not discovered elsewhere in the selection process. The references chosen by a job applicant can also add to one's credibility if they include a legitimate and even prestigious list of persons.

Physical Examinations

Some organizations ask job applicants to take a physical examination. This health check helps ensure that the person is physically capable of fulfilling job requirements. It may also be used as a basis for enrolling the applicant in health-related fringe benefits such as life-, health-, and disability-insurance programs. A recent and controversial development in this area is the emerging use of employee drug testing. Some organizations do this as part of pre-employment health screening and as a basis for continued employment.

Final Analysis and Decisions to Hire or Reject

Final responsibility for analysis of all the data and for the decision to hire or reject usually rests with the manager. This may be done with or without the counsel of the personnel specialists, or other persons with or for whom the job applicant would work. However, it is generally best to allow as many other relevant persons as possible to offer their inputs. This helps to ensure that all factors are considered before a hiring decision is made. The best selection decision is likely to be one made with the consultation of several persons, and based on information obtained from a variety of screening devices.

ORIENTATION

When people join an organization, they need to "learn the ropes" and become familiar with "the way things are done" in their new setting. Managers can and do take steps to help fit newcomers into the work environment. The underlying issue is **socialization,** the process of systematically changing the expectations, behavior, and attitudes of a new employee in a manner considered desirable by the organization.[17] The intent of socialization is to achieve the best possible match between the individual and the job, and between the individual and the organization. At risk is overconformity and loss of creativity.

Socialization of newcomers begins with initial orientation and continues during later training and development activities, as well as in day-to-day supervisor–subordinate relationships. **Orientation** is

HANDLING
THE NEWLY HIRED

An organization may be deservedly pleased with itself for having picked the plums of the annual crop: bright, energetic graduates who are eager to work hard and anxious to go far. But unless new recruits are appropriately dealt with during their first half-year, say experts in corporate culture, these newcomers are as likely to leave as to stick around.

A complete and careful orientation is the key to ensuring that new hires begin their jobs on an enthusiastic note. Nothing distresses a new employee—especially a would-be manager—more than the sensation of being left outside, a virtual stranger to corporate culture. What this means is that management must keep in close contact with recruits during the first weeks of their tenure, taking active steps to guide them

not only in their jobs but also in the ways of the organization itself. Says Joyce Watts, placement director of Northwestern's business school: "if you don't pay attention to [managerial trainees], you lose them easily."

Introductions of new employees to senior staff on the first day are a must. In some organizations, mentors are assigned to recruits to ensure that they receive personal attention on a regular basis; if the mentor if committed and concerned, this arrangement can be a highly successful means of training new hires and strengthening their links to the organization's culture. Large organizations often make use of formal training programs for up-and-coming managers. These programs work best, say experts, when they treat recruits as individuals, not standardized products.

Along with attention, providing the most promising new hires with a reasonable amount of freedom and responsibility right from the start is crucial. They will feel respected for what they have to offer and will be more likely to persevere over the long haul. Finally, frequent performance reviews—in which positive as well as negative behavior is noted—are recommended. Reviews are a good way of checking on the progress of newcomers and letting them know they're watched over—and wanted.

Source: As reported in Walter Kiechel III, "Love, Don't Lose, the Newly Hired," *Fortune* (June 6, 1988), pp. 271–272.

---

a set of activities designed to familiarize new employees with their jobs, co-workers, and key aspects of the organization as a whole. This includes the introduction of the organizational mission and culture, explanation of operating objectives and job expectations, communication of important policies and procedures, and identification of key persons in the hierarchy of authority. One place where special attention is given to employee orientation is

at Disneyworld   where newly hired employees go through an extensive and detailed orientation pro-

gram that teaches them the corporate culture into which they are entering. They are taught that everyone employed by the company, regardless of their specific job—be it entertainer, ticket seller, or groundskeeper—is there "to make the customer happy." They are taught the corporate values embodied in the legacy of the company's founder Walt Disney. And they are taught strict rules in terms of attire, attitude, and personal conduct as a Disney employee.

The unfortunate fact is that employee orientation is too-often neglected as a managerial responsibility. Newcomers are sometimes left to fend for themselves, and learn job and organizational routines on their own or through casual interactions with co-workers. Otherwise well-intentioned and capable persons may learn inappropriate attitudes and/or behaviors as a result.

Newsline 9.2 offers some advice on how to manage the orientation of new hires. This is important, since we know that the first six months of employment are often crucial in determining how well someone is going to perform over time. When done right, orientation enhances a person's understanding of the organization and adds purpose to their daily job behaviors. Increased performance, greater job satisfaction, and more work commitment are the desired results. In addition, it should be remembered that proper new-employee orientation can:

1. *Lower startup costs and time*   Orientation helps a newcomer reach performance standards in minimum time by learning about the job, supervisory expectations, and organizational facilities and work routines.
2. *Reduce anxiety*   The information made available during orientation helps reduce fears of failure and builds the newcomer's job confidence and competence.
3. *Decrease turnover*   Like realistic recruiting, proper orientation helps reduce premature turnover otherwise caused by high anxiety and unmet expectations.
4. *Strengthen the culture*   By communicating basic values, goals, and a clear sense of purpose, orientation helps build and maintain strong organizational cultures.

TRAINING AND DEVELOPMENT

Training is a set of activities that provides learning opportunities through which people acquire and improve job-related skills. These skills, in turn, fall into two general categories. On the one hand, managers are interested in helping the new job holder learn what is required to do a specific job. On the other hand, managers must also be concerned with helping job holders develop additional skills as needed over time. The former responsibility relates more to the initial training of an employee, while the latter involves upgrading or improving skills to meet changing job requirements.

What Constitutes Good Training?

All managers should be concerned about the initial and continued training and development of their subordinates. Good training and development addresses the five steps depicted in Figure 9.9.

Step 1: Assess Needs

Good training begins with a careful needs analysis. This may range from reviewing training needs on an organization-wide basis, to reviewing them for a single job or individual.

Step 2: Set Objectives

A needs analysis helps specify training objectives or desired end results for the training program. This should include the criteria against which final results are to be measured.

Step 3: Select Methods

Training objectives establish a frame of reference for choosing appropriate instructional methods. A number of these will be reviewed here shortly.

Step 4: Implement Program

Actual training activities can then be made available in accordance with choices made in Steps 2 and 3.

Step 5: Evaluate Program

Training outcomes should always be compared to desired results as a measure of actual performance success. Participants can and should be queried for their personal assessment of program content and quality of instruction.

Speaking more generally, good training can only occur when managers establish an overall climate within which

■   *Trainees want to learn*   There is no substitute for training a person who wants to learn and improve. Indeed, willingness to learn is an important criterion that should be used when selecting persons to fill job vacancies.

■   *Trainees are reinforced for learning*   Training accomplishments and the willingness to learn through active participation in future training opportunities must be maintained. This requires reinforcement and reward for individual learning efforts and demonstrated performance results.

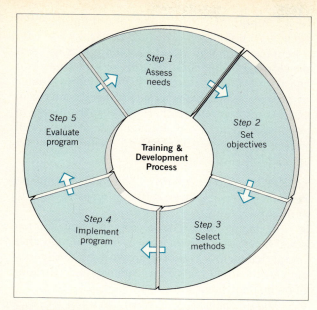

FIGURE 9.9 *Five major steps in the training and development process.*

ILLUSTRATIVE CASE:
PROCTOR & GAMBLE'S LEARNING CENTER

Top management at Proctor & Gamble takes the training and development of its managers very seriously.[18] The company recently published a "Catalog of Learning Opportunities" sponsored by its Corporate Training and Development Department. Offered through P&G's Learning Center were programs on a broad variety of topics. A sample includes interpersonal skills, personal growth, leadership, creative problem-solving, writing skills, stress management, time management, and employee relations.

In addition to providing the programs, however, the company expects its managers to take responsibility by actively planning for their training and how it will be applied back on the job. The catalog states, "This new learning should directly enhance effective performance." To best do so, the individual is asked to work directly with his or her supervisor to develop a *training and development plan*. This plan is supposed to:

■ Describe specific performance areas/skills that will be acquired or strengthened through training.

■ Identify available resources to help acquire or refine the target skills.

Consider how any special needs for coaching and feedback to support skill acquisition will be met.

The training and development plan, furthermore, includes responsibilities for both the individual and the supervisor. The individual is responsible for: an honest self-assessment of needs, taking initiative to pursue training and improve performance, and taking an active role in managing personal career interests. The supervisor is responsible for: describing what's expected for effective performance, identifying areas where improved skills will enhance performance, and providing access to the best ways of developing these skills—both through formal training and through on-the-job coaching. As stated by the company's vice-president, "Formal training programs can play an important role in helping us grow, but they should be viewed only as a supplement to on-the-job training, which should continue to be the primary source of learning and development for all of us."

Types of Training

As suggested in the prior case, the design of training programs varies between on-the-job or off-the-job training locations and among the alternative instructional methods that may be used.

On-the-job training occurs in the work setting and during actual job performance. Basic instructional approaches include job rotation, formal and informal coaching, apprenticeship, and modeling. **Job rotation** was discussed as a job design strategy in Chapter 8. As a training device, it offers opportunities for persons to spend time in different jobs and expand the range of their job capabilities. **Coaching** is the communication of specific technical advice to an individual. It can be done on a formal and planned basis by a supervisor or coworkers. It can also occur more spontaneously or on an informal basis as help offered by other persons when the need arises. **Apprenticeship** involves an assignment to serve as understudy or assistant to a person already having the desired job skills. Through this relationship an apprentice learns the job over time and eventually becomes fully qualified in his or her own right. Although most common to technical trades such as welding or machining, apprenticeship training is becoming more common for persons moving into new managerial jobs for the first time. **Modeling,** as a process of demonstrating through personal behavior what is expected of others, is also an influential means for building appropriate job skills. When persons in supervisory capacities work for good managers, for example, their managerial skills can be enhanced by simply practicing those things practiced on them.

Off-the-job training is accomplished away from the work setting. It may be done within the organization but in a separate training room or facility. It may also be done at a location remote from the organization. Examples of the latter include attendance at special training programs sponsored by universities, trade or professional associations, and consultants.

Figure 9.10 summarizes some of the instructional methods that are employed in off-the-job training: lectures, discussions, demonstrations, case studies, simulations, and role playing. You are probably familiar with most of them through your educational experiences. From a training perspective, two special features about these alternative techniques are worth highlighting. First, the role of the trainee becomes increasingly active as one moves away from lectures and toward role playing. Second, this more active involvement of the learner offers a greater chance for realizing more skills-oriented learning effects. Lecture methods, by contrast, involve a more passive role for the learner and are more knowledge oriented.

Management Development

Training specifically targeted to improve a person's knowledge and skills in the fundamentals of management is referred to as **management development.** If you are truly serious about a managerial career, management development activities should be an important part of your continuing personal agenda. Although some organizations, like P&G, do a better job than others of providing management development opportunities, this is something you can always attend to personally by taking advantage of programs or short seminars always available in the marketplace. Remember, too, that the nature of your management development needs may well vary as you progress through different levels of responsibility. For example,[19]

at IBM the "high potentials" identified in human resource audits are given different types of training at different points in their careers.

■ *Beginning managers* get training that emphasizes delegating duties, since the company has found that technical people promoted into supervision for the first time have a tendency to do the jobs of their subordinates.

■ *Middle managers* receive training with a broader perspective that emphasizes judgmental exercises and refines their capabilities as "managers of managers."

■ *Top managers* attend a special advanced management school that emphasizes case studies to sharpen their decision-making and negotiating skills, and to expand their awareness of corporate strategy and direction.

One increasingly popular form of management development activity is the **management simulation game.** Such simulations place participants in "real-life" organizational situations that involve problem solving and decision making in a hectic setting of frequent meetings, phone calls, and interruptions. The attempt is to simulate a typical day or two in the life of a true manager, and to give participants the opportunity to examine their managerial behavior in a learning environment. For example,[20]

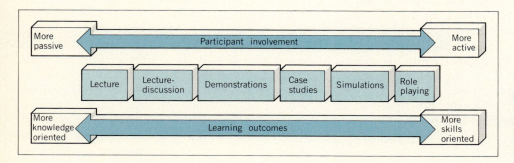

FIGURE 9.10 *A variety of instructional techniques and their training applications.*

at the Center for Creative Leadership William Clabby, a vice-president at Dow Jones, attended one such simulation called "Looking Glass." At the office he was known as a hard charger and intimidating boss who challenged the details of subordinates' work and even disciplined some by timing their lunch hours. Clabby played the role of company president in the simulation, drove his team hard for the day-long exercise, and was triumphant to learn that they had increased return on equity by 12.6 percent at the end of the day. But then it was time to debrief the exercise and learn how his team members felt. To his dismay, they accused him of cutting them out of decisions and being unaware of the complexity of problems they faced. Furthermore, they indicated he didn't do enough to try and help them with these problems. Back at Dow, Clabby's coworkers claimed he came back from the simulation mellower, more interested in subordinates' views, and less likely to explode when things went wrong. "People say I learned," Clabby says of the experience, "You can look in the mirror but you don't see yourself. People have to say how you look."

Mentoring, the act of sharing experiences and insights between a seasoned executive and junior manager, is another increasingly important form of management development. It sets a new or early-career manager up as protégé to the senior person who then coaches, models, and otherwise assists the junior person in efforts to develop his or her man-

agement skills to their highest potential. All indications are that mentor programs will continue to multiply in the future. They are applauded by many past and present executives for helping aid their careers, and for helping attract bright young people to their organizations. For example,[21]

at Ortho Pharmaceutical mentors are assigned to college graduates hired by the company. The firm actively sells the program as part of its on-campus recruiting strategy.

at Pacific Bell the 75 summer management interns hired after their junior year in college get mentors. Later these mentors help decide who will get offered permanent jobs.

REPLACEMENT

The several steps in the staffing process both conclude and recycle with **replacement,** the act of removing a person from an assigned job. Sometimes called "decruiting," replacement relates to the management of promotions, transfers, terminations, layoffs, and retirements as depicted in Figure 9.11.

Any replacement situation offers potential benefits and costs. To restaff a position, the entire selection process must often begin anew. Although costly, this is also a great opportunity to review human-resource plans, update job analyses, re-

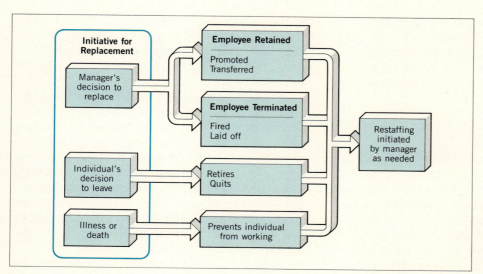

FIGURE 9.11
Dimensions of replacement as part of a manager's staffing responsibilities.

In recent years more than a million mid-level American mangers have lost their jobs to downsizing—the needed reductions of staff that have resulted from major restructurings in many organizations. The necessity of trimming has posed new challenges for managers who remain: they have had to learn the best ways to alert staff to downsizing decisions, conduct layoffs, and maintain the morale of employees surviving staff contractions.

Experts agree that the essence of successful downsizing is ongoing and honest communication between senior management and all employees, managerial and other. Without this, rumors fly and emotions seesaw, causing needless dips in productivity. Nothing injures morale more than hearing of layoffs before they happen—and nothing improves it more than hearing a top manager speak in person about corporate strategy and the reasons for downsizing. Moreover, once layoffs have occurred, senior managers must continue to communicate the vision that impelled the downsizing decision—to ensure "survivor loyalty."

Mass firings are always demoralizing; therefore, it is the manager's task to discharge individuals, never groups, in an honorable way—for the sake of those who remain as well as those laid off. It is especially important, say some experts, to convince managers seen as having a promising track record to stay. They need to be told explicitly that they are valued—or they may be tempted to look elsewhere.

Done right, downsizing leaves the organization not just leaner but also more cohesive and better equipped for competing—but the process requires careful handling throughout its duration.

Source: As reported in Anne B. Fisher, "The Downside of Downsizing," *Fortune* (May 23, 1988), pp. 42–52.

write job descriptions and job specifications, and make sure the best people are selected to next perform the required tasks. Thus, a manager must be ever vigilant in monitoring jobs under his or her control to recognize when replacement actions should be initiated.

Promotions and Transfers

One set of replacement decisions retains persons for employment within the organization, but moves them out of their present jobs. **Promotion** is movement to a higher-level position; **transfer** is movement to a different job at the same or similar level of responsibility. Promotions and transfers are key parts of succession planning as introduced in the prior IBM case. Well-managed organizations combine appropriate training and development activities with planned promotions and transfers to ensure that a talented group of human resources is always ready to move into advanced responsibilities as needed.

Promotion ideally occurs on a performance basis; that is, a person is advanced in responsibility because of demonstrated capabilities for the new job. Some organizations promote by seniority, either by preference or because of union rules. Promoting by seniority eliminates ambiguity regarding why a particular person is chosen for advancement, and it does encourage people to remain on the job in the expectation that their "time will come." However, it can result in the promotion of persons who are less competent than others available.

Job transfers can be growth opportunities for

the persons involved. They offer chances to broaden one's work experience, learn new skills, and become more familiar with other parts of the organization. In this sense the transfer is a personal development opportunity given as a reward for a job well done. Managers can also use the transfer to get rid of a poor performing employee. In order for such "problem-solving" transfers to work out well for all concerned, however, a proper match between the transferred person's capabilities and the new job requirements must be found.

Retirements

Retirement is something most people look forward to . . . until it is actually close at hand. Then the prospect of being retired can raise many fears and apprehensions. Still, retirement is inevitable, and many organizations are taking action to help their employees prepare for it. Many organizations now offer preretirement seminars to employees. These seminars assist workers with company benefits, money management, estate planning, and use of leisure time, all in relation to retirement. Counseling and just being a good listener are also among many things that managers can do to facilitate the successful retirement of subordinates.

Terminations

Downsizing or reducing the size of an organization by eliminating workers is one type of replacement that sometimes reaches sensational and controversial proportions. AT&T, for example, once announced that it was cutting 24,000—that's right, twenty-four *thousand*—jobs as part of a competitive retrenchment. Among the many complications of such acts are managing both the termination of those workers to be replaced, and the morale of those who remain. *Newsline 9.3* addresses these issues.

Layoffs created by downsizing and business downturns are always difficult, and managers seem increasingly sensitive to the need to treat employees fairly under such circumstances. *Work sharing*, described in Chapter 8 is one way to temporarily reduce the number of persons that need to be laid off during a downturn. **Early retirement,** or retirement before formal retirement age but with special financial incentives, is another available option with longer-term impact. AT&T and many other firms have used this strategy to good advantage. Such programs have proven very popular with employees, and employers feel that they help remove from the work force persons who are least satisfied with their jobs and/or the organizations.

In cases where early retirement is not possible, a growing number of organizations provide outplacement services for terminated employees not eligible for retirement options. These services range from personal counseling to direct assistance in seeking alternative employment. When AT&T was forced to lay off so many workers, its methods were applauded by outside observers and former employees. First, the company asked for volunteers who were offered an incentive to leave. Second, it tried to relocate as many as possible within the company. Third, AT&T paid for a full package of outplacement services and career counseling for the rest.

The most extreme form of termination is **firing,** the involuntary and permanent dismissal of an employee. Firing is painful to everyone involved, but there are times when employees must be dismissed. When the dismissal is based on a true mismatch between what a job requires and what a person wants to and/or is capable of doing both the dismissed employee and the organization should benefit from correcting the mismatch.

It may help to share some thoughts on this issue from the perspective of both the person being dismissed and the person doing the dismissing. Exploring these ideas should increase your sensitivity to this very difficult part of the staffing process.[22]

Questions the Dismissed Employee May Ask

Accepting the fact of being terminated is difficult. Often, the notice of dismissal is a surprise. It catches the person off-guard and without any preparation for either the personal or the financial shock. The expert's advice, though, is for the dismissed employee to brace up and stay rational. It's time for them to ask some tough questions of their ex-boss.

1.   *Why am I being fired?*   They have a right to know why. Knowing why can help them decide what to do next. Knowing why can also help them avoid a similar fate in the future.
2.   *What are my termination benefits?*   These benefits can help immeasurably. They range from

severance pay and vested pension rights, to the outplacement services mentioned earlier.

3. *Can I have a good reference?* A good reference can help in the coming job search. A direct personal recommendation might help place the person quickly with an appropriate employer.

What to Do When an Employee Has to Be Dismissed

Certain basic rules should be kept in mind by the manager who must do the firing. A good deal of common sense is called for. In addition, the manager should remember that

■ There is more to firing than giving condolences and severance pay.

■ Firing should always be handled delicately and in full recognition that it can be as personally devastating as divorce or death of a loved one.

■ Firing should always be done in complete compliance with organizational policies and in a manner legally defensible under governing legislation.

■ Firing should not be postponed; it is best done as soon as the inevitability of the dismissal is known.

■ It is best to be clear, frank, and short in communicating the dismissal.

■ There should always be some offer of assistance to help the fired employee reenter the labor market.

Summary

This chapter on staffing concludes our coverage of organizing, the second of four basic managerial functions. Organizing involves the design of appropriate structures to guide and coordinate work activities, the design of jobs to ensure the accomplishment of essential tasks by individuals and groups, and the staffing of these jobs with qualified human resources. The staffing process is a responsibility often shared by line managers and staff specialists in personnel or human resource departments.

Good staffing begins with a human resource planning program. Such programs maintain awareness of labor market trends and organizational needs. Recruitment involves communicating job vacancies and attracting a pool of qualified candidates. Whether done inside or outside the organization, recruiting is best accomplished through realistic job previews. Good recruiting, in turn, creates a foundation for the selection of candidates whose capabilities best match job specifications. These new employees require an orientation to their jobs and continued training and development to further improve and/or expand job skills. The informed manager will be diligent in assessing training needs and then providing on-the-job and off-the-job training opportunities to satisfy them. Management development is a special case of training that is concerned

with the growth of managers to their highest potential. As a manager, you will want to take advantage of management development opportunities to maintain personal growth, as well as to make sure that such opportunities are available to persons working under your supervision.

Replacement is the final stage in the staffing process. When the need to replace arises through promotion, transfer, firing, layoff, retirement, illness, or death, the staffing process is recycled again. Although there will always be times when you regret losing a valued employee, replacement is an opportunity as well. It is a chance to reanalyze job designs and specifications and to fill jobs with persons whose abilities offer maximum performance potential. Succession planning is vital to insure the effective replacement of all employees over time.

In summary, staffing is the process of matching capable people and job requirements. It responds directly to the ability variable in the individual performance equation: performance = ability × support × effort. If staffing helps ensure ability, and organizational and job design help ensure support, what is now left to study is how the manager ensures effort. This leadership challenge is the subject of the four chapters in Part 4 on—*Leading for Productivity*.

Thinking Through the Issues

1. State the individual performance equation. Give an example of how a manager can influence each key variable in the equation.

2. Identify and illustrate each of the key elements in the staffing process. Why is human resource planning an essential first step in this process?

3. Refer back to the illustrative case of Diamond Star Motors. What is unique about this company's approach to the staffing process? Would you recommend that other organizations follow their model? Why or why not?

4. What is "human resource management," and what role does a human resource department play in organizations? Why do most organizations employ persons in various capacities as staff human resource or personal specialists?

5. What guidelines can you offer to a job candidate in order to help him or her succeed in an interview with a prospective employer? What advice would you give to a corporate recruiter in order to help him or her get the right information from a job candidate in an interview?

6. What is a realistic job preview? How can it benefit organizations? How can it benefit the newly-hired employee?

7. Explain how an assessment center might be used to screen applicants for a vacant management position. What are the advantages of this approach compared to other selection techniques?

8. How does orientation differ from training as a managerial responsibility? Why is it important to the staffing process?

9. Describe why replacement should be considered an opportunity for the manager who must now fill a job vacancy.

10. What advice would you give to a manager who has to terminate someone who just can't do the job? Why?

The Manager's Vocabulary

Affirmative-action program
Apprenticeship
Assessment center
Bona fide occupational qualifications
Coaching
Downsizing
Early retirement
Equal employment opportunity
External recruitment
Firing

Human resource audit
Human resource inventory chart
Human resource planning
Human resource management
Internal recruitment
Job analysis
Job description
Job rotation
Job specification

Management development
Management simulation game
Mentoring
Modeling
Off-the-job training
On-the-job training
Orientation
Personnel planning
Promotion
Realistic job previews

Recruitment
Reliable test
Replacement
Replacement chart
Selection
Socialization
Staffing
Succession planning
Training
Transfer
Valid test
Work sampling

HOW GE GROOMS TALENT

CAREER PERSPECTIVE

Twenty years ago it dawned on GE executives that their biggest obstacle to further company growth would be the unavailability of general management talent. They decided to do something about it.[23] And GE's Crotonville Management Development Institute, with its campus-like facilities and extensive programs, has since achieved wide acclaim as one of the best in industry. The firm's commitment to management development has also proven essential to the company as it continues to grow and diversify in a complex business world. GE's approach to grooming management talent is based on the following three-pronged system.

First, a special executive management staff has the job of identifying, assessing, developing, and assisting in selecting people for the company's top 500 jobs. This unit is headed by a senior vice-president reporting directly to the CEO. Second, an annual organization and staffing review takes place for all of the firm's 80,000 salaried employees. Each person meets with his or her boss to complete a form that identifies the individual's performance, strengths and weaknesses, objectives, and needs for development. These reports are evaluated as successive levels all the way to the chief executive's office. Third, a systematic selection process is followed whenever a vacancy arises in one of the 500+ top jobs. A slate of candidates is prepared by the executive management staff, with personal qualifications and any needed development actions identified for each. This slate is then reviewed by the CEO and other senior executives for approval, before the actual hiring manager gets the authority to make his or her decision.

Overall, GE tries to keep its talented and high-potential people challenged and on the move. The company's basic job philosophy is summed up this way by one GE veteran: "The way people grow best and fastest is to keep them in tough, demanding jobs, always stretching them, and to try to keep them working for effective managers."

Questions
1.   What general lessons does this example offer for executives who want to do the best possible job of developing management talent throughout their organizations?
2.   Would you feel comfortable working in the managerial environment of GE as described in this perspective? What would be your major sources of discomfort, if any? What would you especially enjoy?
3.   Based on your response to #2, what personal career planning insights can you now list? Explain what these insights might imply in terms of your continued personal and professional development activities.

Case Application
ED'S STORY

Ed went east to get an MBA, after graduating with a psychology major from a state university in the Midwest.[24] In graduate school he majored in management and marketing. During his second year of the MBA program, Ed interviewed with six different companies on campus and was invited back to three of them for further assessment. Prior to the campus interviews he had gone to a couple of "crash courses" the school offered on how to prepare for job interviews. He was given pointers on what to wear, what questions to expect, what questions to ask, and what information about the company he should obtain. At the end of the courses, he participated in a "mock interview" before a videotape machine. He saw himself on television for the first time and carefully listened to the "pointers" given him by the instructor. By the time Ed went to his first interview, he felt prepared. He had talked with other students about their experiences, read the three most recent annual reports for each company, and rehearsed answers to the "open-ended" questions he anticipated.

Two companies offered Ed a job as a "management trainee." There were differences between the two positions in terms of geographic location, starting salary, general reputation as a desirable place for the new college graduate, and initial job assignment. Ed accepted a position with a large, multinational corporation that sold business machines as its main product. His long-term goal was to enter general management, not to spend his whole career in sales. However, in this particular company, going into sales was regarded by most as the fastest route to district-level management.

The initial training period lasted about three months and was held in a special campus-like location devoted to "corporate training and management development." Although the program was well conceived, organized, and interesting, Ed felt that he still hadn't learned "how things really work" in the company. The next six months of initial field sales experience helped to correct this deficiency. During this period Ed was placed under the mentorship of an experienced sales representative.

After the nine-month mark and a formal appraisal by his mentor, Ed was on his own in the field. For the first nine months, Ed had been on a straight salary. Now he was on a small base salary plus sales commission. The formula for computing it was fairly complicated and had one striking feature. If a company decided not to renew a machine rental contract, a portion of the lost revenue was "charged back" to the sales division and subtracted from Ed's commission. This was designed to force sales personnel to give good, attentive service to their customers. In practice, however, some decisions to terminate rentals were completely out of the control of the salesperson, and Ed's income was not as predictable as it had been. Further, Ed soon learned that the charge-back system was considered a threat by many new sales representatives and was resented by others. The full impact of this compensation system was completely unanticipated by Ed. The previous explanation given to him had seemed abstract at the time—living with the system was another matter altogether.

After about six months in the field, Ed left for another company. Before leaving, he had made a few small deals, but did not generate more than $3000 a month—barely enough to "cover" what he had been paid up to that point. When he quit, the company was out over $30,000 it had spent in the first nine months to recruit, hire, and develop him as an employee. At least another $30,000 would have to be spent on his replacement—with no guarantee to the company that there would be a solid return on the next "human capital" investment.

Questions

1. Analyze "Ed's Story" from the perspective of each element in the staffing process. What mistakes did the company make?

2. What could Ed have done to ensure a better person-job match in his first full-time job?

3. What should the company do to improve its staffing approach in the future? Why?

Class Exercise: The *Unlawful* Interview

1. Assume you are interviewing a candidate for a job vacancy in your work unit. Mark in the space provided whether or not it is legal for you to ask the listed questions.

Interview Questions	Legal	Illegal
How old are you?	—	—
Are you married or divorced?	—	—
Do you have any dependents?	—	—
What was your last job?	—	—
Why did you leave it?	—	—
Do you have a criminal record?	—	—
Are you a U.S. citizen?	—	—
What is your education?	—	—
Why do you want this job?	—	—
Do you own a home?	—	—
Who are your personal references?	—	—
How long do you plan to stay on this job?	—	—
Will any health problems interfere with your job performance?	—	—
Do you take drugs?	—	—
Have you ever been arrested?	—	—

2. Share your responses with those of a nearby classmate. Discuss and resolve any discrepancies. Await further class discussion.

References

[1] See Boris Yavitz, "Human Resources in Strategic Planning," p. 34 in Eli Ginzberg (ed.), *Executive Talent: Developing and Keeping the Best People* (New York: Wiley, 1988).

[2] Information for this case is reported in "Auto Firm Taking No Chances," *Southern Illinoisan* (January 31, 1988), p. 9. See also, "Why Mitsubishi is Right at Home in Illinois," *Business Week* (May 30, 1988), p. 45.

[3] A timely perspective on human resource planning is provided by Yavitz, op. cit., 1988.

[4] For a good discussion of this issue see Richard E. Walton and Gerald I. Susman, "People Policies for the New Machines," *Harvard Business Review*, Vol. 65 (March–April 1987), pp.98–106.

[5] See Ernest McCormick, "Job and Task Analysis," in Marvin Dunnette (ed.), *Handbook of Industrial and Or-*

ganizational Psychology (Chicago: Rand McNally, 1976), pp. 651–696.

[6]Information from James Braham, "Cultivating Tomorrow's Execs," *Industry Week* (July 27, 1987), pp. 33–38.

[7]For a recent article on Succession see Richard E. Vancil, "A Look at CEO succession," *Harvard Business Review,* Vol. 65 (March–April 1987), pp. 107–117.

[8]See the report by Leonard M. Apcar, "Wal-Mart's Sam Walton Turns Over Chief Executive Post to David Glass," *The Wall Street Journal* (February 2, 1988), p. 31.

[9]Braham, op cit.

[10]Information from "GM Picks a Winner," *Time* (August 5, 1985), pp. 42–43.

[11]This example is found in the description of the Proctor & Gamble Company provided in Robert Levering, Milton Moskowitz, and Michael Katz, *The 100 Best Companies to Work for in America* (New York: Plume, 1985), pp. 286–290, emphasis added to quote.

[12]This section based on John P. Wanous, *Organizational Entry: Recruitment, Selection, and Socialization of Newcomers* (Reading, Mass.: Addison-Wesley, 1980), pp. 34–44.

[13]This example is reported in Larry Reibstein, "Crushed Hopes: When a New Job Proves to be Something Different," *The Wall Street Journal* (June 10, 1987), p. 25.

[14]Information from Stew Leonard, "Love Your Customer," *Management Digest Quarterly,* Vol. 2 (1988). Published by the American Management Association.

[15]See Dale Yoder and Herbert G. Heneman (eds.), *ASPA Handbook of Personnel and Industrial Relations,* Vol. 1 (Washington: Bureau of National Affairs, 1974), pp. 152–154; and Walter Kiechel III, "How to Pick Talent," *Fortune* (December 8, 1986), pp. 201–203.

[16]For an excellent review of the legal aspects of job interviewing see Marisa Manley, "Employment Lines," *Inc.* (June 1988), pp. 132–135.

[17]For a scholarly review see John Van Maanen and Edgar H. Schein, "Toward a Theory of Socialization," pp. 209–264 in Barry M. Staw (ed.), *Research in Organizational Behavior,* Vol. 1 (Greenwich, Conn.: JAI Press, 1979); for a practitioner view see Richard Pascale, "Fitting New Employees Into the Company Culture," *Fortune* (May 28, 1984), pp. 28–42.

[18]Information for this case is from "Catalog of Learning Opportunities March–December 1987," *Proctor and Gamble Learning Center* (Cincinnati: Proctor & Gamble Company, 1987).

[19]Braham, op cit.

[20]This case and a description of the "Looking Glass" simulation are reported in Peter Petre, "Games that Teach you to Manage," *Fortune,* (October 29, 1984), pp. 65–72.

[21]Both examples are from "Mentor Programs Now are Used to Attract Quality Young Managers," *The Wall Street Journal* (February 23, 1988), p. 1.

[22]See Ronald Alsop, "Some Basic Rules for Managers to Follow When an Employee has to be Dismissed," *Wall Street Journal* (October 23, 1980), p. 25; Robert Coulson, "Questions You Hope You'll Never Have to Ask," *Wall Street Journal* (January 25, 1982), p. 18; and William E. Fulmer, "How Do You Say, 'You're Fired'?" *Business Horizons,* Vol. 29 (January–February 1986), pp. 31–38.

[23]Information from Braham, op. cit.; and, Janet Guyon, "Culture Class: GE's Management School Aims to Foster Unified Corporate Goals," *The Wall Street Journal* (August 10, 1987), p. 25.

[24]This case is developed from pp. 2-4 of *Organizational Entry: Recruitment, Selection, and Socialization of Newcomers,* by John P. Wanous. Copyright © 1980, by permission of Addison-Wesley Publishing Company, Reading, MA.

PART 3

Northside Child Health Center

A few years ago comprehensive health care facilities for children from low income families were established by grants from the federal government. While the primary objective of the program was the provision of health care to children, individual centers had the prerogative of adding other activities. Listed below are the objectives for the Northside Center at its founding.

A. *Objectives established by federal government—*

1. To provide comprehensive health care to children and youths from low-income families in major cities, to include:
    a. Promotion of health
    b. Medical care
    c. Case finding
    d. Preventive health services
    e. Diagnosis
    f. Treatment
    g. Correction of defects and aftercare
    h. Dental care
    i. Emotional care
2. To develop better methods for delivery of care.
3. To improve quality of health services.
4. To reduce preventable and disabling illnesses.
5. To more efficiently coordinate health services to children.

B. *Subobjectives established by the center—*

1. To develop better procedures and mechanics for the delivery of comprehensive medical care.

Source: The original source for this case could not be located.

2. To coordinate existing health services for children, to bridge gaps, and to avoid duplication.
3. To increase efficiency of the delivery of service.
4. To reexamine concepts of pediatric care—Can excellence and continuity reside in a health team, rather than in a doctor-oriented service?
5. To determine to what extent medical health professionals or other newly defined health workers can provide services traditionally given by the physician.

The Northside Center was organized to provide a facility and extend

---

The Northside Center was organized to provide services to an estimated 5000 children

---

services to an estimated 5000 children in one area of the city. The government required that the agency supply one third of the funds and that the center director be a board-certified pediatrician. No administrative experience was required. The figure illustrates the organization structure.

The center director, Dr. Regina Neal, is an extremely intelligent, aggressive pediatrician who is totally dedicated to improved health care for children. She sees health as including education, housing, employment of

parents, day care, and the many other variables which affect the physical and mental health of children. She had been in private practice for a number of years and was actively engaged in the health rights movement.

Dr. Neal has definite opinions regarding ways in which services could be improved. She states that patient care is a team effort of pediatrician, nurse, and paraprofessional workers. For staff members who are accustomed to traditional health care systems, she provides a stimulating environment in which to work. For example, she maintains that nurses can assume many of the responsibilities for well-child care, which comprises 80 percent of a pediatrician's work load. Costs could be reduced by hiring fewer pediatricians and adding paraprofessional workers to take on the routine managerial and technical duties.

Dr. Neal insists on treating patients two or three days a week in the pediatric care walk-in clinic. In effect, she acts as center director, Pediatric Section head (because this position was never filled), and physician. She is a whirlwind of energy and an inspiring person. Nonetheless, some staff complain about her tendency to utilize favored personnel rather than those on duty. For example, she will bypass the duty nursing supervisor to communicate normal doctor's orders directly to the director of nursing services. Some registered nurses especially complain that Dr. Neal treats them according to the old stereotype of the nurse as doctor's handmaiden rather than as professional colleagues.

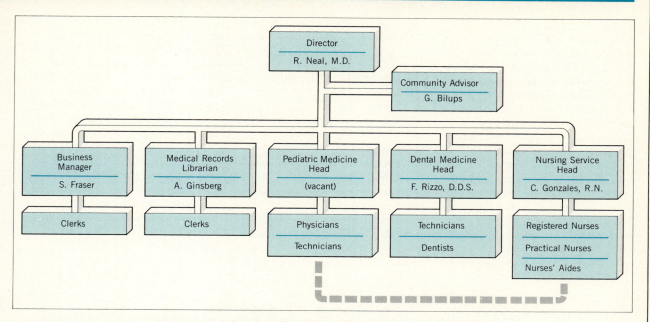

FIGURE IC.1 *Organizational chart of the Northside Child Health Center before its mission was expanded.*

The center has been quite successful in treating children brought to the clinic. However, many staff are dissatisfied for two reasons: (1) they aren't seeing all the children they should because some aren't being brought in, and (2) some illness is so family related that treatment of the child requires family treatment. For example, one child was treated several times for an infection of unknown origin; in fact, it was caused by a chronic disease afflicting her mother of which the center knew nothing.

Consequently, the center has decided to expand its services to include adult care. Dr. Leonard Warren, an internist, has recently left a lucrative suburban practice to accept a position as adult care director and co-director of the center. He in turn is engaging various physicians and staff technicians. A walk-in adult clinic service is to be provided, although it has not been decided yet whether or not this should be physically separate or integrated with the child care clinic.

In addition, the staff feels they must do more than just wait for pa-

---

The center has been quite successful . . . however, many staff are dissatisfied

---

tients to come in; they want to get out into the community. Therefore a new section of Social Work and Community Services is being established. Social workers and psychologists from the new section, along with nurses form the Nursing Services Section, are supposed to cooperate to locate illness and encourage treatment. More important, they hope to edu-cate families to modify conditions and behavior that support illness.

A government community medicine consultant suggests that the center organize family health teams composed of a physician, a community health nurse, a family social worker, and several paraprofessional aids. These teams could become intimately familiar with specific families and their problems. They could draw on the specialized physicians, psychiatrists, and dentists when necessary.

Many staff physicians don't like this proposal because they fear they will waste much precious time trav-

---

The center has decided to expand its services to include adult care

---

eling outside the clinic center. The medical records administrator wonders if she must maintain records for the new adult care section and family care activities without new clerks. The Dental Section director is similarly concerned. The director of nursing services is worried about whom the proposed teams would report to, how they would be controlled, and how she could supply nurses to the teams as well as the new adult care clinic. Dr. Neal feels that the teams could simply report directly to her, so she would be sure of cooperation from the physicians.

Source: Information for this case is from David L. Fortney, "The Little Steel Company That Could," Nucor Corporation document, no date; John A. Savage, "Growth and Success through Employee Involvement," Nucor Corporation document, no date; John Grossman, "Ken Iverson: Simply the Best," *American Way* (August 1, 1987), pp. 23–25; Richard E. Hattwick, "Business Leadership: Kenneth Iverson of NUCOR," *The Journal of Behavioral Economics*, Vol. XVI (Fall 1987), pp. 99–104; and, "U.S. Minimills Launch a Full-Scale Attack," *Business Week* (June 13, 1988), pp. 100–102.

> **A consultant suggests that the center organize family health teams**

Questions

1. What are the major problems of Northside Child Health Center? What are the major causes of each of these problems? Which of these problems might be addressed through possible changes in the organization structure?

2. What specific changes in the organization structure of the center would you recommend? Why? In what ways would your structural changes allow the center to better fulfill its mission? Explain your answer.

3. In what ways does your proposed change in structure implement the "family health team" concept discussed in the case? Explain the potential advantages and disadvantages of operating with these teams. What recommendations can you give to help the center gain the benefits of teams without suffering too many problems? ■

Growth Challenges Nucor Corporation

Nucor Corporation is in the business of making steel and related products. It is one of the pioneers with the "minimill" concept. Such mills usually confine their sales to customers in a 300–400 mile radius from the plants, and recycle junk cars and other scrap to get their steel. The president and chief executive officer of Nucor is F. Kenneth Iverson, who assumed these responsibilities in 1965. At the time, Nucor's parent company was drifting toward bankruptcy. Iverson, a group vice-president in charge of the only division in the firm that was making a profit, was selected to take command.

To keep Nucor solvent, Iverson sold off or closed more than half the

> **"I'm a firm believer in having the fewest number of management levels . . . says Iverson.**

existing divisions. He cut the corporate staff from 12 to 2—himself and a vice-president of finance. He relocated the company headquarters from Phoenix, Arizona, to Charlotte, N.C. In three years he also had the company making a profit. It hasn't failed to do so since. Under Iverson's leadership, Nucor has achieved steady growth, remained union-free in a traditionally unionized industry, and achieved prominence as a benchmark for success as a "minimill" in a lagging U.S. steel industry.

The American steel industry's decline over the last twenty years has been dramatic, as production and jobs fell at the largest firms—Bethlehem, USX, LTV, and Inland—in face of foreign competition. But the minimills offer a different story. Using new technology and focusing on profitable market niches they carved out a place for themselves in the industrial landscape. The combined market share of America's minimills quadrupled to 22 percent . . . and is still growing. Presently, they are threatening the giant integrated producers to the point where the spokesperson for one says: "We're heading into a war." Nucor Corporation, with its emphasis on technology and innovative management and organization practices, is among the leaders in the charge.

The Nucor organization chart is shown in the figure. It is one of Iverson's trademarks—only four levels of management are found in the company, in contrast to the eight or nine management levels found in the larger steel companies. "I'm a firm believer in having the fewest number of management levels and in delegating authority to the lowest level possible," says Iverson. He describes this way how the system works.

> In our case, we move from a foreman, our first line of management, to a department head. In a steel mill, this would be a manager of rolling or melting and casting. From there, authority passes to a general manager of that facility. That general manager reports directly to the corporate office, to myself or Dave Aycock [chief operating officer]. Four levels of management.

This structure coordinates the activities of over 4300 employees spread across the companies facilitates in several states. The corporate staff has grown over the years—it now numbers 17. There are no engineering, manufacturing, marketing or purchasing people in this group.

Nucor operates without any corporate jets, company cars or limosines, or reserved parking spaces.

Iverson's guiding philosophy is to place day-to-day decision making in the hands of the operating people. Each general manager is a vice-president of the corporation, and is responsible for the division as a business unto itself. The company is proud to note that, with the exception of financial management, each of these plants could operate as a separate and independent company at a moment's notice.

In Nucor's home office, a nondescript building located next to a Hardee's restaurant, incoming calls go straight from the switchboard to Iverson's telephone. There's no secretary to intercede. He dials his own outgoing calls. And he enters the weekly production figures directly into the computer, claiming that "by keying in the numbers, you're forced to look at every figure for every division every week. That's the value."

From the beginning Nucor's approach stressed labor productivity and loyalty, along with a deemphasis on status differences between "managers" and "workers". All levels of management, including Iverson, were placed on a bonus system comparable to the one hourly workers have. In addition, managers were expected to eat in the same cafeterias as hourly workers, receive the same fringe benefits, and do things in the "least cost" ways (for example, air travel is by economy rather than first class). And, hourly workers have al-

---

Technology and world-wide awareness are at the forefront of Nucor's growth

---

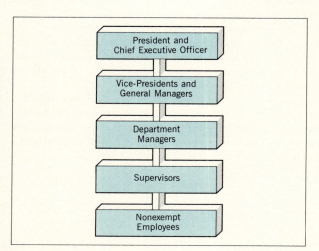

FIGURE IC.2 *Nucor Corporation—organization chart.*

ways been able to take problems with their managers directly to Iverson, who claims to get 10 to 20 such cases a year.

At least one industry expert wonders if doubling in size might not damage the company . . .

Today, Nucor has facilities in eight states and generates some $750 million of sales. It still does so without any corporate jets, company cars or limousines, or reserved parking spaces. In fact, when Nucor recently acquired Genbearco Manufacturing, one of the first things Iverson did was to sell its company cars which had been "perks" for the company's executives. Silvia Matthews, however, doesn't seem to mind losing the use of a company car. "Everybody here is totally Nucor," she says, "People here feel we're with a stable, growing company that knows where it's going." Iverson says in return, "We're trying to get our employees to feel they're a real part of the company and that what they do makes the company successful. . . . And so we've tried to eliminate any differences between management and the rest of our employees."

As another indicator that Iverson means what he says, he recently directed that everyone in the plants wear the same color hard hats. When some of the foremen complained be-

cause of lost status (they previously got white hats and the other workers green ones), Iverson responded: "Your real authority comes not from the color hat you wear. It comes from your leadership abilities."

And lead the company Iverson does. He is now building two more plants, one of which will place Nucor in a new and untried market for flat-steel products. Together they could boost Nucor's daily production by up to 80 percent. "It's a huge step," says Iverson. "Again, we'd be invading an area dominated by the integrated producers. It could change the steel industry dramatically, both here and around the world."

Technology and a world-wide awareness are at the forefront of Nucor's growth strategy. Its new Blytheville, Ark., plant is a joint venture with Yamato Kogyo of Japan. Using Kyogyo's casting technology, the plant will produce large structural beams at 14 percent less cost than USX, Bethlehem, or LTV. Nucor has also adopted a West German thin-slab steel-casting process for making flat-rolled steel. When in place at its new Crawfordville, Ind., plant the firm will have a two-year technology edge on its competitors, and manufacture the cold-rolled steel for 19 percent less than the major producers now achieve. A new computer-controlled rolling technology will slash energy costs by 40 percent, and allow Nucor to make a ton of steel in half the man-hours needed at the best of its larger competitors.

By the late 1990s the minimills as a group are expected to hold 40-50 percent of the domestic steel market. Nucor is expected to boost its annual

sales into the $1-2 billion range. But at least one industry expert wonders if doubling Nucor's size might not damage the company and threaten its successful approach to management and organization.

The optimistic Iverson responds, "I think we can do it." But he admits that organizational changes may be necessary. He'd like to do it without adding more levels of management. Yet, he also suggests that a new level between himself and the steel mills may be necessary. About this kind of "group vice-president"—a position he had long-ago abolished when restructuring the company—Iverson admits: "I hate those words."

Questions

1. What are the major strengths of Nucor's organization chart as presented in the figure? Why is it that Nucor can operate with so few levels of management, a limited number of staff personnel, and virtually no executive "perks" while so many other organizations seem unable to?

2. What are the major problems you feel the added growth of the company will cause for Ken Iverson? Can Nucor's present "organization chart" withstand the pressures of added growth? Where would the "group vice-president" fit in this chart?

3. What do you feel will be required if Nucor is to retain its successful and unique organizational approach in the future?

4. Are the "lessons" of Ken Iverson's approach to "organizing" as a management function applicable to other organizations? . . . other managers? Explain your answer. ∎

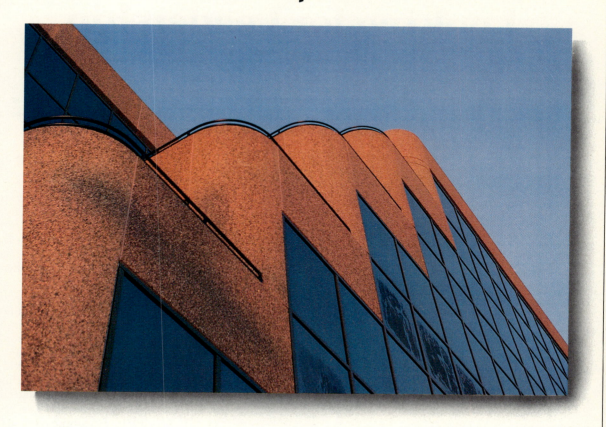

LEADING FOR PRODUCTIVITY

Looking for Leadership

In reaction to the fast-paced, unpredictable nature of modern management, there has been much talk of the need for dynamic leadership—for people who can meet the challenges posed by a competitive environment in constant flux. Inevitably, such talk is informed by popular images of the leader: a strong-looking, somewhat bigger-than-life individual able to motivate masses of people with seeming ease. What does this stereotype reveal about what we expect from our leaders, particularly corporate ones? The answer is many-sided. It includes such apparent contradictions as power and sensitivity, independence and accountability—to name just a few.

While everyone agrees that today's organizations urgently need more and better leaders, there is still considerable debate over what makes a leader successful—and over how to develop leadership in managers.

"QUALITIES FREQUENTLY ADMIRED . . . INCLUDE HONESTY . . . AND BEING ABLE TO INSPIRE."

NOTES
1. Abraham Zaleznik, "Managers and Leaders: Are They Different?" *Harvard Business Review* (May–June 1986), p. 48.
2. Tom Peters and Nancy Austin, "A Passion for Excellence," *Fortune* (May 13, 1985), p. 20.
3. James M. Kouzes and Barry Z. Posner, *The Leadership Challenge: How to Get Extraordinary Things Done in Organizations* (San Francisco: Jossey-Bass, 1987).
4. Noel Tichy and Mary Anne Devanna, *The Transformational Leader* (New York: Wiley, 1986), pp. 4–6.
5. John Case, "Desperately Seeking Leadership," *Inc.* (December 1987), pp. 20–22.
6. John W. Gardner, "The Moral Aspect of Leadership," *New Management*, pp. 11–16.
7. Peter Drucker, "The Mystery of the Business Leader," *Wall Street Journal* (September 29, 1987), p. 30.

Chapters 10 through 13 explore the issues by presenting various theories of leadership and the processes by which it is developed and sustained. We will see that leading, like other managerial functions, is multi-faceted; its ingredients often vary from one situation to the next. Let's begin by looking, in this Perspective, at some new thinking on the crucial topic of leadership, touching on issues and questions that will be addressed later in more detail.

THE LEADERSHIP DIFFERENCES

One element of the controversy is the claim, advanced most forcefully by Professor Abraham Zaleznik of the Harvard Business School, that leaders and managers are temperamentally (hence fundamentally) different breeds. Managers "view work as an enabling process," Zaleznik writes, whereas leaders are "disposed to seek out risk and danger." Managers need order; leaders flirt with disorder, searching out "opportunities for change."[1]

Zaleznik's view may not be universal, but it has occasioned some interesting responses. Authors Tom Peters and Nancy Austin, in apparent agreement with Zaleznik, hold that management "connotes controlling and arranging and demeaning and reducing"; in contrast, leadership implies liberation and growth. However, in proposing a new model of leadership, these authors argue that leaders can be developed—*must* be, in fact, if superior performance is to be sustained over the long haul.[2] Another pair of authors, James Kouzes and Barry Posner, also affirm the need to develop new leaders. Organizations of all kinds, they claim, face a momentous challenge: "We're going through wrenching change, and we don't have enough leaders to deal with crises."[3] Kouzes and Posner studied more than 500 business, community, and military leaders and concluded that over half of them shared certain essential traits. Among these are the ability to "challenge the process," to inspire a shared vision, and to enable others to act. (This last trait echoes Zaleznik's description of a manager, not a leader—proof that it is indeed difficult to pin down the essence of either.) The qualities most frequently admired by the followers of these leaders (also surveyed by Kouzes and Posner) include honesty, competence, being future-oriented, and being able to inspire.

LEADERS AS CHANGE AGENTS

The hue and cry over leadership is encouraged by a perception shared by all observers: intense competitive pressures have called into question the usual ways of running an organization. As stated by authors Noel Tichy and Mary Anne Devanna, a new kind of person—the "transformational leader"—is needed to revitalize flagging organizations. "Traditional managerial skills," these authors write, "are important ingredients in most organizational success stories but not sufficient for organizational transformation." They argue that the new leader, acting as a change agent, must first see the need for revitalization, then come up with a new vision, and finally "institution-

alize" change so it will outlast the individual leader.[4]

Of course, vision alone is not a cure-all for organizations. There are many instances of imaginative and promising business ventures that just didn't work. What, then, separates leadership success from failure?

Sound and reliable judgment is arguably more important than a host of

> "Leadership . . . is too complex to be reduced to a set of rules . . . It has to be learned and practiced in real situations."

other leadership qualities, maintains author John Case. He points to Apple Computer's Steven Jobs as an example of a talented leader whose star rose fast—but whose vision was unable to sustain the organization over time. Jobs was ultimately pushed out by Apple's next CEO, John Sculley. Similarly, Donald Burr, founder of Peoples Express Airlines, made a decision to do what had worked so well for Scandinavian Airlines System—

giving more responsibility to first-line personnel. But People Express ended up going out of business. "What undermined Burr," says Case, "wasn't his innovative approach to managing people, it was the fact that he tried to expand his company too quickly." It is good judgment that ensures realizable goals: "The difference between leaders and everybody else isn't what kind of people they are, it's what they accomplish."[5]

But many other observers maintain that the kind of person a leader is *does* matter. Peters and Austin bemoan the alienation of managers from the employees they work with, citing this as a key reason for the absence of dynamic leadership. And Tichy and Devanna, describing the transformation of an organization as a "human drama," argue that the new leader must learn to handle fairly "the anxieties and criticisms of both managers and employees" who participate in change.

MORAL ASPECTS OF LEADERSHIP

Former Health, Education and Welfare Secretary John Gardner, writing about what he calls the "moral aspect" of leadership, has several noteworthy things to say. Both leaders and teachers, Gardner claims, know

A challenge of leadership includes changes. For women, success can include others' willingness to see them as leaders.

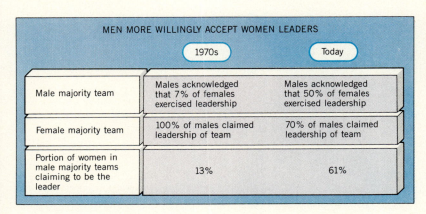

MEN MORE WILLINGLY ACCEPT WOMEN LEADERS		
	1970s	Today
Male majority team	Males acknowledged that 7% of females exercised leadership	Males acknowledged that 50% of females exercised leadership
Female majority team	100% of males claimed leadership of team	70% of males claimed leadership of team
Portion of women in male majority teams claiming to be the leader	13%	61%

that high expectations tend to generate high performance. It is the leader's job to remove "obstacles to our effective functioning—to help individuals "see and pursue shared purposes." In this view, the leader recognizes "the mutual dependence between individual and group" and knows how to balance the two so that passive followers cease to be the norm.[6]

Gardner is concerned about a general lack of momentum in organizational life. "Most people in most organizations most of the time," he writes, "are more stale than they know, more bored than they care to admit." Leaders supply the necessary spark to awaken the potential of each individual—to urge each person "to take the initiative in performing leaderlike acts." In this regard, Gardner's view is shared by Peters and Austin, who believe that people who "own"

their jobs will naturally outperform those who feel they are on the margins. But instilling "ownership" means being the kind of leader who is willing to let others do *their* best— a trait that not all managers possess. "Why in the world," Peters and Austin ask managers, "would you expect [your employees] to be interested in comparative plant profitability if you never tell them how they're doing?"

> It is the leader's job to remove "obstacles to our effective functioning—to help individuals "see and pursue shared purposes."

A successful leader is able, for reasons we may never understand, to motivate and guide others. He or she has excellent communcation skills and an instinct for forging ahead and ignoring, when necessary, the opinions of others. The line between confidence and over-confidence, suggests John Case, is a thin one: "The unsettling truth is that leadership . . . is too complex to be reduced to a set of rules . . . It has to be learned and practiced in real situations."

We'll end with a final statement on the thorny issue of leadership—this one from acclaimed management theorist Peter Drucker. His focus on the human side of leadership is worth remembering: "Leaders in an organization need to impose on themselves that congruence between deeds and words, between behavior and professed beliefs and values, that we call 'personal integrity.' "[7] ■

Fundamentals of Leading

Leaders Who Can Make a Difference

Management alone just won't do the trick; something more is needed. Organizations of all kinds are waking up to the fact that they need *leaders*—people who combine a strong personal presence with a knack for communicating exciting visions. The leader doesn't have to be a CEO; managers can be leaders, too. But they must begin with certain basic instincts, and they have to work at cultivating leadership skills. Chief among these are a sensitivity to the concerns of others, a willingness to innovate, and a commitment to quality and integrity.

The new leader is unafraid of change. He or she is preoccupied with people as much or more than with process and is able—and eager—to influence the entire tenor of an organization. Noel Tichy and Mary Anne Devanna, authors of *The Transformational Leader,* distinguish "transformational" leaders, who make a substantive difference in the way things get done. Tichy estimates that 80 percent of a leader's growth occurs on the job, but the rest can be enhanced by study and training. Given plenty of freedom and responsibility early on in his or her career, a manager with leadership potential stands a better chance of realizing that potential than does one locked into the wrong kinds of job experiences.

One vice-president of Johnson & Johnson summarized his company's aggressive approach to encouraging new leaders: "We believe in keeping the units small and recruiting the best people we can find, giving them as much responsibility as early as we can, moving them up rapidly, and keeping track of them." Those sound like ideal conditions for growth, but not all organizations are as ready to make such efforts to cultivate leadership in their managers. Moreover, leaders learn from failures, from mentors, and from training programs—factors that aren't always viewed sympathetically by many organizations, even small ones.

Nonetheless, organizations taking the long view are starting to see the advantages of developing transformational leadership. General Foods CEO Philip Smith noticed what he called "dramatic changes" in several divisions' performances when "the only thing that had changed [in each division] was the leader." He initiated a series of corporate retreats for high-level GF managers, each of whose leadership had been assessed by subordinate staff in anonymous questionnaires. During the retreats, these managers worked with counselors on identifying ways to improve their leadership skills. Even Smith was assessed—and he decided, after seeing the results, that he needed to become a more open listener. Smith sees his organization's leaders as "the foundation for all growth at General Foods." ■

Source: Information from Jeremy Mains, "Wanted Leaders Who Can Make a Difference," *Fortune* (September 28, 1987), pp. 92–102.

"Manager" . . . "leader" . . . or both? This issue highlights once again the challenges faced by managers in their work. This chapter introduces you to leadership through the following topics.

Leadership Concepts
Power: A Leadership Resource
Approaches to the Study of Leadership
Fiedler's Contingency Theory
House's Path-Goal Theory
The Vroom-Yetton Leader-Participation Theory
Directions in Leadership Theory and Practice

S uch quotes and admonitions on the subject of "leadership" abound in today's world.[1] We are at once enamored of the concept and slightly unsure of how to deal with it. And, of course, "leading" is one of the most talked about of the four management functions. Acting as a leader, it is a manager's responsibility to ensure that work efforts of other persons are enthusiastically directed toward the accomplishment of organizational objectives. **Leading** is just that. It is the process of creating vision, inspiring commitment, and directing human-resource efforts toward organizational objectives. *Great leaders,* it is said, "get extraordinary things done in organizations by inspiring and motivating others toward a common purpose."[2] To succeed as a leader, therefore, a manager requires knowledge and skills in all aspects of interpersonal relations, including communication, motivation, and group dynamics.

> "Leaders, in a special way, are liable for what happens in the future, rather than what is happening day-to-day."
> *Max De Pree,* chairman of the board and CEO of Herman Miller, Inc.

> "Being effective isn't enough, leaders must also have moral goals."
> *John W. Gardner,* author and former Secretary of Health, Education, and Welfare

> "In any case, leadership is finally a collaborative endeavor."
> *Warren Bennis,* author and leadership scholar

> "With leadership, you either use it or lose it."
> *Lee Iacocca,* chairman of the board of Chrysler Corporation

Leading and managing, however, are not one and the same thing. There are two sides to this issue. To begin, leading is only a part of managing. Managers must act effectively in the comprehensive sense of planning, organizing, leading, and controlling. Success as a leader is a necessary but not sufficient condition for managerial success. A good manager is always a good leader, but a good leader is not necessarily a good manager. As shown in Figure 10.1, success in the latter respect requires that the capacity to lead be complemented by the capacity to plan, organize, and control.

The second side of this issue is that many managers are not effective, in part at least, because they are not good leaders. This point is being made more and more frequently by scholars and consultants, and it underlies the viewpoints already reported in the chapter opener. Abraham Zaleznick is a Harvard Business School professor who often speaks on the differences between "leaders" and "managers." Consider this description of his speech to a group of business executives in Philadelphia.[3]

Leaders, he told the audience, can be dramatic and unpredictable in style. They "are often obsessed by their ideas, which appear visionary and consequently excite, stimulate and drive other people to work hard and create reality out of fantasy." They often create an atmosphere of change. Lee Iacocca of Chrysler, Zaleznick says, is a classic leader. *Managers,* he told them, are usually hard-working, analytical, and fair. They often have a strong sense of belonging to the organization and take pride

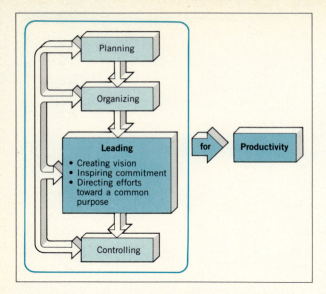

FIGURE 10.1 *Leading for productivity—viewed in relationship with the other management functions.*

maintaining and improving the status quo. They tend to focus on "process," while leaders focus on "substance." The late Alfred Sloan, the driving force behind the great days of General Motors, he says, was a classic manager.

Perhaps nothing frames the problem Zaleznick addresses any better than the responses of the audience to his Philadelphia speech. When it was over, five top executives stepped to the microphones to argue that they were combination "leader–

managers." By the time they finished, it is reported, some of their cohorts in the audience felt they had listened to five managers . . . but no leaders.

LEADERSHIP CONCEPTS

This chapter focuses on the essence of **leadership** as the manager's use of power to influence the behavior of other persons in the work setting. **Power,** in turn, is the ability to get someone else to do something you want done. Said differently, power is the ability to make things happen the way you want. As leaders, managers should be good at using power in ways that influence others to work hard and willingly apply their efforts toward the accomplishment of organizational objectives.

Formal leadership occurs when a manager leads by exercising formal authority. This right to command or to act derives from the manager's official position within the organization's hierarchy of authority. Anyone appointed to the job of "manager" has the opportunity to exercise formal leadership in relationships with subordinates. Some people, like the example in *Newsline 10.1*, do a much better job than others at taking advantage of this opportunity. They are more influential in ensuring that subordinates' work efforts are highly productive over time. This chapter offers a knowledge base that will help you to perform well in any formal leadership capacity.

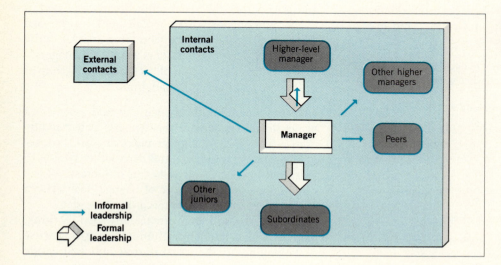

FIGURE 10.2 *A manager's formal and informal leadership roles.*

PUTTING PEOPLE AND POSSIBILITIES FIRST

Ronald J. Burns is the 34-year-old president of Enron Corp.'s Enron Gas Transportation Co., which manages the flow of the country's largest natural gas pipeline system. He is known for being smart, aggressive, and—perhaps most important to his colleagues—very easy to get along with. Burns himself feels that a manager's most important quality is the ability to interact well with others.

Although he is naturally affable, Burns has put time into studying the traits of the individuals who have managed him—to better learn what works and what doesn't. He believes that respect for people is crucial even in high-stress environments. In Burns's view, most young managers aren't sufficiently attuned to the long term; they pay too much attention to what is happening at the moment. To make sure that he avoids this pitfall, Burns spends around a third of each week brainstorming with his staff.

Burns dismisses the notion that executives need special treatment in the form of personal secretaries. What he needs, he says, is "to be stimulated, challenged, and rewarded;" if these criteria were not met in his present position, he would pursue other options. Burns exemplifies a breed of managers who see people as an organization's most valuable asset and think about situations in terms of their possibilities. Tomorrow's managers, he says, will have to be flexible: the future is neither black nor white, and rules that were once clear are changing fast. His own strategy is to push forward energetically—and keep smiling.

Source: As reported in "An Oil-Patch Manager Who Puts People First," *Business Week* (November 10, 1986), p. 96.

Informal leadership arises when a person without formal authority proves influential in directing the behavior of other persons. We know informal leaders best as the people who spontaneously take charge in a group situation. Although not formally appointed or elected, they become leaders through their actions and/or personal attractiveness. They "emerge" in situations as the persons others turn to for guidance, advice, and direction.

Formal and informal leadership coexist in almost every work situation. There are many times when managers have to work with subordinates who defer to a strong informal leader within their peer groups. At other times, managers may find themselves acting as formal leaders in some situations and as informal leaders in others. Figure 10.2 portrays various formal and informal leadership roles that managers may play. Formal leadership follows the chain of command and flows downward in the hierarchy of authority from superior to subordinate. Informal leadership, by contrast, involves participation in networks of interpersonal relationships that exist outside the chain of command. It also includes the capacity to influence one's superior.

POWER: A LEADERSHIP RESOURCE

Speaking of influence and the process of leadership, let's get down to the real world. The following short case presents a typical leadership dilemma. Read the case and think about what you would have done.

Better yet, think about what you *will* do when faced with similar situations in the future.

ILLUSTRATIVE CASE:
THE ENGINEERING PROJECT

Ann Pool is the project engineer in the model shop of a medium-sized technology firm.[4] She has just received a rush assignment on Friday afternoon. It requires that a set of difficult engineering drawings be completed as soon as possible. This will allow the model shop to begin construction of a new device needed to impress a valued customer.

The Manager's Point of View   Ann feels the only drafter who can do this complex task—and do it so there will be no likelihood of problems—is Phil Firenzi, her most senior, experienced employee. Ann knows Firenzi is somewhat of a prima donna, smug in his competence, independent, and outspoken. The job will require at least five hours of work, and since it's almost 3 PM, that means three hours of overtime. Ann also knows that overtime is not compulsory, and is especially unappealing on a Friday.

The Subordinates Point of View   If he is approached by Ann with a request for overtime, Firenzi will be outraged. Instead of feeling rewarded to be chosen the most able and most senior employee, he senses it as a "damn curse." He sees this "crazy" company and "inefficient" middle management as so poor at planning that they are always late, always coming up with emergencies and crises that "can't wait." The last thing he wants is more overtime just before a weekend—and particularly this weekend. He has promised his wife he would be home early to go to an important family function (his daughter's wedding rehearsal). He's sick and tired of being asked to sacrifice his personal life for job requirements "for the good of the company"—and unnecessary ones at that. The company just isn't managed sensibly. As further evidence of management ineptitude, he notes that his boss has never taken the time or had the foresight to train one of her more junior colleagues to handle the complex drawings. The company is either too cheap to invest in training or too foolish.

The Manager's Possible Responses   Ann, the manager, basically wants Firenzi to do something that

is, in part at least, above and beyond the explicit duties of the job. Further complicating the situation, although she may not realize this, is the fact that the employee is already in a negative frame of mind. As a result, we can almost predict that the manager will make the request, get flatly refused, and then become upset by the threat posed to her managerial position. Ann probably will ask herself, "What will *my* boss say if I don't get this job out after having been told how critical it is?" In response, she may try to pressure Firenzi to comply by resorting to one of the following strategies:

Threats   Ann could say: "Remember how much I've done for you—extra time off when you wanted it, and high merit increases. Is this how you pay me back? How much do you think I'll feel like asking for another raise or giving you your way when *you* want something?"

Rewards   Ann could say: "I know this is rough on you, but do a good job and I'll use this when I talk with the superintendent to get you a much bigger raise than you expected at salary-review time," and/or, "I'll try to get you better vacation time, new office space, double time instead of time-and-a-half, or one of a dozen other things if you do what I ask."

Dominance   Detecting the unwillingness of her subordinate, Ann may launch into a long speech about the importance of the drafting assignment: "It will show your skill—only you are good enough to do it and that's why I turn to you," she might say. Or, "It's for the good of the company; it could mean an important new order, lots of new jobs, and more job security for everyone."

The Problems Created   A number of obvious problems are created by this situation, and by the manager's various responses. First, Firenzi is almost certain to be frustrated. He is placed in a position where he is torn between what he wants to do and feels is his "right," and the pressures of the boss. If he gives in, there will be resentment; if he doesn't, the boss–subordinate relationship has been injured. Even if he changes his mind, there is bound to be anger and a lingering feeling that the all-powerful boss has manipulated the weak subordinate.

Second, Ann spent a lot of time seeking to influence Firenzi based on what she *assumed* his needs to be—money, admiration, pride, a good relationship with supervision. She never uncovered what Firenzi *really* may have needed—for example, assurance that this repeating problem would be solved by training someone else to do the work in the future.

Third, Firenzi received no message suggesting that the boss cared about him as a person. He appeared only to be an instrument through which Ann could accomplish her goal of looking good to the superintendent.

The tragedy in all this is that the manager in this case would not only be failing as a formal leader, she probably would also end up distrusting her "unresponsive," "too-independent" subordinate as a result. From the manager's point of view, the blame for missing the order would be his, not hers. Obviously, many things are at issue here—trust, commitment, ego, and responsibility are but a few. Also at issue is *power,* something that author, scholar and consultant Rosabeth Moss Kanter has called "America's last dirty word."[5] It is time to examine and study power for its managerial implications.

Managerial Perspectives on Power

Power is an essential leadership resource. Managers use power to achieve the interpersonal influence through which leadership is ultimately exercised. Power is a force or capability that, when successfully activated, makes things happen. For many people, though, the word power carries a negative connotation that includes undertones of manipulation or political action. Isn't this your reaction to the impression conveyed in the following headline?

> WILLIAM SMALL QUITS
> AS NBC NEWS CHIEF
> AMID POWER STRUGGLE

There is another side to the story. Most people, for example, like to work for someone who has "clout." In practice this term identifies someone who is successful at getting things done, and able to get support for the people and work unit he or she represents. "Clout" in this sense is "power." A manager with clout gets such things as[6]

- Good jobs for talented subordinates.
- Approvals for expenditures beyond budget.
- Above-average pay raises for subordinates.
- Items on the agenda at higher-level meetings.
- Preferred access to top decision makers.

- Early information on policy shifts.

Power is a very "good" thing when used properly by the manager. Recent research recognizes that a need for power is essential for executive success.[7] But this need for power is not a desire to control for the sense of personal satisfaction, it is a desire to influence and control others for the good of the organization as a whole. With power viewed in this more positive way, the stage is set for you to learn more about its role as a foundation for effective leadership. To begin, we should answer three questions regarding how power becomes an essential leadership resource of managers.

1. What are the sources of managerial power?
2. How do managers acquire and use power?
3. What are the limits to a manager's power?

Sources of Power

Figure 10.3 divides the sources of power into those based in the position and those based in the person of the manager.[8] Effective managers acquire and use power from both sources to achieve influence over others in the work setting.

Position Power

Three bases of power relate to a manager's official position in a hierarchy of authority—reward, coercive, and legitimate power. They are defined as follows.

Reward power is the capability to offer something of value, a positive outcome, as a means of controlling other people. Examples of such rewards include raises, bonuses, promotions, special assignments, and verbal or written compliments. To mobilize reward power, a manager says, in effect, "If you do what I ask, I'll give you a reward."

Coercive power is the capability to punish or withhold positive outcomes as a means of controlling other people. A manager may attempt to coerce someone by threatening them with verbal reprimands, pay penalties, and even termination. To mobilize coercive power, a manager says, in effect, "If you don't do what I want, I'll punish you."

Legitimate power is the capability to control other people by virtue of the rights of office. Legitimate

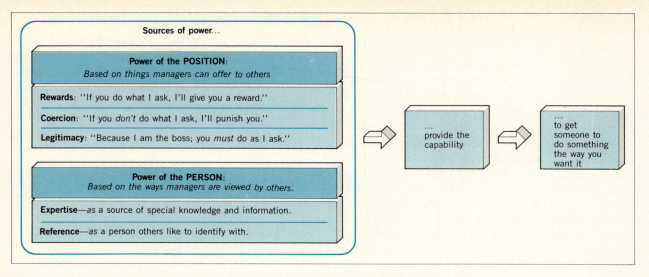

FIGURE 10.3 *Important sources of power for managers: power of the position and the person.*

power is formal authority, the right to command and to act in the position of managerial responsibility. To mobilize legitimate power, a manager says, in effect, "I am the boss and therefore you must do as I ask."

Any person appointed to a managerial position in an organization theoretically has legitimacy and access to both rewards and punishments. How well this position power is used, however, will vary from one person to the next. Leadership success will vary as well.

Personal Power

Another source of power is the person and what he or she brings to the situation in terms of unique personal attributes. Two bases of personal power are expertise and reference.

Expert power is the capability to control other people because of specialized knowledge. Expertise derives from the possession of technical know-how or information pertinent to the issue at hand, which others do not have. It is developed by acquiring relevant information and competencies. It is maintained by protecting one's credibility and not overstepping the boundaries of true expertise.

Reference power is the capability to control other people because of their desires to identify personally

and positively with you. Reference is a power derived from charisma or interpersonal attractiveness. It is developed and maintained through good interpersonal relations which encourage the admiration and respect of others.

A Power Inventory

Table 10.1 summarizes the basic characteristics of these five sources of position and personal power. To maximize power in any leadership situation, a manager should take full advantage of power available in the position—that is, power based on legitimacy and access to rewards and punishments, as well as personal power based on expertise and reference. A basic equation serves as a reminder of these two components of managerial power.

$$\frac{\text{Managerial}}{\text{power}} = \frac{\text{position}}{\text{power}} + \frac{\text{personal}}{\text{power}}$$

Acquiring and Using Managerial Power

Managers need power to succeed in both their formal and informal leadership roles. Leadership, in turn, depends on an ability to acquire and use power from both position and personal sources. Things to keep in mind include.[9]

1. *Don't deny your formal authority.* Good managers use their position power well. They act as the

TABLE 10.1 *Characteristics of Various Power Sources Used by Managers*

Power Source	How Accessed by Managers	Practical Considerations
Rewards	Control over rewards	Continued reward necessary to maintain influence; temporary effects.
Coercion	Control over punishments	Continued punishment or threat of punishment necessary to maintain influence; temporary effects
Legitimacy	Position of formal authority	Limited by extent of others' respect for the position
Expertise	Possession of knowledge, useful information	Limited by exent to which expertise is real or credible; more lasting effects
Reference	Possession of appealing personal traits	Dependent on interpersonal attractiveness; more lasting effects

"boss," but with discretion and sensitivity for the feelings of others. Rewards, punishments, and legitimacy are not guaranteed to work, but they are necessary and important power resources based in the manager's formal authority.

2. *Don't be afraid to create a sense of obligation.* Some managers are highly skilled at doing favors that cost very little but that other people appreciate a lot. The manager's power expands as a result.

3. *Create feelings of dependence.* The more people perceive themselves as dependent on the manager, the more inclined they will be to cooperate with his or her wishes. The best way to maintain dependency is to do a good job of finding and acquiring the resources other persons need.

4. *Build and believe in expertise.* Managers gain power by building reputations for technical expertise. Concrete and visible achievements in areas of task and/or organizational relevance are the foundations on which such reputations are established.

5. *Allow others the opportunity to identify with you as a person.* When others know and respect a manager as a person, they tend to behave and act consistent with the manager's desires. This requires regular contacts and good interpersonal skills to create the sense of positive identification.

The Limits to Power

Power is the potential to control the behavior of other people. But we all know that persons who have access to position and/or personal power don't always get their way. Almost every manager from the president of the United States, to the head teller at your local bank, the instructor in your classroom has, at one time or another, given an order that wasn't obeyed. The question is, "Why?"

The Acceptance Theory

Figure 10.4 shows that one of two things can happen when a manager issues a directive or makes a request of someone else. The person either responds as desired or doesn't respond at all. When a manager issues the directive or makes the request, he or she is attempting to exercise power. The power is only realized when the other person responds as desired—that is, when he or she "accepts" the directive or request. Acceptance therefore establishes the limits to power.

This logic constitutes the acceptance theory of power developed by Chester Barnard based on his many years of executive experience.[10] Barnard identifies four conditions which determine whether or not a manager's directives are likely to be followed. A subordinate is most likely to accept an order or request when he or she—

- Truly understands the directive.
- Feels capable of carrying it out.
- Sees it as in the organization's best interests.
- Believes it is consistent with personal values.

The Zone of Indifference

Power in organizations is also limited by the range of tasks people consider appropriate to their basic

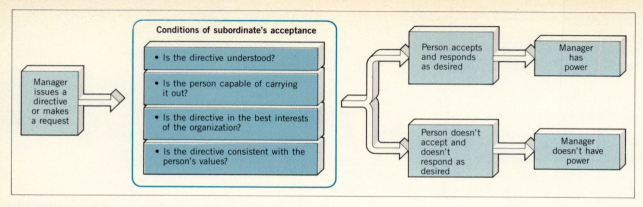

FIGURE 10.4 *Barnard's "acceptance" view of managerial power.*

employment or psychological contracts with the organization. This range defines a **zone of indifference.** Managerial directives and requests falling within this zone tend to be accepted and followed automatically; those falling outside the zone are more likely to be rejected. Take Firenzi again, the drafter in the case mentioned earlier in this chapter. He probably considered the manager's request to work special overtime as falling outside his zone of indifference.

Figure 10.5 diagrams the zone of indifference as it relates to the situation depicted in this case. Note that the manager's request for Firenzi to work overtime on a Friday falls outside of his zone of indifference. Such requests in any situation, if they are to be successful, typically require extraordinary initiatives by a supervisor. This often includes the backing of considerable personal power. For requests that fall inside someone's zone of indifference, position power is usually sufficient to achieve the desired effect. As the example shows, however,

any manager should recognize the limits of position power and be prepared to supplement it with personal power when the need arises. The ability to gain and use personal power may be the ultimate test of a manager's leadership potential.

Ethical Limits and Disobedience: Saying "No" to Higher Authority

This discussion of the acceptance theory of power and the zone of indifference takes the viewpoint of a manager striving to influence someone else. As employees and subordinates in their own rights, however, managers will also be on the receiving end of influence attempts from their supervisors and other persons from both inside and outside of the organization. Indeed, through socialization and other processes, organizations encourage loyalty and conformity among members. Unfortunately, the risk is that the loyalty will extend too far . . . perhaps even to the point of being willing to look

FIGURE 10.5 *A person's "zone of indifference": the case of the engineering project.*

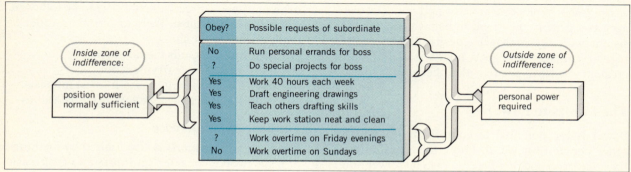

the other way when seeing things that are wrong, or acquiesce when asked to do something unethical and/or illegal.

In fact, there has been a great deal of recent attention given to the ethical and moral aspects of behavior in the workplace. No longer is it acceptable to simply do what one is told, even though it is wrong. Society is now holding organizations and their employees more accountable for misdeeds, and it provides increasing protection for those who are willing to speak up for what is right. For example,[11]

at Beech-Nut it took years to discover that the firm sold a "chemical cocktail" to its unknowing customers, who thought they were buying 100 percent apple juice. Two officers of the company were later tried, convicted of felony crimes, and sentenced to prison. Evidence presented at the trial, however, showed that company officials knew about the problem long before it was uncovered. Even then, it took the courage of the company's former director of research and development who finally "blew the whistle" on the operation.

at Lockheed a former software analyst is suing under protective federal legislation that she was unjustly fired by the large defense contractor for "speaking up" about malpractices at the firm. "The abuses are incredible," she says, alleging that workers did everything from personal business to playing football pools while awaiting security clearances. A government investigation pins the waste to the taxpayers at the tune of $3.5 million per year.

The question you should be asking is, "Where do (or will) I draw the line, at what point do (or will) I refuse to comply with inappropriate requests?" Recently, for example, we have been shocked by insider-information scandals in the financial and defense contracting industries. Someday you may face the situation of being asked to do something in violation of personal ethics and/or even the law. Can you . . . will you . . . when will you . . . say no"?

Of course there are many dilemmas involved in saying "no" to a higher authority. You can't be expected to know when, how, or even why you may refuse to follow an order. But we would be sorely remiss in failing to discuss this flip side of the power coin. There will probably be times when you can and should say "no." Think about it. We'll have more to say on this and related issues in an extended discussion of managerial ethics and social responsibility in Chapter 20.

APPROACHES TO THE STUDY OF LEADERSHIP

For centuries people have recognized that some persons serve well as leaders, while others do not. The inevitable question is "Why?" A correct answer to this question could greatly assist managers in developing personal leadership capabilities to their maximum potential—and would help ensure that all supervisory positions in organizations are staffed with people of appropriate leadership skills. These desirable outcomes, in fact, nicely state the ultimate goal of all leadership theories and research.

Management theory includes the three major directions in the study of leadership as presented in Figure 10.6—the trait, behavioral, and contingency approaches. Each takes a slightly different focus in an attempt to understand and predict leadership success. In general, leadership theories have become more sophisticated as attention shifted over time from leader traits to leader behaviors to situational contingencies.

FIGURE 10.6 *Three directions in the history of leadership research: the trait, behavioral, and contingency approaches.*

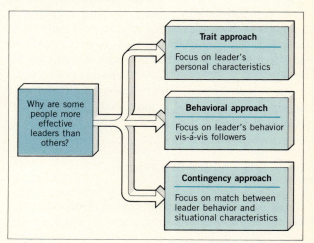

The Search for Leadership Traits

The earliest research on leadership focused on personal **traits** or relatively stable and enduring characteristics of the leader. The trait approach involves the assumption that a leader's personal characteristics determine leadership success. The goal of research in this tradition was to find the set of universal traits that separate effective and ineffective leaders. Given such a list, it would then be easy to select for leadership positions only those people whose characteristics matched the profile and who would therefore surely succeed.

Overall, researchers have been unable to isolate a *definitive* profile of effective leadership traits. The results of many years of research can be summarized as follows.[12] Physical traits such as a person's height, weight, physique, and appearance appear to make *no* difference in determining leadership success. However, certain personal skills and competencies can be of some importance. These include such things as the leader's sense of independence, self-assurance, decisiveness, intelligence in respect to exercising judgment, verbal skills, initiative and concern for self-actualization, as well as supervisory ability.

Such attributes can contribute to someone's development and eventual success as a leader.[13] *Newsline 10.2* offers one perspective on this issue. Consider, too, the point that "followers" appear to admire certain things about leaders and that these positive feelings can enhance a leader's effectiveness. In one study of over 3400 managers from around the United States, for example, the most respected leaders were described as honest, competent, forward-looking, inspiring, and credible.[14] Even these attributes, however, do not apply in a universal manner. There is no way to guarantee that possessing them will result in leadership success in all situations. As the rest of this chapter points out, modern management theory recognizes that leadership success depends on more than one's personal attributes alone.

Focus on Leader Behaviors

In the historical development of leadership research, the inability of researchers to isolate a set of universal traits led to a subsequent focus on actual leader behaviors. This leadership approach involves the assumption that a leader's behavior vis-à-vis followers determines leadership success.

Central to leader-behavior research is the notion of **leadership style,** a term used to describe a recurring pattern of behaviors exhibited by a leader. Although all leadership involves the use of power to exert influence over others, leaders vary in the "style" they use to accomplish this result. The various components of leader-behavior research attempt to both identify various leadership styles and determine which ones work best.

Basic Leadership Styles

Underlying most leader-behavior research is a focus on the degree to which a leader's behavior vis-à-vis followers evidences (1) concern for the task to be accomplished and/or (2) concern for the people doing the work. The terminology used by researchers to describe these two dimensions of leader behavior varies. Concern for task is sometimes addressed under the labels of initiating structure, job-centeredness, and task orientation; concern for people is also referred to as consideration, employee-centeredness, and relationship orientation. Regardless of the terminology used, the behaviors characteristic of each style are quite clear.

1. *A leader high in concern for task emphasizes behaviors that:*
   - Plan and define work to be done.
   - Assign task responsibilities.
   - Set clear work standards.
   - Urge task completion and monitor results.

2. *A leader high in concern for people emphasizes behaviors that convey:*
   - Warmth and social rapport with subordinates.
   - Respect for the feelings of others.
   - Sensitivity to other's needs.
   - Mutual trust.

In practice, leaders emphasize concerns for task and people in the different combinations shown in Figure 10.7. They are:

Abdicative or laissez-faire leadership shows low concern for both people and task. A manager with this style turns most decisions over to the work group and shows little interest in the work process or its results.

DEVELOPING NEW LEADERS

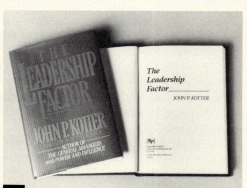

Looking back on management in the 1950s, John P. Kotter, author of *The Leadership Factor,* sees the beginnings of a failure of leadership in American business—a failure that has hampered many organizations' efforts to compete internationally. Kotter maintains that leaders in that decade were actually counterproductive because their ideas tended to disrupt the status quo. Their creativity threatened the bureaucratic style embraced by most businesses until the stormy 1970s.

The new leaders we need, claims Kotter, cannot run complex organizations single-handedly. However, they can and must provide a vision and assemble a network of resources and people to make that vision real. Not all managers can lead, and developing leaders is harder than developing managers. Management is a matter of skills and tools, says Kotter. Leadership involves the less common ability to notice possibilities, and to encourage continual cooperation and initiative in subordinates. It draws on intuition as well as reason, and it demands high levels of energy. For Kotter, leadership is more essential than management—although solid managers can keep leaders from becoming too ego-driven or unpredictable.

Kotter believes that leadership potential is a matter of innate traits fortified by childhood, school, and work experiences. Unfortunately, businesses have been largely unsuccessful in cultivating leadership; an "unresponsive bureaucracy" often discourages talented young leaders. The challenge confronting American organizations is to accept the need for flexible, responsive structures run by leaders—and to develop those leaders from managerial and other ranks.

Source: As reported in Warren Bennis, "Leadership from Inside and Out," *Fortune* (January 8, 1988), pp. 173–174, and Scott DeGarmo, "The Leadership Factor," *Success* (April 1988), p. 2.

FIGURE 10.7 *Leadership styles resulting from different combinations of concerns for task and people.*

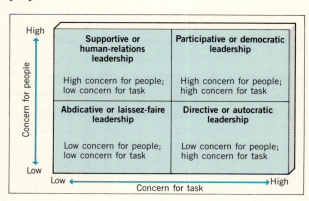

Directive or autocratic leadership shows high concern for the task and low concern for people. A manager with this style makes most decisions for the work group, issues orders, and expects them to be carried out.

Supportive or human relations leadership shows high concern for people and low concern for task. A manager with this style is warm in interpersonal relationships, avoids conflict, and seeks harmony in decision making.

Participative or democratic leadership shows high concern for both people and task. A manager with this style shares decisions with the work group, encourages participation, and supports the task efforts of others.

Research on Leadership Behaviors

Research on leadership behaviors has generally tried to determine which particular combination of behaviors, that is which *style,* is "best." This goal has a very practical appeal. After all, if one best style could be identified from the prior list, it would be possible to train people to use this style and achieve leadership success.

Beginning in the 1940s, the work of scholars at Ohio State University and the University of Michigan was especially important in examining these provocative research directions.[15] The results of their efforts at first suggested that subordinates of more people-centered leaders would be more productive and satisfied than those working for more task-oriented leaders. That is, successful leadership was thought to be associated with a supportive or human-relations style of behavior. Later results, however, suggested that truly effective leaders combined both task and people orientations into a more participative or democratic leadership style.

One of the more popular leadership models to emerge from this latter perspective is the managerial grid concept described by Robert Blake and Jane Mouton.[16] They developed instruments for measuring someone's concern for people and task. Once it is determined where you, for example, would fall on the grid shown in Figure 10.7, they would design an appropriate training program. The purpose of this training would be to help shift your leadership style in the preferred direction of high concern for task and high concern for people—that is, a democratic or participative style which integrates task and people concerns to the benefit of the organization and its members.

Although Blake and Mouton's managerial grid concept is intuitively appealing, most scholars now consider it an oversimplification. Research does not support their universal call for participative or democratic management. While good leaders need the abilities to be both task-oriented and considerate in their relationships with others, they must be able to apply them in a variety of ways—sometimes being directive and showing a concern for production, sometimes being supportive and showing a concern for people, and other times being participative while combining concerns for both production and people.[17] Consider, for example, this series of statements made by managers.[18] What do they have in common?

■ "I put most problems into my group's hands and leave it to them to carry the ball from there. I serve merely as a catalyst, mirroring back the people's thoughts and feelings so that they can better understand them."

■ "It's foolish to make decisions oneself on matters that affect people. I always talk things over with my subordinates, but I make it clear to them that I'm the one who has to have the final say."

■ "Once I have decided on a course of action, I do my best to sell my ideas to my employees."

■ "I'm being paid to lead. If I let a lot of other people make the decisions I should be making, then I'm not worth my salt."

■ "I believe in getting things done. I can't waste time calling meetings. Someone has to call the shots around here, and I think it should be me."

The answer to the question is "success." Each of these manager's behaviors proved effective in its situation. And because of this, most leadership theorists no longer ask "which is the *best* leadership style?" They focus on the question—"when and under what circumstances is a particular style preferable to others?" This is the essence of the contingency approach to leadership. Instead of searching for the one best way to behave in all situations (as the leader-behavior researchers have done), contingency researchers try to determine when a particular behavior is the most appropriate way to achieve leadership effectiveness. They seek the answer by examining the proper matches between situational needs or demands and the leader's behaviors. We will review three leadership theories having this contingency theme—Fiedler's contingency theory, House's path–goal theory, and the Vroom and Yetton leader-participation theory.

FIEDLER'S CONTINGENCY THEORY

The first of the contingency theories was developed by Fred Fiedler in response to what he considered basic deficiencies in the leader-behavior approach.[19] His theory is that successful leadership depends on a good match between the style of the leader and the demands of the situation. Specifically, a leader's basic task or relationship orientation should be consistent with the amount of situational control available to the leader. **Situational control** is defined as the extent to which a leader can determine what a group is going to do and what the outcomes of its actions and decisions are going to be. In situations of high control, leaders can usually predict what will happen when they want something done; in situations of low control, uncertainty exists.

The essence of Fiedler's extensive research can be summarized in the following propositions.

Proposition No. 1   A task-oriented leader will be most successful in situations of either high or low control.

Proposition No. 2   A relationship-oriented leader will be most successful in situations of moderate control.

You can readily see the contingency logic now being pursued. Neither the task-oriented nor relationship-oriented leadership style is predicted most effective all of the time. Instead, each style is effective when used in the right situation. Fiedler's challenge to the manager or aspiring leader is threefold: (1) to understand one's predominant leadership style, (2) to diagnose situations in terms of the amount of control offered the leader, and (3) to achieve a good match between style and situation.

Understanding Leadership Styles

Before reading on, complete the questionnaire presented in Table 10.2. This Least-Preferred Co-Worker Scale, or the LPC scale, is used by Fiedler to determine a person's leadership style.

Score the instrument as follows. Write the numbers you checked for each adjective pair in the space to the right of the page. Add these up to get a total LPC score. If your LPC score is 64 or higher, you are a *high LPC leader* who tends to view even your least preferred co-worker in relatively favorable terms. Fiedler equates this tendency to a *relationship-oriented leadership style*. A score of 57 or lower depicts a *low LPC leader* who views the least-preferred co-worker in less favorable terms. This equates to a *task-oriented leadership style*. If you scored in the 58–63 range, Fiedler leaves it to your best judgment as to which direction your leadership style is weighted.

Diagnosing Leadership Situations

The next step in applying Fiedler's leadership theory is to diagnose the amount of control a situation allows the leader. Three situational variables are important in this regard: (1) **leader-member relations** (good or poor)—the degree to which the group supports the leader; (2) **task structure** (high or low)—the extent to which task goals, procedures, and guidelines are clearly spelled out; and (3) **position power** (strong or weak)—the degree to which the position gives the leader power to reward and punish subordinates.

Figure 10.8 shows eight combinations of these variables. The figure also summarizes the results of Fiedler's extensive research on the contingency relationships between situational characteristics, leadership style, and leader effectiveness. Let's further clarify his approach by example.

Assume you are the supervisor of a group of bank tellers. Your subordinates seem highly supportive. The teller's job is well defined in respect to what tasks need to be done when and how. You have the authority to evaluate the tellers' performance, and make pay and promotion recommendations. This is a high-control situation consisting of good leader–member relations, high task structure, and high position power. The figure shows that you should be a task-oriented leader to be most effective.

Take another example. Suppose that you are chairperson of a committee asked to improve labor–management relations in a manufacturing plant. Although the goal is clear, no one can say for sure what activities will actually result in "improved labor–management relations." Task structure is low. Because the other committee members are free to quit anytime they want, you also have little position power as chairperson. Furthermore, you perceive poor leader–member relations because some members resent your appointment as chairperson. Figure 10.8 shows that this low-control situation also calls for a task-oriented leader.

Finally, assume you are the new head of a retail unit in a large department store. Because you were selected over one of the popular sales clerks you now supervise, the result is poor leader–member relations. Task structure is high since the clerk's job

TABLE 10.2 *Fiedler's Least-Preferred Co-worker Scale*

Throughout your life you will have worked in many groups with a wide variety of different people—on your job, in social groups, in church organizations, in volunteer groups, on athletic teams, and in many other situations. Some of your co-workers may have been very easy to work with in attaining the group's goals, while others were less so.

Think of all the people with whom you have ever worked, and then *think of the person with whom you could work least well.* He or she may be someone with whom you work now or with whom you have worked in the past. This does not have to be the person you liked least well, but should be the person with whom you had the most difficulty getting a job done, the *one* individual with whom you could work *least well.* Describe this person on the scale by placing an X in the appropriate spaces.

Look at the words at both ends of the line before you mark your X. *There are no right or wrong answers.* Work rapidly; your first answer is likely to be the best. Do not omit any items, and mark each item only once. Now describe the person with whom you can work *least* well.

										Scoring
Pleasant	8	7	6	5	4	3	2	1	Unpleasant	___
Friendly	8	7	6	5	4	3	2	1	Unfriendly	___
Rejecting	1	2	3	4	5	6	7	8	Accepting	___
Tense	1	2	3	4	5	6	7	9	Relaxed	___
Distant	1	2	3	4	5	6	7	8	Close	___
Cold	1	2	3	4	5	6		8	Warm	___
Supportive	8	7	6	5	4	3	2	1	Hostile	___
Boring	1	2	3	4	5	6	7	8	Interesting	___
Quarrelsome	1	2	3	4	5	6	7	8	Harmonious	___
Gloomy	1	2	3	4	5	6	7	8	Cheerful	___
Open	8	7	6	5	4	3	2	1	Guarded	___
Backbiting	1	2	3	4	5	6	7	8	Loyal	___
Untrustworthy	1	2	3	4	5	6	7	8	Trustworthy	___
Considerate	8	7	6	5	4	3	2	1	Inconsiderate	___
Nasty	1	2	3	4	5	6	7	8	Nice	___
Agreeable	8	7	6	5	4	3	2	1	Disagreeable	___
Insincere	1	2	3	4	5	6	7	8	Sincere	___
Kind	8	7	6	5	4	3	2	1	Unkind	___

Total ___

Source: Adapted from Fred E. Fiedler, Martin M. Chemers, and Linda Mahar, *Improving Leadership Effectiveness* (New York: Wiley, 1976), p. 7. Used by permission.

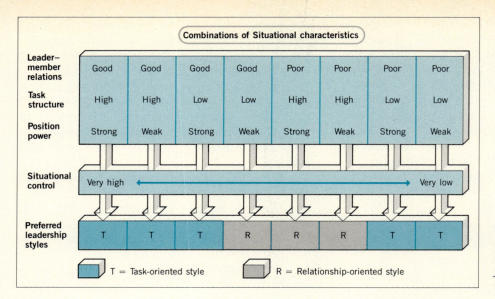

Combinations of Situational characteristics

Leader–member relations	Good	Good	Good	Good	Poor	Poor	Poor	Poor
Task structure	High	High	Low	Low	High	High	Low	Low
Position power	Strong	Weak	Strong	Weak	Strong	Weak	Strong	Weak

Situational control: Very high ⟵——————⟶ Very low

Preferred leadership styles	T	T	T	R	R	R	T	T

☐ T = Task-oriented style   ☐ R = Relationship-oriented style

FIGURE 10.8 *Matching leadership style and situation: predictions from Fiedler's contingency theory.*

is well defined. Your position power is low because the clerks work under a seniority system with a fixed wage schedule. The figure shows that this moderate-control situation requires a relationship-oriented leader.

Matching Leadership Style and Situation

Fiedler basically disagrees with leadership training that attempts only to change a person's leadership style in a preferred direction. Rather, Fiedler believes people should be taught how to understand their personal styles, analyze situations for their leadership implications, and to then *match* style and situation to maximize leadership effectiveness. To begin with, this means that prospective leaders should actively seek situations for which their predominate style, that is, a task-oriented or relationship-oriented approach, is most appropriate. When a mismatch is recognized, it should be corrected by either of the two following strategies:

1. Change situational characteristics to better align them with one's leadership style.
2. Change one's leadership style to better fit the requirements of the situation.

Since Fiedler believes that leadership style is strongly tied to basic personality factors and is therefore not easy to change, he advocates option

one as first priority. Through appropriate "situational engineering," he suggests, the characteristics of situations can often be modified to increase or decrease situational control to achieve a "best fit" with the individual's leadership style.

As with many other management theories, there is controversy surrounding Fiedler's work, and it is easy to find research that is both pro and con. Nevertheless, this theory represents an important turning point in the history of leadership studies. It introduced for the first time the logic of situational factors influencing the success of alternative leadership styles. This step "beyond" the leader-behavior theories has led Fiedler and many others to continue working on contingency models of leadership effectiveness. Fiedler's current work, for example, focuses on the leader's cognitive capabilities as a further contingency issue.[20] His basic point in this *cognitive resource theory* is that the more task-relevant a leader's competencies, intelligence, and experience are, the more directive the leader can be. Otherwise, a more participative style works best.

HOUSE'S PATH–GOAL THEORY

A second useful contingency approach to leadership is the path–goal theory advanced by Robert House.[21] This theory indicates that an effective leader clarifies the paths through which subordinates can achieve both work-related and personal goals, assists them to progress along these paths, and removes any barriers that may inhibit goal accomplishment. To do all this, House believes a leader must utilize four distinct types of leader behaviors—directive, supportive, participative, and achievement-oriented. In addition, his contingency theory suggests that an effective leader uses different behaviors depending on the nature of the situation. Before discussing the contingency issues involved in making such choices, let's examine the four leadership styles in some detail.

1. *Directive leadership.*
   ■ Letting subordinates know what is expected.
   ■ Giving directions on what to do and how.
   ■ Scheduling work to be done.
   ■ Maintaining definite standards of performance.
   ■ Clarifying the leader's role in the group.

2. *Supportive leadership.*
   ■ Doing things to make work more pleasant.
   ■ Treating group members as equals.
   ■ Being friendly and approachable.
   ■ Showing concern for the status, well-being, and needs of subordinates.

3. *Achievement-oriented leadership.*
   ■ Setting challenging goals.
   ■ Expecting subordinates to perform at their highest level.
   ■ Emphasizing excellence and continuous improvement in performance.
   ■ Displaying confidence that subordinates will meet high standards.

4. *Participative leadership.*
   ■ Involving subordinates in decision making.
   ■ Consulting with subordinates.
   ■ Asking for suggestions from subordinates.
   ■ Taking these suggestions seriously into account before making a decision.

Predictions and Managerial Implications

A contingency theorist, House suggests there is no one best way to lead. Path–goal theory advises leaders to vary style or behavior according to situational contingencies, including subordinate characteristics and task demands. In all cases, the actions taken should be useful in helping clarify paths to existing rewards and/or increase the availability of more valued ones. The actions should not simply add to the situation things that are already present by virtue of task designs or the type of people doing them.

House's theory is summarized in Figure 10.9. The research version is quite complex in elaborating a number of possible contingency variables on the one hand and the four leadership behaviors on the other. Briefly, some of the theory's basic predictions are:

■ Supportive leadership complements routine and highly structured tasks.

■ Directive leadership complements ambiguous and unstructured tasks.

■ Achievement leadership complements growth-oriented workers.

■ Participative leadership complements highly capable workers.

Look again at the prior predictions, and note in particular that path–goal theory advises a manager to use leadership styles that *complement* situational contingencies. An effective leader brings to a situation things that are *not* already present; she or he specifically avoids doing things that are redundant. For example, someone who feels unsure how to perform a task is likely to be grateful for a manager's directive leadership; someone working at a machine-paced assembly-line job, by contrast, is likely to resent directive leadership as totally unnecessary. When someone is using an inappropriate leadership style, such as in the last example, House's theory

FIGURE 10.9 *Contingency relationships in the path–goal theory of leadership effectiveness.*

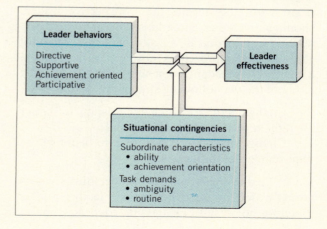

warns that the negative consequences may include reduced effort, poor attitudes, and generally lower performance.

House's path–goal model has strong ties to the expectancy theory of motivation to be discussed in Chapter 12. Continuing research supports it as among the more promising contingency leadership approaches.[22] Some additional examples of proper path-goal leadership responses to common managerial situations include:

1. *Unclear job assignments* The effective manager provides directive leadership to clarify task objectives and expected rewards.
2. *Low worker self-confidence* The effective manager provides supportive leadership to clarify individual abilities and offer any needed task assistance.
3. *Poor performance incentives* The effective manager provides participative leadership to clarify individual needs and identify rewards appropriate to them.
4. *Insufficient task challenge* The effective manager provides achievement-oriented leadership to clarify higher goals and raise performance aspirations.

Substitutes for Leadership

Path-goal theory has also contributed to the recognition of what some theorists call **substitutes for leadership.** These are aspects of the work setting and the people involved that already provide task direction without a leader's personal involvement.[23] To the extent such "substitutes" for leadership are present, they decrease the need for similar managerial responses. As suggested by path-goal theory, managers should avoid such redundancies and con-

centrate their leadership contributions in areas that truly require attention. In general, the more structured a work situation, the less task-oriented leadership is necessary; the more enriched the tasks and the more teamwork involved in their performance, the less people-oriented leadership is necessary. Some of the more common substitutes for leadership that make a difference in each regard are:

■ *subordinate characteristics* for example, ability, experience and independence.
■ *task characteristics* for example, routineness, availability of feedback and intrinsic satisfaction.
■ *organizational characteristics* for example, clarity of plans, formalization of rules and procedures, and the size and influence of staff functions.

THE VROOM–YETTON LEADER-PARTICIPATION THEORY

Victor Vroom and Phillip Yetton offer a contingency theory that centers on how leaders make decisions.[24] This theory builds on the premise that various problems have different characteristics and should therefore be solved by different decision methods.

Alternative Decision-Making Methods

As highlighted throughout this book, decision making is a key activity for managers. The way decisions are made is an important element in a manager's leadership style. Figure 10.10 depicts the three decision methods originally introduced in Chapter 3—the individual or authority decision, the con-

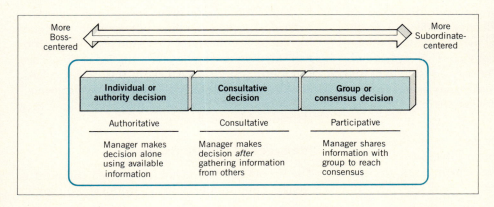

FIGURE 10.10 *A continuum of decision methods and related leadership styles.*

sultative decision, and the group or consensus decision. The figure also relates each decision method to a continuum of leadership styles ranging from authoritative at the extreme where all decisions are made by the manager, to participative at the other extreme where decisions are made by the group as a whole. The differences among these decision-making methods are important.

1. An **authority decision** is made by the manager and then communicated to the group. No input is asked of group members other than to provide specific information on request.
2. A **consultative decision** is made by the manager asking group members for information, advice, or opinion before making a final decision on behalf of the group. Consultative decisions take two forms. In one, group members are consulted individually; in the other, consultation occurs in a meeting of the group as a whole.
3. In a **group decision** all group members participate with the manager and finally agree by consensus on the course of action to be taken. The group-decision process is successful to the extent that each member is ultimately able to accept the logic and feasibility of the final group decision. Complete unanimity is not the goal. Instead, consensus is achieved when any dissenting member is able to say[25]

> I understand what most of you would like to do. I personally would not do that, but I feel that you understand what my alternative would be. I have had sufficient opportunity to sway you to my point of view but clearly have not been able to do so. Therefore, I will gladly go along with what most of you wish to do.

Choosing a Decision Method

A single contingency proposition underlies the Vroom–Yetton model: effective leadership results when the decision method used in problem solving matches problem characteristics. This means there will be times when authority, consultative, and group forms of decision making are each appropriate. For any leader and manager, therefore, the challenge is twofold:

1. To know when each decision method is the best approach for the problem at hand.
2. To know how to implement each decision method well when required.

Let's work on your ability to handle the first of these challenges. Take a moment to solve the following problem.[26]

CASE OF THE EMPLOYEE TRANSFERS

Assume you are supervising the work of 12 engineers. Their formal training and work experience are similar, permitting you to use them interchangeably on projects. Yesterday, your manager informed you that a request had been received from an overseas affiliate for four engineers to go abroad on extended loan for a period of six to eight months. For a number of reasons, the manager argued—and you agreed—that this request should be met from your group.

All your engineers are capable of handling this assignment, and from the standpoint of present and future projects there is no particular reason why any one should be retained over any other. The problem is somewhat complicated by the fact that the overseas assignment is in what is generally regarded in the company as an undesirable location.

How should this decision be made—by an *authority, consultative,* or *group* decision?

Your response to the problem is a ''gut'' reaction. It represents how you would act in this leadership situation without any special guidance. The Vroom and Yetton leadership model offers a more systematic way of making good problem-solving decisions. A *good* decision in this sense is (1) high in quality, (2) accepted by the people who have to implement it, and (3) timely.

The model is depicted in Figure 10.11 and works as follows. Listed across the top of the figure are seven diagnostic questions designed to identify key problem attributes. Asking and answering these questions in sequence for any problem situation leads you through the branches of the decision tree to an ideal decision method. For example, the figure highlights Vroom and Yetton's analysis of the problem situation to which you responded earlier. They feel a group decision is best in this case. Go back and compare your answer to theirs. Work through the decision-tree analysis to understand how they arrived at this conclusion.

Managerial Implications

The Vroom and Yetton model has been criticized as complex and cumbersome. Obviously, you aren't

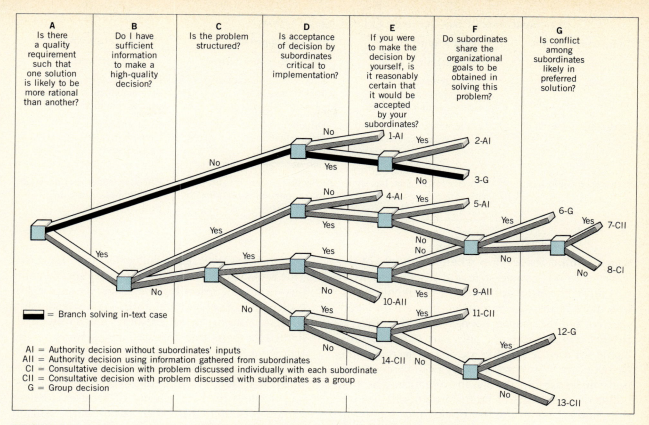

A
Is there a quality requirement such that one solution is likely to be more rational than another?

B
Do I have sufficient information to make a high-quality decision?

C
Is the problem structured?

D
Is acceptance of decision by subordinates critical to implementation?

E
If you were to make the decision by yourself, is it reasonably certain that it would be accepted by your subordinates?

F
Do subordinates share the organizational goals to be obtained in solving this problem?

G
Is conflict among subordinates likely in preferred solution?

■ = Branch solving in-text case

AI = Authority decision without subordinates' inputs
AII = Authority decision using information gathered from subordinates
CI = Consultative decision with problem discussed individually with each subordinate
CII = Consultative decision with problem discussed with subordinates as a group
G = Group decision

FIGURE 10.11 *The Vroom–Yetton decision tree: the case of the employee transfer.*

Source: Slightly adapted and reprinted by permission of the publisher from "A New Look at Managerial Decision-Making," Victor H. Vroom, *Organizational Dynamics,* Spring 1973, pp. 69–70. Copyright © 1973 by AMACOM, a division of the American Management Associations. All rights reserved.

expected to work through the decision tree in Figure 10.11 for every problem you face as a manager. Yet there is a basic discipline to the approach that is most useful. When confronted by future problems, the model reminds you that each of the three alternative decision methods—individual, consultative, and group—is important and useful. The key is to use each method well and only in those problem situations for which it represents the best leadership response.[27] In general,

Managers should use a more participative style and a group decision method when:
■ They lack sufficient information to solve a problem by themselves.
■ The problem is unclear and help is needed to clarify the situation.
■ Acceptance of the decision by others is necessary to achieve successful implementation.

■ Adequate time is available to allow for true participation.

Managers should use a more authoritative style and an individual decision method when:
■ They have greater expertise on a problem.
■ They are confident and capable of acting alone.
■ Others are likely to accept the decision.
■ There is little or no time for discussion.

DIRECTIONS IN LEADERSHIP THEORY AND PRACTICE

Current and popular thinking seeks to further extend leadership thinking beyond the major contingency approaches summarized once again in Table 10.3. The theories discussed so far tend to focus on

A Comparison of Three Contingency Leadership Theories

Comparison Points	Fiedler's Approach	House's Approach	Vroom–Yetton Approach
Concern	Situational control	Situational characteristics	Problem attributes
Diagnostic focus	Task structure Position power Leader-member relations	Subordinate characteristics Task demands	Decision quality, subordinate acceptance, information and time availability
Leadership styles	Task motivated Relationship motivated	Directive Supportive Participative Achievement oriented	Authoritative Consultative Participative
Managerial implication	Effective leader matches style with situation	Effective leader chooses style to complement situational characteristics	Effective leader uses decision method best fitting the problem at hand

transactional leadership wherein the role of the leader is to orchestrate style and situation so as to best direct the efforts of others in productive ways. In today's terms—as introduced in the Part 4 Perspective and the chapter opener—however, this capability still accounts for only part of the requirements for true leadership success. The remaining elements are best represented by two current directions in leadership theory and practice. The first builds on the theme of "transformational" leadership, and relates to the identification of highly inspirational "superleaders." The second, best illustrated through the work of Peter Drucker, has a more traditional thrust. It addresses the old-fashioned view of the "hard work" of being a leader.

Transformational Leadership

"Superleaders?" What is meant by the term? "Charisma," is one possible response. But the concept is really broader than this term allows. When people talk about superleaders today, they are talking about persons who, through vision and strength of personality, are truly inspirational in their impact on other persons.[28] For example, Bernard Bass, a noted leadership scholar, singles out Lee Iacocca and his success in revitalizing the Chrysler Corporation.[29] He sums it up this way: "What does Lee Iacocca have that many other executives lack? Charisma. What would have happened to Chrysler without him? It probably would have gone bankrupt."

Iacocca is what Bass calls a **transformational leader**—someone able to get people to do more than they originally expected to do. Achieving this "transformation" involves moving people from doing what is expected to doing *more* than expected. This is made possible, in turn, by very special abilities—a line of reasoning that takes us once again back to the role of individual attributes in leadership success. Among those attributes currently highlighted for their "transformational" qualities are the following.[30]

■ *Vision* Having ideas and a clear sense of direction, being able to communicate visions to others, and develop in them a sense of great excitement about working hard to accomplish shared "dreams".

■ *Charisma* Arousing others' enthusiasm, faith, loyalty, pride, and trust in themselves through the power of personal reference and appeals to emotion.

■ *Symbolism* Identifying "heroes," offering special rewards and holding spontaneous and planned ceremonies to celebrate excellence and high achievement.

■ *Empowerment* Maintaining a development orientation toward others, removing performance obstacles, sharing responsibilities, and delegating truly challenging work.

■ *Intellectual stimulation* Enhancing the mental involvement of others by creating awareness of problems and stirring their imagination to create high quality solutions.

■ *Integrity* Being honest and credible, acting consistently out of a sense of personal conviction, and above all meeting commitments by following through—doing what you said you would do.

The concept of transformational leadership offers a new and distinct challenge to managers. This challenge is to not just diagnose a situation and

SOME PRACTICAL
ADVICE ON LEADERSHIP

NEWSLINE 10.3

Observing a divisional marketing manager for Intel Corporation make a presentation to corporate sales managers, Intel CEO Andy Grove noticed that the marketing manager had trouble defending his group's line of products against the criticisms of the salespeople. Grove felt that the sales staff was probably trying to avoid being saddled with hard-to-move products—and that the marketing manager was so intent on appeasing them that he ended up looking uncommitted to his wares. In Grove's view, the manager had missed a good opportunity to display genuine leadership—the ability "to make ordinary people do extraordinary things."

In a future similar situation, Grove says, his manager needs to "blend altogether different skills"—logic and emotional forcefulness—"but does not need to be superhuman." This combination is the essence of leadership. The manager must work on developing a keen sense of timing, Grove says, so that he or she can inject emotion into a business situation at the right moment, thus quelling negative reactions or undue criticism. The knack for timing may not be innate, but we can learn it and other ineffables "by studying the behavior of people who have made a success of it and modeling ourselves after them."

Source: As reported in Andrew S. Grove, "Taking the Hype Out of Leadership," *Fortune* (March 28, 1988), pp. 187–188.

transact a leadership style that matches its demands. The real challenge is to do so with a leadership aura and contagious enthusiasm that substantially raises subordinates confidence, aspirations, and commitments to the manager and collective purpose. The benefits include having subordinates who are highly dedicated, more satisfied with their work, and who are more willing to put forth extra efforts.

Good "Old-Fashioned" Leadership

In a *Wall Street Journal* editorial, Peter Drucker describes a telephone conversation with the human resources vice-president of a big bank.[31] "We'd want you to run a seminar for us on how one acquires charisma," she said. Drucker's response was not what she expected. He advised her to tell the VP that there's more to leadership than the popular emphasis on personal qualities that offer a sense of personal "dash" or charisma. In fact he says that leadership ". . . is work."

Drucker's observations on leadership offer a fitting complement to the concept of transformational leadership just advanced. Consider his points on the requirements of leadership.

1. *The foundation of effective leadership is defining and establishing a sense of mission.* A good leader sets the goals, priorities, and standards. A good leader keeps them all clear and visible, and maintains them. Drucker says, "the leader's first task is to be the trumpet that sounds a clear sound."

2. *The effective leader sees leadership as a "responsibility" rather than a rank.* Good leaders surround themselves with talented persons. They aren't afraid to develop strong and capable subordinates. And they don't blame others when things go wrong. As Drucker says, "the buck stops here" is still a good adage to remember.

3. *An effective leader earns and maintains the trust of others.* The key here is "integrity." The followers of good leaders trust the leader, even if they don't

necessarily like him or her. This means they believe the leader means what is being said and that actions will be consistent with what is being said. In Drucker's words again, "Effective leadership . . . is not based on being clever; it is based primarily on being consistent."

Final Advice

There is no getting around it. To be an effective manager, it is necessary to be a good leader. In the final analysis, as suggested by *Newsline 10.3,* you and you alone are responsible for developing and demonstrating *your* leadership skills. Although there are many useful ideas available from research and popular thinking, there is no one hard and fast rule that can be followed to achieve leadership success. A leader certainly requires the capabilities to show support, provide direction, allow participation and inspire followers to pursue extraordinary efforts. To do all of this, a leader must be able to achieve influence over others by using power from both position and personal sources. And a leader must be able to understand situational contingencies and act accordingly.

This final advice leaves a lot of responsibility up to you. It encourages you to take maximum advantage of insights from each leadership theory and viewpoint reviewed in this chapter. It also encourages you to seriously examine the coming chapters on leading through communication, motivation and group dynamics.

SUMMARY

Power is a foundation for leadership. It is a capacity to control or influence the behavior of other persons. Power becomes available to the manager through position (legitimacy, rewards, punishments) and through personal attributes (reference, expertise). Leadership is the use of power to enthusiastically direct the behavior of others toward organizational objectives.

Leadership research historically includes an interest in personal traits, leader behaviors, and situational contingencies. Trait researchers have generally been unable to find one profile of personal characteristics that universally separates effective from noneffective leaders. Leader-behavior researchers, likewise, have been unable to determine that one style or pattern of leader behaviors is consistently superior to others. Fiedler's contingency theory, House's path–goal theory, and the Vroom–Yetton leader-participation theory share the common contingency point of view that there is no one best way to lead. Each offers a slightly different approach for achieving the best match between personal leadership style and situational demands.

Current directions in leadership theory and practice direct a leader's attention toward attributes and behaviors that have a "transformational" quality. The effective leader is depicted as one who is able to truly inspire other people to accomplish more than they ever thought was possible. In addition, Peter Drucker cautions us not to forget that leadership success entails good old-fashioned "hard work." This work includes being able to help establish a sense of mission and earning the respect of others as this mission is collectively pursued.

You have much to gain by reflecting on the full tradition of leadership research. Underlying the success of any true leader is probably the capability to be task-oriented and/or people-oriented as the situation requires. This demands that you know not only *when* to use various styles, but also *how* to use them. Many ideas are found throughout this chapter on the relative advantages of various leadership styles. What remains to be learned are the basic concepts and issues of communication, motivation and group dynamics that affect a manager's ability to use the ideas in the work setting. The next three chapters address these topics.

Thinking Through the Issues

1. What is leadership? How does being a good "leader" differ from being a good "manager"?
2. What is the difference between a formal and informal leader? Is a manager only one or the other? Explain your answer.
3. Name five sources of power available to man-

agers. Give an example of each power source and explain whether it is a source of personal or position power.

4. Of what significance to would-be leaders is the zone of indifference and the acceptance theory of power? Explain your answers.

5. Why did scholars shift away from trait-leadership theory? In what way does this tradition of research relate to some of the current directions in leadership?

6. How have we benefited most from research into leadership behaviors? Explain and give examples of the major leadership "styles" common to this perspective.

7. How do the contingency theories of Fiedler and House differ in concept, and their managerial implications?

8. Explain the concept of "substitutes for leadership," and give some examples of these substitutes. Why would a manager want to be aware of leadership substitutes?

9. Can the Vroom–Yetton model help managers to handle real problem situations successfully? Why or why not?

10. What is transformational leadership? What implications does it hold for the manager who desires true success as a leader?

The Manager's Vocabulary

Abdicative leadership
Authority decision
Autocratic leadership
Coercive power
Consultative decision
Democratic leadership
Directive leadership
Expert power
Formal leadership
Group decision

Human relations
  leadership
Informal leadership
Laissez-faire
  leadership
Leader-member
  relations
Leadership
Leadership style

Leading
Legitimate power
Participative
  leadership
Position power
Power
Reference power
Reward power
Situational control

Substitutes for
  leadership
Supportive leadership
Task structure
Traits
Transactional leader
Transformational
  leader
Zone of indifference

HOW TO WIN THE CORPORATE GAME, OR AT LEAST TIE THE SCORE

CAREER PERSPECTIVE

Bob Cressor was a vice president of one of the largest corporations in America when he retired at 62. He admits he was a game player.[32] "I played the corporate game for many years and left the field with a smile on my face," Cressor says. The smile indicated he'd won. Oh, he didn't pitch a shutout or go undefeated. He didn't demoralize the opposition with one slam-dunk after another.

"I suffered my share of interceptions, fumbles, strikeouts, and roughing-the-wrong-guy penalties," Cressor says candidly, "but I hung tough and gained the eventual victory by discovering very early that it's how you play the game that determines whether you win or lose."

When he trotted away early this year from Sun Co., after 34 years in the game, he was vice-president for constituency relations. By some yardsticks, Cressor would be measured a success. He didn't simply survive; he prospered. He became a company star principally because he kept telling himself it wasn't life or death, only a game, and that there were other games on other fields in which he could play. "You might say I played relaxed, recognizing I'd do okay if I learned the rules and could discipline myself to stay within them," Cressor explains.

A lot of the rules Cressor ad-libbed. Don't work for the boss is one of them. "I had 27 bosses in 34 years," he explains.

A lot of them were great, but a few were so intimidated by their bosses they became monuments to inertia. A couple were plain incompetent.

"I have a gut feeling that a great many bosses are sitting one level above their competence quotient. You can't for the boss; you must work for the company. The boss will pass; the company won't."

Cressor warns it's a mistake to focus on the boss from one end of the day to the other, ignoring everyone else in the organization. "The world turns," he says, "and when it does the boss falls off, leaving you without any support at all from others in the game."

It's important to build an influence network, Cressor emphasizes—a network that includes persons in top management, your peers, and those on lower levels. "At some point, you are going to be dependent on someone up above—with muscle. But it's essential that you have support laterally and from below," he says.

Cressor started his business career as salesman, and though he did very well for himself, he didn't get rich. "Too many young people see stories about six-digit executive salaries and decide to go for it. Don't. One look at the organization chart should convince you the odds are stacked heavily against you. You'll make a living—but a winter place in Palm Beach? Hardly."

Questions

1. What does Bob Cressor mean by the statement—"You can't work for the boss . . . the boss will pass . . ." Is this a realistic way to approach one's job? Please explain.
2. What are the leadership implications of the managerial survival skills advocated by Bob Cressor?
3. Are you prepared to follow the "rules of the game" as described by Bob Cressor? Why or why not?

Case Application

HEAD NURSE AT GENERAL HOSPITAL

Floor A at General Hospital has about 30 private and semiprivate beds. Medical patients and surgical patients are cared for by graduate nurses, student nurses, nurses aides, and maids.

On Floor A, people speak in hushed voices. Conversation is at a minimum. Pat Smith, the head nurse, spends almost all her time at her desk. She gives instructions firmly and unambiguously. The nurses go from room to room caring for patients in a businesslike impersonal manner, and there is little give-and-take between them and the patients.

1. *The Head Nurse* Smith's supervisor said of her: "Pat Smith is of the old school. She's really very stern and rigid. She runs an excellent floor from the standpoint of organization and system. It's beautifully organized. She has all her supplies in perfect condition, but she can't handle human relations. Her graduates claim that she treats them like students, watches everything they do, checks up on them all the time, and won't allow them any responsibility. The students claim that Smith gives them only routine, only the small details."

It is generally agreed that Smith is fair and not arbitrary. For example, she makes a conscious effort to grant nurses' requests for time off whenever possible, but is strict and uncompromising with nurses who violate regulations. She is uniformly courteous in a formal manner. The following conversation with a member of the dietary department is typical: "I am calling for Miss Wilson, a patient in Room 413, a diabetic case. She would like coffee with every meal. Is that all right? Thank you."

She observes the same rather starchy courtesy whether the pressure of work is relaxed or at its height, and expects the same formal courtesy from her subordinates.

2. *The Assistant* Smith delegates almost no authority to Lee Green, her assistant. When Smith is on the ward, Green shares floor duty with the other nurses and does not work at the desk. When Green is in charge, there is a marked change in the atmosphere. People talk to each other more naturally, and sit around when the work is slack. There is also considerable confusion on the ward.

3. *Graduate Nurses* The attitude among the younger graduates toward Smith's supervision is

expressed in the following quotations:

> . . . she runs a very strict floor, and the nurses resent her because she treats them like students.
>
> . . . When I came here, she checked up on everything I did, and that was hard to adjust to. You felt you were a student all over again.
>
> . . . she is off, and the doctors who come here are in a more sociable frame of mind. The whole atmosphere seems to relax. Often we have a nurses' aide mix up a pitcher of lemonade and we have it sitting right down at the desk. If you tried that in the daytime, she would have a stroke.
>
> . . . I don't pay any attention to her any more, and I don't think the others do either. You just let what she says go in one ear and out the other. At first it bothered me, and I think it annoyed most of the others that she treated us like students. All I say is, 'Yes', and go ahead and do what I would have done anyway. We sit around and talk to each other when the work is done, and if she asks us to be a little quiet we lower our voices, but we don't attempt to slink around or anything. There was a tendency to do that for a while, but you soon get over that.

The attitude of the older nurses is different as the following quotations show:

> . . . I like working with her. I know a lot of the others complain about her because she's fussy and checks on them. Personally I'd rather work on this floor than anywhere else for exactly that reason. Everything here is done properly. The doctors prefer this floor because this is where the patients get the best care. The other nurses aren't impressed by that. They insist they wouldn't work here because she is a fussbudget. They don't seem to care whether the patients get good care or not.
>
> . . . I picked this floor because I liked the supervision here. I've worked with her while I was a student and I knew what to expect. I honestly feel I still need a responsible person nearby to supervise. I need guidance, and therefore I prefer to work on a floor where there is a fairly strict supervisor. On some of the other floors things are too slipshod. . . . The head nurse has to be strict in order to get the work done. Isn't that right?
>
> . . . Some of the others are lovely to work with, but just aren't good at supervising. They don't know how to express themselves. Now when she is on, it is altogether different. She knows how to get things done the first time.

4. *Student Nurses* Smith keeps her students under rigid discipline, and they complain to their supervisor that she gives them only routine work and doesn't allow them to take any responsibility. They feel they learn much less than on other floors. The students ask few questions either of Smith or of the graduate nurses. They rarely talk to anyone.

5. *Relationships among Workers* All relationships on Floor A tend to be formal and impersonal. There is very little give and take or development of camaraderie. Nurses' aides complain that the nurses never teach them anything. Smith divides up the work equally and assigns it clearly, and there is no complaint that some members of the group are slack in carrying out their duties. Yet when Smith is off the floor there is evidence of antagonism among the different workers. The aides say that if they had problems they would take them up with their housekeeping supervisor.

6. *Patient Care* The relationship between nurses and patients is rather formal and distant. Patients remain in their rooms, and very few walk about on the floor. Requests by patients and visitors are taken care of promptly and efficiently. The charts are in excellent order, but there is some evidence of slipups in nursing care. In one case, a patient was given the wrong drug and had a severe reaction. During the period when the ward was observed there were three instances of postoperative fever. Once when an intern removed a drainage catheter and forgot to replace it, the error was not corrected for five hours.

Floor B, just one flight up from Floor A in the new hospital wing, is similar in all external features. It has the same number of beds, and the same types of patients are cared for by the same mix of nurses and support staff. But, the Head Nurse on Floor B is supposed to operate quite differently than Pat Smith. The atmosphere is warm and informal there, and many patients who have previously been on the floor ask to be sent back again at the time of a second admission. Some of the doctors request that their patients be admitted to this floor because of the good psychological care which they receive.

Questions

1. Analyze the leadership behaviors exhibited by Pat Smith. Using Figure 10.7 as a guide, what is her predominate style? Give examples to justify your answer.

2. Analyze the leadership *situation* faced by Pat Smith as a head nurse on Floor A. Do this using

Fiedler's contingency theory and House's path–goal theory. Is she achieving a good leader-situation match from the perspective of each theory? Why or why not?

3.　Is Pat Smith an effective manager? . . . an effective leader? Why or why not?

4.　Based on the information in the case, what specific recommendation would you make to Rose to improve her managerial and leadership effectiveness. Why?

Class Exercise: The Meaning of Leadership

This exercise is an opportunity for you to examine your personal approach to leadership, and to compare this approach to ones held by your peers.

1.　Complete the following *leadership questionnaire*.[34]

Instructions

For each of the following 10 pairs of statements, divide 5 points between the two according to your beliefs, perceptions of yourself, or according to which of the two statements characterizes you better. The 5 points may be divided between the A and B statements in any one of the following ways: 5 for A, 0 for B; 4 for A, 1 for B; 3 for A, 2 for B; 1 for A, 4 for B; 0 for A, 5 for B, but not equally $2\frac{1}{2}$ between the two. Weigh your choices between the two according to the one that characterizes you or your beliefs better.

1.　＿＿ A　As leader I have a primary mission of maintaining stability.

　　＿＿ B　As leader I have a primary mission of change.

2.　＿＿ A　As leader I must cause events.

　　＿＿ B　As leader I must facilitate events.

3.　＿＿ A　I am concerned that my followers are rewarded equitably for their work.

　　＿＿ B　I am concerned about what my followers want in life.

4.　＿＿ A　My preference is to think long range: What might be.

　　＿＿ B　My preference is to think short range: What is realistic.

5.　＿＿ A　As a leader I spend considerable energy in managing separate but related goals.

　　＿＿ B　As a leader I spend considerable energy in arousing hopes, expectations, and aspirations among my followers.

6.　＿＿ A　While not in a formal classroom sense, I believe that a significant part of my leadership is that of teacher.

　　＿＿ B　I believe that a significant part of my leadership is that of facilitator.

7.　＿＿ A　As leader I must engage with followers at an equal level of morality.

　　＿＿ B　As leader I must represent a higher morality.

8.　＿＿ A　I enjoy stimulating followers to want to do more.

　　＿＿ B　I enjoy rewarding followers for a job well done.

9.　＿＿ A　Leadership should be practical.

　　＿＿ B　Leadership should be inspirational.

10.　＿＿ A　What power I have to influence others comes primarily from my ability to get people to identify with me and my ideas.

　　＿＿ B　What power I have to influence others comes primarily from my status and position.

2.　Score the questionnaire by making the points you assigned to each item in the spaces now provided.

Column I		Column II	
1. B	_____	1. A	_____
2. A	_____	2. B	_____
3. B	_____	3. A	_____
4. A	_____	4. B	_____
5. B	_____	5. A	_____
6. A	_____	6. B	_____
7. B	_____	7. A	_____
8. A	_____	8. B	_____
9. B	_____	9. A	_____
10. A	_____	10. B	_____
Total:	_____	Total:	_____

3.　Depending on which column total is higher, you see yourself as a somewhat different type of leader. Column I is indicative of your tendencies toward transformational leadership; column II is indicative of your tendencies toward transactional leadership. Refer back to chapter discussion if needed to check the meaning of these terms.

4.　Share your scores with a nearby classmate. Discuss how accurate you think the description is, and what its future implications might be for your managerial career. Help your classmate to explore similar issues. Await further class discussion lead by your instructor.

References

[1] All quotes are from the following articles published in the "Special Section on Leadership," James O'Toole (ed.), *New Management: The Magazine for Innovative Managers,* Vol. 5 (1988), pp. 2–31: Max De Pree, "Leadership and the Art of Performance Appraisal," pp. 5–9; John W. Gardner, "The Moral Aspects of Leadership," pp. 10–16; Warren Bennis, "The Dreamless Society," pp. 17–24; and Lee Iacocca, "Listen-Up, Kid: The Requirements for World Leadership in the 21st Century," pp. 25–31.

[2] James M. Kouzes and Barry Z. Posner, "The Leadership Challenge," *Success* (April 1988), p. 68. See also their book, *The Leadership Challenge: How to Get Extraordinary Things Done in Organizations* (San Francisco: Jossey-Bass, 1987).

[3] Bernard Wysocki, Jr., "The Chief's Personality Can Have a Big Impact—For Better or Worse," *The Wall Street Journal* (September 11, 1984), p.1.

[4] This case and subsequent discussion slightly adapted from *Leadership* by Leonard Sayles, pp. 46–49. Copyright © 1979 by Leonard Sayles. Used with permission of the Mc-Graw-Hill Company.

[5] Rosabeth Moss Kanter, "Power Failure in Management Circuits," *Harvard Business Review,* Vol. 47 (July–August 1979), pp. 65–75.

[6] Adapted from Kanter, op. cit., p. 67.

[7] David C. McClelland and David H. Burnham, "Power is the Great Motivator," *Harvard Business Review,* Vol. 54 (March–April 1976), pp. 100–110.

[8] See John R. P. French, Jr. and Bertram Raven, "The Bases of Social Power," in Darwin Cartwright (ed.) *Group Dynamics: Research and Theory* (Evanston, Ill.: Row, Peterson, 1962), pp. 607–613. For managerial applications of this basic framework, see Gary Yukl and Tom Taber, "The Effective Use of Managerial Power," *Personnel,* Vol. 60 (1983), pp. 37–49; and, Robert C. Benfari, Harry E. Wilkinson, and Charles D. Orth, "The Effective Use of Power," *Business Horizons,* Vol. 29 (1986), pp. 12–16.

[9] Adapted from John R. Kotter, "Acquiring and Using Power," *Harvard Business Review,* Vol. 55 (July–August 1977), pp. 130–132.

[10] Chester Barnard, *The Functions of the Executive* (Cambridge: Harvard University Press, 1938), pp. 165–166.

[11] Information from "What Led Beech-Nut Down the Road to Disgrace," *Business Week* (February 22, 1988), pp. 124–128; and, "Squealing for Dollars," *Business Week* (July 25, 1988), p. 38.

[12] The early work on leader traits is well represented in Ralph M. Stogdill, "Personal Factors Associated with Leadership: A Survey of the Literature," *Journal of Psychology,* Vol. 25 (1948), pp. 35–71. A well-respected empirical study providing the conclusions summarized here is Edwin E. Ghiselli, *Explorations in Management Talent* (Santa Monica, CA: Goodyear, 1971).

[13] See John W. Gardner's article, "The Context and Attributes of Leadership," *New Management,* Vol. 5 (1988), pp. 18–22; and, John P. Kotter, *The Leadership Factor* (New York: The Free Press, 1988).

[14] Kouzes and Posner, op. cit.

[15] See Rensis Likert, *New Patterns of Management* (New York: McGraw-Hill, 1961); and Bernard M. Bass, *Stogdill's Handbook of Leadership* (New York: Free Press, 1981).

[16] Robert R. Blake and Jane Srygley Mouton, *The New Managerial Grid* III (Houston: Gulf Publishing, 1985).

[17] This position is well summarized by Jan P. Muczyk and Bernard C. Reimann in their article, "The Case for Directive Leadership," *The Academy of Management Executive,* Vol. 1 (1987), pp. 301–311.

[18] Robert Tannenbaum and Warren H. Schmidtt, "How to Choose a Leadership Pattern," *Harvard Business Review,* Vol. 51 (May–June, 1973), pp. 162–175, 178–180.

[19] For a good discussion of this theory see Fred E. Fiedler, Martin M. Chemers, and Linda Mahar, *The Leadership Match Concept* (New York: Wiley, 1978).

[20] Fiedler's current contingency research with the cognitive resource theory is summarized in Fred E. Fiedler and Joseph E. Garcia, *New Approaches to Effective Leadership* (New York: Wiley, 1987).

[21] See, for example, Robert J. House, "A Path–Goal Theory of Leader Effectiveness," *Administrative Sciences Quarterly,* Vol. 16 (1971), pp. 321–338; Robert J. House and Terence R. Mitchell, "Path–Goal Theory of Leadership," *Journal of Contemporary Business* (Autumn 1974), pp. 81–97.

[22] The path–goal theory is reviewed by Bernard M. Bass in *Stogdill's Handbook of Leadership,* op. cit., and by Gary A. Yukl in *Leadership in Organizations* (Englewood Cliffs, N.J.: Prentice-Hall, 1981). A supportive review of research is offered in Julie Indvik, "Path–Goal Theory of Leadership: A Meta-Analysis," pp. 189–192 in John A. Pearce II and Richard B. Robinson, Jr. (eds.), *Academy of Management Best Paper Proceedings 1986.*

[23] See Steven Kerr and John Jermier, "Substitutes for Leadership: Their Meaning and Measurement," *Organizational Behavior and Human Performance,* Vol. 22 (1978), pp. 375–403; and, Jon P. Howell and Peter W. Dorfman, "Leadership and Substitutes for Leadership

Among Professional and Nonprofessional Workers," *Journal of Applied Behavioral Science,* Vol. 22 (1986), pp. 29–46.

[24]Se Victor H. Vroom, "A New Look in Managerial Decision-Making," *Organizational Dynamics* (Spring 1973), pp. 66–80; Victor H. Vroom and Phillip Yetton, *Leadership and Decision-Making* (Pittsburgh: University of Pittsburgh Press, 1973). For a recent development with this approach see Victor H. Vroom and Arthur G. Jago, *The New Leadership: Managing Participation in Organizations* (Englewood Cliffs, NJ: Prentice Hall, 1988).

[25]Edgar H. Schein, *Process Consultation: Volume I Its Role in Organization, Development,* Second Edition (Reading, Mass.: Addison Wesley, 1988), p. 73.

[26]This case is from Vroom and Yetton, op. cit.

[27]For a good discussion of research on participation in decision-making, see Edwin A. Locke, David M. Schweiger, and Gary P. Latham, "Participation in Decision Making: When Should it be Used?", *Organizational Dynamics,* Vol. 14 (1986), pp. 65–79.

[28]Among the popular books addressing this point of view are Warren Bennis and Burt Nanus, *Leaders* (New York: Harper & Row, 1985); Max De Pree, *Leadership is an Art* (Lansing, MI: The Michigan State University Press, 1987); Kotter, op. cit.; Kouzes and Posner, op. cit. A number of the issues are well summarized in the "Special Section on Leadership," James O'Toole (ed.), *New Management: The Magazine for Innovative Managers,* Vol. 5 (1988), pp. 2–31.

[29]Bernard M. Bass, "Leadership; Good, Better, Best," *Organizational Dynamics,* Vol. 13 (Winter 1985), pp. 26–40.

[30]This list is based on Kouzes and Posner, op. cit.; and, Gardner, op. cit.

[31]Peter F. Drucker, "Leadership: More Doing Than Dash," *The Wall Street Journal* (January 6, 1988), p. 16.

[32]Excerpted from Robert E. Finucane, "How to Win the Corporate Game, or at Least Tie the Score," *Sun Magazine* (Spring 1982), pp. 27, 28. Used by permission.

[33]This case is abridged by permission from the case "Two Head Nurses: A Study in Contrast," written by George Strauss.

[34]This questionnaire is © by W. Warner Burke, PhD. Reproduced by permission.

Leading Through Communication

Learn
How to Listen

Listening: we all do it, but how well? As it happens, a great many managers lack the right attitude toward listening, and their communication skills aren't put to good use—a fact with unfortunate performance implications. Managers who like best to hear themselves talking, or who resent the time and energy it takes to listen well, run some real risks. Failed negotiations, poor interpersonal relations, and on-the-job encounters with unpleasant truths are among the likely consequences of a tin ear. Especially during crises, the price of a poor attitude is high; ambitious managers simply can't afford to jeopardize their prospects for advancement by developing bad listening habits.

To be sure, listening is in a sense an art, one that involves a delicate balance between readiness and spontaneity. Along with the art is a fair bit of craft, honed by practice. A good listener has some idea of what he or she is listening for but doesn't anticipate too much. The listener's task is to create what experts refer to as an "internal paraphrase" or summary of the speaker's words and to resist editing or reacting prematurely to that paraphrase. Asking open-ended, tonally neutral questions is a good way to check the accuracy of the paraphrase—to learn if the message received is the one intended. A quick verbal playback is also a good insurance policy against misunderstanding. Only after such checking measures have been taken is a response appropriate.

Poor listening habits tend to be reinforced by a distracting environment, which is why some listeners pick places to talk where phones or people won't interrupt. Physical surroundings can send subtle messages; a subordinate may feel uneasy talking in his or her boss's office with the listener safely seated behind a big desk. It helps to pick neutral territory for important talks so that both speaker and listener can relax.

The manager who listens well must also be able to act on what he or she has heard. Otherwise, the speaker may feel that the process of communicating has been a waste of time. But action should follow reflection; "ready, fire, aim" is the behavior of the careless listener. The good listener allows time for the message to sink in. And if the message is not what was hoped for, the listener is ill served by off-the-cuff anger. Better by far to cool off and resume communication when both parties are aware of the need for carefully chosen words—and careful listening. ▪

Source: Information from Walter Kiechel III, "Learn How to Listen," *Fortune* (August 17, 1987), pp. 107–108.

The ability—and willingness—to listen is essential to effective communication. This chapter reviews communication as one of the means through which managers accomplish leadership.

Communication and the Manager
Communication as an Interpersonal Process
Barriers to Effective Communication
Perception and Communication
Organizational Communication
Guidelines for Effective Communication

This really happened.[1]

A memo was sent by top management at General Motor's Inland division plant. It said that because GM's market share was falling, it didn't look good for salaried employees who owned non-GM cars to park them in the *salaried* employee's parking lot. The memo reasoned: "This condition does not convey a positive image to other salaried employees or guests who visit our plant." It went on to say, ". . . and it has a negative impact on our share of the car market." Thus, the memo stated that in the future all such cars would have to be parked in the *hourly* employee's parking lot.

Well, the memo upset the "hourly" workers at the plant. They didn't like the idea that the offending cars of the "salaried" workers were to be banished to their parking lot. An official of the United Automobile Workers Union complained, "They're punishing these guys by telling them to go out there and park with the rest of the dogs." He added: "What does that say about us? A lot of us considered it offensive." Another union worker said: "We didn't want salaried workers parking their non-GM cars in our spaces. We were mad and we complained."

Their complaints got results. The new plant manager, Bill Terry, called the whole affair "like a lot of things, a misunderstanding." Another GM spokesperson further clarified that "It has never been Inland's practice to restrict the kinds of cars our employees drive."

This example shows that the thing we call "communication" is not always easy to accomplish. In the complex setting of the workplace, even the most well-intentioned efforts to communicate sometimes run into trouble. The situation at this GM plant seemed to correct itself once the people disturbed by the memo—both salaried and non-salaried workers—got a chance to express their concerns. But with a better understanding of the communication process to begin with, plant management might have avoided the resulting problems altogether.

Communication is an interpersonal process of sending and receiving symbols with meanings attached to them. Communicaton is the way meanings are transferred among people. And it is an essential foundation for managerial success. This chapter examines the communication process from an applied managerial perspective. Of special interest to you will be the requirements for communicating effectively with others in the workplace, helping them to communicate with you in return, and establishing organizational mechanisms within which open communication becomes a routine and normal part of daily operations.

COMMUNICATION AND THE MANAGER

Ask someone what lies at the root of most problems in their organizations. Nine times out of ten, the answer will be poor or insufficient communication. This popular response is tied to the fact that it is through communication with others that managers get the information they need to make decisions and solve problems. When poor decisions are made and the organization falters, bad communication is frequently to blame.

Any manager's job, therefore, builds around the need to communicate. It is through communication that vital information for decision making is gained and the results of those decisions conveyed to others. Communication makes other people aware of a manager's desires and intentions and thereby sets the foundation for influence to take place. Leadership, in a word, is impossible without communication.

Communication and the Managerial Role

Chapter 1 introduced the importance of "networking" to the managerial role. An effective manager was portrayed as someone who developed and maintained a variety of interpersonal networks, and through these networks was able to implement many action agendas. One way to view the managerial role is as a nerve center of information flows. Figure 11.1 portrays the manager as center point in a complex information-processing system. Success in this role depends on a manager's ability to send and receive information while acting as a monitor, disseminator, spokesperson and decision maker. To fulfill these responsibilities, a manager must be good at gathering appropriate information from sources

inside and outside the work unit (monitor role), distributing information within the work unit (disseminator role) and through external contacts (spokesperson role), and using information to solve problems and explore opportunities (decision-maker role). These roles are largely accomplished through direct contacts between managers and others in their interpersonal networks.

Research indicates that up to 80 percent of a manager's time is spent in oral communications.[2] Executives studied by Henry Mintzberg, for example, distributed their time among various communication activities as follows: scheduled and unscheduled meetings (69 percent), telephone calls (6 percent), and walk-around tours (3 percent). Only 22 percent of their time was spent doing desk work. Obviously, this group of executives spent most of their time on the telephone or in direct face-to-face communications with other persons.

Communication and the Management Functions

Communication is essential to each of the four basic management functions. In order to plan, organize, lead, and control, managers must be able to communicate with other persons—and communicate well. At the heart of all this lies the information processing network just described in the figure. By developing, maintaining, and utilizing a complex network of interpersonal relationships, managers are able to gather and transmit information needed

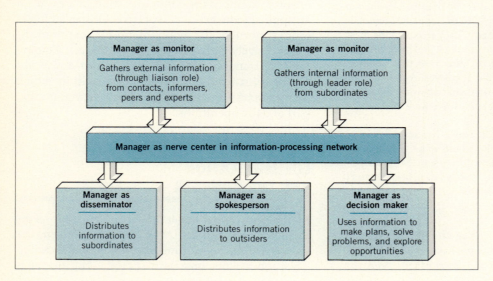

FIGURE 11.1 *The manager as a nerve center in an information-processing network.*

Source: Abridged and adapted text from chart on p. 72 of *The Nature of Managerial Work* by Henry Mintzberg. Copyright © 1973 by Henry Mintzberg. Reprinted by permission of Harper & Row Publishers, Inc.

for problem solving and decision making.[3] Information exchanged with others helps formulate plans, define job assignments and organize work; information on standards, progress, and personal factors fulfills the leadership function; while information in the form of written and oral progress reports is a fundamental element in controlling. Communication is an interpersonal process through which each of the basic management functions is carried out.

COMMUNICATION AS
AN INTERPERSONAL PROCESS

Earlier we defined communication as an interpersonal process of sending and receiving symbols with meanings attached to them. Now it is time to look in detail at the elements in this process, which is supposed to result in information exchange and shared understandings.

Elements in the
Communication Process

The key elements in the communication process are diagrammed in Figure 11.2. They include a *sender,* who is responsible for encoding an intended meaning into a *message.* It is sent through a *channel* to a *receiver,* who then decodes the message into a perceived meaning. *Feedback* from receiver to sender may or may not be given. Another way to view the communication process is as a series of questions. "Who?" (sender) "says what?" (message) "in what way?" (channel) "to whom?" (receiver), "with what result?" (perceived meaning).

To communicate with the receiver, the sender translates his or her intended meaning into symbols. This translation is an encoding process that results in a message that may consist of verbal or nonverbal symbols, or some combination of both. The receiver decodes the message into perceived meaning. This interpretation may or may not result in the same meaning intended by the sender. How would you react, for example, to this well-intentioned sign posted outside a nightclub?[5]

> CLEAN AND DECENT DANCING
> EVERY NIGHT EXCEPT SUNDAY

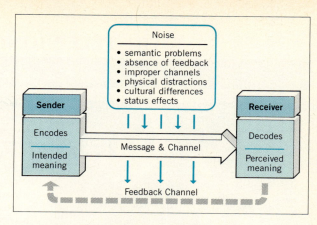

FIGURE 11.2 *Elements in the process of interpersonal communication.*

An alert patron penciled in this unsolicited comment—"You must do a big business on Sundays!"

Effective versus
Efficient Communication

Effective communication occurs when the intended meaning of the sender and the perceived meaning of the receiver are one and the same. This should be the manager's goal in any communication attempt, but it is not always achieved. Even now, I worry whether or not you will interpret these written words as I intend. My confidence would be higher if I were together with you in class, and you could ask clarifying questions. The opportunity to question (that is, offer feedback to the source) is one advantage of face-to-face communication. It is also something denied readers of written memos, letters, or posted bulletins, and the like.

Efficient communication occurs at minimum cost in terms of resources expended. Time is an important resource in the communication process. Picture your instructor taking the time to communicate individually with each student. It would be virtually impossible to do, and, even if it were possible, it would be costly. For similar reasons, managers often send written messages rather than visit their employees personally, or hold group rather than individual meetings.

Efficient communications are not always effective. A low-cost communication such as a posted bulletin may save time for the sender. But, it doesn't

Face-to-face deals are arguably the best kind—but the fact is that considerable business takes place over the phone. And familiar as they are, telephones are tricky instruments of negotiation. They require special handling if they are to be used to persuasive effect.

George R. Walther, a Seattle businessman, insists that someone "who masters the phone rules business." Walther urges phone users to think carefully about what they want to say and accomplish before picking up the phone. Being prepared and initiating the call are two immediate advantages. Negotiating over speaker-phones is a mistake, says Walther; talking with only one person makes it much easier to establish an easy, productive back-and-forth.

Walther cautions those who wish to cut successful deals over the phone to behave professionally and politely by adjusting their speaking style and using "verbal nods" to make their counterparts comfortable. The careful deal maker also takes notes—separating facts from emotions—during the phone conversation. It is important to offer a common ground for negotiating before springing a large demand on the person one has called, says Walther. It is important that the other person "taste the deal" and want to consummate it.

Once the conversation is over and a tentative agreement reached, the caller should quickly write up a summary memo recording the substance of the discussion. This memo should then be transmitted without delay to the other party. "Never trust your memory, or your counterpart's," says Walther. "Documentation prevails."

Source: As reported in George R. Walther, "The Deal Maker's Secret Weapon," *Success* (April 1988), p. 12.

---

always achieve the desired results in terms of having the intended meaning equal the perceived meaning. Similarly, an effective communication may not be efficient. For a manager to visit each employee and explain a new change in procedures may guarantee that everyone truly understands the change. It may also be very expensive in terms of time requirements. Good managers know how to maximize the effectiveness of their communications while still maintaining reasonable efficiency in the process. *Newsline 11.1* develops this issue in specific respect to persuasive telephone communications.

BARRIERS TO EFFECTIVE COMMUNICATION

Noise, as suggested earlier in Figure 11.2, is anything that interferes with the effectiveness of the communication process. Major sources of noise that can threaten communication in work settings include semantic problems, the absence of feedback, improper choice or use of channels, physical distractions, cultural differences, status effects, and perceptions. Because noise threatens the success of any communication attempt, its possible sources—and ways of dealing with them—should be understood by managers.

Semantic Problems

Semantic barriers to communication occur as encoding and decoding errors, and as mixed messages. Symbols, such as the words written in a letter, are selected by the source and interpreted by the receiver. Communication will only be effective to the extent that the source encodes a message into symbols easily and clearly understood by the receiver. This is a semantic challenge.

We generally don't realize how easily encoding and decoding errors occur. They abound, however, as the following examples illustrate. Consider first this classified ad from a newspaper.

```
FOR SALE:
LARGE GREAT DANE
REGISTERED PEDIGREE.
WILL EAT ANYTHING.
ESPECIALLY FOND OF CHILDREN.
```

Consider, too, the following "bafflegab" found among some executive communications.[6]

Example 1: We solicit any recommendations that you wish to make and you may be assured that any such recommendations will be given our careful consideration.

Translation: Please give us your suggestions. We will consider them carefully.

Example 2: Consumer elements are continuing to stress the fundamental necessity of a stabilization of the price structure at a lower level than exists at the present time.

Translation: Consumers keep saying that prices must go down and stay down.

Example 3: The finance director claimed that substantial economies were effected in his division by increasing the time interval between distribution of data-eliciting forms to business entities.

Translation: The finance director said his division was saving money by sending fewer questionnaires to employers.

The Absence of Feedback

Letters, memos, written reports, and posted notices are one-way communications that allow no immediate feedback from receiver to source. Two-way communications, such as interactive conversations, allow for feedback. Because of this opportunity, two-way communication is typically more accurate and effective than one-way. One-way communication, by contrast, is usually more time efficient. Many student interactions with instructors are frustrating because of one-way communications. Examinations are a good example. How often have you labored over the interpretation of a question and wished you could get clarification from the instructor? Sometimes you can't even ask; sometimes you can ask, but still don't get clarification.

One-way communications are frequent in work settings. Sometimes they protect the source from the threat or discomfort that may accompany feedback; many times they result in the receiver being somewhat unsure as to the source's actual intentions. Here is a case in point.

A vice-president in a large U.S. corporation, for example, was having trouble with division managers who occasionally responded inappropriately to his memos.[7] He hired a consultant for a training session to address the problem. During the meeting, several memos from the vice-president to the division managers were selected to be shown on a screen via a projector. After reading each memo on the screen the division managers were asked three questions: (1) What do you think the message says? (2) What priority would you give to the message? (3) What action would you take? Numerous differences appeared in the responses. Later, the vice-president explained what he meant the memo to say, what priority he desired, and what action he wanted. As might be expected, a number of misunderstandings were corrected.

Poor Choice or Use of Communication Channels

A **communication channel** is the medium through which a message is conveyed from sender to receiver. Managers typically use oral, written, and nonverbal channels of communication. Some advantages and disadvantages of the various channels are summarized in Table 11.1. Effective communication depends on a manager choosing the right channel for a given situation, and then being able to implement it well.

Oral and Written Channels

Oral communication takes place via the spoken word. Examples are telephone calls and face-to-face meetings. It takes skill to communicate orally. When done well, though, oral communication allows for feedback, encourages spontaneous thinking and conveys personal warmth.

Written communication also takes skill. We all know how hard it can be to write a good concise letter, or to summarize our thoughts in a formal

TABLE 11.1 *Oral, Written, and Nonverbal Communication Channels Used by Managers*

Channel	Examples	Advantages	Disadvantages
Oral communication	Telephone calls, personal contacts, meetings, speeches and presentations	Allows immediate feedback; more personal; chance for spontaneous ideas, questions, solutions to arise	Can be time consuming and cause conflict; may be no formal record; message may be distorted as passed from person to person
Written communication	Letters, memos, formal reports, posted notices, newsletters, policy manuals	Formal record exists; can be widely distributed; can save time when many persons must be contacted; can appear formal, authoritative	Interpretations can vary; no feedback opportunity; very dependent on writing skills; can be time consuming to prepare lengthy reports
Nonverbal communication	Eye contact, facial expressions, gestures, intonation of voice, office layouts and appearance, personal dress	Can enhance what is being said orally; may reduce need for other communications	Not always consistent with oral message; may be done without sender knowing or desiring it

report. When done poorly, a written message can easily be misunderstood. When done well, the written message can be advantageous. It provides a historical record, can reach a large number of people easily, and appears formal and authoritative.

A key choice you will routinely make as a manager is whether to communicate something orally, in writing, or both, in a given circumstance. Some ideas on making these choices follow.[8]

1. *Use oral communication*
   - To initially point out someone's poor work.
   - To settle a dispute among employees.

2. *Use written communication*
   - To send information requiring future action.
   - To send things "for information only."

3. *Use oral communication followed by written communication*
   - To send information for immediate action.
   - To communicate a directive or order.
   - To communicate an important policy change.
   - To advise a supervisor about work problems.
   - To reprimand an employee for poor work.
   - To commend an employee for good work.

Nonverbal Channels

Nonverbal communication takes place through such things as hand movements, facial expressions, body posture, eye contact, and the use of interpersonal space. It can be a powerful means of transmitting messages. Eye contact or voice intonation can be intentionally used, for example, to accent special

parts of an oral communication. The astute manager also observes "body language" unknowingly expressed by other persons. Watch how people behave in a meeting. A person who feels under attack may move in a back chair, or lean away from the presumed antagonist; a person pleased with what is taking place is prone to lean forward, smile, and nod agreement. All of this is done quite unconsciously, but it still sends a message to those quick enough to pick it up. A **mixed message** occurs when a person's words communicate one message while actions, body language, or appearance communicate something else.

Nonverbal considerations probably play a more important part in communications than most people recognize. In fact, one potential side-effect of the growing use of electronic mail, computer networking, and advanced telecommunications technologies is that one's ability to send and receive nonverbal signals may be lost. For example,

at NASA one review of the events leading up to the decision to launch the ill-fated space shuttle Challenger includes such reasoning. Karl Weick, a noted social psychologist, observes[9]

> . . . communication between Morton Thiokol and NASA about the wisdom of launching Challenger in unusually cold temperatures was made by a conference telephone call, a medium with less variety than face-to-face conversation. With only voice cues, NASA did not have visual data of facial expressions and body cues which might have given them more vivid information about the intensity of Thiokol's concerns.

The placement of furniture in a manager's office sends a nonverbal message to visitors that can facilitate or impede effective communication.

Another aspect of nonverbal communication involves **proxemics,** or the use of interpersonal space.[10] Persons can use space to increase or decrease distance between themselves and others. This distance, in turn, conveys varying intentions in terms of intimacy, openness and status. The proxemics or physical layout of an office, for example, is an often overlooked form of nonverbal communication. As the two accompanying photographs show, various office arrangements convey quite different things to an office visitor. Check the layouts in the photos against those in your office, your instructor's office, or other offices with which you are familiar. What do these layouts "say" to the visitor?

Physical Distractions

Any number of physical distractions can interfere with the effectiveness of a communication attempt. Some of these distractions are evident in the following conversation between an employee, George, and his manager.[11]

> Okay George, let's hear your problem [phone rings, boss picks it up, promises to deliver a report "just as soon as I can get it done"]. Uh, now, where were we— oh, you're having a problem with your technician. She's [manager's secretary brings in some papers that need immediate signature, so he scribbles his name where indicated; secretary leaves] . . . you say she's over stressed lately, wants to leave . . . I tell you what, George, why don't you [phone rings again, lunch partner drops by] . . . uh, take a stab at handling it yourself. . . . I've got to go now.

Besides what may have been poor intentions in the first place, the manager in this example suffered from a number of physical distractions that created information overload. Too many things were occurring at once; the communication with George suffered as a result. This problem can easily be corrected by setting priorities and planning. If George has something important to say, the manager should set aside adequate time for the meeting. Additional interruptions such as telephone calls and drop-in visitors should be avoided by issuing appropriate instructions to the secretary. Many such distractions can be avoided or at least minimized through proper managerial attention.

Cultural Differences

Differences in cultural backgrounds between senders and receivers can also cause communication breakdowns. As pointed out in *Newsline 11.2,* when messages cross cultural boundaries, the effectiveness of a communication attempt can be compromised. This can occur when communications involve persons of different ethnic backgrounds or national origins, or even from different geographic regions within a country.

Cross-cultural communication problems often include a language factor. The most obvious example is in the international arena where managers may experience difficulty when a message that works well in one language is translated into another. The following advertising miscues are one illustration of this pitfall.[12]

ONE CULTURE'S FRIENDLY SALUTE...

Doing business in a foreign country poses a special challenge for the American business-person, who must negotiate not just deals but often entirely different ways of interacting, gesturing, entertaining, and speaking. Behavior that is socially or professionally inappropriate—even if unintentionally so—can jeopardize a business opportunity, as some have learned from unfortunate or embarrassing experiences abroad. Increasingly, representatives of American businesses are discovering that they must acquaint themselves, well before traveling, with the cultural rules of the countries they visit—or suffer the consequences.

Writing on a Japanese person's business card is like writing on his or her hand, and making the "OK" sign with one's fingers is an insult to a Brazilian. In Greece and Bulgaria, a nod of the head means no, and in Hong Kong, wearing blue and white indicates mourning. These and many other customs create potential pitfalls for the American abroad, whose duty it is to respect and follow the norms of the host country—and to make sure not to give or receive the wrong signals. "Diplomacy," writes business-man and frequent flyer Roger Axtell, "isn't just for diplomats. How you behave in other people's countries reflects on more than you alone. It also brightens—or dims—the image of where you come from and whom you work for."

Source: Roger E. Axtell, *Do's and Taboos Around the World* (New York: Wiley, 1985), and Judy Hevrdejs, "One Culture's Friendly Salute Is Another's Obscene Gesture," *Chicago Tribune* (May 10, 1987), p. 12–3.

At Pepsico the firm's popular U.S. ad "Come Alive with Pepsi" had problems in Germany. The translation was "come alive out of the grave with Pepsi." ***At General Motors*** the firm's well-known "Body by Fisher" label translated into Flemish as "Corpse by Fisher." This was not something conducive to car sales.

There is another even more subtle aspect of cross-cultural communication—it is the "silent language" that often differentiates one culture from the next.[13] Indeed, a manager's success in dealing with people across cultures might well depend on the ability to understand and deal with differences in the languages of time, space, things, and contracts. Consider these examples.

■ *Language of time.* Time and how it is used are viewed differently around the world. In the United States, assigning a deadline to something is accepted practice; elsewhere in the world it may convey rudeness. In Latin America, waiting in someone's office for a visit is normal; in the United States, being kept waiting is viewed as disrespect or disinterest.

■ *Language of space.* Proxemics is an important aspect of nonverbal communications. Earlier we used the example of personal space in the office setting. Another case in point is cross-cultural differences in the way people use space during conversations. An American business traveler may be quite surprised at how close a counterpart from the Middle-East may stand when engaged in serious business talk.

■ *Language of things.* The use and significance of material possessions varies across cultures. A casual American visitor might be surprised to find a management consultant in Thailand very concerned about the type of watch, tie, and suit worn—and even the type of pen carried—when working with corporate clients. When questioned, however, the consultant will reply that such "things" are important symbols that help provide desired status in the eyes of clients.

■ *Language of contracts and agreements.* In the United States, a contract is viewed as a final and binding statement of agreements. Elsewhere in the world, including the People's Republic of China, it may be viewed as more of a starting point. Once in place, it will continue to emerge and be modified as the parties work together over time. Also in the United States, contracts are expected to be in writing. Requesting a written agreement from a Moslem who has given his "word" may be quite disrespectful.

Status Effects

"Criticize my boss? I don't have the right to."
"I'd get fired."
"It's her company, not mine."

As suggested in the prior dialogue, the hierarchy of authority in organizations creates another potential barrier to effective communications. The noise created by such status effects can be disastrous. Consider the following examples of "corporate cover-ups" reported by the *Wall Street Journal*.[14]

Example 1   The president of a large machinery producer ordered work to begin on a new kind of photocopying machine. Although those with direct responsibility for the machine knew the job would take two years, a report to the president stated that the machine could be developed in a matter of months. The reason: each layer of management shaved a few weeks off the original estimate to please superiors. Working day and night, the staff managed to construct a prototype to meet the truncated timetable. The president inspected it and left with assurances it was "ready to roll." Hardly had he left the lab when the prototype burst into flames and was destroyed.

Example 2   The chief executive of an electronics company on the West Coast discovered that shipments were being predated and papers falsified to meet sales targets that his managers knew were unrealistically high. At least 20 persons in the organization cooperated in the deception, but it was months before the top found out.

What happened in both these cases is **filtering**, the intentional distortion of information to make it appear most favorable to the recipient. Tom Peters, the popular management author and consultant, calls such information distortion "Management Enemy Number 1." Simply put, it most often involves "telling the boss what he or she wants to hear."

The filtering of information in organizations is often caused by status differentials and their tendencies to create special barriers between managers and their subordinates. Given the authority of their positions, managers may be inclined to do a lot of "telling," but not much "listening." Subordinates, on the other hand, may be willing to communicate only what they expect the boss wants to hear. Whether the reason is a fear of retribution for bringing bad news, an unwillingness to identify personal mistakes, or just a general desire to please, the end result is the same. The manager receiving filtered communications makes poor decisions because of a biased and inaccurate information base. A bit later in this chapter we will discuss "management by wandering around" (MBWA) and other techniques for improving upward communication between subordinates and their managers.

PERCEPTION AND COMMUNICATION

Although the term has been used in this chapter and elsewhere in the book without anything specific said about it, *perception* is an extremely important aspect of communication and other interpersonal relationships. **Perception** is the process through which

FIGURE 11.3 *Perception as an information screen or filter between an individual and the environment.*

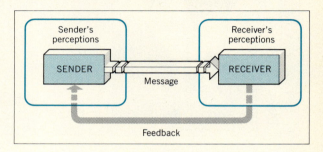

people receive and interpret information from the environment. It is the way we form impressions about ourselves, other people, and daily life experiences. It is the way we process information into the decisions that ultimately guide our actions.

Figure 11.3 depicts perception as a screen or filter through which information must pass before it impacts individual decisions and actions. Depending on individual values, needs, cultural background, and other circumstances of the moment, information will pass through this screen with varying interpretations and degrees of accuracy. Thus perception also introduces potential noise into the communication process.

Understanding Different Perceptions

Look at the two illustrations in Figure 11.4. What do you see? Some people see a young woman in the first picture; others see an old woman. Some people see a vase in the second; others see two faces. What this exercise demonstrates is that people can perceive the same things quite differently. This fact has the potential to complicate a manager's task a great deal. Not only must you be on guard to make your own perceptions as accurate as possible, you must also anticipate, recognize, and be prepared to react to the perceptions of others.

Perceptual differences sometimes occur as contrasts between the way others perceive us and our self-perceptions. A manager's leadership style, as discussed in the last chapter, is one area where such differences can easily arise. These descriptions of persons once identified by *Fortune* magazine as among "the toughest bosses" in America provide interesting examples.[15]

John Welch Jr., Chairman, General Electric
Perceived by others as "abrasive and not wanting 'I think answers' . . . [someone who] misses the opportunity to get input from people."
Self perception Someone who is "demanding" and sets "an atmosphere of rigor at GE but not fear."

Andrew Grove, President, Intel Corporation
Perceived by others as "merciless with people who tell him less than the truth . . . doesn't let anything fall between the cracks."
Self perception "I may be blunt," he says, "but I don't think I'm abrasive."

Martin Davis, Chief Executive, Gulf & Western
Perceived by others as someone who "yells, curses when he chews people out . . . employees all scared to death of him."
Self perception "I am tough . . ." he says, adding, "I am a team player."

Consider, also, the data in Table 11.2. They illustrate that managers and their subordinates may sometimes perceive the same situation quite differently. In this particular case, what's at issue is the frequency with which recognition is given as a reward for work performance. Managers were asked: "How frequently do you give recognition for good

FIGURE 11.4
Contrasting perceptions: What do you see in these illustrations?

TABLE 11.2 *Perceptual Differences between Managers and Subordinates Over Recognition for High Performance*

Ways in which Supervisors May Recognize Subordinates for High Performance	Supervisors' Said Given "Very Often"	Subordinates' Said "Very Often" Received
"Gives privileges"	52%	14%
"Gives more responsibility"	48	10
"Gives a pat on the back"	82	13
"Gives sincere and thorough praise"	80	14
"Trains for better jobs"	64	9
"Gives more interesting work"	51	5

Source: Developed from Rensis Likert, *New Patterns of Management* (New York: McGraw-Hill, 1961).

work done by employees in your work group?" Subordinates were asked: "How frequently does your supervisor give recognition for good work done by employees in your work group?" As the table shows, the managers *perceived* they gave recognition frequently; subordinates *perceived* recognition as less frequently available as a work reward.

Through perception, each of us forms impressions about the world in which we live—including ourselves, other people, and the situations we share. These impressions affect our decisions and actions. Inaccurate impressions can lead to biased decisions and inappropriate actions. A critical question remains—as a manager, can you afford to make perceptual errors when dealing with events and other persons in the work setting?

Avoiding Perceptual Distortions

Four common perceptual distortions that can have a significant impact on the quality of a manager's decisions and actions are: stereotypes, halo effects, selective perceptions, and projections. Because these distortions can prevent managers from drawing an accurate impression of a person or situation, they can interfere with effective communication and cause problems in decision making.

Stereotypes

A **stereotype** occurs when an individual is identified with a group or category, and then the attributes associated with the group or category are assigned to the individual in question. Common stereotypes are those of young people, old people, teachers, students, union members, males, and females, among others. The phenomenon, in each case, is the same. A person is classified into a group on the

basis of one piece of information—age, for example. Characteristics common associated with the group (i.e., "young people dislike authority") are then assigned to the individual. What is generalized about the group as a whole may or may not be true about the individual. Thus stereotypes tend to obscure individual differences.

Stereotypes based on such factors as gender, age, and race can and, unfortunately still do, bias perceptions of people in some work settings. Back in Chapter 2, a newsline introduced you to the "glass ceiling" as an invisible barrier that can inhibit the progress of women into top management positions in organizations.[16] Although employment barriers caused by gender stereotypes are falling, women may still suffer from false impressions and biases tied to them. Think about these examples of how the behavior of female workers may be misinterpreted in comparison to their male counterparts.[17]

Situation	Interpretation
He's having lunch with the boss.	He's on his way up.
She's having lunch with the boss.	They must be having an affair.
He's not in the office.	He's meeting customers.
She's not in the office.	She must be out shopping.
He's talking with co-workers.	He's discussing a new deal.
She's talking with co-workers.	She's gossiping.

Age stereotypes also exist in the workplace. The following example shows how the inappro-

BLACK EXECUTIVES: A STATUS REPORT

Although blacks make up about 12 percent of the nation's population, their numbers in the executive ranks of American corporations remain disappointingly low—despite clear advances on the equal-opportunity front over the past two decades. Less than 7 percent of the MBAs in a recent graduating class of leading American business schools were black, and an even smaller percentage of blacks earned bachelor's or higher degrees in engineering, computer programming, or the hard sciences—areas in which the opportunities for advancement are greatest.

The underlying causes of this lag in black achievement vary. They include uneven support for affirmative action, difficulties in acquiring the necessary education and experience, and pervasive (if often subtle) racism in corporate culture. Black and white executives alike are distressed by the tokenism of workplaces in which less qualified blacks are promoted only to fill quotas and then are inevitably criticized for poor performance. Some executives worry that affirmative action may be inherently problematic. Says one black director of Salomon Brothers, a New York investment firm: "All I ask is the ability to play on a level field." Yet this same manager notes that blacks' successes and failures are magnified because of their race: "Everybody always knows how we're doing."

For all the need for concern and action, blacks who have attained executive-level positions remain convinced that others can do it, too. They stress the need for solid performance, and they have cultivated the ability to deal with racism without either denying it or surrendering to the burden it represents. Frank Savage, an Equitable Life Insurance executive, sums up his position in unambiguous terms: "If I hadn't worked, I wouldn't have made it. . . . The world I live in is the international world of high finance. Most of the time, I'm the only black. That's unfortunate, but I live with it."

Source: As reported in Colin Leinster, "Black Executives: How They're Doing," *Fortune* (January 18, 1988), pp. 109–120.

---

priate use of age stereotypes by managers may place older workers at a disadvantage in various work situations.[18]

Problem   Individual work performance is observed to be declining.

> *Impact of stereotype*   Manager assumes older workers are resistant to change and reassigns the older worker, instead of encouraging improvement in the present job.

Problem   Someone must be promoted to fill an important challenging job.

> *Impact of stereotype*   Manager assumes older workers lack creativity, are cautious, and tend to avoid risk; the older worker is not selected for promotion.

Problem   An older individual requests reassignment to a job requiring substantial physical strength.

> *Impact of stereotype*   Manager assumes older workers are weak because their physical strength has declined with age; the older worker is asked to withdraw the request for transfer.

Racial discrimination is the source of additional stereotyping that sometimes confounds the activities and opportunities of the workplace. *Newsline 11.3* raises questions relating to the progress of black executives in America's corporate mainstream. The end-of-chapter Career Perspective also addresses this issue. Like any stereotype, the bias of race prevents managers from accurately assessing individual differences at work. On a strict organizational criterion, this can result in poor decisions and an underutilization of human resources. But a broader criterion of basic human rights must also be recognized. Gender, age, and racial stereotypes are most unfortunate in a day and age when equal employment opportunity for all persons is not only the law, but a respected social value as well.

Halo Effects

A **halo effect** occurs when one attribute is used to develop an overall impression of a person or situation. This involves generalization from only one attribute to the total person or event. When meeting a new person, for example, the halo effect may cause one trait such as a pleasant smile to result in a positive first impression. By contrast, a particular hairstyle or manner of dressing may create a negative reaction.

Halo effects cause the same problem for managers as do stereotypes—individual differences become obscured. This is especially significant in respect to a manager's views of subordinates' work performance. One factor, such as a person's punctuality, may become the "halo" for a total performance evaluation. Just as it is not enough to assume that anyone who comes to work early is a good performer, occasional lateness may not equate with poor overall performance. Even though the general conclusion seems to make sense, it may or may not be true in a given circumstance. The manager's job is to get true impressions and not allow halo effects to result in biased performance evaluations.

Selective Perception

Selective perception, introduced in Chapter 3, is the tendency to single out for attention those aspects of a situation or person that reinforce or appear consistent with one's existing beliefs, values, or needs. Like the other perceptual distortions, selective perception can bias a manager's views on situa-

tions and individuals. One way to reduce its impact is to gather additional opinions from other people. This adds multiple perceptions to the singular point of view of the manager. When the alternative perceptions prove contradictory, efforts should be made to check the original impression and determine the most appropriate basis for decision making and action.

Projection

Projection is the assignment of personal attributes to other individuals. A classic projection error is assuming other persons share our needs, desires, and values. Suppose, for example, that you enjoy a lot of responsibility and challenge in your work. Suppose, too, that you are the newly appointed supervisor of persons whose work seems dull and routine. You might move quickly to start a program of job enrichment to help your subordinates experience more responsibility and challenge. Why? Because you want them to experience those things that you personally value. This may not be a good decision. Instead of designing the subordinates' jobs to best fit *their* needs, you have designed their jobs to fit *yours*. In fact, they may be quite satisfied and productive doing jobs that, to you, seem dull and routine. It is an error to project your desires onto them, and then change a situation from good to bad as a result.

Projection is another perceptual distortion that compromises a manager's ability to respond to individual differences in the work setting. It can be controlled through a high degree of self-awareness and by a willingness to empathize with other persons and try to see things through their eyes.

Managing the Perception Process

Successful managers understand the importance of perception in the communication process and as an influence on behavior, and they act accordingly. They are aware of perceptual distortions, and they know that perceptual differences are likely to exist in any situation. As a result they try to make decisions and take action with a true understanding of the work situation as it is viewed by all persons concerned. A manager who is skilled in the perception process will:

1. *Have a high level of self-awareness.* Individual needs, experience, and expectations can all affect perceptions. The successful manager knows this and is able to identify when he or she is inappropriately distorting a situation because of such perceptual tendencies.

2. *Seek information from various sources to confirm or disconfirm personal impressions of a decision situation.* The successful manager minimizes the biases of personal perceptions by seeking out the viewpoints of others. These insights are used to gain additional perspective on situations and the problems or opportunities they represent.

3. *Be empathetic—that is, be able to see a situation as it is perceived by other people.* Different people will define the same situation somewhat differently. The successful manager rises above personal impressions to understand problems as seen by other people.

4. *Avoid common perceptual distortions that bias our views of people and situations.* These distortions include the use of stereotypes and halo effects, as well as selective perception and projection. Successful managers are self-disciplined and sufficiently self-aware that the adverse impacts of these distortions are minimized.

5. *Influence the perceptions of other people when they are drawing incorrect or incomplete impressions of events in the work setting.* People act in terms of their perceptions. The successful manager is able to influence the perceptions of others so that work events and situations are interpreted as accurately as possible and to the advantage of all concerned.

Closely related to the latter point is the concept of **impression management,** the systematic attempt to behave in ways that create and maintain desired impressions of one's self in the eyes of others.[19] It is a conscious effort to infuence the perceptions of other people and thereby encourage favorable responses or outcomes. Impressions are managed through a person's verbal and nonverbal communication, as well as by contextual factors such as dress and appearance. An informed manager recognizes the importance of perceptions as people convey information about themselves to one another. This involves being alert to possible mistaken impressions when making judgments about other people, and taking care to convey accurate and positive personal impressions to others.

ORGANIZATIONAL COMMUNICATION

Organizational communication is the specific process through which information is exchanged among persons inside the organization.[20] We noted in Chapter 7 that organizational structures are communication networks formally linking people and groups to one another. The networks may be arranged in different configurations—the wheel or all-channel networks, for example—depending on the information processing requirements of the tasks or problems at hand. Now it is time to examine how messages flow in these networks of organizational communication. The channels can be formal or informal, and the direction of information flows can be downward, upward, or lateral.

Formal and Informal Communication Channels

Formal communication channels follow the chain of command established by an organization's hierarchy of authority. An organization chart, for example, indicates the proper routing for official messages passing from one level or part of the hierarchy to another. Because formal communication channels are recognized as official and authoritative, it is typical for written communications in the form of letters, memos, policy statements, and other announcements to adhere to them.

Informal communication channels exist outside of the formal channels and do not adhere to the organization's hierarchy of authority. They coexist with the formal channels, but frequently diverge from them by skipping management levels and/or cutting across vertical chains of command. Figure 11.5 shows the informal channels that developed alongside the formal communication system of a small community hospital. Note that the informal channels do not coincide with working relationships formally specified by the hospital's hierarchy of authority.

The importance of informal communication channels in organizations is highlighted in the best-selling book *In Search of Excellence.*[21] Thomas J. Peters and Robert H. Waterman, Jr., the book's authors, report their study of successful companies found: "The excellent companies are a vast network

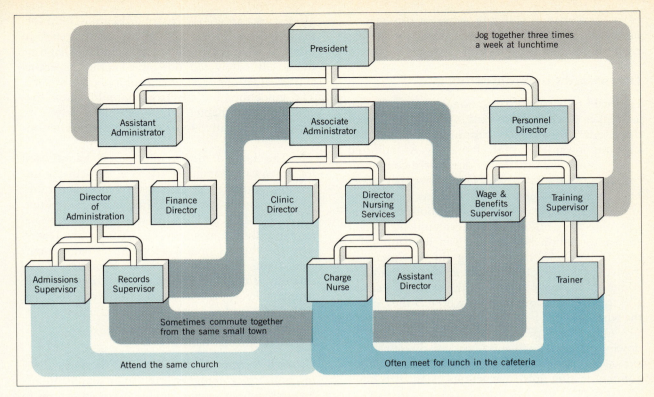

Inside the figure:

President

Jog together three times a week at lunchtime

Assistant Administrator

Associate Administrator

Personnel Director

Director of Administration

Finance Director

Clinic Director

Director Nursing Services

Wage & Benefits Supervisor

Training Supervisor

Admissions Supervisor

Records Supervisor

Charge Nurse

Assistant Director

Trainer

Sometimes commute together from the same small town

Attend the same church

Often meet for lunch in the cafeteria

FIGURE 11.5 *Formal and informal communication channels in an organization: the case of the community hospital.*

of informal, open communications. The patterns and intensity cultivate the right people's getting into contact with each other." Some of the interesting examples they cite include:

Walt Disney Productions Everyone from the president on down wears a tag with only his or her first name on it.

Levi Strauss Calls its open-door policy the "fifth freedom."

Corning Glass Installed escalators instead of elevators in a new engineering building to increase opportunities for face-to-face contact.

3M Sponsors clubs for groups of 12 or more employees in hopes of increasing the probability of spontaneous problem-solving sessions.

A group of people linked together in an informal communication network is sometimes referred to as a **grapevine.** These grapevines have both advantages and disadvantages to organizations and their managers. Among the advantages of grape-

vines are their abilities to transmit information quickly and efficiently. Experienced managers know that a message well placed in a grapevine can travel faster—and often with greater impact—than the same message passed along through formal channels. Grapevines also help fulfill needs for people involved in them. In a grapevine, for example, someone can feel secure and important by being "in the know" when important things are going on. A grapevine can also provide social satisfactions through interpersonal contacts in the give and take of information.

The primary disadvantage of grapevines occurs when they transmit incorrect or untimely information. There is no doubt that rumors can be disruptive and prematurely released information can be easily misinterpreted. Managers should come to know the grapevines operating in their work settings and use them as complements to formal channels. Instead of trying to eliminate grapevines, the advice is to make them work for you. After all, one of the best ways of avoiding incorrect rumor is to make sure the key persons in a grapevine get the right information to begin with.

Downward Communication

Figure 11.6 depicts organizational communication as it takes place in downward, upward, and lateral directions. **Downward communication** flows from higher to lower levels in the hierarchy. As indicated in the figure, one function of downward communication is to be informative. Lower-level personnel have the need to know what higher levels are doing and to be regularly reminded of key policies, strategies, objectives, and technical developments. When such information is shared, it can help minimize fears and suspicions regarding the intentions of higher-level personnel. Informative downward communication also increases the sense of security and involvement for receivers who feel they know the whole story.

Other, and perhaps more difficult, sides to downward communication are its directive and evaluative functions. Managers are responsible for communicating job instructions, standards, and other work expectations to subordinates. This information defines roles and assists subordinates in knowing what is expected of them and in what time frame. Ultimately, too, downward communications carry evaluations of past behavior and performance. The guidelines for effective communication that conclude this chapter can be especially helpful in these more sensitive types of downward communication.

The choice of the communication channel used for downward communications is particularly important. Although newsletters, memos, and other written messages are useful, there is little doubt that the face-to-face and one-on-one communications are typically the most effective. This is one reason why the themes of today's popular management consultants often stress the value of managers getting out of their offices and talking directly to the people they supervise. Such efforts can improve both downward and upward communication.

Upward Communication

Upward communication involves messages flowing from lower to higher levels in an organization's hierarchy of authority. Two important questions in this regard are: What should be communicated upward, and, how can effective upward communication be facilitated?

What Should Be Communicated Upward

Figure 11.6 shows that organization members engage in upward communication for a variety of reasons. These include keeping superiors informed about lower-level activities, sharing feelings and needs, reporting progress, and requesting resource support. For example,[22]

at Johnson & Johnson a company task force concluded that upward communication should keep higher-level managers informed about:

1. *What subordinates are doing.* Highlights of their work, achievements, progress, and future job plans.
2. *Unsolved work problems.* Outlines of ongoing problems, and the help subordinates may need to resolve them at present and/or in the future.
3. *Suggestions for improvements.* Ideas on ways to do things better at individual, work-unit, and/or organizational levels.
4. *How subordinates think and feel about their jobs,*

FIGURE 11.6 *Three directions of organizational communication: downward, upward, and lateral.*

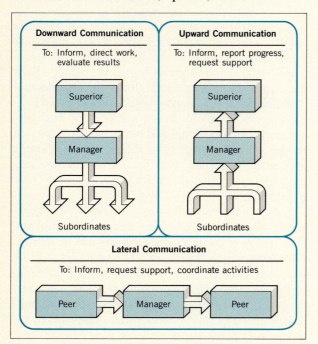

their associates, and the organization. Personal feelings and attitudes relating to the emotional and interpersonal qualities of the work setting.

The first three items on the list are work centered. They are things about which the Johnson & Johnson people felt the "alert" manager would normally try to stay informed. But the fourth item dealing with personal feelings and attitudes was one that seemed to receive less attention. It also appeared of equal and perhaps greater importance to the others. When managers take the time to learn valuable things about subordinates' feelings, they end up with additional information on which to make subordinate-related decisions. The subordinate also has added opportunity to satisfy basic human needs and release emotional stress as a result of expressing feelings to a higher level of management.

Facilitating Upward Communication

Status effects were discussed earlier for their potential to limit the effectiveness of communication between subordinates and superiors. There are a variety of strategies available to try and minimize their negative consequences. One approach, again popularized by the authors of *In Search of Excellence,* is called **management by wandering around,** or MBWA for short. This means dealing directly with subordinates by regularly spending time walking around and talking with them about a variety of work-related matters. Instead of relying on formal channels to bring information to your attention, MBWA involves finding out for yourself what is going on. The basic objectives are to break down status barriers, increase the frequency of interpersonal contact, and get more and better information from lower-level sources. Of course, this requires that the manager establish a trusting relationship with the people being spoken with. This occurred—[23]

at Greyhound as CEO John C. Teets practiced MBWA. He tried to spend a day or more each week in the field talking with plant managers, supervisors, and operating personnel. "You can't follow the chain of command and know what's really going on in your company," he says. "The information that comes in monthly reports has been screened several times; it often doesn't get to the core of the problems." In addition, he adds this warning: "lots of people who surround the boss operate from the assumption—'if he doesn't ask, don't tell him.' They know nobody likes surprises."

There are other ways to create good opportunities for upward communication. Several are illustrated—[24]

at Rutland Hospital where a comprehensive approach to improving communication involved:

Open office hours The hospital director holds open office hours every Wednesday afternoon from 4:00 P.M. to 5:00 P.M. Any employee wishing to speak in private with the director may do so at that time.

Employee meetings Each week, the hospital director holds a 60-minute morning meeting and a 90-minute evening meeting for 25–30 hospital employees who are selected at random from departments and divisions throughout the hospital. These meetings have a fairly structured format that includes reports from the director on current and future programs to improve services. Most of the time is given to employees who wish to ask questions or talk about their concerns or ideas.

Employee advisory council An employee advisory council is composed of 30 employees who are elected by their fellow employees. The council acts in an advisory capacity to the hospital director, who holds monthly meetings with the group's executive committee to discuss issues raised by the council. The director also asks for reactions to policies or programs currently being developed by top management that will affect hospital employees.

Suggestion box Employees are encouraged to submit their ideas to the director's office. Employees who identify themselves receive a letter of acknowledgment. Staff then review ideas that seem promising. Employees whose ideas for improving service are implemented are given public recognition; when these ideas lead to savings in dollars or to increased revenues, they may receive cash awards.

Lateral Communication

Lateral communication occurs among persons working at the same level in the hierarchy of authority, but typically representing different departments or work units. Since lateral communications fall outside the formal chain of command, they tax the full extent of a manager's interpersonal and communication skills. Figure 11.6 shows the function of lateral communication as frequently to inform, but also to request support and coordinate activities. Common mechanisms for achieving lateral communication through formal channels are direct contact, cross-departmental committees, teams or task forces, and the matrix organization. These were discussed in Chapters 6 and 7 as ways for facilitating horizontal coordination among subsystems whose activities are important to one another. Informal channels are also important in the context of lateral communications. Given its ability to cut across vertical hierarchies, the grapevine typically emerges as a key element in this regard.

A special application of lateral communication occurs in the relationships between members of the organization and representatives of its external environment. The best managers are "curious" about what outsiders are thinking, recognize the need to get good information from their suppliers and customers in particular, *and* are willing to listen in turn to what these people have to say. These managers work hard to establish communication channels with key outsiders that can let them know what is really happening—even if that sometimes means hearing about the "bad" news. For example,[25]

at Quad/Graphics   here's what CEO Harry Quadracci is doing to promote lateral communications that help keep himself and his staff in touch with reality.

■   He had the visitor's waiting area placed between his office and the washroom—this way he was forced to mingle with whoever was out there when he passed by. He spends time now talking to the company's customers, equipment repair people, employee's relatives, and the like. For the same reason, his executives' offices are clustered around the main reception lobby.

■   He runs "Quad Camp." Customers are invited to come to town for the night and spend time with people from the plant. They arrive in time for an evening dinner and stay at the homes of Quad executives. The next day is spent in the plant, working through the production process and meeting with workers, who they join again for dinner. Quadracci says it puts his employees "in touch with their counterparts in the client companies, so they don't have to go up and down the hierarchy to solve problems."

Communication of Roles

The term *role* has often been used in this book. A **role** is a set of activities expected of a person in a particular job or position within the organization.[26] One of the most important of a manager's communications is sending and receiving role expectations. On the sending side, the manager's responsibility is to define what he or she expects of subordinates. On the receiving side, the manager must be able to understand what his or her immediate supervisor and other key persons are expecting as well.

Breakdowns or ineffectiveness in the communication of roles can result in role ambiguity, role conflict and/or role overload. Figure 11.7 shows their potential to influence individual performance and job satisfaction. **Role ambiguity** occurs when the person in a role is uncertain about what others expect in terms of his or her behavior. To do a job well, a person needs to know what is expected. Job expectations may sometimes be unclear because the manager has not even tried to communicate them to the subordinate. Other times the manager may have tried, but done so inadequately. Role ambiguity may also result from a failure of the subordinate to listen to what the supervisor is saying.

Role conflict occurs when the person in a role in unable to respond to the expectations held by one or more others. In this case, the role expectations are understood; that is, effective communication has taken place. But, for one reason or another, all of the expectations cannot be fulfilled. A common form of conflict between work and family roles is illustrated,[27]

at Bell & Howell   where president Robert Huff works from 7 A.M. to 7 P.M. weekdays, travels two days per week, and works every other Saturday. "What bothers me," he first says, "is that the family doesn't have dinner together." Yet he then goes on to refer to taking time off during the workday to watch his son play ball as "sneaking out."

Another role conflict occurs when the same source communicates two different sets of performance expectations to a recipient. As another form of the *mixed message* referred to in earlier discussion, this type of role conflict can be highly stressful. A recent example shows, unfortunately, how personal ethics may be compromised by persons caught in such circumstances. This occurred[28]

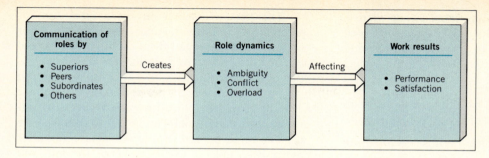

FIGURE 11.7 *Breakdowns in communication can create role ambiguity, role conflict, and/or role overload.*

at McDonnell Douglas Corp. the large aerospace firm whose actions were targeted by FBI investigations in a major defense contractor scandal. One report indicates that top company officials may have been sending mixed signals to lower-level employees. On the one hand they sponsored a comprehensive ethics education program; on the other hand they required adherence to very tight "bottom line" performance standards—ones described as "seemingly impossible" to attain. By implication, the report suggests that ethics were compromised as some employees improperly obtained bidding data and government contracts in order to reach the unrealistic goals.

Role overload occurs when too many role expectations are being communicated to a person at a given time. There is too much work to be done and too little time to do it. Managers who rely on one-way communications are especially prone to create role overload for their subordinates. Cut off from valuable feedback, it is hard for these managers to learn when or why a subordinate is being asked to do too much.

Role dynamics in the form of ambiguities conflict, and overloads can create tensions that have adverse effects on work attitudes and performance. As a manager, you can be the cause of these tensions in others. You may also experience them yourself. In either case, good communication skills can help resolve any difficulties encountered.

GUIDELINES FOR EFFECTIVE COMMUNICATION

Being an effective communicator is a skill. Part of the skill lies in recognizing and overcoming the communication barriers we have already discussed.

Another lies in encouraging a flow of accurate and sufficient information in your direction—that is, being the "active listener." One more lies in being able to give constructive feedback or criticism to others in a nonthreatening way. Through these interpersonal skills the manager can participate effectively in the full range of responsibilities included in organizational communication.

Active Listening

Active listening is a term popularized by the work of *Carl Rogers* and advocated by counselors and therapists.[29] The concept recognizes that when people "talk," they are trying to communicate something; that "something" may or may not be what they are saying. It means taking action to help the source of a message say what he or she really means. There are five guidelines to becoming an active listener.

1. *Listen for message content.* Try to hear exactly what is being said in the message.
2. *Listen for feelings.* Try to identify how the source feels in terms of the message content.
3. *Respond to feelings.* Let the source know that his or her feelings, as well as the message content, are recognized.
4. *Note all cues, verbal, and nonverbal.* Be sensitive to nonverbal messages as well as verbal ones; identify mixed messages that need to be clarified.
5. *Reflect back to the source, in your own words, what you think you are hearing.* Restate or paraphrase the verbal and nonverbal messages as feedback to the source; allow the source to respond with further information.

The last guideline is one of the most powerful of the active listening techniques. It helps the listener avoid passing judgment or giving advice, and encourages the source to say more about what is really the trouble. The following contrasts between how a passive listener and an active listener respond to someone's direct questions illustrate this aspect of active listening.

Question Just whose responsibility is it to maintain security in the computer room?

> *Passive listener's response* Whose do *you* think it is?

> *Active listener's response* Do you feel someone is challenging your authority there?

Question Don't you think capable people should be promoted before senior but less able ones?

> *Passive listener's response* No I don't!

> *Active listener's response* It seems to you that they should, I take it?

Question What does the supervisor expect us to do about these broken-down machines?

> *Passive listener's response* Just do the best we can, I guess.

> *Active listener's response* You're pretty disgusted with those machines aren't you?

The *passive* listener in these examples responded to questions in such a way that the other person was discouraged from saying more, except defensively. The *active* listener left the situations open by encouraging the questioner to say more and communicate further on the issues. As a result, the active listener gains the advantage of receiving important information that can be put to constructive use. The other person should also feel better after having been able to say what he or she felt, and being heard.

Table 11.3 lists 10 additional rules for good listening. Note that good listening begins and ends in the ability to stop talking!

The Art of Giving Feedback

Feedback is the process of telling other people how you feel about something they did or said, or about the situation in general. Managers regularly give feedback to other people. Frequently, this is performance feedback given in the form of evaluations and appraisals. There is an art to giving feedback so that it is accepted and used by the receiver. Feedback that is poorly given can be threatening and cause resentment instead of constructive change.

The first requirement in giving feedback is recognizing when it is truly intended to benefit the

TABLE 11.3 *Ten Rules for Good Listening*

Listening Rule	Reasoning Behind the Rule
1. Stop talking	You cannot listen if you are talking
2. Put the person at ease	Help a person feel free to talk; create a permissive environment
3. Show the person you want to listen	Look and act interested; listen to understand, not to oppose
4. Remove distractions	Don't doodle, tap, or shuffle papers; shut the door if necessary to achieve quiet.
5. Empathize	Try to see the other person's point of view
6. Be patient	Allow plenty of time; do not interrupt; don't start for the door or walk away
7. Hold your temper	An angry person takes the wrong meaning from words
8. Go easy on argument and criticism	Don't put people on the defensive and cause them to "clam up" or become angry; do not argue—even if you win, you lose
9. Ask questions	This encourages a person and shows that you are listening; it helps to develop points further
10. Stop talking	This is first and last, because all other guidelines depend on it; you cannot do an effective listening job while you are talking

Source: Adapted from *Human Behavior at Work,* Fifth Edition, by Keith Davis. Copyright © 1977 by Keith Davis. Used with the permission of McGraw-Hill Book Company.

receiver and when it is purely an attempt to satisfy a personal need. A manager who berates a computer operator for data analysis errors, for example, may actually be mad about personally failing to give clear instructions in the first place.

Assuming that one's original intention is correct—that is, to give feedback helpful to the receiver—a manager should also recognize that constructive feedback meets three additional tests. It should be: (1) understandable, (2) acceptable, and (3) plausible from the recipient's point of view. Specific guidelines for meeting these criteria require that feedback be[30]

■ Given directly and with real feeling, and based on a relationship of trust between the giver and the receiver.

■ Specific rather than general, with good, clear, and preferably recent examples.

■ Given at a time when the receiver appears to be in a condition of readiness to accept it.

■ Checked with others to be sure they support its validity.

■ Concerned with things the receiver might be expected to be able to do something about.

■ Given in small doses, and not more than the receiver can handle at any particular time.

ILLUSTRATIVE CASE:
THE CRITICISM SESSION

The criticism session may well be the toughest test of a manager's communication skills. Picture the setting—you and a subordinate, meeting to review a problem with the subordinate's performance. The question is—how to discuss and resolve the problem in a positive manner that encourages improved performance? This situation requires the skill to give performance feedback to the employee, and to actively listen and respond to the other person's concerns in return. Even the most experienced manager can have difficulty doing this. What is supposed to be a constructive and positive event can easily become a futile gripe session that ends in hard feelings.

The following are five suggestions for making criticism sessions more productive. Note that they involve use of the techniques for effective communication just discussed.[31]

Step 1: Get to the Point

Don't evade the issue. Skip the small talk and go straight to the target: "Bob, I want to talk to you about your late reports," or "Barbara, I called you in to discuss your personality conflict with the director of sales."

Step 2: Describe the Situation

Use a descriptive opening that is specific, not general. Avoid evaluative openings at all costs. Evaluative: "Bob, I can no longer deal with your late, sloppy reports." Descriptive: "Bob, you've been late on three reports in the last two weeks. That caused us two shipping delays and cost us $5000."

Step 3: Use Active Listening Techniques

Encourage the subordinate to tell his or her side of the story. It will reduce defensiveness, clarify the situation, and provide both parties with an opportunity to think the problem through. It helps to ask open-ended questions that invite discussion and cannot be answered with a simple "yes" or "no." Begin questions with *what* or *how,* or sometimes *tell me* or *describe.* Bad: "Do you like our new computer system?" Good: How do you feel about our new computer system?"

Step 4: Agree on the Source of the Problem and Its Solution

It's essential that the subordinate agree that there is in fact a problem. If not, there's little likelihood the problem will be solved. Once you and the subordinate have identified and agreed on the problem, work together to identify the source. Then let the subordinate get involved in coming up with a potential solution.

Step 5: Summarize the Meeting

Have the subordinate summarize the discussion and the agreed solution. Both subordinate and manager should leave the session with the same understanding of what was decided. Establish a follow-up date that allows the subordinate reasonable time to correct the situation.

Ten Commandments
of Good Communication

Effective communication is a two-way process that requires effort and skill by both sender and receiver. As a manager you will at times assume each of these positions in the communication process. This demands an ability to establish good interpersonal rapport with others, to empathize with them and understand the situation from their points of view, and to know yourself well enough to recognize where personal biases may be interfering with what is taking place.

The American Management Association published the following "ten commandments of good communication."[32] If you put these commandments together with your basic understanding of the communication process itself, you will have a good foundation for building and maintaining an effective set of interpersonal communication skills. The ten commandments of good communication are:

1. *Clarify your ideas before communicating.* Good communication requires good planning. Think through the message and consider who will be receiving and/or affected by it.

2. *Examine the true purpose of each communication.* Ask yourself what you *really* want to accomplish—obtain information, initiate action, or influence someone's behavior. Then prepare your message around the objective.

3. *Consider the total physical and human setting.* Meaning and intent are conveyed by more than words. Take into account not only what is to be said, but also the timing, physical setting, and social climate involved.

4. *Consult with others in planning communications.* Allowing others to participate in planning and developing facts can yield useful insights. Those who have helped you plan a communication are also likely to give it their active support.

5. *Be aware of the overtones as well as the basic content of your message.* Your tone of voice, expression, body language, and apparent receptivity to the receiver have a tremendous impact on those you wish to reach.

6. *Take every opportunity to communicate something of help or value to the receiver.* Get in the habit of looking at things from the other person's point of view. People respond best to managers whose messages take their interests into account.

7. *Follow up your communication.* Ask questions and encourage questions to learn if you have succeeded in expressing your true meaning and intentions. Allow for good feedback in all communications.

8. *Communicate for tomorrow as well as today.* Plan communications to serve immediate needs as well as long-run interests and goals. Remember that postponing disagreeable communications makes them more difficult.

9. *Be sure your actions support your words.* The most persuasive communication is not what you say but what you do. Don't let your actions contradict your words.

10. *Be a good listener.* When we start talking, we often cease to listen. Listening demands that you concentrate on what is being said, and recognize overtones as well as context.

Summary

Communication is fundamental to organizations and to the activities of managers. Without an ability to communicate with others successfully, a manager will be unable to give and get the information needed to fulfill planning, organizing, leading, and controlling responsibilities. Especially when acting in a leadership capacity, the manager depends on communication to make performance desires known, and to inspire and support the persons who must satisfy them.

Communication is an interpersonal process of sending and receiving symbols with meanings attached. These symbols can be transmitted as messages through written, oral, or nonverbal communication channels. It is up to the manager to choose wisely among possible symbols and channels to ensure that effective communication occurs. This is achieved only when the intended meaning of the sender and the meaning perceived by the receiver are one and the same.

Noise is anything that interferes with the effectiveness of communication. The potential sources of noise are many, and the concerned manager is always on guard to minimize their negative consequences. One potential source of noise is perception, the process through which people receive, organize, and interpret information received from their environments. Because people may perceive the same situation differently, the manager must try to understand the perceptions of others. Among the perceptual distortions that tend to operate in work settings are stereotypes, halo effects, selective perceptions, and projections.

Organizational communication takes place in downward, upward, and lateral channels through which people transmit and receive information with one another. This includes both formal channels representing the chain of command and informal channels such as the grapevine. In the final result, effective communication depends on both a sound framework for organizational communication and strong interpersonal communication skills among organizational members. As a manager you will have to take the lead in demonstrating these skills and helping your subordinates develop them as well. Foremost among these are active listening and the art of giving feedback.

Thinking Through the Issues

1. Describe and give examples of why communication is essential to the management functions of planning, organizing, leading, and controlling.

2. Draw a diagram of the communication process and label the key components. Use an example to place each in a managerial perspective.

3. State five possible sources of noise in the communication process. Give an example of each type of noise as it might interfere with communications between (a) a manager and subordinate, and (b) you and your boss in a past or present job.

4. What is perception? How does perception influence communication? Be specific in describing the major perceptual distortions and their implications.

5. Describe the difference between formal and informal communication channels in organizations. What is a communication "grapevine?" How it works to a manager's advantage and disadvantage?

6. In organizational communication, what are the special demands on a manager as *sender* of downward and upward communication? What are the special demands on a manager as *receiver* of each type?

7. What are some ways of facilitating upward communications in organizations? Explain "management by wandering around" as it relates to the communication process.

8. What is a manager's responsibility for effective communication of roles? In particular, how can the adverse impact of role ambiguities, overloads, and conflicts among a manager's subordinates be avoided?

9. What is "active listening"? Can it really be used to advantage by a manager? Why or why not?

10. State and defend four guidelines for giving constructive feedback to a subordinate in a performance review session.

The Manager's Vocabulary

Active listening
Communication
Communication
   channel
Downward
   communication
Effective
   communication
Efficient
   communication

Feedback
Filtering
Formal channels
Grapevine
Halo effect
Impression
   management
Informal channels
Lateral
   communication

Mixed message
Noise
Nonverbal
   communication
Organizational
   communication
Perception
Projection
Proxemics
Role

Role ambiguity
Role conflict
Role overload
Selective perception
Stereotype
Upward
   communication
Management by
   wandering around

TOMORROW'S CHIEF EXECUTIVE

When Jerry Williams was growing up poor in Indianapolis, his father had a fifth grade education and drove a truck for a scrap iron company. But his family was close and they set high goals. Jerry had a newspaper route at the age of eight. He's worked hard since to become president of Chicago's AM International at the age of 49. But the story of Jerry Williams doesn't stop there. *Fortune* magazine featured him as likely to become the first black chief executive of a Fortune 500 company. Williams says,"One thing about corporations is that you can make a decision and get things done. I just want to be one of the top 500 CEOs in the country."

Reaching this goal is consistent with ambitions nurtured long ago by Williams' mother. "She was a great inspiration for us," he says, "The word 'can't' wasn't allowed in our house." This lesson has stuck with Williams as he's worked his way up the corporate ladder, changing jobs several times along the way. He moved to AM International from GE, which he describes as "a great place to learn things, but I prefer a smaller environment."

People who work for him describe Williams as a "textbook manager" who helps them set objectives, and then stays out of their way. One subordinate says, "He gives you the latitude you need, but he's not so far away that he can't challenge you when you need to be challenged."

But even as a top manager, Williams has faced difficulties because of his race. The man who hired him at AM says it this way: "One of the problems black executives have is that they rise up too high in staff jobs and they can't break out." In a prior job a lot of skepticism was reported about Williams. The problems multiplied when he had to downsize the operation. After he tripled profits, however, his former boss says, "his status went up quite a bit."

For now, the future looks bright for Jerry Williams. He might just be the first black to head a Fortune 500 firm. After all, as they say at AM International, "Jerry has managed his career just like he's managed his job—very well."

Questions

1.   What strategy seems to have worked for Jerry Williams in overcoming inappropriate and limiting stereotypes? Would this same strategy work for other persons suffering from similar biases? Why or why not?
2.   Suppose you reach a point in your career someday where you seem earmarked for "staff jobs only." Will this be satisfactory, or not? If not, what might you do to prevent getting stuck in a position with no route out to the top?
3.   What general lessons for your personal career planning can you derive from this brief look at Jerry Williams and his career? Please explain.

Case Application

"My Door is Always Open[34]

Setting: The Production Manager's Office
Participants: Gilbert Steiner, Manager
  Harold Terry, Scheduler
Time: Monday morning
Steiner: Good morning, Hal. Have a nice weekend?

Terry: Great, Mr. Steiner . . . took the family to the beach.
Steiner: Fine weekend for it . . . bet your kids enjoyed it.
Terry: They certainly did. My oldest boy loves the ocean.

Steiner:	Billy!
Terry:	(surprised) Yes, Billy. I didn't know you knew his name.
Steiner:	You probably told me once.
Terry:	You have a good memory
Steiner:	Thank you. Frankly, it's something I developed a long time ago. It's good management practice to get to know a little about your employees . . . their families . . . it brings you closer to them.
Terry:	I can't argue with that.
Steiner:	Sounds a little phony at first. . . . I mean someone could sound like a fool overplaying the concerned boss and carrying on about an employee's arthritic dog, Jasper . . . but I mean real interest and concern in the person and family.
Terry:	I'm sure it pays dividends in employee loyalty and productivity.
Steiner:	It certainly does. When you become a supervisor, I'm sure you'll realize it even more. . . . (pause) Well, we'd better get started before the week is over.
Terry:	Right. I've already checked the Final Assembly Department, and we should be able to ship the Fedderson order by Wednesday and the A-B-N Industries order by Thursday or Friday.
Steiner:	Good. I'll hold you to that. . . .
Terry:	We do have a couple of problems, though, which I want to talk to you about.
Steiner:	Yes?
Terry:	We can't ship to Ellis Industries as planned this week because . . .
Steiner:	(angrily) What?
Terry:	The parts we need still haven't arrived.
Steiner:	Dammit, man! You told me that last week didn't you?
Terry:	Yes, I did but . . .
Steiner:	And do you recall what I told you?
Terry:	You said it was my responsibility to make sure the parts came in.
Steiner:	And you blew it!
Terry:	Well, I did review the problem

	with Purchasing and they suggested . . .
Steiner:	To hell with Purchasing! Those paperwork clerks only help foul up things worse. You should have contacted the vendor directly and . . . (pausing and composing himself). Look, Hal, you're a big boy. I don't have to do your job, do I?
Terry:	Of course not, Mr. Steiner.
Steiner:	Then you will get those parts this week won't you?
Terry:	Yes, I'll get the parts.
Steiner:	And you'll ship by Friday?
Terry:	We'll ship by Friday.
Steiner:	(smiling) Good. Management by results is the only thing that counts . . . don't you agree?
Terry:	Yes, sir.
Steiner:	(serious) Look, Hal, I guess I come down hard on you sometimes but it's because I expect a lot from you. How can you grow without challenge . . . without difficult objectives to reach?
Terry:	I suppose you're right.
Steiner:	I know I'm right. It's a philosophy I learned from my father years ago . . . results count, not words.
Terry:	True.
Steiner:	Anything else I should know? I don't care for lots of detail, but, at the same time, a person can easily get cut out of the communications loop by getting too far from the action. And I don't like to get cut out of the loop.
Terry:	Not really. Everything else is moving according to schedule. (pauses) The people in Shipping are a little upset, though, over late Friday afternoon shipping and were asking me if we in Manufacturing might not work out a more sequential shipping schedule. I thought that was

information we could use, particularly with the planned production increase for next quarter . . .

Steiner: Ignore them. Those people are always complaining, and they'll bend your ear all day if you let them. That's not information, Hal, that's *noise* you're getting. When the shipping clerks stop complaining it means they're dead.

Terry: Yes sir.

Steiner: Anything else?

Terry: No. As far as I know we've covered everything.

Steiner: Hal, you know I like you. You've got tremendous potential in this department. I want to help you learn this business inside and out . . . I want to see you grow and develop.

Terry: Yes?

Steiner: Well, what I mean is . . . don't be reluctant to come to me if you have any problems which I can help you with . . . anything that you want to sit down and talk about . . . my door is always open.

Terry: Thank you, Mr. Steiner. (turns to leave)

Steiner: About that Ellis order . . . you did hear me didn't you?

Terry: Yes, sir, I heard you. We'll ship by Friday.

Questions

1. Is effective communication taking place between Steiner and Terry? What communication errors are present?
2. Where do upward, downward, and lateral communication responsibilities impact Terry's role?
3. What would you do in this situation if you were Terry? Why?
4. What recommendations would you make to Steiner? Why?

Class Exercise: Assumptions and Inferences

1. Read this story.[35]

The lights in a store had just been turned off by a businessman when a man appeared and demanded money. The owner opened a cash register. The contents of the cash register were scooped up, and the man sped away. A member of the police force was notified promptly.

2. Take the following quiz.

Answer the following questions abut the story by circling T for true, F for false, or ? for unknown.

1. A man appeared after the owner turned off his store lights.   T F ?
2. The robber was a man.   T F ?
3. The man who appeared did not demand money.   T F ?
4. The man who opened the cash register was the owner.   T F ?
5. The store owner scooped up the contents of the cash register and ran away.   T F ?
6. Someone opened a cash register.   T F ?
7. After the man who demanded money scooped the contents of the cash register, he ran away.   T F ?
8. While the cash register contained money, the story does not state how much.   T F ?
9. The robber demanded money of the owner.   T F ?
10. A businessman had just turned off the lights when a man appeared in the store.   T F ?
11. It was broad daylight when the man appeared.   T F ?
12. The man who appeared opened the cash register.   T F ?

13. No one demanded money.   T F ?

14. The story concerns a series of events in which only three persons are referred to: the owner of the store, a man who demanded money, and a member of the police force.   T F ?

15. The following events occurred: someone demanded money, a cash register was opened, its contents were scooped up, and a man dashed out of the store.   T F ?

3. Share your answers with a nearby classmate. Try to resolve any differences of opinion. Await further class discussion led by your instructor.

References

[1] Information from Bradley A. Stertz, "Management Lesson for Today," *The Wall Street Journal* (May 19, 1988), p. 29.

[2] Henry Mintzberg, *The Nature of Managerial Work* (New York: Harper & Row, 1973).

[3] See for example John P. Kotter, "What Effective General Managers Really Do," *Harvard Business Review,* Vol. 60 (November–December 1982), pp. 156–167; and Daniel J. Isenberg, "How Senior Managers Think," *Harvard Business Review,* Vol. 62 (November–December 1984), pp. 81–90.

[4] Portions of the following originally adapted from John R. Schermerhorn, Jr., James G. Hunt, and Richard N. Osborn, *Managing Organizational Behavior* (New York: Wiley, 1982), pp. 441–448. Used by permission.

[5] This and the subsequent example are from William J. Haney, *Communication and Interpersonal Communication: Text and Cases,* Fourth Edition (Homewood, IL: Richard D. Irwin, 1979), p. 316, 317.

[6] Reported in *Business Week* (July 6, 1981), p. 107.

[7] This incident is reported in W. Warner Burke and Warren H. Schmidt, "Management and Organization Development: What is the Target of Change?" *Personnel Administration* (March–April 1971), pp. 44–57.

[8] Developed from Dale Level, Jr., "Communication Effectiveness: Method and Situation," *Journal of Business Communication,* Vol. 10 (Fall 1972), pp. 19–25.

[9] Karl E. Weick, "Organizational Culture as a Source of High Reliability," *California Management Review,* Vol. XXIX (1987), pp. 112–127.

[10] A classic work on proxemics is Edward T. Hall's book, *The Hidden Dimension* (Garden City, NY: Doubleday, 1986).

[11] Slightly adapted from Richard V. Farace, Peter R. Monge, and Hamish M. Russell, *Communicating and Organizing* (Reading, Mass.: Addison-Wesley, 1977), pp. 97–98.

[12] David A. Ricks, Marilyn Y. C. Fu, and Jeffrey S. Arpan, *International Business Blunders* (Columbus, Ohio: Grid, 1974), p. 11.

[13] The classic work in this area is also found in one of Edward T. Hall's books, *The Silent Language* (Greenwich, CN: Fawcett Publications, 1959).

[14] The examples are from John and Mark Arnold, "Corporate Coverups," *Wall Street Journal* (June 5, 1978), p. 18.

[15] Information from Steven Flax, "The Toughest Bosses in America," *Fortune* (August 6, 1984), pp. 18–23.

[16] See Ann M. Morrison, Randall P. White and Ellen Van Velsor, *Breaking the Glass Ceiling* (Reading, MA: Addison-Wesley, 1987). For a criticism and more positive view of the progress of women in management see Regina E. Herzlinger's editorial, "Dancing on the Glass Ceiling," *The Wall Street Journal* (February 17, 1988), p. 22.

[17] These examples are from Natasha Josefowitz, *Paths to Power* (Reading, MA: Addison-Wesley, 1980), p. 60.

[18] These examples are from Benson Rosen and Thomas H. Jerdee, "The Influence of Age Stereotypes on Managerial Decisions," *Journal of Applied Psychology,* Vol. 61 (1976), pp. 428–432.

[19] For research on impression management see William L. Gardner and Mark J. Martinko, "Impression Management: An Observational Study Linking Audience Characteristics with Verbal Self-Presentations," *Academy of Management Journal,* Vol. 31 (1988), pp. 42–65.

[20] For a compendium of current scholarly thinking on organizational communication see Frederic M. Tablin, Linda L. Putnam, Karlene H. Roberts, and Lyman W. Porter (eds.), *Handbook of Organizational Communication: An Interdisciplinary Perspective* (Beverly Hills, CA: Sage Publications, 1987).

[21] Thomas J. Peters and Robert H. Waterman, Jr., *In Search of Excellence* (New York: Harper & Row, 1983).

[22]Earl G. Planty and William Machaner, "Stimulating Upward Communication," Johnson & Johnson Company Report, undated.

[23]This example is reported in George H. Labovitz, "Want to Find Out What's Going On? Take a Walk," *The Wall Street Journal* (December 20, 1982), p. 12.

[24]Information from Robert B. Smith, "Bridging the Management Employee Gap," *Health Care Management Review,* Vol. 2 (Spring 1977), p. 910.

[25]Information from "How the Best Get Better," *Business Week* (September 14, 1987), pp. 98–120. See also Robert H. Waterman, Jr.'s book, *The Renewal Factor* (New York: Bantam Books, 1987).

[26]See Robert L. Kahn, Donald M. Wolfe, Robert F. Quinn, and J. Diedrick Snoek, *Organizational Stress: Studies in Role Conflict and Ambiguity* (New York: Wiley, 1964).

[27]This example is reported in Walter Kichel III, "The Guilt-Edged Executive," *Fortune* (May 28, 1984), pp. 219–220.

[28]Information from Eileen White Read, "Defense Contractor's Ethics Programs Get Scrutinized," *The Wall Street Journal* (July 21, 1988), p. 4.

[29]This discussion is based on Carl R. Rogers and Richard E. Farson, "Active Listening" (Chicago: Industrial Relations Center of the University of Chicago).

[30]Developed from John Anderson, "Giving and Receiving Feedback," in Paul R. Lawrence, Louis B. Barnes, and Jay W. Lorsch, *Organizational Behavior and Administration,* Third Edition (Homewood, Ill.: Richard D. Irwin, 1976), p. 109.

[31]Excerpted from J. Stephen Morris, "How to Make Criticism Sessions Productive," *Wall Street Journal* (October 12, 1981), p. 24. Reprinted by permission of the *Wall Street Journal.* Copyright © 1981 Dow Jones & Company, Inc. All rights reserved.

[32]Adapted, by permission of the publisher, from "Ten Commandments of Good Communication," *Management Review,* Vol. 44 (October 1955), pp. 704–705. © 1955 by AMACOM, a division of American Management Associations. All rights reserved.

[33]Information from Alex Taylor III, "Tomorrow's Chief Executives," *Fortune* (May 9, 1988), pp. 30–42.

[34]From Robert D. Joyce, *Encounters in Organizational Behavior: Problem Situations* (New York: Pergamon Press, 1972), pp. 2–5. Reprinted by permission of the publisher.

[35]William V. Haney, *Communication and Interpersonal Relations: Text and Cases,* Fourth Edition. (Homewood, IL: Richard D. Irwin, 1979), pp. 250–251. Copyright © Richard D. Irwin, Inc., 1960, 1967, 1973, 1979. All rights reserved. Used by permission.

Leading Through Movitation

Insights
from the 100 Club

Does recognizing good performance lead to increases in productivity? Daniel Boyle, vice-president and part owner of Diamond Fiber Products, an egg carton manufacturing company, thinks so. He came up with the idea for a program dubbed "The 100 Club" after he realized that efficiency and morale at the manufacturing facility were far too low. A survey showed that more than 75 percent of the plant's rank and file felt they weren't rewarded for good performance. Boyle decided then that things had to change.

The 100 Club was designed to recognize worker attendance, punctuality, and safety. It focuses not only on individual performance but also on teamwork to increase productivity. Employees earn points for having perfect attendance and for avoiding disciplinary action and lost-time injuries. They also gain points for community service and for generating cost-saving ideas that the company can implement. Points are subtracted for missed work. In addition, employees win points for group participation, which encourages ongoing teamwork.

After a 15 percent increase in productivity during the Club's first year, the plant has enjoyed average increases of 3 percent annually—largely, Boyle believes, because of the Club's strong focus on group effort. Boyle noticed a definite decline in competition among workers in maintenance after departmental goals had been set. To improve both safety and efficiency, workers found that they had to cooperate. "When a machine goes down now," says Boyle, "the crew works swiftly to get it running again."

Significantly, the Club is not an incentive program. Employees who pass 100 points are given a "100 Club" jacket—a very modest prize—and those amassing between 150 and 600 points can select from among small non-cash prizes such as cameras and luggage. For many Diamond employees, it's the gesture that counts; one employee showed off her new jacket to a local bank teller and said, "It's the first time in the 18 years I've been there that [Diamond] recognized the things I do every day."

The idea, says Boyle, is to let employees know that good performance is valuable and to involve them in boosting productivity. The Club has the effect of drawing everyone into the future of Diamond's business. In Boyle's words, "it's in management's interest for employees to know, for instance, how much it costs when a person is absent. . . . Information like this is vital if people are going to act like a team." ■

Source: Information from Daniel C. Boyle, "The 100 Club," *Harvard Business Review* (March–April 1987), pp. 26–27.

Managers in all organizations must create work environments within which people are willing and able to work hard to achieve high performance results. Key topics in Chapter 12 address this leadership challenge. They include

The Concept of Motivation
Motivation and Rewards
Understanding Individual Needs
Equity Theory
Expectancy Theory
Goal-Setting Theory
Reinforcement Theory
Managing Motivational Dynamics

Why do some people outperform others in their work? What can be done to ensure that maximum performance is achieved by each and every employee? These questions are asked by managers in all organizations. You must answer them if you are to master the manager's challenge as it was originally described in Chapter 1 — to satisfy a performance accountability to a higher level of authority while being dependent on subordinates to produce the desired performance results. This "dependency" on other people is what makes the prior questions so relevant to managers. And good answers to them begin with an understanding of and respect for people as the human resources of organizations. Such awareness is evident in the chapter opening example of Diamond International's "100 Club." It is also clearly presented in these statements of corporate policy from two well-respected organizations whose successes stem, in part at least, from a focus on "productivity through people."[1]

At Nucor Corporation the corporate philosophy states:

■ Management's first and foremost obligation to employees is to provide them the opportunity to earn according to their productivity.

■ We are obligated to manage our company in such a way that employees can feel that if they are doing their job properly they will have a job tomorrow.

■ Employees must believe that they are being treated fairly.

■ Employees have an avenue of appeal if they believe they are being treated unfairly.

At Dana Corporation the corporate philosophy states:

■ People . . . We are dedicated to the belief that our people are our most important asset.

■ We will encourage all of them to contribute and to grow to the limit of their desire and ability.

■ We believe people respond to recognition, freedom to contribute, opportunity to grow, and to fair compensation.

■ We believe that higher pay follows job performance and endorse an above average base compensation with a high incentive potential.

■ We believe in the philosophy of continued employment for all Dana people.

This chapter contains many ideas on how to exercise leadership in ways that encourage high performance on the part of other people. The concept of motivation is central to our investigation.

THE CONCEPT OF MOTIVATION

Suppose that a manager is fortunate enough to have subordinates whose abilities closely match task demands. Suppose, too, that these people have all the support required to do their jobs well. Can we predict that the subordinates will be high performers? If the answer to this question were yes, your job as a manager would be greatly simplified. To ensure performance results, the advice would go, select persons of ability for the jobs to be done and make sure they get the necessary resource support.

Unfortunately, a manager's job isn't quite so easy. The reason traces to the willingness of people to exert work effort. You should remember effort as a critical variable in the individual performance equation introduced in Chapter 9:

$$Performance = ability \times support \times effort$$

In order to achieve high performance, even people with ability and support must *try* to perform. That is, they must put forth adequate work effort. Willingness to exert effort, in turn, reflects **motivation to work.** This term is used in management theory to describe forces within the individual that account for the level, direction, and persistence of effort expended at work. A highly motivated person works hard in a job; an unmotivated person does not.

Leading through motivation, in respect to the manager's challenge depicted in Figure 12.1, requires an ability to create work environments within which other people feel inspired to work hard. A truly motivational environment, in turn, makes the right kinds of rewards available to persons whose work efforts contribute to the achievement of organizational objectives. While this idea is fresh in your mind, consider these examples of managers who did just that—albeit in quite different ways.[2]

■ *At EMC Corporation* a manufacturer of computer enhancements, the senior vice-president had a problem. Over half of the firm's projects were running late, a potentially disastrous situation in a highly competitive industry. His response was an incentive pay plan that works like this. He sets a royalty for all new projects when they begin, based on their size and complexity. He also sets two dates—the first is the date the product should be ready to market; the second is the date (usually six to 12 months later) when the project team will stop receiving its royalty. Of course, the earlier the product gets to market, the longer the team will earn its royalties. Now, only 10 percent of projects are late, and up to 20 percent come in early.

■ *At New England Rock Quarry* the new owner was told of a quarryman who had cut an enormous amount of rock the day before. Spontaneously, the owner picked up a walkie-talkie, contacted the quarryman as he worked, and gave him congratulations and praise for his accomplishment. Sometime later he was told by a coworker that the quarryman had stayed on "cloud nine" for days after getting the call. It turns out that this veteran of 25 years in the quarry had never before been praised by his boss.

MOTIVATION AND REWARDS

A **reward** is formally defined as a work outcome of positive value to the individual. Many types of rewards are available to people at work, but they can be divided into two categories. **Extrinsic rewards** are externally administered. Like incentive pay and verbal praise in the prior examples, they are given to someone by another person—typically, a super-

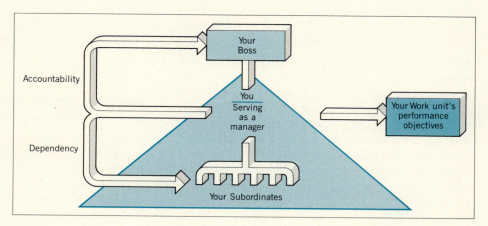

FIGURE 12.1 *The "manager's challenge"— where you must succeed at leading through motivation.*

visor or higher-level manager. The motivational stimulus of extrinsic rewards thus comes from outside the individual. Its strength and durability depends on the continued presence of this external force. Common examples of extrinsic rewards available in the workplace are pay, promotion, time off, special assignments, office fixtures, benefits, awards, praise, and the like.

Intrinsic or natural rewards are *self*-administered. They occur "naturally" as a person performs a task. They are, in this sense, built directly into the job itself. The major sources of intrinsic rewards are the feelings of competency, personal development, and self-control people experience in their work.[3] The motivational stimulus of intrinsic rewards is therefore internal, and does not depend for its continuation on the activities of some external force. Informed managers understand the value of intrinsic rewards and take every opportunity to design jobs that in themselves are motivational to the incumbent.[4] *Job enrichment* and *autonomous work grouping,* as already pointed out in Chapter 8, are both job-design strategies that can provide people with opportunities for more intrinsic rewards. *Newsline 12.1* comments further on the importance of this "motivation from within."

MOTIVATION FROM WITHIN

N E W S L I N E 12.1

As the global marketplace evolves, it becomes clear that the nature of work—all kinds of work—is changing profoundly. In reaction, new theories of motivation are being developed; many are based on the premise that "working smart" is the key to a competitive edge. A growing group of experts believe that today's organizations need employees who can use their judgment as well as their hands or machines, and who display courtesy and cooperation in dealing with peers and customers. Perhaps most important, employees must feel motivated by their jobs themselves, not merely by threats of punishment or promises of outside rewards.

In the view of business consultant Michael Macoby, eliciting solid performance involves more than using a set of sticks and carrots. It entails understanding the basic nature of individual workers and discovering how to encourage their best efforts from within. For this, each person's interests and values are crucial, says Macoby in his book, *Why Work: Leading the New Generation* (Simon & Schuster). Employees who like doing a superior job differ from those who like best to collaborate with others, or those who seek to develop themselves through work—and all such diverse needs must be respected by managers.

Getting to know one's workers and finding ways for them to participate in enhancing their jobs are a manager's main tasks in motivating subordinates, according to Macoby. When people see how their own goals tie in with organizational ends, they are more likely to take the initiative on the job. Macoby issues a challenge to managers: accept your workers for who they are, and tailor your motivating tactics to their natures. The consequences aren't straightforward; a bonus system won't motivate everybody, for instance, and reprimands may spur some and antagonize others. But Macoby suggests that the competitive advantages that result when people are truly satisfied at work are well worth the difficulties encountered in learning how to motivate employees.

Source: As reported in John Case, "Why Work?" *Inc.* (June 1988), pp. 25–28.

Rewards and Performance

Both extrinsic and intrinsic rewards, if used well, can assist managers to lead effectively through motivation. The key phrase in the prior sentence is *if used well.* The manager's basic goal in this regard is to achieve a proper match between available rewards and workers' personal needs. The following parable suggests that this isn't always easy.[5]

A PARABLE

Once upon a time there was a donkey standing knee-deep in a field of carrots, contentedly munching away. A wise farmer wanted the donkey to pull a loaded wagon to another field, but the donkey would not walk over to the wagon. So the wise farmer stood by the wagon and held up a bunch of carrots for the donkey to see. But the donkey continued to munch contentedly on carrots in the field.

Unfortunately, many managers' attempts to encourage subordinates to put forth maximum effort in their work are no more successful than the farmer's efforts in the parable. To utilize rewards successfully, that is, to achieve maximum motivational impact, it is necessary to:

1. Understand clearly what people need from their work activities.
2. Know how to create and distribute rewards so that these needs are met at the same time that the organization's interests are served.

Fortunately managers have access to a number of motivation theories that offer insights relevant to both of these objectives. Each theory is largely grounded in the field of psychology and the philosophical tradition of hedonism. The latter asserts that people act to minimize pain and maximize pleasure in their lives. The motivation theories developed out of this tradition offer considerable assistance to the manager who wants to create a work environment within which people can achieve job satisfaction while facilitating high productivity for the organization.

Types of Motivation Theories

We will examine the managerial implications of three types of motivation theories in more detail—content, process, and reinforcement theories.[5] Each of these theories offers its own special explanation of individual behavior at work.

Content theories of motivation offer ways to profile or analyze individuals to identify their needs. These theories lend insight into various human needs and how they vary among people at work. The theories of Abraham Maslow and David McClelland are singled out in this chapter as two of the better-known examples of this content orientation in motivation theory.

Process theories address the thought processes through which individuals give meaning to rewards and allow them to influence their behavior. They provide guidance on the actual allocation of rewards in specific work circumstances. We will discuss the equity, expectancy, and goal-setting theories within this managerial frame of reference.

Reinforcement theory examines how people learn patterns of behavior based on environmental reinforcements. Using principles developed by B. F. Skinner, reinforcement theorists suggest ways of improving performance by clarifying goals, providing performance feedback, and properly administering rewards.

The content, process, and reinforcement approaches to motivation theory complement rather than compete or contradict one another. We will ultimately draw together the major insights of each into an integrative view of motivation that will prove useful to you as a practicing manager. As we turn to examine this carefully selected group of motivation theories, remember that you must not only master the elements of each theory, but also understand their managerial implications.

UNDERSTANDING INDIVIDUAL NEEDS

Content theories of motivation use individual needs to explain the behavior and attitudes of people at work. **Needs,** in turn, are physiological or psychological deficiencies that an individual feels some compulsion to eliminate. You will sometimes find the terms *needs, motives,* and *drives* used interchangeably. Although each content theory discusses a slightly different set of needs, all agree that managers must understand them because needs cause tensions that influence attitudes and behavior.

Maslow's Hierarchy-of-Needs Theory

Chapter 2 introduced Abraham Maslow's theory of human needs as a foundation element in the behavioral approach to management. His theory includes the hierarchy of needs depicted once again in Figure 12.2. The five needs fall into two general categories.[7] **Lower-order needs** include physiological, safety, and social concerns; **higher-order needs** include esteem and self-actualization concerns. The higher-order needs are placed in a separate category because they represent desires for psychological development and growth, as opposed to lower-order concerns for social and physical well-being.

The Deficit and Progression Principles

The deficit and progression principles are central to Maslow's theory. For review purposes, we can summarize the two principles as follows.

1. *The deficit principle* holds that a satisfied need is not a motivator of behavior. People are expected to act in ways that satisfy deprived needs—that is, needs for which a "deficit" exists. In the parable, for example, the farmer failed to recognize the deficit principle. He was offering a reward (carrots) that appealed to an already satisfied need (hunger).

2. *The progression principle* holds that the five needs exist in a strict hierarchy of prepotency. A need at one level doesn't become activated until the next lower-level need is already satisfied. People are expected to advance step by step up the hierarchy in their search for need satisfactions.

In summary, Maslow's theory suggests that managers should recognize that deprived needs will dominate the attention of people at work and determine their attitudes and behavior. Once a need is satisfied the individual's attention progresses up to the next higher level in the hierarchy. Only when the level of self-actualization is reached do the deficit and progression principles cease to operate. The more self-actualization needs are satisfied, the stronger they are predicted to grow. According to Maslow, an individual should continue to be motivated by opportunities for self-fulfillment as long as the other needs remain satisfied.

Managerial Implications

Research has not been able to verify the strict deficit and progression principles central to Maslow's theory. There is no consistent evidence, for example, that the satisfaction of a need at one level decreases its importance to the individual and increases the

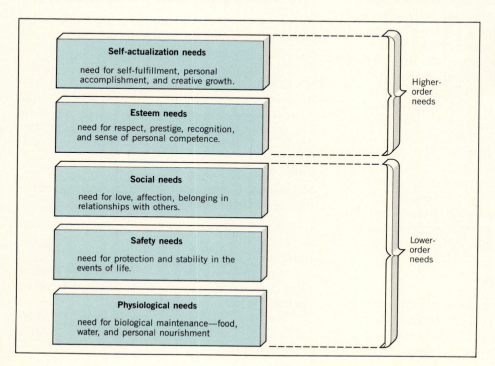

FIGURE 12.2 *Maslow's hierarchy of human needs: the distinction between higher-order and lower-order needs.*

TABLE 12.1 *Opportunities for Individual Need Satisfaction: Things People May Want from Their Work*

Needs	What a Person Wants
Higher-order needs	
Self-actualization	Creative and challenging work
	Participation in decision making
	Job flexibility and autonomy
Esteem	Responsibility of an important job
	Promotion to higher-status job
	Praise and recognition from boss
Lower-order needs	
Social	Friendly co-workers
	Interaction opportunities
	Compatible supervisor
Safety	Safe working conditions
	Job security
	Good compensation benefits
Physiological	Rest and refreshment breaks
	Physical comfort on the job
	Reasonable work hours

importance of the next higher need. Scholars, therefore, are continuing their efforts to modify Maslow's theory and improve its application to day-to-day individual behavior.

Overall, however, Maslow's ideas are helpful for understanding the needs people bring with them to their work *and* determining what can be done to satisfy them. Table 12.1 shows how each of the five needs in Maslow's theory translates into things managers can try to provide in response to the needs of subordinates. Notice that the higher-order needs of self-actualization are unique, in part, because they are served entirely by intrinsic rewards. The esteem needs are served by both intrinsic and extrinsic rewards. The satisfaction of lower order needs, by contrast, is tied directly or indirectly to extrinsic rewards. By paying good attention to people and the work environment, a manager should be able to minimize deficiencies in lower-order need satisfaction and provide growth opportunities for satisfying higher-order needs.

Alderfer's ERG Theory

One of the most promising efforts to build on Maslow's work is the ERG theory of Clayton Alderfer.[8] His theory differs from Maslow's in three basic respects. To begin, ERG theory collapses Maslow's five need categories into three—**existence needs** pertain to people's desires for physiological and material well-being; **relatedness needs** represent desires for satisfying interpersonal relationships; **growth needs** are desires for continued psychological growth and development. Second, ERG theory does not assume that lower-level needs must be satisfied before higher-level needs become activated. Finally, ERG theory includes a unique "frustration–regression" principle whereby an already-satisfied lower-level need becomes reactivated when a higher-level need cannot be satisfied.

Alderfer's personal research demonstrates support for the ERG theory. When used in conjunction with Maslow's ideas, the theory offers an additional means for understanding and responding to the needs of people at work. The growth-need concept is especially useful. In fact, we have already used it in Chapter 8 as a key issue in job design. For example, job enrichment seems most appropriate for persons with strong desires for growth-need satisfaction. Persons with high-growth need strength tend to seek opportunities to gain intrinsic rewards from their work.

McClelland's Acquired-Needs Theory

Another useful theory of human needs is offered by David McClelland.[9] In the late 1940s, McClelland and his co-workers began experimenting with the Thematic Apperception Test (TAT) as a way of examining individual needs. The TAT procedure is to ask people to view pictures and write stories about what they see. The stories, or fantasies, are then content analyzed for themes representing various needs.

Three Acquired Needs

McClelland's approach to motivation emphasizes the importance of three needs. These are:

1. *Need for Achievement (nAch)* The desire to do something better or more efficiently, to solve problems, or to master complex tasks.
2. *Need for power (nPower)* The desire to control other persons, to influence their behavior, or to be responsible for other people.
3. *Need for affiliation (nAff)* The desire to establish and maintain friendly and warm relations with other persons.

TABLE 12.2 *Work Preferences of Persons High in Needs for Achievement, Affiliation, and Power*

Individual Need	Work Preferences	Example of an Appropriate Job Assignment
High need for achievement	Individual responsibility for results Achievable but challenging goals Feedback on performance	Computer scientist responsible for software design and technical problem solving in support of a management information system.
High need for affiliation	Interpersonal relationships Companionship Social approval	Human resources specialist responsible for employee relations, college recruiting, and management development programs.
High need for power	Control over other persons Impact on people and events Public recognition and attention	Audit manager in charge of a group of newly-hired junior accountants assigned to complete a complex audit of a bank.

According to McClelland, people develop needs for achievement, power, and affiliation over time as a result of individual life experiences. In turn, they are motivated by these needs. McClelland thus encourages managers to learn how to recognize the strengths of each need in themselves and in other people. Attempts can then be made to fulfill the needs by responding to preferences such as those described in Table 12.2. Let's consider the three needs more specifically.[10]

Need for Achievement (nAch) High-need achievers like to put their competencies to work; they take moderate risks in competitive situations; they are willing to work alone with success at a task serving as its own reward. As a result, a person high in nAch can be expected to respond well in work situations offering explicit and challenging goals, feedback on task performance, and individual responsibility. In jobs with diffused group responsibility, ambiguous goals, and little or no performance feedback, they are likely to be frustrated and even demotivated.

Effective managers may reasonably be expected to be high in nAch. But while an achievement orientation is certainly important, the issue is more complex. In a study of the careers of AT&T executives, for example, McClelland reports that high-need achievers advanced quickly in technical fields where individual skills and creativity were required.[11] But their careers tended to peak rather early, whereas those persons who advanced to senior management displayed a broader profile of needs that seemed more consistent with their advanced responsibilities. He concludes that success in top management isn't based on a concern for individual achievement alone. It requires an achievement orientation that can be satisfied through the use of power to influence the success of other persons.

Need for Power (nPower) Someone with a high need for power is motivated to behave in ways that have a clear impact on other people and events. They enjoy being in control of a situation and being recognized for this responsibility. A high nPower subordinate is likely to respond well to jobs that include designated opportunities to supervise and direct the work activities of others.

Our discussion of leadership in Chapter 10 highlighted the centrality of power to the managerial role. It only makes sense, therefore, that a high need for power should appear in McClelland's profiles of successful executives. McClelland distinguishes, however, between two forms of the power need. One is exploitative and concerned with manipulation and power for the pure sake of personal gratification. This need for *personal* power is not successful in management. The second form is the need for *institutional* or *social* power. It is very essential to leadership and managerial success. McClelland reports that successful top managers are comfortable with power and enjoy the ability and responsibility to influence other persons' behaviors. But they do so in a socially responsible way that is directed toward organizational rather than personal objectives.

Need for Affiliation (nAff) The need for affiliation is essentially the same as Maslow's social need and Alderfer's relatedness need. It is a desire for companionship, social approval, and satisfying interpersonal relationships. Probably the most important job design requirement of the high nAff person is to work in a setting that requires or at least allows for continuing social interactions during task accomplishment.

McClelland's approach indicates that people

very high in nAff alone may not make the best managers.[12] This is true if the desires for social approval and friendship complicate managerial decision making. There are times when managers must decide and act in ways that other persons are likely to disagree with and even resent. To the extent that high nAff interferes with someone's ability to make these decisions, managerial effectiveness will be sacrificed. The successful executive in McClelland's view is likely to possess a high nPower that is greater than nAff.

Managerial Implications

Two applications of McClelland's theory are especially relevant to managers. First, nAch, nAff, and nPower complement the needs identified in the theories of Maslow and Alderfer. They add to your ability to understand people in their work settings. Acquired needs theory is especially useful in this respect because each need is directly associated with the set of individual work preferences indicated in the last table. Second, if these needs are truly acquired, it may be possible to teach people to adopt the need profiles required to be successful in various types of jobs. McClelland reports some success in stimulating people's needs for achievement, and he is currently working on a program to help managers adopt need profiles he believes are associated with executive success.

Questions and Answers on Individual Needs at Work

The content theories focus on human needs as a way to understand and predict the attitudes and behaviors of people at work. Even though the terminology differs, there is a substantial similarity in the insights these theories offer managers. Figure 12.3 shows how the human needs identified by Maslow, Alderfer, and McClelland compare to one another. By way of further summary, let's answer some questions you may have regarding the content theories and their managerial implications.[13]

"How many different individual needs are there?" Research has not yet determined the complete listing of work-related individual needs. Each of the needs previously discussed has been found useful by management scholars and practitioners alike. As a manager, you can use the ideas of Maslow, Alderfer, and McClelland as a point of departure for understanding the various needs that people may bring with them to the work setting.

"Can a work outcome or reward satisfy more than one need?" Yes, work outcomes or rewards can satisfy more than one need. Pay is a good example. It is a source of performance feedback for the high need achiever. It can be a source of personal security for someone with strong existence needs. It can also be used as a way to satisfy social needs and ego needs.

FIGURE 12.3 *A comparison of human needs identified in Maslow's, Alderfer's, and McClelland's theories of motivation.*

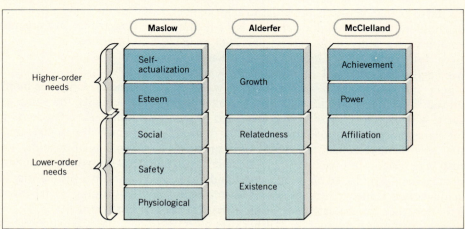

"Is there a hierarchy of needs?" Research does not support the precise five-step hierarchy of needs postulated by Maslow. It seems more legitimate to view needs operating in a flexible hierarchy, such as the one in Alderfer's ERG theory. However, it is useful to distinguish between the motivational properties of lower-order and higher-order needs.

"How important are the various needs?" Research is inconclusive as to the importance of different needs. Individuals vary widely in this regard. They may also value needs differently at different times and at different ages or career stages. This is a major reason why managers should take advantage of all the content theories in attempts to understand the differing needs of people at work.

"What is the manager's responsibility from the perspective of the content theories?" Although the details vary, each content theory considers managers as responsible for allocating rewards in such a way that individuals find opportunities to satisfy important needs on the job. To the extent that some needs are acquired, the manager's responsibility also includes stimulating those needs to which the work setting is best able to respond in a positive manner.

EQUITY THEORY

Do you remember the first parable? It said something about farmers, donkeys, and carrots. Let's spin the parable around in another version.

A SECOND PARABLE

Once upon a time there were six donkeys hitched to a wagon pulling a heavy load up a steep hill. Two of the donkeys were not achievement oriented and decided to coast along and let others do most of the pulling. Two others were relatively young and inexperienced, and had a difficult time pulling their share. One of the remaining two suffered from a slight hangover from consuming fermented barley the night before. The sixth donkey did most of the work.

The wagon arrived at the top of the hill. The driver got down from his seat, patted each of the donkeys on the head, and gave six carrots to each. Prior to the next hill climb, the sixth donkey ran away.

From a donkey's perspective, the moral of the story is to never be the sixth donkey if everyone gets the same number of carrots! From a manager's perspective, the point is that equity problems in the allocation of rewards can affect behavior in the work setting. How would you like to lose your best worker under conditions such as those described in the parable? Motivation theory offers guidance that can help managers avoid such undesirable consequences.

The Equity Comparison

Equity theory is a process theory of motivation known best through the work of J. Stacy Adams.[14] The essence of the theory is that felt inequity is a motivating state. That is, when people feel they have been inequitably treated in comparison to others, they will try to eliminate the discomfort and achieve a sense of equity. Inequities occur whenever people feel the rewards they received for work inputs are unequal to the rewards other persons appear to have received for theirs. The *comparison others* may be co-workers in the immediate situation, workers elsewhere within the organization, and even persons employed elsewhere.

The equity comparison is shown in Figure 12.4. When perceived inequity results, Adams predicts people will respond in one or more of the following ways.

■ Change their work inputs.
■ Try to change rewards received.
■ Use different comparison points.
■ Rationalize the inequity.
■ Leave the situation.

FIGURE 12.4 *The equity comparison: perceived inequity as a motivating state.*

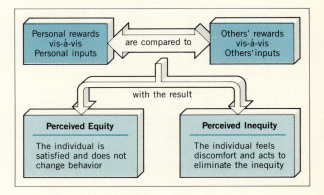

The research of Adams and others, largely accomplished in laboratory settings, lends tentative support to this prediction. People who feel overpaid—that is, who perceive felt *positive* inequity—have been found to increase the quantity or quality of their work. Those who feel underpaid—that is, who perceive felt *negative* inequity—reduce their work efforts to compensate for the missing rewards. The research is most conclusive in respect to felt negative inequity.

Managing Equity Dynamics

An equity comparison typically intervenes between a manager's allocation of rewards and their impact on the work attitudes and behavior of subordinates. Rewards perceived as equitably given can foster job satisfaction and performance; rewards perceived as inequitable can inhibit these key work results. The burden lies with the manager to make sure that any negative consequences of the equity comparison are avoided, or at least minimized, when rewards are allocated. To do this a manager should:

1. Recognize that equity comparisons are likely whenever especially visible rewards such as pay or promotions are allocated.
2. Anticipate felt negative inequities, particularly as co-workers compare one another's rewards and performance accomplishments.
3. Carefully communicate the intended value of the reward being given, an appraisal of the performance on which it is based, and the appropriate comparison points.

Remember, too, that feelings of inequity are determined by individual *perceptions*. It is not how a manager feels about the allocation of rewards that counts; it is how the recipients feel or interpret things that will determine the motivational outcomes of the equity dynamic.

One current and controversial equity question in the United States is presented in the issue of **comparable worth.** This is the principle that people doing jobs of similar value should receive similar pay. Advocates of comparable worth claim that it corrects inequities and is a natural extension of the "equal pay for equal work" concept. Critics claim that "similar value" is too difficult to define, and that the dramatic restructuring of wage scales would have a negative economic impact for society as a whole. An increasing number of states and localities are now using comparable worth as a basis for raising the pay levels of public-sector jobs usually held by women.

EXPECTANCY THEORY

Victor Vroom introduced an expectancy theory of work motivation that has made an important contribution to management literature.[15] The theory seeks to predict or explain the task-related efforts expended by people at work. It asks the central question: What determines the willingness of an individual to exert effort on tasks that contribute to the production purposes of the work unit and the organization? This question, of course, constitutes the heart of a manager's interest in any motivation theory.

The Theory

Expectancy theory argues that work motivation is determined by individual beliefs regarding effort–performance relationships and the desirabilities of outcomes associated with various performance levels. The theory is based on the logic: "People will do what they can do when they want to." It helps to keep expectancy theory in a proper managerial perspective by remembering that, in general, people exert work effort to achieve task performance and receive rewards.

Recall that the theory inquires as to when and under what conditions people will decide to put forth maximum work efforts in support of organizational objectives. To answer such a question in any given circumstance, Vroom suggests that a manager must know the three things highlighted in Figure 12.5.

1. **Expectancy** The person's belief that working hard will enable various levels of task performance to be achieved.
2. **Instrumentality** The person's belief that various work-related outcomes will occur as a result of task performance.
3. **Valence** The value the individual assigns to these work-related outcomes.

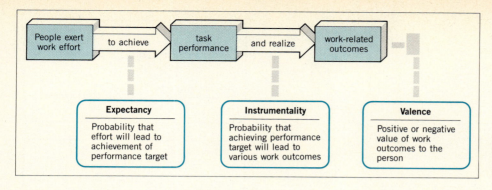

| People exert work effort | to achieve | task performance | and realize | work-related outcomes |

Expectancy

Probability that effort will lead to achievement of performance target

Instrumentality

Probability that achieving performance target will lead to various work outcomes

Valence

Positive or negative value of work outcomes to the person

FIGURE 12.5 *Elements in the expectancy theory of motivation.*

Multiplier Effects

Expectancy theory further posits that motivation (M), expectancy, (E), instrumentality, (I), and valence (V) are related to one another in a multiplicative fashion. That is,

$$M = E \times I \times V$$

In words, this equation states that motivation is determined by expectancy times instrumentality times valence. This multiplier effect in the expectancy theory has important managerial implications. It clearly points out that managers must take action to maximize all three components—expectancy, instrumentality, and valence—when seeking to create high levels of work motivation through the allocation of rewards. Mathematically speaking, a zero at any location on the right side of the expectancy equation ($M = E \times I \times V$) will result in zero motivation.

Suppose, for example, that a manager is wondering whether or not the prospect of earning a promotion will be motivational to a subordinate. Expectancy theory predicts the subordinate's motivation to work hard in the prospect of earning a promotion will be *low* if:

1. *Expectancy is low.* A person feels that he or she can't achieve the necessary performance level.
2. *Instrumentality is low.* The person is not confident that a high level of task performance will result in being promoted.
3. *Valence is low.* The person places little value on receiving a promotion; the promotion is not perceived as a valued reward.

Multiple Outcomes

Expectancy theory also recognizes that more than one outcome can be associated with a given work path. Again, take an example. A typical assumption made by managers is that people will be motivated to work hard if given the prospect of earning a promotion. But . . . will they?

Look at the example as diagrammed in Figure 12.6. The individual in the case faces a decision of how much effort to put forth. The decision may be to work hard to achieve a superior performance target (follow path A), or work less hard and achieve an average performance target (path B). A manager would obviously like to encourage (that is, motivate) this person to pursue the high effort path.

Expectancy theory predicts that the first question the individual will ask is, "Can I achieve the superior performance target?" The answer to this *expectancy* question will depend on the individual's sense of competency in terms of ability, and the amount of support available for achieving high performance. Given a positive response, attention will shift to *instrumentality* and the outcomes that may be associated with each performance level. In the example, promotion and an overtime workload might both result if superior performance is achieved. By contrast, an average performance level will result in continuation of the present job and more leisure time.

To make the final decision whether to pursue path A or path B, the individual next evaluates the *valences* associated with the multiple outcomes of each path. Looking first at the high-effort path, the positive valence of the expected promotion is probably offset by the negative valence of added time commitments. On the path of less effort, expectations of doing the same job and having extra leisure time both probably have modest positive valences. Expectancy theory predicts the person is most likely to work on the low-effort path and seek only an average performance level. Thus, an informed man-

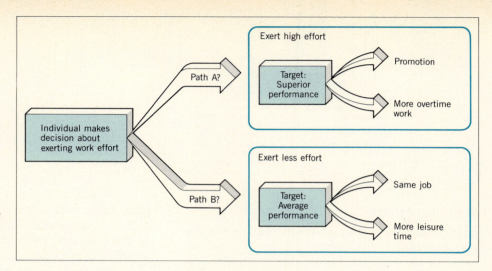

FIGURE 12.6 *An example of applied expectancy theory: the case of the possible promotion.*

ager will always try to identify and understand multiple outcomes from the other person's point of view, and adjust the use of rewards accordingly.

Managerial Implications

Expectancy theory helps managers to better understand and respond to individual points of view in the work situation. This includes trying to maximize expectancies, instrumentalities, and valences that support the organizational objectives. Said differently, a manager should strive to create a work environment within which task contributions serving the organization's needs are also viewed by subordinates as paths toward highly desirable rewards. This argument should sound familiar to you. It is consistent with House's path–goal theory of leadership described in Chapter 10.

Table 12.3 shows that a manager can influence expectancies by selecting individuals with proper abilities, training them to use these abilities, supporting them with appropriate resources, and clarifying performance goals. Instrumentality can be influenced by clarifying expectations and responsibilities in the psychological contract, by communicating performance-outcome possibilities specific to a given situation, and by demonstrating that desired rewards do follow high performance once it occurs.

TABLE 12.3 *Managerial Implications of Expectancy Theory: Understanding and Responding to the Individual's Point of View*

Individual's View	Manager's Objective	Managerial Implicatons
Expectancy—"Can I achieve the desired level of task performance?"	Make the person feel competent and capable of achieving the desired performance level.	Select workers with ability Train workers to use ability Support work efforts Clarify performance goals
Instrumentality—"What work outcomes will be received as a result of the performance?"	Make the person confident in understanding which outcomes will follow performance accomplishments.	Clarify psychological contracts Communicate performance → outcome possibilities Demonstrate that rewards are contingent on performance
Valence—"How highly do I value the work outcomes?"	Make the person understand the value of various possible work outcomes.	Identify individual needs Adjust rewards to match these needs

Finally, managers can influence valence by being sensitive to individual needs. This is where the content theories of motivation are of great benefit. They help managers to understand individual needs and adjust rewards to them.

GOAL-SETTING THEORY

Task goals, in the form of clear and desirable performance targets, are very relevant to the expectancy theory. They also form the basis of a related approach to motivation known as goal-setting theory. Developed by Edwin Locke, the theory's basic premise is that well-set task goals provide important sources of motivation. They give direction to people in their work, assist in energizing work efforts, and encourage persistent efforts over time. In addition, Locke believes that goals can clarify performance expectations, provide a basis for task feedback, and more generally enhance individual work performance and job satisfaction.

Research by Locke and his associates indicates that these results can be achieved through goal-setting.[16] To do so, however, a manager must be able to set the *right* goals for subordinates in the *right* ways. The key issues are:

■ *Goal specificity* Specific goals, such as "increase sales by 6 percent over the next three months," lead to higher performance than more generally stated ones, such as—"do your best."

■ *Goal difficulty* More difficult goals, as long as they are viewed as realistic and attainable, lead to higher performance than easy goals.

■ *Goal acceptance and commitment* People work harder toward goals which they accept as their own and truly believe in; they tend to resist goals that seem inappropriately forced on them.

A key issue in goal-setting is the role of participation. On the one hand, it has not been demonstrated that participation in goal-setting is always a prerequisite for high performance. Not everyone wants to participate to begin with, and situational demands sometimes don't always allow for it to occur. Furthermore, research suggests that people will accept and commit to accomplishing imposed goals *if* the persons assigning them are trusted, and *if* the recipients believe they will be adequately sup-

ported in attempts to achieve them. On the other hand, participation can be a great source of satisfaction for the individuals involved and also contribute to higher performance. Research indicates that these positive results are most likely to occur when the participation (1) allows for increased understanding of specific and difficult goals, and (2) provides for greater acceptance and commitment to them. Managers should also be aware of the participation options. It may not always be possible to allow participation in selecting exactly *which* goals need to be pursued, but it may be possible to allow participation in determining *how* to best pursue them.

The concept of management by objectives (MBO), first introduced in Chapter 5, is a good illustration of a participative approach to goal-setting. We will return to this concept again in Chapter 14 to look at its role as an integrated planning and controlling technique. For now, *Newsline* 12.2 provides an example of how goal-setting and MBO can be used in actual practice.

REINFORCEMENT THEORY

All of the prior motivation theories rely on cognitive explanations of behavior. That is, they are concerned with explaining "why" people do things in terms of satisfying needs, resolving felt inequities, and/or pursuing positive valences and task goals. Reinforcement theory, by contrast, views human behavior as determined by its environmental consequences. It avoids looking within the individual and examining thought processes, and focuses instead on the external environment and the consequences it holds for the individual.

Consider the following example.[17] A person walking down the street finds a $10 bill. Thereafter this person is observed to spend more time looking down when walking. The question is, "Why is the person so motivated?"

Cognitive explanation The person continues to look down frequently because of the high value held for money. Because the person reasons that more money may be found in the streets, he or she decides to look down more frequently when out walking in the future.

Reinforcement explanation When the initial behav-

GO-GETTERS
AND GOAL-SETTERS

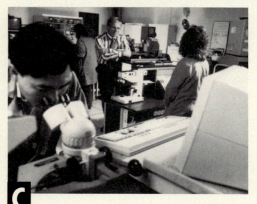

Cypress Semiconductor Corporation's CEO, T. J. Rodgers, is proud of what he refers to as his company's "Turbo MBO"—a high-powered, computerized management by objectives system that coordinates and tracks the weekly objectives established by 670 employees. "A semiconductor is a very unforgiving entity," says Rodgers. "My system makes sure nothing falls through the

cracks." And if something does, Cypress's system alerts its 45 managers to the need for corrective action or shifts in priorities.

While detractors claim that MBO is too machine-like, supporters argue that goal-setting systems allow for flexibility and fast decision making by giving managers timely, accurate information. Moreover, say supporters, goal-setting motivates employees: because they set their own goals, they feel more invested in the outcome of their efforts.

Cypress's employees set new objectives each Monday, and by Wednesday managers must give a status report of their groups' progress in attaining those goals. Accountability is a valued quality at Cypress, and employees take seriously the benchmarks they set for themselves and their work units. Rodgers believes that the system works wonders for his company, and Cypress's high earnings—despite a slump in the industry—corroborate his conviction.

Source: As reported in Steve Kaufman, "Going for the Goals," *Success* (January–February 1988), pp. 39–41.

---

ior of looking down occurred, it was reinforced by the presence of a $10 bill. Having once been reinforced by this environmental consequence, the behavior becomes more likely to occur in the future.

The Law of Effect

The preceding example shows how the reinforcement orientation avoids making assumptions about individual thought processes in order to explain behavior. Instead of looking at "values," "reasons," and "decisions," reinforcement theory views present behavior (e.g., looking down while walking) as determined by environmental responses to past behavior (e.g., finding a $10 bill after looking down while walking). The basis for the argument and the foundation for reinforcement theory is Thorndike's **law of effect.**[18]

LAW OF EFFECT

Behavior that results in a pleasant outcome is likely to be repeated; behavior that results in an unpleasant outcome is not likely to be repeated.

Organizational Behavior Modification

Operant conditioning, a term popularized by the noted psychologist B. F. Skinner,[19] is the process of controlling behavior by manipulating its consequences. You may think of operant conditioning as learning by reinforcement. It is learning that occurs via the law of effect. **Organizational behavior modification** ("OB Mod" for short) is a term that describes the application of operant conditioning techniques to influence human behavior in work settings.[20] Its basic purpose is to systematically reinforce desirable behavior and discourage undesirable behavior by people in organizations.

There are four basic OB Mod strategies:

1. *Positive reinforcement* Increases the frequency of or strengthens desirable behavior by making a pleasant consequence contingent on the occurrence of the behavior.

> *Example* A manager nods to express approval to a subordinate making a useful comment during a staff meeting.

2. *Negative reinforcement* Increases the frequency of or strengthens desirable behavior by making the avoidance of an unpleasant consequence contingent on the occurrence of the behavior.

> *Example* A manager who has been nagging a worker every day about tardiness doesn't nag when the worker comes to work on time one day.

3. *Punishment* Decreases the frequency of or eliminates an undesirable behavior by making an unpleasant consequence contingent on the occurrence of the behavior.

> *Example* A manager docks the pay of an employee who reports late for work one day.

4. *Extinction* Decreases the frequency of or eliminates an undesirable behavior by making the removal of a pleasant consequence contingent on the occurrence of the behavior.

> *Example* A manager observes that a disruptive employee is receiving social approval from co-workers. The manager counsels co-workers to stop giving this approval.

The four OB Mod strategies are illustrated in Figure 12.7. Note how the supervisor uses each of the strategies to influence employees toward desirable quality-assurance practices. Note, too, that both positive and negative reinforcement are used to strengthen desirable behavior when it occurs. Punishment and extinction are used to decrease the frequency of undesirable behaviors. Because positive reinforcement and punishment are so fundamental to any manager's motivational strategy, we'll single them out for further attention.

Positive Reinforcement

Positive reinforcement is an OB Mod strategy highly advocated by Skinner and his followers. To apply positive reinforcement well in the work setting, you

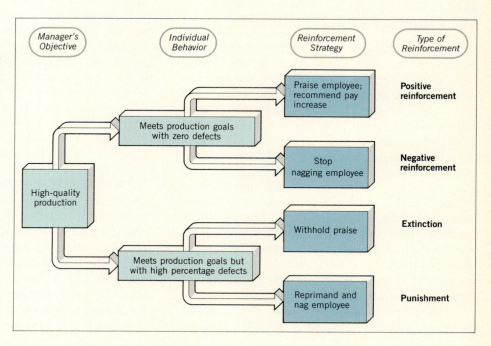

FIGURE 12.7 *Four strategies of organizational behavior modification: the case of the quality improvement program.*

must first be aware of the many things in organizations that have potential reward value. Then you must know how to allocate them in ways that achieve the desired performance effects. Two laws should guide your actions in this latter regard: the **law of contingent reinforcement** and the **law of immediate reinforcement.**[21]

LAW OF CONTINGENT REINFORCEMENT

In order for a reward to have maximum reinforcing value, it must be delivered only if the desired behavior is exhibited.

LAW OF IMMEDIATE REINFORCEMENT

The more immediate the delivery of a reward after the occurrence of a desirable behavior, the greater the reinforcing value of the reward.

Taken together, these two laws suggest that managers should give rewards as immediately as possible, and contingent on desired behavior. Only then will they serve to maximum advantage as positive reinforcers in the work setting. Try applying this advice in the following example.

ILLUSTRATIVE CASE:
THE ASSEMBLY-LINE SUPERVISOR

A new young manager was in charge of a group of workers on an automobile assembly line.[22] This work unit was expected to produce components at a standard rate of 72 per hour. Actual performance was running around 45 per hour, and the manager's boss was holding her accountable for the production discrepancy.

The manager called her subordinates together and asked them what could be done to get production up to standard. They decided that an extra "break" might justify the increased effort. A deal was made. *If* the workers produced 72 units within an hour's time, then they could use the remaining time in the hour as a break. The results were immediate and positive. Within a week the work unit was producing up to standard and taking a 25-minute break every hour!

Sometime after these results were realized, however, it became obvious to both the manager

and her subordinates that the situation couldn't continue. Higher management and the other work units would not tolerate this group taking a 25-minute break every hour. Another deal was made. When the group reached 90 units an hour, the remaining time in the hour could be used as a break. As a result of this agreement, the work unit was soon able to take a 10-minute break almost every hour.

This manager used her reinforcement theory well. She was able to associate a desirable consequence — the work break — with behavior appropriate to organizational objectives — the desired per hour production rate. It is also significant that the break was only one of a number of possible rewards the manager might have tried to use as a positive reinforcer. She wisely obtained information from the workers before choosing among the alternative rewards. The break was highly valued by the workers and proved a powerful positive reinforcer as a result.

Shaping

The supervisor in the previous example could have used another version of positive reinforcement to achieve the desired results. **Shaping** is the creation of a new behavior by the positive reinforcement of successive approximations to the desired behavior. Recall that the work unit in the example originally produced only 45 units per hour when 72 per hour was the goal. A shaping strategy would have rewarded subordinates with verbal praise and recognition each time they produced more than 45 units in an hour. As production continued to increase, reinforcement would be given only when production surpassed the previous high level. Once production reached 72 units, intermittent positive reinforcement would then be used to stabilize behavior at this new performance level.

Scheduling Reinforcement

The timing of positive reinforcement can be varied according to continuous and intermittent schedules. To succeed with a shaping strategy, for example, reinforcement should be given on a continuous basis until the desired behavior is achieved. Then an intermittent schedule should be used to maintain the behavior at the new level. **Continuous reinforcement** administers a reward each time a desired behavior occurs. **Intermittent reinforcement** rewards behavior only periodically. In general, a manager can expect that:

1. Continuous reinforcement will draw forth a desired behavior more quickly than intermittent reinforcement.
2. Behavior acquired under an intermittent schedule will be more permanent than behavior acquired under a continuous schedule.

Guidelines for Positive Reinforcement

To use operant conditioning properly and to ensure that rewards are allocated with the desired positive reinforcement effects, a manager should:[23]

1. *Clearly identify the desired behaviors* that is, determine what specific behaviors will result in the desired performance.
2. *Maintain an inventory of rewards* that have the potential to serve as positive reinforcers.
3. *Recognize individual differences* as to which rewards will actually have reinforcement value for subordinates.
4. *Let subordinates know exactly what must be done to receive a reward* that is, set clear targets and give performance feedback.
5. *Administer rewards contingently and immediately upon the appearance of the desired behaviors* that is, make sure a reward is given only if the desired behavior occurs.

Punishment

Punishment is a means for eliminating undesirable behavior by administering an unpleasant consequence upon the occurrence of that behavior. To punish an employee, a manager may deny the individual a valued reward such as verbal praise or merit pay, or the manager may administer an adversive or obnoxious stimulus such as a verbal reprimand or pay reduction.

It is just as important to understand punishment as an OB Mod strategy as it is to understand the principles of positive reinforcement. Like the other reinforcement strategies, punishment can be done poorly or it can be done well. Your goal, of course, is to know when to use this strategy, and then to know how to do it well.

Problems with the Punishment Strategy

Let's look first at three problems that may accompany a manager's use of punishment.

1. *Although a behavior may be suppressed as a result of punishment, it may not be permanently abolished.* An employee, for example, may be reprimanded for taking unauthorized work breaks. The behavior may stop, but only when the manager is present. As soon as the threat of punishment is removed from the situation, such as when the manager is no longer present, the breaks may occur once again.
2. *The person who administers punishment may end up being viewed negatively by others.* A manager who frequently punishes subordinates may find that he or she has an unpleasant effect on others, even when not administering punishment.
3. *Punishment may be offset by positive reinforcement received from another source.* A worker may be positively reinforced by peers for the same behavior that is punished by a supervisor. The positive value of such peer support may sometimes be strong enough that the individual puts up with the punishment while continuing to misbehave.

Does all of this mean you should never punish? No; the important things to remember are to do punishment selectively, and then to do it right. Consider the following case.

ILLUSTRATIVE CASE:
WAREHOUSE SAFETY

Peter Jones was employed as a forklift operator in a warehouse.[24] He was the highest-paid nonsupervisory employee in the firm, and his job was considered of high status. It took Pete 5½ years to work himself into the position. Unfortunately, he was prone to "show off" by unsafe driving that violated federal safety codes. Pete's supervisor chewed him out regularly, but the unsafe driving continued.

Finally, the supervisor analyzed the situation from a reinforcement perspective and tried to identify the environmental consequences associated with Pete's unsafe driving habits. As you may have predicted, the undesirable behavior was typically followed by laughter and special attention from the other warehouse workers.

The next time Pete was observed to drive unsafely, Pete's boss took him off the forklift truck and reassigned him to general warehousing duties for a period of time. When allowed back on the forklift,

Peter drove more safely. Finally, a true punishment had been found.

Guidelines for Punishment

The following guidelines should be followed by managers when using punishment as an OB Mod strategy.[25]

■ *Tell the individual what is being done wrong.* Clearly identify the undesirable behavior that is the reason for being punished.

■ *Tell the individual what is right.* Clearly identify the desirable behavior as a preferred alternative to the behavior that is being punished.

■ *Punish in private.* Avoid embarrassing people by punishing them in front of others.

■ *Follow the laws of contingent and immediate reinforcement.* Make sure the punishment is contingent on the undesirable behavior and timely.

■ *Make the punishment match the behavior.* Be fair in equating the magnitude of punishment with the degree to which the behavior is truly undesirable.

Punishment and Positive Reinforcement

Remember that punishment can also be combined with positive reinforcement. In the warehouse safety case, Pete should be positively reinforced in the future when observed to drive safely. He will then know exactly what is wrong and the unpleasant consequences associated with it, and know what is right and the pleasant consequences that may be associated with it. This combined strategy may help avoid the first problem of punishment identified earlier—having an undesirable behavior suppressed for awhile but not permanently abolished.

Accolades, Criticisms, and Value Dilemmas

You have now been introduced to reinforcement theory, its supporting concepts, and its possible work applications through the concept of OB Mod. Testimony to the potential payoffs associated with the use of reinforcement techniques in work settings incudes "success stories" from such corporations as General Electric, B. F. Goodrich, Michigan Bell, and Emery Air Freight among others. The reported results include improved safety, decreased absenteeism and tardiness, as well as higher productivity.[26] Critics argue that such positive results may be due only to the fact that specific performance goals were clarified, as in goal-setting theory, and workers held individually accountable for results.[27]

The history of reinforcement theory is also replete with debates over the ethics of controlling human behavior. From the manager's standpoint, there is concern that a use of operant conditioning principles ignores the individuality of people, restricts their freedom of choice, and ignores the fact that people can be motivated by other than externally administered rewards.

Advocates of the reinforcement orientation attack the problem straight on. They agree that it involves the control of behavior. But they argue that behavior control is an irrevocable part of every manager's job. Our view of managerial work is similar. It's inevitable that managers influence the behavior of other people. In fact, this influence must be done well if the manager's challenge is to be met successfully. The real question may be not whether it is ethical to control behavior, but whether it is ethical *not* to control behavior well enough that the goals of both the organization and the individual are well served. Thus even as research continues, the value of reinforcement techniques seems confirmed. This is especially true when they are combined with the insights of the other motivation theories discussed in this chapter.

MANAGING MOTIVATIONAL DYNAMICS

Broadly speaking, the motivational approaches discussed in this chapter address or seek to explain individual motivation to work from two alternative vantage points. The content and process theories take an internal view and try to understand individual needs and thought processes. Reinforcement theory takes an external view and focuses on the environmental consequences of behavior. As you might expect, current thinking pursues a balanced view that recognizes that the best explanation isn't limited to one or the other perspective, but represents some combination of both. Indeed, the tendency is to view motivation as the outcome of a complex process of **social learning,** that is, the learning achieved by people as they behave and interact with others in their social environment.[28] This suggests that people "learn" to work hard—or not—by responding to external rewards and reinforcements, by evaluating their experiences in re-

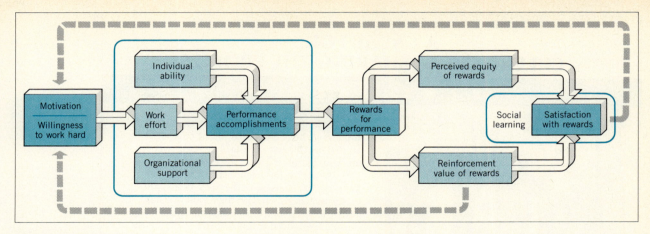

FIGURE 12.8 *Motivational dynamics: an integrated approach to individual motivation to work.*

spect to goals pursued and satisfaction achieved, and by observing what others are doing in the same situations.

An Integrated View of Motivation

Figure 12.8 integrates the logic of the content, process, and reinforcement theories into one model of individual motivation to work. This model builds on an integrative approach first advanced by Lyman Porter and Edward Lawler.[29] As shown in the large inner box of the figure, performance is influenced by individual ability, work effort, and organizational support. Of these three variables from the individual performance equation (first identified in Chapter 9), work effort is directly affected by an individual's level of motivation. Motivation derives from reinforcement, satisfaction, and social learning, and affects performance through its impact on someone's willingness to exert work efforts.

From a manager's perspective, the logic underlying this figure is straightforward. An important key to leading through motivation lies in the ability to reward people in a way that encourages them to work hard to accomplish assigned tasks. This "social learning" process begins with the selection of appropriate rewards. Here, the content theories can be used to better understand individual needs and the types of rewards that will be valued in response to them. The process continues with the manner in which rewards are distributed. Rewards allocated according to reinforcement principles and in a way

that is perceived as equitable should provide satisfaction with past performance, and increase motivation to perform well in the future. Before closing this chapter, let's apply this thinking to an important and special managerial concern.

Motivation and Compensation

Take a look at *Newsline 12.3*. It introduces some of the benefits and opportunities to be gained from truly motivational compensation schemes. In general, the success of any such scheme rests with its ability to tie pay to performance—and to do so in a positive and credible way. The link between motivation and compensation is forged when pay is allocated in a performance contingent and equitable manner. Among the applications to consider are merit pay, a variety of incentive compensation systems, and some additional creative pay practices.[30]

Merit Pay

Merit pay ties increases in base compensation to some measure of individual performance. It is perhaps the most common pay-for-performance system. For example,[31] employees are told:

at IBM employees are told: Merit-based pay and promotion are key components of IBM's merit system to reward superior performance. Employees directly influence their earnings through sustained or improved job performance. Job openings generally are filled by promotion from within. Advance-

A CAUSE FOR
CELEBRATION: SHARING THE PROFITS

N E W S L I N E 12.3

Each year in Bayport, Minnesota, all 3700 employees of Andersen Corporation, a leading maker of windows and doors, celebrate a happy event: the distributing of corporate profits. Last year, Andersen's chairman, Arvid Wellman, astonished everyone by announcing that profit-

sharing for the year would amount to over $105 million—a huge 84 percent of the company's annual payroll and a ten-fold increase over the amount distributed a decade earlier.

Andersen has been disbursing profits among its workers since the early 1900s. The company has grown with the recent housing construction boom, and some employees have never experienced troubled years at Andersen. But even in less ample times, the corporation has always distributed at least 10 percent of its profits. Its employees praise Andersen's management for its consistent sharing of the wealth and for listening to employees' ideas. Says one long-time worker: "It's always a fair factory. That's why everybody gives 100 percent." Adds his wife, also an Andersen employee: "I'd say it's the American dream."

Source: As reported in "Andersen Profits Have Workers Rejoicing," *Southern Illinoisian* (January 19, 1988), p. 14.

---

ment is based on the person's qualifications, job performance, the ability to accept additional responsibility and the availability of openings.

By allocating pay increases and other important rewards on a merit basis, managers hope to recognize high performers for their achievements, and encourage similar and even greater accomplishments in the future. Managers also hope to remind low performers of their lack of achievement and encourage them to do better in the future. Disagreements over performance evaluations and difficulties in giving meaningful differences in merit pay to persons performing at high versus low levels, however, often compromise the effectiveness of merit pay plans. One survey, for example, reports that only 28 percent of U.S. workers questioned in a national sample saw any clear tie between their work performance and the pay increase received. And even at IBM, traditions may be changing. A former director of sales compensation remarked,

"When we began to ask ourselves why Digital Equipment had salespeople who are tough competitors, on straight salary, we decided perhaps we'd gone overboard a bit."[32]

Incentive Compensation Systems

Many of the most exciting new developments move beyond the concept of merit pay. It has traditionally been the case, for example, that executives in many industries had access to special incentives in the form of bonuses, profit-sharing, and related schemes. What is especially exciting about current trends is that such incentive compensation plans aren't just for executives anymore. Employees at all levels in more and more organizations are benefiting from them. Some promising examples of incentive pay and reward systems follow.[33]

■ *Bonus pay plans* provide bonuses to employees based on the accomplishment of performance targets. Bonuses have traditionally been most common at the executive level, but they are now being used more extensively in many settings. At Nucor Corporation, production crews are divided into bonus groups consisting of 25–35 workers and their supervisors. Standards of performance are carefully defined, as for example to produce a certain tonnage of high quality steel in a day. Bonuses are earned by exceeding standards, and workers don't wait more than a week to receive them in their paychecks. This is the firm's attempt to keep them motivated. It works. Many Nucor employees double their pay through bonuses.

■ *Profit sharing plans* distribute to some or all employees a proportion of net profits earned during a stated performance period. The exact amount each individual receives varies according to the level of profits and his or her base compensation level. At Lincoln Electric the emphasis of profit sharing is on creating a loyal and highly motivated workforce that works hard as a team to achieve results. The company has remained profitable over the years while paying profit-sharing awards ranging from 20 percent to 120 percent of their base salaries.

■ *Gain sharing plans* extend the profit-sharing concept by allowing groups of employees to share in any savings or "gains" realized through their efforts to reduce costs and increase productivity. Specific formulas are used to calculate both the performance contributions and gain-sharing awards. A classic example is the *Scanlon Plan* which usually results in 75 percent of gains being distributed to workers and 25 percent being kept by the company. At Herman Miller, the Scanlon Plan involves everyone from the president to the salesperson to the newest production worker.

■ *Employee stock ownership plans* involve employees in ownership through the purchase of stock in the companies that employ them. While they can be used primarily as financing schemes, employee stock ownership plans can be important performance incentives. At Herman Miller again, 100 percent of full-time employees with at least two years of service in the company are stockholders. They buy the stock and thus participate in not only the rights but also the risks of ownership. In effect, stock ownership and the right to dividends creates another incentive to work hard to ensure that sufficient profits will be available for sharing in this manner.

Creative Pay Practices

Beyond the examples just given, other creative pay schemes are being tried in various settings. While different in approach, they share the objective of encouraging high performance through special compensation. For example, Honeywell and TRW, Inc. use **skills-based pay,** which pays workers according to the number of job-relevant skills they master. Such programs are often found in autonomous work groups where part of the "self-management" includes the training and certification of co-workers in job skills. Another new approach is **entrepreneurial pay** where individuals put part of their compensation at risk in return for the rights to pursue entrepreneurial ideas within the corporate umbrella and participate in any resulting profits. AT&T encourages new venture development through such a plan. Interested employees have contributed from 12–15 percent of their salaries for the opportunities to apply their efforts in this way, and in the prospect of future income gains.

Summary

A major part of any manager's leadership role is to enhance the willingness of people to exert work efforts to help accomplish organizational objectives. One approach to this goal is through the concept of motivation, a term defined as forces within the individual that account for the level, direction, and persistence of effort expended at work.

To help others experience a sense of motivation, part of a manager's leadership responsibility is to provide a work environment within which individual needs become satisfied through efforts that also serve organizational objectives. Major elements in any work environment are the extrinsic and intrinsic rewards made available to the individual in return for work contributions and accomplishments. Motivation theories offer insights to the manager who wishes to allocate rewards in such a way that individual needs are satisfied and high levels of task performance result.

Three types of motivation theories were reviewed—content, process, and reinforcement theories. Although the theories differ, each offers useful implications for management practice. They are most useful when integrated and applied through the comprehensive viewpoint just summarized. The management of motivational dynamics begins with an ability to identify and understand individual needs. The content theories of Maslow, Alderfer, and McClelland are helpful in this regard. The process theories of equity, expectancy, and goal-setting offer still further insight by helping us understand how people interpret various rewards and make decisions regarding the application of work efforts to achieve task goals. Equity theory introduces the important dynamic of social comparison in an individual's perceptions of rewards received for efforts contributed. Expectancy theory gives attention to how expectancies, instrumentalities, and valences affect motivation to work. Goal-setting theory identifies the motivational properties of well-set task goals. Finally, reinforcement theory offers ideas on how to administer rewards contingent on performance and with maximum positive impact on individual behavior.

Since we've relied on parables at points earlier in the chapter, let's close with one. The moral of this last story should now be quite clear.

A FINAL PARABLE

Once upon a time a farmer had six donkeys and a barn full of carrots, which she kept under lock and key. At the end of a day of wagon pulling, the farmer looked back over the day's performance of each donkey. To one of the donkeys she said, "You did an outstanding job; here are six carrots." To four of the others, she said, "Your performance was average; here are three carrots." To the remaining donkey she said, "You didn't pull your share of the load; here is one carrot."

Another day of wagon pulling dawned. The top donkey, having been properly rewarded, began the day in high spirits. The thoughts of the remaining donkeys were consumed with how they might earn more carrots through their efforts that day. The farmer had carrots available, but they had to be earned.

Thinking Through the Issues

1. What is "motivation" as the concept applies to people at work? Where does it fit into the individual performance equation? Will a highly motivated worker necessarily be a high performer? Why or why not?

2. What is the key difference between the content and process theories concerning their explanations of motivation to work?

3. Suppose you are a manager and find yourself with one group of subordinates who apparently seek higher-order need satisfactions at work, and another group that seems concerned only with lower-order needs. What would you do to help motivate each group of subordinates? Why?

4. Give an example of how the equity dynamic can adversely affect a person's performance on the job. What should a manager do to minimize these negative consequences?

5. Define three key terms in expectancy theory. How do they explain the level of motivation that a person may display at work?

6. Explain Locke's goal-setting theory. What are its managerial implications?

7. How does reinforcement theory explain individual behavior? What are the managerial implications of Thorndike's "law of effect"?

8. State four guidelines for positive reinforcement. Give an example of how each might apply in a work situation familiar to you.

9. How do merit pay plays try to increase individual motivation to work? What are some of the problems with them? Explain the motivational foundations of three incentive compensation systems of potential value in the workplace.

10. What is the managerial significance of the final parable?

The Manager's Vocabulary

Bonus pay plans
Comparable worth
Content theories
Continuous
  reinforcement
Deficit principle
Employee stock
  ownership plans
Entrepreneurial pay
Existence needs
Expectancy
Extinction
Extrinsic rewards
Gain sharing plans

Growth needs
Higher-order needs
Instrumentality
Intermittent
  reinforcement
Intrinsic rewards
Law of contingent
  reinforcement
Law of effect
Law of immediate
  reinforcement
Lower-order needs
Merit pay
Motivation

Motivation to work
Natural rewards
Need
Need for achievement
Need for affiliation
Need for power
Negative
  reinforcement
Operant conditioning
Organizational
  behavior
  modification
Positive reinforcement
Process theories

Profit sharing plans
Progression principle
Punishment
Reinforcement theory
Relatedness needs
Reward
Shaping
Skills-based pay
Social learning
Task goals
Valence

CORPORATE HUMANIST

C A R E E R   P E R S P E C T I V E

They used to refer sneeringly to Pillsbury Company's distribution department as the "elephant's graveyard."[34] The work was uninviting, just taking orders and shuffling invoices, they said. But all that was before Becky Roloff, 32, took over. Now, 30 or 40 people apply to join her department whenever a job vacancy occurs. What's the reason for her success? Roloff credits it to her "people skills." Her husband adds, "She believes that if you take care of people first, then you'll be taken care of too."

It's been over two years since Roloff took over as distribution director, and assumed responsibility for the work of 450 mostly uninspired people. After identifying that 25 percent or more of sales could be based on the company's record for timely and correct shipments, she redefined the department's task to be more vital to Pillsbury's corporate mission. Distribution became a sales support function rather than a freight expediting one, and workers' objectives were reformulated to emphasize service.

Roloff also rewarded her employees with recognition. She started a program in which people were to try and catch one another "in the act" of excellent performance. Someone who is "caught" gets a plaque and becomes part of another award program which can lead to their being brought to company headquarters as "king or queen for a day." About it all, a Pillsbury vice-president says this: "Becky has the ability to make people more productive than they would ever expect themselves to be."

Questions
1.   What is the motivational value of the redefined sense of mission Becky Roloff created for the distribution department? Do you feel its value would last even if Roloff gets promoted and someone else comes in to take her place? Explain your answer.
2.   What is the motivational value of the special recognition program Roloff also created? Can its positive effects last, even if she moves on? Explain your answer.
3.   What is the likelihood that you, like Roloff, can achieve managerial and leadership effectiveness by acting as a "people person"? Why?

Case Application

GENERAL MOTORS TIES PAY TO PERFORMANCE

When Ford Motor Company announced that its workers would be receiving about $3700 apiece from record corporate earnings in the prior year, General Motors was announcing that it wouldn't be paying profit-sharing bonuses to eligible hourly and salaried workers.[35] The reason given was poor earnings from GM's domestic vehicle operations, the group to which their profit-sharing is pegged. Yet about 5000 GM "executives" divided up about $157 million in stock awards. Their payouts were pegged to corporate-wide earnings, not just to the unprofitable North American automotive group.

Owen Beiber, president of the United Automobile Workers Union, reacted strongly. He called the executive bonuses, "an insult to common sense and fairness." He added: "In this context of hard times and weak performance at GM, we believe the executives should forgo all increases and supplementary awards in the spirit of shared sacrifice." GM Executive Vice-President Elmer W. Johnson, one who received a bonus, indicated that in the future things should be changed so that management bonuses like those of the hourly workers were tied to the performance of their specific units.

GM is trying to reform its incentive pay and compensation systems. One new program that GM hopes can make a difference provides for "special recognition awards" for salaried workers. This will allow high performers to receive special lump-sum payments for their achievements. Managers are also being encouraged to pass out immediate and "spontaneous" awards like theater tickets or trips in return for employee's great work or ideas.

The merit pay system of salaried workers is a target for change as well. In the past, merit raises for managers had become almost automatic. Just about everyone was rated as "superior" or "outstanding" at performance appraisal time. Now, "A merit increase . . . is something you have to earn," says the corporate vice-president for personnel. He adds that the company is taking on a new and "enlightened sensitivity" to the option of firing incompetent workers. "If you are a poor performer," he says, "we're going to work with you to try and make you a better performer. If you cannot do that over time, we'll have to ask you to leave the team."

Questions

1. What is your evaluation of the "motivational properties" of GM's profit-sharing plan for its executives? . . . hourly and salaried workers? Explain your analysis using insights from one or more of the motivation theories discussed in this chapter.
2. What is the "motivational" value of GM's new "special recognition awards" program as viewed from the perspective of reinforcement theory? What recommendations can you offer based on the theory that would help make the program truly valuable? Why?
3. How do you think GM's managerial workers will respond to the changes in their merit pay system? Will the changes be motivating or not? . . . and, if so, to whom in particular—the high performers, low performers, or both?
4. Overall, do you think the proposed changes in GM's incentive compensation scheme will significantly improve the company's performance? Explain your answer.

Class Exercise: What Motivates You?

1. Here is a list of 15 things which people sometimes find important in helping to motivate them to do their best work for their organizations. Read the list of items and think which ones best apply to you.

- having job security
- respect for me as a person
- knowing I'm responsible for things
- good pay
- good working conditions
- getting along with co-workers
- chance to get promoted
- opportunity to do interesting work
- working under close supervision
- knowing what's going on in the organization
- being complimented by my boss for good work
- having a competent supervisor
- opportunity for self-development

- good fringe benefits
- feeling my job is important

2. Go back and select the *five* items from the prior list that you personally find most important in motivating you to do your best work.

3. Share your list with a nearby classmate, and explain to him or her the specific work setting to which your thoughts applied. Examine with the classmate what the items might suggest about the

"needs" which are important for you to fulfill at work. Do the same for your classmate's list.

4. Consider whether or not others in the class as a whole will have selected the same items. Why might they choose different sources of motivation than you did? Be prepared to answer this question and others in general class discussion led by your instructor.

References

[1]Dana is discussed in Thomas J. Peters and Robert H. Waterman, Jr., *In Search of Excellence* (New York: Warner Books, 1982); information on Nucor Corporation from John A. Savage, "Growth and Success through Employee Involvement," Nucor corporate document, undated.

[2]Information from "Wake Up Call," *Inc.* (May 1988), p. 110; and, Tom Peters, "Letter to the Editor," *Inc.* (April 1988), pp. 80–82.

[3]For a research perspective see Edward Deci, *Intrinsic Motivation* (New York: Plenum, 1975); and, Edward E. Lawler III, "The Design of Effective Reward Systems," pp. 255–271, in Jay W. Lorsch (ed.), *Handbook of Organizational Behavior* (Englewood Cliffs, NJ: Prentice-Hall, 1987). A practical perspective on this issue is also found in Peters, op. cit., 1988.

[4]Michael Maccoby's book *Why Work: Leading the New Generation* (New York: Simon & Schuster, 1988) deals extensively with this point of view.

[5]This and subsequent parables are adapted from Dale McConkey, "The 'Jackass Effect' in Management Compensation," *Business Horizons,* Vol. 17 (June 1974), pp. 81–91. Copyright 1974 by the Foundation for the School of Business at Indiana University. Used by permission.

[6]Portions of this chapter originally adapted from John R. Schermerhorn, Jr., James G. Hunt, and Richard N. Osborn, *Managing Organizational Behavior* (New York: Wiley, 1982), pp. 107–126, 138–156. Used by permission.

[7]See Abraham H. Maslow, *Eupsychian Management* (Homewood, IL: Richard D. Irwin, 1965); Abraham H. Maslow, *Motivation and Personality,* Second Edition (New York: Harper & Row, 1970).

[8]See Clayton P. Alderfer, *Existence, Relatedness, and Growth* (New York: Free Press, 1972).

[9]For a collection of McClelland's work see David C. McClelland, *The Achieving Society* (New York: Van Nostrand, 1961); "Business Drive and National Achieve-

ment," *Harvard Business Review,* Vol. 40 (July–August 1962), pp. 99–112; David C. McClelland and David H. Burnham, "Power is the Great Motivator," *Harvard Business Review,* Vol. 54 (March–April 1976), pp. 100–110; and, David C. McClelland, *Human Motivation* (Glenview, Il.: Scott, Foresman, 1985).

[10]McClelland, op. cit., 1985, devotes a separate chapter to each need. For a good discussion of the research see Martin L. Maehr and Larry A. Braskamp, *The Motivation Factor: A Theory of Personal Investment* (Lexington, MA: Lexington Books, 1986), pp. 18–26.

[11]David C. McClelland and Richard E. Boyatsis, "The Leadership Motive Pattern and Long Term Success in Management," *Journal of Applied Psychology,* Vol. 67 (1982), pp. 737–743.

[12]McClelland and Burnham, op cit.

[13]Developed from Edward E. Lawler, III, *Motivation in Work Organizations* (Monterey, Cal.: Brooks/Cole Publishing, 1973), pp. 30–36.

[14]See, for example, J. Stacy Adams, "Toward an Understanding of Inequity," *Journal of Abnormal and Social Psychology,* Vol. 67 (1963), pp. 422–436; J. Stacy Adams, "Inequity in Social Exchange," in L. Berkowitz (ed.), *Advances in Experimental Social Psychology,* Vol. 2 (New York: Academic Press, 1965), pp. 267–300.

[15]Victor H. Vroom, *Work and Motivaton* (New York: Wiley, 1964).

[16]The work on goal-setting theory is well summarized in Edwin A. Locke and Gary P. Latham, *Goal Setting: A Motivational Technique that Works!* (Englewood Cliffs, NJ: Prentice-Hall, 1984). See also Edwin A. Locke, Kenneth N. Shaw, Lisa A. Saari, and Gary P. Latham, "Goal Setting and Task Performance 1969–1980," *Psychological Bulletin,* Vol. 90 (1981), pp. 125–152; and, Mark E. Tubbs, "Goal Setting: A Meta-Analytic Examination of the Empirical Evidence," *Journal of Applied Psychology,* Vol. 71 (1986), pp. 474–483.

[17]Deci, op. cit., pp. 7–8.

[18]E. L. Thorndike, *Animal Intelligence* (New York: Macmillan, 1911), p. 244.

[19]See B. F. Skinner, *Walden Two* (New York: Macmillan, 1948); *Science and Human Behavior* (New York: Macmillan, 1953); *Contingencies of Reinforcement* (New York: Appleton-Century-Crofts, 1969).

[20]OB Mod is clearly explained in Fred Luthans and Robert Kreitner, *Organizational Behavior Modification* (Glenview, IL: Scott, Foresman, 1975); and, Fred Luthans and Robert Kreitner, *Organizational Behavior Modification and Beyond* (Glenview, IL: Scott, Foresman, 1985).

[21]Keith L. Miller, *Principles of Everyday Behavior Analysis* (Monterey, Cal.: Brooks/Cole Publishing, 1975), p. 122.

[22]This case is reported in Harry Wiard, "Why Manage Behavior? A Case for Positive Reinforcement," *Human Resource Management* (Summer 1972), pp. 15–20.

[23]Developed from W. Clay Hamner, "Using Reinforcement Theory in Organizational Settings," in Henry L. Tosi and W. Clay Hamner (eds.), *Organizational Behavior and Management: A Contingency Approach* (Chicago: St. Clair Press, 1977), pp. 388–395.

[24]This example is from Luthans and Kreitner, op. cit., pp. 127–129.

[25]Developed from Luthans and Kreitner, op. cit., 1973; and Hamner, op. cit.

[26]For a good review see Lee W. Frederickson (ed.), *Handbook of Organizational Behavior Management* (New York: Wiley-Interscience, 1982).

[27]Edwin A. Locke, "The Myths of Behavior Mod in Organizations," *Academy of Management Review,* Vol. 2 (October 1977), pp. 543–553.

[28]The social learning perspective is described by Luthans and Kreitner, op. cit., 1985.

[29]Lyman W. Porter and Edward E. Lawler III, *Managerial Attitudes and Performance* (Homewood, IL: Richard D. Irwin), 1968.

[30]For an excellent discussion of compensation and performance see Rosabeth Moss Kanter, "The Attack on Pay," *Harvard Business Review,* Vol. 65 (March–April 1987), pp. 60–67.

[31]*IBM . . . Yesterday and Today* (Armonk, NY: IBM Corporation, undated), p. 3.

[32]The quote is from Kanter, op. cit., p. 63. The survey is reported by *The Wall Street Journal* (February 8, 1988), p. 1.

[33]These examples are reported in Max De Pree, "Theory Fastball," *New Management,* Vol. 1 (1984), pp. 29–34; Bruce G. Posner, "Pay for Profits," *Inc.* (September 1986), pp. 57–60; Kanter, op. cit., 1987; and, John Grossman, "Ken Iverson: Simply the Best," *American Way* (August 1, 1987), pp. 23–25.

[34]Information from "Fast-Track Kids," *Business Week* (November 10, 1986), pp. 90–104.

[35]Information from "GM 'Recognition Awards' Set for Salaried Workers," *The Wall Street Journal* (December 14, 1987), p. 14; Jacob M. Schlesinger, "GM's New Compensation Plan Reflects General Trend Tying Pay to Performance," *The Wall Street Journal* (January 26, 1988), p. 33; "Ford Workers to Get Profit-Sharing Checks That Average $3700," *The Wall Street Journal* (February 2, 1988), p. 22; and, Jacob M. Schlesinger, "GM Officials Get Short-Term Incentives Despite Plan to Emphasize Long Term," *The Wall Street Journal* (April 18, 1988), p. 4.

Leading
Through Group
Dynamics

Meetings
Are Here to Stay

Poorly run meetings are the bane of corporate existence—and an unfortunately common occurrence. Senior executives report spending an average of 23 hours a week in them; middle managers spend 11. Only a bit more than 50 percent of the meetings are rated as productive. Yet despite the frustration that they often evoke, meetings serve a vital purpose in the life of an organization. Likeable or not—meetings are here to stay.

A meeting defines the work group; allows a group to refine or add to what it knows; and lets the individual understand the group's aims and how his or her efforts contribute to those aims. Meetings also encourage individuals to commit to the decisions taken by the group. These are functions that even highly sophisticated telecommunications simply cannot undertake to equal effect; they hinge completely on human interaction.

Often, a meeting is the only place where the group really exists and takes action as a group, not just as separate individuals—and where the leader acts as a real guide, not just another member of the team. Meetings must also be seen as status arenas, where individuals play out concerns relating to the pecking order and display particular kinds of "arena behavior."

Consultant and author Anthony Jay believes that a meeting leader's self-indulgence is the largest obstacle to success in most meet-ings. The role of the leader is to clarify the issues at hand and guide participants toward a set of shared objectives. The result of a productive meeting, he claims, should be the affirmation of the "will of the meeting" by everyone present—even if that affirmation has been preceded by heated discussion and disagreement. In fact, a conflict of ideas is desirable, although a clash of personalities is not. The meeting leader must encourage what Jay calls "a cross-flow of discussion and debate," occasionally intervening by "mostly letting the others thrash ideas out." In the best cases, not just information and opinion but also creative suggestions are the result of this give-and-take—and as Jay points out, suggestions "contain the seeds of future success."

Consensus does not come easily in many meetings. Cost-conscious managers are increasingly unafraid to remind participants that side-tracked discussions or forays into irrelevance can get expensive. "Let's move on" is the familiar refrain of meeting leaders with their eyes on the clock, the agenda, and the bottom line. ■

Source: Information from Antony Jay, "How to Run a Meeting," *Harvard Business Review* (March–April 1976), pp. 43–57; "Making the Most Out of Meetings," *Business Week* (July 13, 1987), p. 120; and, "They're in a Meeting," *The Wall Street Journal* (June 21, 1988), p. 33.

Individuals and groups are the human-resource foundations of organizations. Up to this point in our discussion of leadership, we have focused mainly on the individual. Now it is time to study individuals as they act collectively in the form of groups. The term *group* causes both positive and negative reactions in the minds of most people. Although it is said that "two heads are better than one," we are also warned that "too many cooks spoil the broth." "A camel is a horse put together by a committee," admonishes the true group skeptic.

Against this somewhat humorous background lies a most important point. Groups offer advantages and disadvantages for their members and for the organizations in which they exist. As far back as the historic Hawthorne studies, discussed in Chapter 2, researchers have noted that employees can develop strong group attachments and that these attachments may prove functional or dysfunctional for the organization. The purpose of this chapter is to examine the dynamics of group behavior in work settings and establish their leadership implications for managers.[1] Said a bit differently, this chapter should help you answer the question: What can managers do to facilitate high productivity by groups?

TYPES OF GROUPS IN ORGANIZATIONS

Suppose there is a street-side demonstration and you join a number of other people gathered to watch. Or suppose you are among several persons waiting for an elevator. Are these "groups"? No, they are not, at least in the way most social scientists define the term. A **group** is a collection of people who regularly interact with one another over time and in respect to the pursuit of one or more common goals. The key elements in this definition are interaction, time, and common goals. Neither the people watching the demonstration nor those waiting for the elevator meet all of these requirements. At best they are aggregations or collections of people.

Groups appear in various forms within the organization. Three of these forms—formal groups, informal groups, and psychological groups—are especially important to you as a manager.

Formal Groups

A **formal group** is created by formal authority to perform one or more tasks that support the accomplishment of organizational objectives. They function as small subsystems operating within the context of the larger organization. In this regard, each formal group is expected to transform resource inputs (such as ideas, materials, and objects) into product or service outputs (such as a report, decision, service, or commodity) of some value to the organization. Formal groups in organizations include various types of command or functional groups, committees and task forces, autonomous work groups, worker involvement groups, and electronic group networks, among others.

Command or Functional Groups

Formal work groups in the form of **command groups** or **functional groups** consist of managers and their immediate subordinates. They are important structural features of organizations and often appear on organization charts as departments (e.g., market research department), divisions (e.g., office products division), or units (e.g., public relations unit). Indeed, it is appropriate to view organizations as interlocking networks of work groups as shown in Figure 13.1. Rensis Likert, a noted management scholar, identifies an important "linking pin" role served by managers in this respect.[2] Because each manager acts as a superior in one work group and a subordinate in another at the next higher level, the resulting "networks" help to integrate groups throughout the organization. In this way, the command or functional group becomes a basic building block of organization structures.

Committees and Task Forces

Other formal groups are created to supplement the work of command or functional groups. Two examples are **committees** and **task forces**, both of which bring people together to apply their collective efforts toward a specific purpose, and sometimes with the expectation of disbanding when that purpose is accomplished. Most committees and task forces operate with specific task agendas and are headed by a designated chairperson or leader who is held accountable for results. For example,

at Ford Motor Company the board of directors has organized itself into several "standing" committees to facilitate their work on selected issues. As shown in Figure 13.2, these committees address a range of important issues, and each is headed by a "chair."

Consider, too, this situation once faced by a national company as its managers struggled to develop an appropriate personnel policy.[3]

> With offices across the country, the company offers starting salaries that vary from place to place. Management is concerned about possible inequities in gauging the cost of living and measuring the labor supply and demand in each location. This problem affects more than one department, and no single person can handle it. The issues need to be carefully explored before making recommendations, and the plan will require a broad base of support for implementation.

This problem calls for a task force, a temporary group that can solve the problem and make appropriate recommendations to top management. To ensure good results, any task force must be carefully established and then monitored for its progress. Some basic task force management guidelines follow.

1. *Select appropriate task-force members.* Select members who will be challenged by the assignment, who have a vested interest in the result, and whose skills and views complement one another.
2. *Clearly define the purpose and goal(s) of the task*

FIGURE 13.1 *The organization as an interlocking network of formal work groups.*

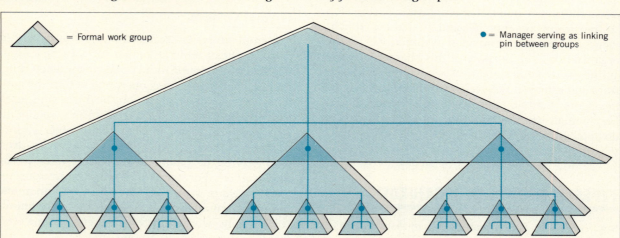

= Formal work group

● = Manager serving as linking pin between groups

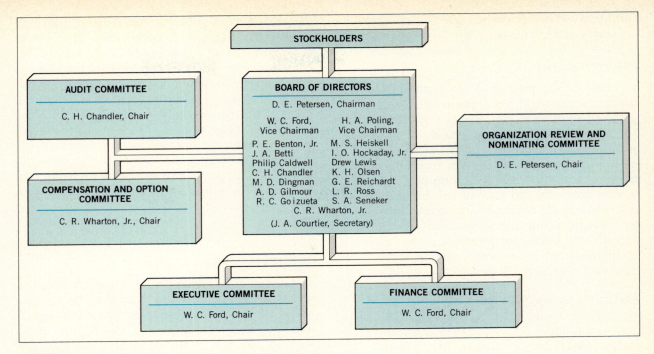

FIGURE 13.2 *Committees in organizations: the case of Ford Motor Company's Board of Directors.*

force. Make sure task-force members and important outsiders know what is expected, why, and on what timetable.

3. *Carefully select the person who will serve as task-force leader.* Make sure this person has appropriate interpersonal skills, can respect the ideas of others, is and will remain prepared for the work that needs to be done.

4. *Periodically review progress.* Make sure task-force members feel a sense of accountability for results, review progress at regular intervals, and provide performance feedback.

Autonomous Work Groups

At many points so far in this book, however, we have noted that the nature of organizations is changing in today's society. An important part of this change is a diminishing emphasis on "command" groups in some organizations, and an increasing use of what we called the **autonomous work group** in Chapter 8. These self-managing work teams emphasize participative decision making, shared tasks, and worker responsibility for many tasks performed by supervisors in more traditional command groups. In such cases, the autonomous work group usually reports to higher management through a "team leader" rather than formal supervisor.

Worker Involvement Groups

Many new and creative developments in today's organizations are taking place in respect to **worker involvement groups** of various types. These are groups or teams of workers brought together to focus the expertise and commitments of members on specific and important workplace issues. Here are two cases in point.[4]

At Phillipps Corporation the Ohio-based building materials producer uses them in a "how-we-can-save-money" program.[4] The program allows groups of five employees to work together for a week to improve Phillipps products and help cut costs. Over 150 teams a year choose to do this. And Bill Roberts, a company vice-president, says that no team effort has yet failed to come up with some savings.

At Averett Express a Tennessee trucking firm, the focus is on "productivity improvement." After the company's 1400 workers were organized into involvement groups of three to ten members, each to focus on the issue, sales shot up 38 percent and earnings by 48 percent. When asked how the groups are managed, the CEO said: "We just play the coach . . . lot's of feedback, lots of encouragement; our people do the rest."

One of the most common forms of worker involvement groups is the **quality circle,** a small group of employees who meet periodically to discuss ways of improving the quality of their task performance. Usually this consists of six to 12 volunteers from a work area. After receiving special training in problem solving, group processes, and quality issues, they try to come up with suggestions that management can implement to raise productivity through quality improvements.[5] This popular approach to worker involvement groups is illustrated by example later in this chapter, and will be discussed in detail in Chapter 16.

Electronic Group Networks

Newsline 13.1 introduces a new form of group that is increasingly common in today's organizations—the **electronic group network.** This is a group in which people interact through electronic computer-based communications rather than face-to-face, in the pursuit of a common purpose. In Chapter 15 on "management information systems" we will examine both *local-area networks* which link computers in offices or buildings close to one another, and *wide-area networks* which link computers across large geographical distances. We will also discuss *group decision support systems* with software which overcomes barriers of space and time to further facilitate group decision making and collaboration. These technologies allow for the formation of new electronic group networks in which people can communicate with one another and solve problems without having to physically be together in the same place. However, the "electronic" groups may encounter problems of their own, particularly when relationships become increasingly depersonalized and traditional advantages of direct interaction among group members are lost.[6] At the very least, their increasing presence will add further complexity to the changing nature of organizations in contemporary society. Here is example of a company that is investing heavily in this new group opportunity.[7]

At Digital Equipment Corporation the firm considers itself to be the best networked company in the world. Using a system of its own design, Easynet, about 60% of DEC's employees have access to a network spanning operations in 26 countries. The emphasis is on "lateral networking" to form teams which share information, help solve problems, and generally speed up operations. For example, teams made up of engineers located in different countries network over Easynet to exchange information, circuit diagrams and software; engineers also team up with sales, marketing and manufacturing people to gain peer support for proposed new products and projects. At present, Easynet costs DEC about $40 million per year.

Informal Groups

In Chapter 6 we discussed the informal structure that exists as a companion or "shadow" to the formal structure of an organization. Just as the organization's formal structure may be viewed as an interlocking network of formal groups, so may the informal structure be viewed as an interlocking network of **informal groups.** These groups emerge within organizations without being formally designated by someone in authority for a performance purpose. They are found as **interest groups** in which workers band together to advance a common cause or special position, such as a concern for poor working conditions. They are also found as **friendship groups** that spontaneously develop within and across formal groups for a wide variety of personal reasons. It is through these groups that the informal channels of communication are set in organizations. Increasingly, opportunities for computer networking are adding a new dimension to such communications.

There are reasons why informal interest and friendship groups emerge. First, they help people in their jobs. Informal groups offer a network of interpersonal relationships with the potential to "speed up" the work flow or "get things done" in ways that the formal structure fails to provide. Second, they can help individuals to satisfy needs that are thwarted or left unmet by formal group affiliations. Among the things informal groups provide their members are:

- *Social satisfactions* Opportunities for friendships and pleasing social relationships on the job.
- *Security* Opportunities to find sympathy for

GROUPWARE
GETS WORKERS TOGETHER

"G"roupware" is what they are calling the latest advance in programming for personal computers. While the technology for linking individual personal computers together—networks—has been around for years, the available software has been designed for people working individually.

Groupware is specifically designed to enhance teamwork on a project. Up to now companies have used computer networks primarily for sending electronic mail. Groupware enables users to move beyond paper creation to paper manipulation. Rather than having a single user produce reports, crunch numbers, and manage all the details of a project in isolation, these new groupware programs enable workers on a network to actively share their work.

Lotus Corporation, developer of the best selling business program in the world, 1-2-3, has announced that it will be introducing a groupware program called Notes. The program is designed to enable workers who have their PCs connected through networks to work together on such things as planning meetings, sharing comments, and tracking project status.

Analysts already expect many advantages from this new technology. Project managers will be able to get input from fellow workers so that all contributions are shown and credited immediately. The time and money saved by eliminating duplicate work could be enormous. With the ability to bring people together to work as a team, groupware represents an important productivity enhancement tool.

Source: As reported in "New Software Helps PC Users Work as Groups," *Wall Street Journal* (February 24, 1988), p. 25; and, Louis S. Richman, "Software Catches the Team Spirit," *Fortune* (June 8, 1987), pp. 125–136.

---

one's feelings and actions, especially as they relate to friction with the formal organization

■ *Support* Opportunities to find help or task assistance from persons other than one's superior.

■ *Identification* Opportunities to achieve a sense of belonging by affiliating with persons who share similar values, attitudes, and goals.

Informal groups are inevitable in organizations, and they often have leaders. Instead of acting in fear of informal groups that may exist in their areas of responsibility, managers should try to understand them, and get to know the influential informal leaders. Given this foundation, informal groups can often be included in an overall management strategy and thereby serve to the organizations's net advantage, not disadvantage.

Psychological Groups

There is another useful perspective on groups in organizations. Some groups are **psychological groups** in the sense that group members are truly aware of one another's needs and potential resource contributions, and achieve high levels of interaction and mutual identification in pursuit of the common purpose.[6] Just as we noted that not all aggregations of people are groups, not all groups are psychological groups. Most informal groups qualify as psychological groups, but many formal groups do not. Just because people are assigned to work together in the same department, for example, does not mean that they actively share and work toward common goals. Managers often wish that their formal work groups would act as psychological groups. Our study of group behavior in organizations should aid you, as a manager and leader, to help your groups make this transition.

USEFULNESS OF GROUPS IN ORGANIZATONS

Figure 13.3 uses the example of a staff auditor to identify some of the ways in which managers get involved with different types of groups. Any manager is likely to serve in many groups at the same time. Consistent with Likert's "linking pin" model, for example, a manager will serve as a supervisor in charge of one command group and as a subordinate in a higher-level one. In respect to temporary task groups, a manager might be the designated head of some committees while serving as a regular member on others. These formal group assignments, in turn, are separate from any informal groups to which the manager may belong. In all cases, managers should be concerned to help make groups function as well as possible.

Group Synergy and Task Accomplishment

The fact of the matter is that many tasks are beyond the capabilities of one person alone. Groups are essential human resources of organizations, and "synergy" is a major benefit that groups can bring to the work setting. **Synergy,** you should recall, is the creation of a whole that is greater than the sum of its parts. When synergy occurs in groups, they accomplish more than the sum total of their members' individual capabilities.

Simply put, groups can be very good for organizations and their members. Groups can make important task contributions to organizational objectives, and they can influence individual work attitudes and behaviors. Among other things, groups can:[9]

- Increase resources for problem solving.
- Promote innovation and creativity.
- Improve quality of decision making.
- Enhance members' commitments to tasks.
- Offer motivation through collective action.
- Control and discipline members.
- Help offset effects of large organization size.

ILLUSTRATIVE CASE: QUALITY CIRCLES AND MANAGEMENT COUNCILS AT AT&T

AT&T's Reading Works is in the business of innovation.[10] Its mission is to manufacture a variety of integrated circuits and electronic devices for company products. But one development at the Pennsylvania plant is neither chip, nor circuit, nor gated diode. It's a participative management process that is helping the factory increase productivity. That accomplishment made the factory's former general manager Mike Turk (now a vice president of manufacturing) something of a hero to his co-workers. But to hear him tell it, the real heroes of this effort in participative decision making are Reading's employees—all 4500 of them. "If people aren't actively and enthusiastically plugged into a management system in which participation and involvement are requisite, it can't work," Turk says.

Central to the Reading-style of participatory management are Reading's "quality circles" made up of nonmanagement volunteers. Members meet once a week to identify, analyze, and solve any problems they perceive as hampering or restricting effective job performance. Utility operator Dottie Hanson, a member of the tool-room quality circle, says: "Before I got involved with the circle, if I noticed a problem I'd think, 'That's wrong; why don't *they* fix it?' But now, working with the circle, I know there's no such thing as 1-2-3 and it's fixed. I've seen, first-hand, the dedication and work it takes to solve even the simplest problems. I have a lot of respect for the people in the quality circles and . . . I also like the fact that, through the circle, management is saying that when it comes to doing my job, I'm the expert, and my ideas are valuable."

Two "management councils" are also involved in the participative process. One includes all levels of management from the engineering community; the other consists of management employees from operating, administrative, and trades departments. These councils, like the quality circles, meet separately once a week; when issues overlap, a joint meeting is held. Except for the joint meetings, there are no written agendas. No attendance records are taken, because serving on a council is strictly voluntary. Members form project teams, based on employees' particular interests, and bring their recommendations back for a final decision and

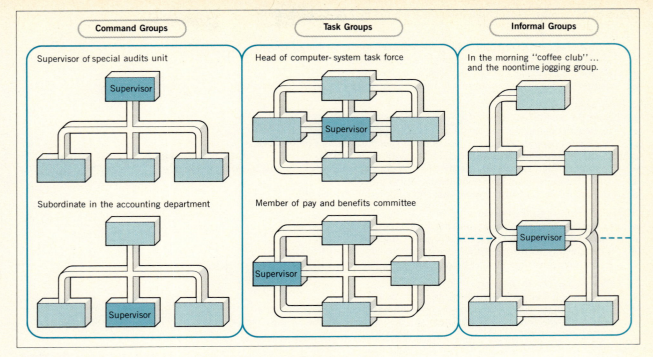

| Command Groups | Task Groups | Informal Groups |

Supervisor of special audits unit

Supervisor

Subordinate in the accounting department

Supervisor

Head of computer-system task force

Supervisor

Member of pay and benefits committee

Supervisor

In the morning "coffee club"... and the noontime jogging group.

Supervisor

FIGURE 13.3 *Formal and informal group involvements of managers: The case of the staff auditor.*

implementation. There are no sacred cows; any subject is fair game for discussion and possible action. Decisions are reached by consensus. The plant manager acts as a facilitator to keep the meetings running smoothly. But while this may sound idyllic, it isn't. "Management by participation is an exacting, hard-nosed system that demands both hard work and thoroughness," says Turk. "When you present a proposal to the council for action, you'd better have done your homework. People don't roll over and say, 'What a great idea!' They fire questions at you. No way is participative management a permissive system; in many ways, it's more demanding than traditional management."

UNDERSTANDING GROUPS IN ORGANIZATIONS

Even though groups often prove superior to individuals in solving problems and accomplishing tasks, you are surely aware of their potential disadvantages as well. Who hasn't encountered "free-riders," the

people who slack off because responsibility is diffused in groups and others are present to do the work? And who hasn't heard comments like these from people heading off to attend what they would call "just another 'time wasting' meeting"?

"Wonder what we are going to do today?"
"Here we go again, another hour down the drain."
"I wonder if Joe will dominate this meeting too?"
"Heck, I don't remember what we did at the last one."

The guidelines in Table 13.1 suggest, however, things don't have to be this way. Meetings and the people who attend them can be well managed. In fact they must be if groups in the many forms just identified are to achieve synergy and make important contributions to organizations. This requires a basic understanding of the complex nature of groups and group dynamics. The first part of a manager's job in dealing with groups is knowing *when* a group is the best choice for applying human resources to a task. The second is to know *how* to work with and manage the group to best accomplish that task.

TABLE 13.1 *Management Guidelines for Conducting Effective Meetings*

I. *Preparing for the meeting*
- Define the purpose and objectives to be achieved by the meeting.
- Prepare an agenda that addresses highest priority items first.
- Distribute the agenda to members *before* the meeting.
- Gather needed information, and consider the major issues *before* the meeting.

II. *Running the meeting*
- Start the meeting on time.
- Review the objectives and agenda, and clarify priorities.
- Stick to the agenda as much as possible, and keep the discussion on track.
- Clarify who is to do what by when for any action decided on.
- Summarize agreements and clarify what happens next *before* closing the meeting.
- Close the meeting no later than the scheduled time.
- Document the meeting by reviewing and completing written notes.

III. *Dealing with difficult members*
- Listen, but don't get into arguments during the meeting.
- Speak with the person privately at another time.
- Look for ways to turn negative behavior into positive contributions.
- Encourage other members to help handle the difficult person.

IV. *Following-up after the meeting*
- Distribute informative written minutes in a timely fashion.
- Stay in contact with members to encourage completion of assigned tasks.
- Add unfinished business and new ideas to the tentative agenda for the next meeting.

Source: Developed from James A. Ware, "A Note on How to Run a Meeting" (Boston, MA: Intercollegiate Case Clearing House, 1977); and, Mike M. Milstein, "Toward More Effective Meetings," in Leonard D. Goodstein and J. William Pfeiffer (eds.), *The 1983 Handbook for Facilitators, Trainers, and Consultants* (San Diego, CA: University Associates, 1983).

Group Effectiveness

Task performance and member satisfaction are two key results of group activity. In the group context, satisfaction relates to the broader concept of **human resource maintenance,** an ability of the group to maintain its social fabric and the capabilities of its members to work well together over time. High member satisfaction suggests a greater capability for human-resource maintenance in a group. An **effective group** can therefore be defined as one that achieves and maintains high levels of *both* task performance and human resource maintenance over time.

The Group as an Open System

Ideally, every manager and group member should work hard to promote group effectiveness. This requires an ability to understand and influence many variables with the potential to affect group behavior. Figure 13.4 portrays the group as an open system that transforms various inputs into the two key outputs—task performance and human resource maintenance—which are ultimate criteria of group effectiveness.

A group's ability to be effective depends, in part, on the strength of its **group process**—the way members work together to transform resource inputs into group outputs. This includes the way members communicate with one another, make decisions, and handle conflicts.

Another important influence on group effectiveness is the nature of the inputs themselves. Even the most positive group process will fail to yield effective results when inputs are inadequate. Among the input factors with the potential to influence group effectiveness are:[11]

- *Organizational setting* affects the degree to which members are able to relate to one another and apply skills toward task accomplishment. A key issue is the amount of support provided by such things as material resources, technology, spatial arrangements and the physical setting, surrounding organization structures, and the available rewards.
- *Nature of the task* affects how well the group can focus its efforts and how intense the group process needs to be. Clearly defined tasks allow for

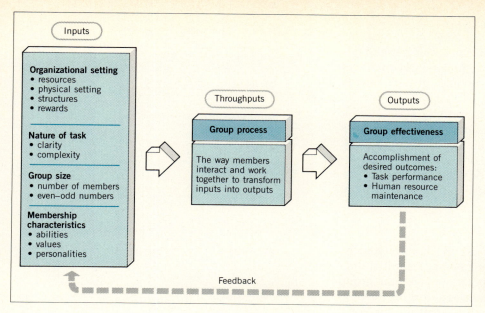

FIGURE 13.4 *The work group as open system: group inputs, throughputs, and outputs.*

better direction of effort than ill-defined ones. Complex tasks require more information exchange and processing than do simpler tasks. Complex tasks thus demand a more intense process, but may result in greater member satisfaction.

- *Group size* affects the ability of members to work well together, handle disagreements, and reach agreements. The number of potential interactions increases geometrically as groups increase in size, and communications become more restricted. Groups larger than about six to seven members are difficult to manage for creative problem solving. Odd numbered groups are often preferred because there cannot be a tie in case voting is required.

- *Membership characteristics* affect the competencies available to perform the group task and the ability of members to work well together for task accomplishment. While heterogeneity in the mix of individual skills, values, and personalities broadens the resource base of the group, it also adds complexity to the group process.

Stages of Group Development

Because the behavior patterns of newly formed groups can be different from mature ones, it is helpful for you to be able to recognize the stage of development of groups in which you participate. Armed with this knowledge, you should be better able to predict what is likely to occur and take action to improve group functioning. A synthesis of the research on small groups suggests that there are four distinct phases of group development: (1) forming, (2) storming, (3) initial integration, and (4) total integration.[12]

Forming Stage

The forming stage involves the initial entry of individual members into a group. At this point individuals ask a number of questions including: "What can or does the group offer me?" "What will I be asked to contribute?" "Can my needs be met while my efforts serve the task needs of the group?"

In the forming stage, people begin to identify with other members and the group itself. They are concerned to establish interpersonal relationships, discover what is considered acceptable behavior, and learn what the real task of the group is. This identification process can be especially complicated in a work group. Such things as prior experience with group members in other contexts, and individual impressions of organization philosophies, goals, and policies may affect how well members come together in newly formed work groups.

Storming Stage

The storming stage of group development is a period of high emotionality. Tension often emerges among members, and there may be periods of hostility and infighting. Coalitions or cliques may form as subgroups emerge. Conflict may develop as individuals compete to impose their preferences on others and become influential in the group's status structure.

Changes occur in the storming stage as task activities are further elaborated, and attention shifts toward obstacles standing in the way of group goals. Members begin to clarify one another's interpersonal styles. Efforts are made to find ways to accomplish group goals while also satisfying individual needs.

Initial Integration

Whereas the storming phase is characterized by differences among group members, the initial integration stage stresses cooperation. Here, the group begins to become coordinated as a working unit and has a clear sense of leadership. Most interpersonal hostilities give way to a precarious balancing of forces.

During initial integration, harmony is emphasized and minority viewpoints may be discouraged. Members are likely to develop an initial sense of closeness, a division of labor, and a sense of shared expectations. All this is designed to protect the group from disintegration. Holding the group together may become more important at this stage than successful task accomplishment.

Total Integration

Total integration characterizes a mature, organized, and well-functioning group. The group is able to deal with complex tasks and to handle conflicts in creative ways. Group structure is stable, and members are motivated by group goals. The primary challenges of this stage are to continue working together as an integrated unit, to remain coordinated with the larger organization, and to adapt successfully to changing conditions over time. A group that has achieved total integration will score high on the criteria of group maturity presented in Figure 13.5.

Group Dynamics

Group dynamics are forces operating in groups that affect task performance and membership satisfaction. When they fail in any way, group effective-

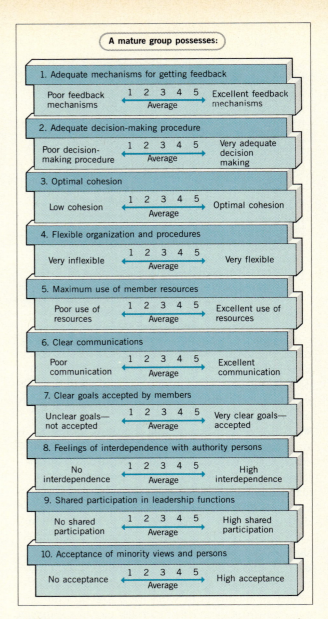

FIGURE 13.5 *Criteria for assessing the maturity of a group.*

Source. Edgar H. Schein, *Process Consultation,* Second Edition, Copyright © 1988, Addison-Wesley Publishing Company, Inc., Chapter 6, pp. 81–82, Figure 6.1, "A Mature Group Possesses." Reprinted with permission.

ness is compromised. The criteria of group maturity listed in the prior figure offer useful insight into good group dynamics. As you read them again, try to anticipate the challenges experienced by managers who seek to create work groups with profiles that score high on each of the items.

A classic view of group dynamics is offered by George Homans, who feels that it is useful to examine the required and emergent forms of the activities, sentiments, and interactions of group members. Homans's model can help you better understand what goes on within groups.[13]

Required and Emergent Behaviors

Required behaviors are formally requested of group members by way of job performance and in return for the right of continued membership. They may include such things as being punctual, treating customers with respect, and being helpful to co-workers. **Emergent behaviors** are what group members choose to do in addition to or in place of what is asked by the organization. Examples include helping out someone who is ill, taking extra time for breaks, and engaging in social activities. In practice, required and emergent behaviors can each have both functional and dysfunctional implications for group effectiveness.

It may help you to think of the system of emergent behaviors as the "shadow" or informal aspect of any required group behaviors. This shadow effect is shown in Figure 13.6 which modifies the open-systems model of groups presented earlier. Ideally, the emergent system supports required operations and enhances group process. Indeed, supportive emergent behaviors are necessary for almost any group or organization to achieve true effectiveness. Rarely, if ever, can the required behaviors be specified so perfectly that they meet all the demands of the work situation. This is especially true in dynamic environments where job demands change over time. In such cases the emergent work behaviors may be more efficient than those required by the rules. This point is perhaps best illustrated when union members choose to "work by the rules" and do only what is formally required of them. Here's one example.[14]

At the U.S. Postal Service route delivery workers are supposed to follow many formal rules and policies. But no one can perform the work satisfactorily while following all of these rules to the letter. In fact, postal employees usually follow rules perfectly only when they wish to "strike" in opposition to federal law against "strikes." In such cases the "strike" is called a "work-by-the-rules-strike." The deliverers leave in the morning, park on the oppo-

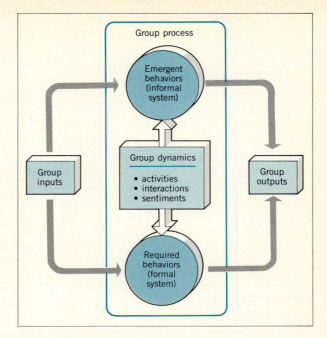

FIGURE 13.6 *Homans' model of group dynamics: emergent behaviors as a "shadow" for required behaviors.*

site side of the street from their postal box (a rule), unlock their trucks, get their bags out, lock the trucks (a rule), go across the street, come back, unlock the trucks, put the mail in, lock their trucks, etc. By following rules perfectly the deliverers come in late from their daily activities with only half the mail delivered . . . and free from any possible prosecution.

Activities, Interactions, Sentiments

Homans further identifies activities, interactions, and sentiments as three basic elements of group dynamics that can have required and emergent forms. **Activities** are behaviors in which group members engage. They are things people do in groups and include efforts directed toward the group task, social activities, and other forms of physical movement. The required activities of a work group are often specified by job descriptions and organizational rules and policies. They formalize what the organization expects individuals to accomplish as group members. Both required and emergent activities will be found in any group.

Interactions are behaviors group members direct toward other persons. The essence of any interaction is communication and information exchange. Interactions also occur in both required and emergent form. Depending upon how well they are accomplished, they can have positive or negative influences on group effectiveness.

Sentiments are feelings, attitudes, beliefs, or values held by group members. They may be brought in from the outside by individuals, or they may be learned from other group members. As you might expect, group sentiments are especially subject to emergent forces. Although it is easy to require positive attitudes toward work, a respect for authority and belief in company rules and procedures, it is difficult to achieve these results in practice. Negative sentiments all too often emerge in groups despite the intentions specified in the required system.

GROUP NORMS AND COHESIVENESS

Two key aspects of group dynamics that relate to the sentiments described in Homans' model are group norms and group cohesiveness. Let's introduce the concepts through the following incident. It involves Frank Jackson, someone who was full of ability and motivation when he joined a new work unit. Soon, however, he was influenced by the group to perform at less than his true level of capability. The factors affecting his decision include group norms and cohesiveness.

ILLUSTRATIVE CASE: FRANK JACKSON

Frank Jackson deftly soldered his last wires in the interconnection.[15] That was 18 for the morning—not bad, he thought. He moved on to the next computer and began to string out the cable for the next job.

"You're new here, aren't you?" The man was standing beside Frank, soldering iron in hand.

"Yeah. I came over from Consumer Products Division—been with the company for 10 years."

"I'm Jim Miller. Been working here in computer assembly for five years."

The men shook hands. Jim walked back to the last job Frank did and looked it over. "Pretty good, Frank, pretty good." He looked back down the assembly floor. "How many have you done this morning?"

"Eighteen."

"Hey, you're quite a rate-buster, aren't you?" Jim laughed. "Most of us here figure 15 interconnections a day is about par for the course."

"Well, these I'm doing are pretty easy."

Jim frowned. "Yeah, but look what happens. You do 20, maybe 25 easy ones, and the others stuck with the hard jobs look bad. You wouldn't want that to happen, would you?"

"Well, no, of course not."

"That-a-boy! You know, the workers here have a bowling team—kind of a company deal. Not everybody is on it—just the interconnection group. Even a few of them don't make it. You know, we like to keep it a friendly bunch." Jim paused. "Like to come next Wednesday?"

"Why, OK. Sure. Jim, what does the supervisor think about the number of jobs a day?"

"Him? He don't know the difference, and if he did, what difference would it make? You can't find good workers right off the street. He goes along—the people upstairs don't know how fast the work should go, and they don't bother him. So he don't bother us."

Frank looked over his next job. He was doing the toughest kind of interconnection, and he knew that any reasonably skilled person should be able to do at least 40 jobs a day on most of the other interconnections. Boy, this was going to be a relaxing job. He didn't like to goof off, but these people were going to be working with him every day—and he wasn't about to get off on the wrong foot with them. Besides, he liked to bowl.

"It's all cost plus anyhow," Jim said. "The company gets plenty from the government for the work. They've got nothing to worry about. Hey, come over to the lounge with me—we can have a break. We got plenty of time."

Norms

A group **norm** is a behavior expected of group members.[17] Norms like those shown in Table 13.2, are "rules" or "standards" that guide the behavior of group members. They are among the sentiments that develop as group members interact with one another. When violated, they may be enforced with reprimands and other sanctions. In the extreme,

TABLE 13.2 *Selected Examples of Work Group Norms: Positive and Negative Versions*

Norms	Positive Version	Negative Version
Organizational and personal pride	It's a tradition around here for people to stand up for the company when others criticize it unfairly.	In our company they are always trying to take advantage of us.
Performance/excellence	In our company people always try to improve, even when they are doing well.	Around here there's no point in trying harder—nobody else does.
Teamwork/communication	Around here people are good listeners and actively seek out the ideas and opinions of others.	Around here it's dog-eat-dog and save your own skin.
Leadership/supervision	Around here managers and supervisors really care about the people they supervise.	In our company it's best to hide your problems and avoid your supervisor.
Profitability/cost effectiveness	Around here people are continually on the lookout for better ways of doing things.	Around here people tend to hang on to old ways of doing things even after they have outlived their usefulnes.

Source: Quotes in the table reprinted by permission of the publisher, from "Confronting the Shadow Organization: How to Detect and Defeat Negative Norms," by Robert F. Allen and Saul Pilnick, from *Organizational Dynamics* (Spring 1973), pp. 6–10. Copyright © by AMACOM, a division of American Management Associations.

violation of group norms can result in expulsion or social ostracism. This concern probably caused Frank Jackson to adopt the group norm of restricted performance in the prior case.

The key point for a manager is whether a group norm has positive or negative implications for the organization. For example, compare and contrast the positive and negative versions of the norms shown in the table. Any manager would clearly prefer to have a work unit in which the positive versions of pride, teamwork, performance, leadership, and profitability norms prevailed. Other norms that emerge as important sentiments in work groups include relationships with supervisors, colleagues, and customers, as well as honesty, quality of work, security, personal development, and change.

One of the most important norms in any group relates to the level of work effort and performance that members are expected to contribute to the group task. This **performance norm** is a key characteristic of work groups, and it can have positive or negative implications for group and organizational productivity. Work groups with more positive performance norms tend to be more successful in accomplishing task objectives than groups, such as Frank Jackson's, with more negative performance norms. Here is another example of this issue in actual practice.[17]

At Steelcase, Inc. the Michigan-based office furniture company, many workers are on "piecework" incentives where they are paid for each item or part completed. This system is designed to encourage higher output while compensating workers for their extra efforts. In some cases, group norms seem to go against the system. Says one worker, "There's an unspoken law. You don't turn in too much." But others like the system, and respond enthusiastically. Larry Graw is one. He builds chairs, and does so faster than anyone else in the plant. He built 101 in a day by skipping breaks, taking short lunches, and working hard. That was 41 more than the rated average. When asked "why?" he replied: "I guess I'm from the old school of hard work."

Cohesiveness

Norms vary in the degree to which they are accepted and adhered to by group members. Conformity to norms is largely determined by a group's **cohesiveness,** the degree to which members are attracted to and motivated to remain part of a group. Persons in a highly cohesive group value their membership and strive to maintain positive relationships with other group members. They tend to conform to group norms as a result. Frank Jackson's work group was highly cohesive. Other members of the team rallied together to withhold their work efforts and adhere to the restricted performance norm. This sense of group belongingness apparently had a strong attraction for Frank. Perhaps it was a need for social affiliation that led him to accept this norm, instead of breaking it and running the risk of being ostracized from the group.

Sources of Cohesion

Group cohesiveness is affected by a variety of personal and situational variables.[18] Cohesion tends to be high in groups whose members share similar attitudes, socioeconomic backgrounds, needs, and other individual attributes. When members respect and hold one another's competencies in high esteem, cohesiveness is also likely to be high. Situational factors that enhance group cohesion include agreement on group goals, small size of membership, tasks requiring a high degree of interdependence, physical isolation from other groups, performance success, and performance failure or crisis.

Cohesion, Satisfaction, and Performance

Cohesive groups are good for their members. Members of highly cohesive groups are concerned about their group's activities and achievements. They tend, as opposed to persons in less cohesive groups, to be more energetic in working on group activities, to be less likely to be absent, to feel happy about performance success, and to be displeased about failures. Cohesive groups generally have stable memberships and foster feelings of loyalty, security, and high self-esteem among their members. Thus they satisfy a full range of individual needs.

Highly cohesive groups are *not* always good for organizations. Frank Jackson's group is one case in point. Even though it was highly cohesive, the group's low-performance norm resulted in restricted outputs by Frank and other members. A basic rule of group dynamics is that the more cohesive the group, the greater the conformity of members to group norms. When the performance norm of a group is positive, high cohesion and resulting conformity to norms has a very beneficial effect. When the performance norm is negative in a cohesive group, however, high conformity can have undesirable results.

Figure 13.7 predicts productivity levels for various combinations of group cohesion and performance norms. Productivity is likely to be highest in a highly cohesive group with positive performance norms. In this situation, competent group members can work hard and reinforce one another's accomplishments while experiencing satisfaction with the group. This situation is highlighted in the shaded cell of the figure.

The worst situation for a manager is a highly cohesive work group with negative performance norms. Here, productivity will probably suffer as

FIGURE 13.7 *Productivity and the relationship between group cohesiveness and performance norms.*

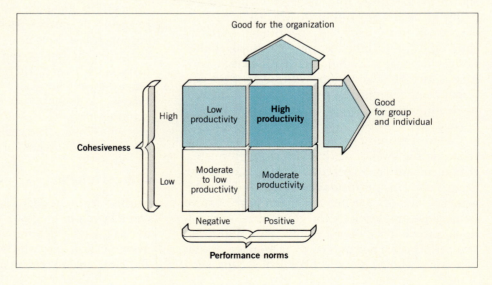

members restrict individual work efforts to levels consistent with the group's negative performance norm. Between these two extremes are mixed situations. Moderate productivity is likely to result from groups with low cohesion under positive performance norms; moderate to low productivity is likely with low cohesion and negative performance norms. In each case, the lack of cohesion fails to rally complete member conformity to the guiding norm.

Influencing Norms and Cohesiveness

The norms and cohesiveness of any group, formal or informal, interrelate with one another to affect the behavior of group members. Managers should therefore be skilled at influencing norms and cohesion in ways that support high levels of task performance and member satisfaction. Group effectiveness will be enhanced as a result.

Building Positive Norms

The appropriate focus for norm-building efforts varies with each of the four stages of group development. In the forming and storming stages, norms relating to membership issues such as expected attendance and levels of commitment are important. By the time a group reaches the stage of total integration, growth-oriented norms relating to adaptability and change become most relevant. Groups that are unable to build norms consistent with the operating problems typical to each stage of development may fail to achieve effectiveness.

Because group norms are largely determined by the collective will of group members, it is difficult for a manager or designated group leader simply to dictate which norms a given work group will adopt. Instead, the concerned manager or leader must use a knowledge of group dynamics to help and encourage group members to adopt norms supportive of organizational objectives. Among the things a manager can do are the following.[19]

■ Act as a positive role model.
■ Reinforce the desired behaviors via rewards.
■ Control results by performance reviews and regular feedback.
■ Train and orient new members to adopt desired behaviors.
■ Recruit and select new members who exhibit the desired behaviors.

■ Hold regular meetings to discuss group progress, and ways of improving task performance and member satisfaction.
■ Use group decision-making methods to reach agreement on appropriate behaviors.

Influencing Cohesion

As was pointed out earlier, there are advantages and disadvantages to high group cohesiveness. It is good in combination with positive group norms; it can be very troublesome in combination with negative norms. Thus, there will be times when a manager will want to build cohesiveness in work groups—for example, when trying to increase conformity to a positive performance norm. There may also be times when the objective is to break down cohesiveness, such as when group members exhibit high conformity to a negative performance norm. A number of things managers can do increase and decrease group cohesion follow.

1. *In order to INCREASE cohesion a manager can:*
■ Induce agreement on group goals.
■ Increase membership homogeneity.
■ Increase interactions among members.
■ Decrease group size.
■ Introduce competition with other groups.
■ Reward group rather than individual results.
■ Provide physical isolation from other groups.

2. *In order to DECREASE cohesion a manager can:*
■ Foster disagreement on group goals.
■ Increase membership heterogeneity.
■ Restrict interactions among members.
■ Increase group size.
■ Reward individual results rather than group.
■ Remove physical isolation.
■ Introduce a dominating member.
■ Disband the group.

"Groupthink"

There is another, more subtle side to group cohesion that can work to a group's disadvantage. Members of highly cohesive groups may publicly agree with actual or suggested courses of action, while privately having serious personal reservations. Strong feelings of loyalty can result in an inability of group members to critically evaluate one another's ideas and suggestions. Desires to retain cohesion, hold the group together, and avoid disagreements can lead to an overemphasis on agreement and biased decision making.

TABLE 13.3 *Symptoms Indicating that "Groupthink" May Be Occurring*

Illusions of group invulnerability. Members of the group feel it is basically beyond criticism or attack.

Rationalizing unpleasant and disconfirming data. Refusal to accept contradictory data or to consider alternatives thoroughly.

Belief in inherent group morality. Members of the group feel it is "right" and above any reproach by outsiders.

Stereotyping competitors as weak, evil, and stupid. Refusal to look realistically at other groups.

Applying direct pressure to deviants to conform to group wishes. Refusal to tolerate a member who suggests the group may be wrong.

Self-censorship by members. Refusal by members to communicate personal concerns to the group as a whole.

Illusions of unanimity. Accepting consensus prematurely, without testing its completeness.

Mind guarding. Members of the group protect the group from hearing disturbing ideas or viewpoints from outsiders.

Irving Janis is a social psychologist who has studied this group tendency in detail. He calls attention to the phenomenon of **"groupthink,"** a tendency for highly cohesive groups to lose their critical evaluative capabilities.[20] Janis ties a variety of well-known historical blunders to groupthink, including the lack of preparedness of the U.S. naval forces for the 1941 Japanese attack on Pearl Harbor, President Kennedy's handling of the Bay of Pigs, and the many roads that led to the United States' involvement in Vietnam.

Groupthink can occur anywhere, and Table 13.3 lists a number of its symptoms. Do you recognize any of these signs in groups with which you are familiar? When and if a group ever does experience groupthink, Janis suggests the following corrective actions.

To avoid groupthink:

1. Assign the role of critical evaluator to each group member; encourage a sharing of viewpoints on all matters facing the group.

2. Avoid, as a leader, seeming partial to one course of action; absent yourself on occasion to allow free discussion.

3. Create subgroups to work on the same problems and then share their proposed solutions.

4. Have group members discuss issues with outsiders and report back on their reactions.

5. Invite outside experts to observe group activities and react to group processes and decisions.

6. Assign one member to play a "devil's advocate" role at each meeting of the group.

7. Hold a "second-chance" meeting after consensus is apparently achieved, to review the decision once again.

GROUP TASK AND MAINTENANCE ACTIVITIES

Activities in Homans's model of group dynamics represent the action contributions of members to the group process. Research on the social psychology of groups identifies two types of activities that are essential if group members are to work well together over time: task and maintenance activities.[21]

Task Activities

Task activities contribute directly to the group's performance purpose. They include efforts to define and solve problems and apply work efforts in support of task accomplishment. Without relevant task activities, groups will have difficulty accomplishing their objectives. Performance success depends on the willingness of group members to contribute activities such as the following.

Initiating   Setting agendas, giving ideas, defining problems, suggesting solutions.

Information giving and seeking   Offering task information, seeking facts, asking for ideas of others.

Summarizing   Pulling ideas together, restating where the group appears to be in its task agenda.

Elaborating   Clarifying ideas by example, making sure meanings and perspectives are shared.

Opinion giving   Giving evaluations of ideas, suggestions, and proposed solutions.

Maintenance Activities

Maintenance activities support the emotional life of the group as an ongoing social system. They help strengthen and perpetuate the group as a social entity. When maintenance activities are performed well, good interpersonal relationships are achieved and the ability of the group to stay together over the longer term is ensured. The maintenance activities listed here can enhance member satisfaction and contribute to group effectiveness.

Gatekeeping   Allowing others to gain "talking time," helping everyone get a chance to speak.

Encouraging   Being warm and receptive to others, drawing forth their contributions.

Following   Going along with the group, agreeing to try out the ideas of others.

Harmonizing   Reconciling differences, getting conflicting parties to agree or compromise.

Reducing tension   Drawing off emotions by changing the subject or being humorous.

Group Task and Maintenance Leadership

Both task and maintenance activities are required for groups to be effective over the long run. They stand in distinct contrast to the dysfunctional activities described in Table 13.4. Activities of this latter type are usually self-serving and detract from rather than enhance group effectiveness. Unfortunately, as you have probably observed, very few groups are

TABLE 13.4   *Nine Common Disruptive Activities Engaged in by Group Members*

1.   *Being aggressive*   Working for status by criticizing or blaming others, showing hostility against the group or some individual, deflating the ego or status of others.

2.   *Blocking*   Interfering with the progress of the group by going off on a tangent, citing personal experiences unrelated to the problem, arguing too much on a point, rejecting ideas without consideration.

3.   *Self-confessing*   Using the group as a sounding board, expressing personal, nongroup-oriented feelings or points of view.

4.   *Competing*   Vying with others to produce the best idea, talk the most, play the most roles, gain favor with the leader.

5.   *Seeking sympathy*   Trying to induce other group members to be sympathetic to one's problems or misfortunes, deploring one's own situation, or disparaging one's own ideas to gain support.

6.   *Special pleading*   Introducing or supporting suggestions related to one's own pet concerns or philosophies, lobbying.

7.   *Horsing around*   Clowning, joking, mimicking, disrupting the work of the group.

8.   *Seeking recognition*   Attempting to call attention to self by loud or excessive talking, extreme ideas, unusual behavior.

9.   *Withdrawal*   Acting indifferent or passive, resorting to excessive formality, daydreaming, doodling, whispering to others, wandering from the subject.

Source: J. William Pfeiffer and John E. Jones, *1976 Annual Handbook for Group Facilitators* (La Jolla, CA: University Associates, 1976), p. 137. Used by permission.

immune from the display of such dysfunctional behavior by members.

Task and maintenance activities are leadership skills. They can and should be learned by all persons, especially managers who wish to be successful in helping groups perform to their highest potential. It is important to remember, though, that any member can assist a group by performing these functions. Although a person with formal authority, such as chairperson or supervisor, will often do them, the responsibility for task and maintenance activities should be shared and distributed among all group members. Everyone in a group has both opportunity and responsibility to participate in the leadership role by helping the group satisfy its task and maintenance needs. This *distributed leadership* responsibility in group dynamics includes the need for every member to:

1.   Correctly diagnose group dynamics and recognize when task and/or maintenance activities are needed.

2.   Respond appropriately by providing or helping others to provide these activities.

TEAM BUILDING: MANAGING GROUP EFFECTIVENESS

When we think of the word *team*, sporting teams often come to mind. And, we know they can have their problems. Members slack off or become disgruntled, and some are retired or traded as a result. Even world champion teams have losing streaks; the most highly talented players are prone to lose motivation at times, quibble among themselves, and go into slumps. When these things happen, the owners, managers, and players are apt to examine their problems and take corrective action to "rebuild the team" and restore what we have been calling group effectiveness.

Work groups are teams in a similar sense. Even the most mature work group is likely to experience problems over time. When difficulties arise from pressures of competition or normal work routines, team-building activities can help. **Team building,** as shown in Figure 13.8, is a sequence of planned activities to gather and analyze data on the functioning of a group and implement constructive changes to increase its operating effectiveness.[22]

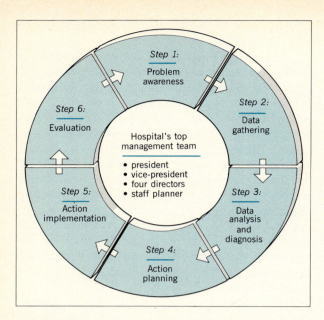

FIGURE 13.8 *Steps in the team building process: the case of the hospital top management team.*

ILLUSTRATIVE CASE:
THE HOSPITAL TOP MANAGEMENT TEAM

The consultant received a call from the hospital's director of personnel. He indicated that a new hospital president felt the top management team lacked cohesiveness and was not working well together as a team. After discussing the matter directly with the president, the consultant agreed to facilitate a team-building activity that would include a day-long retreat at a nearby resort hotel.

The process began when the consultant conducted interviews with the president and other members of the executive group. These interviews surfaced a number of common views about the team's lack of cohesion, but also revealed some contradictions. During the retreat, the consultant reported these results to the group as a whole. She indicated that hospital goals were generally understood by all, but that they weren't clear enough to allow agreement on action priorities. Furthermore, she reported that interpersonal problems between two team members—the directors of nursing services and administration—were making it difficult for the group to work comfortably together.

These and other issues were addressed by the group at the retreat. Working sometimes in small subgroups, and other times together as a whole, they agreed first of all that action should be taken to clarify the hospital's overall mission and create a priority list of objectives for the current year. Led by the president, activity on this task would involve all group members and was targeted for completion within a month. In addition, it was decided that friction between lower-level personnel in the nursing services and administration departments was causing the two directors difficulty in relating to one another. During the retreat they both voiced mutual respect. It was suggested by someone else that the consultant might work with the two departments in an attempt to resolve the intergroup problems, and perhaps even hold a special retreat for them. Both directors agreed to this approach.

The president asked that progress on the action plans agreed to at the retreat be reviewed at each of the next three monthly executive staff meetings. Everyone supported the idea, but one person suggested that it might be helpful for the group as a whole to meet with the consultant to review progress after three months. This was enthusiastically agreed upon. The president, however, issued one final challenge to the group. "Let's be sure," she said, "that after the follow-up retreat we are ready to assume responsibility for our own continued group development." The retreat ended with everyone expressing commitment to this goal.

The Team Building Process

Like the previous example, most systematic approaches to team building follow the steps described in Figure 13.8. The cycle begins with sensitivity that a problem may exist or might develop in the future within the group. Group members then work together to gather and analyze data so that the problem is finally diagnosed. Plans are made and corrective action implemented. Results are then evaluated and any difficulties or new problems that are discovered can serve to recycle the team-building process.

Team building is a data-based way of assessing a work group's functioning and taking corrective action to improve group effectiveness. This can be done with or without consulting assistance, and it can become a regular part of a group's continuing work routine. There are many ways to gather data on group functioning. Structured and unstructured interviews, questionnaires, group meetings, and

TEAM BUILDING:
THE ATHLETIC APPROACH

When Mentor Graphics Corp. sent 17 top executives on a weeklong rafting trip, the purpose wasn't just pleasure. They were on an Outward Bound team building experience designed to help them learn more about themselves, about leadership, about trusting others, and about teamwork. The trip was proposed by Thomas Bruggerre, chairman of the computer maker; most of the others were reluctant participants. About them, Bruggerre said, "We had people who had never slept outside before and whose idea of roughing it was showing up at the Hyatt on Maui without a reservation."

But during the trip Bruggerre himself learned about what it means to lead . . . and follow. The demanding trip and structured team experiences ended up with almost everyone surprising themselves and enjoying it. They were asked to rappel down a 150-foot high cliff, and jump from a high rock into the river and float through rapids in a life-vest, among other things. A nonswimmer made the rapids trip; someone afraid of heights took the rappeling journey.

The group as a whole practiced teamwork, away-from-the-office style. They were asked to make a river traverse. Bruggerre took the lead and the group charged ahead with a plan that he says, "sent most of our expertise over to the wrong side of the river." What should have taken only a few hours, took them until after dark to complete. When it was over, Bruggerre conceded around the campfire that maybe he and the firm's management tended to—"ready, fire, aim" as they addressed problems. He added that the exercise taught participants that "it's important to know what you do well, and what you don't, and rely on other people."

Across the Atlantic, the top management group from the Waldorf Hotel trudged together through the dense woodlands of High Wycombe, England. In a course sponsored by Action Development, they engaged in a number of outdoor exercises to test their teamwork abilities. After a day of many frustrations and a few successes, everyone sat down to share personal feelings. One said: "We all know that working with a team is not for your own benefit." Another added, "There is a subtle feeling of turning over a new leaf." The message seemed clear to all. It's easy to loose sight of similar objectives in a competitive workplace. It's important to remember the strengths of being a team.

Source: As reported in Ken Wells, "The Athletic Approach," *The New York Times* (February 26, 1988), pp. 9D–11D; and, Victoria Schofield, "Management Shoot-Out," *Success* (June 1988), pp. 57–58.

written records are all examples. Regardless of the method used, the principle of team-building requires that a careful and collaborative assessment of the group be made. All members should participate in the data-gathering process, assist in the data analysis, and collectively decide to take action to resolve and/or prevent problems that interfere with group effectiveness.

We will examine team building again in our discussion of organization development in Chapter 17. Of course, it should be remembered that the ultimate goal of team building is create more and better *teamwork* among members of a group. Another way to accomplish this is to send group members to special training and development programs. As illustrated by the example in *Newsline 13.2,* teamwork can be improved when people share the team-building challenges of unusual and sometimes physically demanding personal experiences while guided by experienced group consultants. Yet, teamwork can be enhanced in many cases by informed managers acting without the assistant of consultants. This fact is probably overlooked far too often by managers and consultants alike. Consider what happened—[23]

at Grove Personnel Services, Inc. when Raejean Fellows was concerned by the lack of growth of her placement agency; it had only three counselors and there just wasn't enough business to add more. Fellows decided the group just didn't share her vision of growth. She addressed the problem by having counselors write their own mission statements. Then they worked together as she asked the everyone to tell her "which goals were most important." They ended up by adopting this statement of mission . . . and ambition: "to be the best—and one of the most profitable agencies . . . have a reputation for producing quality results . . . *and* [for the counselors] to have professionally and financially rewarding jobs." By working together to create this shared commitment, the group found a soul. And Fellow's agency became a thriving business with 23 counselors on staff.

INTERGROUP DYNAMICS

As groups mature and take control of their internal processes, attention eventually shifts to working relationships with other groups. Intergroup relations are an important element in organizations, which we have already described as complex networks of interlocking groups. Coordination among the diverse activities of many groups is needed to achieve productivity. Unfortunately, there is a tendency for groups to develop rivalries and antagonisms that detract from this goal of intergroup cooperation and coordination. The net result is a sense of competition that can have negative consequences for the organization. Think about the following comments from the marketing and manufacturing departments in one company.[24]

Issue Capacity planning.

> *Marketing says* "Why don't we have enough capacity?"

Manufacturing says "Why didn't we have accurate sales forecasts?"

Issue Delivery and distribution.

> *Marketing says* "Why don't we ever have the right merchandise in inventory?"

> *Manufacturing says* "We can't keep everything in inventory."

Issue New products.

> *Marketing says* "New products are our life blood."

> *Manufacturing says* "Unnecessary design changes are prohibitively expensive."

Intergroup Competition

Perhaps the most common example of intergroup competition is that which takes place between labor unions and management groups. We will examine this situation quite thoroughly in Chapter 18, on labor-management relations. Yet, all types of groups in organizations compete with one another for rewards, status, resources, top management attention, and the like. What typically happens is that:[25]

1. *WITHIN* each competing group—
■ Members become closer knit and more loyal; group cohesion increases.
■ Concern for group effectiveness grows; members become more task oriented.
■ Group members become more willing to accept a single leader; authority becomes more centralized.
■ Activities become more tightly organized; structure assumes a more mechanistic form.

2. *BETWEEN* the competing groups—
■ Each group views the other as an enemy.
■ Each group develops positive images of itself and negative images of the other; one's own strengths are overestimated and the other's underestimated.
■ Hostilities increase and communications decrease between the groups.
■ When forced into interaction with the other group, members listen only to what reinforces their original predisposition toward one another.

You can the imagine dilemma managers face in respect to the intergroup dynamics just described. On the one hand there are potential advantages to

SYNERGY VS. CONTEST:
THE CASE AGAINST COMPETITION

Companies are rethinking the methods they've used to motivate workers. A number of recent studies show that encouraging cooperation rather than competition among workers not only enhances productivity but pays long-term dividends in employee satisfaction.

For years copanies devised programs to foster competition. But the experience of Chase Manhattan Bank illustrates one of the problems created by competition. Employee bonuses were linked to their division's performance. With the emphasis on "production now," volume won out over other concerns such as creditworthi-ness. One division built a huge portfolio with a new company that defaulted and left Chase with a $117 million write-off.

Studies have shown that competition tends to increase anxiety levels and often results in hostility and distrust among workers. These studies conclude that shared group identity is good motivation when cooperation between individuals and intracompany divisions is encouraged.

Contrast the win–win philosophy in a cooperative structure with the competitive win–lose approach. In the latter case, workers see their benefit coming only from failure on the part of others. In the former, everyone wins if someone wins. American Express, one of the most dynamic corporations in the country, actively encourages cooperation among its divisions. It rewards executives who actively seek out and promote cross-selling opportunities and other synergies among the company's divisions.

Bringing people together to work on a company's goals rather than individual successes produces results. Cooperation in the workplace is an idea whose time has come.

Source: As reported in "Synergy Works At American Express," Monci Jo Williams, *Fortune* (February 16, 1987); "No Contest," Alfie Kohn, *Inc,* (November 1987).

---

be gained from establishing competitive relations among groups in an organization. But the resulting price might also be quite high as the disadvantages come into play. It is largely the latter concern that underlies the emphasis in *Newsline 13.3* on *cooperation* rather than competition.[36] Most higher-level managers in particular, walk a thin line as they try to realize some of the advantages of intergroup competition while minimizing its disadvantages.

Managing Intergroup Competition

There are two approaches to managing intergroup competition. One is to deal with the competition after it occurs; the second is to prevent its occurrence in the first place.

Controlling Existing Competition

Managers sometimes have to try to reconcile differences among groups that should be cooperating but are already having serious problems working together.[27] Strategies for minimizing the negative consequences resulting from groups already in competition include:

1. Identifying a common enemy (for example, another company to be outperformed).
2. Appealing to a common goal (for example, profits or customer satisfaction).
3. Bringing representatives of the groups into direct contact with one another (for example, setting up face-to-face negotiations).
4. Training members of the competing groups in

group process and interpersonal skills (for example, engaging them in exercises to increase interpersonal awareness and promote harmony).

Preventing Future Competition

Action guidelines that managers may follow to prevent destructive intergroup competition from occurring in the first place include:

1. Rewarding groups on the basis of their performance contributions to the organization as a whole.
2. Rewarding groups for the help they give one another.
3. Stimulating frequent interaction between members of various groups.
4. Avoiding tendencies for groups to withdraw and become isolated from one another.
5. Rotating members among groups whenever possible.
6. Avoiding win-lose competition among groups to obtain desired organizational rewards.
7. Emphasizing the sharing of resources for the maximum benefit of the organziaton as a whole.

This discussion of intergroup competition brings us to the point of once again recognizing that the management functions of planning, organizing, leading, and controlling are highly intertwined. Plans should be set and organizations designed to encourage cooperation among individuals and groups, and to minimize destructive competition. These structures should be staffed with persons whose attitudes, goals, and interpersonal skills support cooperation. Then, good leadership should encourage everyone to fulfill the opportunity to achieve group synergy through cooperative efforts. When all this is done, effective control can be exercised to ensure the desired results. Part 5—*Controlling for Productivity* is devoted to the latter concerns.

Summary

Groups are an essential human resource of organizations. Formal groups are officially designated to serve an organizational purpose. They include command, functional, and autonomous work groups, as well as committees and task forces. Informal interest and friendship groups spontaneously arise from the work setting. They exist in any organization and help satisfy the individual needs of members. Informal groups can also be functional or dysfunctional in respect to the accomplishment of organizational objectives.

An effective group achieves high levels of task performance and human resource maintenance over time. Managers must be concerned to increase and/or maintain effectiveness in groups where they are a formally designated leader or general participant. This requires an understanding of group-development stages and the essence of group and intergroup dynamics.

Group dynamics are those forces within groups that affect task performance and membership satisfaction. They are the components of the group process that help transform inputs into outputs. Group norms and cohesiveness emerge as especially important to any group process. Norms are behaviors expected of group members. Cohesiveness is the degree to which members are attracted to and motivated to remain part of the group. A key capability for any manager is to know how to influence norms and cohesion in ways that increase the productivity of groups. Along with this comes the responsibility to facilitate important task and maintenance activities. Task activities directly assist performance accomplishment; maintenance activities maintain the social fabric of the group over time.

To succeed over the long term, any group must periodically take stock of itself and make constructive modifications in its operations. Team building is a data-based approach that can help in this process. An additional leadership challenge for any manager is to facilitate team building to ensure group effectiveness. Finally, groups in organizations must work cooperatively together to accomplish organizational objectives. Successful managers minimize the destructive potential of intergroup competition, while taking advantage of its potential benefits.

Thinking Through the Issues

1. Define and give examples of formal and informal groups in a work setting. What is the difference between an "autonomous work group" and a "worker involvement group"?

2. List and explain some of the advantages and disadvantages of informal groups for (a) their members and (b) their host organizations. How should a manager deal with informal groups in the workplace?

3. When does a formal group become a psychological group? Should every work unit become a psychological group? Why?

4. What is group effectiveness? Explain how it differs from the concept of human resource maintenance in the group setting.

5. Explain the difference between group norms and cohesiveness. How do they interrelate with one another to affect group performance results?

6. Suppose you are manager of a group with a negative performance norm. What can be done to overcome its adverse effects?

7. List the four stages of group development. How does a manager know when a group is finally at the total integration stage?

8. What is "groupthink"? How can it be prevented?

9. What is team building and how can it help managers fulfill leadership responsibilities?

10. What can a manager do to reduce competition between two groups who need to work more cooperatively together?

The Manager's Vocabulary

Activities
Autonomous work group
Cohesiveness
Command group
Committee
Effective group
Electronic group networks
Emergent behavior
Formal group

Friendship group
Functional group
Group
Group dynamics
Group process
Groupthink
Human resource maintenance

Informal group
Interaction
Interest group
Maintenance activities
Norm
Performance norm
Psychological group
Quality circle

Required behavior
Sentiments
Synergy
Task activities
Task force
Team building
Worker involvement group

IN THE HANDS OF OTHERS

CAREER PERSPECTIVE

Think about it. Surely you've been there before. And by the way, you'll probably be there again one day soon. What are we talking about? Oh you know . . . the dreaded committee or task force assignment! Yes, one of the most terrifying organizational experiences known is having to give up individual responsibility for what you do and put your next performance evaluation, pay raise, and maybe even career progress *in the hands of others* . . .

As if it isn't bad enough to have to depend on others to do their fair share of the work, think of some of the people you're likely to encounter. But then again, perhaps you've seen these group members before—[28]

The Backseat Driver very vocal, thinks the group is going in the wrong direction, thinks he/she knows the *right* direction.
The Slow Rider competent, responsible, willing to work, but sl*ooo*w, oh so slow in getting the job done.
The Hitchhiker usually present but just along for the ride; maybe bored, maybe just lazy, maybe even capable, but who knows?
The Freeloader seldom seen or heard, appears too busy or disinterested to bother with the group project.
The Squeaky Wheel prone to making annoying, irrelevant, but continual remarks during group meetings; always talking, but never saying anything.

Questions

1. Which of these "types" have you encountered before in group situations? In what ways did they affect, positively or negatively, the overall *effectiveness* of the group?

2. Suppose you are (a) just another group member, and (b) the assigned "head" of the group. How would you deal with each of the prior types of group members? Explain both your action strategies and the goals you hope to achieve in each case.

3. Are you comfortable working in group situations when you are (a) another group member, and (b) the designated head? What can you do to further develop your skills and competencies in working successfully in both capacities?

Case Application

OZYX CORPORATION

The Ozyx Corporation is a relatively small industrial company.[29] The president has hired a consultant to help discover the reasons for the poor profit picture of the company in general, and the low morale and productivity of the research and development division in particular. During the investigation, the consultant becomes interested in a research project in which the company has invested a sizable proportion of its R&D budget.

When asked about the project by the consultant in the privacy of their offices, the president, the vice-president for research, and the research manager each describe it as an idea that looks great on paper but will ultimately fail because of the unavailability of the technology required to make it work. Each also acknowledges that continued support of the project will create cash-flow problems that will jeopardize the existence of the total organization.

Furthermore, each individual indicates he or she has not told the others about these reservations. When asked why, the president says he can't reveal his "true" feelings because abandoning the project, which has been widely publicized, would make the company look bad in the press. In addition, it would probably cause his vice-president's ulcer to kick up or perhaps even cause her to quit, "Because she has staked her professional reputation on the project's success."

Similarly, the vice-president for research says she can't let the president or the research manager know her reservations because the president is so committed to it that "I would probably get fired for insubordination if I questioned the project."

Finally, the research manager says he can't let the president or vice-president know of his doubts about the project because of their extreme commitment to the project's success.

All indicate that in meetings with one another, they try to maintain an optimistic facade so the others won't worry unduly about the project. The research director, in particular, admits to writing ambiguous progress reports so the president and vice-president can "interpret them to suit themselves." He says he tends to slant them to the "positive" side, "given how committed the brass are."

Questions

1. What is the problem in this case?

2. Are group norms and cohesiveness contributing to the problem? Explain your answer.

3. What would you recommend as an action plan to resolve the problem and prevent it from happening again in the future? Why?

Class Exercise: Analyzing Group Effectiveness

1. Think of a group to which you belong. Try to choose a work group at your place of employment, or choose a student course project group. Rate the effectiveness of this group by now circling *one* of the following choices—very highly effective . . . about average effectiveness . . . not very effective.

2. Now read the *criteria of group effectiveness* that follow.[30]

Goals: Degree to which they are shared and held important by all group members.

Not at all   1   2   3   4   5   6   7   8   9   10   Completely

Participation: Degree to which all members are listened to and able to participate in discussions.

Not at all   1   2   3   4   5   6   7   8   9   10   Completely

Feelings: Degree to which feelings are openly expressed and treated with respect by everyone.

Not at all   1   2   3   4   5   6   7   8   9   10   Completely

Problem-solving: Degree to which problems are carefully diagnosed before actions are taken.

Not at all   1   2   3   4   5   6   7   8   9   10   Completely

Leadership: Degree to which everyone assists in group leadership needs as they arise.

Not at all   1   2   3   4   5   6   7   8   9   10   Completely

Decision-making: Degree to which decisions get made when needed, and all members assist in making these decisions.

Not at all   1   2   3   4   5   6   7   8   9   10   Completely

Trust: Degree to which members of the group trust one another and feel free to express negative reactions to ideas.

Not at all   1   2   3   4   5   6   7   8   9   10   Completely

Creativity: Degree to which the group is flexible, seeks new ways of doing things, and achieves creative growth over time.

Not at all   1   2   3   4   5   6   7   8   9   10   Completely

3. Think again about the group you rated in step #1 above. Now evaluate this group formally on each of the prior criteria. Add up the group scores for all criteria by circling the appropriate numbers. Check where the group rates on this profile of effectiveness.

Average score	Level of effectiveness
10–30	Not very effective
40–70	Average effectiveness
80–100	Very highly effective

4. Compare how your group evaluated in steps 1 and 3. How do you account for any differences in the two evaluations?

5. Reread your rating of the group in step 3. What suggestions do you have for improving the group's performance on each criterion, and therefore improving its overall effectiveness?

6. Share your results from this exercise with a nearby classmate. Help each other to answer the questions posed in steps 4 and 5. Be prepared to participate in further class discussion led by your instructor.

References

[1]Portions of this chapter were originally adapted from John R. Schermerhorn, Jr., James G. Hunt, and Richard N. Osborn, *Managing Organizational Behavior* (New York: Wiley, 1982), pp. 213–223, 242–251, 261–267, 275–279, 281–287. Used by permission.

[2]The "linking pin" concept is introduced in Rensis Likert, *New Patterns of Management* (New York: McGraw-Hill, 1962).

[3]Case and subsequent guidelines developed from Susan D. Van Raalte, "Preparing the Task Force to Get Good Results," *S.A.M. Advanced Management Journal*, Vol. 47 (Winter 1982), pp. 11–16.

[4]Information for these two examples if from "Management for the 1990s," *Newsweek* (April 25, 1988), pp. 47–48; and, "The 21st Century Executive," *U.S. News & World Report* (March 7, 1988), pp. 48–51.

[5]For a good discussion of quality circles see Edward E. Lawler III and Susan A. Mohrman, "Quality Circles after the Fad," *Harvard Business Review,* Vol 63 (January–February 1985), pp. 65–71; and, Gregory P. Shea, "Bottled Change," *Sloan Management Review,* Vol. 27 (Spring 1986), pp. 33–43.

[6]See William L. Gardner and John R. Schermerhorn, Jr., "Computer Networking and the Changing Nature of

Managerial Work," *Public Productivity Review,* Vol. XI (Summer 1988), pp. 85–99.

[7]Information from Leslie Helm, "How the Leader in Networking Practices What it Preaches," *Business Week* (May 16, 1988), p. 96.

[8]See, for example, Edgar H. Schein, *Organizational Psychology,* Second Edition (Englewood Cliffs, NJ: Prentice-Hall, 1970), p. 81.

[9]See Marvin E. Shaw, *Group Dynamics: The Psychology of Small Group Behavior,* Second Edition (New York: McGraw-Hill, 1976); and, Harold J. Leavitt, "Suppose We Took Groups More Seriously," in Eugene L. Cass and Frederick G. Zimmer (eds.), *Man and Work in Society* (New York: Van Nostrand Reinhold Company, 1975), pp. 67–77.

[10]Information from Maureen Lynch, "They Becomes Us," *AT&T Magazine,* Vol. 1, No. 2 (1985), pp. 29–30; and, "Quality: The Competitive Advantage," *Business Week,* Special Advertising Supplement (March 31, 1988). Excerpts from Lynch used by permission.

[11]For a review of research on group effectiveness see J. Richard Hackman, "The Design of Work Teams," pp. 315–342, in Jay W. Lorsch (ed.), *Handbook of Organizational Behavior* (Englewood Cliffs, NJ: Prentice-Hall, 1987).

[12]J. Steven Heinen and Eugene Jacobson, "A Model of Task Group Development in Complex Organizations and a Strategy of Implementation," *Academy of Management Review,* Vol. 1 (1976), pp. 98–111.

[13]This classic model is found in George C. Homans, *The Human Group* (New York: Harcourt, Brace, and World, 1950).

[14]Slightly adapted from Burt Scanlan and J. Bernard Keys, *Management and Organizational Behavior,* Second Edition (New York: Wiley, 1983), p. 294.

[15]From Dorothy N. Harlow and Jean J. Hanke, *Behavior in Organizations* (Boston: Little, Brown, 1975), pp. 244–245. Original source unknown.

[16]See Edgar Schein, *Process Consultation: Its Role in Organization Development* (Reading, MA: Addison-Wesley, 1988), pp. 76–79.

[17]Information from Bob Cohn, "A Glimpse of the 'Flex' Future," *Business Week* (August 1, 1988), pp. 38–40.

[18]See Shaw, op. cit. for a research summary on group cohesiveness.

[19]Robert F. Allen and Saul Pilnick, "Confronting the Shadow Organization: How to Detect and Defeat Negative Norms," *Organizational Dynamics* (Spring 1973), pp. 13–17.

[20]See Irving L. Janis, "Groupthink," *Psychology Today* (November 1971), pp. 43–46; *Victims of Groupthink,* Second Edition (Boston: Houghton Mifflin, 1982).

[21]The following discussion is based on Rensis Likert, op. cit., pp. 166–169; and, Schein, op. cit., pp. 49–56.

[22]See William D. Dyer, *Team-Building* (Reading, Mass.: Addison-Wesley, 1977).

[23]Information from Sandra Dark, "Let the Spirit Move You," *Success* (May/June 1988), pp. 34–36.

[24]Benson S. Shapiro, "Can Marketing and Manufacturing Coexist?" *Harvard Business Review,* Vol. 55 (September–October, 1977), pp. 104–114.

[25]This discussion is based on Schein, op. cit., pp. 96–103.

[26]For an informative debate on the "competition-cooperation" issues, see Alfie Kohn, "Incentives Can Be Bad for Business," *Inc.* (January 1988), pp. 93–94; and, Tom Peters, "Letter to the Editor," *Inc.* (April 1988), pp. 80–82.

[27]See the discussion by Robert R. Blake and Jane S. Mouton, *Solving Costly Organizational Conflicts: Achieving Inter-group Trust, Cooperation and Teamwork* (San Francisco: Jossey-Bass, 1984).

[28]These profiles are described in Robin De Rieux, "Brewing Up a Great Group Project," *Psychology Today* (August–September 1984), pp. 10–14.

[29]This case is reported in Jerry Harvey, "Managing Agreement in Organizations: The Abilene Paradox," *Organizational Dynamics* (Summer 1974), pp. 1–14. Copyright © 1974 by AMACOM, a division of American Management Associations. All rights reserved.

[30]These criteria of group effectiveness are developed from Schein, op. cit., 1988, pp. 57–58.

PART 4

MacGregor

My encounter with MacGregor came about during the course of a study of the extent to which operating managers actually use participative management techniques in their dealings with subordinates. MacGregor, who at the time was manager of one of the largest refineries in the country, was the last of more than 100 managers I interviewed in the course of the study. Although the interview had been scheduled in advance, the exact time had been left open; I was to call MacGregor at his office early in the week that I would be in the vicinity and set up a specific date and time.

Here's how that phone call went. The switchboard operator answered with the name of the refinery. When I asked for MacGregor's office, a male voice almost instantly said, "Hello." I then asked for MacGregor, whereupon the voice responded, "This is he." I should have recognized at once that this was no ordinary manager; he answered his own phone instantly, as though he had been waiting for it to ring. To my question about when it would be convenient for me to come see him, he replied, "Anytime." I said, "Would today be all right?" His response was, "Today, tomorrow, or Wednesday would be O.K.; or you could come Thursday, except don't come between 10:00 A.M. and noon; or you could come Friday or next week—anytime." I replied feebly, "I just want to fit in with your plans." Then he said, "You are just not getting the message; it makes no difference to me when you come. I have nothing on the book except to play golf and see you. Come in anytime—I don't have to be notified in advance, so I'll be seeing you one of

Source: Adapted from Arthur Elliott Carlisle, *Organizational Dynamics,* Vol. 5 (1976), pp. 50–62. © 1976 by AMACOM, a division of American Management Association, New York. All rights reserved. Used by permission.

> I should have recognized at once that this was no ordinary manager; he answered his own phone . . .

these days," and he then hung up. I was dumbfounded. Here was a highly placed executive with apparently nothing to do except play golf and talk to visitors.

I took MacGregor at his word and drove over immediately to see him without any further announcement of my visit. MacGregor's office, in a small building at one corner of the refinery, adjoined that of his secretary—who, when I arrived, was knitting busily and, without dropping a stitch, said to me, "You must be Mr. Carlisle; he's in there," indicating MacGregor's office with a glance at a connecting door.

MacGregor's office was large and had a big window overlooking the refinery, a conference table with eight chairs arranged around it (one of which, at the head, was more comfortable and imposing than the rest), an engineer's file cabinet with a series of wide drawers, two easy chairs, a sofa, a coffee table with a phone on it, and a desk. The desk had been shoved all the way into a corner; there was no way a chair could be slipped in behind it, and it was covered with technical journals. A lamp stood on the desk, but its plug was not connected to an outlet. There was no phone on the desk. MacGregor, a tall, slender man with a tanned face, stood by the window peering absently into space. He turned slowly when I entered his office and said, "You must be Carlisle. The head of-

fice told me you wanted to talk to me about the way we run things here. Sit down on the sofa and fire away."

MacGREGOR'S MODUS OPERANDI

"Do you hold regular meetings with your subordinates?" I asked.

"Yes, I do," he replied.

"How often?" I asked.

"Once a week, on Thursdays between 10:00 A.M. and noon; that's why I couldn't see you then," was his response.

"What sorts of things do you discuss?" I queried, following my interview guide.

"My subordinates tell me about the decisions they've made during the past week," he explained.

"Then you believe in participative decision making," I commented.

"No—as a matter of fact, I don't," said MacGregor.

"Then why hold the meetings?" I asked. "Why not just tell your people about the operating decisions you've made and let them know how to carry them out?"

"Oh, I don't make their decisions for them and I just don't believe in participating in the decisions they should be making, either; we hold the weekly meeting so that I can keep informed on what they're doing and how. The meeting also gives me a chance to appraise their technical and managerial abilities," he explained. "I used to make all the operating decisions myself; but I quit doing that a few years ago when I discovered my golf game was going to hell because I didn't have enough time to practice. Now that I've quit making other people's decisions my game is back where it should be."

"You don't make operating decisions any more?" I asked in astonishment.

MacGregor refused to make decisions related to the work of his subordinates.

"No," he replied. Sensing my incredulity, he added. "Obviously you don't believe me. Why not ask some of my subordinates?"

PETERSON'S VIEW OF MacGREGOR

I picked Peterson who, when phoned to see whether he was available, said that he had nothing to do. So I went to Peterson's office.

Peterson was in his late twenties. He asked me what I thought of MacGregor. I said I found him most unusual. Peterson replied, "Yes, he's a gas." MacGregor refused to make decisions related to the work of his subordinates. When Peterson got into a situation he could not deal with, he said he called one of the other supervisors, usually Johnson, and together they worked it out. At the Thursday meetings, he reported on the decision and gave credit to his helper. "If I hadn't," he added, "I probably wouldn't get help from that quarter again."

In reply to a query on what the Thursday meetings were like, he said, "Well, we all sit around that big conference table in MacGregor's office. He sits at the head like a thinned-down Buddha, and we go around the table talking about the decisions we've made, and if we got help, who helped us. The other guys occasionally make comments—especially if the particular decision being discussed was like one they had to make themselves at some point or if it had some direct effect on their own operations." MacGregor had said very little at these past few meetings, according to Peterson, but he did pass on any new developments that he heard about at the head office.

JOHNSON'S VIEW OF MacGREGOR

I also walked over to Johnson's unit and found him to be in his early thirties. After a couple of minutes of casual conversation, I discovered that MacGregor and all eight of his subordinates were chemical engineers. Johnson said, "I suppose MacGregor gave you that bit about his not making decisions, didn't he? That man is a gas."

"It isn't true though, is it? He does make decisions, doesn't he?" I asked.

"No, he doesn't; everything he told you is true. He simply decided not to get involved in decisions that his subordinates are being paid to make. So he stopped making them, and they tell me he plays a lot of golf in the time he saves," said Johnson.

"The supervisors are a lot more self-reliant, and we don't have to do their work for them."

Then I asked whether he tried to get MacGregor to make a decision and his response was: "Only once. I had been on the job for only about a week when I ran into an operating problem I couldn't solve, so I phoned MacGregor. He answered the phone with that sleepy 'Hello' of his. I told him who I was and that I had a problem. His response was instantaneous: 'Good, that's what you're being paid to do, solve problems,' and then he hung up. I was dumbfounded. I didn't really know any of the people I was working with, so because I didn't think I had any other alternative, I called him back, got the same sleepy 'Hello,' and again identified myself. He replied sharply, 'I thought I told you that you were paid to solve problems. Do you think I should do your job as well as my own?' When I insisted on seeing him about my problem, he answered, 'I don't know how you expect me to help you. You have a technical problem and I don't go into the refinery anymore. Ask one of the other managers. They're all in touch with what goes on out there.'

'I didn't know which one to consult, so I insisted again on seeing him. He finally agreed—grudgingly—to see me right away, so I went over to his office and there he was in his characteristic looking-out-the-window posture. When I sat down, he started the dirty-shirt routine—but when he saw that I was determined to involve him in my problems, he sat down on the sofa in front of his coffee table and, pen in hand, prepared to write on a pad of paper. He asked me to state precisely what the problem was and he wrote down exactly what I said. Then he asked what the conditions for its solutions were. I replied that I didn't know what he meant by that question. His response was, 'If you don't know what conditions have to be satisfied for a solution to be reached, how do you know when you've solved the problem?' I told him I'd never thought of approaching a problem that way and he replied, 'Then you'd better start. I'll work through this one with you *this* time, but don't expect me to do your problem solving for you because that's *your* job, not mine.'

I stumbled through the conditions that would have to be satisfied by the solution. Then he asked me what al-

"My subordinates compete with one another in helping anyone with a problem . . ."

ternative approaches I could think of. I gave him the first one I could think of—let's call it X—and he wrote it down and asked me what would happen if I did X. I replied with my answer—let's call it A. Then he asked me how A compared with the conditions I had established for the solution of the problem. I replied that it did not meet them. MacGregor told me that I'd have to think of another. I came up with Y, which I said would yield result B, and this still fell short of the solution conditions. After more prodding from MacGregor, I came up with Z, which I said would have C as a result; although this clearly came a lot closer to the conditions I had established for the solution than any of the others I'd suggested, it still did not satisfy all of them. MacGregor then asked me if I could combine any of the approaches I'd suggested. I replied I could do X and Z and then saw that the resultant A plus C would indeed satisfy all the solution conditions I had set up previously. When I thanked MacGregor, he replied, 'What for? Get the hell out of my office; you could have done that bit of problem solving perfectly well without wasting my time. Next time you really can't solve a problem on your own, ask the Thursday man and tell me about it at the Thursday meeting."

I asked Johnson about MacGregor's reference to the Thursday man.

"He's the guy who runs the Thursday meeting when MacGregor is away from the plant. I'm the Thursday man now. My predecessor left here about two months ago."

"Where did he go? Did he quit the company?" I asked.

"God, no. He got a refinery of his own. That's what happens to a lot of Thursday men. After the kind of experience we get coping with everyone's problems and MacGregor's refusal to do what he perceives as his subordinates' work, we don't need an operating superior any more and

we're ready for our own refineries. Incidentally, most of the people at our level have adopted MacGregor's managerial method in dealing with the supervisors who report to us, and we are reaping the same kinds of benefits that he does. The supervisors are a lot more self-reliant, and we don't have to do their work for them."

MacGREGOR'S "THURSDAY MAN"

I went back to the refinery with a few last questions for MacGregor. His secretary had made considerable progress on her knitting and her boss had resumed his position by the refinery window.

"Let me ask you a couple of questions about the Thursday meeting," I continued. "First of all, I understand that when you are away, the 'Thursday man' takes over. How do you choose the individual to fill this slot?"

"Oh, that's simple. I just pick the man who is most often referred to as the one my subordinates turn to for help in dealing with their problems. Then I try him out in this assignment while I'm off. It's good training and, if he proves he can handle it, I know I have someone to propose for any vacancies that may occur at the refinery manager level. The head-office people always contact me for candidates. As a matter of fact, the Thursday-man assignment is sought after. My subordinates compete with each other in helping anyone with a problem because they know they'll get credit for their help at the Thursday meeting. You know, another development has been that jobs on the staff of this refinery are highly prized by young people who want to get ahead in the corporation; when junior management positions open up here, there are always so many candidates that I often have a tough time making a choice."

QUESTIONS

1. How do you describe MacGregor's leadership style in terms of Fiedler's contingency theory, House's path–goal theory, and Vroom and Yetton's leader-participation theory? Is his leadership style effective? Why or why not?

2. Does MacGregor make good use of communication, motivation, and group dynamics in his leadership efforts? Explain your answer.

3. Is MacGregor a good manager? Would he be a good manager in a different setting, for example, as head of an advertising firm . . . a large urban branch bank? Why or why not? ∎

Wal-Mart
Steps into the Future

Fortune magazine calls *him* an American "superman" of specialty stores; *Forbes* reports him as the richest man in America. *He* lives with his wife Helen in a modest ranch-style house in Bentonville, Arkansas, drives an old pick-up truck, and tells the employees in his Wal-mart stores to simply call him "Mr. Sam." We know him as *Sam Walton*, founder and chairman of the board of Wal-mart stores, one of the largest and fastest growing of the nation's retail chains.

PART I—WAL-MART'S ROOTS

The sprawling gray building with its dozens of trucks parked just off U.S. Highway 71 in a rural corner of northeastern Arkansas looks like any ordinary, busy warehouse.

Busy it is, but ordinary it's not. The distribution warehouse and adjoining offices are headquarters of Wal-Mart Stores Inc., the fastest-growing and one of the most profitable and innovative retailers in the country. . . .

For the past decade, Wal-Mart has outpaced all other discounters with compounded annual growth rates near 40 percent. . . .

The Wal-Mart strategy: Sell brand-name goods in small-town USA at the

Source: Part I from Lorraine Cichowski, "Small-Town Roots Make Wal-Mart Big," *USA Today* (March 8, 1985), pp. 1B, 2B. Used by permission. Part II information from "Make That Sale, Mr. Sam," *Time* (May 18, 1987), pp. 54–55; "Power Retailers," *Business Week* (December 21, 1987), pp. 86–92; Leonard M. Apcar, "Wal-Mart's Sam Walton Turns Over Chief Executive Post to David Glass," *The Wall Street Journal* (February 2, 1988), p. 31; and, "Sam Walton Chooses a Chip Off the Old CEO," *Business Week* (February 15, 1988), p. 15.

> *"Wal-Mart's expansion and merchandising strategies are carefully thought out and executed with skill and precision."*

lowest prices. Do it while being nice to the employees—who number nearly 90,000—and nice to the customers. And keep a tight rein on expenses.

Its source and inspirational leader: Sam Walton says a Wal-Mart executive, "When Sam started the business, he had an overriding philosophy that said if everybody in the business were partners and you had that type of relationship as opposed to an employer–employee relationship, that it would work a lot better. It's ingrained in Wal-Mart."

It sounds self-serving and, Wal-Mart executives fear, a bit hokey. But Wal-Mart rated several mentions in *In Search of Excellence,* the book about America's best-run companies. And analysts generally credit Wal-Mart's success to the leadership and business principles of the effervescent Walton—who shies away from interviews—and the management team he has hired since opening his first Ben Franklin variety store in Newport, Ark., in 1945.

The first of the Wal-Mart discount stores—big, flat warehouse-type buildings similar to K marts, packed with everything from apparel to automotive supplies and small appli-

ances—was opened by Walton and his brother, Bud, in nearby Rogers, Ark., in 1962. By now there are over 1000 Wal-Marts in 23 states across the south from Florida west to New Mexico and as far north as Iowa and Nebraska. Their Ben Franklin stores have been closed.

"As investors, suppliers and others close to the company know, Wal-Mart's expansion and merchandising strategies are carefully thought out and executed with skill and precision," writes Joseph Ellis, an analyst with Goldman Sachs, in an analysis of Wal-Mart." . . . The company's true competitive edge derives from the clear perception and 'levelheadedness' of top management and the unique 'corporate culture' that results throughout the organization."

Admirers generally point to these reasons for the company's success:

Listening Managers spend lots of time in stores—their own and competitors'—talking to customers and employees. Every corporate executive is required to spend at least one week a year working in a Wal-Mart store, not supervising but unloading boxes and waiting on customers.

There's a direct link between the field and corporate headquarters because the 10 regional vice presidents all live in or near this small town in the heart of poultry-raising country in the Ozark Mountains. The vice presidents are flown to their districts by corporate jet each Monday morning and returned each Thursday afternoon.

Corporate executives, too, get involved in merchandising by picking a favorite item and championing its cause for a year, such as thinking of new ways to display it in stores to attract customer attention. The executive whose product shows the best sales gain for the year wins the "contest" and the recognition of his peers.

Ellis credits customer contact for Wal-Mart's decision to stress brand names, higher quality and quicker checkout and to add pharmacy and auto repair services. Glass says customer confusion about continuous promotions at many other discounters and retail stores convinced it to limit its promotions to one sale circular per month and a promise that its regular prices are as low as possible.

Distribution Unlike many other retailers, Wal-Mart stores get few deliveries direct from suppliers. Instead, deliveries go to one of seven highly automated distribution centers, then on to the stores in Wal-Mart-owned trucks. The central distribution helps Wal-Mart control shipping and inventory costs. Ordering is computerized.

Flexibility Depending on market size, Wal-Mart stores vary from less than 30,000 to nearly 100,000 square feet, and managers cater merchandise to local demands. Wal-Mart is always testing new concepts to complement its discount stores.

Employee relations Right down to part-time clerks, all employees—called associates since the early days of the company—are encouraged to buy company stock and participate in the profit-sharing plan. In addition, they can qualify for special bonuses

for doing things like offering ideas on how to reduce pilferage. Workers are continually asked for suggestions, and a senior executive comments: "Most of the good ideas come from the bottom up."

Don Spindel, an analyst with A. G. Edwards in St. Louis, says this of Walton: "His management style is one of utilizing praise and recognition as opposed to managing by intimidation. Therefore, he's been able to get a lot out of people."

"The team spirit is important. You couldn't evaluate Wal-Mart without saying that the people make the difference," says one company executive.

There's also no mandatory retirement age, so it's common to find long-time employees working well into their 60s and 70s. Elvena Walter, 62, worked in the Rogers store for 16 years—more than half of those as a manager in the men's apparel department. "I've always enjoyed it," she says, adding hesitantly, however, "There are times when I think they expect too much. There are a lot of things they want all at one time."

Capturing the spirit of Wal-Mart best may be its famous "Saturday morning meetings." As many as 300 top and middle-managers, store personnel and buyers crowd a sparse auditorium behind the general offices to review the week's sales, talk about products and recognize—through applause and cheering—any individual accomplishments. Even a store clerk whose display might have boosted sales of an item could be singled out for praise. The meeting is often chaired by Walton, who lives less than five minutes away.

Wal-Mart executives reject the notion that continued growth ("Someday we'll reach California," Glass says) will cause Wal-Mart to lose its small-town values and take its busy managers out of contact with its customers.

Says Jim Von Gremp, corporate public affairs director, "Just because

you're bigger doesn't mean you're different. You've just done the same thing more times."

PART II—WAL-MART'S FUTURE

Wal-Mart ranks as the third largest U.S. retailer, having moved past J.C. Penney in sales, and gaining fast on the industry giants—K-mart and Sears. But the company is also at a turning point. It's expanding beyond its regional base in the sun-belt states to become a truly national operation.

Presently in 23 states, Wal-Mart is expected to keep expanding to cover the map from California to New York. It's also expanding in other ways. There are now over 50 Sam's Wholesale Clubs that operate in warehouse-style stores, and cater to volume purchasers. The company has also opened its first "hypermarket" or combination discount store and supermarket.

To help manage the growth, the company is investing in a satellite communications system. This will allow a continual stream of sales and inventory data to flow between every store and corporate headquarters. This headquarters, by the way, remains located in plain red brick offices in Bentonville. The building is frugal, up to and including the chairman's office.

But through it all, Wal-Mart has shown great momentum over the years, and great ideas. Sam Walton, described by *Time* magazine as someone with an "uncanny ability to motivate employees and slash expenses," has been the central force. With his heavy travel schedule of visiting as many as six stores a day, he has had a personal impact throughout the organization. He has inspired Wal-Mart employees and created what one industry analyst calls "the best-managed company I've ever followed, and I've looked at hundreds."

For some time, though, a worrysome question has nagged the company—what will happen after Mr. Sam is no longer in charge. The question has been called. Sam Walton has finally given up his title of chief executive officer and handed the job to David D. Glass. At the age of 52, Glass moved up from president to take over the top slot. With an educational background in finance, and broad merchandising experience, he has been a driving force behind the company's experiment with hypermarkets. He was praised by Walton as someone who "has exhibited excellent leadership and management skills." In his own behalf, Glass indicates that he shares the same retailing principles with Walton, and doesn't plan any major changes at Wal-Mart. Glass also concedes, however, that he doesn't have Mr. Sam's "flair." He adds, "Sam's one of a kind."

> **Glass also concedes, however, that he doesn't have Mr. Sam's "flair." He adds, "Sam's one of a kind."**

Most outsiders agree that Glass will probably make few changes. They also acknowledge that while Walton has given up his title, he hasn't given up being a part of the company. He retains the title of chairman, and will continue to preside over the regular Saturday morning management meetings. He's also expected to continue visiting Wal-Mart's many stores, just as he's done in the past. "Sam's only hobby besides bird hunting is working," Glass says, "Sam will still be involved. The change will be gradual."

QUESTIONS

1. Use the leadership theories introduced in Chapter 10 to analyze and explain Sam Walton's leadership approach. In what way do his leadership and Wal-Mart's corporate strategy complement one another?

2. How has Walton made good use of basic concepts of communication, motivation, and group dynamics in his leadership of Wal-Mart? Are these things that David Glass should be easily able to continue? Explain your answer.

3. What pressures will continued growth in size put on the current leadership approach at Wal-Mart? What should Glass do to maintain leadership effectiveness throughout the company as it grows? Why? ■

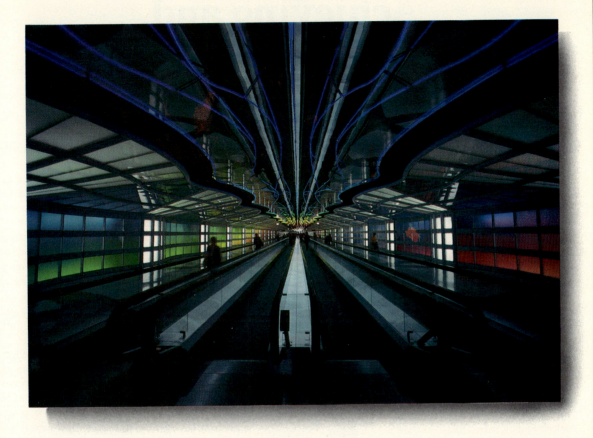

CONTROLLING FOR PRODUCTIVITY

Achieving and Sustaining the Competitive Edge

The last decade has been a test of sorts for American industry—a make-or-break-it period in which managers everywhere had to confront certain unpleasant economic realities. The rising and burdensome cost of credit and a soaring dollar, coupled with intense, fast-growing international competition, knocked numerous companies for a loop. Some went under; others could not survive a wave of mergers and conglomerations. A good many of the companies that didn't pull through these hard times were paying the ultimate price for a habitual lack of managerial control. Far-sighted leaders in both manufacturing and service sectors saw the writing on the wall: obviously, things had to change.

And they have been changing, to everyone's relieved surprise. American organizations have much to be proud of as they set their sights on regaining their competitive edge in the 1990s and beyond. The United States is still the biggest producer in major industries and the technologi-

cal leader in such areas as telecommunications, scientific instruments, and computers. Overall American industrial production has been rising faster than that of most other nations, and in the manufacturing sector, productivity is growing.[1]

"COST AND QUALITY CONTROL . . . BY-WORDS OF LARGE AND SMALL ORGANIZATIONS."

It seems clear that the steps some organizations took to reverse the negative trends—steps that ranged from severe cost-cutting measures and financial restructuring to worker retraining and improved quality assurance—have left those organizations in a much stronger competitive position. What began as a self-rescue mission spawned basic, much-needed changes in managerial philosophy, and those changes will undoubtedly have positive ripple-effects in the years to come.

The fight for a competitive edge is far from over, however. Quality and production control problems persist; poor worker–management relations continue to plague many organizations and reduce operational efficiency; and a narrow view of the competition has left some organizations unprepared for the challengers abroad. In light of these and other factors, the topic of managerial control has become increasingly hot.

Cost and quality control in particular are the by-words of large and small organizations alike. For a growing number of managers, moreover, quality control *is* cost control; improvements in quality inevitably lead to fewer wasteful expenditures of time and energy. And with a sustained focus on quality, the responsibility for control is more effectively distributed throughout the organization. Weyerhaeuser Company's president, George H. Weyerhaeuser, described what happened at his firm: "Because of our quality improvement efforts, hourly workers, working as

NOTES

1. Sylvia Nasar, "America's Competitive Revival," *Fortune* (January 4, 1988), pp. 44–52; and, "The Productivity Paradox," *Business Week* (June 6, 1988), pp. 100–114.
2. "Making Brawn Work with Brains," *Business Week* (April 20, 1987), pp. 59–60.
3. George Melloan, "Manufacturing's New Window of Opportunity," *Wall Street Journal* (April 19, 1988), p. 27.
4. Bill Saporito, "Cutting Costs without Cutting People," *Fortune* (May 25, 1987), pp. 27, 31.

teams, are now able to do much of the planning and control formerly imposed upon them, and they are doing it better."

Chapters 14 through 16 explore in detail the various facets of managerial control. In this Perspective we'll look at how some companies are successfully handling competitive pressures by making advances in cost and quality control. As we will see, such control need not be achieved at the expense of an organization's greatest resource—its people.

RESPONDING TO THE JAPANESE CHALLENGE

It wasn't too long ago in a now familiar story that Japanese car makers ousted the American car industry from its traditional position of dominance. Japan went for the Achilles heel of mass production, offering a broader array of cars and creating an infrastructure that could respond rapidly to market demands and new opportunities. Japanese management organized car factories by product, not function, thereby enhancing flexibility. Each worker was expected to maintain quality—and each one did. The near-legendary cooperation and teamwork of Japanese employees left their American counterparts temporarily in the dust.

This tale offers lessons in cost and quality control that have not been lost on American managers. General Electric Corporation, for instance, has invested billions of dollars in efforts to boost competitiveness. According to Fred Garry, vice-president for manufacturing, the corporation was forced to begin "looking at things from a total-cost point of view." GE has adopted a Japanese-style approach to managerial control. At its plant in Erie, Pennsylvania, engineers solicit suggestions from workers for improving productivity, and drastic cost reductions for some products have been achieved. Similarly, after Westinghouse created its Productivity & Quality Center, thousands of employees began working in teams that supervise themselves and monitor quality. The corporation invested several billion dollars in improved manufacturing methods; in a few years its income rose 50 percent.[2]

A PLACE FOR NEW TECHNOLOGIES

Milwaukee-based Allen-Bradley, owned by Rockwell International, is a prime example of an automated manufacturing company—what its CEO, J. Tracy O'Rourke, calls a "computer-enabled enterprise." Allen-Bradley makes over 300,000 different items of varying types and prices, and its engineers are

"hundreds of times more productive" because they make use of computers in all facets of their work. O'Rourke claims that a successful computer-enabled enterprise is one with virtually no expensive investory or rejects. He cautions that the quality of automated manufacturing systems must be extremely high, or "the whole thing just shuts down. If you go in this with a lack of understanding, you can get yourself into a lot of trouble."

Yet Allen-Bradley indicates the potential: its sales more than doubled during the decade in which automated manufacturing was put in

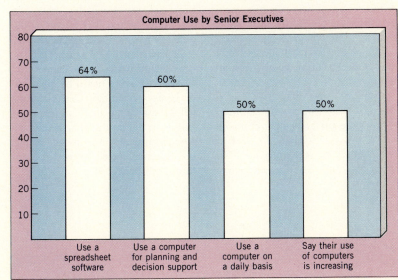

Computer Use by Senior Executives

64% Use a spreadsheet software
60% Use a computer for planning and decision support
50% Use a computer on a daily basis
50% Say their use of computers is increasing

Source: *Wall Street Journal Reports.*

place. One big challenge facing managers, O'Rourke says, is to rethink assumptions about cost control; if they are outdated, they may distort return-on-investment calculations, making this form of manufacturing seem more expensive than it is. Another control-related task is to integrate manufacturing and sales. Says O'Rourke: "We're probably going to be able to design, test, and be ready to go to market with a product faster than our sales force can handle it. That's going to be the next challenge."[3]

New cost-cutting technologies *are* expensive in many industries, and managers may have difficulties justifying their introduction. Yet as Allen-Bradley's O'Rourke suggests, that difficulty sometimes stems from budgeting and accounting systems that are no longer suited to the environment. In particular, cost-accounting methods have typically depended on savings from direct labor to recoup capital investments, but labor costs have been significantly reduced in many industries. Says John J. Clancy, president of McDonnell-Douglas Manufacturing and Engineering Company: "The nondirect cost areas—inventory requirements, product flow-through, and quality—have to be considered more closely. The normal capital-budgeting process using discounted cash flow based on hard savings has gotten in the way" of modernizing.

Manufacturing is not the only sector of the economy to face the music and initiate technological change. Increasingly, retailers have recognized that integrated information systems can help create the highly efficient store environments that attract busy customers. High-tech systems can deliver instant sales-trend data from across the nation, linking retailers and manufacturers in a tight communication chain that gets the right products where they need to be, on time. Levi Strauss, the jeans maker, is among the suppliers that have put bar codes on their merchandise to speed inventory control. In the stores of national retailers such as Sears, J.C. Penney, and Wal-Mart, optical scanners read the codes, which cuts down on processing time and enhances responsiveness to customers' needs—a key to success in the retail sector.

All this, of course, stands in addition to the more general managerial use of new computer technologies and software. Although not all executives are yet on board, data reported in the figure show that personal computer usage in the senior managerial ranks is now high and increasing. Particularly valuable are the assistance offered in planning and controlling activities.

PEOPLE COUNT TOO

A renewed emphasis on how work gets done is spreading fast, but it must be remembered that people count too. Productivity can and must mean more than how many hands are busy.

One company that tries *not* to change basic tenets is Hallmark Cards. The privately held company hasn't imposed a layoff for lack of work since its inception in 1910. What Hallmark has done, however, is to redeploy workers. Says Lowell Malone, Hallmark's vice-president for personnel: "If we have too many people, we consider it a management problem, not an employee problem." Hallmark has an ongoing retraining program, and its redeployed workers end up with a broad repertoire of skills—which translates into value added for their employer. With retraining, Hallmark has removed 1300 positions (out of some 20,000 worldwide) from its rolls since 1985; this means that 1300 people have been moved to new jobs within the company. And in the creative area, artists, writers, and marketers work together on a line of cards. Teamwork is seen as the key to productivity and a high-quality product.

Irvine Hockaday, Jr., Hallmark's CEO, reduces its corporate philosophy to two elements: "commitment to excellence and, because I can't think of a better word for it, a commitment to brotherhood. Maybe it's more aptly put as recognition of the value of people to an organization." He feels very strongly about both elements. "As soon as people can no longer dream of some progress, and in a business context, of career progress," says Hockaday, "then you lose hope. When that happens, the quality of work, the inspiration necessary, particularly in a creative business, begins to diminish."[4]

A theme we've heard before—but it bears repeating. Organizations whose managers that engage their people in the task of sharpening the competitive edge are finding themselves better placed for present and future prosperity. ∎

Fundamentals of Controlling

"Congenial Controls"

Controls may sound ominous to managers attempting to be flexible and creative in their work, but as everyone who has prepared a budget knows, they do serve a purpose. What purpose, and how served? These are the important questions, suggests Bob Waterman, author of *The Renewal Factor*. He speaks of "friendly facts and congenial controls"—not numbers for their own sake, but useful information that provides real guidance. Speaking of his earlier book, *In Search of Excellence* (co-authored with Tom Peters), Waterman concedes that too much was made of managers who overcontrol and overanalyze. In fact, a balance is needed between controls and autonomy, and Waterman is confident that organizations can find this meeting ground.

Waterman tells the story of the struggle of Cummins Engine Company, a truck-engine maker, to defend its market share against Japanese encroachments. CEO Henry Schacht saw the need for controls in the form of "friendly facts"—which aren't, as it happens, always cheering ones. In Schacht's words, "facts that reinforce what you are doing . . . are nice, because they help in terms of psychic reward. Facts that raise alarms are equally friendly, because they give you clues about how to respond, how to change, where to spend the resources." In Schacht's view, controls help managers contain risk. They provide the best

possible weapon against the competition: awareness of what's really going on. For Cummins, good controls enabled management to cut material costs by 18 percent over a three-year period and to reduce inventory supplies to just three or four days.

Waterman warns against "analysis paralysis"—the bogging-down of inefficient control systems. Clearly, too much complexity makes controls counterproductive, as one GE senior vice-president, Roger Schipke, admits. GE's Louisville-based Appliance Park tied itself into control knots at one point. Having broken down refrigeration into five different businesses, GE "made $2 billion of white boxes and no profit," says Schipke. Once the process of control was simplified, a turnaround commenced.

Congenial controls, as Waterman dubs them, serve those who develop them—and not the other way around. When viewed as "benign checks and balances," not as numerical balls-and-chains, controls are one of management's best ways of keeping tabs on the competitive reality. ■

Source: Information from "*The Renewal Factor:* Friendly Fact, Congenial Controls," *Business Week* (September 14, 1987), p. 105, and "How the Best Get Better," *Business Week* (September 14, 1987), pp. 98–100.

This chapter reviews controlling as what managers do to prevent things from going wrong in the first place, and/or to identify and correct problems as they occur. Key topics are

Controlling as a
   Management Function
Organizational Control
   Systems
Performance Appraisal
   Systems
Compensation and Benefit
   Systems
Employee Discipline
   Systems
Management by
   Objectives: An
   Integrated Planning and
   Control System
Making Controls Effective

"Keeping in touch . . . Staying informed . . . Being in control." These are important responsibilities for every manager. But, *control* is one of those words like *power*. If you aren't careful when it is used, it leaves a negative connotation. While this value judgment may be quite appropriate in certain contexts, (e.g., control that is malicious), control plays a positive and necessary role in the management process. This more positive perspective on the issue is quite evident in the chapter opener. To have things "under control" at work is good; for things to be "out of control" is bad. This chapter introduces the fundamentals of controlling as an essential management function. It considers effective control an important means for coordinating multiple and varied activities in organizations to ensure that organizational objectives are met.

CONTROLLING AS A MANAGEMENT FUNCTION

Controlling is a process of monitoring performance and taking action to ensure desired results. Its purpose is to make sure that actual performance is consistent with plans. Its basis is information well used by managers for decision making and problem solving.

The Importance of Controlling

Controlling acts in relation to the other management functions. Planning sets the directions and allocates resources. Organizing brings people and material resources together in working combinations. Leading directs people in the utilization of these resources. Controlling sees to it that the right things happen, in the right way, and at the right time as a result. In other words, proper controls help managers make sure that people in organizations do *what* is necessary, *when* it is necessary, and in the *way* it is required.[1]

Controls thus fulfill at least three purposes in organizations. First, control helps make sure overall direction is consistent with short- and long-range plans. Control provides a means for monitoring performance under plans as time passes. Second, control helps ensure that objectives and accomplishments throughout an organization are consistent with one another in proper means-end fashion. Objectives pursued at one level (e.g., work group), should be the means to achieving ends represented by objectives at the next higher level (e.g., division). Third, control helps ensure individual compliance with basic organizational rules and policies. This involves not only direct task requirements such as attendance and work hours, but also basic rules of propriety and respect for individual rights. A good example is the right to freedom from sexual harassment at work.

Figure 14.1 shows the relationship between controlling and the other management functions. Its importance is further enhanced by the following forces common to most work situations.

1. *Uncertainty* Plans and objectives deal with the future, and the future is always uncertain. There is a need for control points and control systems that allow for constructive adjustments in activities, plans, and even the objectives themselves over time.

2. *Complexity* As organizations grow in size and diversity, they become increasingly complex. Adequate controls are required to help coordinate activities and accomplish integration in the face of such complexity.

3. *Human limitations* People make mistakes. Forecasting errors are common in complex and unpredictable environments; errors of judgment can occur in any problem situation. Control helps spot such mistakes.

4. *Delegation and decentralization* Delegation and decentralization increase the decision-making authority of lower-level personnel. As authority to act moves down the hierarchy, control mechanisms are required to ensure that accountability for results flows back up. Controls help managers delegate and decentralize while maintaining accountability for results.

FIGURE 14.1 *Controlling for productivity—viewed in relationship with the other management functions.*

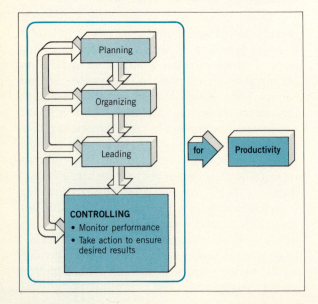

Elements in the Control Process

The emphasis of control is on action designed to prevent problems, correct problems, and/or explore opportunities. The classic example, and the purest form of the control process, is a home thermostat. We set the thermostat to a desired temperature. When actual conditions in a room deviate from the setting, the thermostat senses the difference and takes corrective action by turning on the furnace or air conditioner. They are automatically turned off again once the desired temperature is achieved.

The thermostat is a **cybernetic control system,** one that is self-contained in its performance monitoring and correction capabilities. Rarely is such an ideal state achieved in management practice. Instead, managers must implement the four steps in the **control process** listed below and depicted in Figure 14.2.

1. Establish objectives and standards.
2. Measure actual performance.
3. Compare results with objectives and standards.
4. Take necessary action.

Step 1: Establishing Objectives and Standards

The control process begins with planning and the clarification of performance objectives, as discussed in Chapters 4 and 5. From a control standpoint any objective should be associated with a measurement standard for determining when the desired end state has been reached. Managers become involved with two basic types of standards. **Output standards** measure performance *results* in terms of quantity, quality, cost, or time. Some examples include percentage error rate, dollar deviation from budgeted expenditures, and the number of units produced or customers serviced in a time period. **Input standards,** by contrast, measure the work *efforts* that go into a performance task. They are used in situations where actual performance outputs are difficult or expensive to measure. Examples include conformance to rules and procedures, efficiency in the use of resources, and even work attendance and punctuality.

Standards can be historical, and use past performance as a benchmark for evaluating correct performance. They can also be comparative—that is, based on how performance measures up to that achieved by other persons, work units, or organizations. Finally, standards can be engineered.

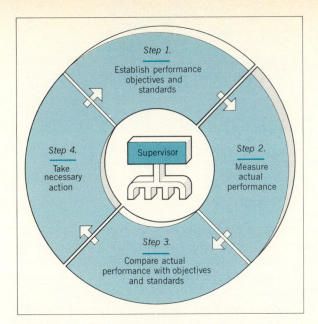

FIGURE 14.2 *Four steps in the control process: the case of the first-line supervisor.*

Through such methods as time and motion studies, for example, some jobs can be precisely analyzed to determine what outputs are possible and/or what inputs are most appropriate.

Step 2: Measuring Actual Performance

Objectives and standards set performance targets and establish a framework for evaluating results. In the measurement stage of the control process, the task is to measure actual performance outputs and/or inputs accurately. The emphasis in the last sentence should be the word *actual*. Measurement must be done well enough to spot deviations or variances between what actually occurs and what is desired.

Step 3: Comparing Actual Performance with Objectives and Standards

Action is the ultimate basis of the control process. And the need for action in any situation is identified by comparing actual performance with desired performance as represented by established objectives and standards. This comparison is summarized in the *control equation*.

Need for action
= *Desired* performance − *Actual* Performance

As shown in Figure 14.3, two outcomes are possible when actual performance is compared with objectives and standards. First, performance may equal the standard. This is a maintenance situation and requires no corrective action. However, managerial effort should still be sufficient to maintain the desired performance in the future. Second, performance may differ from the standard. This is the "exception" case and deserves immediate attention. The responsible manager should be prepared to make a decision as to what action should be taken in response to the problem or opportunity involved.

Step 4: Taking Necessary Action

Management by exception focuses a manager's attention on situations showing the most significant

FIGURE 14.3
Management by exception in the control process.

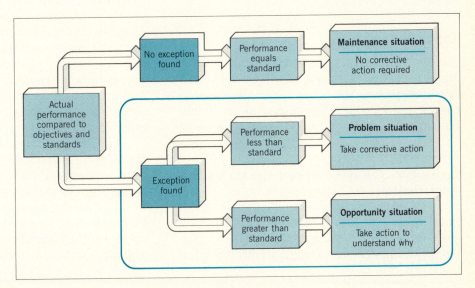

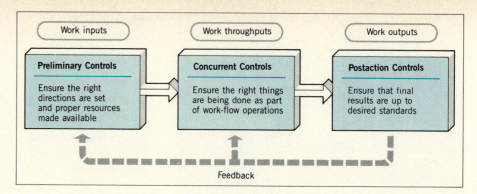

FIGURE 14.4 *Three types of controls: preliminary, concurrent, and postaction controls.*

deviations between actual and desired performance. This facilitates action while saving valuable time and energy, and allowing work efforts to be concentrated on areas of greatest need. As suggested by the control equation, the larger the observed difference between desired and actual performance, the greater the need for action. Looking again at the figure, two types of exceptions are significant—problems and opportunities. A *problem situation* is one in which actual performance is less than desired. This indicates a need for corrective action to restore performance to the desired level. Equally important, though, is the exception signaled when actual performance is above standard. This is an *opportunity situation*. The need for action is to discover why desired performance was exceeded, and learn what can be done to continue this higher level of accomplishment in the future. It is also a chance to review established objectives and standards to determine if they should be improved.

Types of Controls

The three major types of controls are classified in Figure 14.4 as preliminary, concurrent, and postaction controls.[2] As the figure shows, each type of control addresses a different part of the input-throughput-output cycle typical to all work settings.

Preliminary Controls

Preliminary controls, sometimes called **feedforward controls,** are accomplished before a work activity begins. They make sure that proper directions are set and that the right resources are available to accomplish them. At McDonald's, for example, preliminary control of food ingredients plays an important role in the company's ability to serve

consistent high-quality meals. As just one case in point, the company requires that suppliers of its hamburger buns produce them to exact specifications, covering everything from texture to uniformity of color.

More and more quality control experts are emphasizing the importance of preliminary controls of this nature. By ensuring that the right quantity of materials is always available in consistent quality, a large step forward is made toward ensuring that outputs will satisfy desired performance objectives. Preliminary controls are designed to anticipate potential problems and take preventative action to avoid their occurrence. This requires the forward-thinking and proactive approach to problem solving stressed in Chapter 3, rather than a reactive and defensive one.

Concurrent Controls

Concurrent controls focus on what happens during the work process. Sometimes called **steering controls,** they monitor ongoing operations and activities to make sure that things are being done correctly. Ideally, these controls allow for corrective actions to be taken while the work is being done. This helps avoid the waste and misfortunes of creating finished products or services that are unacceptable.

Looking at McDonald's again, the ever-present shift leaders exercise concurrent control through direct supervision. They constantly observe what is taking place, even while often helping out with the work. When something is not done right, they are trained to immediately intervene and correct things on the spot. Detailed instruction manuals that, for example, specify which machine or part of the facility is to be cleaned each day of the week, also "steer" workers in the right directions as their jobs are performed. They, too, function as concurrent controls helping to make sure things are done in the right ways all of the time.

Postaction Controls

Postaction controls, sometimes called **feedback controls,** take place after an action is completed. They focus on end results, as opposed to inputs and activities. Restaurants ask how you like a meal . . . after it is eaten; a final exam grade tells you how well you performed . . . after the course is over; a final budget summary informs managers of any cost overruns . . . after a project is completed. Going back to McDonald's, employees at each location never know when a corporate evaluator may stop in to sample the food and the service. When this happens, though, the evaluator provides feedback with the goal of helping to further improve operations.

In these and related ways, postaction controls provide feedback or information which can be used to evaluate existing plans and activities, and better prepare future ones. They also can contribute to better preliminary and concurrent controls by helping to identify where changes in resource inputs and/or workflow operations might improve final results. In addition, postaction controls provide a basis for formally documenting accomplishments and making decisions on the allocation of performance-contingent rewards. Look around the next time you're in a McDonald's restaurant. Many proudly display wall plaques indicating special corporate recognition for the store's outstanding accomplishments; at others, you're likely to see an "employee-of-the-month" singled out for similar recognition.

Internal and External Control Strategies

Managers can approach their controlling responsibilities in two ways. First, they can rely on other persons to control their own behavior. This is an **internal control** strategy that allows motivated individuals and groups to exercise self-discipline in fulfilling job expectations. Second, managers can take direct action to control the behavior of other persons. This **external control** strategy occurs through personal supervision and the use of formal administrative systems. As shown in Figure 14.5, effective control typically involves using both strategies to good advantage.[3]

Internal Control

Internal control is self-control. It is exercised by people motivated to take charge of their own behavior on the job. Douglas McGregor's Theory Y perspective, introduced in Chapter 2, recognizes a willingness for people to exercise self-control in their work.[4] Of course, he also notes that people will do this only for those matters to which they are truly committed. Any manager who expects others to exercise internal control should be willing to let them participate in setting performance objectives and standards. Reliance on an internal control strategy also requires a high degree of trust from the manager. When people are left to perform on their own, managers must trust them to fulfill their obligations. McGregor would probably argue that managers should trust others to exercise self-control wherever possible. When and if the trust proves unjustified, alternative measures can be taken. Unfortunately, many managers begin with the assumption that others *can't* be trusted. This is a limited view of human nature that may well inhibit the personal growth of subordinates.

The potential for self-control is enhanced when highly competent people have clear performance objectives and proper resource support. It is also enhanced by the internal motivation associated with participative work cultures in which people are treated with respect and consideration, are allowed to exercise personal initiative, and have ample opportunities for intrinsic rewards for job performance.[5]

Many of our thoughts on enriched job designs and autonomous work groups in Chapter 8 are based on increased individual responsibility and self-control. As these cases show, internal control is finding its way into the new work scene with positive results.[5]

At NUMMI the GM-Toyota joint venture in California, officially called New United Motor Manufacturing, Inc., teamwork leads the way. Workers are organized into six to eight persons teams each headed by an hourly worker. Each team member is responsibile for a variety of tasks, and gets assistance

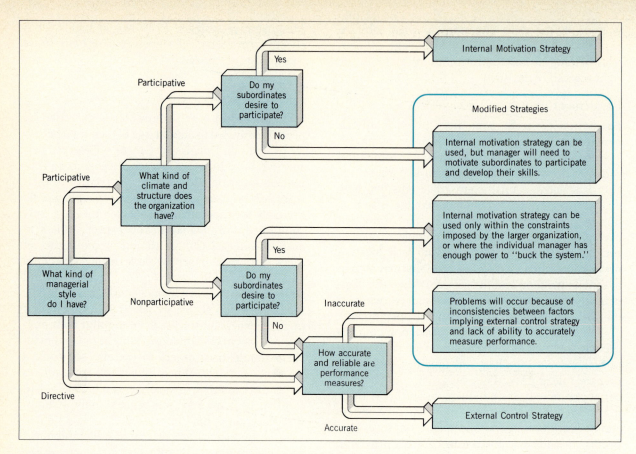

FIGURE 14.5 *Decision tree for choosing a managerial control strategy.*

Source: Permission of the *Harvard Business Review.* Exhibit from "Fit Control Systems to Your Managerial Style" by Cortlandt Cammann and David A. Nadler (January–February 1976), p. 71. Copyright © 1976 by the President and Fellows of Harvard College. All rights reserved.

from others when needed. Everyone has the power to stop the assembly line any time a machine malfunctions or a defective part is produced. The plant is acclaimed for productivity and the quality of its products.

At Huffy Corporation the bicycle maker's new production methods and a cooperative work climate have boosted productivity about 30 percent in five years. Employees get involved in decisions, are expected to inspect their own work, and work with one another as mutually-helpful quality controllers. In this way most problems are corrected before a whole batch of defective bikes is produced. Individual commitment is bolstered by a gain-sharing plan in which workers receive separate monthly checks for their shares of any cost savings realized in the prior month.

External Control

External control supplements internal control to further direct behavior in organizations toward a common purpose. It extends the control process in several ways. To begin, managers can and do exercise control by directly supervising the work of subordinates and taking any required action to ensure desired results. Job technology can also play an important role in external control. *Newsline 14.1* on the "silent supervisor" gives an extreme example of how advanced computer technologies can be used to control individual work performance in some jobs. Less controversial is the technological control that comes from the predictability of performance provided by some machine-intensive operations, such as computer assisted manufacturing to be discussed in Chapter 16. In addition, external control

SILENT SUPERVISOR:
THE BOSS THAT NEVER BLINKS

Is "Big Brother" in your office? According to Congress's Office of Technology Assessment, over six million workers are monitored daily via their computers, which are able to tally keystrokes, phone calls, and other measures of productivity. Monitoring techniques vary depending on the job being assessed, but most electronic supervision requires only the straightforward installation of special computer software. This software records and tabulates details of individual workers' efficiency, providing managers with up-to-date productivity information.

Not surprisingly, computer surveillance has both staunch supporters and fierce critics. "We are letting management make better, quicker decisions based on facts, not emotions," says R. Douglas MacIntyre, a vice-president at Management Science America, which develops monitoring programs. Such programs are employed in a variety of ways. Pacific Southwest Airlines, for example, records how long each reservations clerk spends on each phone call and how much time elapses between calls—and then assigns negative points for each call in excess of an average 109 seconds. Too many points can lead to a clerk's dismissal.

In contrast, Automatic Data Processing combines its monitoring system with pay-for-performance programs, allowing highly efficient data-entry typists to increase their pay by up to 40 percent. At Citicorp Latino, Inc., the South Florida subsidiary scans employee calls using a personal computer hooked up to its digital PBX. When a software developer was discovered to spend half his day working on the phone with an overseas bank, management looked in. Instead of the developer trying to correct problems via long distance, the software manual was rewritten and a new staff training program initiated for the bank.

While some workers respond positively to objective measures of their activity, many others find computer surveillance stress-inducing and counterproductive. One study by 9 to 5, a working women's organization, found that monitored workers were especially likely to report health problems such as headaches, depression, and digestive ailments. Karen Nussbaum, 9 to 5's director, claims that "the potential for corporate abuse (of such monitoring) is staggering." Various experts as well as labor and governmental representatives share Nussbaum's concern about invasion of privacy and dehumanization. In addition, critics increasingly argue that computer monitoring is no more than a new spin on the old idea of output quotas—and that the working speeds established are unrealistically high.

The question is whether some computer surveillance coupled with old-fashioned personal supervision can improve productivity without jeopardizing product quality. Labor and technology specialist Harley Shaiken expresses his doubts: "(Monitoring) seems to address workplace problems technologically when they perhaps should be addressed through better worker-manager relations."

"Big Brother" may be watching, but someone with a human face has to watch, too.

Source: Information from "Memo to Workers: Don't Phone Home," *Business Week* (January 28, 1988), pp. 88–89; and, Stephen Koepp, "The Boss that Never Blinks," *Time* (July 28, 1986), pp. 46–47.

is accomplished when managers create and implement appropriate management systems. Well chosen policies and procedures, organization structures, and the like, all have the potential to guide behavior in desired directions. Many ideas on this important aspect of organizational control systems are found in the remainder of this chapter.

ORGANIZATIONAL CONTROL SYSTEMS

Figure 14.6 classifies the essential components of organizational control systems into two groups. Controls in the first group derive from planning, organizing, and leading as management functions. The second group includes comprehensive controls which are new directions for us to study.

Planning and Controlling

Good planning facilitates control. Planning gives direction to the organization as a whole and to the individuals and groups that are its working components. Control via strategy and objectives occurs when work behaviors are directed toward the right end result. When goals are clear to begin with, performance deviations caused by a lack of direction in one's work efforts are less likely to occur.

Control via policies and procedures occurs in similar fashion. They offer guidelines for behavior that help ensure people act uniformly and respond in the same ways to defined problem situations. Reflecting on past experience and then planning ahead by specifying policies and procedures to guide future behavior in similar circumstances are important aspects of control in any organization.

Organizing and Controlling

Good organizing facilitates control. Throughout this book we have emphasized the necessity of providing adequate support for people's work efforts in organizations. Control via staff selection and training involves the maintenance of a qualified workforce. This means staffing an organization with qualified personnel and providing them with adequate training to enhance their skills over time. The closer the match between skills and job requirements, the greater the probability that work efforts will be appropriate to performance objectives. This reduces the need for external controls and facilitates internal or self-control.

The design of organizational structures and jobs is also important. Control via structural and job design occurs when a good match is achieved between the tasks to be accomplished, the people who do them, and the structure within which the work takes place. The contingency approaches to organizational design discussed in Chapter 7 and the diagnostic approach to job enrichment covered in Chapter 8 capture this logic well.

Leading and Controlling

Good leading facilitates control. Leadership is a use of power to influence other people to act in ways that serve organizational objectives. Control via authority relations occurs when a manager directly supervises the work activities of someone else. This is one of the external forms of administrative control discussed earlier. By formally overseeing work, deviations from standard can be prevented and/or corrected through direct superior–subordinate communications.

Control via group norms may support or hinder a manager's efforts. The best situation is when group norms support organizational objectives. Ideally, too, the commitment to positive norms extends throughout an organization and is manifested by a strong and supportive culture. When a manager assists in the development of a positive culture and norms, good leadership also facilitates control.

Comprehensive Controls

Each of the prior aspects of organizational control builds directly from one of the other management functions. As you can see, these topics have been covered elsewhere in this book. Now, it is time to shift our attention to the other six "comprehensive" controls identified in the figure. Performance-appraisal systems, pay and reward systems, management-by-objective systems, and employee-discipline systems will be reviewed in the present chapter. Control by management information systems and budgets is covered in Chapter 15. Operations management and control is covered in Chapter 16.

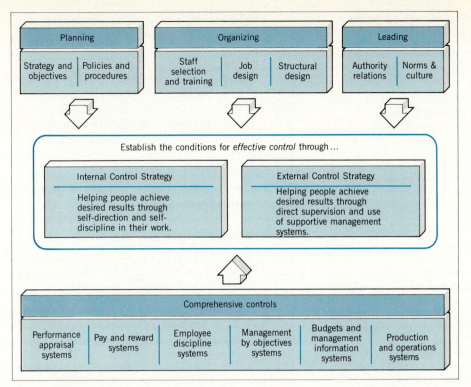

FIGURE 14.6 *Components of organizational control systems: foundations for effective internal and external control.*

The diagram contains the following elements:

Planning
- Strategy and objectives
- Policies and procedures

Organizing
- Staff selection and training
- Job design
- Structural design

Leading
- Authority relations
- Norms & culture

Establish the conditions for *effective control* through...

Internal Control Strategy
Helping people achieve desired results through self-direction and self-discipline in their work.

External Control Strategy
Helping people achieve desired results through direct supervision and use of supportive management systems.

Comprehensive controls
- Performance appraisal systems
- Pay and reward systems
- Employee discipline systems
- Management by objectives systems
- Budgets and management information systems
- Production and operations systems

PERFORMANCE APPRAISAL SYSTEMS

Performance appraisal is a process of formally evaluating someone's work and providing feedback on their performance. Comprehensive control in any organization is enhanced by a good performance appraisal system that is well implemented by managers at all levels.[6]

Purposes of Performance Appraisal

The basic intent of any performance appraisal system is to provide information about work performance. This information, in turn, may be used for two quite different purposes: (1) *evaluation*—letting people know where they stand relative to objectives and standards, and (2) *development*—assisting in the training and continued personal development of people. Table 14.1 shows how these purposes differ in several respects. Note that a manager acts in more of a judgmental role when using performance appraisal for evaluation, and in more of a counseling role when using performance appraisal for development.

Each role is important and both require good communication skills of the types discussed in Chapter 11. But, the required communications are quite different in each case. Success as a counselor requires active listening skills and the ability to guide and help another person. Success as a judge and evaluator requires the ability to give constructive feedback that is often critical of someone else's accomplishments. This distinction was found to be quite important—[7]

at American Cyanamid where a survey revealed that employees viewed the company as "conservative, bureaucratic, and not sufficiently people-oriented." Part of the problem traced to a performance appraisal system in which managers had to compare the performance of subordinates with one another, and were required to discuss their subordinate's shortcomings in formal "progress reviews." Under a more popular new system, supervisors are specifically focused on complimenting subordinates on their strengths and accomplishments. They refer to shortcomings only if serious

TABLE 14.1 *Two Purposes Served by Performance Appraisal Systems: Evaluation and Development*

I.   In respect to *evaluation*, performance appraisal—

■   Focuses on *past* performance and the measurement of results against standards.
■   Provides a basis for allocating performance-contingent rewards and documenting performance for the record.
■   Involves the manager in the *judgmental role* of giving a direct evaluation of another person's performance accomplishments.
■   Requires good communication skills and the ability to offer constructive, often critical, feedback to someone else.
■   Often creates a passive and even defensive role for the person being judged.

II.   In respect to *development*, performance appraisal—

■   Focuses on *future* performance and the clarification of the standards of success.
■   Provides a way of discovering any performance obstacles, and identifying training and development opportunities.
■   Involves the manager in the *counseling role* of being helpful and offering advice on another person's developmental needs.
■   Requires good communication skills and the ability to actively listen to someone else's concerns and feelings.
■   Often creates an active and involved role for the person being counseled.

Source: Developed in part from Larry L. Cummings and Donald P. Schwab, *Performance in Organizations: Determinants and Appraisal* (Glenview, IL: Scott, Foresman, 1973).

and within the individual's capacity to change. Now, the progress reviews are supposed to be ego-supporting now rather than ego-damaging.

When done well, performance appraisal facilitates control through both its evaluation and its development purposes. The benefits apply to the individual and the supervisor, as well as the organization as a whole. For example,[8]

1.   The individual benefits from *improved*—
■   *Understanding* of past achievements, the methods of evaluation, and future performance expectations.
■   *Opportunities* to communicate concerns, ideas, needs, and plans to a supervisor.
■   *Confidence* that performance is taken seriously by higher management.

2.   The supervisor benefits from *improved*—
■   *Understanding* of the support subordinates need to do their jobs well.
■   *Human-resource planning* which helps identify staffing needs.

■   *Confidence* that subordinates know how they have done and what is expected in the future.

3.   The organization benefits from *improved*—
■   *Performance* as the consistency and predictability of performance is increased throughout the organization.
■   *Personnel decisions* on matters such as salary increases, staff selection, promotions, terminations, or transfers.
■   *Training and development* as programs are planned with good information about personnel strengths and weaknesses.

Performance Appraisal Methods

Managers use a variety of methods to formally appraise individual performance. These include graphic rating scales, behaviorally anchored rating scales, critical-incident techniques, free-form narratives, and multiperson comparisons. Regardless of the approach used, any appraisal must be[9]

1.   *Relevant* The measures must be as closely related to actual job requirements as possible.
2.   *Unbiased* The measures must be of performance-related factors; they should not measure nonperformance factors.
3.   *Significant* The measures must relate to performance outcomes that are important to the accomplishment of organizational objectives.
4.   *Practical* The measures must be capable of being accurately and efficiently taken in the actual work setting.

Two specific criteria of the strength of a performance-appraisal method are **reliability** and **validity.** For a performance-appraisal method to be *reliable,* it must be consistent in yielding the same result over time and/or for different raters. For it to be *valid,* it must be relevant to the job at hand and unbiased—that is, it must measure only factors directly relevant to performance. Both these criteria are especially important given legal concerns for the impact of performance appraisal practices on age, sex and other forms of discrimination in the workplace. A manager who hires, fires, or promotes someone is increasingly called upon to defend such actions—sometimes in specific response to lawsuits alleging that the actions were discriminatory. At a minimum, written documentation of performance appraisals and a record of consistent past actions will be required to back up any contested decision.[10] The informed manager understands not only the various performance appraisal methods, but also their strengths and limitations.

Graphic Rating Scales

Graphic rating scales, like the one in Figure 14.7, list a variety of traits or characteristics that are thought to be related to high performance outcomes in a given job. A manager then rates the individual on each trait to indicate a range of unsatisfactory to outstanding accomplishments. These ratings are sometimes given point values to allow for a summary numerical rating. The primary appeal of graphic rating scales is that they are relatively easy to complete, and are efficient in the use of time and other resources. Their reliability and validity, however, are easily questioned.

FIGURE 14.7 *Example of a graphic rating scale for performance appraisal.*

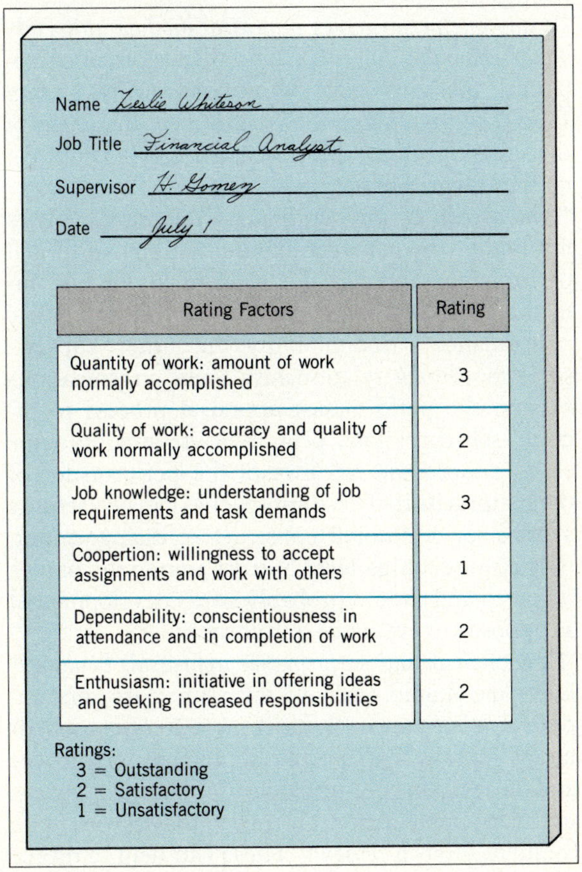

Name _Leslie Whiteson_

Job Title _Financial Analyst_

Supervisor _H. Gomez_

Date _July 1_

Rating Factors	Rating
Quantity of work: amount of work normally accomplished	3
Quality of work: accuracy and quality of work normally accomplished	2
Job knowledge: understanding of job requirements and task demands	3
Coopertion: willingness to accept assignments and work with others	1
Dependability: conscientiousness in attendance and in completion of work	2
Enthusiasm: initiative in offering ideas and seeking increased responsibilities	2

Ratings:
3 = Outstanding
2 = Satisfactory
1 = Unsatisfactory

Behaviorally Anchored Rating Scales

A **behaviorally anchored rating scale (BARS)** is based on explicit descriptions of actual behaviors that exemplify various levels of performance achievement. Look at the case in Figure 14.8. "Extremely poor" performance is clearly defined as when a customer-service representative can be "expected to treat a customer rudely and with disrespect." Because performance assessments are anchored to specific descriptions of work behavior, the reliability and validity of a BARS are improved over the graphic rating scale. This is also helpful in training people to master job skills of demonstrated performance importance. Even though somewhat complex to develop and administer, the BARS method of performance appraisal is growing in popularity.

Critical-Incident Techniques

The **critical-incident technique** involves a running log or inventory of effective and ineffective job behaviors. By creating a written record of positive and negative performance examples, the critical-incident method documents success or failure patterns that can be specifically discussed with the individual. A good critical-incident log is complete and unbiased; a manager must be observant, diligent, and fair when selecting incidents for the record. Using the case of the customer service representative again, a critical incidents log might contain—

a Positive example Took extraordinary care of a customer who had purchased a defective item from a company store in another city.

a Negative example Acted rudely in dismissing the complaint of a customer who felt that a "sale" item was erroneously advertised.

Free-Form Narratives

The **free-form narrative** is a written essay description of someone's job performance. The commentary typically includes actual descriptions of performance, discusses an individual's strengths and weaknesses, and provides an overall evaluation. Free-form narratives are sometimes used in combination with other performance appraisal methods, such as the graphic rating scale. Because of their essay character, free-form narratives require good written communication skills on the part of the person doing the evaluation.

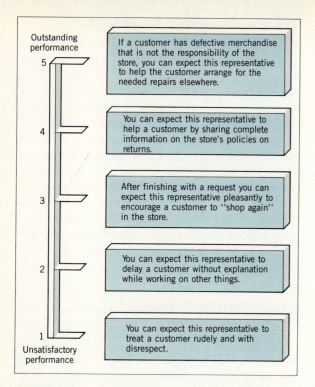

Outstanding performance

5

If a customer has defective merchandise that is not the responsibility of the store, you can expect this representative to help the customer arrange for the needed repairs elsewhere.

4

You can expect this representative to help a customer by sharing complete information on the store's policies on returns.

3

After finishing with a request you can expect this representative pleasantly to encourage a customer to "shop again" in the store.

2

You can expect this representative to delay a customer without explanation while working on other things.

1

You can expect this representative to treat a customer rudely and with disrespect.

Unsatisfactory performance

FIGURE 14.8 *Example of a behaviorally anchored rating scale for performance appraisal: the case of a customer-service representative.*

Multiperson Comparisons

Multiperson comparisons formally compare one person's performance with that of one or more others: Three of the more common techniques are:

1. *Rank ordering* All persons being rated are arranged in order of performance achievement. The best performer goes to the top of the list, and the worst performer goes to the bottom, with no ties allowed.

2. *Paired comparison* Each person is formally compared to every other person, and is rated as either the superior or weaker member of the pair. After all paired comparisons are made, each person is assigned a summary ranking based on the number of superior scores achieved.

3. *Forced distribution* Each person is placed into a specified frequency distribution of performance classifications. For example, General Motors managers now have to identify which of their subordinates fall into these performance categories: top 10 percent, next 25 percent, next 55 percent, and bot-

tom 10 percent. They are also required to enforce pay differences between categories.[11]

Multiperson comparisons can also be combined with one or more of the other methods. They are an additional point of comparative reference that can add rigor to the performance appraisal process.

Questions and Answers on Effective Performance Appraisal

A good performance appraisal system facilitates managerial control in a positive manner. This includes adequate attention to the needs of individuals as well as the organization. Some questions and answers to keep in mind on the challenges of doing effective performance appraisals are the following.

"Should performance appraisals be done at all?" The answer to this question is "yes." As indicated earlier, performance appraisals offer numerous benefits that play an important and necessary role in the management process.

"Is any one performance appraisal method uniformly better than the others?" No, all performance appraisal methods have weaknesses. Any system should be designed or chosen to meet the needs of the situation. Often, an approach involving multiple methods works best.

"Who should do the performance appraisal?" At a minimum, the manager should complete a formal performance appraisal for each of his or her immediate subordinates. This establishes a basic performance accountability in the supervisor–subordinate relationship. Some organizations expand the performance appraisal process to include self-appraisals, peer reviews, and, in some cases, subordinate reviews of the performance of their supervisors. These approaches can be useful as a basis for additional constructive dialogue. But, they require a high level of trust among the parties involved and should probably stress developmental as opposed to evaluative purposes.

"How often should performance appraisals be done?" Everyone should receive a formal performance appraisal at least once a year. A more frequent schedule of appraisals is appropriate for new employees and those having performance problems. It is always useful to supplement the formal appraisal with more frequent interim reviews. These can help reinforce

performance targets, modify plans and initiate support activities where needed.

"Is there any special advice for conducting effective performance appraisal interviews?" The actual performance appraisal interview, as noted in our discussion of communication in Chapter 11, may be one of the most difficult events managers must deal with. It can be a stressful, emotional, and even hostile situation. Performance reviews challenge the interpersonal and communication skills of all parties concerned. As a manager, you must take the lead in preparing for and conducting such interviews in an effective manner. Table 14.2 lists several helpful guidelines.

COMPENSATION AND BENEFIT SYSTEMS

Any organizational control system should improve the consistency and predictability of desired behavior. Important and most useful in this regard are compensation and benefit systems. When properly designed and implemented, they help (1) attract people to the organization and retain them, (2) motivate them to exert maximum effort in their work, and (3) signify for them the value of their contributions to the organization. There is an element of control in each of these purposes. Although we discussed the motivational aspects of incentive pay and rewards in Chapter 12, compensation deserves special attention here for its role in the overall control process. We'll begin with an example taken from a perspective offered in the *Wall Street Journal*.[12]

ILLUSTRATIVE CASE:
HIGH WAGES DON'T NECESSARILY MEAN HIGH COSTS

Most business people thought Henry Ford was a madman when he announced, in 1914, that he was raising the minimum wage for plant workers from $2.34 to a hitherto unheard of $5 a day. It simply wouldn't work, they said. Labor costs would be too expensive. The employees would simply take the extra money and stay drunk. But Ford Motor Co. has lasted longer than most of its detractors. Henry

TABLE 14.2 *How to Prepare for and Conduct a Performance Appraisal Interview*

Preparing for the Interview
1. Make sure that everyone understands the performance appraisal system and performance standards being used for their appraisals.
2. Clarify any differences in language between the formal written appraisal and the one you plan to use in the interview.
3. If you are angry with an employee, talk about it before the interview, not during the interview.
4. Be aware of your own biases in judging people.
5. Review the employee's compensation plan and be knowledgeable of his or her salary history.
6. If you have already given the employee a number of negative appraisals, be prepared to take corrective action at this point in time.

Conducting the Interview
1. Be thoroughly prepared.
2. Take enough time for the interview.
3. Focus on positive work performance; don't be overly negative.
4. Remember that strengths and weaknesses usually spring from the same general characteristics.
5. Admit that your judgment of performance contains some subjectivity.
6. Make it clear that the individual holds primary responsibility for development.
7. Be specific when citing examples; never generalize problem behavior.
8. Summarize agreements in writing and keep them on file for future reference.

Source: Adapted by permission of the publisher from "A Human Factors Approach to Appraisals," by John Cowan, from *Personnel* (November–December 1975), pp. 49–56, © 1975 by AMACOM, a division of American Management Associations. All rights reserved.

Ford later said: "The payment of the $5 a day for an eight-hour day was one of the finest cost-cutting moves we ever made, and the $6 day was cheaper than the $5."

Unfortunately, Ford's insight into labor costs still eludes many management people today. Low wages do not necessarily mean low costs. In fact, all too often exactly the opposite is true. Consider Eclipse Inc., a Rockford, Illinois-based manufacturer of industrial heating equipment with some 650 employees. At one time employee turnover was 95 percent per year, daily absenteeism was running at about 10 percent and there had been a five-year slide in earnings. The company decided to offer wage incentives based on individual and overall company performance, and scheduled merit reviews of all employees, including supervisors.

Wages rose by 34 percent over three years, employee turnover was reduced to 20 percent per year and absenteeism to less than 3 percent. Meanwhile, shipping volume per employee rose 65 percent and company profits jumped 600 percent.

For companies the advantages are clear. With good wages accompanied by controls and standards of accountability, a company is in a position to:

■ Attract better employees, pay them better than average wages, and expect more from them.

■ Motivate people to produce because they want to produce.

■ Insist on high productivity and refuse to tolerate anything but good overall quality and performance.

Put another way, for average wages a company will normally obtain average productivity. For high wages a company might expect to get high productivity. But it doesn't. It gets *exceptionally* high productivity.

Base Compensation

Base compensation in the form of salary or hourly wages is one means of attracting and retaining a qualified workforce. It can make the organization very desirable as a place of employment and thus help get the right people into the jobs that need to be done. The more capable a person is, the more self-control one can expect them to exercise over the tasks at hand. Unless an organization's prevailing wage and salary structure is attractive and competitive in the labor market, it will be difficult to attract and retain a staff of highly competent workers. And the less capable the workforce is to begin with, the greater the burden on external controls.

A proper base compensation system attracts a qualified workforce to an organization and increases opportunities for self-control. A basic rule of thumb should be—pay at least as much, and perhaps a bit more, in base wage or salary than what competitors are offering.

The way in which "merit" increases to base compensation are handled can also be significant to the control process. The motivation theories in Chapter 12 strongly support the notion of "pay-for-performance" or "performance-contingent" pay plans. One corporate executive summarized the implications of this thinking as follows.[13]

Pay very poorly for poor performance, pay poorly for average performance, pay good for above-average performance, pay obscenely for outstanding performance.

In practice, this advice is hard to follow and the pay-for-performance relationship often becomes obscured. *Newsline 14.2* reports on continuing criticisms about the lack of relationship between the compensation of chief executives and the performance of the companies they head. Other consulting reports document the tendencies of many organizations to treat their "fast-trackers" or high performers pretty much the same as the rest of the crowd.[14] In one survey by the Hay Group, a specialist in compensation and related matters, high achieving managers were receiving 8.7 percent increases while average performers were getting 5.5 percent. For those earning $40,000, this turns out to be a $67 per week raise for the fast-trackers versus $42 for their run-of-the-mill counterparts. Hay consultants point out that this is too little difference to have a motivating impact on work behavior. They recommend that "stars" should get 12 percent increases, that underachievers get no increases, and that average performers get 3 to 4 percent raises.

Fringe Benefits

The overall employee-benefit program of an organization also plays a role in the attraction and retention of capable workers. Fringe benefits can add 10 to 40 percent to a person's base salary. Typical benefit packages include various options on disability protection, health and life insurance, and retirement plans. At the executive level these benefits may extend into such additional "perks" as being provided with a company car and expenses, club memberships, deferred compensation, supplemental retirement benefits, and personal tax and financial planning. Regardless of the employee's level in the organization, however, the basic importance of the benefits program remains the same. When benefits are attractive or at least adequate, the organization is in a better position to employ highly qualified people and realize the advantages of self-control through staff competency.

The costs of employee benefit plans are rising at a fast pace. Health care insurance costs, in particular, are rising; and such new options as long-term-

THE 10 LARGEST GOLDEN PARACHUTES

	Company	Reason for payment	Total package** Thousands of dollars
1. **TERRENCE A. ELKES**, CEO	Viacom	Sumner Redstone takeover	$25000
2. **ROBERT FOMON**, Chmn.	E.F. Hutton	Shearson merger	16600
3. **RICHARD J. JACOB**, Chmn.	Day Intl.	M.A. Hanna merger	16000
4. **J. TYLEE WILSON**, CEO	RJR	Nabisco merger	15000
5. **LEONARD LIEBERMAN**, CEO	Supermarkets Genl.	Leveraged buyout	10700
6. **HOWARD GOLDFEDER**, Chmn.	Federated	Robert Campeau takeover	9900
7. **KENNETH F. GORMAN**, Exec. V-P	Viacom	Sumner Redstone takeover	9500
8. **ERNEST F. DOURLET**, Pres.	Day Intl.	M.A. Hanna merger	9100
9. **PAUL G. STERN**, Pres.	Unisys	Resignation	6800
10. **THOMAS B. KELLEY**, CEO	BA Investment	Monarch Capital merger	5800

* Chairman of Chrysler Motors   ** Includes final salary, bonus, long-term compensation, certain retirement benefits, and estimated future annuity payments as well as parachute

The pay of America's chief executives is rising at a rate more than double that of middle managers' average merit increases—to levels that stun and distress many observers. Last year the top ten best-paid CEOs made between $8.8 and $26.3 million in salaries, bonuses, and stock options—and many more are making in the lower millions, sparking questions about CEOs' performance. Critics such as Tom Peters claim that such compensation "has no coherence, makes no sense, and, at a time when there's a requirement for violent restructuring in companies, has a very negative impact" on employees. But supporters argue that, in the words of Robert Topel of the University of Chicago's business school, "competition is going to dictate what people make."

The debate turns on several issues: the dangers to worker morale of huge CEO salaries; the appropriateness of stock options as a performance incentive; and the validity of measuring a CEO's performance only in the stock market, whose cycles arguably reward executives unfairly. The effect of corporate size, too, is a problem; for CEOs of large firms, "total pay is going to be larger," although size alone has "little to do with how much value [the CEO can] create for the owners of the business," according to Alfred Rappaport of Northwestern University.

Some CEOs, such as Genentech's Robert Swanson, point to high shareholder returns as proof that their salaries are warranted. Yet Rappaport and others worry that too many CEOs are compensated more for short-term than long-term performance—and that when the going gets rough or a takeover occurs, excessively lavish "golden parachutes" will unfurl.

Source: As reported in "Who Made the Most—And Why," *Business Week* (May 2, 1988), pp. 50–56, and Amanda Bennett, "Corporate Chiefs' Pay Far Outpaces Inflation in the Gains of Staff," *Wall Street Journal* (March 28, 1988), p. 1.

---

care insurance are only adding to the complexity. Employers are struggling not only to keep up with increasing benefits costs, but also to respond to a complex mix of employee needs. As benefits managers struggle with this important set of issues, **cafeteria benefits** plans are growing more common. Such programs allow employees to select within a given monetary limit that combination of benefits best meeting their needs. Single workers, for example, may well elect different combinations of vacation, insurance, and retirement packages than someone closer to retirement. By providing flexibility, cafeteria benefit plans are designed to appeal to a wider range of individual needs and thus provide further satisfaction in the individual-organization relationship. For example, [15]

at Steelcase Incorporated a growing number of two-career couples and intense competition for labor has contributed to the firm's emphasis on flexibility in employment relationships. Take the case of Cindy and Scott Keech, both of whom work at the firm. Each December they sit down together to plan their selection of cafeteria benefits for the coming year. They choose a mix of medical-, dental-, life-insurance and disability coverage from a range of options offered in the company's flexible benefits package. Through piggy-backing on her husband's coverage, Cindy is sometimes able to bring home as much as an extra $900 in annual income gained from her unused benefit allowance.

EMPLOYEE DISCIPLINE SYSTEMS

"Absenteeism . . . tardiness . . . sloppy work . . . temper tantrums" . . . and the list could go on. These are all common examples of things that can be disruptive and interfere with work performance. Employee theft, as introduced in *Newsline 14.3*, is a much more extreme example of what can go wrong. All are among the types of behaviors that are frequently addressed in formal employee discipline systems. **Discipline** can be defined as influencing behavior through reprimand. In its managerial application, discipline is one way of enhancing control over the behavior of people at work. Ideally, such discipline is handled in a fair, consistent, and systematic way. Two approaches to consider are progressive discipline and positive discipline.

Progressive Discipline

Progressive discipline ties reprimands to the severity and frequency of the employee's infractions. The penalties or punishments vary in severity according to the number of times a disruptive behavior has occurred and/or its significance. For example, the progressive-discipline guidelines of one university state, "The level of disciplinary action shall increase with the level of severity of behavior engaged in and based on whether the conduct is of a repetitive nature." Details of this program are shown in Table 14.3.

Note in the table, that the ultimate penalty of "discharge" is reserved for the most severe behaviors (e.g., any felony crime) or for continual infractions of less severe behaviors. Someone who is continually late for work, for example, would be discharged only after failing to respond to a series of written reprimands and/or suspensions.

Progressive-discipline systems seek effective disciplinary control at minimum cost to individuals and the organization. The goal is always to achieve compliance with organizational expectations through the least extreme reprimand possible—that is, without reaching the more extreme penalties. But even a progressive discipline system can have unpleasant consequences. Sometimes the relationships between management and workers take on an adversarial character; sometimes managers wait too long and fail to take disciplinary action until a problem is severe; and, sometimes poor attitudes develop among persons who can't seem to change and keep receiving ever-harsher punishments.

Positive Discipline

Positive discipline is an approach which tries to involve people more positively and directly in making decisions to improve their behavior. Sometimes called the *commitment approach to discipline,* this process begins by clearly identifying for an individual the difference between actual and desired behaviors.[15] Then a series of progressive reminders are given to make the person aware that he or she alone is responsible for doing things correctly. The next step is "paid" time off to think about one's behavior and its consequences. This time it is given with the understanding that it is a positive opportunity for constructive change. The final step for continued misbehavior is discharge.

For example, someone who starts to come in late quite often will first get an oral "reminder" that promptness is expected. Upon being late in the future, the reminder is given in writing. Finally, further tardiness results in a "decision-making leave day." While not suffering a loss in pay, the person knows this paid day off is a last chance to reform. The next step is discharge.

Many organizations are now adding elements of positive discipline to their progressive discipline programs, and they are reporting good results. Employers tend to like the approach because it helps reduce an adversarial relationship between management and workers. Some union leaders disagree, feeling it is simply another way to get workers pushed out of a company. But positive discipline seems to be working—[17]

at the Pinnelas Highway Department where one construction worker who was given a paid day off because of absenteeism sums it up this way. "It got me to change my attitude," he says, "I was embarrassed in front of everyone when they told me I had the day off. I didn't want that to happen again." Since having the day off, by the way, the same worker has gotten two promotions and pay raises totalling 50 percent.

Guidelines for Disciplinary Action

The guidelines for handling punishment, as developed in Chapter 12 from reinforcement principles,

EMPLOYEE THEFT: EVEN THE BEST CAN BE RIPPED OFF

THE WALL STREET JOURNAL

"I took at the office."

It can happen to anyone and often does: employee theft amounts to over $40 billion a year. In one organization, Philip Crosby Associates (PCA), founder Crosby (author of the bestselling *Quality Is Free*) worked hard to create an atmosphere of mutual respect and trust among his employees. Despite the firm's close-knit environment, the inconceivable happened: employee embezzlement. PCA's director of finance, John C. Nelson, managed to embezzle nearly $1 million before his activities were detected. Even then, his scheme was uncovered only by accident. In Crosby's words, "when a company approaches $50 million in sales, it runs into control problems that are not well understood."

PCA's mistake was a common one. Every company needs internal controls that will reduce or eliminate employee theft. Among these are separation of financial duties so that bookkeepers do not have payment authority, careful screening of applicants for positions with fiduciary responsibility, and clear communication with all employees so that they understand that theft costs everyone in the organization.

Recognizing warning signs can help head off problems. Managers alert to inconsistencies in financial records or to obvious changes in an employee's lifestyle can more readily detect theft. But the keys to prevention are knowledge of one's employees and creation of a sense of teamwork. Because employee dishonesty often stems from dissatisfaction, it is imperative to keep open all lines of communication and to address any complaints about working conditions or processes.

Employee theft is a widespread problem, and it won't go away simply by being downplayed. Says Crosby: "Everyone does not need to learn as we did."

Source: As reported in Joshua Hyatt, "Easy Money," *Inc.* (February 1988), pp. 91–99.

---

are a good starting place for managers seeking advice on handling day-to-day disciplinary situations. Remembering the analogy of the "hot stove" can also help. Everyone should know the following rule—when a stove is hot, don't touch it. We also know that when this rule is violated you get burned—immediately, consistently, and usually not beyond the point of repair. From this analogy the following "hot stove rules" for using reprimands in disciplinary action have been developed.[18]

1. *A reprimand should be immediate.* A hot stove burns the first time you touch it.

2. *A reprimand should be directed toward someone's actions, not their personality.* A hot stove doesn't hold grudges, it doesn't try to humiliate people, and it doesn't accept the excuse of being "sorry." It simply burns those people who touch it.

3. *A reprimand should be consistently applied.* A hot stove burns everyone who touches it, and it does so consistently over time. Anyone who touches a hot stove anytime gets burned.

4. *A reprimand should be informative.* A hot stove lets the person who touches it know what to do to avoid getting burned in the future—don't touch.

5. *A reprimand should occur in a warm and suppor-*

TABLE 14.3 *A Progressive Discipline Program for University Employees*

	Level I	Level II	Level II	Level IV	Level V
Employee Infractions	Tardiness Disregard of safety regulations Loafing or wasting time Horseplay or scuffling Insolence	Leaving work without authority Misrepresentation of absence Sleeping during work hours Insubordination Sexual harassment of co-worker	Falsifications of documents or records Drinking intoxicating beverages Unauthorized absence of 5–19 work days Sexual harassment by a supervisor	Fighting Immoral or indecent conduct Any criminal misdemeanor	Any criminal felony Theft Bribery Unauthorized absence of 20 or more assigned workdays
Disciplinary Actions					
First time	Verbal or written reprimand or warning	Written reprimand or 1–5 workday suspension	1–10 workday suspension	15–20 workday suspension	Discharge
Second time	Written reprimand or 1–5 workday suspension	1–10 workday suspension	15–20 workday suspension	Discharge	
Third time	1–10 workday suspension	15–20 workday suspension	Discharge		
Fourth time	15–20 workday suspension	Discharge			
Fifth time	Discharge				

tive setting. A hot stove conveys warmth and pleasure to people. It just operates with an inflexible rule—don't touch.

6. *A reprimand should support realistic rules.* The don't-touch-a-hot stove rule isn't a play for power, or something based just on a whim or emotion of the moment. It is a real and necessary rule of reason.

MANAGEMENT BY OBJECTIVES: AN INTEGRATED PLANNING AND CONTROL SYSTEM

A basic premise of this chapter is that controlling works hand in hand with the other management functions. This is especially evident in the relationship between planning and controlling. One useful technique for integrating these two functions is **management by objectives,** or MBO. As first defined in Chapter 5, MBO is a process of joint objective setting between a supervisor and subordinate. MBO is also known by the terms *management by* *results, management by goals,* and *work planning and review.*

The Concept of MBO

In its simplest terms, MBO involves a formal agreement between a supervisor and subordinate concerning (1) the subordinate's performance objectives for a given time period, (2) the plans through which they will be accomplished, (3) standards for measuring whether or not they have been accomplished, and (4) procedures for reviewing results. Figure 14.9 clarifies this view of MBO.

Note the distinction in the figure between "joint" and "individual" responsibilities. The supervisor and subordinate *jointly* establish plans and *jointly* control results in any good MBO action framework. This full involvement of subordinates in the MBO process enables and encourages self-control. The end product of MBO is a written agreement that documents work objectives for a subordinate. This includes a timetable and a set of evaluation criteria. MBO thus offers the advantage

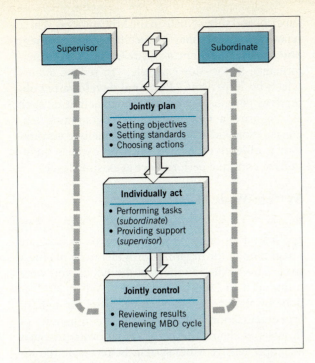

FIGURE 14.9 *The management by objectives (MBO) process: an integrated planning and controlling system.*

of clearly focusing the subordinate's task efforts and the supervisor's support efforts on specific performance objectives. Because the process involves direct face-to-face communication between supervisor and subordinate, MBO also fosters understanding and gives the subordinate a chance to participate in decisions that affect his or her work.

ILLUSTRATIVE CASE:
MBO IN ACTION

The process through which MBO is accomplished is very important. Here's how the MBO sequence has worked at Alcoa.[19]

Step 1

Individual lists key performance objectives for the coming period with target dates for accomplishing them.

Step 2

Objectives are submitted to the supervisor for review. Discussions between the supervisor and subordinate result in an agreed-upon set of objectives.

Step 3

The supervisor and subordinate meet on a quarterly basis to review progress, and make revisions or update objectives as needed.

Step 4

At the end of the year, the individual prepares a "performance report" that lists major accomplishments, and comments on discrepancies between expected and actual results.

Step 5

This self-appraisal is discussed with the supervisor. The reasons for objectives not being met are explored in depth.

Step 6

A new set of objectives is established for the next year, as in Step 1. The MBO cycle begins anew.

Note that the six steps in the Alcoa approach to MBO convey the sense of "participation" referred to earlier. This is a distinct contrast to the "one-way" or "top-down" approach often encountered in management practice. Consider, for example, this observation by Richard Beeson, once president of Canada Dry, about a conversation held with his boss at the time, David Mahoney. It aptly illustrates the type of situations MBO is designed to avoid.[20]

"I had been on the job only a couple of weeks," Beeson says, "when we had a Canada Dry board meeting. I said to Mahoney, 'Dave, we're a little bit below budget now, and I think we can hold that for the rest of the year.'

"Dave looked at me, smiled, and said, 'Be on budget by the six-month mark; be on by the year.'

" 'But Dave,' I said, 'there isn't enough time to get on by the *half*. I inherited this situation, after all.'

"Still smiling, Dave looked at me and said, 'Do I pay you a lot of money? Do I argue with you over what you want to spend? Do I bother you? Then don't tell me what the goals should be. Be on by the half; be on by the end of the year.'

" 'What if I can't, Dave?'

[Mahoney replied] " 'Then clean out your desk and go home.' "

Performance Objectives in MBO

Establishing performance objectives is an essential part of the MBO process. For purposes of MBO, a *good* performance objective

- Expresses a commitment to action.
- Specifies a key result to be accomplished.
- Identifies a target date for achieving results.
- Is specific and as quantitative as possible.
- Presents a challenge while still being realistic and attainable.

One difficult aspect of MBO relates to the desire to have performance objectives stated as specifically and as quantitatively as possible. Ideally this occurs as agreement on a *measurable end product.* But some jobs, particularly managerial ones, involve objectives that are hard to quantify in terms of a measurable end product. Rather than abandon MBO in such cases, it is often possible to agree on a set of *verifiable work activities* whose accomplishment indicates progress under the objective. The following examples show performance objectives stated in each format for the housekeeping supervisor in a hospital.

1. *Measurable end product* "To reduce housekeeping supply costs by 5 percent by the end of the fiscal year."
2. *Verifiable work activities* "To improve communications with my subordinates in the next three months by holding weekly group meetings."

Performance objectives are usually written and should always be formally agreed to by both the superior and subordinate in the MBO process. Three types of objectives may be specified. **Improvement objectives** document a desire to improve a performance factor—for example, "to reduce quality rejects by 10 percent." **Personal development objectives** pertain to personal growth activities, such as "to learn a new computer programming language." Some MBO contracts also include **maintenance objectives,** which formally express intentions to continue performance at existing levels.

System-Wide MBO

Figure 14.10 shows how the concept of MBO can be applied on an organization-wide basis to facilitate integration in the organization's hierarchy of objectives. This is the rationale under which you were introduced to MBO in Chapter 5. When MBO is done by all superior–subordinate pairs throughout an organization, system-wide coordination of means-end chains can enhance performance. Such a comprehensive MBO system helps create the interlocking network of groups that organizations depend on for true accomplishment of a common purpose.

MBO Pros and Cons

MBO is one of the most talked about and debated management concepts of the last 25 years. It is the subject of books and a target of research criticism.[21] This criticism helps identify things to be avoided and done to take maximum advantage of MBO as a management technique.

FIGURE 14.10 *System-wide MBO: integrating objectives from top to bottom in an organization.*

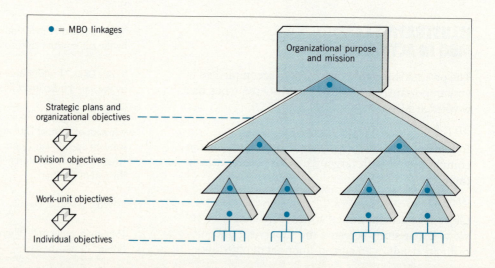

Things to Avoid

Five things above all others seem to detract from the success of MBO.[22]

1. *Tying MBO to compensation.* When MBO is linked to pay, there is a tendency for objectives to become ends in themselves.
2. *Focusing too much attention on objectives that are easily quantified.* This tends to direct work efforts toward limited and sometimes inappropriate ends.
3. *Focusing too much on written documentation and forms.* Excessive paperwork is a characteristic of MBO programs that fail, especially on a system-wide basis. Although it is important to state objectives in writing, little additional paperwork is required for MBO to work to advantage.
4. *Using a prepackaged program.* MBO is often implemented by external consultants who install a similar set of MBO procedures for all their clients. Any MBO "package" usually requires substantial modification to fit the unique needs of a given organization.
5. *Telling subordinates their objectives.* This is the top-down approach exemplified earlier in the conversation between Beeson and Mahoney. It violates the very essence of the MBO concept.

Things to Do

Certain guidelines or things to be done can help make MBO work well for individuals and the organization.

1. *Ensure top management support.* MBO works best when managers from top to bottom in the organization commit themselves to the process, do it right, and reinforce it in their day-to-day work with subordinates.
2. *Don't let MBO become the responsibility of a personnel director or human resource department.* MBO is a managerial tool and responsibility. Staff personnel cannot *do* MBO for managers elsewhere in the organization. Managers must *do* MBO for themselves and in direct person-to-person relationships with subordinates.
3. *Emphasize significant and well-stated objectives.* To serve their purpose in MBO, objectives should be specific, time defined, understandable, verifiable . . . and challenging.
4. *Emphasize regular and direct superior–subordinate interactions.* The essence of MBO is

regular task-oriented communication between superior and subordinate. If MBO is to work, this must occur throughout the organization . . . over and over and over again.

MAKING CONTROLS EFFECTIVE

All control systems share the common goal of helping to ensure and coordinate performance contributions within organizations. The managerial emphasis in controlling is on objectives and results. To make controls effective, however, it helps if managers recognize potential human reactions to them.

Human Reactions to Controls

Some time ago, the Boy Scouts of America had a problem.[23]

> Membership figures coming in from the field had been falsified. In response to the pressures of a national membership drive, people within the organization had vastly overstated the number of new Boy Scouts. To their chagrin, the leaders found something that other managers have also discovered: organizational control systems often produced unintended consequences. The drive to increase membership had motivated people to increase the number of new members reported, but it had not motivated them to increase the number of Boy Scouts actually enrolled.

The case of the Boy Scouts clarifies a dilemma sometimes faced by managers. At the same time that control systems are designed to ensure performance, human reactions can render them ineffective and even dysfunctional. Truly effective control systems channel human energies toward improved work performance instead of toward "beating the system."

Among the human reactions to controls that can lead to such unintended consequences are resentment of the act of measurement, defensiveness about one's true performance, and rejection of the performance targets stated in objectives. These reactions are especially likely in high stress situations where resources are scarce and/or performance competition is intense.

Characteristics of Effective Control Systems

To help managers avoid problems, the literature offers a number of guidelines for making controls effective. An effective control system is:[24]

1. *Strategic and results oriented.* It supports strategic plans and focuses on what needs to be done, not just on the act of measurement itself. The focal points are significant activities—that is, activities really making a difference to the accomplishment of organizational objectives.

2. *Information based.* It supports problem solving and decision making. A good control system does more than point out differences between actual and desired performance levels. It lends insight as to why the variance occurs and what might be done to correct it.

3. *No more complex than necessary.* It is tailored to fit the people involved, task requirements, and situation. A rule of thumb is to keep controls as simple as possible. Overcontrol can be costly, and it raises the prospect of adverse human reactions.

4. *Prompt and exception oriented.* It reports deviations quickly enough that trends can be corrected before too much harm is done. Ideally, control is triggered before anything actually goes wrong, reports deviations in a manner appropriate to the task at hand, and highlights exceptions instead of standard practices.

5. *Understandable.* It presents data in understandable terms. Good control systems present data to decision makers in a concise and easy-to-understand fashion. Unnecessarily complex computer printouts and statistics, for example, may detract from, not add to, the usefulness of a given control.

6. *Flexible.* It leaves room for individual judgment and is modified to fit new circumstances as they arise. Good control systems allow for human judgment in response to unique situations and changing circumstances.

7. *Consistent with the organization structure.* It complements the hierarchy of authority. Control systems should get data into the decision-making system at points where authority to act exists. Until such information gets processed at the right place in the hierarchy, the probability of corrective action being taken is slight.

8. *Designed to accommodate self-control wherever possible.* It recognizes the capacity for self-control and allows for mutual trust, good communication, and participation among all parties involved. Self-control is enhanced by appropriate job designs and the selection of capable people for the jobs to be performed.

9. *Positive in nature.* It emphasizes development, change, and improvement; it minimizes penalty and reprimand. Commitment to controls is enhanced by a focus on developmental rather than evaluative concerns. When disciplinary measures are necessary, they should be handled with due respect to the people involved.

10. *Fair and objective.* It is viewed as impartial and accurate by all parties concerned. When the control system stands above criticisms of partiality and subjectivity, it is likely to be respected for its fundamental purpose—performance enhancement.

Summary

Controlling is the fourth of the management functions. As a process of monitoring performance and taking corrective action, it is a responsibility of all managers at all levels in organizations. This chapter introduced the concept of control, discussed the various types of controls, and looked in some depth at the difference between internal and external control.

There are four elements in the basic control process: (1) establish objectives and standards, (2) measure performance, (3) compare actual performance with standards, and (4) take necessary action. These elements are common to the control systems discussed in this chapter, as well as those to be examined in Chapters 15 and 16.

Performance appraisal is an important means for controlling individual behavior in organizations. A manager can use a variety of methods to accomplish performance appraisals. The process will always be challenging, but there are guidelines on how to make performance appraisals constructive and effective. Compensation systems contribute to control when properly implemented. Appropriate base pay and benefits, for example, can bring qualified people capable of considerable self-control to an organization. When deviations from standards occur or when basic rules of organizational propriety are broken, progressive and positive discipline can serve as an important additional control system.

Planning and controlling come together in management by objectives (MBO) systems. MBO involves joint objective setting and performance review by a supervisor and subordinate. MBO helps direct behavior toward important objectives and control results. Because it allows participation by subordinates, it encourages self-control. This element of participation is one of several characteristics of effective controls pointed out in the last section of this chapter. Keep these characteristics in mind as you study other control techniques and eventually take action to implement them in management practice.

Thinking Through the Issues

1. Define control as a management function. What is its basic relationship with the other management functions?

2. What is the difference between external and internal control in the work setting?

3. Identify and explain the four steps in the control process.

4. Define and give examples of preliminary controls, concurrent controls, and postaction controls.

5. What is "management by exception?" Explain how it can help a manager in the control process.

6. Define and give examples of three different performance appraisal methods. Which method do you think is best, and why?

7. How can both base compensation and fringe benefits be justified as components in a comprehensive organizational control system?

8. What is progressive discipline in the context of managerial control? How does it differ from the concept of "positive" discipline?

9. Is MBO essentially a planning or control technique, or is it both? Why?

10. If you could give someone only three pieces of advice on how to make control systems effective, what would you tell them? Why?

The Manager's Vocabulary

Behaviorally anchored
  rating scale (BARS)
Cafeteria benefits
Concurrent control
Control process
Controlling
Critical-incident
  technique
Cybernetic control
  system

Discipline
External control
Feedback control
Feedforward control
Free-form narrative
Graphic rating scale
Improvement
  objectives
Input standards
Internal control

Maintenance
  objectives
Management by
  exception
Management by
  objectives (MBO)
Multiperson
  comparison
Output standards
Performance appraisal

Personal development
  objectives
Postaction control
Positive discipline
Preliminary control
Progressive discipline
Reliability
Steering control
Validity

THE POSITIVE SIDE OF MISTAKES

When was the last time you made a mistake? Did you tell anyone about it? Did you try to conceal it? Did you worry that if someone found out, you would really look stupid? Well, don't worry. If you've done one of more of these things, you're just like most of the rest of us . . . absolutely human!

But there's a problem in all this that can work to the detriment of organizations and their managers.[25] John Cleese, the former British comedian of Monty Python fame, now makes a living doing corporate training seminars that try to teach participants "the importance of mistakes."

Clesse's message is simple enough. If you're not willing to risk mistakes you'll never do anything, let alone make a creative contribution to the organization. In order for a group to function well, its members must be willing to contribute spontaneously to discussion. If they're afraid to make mistakes at the risk of looking foolish, the group loses creativity and the organization does too.

If the culture of an organization is anti-mistake, bad things can happen. Mistakes made by people at the top get rationalized or explained away. Mistakes made by people at the bottom get concealed. They are hidden for fear that the top will find out and penalize the perpetrators for them. In the best organizations, by contrast, the taboos are not against making mistakes—they are against concealing them. One former head of British Rail illustrates the point perfectly. "The hardest thing in management is the mistake concealer. If someone comes into my office saying, 'I screwed up,' I say, 'Come on in.' "

Remember, the best results are sometimes achieved through some mistakes and the risks of making many others. You need to be more willing to learn from mistakes, and persuade yourself that mistakes are okay to make and to own up to. Only then can you be the role model others in the organization will need in order to develop the same positive attitude toward mistakes.

Questions

1. Is a positive attitude toward mistakes inconsistent with the concept of control as discussed in this chapter? Explain your answer.
2. Why is it that many people are hesitant to take risks in their work settings? What is required to establish an organizational culture in which mistakes are "okay?"
3. What is your willingness to take risks and make mistakes in public situations? Will your willingness to take risks and make mistakes be an asset or liability in your career? Why?

Case Application

BARNETT BANKS

Charlie Rice is a vigilant CEO. His monitoring system helped make Barnett Banks first in Florida. In eight years since Rice became CEO, Barnett has doubled its share of bank deposits in the state while profits have risen nearly seven-fold. A bank holding company, Barnett has grown under Rice's management to include over 30 subsidiary banks with some 450 branches. The company just bought its first out-of-state bank in suburban Atlanta county of Georgia.[26]

"The president of each bank is at risk for its performance," Rice says in expressing one of his principles of management. He believes you should immediately turn problems over to the executive in charge, and offer them generous rewards for solving them and certain punishment if they don't. Each bank under his control gets a monthly "performance ranking" based on its market share, and other indicators. Banks receiving low rankings are visited personally by Rice to find out what's going on. The next step is a visit by a team of experts—five or six persons gathered from headquarters staff and other banks. Some call them "SWAT" teams, Rice prefers to view them as "internal consulting teams" who help to solve local bank problems. "We devote considerable energy to dealing with these situations," he reports. Everyone understands that no bank stays at the bottom of the list for long. "Morale is very high," Rice says, "We have evolved a group of leaders who thrive on our entrepreneurial system."

Barnett's basic management approach begins in May each year when performance targets are set for each bank. Under Rice's "delivery systems planning," he and a five-person senior executive group analyze a variety of market data for each bank. The data include average age, income, employment, family status, and housing in each bank's neighborhood, along with the population growth rate. The bank's deposit base, and number of accounts and loans is also reviewed. This information is used to set tentative performance targets covering market share, deposit growth, and other objectives for each of the 33 subsidiary banks. These targets are presented to the bank presidents by two of Barnett's senior executives. The presidents negotiate with them to make final performance commitments. The negotiations are important and delicate. "Some bank presidents will stretch to promise more than they should," says one of Rice's executives, "and some will sandbag the hell out of you."

Presidents of banks who surpass the targets are eligible for bonuses as high as half of their base compensation level. To get the maximum bonus usually requires being at least 20 percent above targeted performance. One of the decisions subsidiary presidents can make on their own is whether or not to have similar performance schemes for their branches and branch managers. Almost all of them do. In this way the subsidiary presidents represent a middle level of management between Rice's headquarters and the branch banks.

If everybody hits their performance targets, Rice doesn't get further involved in operations. He stays in touch with things through a computerized flow of data. "If you're not well informed here, it's your own fault," he says. He interacts mostly with his immediate executive staff, and expects the executives reporting to him to make decisions based on the policies he establishes. One comments that "it's hard to appreciate how intelligent somebody is when all he's doing is enunciating general principles."

Questions

1. How do you evaluate Charlie Rice's performance in fulfilling his "controlling" responsibilities? Explain your answer. Is he an effective manager? Why or why not?
2. Is the "delivery systems planning" approach of Barnett Banks really a form of management by objectives (MBO). Why or why not? Is it an effective planning and controlling approach? Explain your answer.
3. Is the bonus compensation scheme an effective control device? . . . an effective motivational technique? Why or why not? How could it be improved in each respect?
4. Are you confident that Barnett Banks will be as successful in the future as it appears to be today? Justify your answer based on the facts of the case as presented.

Class Exercise: The MBO Contract

1. Figure 14.11 shows an MBO contract for a production manager by the name of Lee Crawford. Column 1 in the figure lists a number of objectives for Crawford. Column 2 shows their priority as A (higher) or B (lower). Column 3 lists projected completion dates. Column 4 provides space for the results to be documented.
2. Study this MBO contract. In Column 4 write one of the following symbols to identify each objectives as an improvement, maintenance, or personal-development objective.

I = Improvement objective

M = Maintenance objective

P = Personal development objective

MANAGERIAL JOB OBJECTIVES

Lee Crawford	7/2	Production Manager
Prepared by employee	Date	Employee's job title
S.K. Worth	7/2	Plant Manager
Reviewed by supervisor	Date	Supervisor's job title

Performance Objectives	Target Date	Outcomes or Results
1. To increase quality on finished products to a 98% standard.	6/30	
2. To reduce waste of materials by 3%.	6/30	
3. To totally eliminate lost time due to accidents.	6/30	
4. To operate within the quarterly budget.	9/30	
5. To computerize the materials inventory records as part of the new management information system.	12/31	
6. To implement at least two skill training workshops on computer-assisted manufacturing.	3/31	
7. To attend a company-sponsored leadership seminar.	3/31	

FIGURE 14.11 *An MBO contract: the case of the production manager.*

Source: *Wall Street Journal Reports*

3. Assume that this MBO contract was actually developed and implemented under the following circumstances. After each statement, write "yes" if the statement reflects proper MBO procedures and write "no" if it reflects poor MBO procedures.
   a. The plant manager drafted the seven objectives and submitted them to Crawford for review.
   b. The plant manager and Crawford thoroughly discussed the eight objectives in proposal form before they were finalized.
   c. The plant manager scheduled a meeting in six months to review Crawford's progress on the objectives.
   d. The plant manager didn't discuss the objectives with Crawford again until the scheduled meeting was held.
   e. The president said that Crawford's annual raise would depend entirely on the extent to which these objectives were achieved.
4. Share and discuss your responses to steps 1 and 2 with a nearby classmate. Reconcile any differences of opinion by referring back to the chapter discussion of MBO. Await further class discussion.

References

[1]Joseph A. Litterer, "Elements of Control in Organizations," in Mariann Jelinek, Joseph A. Litterer, and Raymond E. Miles (eds.), *Organization by Design: Theory and Practice* (Plano, Texas: Business Publications, 1981), p. 439.

[2]See William Newman, *Constructive Control: Design and Use of Control Systems* (Englewood Cliffs, NJ: Prentice-Hall, 1975).

[3]For a good discussion see Cortlandt Cammann and David A. Nadler, "Fit Control Systems to Your Management Style," *Harvard Business Review,* Vol. 54 (January–February 1976), pp. 65–72.

[4]Douglas McGregor, *The Human Side of Enterprise* (New York: McGraw-Hill, 1960).

[5]Information from *NYU Business* (Fall/1986/Winter 1987), pp. 7–15; and, Ralph E. Winter, "Delayed Future: Upgrading of Factories Replaces the Concept of Total Automation," *The Wall Street Journal* (September 30, 1987), pp. 1, 8.

[6]For a good review see Edward E. Lawler III, Allan H. Mohrman, Jr., and Susan M. Resnick, "Performance Appraisal Revisited," *Organizational Dynamics,* Vol. 13 (Summer 1984), pp. 20–35.

[7]Reported in Saul W. Gellerman and William G. Hodgson, "Cyanamid's New Take on Performance Appraisal," *Harvard Business Review,* Vol. 66 (May–June 1988), pp. 36–41.

[8]Developed from Edgar F. Huse, *Management,* Second Edition (St. Paul: West Publishing, 1982), p. 204.

[9]Patricia Smith, "Behaviors, Results, and Organizational Effectiveness," in Marvin Dunnette (ed), *Handbook of Industrial and Organizational Psychology* (Chicago: Rand McNally, 1976), pp. 745–775.

[10]See Wayne F. Cascio and H. John Bernardin, "Implications of Performance Appraisal Litigation for Personnel Decisions," *Personnel Psychology,* Vol. 34 (1981), pp. 211–226.

[11]Information from Jacob M. Schlesinger, "GM's New Compensation Plan Reflects General Trend Tying Pay to Performance," *The Wall Street Journal* (January 26, 1988), p. 33.

[12]Excerpted from John A. Patton, "High Wages Don't Necessarily Mean High Costs," *Wall Street Journal* (November 8, 1982), p. 22. Reprinted by permission of the *Wall Street Journal.* Copyright © 1982 Dow Jones & Company, Inc. All rights reserved.

[13]Reported in James O'Toole, *Vanguard Management* (New York: Doubleday, 1986).

[14]Information from "The Fast Track May Not Be So Fast After All," *The Wall Street Journal* (June 9, 1987), p. 1.

[15]See Eric L. Harvey, "Discipline vs. Punishment," *Management Review,* Vol. 76 (March 1987), pp. 25–29.

[16]Information from Bob Cohn, "A Glimpse of the 'Flex' Future," *Newsweek* (August 1, 1988), pp. 38–39.

[17]This example is reported in "Punishing Workers with a Day Off," *Business Week* (June 16, 1986), p. 80.

[18]The "hot-stove rules" are developed from R. Bruce McAfee and William Poffenberger, *Productivity Strategies: Enhancing Employee Job Performance* (Englewood Cliffs, NJ: Prentice-Hall, 1982), pp. 54–55. They are originally attributed to Douglas McGregor, "Hot Stove Rules of Discipline," G. Strauss and L. Sayles (eds.) in *Personnel: The Human Problems of Management,* (Englewood Cliffs, NJ: Prentice-Hall, 1967).

[19]Walter S. Wikstrom, *Managing by-and-with Objectives,* Studies in Personnel Policy, No. 212 (New York: Conference Board, 1968), p. 3.

[20]This conversation is reported in "The Way I Make My Numbers is for You Guys to Make Your Numbers," *Forbes* (February 15, 1972), p. 26.

[21]See for example, Dale D. McConkey, *How to Manage by Results,* Third Edition (New York: AMACOM, 1976); Stephen J. Carroll, Jr., and Henry L. Tosi, Jr., *Management by Objectives: Applications and Research* (New York: Macmillan, 1973); Anthony P. Raia, *Managing by Objectives* (Glenview, IL: Scott, Foresman, 1974).

[22]Steven Kerr, "Overcoming the Dysfunctions of MBO," *Management by Objectives,* Vol. 5, No. 1 (1976).

[23]Excerpt from Cammann and Nadler, op cit. p. 65.

[24]Developed from Harold Koontz and Cyril O'Donnel, *Essentials of Management* (New York: McGraw-Hill, 1974), pp. 362–365; and, Howard M. Carlisle, *Management: Concepts, Methods, and Applications,* Second Edition (Chicago: Science Research Associates, 1982), pp. 297–300.

[25]Information from "No More Mistakes and You're Through!" *Forbes* (May 16, 1988), pp. 126–128.

[26]Information from Martin Mayer, "The Watchful Eye of Charlie Rice," *Business Month* (September 1987), pp. 34–40.

Control
and Management
Information Systems

Mrs. Fields' Secret Ingredient

Cookies and control are what distinguish operations at Mrs. Fields' Cookies. The company has over 500 retail stores, and its headquarters retains direct daily control over each one—none are franchised. That may sound like a recipe for a flop, not a description of a profitable cookie-making company. The secret lies in the airtight management information system that the husband–wife team of Randy and Debbi Fields has put in place. "MIS in this company," explains Randy, "has always had to serve two masters. First, control. Rapid growth without control equals disaster. . . . And second, information that leads to control also leads to better decision making."

Mrs. Fields Cookies' information system operates on unfancy hardware, but Randy Fields, its architect, takes considerable pride in the software's elegance. Each store manager's computer is interactive and in constant communication with headquarters; the system allows each manager to schedule crew, interview new applicants, help with personnel administration, and even help with maintenance. Randy Fields designed the system so that his wife, a quintessential "people person," can stay in two-way communication with hundreds of managers. The idea, they both claim, is to use appropriate technology to keep the organization as flat as possible.

The company has seven "store controllers," individuals who form a kind of control safety net. They watch over daily and weekly store reports and follow up, in person, on any discrepancies. Store controllers relieve managers of responsibility for numbers and let them do what they're good at—working with people. "We want managers to be with people, not with problems," says Debbi Fields.

Too much of the wrong kind of information technology is potentially as damaging as none at all, and the organization keeps things simple. Mrs. Fields' Cookies has only one database, and everything from sales reports to utility charges goes into it. This makes it possible for the system to do lots of work that people used to do—like ordering chocolate when the database indicates that supplies are low.

It is crucial, Randy Fields stresses, to have a vision of what one wants to accomplish with a management control system. "If you don't have your paradigm in mind, you have no way of knowing whether each little step is taking you closer to or further from your goal." With profits approaching $90 million, Mrs. Fields' Cookies is clearly taking big steps forward. ■

Source: Information from Tom Richman, "Mrs. Fields' Secret Ingredient," *Inc.* (October 1987), pp. 65–72.

All organizations require systems for gathering and processing information for decision making. This chapter focuses on management information systems and their role in the control process. Key topics include:

Management Information

Management Information
  Systems (MIS)

Decision Support Systems
  (DSS)

Advances in Information
  Technologies

Information and Systems
  Effectiveness

Information and the
  Budgeting Process

Achieving Budgetary
  Control

The chapter opener on Mrs. Field's Cookies broadly introduced the value of computer-based information and control systems. Here are three additional illustrations of organizations that have benefited from improvements of a related nature.

At a prominent insurance company computer files were reorganized by customer name rather than by policy number. This allows salespersons to easily review a customer's entire portfolio of policies to spot ones going out of date and/or the possible need for new holdings. They can now stay in close contact with customers to monitor their needs and pursue sales opportunities. A new incentive scheme rewards them for building successful long-term customer relationships; the information system helps make such relationships possible. In an industry characterized by large and inflexible data files, this company achieved a strategic edge and its competitors are now trying to catch up.

At a big supermarket company computer scanners are now used at check-out counters. The scanners log every item leaving the store, post inventory records instantly, and update a central data base used by store managers to make a variety of purchasing and merchandising decisions. Employees used to physically count stock to gather similar information. Managers often learned about changes in sales patterns items too late to take advantage of trends, and they frequently over-ordered by relying on suppliers' advice. Now store managers carry lower inventories and offer more timely promo-

tions. Armed with accurate data on product sales trends, they have more bargaining power over suppliers and are less prone to order in response to sales pressure.

At a passenger elevator company branch offices used to oversee contract maintenance services. They handled service calls and submitted monthly activity reports to the head office. But the reports passed through four levels of management and often failed to clearly identify customer complaints. A new information system now enters all service reports into a central data base that is used for a variety of management reports. When the system was first implemented, it was discovered that many elevators were breaking down far more often than realized. Now, service personnel receive computer-prompted messages to schedule preventative maintenance visits. A better knowledge of breakdown patterns also helps management make staff assignments and plan training.

These are but some of the many ways that new information technologies are becoming invaluable to organizations and their managers. In particular, they add power to control systems by:

■ Helping managers acquire and utilize resources more efficiently.

■ Helping integrate the many parts of an organization with system-wide objectives.

■ Helping collect more immediate and complete data for making strategic and operating decisions.

A further illustration of the significance of information to management rests with the increasing prominence of what is called the **chief information officer** or CIO.[2] The CIO typically reports to the chief executive and fulfills these functions: oversees computer-based information and data processing systems, as well as office and telecommunications systems; plays a key role in long-range and strategic decisions; and manages the information applications of computer technology within the organization.

The end-of-chapter career perspective offers further insight into career opportunities you might pursue in this direction. For now, our specific interest is on current developments in the area of control and management information systems. Through an examination of key issues and concepts, and the use of other timely examples, this chapter will review the managerial implications of information utilization in organizations.

MANAGEMENT INFORMATION

"Information enlightens"

"Information aids decision making"

"Information is power"

Any control system requires communication of the *right* information at the *right* time and among the *right* people if it is to function effectively. People must know what is expected of them in terms of task performance; managers and other decision makers must have useful information regarding actual performance in order to make plans and take appropriate action. This information-processing component of the managerial role was initially discussed in Chapter 1. Since then it has remained a background theme as we have studied various facets of managerial problem solving and decision making.

Figure 15.1 more formally reminds you of the information foundations of the manager's job.

Data, Information, and Information Systems

Data consist of raw facts such as figures and other symbols used to represent people, events, and concepts.[3] In the management context, **information** is data made useful for decision making and problem solving. An **information system,** accordingly, collects, organizes, and distributes data in such a way that they become meaningful as information. Good information systems greatly facilitate each of the management functions, but they are especially beneficial when it comes to planning and controlling.

Because they provide a historical data base, information systems facilitate planning by assisting in the establishment of objectives and standards, as well as providing support for the formulation of related budgets. Information systems are also essential elements in the control process. They provide the basis for documenting, storing, and disseminating performance results. Depending on their level of sophistication, they may also identify deviations from plans and even suggest what actions should be taken under the circumstances.

Information Needs of Managers

Information systems serve the needs of managers in two main ways. First, they assist in the management of the complex relationship between an organization and its environment. In general, managers need information to help them deal effectively with such outside parties as competitors, government agencies, creditors, suppliers, and stockholders. To formulate objectives and strategy, for example, data on

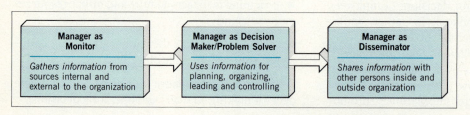

FIGURE 15.1 *Information foundations of the managerial role.*

consumer tastes, competitor activities, and related matters is of high priority. A good information system facilitates the gathering of such data and processes it into *intelligence information* for use by key decision makers. In addition, the environment needs information from the organization for a variety of purposes, ranging from image building to product advertising to financial reporting for taxes. A good information system facilitates the gathering of internal data for dissemination to environmental elements as *public information.*

Second, managers at various levels in the organization's hierarchy of authority need information to make decisions and solve problems in the conduct of daily operations. Figure 15.2 reminds you that the information needs of managers vary by level of responsibility and according to the purpose to be served. Higher-level managers tend to emphasize strategic planning, while middle-level and lower-level managers focus more on operational considerations dealing with the implementation of these plans. As the following examples help to show, effective managers at all levels of responsibility benefit greatly from supportive information systems.[4]

A top management perspective   More and more frequently, information systems are becoming important tools for helping organizations achieve a *competitive advantage* over their rivals. Michael Simmons, as chief information officer at Fidelity Investments Corporation, noticed increasing concern among brokers that their customers were unhappy about ups and downs in the mutual fund markets. Customers were unable to get price quotes except at the end of the day. Simmons worked out a way to provide hourly quotes using the existing computer system. Fidelity was the first U.S. mutual fund firm to do so, and Simmons' innovation created major business opportunities for the company.

A first-level management perspective   At the city garage, Salinas, California six mechanics and two supervisors use a computer to help manage repair and maintenance data on over 150 vehicles and 300 engine-driven devices. The mechanics used to spend countless hours filling out slips and keeping manual records; it took over 176 hours to gather data for the annual budget. Now the mechanics enter and retrieve maintenance data through computer terminals. This computerized information system helps with scheduling maintenance and repair. It also allows data to be gathered for the annual budget in under 15 minutes.

FIGURE 15.2 *Information systems serve multiple needs of managers.*

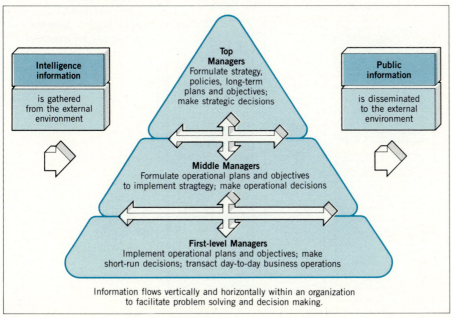

MANAGEMENT INFORMATION SYSTEMS (MIS)

A **management information system,** or MIS, collects, organizes, and distributes data in such a way that it meets the information needs of managers. It does this by getting the right information into the hands of the right persons on a timely, and cost-efficient basis.

The basic foundations for most management information systems include these major components.[5]

1. *Data gathering*   Data pertinent to operations of the organization and gathered from both internal and external sources are entered into the system.
2. *Data entry*   This data is entered and stored in data bases at the information processing core of the system.
3. *Data transformation*   The data are transformed into useful information through the assistance of computer software programs and judgments made by technical support staff and other systems users.
4. *Information utilization*   This information is retrieved as needed by management personnel and used to make a wide variety of decisions relating to the conduct of operations and their improvement.

Figure 15.3 uses the example of a human resource or personnel information processing system to demonstrate these components of a MIS. In this model, personal, financial, and job data are the basic inputs. They are combined into data bases that include wage and salary, fringe benefits, and career and equal employment opportunity files. When accessed and processed, these data files provide information useful to managers who have to make a variety of personnel decisions. The MIS helps them make the decisions on a timely and efficient basis using accurate and appropriate information. Specifically, a MIS can be utilized to:

■ *Provide early warnings of problems and opportunities*   both internal and external to the organization.

■ *Make programmed decisions*   that require the simple application of decision rules to standard information.

■ *Prepare automatic reports*   of a recurring nature, and which require the simple organization of information into standard report formats.

■ *Facilitate problem solving*   that requires analysis of complex information and the exercising of judgment to reach a final decision.

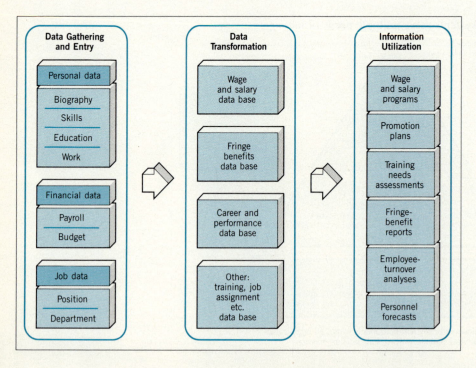

FIGURE 15.3 *Basic elements in a computer-based personnel or human-resources information system.*

ILLUSTRATIVE CASE:
MRS. FIELD'S STORE AT PIER 39

The first thing Richard Lui, store manager at Pier 39 Mrs. Field's in San Francisco, usually does in the morning is call up the Day Planner Program on his microcomputer.[6] He enters the day's sales projections, plus some requested information—for example, this is a Tuesday on a school day. The computer reviews the store's performance on similar days in the past and prepares an hour-by-hour sales plan. It tells him how many customers he'll need each hour to meet the sales projections and then tells him how many cookie batches of each product to mix and when to do it. Of course Richard could do this himself. He used to in fact, but this saves time and is more accurate.

As the day wears on, Richard updates the computer each hour to report on progress. The computer updates the sales plan and makes suggestions—for example, offer some free samples to passers-by. How does Richard feel about having a computer set sales goals by the hour and then keep track of how well he's doing? "It's a tool for me," he says. And this is the way founder Debbi Fields always did things when she was running her own store.

Now that Debbi is running the company and its over 500 retail stores, she still keeps an active hand in what's going on. She does it through the same computer-based information system. Several times a week, for example, Richard Lui telephones headquarters in Park City, Utah to check his computerized phone messages. Often there's one from Debbi expressing a new idea, commenting on a question asked previously, or expressing her dismay about a problem. If Richard wants to say something to Debbi, he leaves a computer message for her.

Back in the store, Richard's computer and the information system help him do a variety of other important things. Among other things, it:

■ *Helps him schedule workers.* He enters daily sales projections for a two-week period, and the computer uses historical data to prepare a suggested staffing plan.

■ *Helps with personnel administration.* He enters data on newly hired workers and a central personnel file is established at corporate headquarters. From this computer file, all subsequent payroll and employment records will be prepared.

■ *Helps with maintenance.* He enters machine problems into the computer and gets back recommended maintenance strategies and a recommended service vendor if the need exists.

Store managers like Richard Lui benefit from the continuous exchange of data and information with the corporate computer-based information system. They are motivated to use the system, in part, because the data they provide comes back to them as useful information of one sort or another. They enter the data, and the computer sorts and processes it into a meaningful form. Randy Fields, the systems designer, is persistent on one point in particular—the maintenance of but *one* data base. Everything from cookie sales to personnel records to utility charges are in the same data base. But from this central repository of information, the work of store managers like Richard Lui is greatly facilitated at the same time that the needs for control by corporate headquarters is satisfied.

Computer Utilization in MIS

Most management information systems, like the one at Mrs. Field's Cookies, rely on computers to process the large amounts and wide variety of data required to keep a modern organization functioning. As just a quick review of some basics, you should recognize the following elements central to any computer-based MIS.

Hardware Equipment required to operate a computer system. This includes data-input devices such as terminals and card readers, central processing units, storage devices such as tape drives and disk units, and output devices such as printers and terminals.

Software Coded instructions in the form of programs that give the computer its capability to perform computational operations on data. These programs are written in special computer languages such as FORTRAN, COBOL, and BASIC. One or more of these languages should be part of a modern manager's repertoire of skills and capabilities.

Central processing unit (CPU) The collection of electronic circuitry that controls the computer and allows it to store and perform a variety of computa-

DESIGNERS RACE
TO BUILD NEW SUPERCOMPUTERS

"Supercomputers are as significant to pioneering research today as calculus was to Newton."

One U.S. firm, Cray Research, sells 60 percent of the world's supercomputers, but Cray's competitors at home and especially in Japan are in hot pursuit of the leading edge. Makers of gigantic supercomputers that are shared by large users are also having to compete with manufacturers of a new, smaller generation known as personal supercomputers, which sell for far less and are accessible to single users— and thus may appeal to entirely new markets. These minisupercomputers, which combine graphic displays with enormous computing power and speed, bring supercomputers to business for the first time.

What the future holds, say some experts, is a new crop of machines that will combine supercomputing with artificial intelligence— allowing for such impressive high-tech developments as typewriters that take dictation. Clearly, those nations with major supercomputer capabilities can expect to reap many positive benefits in the Twenty-First century. The stakes are high, and the race is nothing if not fast.

Supercomputers—a group of high-speed, extremely powerful computers that can crunch numbers in milliseconds and create dazzling graphics—are becoming increasingly available not just to large institutional users but also to many elements in the private sector. And as ongoing technological advances cause international competition to heat up, supercomputer manufacturers keep pushing for the next breakthrough—the effects of which will be felt in such varied areas as fluid dynamics, astrophysics, and automated manufacturing. Says Ron Bailey of NASA's Ames Research Center:

Source: As reported in "Fast and Smart," *Time* (March 28, 1988), pp. 54–58, and Lawrence M. Fisher, "The Shrinking Supercomputer," *New York Times* (February 26, 1988), p. D-1.

---

tional operations on data according to the instructions of programs. A CPU will include a central memory for storing data and instructions. This memory is often supplemented by external storage on magnetic tapes and disks.

Continuing advances in microelectronics have dramatically changed the computer industry and the role of computers in the modern world. Computer makers are increasingly adopting standards that allow computers of different vendors to exchange information with one another; computer users are increasingly found in the managerial and executive ranks, not just in technical positions; computers are becoming increasingly powerful. Indeed, *Newsline 15.1* introduces developments in the area of **supercomputers** which operate with speeds in the milliseconds range to manage vast amounts of data and solve extremely complex problems. But even as these new powerhouse computers emerge, the **microcomputer** continues to advance in power and prominence. This small, self-contained personal computer system offers desk-top capability to handle a wide variety of information-based jobs for the manager. These include writing, calculating, storing, organizing and analyzing data, drawing graphs, and transmitting messages.

Applications software, programs which are already written and tested, and which allow the user to perform a variety of tasks without writing his or her own programs, provides these capabilities to anyone with access to a microcomputer. Specific-purpose applications software assists in a wide range of occupational and personal tasks. These include applications in accounting (e.g., order processing, inventory control), manufacturing (e.g., purchasing, material requirements planning), personal finance (e.g., income tax, investments management), among many others. In addition to being familiar with applications software for specific personal and occupational needs, the modern manager should also be able to use the major types of general-purpose applications. These include word processing, electronic spread sheet, computer graphics, data base and file management, and communications software.

Evolution of MIS

Early developments in information systems resulted in computerized **transaction processing systems.** These systems use the computer to organize and sort the data needed to complete routine transactions such as inventory management, payroll preparation, customer billings, and the like. Transaction processing systems bring added efficiency and accuracy to these recurring tasks. They can also assist in areas where a great deal of standard information must be continually transmitted back and forth between remote terminals and a central computer. A good example is an airline reservations system. Today, the developments in management information systems extend well beyond this transactions processing capability. Of particular interest are the opportunities now found in decision support systems.

DECISION SUPPORT SYSTEMS

A **decision support system (DSS)** allows users to interact directly with a computer to create information helpful in making decisions to solve complex and sometimes unstructured problems. Its capability to *interact* with a user in addressing problems makes the DSS a special and more advanced type of management information system. Only when the MIS is extended to allow users to interact with the information base in a way that directly assists in making judgments about complex decision situations, does it become a true DSS.

Decision Support Systems Applications

Decision support systems are available to assist in such business decisions as mergers and acquisitions, plant expansions, new product developments, and stock portfolio management, among many others. Perhaps the best way to clarify the essence of any DSS is by illustration. Consider these reports of how decision support systems are used in two quite different settings.[7]

At IBM the firm uses a decision support system in the purchasing department of one of its manufacturing facilities. The system is designed to help make an optimum choice among vendors supplying various parts needed by the plant. The goal is to have the needed parts arriving on schedule and in the right combinations. Some vendors can supply multiple parts, but the prices, shipping times, and transportation costs vary. Managers use the DSS to enter requirements and arrive at an optimal combination of vendors, parts, order quantities, and order times that will minimize all relevant costs over multiple time periods.

At Topeka & Santa Fe Railway the company uses a decision support system to help manage freight car scheduling. Each day an operator at headquarters types a password into the terminal and logs onto the "operations expediter" (OX) software system. It quickly provides the operator with information on which freight cars are scheduled for use that day all over the United States, which ones are idle, and which ones are in transit as empty cars. By entering a few commands, the operator can trace the effects of moving some cars from one point to another. But OX might respond by suggesting the cars would be better used by transferring them from and/or to different locations. Thousands of dollars are saved this way each day.

Group Decision Support Systems

One promising current development in DSS lies in the area of **group decision support systems**

(GDSS). A GDSS is an interactive computer-based information system that facilitates *group* efforts at solving complex and unstructured problems.[8] It utilizes special GDSS software to facilitate information retrieval, information sharing, and information use among members of a group—whether the members are geographically proximate or distant from one another. The continued efforts to refine GDSS technology are especially important given increasing awareness of the value of groups for problem solving and decision making. This is a useful evolution of decision support systems with the potential to further assist in improving decision making in organizations.

Figure 15.4 describes four scenarios for group-decision support systems. Note that the purpose and design of the GDSS varies according to the duration of the required decision-making sessions and the physical proximity of group members. In the *decision room*, the GDSS adds interactive computer support to a traditional decision making meeting. The public display screen can present various types of data, as well as special summaries and the results of analyses. The *local decision network* allows persons who work in close proximity to interact with one another and an information base through the GDSS. This helps deal with recurring problems without the necessity of face-to-face meetings. In *teleconferencing* two or more decision rooms connect geographically distant groups of problem solvers. This can save travel costs and speed up decision making. Finally, *remote decision-making* links together several individuals at geographically distant work stations. The GDSS electronically brings them together as desired to deal with shared problems.

One of the advantages noted for groups using a GDSS is the tendency of members to focus more intently on the data displayed on their computers or a common screen. This can help overcome what some call the problem of "dualing egos" where people concentrate more on the people making points, than the substance of the points themselves. In addition, a meeting guided by a GDSS has quick access to important data bases, and a built-in capability to document what takes place and any conclusions reached. Of course disadvantages may occur as members lose "personal" touch with one another, are unable to read nonverbal messages, and miss the shared exuberance from which spontaneous and creative thinking sometimes emerges.

Executive Information Systems

Among the newest developments in information systems is their special application to the needs of senior management. **Executive information systems** (EIS), sometimes called *executive support systems,* offer special capabilities in helping top managers access, process and share information needed to make a variety of operational and strategic decisions. Among all managerial levels, top management has been the slowest to take advantage of microcomputers. In part this was due to an availability of staff aides who could either do the computer work themselves, or gather the needed data manually; in part it was also due to the inability of software support to directly meet the needs of the executive decision maker. But today, new cost consciousness, reduced staff, and a wave of new software have combined to make computer-based executive support systems a mainstay in many organizations.

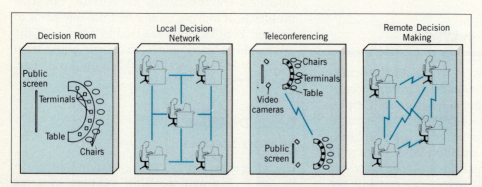

FIGURE 15.4
Frameworks for utilizing group decision support systems (GDSS).

Source: Gerardine De Sanctis and Brent Gallupe, "Group Decision Support Systems: A New Frontier," *Data Base* (Winter 1985), p 6.

One of the distinguishing features of an EIS is the type of computer support relied upon. The emphasis is on multi-color displays of charts and graphs, big screen projections for conference use, and easy-to-use touch-sensitive monitors or mouses instead of keyboards for computer control. They are designed this way in response to the executive's need to look at and consider information, rather than to manipulate it. Often, the executive's interest is management by exception, with a special concern for numbers that fall outside of boundaries set by objectives and plans.

The advantages of EIS include more immediate access to a more accurate and complete set of data than may otherwise be available. The data is also easily arranged and displayed in meaningful forms that further assist individual and group decision making. Some EIS programs even color-code exceptions—red for below target and green for above target—to help executives focus on trouble spots and opportunities. Furthermore, this new data rich environment allows executives in many cases to probe more deeply than ever before down through the levels of an organization and into day-to-day operations. To further introduce you to developments in EIS, some examples help complete the story.[9]

At Kraft, Inc. it has been difficult to keep track of business in the complicated Grocery Products Group. It sells over 500 products to 33,000 stores. The group's president used to receive stacks of paper with the previous day's sales results at 3 pm in the afternoon. Today, an EIS makes the same information available at 8:30 am, on the computer screen, and neatly organized by territory and product line. Together with other senior executives, the president can spot and solve problems more quickly than ever before.

At Unum, Corporation a Portland, Maine, insurer, Chairman James Orr recently asked for a daily count on the number of company employees. He couldn't get it. The needed data were kept at the division level, in different forms, and in some cases in a data base accessible only by programmers. Now, he gets this and other information when he wants it. A new EIS links personnel data to a desk-top computer in his office. Orr is able to watch the staffing levels, and his managers know it. "Believe me, they don't add staff carelessly," he says.

ADVANCES IN INFORMATION TECHNOLOGIES

Information systems and computers are dramatically changing the way information flows and is utilized in organizations. *More* information about *more* things is being made available to *more* people in organizations *more* quickly than ever before. And continuing new developments in information technologies only keep further accenting the "more" as it was used each time in the prior sentence. Some of the key things you will want to become increasingly familiar with relate to ongoing developments in expert systems, office automation and computer networking.

Expert Systems

Among the most striking developments in information technology is continuing progress in the area of **artificial intelligence (AI)**. This is a field of study concerned with building computer systems with the capabilities to reason the way people do, even to the point of dealing with ambiguities and difficult issues of judgment. The managerial applications of this attempt to give computers human-like capabilities lie in the realm of **expert systems (ES)**.[10] These are decision-support systems that mimic the thinking of human experts and, in so doing, offer consistent and "expert" decision-making advice to the user. Examples are found—[11]

at Ford Motor Company where an expert system is being developed that will allow Ford dealers around the country to access computer-based expertise for solving tricky and hard-to-diagnose engine problems. Up until now, the dealers would call company expert Gordy Kujawski each time they ran into a problem they couldn't handle. Ford is about ready to unveil an ES that taps Kujawski's expertise and duplicates the reasoning he uses to solve even the thorniest of engine problems.

at American Express where groups of specialists used to field inquiries from the field for approval of unusual credit requests by cardholders. Since the Amex card has no credit limit such approvals give the firm a competitive advantage, but determining the limits to approval was a tricky administrative problem. Various data bases had to be checked on the cardholder, and a judgment made as to whether the current request seemed okay given the person's credit history. Now the Authorization Assistant Expert System performs the required searches of company data bases on the customer and makes the authorization decision in seconds, and while the merchant is still on the telephone.

As implied by the prior examples, ES serve in the capacity of "expert consultants" to their users. In fact, most of the ones currently used are "rule-based" systems that use a complicated set of "if . . . then" rules to analyze problems. These rules are determined by working with actual human experts in a certan problem area, like Ford's Gordy Kujawaski, and then building their problem-solving rules and routines into a computer program. This program can then be applied through direct interaction between the ES and a data base, or interaction between the ES and inputs provided by the human user—as in the American Express example.

In general, expert systems benefit organizations and their users in several ways. These include:[12]

- Reducing the need for highly paid experts.
- Making these experts even more productive.
- Allowing novices to perform expert tasks.
- Improving the consistency of decision making.
- Documenting the rationale for decisions.

Finally, it is important to note that existing expert systems are useful only for problems within their specific and limited ranges of expertise. They work best when narrowly applied to the specific type of problem they were designed to handle. The next wave of ES will certainly be more powerful and broadly applicable. Their availability, however, awaits further advances in the field of artificial intelligence and the technology needed to support them.

Office Automation

One of the most immediately relevant examples of the everyday impact of computers and information systems on the work setting lies with **office automation.** This term refers to the use of computers and related technologies to facilitate operations in the office environment. Take a moment to consider the office you are likely to become part of tomorrow.

First of all, people will have individual work stations centered around desk-top personal computers or terminals that allow sophisticated voice, image, text, and other data handling operations.

Voice messaging will utilize the voice recognition capabilities of computers to take dictation, answer the telephone, and relay messages. Other documents will be drafted via word processing software on the computer. Once finished a copy of any document will be sent via *electronic mail* or *facsimile transmission* to other persons, while additional copies are automatically printed and/or stored in the computer database for later retrieval and use as desired.

Gone will be the large number of filing cabinets that once typified the office; gone, too, will be most of the paper. In this office of tomorrow mail will arrive electronically, be routed to its destination via computer, and get posted to *electronic bulletin boards* to be prioritized and accessed according to importance. Telephone calls will be received at the work station, and the recipient will identify the caller before deciding to respond directly or have a voice message stored for later retrieval. Travel will be diminished as more *computer conferencing* and *videoconferencing* take place, often with the assistance of GDSS. In general, productivity will be enhanced by the improved information processing available to all members of the computer-coordinated office network.

Computer Networking

Central to the automated office is the integration of computers and communication. **Local-area networks** are sets of two or more computers that can communicate with one another from locations within an office, building, or group of buildings in close physical proximity. **Wide-area networks** extend this communication capability to link computers together across large geographical distances. *Newsline 15.2* shows that computer networks are now taking on truly "global" proportions.

The convergence of computer and communications technologies makes networking in its various forms possible. The basic concept is to allow information to be moved in digitized form through telecommunication linkages between computers. This direct information transmission not only eliminates delays, it can also avoid the errors that may occur when information gets filtered and interpreted by human intermediaries.

Figure 15.5 depicts how network information systems can create **enterprise-wide networks.** When the total enterprise is fully integrated in com-

GLOBAL NETWORKS
LINK OPERATIONS WORLD-WIDE

Like many others, Merrill Lynch has been spending heavily on its world-wide communications and computer networking capabilities. It won't be long before a stockbroker in Chicago can buy shares on the London Stock Exchange directly, without going through a New York-based trader. Even now, a broker in one of the company's many U.S. offices—say Albuquerque—can respond quickly to a local client's inquiry regarding a stock. Working from a desk-top terminal, a few commands instruct a satellite dish antenna on the office roof to pick up data from Merrill's computer center in downtown New York City. Just seconds after making the computer request, the broker is able to review corporate research on the stock and answer the client's questions.

Organizations with expanding international business ties are rapidly extending themselves to create global networks that break the boundaries of time and distance around the world. Hewlett Packard executives use global networking to conduct meetings involving California and Geneva, Switzerland staff—without anyone having to travel. American President Companies, a worldwide shipper, uses satellite links to keep track of cargo movements. A customer can call a toll-free number, enter a code, and receive a message in 10 seconds pinpointing the location of their shipment. The same system also is used to help managers make decision routing the company's ships, trains and trucks.

Honda is in the act too. A parts clerk in a Long Island, N.Y., dealership can use a computer terminal to scan stocks in 10 regional warehouses. These are tied to Honda's U.S. headquarters, which is in turn tied to the parent firm's Tokyo offices. About such global networks, Merrill Lynch's executive vice president for information systems and telecommunications says, "This is becoming a worldwide trading environment. Instantaneous communications is vital." Westinghouse's telecommunications director says that with an international network, "A business can act very nimbly."

Source: As reported in "A Scramble for Global Networks," *Business Week* (March 21, 1988), pp. 140–148.

puter-communication linkages, major efficiencies and other advantages are gained as information moves quickly and accurately from one point to another.[13] In the future it will probably be possible, for example, for a field salesperson to pass on a customer's suggestion for a product modification via electronic mail. This mail arrives at the computer used by a product designer at company headquarters. After working on computer designs for the product, the designer can pass the new prototype on simultaneously to engineering, manufacturing, finance and marketing for their preliminary analyses. The results of these analyses may be pooled through a GDSS to allow further consideration of the prototype's business potential. From there—well, let's just say the procedure can continue—always guided by the support of computers and the communications that allow them to "talk" to one another.

INFORMATION UTILIZATION AND SYSTEMS EFFECTIVENESS

The basic purpose of any information system is to facilitate the accomplishment of objectives through

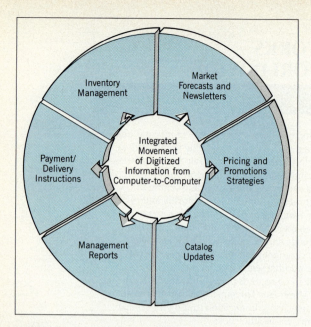

FIGURE 15.5 *Enterprise-wide networks: potential applications in many industries.*

improved information utilization. Ideally, computer-based information systems will increase performance efficiency and effectiveness. Practically speaking, they will do so only if the systems are properly designed for users who (1) understand their management and organizational implications and (2) are committed to their effective utilization.[14]

Management and Organizational Implications

The future is now when it comes to the rapidly changing state of computer and information technologies. Even today, a manager somewhere might be sitting at a terminal performing an old task in a radically new way—a way that is changing not only the nature of the manager's job, but the very essence of the organization iteself. Consider this scenario.[15]

A manager turns on her desk-top computer and is reminded that one of her subordinates is due for a salary review. Entering a password links the manager's desk-top computer with the firm's mainframe. The person's employment file is retrieved and a program run to compare his present salary with peers. Results are dis-

played in a bar chart with a window summarizing the latest performance evaluations. The manager decides how big a raise she wants to give, enters it into the computer, and electronically notifies the personnel and payroll departments. Net time elapsed—about five minutes.

Such advances in the managerial applications of new information and computer technologies can and should provide a *strategic advantage* to those who employ them to full advantage. However, it is also important to recognize that the nature of management and organizations may also be changing in the process. In addition to the benefits of increased efficiency and improved information foundations for decision making, trends such as the following are accompanying the growing utilization of computer-based technology in organizations.

1. *Organization structures are changing* as the new information technologies exert their influence.[16] On the one hand, *hierarchies are becoming flatter,* as fewer management levels are required. The new organizations rely increasingly on computers rather than people to move information from one part of the system to another. But on the other hand, *new information departments or centers are appearing* along with new staff personnel in the information career fields. As depicted in Figure 15.6, these new units can complicate organization structures at the same time that they provide technical expertise to support utilization of information systems and computers. Many such units are headed by a chief information officer who serves as a member of the top management team, and they often include a steering committee composed of other functional managers to advise on user needs.

2. *The nature of managerial work is changing* as managers adapt to the new information-rich environment of organizations.[17] The presence of advanced decision support systems allows for *more decentralization of decision-making,* and empowers lower-level personnel with information needed to make operating decisions. At the same time, the systems provide managers with timely information on performance that allows for *improved control and accountability.* As electronic groups form around computer networks, individual decision makers may remain more anonymous as *decisions become more data-based* and less subject to the influence of group dynamics. The leadership process itself may

change in this more depersonalized work setting, where *information is power* and the influence of a manager's interpersonal presence may be diminished.

3. *Job designs are changing* as new opportunities put even more pressure on managers to utilize both human and technological resources to full advantage, and in combination with one another. This is leading to renewed interest in *highly integrated sociotechnical systems*. Job designs are increasingly challenged to match people and machines, if the machines are to be used to full advantage. This case in point helps to illustrate what can go wrong, and what can be done about it.[18]

At Shenandoah Life Insurance Company a new computer integrated information system was installed. But management discovered it still took 27 working days and the actions of 32 employees to process a new policy. The problems turned out to be, not the new system, but the fact that clerks still worked in assembly-line fashion just as they had when all tasks were manually performed. The job design was changed to reduce the specialization of tasks and put clerks together in teams working with the support of the computer system. This reduced processing time on a new policy to two days and increased the number of transactions processed by 28 percent.

Achieving Information Systems Effectiveness

The basic purpose of any information system is to facilitate the accomplishment of organizational objectives through improved information utilization. An effective information system achieves this purpose. The success of a specific MIS, DSS, or EIS, however, is not guaranteed. To achieve effectiveness, the information system must be well designed and then be actually *used* by people in the organization to accomplish important tasks. To begin, it is always beneficial to have favorable user attitudes.

FIGURE 15.6 *Organization chart for the information systems department in a large organization.*

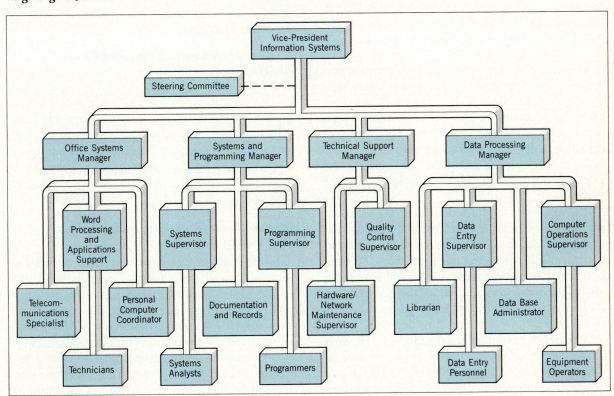

Things to remember include the following.

1. An information system of higher technical quality produces more favorable user attitudes.
2. Strong management support in systems development and implementation results in more favorable attitudes.
3. Individual involvement in systems design and operation results in more favorable user attitudes.

In addition to these points, a number of behavioral factors are known to influence the success of information systems. It is important for a manager to understand these factors, as well as some of the common mistakes which can limit information systems effectiveness.

Behavioral Factors in Information Systems Success

A well-designed information system may fail in one organization when it could easily succeed in another. The difference often traces to behavioral factors. People who view an information system favorably can make it work, even if design flaws exist. By contrast, even the most sophisticated and state-of-the-art system will fail if people within the organization don't correctly and diligently use it.

Different groups in organizations are affected differently by an information system. Operating personnel become involved as the system places substantial responsibility on them to provide accurate and timely data inputs. This aspect of their jobs can become much more structured and less tolerant of deviation with the advent of a new system. If the systems-development group fails to consider the impact of this additional burden, outright resistance to the system is possible.

Managers also resist information systems at times. Among the reasons for this is that any system changes life for the manager, but not always for the better. An MIS, for example, makes more information available to both the manager and his or her immediate supervisor. Some of this information may not be favorable. An MIS can increase the visibility of the *bad* as well as good decisions. Other sources of potential discomfort include the fact that an MIS usually allows managers more time to deal with creative and troublesome issues. This is not necessarily a plus if the manager must learn new ways of doing things and knows he or she will be held accountable for them in return.

Important, too, are people's expectations regarding the role, contributions, and limitations of information systems in the organization. Expectations must be realistic among all personnel who will use and/or be affected by the system. Users must be realistic in their expectations, as to what the MIS can do. Specialized information systems personnel must be careful not to promise more than can be delivered and see to it that they understand the limitations of the available system.

Common Information Systems Mistakes

Information systems of many types will be encountered in your career. Sometimes you may be the designer of a new system and you may serve on an information steering committee, but always you will be a *user*. The task is to use any information system well to facilitate your success in all aspects of the management process—and to enhance organizational productivity as a result. As you look forward to this challenge, keep the following seven common mistakes in mind. Any information system is destined to fail if the designers and users act under the following assumptions.[19]

Mistake 1: Assume more information is always better

It is common to assume that managers suffer a lack of relevant information. While many managers lack a good deal of information that they should have, they may suffer even more from an overabundance of irrelevant information. Most managers receive much more data (not necessarily "information") than they can possibly absorb even if they spend all of their time trying to do so.

Mistake 2: Assume managers need all the information they want

Systems designers typically determine what information is needed by asking managers what they would like to have. This assumes managers know what information they need. But the manager who does not understand a phenomenon is prone to play it safe and, with respect to information, want "everything." The systems designer, with even less understanding of the phenomenon, can easily increase what is already an overload of irrelevant information by trying to provide even more of everything.

Mistake 3: Assume that if managers are given all the information they need, their decision making will improve

It is frequently assumed that managers who have the information they need will use it effectively. This is not especially true. Having information is one thing; using it well is quite another.

Mistake 4: Assume more communication means better performance

An information system usually provides managers with better current information about what other managers and their departments and divisions are doing. Underlying this provision is the belief that better interdepartmental communication enables managers to coordinate their decisions more effectively and hence improves the organization's overall performance. This is not necessarily so.

Mistake 5: Assume managers do not have to understand how an information system works to use it well

Systems designers try to make the systems as accessible as possible for managers and to assure them that they need to know nothing about it. It is easy for managers to stay ignorant. This leaves them unable to evaluate the information system as a whole and with a tendency to delegate much of the control process to the system's designers and operators. The system users should always be trained to evaluate and control it, instead of the system controlling its users.

Mistake 6: Assume the computer can do everything

High technology has brought computers directly into the day-to-day world of management. Micro or personal computers are lending technical sophistication to management and information systems in situations where the costs of such advances were prohibitive until just recently. Along with the growing role of the computer in information systems is the tendency to assume that it can do everything. This is not true; managerial judgment is still a required element in any computer-based information system. Information problem-solving, and decision-making needs within organizations are much broader than what computers alone can supply.

Mistake 7: Assume nothing will ever go wrong with your computer.

Reliance on computers to store important data bases and execute programs governing essential organizational systems and routines has become a way of life. One reports shows a little over 85 percent of surveyed companies were "heavily dependent" on their computer facilities. But computers and electronic data bases must be protected from a variety of threats. They can and do fail . . . and the results can be chaotic and costly. Among the things to be concerned about are the "computer viruses" described in *Newsline 15.3,* as well as:[20]

■ Power outages caused by weather disturbances or other unexpected breakdowns in an organization's electrical systems.

■ Sneak attacks by "hackers," outside computer buffs who make a hobby out of trying to penetrate and sometimes disrupt the computer systems of others.

■ Employee tampering in which disgruntled or simply malicious employees use their access to computer systems to damage data bases and otherwise interfere with operations.

■ Electronic eavesdropping where special means are used by outsiders to intercept computerized telecommunications to gather data and learn vital inside information.

INFORMATION AND THE BUDGETING PROCESS

One important role for management information in organizations is to support budgetary control. Effective managers are comfortable working with budgets and with the information systems upon which they are based.

Budgets

Budgets are quantitative and usually financial expressions of plans; that is, they allocate resources to activities. Think what this means. As the manager of a work unit—the information systems department of a bank, for example—an operating budget allocates to you those resources necessary to accomplish the department's daily responsibilities. Without the budget you wouldn't know how much you

A COMPUTER
VIRUS CAN BE FATAL

"Safe computing" is more and more in the news these days. It means—don't use software of questionable origin, or download software from a networked system. What's at risk is the possibility of becoming infected with a *computer virus*—a troublesome software program that uses computer codes to enter other programs and alter or destroy them. Many of these viruses are especially deadly because they can "reproduce" once on a host computer and pass offspring along to others tapping into the main system.

Viruses often begin with disgruntled employees who have something to grieve against a particular organization. A former employee of USPA & IRA Co., a securities trading firm, entered a virus that destroyed over 168,000 sales commission records before it was eliminated. A British programmer once put three viruses into a program he wrote for a company. Then he demanded a ransom to eliminate them. Some viruses are done just for a stunt or for the thrill of it. A University of Arizona student began one that ended up sending messages of "World Peace" to software users.

The process usually begins when someone inserts a virus program into a normal piece of software. This is its carrier or "Trojan Horse." It can reside on the carrier for years operating with a built-in time clock, only to attack at a preset time. The virus spreads when the host program is transferred among users, and the more swapping takes place the more the virus multiplies. When the damage occurs, the virus activates to take control of the program and do its mischief. Some are known to taunt their victims with messages like "Gotcha!"

"Gotcha" indeed. One virus expert says there have already been more than a quarter of a million reported cases. Forty of the country's largest industrial companies have been afflicted. No one knows how many other viruses have been planted and loom ready to do their dirty work at any time.

Source: As reported in "Is Your Computer Secure," *Business Week* (August 1, 1988), pp. 64–71; and, Peter H. Lewis, "A Virus Carries Fatal Complications," *The New York Times* (June 26, 1988), p. F11.

---

could or should spend on people, supplies, telephone, equipment, etc. Furthermore, your supervisor wouldn't have a basis for evaluating how efficiently the department performs in terms of resource utilization.

Why Budgets are Important

As suggested in the last example, budgets give managers the resources needed to implement plans in their areas of work responsibility. They also become a foundation for exercising management control over how well resources are utilized to accomplish those plans. Budgets are preliminary controls in that they allocate the resources considered necessary to achieve performance objectives. When they allow interim reporting of performance, such as monthly status reports, budgets also serve responsibility-center managers as concurrent controls. Finally, because budgets formally commit the manager to targeted levels of resource utilization and/or performance accomplishment, they serve as benchmarks for postaction controls once actual results are in.

As a manager, you must be comfortable working with budgets, supervising people with assigned budgets, and participating in the budgeting processes of the organization as a whole. In any organization, you can expect to find that[21]

1. *Budgets are stated in monetary terms.* Resources are allocated to activities in specific monetary amounts.
2. *Budgets contain an element of management commitment.* Managers agree to accept the responsibility for attaining the budgeted objectives.
3. *Budgets are based on proposals.* These proposals are usually reviewed and approved by someone in higher authority.
4. *Budgets can be changed only under specific conditions.* They are usually modified only after formal review and approval by higher authority.

Budgets and Responsibility Centers

A good budget translates into financial terms the resources assigned by the organization to a specific area of performance responsibility. If you think about it, in fact, managers are persons in organizations who are "responsible" for using resources efficiently and effectively in pursuit of task accomplishments. Look at the manager's challenge depicted in Figure 15.7. It once again acknowledges that every manager is held accountable by a higher-level supervisor for the task performance of a work unit. Now, however, our figure ties this performance responsibility to a budgetary responsibility as well. An effective manager not only gets the task accomplished; he or she does so within the assigned budget.

From this logic emerges the concept of a **responsibility center,** or work unit formally charged with budgetary responsibility for carrying out various activities. Any responsibility center includes a manager who is held formally accountable by higher authority for achieving performance objectives while remaining *within the budget.* One way of viewing an organization, in fact, is as a hierarchy of responsibility centers ranging from sections, shifts, or other small units at lower levels to larger aggregations such as departments or divisions at higher levels. The development of interlocking budgets for such a hierarchy of responsibility centers is called a **responsibility accounting system.** It is common to find responsibility centers in these systems separated into one or more of the following types.

Revenue centers in which budgets and performance targets concentrate on the product or service outputs of a responsibility center measured in monetary terms. A revenue center is typically controlled on the basis of sales of products or services.

Cost centers or **expense centers** in which the utilization of resource inputs is measured in monetary terms as an expense. No attempt is made to measure outputs in monetary terms. A cost or expense center is controlled on the cost of resources consumed in operations.

Profit centers in which budgetary responsibility is measured on the difference between the revenues and expenses of operations—that is, on the amount of profits realized. A profit center is controlled on the basis of contributions made to the overall profit of an organization.

Investment centers in which budgetary responsibility includes the expenditure of resources for capital equipment. An investment center is controlled

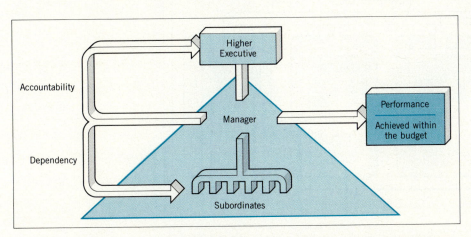

FIGURE 15.7 *The manager's challenge: meeting performance objectives while staying within the budget.*

not only on the amount of profits generated, but also on the capital investment required to produce those profits.

The Budgeting Process

All budgeting directs attention to both performance objectives and anticipated resource requirements. An important concern of most manages is the short-range budget covering periods of one year or less. These are of two general types. **Operating budgets** assign resources to a responsibility center on a short-term basis. **Master budgets** are comprehensive short-term budgets for the organization as a whole. They summarize the approved operating budgets for all the responsibility centers in the organization.

The master budget helps upper-level managers coordinate the activities of many responsibility centers on a short-term basis. As shown in the case of the city bank in Figure 15.8, operating budgets for many separate responsibility centers combine to create the master budget for the organization as a whole. Of course, responsibility centers will also be involved in activities that extend beyond relatively short time horizons. These longer-term activities, both contemplated and in progress, form the basis of the organization's long-range budgetary system.

The budgeting process itself involves the establishment of budgets that achieve a "best fit" between the needs of a work unit or project and the resource capabilities of the organization. Of managerial concern are basic differences between top-down and bottom-up approaches, as well as the concept of zero-based budgeting.

Top-Down versus Bottom-Up Budgeting

Top-down budgeting is a process initiated, controlled and directed by top management. Budgets are set in a manner which is presumed to best allocate available resources among alternative uses within the organization. These budgets are then imposed on middle- and lower-level managers whose responsibilities are to meet the demands conveyed in them. Because top managers are well informed about organizational objectives, strategic plans, current performance, and forecasted conditions, a top-down approach can tailor budgets to overall organizational needs and opportunities. However, due to a lack of involvement of lower-level personnel, the commitments needed to fulfill the imposed budgets are sometimes lacking.

Under Harold Geneen's leadership, ITT used to operate with a top-down budgeting process. In his words, this is how it worked.[22]

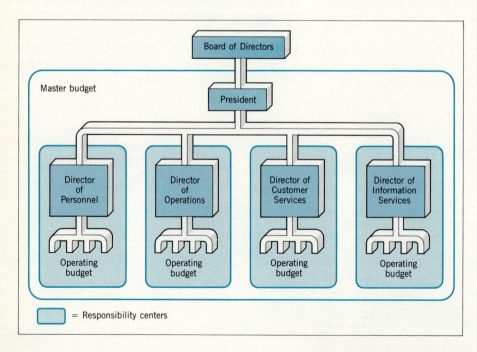

FIGURE 15.8 *Multilevel budgetary control: the case of the city bank.*

At ITT the budgets, which contained the business plans for the following year were drawn up in February and March, reviewed and revised at the local level, and then reviewed and revised at headquarters. We sat face to face with each and every managing director and his own senior staff, division by division, unit by unit. The plans and budgets were discussed and revised and agreed upon in the last quarter of the year, and then they served as the benchmark of performance for the following year. Each division manager and his own management staff had negotiated an agreement with headquarters on his budget and business plan for the following year. He had made a firm commitment to ITT. His subordinates down the line had made their commitments to him for the integral parts of his budget. He would hold them to their word as we would hold him to his commitment—or know the reason why.

Bottom-up budgeting, by contrast, begins with the needs and suggestions of lower-level personnel. With an understanding of department-level needs and opportunities, budgets are tentatively prepared and passed up to the next higher-level for analysis and review. After modification, the budget is combined with others at that level as a proposal to the next higher level. This process is followed until an organization-wide budget is developed. One problem with the approach is the difficulty of achieving a final budget that adequately reflects the budgetary requirements of overall organizational objectives and strategies. But, it creates a high level of commitment among lower-level personnel who have been involved in the process from its beginning.

One example of where a change from top-down to more of a bottom-up process benefited an organization occurred—[23]

at ABC Television where a senior financial team used to create and control every manager's budget. Now, the managers write their own budget proposals. Once budgets are approved, they can do basically whatever they want as long as the budget isn't exceeded. Rick Kaplan, executive producer of *Nightline,* likes this arrangement. It used to be difficult to get approvals for special programs. Under the new system he has successfully done several. "Everything gets done more efficiently," he says, "and we can actually produce more quality on the air because we can plan better."

Because there are advantages and disadvantages of both top-down and bottom-up budgeting, most organizations use some combination of the two. Within broad priorities set by senior management and subject to their final approval, middle- and lower-level managers initiate and negotiate their budget commitments. As suggested in the prior example, two issues are central to the success of any such approach. First, the budgeting process must provide an adequate basis for constructive dialog between the needs of senior management and persons in more operational positions. Second, the process should satisfy higher level needs for budgetary accountability while still providing sufficient flexibility of action at lower-levels.

Zero-based Budgeting

First introduced in Chapter 4, in a discussion of budgets as planning devices, **zero-based budgeting** requires that a budget be justified in its entirety at the beginning of each new funding cycle. There is no automatic roll-over or continuation of the prior level of funding for a department or project; each responsible manager starts from "zero" in building and then justifying a budget request for the new cycle. A major advantage of the approach is the rigor it imposes on managers to carefully evaluate their budget needs and related activities. The time consuming nature of the process and some budgetary uncertainty are among its disadvantages. Originally developed for government use, zero-based budgeting takes place in many organizations of all types. In each case, it is designed to keep current budget allocations in line with the true needs and opportunities of the moment.

ACHIEVING BUDGETARY CONTROL

Planning facilitates control. Good budgets, by specifying in financial terms what is *supposed* to happen, have the potential to help managers effectively fulfill their controlling responsibilities. Achieving budgetary control, however, requires budgets that are both well prepared and well utilized. Three areas of attention are of special managerial significance in this regard: (1) the use of break-even points, (2) financial-ratio analysis, and (3) organizing for budgetary control.

Break-Even Points

Budgets and the budgeting process make a variety of information available to managers. This information can be used in the control process to identify when a system is not achieving its objectives and is therefore in need of corrective action. Among the techniques managers use to do this, at the sub-unit and organization-wide levels, is break-even analysis.

A **break-even point** occurs where total revenue from sales of goods or services is just sufficient to cover total costs. The formula used to calculate a break-even point follows.

In words:

Break-even point = fixed costs divided by (sell-ing price per unit minus the variable cost per unit)

In mathematical symbols:

$$BEP = \frac{FC}{SP - VC}$$

where,

BEP = break-even point
FC = fixed costs
VC = variable cost per unit
SP = selling price per unit

Break-even analysis is the study of the rela-tionship between budgeted revenues and costs to determine how changes in each affect profit. Sup-pose a firm can produce 800 units of product during a year and incurs a fixed cost of $5000. The variable costs of production are $5 per unit and units can be sold for $10 per unit. Break-even analysis asks, "Can this firm make a profit during the year?"[24]

A graphic illustration of the problem is shown in Figure 15.9. Break-even analysis is often por-trayed in this fashion to facilitate decision making. The first step is calculation of a break-even point. Using data provided in the example, it can be deter-mined that

$$\text{Break-even point} = \frac{\$5000}{\$10 - \$5} = 1000 \text{ units}$$

This means that the firm must sell 1000 units to reach the break-even point and start making a profit.

The second step in break-even analysis is to compare the break-even point with projected oper-ations. Because this firm can only produce 800 units, it would be impossible to make a profit. The responsible manager in this case should not proceed with the product under study unless fixed and vari-able costs can be reduced and/or the selling price increased. It is in this way that break-even analysis facilitates precontrol and helps managers avoid situ-ations where performance objectives will not be realized.

Financial Ratio Analysis

The financial projections allowed by the master-budgeting process enable calculation of a number

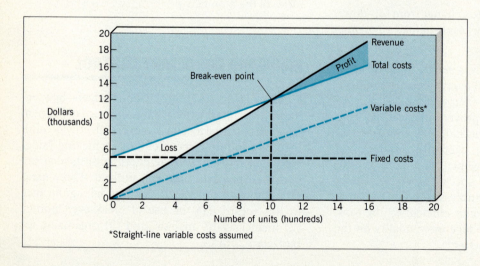

FIGURE 15.9 *A graphic approach to break-even analysis.*

*Straight-line variable costs assumed

of financial ratios that further facilitate managerial control. Among the most common measures of an organization or subunit's financial performance are:

Profitability ratios which measure the ability to earn income. These include *return on equity (ROE)* and *return on investment (ROI)*.

Liquidity ratios which measure the ability to meet short term financial needs. The most popular focus here is on the *current ratio* and the *quick ratio*.

Efficiency ratios which measure the ability to use assets well. The most popular focus here is on the *asset turnover ratio*.

Leverage ratios which measure the extent of debt financing by the firm. This includes the *debt-to-asset ratio* and *debt-to-equity ratio*.

Table 15.1 adds additional details on these ratios as they are used by managers to achieve budgetary control. Top managers find them useful in analyzing enterprise performance against historical and industry standards. But managers at all levels should understand their meanings and performance implications. For example, you will often see or hear

ROE being used to evaluate a firm's performance and/or compare it with others. Frequently, too, specific ROE targets—such as, to achieve a return on equity of 15 percent or better—will be found among a firm's financial objectives. In general, the key to improving ROE lies with increasing profits. This typically involves strategies for achieving revenue growth and cost control.

Organizing for Budgetary Control

The organization of a budgetary control system often involves the participation of a separate budget department staffed by specialists and headed by a budget director. In addition to such a formal staff unit, an organization may have a budget committee consisting of top management and including the chief financial officer or budget director. This committee typically reviews and either approves, disapproves, or adjusts each component in the master budget. Very large organizations have separate budget committees responsible for reviewing the budget submissions of subunits such as departments or divisions.

TABLE 15.1 *Common Financial Ratios Used in Budgetary Control*

Ratios	Calculation	Implication
Profitability ratios		
Return on equity (ROE)	$\dfrac{\text{Net income}}{\text{Sales}}$	Show the efficiency of operations in generating actual or projected profits
Return on investment (ROI)	$\dfrac{\text{Net income}}{\text{Total assets}}$	
Liquidity ratios		
Current ratio	$\dfrac{\text{Current assets}}{\text{Current liabilities}}$	Show actual or projected financial health in terms of assets that can easily be converted into cash
Quick ratio	$\dfrac{\text{Current assets-inventory}}{\text{Current liabilities}}$	
Efficiency ratios		
Asset turnover	$\dfrac{\text{Sales}}{\text{Total assets}}$	Show actual or projected efficiency of asset utilization
Inventory turnover	$\dfrac{\text{Sales}}{\text{Inventory}}$	
Receivables turnover	$\dfrac{\text{Sales}}{\text{Accounts receivable}}$	
Leaverage ratios		
Debt to equity	$\dfrac{\text{Total debt}}{\text{Stockholder's equity}}$	Show extent of debt financing used by organization
Debt to assets	$\dfrac{\text{Total debt}}{\text{Total assets}}$	

In addition to approving initial budgets, budget directors and/or budget committees are responsible for approving changes in budgets. Since any budget represents a commitment to action that is part of an organization-wide plan for resource utilization, budget changes should not be made purely at the discretion of the responsibility-center managers. Indeed, such alterations should be carefully analyzed and limited to situations where changing circumstances have made the original budget so unrealistic that it no longer serves a useful purpose as a planning or controlling device.

At the conclusion of Chapter 14, we presented 10 characteristics of effective control systems. Now it is time to conclude here with counterpart thoughts on the characteristics of effective *budgetary* control systems. In general, we can say that successful budgetary controls are

- Strategic and oriented to results.
- Based on information.
- Simple and understandable.
- Prompt and oriented to exceptions.
- Flexible.
- Based on controllable factors.
- Fair and objective.
- Positive and conducive to self-control.

Summary

Information, or data made meaningful for decision making and problem solving, is the foundation for managerial work. Information systems are designed to collect, organize, and distribute data in such a way that they become meaningful as information. A management information system, or MIS, does this in such a way that the information needs of managers are met. Decision support systems (DSS) are advanced forms of MIS that try to meet manager's specific needs for information of use in decision making. Expert systems are even more advanced and try to meet these needs through artificial intelligence and the capacity of the computer to reason as a human "expert" in respect to particular types of complex problems.

Computer utilization is critical in most information systems. This includes a variety of applications software packages for gathering, storing, and processing data. The personal or microcomputer is increasingly important to the manager as a component in information systems. It makes available at the manager's desktop a variety of information-reporting and decision-support capabilities.

All information systems require the support of people to serve as effective control devices. Poor systems design and/or implementation can discourage, frustrate, and even alienate the persons required to work with the system. Good managers avoid common information systems mistakes. They also recognize that, like all other managerial tools and techniques, such systems can only facilitate the management process—they cannot guarantee its success.

Every manager has to deal with budgets as well as information systems. A budget both commits resources to plans and establishes the framework through which managers are held accountable for using these resources well for task accomplishment. The responsibility-center concept formalizes budgetary responsibility for managers at all levels and sub-units within organizations. Responsibility centers can be defined on a revenue, cost/expense, profit, or investment basis. In each case the related budgets encourage activities that improve planning and make control more effective.

Most managers work with short-range operating budgets covering periods of a year or less. The master budget integrates all operating budgets for the organization as a whole. When preparing budgets for the long and short range, careful consideration must be given to the process through which programs or activities are proposed, evaluated, and eventually approved or disapproved for resource allocations. Budgetary control is facilitated by such techniques as break-even point and financial-ratio analysis, proper organization and adherence to basic characteristics of successful budget systems.

Thinking Through the Issues

1. What is the difference between data and information? Give an example. What is the difference between an information system and a "management" information system?

2. What is a decision-support system (DSS)? In what ways can the use of a DSS benefit managers and organizations?

3. What is the difference between a group decision support system (GDSS) and an executive information system (EIS)? Use examples to explain your answer.

4. What is an expert system? In what ways can the use of expert systems benefit managers and organizations?

5. Explain the difference between "local" and "wide" area networks. How do they bring together computer and communications technologies to serve the needs of managers?

6. What is "applications software"? What types of applications software could a manager make good use of on a desk-top personal computer?

7. Why might managers resist the development and implementation of a new information system? What can be done to prevent this resistance?

8. Why are budgets important to managers? . . . to organizations? What is the basic difference between a "master" budget and an "operating" budget?

9. Identify four types of responsibility centers. Define and give an example of each.

10. "A manager's performance should be evaluated solely on ability to meet budgeted figures." Critically discuss this statement and indicate why you agree or disagree with it.

The Manager's Vocabulary

Applications software
Artificial intelligence
Bottom-up budgeting
Break-even analysis
Break-even point
Budget
Central processing
  unit
Chief information
  officer
Cost center
Data
Decision support
  systems

Efficiency ratios
Enterprise network
Executive Information
  Systems
Expense center
Expert systems
Group decision
  support systems
Hardware
Information
Information reporting
  system
Information system
Investment center

Leaverage ratios
Liquidity ratios
Local-area network
Long-range budget
Management
  information system
Master budget
Office automation
Operating budget
Personal or
  microcomputer
Profit center
Profitability ratios
Responsibility
  accounting system

Responsibility center
Revenue center
Short-range budget
Software
Structured decision
  system
Supercomputer
Top-down budgeting
Transaction
  processing system
Wide-area network
Zero-based budget

INFORMATION SYSTEMS AND YOU

C A R E E R   P E R S P E C T I V E

One offshoot of the great computer revolution is that careers in information systems and related fields are among the fastest growing opportunities available to college graduates. Not all information systems jobs require a technical background in computer programming. Have you ever considered pursuing job opportunities in this area? Here are just a few jobs that you will probably find available if you decide to look.

Systems analyst Works with users to analyze information requirements and design supporting information systems. Serves as an intermediary between the users and the programmers.

Programmers Write and maintain the programs that control the computers. Applications programmers write programs to fit the needs of specific users; systems programmers write programs for the machine operating systems.

Database managers Design and control the various data bases maintained in the organization. Work with programmers, analysts and users to ensure that data bases are well maintained and best utilized.

Computer coordinator Develops policies and procedures to ensure efficient use of personal computers throughout an organization. Knows the computers and their capabilities, and helps others choose and use them well.

Data processing supervisor Supervises operators responsible for entering data into computers, operators responsible for running mainframe and minicomputers, and librarians responsible for storing programs and data files.

Data processing auditor Reviews computer controls, including the safety of and access to data bases. Assists regular auditors in producing audit information through use of computers.

Questions

1. To what extent are you familiar with computers—both mainframe and desktop?

2. Do you suffer from any "computer anxiety," that is, a fear of working with computers and a reluctance to learn more about them? What steps are you taking to make sure that your computer expertise continues to develop as an asset to your personal career?

3. Is a career in one of the information systems areas of any interest to you? If so, what can you do to increase your attractiveness to a potential employer as a job candidate?

Case Application

ONE PERSON BUILDS A BUSINESS

Alan Cadan is the entrepreneurial equivalent of the one-man band.[25] He is the owner, founder, and chief executive of Alynn Neckwear, Inc., as well as its head designer, bookkeeper, salesman, order taker, typist, shipping clerk, and telephone operator.

His four-year-old necktie business booked sales of $1 million. Cadan runs the business from his house in Stamford, Connecticut. He is the only full-time employee. He manages that because he is well organized. He's probably that way, he says, because he admired an uncle who was a compulsive organizer. The uncle wrote his own obituary and died on a weekend, his family says, so as not to inconvenience his loved ones.

"The only way you can run a business by yourself is to be organized," Cadan says. "You have to be on top of things." Working at home saves him commuting time, but the trade-off, he says, is that the office is always present "to remind you of all the work there is to do. You forget to take time to play."

His wife, Lynn, and their four children, ages 11–15, help out. Mrs. Cadan does some bookkeeping and mailing chores and tones down some of her husband's ideas for tie designs, which tend to be clever. A rodent in a jogging outfit is the figure on the Rat Race tie; a design of thumb tacks is sold as the Tacky Tie.

Cadan's fabrics are made in U.S. and European mills; a New York City factory turns them into ties. But all of Alynn Neckwear's shipments are from the Cadans' home.

Packing and shipping are the most time-consuming tasks. Everyone in the family packs ties, a chore that extends into the late hours during the Christmas season, when the company ships 50 percent of its annual volume. Cadan's 79-year-old mother drove 40 miles a day to help out last year." "It's a one-person business," Cadan says, "with a lot of elves."

It's also a no-frills business. The shipping department is in the basement, where boxes of ties—there are 62 designs—sit on tables made of doors and sawhorses. It is equipped with an old, hand-operated tape machine and a worn bathroom scale.

Cadan's desk is a door covered with blotting paper that rests on two sawhorses. His office used to be the garage. A $10,000 computer system was acquired, but he prefers to use clipboards to keep track of things. The clipboards hang in neat rows on the wall behind the desk. One holds orders to be shipped; another has documents that show when fabric went from the mills to the New York tie makers. The computer could track the inventory, but it is simpler and quicker to subtract each day's shipments from what's on hand to keep a continuous inventory count, Cadan says.

The inventory data are on one of the clipboards on the wall. Cadan can reach it without putting down the phone. "You have to be able to save time if you're doing everything yourself," he says.

The computer is used mostly to make out invoices. Previously, with nearly 1,000 retail stores, 36 mail order houses, and 196 corporations buying his ties, Cadan sometimes had to spend entire days typing invoices. The computer also tabulates accounts receivable and prints monthly statements.

But Cadan uses a manual system to track accounts receivable. A file at his desk contains unpaid invoices grouped by customer. He says he can update the file faster than he could if the information were in the computer. He also can get current information about the account quicker by pulling the unpaid invoices than he could if he had to depend on the computer.

Questions

1. To Alan Cadan, "being organized" seems to mean having an orderly flow of the information required to maintain the business. What specific information needs does he have?
2. How confident are you that Cadan's current information system is truly best? What changes would you recommend and why?
3. Suppose the opportunity existed to triple the size of this business. What would need to be done by way of budgets and information systems to provide for growth while allowing Cadan to remain "in control"? Explain your answer.

Class Exercise: Measuring Corporate Performance

Managers, especially senior managers in a large firm and owner-managers in smaller ones, sometimes wonder just what financial indicators they should be monitoring for control purposes. Their concerns include: (a) profitability, (b) liquidity, (c) efficiency, and (d) leverage.

1. Which of the following financial ratios would you use as indicators of performance in each of the above areas? Use the spaces provided to mark letters from the list of concerns above to properly identify the best use of each ratio.

_____ Asset turnover
_____ Current ratio
_____ Return on equity
_____ Debt to equity
_____ Return on investment
_____ Debt to assets
_____ Quick ratio

2. Listed here are a series of figures taken from the balance sheet and income statement of a retail store. Sort through them to locate the information needed to calculate each of the ratios listed above. Make those calculations.

Net sales	$2,160,000
Stockholder's equity	95,600
Total assets	167,600
Inventory	24,000
Current assets	67,600
Current liabilities	44,000
Net income	30,400
Total debt	36,000

3. Share your results in Steps 1 and 2 with a nearby classmate. Compare answers and check one another's accuracy.
4. Working with your classmate, answer this additional question—What additional information would be helpful in order to use the prior ratio calculations to best advantage in this situation? After discussing this question, await further class discussion led by your instructor.

References

[1] These examples are from William J. Burns, Jr., and F. Warren McFarlan, "Information Technology Puts Power in Control Systems," *Harvard Business Review,* Vol. 65 (September–October 1987), pp. 89–94.

[2] This role is reviewed in Mark Mehler, "The New Corporate Chieftain?" *Success* (May 1988), pp. 58–61.

[3] John G. Busch, Jr., Felix R. Strater, and Gary Gundnitski, *Information Systems: Theory and Practice,* Third Edition (New York: Wiley, 1983), p. 4.

[4] Information from *Fortune* (April 15, 1985), advertising supplement; and, Mehler, op cit., 1988.

[5] For a related scheme see Raymond McLeod, *Management Information Systems,* Third Edition (Chicago: SRA, 1986).

[6] Information from Tom Richman, "Mrs. Field's Secret Ingredient," *Inc.* (October 1987), pp. 65–72.

[7] Theses examples are from Paul S. Bender, Richard W. Brown, Michael H. Isaac, and Jeremy F. Shapiro, "Improving Purchasing Productivity at IBM with a Normative Decision Support System," *Interfaces,* Vol. 15 (May–June 1985), pp. 106–115; Stan Kolodziej, "Bringing DSS into Focus," *Computerworld Focus* (September 16, 1985), pp. 47–49; and, "At Today's Supermarket, the Computer is Doing it All," *Business Week* (August 11, 1986), pp. 64–65.

[8] See Gerardine DeSanctis and Brent Laaupe, "Group Decision Support Systems; A New Frontier," *Data Base* (Winter 1985), pp. 3–10.

[9] Information from William M. Bulkeley, "Special Systems Make Computing Less Traumatic for Top Executives," *The Wall Street Journal* (June 20, 1988), p. 15; and "The Computer Age Dawns in the Corner Office," *Business Week* (June 27, 1988), pp. 84–86.

[10] The article by Dorothy Leonard-Barton and John J. Sviokla, "Putting Expert Systems to Work," *Harvard Business Review,* Vol. 66 (March–April 1988), pp. 91–98, provides a very practical overview of expert systems and their management applications.

[11] These examples are from Leonard-Barton and Sviokla, op. cit.; and, "Putting Knowledge to Work," *Time* (March 28, 1988), pp. 60–63.

[12] Developed from James O. Hicks, Jr., *Management Information Systems: A User Perspective,* Second Edition (St. Paul, MN: West, 1987), p. 443; and, Leonard-Barton and Sviolka, op. cit., 1988.

[13] See "Enterprise Networking: Key to Your Company's Future," special advertising section in *Business Week* (March 21, 1988).

[14] See the book by Shoshana Zuboff, *In the Age of the Smart Machine: The Future of Work and Power* (New York: Basic Books, 1988)

[15] This example is suggested by Stuart Gannes, "Tremors from the Computer Quake," *Fortune* (August 1, 1988), pp. 42–60.

[16] For a discussion of the structural implications of new information technologies see John Child, "New Technology and Developments in Management Organization," *Omega,* Vol. 12 (1984), pp. 211–223; and George P. Huber, "The Nature and Design of Post-Industrial Organizations," *Management Science,* Vol. 30 (1984), pp. 928–951.

[17] The managerial implications of new information technologies are examined in William L. Gardner and John R. Schermerhorn, Jr., "Computer Networks and the Changing Nature of Managerial Work," *Public Productivity Review,* Vol. XI (Summer 1988), pp. 85–99.

[18] This case is reported in David Wessel, "Service Industries Find Computers Don't Always Raise Productivity," *The Wall Street Journal* (April 19, 1988), p. 29.

[19] Developed in part from Russell L. Ackoff, "Management Misinformation Systems," *Management Science* (December 1967), pp. 147–156.

[20] See for example, "Is Your Computer Secure?" *Business Week* (August 1, 1988), pp. 64–71.

[21] Robert Anthony and John Dearden, *Management Control Systems,* Fourth Edition (Homewood, IL: Richard D. Irwin, 1980), pp. 368–369.

[22] Harold Geneen with Alvin Moscow, *Managing* (Garden City, New York: Doubleday, 1984), p. 88.

[23] Information from Patricia Sellers, "Lessons from TV's New Bosses," *Fortune* (March 14, 1988), pp. 115–130.

[24] Example from Burt Scanlan and Bernard Keys, *Management & Organizational Behavior,* Second Edition (New York: Wiley, 1983), p. 487.

[25] Sanford L. Jacobs, "By Being Organized, One Man Builds a Thriving Tie Business," *Wall Street Journal,* February 14, 1983, p. 19. Reprinted by permission of the *Wall Street Journal.* © Dow Jones & Company, Inc., 1983. All Rights Reserved.

UNITED AIRLINES

Operations Management and Control

The Push for Quality

Many American executives were looking the other way when quality experts W. Edwards Deming and J. M. Juran went east in the 1950s and 1960s to teach Japanese executives about managing for quality. Frederick Z. Herr, a divisional vice-president at Ford Motor Company, admits that "American industry went to sleep"—and Japanese industry, car manufacturers in particular, profited handsomely from this complacency. American auto makers are still paying the price for ignoring quality. "It takes a long time to change a reputation," says Robert D. Knoll of *Consumer Reports* magazine's auto-testing group.

A stunning 20 to 25 percent of a typical factory's operating budget goes to finding and fixing mistakes—and about the same percentage of workers spend their time reworking products instead of making new ones. Given such dispiriting news, many companies are rethinking their entire approach to quality. Says Myron Tribus of the American Quality & Productivity Institute, they now realize that: "Quality is never your problem. It is the solution to your problem."

Having been forced to accept their slip down the quality ladder, American car manufacturers are working hard to better the Japanese competition—and are encountering success. Several years ago Ford brought in Deming to implement statistical process control, in which the performance of a particular manufacturing process is measured by monitoring variations in its products. Such on-the-spot quality checking was difficult medicine for Ford managers to swallow at first—yet now, claims Ford's Herr, "we think of quality and cost in one breath." The ability to improve quality has become a significant criterion against which upper-management performance is measured at Ford. And GM, following suit, has experimented with dividing workers into teams that monitor the quality of their output and conduct daily quality audits—a task that was formerly the responsibility of separate inspectors.

In many other industries, manufacturing innovations—changes with big implications for quality—are being generated not just by management but by workers on the shop floor. Whirlpool's workforce at its Clyde, Ohio, washing-machine plant suggested an entirely new workflow direction for their production line, and now inspect machinery before it is purchased from suppliers. Moves such as these, which make quality everyone's responsibility, are ones which Deming and Juran would undoubtedly approve. ■

Source: Information from "The Push for Quality," *Business Week* (June 8, 1987), pp. 130–136, and "Why Image Counts," *Business Week* (June 8, 1987), pp. 138–140.

The chapter opener introduces some of the issues and current developments in the area of **operations management (O/M)** This is a branch of management theory specifically concerned with the activities and decisions through which organizations transform resource inputs into product outputs. Broadly stated, the *product outputs* can be either goods or services. The *resource inputs,* or factors of production, include the wide variety of materials, technologies, capital, information, and people needed to create finished goods or services. The **transformation process,** in turn, is the actual set of operations or activities through which various resources are utilized to create a finished product of value to a customer or client in the organization's external environment.

The notion of *value-added* is very important to operations management. *If* operations add value to the original cost of resource inputs, *then:* (1) a business organization can earn a profit—that is, sell a product for more than the cost of making it (e.g., fast food restaurant meals); or, (2) a nonprofit organization can add wealth to society—that is, provide a public service that is worth more than its cost (e.g., fire protection in a community). To achieve such ends, the operations of all organizations—manufacturing and service—must be well managed. Ideally, this will ensure that all resources—human and material—are combined in the right way and at the right time in order to create a product at minimum cost and of high quality.

Think for a moment what this last statement means. Abbott Laboratories produces some 750 health-care products. The production process involves obtaining the raw materials, either liquid or dry, mixing them, filling containers, sterilizing the containers, and packaging. The 2000 customers are primarily hospitals who expect one-day delivery. Imagine trying to coordinate all these activities and still satisfy the one-day delivery time.

To accomplish this challenge, managers use a variety of modern operations management techniques. In the remainder of this chapter, you will learn more about these techniques and how they are used either by manufacturing companies like Abbott Labs or by service organizations like the hospitals who buy Abbott's products.

OPERATIONS MANAGEMENT IN ORGANIZATIONS

To create a finished good or service by successfully combining labor, materials, and other resource inputs, any organization must satisfactorily perform three basic activities. As shown in Figure 16.1, these activities or components of operations management are: (1) obtaining and storing raw materials, (2) scheduling the utilization of these materials, and (3) creating finished goods and/or services through the combined efforts of people and technology.

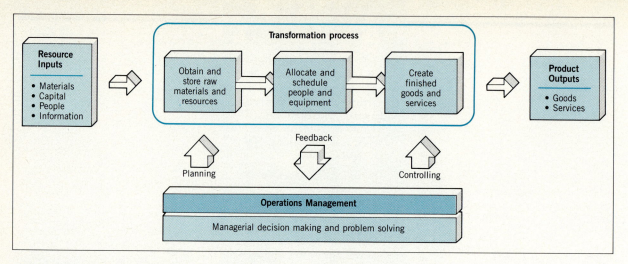

FIGURE 16.1 *Operations management: managing the transformation of resource inputs into product outputs.*

ILLUSTRATIVE CASE:
HUFFY CORPORATION UPGRADES ITS OPERATIONS

The totally mechanized factory isn't in yet at Huffy Corporation, the bicycle manufacturer.[1] And it isn't likely to be for a long time to come. But Huffy has dramatically upgraded its operations at the 32-year-old Celina, Ohio, plant, and turned it into a model of how U.S. firms can meet the challenges of foreign competition.

In years past the firm faced the test with imported bikes taking an ever larger share of the market, and its newest plant with automated equipment wasn't living up to expectations. Huffy's senior management decided to close the new plant and make a major investment in upgrading the Celina facility. At the time, 2200 workers at Celina were turning out 10,000 bikes per day. Now, 1700 workers there make 15,000 bikes a day. The company claims it is the most productive bicycle factory in the world—requiring only 42 minutes to make a bike.

The new plant gives special attention to quality, production, and inventory management. Every attention is given to creating defect-free products, and to making sure parts and assemblies flow smoothly and rapidly throughout the plant. Suppliers furnish materials and parts just as they are needed, and must certify that they meet specifications. Those who can't are immediately dropped.

They are also required to ship frequently. For example, Huffy receives steel daily from an Ohio company. It doesn't take longer than a week for the steel to be turned into a bicycle; five years ago it took three. A plant manager says, "Our goal is to have things come in in the morning and go out that evening."

Plant employees get involved in making decisions affecting their work. Management expects workers to inspect the results of their own labor and correct any problems before passing the in-process product along to the next work station. A quality inspector randomly takes a completed bike completely apart. "Most of the time there are no defects," he says. "The company has trained the employees to do a better job and we're part of a team." Exactly. Huffy employees apply a team approach to many jobs, organizing groups of people and machines into work cells. In one such cell, several workers make the forks that hold bike wheels. They use machines to shape, grind, weld, and drill the forks to specifications. They share the tasks and inspect the finished products. Of course, they're responsible for correcting anything that goes wrong in the cell.

People and machines blend together at Huffy in optimum combinations. An electrostatic painting system puts the base coat on all bike frames. But experienced workers apply touch-up paint using hand-held spray guns. The painter robots just aren't smart enough to do that.

Essentials of Operations Management

It is important to understand that the elements of operations management apply to both manufacturing and service organizations. It is just as important for banks, public agencies, hospitals, stores, and schools to manage their service operations as it is for a manufacturing firm to manage its production function. Products constantly move through a manufacturing facility; clients continually flow through a service operation. Performance success in each case requires that all facets of the transformation process be well managed. As Figure 16.1 originally showed, finished goods and services are the result of decisions that exercise good operations control. If the environment were always certain and the future always predictable, these decisions would be easy and routine. But this is not the case in today's world. Operations management and control is thus an essential and exciting managerial task. It places a premium on the manager's ability to plan well enough in the first place so that operations can be effectively controlled to ensure desired results in the final analysis.

The field of operations management is dedicated to helping managers create and improve upon operations. Ideally, this ensures that the needs of any organization or subunit and its customers are best satisfied. Typical operations management decisions, and ones that we will be addressing in this chapter, include:[2]

1. *Capacity decisions*
- How much production capacity is needed?
- How flexible should this capacity be?

2. *Facilities decisions*
- Where should facilities be located?
- How many are needed and of what sizes?

3. *Workflow and technology decisions*
- What workflow layouts are best?
- What technologies should be used?

4. *Materials and inventory decisions*
- How often should materials be obtained?
- How large should inventories be?

5. *Quality decisions*
- What level of product quality is needed?
- How do we achieve the desired quality?

STRATEGIC ISSUES IN OPERATIONS MANAGEMENT

The context for making good operations management decisions is set by overall organizational objectives and strategy. *Strategy* was defined in Chapter 5 as a long-term plan that sets critical direction for the enterprise. Up until recently, the important and vital link between strategy and operations management was relatively neglected by managers in many industries.[3] Finally, the competitive pressures of global markets and a volatile economy have reawakened managers to the significance of productivity improvement through better operations management. This quest, highlighted in *Newsline 16.1*, is proceeding at a fast pace in both manufacturing and service enterprises. Its success depends on the foundations of operations management to be presented in this chapter, as well as a number of "strategic issues" now viewed as essential components of enterprise strategy and total systems success. These include concerns for competitive advantage, customer orientation, product design, technology utilization, and the role of the human factor.

Competitive Advantage

Any strategy should contribute to an organization's ability to create a *competitive advantage* or *distinctive competency,* something that sets it clearly apart from competitors. Perhaps the best continuing example of how operations management can be used to strategic advantage still rests with the successes of Japanese industry. Consider these data reported in a study conducted by a consultant working for the Massachusetts Institute of Technology's International Vehicle Program. The consultant measured productivity and quality at 38 automobile plants around the world, and found that:[4]

1. *The Japanese plants were the most productive.* The average Japanese plant is 39 percent more productive than plants of the American automakers, and 88 percent better than those of the Western Europeans.

2. *The Japanese built the highest quality cars.* Japanese cars sold in the United States averaged 44 assembly defects per 100 cars; American cars had 87 per 100; European cars had 90 per 100.

U.S. TEXTILE MAKERS
CHALLENGE FOREIGN RIVALS

After experiencing troublesome setbacks when hundreds of plants were forced to close in the face of heavy Asian competition, American textile manufacturers are working to regain their former edge. One new synthetic-fiber maker, Fiber Industries, is using communications and data technology to give its customers—purchasers of fabric for clothing, home furnishings, and car interiors—better inventory at a faster and more reliable pace.

In addition to high-speed spinning machines, Fiber Industries' employees use computers on the shop floor to monitor the quality of polyester fiber before it is made into fabric. Because Fiber can offer nearly defect-free goods, over two-thirds of its clients have granted the company "certified" status: they believe Fiber will supply just what they want, when or before they need it. One client, Milliken & Co., simply computer-checks the quality data for each batch of fabric it receives from Fiber, rather than testing samples—thus saving itself considerable time and money. Milliken's director of raw materials calls Fiber's quality-control program "a major step forward."

Fiber Industries is able to route invoices and order changes electronically, and its computers check inventory and automatically send fiber bales to its mills when stock is low. These capabilities appeal to retailers, many of whom will pay more for such efficiency—and for the assurance of prompt deliveries, which many Asian rivals cannot make.

Fiber's chief executive, Anthony Champ, is pleased with the combination of savings and worker participation that have resulted from his introduction of high technology into his company's operations. Champ sees big improvements, not only "in the bottom line but in the morale" of his workers.

Source: As reported in "Putting Pep Back into Polyester," *U.S. News & World Report* (March 7, 1988), p. 53.

Distinctive competency indeed! The ingredients of the Japanese success lie with a manufacturing system that begins on the shop floor with workers who maintain their own machines, ensure the quality of their work, and continually work to improve the production process itself. This "culture" is closely tied, furthermore, to a smooth blend of high technology with human effort, support systems like "just-in time" delivery of parts that help to control costs, and a commitment to "total quality" ranging from initial design and raw materials right down to finished product.

Today, progressive organizations in America and elsewhere in the world are making the commitments necessary to achieve competitive advantages through operations. They are changing the operations management approaches of the past and updating them in creative and productive ways—some by selectively learning from Japanese examples, and some by developing their own unique capabilities. Many of these foundations for high performance through effective operations management are introduced in this chapter.

Customer Orientation

Question: "What's your job?"
Answer: "I run the cash register and sack groceries."
Question: "But isn't your job to serve the customer?"
Answer: "I guess, but it's not in my job description."

The prior conversation betrays what is often a major missing ingredient in attempts to link strategy and operations management—concern for the customer or client.[5] And the issue is much too common to deny. How many times have you asked this question of a passing waiter in a restaurant? *You:* "Can we have some more water, please?" *Passing waiter:* "Sorry, but it's not my table." Or, how about this conversation in an airline terminal? *You:* "Excuse me, but could you tell me where to find Flight #142 to Los Angeles?" *Uniformed airline employee:* "Sorry, I'm going off duty right now."

Notwithstanding the fact that the *disservice* represented in the prior conversations can and does happen, customer or client service lies at the heart of efforts to improve operations management in organizations. And what the customer in a grocery store wants—"service" from the check out clerk—is quite generalizable to customers in almost any setting. The key objectives of operations management include providing customers with—(1) high-quality products, (2) low-cost products, (3) short waiting times, and (4) flexible responses to individual needs.[6]

One of the major accomplishments of operations management today, however, is broadening this customer orientation to include "internal" as well as external customers. The concern for service holds true whether the customer is someone external to the organization, or another employee who works at a later stage in the production process. In both cases, the concern for customer requirements is critical to the success of operations management and the total organization. Figure 16.2 depicts this focus on both internal and external customers. Consider, too, this example.[7]

At Hewlett-Packard a new quality-control system is designed to make sure that things are done right at every step in the production process. Management has told everyone who works for the company that he or she is both a customer and a supplier. For someone assembling circuit boards, for example, her supplier is the person making chips and her customer is the person who puts boards into finished components. Each person in the workflow works directly with their "suppliers" and "customers" to make sure everyone has the quality materials they need to pass a quality product on to the next work station. This provides accountability for results to one's co-workers, not just supervisors. The results, as you might expect, are very positive.

Product Design

Newsline 16.2 introduces another timely and important strategic issue in operations management—the role of product design. We're all aware of design differences among products, be they cars, stereos, clothes, or watches. But what might not be recognized is that design makes a difference in how things are produced, and at what level of cost and quality. As suggested in the newsline, a good design has eye appeal to the target consumer *and* is easy to manufacture. This point is increasingly recognized as central to operations management, and many companies turn to design experts for help. For example,[8]

At David Kelley Design a Palo Alto based consulting firm, the customers are major corporations who

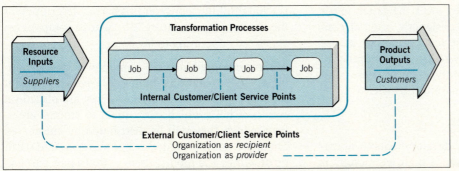

FIGURE 16.2 *The importance of customer or client orientation to operations management.*

After surrendering its lead in product design to Europe and Japan, American industry has awakened to the "design crisis." It is once again designing for quality, ease of production, and high style. Ford's Taurus and Tandem Computers' NonStop CLX computers are examples of the new look in American products: smooth, sleekly curved, and high quality. These and many other new products are designed with users in mind, and they bring in big profits for their manufacturers.

Simplicity is the watchword in current design: products that are readily identified, safe, and straightforward to use. Another important trend is "design for assembly"—styling products that can be made cheaply because they have few complex parts. Computer programs now aid designers in such streamlining, and companies such as GE and IBM have found that they can greatly reduce assembly time using "leaner" designs.

Teamwork in design is crucial, and independent design firms often combine their clients' marketing and manufacturing staffs right from the start—to make sure everyone's input is reflected in the final product. Cosmetic changes are no longer the name of the game in American design; substance is as important as surface appearances, and it definitely enhances profitability. As Philips Corporation designer Robert Blaich puts it, "design is a strategic weapon for business."

Source: As reported in "Smart Design," *Business Week* (April 11, 1988), pp. 102–117; and, "Quality is not Accidental—It is Designed," *The New York Times* (June 26, 1988), p. 2F.

come to David Kelley for ideas on how to get new products to work, both in the marketplace and in the factory. They usually come to Kelley with designs in hand, but need help in translating the design into something that's workable for production. Kelley and his team try to meet the latter needs while still preserving the designer's original concept. A good example is the point-and-click mouse for Apple computers. They reduced the number of parts from the original prototype, made it less complex, and thus made final manufacturing easier.

Technology Utilization

Among the many strategic developments in operations management, the role of high technology is among the most visible. Computers and information technologies are being used with increasing frequency and sophistication in all aspects of operations. **Automation,** the accomplishment of work via machines, lies at the heart of the issue. Just to get you thinking, consider this partial description of the "factory of the future" . . . whose components are already operating today.[9]

At the automated factory computer networks handle diverse operations. Materials are checked in at the loading dock by computer. They are placed on conveyor belts which carry them to storage areas, from which they will be distributed by automated carriers. Computer-aided design systems (CAD) call up drawings and modify them so that a new part can be produced on a computerized numerical control (CNC) machine. A bill of materials is extracted from the design and transferred to the materials requirements planning (MRP) system, and then translated for further input to the computer-aided process planning (CAPP) system . . . and so on until the finished part is available for use and all cost records updated for input to the financial reporting systems.

No modern manager can fail to be informed about the increased opportunities for computer utilization in all aspects of operations. Figure 16.3 presents a sample of the ways in which computers are now being used to accomplish **computer integrated manufacturing.** This is manufacturing that uses a variety of computer applications to automate and integrate activities. It is also manufacturing that is well supported by appropriate information systems—both *decision support systems* and *expert systems.* Briefly highlighted here are several terms that are now part of the operations management vocabulary.[10]

■ *Automated guided vehicles (AGVs)* driverless transports that use computer control to guide them in moving materials from one work location to another.

■ *Computer-aided design (CAD)* uses computers to help create engineering designs and to rapidly change them as needed.

■ *Computer-aided manufacturing (CAM)* uses computers to monitor the production process, link various machines and operations to one another, and provide feedback for control purposes.

■ *Computer-aided process planning (CPP)* uses computers to plan operations and determine the best routings of parts through a series of machines.

■ *Computer numerical control (CNC)* uses computers to store instructions on various machine operations, and control changes in machine settings and movements.

■ *Group technology (GT)* uses computers to help code and classify parts into families that require similar handling in respect to storage and manufacturing utilization.

■ *Robotics* uses computers to guide multifunctional robots in the performance of work tasks previously performed by human operators.

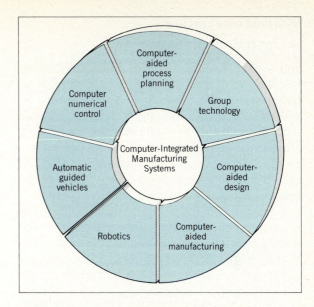

FIGURE 16.3 *Typical components in computer-integrated manufacturing.*

The Role of the Human Factor

Our review of job design in Chapter 8 stressed the importance of combining people and machines into effective *socio-technical systems.* Thus even as we talk about the great advantages and potential of high technology in management, it is necessary to remember that human resources are still essential to the success of any operations process. If anything, effective operations in the 1990s will be true partnerships between people and machines.[11]

In the midst of technological developments, however, managers must understand their potential job design and staffing implications. Workers of tomorrow will need advanced technical skills to work with a variety of information-based computer systems, and they will need the skills to work together in more flexible and adaptive organization structures. The success of computerized operations will depend not only on the quality of the underlying technology and its design, but also on the continued involvement of the human factor. Computers and automated machines will be but one part of a workplace in which quality circles, autonomous work groups, job enrichment, and the many other innovations discussed elsewhere in this book bring human skills and contributions to bear on operations.

Systems Integration in Operations Management

You should recall from earlier discussion that the essentials of operations management rest with its critical role in the transformation process—that is, as the set of activities through which resource inputs are transformed into product outputs. Figure 16.4 presents the basic elements in a systems perspective on operations management. Managerial effectiveness begins with an understanding of each of the responsibilities in the figure. Notice that computers and information technologies, quantitative decisions techniques (such as those reviewed in the Management Applications Module at the end of the book), and the indispensable human factor all play central roles. They support, in turn, these operations management foundations to which our attention is now directed.

1. *Designing manufacturing and service operations* capacity planning, process planning, facilities location, and facilities layout.
2. *Allocating and scheduling resources* aggregate planning, master scheduling, materials requirements planning (MRP), manufacturing resources planning (MRPII), just-in-time scheduling (JIT), and project management.
3. *Controlling costs of materials and inventories* materials management, lot-sizing, and inventory models.

4. *Managing for total quality control* quality analysis and quality assurance.

DESIGNING MANUFACTURING AND SERVICE OPERATIONS

Like the management process in general, operations management begins with planning. In order to set the stage for an effective blend of people and machines, both manufacturing and service operations must be designed for maximum opportunity of success. Four key decisions are central to this planning process. They include decisions on: (1) how much production capacity is needed, (2) where to locate facilities, (3) what operations processes to employ, and (4) how to layout the facilities so people and machines can perform the actual work.

Capacity Planning

Capacity planning is the process of deciding how much production or service "capacity" is needed to meet the forecasted demand for an organization's goods and/or services. Airlines, for example, measure capacity in available passenger seat miles; hospitals use available beds; manufacturing firms may use available machine time. The capacity planning problems for any manager is to have the most economical amount of capacity available to meet

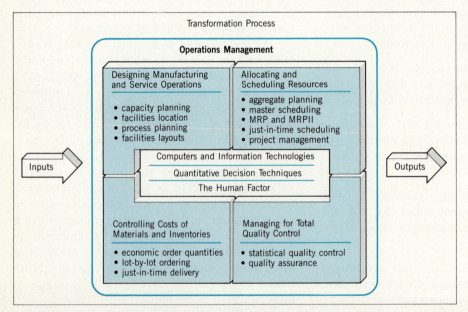

FIGURE 16.4 *Essentials of operations management: a systems integration approach.*

production or service demands. This isn't always easy. Think about the situation in a bank. Sometimes you can walk in and a teller is free or you have to wait only a short time. Those times there is sufficient capacity. There may even be overcapacity if extra tellers are available with no one to wait on. At other times, such as Friday after work or Saturday morning, you've probably experienced the irritation of a long wait just to cash a check or make a deposit. Those times there is insufficient or undercapacity. The bank manager wants to maintain sufficient capacity to meet service demands, and minimize both over- and undercapacity.

The capacity of any operation should be planned on the foundations of a good forecast of customer demands. **Demand forecasting** is the process of estimating future demand for an organization's products or services. The demand forecast in a manufacturing firm may involve projecting the number of product units to be made each week. For a hospital the same goal becomes one of projecting how many patients will be served each day. Meeting this demand generates requirements for people, equipment, raw materials, and other resources.

A demand forecast can help managers anticipate and prepare for times when more capacity must be added for too much demand, or excess capacity should be reduced because of too little demand. If a bank manager knows that every Saturday morning will be busy, he or she can plan to add extra tellers and increase capacity. If a hospital administrator expects an emergency room to be busier on holiday weekends, plans can be made to schedule extra staff on those days. When properly done, demand forecasting helps managers plan capacity by:

1. *Deciding whether demand is sufficient to generate the desired returns for the organization.* If demand exists but at too low a "price" to cover the "costs" that will be incurred, the organization should reject the opportunity. This is an essential principle in break-even analysis, as discussed in Chapter 15.

2. *Identifying short-term fluctuations in demand for use in production planning, workforce scheduling, materials planning, and so forth.* These weekly to monthly forecasts are of special importance and crucially affect workflow bottlenecks, master scheduling, promised delivery dates, and other such issues of concern to top management and the organization as a whole.

3. *Determining long-term capacity needs for facility design.* An accurate projection of demand for a year or more in the future can save the organization great expense in expanding or contracting capacity to accommodate future conditions.

Facilities Location Planning

Facilities location planning involves the choice of a preferred location for a manufacturing or service facility. This is a complex decision that can have a very significant impact on the success of the organization. Key considerations will vary, of course, depending on the exact nature of the operation under consideration. Generally speaking, however, most facilities locations planning takes into account:

- Availability of skilled workers.
- Cost of labor.
- Government incentives and services.
- Access to needed raw materials suppliers.
- Taxes, utilities, and other expected costs.
- Transportation and communication systems.
- The availability of customers.

Advanced computer models are now available to help support managerial decision making on these matters. However, "rules of thumb" are still used in some industries. This may be especially true in retail businesses where the value of a location in respect to customer traffic flow is critical. When asked how locations were chosen for Pizza Hut restaurants, for example, entrepreneur Frank Carney once replied that he built as close to McDonald's as possible.

Process Planning

The design of manufacturing and service operations is always based in part on the approaches used to produce a good or service. Figure 16.5 shows a continuum of choices in the processes organizations can use to accomplish work. At the two extremes are "repetitive" and "batch" processing. Although the terms may be new to you, the essence of each is quite familiar.

1. *In repetitive processing* the raw materials flow continuously through an operation, as they are transformed into finished products. There are two basic types of repetitive processes:
Continuous process involves the transformation of raw materials that enter the system as "flows" or

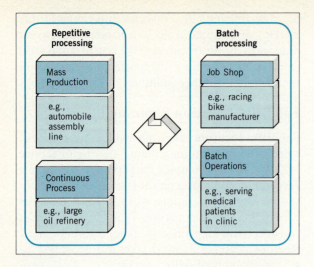

FIGURE 16.5 *A continuum of operations processes: repetitive and batch processing alternatives.*

"fluids" and exit the system in various product forms. These processes are often capital intensive. Two examples are an oil refinery that continuously processes crude oil into a variety of petroleum products, and an electric utility that continually processes various forms of energy into electricity.

Mass production takes place in an assembly-line format with items or customers being systematically and repetitively passed from one work station to another until the good is completed or service delivered. A good example is in automobile manufacturing where machine-paced assembly lines structure the flow of work from station-to-station in a fixed and repetitive sequence.

2. *In batch processing* raw materials are worked on in "batches" to create a finished product. In manufacturing this may involve the creation of a unique commodity tailored to one customer's needs; in services it involves treating an individual client in a unique way. There are also two basic types of batch processing:

Job shops are specialty operations where customers and products get individual attention in the production process. Restaurants are job shops in the service sector; a specialty racing bicycle factory is a job shop in the manufacturing sector.

Batch operations are common where low volume and the need for flexibility prevents a mass production approach, but some economies of scale can be gained by "batching" items together for similar pro-

duction runs. Batch processing is common in "project" environments such as marketing and research and development; it is also the basis for new flexible manufacturing systems.

Facility Layout Planning

Facility layout planning deals with the way work space is arranged in a given situation. It involves decisions on how to arrange work stations and the flow of work from station to station. The exact choice of layout will have to be determined in respect to situational needs and variables. Operations management typically deals with these four types of facilities layouts.[12]

Process layouts where facilities group together people to employ the same process or perform a similar function. Sometimes called *functional layouts,* such arrangements facilitate cross-training and supportive relationships among persons doing the same work. They are common in job shop settings.

Product layouts where facilities are arranged in accord with the flow of a product from inception to finished good or service. Production efficiency is achieved as the same activities are performed over and over at each work station in routine fashion. The *mass production* common to assembly line situations represents a product layout in manufacturing; in services, product layouts are found in government agencies where clients move from one office to another to process applications.

Fixed-position layouts where the product or customer is fixed and the necessary workers and supporting facilities are brought to it. Construction is one example; the manufacture of very large vehicles such as railroad locomotives is another. In such cases the product is simply too large or heavy to be moved from one location to another. Instead, work is arranged around the product as it is built in a fixed position.

Cellular layouts where workstations are arranged in "cells" dealing with "families" of activities that can be performed together. Within a **work cell,** machines and operators cluster together to lend an integrated socio-technical team focus to all work within the cell. This allows team members to become very product and process oriented, and develop commitments to continued high-quality production. It also adds considerable efficiency to materials handling and other workflow related matters. Work cells are used in the new plant—[13]

at Huffy Corporation where a team of eight people assembles bicycle wheels. They switch jobs among themselves, sharing tools, equipment and work stations. They also handle their own inspection and quality control. Boredom is avoided. Joann Wilkins, an 11 year veteran familiar with the way things used to be done, says: "I like working in a group a lot better than doing one job by myself."

Flexible manufacturing systems use computer-based group technology to integrate resources and activities in more complex cellular layouts.[14] This creates, in a sense, "minifactories" within a larger facility to perform work on separate products or product components.

ALLOCATING AND SCHEDULING RESOURCES

When operations are well planned initially, control is facilitated in the final result. The purpose of scheduling is to ensure that the *right things* are done at the *right time* with the *right items and/or people* to create the *desired product or service output* through the most *efficient utilization of resources.*[15] Managers work with the results of the basic scheduling activities depicted in Figure 16.6. They include aggregate and master scheduling, material-requirements planning (MRP), manufacturing resources planning (MRPII), just-in-time systems (JIT), and the special techniques of project management including CPM, and PERT.

Aggregate Scheduling

Aggregate scheduling is the process of making a rough cut or first approximation to a production/operations schedule based on a demand forecast. Manufacturing organizations, for example, need to decide in general whether to produce early and store

products in inventory until demanded, or to delay production until the product is actually demanded and then supply it later. Service organizations such as a hospital must decide if they will staff to meet any demand that occurs (e.g., emergencies) or staff on the basis of demand that is controlled on the basis of selective admissions policies. In both cases, aggregate planning is a first approximation or approach to making resources available to satisfy forecasted demand.

Because aggregate planning is a first approximation to a production or service schedule, it is not usually very detailed. Yet it does help to set a longer-term perspective on resource utilization that will satisfy product or service demands with minimum cost. To do this, aggregate scheduling focuses on groups of products or services and determines in broad terms what resources will be needed in the associated production/operations processes. It helps managers look ahead and broadly choose resource-utilization strategies most preferable to the organization as well as capable of satisfying the demand forecasts.

Master Scheduling

Master scheduling specifies in detail exactly what goods or services will be produced during the short term. It makes an aggregate schedule operational and guides the production or service delivery processes on a weekly or even daily basis. Some organizations go even further. The Anheuser-Busch Brewery in St. Louis, for example, plans the production of its beers on an *hourly* basis. Hospitals may also schedule operating rooms, special equipment, and other facilities hourly.

There are really no hard and fast rules for master scheduling. It always involves making trade-offs between different resource requirements and the constraints of various demand forecasts. A look at how master scheduling is done by one company will give you the flavor of what it entails.[16]

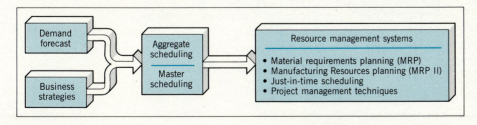

FIGURE 16.6 *Basic operations management approaches to allocating and scheduling resources.*

At Black & Decker the Hampstead, Maryland, plant manufactures over $200 million worth of power tools each year for its customers, mostly distributors and wholesalers who demand one-week delivery. To handle all this, B&D prepares a master schedule on a week-by-week basis for each of the 3100 end products over a 12-month time span. Both marketing and manufacturing are involved in master scheduling. A "logistics group" in marketing identifies marketplace requirements. The master schedule is the result of their needs being integrated with factory capabilities and constraints. This integration is accomplished by a continuing dialogue between inventory-planning analysts in marketing and production-planning analysts in manufacturing. Adjustments in both production quantity and timing are negotiated so that market needs are satisfied and plant profitability is maximized. At the end of each month, a new month is added to the 11 remaining in the master schedule. The production schedule in that month is somewhat imprecise, but becomes more clearly defined as the time draws closer to the present.

Material Requirements Planning (MRP)

The master schedule plans the production of each finished product or service. To fulfill this schedule, all component parts and resources must be brought together at the specified time and in the right place. This is difficult to achieve in practice. A good ex-ample is automobile manufacturing, where it takes time to make or order the various components of a final car assembly. This adds additional complication to any production/operations process.

Material requirements planning (MRP) is an integrated production planning and control technique that schedules materials needed to create a product. As shown in Figure 16.7, an MRP computer system achieves this integration by utilizing production and inventory information to schedule and release production orders. The primary inputs to this system are:

1. *The master production schedule* which is developed from demand forecasts and firm orders, and indicating the quantities of finished goods to be produced in a given time period. This schedule tells the system when products of a certain type must be completed.
2. *The bill of materials* computer file which contains the lists of components required to complete each of the subassemblies which together comprise the finished good. This file tells the system which components are needed to fulfill the master production schedule.
3. *The inventory records* computer file which identifies the current availability of any required components, as well as the timing of replenishments. This file tells the system how many components are available at the times they will be scheduled for use.

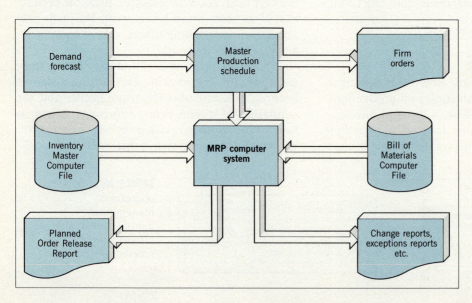

FIGURE 16.7 *A schematic view of a computer-based material requirements planning (MRP) system.*

Source: Jack R. Meredith, *The Management of Operations,* Third Edition (New York: John Wiley & Sons, 1987), p. 456. Used by permission.

With this information available, the MRP system is able to perform a series of calculations to best coordinate inventories and production requirements under the master schedule. It is able to ensure a smooth and efficient flow of materials throughout the necessary production processes. It is also able to update planning as changes, such as modifications to the master schedule, are made.

As you can tell, MRP is a powerful managerial tool that quickly increases in complexity when applied to operations involving the multitude of finished goods or services and component parts suggested earlier in the Black & Decker example. Fortunately, computers make the required calculations easy. They can readily supply the managers of even very complex operations with good MRP information that helps anticipate materials needs, analyze lead times, release purchase orders, and plan production runs in accord with the master schedule. The latest versions of MRP extend its coverage to all types of resources used in the production process, not just the material ones. Called *resources requirements planning,* or RRP, it further assists operations management and control.

Manufacturing Resources Planning (MRPII)

Manufacturing resources planning (MRPII) extends the computerized form of MRP just described to include linkages with purchasing, accounting, sales, engineering, and other business functions.[17]

Figure 16.8 describes a typical MRPII system and its components. Notice that a master schedule still drives the production process. But now there are additional inputs received from engineering and purchasing to add further detail to production planning. Once the process proceeds to the actual manufacturing stages, data is collected through the computerized information system to support cost accounting, plant maintenance, and distribution planning, among other possible uses.

Because MRPII integrates so many functions, it adds considerable efficiency to the operations planning and control processes. It allows for better utilization of financial and human resources, as well as the physical plant and equipment. Among the many computer software packages available to support MRPII, a popular one is the Production Information and Control System (PICS) designed by IBM. It not only handles the elements described in Figure 16.7, but also allows for "changes" to be factored into the system as they arise. For example, when a rush order is received the program steps backwards into the process and adjusts schedules and resources to accommodate the request. MRPII is a good example of where computers and information systems can work together to streamline and increase the efficiency of many interrelated operations and business functions.

Just-in-Time (JIT) Scheduling

Newsline 16.3 helps to introduce one of the more talked about recent developments in operations

FIGURE 16.8 *A typical manufacturing resource planning system (MRPII) and its component modules.*

Source: Jack R. Meredith, *The Management of Operations,* Third Edition (New York: John Wiley & Sons, 1987), p. 379. Used by permission.

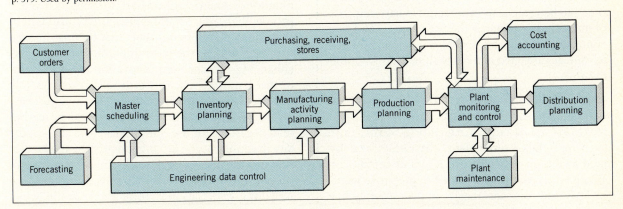

SMALL COMPANIES
ADOPT "JUST-IN-TIME" TECHNIQUES

Just-in-time manufacturing techniques are proving useful to companies that seek to simplify production and keep costly inventories low. JIT management involves redesigning the production process so that every component arrives on the assembly line when needed—and no sooner. Large production runs are replaced by smaller ones, and often the line is shortened and streamlined. Small companies in particular can benefit from JIT management, as they tend to have flatter management structures, smaller labor forces, and less complex planning and accounting systems.

One small maker of medical-electronic equipment, Lifeline Systems Inc. of Watertown, Mass., is using JIT principles to deal with a slump in profits. Lifeline's employees assemble and test electronic relay devices individually, and they are able to spot defects before entire production lots are finished. Another company, California-based Fireplace Manufacturers, has used JIT techniques for standardizing products to scale down inventory and reduce assembly set-up time. Don Bowker, vice-president for manufacturing, credits JIT management with resolving the company's serious cash-flow difficulties, which stemmed from continuously carrying too much stock.

Moving, inspecting, or storing products or supplies is expensive—and often unnecessary, claim JIT supporters. According to one Connecticut-based consultant, Kenneth McGuire, JIT is really nothing more than "the fanatical application of common sense" to manufacturing—and it has made a noticeable difference for a growing group of companies both large and small.

Source: As reported in Steven P. Galante, "Small Manufacturers Shifting to 'Just-in-Time' Techniques," *Wall Street Journal* (December 21, 1987), p. 21.

---

management—**just-in-time scheduling (JIT).** JIT systems were popularized by the productivity of Japanese industry. They involve attempts to reduce costs and improve workflows by scheduling materials to arrive at a work station or facility "just in time" to be used. This can cut down carrying costs of inventories, maximize the use of space, and even contribute to improved quality of results. These advantages are cited in the newsline. Here's another example.[18]

At Chrysler Corporation a JIT system operates at the Sterling Heights, Michigan, factory. A supplier makes automobile seats at a facility located 75 miles away from the Chrysler plant. These seats are delivered to the plant within two hours of completion. When received, they are placed in proper sequence by style and color for transfer to the assembly line.

A continuous flow of seats arrives just in time for final installation.

Managers in organizations using JIT scheduling generally find it worthwhile, and a growing number of American firms are turning to this approach. Richard J. Schonberger, noted consultant in operations management, says that the just-in-time approach may be the most important productivity-enhancing management innovation since the turn of the century.[19] All this is true, he says, merely because the system allows production and purchasing to be done in small quantities and no earlier than necessary for use. But, JIT can also add important discipline to the production process and further support the use of teamwork. In the absence of backup inventories, materials scheduling must be well done, materials must be of usable quality when they arrive, and the workers must continually strive to use them well in the ongoing production process.

Still, it would be unfair not to point out that the just-in-time approach does require special support if it is to work right. Factors that are essential if this system is to succeed include[20]

1. *Geographic concentration* Relatively short transit times from vendor plants to customer plants—less than one day—are necessary to get the materials required "just in time." In Japan, for example, Toyota, has most of its suppliers located within 60 miles of its plants.
2. *Dependable quality* The users must be able to receive only *good* parts from suppliers. This places a strong emphasis on having relationships with very dependable, high-quality suppliers.
3. *Manageable supplier network* A minimum number of suppliers working under long-term contracts helps make just-in time systems work. Most Japanese auto companies use fewer than 250 parts suppliers; General Motors uses about 3500 suppliers for its assembly operations alone.
4. *Controlled transportation system* The key to this is short, reliable transit lines between suppliers and users.
5. *Efficient receiving and materials handling* Parts must be delivered as close as possible to points of use.
6. *Strong management commitment* Management must make sufficient resources available to ensure that the system works. This commitment must stand firm during periods of conversion to just-in-time systems when problems may initially be encountered.

Project Management

The term **project** is used to describe an entire set of actions needed to create single products (goods or services) that are not complete until many—perhaps hundreds—of individual tasks are finished in a particular sequence. **Project management** is the responsibility for making sure that the various phases are completed on time, in the order specified, and with a level of quality sufficient to guarantee the success of the final product. Among the techniques used to facilitate project management are Gantt charts and PERT/CPM network models. They are scheduling techniques that facilitate operations control by allowing managers to make sure that all required tasks are completed by the desired dates.

Gantt Charts

Gantt charts were introduced in Chapter 3 as basic aids to managerial decision making. They graphically depict the routing or scheduling of project activities from start to conclusion. This provides a visual measure of the progress of each activity against the time schedule.

Gantt charts are most useful in situations where there aren't many tasks, where task times are relatively long (days or weeks rather than hours), and where the job routings are short and relatively simple. Many mechanical and magnetic-board devices are available to facilitate the use of Gantt charts. They are common fixtures in many offices and help managers exercise postaction or feedback control over projects.

PERT/CPM Network Models

Network models such as **PERT (program evaluation review technique)** and **CPM (critical path method)** assist in identifying and controlling the many separate events required to complete more complex projects. Although they originated separately, usage of PERT and CPM has converged to the point where they now pretty well represent one technique.

The network chart is fundamental to both PERT/CPM. It is developed by breaking a production/operations project into a series of small subactivities, each of which has a recognizable beginning and ending point. These points in time are called "events," and they are often shown on a network diagram as circles or "nodes." One such diagram is depicted in Figure 16.9. It is drawn to show the necessary relationships among the activities which must occur for a sub-assembly to be completed on time. The model makes it possible to plan for effective completion of a project by ensuring that activities get done in proper sequence. Because delay or interruption of any activity can affect what will happen in later project stages, PERT/CPM techniques allow for precontrol or feed-forward control as well as postaction or feedback control.

Look at the figure again. The time required to traverse the path between each activity is computed by adding up all required activity times along the path. Among all paths required for the project, the path having the longest time is designated the *critical path*. It represents the shortest possible time in which the entire project can be completed. For the

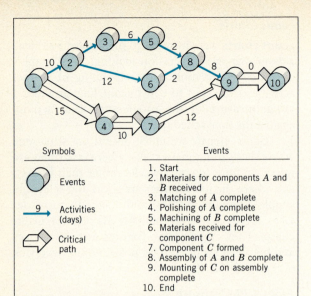

FIGURE 16.9 *A PERT/CPM network model: finding the "critical path" for a subassembly project.*

Source: Lawrence J. Gitman and Carl McDaniel, Jr., *Business World* (New York: John Wiley & Sons, 1983), p. 241. Used by permission.

sample PERT network in Figure 16.9, the highlighted critical path consists of events (1–4–7–9–10), requiring a total time of 37 days (15 + 10 + 12 + 0).

PERT/CPM network models are best suited to situations in which the interrelationships of activities and reasonable time estimates can be established. One important feature of these models is that they permit the manager to exercise control by determining the overall effects of a delay in the completion of a particular task. It also makes it possible to figure the effect on the schedule of a reallocation of resources from one task to another. Good computer programs are now available to help managers with PERT/CPM schedules for even very complex projects. Computers can be used to determine and draw network paths, and to update these networks as work progresses.

CONTROLLING COSTS OF MATERIALS AND INVENTORIES

There are many points of attention in operations control systems. Among them, however, controlling costs of materials and inventories are highly important. **Inventory** is the amount of materials or products kept in storage. Organizations keep inventories to maintain flexibility in their production/operations processes, smooth out periods of excess or undercapacity, meet periods of unusual demand, and/or achieve economies from large-scale purchases. Because inventories can represent major resource investments, they must be well managed. The basic objective of inventory control is to make sure that any inventory is neither too large nor too small for the tasks at hand.

Types of Inventories

It is common for organizations to maintain inventories of raw materials, work in process, and/or finished goods. Recall that in talking about MRP we mentioned that component parts could be kept in inventory. This *raw-materials inventory* is used or "drawn down" when the components are assembled into a finished product. *Work-in process inventories* represent goods in all but the final stage of production. Most manufacturing companies also maintain *finished-goods inventories* of completed but unsold products.

Although all inventories may seem the same to you, there are big differences among them. The use of finished goods can follow a pattern of *independent demand*. Imagine the demand for cartons of milk in a grocery store. Most customers buy only a few cartons, two or three at the most. As a result, the level of inventory falls gradually over time. There are usually no big drops, and inventory decreases at an approximately uniform rate. Work-in-process inventory for component parts can easily follow a different pattern. Most manufacturers produce finished products in batches or lots. Requirements from inventories tend to follow the lot sizes. This is called *dependent demand* because it depends on orders for finished items. Dependent inventory demand follows a "lumpy" pattern and causes inventory levels to fall in bunches over time.

The dependent and independent demand patterns require different approaches to inventory control. Independent demand can be controlled by orders based on economic-order quantity; dependent demand is controlled via lot-by-lot orders using MRP.

Economic Order Quantity

Two major costs are associated with inventory: ordering costs and carrying or holding costs. **Ordering costs** are the costs of arranging the procurement of items for inventory from outside suppliers as well as the costs of any internal procurement (e.g., manufacture) of such items. They do *not* include the cost of the items themselves; they only include such things as the cost of labor and materials required to place the orders and arrange for their subsequent shipment and receipt. **Carrying or holding costs,** by contrast, include the costs of storing and insuring the items in inventory against loss plus the opportunity cost of the funds tied up in inventory.

These two inventory costs, carrying and ordering, are constantly balancing each other. If the number of orders per year is high, ordering costs are high and both average inventory and carrying costs tend to be low. Given few orders, average inventory will be high and costs follow the reverse pattern. The total of these two costs is minimized when the two are *equal;* that is, the cost of inventory is minimized when carrying cost equals ordering cost. This principle underlies the control of inventories subject to dependent demand and allows for use of economic order quantities.

The **economic order quantity** (EOQ) is a method of inventory control that involves ordering a fixed number of items every time an inventory level falls to a predetermined point. When this point is reached, a decision is automatically made, more and more frequently now by computer, to place a standard order. The best example is the supermarket, where hundreds of daily orders are routinely made on this basis. These standard order sizes are calculated according to a mathematical formula that results in minimum total inventory cost.

The formula for determing the *economic order quantity (EOQ)* in any situation is expressed as follows.

In words

Economic order quantity = the square root of (two times actual demand for inventory use times ordering cost) divided by carrying cost

In mathematical symbols

$$EOQ = \sqrt{\frac{2DO}{C}}$$

where,

D = actual demand for inventory use
O = ordering cost of inventory
C = carrying cost of inventory

Suppose independent demand for inventory is 100 units per year, the cost for each order is $80, and carrying cost is $10 per unit per year. The EOQ in this case comes out to be 40—that is, $\sqrt{2(\$80 \times 100)/10}$. The manager should order 40 units each time to minimize inventory cost. Of course, this order must be placed with sufficient lead time (i.e., time between placing and receiving the order) that enough inventory remains on hand to meet demand in the interim. Figure 16.10 shows the cycle of orders and reorders characteristic of an EOQ-controlled inventory. The objective is always to have new inventory arrive just as old inventory runs out. This minimizes the cost of an independent demand inventory.

Lot-by-Lot Orders

In situations of dependent inventory demand, such as when dealing with in-process inventories of component parts, planned orders are based on the MRP schedule. In that case, planned orders were the same as net requirements. They were just offset by the lead time. This approach to inventory control is called **lot-by-lot-ordering** because the planned orders are based on the net requirements in each time period, as they appear "lot by lot" in the MRP schedule.

Just-in-Time Delivery

Just-in-time scheduling has important inventory control implications, since it minimizes the amount of on-hand materials and requires careful planning for just-in-time deliveries of component parts and supplies. This approach to inventory control involves minimizing carrying costs and maintaining almost no inventories by ordering or producing only as needed. It usually occurs in extremely small lots, possibly even on a unit-by-unit basis. The trade-off, however, is high ordering costs.

Kanban is a Japanese word for the piece of paper that accompanies, for example, a bin of parts in a camera factory. When a worker first takes parts

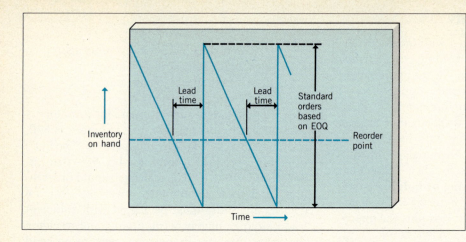

FIGURE 16.10 *Inventory control by Economic Order Quantity (EOQ).*

from a new bin, the *kanban* is routed back to the supplier and serves as an order for new parts. Contrast this direct approach to inventory control with the EOQ and lot-by-lot ordering techniques just discussed. It is easy to see the allure in the Japanese system.

MANAGING FOR TOTAL QUALITY CONTROL

Every organization should be concerned with the quality of its outputs. **Quality control** is the process of *checking* products or services to ensure that they meet certain standards. The importance of quality control is increasingly evident in the slogans of U.S. companies. Ads for Ford Motor Company say, "If it's not right, we won't ship it."; those of the General Electric Company intone, "Quality is our No. 1 focus."

The purpose of quality control is to ensure that the finished good or service produced by an organization is of high standards. The process of quality control, however, is applied to all aspects of production and operations from the selection of raw materials and supplies right down to the last task performed on the finished good or service. Properly done, quality control improves productivity by reducing waste on the input side and reducing rejects on the output side.

More and more frequently these days, the emphasis is on something called **total quality control.** This term has generally been defined as meeting customer requirements by doing things right the first time.[21] As indicated in our discussion of stra-

tegic issues in operations management earlier in the chapter, furthermore, the "customer" in this definition may be the ultimate consumers of finished products or co-workers who depend on one another's efforts to make these products possible. "Total quality control" in this sense permeates the system and applies to everyone's efforts at every stage in production or service operations. In terms used by quality consultant Philip B. Crosby, the "four absolutes" of management for total quality control are:[22]

1. *Quality means conformance to standards.* Workers must understand exactly what the requirements are, and the performance standards they are expected to meet.
2. *Quality comes from defect prevention, not defect correction.* The key to quality is to present defects in the first place. This depends on proper leadership, training and discipline.
3. *Quality as a performance standard must mean zero defects.* The only acceptable quality standard is perfect, defect free work.
4. *Quality saves money.* Doing things right the first time saves the cost of correcting poor work; manufacturers spend up to 25 percent of sales correcting mistakes, while service companies spend 40 percent.

ILLUSTRATIVE CASE: TENNANT COMPANY MAKES IT RIGHT THE FIRST TIME

There was a day that Tennant Company was threatened with a survive or fail situation.[23] Word arrived at company headquarters that the motorized floor sweepers it was shipping to Japan had potentially disastrous defects. They were leaking oil, something that the Japanese customers wouldn't tolerate. And to make things worse, Toyota announced that it was coming out with a competing product.

Well that was almost ten years ago. Today Tennant Company has sales of $160+ million compared with $98 million at the time. It owns 60 percent of the North American market for floor maintenance equipment, has 40 percent of the world market, and has forestalled Toyota's expansion in the United States. What began as a potential disaster, was turned into an opportunity to undertake a quality improvement program that is a textbook case today.

Tennant's president, Roger Hale, started the process by turning to consultant Philip Crosby. He pointed out that the product had to be made right the first time, and recommended that the firm eliminate the rework area where 18 of its best mechanics were assigned to fix any defective sweepers that rolled off the assembly line. This meant that assembly workers had to make fewer errors, and had to catch any they did make. Managers and workers met in small groups to brainstorm ideas of how to improve quality. They ended up changing the shape of the assembly line, rerouting deliveries of parts, and revising some production procedures. They were taught statistical quality control techniques to help monitor defects and establish goals for reducing their frequency.

One group discovered that the oil leaks were caused by failures to use the latest hydraulic technology, poor training of some assembly workers, and use of fittings from different suppliers that failed to meet common specifications. All this has been corrected. President Hale says proudly, "The leadership on the quality program has come from the factory floor." Every 18 months now, just to keep quality in sharp focus, the company sponsors a Zero Defect Day complete with a magic show and live entertainment. At the end of the day everyone agrees once again to make a personal commitment to do his or her work right the first time.

Statistical Quality Control

One foundation of any quality improvement program is statistical quality control. To illustrate how the process might work, consider the case of an engine crankshaft for an automobile. These crankshafts are first molded, then machined to the correct dimensions. Because of variation in the parts, wear on the equipment, and/or differences among the skills of machine operators, not all crankshafts will have exactly the same dimensions after machining. That's not totally bad in itself because the crankshaft will still perform properly so long as its dimensions are within certain limits. For instance, the diameter at a certain point on a crankshaft should be 1.28 inches; the part will still function if the diameter is between 1.26 inches (the lower control limit) and 1.30 inches (the upper control limit).

The quality of these crankshafts might be checked by measuring each one as it is completed. If the diameter of a crankshaft is within the upper and lower control limits, it passes; otherwise it fails and must be reworked. An occasional crankshaft falling outside the limits would not be cause for managerial concern, it would simply be rejected. However, several rejects might mean the machining process is out of control and requires correction. It is often helpful to keep track of trends graphically, such as with the **control chart** in Figure 16.11. The basic purpose of a control chart is to display work results on a graph that clearly delineates upper control limits (UCL) and lower control limits (LCL). A process is in or out of control depending on how well results remain within these established limits. The trend shown by the data in the figure indicate that the production process should be halted to reset or repair the machine in question, or retrain the operator.

This same concept can be extended using statistical concepts to set upper and lower control limits and monitor product performance in respect to them. In such cases, instead of checking every part, batches of a product or service are checked by taking a random sample from each. This is called inspection by statistical sampling. Because of the inherent difficulty of carefully inspecting every raw-material input or product/service output, most quality control is accomplished via statistical sampling procedures. The information made available for managerial control is of equal significance, but, is more efficient in larger and more complex operations.

Quality Assurance

Total quality control depends on **quality assurance,** the process of *preventing* the production of defective products or services. This is among the

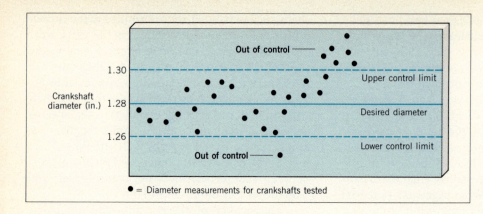

FIGURE 16.11 *Control chart: the case of engine crankshaft production.*

quality-control concepts that have been given new impetus by the successes of Japanese industry. Interestingly, the ideas on which these accomplishments are based were first introduced to the Japanese over 25 years ago by American professors.

One of them, W. Edwards Deming was invited to Japan in 1950 to share the quality-control techniques developed in the United States just prior to World War II.[24] What resulted was a lifelong relationship now epitomized in the "Deming" prize for quality control. This annual award is so important in Japan it is broadcast on national television. The principles Deming taught the Japanese are basically straightforward: tally defects, analyze and trace them to the source, make corrections, and keep a record of what happens afterward. These are good basic precepts for any managerial control system. Consider this example:[25]

At Genesco the managers of a middle-sized hosiery plant in Tennessee decided they had to change the ways they had grown used to in the previous 65 years. A preliminary study showed one source of defects was the "looping" department, which performed the task of closing toes. Inspectors soon found that a few of the workers produced most of the defects. An older worker responsible for 20 percent of the faulty loops was persuaded to take early retirement. A dozen others did fine once they got new glasses. Another said she paid little attention to what she was doing because no one had shown concern for quality; when management did, she easily improved her work. So it went. In seven months, the plant cut its rejects from 11,500 to 2,000 stockings out of a total weekly output of 120,000 pairs. To put it another way, productivity climbed 4 per cent virtually costfree. Until recently

few American companies bothered with that kind of analysis.

The essence of Deming's approach to quality control is illustrated in the preceding case. His basic proposition is that the cause of a quality problem may be some component of the production/operations process, like an employee or a machine, or it may be intrinsic to the production/operations system itself. If it is caused by an employee, that person should be retrained or replaced. Likewise, a faulty machine should be adjusted or replaced. If the cause lies within a system, blaming an employee only produces frustration. Instead, the system must be analyzed and constructively changed.

Out of this type of thinking emerged the popular *quality circle* concept. As defined in Chapter 13 in our discussion of worker involvement groups, a **quality control circle** is a group of employees (usually no more than 10) who meet regularly to discuss ways of improving the quality of their products or services. The objective of using quality circles is to build a sense of employee responsibility for quality assurance and to unlock the potential of every employee to contribute useful ideas and information. In addition to direct monetary savings, the advantages of quality control circles include increased morale and commitment among employees. Consider these remarks from one company[26]

"This is the best thing the company has done in 15 years," an hourly worker told his supervisor.

"The program proves that superiors have no monopoly on brains," an operational employee said.

"It gives me more pride in my work," an assembler remarked.

As with any managerial technique, the quality control circle must be carefully analyzed for its applicability in any given work situation. Quality control circles work best with a knowledgeable work force, groups that possess a true "team spirit," managers who are willing to trust workers with necessary information, and situations where quality goals are embraced by the entire organization.

Today, American manufacturers are increasingly turning to another Japanese import, the *Taguchi method* for an integrated approach to statistical quality assurance.[27] Developed in Japan by Genichi Taguchi, this method combines engineering and statistical methods to speed up the process of locating the source of defects in highly complex manufacturing operations. In addition, Taguchi also teaches that just because products fall within the range of preset statistical tolerances, that doesn't mean things are acceptable. He seeks commitments to "robust quality" that is achieved through continuous operations improvements and product designs that are able to withstand fluctuations in the production process.

Quality and the Operations Management System

The messages of Crosby, Deming, Taguchi and other quality experts have been heard by managers around the world, and are being pursued with increasing vigor in their organizations. When these efforts are applied together with the operations management foundations described throughout this chapter, the lofty goals of "total quality" have the potential to be achieved. As a symbol of operations management success and responsibility, quality occurs when the total system functions as it should—from the point of accepting resource inputs, through the various stages of the transformation processes, all the way to delivery of the finished good or service to the customer. Increasingly, this quest for quality is based on mutual commitments between the suppliers of essential resources and the organizations who consume them in operations. Here's one final example.[28]

At Wrayco the small 50-person Ohio firm ships parts on a just-in-time schedule to Caterpillar. It puts bar codes on the parts so they can be scanned by computers in receiving which, in turn, notify computers in accounting to order payments to Wrayco by wire transfer. On its own initiative, Wrayco cut costs by redesigning a fuel tank, and now makes it for Caterpillar for $950 instead of almost $5,000. The large customer trusts Wrayco to assure quality and doesn't even inspect parts received. In this way, Wrayco has earned the label of being one of Caterpillar's "certified suppliers."

Summary

This chapter introduces the fundamentals of operations management and control. This subject can fill a whole book by itself, and you may well have access to specialized O/M courses elsewhere in your program of study. For our purposes in the introductory study of management, this chapter gives you an essential overview.

The chapter began by describing the functions that any organization must perform to produce a good or service: (1) obtaining and storing raw materials, (2) scheduling people and equipment, and (3) creating finished goods or services from the combined efforts of people and equipment. Operations management is concerned with ensuring the productivity of these resource-transformation processes in organizations.

A number of strategic issues in operations highlight current trends and developments in this area. They include the role of operations in establishing competitive advantage, the emergence of a strong customer orientation, product design considerations, technology utilization, and the role of the indispensable human factor. Beyond these issues, lie a number of operations management foundations supported by related quantitative techniques and computer applications. Addressed in this respect were demand forecasting, aggregate scheduling, master scheduling, material requirements planning, manufacturing resources planning, just-in-time scheduling, capacity planning, project management and inventory control. A final emphasis on the integration of all activities around total quality control suggested how the effective coordination of all operations management activities is essential to any organization.

Thinking Through the Issues

1. Explain why operations management control is extremely important to any organization—be it manufacturing or service oriented. List the three major operations activities involved in any organization. Give examples of each in (a) a manufacturing setting and (b) a service setting.

2. What does "customer orientation" mean in the context of operations management? Why is it an important focus for organizations seeking "competitive advantages" in today's complex environments?

3. Are we at the stage where technology dominates and the human factor is no longer of much significance from a production/operations perspective? Explain your answer.

4. What is the significance of (a) "capacity planning" and (b) "process planning" to the design of operations? What are some of the major alternatives in respect to "facilities layout planning?"

5. Explain the purpose and focus of aggregate scheduling. How does it differ from master scheduling?

6. What is MRP, or material requirements planning? Give an example of its application in a manufacturing firm. What is MRPII?

7. Why is "just-in-time" scheduling an important operations management approach in respect to the allocation and scheduling of resources? What are its potential advantages . . . and disadvantages?

8. Explain the difference between a Gantt chart and a PERT/CPM network model. In what ways are they useful in project management?

9. What is the "economic order quantity" method of inventory control? How does it differ from a "just-in-time" inventory delivery system?

10. How does the concept of "total quality control" attempt to integrate the entire organization around high-quality goals? What is required for an organization to be achieving "total quality" goals? Please explain.

The Manager's Vocabulary

Aggregate scheduling
Automation
Automatic guided vehicles
Batch operations
Capacity planning
Carrying costs
Computer aided design (CAD)
Computer aided manufacturing (CAM)
Computer aided process planning (CPP)

Computer-integrated manufacturing (CIM)
Computer numerical control (CNC)
Continuous processing
Control chart
Critical Path Method (CPM)
Demand forecasting
Economic order quantity (EOQ)
Facilities location planning

Flexible manufacturing systems
Gantt chart
Group technology (GT)
Inventory
Job shop
Just-in-time scheduling
Lot-by-lot ordering
Master scheduling
Material requirements planning (MRP)
Manufacturing resources planning (MRPII)

Mass production
Ordering costs
Operations management (O/M)
Program Evaluation and Review Technique (PERT)
Project
Project management
Quality assurance
Quality control
Quality control circle
Robotics
Total quality control
Transformation process
Work cells

TRADING A DESK
JOB FOR THE FACTORY FLOOR

Thomas W. Gorman has an MBA degree from the University of Michigan.[29] At the time of this report he is one month into a new job with Dana Corporation. His job title is area production manager for the automotive gaskets division. Prior to taking the new assignment, Gorman spent three years as a divisional marketing manager. Now, his superiors are anticipating that his willingness to work in production will make him a fine candidate for senior management someday.

Gorman plans to remain at Dana for his entire career. He likes the corporate culture and the firm's record in promoting from within. With the aspiration of moving to the top, Gorman wants to learn as much as he can about the entire operation so that he can prosper in the firm. "I'm not vain enough to believe I can manage the whole company until I get down to the bottom level," he says.

But even in the job, he's not afraid to step in and try to do things better. He's trying to raise product quality by giving workers more responsibility on the assembly line. He also tries to work with both shifts each day, even though it means getting up at 4:30 AM and not returning home until after 7:00 PM. This is all part of living out his goal of working in a mainstream manufacturing company. "I wanted to be part of mature American industry and make a difference," is how Gorman puts it. His superiors have confidence that he will make it.

Questions

1. What do you think about Gorman's desire to stay with one company until retirement? Is it realistic? Is it too limiting in terms of career opportunities? Would you pursue a similar choice?
2. Is Gorman going about things in the right way in his attempt to find a path to the "top" at Dana? Explain your answer.
3. Where does the possibility of work in manufacturing fit into your career plans? What advantages might it offer in making you more competitive for higher-level promotions? Is it for you, or not? Why?

Case Application
MULTI-CHEM'S MRPII SYSTEM

The U.S. chemical industry is highly competitive and tightly controlled. Multi-Chem, a multinational chemical and pharmaceutical manufacturing firm with three U.S. divisions, tries to maintain a competitive edge by maximizing its efficiency in the manufacturing process. One strategy is to have all of its divisions adopt an integrated manufacturing resource planning system (MRPII).[30]

The steps involved in turning raw materials into finished chemical products are relatively simple. However, almost anyone in marketing, production, finance, product development, or management can affect the production schedule. A single change in schedule for one product at one plant may cause a "ripple effect" on products, intermediates, and raw materials at another plant. Stresses placed on processes by conflicting business and production demands can result in costly inefficiencies—excess inventory on the one hand and failure to meet customer demands on the other. Production schedules and plans must be continually adjusted to meet the changing business environment.

Like other manufacturers, Multi-Chem tries to minimize these inefficiencies by using a production plan and master schedule to tie all of the manufacturing activities together. The production plan establishes monthly rates of production and is developed to meet the sales plan. The master schedule converts the monthly production rates into a weekly schedule and plans the necessary material and capacity based on anticipated customer demand. A final production schedule, reflecting the availability of material and plant capacity, responds to actual customer orders. The daily production schedule tracks production and shipments on a daily basis to ensure that both production and business plans are met.

Multi-Chem's MRPII system helps to meet these planning needs by providing a scheduling system to show what is required by a particular process and when. The system plans all levels of a product from raw materials through finished goods and tracks information to ensure that tasks can be completed quickly and profitably. The MRPII system shows today's balance for every product, intermediate, and raw material it tracks. It can project what the balance will be on any future date, given expected sales, shipments, production, and purchases. It can recommend changes in shipping or manufacturing schedules based on its calculation of shortfalls and excesses.

The system is used at many locations by employees whose positions range from inventory clerks to production planners to divisional managers. Some of these users need exact, detailed answers at once. Others expect to see an overall picture once a quarter. The following examples are illustrative:

■ Multi-Chem's agricultural chemical products are manufactured at plants in Illinois and Alabama, and about 15 by outside processors under contract. A vendor has shipped defective bottles to an outside processor that produces Ag Chem No. 1. The inventory control clerk in the Contract Manufacturing Department knows that Ag Chem No. 1 is also produced at the Alabama plant. He wants to find out if some bottles can be transferred to the outside processor (in Memphis) without too much impact on the Alabama plant's schedule.

■ The director of production is preparing for the quarterly planning meetings with his counterpart in world headquarters. He needs to know the net inventories of Ag Chem No. 5, together with export and marketing plans for the next five quarters.

■ Marketing has changed plans for Ag Chem No. 7 (made at the Alabama plant), causing an increased demand for Ag Chem No. 11 (made at the Illinois plant). This change, in turn, may affect the schedule for HCN (an intermediate product made at the Illinois plant). The Illinois plant needs to know how to adjust HCN production. It may also need to rework the schedules for raw materials and labor.

The MRPII system runs on the central mainframe computer at Multi-Chem's U.S. corporate headquarters. A network of terminals with telecommunications links to the central computer ties in divisional headquarters, plant sites, and departments. Inquiries such as that of the inventory clerk for the number of bottles on hand can be serviced directly on-line through these terminals. However, the requests for information in the other two examples require much more complex totaling, analysis, and manipulation of data. Computer jobs to provide the answers must be batched together and run later or overnight.

Since the MRPII system was installed, Multi-Chem has reported inventory reductions of up to $2 million, with annual savings of $240,000 in inventory carrying costs and a 98 percent inventory accuracy.

Questions

1. What people representing which functions does this MRPII system serve and in what ways? What are the information systems upon which it is based?
2. Explain the basic elements of MRPII as they are illustrated in this case. Why is this an MRPII instead of an MRP system? Please explain.
3. How important is this MRPII system to Multi-Chem? What other operations management systems, if any, might top management consider using? Why?

Class Exercise: In Or Out of Control?

1. Control charts were introduced in the discussion of statistical quality control. Good managers use control charts to spot undesirable trends. Problem solving can then be done to correct any operations representing a source of potential trouble.

2. Study the four control charts presented in Figure 16.12.

3. Decide which, if any, of these charts suggest the existence of a problem. Which charts suggest a production or operations process that may be going "out of control"? Why?

4. Share your decisions with a nearby classmate. Be sure to examine the rationale behind each other's conclusions carefully. Await further class discussion.

FIGURE 16.12 *Four control charts: which ones indicate potential quality problems?*

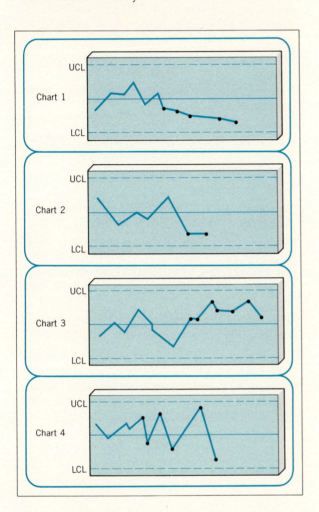

References

[1]Information from Ralph E. Winter, "Delayed Future: Upgrading of Factories Replaces the Concept of Total Automation," *The Wall Street Journal* (September 30, 1987), pp. 1, 8.

[2]This list is developed from Mark A. Vonderembse and Gregory P. White, *Operations Management: Concepts, Methods, and Strategies* (St. Paul, MN: West, 1988), pp. 339–344.

[3]Wickham Skinner, "Manufacturing—Missing Link in Corporate Strategy," *Harvard Business Review*, Vol 47 (May-June 1969), pp. 136–145; and, "Business Refocuses on the Factory Floor," *Business Week* (February 2, 1981), p. 91.

[4]See Alex Taylor III, "Japan's Carmakers Take on the World," *Fortune* (June 20, 1988), pp. 67–76.

[5]From Richard J. Schonberger and Edward M. Knod, Jr., *Operations Management: Serving the Customer,* Third Edition (Plano, TX: Business Publications, Inc., 1988), p. 4.

[6]Ibid., p. 5.

[7]Information from Bob Waterman, "Start Your Own Quality Revolution," *Success* (April 1988), p. 16.

[8]Information from "Taking Ideas from Plan to Plant," *Business Week* (April 11, 1988), p. 106.

[9]This composite is developed from Winter, op cit.; and, "Enterprise Networking," a special advertising supplement to *Business Week* (March 21, 1988), pp. 161–162.

[10]This listing is developed from Vonderembse and White, op. cit., pp. 41–58.

[11]The human resource issues in technology utilization are addressed by Richard E. Walton and Gerald I. Susman, "People Policies for the New Machines," *Harvard Business Review,* Vol. 65 (March–April 1987), pp. 98–106.

[12]See Schonberger and Knod, op. cit., pp. 718–721.

[13]Information from Winter, op cit.

[14]Flexible manufacturing systems are discussed in Richard J. Schonberger, "Frugal Manufacturing," *Harvard Business Review,* Vol. 65 (September–October 1987), pp. 95–100.

[15]Jack R. Meredith, *The Management of Operations,* Third Edition (New York: Wiley, 1987).

[16]William Berry, Thomas Vollmann, and D. Clay Whybark. *Master Production Scheduling: Principles and Practice* (Washington, D.C.: American Production and Inventory Control Society, 1979).

[17]For an explanation of MRPII see Ibid., pp. 378–383.

[18]Example reported in Dexter Hutchins, "Having a Hard Time with Just-in-Time, *Fortune* (June 9, 1986), pp. 64–65.

[19]Richard J. Schonberger, "A Revolutionary Way to Streamline the Factory," *Wall Street Journal* (November 15, 1982), p. 24.

[20]John D. Baxter, "Kanban Works Wonders, But Will It Work in U.S. Industry?" *Iron Age,* Vol. 225, No. 16 (June 7, 1982), pp. 44–48.

[21]Philip Crosby's approach to total quality control is described in his books *Quality is Free* (New York: McGraw-Hill, 1979); and, *The Eternally Successful Organization* (New York: McGraw-Hill, 1988).

[22]See Philip B. Crosby, "Lead Your Employees to Quality," *Success* (June 1988), pp. 60, 61.

[23]Information from "What America Makes Best," *Fortune* (March 28, 1988), p. 41–48.

[24]See Jeremy Main, "The Curmudgeon Who Talks Tough on Quality," *Fortune* (June 25, 1984), p. 118; and, Jeremy Main, "Under the Spell of the Quality Gurus," *Fortune* (August 18, 1986), pp. 30–34.

[25]Main, op. cit., 1986.

[26]Arnold Kanarick, "The Far Side of Quality Circles," *Management Review,* Vol. 70 (October 1981), pp. 16–17.

[27]For more on the Taguchi method see "How to Make It Right the First Time," *Business Week* (June 8, 1987), pp. 142, 143; and, John Holusha, "Improving Quality, the Japanese Way," *The New York Times* (July 20, 1988), p. F3.

[28]Information from Myron Magnet, "The Resurrection of the Rust Belt," *Fortune* (August 15, 1988), pp. 40–46

[29]Information from "Fast Track Kids," *Business Week* (November 10, 1986), pp. 90–104.

[30]Kenneth C. Laudon and Jane Price Laudon, *Management Information Systems* (New York: Macmillan, 1988), pp. 24–25. Used by permission.

PART 5

MBO at American Digitron

Greg Davis was one of the most vocal opponents of American Digitron's management-by-objectives (MBO) program, but his warnings had not been heeded. Now he found himself having to fire Gus Kaplan, a top salesman, as a result of MBO's implementation.

American Digitron is one of the top seven firms in the rapidly expanding data-processing industry. It manufactures, installs, and services information-processing systems worldwide, and carries one of the broadest hardware and software product lines in the industry. Digitron offers a complete line of peripherals, communications networks, data centers, training centers, field maintenance, engineering, and other services.

Greg Davis was the ranking administrative manager in American Digitron's Southwest U.S. district. The district was broken down into four departments: sales, systems engineering, field engineering, and administration. The MBO plan was designed to treat each department except administration as an individual profit center. Using a complex formula called the flexible expense budget, the MBO system attempted to balance revenues against expenses in each of these three business areas. Administrative managers, such as Davis, were not subject to this formula, but were evaluated annually according to a different but equally detailed set of objectives. Performance on these objectives was a major criterion in annual performance evaluations of the administrative managers.

Davis was especially upset about his performance on one such measure known as assigned inventory. A few months after American Digitron implemented its MBO program, Gus Kaplan, one of the South-

> The MBO plan was designed to treat each department except administration as an individual profit center.

west district's leading salesmen, had come to Davis to persuade him to keep a very expensive computer system in inventory at that district. Kaplan had assured Davis that a major long-time customer had already signed an order for it. While having such an expensive system on hand would look bad on Davis's assigned inventory performance, he agreed to hold on to the system as a favor to Kaplan.

Unfortunately for both Davis and Kaplan, the proposed sale fell through, and Davis's inventory objectives were not met because of the additional inventory on hand. Upon questioning Kaplan about the order, Davis was told that the customer had never really signed one; Kaplan had

only wanted to be sure that the system would be readily available as an additional selling point to the customer. The net result was a lower MBO rating for Davis and the subsequent firing of Kaplan.

Such an occurrence, while having more severe consequences than most, has not been unusual since American Digitron embraced MBO. In the early years of the company's history, when it sold accounting machines, a salesperson wrote the complete order, programmed the machine's tabs and accumulators, and occasionally made minor mechanical adjustments. Today, the computer salesperson depends on an administrative assistant to prepare all the paperwork, a field engineer to install, test, and adjust the equipment, and a systems engineer to get the computer system up and running. At times it was very difficult to find who was to blame when the customer later com-

> Performance on these objectives was a major criterion in annual performance evaluations . . .

plained about system malfunctions or other service needs.

Davis predicted all along that the MBO plan and its accompanying rewards system would reduce cooperation among departments in his dis-

Source: This case was prepared by Daniel Robey in collaboration with Alberto de Solo and Todd Anthony. It is found in Daniel Robey, *Designing Organizations: A Macro Perspective* (Homewood, Ill.: Richard D. Irwin, 1982), pp. 431–433. Used by permission.

trict, and the Kaplan incident had convinced him. As people sought to meet their own individual objectives, they would become less sensitive to the needs of others, even when they all had to work together to satisfy the customer. Davis was perfectly willing to dismiss disruptive individuals like Kaplan who resorted to outright dishonesty to get their way. But it

---

At times it was very difficult to find who was to blame when the customer later complained . . .

---

seemed that MBO had even more problems than just motivating selfishness.

Timeliness of reports was one of the most heavily weighted criteria for judging Davis's performance as a district administrative manager. The Revenue Action Plan was one report that absolutely had to be submitted on time because it was used by upper management to forecast American Digitron's revenues for each upcoming month. However, it was the *sales*

Davis felt he and many others had been unjustly victimized by the MBO program.

---

manager's duty to keep track of orders and billing, both of which were required inputs to the report Davis submitted. Timeliness of reports is not among sales managers' performance objectives in the MBO system, though. As a result they often come to Davis's desk late, and the Revenue Action Plan is submitted late. Lately, Davis's own MBO ratings had suffered a great deal because of late filing of these reports.

Davis felt that he and many others had been unjustly victimized by the MBO program. On top of problems like those described, the system multiplied his already substantial load of paperwork. The time had come to voice his complaints. He was certain that other department managers must be experiencing similar difficulties, and he intended to make his views clear at an upcoming meeting of managers at the district level and above. He had already begun to itemize a list of specific complaints.

QUESTIONS

1. Why is the MBO system causing difficulty?
2. What specific points do you think Davis will be prepared to voice at the meeting?
3. What modifications should be made to increase the effectiveness of the MBO system? Why?
4. What additional recommendations do you have to improve the management and organization of Digitron's Southwest District? Please explain. ■

Segal
Electric's Quality Crusade

George Mansfield poured himself another cup of coffee and walked down the hall to Pete Jameson's office. He'd spent half the night agonizing over how to broach a problem with Pete, the general manager who had hired him a month ago to run Segal Electric's quality operation as director of quality assurance.

George had always thought that anything worth making was worth making right. That's one reason he advocated generous warranty programs. He knew that if operations were running as they should, the company wouldn't have to worry about warranty costs because there wouldn't be any. His high standards had served him well at his last job, where he was perceived as a real

Source: Frank S. Leonard, "The Case of the Quality Crusader," *Harvard Business Review,* Vol. 66 (May–June 1988), pp. 12–14. Used by permission.

George: "[I] had always
thought that anything worth
making was worth
making right."

comer and had been promoted several times.

Segal was once the top manufacturer of high-quality electrical products, but for a combination of reasons its reputation had fallen steadily over the last few years. George welcomed the chance to help turn the company around. The hefty salary and direct reporting relationship to Pete Jameson had persuaded him that Segal was serious about regaining its position in the market. George was given much of the responsibility to help reach that goal.

"Come on in, George, and have a seat," Pete began. "So you've run into some trouble in the plant already. I told you this job would be tough. What's the problem?"

"There was a mix-up in the plant while I was gone last week. I think it might happen again, so I want to discuss it with you now."

"Of course, go ahead."

"Last week when I was at that quality seminar in Milwaukee, Gene Davis was overseeing the quality control team for me. Early in the week, they kept running into trouble with the 5051 fans. The end play of the fan blades on the shaft wasn't right. They had to reject five pallets of fans.

"Apparently there was a big rush order, so some people were pulled off other lines to assemble the fans. But nobody told them all the specs. So they were loading up as many thrust washers as they could fit on the shaft, and instead of getting ten-thousandths clearance, they got zero.

There was no end play at all.

"Following quality procedures, Gene red-tagged them and put them aside for rework, but then Sharon Morse got involved. She decided it would take too long to fix the fans, so she plugged the darn things in and ran them full speed to burn the washers down to the right clearance. Now, you and I both know that doing that pushes the spec strength of those washers."

"Well, in theory, yes. But I don't know how much difference it really makes. Still, I get your point, George. That's not the way it ought to be."

"No sir, as far as I'm concerned it isn't. I guess Gene tried to talk to Sharon about it. He knows how I feel about quality, and he was trying to do what I would expect. But Sharon took charge of the situation. As production superintendent she outranks Gene, and he finally deferred to her. Well, don't you know, those fans were shipped last Thursday."

"Have you discussed this with Sharon?" Pete asked.

"No, I haven't. Gene just told me about it yesterday. I'm perfectly willing to talk to her, but I want to make sure I'm right first. Doesn't my department have the last word about what gets out the door?"

"George, we're like every other company. We've got production quo-

Sharon: It's on-time delivery
that gets us business."

tas, we've got budgets, we've got marketing plans. Sure, we want to make a good product, but we don't want to lose our shirts doing it. Sounds to me like you and Sharon will have to work it out. I think you can handle it."

George was disappointed by Pete's response. After all, in the job interview Pete assured him that Segal was serious about the renewed emphasis on quality. But it didn't seem as if the idea had filtered down to the factory floor—where priorities are really set.

The people in the plant were very loyal to Sharon. According to Gene Davis, they had often helped her patch up rejected products and rush them onto the shipping dock to help make quotas. George was anxious to confront her. Later that day when he saw her on the plant floor, he made a point of starting a conversation. He didn't want to come on too strong, but he wanted to let her know he wasn't happy about what had happened last week and that he didn't want it to happen again.

"Say, how did things go when I was gone?" he asked.

"It was touch and go for a while there, but we managed to fill a couple of big, important orders."

"I understand you were short of assemblers."

"We're always short of assemblers. But you're right. Last week absenteeism was especially high, and we had to do a lot of juggling to meet our quotas. You know about the special promotions?"

"I've heard of something, but no details."

"Sales is running a special seasonal promotion for both trade and retail. It's in response to a new product that some competitor is coming out with. We're trying to preempt that market share."

"Gene tells me we ran into some trouble with the 5051s."

"Yes, sales was leaning all over us for them. All I kept hearing all week was 'Delivery! Delivery!' "

"But some of the products were rejected?"

"Well, the thrust washers were tight. But you know, if you run them tight for a little while, it frees them up just the right amount. You should have seen this place with all those fans running. It was quite a sight."

"But doesn't running them tight like that burn the washers and stress the metal?"

"Well, I'm not so sure about that."

George was annoyed by Sharon's skepticism, especially since he felt sure of himself on technical matters.

Sharon: "We're lucky if we have *one* person who knows how to do the job.

After all, he had been trained as an engineer. Sharon had started as a production worker and come up through the ranks. Despite the fact that George had been at Segal for only a month, he was sure Sharon didn't understand the product as well as he did.

"I don't want to make a big deal of something that's already happened, but it's not such a good idea to burn the washers into spec. We should be putting the product together correctly in the first place."

"Oh boy, you won't get any disagreement from me there. I had some people who started work on Monday and were on their own assembling parts that afternoon. I barely had time to show them where to hang their coats."

"Don't new employees get any training? At my old company everyone was cross-trained so they could do at least a couple of different tasks. That way, people could be moved from one job to another."

"Do you know how big our training department is? Do you know what our turnover is? We're lucky if we have *one* person who knows how to do the job. But you know, sometimes the problem is with the parts we get—not so much the ones we get from our shop but the ones we get through purchasing. I don't know whether they're mixing up part numbers or what, but those washers aren't all the same."

"What makes you say that?"

"When you put them on the fan shaft, you can tell. One fan has five washers and twenty-thousandths clearance. Another fan has five washers and five-thousandths clearance. If you ask me, they're getting the cheapest washers they can find."

"Of course, if it's just a slight variation, the assemblers can adjust for it when they're putting the fan together," George conceded.

"Are you kidding? We can't pull out a micrometer every time we throw a few thrust washers onto a shaft. We'd never get our orders out. The bill of material and assembly specs for a 5051 fan call for five thrust washers, so that's what we use. Every once in a while a worker forgets that. Like last week, when we were in such a rush. Some of the people hadn't worked on that line for months, so they were putting on five, six, seven of them—however many they could fit on the shaft. But normally it's five

---

Pete: "Sure we want to make a good product, but we don't want to lose our shirts."

---

washers. Look George, if you want to measure those washers, I'd be real happy. I'm all for anything that will help me meet my objectives."

"I'm not interested in measuring washers, but we should be checking that clearance before the fans get to final test. It would take just one second to make the adjustment during assembly, and you know how long it takes to pull the thing apart and remake it."

"It's not that I don't have a mind of my own, but I follow the process orders that come from engineering. That's my job. I'm not going to arbitrarily change the procedure. Besides, five washers is usually right, so there's really not a problem. Do you know we ship 95 percent of our orders on time? We're pretty proud of that record. Sales tells me that it's our delivery performance that gets us business. I don't want to mess with that."

The conversation with Sharon ended on a friendly note, but George knew he hadn't won her over. He walked back to his office to decide what to do next.

QUESTIONS

1. What went wrong with quality control at Segal Electric and how can the situation best be resolved?

2. What specific criticisms do you have of a) George, and b) Sharon in this case? Explain and justify your criticisms. As a consultant, what would you recommend be done to improve their working relationship?

3. Is Pete an effective general manager? Why or why not? What advice would you give Pete to improve both his performance as a manager and that of Segal Electric Company as a whole? Why? ■

PRODUCTIVITY IN THE CONTEMPORARY ENVIRONMENT

How the Best Get Better

On a world at once vast and small, everything is interdependent—people, organizations, and economies. This is the world in which modern managers do their work. The best managers are unafraid to step back and look at the big picture—to examine creatively and with enthusiasm all the conditions that affect their jobs and their organizations. They find that thinking about how to deal with a highly complex world is perhaps the most stimulating part of what they do.

The chapters in Part 6 explore some of the major challenges of the modern environment—in particular, the fast pace of change and the need for innovation, shifts in labor–management relations, the globalization of business, and the importance of ethics and social responsibility in organizational life. This Perspective surveys each of these challenges.

Taken together, Chapters 17 through 20 stress a crucial fact: the context within which managers must

" . . . MANAGERS CONFRONT CHALLENGES OF FAST-PACED CHANGE, AND GLOBALIZAITON . . . "

function is dynamic and unpredictable. Those organizations able to exploit this context—to ride the waves of change rather than resisting them—are likely to go far; those too invested in habitual ways of operating will find it difficult to chart a course on such transient seas.

LOOKING AND THINKING AHEAD

To respond successfully to the challenge of rapid change, says management authority Tom Peters, organizations must concentrate on attaining "world-class quality and service, enhanced responsiveness through greatly increased flexibility, and continuous, short-cycle innovation and improvement" to create new markets.[1]

Signs abound that Peters's advice is being taken seriously. There is a marked trend toward decentralization as companies divest themselves of soft acquisitions and focus on the areas in which they excel. Some organizations are even trading units—acquiring a strong division in exchange for a weak one. Others are entering into joint ventures to spread the risks and increase the benefits of new-product introductions.[2] These and other creative responses to a fiercely competitive environment are seen by a growing number of observers as both necessary and good. Organizational strategy has to be based on a context in flux; constant product and service innovation and shorter product cycles are prerequisites for success. Alan Hassenfeld, president of Hasbro, Inc., maintains that his company must be able "to stop on a dime" if it anticipates trouble with a new product. His attitude typifies that of many managers who recognize that responsiveness is crucial. And Kirby Warren of the Columbia Business School points out that time has become a rare luxury. "In the past, you could enter markets at your own pace," he notes. "Today, you

NOTES
1. Judith H. Dobrzynski, "Tom Peters: Now There Are No Excellent Companies," *Business Week* (December 21, 1987), pp. 20–22.
2. Susan Lee and Christie Brown, "The Protean Corporation," *Forbes* (August 24, 1987), pp. 76–78.
3. U.S. Industry's Unfinished Struggle," *New York Times* (February 21, 1988), pp. 3-1–3-7.
4. "The 21st Century Executive," *U.S. News & World Report* (March 7, 1988), p. 50.
5. Richard I. Kirkland Jr., "We're All in This Together," *Fortune* (February 2, 1987), pp. 26–29.
6. "The 21st Century Executive," *U.S. News & World Report* (March 7, 1988), p. 50.
7. Tad Tuleja, *Beyond the Bottom Line* (New York: Penguin, 1987), p. 14.

have to learn what customers want, make it, and sell it, or someone else will."[3]

A NEW LABOR–MANAGEMENT COLLABORATION

To keep pace with all this upheaval, labor and management are having to renegotiate not just contracts but an entire way of working together. In this realm, where a host of historical antagonisms must be overcome, achieving positive results is not simply a matter of upgrading machinery or health insurance. A radical restructuring of hierarchies and shifting of responsibility has been neces-

sary. According to labor scholar Shoshana Zuboff, without a constant give-and-take of the information that makes smooth operations possible, those on the front line won't be able to serve customers fast and flexibly.[4]

GLOBAL BUSINESS

"We have entered the age of alliances," claims Olivetti Chairperson Carol De Benedetti, whose firm has entered joint ventures with Volkswagon and AT&T. Indeed, the internationalization of business is one of the most striking aspects of the contemporary environment. Despite debates over protectionism and "economic nationalism," American businesses are aware that consumer desires constantly cross national borders—and that, in the words of Sony Chairperson Akio Morita, "the economic system is more and more like one single interacting organism."

The United States is likely to export services—banking, consulting, engineering, and so on—at a growing rate to help service its foreign debt, according to Data Resources Inc., an economic forecasting firm. Certain

American industries (notably telecommunications, electronics, computers, specialty chemicals, and pharmaceuticals) are sure to press their current lead in world markets— but international competition will only stiffen as technological advances multiply.[5]

The global context is sure to become more complex as growing numbers of businesses manufacture

and market their products in multiple locations and as joint ventures spring up in response to competitive pressures. A recent report by McKinsey & Company concludes that

Source: Data from *Wall Street Journal/NBC News Survey.*

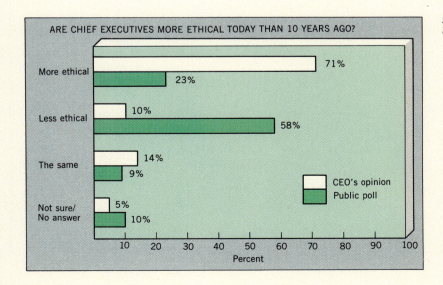

ARE CHIEF EXECUTIVES MORE ETHICAL TODAY THAN 10 YEARS AGO?

More ethical: 71% (CEO's opinion), 23% (Public poll)
Less ethical: 10% (CEO's opinion), 58% (Public poll)
The same: 14% (CEO's opinion), 9% (Public poll)
Not sure/No answer: 5% (CEO's opinion), 10% (Public poll)

in this realm, success is "the product of the CEO's vision: A perception early on that international expansion is not a sideline but integral to the future." Lester Thurow, dean of MIT's Sloan School of Management, neatly sums up the challenge for managers at home: "To be trained as an *American* manager is to be trained for a world that is no longer there."[6]

DOING WELL AND DOING GOOD

As managers confront the challenges of fast-paced change, new labor–management relations, and globalization, they must also deal with an issue that permeates everything an organization undertakes: corporate ethics and social responsibility. When so much is in flux, once-adequate standards of corporate behavior are proving insufficient or irrelevant. Increasingly, managers are charged with the task of determining new ethically and socially appropriate norms of corporate activity.

Ethicist Tad Tuleja argues that the manager's job is not to get the right answer but rather to consistently ask the right questions about what constitutes ethical behavior. Although all people are morally fallible, every manager can develop a "moral attitude" to guide his or her perceptions of right and wrong, says Tuleja.[7] This is a serious personal as well as professional challenge—and one to which even seasoned managers must give much thought.

What kind of manager can juggle so many balls at the same time? It

> "To be trained as an *American* manager is to be trained for a world that is no longer there."

seems clear that a person who can meet these challenges will have to be someone who finds opportunity in problems and pays attention to the unexpected—be it a success or a failure. Professor John Kotter of the Harvard Business School points out that until recently, most managers were not trained to think in terms of an ever-changing environment. And even if a manager accepts the need for changes in work styles, getting others to do the same "demands skills and approaches that most managers simply did not need" in earlier times." Perhaps the first hurdle to cross is admitting that management takes place under conditions of uncertainty and surprise. The second hurdle is harder: making the necessary adjustments in thinking. Many individuals are understandably reluctant to do so—but reluctant or no, they must react or else face large difficulties. "Being good just isn't good enough any more," insists DuPont Chairman R. E. Heckert. "We must be better." ■

Managing Innovation, Change and Conflict

Post-It Notes and Other Great Notions

Fads may be fun, but they have a short shelf-life. Most experienced businesspeople agree that innovation—the development of new products or services that bring in profits over the long haul—is more important than ever in a high-tech environment. Yet the authors of one study, *Breakthroughs!,* found that innovation doesn't usually occur because an organization encourages it; rather, it happens because individuals become intensely curious about something and pursue their fascination even in the face of corporate opposition. Of course, organizational support of breakthroughs helps—but not all companies recognize the potential of new ideas, and even savvy organizations may overlook (and sometimes ruin) great opportunities for innovation.

"Post-It" notepads and CAT scanners are two innovations that became exceptional successes despite the misgivings and miscalculations of the organizations in which they were conceived. Spencer Silver, a chemist at 3M, invented the now-famous Post-It adhesive by accident, and it wasn't initially popular. For several years 3M's management was worried about applications and gave the product team little backing. Eventual test marketing warmed their reception. Not long after, 3M began to be flooded by orders for its new offering.

Godfrey Hounsfield, a computer designer and electrical engineer working for England-based EMI, Ltd., encountered similar organizational obstacles after introducing his inspiration—CAT scanners, which use computerized tomography to "see" parts of the body with far greater clarity than X rays can provide. Hounsfield was a brilliant designer who had a vision of a new product: an imaging device that would work well and be commercially successful. Aided by John Powell, an EMI manager who effectively marketed CAT scanners, Hounsfield was finally able to bring his idea to fruition. Powell persuaded EMI's top management to commit $15 million to the product, and the field of medical imaging was changed forever.

Silver, Hounsfield and people like them are driven by the power of ideas, not by hopes of financial reward. They seek the pleasures of invention, and they are undaunted by corporate hesitation. For them, say the authors of *Breakthroughs!,* innovation is a matter of "a problem to be solved, not a fortune to be made . . [or] a market to be exploited." ■

Source: P. Ranganath Nayak and John M. Ketteringham, *Breakthroughs!* (New York: Rawson Associates, 1986).

All organizations and their managers depend on adaptation and renewal to succeed over time. This chapter addresses the challenges of managing innovation, change, and conflict. Key topics of study include:

Creativity, Innovation and Entrepreneurship
Innovation in Organizations
Organizational Change
Managing Planned Change
Organization Development (OD)
Conflict in Organizations
Conflict Management

*M*egatrends, The Change Masters, Re-Inventing the Corporation, Thriving on Chaos, The Renewal Factor—these titles of recent bestselling books communicate the urgency of dealing with our dynamic society in creative and progressive ways.[1] Read the newspapers and you'll get another feel for the issue. Even some of the terms used to describe organizational responses to new and demanding circumstances have a sensational quality—"downsizing," "restructuring," "leveraged buyouts," and "divestitures" are just a few. The more mundane descriptions of "plant closings," "mergers," "acquisitions," and the like, are just as significant in their impact on the organizations and people involved.

The words of the day are, and will remain for quite some time to come, *innovation, change,* and *conflict.* Organizations and their managers must continually adapt to new situations if they are to continue to survive and prosper over the long run. To do this, in turn, they must be capable of managing in a progressive way. Max DePree, Chairman and CEO of Herman Miller Company—widely acclaimed for its continued creativity and accomplishments—says it well: "you have to have an environment where the body of people are really amenable to change and can deal with the conflicts that arise out of change and innovation."[2]

The very nature of the dynamic, complex, and at times unpredictable environment in which we live demands this. People change, their tastes and values change, governments and laws change, technologies change, and knowledge changes. Unless organizations also change, they risk stagnation, decline, and even death. Some important *external forces for change* include:

■ *Competitive pressures* in the form of changes in the industry and marketplace, and in the nature and the accomplishments of competitors.

■ *Government laws and regulations* in the form of changing legislation and/or policies which affect the legal–political environment and government–business relations.

■ *Economic conditions* in the form of changes in economic trends affecting financial markets as well as the well-being of populations served by the organization and locations in which they operate.

■ *Labor markets* in the form of changes in the supply of and demand for human resources with skills and qualifications desired by the organization.

■ *Technological advancements* in the form of new scientific knowledge and technological developments relevant to the organization and its competitors.

Enlightened management can maintain pace with these and other environmental challenges over time. This chapter examines how this process is facilitated by sound management of innovation, change, and conflict. When done well, these processes help people and organizations achieve creativity and renewal in the contemporary environment.

CREATIVITY, INNOVATION AND ENTREPRENEURSHIP

Creativity is ingenuity and imagination that results in a novel approach to things or a unique solution to a problem. As first discussed in Chapter 3, our interest is with the stimulation of individual and group creativity in organizations. Our concern is that the inherent creative potential of people may often be blocked by poor management and organizational practices. A case in point are these words penned by a Unilever executive trying to put his frustrations into rhyme.[3]

> *Along this tree*
> *From root to crown*
> *Ideas flow up*
> *And vetos down.*

This verse leaves the impression of an organization with the advantages of alertness and imagination at its lower levels, but suffering from rigidity, resistance to change and a lack of foresight at the top. Whereas Unilever had the internal resources for creativity, top management was apparently discouraging instead of encouraging it. The ability to facilitate creativity is among the most basic of a manager's work responsibilities. After all, creativity is the foundation for innovation.

Innovation

Innovation is the process of creating new ideas and putting them into practice as part of the organization's normal operating routines. It is the act of converting new ideas into usable applications. In organizations, these applications occur in the form of **process innovations,** which result in better ways of doing things, and **product innovations,** which result in the creation of new or improved goods and services.

A good way to remember the essence of innovation is this equation.[4]

$$\text{Innovation} = \text{Invention} + \text{Application}$$

"Invention" in this equation relates to the development of new ideas. Managers need to be concerned about creating work environments that stimulate creativity and an ongoing stream of new ideas. "Application," on the other hand, deals with the utilization of inventions to exploit or take advantage of their value. Managers need to be concerned in this respect with two major tasks. First, they must make sure that good ideas for new or modified work processes are actually implemented. Second, they must make sure that the commercial potential of ideas for new products or services is fully realized. In these ways the management of innovation includes responsibilities for attending to both invention—the act of discovery—and application—the act of use.

Entrepreneurship

Entrepreneurship is a term used to describe behavior that is dynamic, risk-taking, creative, and oriented toward innovation. An **entrepreneur** is a person who displays these characteristics and is willing to take action to pursue opportunities in situations others may view as problems or threats. An international view of entrepreneurship in small business and new venture development is highlighted by *Newsline 17.1.* Here, we are more generally interested in what entrepreneurial behavior offers to established organizations—creative ideas and potential for the innovation that is so important to their continued success.

Managers have a major responsibility to develop entrepreneurial behavior in organizations, and to be as entrepreneurial as possible themselves. Again, let's reinforce this point with two examples—both from the same well-respected company, but one a positive case and one negative.[5]

At Hewlett-Packard the year was 1966 and calculators were mostly mechanical and bulky devices. A young man employed by another company created an electronic calculator, but his firm wasn't interested because they weren't into electronics. He took the model to Hewlett-Packard. Although the market research cast an unfavorable light on the project, William Hewlett felt it was a winner. He personally championed the project. The success of the "HP" calculators is now legendary. . . . *The year was 1980* and one of Hewlett-Packard's own employees tried to persuade the company's new product people to get into biotechnology. He reports: "I was laughed out of the room." But the venture capitalists didn't laugh. They staked him $5.2 million to start a new company to make gene machines. Less than three

EUROPE'S NEW ENTREPRENEURS

NEWSLINE 17.1

Small businesses are booming all across Europe, which is experiencing a marked rise in vigorous entrepreneurial activity—and in numbers of millionaires. In England, young small businesses have created nearly a million new jobs in recent years; in Italy, start-ups have tripled in five years and in Holland, a $650-million venture-capital pool is helping new businesses take off and grow at a remarkable rate.

The European entrepreneurs are energetic, highly market conscious, and very good at motivating their employees, often by offering stock options. They want their companies to grow fast, and they push for listings on over-the-counter stock markets to swell their profits. France's OTC market alone sports close to 200 companies worth a total of $16 billion—and other European nations boast similarly healthy OTC trading.

"Until a few years ago, entrepreneur was almost a dirty word" in Europe, says England's Richard Branson, the young CEO of the $450-million-a-year Virgin Group, a multinational leisure and entertainment conglomerate. But no longer: Europe has seen the value of encouraging entrepreneurial activity. Even large, established firms such as Olivetti and Philips are backing start-ups, aware that they need fresh players and ideas to compete in the technology race with the United States and Japan. And buyouts by managers seeking to run their own shows are increasingly common. As one successful young entrepreneur put it, "Too many big European companies get old . . . before they realize it. Buyouts . . . are often the best way to prune these giant oaks."

Source: As reported in Richard I. Kirkland Jr., "Europe's New Entrepreneurs," *Fortune* (April 27, 1987), pp. 253–262.

---

years later HP was forming a joint venture with a rival firm Genentech to develop—you guessed it—gene machines.

Figure 17.1 distinguishes between two types of managers—the "entrepreneurial manager" and the "trustee."[6] The entrepreneurial manager is a proactive person confident of his or her ability. This manager seizes opportunities for innovation, and not only expects surprises but capitalizes on them. The trustee, by contrast, is reactive. He or she is likely to feel threatened by change and uncertainty,

FIGURE 17.1 *The entrepreneurial manager and the trustee: contrasting implications for creativity and innovation.*

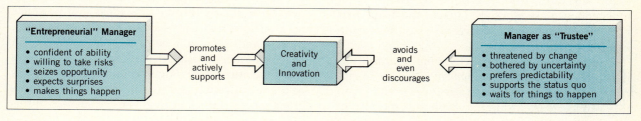

and is inclined to maintain the status quo. Obviously, the need for responsive organizations in today's environment depends on entrepreneurial managers willing to assume risk and encourage creativity and innovation on the part of others.

Intrapreneurship

All managers have a responsibility to promote entrepreneurial behavior. This can be especially challenging in very large and complex organizations whose natural tendencies may be toward stability, rigidity, and the avoidance of risk. **Intrapreneurship** is a term now used to describe entrepreneurial behavior on the part of people and subunits within large organizations.[7]

What is at stake in the quest for intrapreneurship is performance excellence in a highly competitive market environment. It took a new product development team at Compaq Computer, for example, just nine months to bring out the Deskpro 386, a powerful PC that set competitor IBM back on its heels. The best IBM has done to date is 13 months—and that was with its original PC. With performance like this, Compaq went from small upstart to Fortune 500 firm in just four years.[8]

Achieving the competitive edge through intrapreneurship requires the ability for large organizations to act in some ways like small ones. To do this some create small subunits, often called *skunkworks,* where groups of people work together in a highly creative setting free of many of the restrictions of the larger organization.

A classic case occurred—

at Apple Computer, Inc. where a small group of enthusiastic employees was once sent off to a separate facility in Cupertino, California. Their mandate was straightforward—create a state-of-the-art user-friendly personal computer. They operated free from the firm's normal product development bureaucracy, set their own norms, and worked together without outside interference. The "jolly roger" was raised over their building as a symbol of independence. It worked. This is the team that brought the now famous MacIntosh Computer into being.

Another approach taken by some organizations is to offer *new venture development programs* to employees. These are designed to encourage and retain new venture ideas within the corporate umbrella. In return for the direct investment of company resources in their projects, participating employees are asked to take some risks themselves. For example,[9]

at AT&T potential intrapreneurs can get projects funded by an internal venture board. They are offered the opportunities to pursue their ideas under three different compensation schemes—(1) to continue on standard salary with expected normal increments, (2) to keep current salary with no increments, but get 150 percent bonuses if the project succeeds, and (3) to contribute payroll deductions to the venture's capitalization and get bonuses of up to 800 percent with its success. Plans #2 and #3 have been the options of choice so far; the company has received over 2000 ideas for new ventures since the program was started.

INNOVATION IN ORGANIZATIONS

While we can admit that innovation is a key operating objective for organizations, we must also recognize that there are many organizations that should be innovating but fail to do so. As dramatic technological, economic, and social changes continue to characterize the world at large, however, the responsibilities of managers in these organizations to stimulate, support, and achieve innovation are becoming inescapable. All informed managers understand the complexities of innovation in organizations and the requirements for its successful accomplishment.

The Innovation Process

Figure 17.2 introduces four basic elements in the process of organizational innovation—idea creation, initial experimentation, feasibility determination, and final application.[10] The figure uses the example of a new product development to highlight the business significance of "commercializing" innovations, that is turning new ideas into products or processes that can make a difference in sales, profits, and/or costs. One of the major features of organizational innovation, as shown in the figure, is that the entire process must be related to the needs of the organization and its marketplace. New ideas alone are not sufficient to guarantee success in this

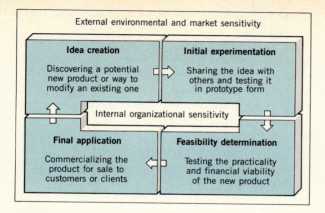

External environmental and market sensitivity

Idea creation

Discovering a potential new product or way to modify an existing one

Initial experimentation

Sharing the idea with others and testing it in prototype form

Internal organizational sensitivity

Final application

Commercializing the product for sale to customers or clients

Feasibility determination

Testing the practicality and financial viability of the new product

FIGURE 17.2 *The process of innovation in organizations: a case of new product development.*

setting. They must be effectively utilized in order to contribute to organizational performance.

Activities common to the four major stages of organizational innovation include:

1. *Idea creation.* This is the stage where new knowledge forms around basic discoveries, extensions of existing understandings, or spontaneous creativity made possible by individual ingenuity and communications with others.

2. *Initial experimentation.* This is the stage of first trial where ideas are tested in concept by discussions with others, referrals to customers, clients, or technical experts, and/or in the form of prototypes or samples.

3. *Feasibility determination.* This is the stage where practicality and financial value are tested in formal feasibility studies, which also identify potential costs and benefits as well as potential markets or applications.

4. *Final application.* This is the stage where a new product is finally commercialized or put on sale in the open market, or a new process is implemented as part of normal operating routines.

ILLUSTRATIVE CASE:
NEW PRODUCT DEVELOPMENT AT 3M

One of the best examples of creativity, innovation, and entrepreneurship in the corporate context is the record achieved by 3M corporation.[11] It is consistently cited as one of America's best-run companies, and it is envied for a sustained record of suc-

cessful new product development. The chapter opener, in fact, introduced what is perhaps the most well-recognized of 3M's new products—"Post-It" notes. The story of how they came into being is worth thinking about, as is the way 3M continues to operate in the quest for future successes of a similar nature.

The story begins with 3M employee Art Fry, whose desire to mark pages in his Sunday hymnal led him to a light adhesive that had been developed in the company's research labs by a colleague Spencer Silver. He thought the adhesive was no good—it wasn't sticky enough. For Art Fry's needs it turned out to be just right.

Fortunately, 3M encourages its technical employees to use 15 percent of their time for "bootlegging"—working on their own projects. Art Fry did this and eventually created the "Post-It" notes as a new product idea. Initial market research wasn't too favorable, and he couldn't catch the marketing department's eye. Fry distributed the notes within the company, where they became popular. He continued to champion the idea while using his bootleg time to work on manufacturing details with the support of other interested company personnel. Eventually, even top management was hooked on the little notes. Further market tests proved successful and "Post-It" notes received full support. The whole process took six years, a good amount of risk, a lot of teamwork, and some conflict. But it paid off. Art Fry's "idea" eventually became one of the five best-selling office products in history.

The real story at 3M, however, is more than about "Post-It" notes alone. Innovation and entrepreneurship are a way of life at the company. With over 6000 scientists and engineers, the quest is always on for both new products and creative variations of existing ones. 3M is relatively decentralized, but clear reporting relationships facilitate the flow of information to the top. Formal practices like "bootlegging" keep the innovative spirit a part of daily operations. Small groups are used to bring together researchers and marketing personnel who work together to get new products through the design the design and development stages. While it took Post-it notes six years to make it through, some products make it in a year. Over 60 percent of the new ideas spawned by the firm's employees don't make it to final application. But current CEO Allen Jacobson says, "Outsiders say we are very lenient in rewarding failure." It's just this type of spirit that keeps the company at the forefront of American industry.

Characteristics of Innovative Organizations

Innovative organizations share many characteristics in common with 3M. They have organized and staffed themselves to achieve innovation, and their managers take active roles in leading the process. Here are some of the ways organizations and their managers do it.[12]

1. *The corporate strategy and culture support innovation.* The strategies of the organization, visions and values of senior management, and the framework of policies and expectations emphasize an innovative spirit. At 3M, we have noted that "bootleg" time is expected by scientists. Divisions are expected, in turn, to earn 25 percent of their profits from the new products it is supposed to produce. But even with such directions in place, failure is accepted at 3M as part of business. At Johnson & Johnson, CEO James Burke echos a similar theme — "I try to give people the feeling that it's okay to fail, that it's important to fail," he says. The key is to eliminate risk-averse climates and replace them with organizational cultures in which innovation is expected, and failure is accepted.

2. *The organization structure supports innovation.* More and more large organizations are trying to capture the structural flexibility of smaller ones. They are reorganizing to create many smaller divisions, to allow "skunkworks" to operate and even to form intrapreneurial new ventures like those reported in *Newsline 17.2*. They are also striving for more organic operations with a strong emphasis on lateral communications. In particular, research and development, historically a separate and isolated function, is being integrated into a team setting. As Peter Drucker points out, "successful innovations . . . are now being turned out by cross-functional teams with people from marketing, manufacturing, and finance participating in research work from the very beginning."[15] These are all means of limiting structural obstacles to innovation and encouraging the freedom and interaction so necessary to creativity.

3. *The organization's staffing supports innovation* Organizations need different kinds of people to ac-

complish innovation. The critical innovation roles to be filled are:[14]

- *Idea generators* who create new insights from internal discovery or external awareness, or both.
- *Information gatekeepers* who serve as links between people and groups within the organization, and with external sources.
- *Product champions* who advocate and push for change and innovation in general, and for the adoption of specific product or process ideas in particular.
- *Project managers* who perform the technical functions needed to keep an innovative project on track with all needed resource support.
- *Leaders* who encourage, sponsor, and coach to keep the values and goals in place, and the all-important psychic energies and commitments to innovation channeled in the right directions.[14]

4. *Top management supports innovation.* Top management sets the tone in innovative organizations. In the case of 3M, Johnson & Johnson, and others, many top managers have been the innovators and product champions of the past. They understand the innovation process, are tolerant of criticisms and differences of opinion, take all possible steps to keep the pressures on, and remove the obstacles to success. Max DePree, CEO of Herman Miller, elaborates.[15] "If you want the best things to happen in corporate life, you have to find ways to be hospitable to the unusual person," he says. DePree's philosophy is to create a relationship with employees in which they understand "it is OK for everybody to do their best." "There are an awful lot of people in management who really don't want subordinates to do their best, because it gets to be very threatening," he points out. Effective managers set the tone for innovation by allowing others to excel through creativity and hard work.

Barriers to Innovation in Organizations

In contrast to the characteristics just identified, there are many organizational and management barriers to innovation. These are the things that too often inhibit the many processes, events, and accomplishments necessary to achieve both continued invention of ideas and their practical applications. Organizations that lack the capacity to innovate may

"Intrapreneurs"
Aid Consumer-Product Giants

NEW From Scott

Instant CAR DRY

$1.00 REBATE On Package

- Soft
- Absorbent
- Convenient
- Disposable

Reg.	$0.00
Sale	$0.00
Less Rebate	$1.00
YOUR COST	**$0.00**

Working as innovators inside large organizations and mostly shielded from bureaucratic interference, "intrapreneurial" employees of such large consumer-product makers as Colgate-Palmolive and Scott Paper are scrambling to come up with new and different products for their marketing-driven employers. The idea behind such corporate sponsoring of intrapreneurs is to spur product development in a small-business setting where the risks are high and the potential winnings large.

Colgate Venture Co. is a small Colgate-Palmolive branch that attempts to come up with core-market-related and even entirely new products for its parent company. Among its non-traditional offerings are cat-litter-box liners and teeth-retainer cleansers for teens. Colgate Venture's 70-person staff forms a close-knit team of five divisions; these employees are reimbursed through bonuses and an incentive program as well as salaries. Scott Paper's "Do-It-Yourself" business, an intrapreneurial unit with 15 products on the market, uses Scott's name to gain entrance to retailers while keeping separate from its large parent. And S.C. Johnson & Sons Inc., makers of wax and insect spray, has set up a $250,000 starter fund for employees with innovative ideas—a push that has led to the test-marketing of a Home Cleaning Service and a product for cleaning fishing line.

Not all these new products fly, but the notion of intrapreneurship has its enthusiasts in large organizations—managers who recognize the need to put some space between groups of innovators and their parent companies. The freedom to pursue ideas without having to wait for market research results marks "a very major change from the mainstream marketing culture" of the other consumer-product makers, says Colgate Venture Co.'s president, Barrie Spelling.

Source: As reported in Ronald Alsop, "Consumer-Product Giants Relying on 'Intrapreneurs' in New Ventures," *Wall Street Journal* (April 22, 1988), p. 19.

---

suffer from one or more of the following difficulties.[16]

- *Top management isolation* which fosters misunderstandings about conditions and people in the organization, and contributes to the emergence of a "risk-averse" climate.

- *Intolerance of differences* which denies people and subunits their individualities, tends to create homogeneity of ideas and thinking, and brands as "trouble makers" those who question the status quo.

- *Vested interests* which create feelings that individual departments are more important than the organization as a whole, and that one's "turf" is to be protected from the encroachment of others and their outside ideas.

- *Short time horizons* which emphasize short-term performance results over the potential for long-term gains, and in the process deny many new ideas the opportunities to "earn" their way into the spotlight.

- *Narrow accounting practices* which limit managerial attention to cost recovery goals based on corporate overheads, and thereby drive development expenses up so high that many new ideas never get a chance to prove their worth.

- *Overly rational thinking* which tries to put what should be a creative and sometimes chaotic process into a systematic and rational sequence, and with the result that true potential often goes unrealized as schedules and commitments take precedence over development needs.

- *Inappropriate incentives* which take the form of reward and control systems that reinforce regularity and routines, and dislike the surprises and differences that often accompany the processes of innovation.

- *Excessive bureaucracy* which gives allegiance to rules, procedures, and efficiency, and compromises innovation through excessive delays and frustrations for the "idea" people and their cohorts.

ORGANIZATIONAL CHANGE

"Change" is an essential part of creativity and innovation in organizations. Some even say that "change is inevitable." But is it necessarily so? Consider what happened—[17]

at BankAmerica after the company announced a large quarterly operating loss. Chairman Samuel Armacost complained about the lack of "agents of change" among his top managers who seemed more interested in taking orders than initiating change. "I came away quite distressed from my first couple of management meetings," he said. "Not only couldn't I get conflict, I couldn't even get comment. They were all waiting to see which way the wind blew."

The Manager's Role as Change Agent

A **change agent** is a person or group taking responsibility for changing the existing pattern of behavior of another person or social system. Change agents make things happen, and part of every manager's job is to act as a change agent in the work setting. This is an entrepreneurial responsibility that requires being alert to situations or people needing change, open to good ideas, and able to support the implementation of new ideas into actual practice.

Figure 17.3 shows six phases through which change may occur in organizations. In this figure, change is depicted as a "top-down" process that is initiated and directed by top management. Strategic and comprehensive changes typically follow this pattern. The transformation of the once ailing Chrysler Corporation under the leadership of Lee Iacocca is one example; the attempted transformation of General Motors Corporation by CEO Roger Smith, as discussed in the Part 6 opening perspective, is another. When done well, top-down change

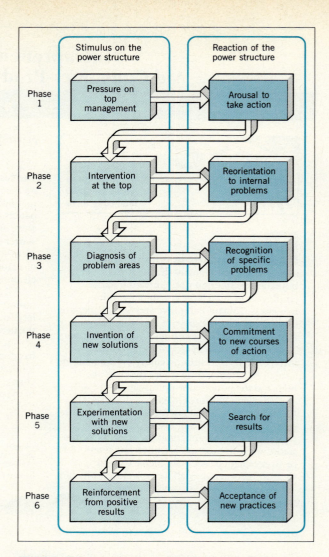

FIGURE 17.3 *Six phases of organizational change.*

Source: Reprinted by permission of the *Harvard Business Review*, "Patterns of Organizational Change," by Larry E. Greiner, *Harvard Business Review*, Vol. 45 (May–June 1967). Copyright © 1987 by the President and Fellows of Harvard College, all rights reserved.

can occur rather rapidly and with a comprehensive impact on the organization. It runs the risk of being perceived as insensitive to the needs of lower-level personnel, and can suffer from implementation problems brought on by resistance and a lack of organization-wide commitment to change. Part of the success of top-down change is usually determined by the willingness of middle and lower-level managers to actively support top-management initiatives.

Change in organizations also occurs in a "bottom up" fashion. In such cases the initiatives for change come from persons throughout an organization, and are supported by the efforts of middle and lower-level managers acting as change agents. Bottom-up change is essential to organizational innovation and is very useful in terms of adapting operations and technologies to the changing requirements of work. Indeed, innovation oriented companies like 3M are organized and managed to facilitate bottom-up change.

Planned and Unplanned Change

Not all change in organizations happens at a manager's direction. **Unplanned changes** occur spontaneously or at random and without a change agent's attention. They may be disruptive, such as a wildcat strike that results in a plant closure, or beneficial, such as an interpersonal conflict that results in a new procedure or rule being established to guide interdepartmental relations. The appropriate goal in managing unplanned change is to act immediately once it is recognized so as to minimize any negative consequences and maximize any possible benefits.

We are particularly interested in **planned change** that happens as a result of specific efforts by a change agent. Planned change is a direct response to someone's perception of a **performance gap,** defined in Chapter 3 as a discrepancy between the desired and actual state of affairs. Performance gaps may represent problems to be resolved or opportunities to be explored. In each case, managers as change agents should spot performance gaps and initiate planned changes to close them.

Organizational Targets and Forces for Change

Organizational change involves some modification in the various components constituting the essence of an organization. The possible *targets* include all of the aspects of organizations already discussed in this book. We can summarize them now as:[18]

■ *Tasks*   Task direction and the nature of work as represented by organizational mission, objectives and strategy, and job designs for individuals and groups.

■ *People*   The attitudes and competencies of the organization's human resources, and the staffing processes used to acquire and maintain high-quality personnel over time.

■ *Culture*   The predominate value system for the organization as a whole, and the norms and values guiding individuals and groups at all levels in the organization.

■ *Technology*   The operations and systems used to support job designs, arrange the flow of work, and integrate people and machines in well-functioning socio-technical systems.

■ *Structure*   The configuration of the organization as a complex system, including its bureaucratic features, forms of departmentation, and other formal aspects of authority and communications.

Performance gaps and the impetus for change in any one or more of these targets can arise from the variety of external forces for change shown in Figure 17.4. As things develop and change over time in an organization's general and specific environments, the organization must adapt as well. This point was made right at the beginning of the chapter. Changes in the external environment often create the need for change in organizations.

Other important forces for change arise from within the organization. Indeed, any change in one part of the organization as a complex system, perhaps a change initiated in response to one or more of the external forces just identified, can often create the need for change in another part of the system. The many targets for change—task, people, culture, technology, structure—are highly interrelated.

MANAGING PLANNED CHANGE

Change is a complicated phenomenon at the heart of which lie people. But people have a tendency to act habitually and in stable ways over time. That is, they may tend *not* to change even when circumstances warrant. As a manager, you will need to recognize and deal with such inertia in the work setting. To begin, it helps to understand the phases of planned change and their managerial implications.

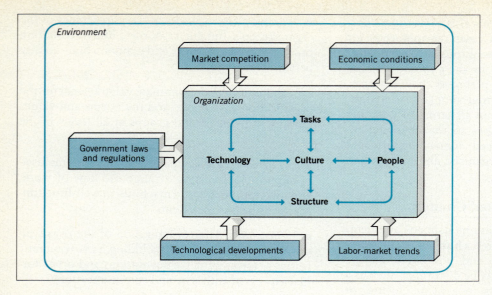

FIGURE 17.4 *Forces and targets for planned organizational change.*

The Phases of Planned-Change

Kurt Lewin, a noted psychologist, recommends that any planned-change effort be viewed as a three-phase process: unfreezing, changing, and refreezing.[19] This process is diagrammed in Figure 17.5.

The Unfreezing Phase

Unfreezing is the stage of preparing a situation for change. This requires that a manager establish a good relationship with the people involved and develop a felt need for change. Planned change has little chance for long-term success unless existing attitudes and behaviors are disconfirmed, and people become open to doing things differently. Unfreezing can be assisted through environmental pressures for change, declining performance, recognition that problems or opportunities exist, and from observing behavioral models displaying alternative approaches. When handled well, conflict can be an important unfreezing force in organizations. It often helps people break old habits and recognize alternative ways of thinking about or doing things.

The Changing Phase

In the changing phase, change is actually implemented. This is the point where managers, for example, initiate changes in the organizational targets of tasks, people, culture, technology, and structure. It is ideally done in response to good problem diagnosis and a careful examination of alternatives.

However, Lewin believes that many change agents enter the changing phase prematurely, are too quick to change things, and therefore end up creating resistance to change. When managers implement change before the people involved feel a need for it, there is an increased likelihood that the attempt will fail.

The Refreezing Phase

The final stage in the planned-change process is refreezing. Here the manager is concerned about stabilizing the change and creating the conditions for its long-term continuity. Refreezing is accomplished by providing appropriate rewards for performance, positive reinforcement, and necessary resource support. It is also important to carefully evaluate results, provide feedback to the people involved, and make any required modifications in the original change. When refreezing is not done well, changes are too easily forgotten or abandoned with the passage of time.

Choosing a Change Strategy

Managers use various strategies for getting other persons to adopt a desired change. Figure 17.6 summarizes these as force-coercion, empirical-rational, and normative-reeducative change strategies.[20]

Force–Coercion Strategies

A **force-coercion strategy** uses the power bases of

legitimacy, rewards, and punishments as primary inducements to change. This can be done in more than one way. In a pure *forcing* strategy the change agent takes direct and unilateral action to "command" that change take place. This involves the exercise of formal authority or legitimate power, offering special rewards, and/or threatening punishment. In a more *political* strategy, the change agent maneuvers indirectly to gain special advantage over other persons and thereby make them change. This involves bargaining, obtaining control of important resources, or granting small favors in return for "IOUs."

In both the forcing and political versions, a force–coercion strategy of planned change has limited results. Although it can be done rather quickly, most people respond to this strategy out of fear of punishment or desire for reward. This usually results in only temporary compliance with the change agent's desires. The new behavior continues only so long as the opportunity for rewards and punishments is present. For this reason, force–coercion is most useful as an unfreezing device that helps people break old patterns of behavior and gain initial impetus to try new ones.

Empirical-Rational Strategies

Change agents using an **empirical–rational strategy** attempt to bring about change through persuasion backed by special knowledge and rational argument. This is an *informational* strategy

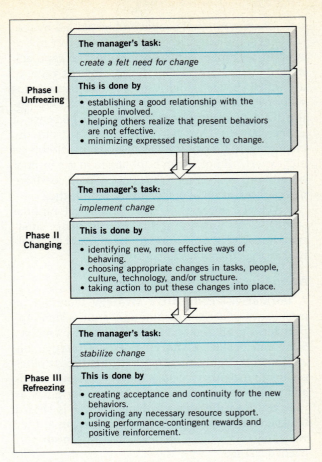

FIGURE 17.5 *The three phases of planned organizational change: an application of Lewin's model.*

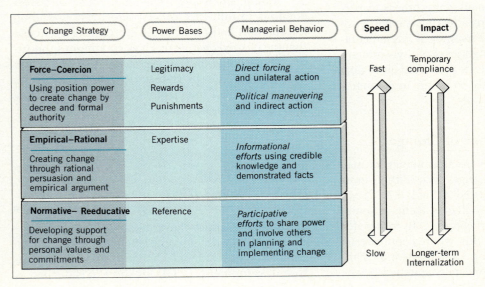

FIGURE 17.6 *Three change strategies and their managerial implications.*

that assumes rational people will be guided by reason and self-interest in deciding whether or not to support a change. A manager using this approach must convince others that the cost/benefit value of a planned change is high, and persuade them that it will leave them better off than before. Accomplishing this depends to a large extent on the presence of expert power. This can come directly from the change agent *if* he or she has personal credibility as an "expert." If not, it can be obtained in the form of consultants and other "outside experts," or from direct observation of demonstration projects.

When successful, an empirical–rational strategy helps unfreeze and refreeze a change situation. It results in a more longer-lasting and internalized change than does force–coercion.

Normative-Reeducative Strategies.

A **normative–reeducative strategy** identifies or establishes values and assumptions from which support for a proposed change will naturally emerge. Sometimes called a **shared power strategy,** this approach is highly *participative* in nature. It relies on involving others in examining personal needs and values, group norms, and operating goals as they relate to the issues at hand. Power is shared between the change agent and other persons as they work together to develop new consensus to support needed change.

Managers using this approach to planned change need reference power and the skills to work effectively with other people in group situations. They must be comfortable allowing others to participate in making decisions affecting the nature of the planned change and its manner of implementation. Because it entails a high level of involvement, a normative–reeducative strategy is often quite time consuming. But, it is likely to result in a longer-lasting and internalized change.

Dealing with Resistance to Change

Some of the common reasons that managers may experience resistance to change, even to their most well-conceived ideas, are listed in Table 17.1. Such resistance is often viewed by change agents as something which must be "overcome" in order for change to be successful. But when people resist change, they are defending something important that—to them at least—appears threatened by the

change attempt. Thus resistance is really a type of feedback that the informed change agent can use to constructively modify a planned change. When resistance is encountered, it usually means something can be done to achieve a better "fit" between the planned change, the situation, and the people involved.

Once resistance is recognized and understood, it can be responded to in constructive ways. This is especially true if the manager has been alert and identified resistance early in the planned change process. Six general approaches for dealing with resistance to change are:[21]

1. *Education and communication.*   Use of one-on-one discussions, presentations to groups, memos, reports, and demonstrations to educate people beforehand about a change and to help them see the logic of the change.
2. *Participation and involvement.*   Allowing others to help design and implement the change; asking individuals to contribute ideas and advice, or forming task forces or committees to work on the change.
3. *Facilitation and support.*   Providing socioemotional support for the hardships of change, actively listening to problems and complaints, providing training in the new ways, and helping overcome performance pressures.
4. *Negotiation and agreement.*   Offering incentives to actual or potential resistors; working out trade-offs to provide special benefits in exchange for assurance that the change will not be blocked.
5. *Manipulation and co-optation.*   Use of covert attempts to influence others; selectively providing information and consciously structuring events so that the desired change receives maximum support.
6. *Explicit and implicit coercion.*   Use of force to get people to accept change; threatening resistors with a variety of undesirable consequences if they don't go along as planned.

ORGANIZATION DEVELOPMENT (OD)

Behavioral scientists have been working since the early 1960s with a comprehensive approach to planned organizational change. Called **organization development,** or **OD** for short, it is defined as

1. *Fear of the unknown.* Being uncertain about the nature of a change; feeling that you do not know what is going on and what the future is likely to hold.
2. *Loss of control.* Feeling that the change is being done *to* you and not *by* you; worrying that you have no say in the situation and the events taking place.
3. *Loss of face.* Feeling embarrassed by the change, and viewing it as a testimony that the way you have done things in the past was wrong.
4. *Loss of competency.* Feeling that existing skills and competencies will no longer be of use after the change, and worrying about your ability to perform effectively after the change.
5. *Need for security.* Worrying about what your role will be, if any, after the change is in place; feeling that your job and/or chance for career advancement is in jeopardy.
6. *Poor timing.* Being caught by surprise with a change that has just been sprung on you; or, being asked to change at a time when you feel already overworked.
7. *Force of habit.* Not liking to change existing ways of doing things; feeling comfortable in present routines and habits . . . things that are just tough to change.
8. *Lack of support.* Lacking important support from your supervisor and/or the organization; not having the resources and other things needed to do the change right and in a timely way.
9. *Lack of confidence.* Lacking in personal confidence that things, once changed, will really be better than they were before; not seeing any direct performance benefit from the change.
10. *Lingering resentment.* Being recalcitrant because of a lack of respect for the people involved and/or because of anger over the way you have been treated during past change efforts.

Source: Developed in part from Rosabeth Moss Kanter, "Managing The Human Side of Change," *"Management Review,* Vol. 74 (1985), pp. 52–56.

the application of behavioral science knowledge in a systematic and long-range effort to improve organizational effectiveness.[22] In particular, OD seeks to help organizations cope with forces for change in their environments, and improve their internal problem-solving capabilities. Thus, it has both outcome and process goals.

■ *Outcome goals of OD* address task accomplishments. They focus on performance improvements by individuals, groups, and the organization as a whole.

■ *Process goals of OD* address the way people work together. They focus improving relationships, and key processes of communications and decision making among organizational members.

Although OD is a planned change process, the existence of both goals helps to make it somewhat distinctive. You might think of OD as "planned change *plus*" if you'd like. That "plus" is the goal of creating change in a way that organization members develop a capacity for continued self-renewal. This means that true OD seeks more than the successful accomplishment of one planned change. It tries to achieve change in such a way that organization members become more active and confident in

meeting their responsibilities to maintain longer-run organizational effectiveness.

What also makes OD unique as a planned change approach is its allegiance to strong humanistic values and several established behavioral science principles. In terms of *core values,* true OD is committed to improving organizations by (1) providing people with choices about matters affecting their work, (2) sharing power and involving them in participative problem solving, and (3) leaving them capable self-renewal and continued development. In terms of *behavioral science principles,* OD recognizes the following.[23]

1. *Principles regarding individuals.*
■ Individual needs for growth and development are most likely to be satisfied in a supportive and challenging work environment.
■ Most people are capable of assuming responsibility for their own actions and of making positive contributions to organizational performance.

2. *Principles regarding groups.*
■ Groups help people satisfy important needs, but can be either helpful or harmful in supporting organizational objectives.

■ Through better collaboration, people can increase the effectiveness of groups in meeting individual and organizational needs.

3. *Principles regarding organizations.*
■ Changes in one part of an organization will also affect other parts.
■ The culture of the organization will affect the nature and expression of individual feelings and attitudes.
■ Organizational structures and jobs can be designed to meet the needs of individuals and groups as well as the organization.

ILLUSTRATIVE CASE:
OD IN AN INDIAN TRIBE

An OD consultant received a request for assistance from the executive director of the tribal council of an American Indian tribe.[24] The council was responsible for utilization of natural resources on the reservation, running the tribal enterprises, managing utilities and services, maintaining general health and welfare, and preserving the tribal culture among other things.

The consultant and a colleague planned and conducted a workshop for 20 key people from the council and other tribal units. Before the workshop, interviews were held with all those who would be attending. They were asked to comment on what they thought was going right for the tribe, and what things were hampering the accomplishment of key objectives. After summarizing the major positive and negative themes expressed to them, the consultants used this information to initiate a week-long organization development workshop. The results of the interviews were "fed back" to the tribal members and they engaged in constructive dialog on the issues. Through additional group activities led by the consultants, more data was collected from council members and addressed by them during the week. Occasional lectures on management topics and skill-oriented experiential exercises further assisted in the personal development of the participants. At one point, everyone worked together to help define roles for the tribal council and its executive director to help increase their effectiveness.

An evaluation questionnaire completed on the last day of the workshop indicated a high level of enthusiasm for the process and its outcomes. The consultants felt everyone was working together with a higher level of mutual trust and support. It was agreed that the consultants would visit the reservation again in about six months time to check on progress. But, this follow-up was held sooner when the consultants learned that action was proceeding more slowly than expected.

They returned to the reservation and interviewed a sample of participants from the initial workshop. The results were reported to the tribal council and discussions held to clarify action expectations. A short time later the council and director asked the consultants to conduct another workshop. It was held over a four-day period. A similar format to the first workshop was followed, with the exception of less time being devoted to lectures and more time to working through differences between key subgroups. Additional time was devoted to role clarification for each individual participant. The workshop ended with the subgroups and individuals feeling better informed about one another's needs and goals. With the consultants' agreement, they decided to schedule two follow-up sessions to facilitate continued progress.

A General Model of OD

Figure 17.7 depicts a general model of OD and shows its relationship to Lewin's three phases of planned change. This is consistent with accepted OD practice as illustrated in the prior case.

To begin the OD process successfully, any consultant or facilitator must *establish a working relationship* with members of the client system. The next step is *diagnosis;* gathering and analyzing data to assess the situation and set appropriate change objectives. This helps to unfreeze an existing situation as well as pinpoint appropriate action directions. Diagnosis leads to active *intervention* wherein change objectives are pursued through a variety of specific interventions, a number of which will be discussed shortly.

Essential to any OD effort is *evaluation*. This is where the process is examined to determine if things are proceeding smoothly and in a desired direction, and if further action is needed. Eventually, the goals of OD are for the consultant or facilitator to *achieve a terminal relationship* with the client system. If OD has been well done, the system and its members should be prepared to better manage by themselves

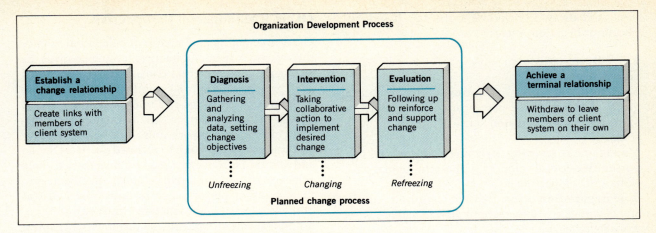

FIGURE 17.7 *Organization development and the planned change process.*

Action Research Foundations of OD

The success or failure of any OD program rests in part with the strength of its action research foundations. Shown in Figure 17.8, **Action research** is a process of systematically collecting data on an organization, feeding it back to the members for action planning, and evaluating results by collecting more data and repeating the process as necessary. It is a data-based and collaborative approach to problem solving and organizational assessment.

The action-research is initiated when someone senses a performance gap and decides to analyze the situation systematically for the problems and opportunities it represents.

Data gathering can be done in several ways. Interviews are common means of gathering data in action research. Formal written surveys of employee attitudes and needs are also growing in popularity. Many such "climate," "attitude," or "morale" questionnaires have been tested for reliability and validity. Some have even been used to the extent that "norms" are available so that one organization can compare its results with those from a broader sample of counterparts.

OD Interventions

OD interventions are activities initiated by consultants or managers in support of a comprehensive OD program. They are ways of facilitating the action-research process and taking action in response to the problems and opportunities it brings to the surface. A list of popular OD interventions focusing on the individual, group, and organizational levels of action follows. You are already familiar with many of them, since they represent management theories and concepts discussed throughout this book. What makes them important here is *how* they are used in OD—selectively, usually in combina-

FIGURE 17.8 *Action research: the methodological foundations of organization development.*

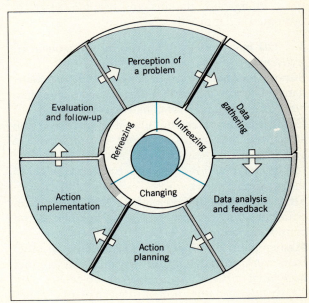

tions, and always in response to the data-based implications of action research.

1. *OD interventions to improve individual effectiveness.*

Sensitivity training (T-groups) Unstructured group sessions where participants learn interpersonal skills and increased sensitivity to other persons.

Management training Structured educational opportunities for developing important managerial skills and competencies.

Role negotiation Structured interactions to clarify and negotiate role expectations among persons who work together.

Job redesign Realigning task components to fit the needs and capabilities of the individual better.

Career planning Structured advice and discussion sessions to help individuals plan career paths and programs of personal development.

2. *OD interventions to improve group effectiveness.*

Team building Structured experiences to help group members set goals, improve interpersonal relations, and become a better-functioning team.

Process consultation Third-party observation of critical group processes (e.g., communication, conflict and decision making), and giving advice on how to improve these processes.

Intergroup team building Structured experiences to help two or more groups set shared goals, improve intergroup relations, and become better coordinated and mutually supportive.

3. *OD interventions to improve organizational effectiveness.*

Survey feedback Comprehensive and systematic data collection to identify attitudes and needs, analyze results, and plan for constructive action.

Confrontation meeting One-day intensive and structured meeting of a sample of employees to gather data on their attitudes and needs, analyze results, and plan for constructive action relevant to the organization as a whole.

Structural redesign Realigning the organization structure to meet the needs of environmental and contextual forces.

Management by objectives Formalizing an MBO framework throughout the organization so that individual-subunit-organizational objectives are clearly linked to one another in means-end chains.

OD in a Managerial Perspective

OD is an exciting application of behavioral science theory to management practice. It often involves the assistance of an external consultant or an internal staff person with special training. But, a manager with appropriate skills and understanding can and should utilize elements of OD in ongoing development efforts with a work unit. As a comprehensive and systematic approach to planned change, OD can and should be routinely used by managers to help achieve and maintain high levels of effectiveness in their areas of performance responsibility. Just as "human-resource development" must be a continuing management concern, so too must "organizational development." There are times when every organization or subunit needs to reflect systematically on its strengths and weaknesses—and on the problems and opportunities it faces. The concepts and ideas of OD can assist managers to introduce planned changes, foster creativity and innovation, and improve organizational productivity.

CONFLICT IN ORGANIZATIONS

The process of innovation and change in organizations are bound to create occasional **conflict** in the form of disagreements between people on issues of substance or emotion.[25] Managers and change agents spend a considerable amount of time on a daily basis dealing with conflicts of various forms. **Substantive conflicts** involve disagreements over such things as goals, the allocation of resources, distribution of rewards, policies and procedures, and job assignments. **Emotional conflicts** result from feelings of anger, distrust, dislike, fear, and resentment, as well as from personality clashes. When managed well, both forms of conflict can be helpful in promoting creativity and innovation. Unfortunately, they can have their destructive sides as well.

Destructive Conflict

Destructive conflict works to the disadvantage of the people and organization involved. It occurs, for example, when two employees are unable to work together because of interpersonal hostilities (a destructive emotional conflict) or when the members of a committee can't agree on group goals (a destructive substantive conflict). There are many circumstances under which conflict can be upsetting to the participants, to others who may observe its occurrence, and to the organization or subunits in which the conflict situation exists.

The disadvantages of destructive conflicts are many. The harm that can be done includes unnecessary or overpowering stress, decreased communication and increased suspicion, reduced cooperation, increased competition, and decreased concern for a common goal. Overall, destructive conflicts can reduce the effectiveness of individuals, groups, and organizations by decreasing productivity and satisfaction.

Constructive Conflict

Constructive conflict is quite a different story. It results in benefits instead of disadvantages for the people and organization involved. The potential benefits include:

1. *Increased creativity and innovation.* As a result of the conflict, the people do things or behave in new and better ways.
2. *Increased effort.* Conflict can overcome apathy and can cause the people to work harder.
3. *Increased cohesion.* Conflict with outsiders can strengthen group cohesion and commitment to the common purpose.
4. *Reduced tension.* Conflict can help people release tensions that, if held back, could cause stress and disrupt work efforts.

Whether conflict works beneficially for the organization or not depends on two factors: (1) the intensity of the conflict, and (2) how well the conflict is managed. The inverted "U" curve in Figure 17.9 shows that conflict of moderate intensity can be good for the organization, whereas very low- or very high-intensity conflict can be bad. Too much conflict overpowers the organization and its people; too little conflict prevents them from achieving a creative performance edge.

Types of Conflict Situations

Managers spend a lot of time dealing with conflict situations of these types: (1) personal conflict (2) interpersonal conflict, (3) intergroup conflict, and (4) interorganizational conflict. Stress is a frequent by-product of conflict, in any of the prior forms. A special section in Chapter 21 examines stress in detail and offers a number of insights that can help you better deal with it. For now, the question becomes, "How well prepared are you to deal with each type of conflict situation as a manager?"

Personal Conflict

Among the more potentially upsetting conflicts are those involving the individual alone. In Chapter 11, for example, we discussed conflicts based on role overloads and person–role incompatibilities. Project yourself ahead a few years. Personal conflicts might develop as you take on too many responsibilities. It might also develop as a conflict between personal ethics and organizational expectations. Some common types of person conflict are:

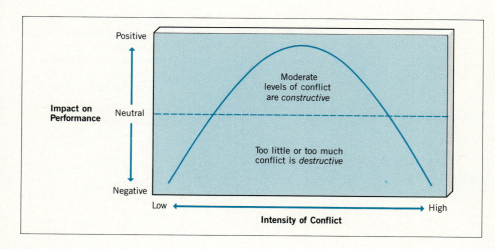

FIGURE 17.9 *The relationship between conflict and performance: constructive versus destructive conflict.*

1. *Approach–approach conflict*   A person must choose between two equally attractive behavioral alternatives.
2. *Avoidance–avoidance conflict*   A person is forced to make a choice between equally unattractive and undesirable goals.
3. *Approach–avoidance conflict*   A person is pushed toward a single goal by a desire to attain it, but is simultaneously pushed away from it by undesirable aspects it also involves.

Interpersonal Conflict

Interpersonal conflict occurs among two or more individuals. It can be substantive or emotional in nature, or both. Everyone has experience with interpersonal conflict, and it is very commonly faced by managers. Because it involves confrontation with one or more other persons, it is also something we sometimes try to avoid.

Learning how to engage in interpersonal conflict without it becoming destructive, and being able to help others do the same, is an important managerial skill. For example,

at Intel Corporation   president Andrew Grove calls this the ability to engage in "constructive confrontation." It is illustrated in this description of what took place during a staff meeting to discuss a vice-president's proposal to use a new statistical indicator of production timeliness.[26]

> Arguments generated rebuttals, numbers collided with other numbers. New ideas began to surface, most of them to be immediately rejected, until eventually the

heated exchanges dissipated. The still-animated group of people in the room suddenly realized, with considerable satisfaction, that they had now come up with the right statistical measure.

Intergroup Conflict

Another type of conflict occurs within the organization as an interlocking network of groups. This topic was first introduced in our look at intergroup competition in Chapter 13. Intergroup conflict is common in organizations, and it can easily make the desired integration and coordination of activities very difficult to accomplish.

Figure 17.10 shows how intergroup conflict can develop in both vertical and horizontal relationships in organizations. A common *vertical conflict* involves representatives of line–staff groups. In a manufacturing firm, for example,

Headquarters staff may emphasize the need for detailed performance reports on a weekly basis, and complain when the reports are submitted late and with incomplete information.
Line personnel in the plant may complain that such reports are time consuming to prepare, and fail to give an accurate picture of long-term accomplishments.

Horizontal conflict often occurs when members of different functional departments have difficulty working with one another. Going back to the example in the figure, for example,

Marketing's objective of customer satisfaction may lead to complaints that faster production schedules

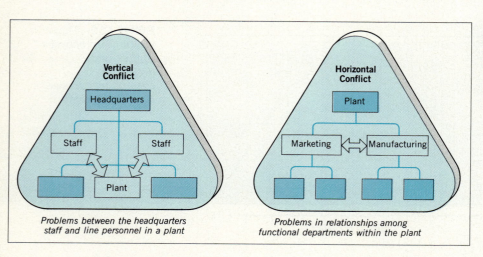

FIGURE 17.10
Intergroup conflicts in organizations: common vertical and horizontal conflicts in a manufacturing firm.

Vertical Conflict

Headquarters

Staff   Staff

Plant

Problems between the headquarters staff and line personnel in a plant

Horizontal Conflict

Plant

Marketing ⟷ Manufacturing

Problems in relationships among functional departments within the plant

UNION AND
MANAGEMENT CLASH OVER TEAMWORK

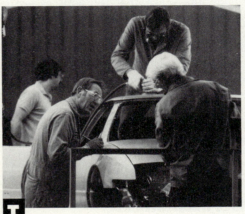

To the managers of America's biggest auto makers, teamwork is an increasingly important weapon in the arsenal against tough competition and the rising costs of production. But organized labor—specifically, the UAW—is not wholly convinced that teams are in the best interests of union members. GM and the UAW have locked horns over the issue, which has strong implications for negotiations over work-rule changes on the local plant level.

The dispute centers on whether teamwork is a ploy to get union labor to work harder for the same price. Some UAW members have complained that GM pits plants against each other in order to force cooperation with the teamwork concept. As evidence, these workers cite the closing of GM's Norwood, Ohio, plant, which made cars more cheaply than did the Van Nuys, California, facility but refused to switch to teams.

Apart from union members, some lower-level managers have tended to resist teams because they replace foremen with union-member team leaders who cannot simply be given orders. For such managers, teams pose a threat to shop-floor power.

The danger, from an upper-management point of view, is that pushing too hard for teams will undercut their potential benefits by causing worker resentment. To skirt this problem, Detroit will need to convince the UAW that job security will be guaranteed—so that teamwork will be perceived as in everyone's interest. But many workers fear long-term job losses and reduced union power.

Source: As reported in "Detroit vs. the UAW": At Odds Over Teamwork," *Business Week* (August 24, 1987), pp. 543–55; and, "GM's New 'Teams' aren't Hitting any Homers," *Business Week* (August 8, 1988), pp. 46–47.

---

are needed along with the ability to make design modifications to fit unique customer preferences. *Manufacturing's* objective of operating efficiency may lead to complaints for better market forecasts and the avoidance of unnecessary design changes so that better production schedules can be set.

Interorganizational Conflict

Conflict also occurs between organizations. Consider, for example, disagreements between unions and organizations employing their members, between government regulatory agencies and organizations subject to their surveillance, and, more generally, between organizations and others that supply them with raw materials. In each setting, the poten-

tial for conflict involves individuals who represent total organizations, not internal subunits or groups. But again, any resulting conflicts must be managed to the benefit instead of the detriment of the organizations and individuals concerned.

Newsline 17.3 highlights interorganizational conflict between the United Auto Workers Union and General Motors. It serves as a prelude to Chapter 18, which is devoted to the topic of managing labor–management relations.

Sources of Conflict

Conflict in any of the prior types may arise for a variety of reasons. To begin, there are certain antecedent conditions present in most organizations most of the time, which make the eventual emergence of conflicts very likely. These sources of potential conflict include:

■ *Role ambiguities.* Unclear job expectations and other task uncertainties increase the probability that some people will be working at cross purposes at least some of the time.

■ *Resource scarcities.* Having to share resources with others and/or compete directly with them for resource allocations makes a situation conflict prone, especially when resources are scarce.

■ *Task interdependencies.* When individuals or groups must depend on what others do in order to perform well themselves, conflicts often occur.

■ *Competing objectives.* When objectives are poorly set or reward systems poorly designed, individuals and groups may come into conflict as they work to one another's direct disadvantage.

■ *Structural differentiation.* Differences in organization structures and in the characteristics of people staffing them may foster conflict due to incompatible approaches toward work.

■ *Unresolved prior conflicts.* Unless a conflict is fully resolved, it may remain latent in the situation as a lingering basis for future conflicts over the same or related matters.

With these antecedent conditions present in most work situations, an informed manager expects conflicts to occur. When they do, Figure 17.11 shows that manifest conflicts can then be either *resolved*—in the sense that the sources are corrected—or *suppressed*—where the sources remain but the conflict behaviors are controlled. Naturally, the aftermath varies in each case. Conflicts that are suppressed tend to fester and reoccur again at some later point in time. They can also contribute to other conflicts over the same or related issues. True conflict resolution reduces the potential for future conflicts of a similar nature. It is an important goal in approaching conflict management.

CONFLICT MANAGEMENT

Managers can be principal parties to conflicts, that is, as persons actively involved in the conflict situation. They may also be called on to act as mediators in the conflicts of others. In each case the manager must be a *skilled* participant in conflict dynamics. Ideally, these skills will help achieve **conflict resolution** through the elimination of underlying causes for a conflict and removal of any lingering conditions which might rekindle the conflict again sometime in the future. Although perfect conflict resolution is not always possible, managers can frequently take action to direct conflict toward constructive rather than destructive results. These actions include both structural approaches and interpersonal styles.

Structural Approaches to Conflict Management

Managers can do several things to try and restructure situations in order to resolve conflicts. There are times when an *appeal to superordinate goals* can focus the attention of conflicting parties on one mutually desirable end state. This offers all parties a common frame of reference against which to analyze differences and reconcile disagreements. Conflicts whose antecedents lie in competition for scarce resources can also be resolved by *expanding*

FIGURE 17.11 *Antecedent conditions and the stages of conflict in organizations.*

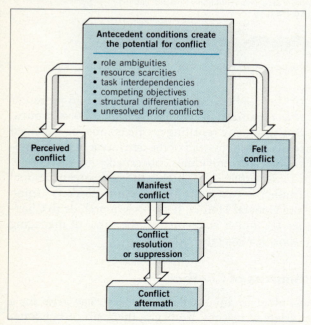

the resources available to everyone. Although costly, this technique removes the reasons for the continuing conflict. By *altering one or more human variables* in a situation—that is, by replacing or transferring one or more of the conflicting parties—conflicts caused by poor interpersonal relationships can be eliminated. The same holds true if a manager can *alter the physical environment,* such as by rearranging facilities, workspace, and workflows to create a setting that decreases opportunities for conflict.

The *use of integrating devices* or coordinating mechanisms introduced in Chapter 7 is another useful approach in many settings. In particular, the use of liaison personnel, special task forces and cross-functional teams, and even the matrix form of organization, can change interaction patterns and assist in conflict management. Finally, *changes in reward systems* may be necessary to reduce the competition among individuals and groups for rewards. Creating reward systems that respond positively to cooperation rather than competition can encourage behaviors and attitudes that keep conflict within more constructive limits.

Interpersonal Styles of Conflict Management

People respond to conflict in different ways. Someone's interpersonal style in conflict situations can be described in terms of relative emphasis on cooperativeness and assertiveness.[27]

Cooperativeness is the desire to satisfy the other party's needs and concerns.

Assertiveness is the desire to satisfy one's own needs and concerns.

Figure 17.12 shows five interpersonal styles of conflict management that result from various combinations of cooperativeness and assertiveness. Briefly stated, these styles involve the following interpersonal behaviors.[28]

Avoidance Being uncooperative and unassertive; downplaying disagreement, withdrawing from the situation, and/or staying neutral at all costs.

Accommodation or smoothing Being cooperative but unassertive; letting the other's wishes rule; smoothing over differences to maintain superficial harmony.

Competition or authoritative command Being uncooperative but assertive; working against the wishes of the other party, fighting to dominate in win–lose competition, and/or forcing things to conclusion through the exercise of authority.

Compromise Being moderately cooperative and assertive, but not to either extreme; working toward partial satisfaction of everyone's concerns; bargaining or negotiating for "acceptable" solutions where each party wins a bit and loses a bit.

Collaboration or problem solving Being both cooperative and assertive; seeking true satisfaction of everyone's concerns by working through differences; finding and solving problems so everyone gains.

The various interpersonal styles of conflict management vary in the outcomes they are likely to produce. In particular, they can be classified as lose–lose, win–lose, and win–win methods.[29]

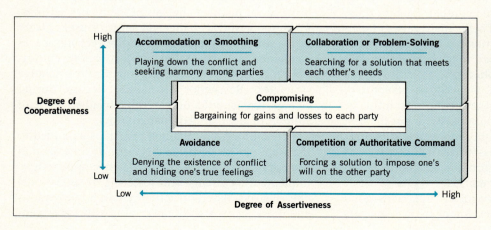

FIGURE 17.12
Interpersonal styles of conflict management: lose–lose, win–lose, and win–win methods.

Lose–Lose Methods

Lose–lose conflict occurs when no one achieves his or her true desires, and the underlying reasons for conflict remain unaffected. Although a lose–lose conflict may appear settled or even seem to disappear for a while, it has a tendency to reoccur in the future. This is common when conflict is managed by avoidance and accommodation or smoothing.

Avoidance is an extreme form of nonattention. Everyone pretends that conflict doesn't really exist and hopes that it will simply go away. *Accommodation or smoothing* plays down differences among the conflicting parties and highlights similarities and areas of agreement. Peaceful coexistence through a recognition of common interests is the goal. Such efforts at smoothing, as suggested by "we run a happy ship here" and "nice people don't fight," may ignore the real essence of a given conflict.

Win–Lose Methods

In **win–lose conflicts** the parties gain at one another's expense. In the extreme cases, one party achieves its desires to the complete exclusion of the other party's desires. Because win–lose methods fail to address the root causes of conflict, future conflicts of the same or similar nature are likely. Competition or authoritative command and compromise are win–lose methods of conflict management.

In *competition* one party wins as superior skill or outright domination allows his or her desires to be forced on the other. In *authoritative command* the forcing is accomplished by a supervisor who simply dictates a solution to subordinates. When the authority figure is an active party to the conflict, it is easy to predict who will be the winner and the loser. *Compromise* occurs when trade-offs are made such that each party to the conflict gives up and gains something of value. As a result, neither party is completely satisfied, and the antecedent conditions for future conflicts are established.

Win–Win Methods

Win–win conflict is resolved to the mutual benefit of all conflicting parties. This is typically achieved by confrontation of the issues and the willingness of conflicting parties to recognize that something is wrong and needs attention.

Collaboration or problem-solving, which tries to reconcile underlying differences, is often the most effective interpersonal style of conflict management. It establishes win–win conditions by eliminating the underlying causes of the conflict. All relevant issues are raised and openly discussed. Win–win methods are clearly the most preferred of the interpersonal styles of conflict management. In actual practice, the ultimate test may be whether or not the conflict participants are willing to say two things to each other.

1. "It is our collective responsibility to be open and honest about facts, opinions, and feelings."
2. "I want a solution that achieves your goals and my goals and is acceptable to both of us."

Summary

This chapter approached the challenges of managing innovation, change, and conflict. Each of these processes is an opportunity for managers to facilitate organizational adaptation to changing environmental circumstances over time. Innovation, defined as "invention + application," is critical in the latter regard. Organizations must be structured, staffed, and managed to attain a continued influx or new ideas and maintain the capacity to put the best of these into practice. Highly innovative organizations share a number of essential characteristics as they pursue innovation through creativity, entrepreneurship, and intrapreneurship.

A good manager recognizes and takes good advantage of opportunities for change. Managers have the responsibility to act as change agents who bring about planned changes in their work settings. To be successful at change, managers must be aware of the unfreezing, changing, and refreezing phases of change, as well as the force–coercion, empirical–rational, and normative–reeducative change strategies. Resistance frequently occurs during change and should be carefully handled to lend support to any planned-change effort.

The process of planned change is extended to the total system level in the form of organization development (OD), a comprehensive approach to implementing change and fostering organizational effectiveness. Based on action research foundations and drawing on a wide range of possible interventions, OD is a relatively new and promising application of behavioral science principles to management practice. Its basic goal is to help organizations keep pace with their environment and achieve productivity while maintaining high-quality work lives for their members.

All innovation and change brings the prospect of conflict. In organizations, conflicts can be constructive or destructive. To manage conflict successfully, a manager must be able to understand conflict situations for the substantive and/or emotional differences they represent. Then the reasons for these differences can be identified and appropriate actions taken. People attend to conflict in different ways, including avoidance, smoothing, competition, compromise, and problem solving. Only the problem-solving approach leads to true conflict resolution.

Thinking Through the Issues

1. What is "innovation"? Why are individual creativity and organizational innovation necessary ingredients of organizational productivity in the contemporary environment?

2. Explain the difference between "entrepreneurship" and "intrapreneurship." What are some of the things managers are doing to establish intrapreneurial capabilities within their organizations?

3. What are the four major steps in organizational innovation? Explain how each step might be engaged in the process of developing (1) a new product or service, and (2) a new work technology.

4. What are Lewin's three phases in the planned-change process? Give examples of what managers can do to accomplish each stage successfully.

5. Define the three basic change strategies and give examples of how a manager might use them in practice. Identify four major sources of resistance to change, and describe what managers can do about them.

6. What is "organization development" (OD)? How does action research work as a foundation element of OD?

7. List and give examples of two OD interventions that address problems at each of the following levels of action: (1) individual, (2) group, (3) organization as a whole.

8. What is the difference between constructive and destructive conflict? Give an example of each from an organizational situation with which you are familiar.

9. Name five possible sources of conflict in organizations. Give examples of each.

10. Identify five interpersonal styles of conflict management. Which one(s) are most prone to result in conflict resolution? Why?

The Manager's Vocabulary

Accommodation
Action research
Authoritative
   command
Avoidance
Change agent
Collaboration
Competition
Compromise
Conflict
Conflict resolution

Constructive conflict
Creativity
Destructive conflict
Emotional conflict
Empirical-rational
   change strategy
Entrepreneur
Entrepreneurship
Force-coercion change
   strategy
Innovation

Intrapreneurship
Lose-lose conflict
Normative-
   reeducative change
   strategy
OD interventions
Organization
   development (OD)
Organizational change
Performance gap

Planned change
Problem solving
Process innovation
Product innovation
Shared power strategy
Smoothing
Substantive conflict
Unplanned change
Win-lose conflict
Win-win conflict

R&D AT SMITH, KLINE & FRENCH LABORATORIES

Smithkline Beckman's new CEO, Henry Wendt, faced a problem.[31] His $4 billion company was falling behind its major competitors in the area of new product development. To survive and prosper in the future, the firm needed to get back on track as one capable of producing a steady stream of wonder drugs. The key, he felt, was in the R&D division of Smith, Kline & French (SKF) Laboratories. It needed a major restructuring to create an organization of world-class scientists who could develop the drugs of tomorrow. Wendt made clear his commitment to make things right again. He also hired a new vice-president for human resources, Thomas Kaney, to help recruit new scientists and support personnel and reshape R&D's culture.

Kaney began with an emphasis on the culture.

The scientists who Kaney felt are independent by nature, needed to be molded together in an environment that allowed them to be creative but also encouraged productivity. His goal was not to change them, but to create broad organizational boundaries under which they could do their science to the firm's best advantage. It was a tricky task since, as Kaney said: "Like it or not, scientists are dedicated to their professional discipline first and only secondarily to their employer. They come to work to optimize their science."

But before he arrived, R&D wasn't giving them much of a chance to do that. If a scientist wanted to work on a Friday night or weekend, they couldn't get access to the locked laboratories. One of the first things Kaney did was to remove such obstacles and set a new operating tone. Along with his human resources staff, he went further to encourage the use of task forces and teams on many projects. The best talent was assigned to projects, regardless of where they were located in the company and in its world-wide operations. A consultant was also hired to help build cohesion among R&D employees. Her goal was to help them recognize that for projects to succeed "requires people to have a knowledge of other people—what they can bring to the group and how they can use one another."

Team-building is now used to help R&D employees work together. A task-oriented approach is used that encourages people to form networks that can help people get work done even if they don't see one another face-to-face that often. Quality circles and problem-solving groups are also being used now. According to Kaney, management is saying: "Department heads, we are willing to act as your counsel and help shape these ideas: here's the broad directions, but how it pans out and how it operates in your own area is really up to you."

This change in direction for R&D caused some anxiety among laboratory employees. Many were apprehensive and confused about how fast the changes were moving. Some left the company, while others complained that it all wouldn't work. Those who've stayed, however, see signs of improvement already. Compared to five years past, the number of major projects in place has risen from five to 30. A new asthma drug is in the final stages of development.

Questions

1. Apply the model of the innovation process introduced in this chapter to the situation at SKF laboratories. In what ways do the reported changes respond to the requirements of this model? What else should Wendt and Kaney be concerned about, if anything, to ensure that the innovation process is well supported at SKF?

2. Take the position of an R&D scientist who worked for SKF labs long before Wendt and Kaney arrived on the scene. Why might the scientist "resist" some or all of the reported changes? What could Kaney do to respond to this resistance in a positive way?

3. Is Kane an effective change agent? Why or why not? Is Kane doing organization development (OD)? Why or why not?

4. What should Kane do next to ensure that the progress made to date at SKF becomes a permanent foundation for future success? Explain your answer.

Class Exercise: Managing a Conflict Situation

1. Think about this situation. You are the supervisor of a work unit in a manufacturing plant. Top management has just announced a change of policy that will allow workers to engage in job rotation and more teamwork, if they so desire. You are very pleased with this opportunity. Upon bringing the matter up in a weekly staff meeting, however, it appears that two of the six employees you supervise are *not* in favor of changing to this type of system. The four others seem to be favorably inclined toward the idea.

2. Listed here are several things you might do to manage this conflict situation.

_____ Simply tell all three subordinates that job rotation will begin immediately.

_____ Convince all three that their good feelings toward one another are more important than any job design; get them to agree to rotate jobs or not, depending on what will maintain harmony in the group.

_____ Work out an arrangement where job rotation occurs for a while, is stopped for a while, and so on; this allows each person to have his or her way part of the time.

_____ Drop the idea about making any job design changes; forget you ever raised the possibility in the first place.

3. Rank order these alternative responses with "1" assigned to the one you most prefer, and "4" assigned to the one you least prefer.

4. Review the alternatives once again. Would you prefer to do something else? If so, make notes describing your alternative course of action. Indicate where in the preference ranking you would place this new approach to the situation.

5. Share your responses with a nearby classmate. Discuss how your preferences may differ and why. Also discuss any new alternatives either of you suggested to deal with the situation. Await further class discussion led by your instructor.

References

[1] John Naisbitt, *Megatrends* (New York: Warner, 1982); Rosabeth Moss Kanter, *The Change Masters* (New York: Simon & Schuster, 1984); John Naisbitt and Patricia Aburdene, *Re-Inventing the Corporation* (New York: Warner, 1985); Tom Peters, *Thriving on Chaos* (New York: Random House, 1987); and, Robert H. Waterman, Jr., *The Renewal Factor* (New York: Simon & Schuster, 1988).

[2] George Melloan, "Herman Miller's Secrets of Creativity," *The Wall Street Journal* (May 3, 1988), p. 23.

[3] Cited in Peter F. Drucker, *Management: Tasks, Responsibilities and Practices* (New York: Harper and Row, 1973), p. 797.

[4] This discussion is based on the thorough review of the concept of innovation provided by Edward B. Roberts, "Managing Invention and Innovation," *Research Technology Management* (January–February 1988), pp. 1–19.

[5] These examples are reported in Robert A. Burgelman, "Designs for Corporate Entrepreneurship in Established Firms," *California Management Review,* Vol XXVI (Spring 1984), pp. 154–166.

[6] Howard H. Stevenson and David E. Gumpert, "The Heart of Entrepreneurship," *Harvard Business Review,* Vol. 64 (March–April 1985), pp. 85–94; and Peter F. Drucker, *Innovation and Entrepreneurship* (New York: Harper & Row, 1985).

[7] Gifford Pinchot III, *Intrapreneuring, Or Why You Don't Have to Leave the Corporation to Become an Entrepreneur* (New York: Harper & Row, 1985).

[8] See Bro Uttal, "Speeding New Ideas to Market," *Fortune* (March 2, 1987), pp. 62–66.

[9] Information from Rosabeth Moss Kanter, "The Attack on Pay," *Harvard Business Review,* Vol. 65 (March–April 1987), pp. 60–67. Kenneth Labich, "The Innovators," *Fortune* (June 6, 1988), pp. 49–64.

[10] This model of the innovation process is adapted from Roberts, op. cit.

[11] Information on "Post-It" notes and the 3M corporation is reported in Tom Peters and Nancy Austin, *A Passion for Excellence* (New York: Random House, 1985); and, Keeping the Fires Lit Under the Innovators," *Fortune* (March 28, 1988), p. 45.

[12] This discussion is stimulated by James Brian Quinn, "Managing Innovation: Controlled Chaos," *Harvard Business Review,* Vol. 63 (May–June 1985). Selected quotes and examples from Labich, op. cit., 1988.

[13] Peter F. Drucker, "Best R&D is Business Driven," *The Wall Street Journal* (February 10, 1988), p. 11.

[14] See Roberts, op. cit., 1988.

[15] Quoted in Melloan, op. cit., 1988.

[16] Developed in part from Quinn, op. cit., 1984.

[17] Reported in G. Christian Hill and Mike Tharp, "Big Quarterly Deficit Stuns BankAmerica, Adds Pressure on Chief, the *Wall Street Journal* (July 18, 1985), pp. 1, 12.

[18] The classic description of organizations on these terms is by Harold J. Leavitt, "Applied Organizational Change in Industry: Structural, Technological and Humanistic Approaches," pp. 1144–1170 in James G. March (ed.), *Handbook of Organizations* (Chicago: Rand McNally, 1965). Another timely approach is described by Ralph H. Kilmann in *Beyond the Quick Fix* (San Francisco: Jossey-Bass, 1984).

[19] Kurt Lewin, "Group Decision and Social Change," in G. E. Swanson, T. M. Newcomb, and E. L. Hartley (eds.), *Readings in Social Psychology* (New York: Holt, Rinehart, 1952), pp. 459–473.

[20] This discussion is based on Robert Chin and Kenneth D. Benne, "General Strategies for Effecting Changes in Human Systems," in Warren G. Bennis, Kenneth D. Benne, Robert Chin, and Kenneth E. Corey (eds.), *The Planning of Change,* Third Edition (New York: Holt, Rinehart, 1969), pp. 22–45; and, Patrick E. Connor, "Strategies for Managing Technological Change," *Harvard International Review,* Vol. X (1988), pp. 10–13.

[21] John P. Kotter and Leonard A. Schlesinger, "Choosing Strategies for Change," *Harvard Business Review,* Vol. 57 (March–April 1979), pp. 109–112.

[22] Two good overviews of organization development are provided by Wendell L. French and Cecil H. Bell, Jr., *Organization Development,* Third Edition (Englewood Cliffs, NJ: Prentice-Hall, 1984); and, W. Warner Burke, *Organization Development: A Normative View* (Reading, MA: Addison-Wesley, 1987).

[23] Developed from Edgar F. Huse, *Organization Development and Change,* Second Edition (St. Paul: West Publishing, 1980), pp. 30–31.

[24] This case is reported in French and Bell, op. cit. pp. 8–11.

[25] Richard E. Walton, *Interpersonal Peacemaking: Confrontations and Third-Party Consultation* (Reading, Mass.: Addison-Wesley, 1969), p. 2.

[26] Andrew S. Grove, "How to Make Confrontation Work for You," *Fortune* (July 23, 1984), p. 73.

[27] See Kenneth W. Thomas, "Conflict and Conflict Management," in M.D. Dunnett (ed.), *Handbook of Industrial and Organizational Behavior* (Chicago: Rand McNally, 1976), pp. 889–935.

[28] See Robert R. Blake and Jane Strygley Mouton, "The

Fifth Achievement," *Journal of Applied Behavioral Science,* Vol. 6 (1970), pp. 413–427; and, Alan C. Filley, *Interpersonal Conflict Resolution* (Glenview, IL: Scott, Foresman, 1975).

[29]This discussion is based on Filley, op. cit.; and, Vincent L. Ferraro and Sheila A. Adams, "Interdepartmental Conflict: Practical Ways to Prevent and Reduce It," *Personnel,* Vol. 61 (1984), pp. 12–23.

[30]The *Wall Street Journal* (March 10, 1982), p. 21.

[31]Information from Barbara Jean Gray, "The Missing Ingredient at SKF," *Human Resource Executive* (March 1988), pp. 32–34.

Managing Labor–Management Relations

A New
Spirit of Cooperation

Labor and management may never see eye to eye on certain issues, but an undeniable spirit of cooperation between the two is developing in some industries. Making a virtue out of necessity—that is, the urgent need to battle imports—unions and management in the automobile and steel industries, among others, are adopting a teamwork approach to the productivity and quality problems that have plagued their plants in recent years. New union contracts in the auto industry are calling for the establishment of labor–management committees in each plant to study ways of improving quality, and guarantees of worker flexibility are being made in exchange for promises of job security.

For years unions fought to preserve jobs at any cost—even obsolete ones. Now, however, the rank-and-file are recognizing that competitive pressures threaten entire plants, and new, more cooperative ways of working are a must. At GM's Buick Reatta plant in Lansing, for example, workers on teams rotate jobs and acquire new skills, and managers work on the factory floor once a month to keep in touch with how the plant actually operates. Each team has a set of tasks to do, and team members divide the work as they see fit. One team leader, praising the system, stated that "this way we have some control over our eight hours. . . . Now we have a say in what we do." Fewer workers are needed to produce a given volume of cars with this approach; however, no jobs are eliminated because of productivity increases, and workers are urged to move around the plant and learn new skills through retraining.

Giving workers more say in how operations are managed is a new trend at Xerox's Rochester facility, where employees order materials, help select their equipment, and schedule their own time. One vice-president of the Amalgamated Clothing and Textile Workers Union, which represents labor at Xerox, said that the same number of workers employed at the plant in the past are "making a lot more machines these days"—and stemming the tide of Japanese photocopier imports. Xerox and other high-tech companies, aware that constant technological advances demand more worker involvement and know-how, are finding that teamwork is the answer. And labor and management experts alike agree that the results, in terms of quality, productivity, and worker morale, are often heartening.

The line between labor and management is shifting, albeit slowly, and some argue that it should be softened further. A changing competitive environment has caused inevitable alterations in the labor–management relationship; and increasingly, both sides see cooperation as the only way to go. In front of GM's Reatta plant in Lansing, the UAW flag flies alongside the corporation's—tangible proof of a new partnership in the making. ■

Source: Information from John Holusha, "A New Spirit at U.S. Auto Plants," *New York Times* (December 29, 1987), pp. D-1, D-5; and, "GM's New 'Teams' aren't Hitting any Homers," *Business Week* (August 8, 1988), pp. 46–47.

A unionized workforce can place special demands on the manager. Increased familiarity with the following topics will help you be more informed about managing labor–management relations.

Labor Unions in Society
Unions as Organizations
The Legal Environment of
    Labor–Management
    Relations
How Organizations
    Become Unionized
Collective Bargaining
Managerial Implications of
    Collective Bargaining
Improving
    Labor–Management
    Relations

Here are the key terms. A **labor union** is an organization to which workers belong and which collectively deals with employers on their behalf. Examples of labor unions frequently in the news are the United Auto Workers (UAW), United Mine Workers (UMW), and the Teamsters. **Labor–management relations** is the ongoing relationship between a group of employees represented by a union and management in the employing organization. The foundation for any labor–management relationship is **collective bargaining**—that is, the process of negotiating, administering, and interpreting a formal agreement or labor contract between a union and the employing organization. **Labor contracts** specify the rights and obligations of employees and management in respect to wages, work hours, work rules, and other conditions of employment. They constitute a major influence on the management process and the managers who implement it in unionized work settings.

Here's what a sampling of headlines from *The Wall Street Journal* suggests the real-world implications of these terms sometimes come to mean.

BROWN & SHARPE WALKOUT GROWS VIOLENT

FIGHTING OFF UNIONS, INGERSOLL-RAND USES A WIDE RANGE OF TACTICS

RAILROADS CONFRONT UNIONS ON CREW SIZE.

But be careful, there is more to labor–management relations today than what is depicted in the prior headlines. For one thing, a new form of assertiveness is appearing on the union side. Did you know that in the U.S. airline industry alone, for example:

- Unions were accused in a lawsuit by Eastern Airlines of trying to drive down the company's market value so that they could buy the stock more cheaply in a take-over bid?

- Unions have found several investors for ailing Pan Am, and have agreed to make special concessions to the new owner?

And yet the story continues . . . there's still more to the complex nature of today's labor–management relations than even this new-form of union assertiveness indicates. *Newsline 18.1* serves as a reminder that old strategies aren't completely fulfilling union's needs anymore. As introduced in the Chapter opener, "cooperation" and "involvement" are also emerging as the passwords to mutual gain in many progressive unions and employment settings. Consider this added example.[1]

At AT&T positive efforts by management and leadership in the Communications Workers of America has resulted in greater cooperation for the common good. The company now runs "common interest forums" in which union and management representatives periodically pour over financial figures normally reserved for the board of directors. They use them as a basis for discussing ways to improve operations, products, and services. When

LABOR'S
ULTIMATE WEAPON IS ON THE WANE

At one time in American labor history, strikes were a union's surefire weapon against an unbudging management. But some labor analysts argue that the strike has outlived its historical utility and needs to be replaced by other tactics that can meet workers' needs for job security and satisfaction.

Two key factors that have significantly altered the ways in which organized labor responds to management are automation and anti-unionism. Both weigh against walkouts. Strikes have not deterred many industries from automating their operations—and strikers risk provoking the hostility of nonunion employees as well as management. Moreover, in some instances unions are wary of further weakening employers already beleaguered by foreign competition, such as clothing manufacturers, by staging walkouts.

And cooperation between unions, once a given, is not as easily forged today.

A few alternatives to strikes have emerged, one of which is the corporate campaign. With this tactic unions apply pressure via the company's lenders or outside directors, or try to embarrass the company publicly. Some labor consultants suggest that a corporate campaign is best waged during collective bargaining. Another tactic sometimes used to varying effect is the "work-to-rule" approach, in which workers disrupt production by not doing tasks that aren't specifically set forth in their contract—for example, "forgetting" to bring their tools to work. Yet such strategies, along with more sophisticated bargaining techniques, haven't consistently given unions what they want.

In light of changing labor and economic conditions, strikers cannot avoid the high risk of unemployment, contend experts who see the strike as outmoded. For many union members, however, a strike is the only way to go, despite its risks. And strikes still sometimes achieve their objectives—as did a recent nine-day walkout of workers at NYNEX Corporation, a major telecommunications firm. The workers forced NYNEX to ease up on its demand that they pay more of their medical expenses. "Old-fashioned unionism still works," said Jan Pierce, a vice-president of the communications workers' union.

Source: As reported in Alex Kotlowitz, "Labor's Ultimate Weapon, the Strike, Is Mostly Failing," *Wall Street Journal* (October 13, 1986), p. 5.

---

the company ran into trouble with its retail operations, for example, they consulted with the unions instead of just closing the unprofitable stores. What resulted was an experiment in which some sales clerks agreed to be paid on commission rather than straight union wages. It worked, and nine endangered stores were kept in business.

Thus, as we begin this study of labor–management relations, let's recognize that there are many complex and dynamic issues involved.

Unions are important forces in the contemporary work environment. And whereas they used to be primarily associated with industrial and business occupations, they are now increasingly found representing public sector employees such as teachers, police officers, and government workers. Any manager in any organization—small or large and public or private—must be prepared to deal successfully with them. This chapter is designed to increase your understanding of unions and the challenges they add to the management process. We'll begin by examining labor unions in general and their changing roles in modern society.

LABOR UNIONS IN SOCIETY

Labor unions have a strong base in American society.[2] But over the years the nature of the labor movement and its membership has changed. It is likely to continue to do so in the future. In order to better understand the present directions, it is helpful to review some historical trends and developments.

Evolution of the American Labor Movement

The first unions were established in the United States around 1800, but there was little activity until the Knights of Labor began in 1869 as an attempt to establish a national labor union. From then until the early 1920s, the labor movement remained quite small. Its appeal was limited, in part, by a number of social, economic, and political forces. These included a steady flow of new immigrants into American industry, ready opportunities for employment, employer resistance to unions, and a court system that tended to restrain union activities.

Beginning with the great depression in the late 1920s, however, unions became popular. Economic hardship and loss of jobs created worker discontent, and tarnished the image of "big" business as an employer. Changes in the legal environment also benefited the union movement. Congress passed laws in the 1930s which protected the rights of workers to join unions and engage in strikes. They also required employers to bargain in good faith with certified unions and to refrain from discriminating against union workers.

Figure 18.1 shows that union membership as a percent of the U.S. *private sector* nonfarm workforce peaked in the early 1950s. Since then the trend has been down. Today less than 15 percent of nonfarm workers are unionized.[3] The unions who represent them are searching for both new members and new identities in the new world of work. Some of the reasons most often cited for this decline in traditional union membership include such external environmental forces as:[4]

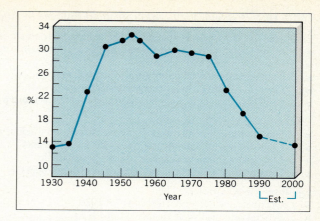

FIGURE 18.1 *Trends in union membership as a percent of the U.S. nonfarm workforce.*

Source: Information from Leo Troy and Neil Shevin, *Union Sourcebook* (West Orange, NJ: Irdis, 1985); and *Business Week* (May 16, 1988), p. 30.

■ *Economic trends.* Globalization of markets and foreign competition have led to structural changes in the U.S. economy. Labor-intensive industries like heavy manufacturing which were traditionally unionized have declined, while new service and knowledge-intensive industries more resistant to unionization have advanced.

■ *Political trends.* Shifting political currents have resulted in trends toward the deregulation of many industries, including transportation and communications. Unions have generally lost ground under deregulation through cost-cutting layoffs, and plant closings by unionized employers, and the emergence of nonunion employers.

■ *Advances in technology* The emergence of high technology on the shop floor and in offices has resulted in further changes in the workplace. Robots, new forms of factory autonomation, and desktop computing have reduced the demand for labor in many settings. Along with this, they have reduced the size of the workforce traditionally composed of potential union members.

■ *Trends in the legal system.* The growing legal protections for workers in general has reduced one of the major original appeals to union membership—protection of individual rights in the workplace. Table 18.1 highlights legislation of this nature that is already in place. It also identifies some of the items now before the courts and having the potential to extend the protections even more.

■ *Changing composition of the workforce.* As work-

TABLE 18.1 *Examples of Legal Protections Enjoyed by American Workers*

Employee rights are being expanded at the federal, state and local level by:
- Right-to-know laws requiring companies to provide information on workplace hazards
- Laws protecting whistleblowers
- Court decisions weakening employment-at-will doctrine
- Laws prohibiting a mandatory retirement age
- Laws requiring notice of plant shutdowns and severance pay for workers

Employee privacy is protected by:
- Laws limiting personal data that government can disclose to employers
- Laws limiting use of polygraph tests for job applicants
- Laws giving employees access to their personal files
- Laws restricting use of arrest records in hiring process

Employee safety is protected by:
- Occupational Safety & Health Act of 1970
- Federal Mine Safety & Health Act of 1977

Employee freedom from discrimination in hiring, promotion, and discharge is protected by:
- Civil Rights Act of 1964
- Age Discrimination in Employment Act of 1967 and 1978 amendment
- Some state and local laws which add protection for marital status and sexual preference

force demography has changed over the years, the pool of traditionally pro-union members has grown smaller. Women and younger workers have historically been less inclined to belong to unions, as have professional and white-collar workers. As these groups have increased in importance in the labor force, the proportion of workers holding union membership has declined.

The Changing Role of Unions

Although new environmental trends have certainly created problems for unions, the situation has been further complicated in some cases by management difficulties within the unions themselves. Some union leaders have been slow reacting to environmental changes and too persistent in clinging to traditional ways.

A historical anchor point for union roles in society rests still with the legacy of Samuel Gompers. He served as president of the American Federation of Labor (AFL) for all but one year during 1886–1924. Under his leadership, the AFL successfully organized many separate labor organizations by applying a set of principles that established guiding philosophy for the U.S. labor movement. In Gompers's words,[5]

> The ground-work principle of America's labor movement has been to recognize that first things must come

first. The primary essential in our mission has been the protection of the wage-workers, now; to increase wages; to cut hours off the long workday; . . . to improve the safety and the sanitary conditions of the workshop; to free workers from the tyrannies, petty or otherwise, which served to make their existence a slavery. These . . . are the primary objectives of trade unionism.

These traditions are now being threatened by trends such as those pointed out earlier. In response, some labor leaders are redefining the roles of unions. They are making progress in organizing *public sector* workers. In the past 20 years, the percent of union membership in this sector has risen from 11 to about 33 percent.[6] They are also asserting themselves to ensure employment security for their members. When Chrysler announced plans to close its Kenosha, Wisconsin, assembly plant, for example, the UAW launched a massive protest that included threats to withdraw from participation in a broad variety of cooperative programs with the company.[7] Chrysler listened, and kept the plant open.

In return for concessions in an increasing number of labor contracts, more and more union members are becoming stockholders. With stock ownership comes a greater responsibility for performance results and a direct voice in management. Unions are now represented on a growing number of corporate boards, including General Motors and the Chrysler Corporation, and they enjoy increasing leverage gained from shared power roles in the management of firms. But the willingness of unions to get directly involved in this way has taken on a new and often aggressive character. As the president of the United Steelworkers says, "We're not going to sit around and allow management to louse things up like they have in the past."[8]

The new wave of union activity involves taking a step beyond representing workers at the bargaining table and into helping to establish them as legitimate organizational "stakeholders." The traditional role of protecting workers by contracting for wages and other conditions of work, and then monitoring these contracts to ensure compliance, is still important. But it appears no longer sufficient to guarantee success. By asserting themselves as representatives of employee interests, as "stakeholders" and not just "workers" in organizations, progressive unions are trying to establish new directions in labor–management relations.

UNIONS AS ORGANIZATIONS

Unions are organizations that, in their own ways, are often as complex as those employing their members. It is helpful to recognize the different types of unions, the structural characteristics of most unions, and some of their managerial dilemmas.

Types of Unions

Craft unions represent workers in skilled trades or occupations—for example, carpenters, plumbers, and electricians. They are concerned with protecting their members' jobs from the competition of other crafts and less skilled workers. Agreements among craft unions establish fairly well-defined **jurisdictions** or task domains within which each craft union retains autonomy to organize and represent workers. Craft unions agree not to organize workers outside their respective jurisdictions and try to negotiate agreements with employers requiring that only members of a particular craft union be assigned to particular types of jobs. **Industrial unions** typically serve a single indusry and represent both skilled and less skilled workers in a wide variety of occupations. Although industrial unions often

organize in many different areas, most limit their organizing activities to a few primary industrial jurisdictions. The UAW, for example, primarily represents employees in the automobile-manufacturing and aerospace industries, while the UMW's primary jurisdiction is coal mining. In terms of total membership, industrial unions currently dominate the U.S. labor movement.

Some unions are organized in a variety of unrelated industries. They are referred to as **general unions** because they lack a specific craft or industry focus. Perhaps the best example is the Teamsters. It is the largetst union in the United States and represents workers in a wide variety of industries and occupations. General unions are likely to gain in strength in the future as weaker unions with overlapping jurisdictions merge and others with dwindling memberships are absorbed by stronger ones.

National and International Unions

The basic organizational unit of the U.S. labor movement is the national or international union. **National unions** have members throughout the United States; **international unions** also have members outside the United States. There are now about 170 national or international unions and about 35 professional and state employee associations active in the United States.

The building block of virtually all national and international unions is the **local,** an administrative unit that services at the local level a particular group of workers represented by the union. There are about 65,000 locals in the United States, most of which are quite small with an average membership of 200.

The affairs of the local union are normally managed by elected officers or, in some cases, full-time business agents. Locals serve as the "voices" or representatives of members in relationships with employers. Their duties typically include negotiating new contracts, administering existing contracts, and handling contract disputes. As shown in Figure 18.2, the president and other officers of locals are normally assisted by **union stewards,** employees who are union officials and who represent fellow workers in resolving disputes with management. The union steward is a person with whom managers frequently interact as part of day-to-day practice in a unionized work setting.

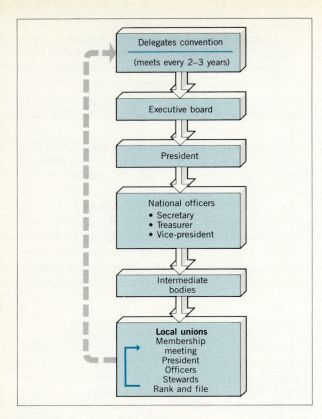

```
        ┌─────────────────────────────┐
    ┌─→ │     Delegates convention    │
    ╎   │   (meets every 2–3 years)   │
    ╎   └─────────────────────────────┘
    ╎                 │
    ╎   ┌─────────────────────────────┐
    ╎   │       Executive board       │
    ╎   └─────────────────────────────┘
    ╎                 │
    ╎   ┌─────────────────────────────┐
    ╎   │          President          │
    ╎   └─────────────────────────────┘
    ╎                 │
    ╎   ┌─────────────────────────────┐
    ╎   │      National officers      │
    ╎   │        • Secretary          │
    ╎   │        • Treasurer          │
    ╎   │        • Vice-president      │
    ╎   └─────────────────────────────┘
    ╎                 │
    ╎   ┌─────────────────────────────┐
    ╎   │        Intermediate         │
    ╎   │          bodies             │
    ╎   └─────────────────────────────┘
    ╎                 │
    ╎   ┌─────────────────────────────┐
    ╎   │        Local unions         │
    ╎   │        Membership           │
    ╎   │          meeting            │
    ╎   │        President            │
    ╎   │        Officers             │
    ╎   │        Stewards             │
    └───│        Rank and file        │
        └─────────────────────────────┘
```

FIGURE 18.2 *Structural features in the organization of a national or international union.*

The next level of authority above the local union is the intermediate body, which coordinates and facilitates the activities of locals. At the upper level of the union organizational structure are the national or international president, officers, and executive council. They are normally accountable to the delegate's convention, at which rank-and-file members are generally represented by delegates chosen by the locals. This convention is a counterpart to the stockholders' meeting for a corporation; the executive board of the union is similar to a corporation's board of directors.

The AFL-CIO

The AFL-CIO, American Federation of Labor—Congress of Industrial Organizations, is not a trade union itself. It is a voluntary association that provides services to its affiliated but independent unions. With an affiliated membership of about 102 unions covering approximately 70 percent of unionized American workers, the AFL-CIO is a dominant force in the American labor movement. Its actions are far-reaching in scope and impact.

Among other things, the AFL-CIO is active in the political arena. Its Committee on Political Education works to elect pro-labor candidates to political office, while its Legislative Department is primarily involved in lobbying activities. Other departments and committees of the AFL-CIO assist affiliate unions in organizing campaigns for new members, preparing for contract negotiations, resolving disputes with other unions, and coordinating with other unions having similar interests.

Unions affiliated with the AFL-CIO retain autonomy in negotiating contracts and administering their internal affairs. While the federation may make recommendations, individual unions are free to conduct their own affairs. However, affiliated unions that engage in activities the AFL-CIO considers contrary to the interests of organized labor can be suspended or expelled from the federation. The Teamsters union was expelled from the AFL-CIO in 1957 for corrupt activities. It was readmitted in 1987. The latter move was generally interpreted as a potential strengthening of organized labor's united front.[9] As *Newsline 18.2* points out, it is also related to the Teamsters' struggle to come to terms with the present-day environment.

Management Problems in Unions

Two management problems relating to the administration of national and local unions have plagued the U.S. labor movement over the years. First, some unions—the Teamsters for one—have allegedly been influenced by organized crime. Some labor "racketeers" have extorted money from employers in return for special labor contracts, and from members in return for work opportunities. Other corrupt union officials have also embezzled and misused union funds. Former Teamster's Presidents Dave Beck, Jimmy Hoffa, and Roy Williams all went to jail; Williams' successor, Jackie Presser, died while under indictment on embezzlement charges.[10]

A second management problem relates to the tendency for some unions to become excessively centralized as they grow and mature. As the union leaders become more distant from and less accountable to the rank and file, they may act in self-serving

A NEW
ROAD FOR THE TEAMSTERS

In late 1987, 30 years after parting company, the International Brotherhood of Teamsters and the AFL–CIO were reunited. Some labor experts believe that the merger will steady the falling membership of the AFL (before the merger, a target of membership raids by the Teamsters) and reduce duplicate organizing drives. The Teamsters themselves hope that being under the AFL umbrella will strengthen their hand at the bargaining table.

Since 1980, when the trucking industry was deregulated, the Teamsters have met adversity—particularly the loss of over 100,000 jobs and wage concessions necessitated by the busi-

ness-grabbing successes of small nonunion carriers. Recognizing that price-cutting wars have weakened some union carriers, the Teamsters have begun permitting carriers to set up profit-sharing or stock-ownership plans in exchange for reduced wages—a move that in turn may let the union tighten rules on casual hires and gain faster wage increases for new hires.

Past Teamsters President the late Jackie Presser, while ill and facing embezzlement charges, proposed the reunion with the AFL in part to protect his union against federal action. Alleging Teamster–mob ties, the Justice Department sued to place the union under court-appointed receivership—a move that AFL President Lance Kirkland took as a possible sign of future similar attacks on other unions. The AFL's executive council was quick to accept Presser's proposal. Although the merger may not work miracles for the rank-and-file, it is likely to encourage greater cooperation among hitherto feuding union members.

Source: As reported in "The Teamsters: A Break in Forty Miles of Bad Road," *Business Week* (March 21, 1988), pp. 91–92, and "Teamsters: The Big Sweep," *Newsweek* (July 11, 1988), p. 33.

---

ways that are inconsistent with the desires of the members.

Senate hearings in the late 1950s highlighted such management problems and led to the passage of the Landrum–Griffin Act of 1959 to regulate the internal affairs of unions. This act requires unions to file annual financial statements with the Department of Labor, to guarantee members certain rights, and to hold periodic elections of union officials. The act also mandates standards for these elections, restricts national and international unions from assuming direct control over local unions, and prohibits corrupt practices by union officers. Although corruption problems still appear on occasion, the legal system is increasingly diligent in monitoring these illicit practices.

THE LEGAL ENVIRONMENT OF LABOR–MANAGEMENT RELATIONS

The preceding discussion highlights the importance of the legal environment of labor–management relations. The cornerstone of this law in the private nonfarm sector is the **National Labor Relations Act (NLRA).** Its coverage extends to about 50 percent of the American workforce. The largest single group not covered by the act consists of public sector government workers. Their situation will be described shortly. First, however, an understanding of the NLRA helps create the foundation for a general understanding of the legal environment of labor–management relations.

National Labor Relations Act

The NLRA as we know it today is a composite of the Wagner Act of 1935 as amended by the Taft–Hartley Act of 1947 and the Landrum–Griffin Act of 1959. This important legal framework for labor–management relations seeks to protect both employee and employer rights.

The Wagner Act of 1935 sets forth a number of employee rights with regard to unions. It specifically gives employees the right to join or form unions, to bargain collectively, and to undertake "concerted" activities or strikes in pursuit of their bargaining objectives. As shown in Table 18.2, the Wagner Act is quite specific in prohibiting several unfair labor practices applicable to employers.

In 1947 Congress passed a landmark piece of legislation known as the Taft–Hartley Act. This act amended the Wagner Act in important ways. To begin, the Taft–Harley Act states that union membership cannot be a condition of employment in those states that prohibit the practice by what are commonly called **right-to-work** laws. States that have such laws are known as "right-to-work" states, and union activities tend to be more restricted there than in states without the laws. As a result, "right-to-work" is a controversial issue and laws both for and against the concept continue to be proposed in state legislatures.

TABLE 18.2 *Selected Examples of Unfair Labor Practices Subject to Provisions of the National Labor Relations Act*

Wagner Act (1935) prohibits *employers* from
- Interfering with the right of employees to join unions (*Example:* Threatening to fire employees who join unions)
- Discriminating against employees to discourage union membership (*Example:* Denying a pay increase to a union activist)
- Refusing to bargain in good faith with a certified union (*Example:* Changing wage levels without discussing the matter with union representatives.)

Taft–Hartley Act (1947) prohibits *unions* from
- Coercing or restraining employees in the exercise of their rights under the NLRA (*Example:* Mass picketing with the intention of intimidating strikebreakers)
- Engaging in certain types of strikes (*Example:* A jurisdictional strike to compel the employer to give work to members of one union as opposed to another)
- Refusing to bargain in good faith with an employer's representatives (*Example:* Striking over something other than wages, hours, and conditions of employment)

In addition, the Taft–Hartley amendments to the NLRA prohibit unions from engaging in such unfair labor practices as those listed in Table 18.2. It also sets forth procedures through which employees can "decertify" or revoke a union's right to represent them, and allows the U.S. president to seek temporary injunctions to suspend otherwise legal strikes that threaten national health or safety.

The final component in NLRA is the Landrum–Griffin Act passed in 1959. As noted earlier, this act regulates internal affairs of unions relating to certain financial matters and administrative procedures. Its goal is generally to minimize corruption and foster democratic practices in unions.

National Labor Relations Board

Under the Wagner Act, the **National Labor Relations Board (NLRB)** was created to generally administer the provisions of the act. Among other things, it supports the NLRA by conducting elections through which employees decide whether or not to unionize, investigating any charges of unfair labor practice. The unfair labor practices defined by the NLRA are not crimes. But when one is alleged to have occurred, the NLRB investigates. If the allegation is substantiated, remedial action will be prescribed. The most common order by the NLRB is for the offending party to refrain from unfair practices in the future and post public notices to that effect. In cases where someone has been injured because of an unfair labor practice, the board may require restitution. For example, if the board determines that an employee was discharged for joining a union, it will normally order that the employee be reinstated and paid any lost wages. The findings of the NLRA may be appealed through the federal court system.

Public Sector Considerations

In the public sector—noted earlier as an area where union membership is on the increase—a variety of federal executive orders and state labor laws, mostly modeled after the NLRA, now govern labor–management relations. Federal workers are given the right to organize, but not to strike, by the Federal Service Labor–Management Statute of 1979. This statute also created the Federal Labor Relations Authority (FLRA), which administers the act and performs functions similar to the NLRB. State and local government employees face a variety of specific statutes, which vary from place to place. Most state government employees, however, do have collective bargaining rights.

HOW ORGANIZATIONS BECOME UNIONIZED

Most unions employ a staff of organizers whose function is to assist people in establishing collective-bargaining agreements with their employers. Often, the initial stimulus to seek union representations comes from employees who are concerned about their working conditions.

ILLUSTRATIVE CASE:
THE UAW MOVES IN AT NISSAN

It was supposed to be blue-collar paradise, this new Nissan Motor Company plant in Smyrna, Tennessee.[11] Workers were promised good benefits, job security, concerned management, and the opportunity of working for a company whose products were selling very well. The company hired about 2400 employees for the facility, and they eagerly turned it into one of the most productive truck and car assembly plants around. But then the United Auto Workers union made Nissan the target of an organizing drive. The UAW hopes to make it the first Japanese car company in the United States to be organized despite management opposition.

UAW President Owen Beiber reports that the union received many complaints from workers regarding injuries, poor working conditions, and sexual harassment. He says, "Anytime a company tries to increase productivity . . . at many times, it's at the expense of the health and safety of the workers." One of the biggest complaints at the Smyrna plant is the speed of the assembly line—63 cars per hour. "I wasn't for the union when I started because I thought that it was a great place to work," said Jackie Payne a 31-year old worker attending a pro-union rally. He went on to add that the work load is too heavy, saying, "I can't see myself working here at 40."

The UAW placed a team of organizers in the plant in response to worker's complaints. But Gail Neuman, the company's vice-president for human resources, speaks for a management group that believes it is still a great place to work. She says, "We continue to believe that the vast majority of our employees don't want a union." In specific response to UAW charges she responds: Nissan has "half the injury record" of other major U.S. auto plants, a line speed that "is slower than that at many other unionized plants," and feels the sexual harassment charges are "without merit."

Once the union persuades 30 percent or more of the workers to sign authorization cards, it can petition for an NLRB-sponsored election. Then it will be up to the workers to decide whether or not to organize and let the UAW represent them.

The Decision to Seek Union Representation

The preceding example introduces some of the reasons why workers may decide to unionize and the process through which this can legally be achieved. A great deal of research has been done in recent years on the attitudes of employees toward unionization.[12] Psychological studies find that attitudes toward unions are more favorable when job satisfaction is low. But the nature of this relationship varies according to the occupational status of the employee. White-collar and professional workers are more likely to favor unionization when dissatisfied with intrinsic rewards of their jobs (e.g., personal autonomy, self-fulfillment); blue-collar workers are more likely to favor unionization when dissatisfied with the extrinsic rewards of their jobs (e.g., pay, fringe benefits, quality of supervision, work conditions). In addition, employees are more likely to favor unionization when (1) they perceive of themselves as having little power to change work conditions for the better, (2) they expect a union to be effective in changing work conditions, and (3) they have only limited employment opportunities elsewhere.

Employer resistance to union organizing activities has clearly increased in recent years, and associated with this trend has been the emergence of management-consulting firms that specialize in "positive-" or "preventive-labor relations." They help employers develop strategies to avoid a decision by employees to seek union representation. Many executives simply act on their own to protect their organizations from unionization. One study of 26 large nonunionized firms found that many of their personnel policies reflected the objective of maintaining nonunion status.[13] These firms implemented modern personnel systems, with considerable emphasis on employee participation (e.g., quality circles), progressive compensation and benefits programs, employment security, and promotion from within.

Certification of Unions

A **certification election** is the means through which employees choose whether or not to be represented by a union. This process is carefully governed by federal and state laws. In the private sector, certification elections are held under the provisions of the NLRA and are supervised by the NLRB. As

FIGURE 18.3 *Steps in the union certification procedure as governed by the National Labor Relations Act.*

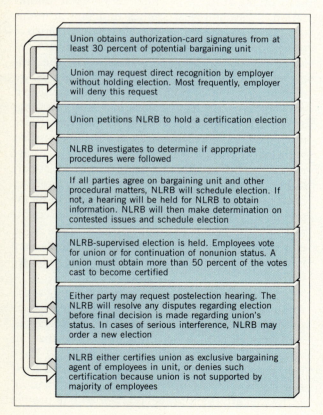

Union obtains authorization-card signatures from at least 30 percent of potential bargaining unit

Union may request direct recognition by employer without holding election. Most frequently, employer will deny this request

Union petitions NLRB to hold a certification election

NLRB investigates to determine if appropriate procedures were followed

If all parties agree on bargaining unit and other procedural matters, NLRB will schedule election. If not, a hearing will be held for NLRB to obtain information. NLRB will then make determination on contested issues and schedule election

NLRB-supervised election is held. Employees vote for union or for continuation of nonunion status. A union must obtain more than 50 percent of the votes cast to become certified

Either party may request postelection hearing. The NLRB will resolve any disputes regarding election before final decision is made regarding union's status. In cases of serious interference, NLRB may order a new election

NLRB either certifies union as exclusive bargaining agent of employees in unit, or denies such certification because union is not supported by majority of employees

mentioned earlier, public sector organization is governed by federal and state laws. But it is generally patterned after the NLRB procedures for certification of unions now detailed in Figure 18.3.

The process of certifying a union formally begins when a petition for an election is filed with the NLRB. This petition must be signed by at least 30 percent of the employees in a potential **bargaining unit**—that is, the organization or sub-unit of an organization that would eventually be subject to union representation. There may be disagreement between a union and the employer over a proposed bargaining unit, since its composition may influence election outcomes. Thus, prior to any election the NLRB may have to determine if the employees in the proposed unit share a "community of interests" and if all of them fall under the jurisdiction of the law. Supervisors, for example, are not covered by the NLRA and may not vote in certification elections. The criteria used by the NLRB in determining if a *community of interests* exists include:

1. The extent to which workers share similar skills, employment interests, work duties, and working conditions.
2. The employer's organizational structure, including the functional integration of departments and the geographic distribution of operations.
3. The history of bargaining in the company or industry.
4. The preferences of the employees regarding the structure of the bargaining unit.

Once the bargaining unit has been determined and any other issues resolved, a date is set for the secret-ballot certification election. Before the election, the union and company normally attempt to influence workers to vote either for or against unionization. Pre-election campaigns are monitored and closely regulated by the NLRB. Both unions and employers are prohibited by law from threatening or bribing employees. They may provide persuasive information regarding what they believe to be the advantages or disadvantages of unionization, but campaign literature and speeches may not contain misrepresentations of fact.

The NLRA requires that a union establish its *majority status* in an election in order to be recognized. This means that a union must receive at least 51 percent of the votes cast to become certified as the employee's bargaining agent. Should a union lose an election, it may not petition for a new election for at least one year. Unions are currently winning less than half of the NLRB supervised certification elections. At their peak in 1937, unions won the right to represent employees 94 percent of the time.[14]

Decertification of Unions

The NLRA also provides employees with a procedure for **decertification**—that is, a means for revoking the certification of a union previously certified as their bargaining agent. A showing of interest by 30 percent or more members of the bargaining unit is required for a decertification election to be held by the NLRB. Decertification elections are sometimes initiated by an outside union that wants to replace an existing union. Such "raiding" is less common today than in the past. Most decertification elections involve the employees' choice between remaining unionized and returning to nonunion status.

Although employers may express opinions during a preelection campaign for decertification, they may neither initiate a decertification campaign nor encourage employees to do so. However, the process of decertification is often controversial. The number of decertification elections held in the United States has been running over 1000 per year. Unions are now losing almost 75 percent of them.[15]

COLLECTIVE BARGAINING

Collective bargaining stands at the heart of the labor–management relationship. This process of negotiating, interpreting, and administering a labor contract establishes the conditions under which managers and their subordinates work together in a unionized setting.

The Bargaining Process

The NLRB oversees the entire collective-bargaining process, from negotiating a new labor contract to resolving disputes that arise under an existing one. In each case the bargaining takes place in face-to-face meetings between labor and management representatives. During this time a variety of demands, proposals, and counterproposals are exchanged. Several rounds of bargaining may be required before an issue or contract is eventually decided.

Most bargaining begins with a statement of position by both management and the union on a given issue. If the initial differences in the two positions are too great, the *bargaining zone* may be too wide to produce any meaningful discussions. The example depicted in Figure 18.4 describes bargaining between the Carpenters union and U.S. Homes on a wage issue.[16] The union starts with an initial demand of $0.90 per hour wage increase, knowing full well that a "final offer" from management of a $0.60 per hour increase is likely and feeling that anything less than $0.40 per hour would be totally

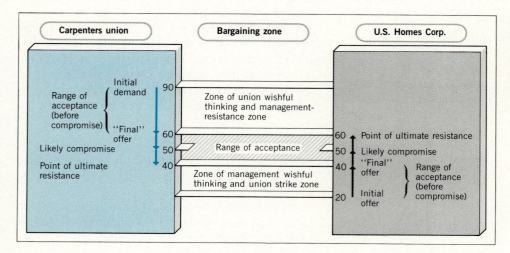

FIGURE 18.4

Bargaining in labor–management relations: the case of the Carpenter's Union vs. U.S. Homes Corporation.

unacceptable. The bargaining representative for U.S. Homes, by contrast, starts by offering $0.20 per hour, would be glad to settle a "final offer" at $0.40 per hour, and in no way will give more than $0.60 per hour for the wage increase.

If both management and labor restrict their demands to the initial offers, no zone exists for realistic bargaining and a strike is possible. Once "final-offer" points are reached in the negotiations, however, true bargaining can take place, with the likelihood that some compromise and agreement will be reached. In this case the likely compromise would be a $0.50 per hour increase. This is why you frequently find that both unions and management settle disputes at something different from their stated "final-offer" points.

What the Bargaining Is All About

Labor contracts are complex, often lengthy and legally-binding written agreements between the management of an organization and the union(s) representing its employees. One agreement between the United Auto Workers and General Motors was 350 pages long. Although the specific provisions of these contracts vary from one organization to the next, the collective-bargaining process and labor agreement typically cover the issues like those listed in Table 18.3. The following examples further describe what is likely to be addressed in any collective bargaining negotiation.

Union Security

An **open shop,** which does not require union membership as a condition of employment, is the least restrictive situation for an employer. But an important issue in most negotiations is the attempt to put some form of *union security clause* in the contract. This is a contract provision that imposes union membership on employees, or at least requires that the union be paid a service fee by any nonunion workers. The most restrictive form of union security is called a **closed shop.** Under this arrangement a person must be a union member in good standing *before* being hired as an employee. The Taft–Hartley Act made the closed shop illegal. The most common union security clause creates a **union shop,** wherein all employees must belong to the union and newly hired employees must join the union within a certain number of days. A third form of union security, the **agency shop,** requires all employees to pay a service fee to the union even though they don't officially have to join.

Job and Employment Security

The traditional concerns for job security focused on the protection of individual workers and dealt mainly with "seniority" issues. **Seniority,** or length of service with an employer, is discussed in most labor contracts and can be used to determine a number of decisions affecting a person's job and employment rights. For example, seniority may be the basis for determining pay increases and wage levels, the order of layoffs during cutbacks and the order of rehiring, and eligibility for benefits such as vacations, holiday privileges, and pensions. It may also be used to determine job assignments among workers for higher-paying jobs, shift work, overtime work, and job transfers. More recently, union concerns have been extended to employment security in the form of job preservation and job creation issues. Such things as retraining for workers displaced by new technology, guarantees on the number of jobs in a company even if sales fall, and overtime limits to create jobs for laid-off workers, are common examples of this trend.

Wages and Benefits

Much bargaining time and effort is devoted to contract provisions for wage increases and fringe-benefit improvements for employees. Wage increases are often stated as (1) across-the-board percentage or cents-per-hour increases, (2) deferred increases based on productivity improvements, and (3) cost-

TABLE 18.3 *Subjects Frequently Covered in a Labor Contract*

Basic Issues	Work Rules
Union security	Job classifications
Job security	Job assignments
Employment security	Job rotation
Length of contract	
	Management Rights
Wages and Benefits	Work hours
Wage levels	Performance standards
Cost-of-living increases	Promotion criteria
Incentive pay	
Insurance programs	*Personnel Practices*
Pensions & retirement	Hiring policies
Sick leave & disability	Disciplinary procedures
Vacations	Seniority rules

of-living adjustments (COLA). Besides wage increases, contracts usually cover various fringe benefits, such as wage rates for overtime and holiday work, insurance programs (life, health and hospitalization, dental care), vacation and sick-leave privileges, and retirement pensions. In some industries, such as steel and auto manufacturing, fringe benefits make up to 40 percent of the total compensation package.

Work Rules

Work rules are labor contract provisions that govern the decisions which assign tasks to employees. Because they can influence job classification schemes, limit what individual employees may be expected to do, and restrict management's use of labor to perform various jobs, work rules are important collective bargaining issues. This is especially true in today's environment when managers often seek productivity increases through basic changes in the ways jobs are distributed in organizations. Typical work rules influence the flexibility with which one worker can temporarily substitute for another in a job—e.g. a plumber moving a wall stud in a construction job, how readily workers can be rotated among several different jobs—e.g. sharing assembly operations in manufacturing setting, and whether or not managerial personnel can temporarily perform nonsupervisory work—e.g. a supervisor pitching in to operate a machine when a production run is behind schedule.

Management Rights

Management groups often seek some security of their own in labor contracts. Many labor contracts address this in the form of **management rights** provisions. A typical clause formally gives the employer all rights to manage the operation except as these rights are modified through specific terms of the labor agreement. For instance, the labor contract might modify the employer's promotion policy by specifying that seniority be considered in making promotion decisions. A common management-rights provision is a lengthy list of specific areas not subject to collective bargaining, such as the right to (1) schedule working hours, (2) hire and fire workers, (3) set production standards, (4) promote, demote, and transfer workers, and (5) determine the number of supervisors in each department.

Other Major Issues

Among other important bargaining issues are the duration of the labor contract, the no-strike and no-lockout clauses, and procedures regarding employee discipline and contract disputes. In private industry the most typical labor contracts have a three-year duration; contracts in the public sector are generally for shorter periods. Under a no-strike clause, the union agrees not to strike during the term of the contract. In turn, the employer gives a no-lockout pledge, which means business will not be shut down and workers forced off their jobs in an attempt to get the union to change its position on some crucial issue. Procedures for handling employee discipline and contract disputes are also covered in most bargaining agreements.

Grievances and Arbitration

A procedure is needed to resolve disputes that arise regarding the implementation and interpretation of a labor contract in daily affairs. In fact, this is the point where a labor contract can have the most direct impact on a manager—as a constraint on the day-to-day working relationship between the manager and subordinates. Two terms are most significant in this regard for their managerial implications—grievance and arbitration.

Grievances

A **grievance** is a complaint from an employee regarding treatment he or she has received in respect to a condition of employment. Most grievances allege that a manager or management in general has violated some provision of the labor contract. The union's mechanism for airing such disputes and policing the terms of the collective-bargaining agreement is a formal grievance procedure specified in the labor contract.

Figure 18.5 illustrates the grievance procedure specified in the UAW contract with International Harvester. The first step in the procedure is taken when the employee discusses a complaint with the supervisor. Things may be resolved here. If not, the procedure passes to the next step where the complaint is formally presented in writing to the supervisor. A second discussion is held and the union steward is usually present. If the dispute is not resolved at this level, further discussions take place between the employee, a chief steward or other local

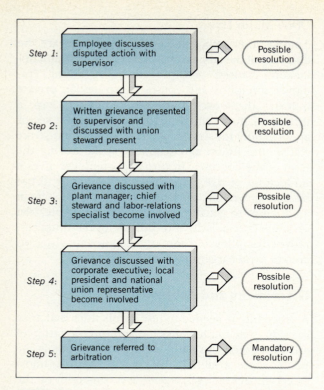

Step 1:	Employee discusses disputed action with supervisor	→	Possible resolution
Step 2:	Written grievance presented to supervisor and discussed with union steward present	→	Possible resolution
Step 3:	Grievance discussed with plant manager; chief steward and labor-relations specialist become involved	→	Possible resolution
Step 4:	Grievance discussed with corporate executive; local president and national union representative become involved	→	Possible resolution
Step 5:	Grievance referred to arbitration	→	Mandatory resolution

FIGURE 18.5 *Steps in processing a grievance under a labor contract: the case of International Harvester.*

union officials, the employee's supervisor and other higher management officials. The latter might include a labor-relations specialist from the human resources department and the plant manager. If the problem is still not resolved, it goes to the next stage where even higher-level union and management officials become involved. This might include the president of the local union and a representative from the national union, as well as the plant manager and a top corporate executive. If there is still no agreement, the matter passes into arbitration.

Arbitration

Arbitration is the process by which parties to a labor–management dispute agree to abide by the decision of a neutral and independent third party called an arbitrator. Arbitrators settle issues for which bargaining impasses have been reached during contract negotiations or, as in the prior case, they settle grievances unable to be resolved through other measures. The courts have granted arbitrators wide powers, and their decisions are usually considered final and binding.

Fact Finding and Mediation

Arbitration is the strongest form of third party dispute resolution under a labor contract. **Fact finding** is an important alternative wherein "fact-finders" are selected by consent of both parties to investigate and report on all the facts surrounding a dispute. Hearings are typically held and the fact-finder's formal report usually includes recommended courses of action. Unlike arbitration, however, the conflicting parties are not bound to follow the fact-finder's recommendations. Each party can accept or reject them.

Mediation and **conciliation** are two additional forms of dispute resolution. In **conciliation** the neutral tries to keep the parties to a dispute focused on the issues of disagreement. He or she acts as a channel of communication for the exchange of information between the parties. In **mediation,** the neutral engages in substantive discussions with union and management negotiators in separate meetings and in joint sessions. He or she makes suggestions to the parties in the hope that concessions and compromise will result in an agreement. Mediation and conciliation might be employed to help resolve a dispute prior to the point of formal arbitration or fact-finding. Both approaches use neutral third parties, but they do not have the right to make final and binding decisions.

ILLUSTRATIVE CASE:
JACK PRITCHARD'S ATTENDANCE RECORD

Most grievances don't go to arbitration. But some problems just can't be settled without it. One such problem for Labconco, a small Kansas City manufacturer of laboratory equipment, involved a worker's attendance record.[17] The company's discipline procedure for workers with attendance problems involves four progressive steps—a verbal warning, a written warning, a three-day suspension, and finally firing. Before a worker is given a warning, though, the company offers counseling. After the disciplinary process has begun, it can be canceled if the worker's attendance improves.

When Jack Pritchard, an assembler, left work early one day to appear as a defendant in court, he was fired. Pritchard filed a grievance the next day. Supporting the grievance, the union claimed he had been fired unjustly because his absence was unavoidable. It asked that he be reinstated. Three months later, having passed unresolved through earlier stages of the grievance procedure, the case was presented before a professional arbitrator, a college dean paid by the company and the union and chosen by them from a list supplied by the Federal Mediation and Conciliation Service. At issue in this case was the discharge clause in the labor contract that says "no employee shall be discharged, suspended, or disciplined without just cause."

The arbitration hearing began with opening statements by the company and the union. The company called its witnesses—the director of administrative services, production manager, and Pritchard's supervisor. Through testimony and exhibits, the company's lawyer presented the following case. Labconco's attendance rules had been formulated with the union's cooperation and implemented with the union's approval. In accordance with the rules, Pritchard had been counseled often, had received many verbal and written warnings, and had even twice been suspended for three days before he'd finally been fired.

The union's witnesses—Pritchard and the union steward for his department—didn't refute the company's testimony. They focused on his personal problems—a large family, and seemingly unending health and financial problems. All these, they argued, made it hard for him to meet the demands of his job. "With all the problems that this person has had," asked the union representative, "why did the company have to take the day to terminate the man when they knew full well he had to be in court?"

The company's position was that the absence was part of a pattern Pritchard apparently was unable to change. So many allowances had been made for him already, explained the production manager, that "we were on the cliff-edge of discriminating against other employees." Further, Pritchard hadn't tried to change the court date or inform the company of it until the day before it was scheduled to take place.

The arbitrator's decision was released more than a month after the hearing. It held that the company's attendance rules were reasonable and that the company had the right to enforce them reasonably, even when absences might seem beyond the employee's control. The union had produced no evidence to show the company had enforced the rules in a "capricious or discriminatory manner."

Though Pritchard's problems invited sympathy, "leniency or clemency is the prerogative of the employer rather than of the arbitrator." The company's action was upheld.

MANAGERIAL IMPLICATIONS OF COLLECTIVE BARGAINING

There is no doubt but that labor unions can have a major impact on their members, as well as on organizations and managers. From a managerial perspective, the influence of unions in contemporary society can be addressed at two levels—the more general social and economic impacts, and the more specific operational impacts.

Social and Economic Impacts of Unions

One of the best available analyses of the overall social and economic impact of unions on contemporary American society is the book *What Do Unions Do?*, by Richard B. Freeman and James L. Medoff.[18] In this book, the author's conclusions lend some insight to two lingering controversies regarding the impact of unions in society—their roles as labor-force monopolies, and their abilities to serve as mechanisms for workers to express a collective voice. The researchers conclude that unions do represent monopoly labor power, which leads to higher wages and benefits for their members. This may cause unionized companies to be less profitable than would otherwise be possible. However, they also conclude that unions have a strong and positive voice-response effect in the work setting. That is, they typically provide unionized workers with an increased voice in decision making.

More specifically, Freeman and Medoff review a wide body of literature and empirical data, and come up with these basic observations regarding the social and economic impact of unions.

■ Unions have a monopoly impact on wages, with union workers outearning nonunion workers by as much as 30 percent.

■ Unions reduce the wage gap between blue-collar and white-collar workers.

■ Unions generally force an equality in the distribution of wages among individual workers.

■ Unions alter the total compensation package of

workers by increasing the proportion of fringe benefits available.

■ Unions reduce the frequency with which workers quit their jobs.

■ Unions reduce wage cuts and terminations affecting employees during business downturns.

■ Unions contribute to increased jurisprudence by management and contribute to improved personnel practices in nonunion work settings.

■ Unions do not reduce productivity overall, but they can reduce business profits.

■ Although corruption does exist in unions, it is mainly concentrated in a few industries and is not as far reaching as generally expected.

Operational Impacts of Unions

At the operational level, a collective bargaining agreement can have a very direct and specific impact on the conduct of managerial work. In nonunion settings, managers make decisions and take action in respect to things like wages, work hours, rest periods, vacations, and disciplinary rules on personal prerogative—always, one hopes, while exercising good judgment. In unionized settings all or much of that is changed. Union and management representatives collectively bargain for a labor contract that stipulates much of what managers and employees are to do at work, and what is to be done when they don't. Simply put, collective bargaining can place limits on managerial decision making in the following and related areas.

Wages and Wage Adjustments

The presence of collective bargaining generally reduces the ability of managers in an organization to tie compensation to worker performance. Incentive pay systems, for example, are less common among unionized firms. When they do exist, they tend to be closely regulated by contract language. Unions also tend to look unfavorably on merit-pay plans in which wage or salary increases are tied to performance measures. In place of pay rates and increases that are specific to the individual, unions normally negotiate standard rates for particular job categories and across-the-board annual increases for all employees of a bargaining unit.

Promotions, Transfers, and Layoffs

Unions generally believe that employees acquire, through service to an organization, a vested interest in their jobs and acquire something akin to property rights with respect to employment. Labor contracts therefore usually define job rights on the basis of seniority and other terms that limit the discretion of managers in making promotion, transfer, and layoff decisions. Seniority instead of performance may be the governing criterion in unionized settings. Managers in such settings must understand the complexities of contract rules governing staffing decisions, and know where and when they have personal discretion on such matters.

Work Rules and Assignments

Decisions through which work is assigned to individuals or groups are frequently an issue in labor–management relations. Union-management conflicts over "work rules" can often arise, and the presence of such rules will limit managerial prerogatives in many cases. As pointed out earlier, they can create complex job classification schemes that limit a manager's ability to ask workers to share tasks, swap jobs, and even do things to help one another out. Peter Drucker, in fact, believes that restrictive work rules are a major reason for the "productivity gaps" experienced by many American and European manufacturers—especially in comparison with their Japanese counterparts. He cites these examples to support his point.[19]

At a Nissan plant in England 24 cars per year are manufactured per worker, and the plant operates with five job classifications. At a Ford plant in England, only six cars per year are manufactured per worker, but the plant operates with 125 job classifications. Each classification restricts Ford workers to doing only one small task.

At Honda, U.S.A. there are only three to five job classifications in the firm's American plants, while competitors GM, Ford and Chrysler still operate with about 60. Productivity is 30–50 percent higher in the Japanese owned plants.

Employee Discipline

Most labor contracts try to limit the disciplinary powers of managers. Actions subject to discipline, as well as the penalties to be assessed, are often incorporated into the labor contract in detail. This was the case, for example, in the Jack Pritchard case described earlier. The principle of **just cause** holds that an employee should not be disciplined without sufficient justification—"just cause"—and that the penalty imposed should not be excessive compared to the offense. If a disciplinary case ends up in a formal grievance or arbitration, management has the obligation of establishing just cause for its actions. While the personnel procedures of many nonunion organizations also mandate that supervisors establish just cause in disciplinary cases, this is not required by law. Disciplinary procedures in nonunion settings usually allow managers greater freedom of action, although the potential for discipline to be misused is increased as well.

Technological Change

Job displacement as a possible result of increased automation and other forms of technological change is a continuing concern of organized labor. This is especially true with the rising use of computer technologies in factory automation. Since technological changes can affect employment opportunities and conditions of work, management is normally obligated by labor contracts to bargain over the decision to implement them. Since competitive pressures often necessitate accommodating new technologies, unions turn their attention to softening the blow of technological change. They try to negotiate contract provisions requiring organizations to retrain displaced workers and/or help them find work elsewhere. Displaced workers often receive substantial severance pay; in return for accepting the changes,

unions may expect the remaining employees to share in the financial benefits of increased productivity.

IMPROVING LABOR–MANAGEMENT RELATIONS

The traditional side of labor–management relations was introduced in the headlines which began this chapter. It is also reflected in the adversarial relationship shown in Figure 18.6. Labor and management are viewed as adversaries, destined to be in conflict and possessed of certain weapons with which to fight one another. As we have noted at several points in the chapter, however, times are changing to some extent.

The Trend Toward Cooperation

Recall the chapter-opening examples of unions and employers trying to work together for the common good. It is all part of enlightened management in both the unions and the employing organizations.

As just one final example, consider a joint effort by the United Steel Workers and industry officials to establish *labor–management participation teams* in American steel companies. The intent of these "LMPTs" is similar to the quality circle concept, that is to tap worker knowledge about their jobs and

FIGURE 18.6 *Traditional adversarial view of labor–management relations.*

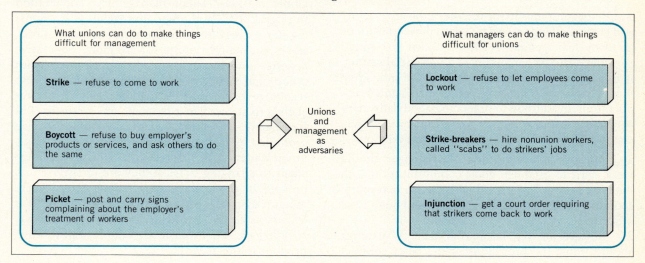

help improve productivity. Many industry and union officials feel this new form of worker participation may make a real difference in helping save the country's ailing steel firms. For example,[20]

at A. O. Smith Corporation the way the system works is through this three-tiered structure for participation.

1. *A policy committee* comprised of senior corporate, plant and union officials. This committee works together to set long-term policy and plan alternatives to employee layoffs.
2. *An advisory committee* comprised of middle managers and local union leaders. This committee develops and coordinates LMPTs and helps to implement their suggestions.
3. *Labor–management participation teams* each comprised of 10–15 workers and a leader in different plant departments. These LMPTs identify and analyze problems and implement solutions.

The history of the A. O. Smith project to date provides a good overview of the issues as labor unions and management try to work together in new and more cooperative ways. Company executives feel the results of participation will help reduce its prices and retain customers. But some union members feel it is just another way to squeeze more work out of them. They are concerned that LMPT suggestions will compromise some of their job protections. As one USW official says, "Workers are reluctant to come up with good ideas that will eliminate jobs."

What the Manager Can Do

The manager stands in the middle of the uncertainty and great challenge associated with these transitions in labor–management relations. Since you might someday serve as a manager in a unionized setting, it is appropriate to point out how the individual manager can help maintain labor–management cooperation. In addition to practicing good daily management, the following personal efforts by managers can foster improved labor–management relations.

1. *Effective communication* A manager should work hard to establish good communication with his or her subordinates and with their union representatives, including union stewards and other local officials.
2. *Respect for the labor contract* A manager should know the provisions of the labor contract and how they apply to the work unit; a manager should also work sincerely with union members to administer the contract on a day-to-day basis.
3. *Support for the grievance procedure* The grievance procedure, like it or not, is the basic mechanism for resolving disputes relating to a labor contract. A manager should make every effort to resolve problems short of a formal grievance being filed. Once filed, however, a grievance should be handled promptly and in strict conformity to procedures.
4. *Sponsorship of the labor–management "team"* A manager is uniquely positioned to sponsor greater labor–management cooperation; by taking advantage of any and all opportunities to promote shared goals, a manager's efforts can help bridge the gap between contest and cooperation in labor–management relations.

Even managers in a nonunion setting can take advantage of this advice. Remember, unions fill a need for their members. This need most typically relates to a deficiency in the treatment they are receiving at work. Good management can go a long way toward reducing such deficiencies and thereby decreasing the need for a union to be certified as a bargaining agent for employees. The final point to be made then, is straightforward. In unionized work settings, successful managers practice good management within the labor contract; in nonunion settings, successful managers practice good management.

Like the steel companies, organizations in most industries need the help of organized labor to achieve and maintain a competitive position in global markets. Labor–management cooperation through LMPTs and other approaches is a promising step in this direction. Economic necessity alone, serves as a major stimulus toward more cooperative postures and away from adversarial ones. Both unions and management seem more willing now to recognize that by working together each has a better chance to succeed in a dynamic environment. But fortunately, the shift toward cooperation is also prompted by new leadership perspectives. Today's union leaders appear to recognize that unions must adapt to changing times if they are to survive and prosper in the years ahead. By the same token, modern managers seem more willing to view labor leaders as equal "partners" in the world of work. *Newsline 18.3* offers one final example of continuing progress in this regard.

LABOR-MANAGEMENT COOPERATION BY NECESSITY

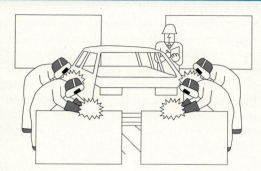

Teamwork may not be the first choice of either labor or management in some industries, but both workers and managers are starting to experience its advantages. In select companies in the steel, auto, and office equipment industries, teamwork is paying off. Reduced job classifications and other work-rule changes, coupled with greater worker participation in managerial decisions, have enhanced profitability at the National Steel Corporation. The chairman of the negotiating committee of the United Steelworkers of America, which represents National's workers, has hopes that even greater gains in productivity will result. At Xerox, teamwork has helped stave off Japanese competition in the photocopying end of the business. And in the auto industry, both GM and Chrysler have endorsed teamwork in some plants—and have managed to bring along unionized labor in the pursuit of higher productivity through cooperation.

At GM's Lansing, Mich., Reatta plant, the union contract requires labor-management committees to study possible quality and efficiency improvements and report to a national committee. J. Robert Thompson, the Reatta program manager, admits that because the plant was in danger of closing, workers were more readily persuaded to adopt a team approach—one not favored by those in the labor movement who fear job losses will result from declassifying jobs. "When you don't have anything to lose . . . I'm not sure you can reach some of the lofty goals" of teamwork, says Thompson.

Yet forced or no, closer labor-management cooperation is becoming a way of life at a growing number of plants. Union members are beginning to acknowledge the advantages it confers—flexibility and greater worker participation being chief among them—and managers are starting to accept that new lines must be drawn between themselves and workers. Says Thompson: "There has to be a sincere demonstration by the plant managers that we do want the barriers broken down so we can operate more efficiently." A UAW official comments, "This is an ongoing process, not a one-shot deal." At the Reatta plant, where workers helped redesign the assembly line, supporters of teamwork are to be found in both camps.

Source: As reported in John Holusha, "A New Spirit at U.S. Auto Plants," *New York Times* (December 29, 1987), pp. D-1–D-5; and, "GM's New Teams aren't Hitting any Homers," *Business Week* (August 8, 1988), pp. 46–47.

Summary

Labor unions are an important force in the contemporary work environment. Although private sector union membership has been declining as a percent of the total U.S. labor force, public sector membership is on the upswing. Some 200 national and international unions represent U.S. workers to their employers. The majority of these unions are affiliated with the AFL-CIO, a labor federation that provides services to its member unions. Locals provide services directly to members and represent them in the workplace. The union steward is the local union representative with whom line managers most frequently interact.

Labor—management relations within the

United States are governed by an elaborate labor–law system, the cornerstone of which is the National Labor Relations Act (NLRA). Originally the Wagner Act of 1935, the NLRA has been modified by the Taft–Hartley Act (1947) and Landrum–Griffin Act (1959). The NLRA establishes basic employee rights with respect to unionization. It provides systems through which employees can certify a union to represent them and to decertify a union which they no longer desire to have represent them. The NLRA is administered by the National Labor Relations Board (NLRB). Counterpart statutes at the federal and state levels govern labor-management relations in the public sector.

Collective bargaining is the process of negotiating, interpreting, and administering a labor contract. The labor contract, in turn, is a formal written agreement stipulating the wages, hours, and other terms of employment for union members working for an organization. During the life of a contract, employees who feel they are being mistreated on a contract issue may file a grievance. This begins a formal procedure for resolving the dispute that may go as far as arbitration.

Recent trends evidence greater cooperation in labor–management relations. Adversarial roles are giving way to enhanced cooperation as a mutual accommodation to changing economic and social realities. While emerging trends support improved labor–management relations in general, the individual manager in both union and nonunion settings can do a great deal to support these improvements in day-to-day dealings with subordinates.

Thinking Through the Issues

1. Define and clarify the distinction between a labor union, labor–management relations, and collective bargaining.

2. Why do people join unions? Are these reasons as relevant today as they were in the early 1900s? Explain your answer.

3. How is the typical international union structured? Where in this structure does the "union steward" fit, and what does this person do? Is the AFL-CIO a union? Why or why not?

4. State and explain two management problems that unions may face.

5. What are the major components of the National Labor Relations Act (NLRA)? Whose rights are protected by each, and in what ways?

6. Explain the steps employees would go through to certify a union as their bargaining agent in a business firm. How can a union be decertified?

7. What are the major issues with which collective bargaining is typically concerned?

8. What is arbitration, and when will a grievance normally end up in formal arbitration? How does arbitration differ from fact-finding and mediation?

9. What are the major social and economic impacts unions appear to be having in the United States? In what ways do they appear to be benefiting their members?

10. What advice would you give to someone taking a managerial job in a unionized setting? What can and should this person do to ensure high productivity and good employee relations within his or her work unit?

The Manager's Vocabulary

Agency shop	Decertification	Labor contract	National Labor
Arbitration	Fact finding	Labor union	Relations Board
Bargaining unit	General unions	Local	(NLRB)
Certification election	Grievance	Management rights	Open shop
Closed shop	Industrial unions	Mediation	Right-to-work laws
Collective bargaining	International union	National Labor	Seniority
Comparable worth	Just cause	Relations Act	Union shop
Conciliation	Jurisdiction	(NLRA)	Union stewards
Craft unions	Labor-management	National union	Work rules
	relations		

A SHOP
STEWARD'S FRUSTRATIONS

Alan Mosley is frustrated as a union steward for the United Steelworkers Local 1010 in East Chicago, Indiana. He handles complaints of the local union members about their employer Inland Steel Company. His frustration reflects a year of talks with company officials over whether or not eight new jobs to be created should go to union or salaried workers. He's reached a tentative agreement with the company people, but now his union members are resisting. Mosely says: "It's total unrest out there. It's a daily battle over jobs."

Inland's management considers Mosely's job critical to its labor–management relationship. They look to him to serve in a critical intermediary capacity—representing the union but listening to the company side as well. "I feel like I'm supposed to be a panacea for both the company and the union," says Mosely. But morale sometimes gets so low in the plant that even minor disputes become emotionally charged. When a supervisor caught two sleepy workers

laying on their workbenches one hot night, they were suspended for a day. Mosely had to file a grievance and then talk to union members about the issue. After the workers were suspended, production dropped on later shifts.

About the eight new jobs, Mosely finally got the company to let the union have four of them. But he adds, "I guess the longer the turmoil goes on, the longer it wears you down. Maybe I'm just getting burned out."[21]

Questions

1.   Why are Mr. Mosely and his job as union steward viewed as so important by Inland Steel's management? Please explain.
2.   What special training would help someone like Mr. Mosely perform this type of job?
3.   Have you ever belonged to a union or worked in a unionized setting? If so, how did your experience compare to Mosely's? If not, how well prepared are you to work in such a setting?

Case Application

A LABOR LEADER SPEAKS OUT

Douglas A. Fraser is unusual among American union leaders of this generation.[22] He started out as a worker, not as a professional union man, during that fervid time of union organization, the Great Depression, and witnessed the founding of his own union. When Fraser retired from the presidency of the United Automobile Workers in 1983, it marked the end of an epoch in the UAW and in American trade unionism. Almost alone among modern union leaders, Fraser knew firsthand what working was like before the union and what it was like after. In the labor negotiations in 1980 with the Chrysler Corporation, Fraser broke new ground in American labor–management relations when, as UAW president, he was named a director of the Chrysler Cor-

poration. The company accepted Fraser, it said, because of its respect for him.

Fraser . . . was interviewed in his office in the Walter P. Reuther Library of Labor and Urban Affairs at Wayne State University in Detroit, where he has been teaching since his retirement.

What was it like working in the plant before the union?
The best way to describe it, to use an old-fashioned word, is that there was no *dignity*. You couldn't question any decisions and you couldn't dissent. Nobody did. If you were lucky, you might have run into a good boss, but in that case he was a benevolent dictator. My boss was an S.O.B. by the name of

Remsnyder, and I'll never forget him. Everybody was really scared of that guy. He never smiled, and I can see him today: he always wore a hat squared on his head, never tilted to one side, and he would just sit at a stool at his desk or stand in the middle of the department floor, and he would look around and once in a while take a walk around the department and never stop and talk to anybody except to chew him out. Or he had his foreman do his dirty work. That was the kind of environment. People feared Remsnyder.

Dignity was the great thing that came out of union organization. When you think of it, wages in the auto industry were not bad, and nobody had benefits of any kind. So you didn't realize what you were missing. But what you gained from the union was the right to talk back, the right to question decisions, the right to dissent, and that's one hell of a feeling. They'll never take the democracy away from us, the right of the individual to speak up in dissent and file a grievance. That was a revolution.

Looking back, is your view of employers any different now from what it was when you were a young man in the DeSoto plant?
Yes. The big employers are different, even though I still get enraged today with the things that used to anger me then. For example, a superintendent or a Remsnyder bawling out a worker in front of his fellow workers—I get just as mad today as I would have in the 1930s. I get as angry about unemployment and deprivation as I did then.

But I think, being objective, that the employers have changed. Not necessarily in their attitudes toward the workers. But they used to think their responsibility began and ended with the stockholders. They had no responsibility to or awareness of the community. That's changed. It was coincidental with the urban riots of the sixties, and I don't know what the motivating factor was—it doesn't matter—but now most of them view their responsibilities differently.

But does it bother you when the auto industry is cutting back, and the workers are losing, and the executives get huge bonuses?
You wonder where the hell their brains are. At one of the last Chrysler board meetings I attended, they fixed up this deal for Lee Iacocca. They gave him one hundred and fifty thousand shares at that day's price—I figure it was a cool four million dollars or

so. Now he's not in the room when this is discussed. So I get into an argument with these guys on the board about the values in society. That money is I don't know how many more times more than I make in fifty years of work, and here he makes it in five minutes. In addition to the money, I said, it's the perception of what the workers feel out there, and the general public.

When I walked out of the board meeting, the first guy I run into is Lee. I told him what I said, and he sort of brushed it off and says, "Well, I'm not going to get any of it anyway, the kids'll get it." When I sat down to lunch, I was still mad, and another board member came up to me and said, "Don't be so upset, Doug. Wouldn't you like to see the look on Henry Ford's face when he reads about this tomorrow?" And lightning strikes. This has nothing to do with money—it's let's get even, show Ford that I'm going to be the richest S.O.B. in the auto industry.

What do you think unions have done for this country?
Unions have civilized the workplace, given the workers dignity and self-respect, and have improved enormously the standard of living of the workers generally, whether you belong to the union or not. The labor movement—or a good section of the labor movement—has played a major role in advancing social causes in our country. We were in the forefront of the civil rights struggle, we were in the forefront of environmental struggles, and all of the others.

I'm not saying the labor movement is without flaws. I look at the Teamsters. I said one time at a press conference—though I shouldn't have said it—that in order to be eligible to be the president of the Teamsters Union you have to be indicted at least twice. But that's the bottom side. I think the labor movement, with all of its flaws, has played a damned constructive role in American society. I think our country is better off for it.

What about those guys at the Chrysler plant fifty years ago? What did they think they were going to get by forming a union?
If I'd say one thing, it would be freedom. Freedom, individuality, respect. That's what they wanted more than anything else. They wanted to be able to stand up to Remsnyder.

Questions

1. What does Fraser mean when he indicates that the major difference between union and nonunion organizations is the "dignity" of employees? In what ways do unions, from his point of view, help create such dignity?

2. Where does labor–management "cooperation" fit in the scheme of things as described by Fraser?

Based on this case, do you feel the future of labor–management relations will be more, or less cooperative? Why?

3. What could an "enlightened" manager learn from Fraser's comments that would help him or her perform more effectively in a) a unionized work setting, and b) a non-unionized work setting? Please explain.

Class Exercise: YOU BE THE ARBITRATOR

1. The following incident actually happened at AT&T. Read and think about it.[23]

Mary is a senior operations clerk. She works in a test room for an operations manager and coordinates administrative duties for the office. Her job requires working with others in the office. She is responsible for processing vouchers and employee phone bills, answering the phone, making out time reports, maintaining the vacation schedule, forwarding payroll inquiries, and performing other duties related to office administration.

Although Mary is considered an efficient worker, she has developed a reputation for being rude and uncooperative. Employees have complained that she is impossible to work with. On several occasions when her fellow employees have asked for information she has scolded them for asking such "dumb questions."

Her appraisals in the past have been satisfactory in every category except "sense of cooperation." Her supervisor characterizes her as a good, productive worker on jobs that do not require her contact with others. However, in her most recent appraisal she receives a "limited" in the category of "sense of cooperation." Her supervisor informs her that improvement is expected in this area or she could face discipline. Mary replies that if employees would stop asking so many stupid questions she wouldn't be so provoked. Her supervisor responds that answering inquiries is part of the job.

A few days later a customer calls to complain about service. At the time, Mary was busy typing a report and she told the customer everyone in the office was busy, so call back later. When the customer later tracks down the operations manager, the customer complains about the rudeness of the clerk. Her supervisor asks Mary about the incident and she ac-

knowledges the conversation but says she couldn't find anybody to talk to the customer. After making other inquiries, the supervisor finds that Mary made no effort to ask anyone in the office about assisting the customer. Consequently, the supervisor suspends Mary for three days for unsatisfactory job performance.

In the following months a series of incidents were documented. Employees continued to complain that Mary was slow to respond to their questions. In one incident, a supplier was not paid promptly because Mary didn't like the supplier's agent. Mary was subsequently given two more suspensions and finally warned that unless her cooperation improved to a satisfactory level, she would be terminated. A few weeks later her supervisor asked her to update a time report. Mary said she was tired of making changes and if the supervisor wanted the change to make it himself.

Mary was fired for poor work performance demonstrated by her repeated lack of cooperation with others. Despite satisfactory performance in all other areas, Mary's continued lack of cooperation was unacceptable.

The union contended in a grievance that Mary worked hard and knew her job and the company could not dismiss an employee for lack of cooperation when all other work performance categories were satisfactory.

2. This case went to an arbitrator who had to decide if Mary's dismissal was with "just cause." If you were the arbitrator in this case, how would you decide?

3. Share your decision with a nearby classmate. Discuss the reasons for each of your decisions. Await further class discussion.

References

[1]Information from "Labor Relations: Reconnecting the Lines," *Business Week* (January 18, 1988), p. 59.

[2]An excellent review of labor unions in America is found in Richard B. Freeman and James L. Medoff, *What Do Unions Do?* (New York: Basic Books, 1984). See also Charles C. Heckscher, *The New Unionism* (New York: Basic Books, 1988).

[3]See "Why Unions Grow and Shrink at the Same Time," *Business Week* (May 16, 1988), p. 30.

[4]For good discussions of the problems facing unions see Richard B. Freeman, "Can American Unions Rebound?" *The Wall Street Journal* (December 8, 1987), p. 30; and, Edward E. Lawler III and Susan A. Mohrman, "Unions and the New Management," *Academy of Management Executive,* Vol. 1 (1988), pp. 293–300.

[5]Samuel Gompers, *Labor and the Common Welfare,* as cited in E. Wight Bakke, Clark Kerr, and Charles Amrod (eds.), *Unions, Management and the Public,* Third Edition (New York: Harcourt, Brace & World, 1967), p. 42.

[6]*Business Week,* op. cit., 1988.

[7]Reported in Jacob M. Schlesinger, "UAW's Chrysler Concessions May be Nearing an End," *The Wall Street Journal* (April 15, 1988), p. 30.

[8]*Business Week* (May 18, 1987), p. 107.

[9]See "The AFL-CIO: A Tougher Team with the Teamsters," *Business Week* (November 9, 1987), p. 110; and, "The Teamsters: A Break in Forty Miles of Bad Road," *Business Week* (March 21, 1988), pp. 91–92.

[10]"Teamsters: The Big Sweep," *Newsweek* (July 11, 1988), p. 33.

[11]Information for this case is reported in "Life at Nissan: Paradise Lost?" *Newsweek* (August 10, 1987), p. 49; and, Jacob M. Schlesinger, "UAW Starts Nissan Organizing Drive in Test of Japanese-Owned U.S. Plants," *The Wall Street Journal* (January 20, 1988), p. 13.

[12]See Thomas Kochan, *Collective Bargaining and Industrial Relations,* (Homewood, Ill.: Richard D. Irwin, 1980), pp. 124–150; Jack Fiorito and Charles Greer, "Determinants of U.S. Unionism: Past Research and Future Needs," *Industrial Relations,* Vol. 21 (Winter 1982), pp. 1–32.

[13]Fred K. Foulkes, *Personnel Policies in Large Nonunion Companies* (Englewood Cliffs, NJ: Prentice-Hall, 1980).

[14]Daniel Seligman, "Who Needs Unions?" *Fortune* (July 12, 1982), pp. 54–66.

[15]Ibid.

[16]Reported in Lawrence J. Gitman and Carl McDaniel, Jr., *Business World* (New York: Wiley, 1983), pp. 214–216.

[17]Adapted from Gitman and McDaniel, p. 217. Used by permission.

[18]Freeman and Medoff, op. cit. For another scholarly perspective see Heckscher, op cit.

[19]Peter F. Drucker, "Workers' Hands Bound by Tradition" *The Wall Street Journal* (August 2, 1988), p. 20.

[20]See "Steelmakers Want to Make Teamwork an Institution," *Business Week* (May 11, 1987), p. 84.

[21]Information from Alex Kotlowitz, "Grievous Work: Job of Shop Steward Has New Frustrations in Era of Payroll Cuts," *The Wall Street Journal* (April 1, 1987), pp. 1, 20.

[22]This interview is excerpted by permission of the author from *American Heritage,* Vol. 36 (February–March 1985), pp. 56–64.

[23]Reported in *Mgr.* (No. 1, 1978), p. 19. Used by permission.

Managing in an International Arena

Soviets Test the Capitalist Waters

"Bolshoi Macs"?—strange but true: McDonald's hopes to be in the Soviet Union before long. In the search for new and lucrative foreign markets for their goods, Western businesses have not typically turned to the Soviet Union; it is not a nation known for flexible business deals. However, all that may be changing. Soviet leader Mikhail Gorbachev has made clear his interest in Western technology and management practices, and his country is beginning to open its doors to interested trade and investment parties.

The Soviet Union has signed dozens of agreements for joint ventures, and this trend is expected to continue. According to the US–USSR Trade and Economic Council, the American industries most keen on such ventures are energy, food, and chemicals. Some big corporate names are already involved: Pepsico, for example, sells its soft drink in the Soviet Union and plans to build two Pizza Hut restaurants in Moscow. McDonald's and Coca-Cola are also formulating investment plans. Recently, Honeywell, Combustion Engineering, and Occidental Petroleum signed on with the Soviets to undertake joint-manufacturing projects.

One West German machine-tool company, Heinemann, has already landed an ambitious deal that involves building a plant in Moscow identical to its Black Forest facility and then employing Soviets in both places. Products will be made for Soviet and Western markets. Expatriating profits can be a problem: Soviet law requires that Western partners export from the Soviet Union in order to bring out their hard-currency returns. But Heinemann, in setting up two plants, is skirting that problem. It will pay Soviet workers in West Germany partly in rubles, thereby saving on labor costs. American firms, too, are end-running the ruble. Occidental, for example, will export one-quarter of the plastics it plans to produce in the Soviet Union. Its aim is to sell its wares to food packagers, vinyl-floor makers, and other manufacturers in Western European and other markets.

Negotiations with the Soviets can be lengthy and complex—a big negative for companies interested in rapid returns. However, a recently passed Soviet law allows 20 ministries and 70 major enterprises to deal directly with foreign partners, which means that negotiations once bottlenecked at one agency should now move along more quickly. Undeniably, the Soviets are proceeding carefully, anxious to ensure that these new ventures make money. But James H. Giffen, president of the US–USSR trade council, believes that where there's a will, there's a way: "Everyone on both sides is being cautious, but the Soviets will do what it takes to make the ventures work." ■

Source: Information from "*Perestroika* to Pizza," *Time* (May 2, 1988), pp. 52–53; "Ivan Starts Learning the Capitalist Ropes," *Business Week* (November 2, 1987), p. 154; "Letting Western Business In," *Business Week* (April 20, 1987), p. 40.

One of the most fascinating of all management challenges involves international dimensions of our world. This chapter examines many facets of international management. Key topics include:

International Management
International Business
Multinational
    Corporations (MNCs)
Environmental Constraints
    on International
    Operations
The Management
    Functions in an
    International
    Perspective
Comparative Management
    Practices

There is no doubt about it; we live in an international world. The supersonic Concorde flies from New York to London or Paris in just over three hours. It is possible to board a plane in Chicago and get off in Japan or Singapore in less than a day's time. These are incredible opportunities for a person to see and become involved in all of the splendor and variety of our world.

It is not only through travel that the average person is increasingly becoming a citizen of the world, but in everyday living as well. Just think how many of your favorite consumer products are made in other countries. We enjoy cars from Germany, cameras from Japan, wines from France, and coffee from Columbia, to name but a few. What you might not realize are some other examples of the increasing globalization of business. Chrysler, GM, and Ford all sell under their names cars that are built in the United States by Japanese firms; AT&T manufactures telephones in Singapore for the American market and Hewlett-Packard has just established a major research center there; Sony is now the proud owner of CBS Records; and the list of newsworthy international business developments goes on and on.

Into this complex and truly *global* arena steps the modern manager. As the world shrinks and the operations of organizations more and more frequently span national boundaries, a new action dimension emerges to challenge a manager's skills and capacities. This is the fascinating international dimension of the practice of management.

INTERNATIONAL MANAGEMENT

International management is a term used to describe management that involves the conduct of business or other operations in foreign countries. Scholars study international management to learn how the management process applies across cultural and national boundaries; practicing managers benefit from these efforts when they learn how to transfer management practices successfully from one cultural setting to another.

Perhaps you are asking at this point, "But when and where will I ever get involved in this thing called 'international management'?" The response is two-fold.

1. *You will always be affected by international events in day-to-day living.* A familiarity with international management can help you to put these worldwide events in perspective and better understand them. The study of international management can help you become a more informed citizen of the world.

2. *The likelihood is high that international management responsibilities will someday enter into your career.* The opportunities to become involved in international management include (1) working overseas in the foreign operation of a domestic firm, (2) working overseas as an expatriate employee of a foreign firm and, (3) working as a domestic employee of a foreign firm operating in your country. While each of these opportunities may well come

A CLASH OF STYLES: JAPANESE COMPANIES AND U.S. WORKERS

NEWSLINE 19.1

Hiring and employing nationals in a foreign country is not always a straightforward undertaking, as many multinationals are finding out. Cultural barriers are not necessarily overcome by assertions of mutual interest, and employees who are local residents sometimes express resentment at what they take to be discrimination on the part of the foreigners who employ them.

A case in point is the situation in some Japanese-owned, American-staffed companies in California, where a large number of the 600 U.S. subsidiaries of Japanese organizations are located. The Japanese owners have hired thousands of Americans, many of whom serve as managers—and some of whom complain that because they aren't Japanese, they cannot reach the top rungs of the corporate ladder. Such charges can lead to litigation; in one lawsuit, filed against NEC Electronics Inc., two high-ranking American executives contended that the parent company in Tokyo didn't trust them and kept a tight hold on every aspect of the subsidiary's operations, thus violating promises that the American managers would be given free operational rein.

Japanese employees of American firms allege similar forms of bias—a fact that leads some businesspeople to question whether and how cultural obstacles can be overcome. Norman Peterson, president of a Fujitsu subsidiary in Silicon Valley, says playing golf is his path to smooth social relations with his Japanese colleagues—yet other Americans claim that Japanese co-workers don't seek them out or encourage socializing. Equal employment opportunity has also been at issue in some instances. Sumitomo and Honda have both been hit with litigation over their U.S. operations. With the number of state-side Japanese firms expected to rise, the issue of cultural clashes is sure to become increasingly prominent.

Source: As reported in Kenneth Noble, "A Clash of Styles: Japanese Companies in U.S.," *New York Times* (January 25, 1988), p. 7; and, Faye Rice, "Should you work for a foreigner?" *Fortune* (August 1, 1988), pp. 123–134.

---

your way someday, it is the latter one, in particular, that may be of most immediate significance. Take a look at *Newsline 19.1* which discusses some of the difficulties encountered by Japanese firms operating in the United States, and by some of the American employees who work for them. As direct foreign investment grows around the world, the implications of the many issues of international management magnify as well.

This chapter focuses primarily on international management from the perspective of businesses and their international operations. This focus was chosen because businesses are visible and active in the international arena, and because they have been studied the most by scholars. As has consistently been true throughout the book, however, the concepts, issues, and guidelines to be developed in the business context readily apply to other types of organizations.

INTERNATIONAL BUSINESS

International business is just what the label implies, the conduct of for-profit transactions of goods and services across national boundaries. It is the foundation for world trade and the movement of raw materials, finished products, and specialized services from one country to another around the globe. Have you ever considered just how international most major business firms have become? Take the Coca-Cola Company, for example.

ILLUSTRATIVE CASE:
COCA COLA COMPANY

The Coca-Cola Company operates in about 150 countries, and commands about 40 percent of the U.S. soft drink market and 33 percent of the market elsewhere in the world.[1] The company now earns more money from soft drink sales in Japan than it does in America. In the past, Coke's international operations involved the sale of syrup to wholesalers and bottlers in other countries. Of late, it has embarked on a new strategy of investing in some bottling operations overseas and spending heavily on foreign plants and distribution systems. The company is betting that foreign markets are its best investments, and is targeting underdeveloped markets in Europe and Asia for special attention.

Of course, the problems of implementing this global strategy vary from country to country. In Germany, Coke is trying to streamline a chaotic bottling and distribution system; in Indonesia, it's trying to increase the number of retail outlets, including the purchase of over 20,000 pushcarts; and in Italy and France it's trying to convince consumers to drink Coke with meals.

Decision making in worldwide markets can also get very complicated. For example, when Coca-Cola first gave an Israeli firm a franchise to bottle and sell Coke in Israel, Coke was promptly boycotted in the Arab countries. However, the company had technology and know-how that the Arab countries needed. Its food division had expertise in agriculture, and the Arabs were interested in developing their agricultural know-how. Consequently, the company had reason to hope that this expertise would maintain sales of Coke in the Arab world.

Another international market decision made by Coca-Cola involved India. The Indian government insists that all multinationals transfer some of their knowledge and ownership to Indian nationals. Coca-Cola refused to make its secret formula known and thus lost the lucrative Indian market. Management decided that disclosure of the secret formula

would be even more adverse to the company's interests than losing India's business.

Coca-Cola has also opened plants in China, where the "cola wars" continue as Coke and Pepsi battle for markets they describe as "limitless." Executives from both firms are serious about competing, but are finding it difficult to get established in this new environment. The operating problems include getting used to the needs and competencies of local workers, working with government-imposed foreign exchange restrictions, and otherwise learning how to deal with the Chinese bureaucracy.

Even if Coca-Cola had no foreign sales or facilities, its operations would still be greatly affected by the international environment. Imports are essential for two of the company's major products—soft drinks and coffee. Almost all coffee must be imported, and about half the sugar used in soft drinks comes from foreign sources.

Reasons for Going International

The Coca-Cola case shows how strongly even one of our most common day-to-day products is tied to international business operations. Business firms engage in international activities for many reasons. NEC, Hitachi, and other Japanese corporations are operating in the United States for a purpose; Coke and Pepsico are operating in China, the Soviet Union, and many other countries of the world for good reasons also. In general, the impetus toward international business is a quest for opportunities not otherwise available in domestic markets, or to solve problems that can't be solved through domestic operations alone. More specifically, international business offers firms the potential for:

1. *Profits.* Organizations often initiate international operations to expand their profit potential.
2. *Expanded markets.* A worldwide sales orientation means that goods can be sold to many markets.
3. *Raw materials.* Businesses operating in many countries have expanded access to raw materials suppliers.
4. *Financial capital.* International operations allow firms to draw on the financial resources of many nations.
5. *Lower labor costs.* International corporations can concentrate labor-intensive operations in countries with lower labor costs.

A good example of how the advantages of international operations are used by business firms is **worldwide sourcing.** This involves the manufacturing and/or purchasing of components from various parts of the world for use in a final product. Take a classic case.

At IBM the firm's original IBM-PC had a total manufacturing cost of about $900. Of this, around $600 was spent overseas. The monochrome monitor came from Korea, the floppy disk drives from Singapore, and the power supply, printer, and keyboard from Japan. The case and semiconductors came from the United States, where the final unit was also assembled. It then sold for $2000 + .

Forms of International Business

International businesses exchange goods, services, technologies, and capital across national boundaries. They do this through the various forms of business described below. In general, the degree of commitment to international business—both in terms of resource commitments and risk—increases as you move further down the list.

Exporting and importing of goods and/or services across national boundaries. Exporting involves selling abroad in foreign markets; importing involves acquiring foreign goods and selling them in domestic markets. Exports, in particular, are considered important to a country's economy. Major interest in the United States of late, for example, has centered on the size of the country's trade deficit as based on export/import relationships like those depicted in Figure 19.1. The end-of-chapter career perspective picks up on this with a special look at America's new "export entrepreneurs."

Licensing agreements wherein a foreign firm pays a fee for the rights to make or sell a foreign company's product. This typically involves obtaining access to a special technology or brand name for which the licenser has proprietary interests. Licensing is one way technology is transferred from one country to the next, and is common in pharmaceuticals, consumer products, and high-technology industries.

Management contracts in which an individual or firm contracts to provide management and technical services to a foreign concern. Such contracts are especially common in the hospitality in-

dustry, where established hotel firms contract to manage hotels in other countries, and in construction where established contractors agree to manage large projects around the world. Emerging nations often use management contracting to gain outside expertise for development projects.

Joint ventures in which investments are made in a foreign operation in cooperation with one or more local partners. As introduced in the chapter opener, the joint venture is often used as a way of establishing a business presence in a foreign country. It can also become an important vehicle for technology transfer. All the major U.S. automakers, for example, now have joint ventures with Japanese firms to manufacture cars and trucks in the United States. The benefits flow both ways, with U.S. firms gaining access to Japanese technology and the Japanese firms gaining further access to U.S. markets.

Subsidiary investments that establish wholly-owned operations in a foreign country. Foreign subsidiaries may be formed through direct investment in start-up operations abroad, or equity investments that acquire major interests in existing ones. Foreign direct investment is very important to the world economy, and is increasingly common in the United States. In just one year alone, overall direct foreign investment in the U.S. rose 19.6 percent while Japanese investments and acquisitions in the United States jumped to over $5.9 billion. This includes the $2 billion Sony paid for CBS Records, as well as the $1.5 billion Aoki paid for Westin Hotels and the $500 million Nippon Life invested in Shearson Lehman Brothers. During the same year, U.S. acquisitions in Japan totaled about $26.3 million.[2]

Each of the prior forms of international business is a strategic option available to managers seeking to pursue overseas initiatives. When you think of the alternatives, however, you might be tempted to picture them as pursued most aggressively by *large* firms. In the United States, the export accomplishments and potential of *smaller* businesses increasingly signal a new and major positive shift in the economy.[3] Indeed, the international commerce of smaller businesses may be a major factor in reducing the trade deficits that result from patterns like the ones depicted earlier in Figure 19.1. The following report on one firm's foray into the world of international business is indicative of what is happening in this sector of the economy.[4]

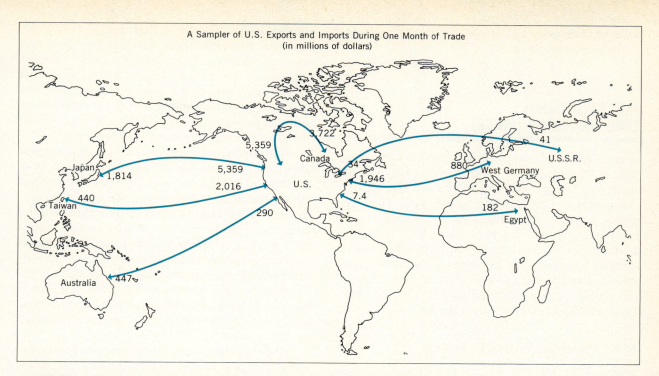

A Sampler of U.S. Exports and Imports During One Month of Trade
(in millions of dollars)

5,359

3,722

Canada

41

U.S.S.R.

Japan

1,814

5,359

2,016

34

880

West Germany

U.S.

1,946

Taiwan

440

7.4

182

Egypt

290

Australia

447

FIGURE 19.1 *Export-import relationships in the global economy: the case of the U.S. trade deficit.*

At Falcon Products, Inc. a small, St. Louis-based manufacturer, the initiative came more by chance than design. Owner Franklin Jacobs was on a tour through Europe. He says: "I discovered that my products were a lot better and a helluva lot cheaper" than those on the market there. He caught export fever, rented exposition space at the U.S. embassy in London, and shipped over a container load of his restaurant furniture and equipment. He received orders for more than $200,000 worth of goods, and now exports through European distributors. It's a modest beginning for the newly *international* Falcon Products, but Jacobs is optimistic in summing up his experience to date—". . . what we have is priced properly, and it will beat them on quality," he says.

Joint ventures are also in the news these days. Think back to the chapter opening example of Mikhail Gorbachev's campaign for *perestroika* or economic reforms in the Soviet Union. One result is heightened interest in East–West cooperation via joint ventures. In any setting, joint ventures offer potential benefits when foreign and local expertise are combined to mutual advantage. In return for its

investment from abroad, the outside partner gains access to a foreign market and the assistance of a local partner who should understand the local business environment. In return for its investment, the local partner often benefits through the transfer of capital goods and technology as well as the opportunity to learn new skills and expertise through participation in joint operations. Consider this example.[5]

At New United Manufacturing, Inc. (NUMMI) a GM–Toyota joint venture in Fremont, California, a plant that had been closed under GM ownership was reopened under the joint venture. It now operates with a higher productivity rate than ever in the past and employs a number of innovative manufacturing techniques learned from the Japanese partner—including just-in-time scheduling, flexible work teams, and careful staffing. GM has transferred many of the new techniques successfully to its other domestic operations. Toyota, meanwhile, has gained valuable experience dealing with U.S. labor unions, suppliers, and other elements in the business environment. Many of these insights are helpful as the firm expands its own operations elsewhere in the United States.

MULTINATIONAL CORPORATIONS (MNCs)

A **multinational corporation (MNC)** is a business firm with extensive international operations in more than one foreign country. MNCs are more than companies that just do "business abroad." They are *global concerns* whose missions and strategies are truly international in scope. These large multinational businesses are complemented by other *multinational organizations* (MNOs) whose non-profit missions and operations also span the globe. Good examples are the International Red Cross, the United Nations, and the World Bank.

MNCs and the World Economy

Many of the premier businesses in the world are found in any listing of MNCs. Table 19.1 shows 10 large MNCs headquartered in the United States and

TABLE 19.1 *Ten Large U.S. and Foreign Multinational Corporations*

Large U.S.-based MNCs
Exxon
Mobil
IBM
General Motors
Ford Motor
Texaco
Citicorp
Du Pont
Dow Chemical
Chevron

Large MNCs based elsewhere
Royal Dutch/Shell Group (Netherlands/UK)
British Petroleum (United Kingdom)
Toyota Motor Corp. (Japan)
IRI-Instituto Reconstruzione Industriale (Italy)
Daimler-Benz (West Germany)
Volkswagen (West Germany)
Hitachi (Japan)
Fiat (Italty)
Siemens (West Germany)
Matsushita Electric (Japan)

Source: "The 100 Largest U.S. Multinationals," *Forbes* (July 25, 1988), pp. 248–249; and, "The International 500, *Fortune* (August 1, 1988), pp. D7–D9.

another 10 headquartered elsewhere in the world. In a time when consumer tastes and product and resource markets increasingly span national boundaries, the actions of multinational firms can substantially impact the world economy and the affairs of individual nations as well. One distinction in the approaches taken by MNCs to their global operations involves the contrasts between:[6]

Ethnocentric corporations—which impose their own philosophies and management practices on foreign operations, and then strictly control them through highly centralized structures. An ethnocentric corporation tries to operate abroad in the same way that it does at home. This rather "colonial" approach to foreign operations generally fails to respect local needs and customs, and often encounters eventual resistance and operating difficulties. Some of the criticisms of Nestlé in the products it has sold in developing countries might be attributed to an inappropriate ethnocentric philosophy toward foreign markets.

Polycentric corporations—which pursue decentralized operations in several different countries. They allow subsidiaries to operate abroad in relatively autonomous ways while pursuing locally-appropriate missions and strategies, but reporting to a common corporate umbrella. Large oil companies like Exxon and British Petroleum are polycentric MNCs that operate around the world through many subsidiary companies. This approach allows greater responsiveness to local needs and conditions, and tends to be quite successful when decentralization is genuinely implemented.

Geocentric corporations—which are dedicated to totally-integrated global operations. Such firms pursue worldwide missions and strategies in both product and resource markets. Ideally, they take on transnational corporate identities, and make strategic decisions from a global perspective. While this extreme is probably difficult to achieve in actual practice, the current directions of Ford Motor Company evidence a "geocentric" posture. The company is trying to build "world" cars for "world" markets using "worldwide" expertise and resources. More on the Ford case will be said later.

MNC/Host-Country Relations

The many possible reasons for pursuing international business initiatives were identified earlier.

They represent what MNCs hope to gain through operations in various countries. Figure 19.2 shows that both the MNCs and the countries that "host" their foreign operations should be able to mutually benefit. From the host country's viewpoint, MNCs can bring a number of advantages. These include expanded tax bases, more revenue, increased employment, technology transfer, capital development, access to special industries, development of local resources, and more. When an MNC prospers, so too should the host country.

If this represents what should happen in MNC/host-country relations, a logical question to ask is, "What then can go wrong?" There are many possible answers to this question, all relating to the potential for MNCs to have adverse impacts on the countries in which they operate. This is particularly true for MNCs operating in developing countries. Perhaps you remember the controversy over the safety and marketing of Nestle's infant formula to third-world countries. You probably didn't know that a U.S. federal judge once ruled that the Consumer Products Safety Commission couldn't prevent a North Carolina carpet mill from exporting

rugs to Africa which were considered unsafe because they didn't meet U.S. flammability standards. But, surely, you didn't miss publicity regarding the tragedy experienced in India when deadly poisonous gas leaked into the city of Bhopal from a Union Carbide subsidiary operating there.

The controversies associated with MNC operations in foreign countries more generally include complaints that they will:[7]

- Extract excessive profits.
- Dominate the local economy.
- Interfere with the local government.
- Fail to help domestic firms develop.
- Divert the most talented of local personnel from domestic enterprises.
- Fail to transfer advanced technologies and know-how into local hands.
- Fail to respect local customs, needs, and government objectives.

Of course, problems in MNC/host-country relations can also emanate from the MNCs' points of view. They sometimes feel exploited as well. Consider for example, the misfortunes of some firms with joint ventures in China. Profits from operations in China are proving elusive to come by and, even when made, foreign exchange restrictions make it very difficult to get them out of the country. Adventurous companies that set up manufacturing and other operations there have also found it difficult to deal with local pressures to buy raw materials at inflated prices, pay above-market wages to local labor, and pay high prices for local services. The complicated nature of business dealings inside this particular country is illustrated—[8]

at one western company which had to pay a government bureau $236 per month to hire a local driver. Of this amount, the driver only received $36. He was allowed to earn from the foreign employer only the standard local wage. But the employer had to pay a premium to the government in order to hire his services.

at American Motors where the company's Beijing Jeep joint venture had to stop assembling vehicles for a two-month period—the reason? The Chinese government refused to allocate the foreign exchange needed by the factory to buy component parts abroad. The problem wasn't resolved until the company appealed directly to China's premier. If anything, AMC executives feel they got into trouble by

FIGURE 19.2 *Contrasts in the working relationships between MNCs and host countries.*

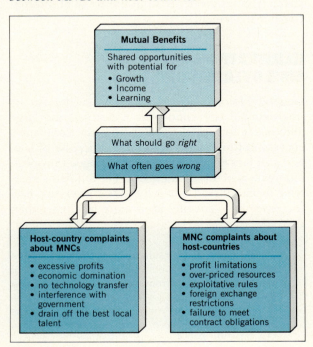

Mutual Benefits

Shared opportunities with potential for
- Growth
- Income
- Learning

What should go *right*

What often goes *wrong*

Host-country complaints about MNCs
- excessive profits
- economic domination
- no technology transfer
- interference with government
- drain off the best local talent

MNC complaints about host-countries
- profit limitations
- over-priced resources
- exploitative rules
- foreign exchange restrictions
- failure to meet contract obligations

rushing too quickly into a situation they knew too little about. The local manager AMC sent in from overseas to head the joint venture said: "Who knew anything about the Chinese auto industry then? Nobody knew how the supply situation would develop or that the foreign exchange crunch would be so severe."

MNC/Home-Country Relations

Another aspect of the MNC story deals with the "home" country's point of view. This is the country in which the MNC is headquartered and from which its international operations are directed. Even at home MNCs are sometimes subject to criticism that they:

- Lose touch with domestic needs and priorities.
- Export jobs by diverting labor-intensive operations to cheaper foreign labor markets.
- Divert capital investments away from domestic opportunities to those abroad.
- Allow and even encourage corrupt practices in their overseas dealings.

The last item on the list deserves special elaboration. The subject of foreign corrupt practices is a source of continuing controversy in the United States. In 1977 the Foreign Corrupt Practices Act became law. This act made it illegal for firms and their managers to engage in a variety of "corrupt" practices, such as giving bribes and excessive commissions in return for business favors abroad. The law specifically bans payoffs to foreign officials to obtain or keep business, provides punishments for executives who know about or are involved in such activities, and requires that detailed accounting records be kept for international business transactions.

At the time the antibribery law was passed, over 300 companies were linked to corrupt foreign practices. Since then, however, substantial lobbies have tried to get the 1977 law repealed. Critics of the law feel that it fails to recognize the "reality" of business as practiced in many foreign nations. They complain that American business suffers a competitive disadvantage as a result, because it can't offer the same "deals" abroad as competitors from other countries can and which locals might expect as standard business practice. At present, we have continuing debate on the issue but also, the continuing presence of the law.[9]

ENVIRONMENTAL CONSTRAINTS ON INTERNATIONAL OPERATIONS

The environment is an important influence on any organization. And as summarized in Figure 19.3, nowhere is the challenge of general environmental characteristics greater than in the arena of international management.

ILLUSTRATIVE CASE:
GM'S OVERSEAS DRIVE

General Motors' lack of complete success in its international operations has concerned the large automaker for years. Even though the company's success in Europe has been on the increase of late, GM still lags behind Ford and the major European automakers in this marketplace. The following ideas have been offered for why GM's overseas performance has generally been more lackluster than desired.[10]

. . . GM's overseas subsidiaries have suffered from a Detroit-always-knows-best syndrome. As a result of constant interference from engineers and designers in the United States, foreign products always seemed to wind up looking more American than European. "The joke was that whenever we'd start out to build a Mercedes, we'd end up with a Cadillac," says David

FIGURE 19.3 *Sample general environmental factors influencing the management of international operations.*

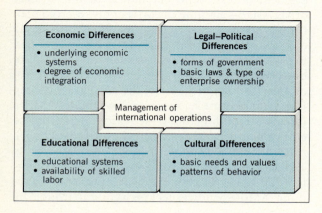

Lewis, a University of Michigan professor who once worked in the chairman's office at GM.

For years, GM treated its foreign subsidiaries like undeserving orphans, forcing them to finance their own expansion through earnings and local borrowings. But the practice, says David Healey, an auto analyst at Drexel Burnham Lambert Inc., not only inhibited foreign growth but also resulted in "some pretty weird items" on GM's worldwide balance sheet. "They had debts in one place at 15 percent interest and debts in another at 10 percent," he says. "It made no sense at all."

GM has had a particularly tough time, for instance, persuading bright young managers to accept overseas assignments. Because the company formerly used its foreign operations as a dumping ground for washed-up executives, some employees still attach that stigma to foreign transfers. "International was like the black hole," says James Bowling, who worked on GM's worldwide staff. "People were sent abroad, and you never heard from them again."

"GM has yet to become a truly multinational corporation," says Peter Drucker, whose organizational study of GM, "Concept of the Corporation," has served as a model for a number of major U.S. companies. "They are an American concern with overseas affiliates" that aren't integrated into the company.

Peter Drucker's closing observations are an interesting commentary on the GM case. He implies that for an organization to be truly "multinational," it must understand and successfully accommodate the intricacies of operating in different countries. Things like language barriers, governmental practices, consumer preferences, and cultural biases—all things which the article implies GM has historically had a hard time dealing with—are but a few of the environmental differences to which international management must adapt. Let's examine some of these differences in more detail.

Economic, Legal–Political, and Educational Differences

To operate successfully in a foreign country, a wise manager recognizes a wide variety of environmental differences in economic, political and educational systems. These differences must be systematically considered if decision making in international management is to meet the demands of local situations.

Economic Differences

Looking around the world, we can see many shared economic concerns, needs, and problems. But there are important differences as well. A basic issue relates to the nature of the foreign economic system itself. In broadest terms, the economic systems of the world fall on a continuum of two extremes—free-market economies and centralized-planning economies. Each presents a different set of challenges to the foreign firm that must operate under its constraints.

Free-market economies characterize most Western nations such as Canada and the U.S. They operate under an economic system governed by laws of supply and demand. Although government policies will influence the free-market system, they do so to a far lesser extent than in **centralized-planning economies.** The latter, characterized by the Soviet Union and China require a central government body to make basic economic decisions for an entire nation. Such centralized systems may determine allocations of raw materials, set product or service output quotas, regulate wages and prices, and even distribute qualified personnel among alternative employers.

The degree of economic integration across countries can also become quite significant. The **European Economic Community,** for example, is an agreement among twelve European nations relating to common policies for trade and tariffs, and the flow of labor and capital among member nations. Sometimes known as the *Common Market,* this form of economic cooperation among nations can become a major force with which international business must contend. *Newsline 19.2* gives a further example from Europe of the growing competitive significance of transnational alliances.

Legal–Political Differences

The legal–political system of any nation is also a major environmental influence on international management. Two broad political extremes are democratic or representative government and totalitarianism. In between both sets of extremes, of course, are the multiple and varied combinations that actually represent the countries of the world at any point in time. **Democratic systems** rely on free elections and representative assemblies of the population to establish a government for the society as a whole. **Totalitarian systems** govern by restricted

BUSINESS IS CREATING EUROPE, INC.

The idea of an integrated European market is not new, but now it is really beginning to come alive as Europe experiences a wave of cross-border mergers, joint ventures, and buyouts. Such moves are on the rise within the 12-nation European Community, and many similar deals are also being struck between EC-based and non-EC companies in Europe.

Jean-Louis Beffa, chairperson of Saint-Gobain, a French glass and building-materials company, summed up efforts by European executives to put aside national and corporate rivalries: "There is no other choice. We are managing American-style, with the emphasis on profits. That logic brings you to thinking along European lines."

A $2-billion joint venture between Britain's General Electric Company and Holland's Philips Corporation has created instant challenges for America's General Electric and Japan's Toshiba Corporation. As Europe shares more markets, especially in key industries such as telecommunications and computers, gobal competition will surely increase. For the European businesses crossing national lines, the challenge is to know the local markets they target. Says McKinsey & Company's Eric Friberg, stationed in Brussels: "Managers have to think through how they can become local insiders in ways that count."

Signs are also growing that countries outside the community will face growing trade restrictions. The newly integrated EC may bring in a new era of European protectionism.

Source: As reported in "Hands Across Europe: Deals that Could Redraw the Map," *Business Week* (May 18, 1987), pp. 64–65; and "How Business Is Creating Europe Inc.," *Business Week* (September 7, 1987), pp. 40–41; and, "Laying the Foundation for a Great Wall of Europe," *Business Week* (August 1, 1988), pp. 40–41.

---

representation in the affairs of government through dictatorship, single-party rule, or the rule of preferred-membership groups. As international operations vary between countries governed at these political extremes, they encounter very different operating constraints.

The legal systems of the nations of the world also vary widely. This is significant because an international operation is expected to abide by the laws of the host country. The more host-country laws differ from those of the home country and/or from other countries in which international operations are conducted, the more difficult and complex it may be to adapt to local ways. Consider this example of how differing laws in various European countries would require the modification of a 30-second Kellogg cereal commercial that was originally produced for showing on British TV:[11]

■ *In the Netherlands* all references to iron and vitamins in the cereal would have to be deleted.

■ *In France* because children are forbidden from endorsing products on TV, a child wearing a Kellogg t-shirt in the commercial would have to be edited out.

■ *In Germany* rules against making competitive claims would require that the line "Kellogg makes their cornflakes the best they've ever been" would have to be cut.

A significant legal issue in international business relations to incorporation practices and business ownership. Some countries, like Egypt, won't allow foreign firms to invest there without at least 51 percent of ownership resting in local hands. In other cases, the prevailing political philosophy makes a difference in the environment for operations. When the socialist François Mitterand was elected president of France, he ushered in a trend to nationalize major French enterprises, even those involving foreign investments. ITT, for example, was forced to negotiate the sale of its telecommunications unit there to the French government. The ultimate legal risk in such cases is when a host country expropriates or takes over foreign assets without payment.

Another important legal consideration in conducting international business rests with trade and copyright laws as they vary around the world. Counterfeit computers and computer software, for example, are prevalent in parts of Asia. But consider what happened—[12]

at Apple Computer, Inc. when the firm brought 34 retailers to court in Hong Kong under the local copyright ordinance. Management was quite disappointed with the results.[13] Instead of heavy fines and possible prison sentences, magistrates levied what company officials considered only "token" fines. They complained that Apple's market share there was being "crushed by clones," and observed, "Overseas companies are not going to set up here if their products are not adequately protected."

Educational Differences

Educational systems also vary from one country to the next, and the level and quality of education achieved by the local populations varies as well. Since international operations usually rely in part on the local labor force, literacy and the level of technical education are important environmental factors. For those operations needing more skilled employees, the better the educational system and the greater the availability of trained persons, the better things will be for the employing organization.

Great pressures are often placed on international operations to train and upgrade the skills of local citizens. At the same time, a firm may have to import qualified personnel from the home or other countries to compensate for local deficiencies, on a short-term or long-term basis. This creates complex situations within the firm and in firm/host-country relations. U.S. and European firms operating in Tanzania, for example, employ large numbers of Asian

expatriates to staff certain technical positions, such as accounting and engineering. The Tanzanian government, in turn, exerts continued pressure for the firms to replace these expatriates as soon as possible with local nationals.

Cultural Differences

Culture is a shared set of beliefs, values, and patterns of behavior common to a group of people. Some aspects of culture that make it significant to international management are that it[13]

- Changes slowly, if at all.
- Is difficult to change.
- Exists in the minds of people.
- Is shared by a number of people.
- Is present in a society's institutions.
- Represents the national character.

Culture in the Traveler's View

Anyone who travels from one country to the next knows that cultural differences exist. **Culture shock,** the confusion and discomfort someone experiences when in an unfamiliar culture, is a reminder that many of them must be mastered to even travel comfortably around the world. But, the important business and managerial implications of cultural differences must be understood too. For example,[14]

In Tokyo an American marketing representative entered a conference room expecting preliminary and superficial discussions with the CEO. Waiting for her instead, were several department heads wanting to know everything in minute detail about her offer. She lost face when unable to answer their very detailed questions. The price for being unprepared in Japan was the loss of the $6 million sale to a German who came in with the facts at hand.
In Riyadh an American exporter went to see a Saudi official. After entering the office, he sat in a chair and crossed his legs. With the sole of his shoe exposed to the Saudi host, an insult had been delivered. Then, he passed documents to the host using his left hand, which Muslims consider unclean. Lastly he refused when offered coffee, suggesting criticism of the Saudi's hospitality. The price for these cultural miscues in Saudi Arabia was the loss of a $10 million contract to a Korean better versed in Arab ways.

Obviously, cultural differences such as these are highly varied and ultimately complex. In general, the informed manager should be as sensitive as possible to what is "different" about a foreign culture, and try to learn as much as possible through personal experience and/or the advice of others with that experience.[15] Remember in particular, that cross-cultural communications may be affected by such basic things as—

1. *Language differences* Languages vary dramatically around the world; even the same basic language (such as English) varies in usage from one country to the next (e.g., from America to England to Australia). This places great emphasis on basic communications skills and points to the advantage of good foreign language training. At the very least, one must be prepared to do business in the language of a host country even if this requires the services of a translator.

2. *Etiquette and custom differences* Local customs vary in terms of dress and interpersonal habits, as well as protocols of time. One must learn in a given culture whether to be on time or to be late, how to dress for business, and how close to get in interpersonal relationships. What is standard and polite in one country may be considered impolite somewhere else.

National Culture in Four Dimensions

There is a pressing need to develop more systematic guidelines on cultural patterns and differences across nations. One advance in this area of management research has been made by Geert Hofstede, a Dutch scholar and international consultant to organizations. Hofstede studied personnel from a U.S.-based MNC operating in 40 countries. He concluded that managers and employees in the organization varied from one country to the next on these four *dimensions of national culture.*[16]

1. *Power distance* The degree to which a society accepts the unequal distribution of power in organizations.
2. *Uncertainty avoidance* The degree to which a society tolerates risk and situational uncertainties.
3. *Individualism* The degree to which a society emphasizes individual self-interests, versus the collective values of groups.
4. *Masculinity* The degree to which a society emphasizes assertiveness and material concerns, versus relationships with others and concerns for feelings.

Figure 19.4 presents a sampling of how various countries in Hofstede's study ranked on each of

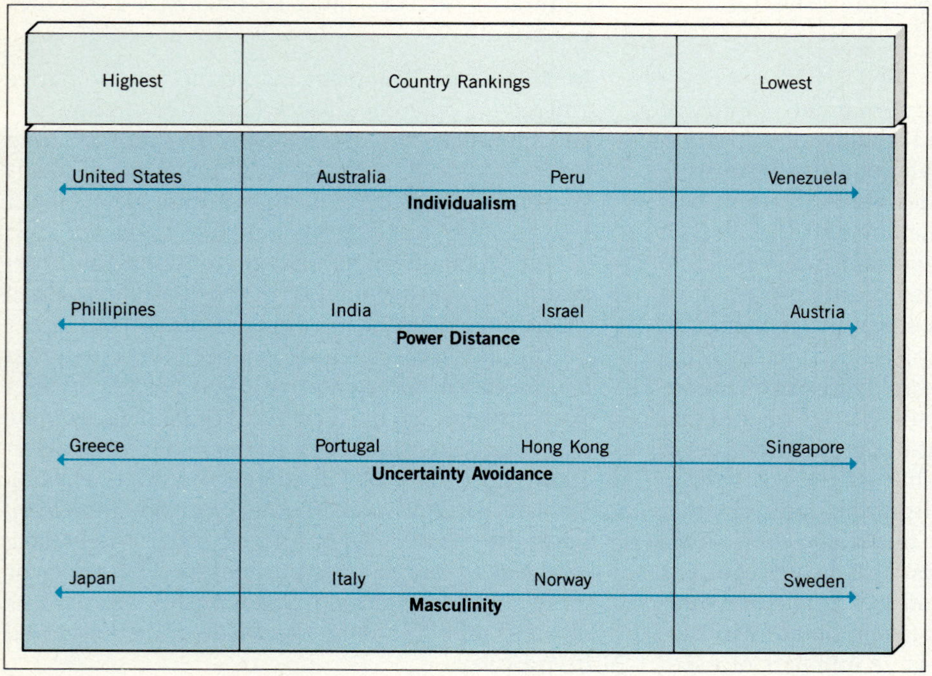

Highest	Country Rankings		Lowest
United States	Australia	Peru	Venezuela
	Individualism		
Phillipines	India	Israel	Austria
	Power Distance		
Greece	Portugal	Hong Kong	Singapore
	Uncertainty Avoidance		
Japan	Italy	Norway	Sweden
	Masculinity		

FIGURE 19.4 *A sampling of differences in country rankings on Hofstede's four dimensions of national cultures.*

Source: Data reported in Geert Hofstede, *Culture's Consequences* (Beverly Hills, CA: Sage, 1984).

these dimensions. For an added comparison, this is how the United States and Japan ranked.

- *Power distance* The United States ranked 15 out of 40 countries, reflecting a moderate tolerance of unequal power distribution. Japan had an intermediate score.

- *Uncertainty avoidance* The United States ranked 9 out of 40, reflecting above-average tolerance for uncertainty. Japan was among the countries showing the lowest tolerance for uncertainty.

- *Individualism* The United States ranked 40 out of 40, being the most individualistic country in the sample. Japan had an intermediate score.

- *Masculinity* The United States ranked 28 out of 40, reflecting values generally stereotyped as "masculine." Japan had the highest masculinity score of any country in the sample.

Hofstede's research is somewhat controversial, but it has gained considerable respect as one framework for understanding cultural differences.[17] It demonstrates that there are important differences among national cultures that have the potential to affect many aspects of international management. Later we will return to this notion when we examine the transferability of management theories and practices from one culture to the next.

THE MANAGEMENT FUNCTIONS IN AN INTERNATIONAL PERSPECTIVE

It goes without saying that the basic management functions—planning, organizing, leading, and controlling—apply to the international arena. It also holds true, though, that international management must accommodate the great diversity among national environments about which we have just been speaking. *Newsline 19.3* talks about this challenge in specific respect to the "global manager."[18] Some additional thoughts relevant to each of the management functions follow.

Planning and Controlling

The complexity of the international operating environment makes planning and controlling, already substantial tasks, even more difficult for managers. Picture a home office somewhere in the United States, say Chicago. Foreign operations are scat-

tered around the globe—Asia, Africa, South America, and Europe. Somehow the planning process must link the home office and foreign affiliates, while taking into account different environments and needs. These same factors add considerable pressure to control systems. Normal routines involving budgets, information systems, and other comprehensive controls are more difficult to maintain and implement in the face of environmental complexity. Distance, alone, adds a significant burden to the control requirements of any international operation.

Strategic Planning and Control

A difficult scenario has just been described. It is logical that local management *should* make decisions consistent with the host country's environment, and that they *should* supply the information corporate headquarters needs for planning and controlling. Perhaps closer to the truth of what often happens is that top management in corporate headquarters makes the strategic choices and sets policy for foreign operations with only sketchy planning inputs from the field. Control may well be left to chance, while local managers remain frustrated by lack of individual attention to their needs by home-office executives. It is unlikely, for example, that any strategic decision made in Chicago on the basis of limited information and perspective can optimally serve the needs of operations located in Asia, or anywhere else in the world.

Strategic planning and control in the international arena require major investments in information systems and sensitivity to all of the environmental issues discussed earlier in this chapter. The SWOT analysis of (1) organizational strengths and weaknesses, and (2) environmental opportunities and threats, reviewed in Chapter 5, is critical in this setting. Strategy formulation and implementation in international business is especially challenging in respect to the environmental considerations. More and more, the large MNCs in particular are realizing that *global strategies* and *global planning* are required. For example,[19]

At Ford Motor Company success has been found lately in world auto markets. And Ford's global strategy is clearly evident in the company's plan to build "centers of excellence" which avoid duplication of efforts and take advantage of expertise among company personnel around the world. Lo-

THE
GLOBAL MANAGER

International competition has given rise to the *global manager*—an individual comfortable with cultural diversity, quick to find opportunities in unfamiliar settings, and able to marshall many conflicting forces—economic, social, technological—for the benefit of the business. Successful global managers have learned the ropes the hard way—by having deals fall through. Experience has taught them how to pick a country for a new plant, how to coordinate production and inventory control, and how to standardize products in ways that will make them sell internationally.

IBM's products, marketed worldwide, are a good example of careful globalization. They are easily modified to meet the needs of local markets, which means that they are at once standardized and customized. Boeing, another globally aware company, adapted its 737 jet to the conditions of airports in underdeveloped countries—and thus was able to revive the flagging sales of a plane that had trouble competing at home. Its management recognized an opportunity and moved quickly to establish a customer base.

An essential key to global management is practice: ample experience working with foreign conditions, people, and markets. Many companies send managers abroad to learn the hows and whys of international business. Some companies have ongoing international research projects staffed by experts with no sales responsibility; others make use of on-site experts who can evaluate foreign marketing and production possibilities.

Roger Johnson of Western Digital, a microcomputer component maker, stresses that American managers of "world product groups," a popular organizational structure for international business, need to work closely with their foreign colleagues to make this structure pay off. "Don't let your people in the U.S. think they know best," he says. "They probably don't."

Source: As reported in Andrew Kupfer, "How to Be a Global Manager," *Fortune* (March 14, 1988), pp. 52–58.

---

cated in different countries, these centers will eventually specialize in the production of the basic "platforms" from which different model Ford cars are assembled. The platforms will be shipped from each center to many assembly points where local tastes can be accommodated through special exterior and passenger compartment styles. As Ford CEO Donald Peterson looks toward the next decade, his global strategy is for—*North America* (U.S.) to build midsize car platforms, *Ford of Europe* (England) to build compact ones, *Mazda* (Japan; 25% Ford owned) to build subcompact ones, and *Asia-Pacific* (Australia) to build them for specialty models.

Political-Risk Analysis

What we didn't tell you in the prior example is that Ford has also explored a joint venture to produce cars in the Soviet Union. However, Ford management was cautious since the project might be hampered by shifts in U.S.–Soviet relations.[20] This brings us to the subject of **political risk analysis,** or forecasting the probability of various events that can threaten the security of a foreign investment. This is a high-level and even glamorous form of forecasting. Organizations that operate seriously in the international arena typically have planning staffs specially trained and assigned to forecast political events and follow worldwide trends. Many ex-diplomats also become private consultants in the field. Henry Kissinger (former U.S. secretary of state) is one that comes immediately to mind. He is part of a growing cadre of "global business diplomats," who not only provide political risk consultations but also may engage in acts of diplomacy in behalf of their organizational clients.[21]

The stakes of political risk are high. It is obvious, for example, that foreign investors suffered in the political turmoil accompanying the fall of the Shah of Iran and the overthrow of Nicaraguan governments. It is less obvious that in one February day, it was possible for a firm to lose 28 percent of its foreign assets overnight. How? Simply because the Mexican government made a decision to allow its currency, the peso, to float in the international money markets. The net result was a loss in the value of Mexican assets valued in U.S. dollars. Not all multinationals were caught by surprise in this case; some took protective measures ahead of time and benefited accordingly. They were the firms that had done their political-risk analysis well.

Among the basic factors that would be considered in a political-risk analysis for operations in a particular foreign country are the following.[22]

1. *Social instability* Potential for local rebellions, subversion, riots, strikes, and spontaneous violence.
2. *Foreign conflict* Potential for the host country to enter into armed or diplomatic conflicts with other nations.
3. *Governmental system* Potential for the governmental system of the country to shift from one extreme to another, or revise its policies toward foreign investors and other nations.
4. *Economic climate* Potential for the local economy to surge or decay, and for economic components such as labor, capital, and regulations to change also.

Organizing and Leading

The same factors that challenge the planning and controlling functions in the international arena also influence organizing and leading. Three areas of special attention can be highlighted in the General Motors case cited earlier in this chapter. If you recall

The article stated "GM has yet to become a truly multinational corporation. They are an American concern with overseas affiliates that aren't integrated into the company."
The implication is GM's *organization structure* is not well suited to international operations.
The article stated "GM has had a particularly tough time, for instance, persuading bright young managers to accept overseas assignments."
The implication is GM has a *staffing* problem in its international operations.

FIGURE 19.5 *Organization designs for international operations: a multinational geographic structure.*

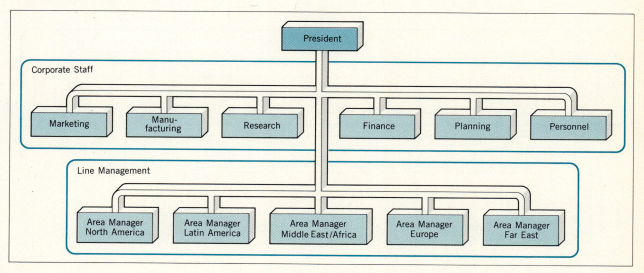

The article stated "A long-term consequence of GM's inability to groom executives overseas is a shortage of international savvy at the top of the corporation."

The implication is GM has a *leadership* problem in its international operations.

Multinational Organization Structures

A basic principle of organization design holds in the international as well as the domestic setting: structure should match environment and context (size, technology, strategy, and people). Multinational organization structures are not all that different from others studied in Chapter 6, they are just more complex.[23]

The usual pattern for an emerging international business is simply to set aside a vice-presidential function and give it the responsibility for overseeing all foreign operations. This structure may be fine for a single foreign country and single product or business line. As operations expand into multinational settings, however, the demands on the organization and the international division manager can easily overload the structure. Two organization designs better adapted to worldwide operations are the multinational geographic and product structures. Each encourages decentralization and flexibility in responding to varying needs and conditions on a worldwide basis.

In the multinational geographic structure shown in Figure 19.5, any given country becomes simply one of a number of world markets. Producing and selling functions are grouped under separate geographic units. Responsibility for all products in a given region is assigned to a single-line executive who reports to corporate management. This structure is strong in respect to area expertise. But it can be cumbersome to coordinate product developments and technology transfers from one area to the next.

In the multinational product structure shown in Figure 19.6, worldwide product responsibility is assigned to separate line-product group managers. Area specialists coordinate product activity in a given area from the corporate staff level. Each product group has operational responsibility on a worldwide basis for its products or services, but operates in any given area under the guidance of the area specialist. This structure facilitates global product strategies. But it works best only when managers representing all geographical regions are part of the product team. Otherwise it may be dominated by the narrow perspectives of home-country managers.

FIGURE 19.6 *Organization designs for international operations: a multinational product structure.*

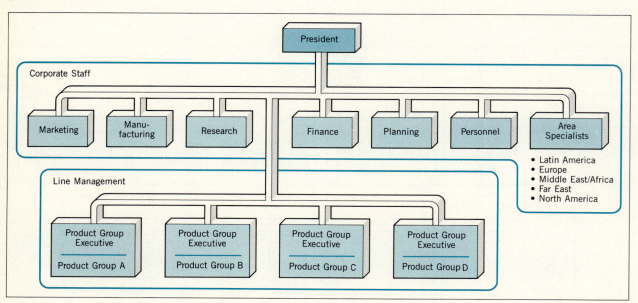

Staffing International Operations

Organizations seeking success on a global scale require the contributions of personnel from the host countries. This is an indispensable requirement and should be taken very seriously as a staffing responsibility. One successful international business owner sums it up this way: "Hire competent locals, use competent locals, and listen to competent locals."[24]

In addition to local hires, organizations with international operations need people capable of handling overseas assignments of short-term or long-term nature. The international dimensions of business are increasingly addressed in U.S. business curricula, and employers keep asking for even further emphasis. Perhaps the most dramatic example of education for international responsibilities comes from Europe, where a number of business schools are gaining reputations for turning out graduates with the potential to become truly global managers.[25] Institut European D'Administration des Affaires—INSEAD (France), London Business School (England), International Management Development Institute—IMEDE (Switzerland), International Management Institute—IMI (Switzerland), and Instituto de Estudios Superiores de la Empresa—IESE (Spain) are the widely respected leaders in this respect. The schools have international student bodies, offer international curricula, expose students to international executives and perspectives, and stress foreign language capabilities.

At the executive level, in particular, success in international operations often depends on having home-office personnel with experience abroad. This helps facilitate planning and control through better corporate staff–foreign affiliate relationships. It also helps ensure that the international arena, with all of its peculiarities and unique demands, is truly represented in strategic decision making.

From an organization's point of view, however, posting staff to foreign locations has many complications. It is costly to transfer home-office personnel abroad and pay moving expenses, cost-of-living allowances, overseas salary supplements, special vacation privileges, and other family support and benefits necessary to maintain an overseas assignment. Such compensation and benefit packages are designed to make an overseas assignment as attractive as possible to the employee and his or her family. Even then, success in overseas assignments generally requires:

- Real desire to live and work for an extended time in a foreign country.
- Active encouragement and support from spouse and family.
- Adaptability and flexibility on the individual's part, as well as by part spouse and family.
- High degree of cultural awareness/sensitivity.
- Technical competence.
- Leadership ability.

Leadership in the International Setting

The last item on the preceding list is fundamental. Good management involves successful leadership, and there is continuing debate on how the practice of leadership applies across cultures. Our discussion on environmental differences from one country to the next clearly suggests that leadership in international management should be highly contingent as well. That is, leadership practices should fit the unique demands of local cultures and situations as much as possible.

But what does this last statement really mean? Does it mean that our prevailing theories of leadership and management really do apply across cultures? Or does it mean that the theories don't universally apply and that new ones specific to alternative cultures, must be developed in their place? These are among the questions addressed by research on comparative management practices.

COMPARATIVE MANAGEMENT PRACTICES

Comparative management, as a field of inquiry, is the study of how management practices systematically differ from one country and/or culture to the next. As the worldwide focus of management expands, the significance of comparative management studies expands as well.

Do American Practices Apply Abroad?

For much of the twentieth century, the United States has been a major source of research on management. U.S. management practices have also been frequently used as appropriate models by managers from other nations around the world. Against this background, however, lies a significant academic question: "Do American theories apply abroad?" Geert Hofstede, whose research was mentioned earlier, feels that they don't; at least he feels they don't apply universally and without modification.[26] Some of his specific concerns deal with leadership, motivation, and organization design.

Leadership Across Cultures

Hofstede critiques popular leadership theories according to how U.S. workers score on the four dimensions of national culture reviewed earlier. He argues, for example, that the U.S. focus on "participation" in the practice of leadership reflects its moderate position on the power-distance scale. France, a country with a higher score, shows less concern for participative management in the U.S. style. Countries with still lower scores, such as Sweden and Israel, are characterized by even more "democratic" management initiatives than the U.S. style.

Another example involves a U.S. consulting firm that analyzed decision-making practices in a large Scandinavian firm. The report criticized the corporation's decision-making style, which was described as "intuitive" and "consensus based." The consultants preferred the approaches more common to their U.S. clients—namely, fact-based instead of intuitive and fast, based on clear individual responsibilities. They appeared to have overlooked that decisions have to be made in a way that corresponds to the values of the environment in which they are to be implemented. This doesn't mean that the Scandinavian corporation's management need not improve its decision making and could not learn from the consultants' experience. But it does suggest that all of this should be done through a mutual recognition of cultural differences, not by ignoring them.

Motivation Across Cultures

Hofstede's critique of the cross-culture applications of motivation theories focuses largely on the assumptions underlying U.S.-based theories. He sees these theories as value-laden and heavily tied to cultures that stress willingness to accept risk and high concern for performance. Hofstede's data show this pattern consistent only with Anglo-American countries such as the United States, Canada, and the United Kingdom.

One of Hofstede's examples acknowledges that even a common value, such as the desire for in-creased humanization of work, has evolved into different management strategies in the American and European traditions. U.S. practice emphasizes job enrichment and a focus on restructuring *individual* jobs; autonomous work groups and restructuring jobs for groups or *teams* are the major focus of European practices.

Organization Design Across Cultures

A third focus for comparative management studies is organization design. Two of Hofstede's propositions on the application of basic structural design alternatives across cultural boundaries follow.

1. *Greater centralization* of decision making is preferred in countries with higher power-distance scores (*example:* France).
2. *Greater formalization* in the form of added rules and procedures is preferred in countries with higher uncertainty-avoidance scores (*example:* Germany).

An interesting insight into these patterns is found in the responses of a group of European MBA students when asked how they would resolve a common organizational problem—a conflict within one company between the sales and production departments. French students would refer the problem to higher authority, while German students would establish written policies governing sales/production relationships. British students by contrast, would use some form of group training to improve interpersonal skills among sales and production personnel.

Commentary

You have just experienced a heavy dose of one person's point of view on the transferability of management practices and theories across cultures. It is a useful review because Hofstede has studied the issue more rigorously than most scholars and his thoughts are both recent and provocative. They are not however, without fault.

Let's concede that there are important differences across cultures, just as the general environment itself varies substantially from one nation to the next. Hofstede's work is worthwhile because he approaches cultural differences in a systematic and empirical fashion. He then uses apparent variations in cultural patterns to explain the different preferences and practices of management in various countries. Cross-cultural research is difficult, though, and Hofstede's work is criticized for methodological shortcomings. He is also faulted for making his arguments on the failure of American management theories abroad too extensive and too general, given the data at hand.[27]

Still, work like Hofstede's research sensitizes us to cultural differences at the very time that interest is high in seeing what managers in one country can learn from the theories and successes of managers in other countries. Nowhere is this more evident than current worldwide interest in Japanese management practices.

American and Japanese Management Practices

Two popular management books of the 1980s are based on a comparison of Japanese and U.S. management practices. *Theory Z* by William Ouchi and *The Art of Japanese Management* by Richard Tanner Pascale and Anthony G. Athos remain on the bookshelves of most informed executives today.[28] The authors of the two books feel that understanding Japanese practices can enlighten other managers as to the essential ingredients of business and organizational success. Many other researchers and managers have followed their lead, with the result that much attention has been given during the last decade to the Japanese approach to management.

There are several unique aspects to the Japanese style that deserve attention.[29] Of fundamental significance is the emphasis on a strong bond between the employing organization and the individual worker. This involves shared loyalties—loyalty of the organization to the needs of the individual employee, and loyalty of the individual to the objectives of the organization. Some of the specific Japanese practices that are highlighted as beneficial in this regard are the following.

1. *Lifetime employment* Many Japanese join a company with the expectation of working there for an entire career. Both the organization and individual grow and mature together over time.
2. *Job rotation and broad experience* Many Japanese managers are rotated through several types of jobs and functions over time. The emphasis is on breadth of experience, not specialized skills; and it is on gradual progress, not speed of career advancement. This results in a management staff well in-

formed about the organization as a whole, and sharing common objectives.
3. *Shared information* Japanese firms emphasize information sharing at all levels of responsibility. A lot of information circulates in respect to performance objectives and accomplishments, and proposed activities and problems. "Networks" of interpersonal relationships built up through job rotation further assist in developing a broad base of information for decision making.
4. *Collective decisions* The Japanese often use a complex group consensus form of decision making that spreads responsibility for results and creates a team feeling among all parties involved. Called the *ringi system,* a typical decision sequence is:
■ After discussing a proposed solution to a problem, members of a work group arrive at a consensus and draft a plan of action.
■ The plan circulates among persons at the same or lower levels if they will be eventually affected; each affixes a formal seal after the review.
■ The plan is passed up the heirarchy gathering more seals at each stop until it reaches the level of final approval.
5. *Quality-control circles* The Japanese make good use of periodic group meetings to discuss possible quality improvements. We discussed the "QC-circle" concept in detail in Chapters 13 and 16.

You can see in these examples some interesting departures from what might be considered standard American practice. Table 19.2 goes further in detailing some generalized characteristics of organization structures and management systems in Japanese firms.

Do Japanese Practices Apply Abroad?

There is still a tendency when reading and thinking about Japanese management practices to view them as highly desirable for application in other countries and cultures. This is essentially the same thing we cautioned against, however, when critiquing the transfer of American management theories abroad a bit earlier. Perhaps Hofstede's words can again help you to put this issue of culture and the transfer of management practices among cultures in a realistic perspective.[30]

The way Americans look to Japan these days closely resembles the way the French, British, and Germans used to look to America 30 years ago. What the Japa-

TABLE 19.2 *Selected Characteristics of Traditional Japanese Management and Organization Practices*

Characteristics	Traditional Japanese System
Organization structure	Hierarchical organization with loose, broad general functions and informal job descriptions with strong reliance on internalized work-group norms of cooperation, consensus seeking, and high group achievement standards. Organization built around groups.
Management philosophy and expectations	People seen as most valuable asset in order to achieve company goals—that is, increasing their share of international markets. Organization and employee group goals are therefore seen as congruent to group goals.
Decision-making system	Decision-making system is highly decentralized, bottom-up, and informal, with verbal communications used to seek consensus and written system (Ringi) used as postconfirmation.
Management-employee relationship and control system	Paternalistic relationship with employees and their families. Lifetime employment with reciprocal employee-company dependency and loyalty. Reliance on high group motivation and standards with social work controls. Joint management–employee problem solving used as way of reinforcing common goals.
Selection, compensation, and promotion	Employees selected directly from school based on academic achievement, corporate examinations, and extensive screening program including familial relationships and school ties for lifetime. Promotion and compensation function of education, tenure, gender, and family responsibility until age 55. Broad group-evaluation criteria.
Human-resources training development	Human resources seen as invaluable lifetime investment. Continuous in-house training and development key to both organization loyalty and technical development. Less job and career specialization with broader skills and management development as team member. Technical adaptation and development traditionally very well developed.

Source: Adapted from Robert R. Rehder, "What American and Japanese Managers are Learning from Each Other," *Business Horizons,* Vol 24 (1981), p. 67. Copyright 1981 by the Foundation for the School of Business at Indiana University. Reprinted by permission.

nese are doing with American ideas resembles what the Americans were doing earlier with European ideas. In several respects, history repeats itself. Disregard of other cultures is a luxury only the strong can afford. . . . [The] consequent increase in cultural awareness represents an intellectual and spiritual gain. And as far as management theories go, cultural relativism is an idea whose time has come.

Support for Hofstede's warning was present in this chapter as far back as Newsline 19.1, which introduced some of the difficulties Japanese firms are finding in the United States and dealing with American workers.[31] Yet the success stories are there too. The most noteworthy may be—[32]

at NUMMI the GM–Toyota joint venture in Fremont, California mentioned earlier. Originally run by GM alone, the plant had been closed after a history of labor–management strife. One worker with 19 years of experience said his job "was boring and tedious because you did the same thing." After working in a job rotation and team-assembly operation set up in the new joint venture, he was more

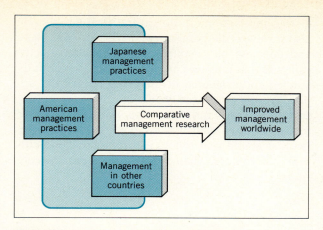

FIGURE 19.7 *Future research directions in comparative management: the emergence of global management theories?*

enthusiastic in these comments: "It's exciting, and the people are really high." One analyst comments: "NUMMI changed the direction of the American automobile industry . . . At G.M., you never admitted there was a problem. The Japanese look at problems as an opportunity and encourage open discussion."

In the final analysis, however, a cautious approach that recognizes not only the potential merits of new practices but the role of cultural variables as well, will prove best. We can and should be using such cross-cultural insights for purposes of provocation and dialog, and for new ideas and the stimulus to innovation. But we should not accept them as universal prescriptions to action. Indeed the intent of comparative management studies is not to provide definitive answers, but to help develop creative

and critical thinking about the way we do things and whether or not we can and should be doing them better.

Future research on Japanese and American management practices will clarify their similarities and differences with not just one another, but with those from many more countries and cultures around the globe. And this is already happening. Chinese students and managers are avid consumers of western know-how and theories; while westerners are studying and writing about how the Chinese do things. Teams of Soviet and Harvard Business School researchers are conducting management studies in each other's countries in an attempt to learn ways to facilitate more successful joint ventures.

Indeed, we live at a fortunate time of growing recognition that managers around the world have much to share with and learn from one another. This is the point made in Figure 19.7. It is also evident in a perspective offered by the noted Japanese management consultant, Kenichi Ohmae. Addressing the fact that the Japanese translation of *In Search of Excellence: Lessons from America's Best-Run Companies* was being widely read in Japan, he observed[33]

> Companies can learn from one another, particularly from other excellent companies, both at home and abroad. That is why the "excellent company" book is selling so well in Japan; Japanese managers find it relevant and useful. The industrialized world is becoming increasingly homogenous in terms of customer needs and social infrastructure, and only truly excellent companies can compete effectively in the global marketplace.

Summary

International management involves the management of organizations with operations in more than one country. As businesses in particular become more and more global in outlook and operations, the challenges of international management are becoming increasingly clear. We live and work in a *global society* that increasingly challenges many organizations to operate on a worldwide basis using *global strategies* and under the leadership of *global managers*.

With operations in several different countries,

multinational corporations (MNCs) are important elements in the world economy. They are controversial for their potential influence on the economies and politics of both their home and host countries. MNCs, like all organizations operating internationally, face a variety of external environmental constraints. These include economic, legal–political, educational, and cultural differences that are most typically encountered when national boundaries are crossed. Each of these differences can create special pressures on planning, organizing, leading, and controlling international operations. Managers with international responsibilities must remain sensitive to these external constraints and adjust their practices accordingly.

Comparative management is the study of how management practices differ across cultures. One of the most common questions asked in the comparative management framework is, do American theories apply abroad? In this chapter we used the empirical research of Geert Hofstede to examine insights into this question and open the debate on the cross-cultural applicability of theories of leadership, motivation, and organizational design. We also reviewed the popular comparison of American and Japanese management practices. Our conclusion was that Japanese practices should be carefully studied and evaluated before being universally applied in other cultures. While we await further research on these and other important comparative topics, the best advice is for every manager to remain alert and sensitive to environmental and cultural differences when managing in the international arena.

Thinking Through the Issues

1. What is international business? Why is it a useful point of reference for studying the key issues of international management?

2. What are the major forms of international business? Why would a business firm be interested in establishing one or more ways of doing international business?

3. How does a "joint venture" differ from a "subsidiary investment?" What are some of the potential advantages and disadvantages of a joint venture?

4. What is a multinational corporation or MNC? What is the difference between MNCs that operate in ethnocentric, polycentric, and geocentric manners?

5. Explain and give examples of how MNCs cause controversies in their relationships with a) host countries, and b) home countries.

6. Identify and give examples of economic, legal–political, and educational differences that make international operations complex and difficult.

7. What is "culture"? Explain the significance to the field of management of Hofstede's research on national cultures.

8. Draw organization charts that show two different ways a corporation might structure itself for worldwide operations. Explain when and why each form might be preferable to the other.

9. Do U.S. management theories apply abroad? Defend your answer.

10. As it was described in this chapter, what do you consider the most appealing aspects of Japanese management practices? Why?

The Manager's Vocabulary

Centralized-planning economy
Comparative management
Culture
Culture shock
Democratic system
Ethnocentric corporation
European Economic Community
Exporting
Free-market economy
Geocentric corporation
Importing
International business
International management
Joint venture
Licensing agreement
Management contract
Multinational corporation (MNC)
Political-Risk Analysis
Polycentric corporation
Subsidiary investment
Totalitarian system
Worldwide sourcing

More and more aggressive American companies are storming foreign markets.[34] They are led by managers of different motivations, but common goals—to seek profits through expanded exports. Some do it because their domestic markets have matured; some because they sense foreign demand for their products; and some because they believe future lies with viewing the world without regard to national borders. Some 95 percent of the world's population lies outside the United States, it's growing 70 percent faster, and it's getting richer all the time. A McKinsey & Company survey indicates most aggressive midsize companies doing business abroad expect their sales to increase 15–20 percent a year for the next five years. James Thorneburg is a North Carolina sock manufacturer. He says: "I looked at the marketplace and convinced myself that you're either going to be global or you're going to be nobody."

But exporting still isn't a mainstream activity for many American companies. Up until recently, it seems, they had plenty of markets at home to deal with. When they did look abroad, it was more likely for surplus products and outdated models. Now, however, times have changed. The federal government encourages exporting through the De- partment of Commerce's "Export Now" program. Many state and local governments do the same. And there's a lot to learn. Language differences, time- tax-customs-transportation differences, plus cultural differences create many obstacles. Financing is sometimes difficult, and negotiations can be lengthy.

Yes, exporting is hard work and it offers some special challenges. But as export entrepreneur Thorneburg found out, it can also pay off—handsomely. In just one year of work he now expects to sell more than $1 million per year of athletic socks in Japan.

Questions
1. Do you agree that American businesses will need to become more and more active as exporters to prosper in the business environment of the future? Please explain your answer.
2. What special knowledge and skills may be necessary to succeed in exporting? Can others, like James Thorneburg succeed without any special training in this area? Why or why not?
3. Are you interested in becoming part of an export/import business? If yes, what special efforts are you making to learn more about it and the opportunities that might be available to you?

Case Application

CLASH OF CULTURES IN AUTO FIRM

When several Americans came to work as depart- ment heads at one of the largest Japanese automo- tive firms in the United States, they had all been reading extensively on Japanese methods.[35] Most of them had come from a major American automotive company, and all had had long experience in the industry. Inevitably, under the pressure of business in this fast-growing organization, they turned in- stinctively to their accustomed Western manage- ment techniques. They looked to the Japanese na- tionals at the top levels of the organization to give them direction, objectives, and priorities. But noth- ing was forthcoming; the Japanese were waiting patiently for initiatives from them.

After a time, on the Americans' initiative, an organization chart was drawn up in an effort to settle where the authority and responsibility for decisions rested. It was a thoroughly American document, showing in neat boxes the various departments— parts, service, sales, marketing, planning, and so on—and the vertical relationships, with the Japa- nese president at the top and the lowest subdepartment on the bottom. The Japanese, who rarely draw up organization charts (and who, if they do, invariably make them read horizontally, like a flowchart), tolerated the American version as a "when in Rome" accommodation. But the chart did not solve the problems; the organization was not functioning well, and decisions were not being made.

For example, there was the simple problem of timing the availability of advertising media for the introduction of new models each year. In the U.S. market this occurs in October; in Japan, new models are introduced in January. From the parent company in Japan, the advertising materials consistently arrived two to three months late for the introduction of new models. Year after year, the U.S. distributors complained about the delay. The American heads of the sales and advertising departments took the problem up the chain of command and requested their Japanese president to contact Japan and straighten the matter out. He did contact Japan—but the problem remained.

By chance, other departments in the organization provided an opportunity for overcoming the difficulty. Some time past, top management began to assign a Japanese "coordinator" to each American department head. The coordinators, usually promising young executives in training for international assignments, were to become acquainted with U.S. business practices. It was not long before they began observing with dismay that the American managers tended to concentrate on their functional roles and to expect coordination between functions to occur at the senior management levels—as is the practice in many U.S. companies. To the Japanese, it appeared, as one put it, "as if the various departments were separate companies, all competing against each other."

As inveterate communicators, some coordinators began to pick up problems that cropped up in one department and share them with their counterparts in other departments. In this roundabout way, the Americans learned what their colleagues were doing. Coordination between departments improved.

Soon the Japanese coordinators became aware of the difficulties typified by the late arrival of the advertising materials. True to their training in the U.S. companies, the Americans were sending a report on every problem up the chain of command. Japanese top management in the United States would listen to each complaint, then send the American manager back for "more information." Translated, this meant "Come back with a proposal." Not comprehending, the Americans became increasingly impatient and frustrated. Occasionally, as in the case of the ads, the problems became so serious that the Americans insisted they be reported to Japan. The Japanese president obliged them, but the parent company remained unresponsive. The reason was simple: since Japanese organizations are unaccustomed to dealing with problems from the top down, the Tokyo organization did not know how to handle the letter from the president of the Japanese subsidiary in the United States to the president of the parent company in Japan.

Once the coordinators understood the nature of the difficulty, remedying the advertising-materials lag and similar problems was easy. A coordinator would simply pick up the telephone and call somebody at his managerial level in Tokyo. In a few days an answer would come back—and in this manner the matter of the ads was resolved.

The coordinators took some time—and the American department heads a somewhat longer time—to realize that the neat boxes in the organization chart were not interacting. By U.S. standards, the Americans were doing a good job. But without American superiors to make decisions and weave the organization together, they found that their effectiveness was diminished. To bridge the gap in managerial styles, the coordinators created a shadow organization. In this manner they not only solved the coordination problem but also involved the parent organization in the process.

Questions

1. Is the "problem" in this case due to poor structure, poor management practice (on whose part?), or both? Defend your answer.
2. What "cultural differences" appear to have affected the working relationships between American and Japanese managers in this case? Are these differences reconcilable? Please explain.
3. Is the stated solution a good one? Does it have the capability to provide for long-term operating success? Why or why not?
4. As a consultant to *Japanese* top management in this case, what would you recommend be done to further improve the situation? Explain and defend your proposals.

Class Exercise: Traveler's Dilemma: Gifts and Bribes

1. "What will I say if he or she asks for a bribe?" This may not be a question you expect to have to answer in the near future, but it might well come your way some day . . . in the course of international business. Most managers and executives are uncertain how to handle sensitive situations when doing business in a foreign country. And, of course, Americans are governed by the 1977 Foreign Corrupt Practices Act in their business dealings abroad.

2. How would you handle the following situations?[36]

(a) You are invited to the home of one of your foreign colleagues. It is supposed to be a palatial villa. What gift should you bring? You'd like to take something that would please both your boss in the home office and smooth business relations with your colleague. What if he thinks your gift is a bribe? Or, suppose he expects your gift to be a bribe? You're uneasy for sure. But what do you do?

(b) Your company's perishable product is on the dock of a foreign port. It may spoil if not released quickly through customs. Would a "gift" help you get it passed through right away? Suppose that's why it is tied up—a "gift" is expected? What if the expectations are for $500 . . . or, $5000 . . . or, $50,000? When does a "gift" become a bribe? While all this is going through your mind, the product may be spoiling. What do you do?

(c) At last the negotiations have been completed and the contract signed. But, what's this? In less than a week a government minister is calling to ask your company for $1 million. The "gift" would be for a hospital and, if given, he says you will surely receive "other valuable considerations." You are worried now that the signed agreement might be held up pending the results of his inquiry. What do you do?

3. Share your responses to each of these dilemmas with a nearby classmate. Explain what you would do and why in each case. Find out how the classmate would respond, and why. Try to understand any differences of opinion.

4. Now consider this question. In responding to such situations, how important are each of the following considerations and why? (a) local customs, (b) your personal ethics, (c) your country's laws.

References

[1] Information for this case from Edgar F. Huse, *Management,* Second Edition (St. Paul, MN: West Publishing, 1982), p. 596; "Things Go Better for Coke," *Hong Kong Sunday Morning Post* (January 19, 1986), p. 4; Louis Kraar, "The China Bubble Bursts," *Fortune* (July 6, 1987), pp. 86–89; and, Richard W. Stevenson, "Coke's Intensified Attack Abroad," *The New York Times* (March 14, 1988), pp. D-1, D-11.

[2] "Japanese Acquisitions in the U.S. Jumped to $5.9 Billion in '87; Strong Yen Cited," *The Wall Street Journal* (January 21, 1988), p. 14; and Jaclyn Fiernan, "The Selling of America (Cont'd)," *Fortune* (May 23, 1988), pp. 54–64.

[3] For information on the role of U.S. small businesses in the world economy see "Made in the U.S.A.," *Business Week* (February 29, 1988), pp. 60–62.

[4] This case is reported in "The Long Arm of Small Business," *Business Week* (February 29, 1988), pp. 63–66 respectively.

[5] For more information about NUMMI, see Ibid.

[6] See David P. Rutenberg, *Multinational Management* (Boston, MA: Little Brown, 1982).

[7] Adapted from R. Hall Mason, "Conflicts Between Host Countries and Multinational Enterprise," Vol. XVII, *California Management Review* (1974), pp. 6, 7.

[8] These examples are reported in Kraar, op. cit.

[9] See "The Antibribery Act Splits Executives," *Business Week* (September 19, 1983), p. 16; John L. Graham, "Foreign Corrupt Practices: A Manager's Guide," *Columbia Journal of World Business,* vol. XVIII (Fall 1983), pp. 89–94; Norman C. Miller, "We Should Not Relax the Corporate Anti-Bribery Law," *Wall Street Journal* (July 15, 1982), p. 26. For an interesting commentary see Jeffrey A. Fadiman, "A Traveler's Guide to Gifts and Bribes," *Harvard Business Review,* Vol. 64 (July–August 1986), pp. 122–136.

[10] Excerpted from John Koten, "Innocents Abroad: GM's Overseas Drive Continues to Sputter After Three-Year Push," *Wall Street Journal* (July 19, 1982), pp. 1, 10. Reprinted by permission of the *Wall Street Journal.*

Copyright © 1982 Dow Jones & Company, Inc. All rights reserved. See also Andrew C. Brown, "A Surprising Ford-GM Faceoff," *Fortune* (June 10, 1985), pp. 148–150.

[11] Ronald Alsop, "Countries' Different Ad Rules are Problem from Global Firm," *Wall Street Journal* (September 27, 1984), p. 25.

[12] This case is reported in "Apple Unhappy with Magistrates," *The South China Morning Post* (January 26, 1986), p. 3.

[13] Geert Hofstede, "Motivation, Leadership, and Organization: Do American Theories Apply Abroad?" *Organizational Dynamics,* Vol. 9 (Summer 1980), p. 43; and, Geert Hofstede, *Culture's Consequences* (Beverly Hills, CA: Sage, 1984).

[14] For a good overview of the practical issues, see Philip R. Harris and Robert T. Moran, *Managing Cultural Differences,* Second Edition (Houston: Gulf Publishing, 1987).

[15] Reported in Neil Chesanow, *The World-Class Executive* (New York: Rawson Associates, 1985).

[16] Geert Hofstede's research is summarized in his *Organizational Dynamics* article, op. cit. It is presented in detail in his book, *Culture's Consequences* (Beverly Hills, CA: Sage, 1984). A recent work by Richard H. Franke, Michael H. Bond, and Geert Hofstede, "Culture's Consequences: Economic Growth and Western and Chinese Cultural Dimensions," *Organizational Dynamics,* forthcoming 1988, compares Eastern and Western perspectives on national culture by presenting data from Bond's "Chinese Values Survey."

[17] Leonard D. Goodstein, "American Business Values and Cultural Imperialism," *Organizational Dynamics,* Vol. 10 (Summer 1981), p. 50.

[18] The concept of the "global manager" is discussed further by Patricia Sanders in her article, "Global Managers for Global Corporations," *Journal of Management Development,* Vol. 7 (1988), pp. 33–44.

[19] Information reported in "Ford's Global Plan: Centers of Excellence," *Business Week* (September 28, 1987), p. 80.

[20] Information from "Ford Motor Co. Explores Joint Venture with Soviets," *The Wall Street Journal* (December 16, 1987), p. 31.

[21] This role is also discussed in Sanders, op. cit.

[22] See, for example, Dan Haendel, *Foreign Investments and the Management of Political Risk* (Boulder, CO: Westview Press, 1979).

[23] For a research report see John R. Daniels, Robert A. Pitts, and Marietta J. Tretter, "Organizing for Dual Strategies of Product Diversity and International Expansion," *Strategic Management Journal,* Vol. 6 (1985), pp. 223–237.

[24] "His Business Knows No Borders," *U.S. News & World Report* (March 7, 1988), p. 52.

[25] See Shawn Tully, "Europe's Best Business Schools," *Fortune* (May 23, 1988), pp. 106–110.

[26] This research critique is based on Hofstede, op. cit. 1980 and 1984.

[27] See Goodstein, op. cit.; and, John W. Hunt, "Applying American Behavioral Science: Some Cross-Cultural Problems," *Organizational Dynamics,* Vol. 10 (Summer 1981), p. 68.

[28] William Ouchi, *Theory Z: How American Business Can Meet the Japanese Challenge* (Reading, MA: Addison-Wesley, 1981); Richard Tanner Pascale and Anthony G. Athos, *The Art of Japanese Management: Applications for American Executives* (New York: Simon and Schuster, 1981).

[29] A useful perspective on Japanese management practices is the teaching note by Stephen E. Marsland, Bert Spector, and Michael Beer, "Note on Japanese Management and Employment Systems," #481-009 (Boston, MA: HBS Case Services, 1980). See also, Shoichi Suzaqa, "How the Japanese Achieve Excellence," *Training & Development Journal,* Vol. 39 (1985), pp. 110–114.

[30] Geert Hofstede, "A Reply to Goodstein and Hunt," *Organizational Dynamics,* Vol. 10 (Summer 1981), p. 68.

[31] See also J. Ernest Beazley, "In Spite of Mystique, Japanese Plants in U.S. Find Problems Abound," *The Wall Street Journal* (June 22, 1988), pp. 1, 14.

[32] Information from Paul Ingrasia and Joseph B. White, "GM Mulls Tough Call in Toyota Venture," *The Wall Street Journal* (June 10, 1988), p. 2; and, John Holusha, "Mixing Cultures on the Assembly Line," *The New York Times* (June 5, 1988), pp. 1F, 8F.

[33] Kenichi Ohmae, "Japan's Admiration for U.S. Methods is an Open Book," *Wall Street Journal* (October 10, 1983), p. 21.

[34] Information from Christopher Knowlton, "The New Export Entrepreneurs," *Fortune* (June 6, 1988), pp. 89–102.

[35] This case is reprinted by permission of the *Harvard Business Review.* Excerpt from "Made in America (under Japanese Management)" by Richard Tanner Johnson and William G. Ouchi, *Harvard Business Review,* Vol. 52 (September–October 1974), pp. 67–68. Copyright © 1974 by the President and Fellows of Harvard College; all rights reserved.

[36] Reported in Fadiman, op. cit., 1986.

Managing with Ethics and Social Responsibility

Getting
Serious about Ethics

Talk may be cheap in organizations, but there's a lot of it on the topic of ethics—especially in the wake of recent scandals in the defense industries and with Wall Street insider-trading. While such acts of moral blindness are justifiably alarming to many people, do they indicate a downhill trend in workplace ethics? Has American business in particular lost its ethical rudder?

A major controversy has developed around such questions. While even the skeptics—those who wonder if ethics and competition are like oil and water—agree that organizational adherence to ethical standards is a must, no one is absolutely clear on how such standards should be devised and enforced. Some observers, noting the increasing role of the business school in instructing would-be managers and executives about corporate ethics, feel that the stress on education is vital. Indeed, John Shad, former chairperson of the Securities and Exchange Commission, believes so strongly in inculcating moral sensitivity in the next generation that he pledged a huge $30 million grant to the Harvard Business School to establish a program to teach Harvard MBAs that "ethics pays."

Some scoff at the notion that ethics can be taught. "You can't take morally disabled people and recreate them," says H. J. Zoffer, dean of the University of Pittsburgh's Business School. Professor David Vogel of the University of Berkeley's Business School notes that the curriculum in workplace ethics tends to address "yesterday's" issues: "Insider trading will doubtless become the focus of many lectures. . . . But it is highly unlikely that this problem will be as salient a decade from now." He believes that the educator's role is to support students with an already well-developed sense of personal morality—and to teach management practices that minimize the likelihood of employees' violating corporate policies or the law.

A special problem is the changing nature of the ethical conflicts that workers encounter—conflicts that neither schools nor management are always going to predict or know how to handle. Doug Wallace, director of the Center for Ethics, Responsibilities, and Values in St. Paul, Minnesota, says that people in organizations face a raft of unexpected moral questions. "It's like changing the rules in the middle of the game," he says. "What's good for the customer, employees, and shareholder isn't necessarily the same."

One thing is clear: the questions aren't going away, and a manager can't pretend they will. The pressure on ethics in business and other aspects of the workplace is here to stay. ■

Source: Information from "Harvard's $30 Million Windfall for Ethics 101," *Business Week* (April 13, 1987), p. 40; David Vogel, "Could an Ethics Course Have Kept Ivan from Going Bad?" *Wall Street Journal* (April 27, 1987), p. 18; and, Eileen White Reed, "Defense Contractor's Ethics Programs get scrutinized," *The Wall Street Journal* (July 21, 1988), p. 4.

CHAPTER 20

PLANNING AHEAD

This chapter examines how a manager's decisions and actions are affected by a sense of ethics and social responsibility. Key topics of study include:

What is Ethical Behavior?
Managerial Ethics
Maintaining High Ethical Standards
Corporate Social Responsibility
Government Regulation of Business
Ethics, Social Responsibility, and the Manager's Challenge

Item AT&T admits lowering phone contract bid after receiving confidential information from a GSA insider that an initial bid "was not good enough to win." [1]

Item Hertz Corporation admits overcharging consumers and insurers more than $13 million for repairs to damaged rental cars.

Item Ocean Spray Cranberries, Inc., is indicted by a federal grand jury on charges that one of its plants is polluting the environment.

Item Beech-Nut executives get prison terms for selling adulterated apple juice—the juice labeled "100% fruit juice" was actually a blend of synthetic ingredients.

Ａnd that's not all. Consider these words from a commencement address delivered a few years ago at the University of California School of Business Administration.[2] "Greed is all right," the speaker said. "Greed is healthy. You can be greedy and still feel good about yourself." The students, it is reported, greeted these remarks with laughter and applause. The speaker was none other than Ivan Boesky, once considered the "king of the arbitrageurs." It wasn't long after his commencement speech that Boesky was arrested, tried, convicted, and sentenced to prison for trading on inside information. Wall Street hasn't been the same since.

Don't you just have to wonder what is happening in a society where such actions are increasingly in the news? And don't you just have to ask—Isn't it about time that everyone gets serious about the moral aspects and social implications of decision making in organizations?

The answer to your question has to be "yes." And this chapter asks you to make just these types of self inquiries. Throughout this book our focus has been on the manager's basic goal of performance accomplishment—that is, to help the organization and its members achieve high productivity. Our thoughts, principles, and suggestions regarding how best to accomplish this goal have been many. Now it is time to think about mastering this challenge while acting ethically and in a socially responsible fashion.

WHAT IS ETHICAL BEHAVIOR?

We will use three words with frequency in the coming discussion—*ethics, moral,* and *ethical.* Let's turn to the dictionary for initial clarity in their respective meanings.[3]

ethics (éth-iks) *n.pl.* The system or code of morals of a particular person, religion, group, profession.
moral (mor-l) *adj.* Relating to, dealing with, or capable of making the distinction between right and wrong in conduct or character.
ethical (éth-ik-l) *adj.* Having to do with ethics or morality; of or conforming to moral standards; conforming to the standards of conduct of a given profession or group.

Ethics—In Concept and In Practice

Ethics is a difficult word when it comes to specifying its meaning. The dictionary definition is a good point of departure. We will consider **ethics** to be the code of morals of a person or group that sets standards as to what is good or bad or right or wrong in one's conduct. In concept, the purpose of ethics is to establish principles of behavior that help people make choices among alternative courses of action.[4] In practice, *ethical behavior* is what is accepted as "good" and "right" as opposed to "bad" or "wrong" in the context of the governing moral code.

There is clearly a legal component to ethical behavior. That is, any behavior considered ethical should also be legal in a just and fair society. This does *not* mean, however, that simply because an action is *not illegal* it is necessarily ethical. In other words, just living up to the "letter of the law" isn't sufficient to guarantee that one's actions can or should be considered ethical. Think about this last statement. Is it truly ethical, for example, for an employee to

- Take longer than necessary to do a job?
- Do personal business on company time?
- Call in sick to take a day off for leisure?
- Fail to report rule violations by a co-worker?

None of the prior acts are strictly illegal. But many people, perhaps you, would consider one or more of them to be unethical. Indeed, most ethical problems arise when people are asked or find themselves about to do something that violates their personal conscience. For some of them, if the act is legal they proceed with confidence; for others, however, the ethical test goes beyond the legality of the act alone. The issue extends to personal beliefs about what is correct on moral grounds.[5]

To thus establish whether a given behavior is ethical or not, we must inquire beyond its legality and probe into whether it is right or wrong in a broader moral sense.[6] The following equation figuratively expresses this expanded view of ethical behavior.

$$\frac{\text{Ethical}}{\text{behavior}} = \frac{\text{legal}}{\text{behavior}} + \frac{\text{"something}}{\text{else"}}$$

"Something else" in this equation represents behavior that conforms to the moral standards gov-

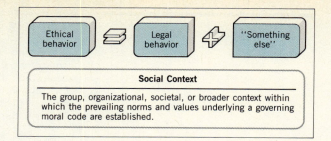

FIGURE 20.1 *The social context of ethical behavior.*

erning the situation. These moral standards, in turn, are usually based on society's prevailing norms and values. Figure 20.1 places the equation in a social context that serves as the source of the norms and values that give meaning to a moral code. Depending on the situation, the relevant social context might be defined at the group, organizational, societal, or even broader levels.

ILLUSTRATIVE CASE:
INDUSTRIAL ESPIONAGE AT THE HARVARD B-SCHOOL

This case is based on events that occurred when a group of MBA students participated in a computer simulation at the Harvard Business School. The "game" is designed to integrate various parts of the graduate curriculum.

Dan Friedman, president of Corporation 2, is working on a plan to protect his company's market share in the shire industry when his executive vice-president informs him that the confidential computer code of Corporation 6, one of their most aggressive competitors, has fallen into their hands. (A shire is a cross between a shirt and a tire.) Since the six companies in the shire business share a central computer, the code could give Friedman instant access to the secret decisions made by Corporation 6, a go-go concern challenging Corporation 2's industry leadership.

Production planning and market timing are all-important in the cut-throat shire business. Knowing what a competitor is up to ahead of time would be a significant advantage. As it is, companies in the industry spend heavily to buy market studies and other publicly available intelligence, called snoop reports, on such things as who's floating bonds or investing in new technology in which regions. For that matter, with Corporation 6's code, Friedman could order all the snoop reports he wanted and simply charge them to his competitor.

The fortuitous discovery comes at a critical time: an unforeseen depression looms over the economy, threatening an imminent shakeout in the shire industry that could well determine market position for a decade.

Friedman has only two days to use the code—if he decides to do so. What should he do as president of Corporation 2?

Here's what happened.

■ Corporation 2 used the code to access Corporation 6's decisions during the game and to charge extra expenses to Corporation 6's financial accounts.

■ Corporation 2 passed on information about Corporation 6 to other companies in the game; the other companies used the information to disadvantage Corporation 6.

■ Based on an anonymous tip, Corporation 6 discovered the sabotage and publicly exposed Corporation 2 just minutes before the game ended.

■ Corporation 2 was assessed a penalty by the course instructor and finished in last place for the game competition.

The whole incident might have ended at this point, but the conduct and "ethics" of the student players became controversial. Consider these contrasting viewpoints on what took place.

Corporation 2 members said . . .
■ "We couldn't believe we had the other company's password; it was such a joke."
■ "We never had a meeting over whether it was right or wrong to use the password. In the context of the game, once you have access to information, it would not make sense not to use it."
■ "It wasn't as though we were cheating. I thought part of the fun was doing things like espionage or collusion."

Corporation 6 members said . . .
■ "We felt let down. . . . This a professional business school and these were the people we'd been in class with for an entire year."
■ "My question was, if there was nothing on the line here and they did this, what would they do when there was money riding on it?"
■ "One of the concerns I have . . . is how the cold, unimpassioned monetary values we learn at Harvard can be applied. If you look at risks against costs in such a case—the possible penalties against the possible gains—you may come out with a positive net present value. That means it may be unethical but it is economically justifiable. I'd hate to read about some classmate in jail ten years down the road who justified his crime by the kind of analysis he learned at the Harvard Business School."

Dan Friedman, President of Corporation 2, said . . .
■ "One of the things that the Harvard Business School teaches is that there are no truths. There are some broad issues here, and a variety of different opinions, and we got a chance to think about them."

MANAGERIAL ETHICS

A classic business quote goes, "Ethical business is good business." The same can be said for all persons and institutions in all aspects of society. As with Dan Friedman in the prior case, it's now time to think seriously about ethics in management. **Managerial ethics** are principles that guide the actions and decisions of managers, and determine if they are "good or bad" or "right or wrong" in a moral sense. **Ethical managerial behavior** is behavior that conforms not only to law, but also to a broader set of moral principles common to society. Managers who act ethically and with a sense of responsibility can have a positive impact on the social good performed by their organizations. Managers who fail to do so make it more difficult for their organizations to perform in moral and socially acceptable ways.

Ethical Dilemmas Faced by Managers

An **ethical dilemma** occurs when someone must choose whether or not to pursue a course of action that, although offering the potential of personal or organizational benefit or both, is also unethical and/or illegal. Illegal behavior, like the insider trading scandals of Wall Street mentioned earlier, is one side of the story. Frankly, we live at a time when more and more persons are suffering judicial consequences for "white collar" crime and other illegal acts in the workplace. But set them aside for the moment and realize that managers face many dilemmas that involve the choice among alternatives of questionable ethical qualities. One engineering manager sums it up this way: "I define an unethical situation as one in which I have to do something I don't feel good about."[8]

What would you do in each of the following cases if you were president of a company? The cases were originally presented in a survey of *Harvard Business Review* subscribers.[9] The respondents opinions are also presented.

Case 1 Foreign payment: The minister of a foreign nation asks you to pay a $200,000 consulting fee. In return for the money, the minister promises special assistance in obtaining a $100-million contract that would produce at least a $5-million profit for your company. The contract will probably go to a foreign competitor if not won by you.

> *Result:* Forty two percent would refuse to pay; 22 percent would pay, but consider it unethical; 36 percent would pay and consider it ethical in the foreign context.

Case 2 Competitor's employee: You learn that a competitor has made an important scientific discovery. It will substantially reduce, but not eliminate, your profit for about a year. There is a possibility of hiring one of the competitor's employees who knows the details of the discovery.

> *Result:* Fifty percent would probably hire the person; 50 percent would not.

Case 3 Expense account: You learn that an executive in your company who earns $50,000 a year has been padding his expense account by about $1500 a year.

> *Result:* Eighty-nine percent feel padding is okay if superiors know about it; only 9 percent feel it is unacceptable regardless of the circumstances.

Table 20.1 summarizes data from this same sample of managers in respect to the ethical dilemmas that they have experienced. The table indicates both the people and issues most frequently involved. Most of the reported dilemmas involve conflicts with superiors, customers, and subordinates. Note that superiors head the list. They were cited for pressuring the managers working for them to support incorrect viewpoints, sign false documents,

TABLE 20.1 *Ethical Dilemmas Reported by Corporate Managers: Conflicts between Personal Ethics and Company Interests*

Conflicts reported by managers most often arise . . .

In working relationships with:
   Superiors
   Customers
   Subordinates
   Competitors
   Regulators
   Suppliers

In respect to issues of:
   Honesty in communication
   Gifts, entertainment, kickbacks
   Fairness and discrimination
   Breaking laws
   Honesty in contracts
   Firings and layoffs
   Pricing practices

overlook their wrongdoings, and do business with their friends. The most frequent issues underlying the ethical dilemmas involved honesty in advertising and in communications with top management, clients, and government agencies. Opportunities to accept special gifts, entertainment, and kickbacks were also reported. Some specific examples of ethical dilemmas faced by these managers follow.

■ *The vice-president of a California industrial manufacturer* "Being required as an officer to sign corporate documents which I knew were not in the best interest of minority stockholders."

■ *A manager of product development from a computer company in Massachusetts* "Trying to act as though the product [computer software] would correspond to what the customer had been led by sales to expect, when, in fact, I knew it wouldn't."

■ *A manager of corporate planning from California* "Acquiring a non-U.S. company with two sets of books used to evade income taxes—standard practice for that country. Do we (1) declare income and pay taxes, (2) take the "black money" out of the country (illegally), or (3) continue tax evasion?"

■ *The president of a real-estate property-management firm in Washington* "Projecting cash flow without substantial evidence in order to obtain a higher loan than the project can really amortize."

■ *A Texas insurance manager* "Being asked to make policy changes that produced more premium for the company and commission for an agent but did not appear to be of advantage to the policy-holder."

Factors Affecting Managerial Ethics

As interesting as the preceding examples may be, we must be careful. It is almost too easy to confront ethical dilemmas in the safety of a textbook or college classroom. In practice, managerial ethics are influenced by a number of forces present in the actual situation within which the manager must perform. At the personal level, greed lowers standards, while professionalism and management education are sources of higher standards. Pressure for profit from within an organization draws standards down, while a climate of social responsibility raises them. Competition, political corruption, and social decay are felt to cause lower standards. Increased public exposure and concern, government regulation, and new social expectations, by contrast, are sources of higher standards.

In between these many and sometimes conflicting forces stands the individual manager. He or she must choose courses of action that demonstrate acceptable managerial ethics in situations where the pressures may be contradictory and great. Increased awareness of the possible sources of pressure may help you to deal with them better in your managerial future. Figure 20.2 divides these forces into influences emanating from (1) the manager, (2) the organization, and (3) the environment.

FIGURE 20.2 *Factors affecting ethical managerial behavior in organizations.*

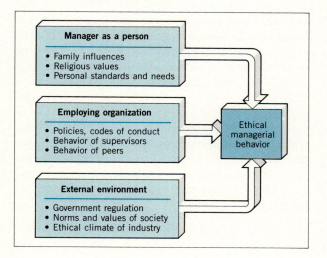

The Manager as a Person

Managerial ethics are affected by the personal experiences and background of the manager. Family influences, religious values, personal standards, and personal needs (financial and otherwise) will help determine the ethics influencing a manager's conduct in any given circumstance. Although other factors are also important, the power of these individual factors as determinants of personal ethical standards is certainly great.

Managers who lack a strong and consistent set of personal ethics will find that their decisions vary from situation-to-situation as they strive to maximize self-interests. By contrast, managers who operate with strong **ethical frameworks**—personal strategies for ethical decision making—display quite a different pattern of behavior.[10] Their decisions and actions are more consistent, since choices are made against a stable set of ethical standards. They also display greater confidence in difficult situations, since their ethical frameworks provide a basis for making tough judgments. And they deal better with competitive stress, since they benefit from the strength of high self-esteem. Just as organizations need strategies to guide them in complex and uncertain environments, so too can managers gain by having ethical frameworks that clearly set forth their ethics and values to guide them through similarly difficult situations.

The Employing Organization

The organization is another important factor with the capability to influence managerial ethics. Formal organizational policies and rules, that is "codes of conduct," are often established to guide behavior and decision making in situations prone to create ethical dilemmas for the people involved. For example,[11] employees

at IBM work under very clear corporate policies in respect to offers of bribes, gifts, and entertainment. They are told, in writing, that[11]

■ *In respect to receiving* neither you, nor any member of your family, may solicit or accept from a supplier money or a gift that may reasonably be construed as having any connection with IBM's business relationships.

■ *In respect to giving* you may not give money or a gift to an executive, official, or employee of any supplier, customer, government agency or other organization if it could reasonably be construed as having any connection with IBM's business relationships.

We noted earlier that managers consider their immediate supervisors as important influences on their behavior. Just exactly what a supervisor requests of a manager, and which of a manager's actions are rewarded or punished, can certainly affect an individual's behavior. The expectations and reinforcement of peers and other insiders are likely to have similar impact. Thus, within any organization, both stated policies and the day-to-day actions of people establish the social context for ethical behavior. We will have more to say on these matters shortly.

The External Environment

Organizations operate within external environments composed of competitors, government laws and regulations, and social norms and values among others. Laws interpret social values to define appropriate behaviors for organizations and their members; regulations help governments to monitor these behaviors and keep them within acceptable standards. But the climate of competition in an industry also sets a standard of behavior for those who hope to prosper within it. Sometimes the pressures of competition contribute further to the ethical dilemmas of managers. Here is one example.[12]

At American Airlines president Robert Crandall once telephoned Howard Putnam, president of Braniff International Airlines. Both companies were suffering from money-losing competition on routes from their home base of Dallas. A portion of their conversation follows.

Putnam: Do you have a suggestion for me?
Crandall: Yes . . . Raise your fares 20 percent. I'll raise mine the next morning.
Putnam: Robert, we . . .
Crandall: You'll make more money and I will, too.
Putnam: We can't talk about pricing.
Crandall: Oh, Howard. We can talk about anything we want to talk about.

The U.S. Justice Department disagreed. It alleged that Crandall's suggestion of a 20 percent fare increase amounted to an illegal attempt to monopolize airline routes. The suit was later settled when Crandall agreed to curtail future discussions with competitors about fares.

MAINTAINING HIGH ETHICAL STANDARDS

Perhaps the most disturbing data in respect to managerial ethics is from a group of college students. When business students at a major American university were queried on the topic, 88 percent said they expected to encounter pressures to compromise their ethics in future jobs; 50 percent implied that they would have no recourse but to conform to the lower standards.[13] Given such expectations, ones that you may in fact share, it is especially appropriate to examine ways of maintaining high ethical standards in management. Some of the most important efforts in this regard involve (1) ethics training, (2) whistleblower protection, (3) top management involvement, and (4) formal codes of ethics.

Ethics Training

Ethics training seeks to help people better understand the ethical aspects of decision making, and incorporate high-ethical standards into their daily behaviors. Workshops and seminars on this topic are growing in popularity in the corporate world, and an increasing number of college curricula now include formal courses on ethics.

The end-of-chapter exercise gives you a sampler of what ethics training often involves. As you consider the issue, however, it is important to keep the purpose of most ethics training in perspective.[14] An executive at Chembank puts it this way: "We aren't teaching people right from wrong—we assume they know that. We aren't giving people moral courage to do what is right—they should be able to do that anyhow. We focus on dilemmas." Many of these dilemmas arise because of the time pressures of decisions, and most ethics training is designed to help people deal with ethical issues while under pressure.

Newsline 20.1 introduces some of the advice typical to ethics training programs. In addition, you may recall that we offered one consultant's suggestions on the ethics of decision making back in Chapter 3. It's useful to revisit this checklist for confronting an ethical dilemma.[15]

1. Recognize and define the dilemma.
2. Get the facts.

UNFUZZING MANAGERIAL ETHICS

N E W S L I N E 20.1

Corporations across the country are addressing ethics in their training programs, and more and more business schools are offering courses in ethics. Beyond these training programs and courses, however, are the managers who need practical advice on how to deal with ethical questions in the workplace. A good approach for managers is to recognize that all their decisions have consequences, usually for a number of different parties. Those consequences can be analyzed to see if they include harming others, not only in the short term but also in the long term.

The first step in an analysis is to recognize a problem. Some ethical questions are obvious; the people involved know they shouldn't be doing what they are doing. The less obvious situations require increased vigilance. These can occur in changing industries, where the rules are changing as well, or where competition is keen enough to make people want to cut corners.

After a problem is recognized, a clear and consistent ethical standard can help managers decide what to do about it. Common ethical equations like "do unto others as you would have them do unto you" serve most cases well, but some experts advise a more stringent test. Professor Thomas W. Dunfee of the Wharton School recommends that managers act to avoid even the appearance of a conflict of interest. And others advocate acting so that other people's freedoms and lifestyles are respected.

The ultimate way to deal with ethical problems is to prevent them from happening. Formal codes of ethics are common, but they are probably not as effective as an atmosphere in which people are encouraged to think about ethics and to express ethical concerns—before problems happen. If managers set the example here, and follow through on their values, their employees will know that their ethics mean business.

Source: As reported in Walter Kiechel III, "Unfuzzing Ethics for Managers," *Fortune* (November 23, 1987), 229–234; and, Amanda Bennett, "Ethics Codes Spread Despite Skepticism," *The Wall Street Journal* (July 15, 1988), p. 13.

---

3. List your options.
4. Test each option—
   Is it legal?
   Is it right?
   Is it beneficial?
5. Make your decision.

As one last check on such a process, another consultant adds this recommendation. Before taking action, double-check your decision by asking two final questions.

1. "How would I feel if my family found out about my decision?"
2. How would I feel if I saw my decision printed in the newspaper?"

Another aspect of ethics training emphasizes your personal responsibility to spot and then be able to deal with some of the reasons why otherwise reasonable people might act unethically in the first place. Think back to examples given already in this chapter—trading stocks on insider information, paying bribes to obtain business, falsifying bills, and so on. "Why," you should be asking, "do people do things like this that may ultimately harm them and/or their organizations?" Ethics training brings attention to four common rationalizations people use to justify their misconduct. They are:[16]

1. *"It's not really illegal."* Believing that the behavior is within acceptable ethical and/or legal limits, especially in an ambiguous situation where it is difficult to draw a clear line between right and wrong. When dealing with situations in which you or someone else is having a hard time precisely defining right from wrong, the advice is quite simple: When in doubt, don't.

2. *"It's in everyone's best interests."* Believing that the behavior taken is in the individual's or the organization's best interests. Overcoming this rationalization depends in part on the ability to look beyond short-run results to address longer-term implications; and, to look beyond results in general, to the ways in which they are obtained. In response to the question, "how far should I go?", the recommended answer is—"don't try to find out."

3. *"No one will ever know about it."* Believing that the behavior is "safe" in the sense that it will never be found out or made public. Unless it is discovered, the implied argument goes, no crime was really committed. Lack of control, pressures to perform, and management that prefers "not to know" reinforce such thinking. In this case, the best deterrent is to make sure that all punishment for wrongdoing is made public for everyone to know.

4. *"The organization will stand behind me."* Believing that the behavior helped the organization and because of this, top managers will condone it and protect the individual from harm. But loyalty to the organization isn't an acceptable excuse for misconduct; everyone should be taught by management example not to put organizational loyalty above the law and social morality.

Whistleblower Protection

Agnes L. Connolly pressed her employer to report two toxic chemical accidents as she believed the law required; Dave Jones reported that his company was using unqualified suppliers in the construction of a nuclear power plant; Margaret A. Newsham revealed that her firm was allowing workers to do personal business while on government contracts.

All three were fired. But they are eligible for redress from their companies under new federal and state laws which offer "whistleblowers" protection against "retaliatory discharge."[17] A **whistleblower** is someone who exposes the misdeeds of others in organizations to preserve ethical standards and protect against wasteful, harmful, or illegal acts.

All signs are that the courts are growing increasingly supportive of efforts by employees to report unethical acts by their co-workers, and to avoid engaging in unethical acts on behalf of their employers. Notwithstanding such legal support, people face barriers that can make it hard for them to expose unethical behavior in the workplace. Three important organizational blocks to exposing unethical practices are:[18]

1. *Strict chain of command.* This makes it difficult to report unethical practices of one's boss to higher-level management. It is even harder to do this when the risk exists that you may have misperceived the situation (i.e., nothing wrong is really taking place), or that the boss may be acting on orders from above. The chain of command can also interfere with exposing that one's boss refuses to take action about subordinates' misdeeds. Once again, the only route for exposing things is to bypass the boss and communicate to a higher management level, perhaps at substantial personal risk.

2. *Task-group cohesiveness.* Group norms are powerful influences on the behaviors of members. There may be times, however, when group norms support behaviors that violate a member's personal standards of ethics. Yet, violating the norms may result in social ostracism and subsequent loss of group-membership privileges. This may result in tendencies to go along with the group and avoid "blowing the whistle."

3. *Ambiguous priorities.* It is not always clear what is "right" or "wrong" according to the internal policies of an organization. Formal policy statements may be inconsistent with what appears as acceptable day-to-day practice; official directives may differ from standard ways for "getting the job done." Such ambiguities make it difficult to determine if a behavior is unethical or not, let alone expose it.

Special attempts must be made to reduce these and other organizational barriers to the exposure of unethical behaviors. Some companies, like Boeing, have staff persons formally appointed to serve as "ethics advisers" and may even have a formal staff unit for processing reported infractions. One novel proposal even goes so far as to suggest the convening of *moral quality circles* to help institutionalize shared commitments for everyone to work at their moral best.[19] The significance of developing good responses to this problem is well highlighted—[20]

at the federal government where a study released by the Merit Systems Protection Board of the federal service reported: "Numerous federal employees are aware of fraud and abuse in federal agencies and departments but are afraid to come forward." In one of the Board's studies, 69 percent of surveyed government workers said they had witnessed waste but didn't report it; 37 percent said they feared some sort of reprisals if they did.

Top Management Involvement

The persons serving in management capacities play crucial roles in the maintenance of high ethical standards in any organization. The individual worker may be honest and of the highest moral character. Yet examples offered by higher levels of authority might cause them to overlook the unethical practices of others and even to adopt some themselves. The key point here is that top management sets an ethical tone for the organization as a whole. For example[21]

■ "If the boss winks," someone once stated, "he or she will find the employees winking back" with illegal, corner-cutting behavior.
■ Communication from the top can subtly suggest that it doesn't want to know about deceptive or illegal practices among employees.
■ When the top management uses company resources for purely personal pleasures, lower-level employees may be expected to do likewise.

There is no doubt that top management has the power to shape an organization's policies and set its moral tone as well. As a result, top managers have a major responsibility to serve as models of appropriate ethical behavior for the entire organization. Not only must they be the epitomy of high ethical conduct, top managers must also communicate similar expectations throughout the organization . . . and reinforce positive results.

This general appeal easily extends to all levels of management. Every manager is in a position to influence subordinates. Care must be taken to do so in a positive and informed manner. The important supervisory act of setting goals and communicating performance expectations is a good case in point. A surprising 64 percent of 238 executives in one study reported feeling under pressure to compromise personal standards to achieve company goals; a *Fortune* survey reports that 34 percent of its respondents felt a company president can create an ethical climate by setting reasonable goals "so that subordinates are not pressured into unethical actions."[22] Clearly, a supervisor may unknowingly encourage unethical practices by exerting *too* much pressure for the accomplishment of goals that are *too* difficult. This may have been part of the problem—[23]

at McDonnell Douglas when the firm was named in a defense contractor scandal. A Conference Board Report suggests that personnel in the company's Aerospace Division may have been confused by an ethics training program that coexisted with seemingly impossible performance objectives. At the same time that senior management was reaching adherence to high ethical standards, it seemed to have been holding lower-level employees accountable for next-to-impossible bottom-line performance.

Formal Codes of Ethics

Formal codes of conduct guide members of such professions as engineering, medicine, law, and public accounting. Indeed, the existence of such codes is part of the very definition of a profession. The codes channel individual behavior in directions consistent with the historical and shared norms of the professional group. The National Association of Accountants, for example, has a code for companies' internal accountants. Among other things, the code requires an accountant to report to superiors within the company any improper behavior that may be observed. Association officials feel the code will give management accountants a standard to point to if asked to "cook the books" or overlook accounting abuses. One says[24]

> Those who call themselves professional will welcome the support provided by this code of conduct in helping them to resist inappropriate demands of a superior or of anyone else.

ETHICS CODES SET—
AND ENFORCE—THE STANDARDS

Formal codes of ethics are being written at more and more organizations. At others, existing codes are being rewritten to clarify old expectations and establish new ones. "The interest today is greater than it's ever been," says Alexander Horniman from the Olsson Center for Applied Ethics at the University of Virginia. A recent Conference Board study sheds additional light on who is involved in preparing these documents, and what penalties they describe for ethics violations.

Source: As reported in Amanda Bennett, "Ethics Codes Spread Despite Skepticism," *The Wall Street Journal* (July 15, 1988), p. 13.

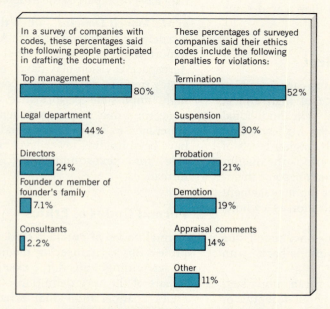

In a survey of companies with codes, these percentages said the following people participated in drafting the document:

Top management — 80%
Legal department — 44%
Directors — 24%
Founder or member of founder's family — 7.1%
Consultants — 2.2%

These percentages of surveyed companies said their ethics codes include the following penalties for violations:

Termination — 52%
Suspension — 30%
Probation — 21%
Demotion — 19%
Appraisal comments — 14%
Other — 11%

More generally, formal **codes of ethics,** which document in writing the commitments to values and ethical conduct that an organization expects of its employees, are now commonplace. In fact, when the CEOs of 200 major corporations met in a Business Roundtable on ethics, their final report was topped by two recommendations: (1) that top management make greater commitments to ethics programs in their firms, and (2) that written codes be established to clearly communicate management expectations to all employees.[25]

Newsline 20.2 adds further perspective on trends in the development of ethics codes. In a related survey of companies with codes of conduct, these items were among those most frequently addressed in them:[26]

- Bribes and kickbacks
- Conflicts of interest
- Political contributions
- Honesty of books or records
- Customer/supplier relationships

- Misappropriation of corporate assets
- Confidentiality of corporate information

While interest in codes of ethical conduct grows and they assume a rightful role in helping more organizations to establish high ethical standards, the codes do have their limits. They can't cover all situations, they aren't an automatic "cure all," and they can't alone create a strong corporate culture and supportive value system. The value of any formal code of ethics still rests on the underlying human resource foundations of the organization—its managers and other employees. There just isn't any replacement for effective hiring practices which staff the organization with honest and moral people to do the work. And there isn't any replacement for having them led by committed managers—at all levels of the organization—who are willing to set the examples and expectations, and then follow-through to ensure desired results. In support of this position, some organizations take a "minimalist" approach to ethical codes. For example,[27]

at Levi Strauss & Co. the firm dropped its 13-page booklet "filled with details and procedures" in favor of a half-page statement of principles that communicates Levi's "respect for customers and employees," and asks everyone to avoid "real or perceived conflicts of interest." This change was made to show the firm's confidence in its employees and their personal senses of right and wrong. When they can't decide on something, a spokesperson says, the firm would rather have them consult a supervisor for advice rather than turn to a written document.

CORPORATE SOCIAL RESPONSIBILITY

It's now time to shift our interest in ethical behavior from the level of the individual to the organization. We begin by once again recognizing that all organizations exist in complex relationship with elements in their external environments. Figure 20.3 depicts how this environment takes meaning for a business firm as a network of other organizations and institutions with which it must interact. In this context, **corporate social responsibility** is defined as an obligation of the organization to act in ways that serve both its own interests and the interests of its

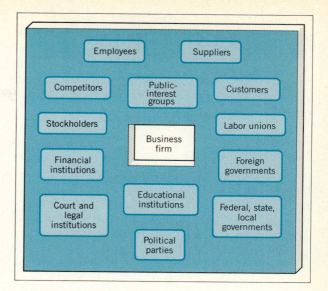

FIGURE 20.3 *Multiple stakeholders in the external environment of a business firm.*

many external publics. As first introduced in Chapter 5, these publics are considered **stakeholders** or persons and groups who are affected in one way or another by the behavior of an organization.

Arguments "Against" and "For" Social Responsibility

You will find in this discussion an underlying presumption that businesses and other organizations *should* act in a socially responsive fashion. However, it is important to understand that there are two contrasting sides to this argument.[28] On the one side is the *classical view* that believes that management's only responsibility in running a business enterprise is to maximize profits. This *stockholder model* is represented by Milton Friedman, a widely recognized advocate of classic free-market economics, who argues against social responsibility. He contends that "few trends could so thoroughly undermine the very foundations of our free society as the acceptance by corporate officials of a social responsibility other than to make as much money for their stockholders as possible." On the other side is a *socio-economic view* that believes that any organization, businesses included, must be concerned for the broader social welfare—not just corporate profits. This *stakeholder model* is supported by Paul

Samuelson, another distinguished economist. He states that "a large corporation these days not only may engage in social responsibility, it had damn well better try to do so."[29] To help you develop a truly informed perspective, the cases against and for corporate social responsibility are now summarized.[30]

Arguments "Against" Corporate Social Responsibility

Major arguments against the assumption of social responsibility by business include:

■ *Loss of profit maximization* Diverting resources to social-responsibility programs undermines the principles of a competitive marketplace and deprives stockholders of economic gain.

■ *Cost* Social obligations can become costly for firms, with the result that some may be driven from business and others forgo attractive investments.

■ *Lack of skills* Many businesses lack the necessary personnel skills to work successfully with social issues.

■ *Dilution of purpose* Pursuit of social goals may dilute the economic productivity of business; society may suffer as both economic and social goals are poorly accomplished.

■ *Too much power* Business already has enough power as a social institution; there is no need to allow it to develop greater social influence.

■ *Lack of accountability* Business has no direct line of accountability to the people; thus, it is unwise to give it further discretion to act where it cannot be held accountable for outcomes.

■ *Lack of broad support* Society is divided in its position on business social involvement; actions in face of such divided support are predisposed to fail.

Arguments "For" Corporate Social Responsibility

Major arguments supporting the assumption of social responsibility by business include

■ *Public expectations* Public opinion in support of business social involvement runs deep; productivity goals are expected to co-exist with quality-of-life goals.

■ *Long-run viability* If business fails to act, other groups will eventually step in to assume the responsibilities and the power that goes with them.

■ *Public image* Socially responsible behaviors improve the public image of business.

■ *Better environment* To the extent business can improve the environment, it will be more conducive to future business prosperity.

■ *Avoidance of government regulation* The more socially responsible business is, costly and restrictive government regulation can be reduced.

■ *Balance of responsibility and power* Because business has so much social power, its sense of social responsibility should be equally large.

■ *Let business try* Other institutions have failed in handling many social problems; it makes sense to let business try to solve them.

■ *Business has the resources* There is a pool of expertise and capital in business that can be used in social service; it is logical to let it try.

■ *Problems can become profits* If the innovative capability of business can be applied to social problems, many might be handled profitably in a traditional business sense.

■ *Prevention is better than curing* Any delays in addressing the social problems of today may magnify problems in the future.

■ *Stockholder interests* In all prior respects, businesses can prosper and benefit from an improved environment; socially responsive behavior is in the best long-run interests of shareholders.

Although the academic debate continues, there is little doubt that the public at large expects businesses and other organizations to act with genuine social responsibility. Indeed, the demands in today's social and economic climate all point toward ever-increasing expectations that organizations will integrate expanded social responsibility into their activities and values. These final comments by Keith Davis, a management theorist who has thought seriously about this debate, sum it up best.[31]

> Society wants business as well as all other major institutions to assume significant social responsibility. Social responsibility has become the hallmark of a mature, global civilization. . . . The business which vacillates or chooses not to enter the arena of social responsibility may find that it gradually will sink into customer and public disfavor.

ILLUSTRATIVE CASE:
JOHNSON & JOHNSON COMPANY

You should remember sensational reports on the tragedy, even if you don't remember the "scare"

Our Credo   Wherever You Start, You Can Make A Difference

We believe our first responsibility is to the doctors, nurses and patients, to mothers and all others who use our products and services ∎ In meeting their needs everything we do must be of high quality ∎ We must constantly strive to reduce our costs in order to maintain reasonable prices ∎ Customers' orders must be serviced promptly and accurately ∎ Our suppliers and distributors must have an opportunity to make a fair profit ∎

We are responsible to our employees, the men and women who work with us throughout the world ∎ Everyone must be considered as an individual ∎ We must respect their dignity and recognize their merit ∎ They must have a sense of security in their jobs ∎ Compensation must be fair and adequate, and working conditions clean, orderly and safe ∎ Employees must feel free to make suggestions and complaints ∎ There must be equal opportunity for employment, development and advancement for those qualified ∎ We must provide competent management, and their actions must be just and ethical ∎

We are responsible to the communities in which we live and work and to the world community as well ∎ We must be good citizens—support good works and charities and bear our fair share of taxes ∎ We must encourage civic improvements and better health and education ∎ We must maintain in good order the property we are privileged to use, protecting the environment and natural resources ∎

Our final responsibility is to our stockholders ∎ Business must make a sound profit ∎ We must experiment with new ideas ∎ Research must be carried on, innovative programs developed and mistakes paid for ∎ New equipment must be purchased, new facilities provided and new products launched ∎ Reserves must be created to provide for adverse times ∎ When we operate according to these principles, the stockholders should realize a fair return ∎

Early responsibility, diversity, and growth characterize the array of functional career opportunities at Johnson & Johnson. Some of our professionals, shown here, discuss their careers later in this brochure.

Johnson & Johnson is the largest and most diversified health care products company in the world. We rank among the top 100 of the *Fortune* 500 U.S. industrial corporations, with sales of about $5 billion. Our products range from the well-known BAND-AID Brand Adhesive Bandage to the most advanced medical diagnostic imaging equipment.

We are a highly decentralized family of 150 companies—each with responsibility for charting its own course for the future. When you work for a Johnson &

company—whether in marketing, sales, engineering, finance, research, or another function—you're part of a relatively small, highly autonomous organization, rich with the vast resources of Johnson & Johnson. That makes you a vital contributor from the beginning. And that's the Johnson & Johnson difference.

We can offer you a unique opportunity to play an important part in an important company—and in an atmosphere in which bright, talented people can make a difference wherever they start.

Johnson & Johnson corporate credo serves as a unifying force that communicates socially responsible values to all employees.

itself—seven deaths resulting from cyanide being maliciously placed in capsules of Extra-Strength Tylenol.[32] Top management at Johnson & Johnson (J & J), the maker of this popular aspirin substitute, moved quickly in deciding to remove all Tylenol from distribution. But in many locations, responsible company employees had already taken action. When poisoned Tylenol was found on some store shelves, they independently made decisions to remove it from sale across the country. This was done at great expense to the company, even though it was quickly determined that the cyanide got into the capsules after they had left J & J manufacturing and distribution centers. But a socially responsive company delivers reasonable and safe products to its customers. By deciding to withdraw all Tylenol from the market, J & J executives and other employees acted with great honor to themselves, and to the company.

Much of the credit is attributed to J & J's "Credo" shown in the accompanying photo. For years senior executives have drilled into subordinates the company's commitments to basic operating principles which stress commitments to—in this

priority order—customers, employees, communities in which the company operates, and shareholders. With over 150 separate operating units the company needs to strike a good balance between management controls and employee autonomy. The value system built and reinforced through the famous Credo serves as a unifying force which helps keep everyone heading in the same direction.

The Credo is central to J & J's corporate culture. So much so in fact, that periodic "challenge meetings" are held to explore the need for change in the 30-year old statement. Seminars are held twice a year at which time selected managers review the values and recommit to the Credo.

Areas of Social Responsibility

Organizations fulfill their social responsibilities in many ways. See, for example, if you can guess what these three people have in common.[33]

Helen Olson worked at Save the Children Federation. She also traveled to Honduras and to the Dominican Republic as financial adviser.
Eric Grey worked in a program to train physically

disabled high-school students at the Rusk Institute for Rehabilitation Medicine at New York University Medical Center.

Norman Steele worked as an adjunct professor of international marketing at Baruch College in New York. He headed a program that places students in jobs related to their business studies.

The common element is that each of these people was an IBM employee working in the company's "community-service" program. IBM spent $20 million in one year on this program, which loans employees to other institutions serving the public interest. The typical loan is for one year, and IBM pays the employee's full salary. The person on leave is guaranteed a job at the same level upon return.

"Why," you might ask, "do companies maintain expensive social-service leave programs? What are the benefits?" Answers to your questions are found in the responses of persons involved in a similar program offered by the Xerox Corporation.[34]

"I came back super-charged-up and proud of the company. I think it helped my career."
—Xerox employee.

"The hope and expectation is that we get back a better employee—one better equipped at problem solving and a lot of other things."
—Xerox vice-president.

"More companies are going to have to be doing this, because you have to put something back into the communities—you can't just extract profits."
—Xerox manager.

Both IBM and Xerox can be considered as acting in socially responsible ways by making paid social-service leaves available to their employees. Table 20.2 lists additional areas of social responsibility common to business firms and other types of organizations. These include ecology and environmental quality, consumerism, community needs, governmental relations, corporate philanthropy, minorities and disadvantaged persons, labor, and stockholder relations, among other possibilities.

At the organizational level, a **social audit** can be used at regular intervals to systematically assess and report on an organization's resource commitments and action accomplishments in these many areas of social responsibility. You might think of social audits as attempts to assess the social performance of organizations, much as financial audits assess their performance in an economic sense. Social audits help managers to better understand what is being done, how well it is being done, what isn't being done, and what should be done in the future. As such they offer the potential benefits of improved internal resource allocations, more complete evaluations of corporate social accomplishments, and documentation of these accomplishments for public-relations efforts. But they also suffer from diffi-

---

TABLE 20.2 *Selected Areas of Corporate Social Responsibility*

Ecology and Environmental Quality	*Minorities and Disadvantaged Persons*
Pollution cleanup and prevention	Training of unemployed
Dispersion of industry	Equal employment opportunity
Land use and beautification	Locating plants and offices in minority areas
	Purchasing from minority businesses
Consumerism	
Truth in lending, advertising, and business	*Labor Relations*
Product warranty and service	Improved occupational health and safety
Control of harmful products	Provision of day-care centers
	Options of flexible work hours
Community Needs	
Use of expertise for local problems	*Stockholder Relations*
Aid with health-care facilities and education	Public seats on board of directors
Service on voluntary groups	Improved financial disclosure
Governmental Relations	*Corporate Philanthropy*
Restrictions on lobbying	Financial support for arts and culture
Control of business political action	Special scholarships and gifts to education
	Financial support for assorted charities

culties of accurately measuring the effectiveness of some social programs.

Overall, there seems to be a growing sensitivity by enlightened management toward the needs of multiple stakeholders as well as the enterprise itself. Indeed, the old controversy over whether or not profits and social responsibility can go hand in hand is increasingly being challenged in new and creative ways. Consider the approach taken—[36]

at American Express where corporate philanthropy takes different forms. In one program, Amex makes contributions to "Project Hometown America." The company plans to make a $1 donation for each new credit card it approves, and 1¢ donations for each purchase charged to its cards to the fund. Grants will then be made to hometown groups proposing to "demonstrate an innovative approach to solving a pressing local human problem."

A Continuum of Social Responsibility

Figure 20.4 describes how organizations can respond with different degrees of commitment to their social responsibilities. The continuum of corporate social responsibility shows a desirable shift in emphasis from acting purely from a sense of obligation at the one extreme, to acting from a sense of progressive citizenship at the other. The three levels of action are:[37]

1. *Social obligation*   Corporate behavior at this level conforms only to legal requirements and competitive market pressures.
2. *Social responsibility*   Corporate behavior at this level is congruent with prevailing norms, values, and expectations of society.
3. *Social responsiveness*   Corporate behavior at this level takes preventive action to avoid adverse social impacts from company activities and even anticipates or takes the lead in future movement beyond current expectations.

This continuum raises an issue similar to the one we addressed in the context of managerial ethics. When it comes to corporate social responsibilities, the law defines what is minimally acceptable on moral grounds. Organizational decision makers, however, must answer an additional question: Should more be done than the law requires? Moving up the continuum in the prior figure from social obligation all the way to social responsiveness requires positive answers to this question. Here's an unfortunate example of failure to do so.[38]

At a toxic waste facility   in northern California, inspections were conducted regularly and the operation was in compliance with all regulations. But a manager noticed a leakage that might endanger nearby ranchers and livestock. The leak was reported to corporate officials. Because it is impossible to know how long a leakage will go before being detected, they took the position that as long as the operation was in compliance with the law, they didn't need to do anything. Eventually, after failing to get the officials to act, the frustrated manager finally took the matter public.

Fortunately, *Newsline 20.3* shows that progressive managers in many other organizations are responding to higher social expectations.

GOVERNMENT REGULATION OF BUSINESS

One argument in favor of corporate social responsibility is to avoid costly and restrictive government

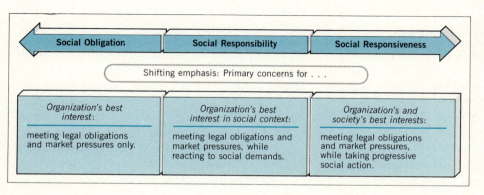

FIGURE 20.4 *A continuum of corporate social responsibility.*

CORPORATE CONSCIENCE AWARDS

N E W S L I N E 20.3

In the second annual granting of Corporate Conscience Awards by the New York-based Council on Economic Priorities, nine corporations were recognized for exemplifying socially responsible corporate behavior. The aim of these awards, according to the Council, is to encourage superior "corporate citizenship."

In the area of animal rights, Procter & Gamble was awarded for leading a search for alternatives to testing with animals. Ben & Jerry's, Inc., was awarded for donating 7.5 percent of its pretax earning to charities and social causes. In a similar vein, Best Western was recognized for a job training program for female inmates, and the South Shore Bank of Chicago received an award for job training as well as for a lending program in a low-income neighborhood.

Socially responsible activity in the areas of education, the environment, the family, the disabled, and fair employment was also recognized. Receiving awards in these categories were the Gannett Company (for adult literacy program aid); 3M Corporation (for waste recovery programs); IBM (for elderly-care referral services); General Mills (for ongoing aid to the disabled); and Xerox and Gannett (for promoting minorities and women, respectively). Finally, the Kellogg Company, which agreed to participate in the Council's corporate studies, was awarded for most improved corporate disclosure.

Source: As reported in "9 Get Corporate Conscience Awards," *New York Times* (March 1, 1988), p. D-21.

---

regulations. If businesses don't act responsibly on their own, the argument goes, government will step in and attempt to regulate the desired behavior. This is but one example of the many ways government regulations constrain and impact the practice of management.

The Complex Legal Environment

Government regulations are an important influence on all organizations. The legal environment of business, in particular, is most complex. Although many laws and regulations are certainly beneficial, business executives often complain that others are overly burdensome. Specific business concerns are that regulations increase costs by creating the need for increased paperwork and staff to maintain compliance, and that the paperwork consumes so much managerial time that attention is diverted from important productivity concerns.

In reality, the legal environment is both complex and constantly changing. Managers must always remain informed about new and pending laws, as well as existing ones. Among the trends in government legislation is a continuing interest in quality-of-life issues. Several themes we have already discussed as key social-responsibility areas are backed by major laws on water pollution, air pollution, consumer protection, and noise control, among others. When we hear or read about such regulations in the news, the report is usually negative. That is, we either hear business complaints about the costs of compliance with the laws, or we hear public outcries protesting spectacular business violations of them.

As a reminder of the positive sides of state and

federal legislation, consider these "quality-of-life" protections enjoyed by American workers.

1. *Occupational health and safety* The Occupational Safety and Health Act of 1970 firmly established the federal government as concerned about worker health and safety on the job. Even though some complain the regulations still aren't strong enough, the act continues to influence the concerns of employers and government policy-makers for worker safety.

2. *Pollution control* Several anti-pollution acts, beginning with the Air Pollution Control Act in 1962, are designed to eliminate careless pollution of the air, water, and land. Many companies have taken steps, in cooperation with or under pressure from governmental agencies, to reduce pollution and clean up their operations. An important concern in this area is the disposal of hazardous wastes, the subject of an earlier example.

3. *Fair labor practices* Legislation and regulations that prohibit discrimination in labor practices by business were discussed in Chapters 9 and 18. The Equal Employment Opportunity Act of 1972 and related regulations are designed to reduce barriers to employment based on race, sex, age, national origin, and marital status. They have clearly had an impact on minority hiring by U.S. firms.

4. *Consumer protection* The Consumer Product Safety Act of 1972 is a broad-based law that gives the government authority to examine, and to force a business to withdraw from sale, any product that it feels is hazardous to the consumer. Children's toys and flammable fabrics are among the great range of products affected by such regulation.

Government Agencies as Regulators

It may not be too farfetched to say that behind every piece of legislation is a government agency charged with the responsibility of monitoring and ensuring compliance to its mandates. You know these agencies best by their acronyms; FAA (Federal Aviation Administration), EPA (Environmental Protection Agency), OHSA (Occupational Health and Safety Administration), and FDA (Food and Drug Administration) are a few examples. Figure 20.5 shows that all such agencies stand at the interface between the public interest, as reflected in laws and legislation, and the activities of organizations and their

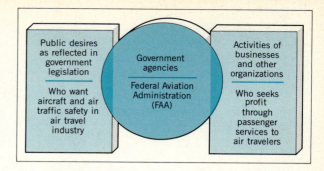

FIGURE 20.5 *Government agencies at the interface of public and organizational interests: the case of the Federal Aviation Administration.*

members. The agencies are staffed and supported from the federal budget to make sure that the public interest is best served. Take one case in point. When you fly, you want to be secure in knowing that you are flying in a safe aircraft and according to safe air traffic procedures. The FAA was established to regulate air travel with just this goal in mind. Backed by a myriad of legislation, the FAA works daily in the public interest.

As with the underlying legislation itself, the activities of government agencies are subject to criticism. Public outcries and political slogans to "dismantle the bureaucracy" and/or "deregulate business" reflect concerns that specific agencies and their supportive legislation are not functional. Many times, it is the agency's interpretation of a law and manner of seeking compliance that is criticized, not the law itself. Businesses sometimes feel that regulating agencies are unclear in telling them how to comply with the laws, require unnecessary paperwork to document compliance, and/or are inconsistent in enforcing the laws.

Political Action by Businesses

Government directly influences business through laws and the regulating efforts of agencies such as the EPA and FAA. But, the line of influence between government and business is not a one-way arrow. Just as government takes a variety of actions to influence organizations, organizations can and do take a variety of actions to influence government.

Figure 20.6 lists five ways in which representatives of businesses attempt to influence government.

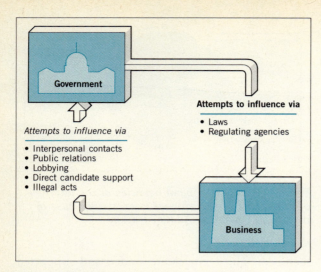

FIGURE 20.6 *The mutual exchange of influence between government and business.*

Such influence takes place

1. *Through interpersonal contacts.* Business executives can persuade government officials or politicians to support pro-business and oppose anti-business legislation. This requires that executives get to know important people in government and develop influential relationships with them.
2. *Through public-relations campaigns.* Businesses can communicate positive images of themselves to the general public. Note how frequently you see the big oil companies explaining in television or magazine ads how hard they work for the social good. Presumably, a better-informed public will be more supportive and pass this feeling along to their elected officials.
3. *Through lobbying.* Businesses can use special staffs or consultants to communicate their preferences directly to legislators. These *lobbyists* try to convince members of congress to vote pro-business on legislation. The "deregulation" theme popular in the early years of the Reagan administration was backed by considerable lobbying for reduced power of "watchdog" government agencies.
4. *Through direct candidate support.* Business executives can individually endorse candidates running for pubic office. They may also run for public office themselves, or accept political appointments to serve in government. Beyond this, they may become involved with **political action committees,**

or PACs, organized to assist in the election of candidates who favor special interests. Under the law, they are allowed to collect money and donate it to the election campaigns of favored candidates. PACs are used not only by businesses, but also by trade associations and labor unions as well. Business executives feel that PACs increase their political influence.

5. *Through illegal acts.* Business representatives can gain special favors from corrupt officials who accept bribes, illicit financial campaign contributions, and/or who succumb to threats of blackmail. While we must acknowledge that illegal acts exist, they are certainly contrary to the high standards of ethical practice and social responsibility that managers should follow.

ETHICS, SOCIAL RESPONSIBILITY, AND THE MANAGER'S CHALLENGE

Throughout this book we have focused on the manager's challenge as depicted, with one new modification, in Figure 20.7. That modification now makes the manager's performance objective subject to qualification by the two themes of the present chapter—high ethical standards and social responsibility. There is no reason that high ethical standards and social responsibility cannot be maintained in the manager's quest for productivity. The argument holds true for managers in any organizational setting, public or private, small or large, located in the United States or anywhere else in the world.

Values are the underlying beliefs and attitudes that help determine individual behavior. Trends in the evolution of managerial values over time suggest that managerial decisions in general increasingly reflect ethical as well as performance values. Although the emphasis certainly varies from person to person in the workplace, we appear to be entering a new fourth phase in the historical emergence of managerial values. On a scale of increasing social and moral commitment, the four phases may be described as:[39]

Phase I Profit-maximizing managers The profit motive was viewed as the predominate managerial focus. Concerns for social welfare in the form of working conditions, preservation of the environ-

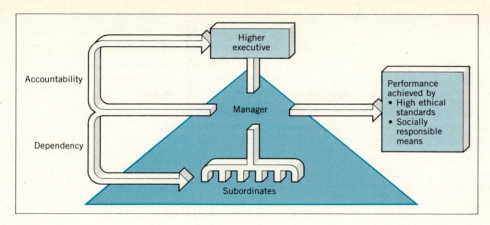

FIGURE 20.7 *Ethics, social responsibility, and the manager's challenge.*

ment, and consumer protection were secondary. The capitalist business system was guided by beliefs in profit maximization and an emphasis on economic growth. The good manager was one who worked hard and contributed to profit maximization and the maintenance of economic growth.

Phase II   Trusteeship managers   The emerence of trusteeship management broadened a manager's self-interest to include concerns for other persons whose contributions were essential to the well being of the organization—including stockholders, employees, customers, suppliers, and the local community. The task of trusteeship was multiple in focus. Profit maximization was asked to find its way along with selected external interests, especially as represented by labor unions and government regulations.

Phase III   Quality-of-life managers   An affluent society helped shift attention further away from the production of goods and services, and toward consideration of the social impact of these goods and services . . . and the organizations producing them. Quality-of-life management reflects broad priorities concerned with poverty, deteriorating cities, air and water pollution, consumer protection and the like. It calls on managers not only to achieve economic success, but also to solve basic social problems.

Phase IV   "Ethical" managers   A new wave of inter-est in the "ethics" of managerial decisions as well as the social responsibilities of organizations is extending managerial values even further. Today's managers—and those of tomorrow—must accept personal responsibility for doing the "right" things in terms of broad social and moral criteria representing multiple stakeholders in a highly complex environment. Decisions are expected to be made and problems solved with ethical considerations standing side-by-side with high performance objectives. As a Conference Board spokesperson says: "This generation of managers will be judged in large measure according to its ability to make sound ethical choices" . . . not just ones that contribute to bottom line performance.[40]

This profile of contemporary management values as "ethics" oriented may be somewhat idealistic, but it does reflect an increasing willingness of managers to subject their decisions and actions to the scrutiny of ethical and social as well as performance criteria. Once again, the manager stands on the boundary as *the* person who must accommodate each of these criteria in his or her decisions and actions. The argument is not that the decisions are getting any easier. Rather, it is that managers are becoming more willing to increase the weight given to ethical and social responsibility considerations when making those decisions.

Summary

Ethical behavior by managers both meets legal obligations and conforms to a broader set of social principles of what is "right or wrong" or "good or bad." There is and probably always will be a lingering philosophical debate on ethics in all reaches of human behavior. Nevertheless, our definition helps to identify ethical dilemmas faced by managers and understand how the resolution of these dilemmas is influenced by a variety of personal, organizational, and environmental factors. Although no precise guidelines exist, managers appear increasingly allegiant to high ethical standards. The efforts of many organizations to provide ethics training and "whistleblower" protections, ensure top management support, and establish codes of ethics illustrates trends in this area.

Organizations are also increasingly subject to social evaluations of their conduct. A socially responsible corporation, for example, acts in ways that serve public interests as well as economic interests of the firm. Social responsibility extends to all segments of society, including customers, employees, stockholders, and local communities. It is often regulated in whole or part by government agencies acting under mandates granted by legislation. All organizations operate under the umbrella of a complex legal environment that causes them to complain at times about the burdens of regulation. Our review of government regulation also recognizes, though, that the public welfare is often well served through the legislation of social responsibility.

The resolution of ethical dilemmas and conflicting social responsibility in any decision situation will never be easy or clear-cut. Underneath it all, the personal value systems of managers will determine how well their decisions and actions satisfy performance, ethical, and social-responsibility criteria. These values, although observed to be evolving in a direction supportive of "quality-of-life" management, remain dynamic and individualized in the contemporary world.

Thinking Through the Issues

1. Define in your own words: ethics, morals, ethical behavior. What is ethical managerial behavior?

2. What was the central issue raised in the Harvard Business School case? Can you identify similar issues in your personal experiences? Give examples.

3. What is an ethical dilemma? What are common sources of ethical dilemmas faced by managers, and what types of issues do these dilemmas most often involve? How do ethics training consultants recommend managers deal with ethical dilemmas facing themselves and others?

4. How can managerial ethics be influenced by (a) the manager as a person, (b) the employing organization, and (c) the external environment? Please explain using appropriate examples.

5. Explain how "codes of ethics" and "top-management support" can help to maintain high ethical standards among managers, and more generally among an organization's workforce.

6. Why aren't more unethical practices exposed by whistleblowers in organizations? What should be done to correct this situation? Why?

7. What is the relationship between the ethics of managers and the social responsibility of organizations? Explain your answer.

8. Identify three major areas within which corporations can display their social responsibility. When it comes to such behavior, what is the difference between social "obligation" and social "responsiveness?"

9. Explain the arguments "for" and "against" corporate social responsibility. Which of these positions do you hold? Why?

10. What is the legal environment of business? Explain the role of government agencies as "regulators" in the contemporary environment. What does the existence of "regulations" mean to managers?

The Manager's Vocabulary

Code of ethics
Corporate social
   responsibility
Ethical behavior
Ethical dilemma

Ethical framework
Ethical managerial
   behavior
Ethics

Ethics training
Managerial ethics
Political action
   committees (PACs)

Social audit
Stakeholders
Values
Whistleblower

TALE OF
A WHISTLEBLOWER

The memo Jerome J. LiCari wrote one August day was to change his life and significantly affect his company.[41] The director of research and development for Beech-Nut Nutrition Corporation, the second-largest U.S. baby food manufacturer and subsidiary of the Swiss food giant Nestle, LiCari had been concerned for some time that Beech-Nut's apple juice products might be adulterated. The labels read "100% fruit juice," but LiCari suspected the concentrate that Beech-Nut was buying to make the product was a blend of synthetic ingredients. Although lab tests were not conclusive, LiCari became convinced and sent a memo to senior executives. In it he pointed out the "tremendous amount of circumstantial evidence" that he felt constituted a "grave case" against the supplier. His superiors took no action. LiCari resigned a few months later.

When a prosecutor eventually presented this memo to a grand jury investigating the company, he termed it a "smoking gun" memo. Beech-Nut later pleaded guilty to 215 felony counts of willfully violating food and drug laws by selling adulterated apple products. The plea was based on the "collective knowledge" of the firm's employees that the juice was impure. One of them, in fact, referred to it in court as a "100% fraudulent chemical cocktail." The president of the company and its operations head pleaded "not guilty" to their own felony indictments. They were later convicted and sentenced to prison.

Business Week magazine headlined the whole matter as a "road to disgrace" for the firm. They noted trial testimony that showed Beech-Nut was under great financial pressure and use of the phony concentrate saved them millions of dollars. Under such pressures, executives characterized as "honest and well respected" fell prey to a "pernicious climate of rationalization, self-delusion, and denial." Their report commented further: "Beech-Nut executives apparently convinced themselves that what they were doing was just a little innocuous cheating."

The prosecutor referred to LiCari as "the conscience of Beech-Nut." During the investigation, one of his performance evaluations was made public. In it his supervisor praised his loyalty and technical ability. But LiCari was also faulted for his judgment that was described as "colored by naivete and impractical ideals." When asked in court if he felt he had been naive, LiCari responded: "I guess I was. I thought apple juice should be made from apples."

Questions

1. What is your feeling about the apparent tendency of Beech-Nut executives to try and rationalize the firm's misconduct in this situation? Can and should we hold organizational leaders accountable for such actions? Why or why not?

2. Are you prepared to face workplace dilemmas as serious as the one confronted by John LiCari? Would you deal with them in a similar fashion? Do you feel he could have handled things differently? Please explain.

3. What are the career implications of LiCari's dilemma? What advice can you now give yourself to help guide your future decisions and actions toward a career that will always be a source of personal pride?

Case Application

THE TONY SANTINO CASE

Tony Santino was a 39-year-old manager facing an ethical dilemma.[42] Three years earlier he had received his MBA from a leading business school, but he had not yet established a stable work history. He lost his first job out of graduate school when he, along with a small band of fellow MBA "hotshots," got caught in the crossfire between two warring executives in an aerospace firm. Tony's mentor left the company as a result of the battle and, shortly after, Tony did, too. He had hoped to find a job with another large firm in the same industry, but at 37 his lack of a private-sector track record seemed to be a liability.

After a prolonged and disappointing job search, Tony was appointed director of marketing for a small firm that manufactured undifferentiated, inexpensive—but critical—parts for industrial equipment. Once again, Tony discovered he was trapped between two warring executives: the company president was displeased with the performance of the current vice-president of marketing. During his job interview, the president said Tony could hope to replace that vice-president, who meanwhile was Tony's direct boss.

One of Tony's first assignments from the vice-president was to acquire information about a competitor by pretending to be an executive recruiter. Tony at first protested, but remembering his recent job search and the fact that the assignment came after only one month on the job, he reluctantly performed the task.

The president and the marketing vice-president were both strong-willed individuals and frequently did not see eye to eye. But they joined forces when Tony expressed some reluctance to sign and distribute what he believed to be an illegal and unethical price list. Tony's employer, as it turned out, had been illegally setting prices in collusion with its major competitors for years, yielding a handsome profit.

One of the competing firms had invested this monopoly profit back into R&D and developed a process for manufacturing the same product line for 40 percent of the current cost. The competitor was passing on the savings to customers and devouring the market, especially for new customers. Tony's firm, anxious to maintain its market share with less competitive goods, developed a fictitious product line that would sell at the competitor's price.

The lower-priced items were exactly the same as the higher-priced products, but were labeled differently and made available only to new customers. The purchasing engineers of old customers were too loyal and lazy to run the certification tests necessary to switch to a new product line or supplier. The deception in Tony's company would involve lab technicians, phone order clerks, and the company sales force.

Tony believed this practice to be a violation of the Robinson–Patman and Sherman Antitrust laws, an opinion he conveyed to his superiors. He suggested that the only way to effectively compete in an industry with an undifferentiated product was by being a cost leader. Tony's bosses, however, defended their proposed action as common industry practice and asked Tony not to be so "negative."

Tony consulted with a local lawyer, a friend who confirmed the illegality of the proposed pricing scheme but also emphasized that "small companies were known for this kind of stuff." The probability of apprehension and any kind of legal action was negligible, the lawyer said.

In addition, Tony hired an outside marketing consultant to advise the company on broad strategic issues. In a meeting attended by the consultant, Tony, and his superiors, Tony asked about the Robinson–Patman violation. His bosses looked on in horror as he described the pricing decision. But they were relieved as the consultant said, "The jails are not big enough to hold all the people who do this sort of thing."

Tony had to obtain forged lab test results from the company's R&D engineers to implement the pricing scheme. Although they complied promptly, one of the engineers commented, "Tony, I know you're just caught in the middle, but I've been around here 39 years and have never been able to like these things any better." One of the sales managers also called Tony to inquire about the rumored new product and asked, "Hey, what's the story on the new 1700s? I've heard that they're just the 1400s with a new name. Since when do we have the capabilities to make these specs?" That call convinced Tony the scheme was as transparent as it was dishonest.

The dilemma was exacerbated when Tony's bosses asked him to sign the cover sheet of the new price list. He confided in a friend: "I still think I know what's right, but with all these other voices telling me to sign the price list, maybe I'm just making a mountain out of a molehill. Then again, maybe I compromised myself through the executive headhunter intrigue. And if I leave, how do I explain my short job tenure to any potential employer?"

After deliberating over these questions, Tony consulted with former MBA classmates. He found a high degree of understanding and support from peers who had faced similar dilemmas, and he resolved not to sign the price list. He asked his secretary to retype the cover letter to allow instead for the signature of his superior, the vice-president of sales and marketing. Along with this letter draft, he sent a note which stated, "After a good deal of consideration, I feel that the announcement of new products would never come from a director. Something this momentous should come from a vice-president to avoid arousing suspicion."

Tony was relieved when the vice-president signed the letter. However, he then asked Tony to present the new products to the sales force at an upcoming retreat. Faced with a dilemma again, Tony told his superior that he was personally opposed to making the presentation at the sales meeting but he would if he was so directed. Tony also wrote a memo to this effect for the office file. After his superiors told Tony that they would instruct R&D to really make two new products, Tony made the sales presentation.

But he doubted his bosses' commitment to changing their behavior, and Tony continued to search for a new job. His mentor from his first job after business school was now a senior executive in a large firm, and he created a staff job for Tony, after warning him that the industry was headed for a downturn and the job could be a casualty. Tony, however, preferred to take that chance rather than stay where he was. Accordingly, a few weeks after Tony had made the sales presentation, he resigned.

Concerned about whether he had changed anything in the firm with his resignation, Tony wrote a letter to the president that was titled "Subject: Unlawful Pricing Tactics" and circulated copies to the company's division managers. The president was furious, called Tony into his office, and yelled, "Who are you to make me answer to my subordinates?" He "fired" Tony, even though he had already resigned the previous week.

Tony's next job did not last long since the industry, as expected, went through a severe downturn. He worked for some time as a free-lance consultant and went through a period of severe economic and personal hardship. Gradually, Tony's consulting business started to get established. He also landed another job as a senior executive with a large high-tech manufacturing company, whose executives admired Tony's career choices. His new boss said, "Only a weak person would have succumbed to the kinds of pressures that you faced." As of this writing, Tony has worked for the company for 5 years.

Questions

1.   What are the sources of the various conflicts and dilemmas Tony Santino experienced in this case? What "signals" might Tony have picked up from the organization, industry environment, and individual behaviors that might have alerted him to the presence of potential dilemmas? In what ways was Tony able to clarify his own values during the course of his experiences?
2.   What tactics did Tony use to try and initiate change in the work situations in which he was confronting ethical dilemmas? What tactics did he use to protect himself in those situations? Were his tactics well chosen and well executed? Why or why not?
3.   Was Tony a success in the case? Why or why not? What lessons can you summarize from Tony's experience that might help others deal with similar situations? Please explain.

Class Exercise: Ethics Training

1.   Read and think about the following situations. Each is taken from an ethics training workshop run by consultants for major corporations.[43]

Budget Maneuver   Dan Calvin, director of community relations for a local utility, has worked for three years with the downtown redevelopment association in the city where his office is located. He was recently selected by the members to chair the association for the coming year. When the news came out, Dan was congratulated by a senior executive who asked him to "go all out" with this work. It wasn't long after, however, that Dan's boss told him that financial difficulties meant that Dan's entertainment budget would be cut 20 percent. This hurt Dan because he had been planning to pick up the

$625 bill for a big public relations banquet to acquaint neighborhood leaders with the association's plans. Given conflicting signals from the senior executive and his immediate boss, Dan put the charges down as "advertising" costs. In this way they were charged to another division's budget. Dan's action was discovered. As the company's personnel director, you must decide how to deal with him. What is your decision?

Secret Envelope Jackie Smith, vice-president of a defense contractor, opened an envelope marked "Confidential and Personal." It contained data that appeared to be from one of her firm's competitors for a Navy contract. It was accompanied by a note from one of Jackie's marketing managers. The note said the data was real. Jackie called in two of her trusted aids to discuss the use of the data, which could dramatically help in preparing their own bid. The head marketing person saw no problem, since it was common in the industry to get intelligence on one another's competitive plans. Jackie, in fact, had recently reminded her managers how important this was. But her executive assistant warned of the risks. The figures might have been purchased with the promise of some eventual quid pro quo. It could also blow up in their faces if the situation became public. What should Jackie do?

2. Decide what you think the personnel director should do in the case of the *budget maneuver,* and what Jackie should do in the case of the *secret envelope.* Make sure you are clear in the reasons why you would act this way in each case.

3. Share your responses to each incident with a nearby classmate and explain the rationales for your proposed actions. Listen to the classmate's responses and rationales in return. Try to determine if either of your responses is better. And, if so, try to determine why.

4. Await further class discussion led by your instructor.

References

[1] These cases are reported in *The Wall Street Journal* (February 9, 1988), p. 2; *Business Week* (February 15, 1988), p. 56; and, *Business Week* (February 22, 1988).

[2] Reported in Adam Smith, "Wall Street's Outrageous Fortunes," *Esquire* (April 1987), p. 73.

[3] All definitions are from *Webster's New World Dictionary of the American Language,* Second College Edition, David B. Juralnik (ed.) (New York: World Publishing, 1972).

[4] For informative practical perspectives on business and managerial ethics see Verne E. Henderson, "The Ethical Side of Enterprise," *Sloan Management Review,* Vol. 23 (1982), p. 38; Barbara Ley Toffler, *Tough Choices: Managers Talk Ethics* (New York: Wiley, 1986); Saul W. Gellerman, "Why 'Good' Managers Make Bad Ethical Choices," *Harvard Business Review,* Vol. 64 (July–August 1986), pp. 85–90; the special section on "Business Ethics: The Need for New Definition," in *New Management,* Vol. 4 (1987); and, the editorial by Irving Kristol, "Ethics, Anyone? Or, Morals?" *The Wall Street Journal* (September 15, 1987), p. 32.

[5] See James O'Toole, "William May: Good Ethics is Good Business," *New Management,* Vol. 4 (1987), pp. 57–61.

[6] For a research perspective on managerial ethics, see George K. Saul, "Business Ethics: Where Are We Going?" *Academy of Management Review,* Vol. 6 (April 1981), pp. 269–276; and, Linda Klebe Trevino, "Ethical Decision Making in Organizations: A Person–Situation Interactionist Model," *Academy of Management Review,* Vol. 11 (1986), pp. 601–617.

[7] This case and related quotes from Thomas Moore, "Industrial Espionage at the Harvard B-School," *Fortune* (September 6, 1982), pp. 70–72 and 76. © 1982 Time Inc. Courtesy of *Fortune* Magazine.

[8] Reported in Barbara Ley Toffler, "Tough Choices: Managers Talk Ethics," *New Management,* Vol. 4 (1987), pp. 34–39.

[9] The cases and subsequent discussion are developed from Steven N. Brenner and Earl A. Mollander, "Is the Ethics of Business Changing?" *Harvard Business Review,* Vol. 55 (January-February 1977), p. 57.

[10] See Robert D. Gilbreath, "The Hollow Executive," *New Management,* Vol. 4 (1987), pp. 24–28.

[11] *Business Conduct Guidelines* (Armonk, NY: IBM Corporation, 1983), pp. 18–19.

[12] William M. Carley, "Antitrust Chief Says CEOs Should Tape All Phone Calls to Each Other," *Wall Street Journal* (February 1983), p. 23. See also "American Air, Chief End Antitrust Suit, Agree Not to Discuss Fares with Rivals," *The Wall Street Journal* (July 15, 1985), p. 4.

[13] John A. Pearce, II, "Newcomer's Need for a Code of Business Ethics," *Collegiate Forum* (Fall 1978), p. 12.

[14] Quotes are from Alan L. Otten, "Ethics on the Job: Companies Alert Employees to Potential Dilemmas," *The Wall Street Journal* (July 14, 1986), p. 17.

[15]Both consulting approaches reported in Ibid.

[16]Saul W. Gellerman, "Why 'Good' Managers Make Bad Ethical Choices," *Harvard Business Review,* Vol. 64 (July–August 1986), pp. 85–90.

[17]Alan L. Otten, "States Begin to Protect Employees Who Blow Whistle on Their Firms," *Wall Street Journal* (December 31, 1984), p. 11; and, "Squealing for Dollars," *Business Week* (July 25, 1988), p. 38.

[18]Information from James A. Waters, "Catch 20.5: Morality as an Organizational Phenomenon," *Organizational Dynamics,* Vol. 6 (Spring 1978), pp. 3–15.

[19]Information from "Back to the Basics: Businesses are Moving to Close the Literacy Gap," *Business Week* (September 21, 1987), pp. 54–56.

[20]*The Wall Street Journal* (January 15, 1985), p. 1.

[21]Harold L. Johnson, "Ethics and the Executive," *Business Horizons,* Vol. 24 (1981), pp. 53–59.

[22]All reported in Charles D. Pringle and Justin G. Longnecker, "The Ethics of MBO," *Academy of Management Review,* Vol. 7 (April 1982), p. 309. See also Barry Z. Posner and Warren H. Schmidt, "Values and the American Manager: An Update," *California Management Review,* Vol. XXVI (Spring 1984), pp. 202–216.

[23]Information from Eileen White Read, "Defense Contractors' Ethics Programs Get Scrutinized," *The Wall Street Journal* (July 21, 1988), p. 4

[24]David B. Hilder, "Accountants' Code Calls Whistle Blowing Inappropriate Unless the Law Requires It," *Wall Street Journal* (July 21, 1983), p. 6.

[25]Information from "Businesses Are Signing up for Ethics 101," *Business Week* (February 15, 1988), pp. 56–57.

[26]See Rick Warttzman, "Nature or Nurture? Study Blames Ethical Lapses on Corporate Goals," *the Wall Street Journal* (October 9, 1987), p. 21; and, Amanda Bennett, "Ethics Codes Spread Despite Criticism," *The Wall Street Journal* (July 15, 1988), p. 13.

[27]Information from Bennett, op. cit.

[28]See Anthony F. Buono and Lawrence T. Nichols, *Corporate Policy, Values and Social Responsibility* (New York: Praeger, 1985).

[29]The Friedman quote is from Milton Friedman, *Capitalism and Freedom* (Chicago: University of Chicago Press, 1962); Samuelson quote is from Paul A. Samuelson, "Love that Corporation," *Mountain Bell Magazine* (Spring 1971). Both are cited by Keith Davis, "The Case For and Against Business Assumption of Social Responsibilities," *Academy of Management Journal* (June 1973), pp. 312–322.

[30]This discussion is developed from Davis, op. cit.; and, Keith Davis and William C. Frederick. *Business and Society: Management, Public Policy, Ethics,* Fifth Edition (New York: McGraw-Hill, 1984), pp. 28, 41.

[31]Quotes from Davis, op. cit.

[32]Information for this case is from Walter Kiechel III, "Unfuzzing Ethics for Managers," *Fortune* (November 23, 1987), pp. 229–234; and, "Businesses are Signing up for Ethics 101," *Business Week* (February 15, 1988), pp. 56–57.

[33]Elisabetta Di Cagno, "IBM: One Corporation's Contribution," *Hermes,* Vol. 8 (Winter 1982), p. 18. The discussion that immediately follows is also based on this article.

[34]Jeffrey A. Tannenbaum, "Paid Public-Service Leaves Buoy Workers, But Return to Old Jobs Can Be Wrenching," *Wall Street Journal* (May 6, 1981), p. 27.

[35]Information from *Business Week,* op. cit., 1987.

[36]Information from "Company Helping Communities: American Express Chips In," *Southern Illinoisan* (October 24, 1985), p. 10W.

[37]S. Prakash Sethi, "A Conceptual Framework for Environmental Analysis of Social Issues and Evaluation of Business Response Patterns," *Academy of Management Review,* Vol. 4 (January 1979), pp. 63–74. For a related discussion see also K. E. Goodpaster and J. B. Matthews, Jr., "Can a Corporation Have a Conscience," *Harvard Business Review,* Vol. 60 (January–February 1982), pp. 132–141.

[38]This case in O'Toole, op. cit., 1987.

[39]The first three phases are described in Robert Hay and Ed Gray, "Social Responsibilities of Business Managers," *Academy of Management Journal,* Vol. 18 (March 1974), pp. 135–143.

[40]Bennett, op. cit.

[41]Information from "What Led Beech-Nut Down the Road to Disgrace," *Business Week* (February 22, 1988), pp. 124–128.

[42]This case is reported in Arvind Bhambri and Jeffrey Sonnenfeld, "The Man Who Stands Alone," *New Management,* Vol. 4 (1987), pp. 29–33. Used by permission.

[43]These incidents are reported in Otten, op. cit.; and, "The Business Ethics Debate," *Newsweek* (May 25, 1987), p. 36.

PART 6

Latino Glass, S.A.

Production superintendent Angel Ramos obviously was upset. Ramos had been with Latino since the company began its operations in his country 12 years ago. He had worked hard during these years and had been recognized for his effort with numerous promotions. He had counted heavily on replacing Roy Webster as plant manager at Latino Glass when he heard that Webster was being promoted to president. Now he waited outside Webster's office, having just learned that an "outsider" was being brought in as the new plant manager. He was unaware that Webster himself was concerned about Ramos's predicament, and that he was discussing it with the company controller at that very moment.

BACKGROUND

Latino Glass was founded as a joint venture in Latino, South America. The parent United States company, Stateside Glass Company, produced a wide variety of glass products for both domestic and foreign markets. Latino Glass, unlike most glass plants, which specialize in a single product, produced two products. Therefore, managers could acquire experience in two product areas simultaneously. The Latino operation was considered by ambitious middle-level managers in Stateside Glass as a good opportunity to gain valuable managerial experience. In addition to the two-product experience, the Latino operation was thought to provide decision-making opportunities that comparable level managers in

Source: Donald D. White and H. William Vroman (eds.), *Action in Organizations,* Second Edition (Boston: Allyn and Bacon, 1982), pp. 367–369. Used by permission.

Stateside did not have. On the other hand, it was generally believed that many of the decisions made by Latino managers were reviewed by corporate-level managers at the home office of Stateside Glass.

> The government declaration stated that all new enterprises begun in Latino must have at least 51 percent Latino ownership.

Latino's primary product was black-and-white . television picture tubes. Competition in the area had been limited for some time as a result of a government decree prohibiting the importation of picture tubes into the country. One Japanese firm did build and operate a similar plant in Latino, however, and gained about 20 percent of the total market. In addition, recent trade agreements among several Latin American countries allowed a Mexican producer of picture tubes to market its product in Latino. To date, Latino has not been hurt seriously by the Mexican competition, and sales outside the country are on the increase.

Approximately one year ago, the company decided to expand its present production and add a line of picture tubes for color television. However, a government declaration made shortly after the decision caused the parent company to hold up any action of the addition on the new line. The original plan had called for Stateside Glass to form a second joint-venture company in Latino for the express purpose of producing the color-television picture tubes. The government declaration stated that all new enterprises begun in Latino must have at least 51 percent Latino ownership. A final decision as to whether or not the company's plans will be nullified by the declaration has not yet been made by the local government.

ROY WEBSTER'S OBSERVATIONS

"When Angel Ramos found out, by way of the grapevine, that we were bringing in Joe Kent to be plant manager, he was quite upset, even somewhat emotional. Indirectly, he threatened to quit. Ramos is a good man and has performed well as production superintendent for three years. He's only 32 years old."

"When I was plant manager, I never had any trouble with him—we always got along pretty well, though he tends to be a little impulsive. I guess when I moved up to president from plant manager, he assumed he would replace me as plant manager. While I was never free to tell him, he was my choice for the job, even though I knew he would have some problems because of lack of experience in the areas reporting to him— plant accounting and industrial relations, especially. I guess Paul Moore (vice-president of Latin American operations for Stateside) felt Ramos's lack of experience would create too many problems. That's on our agenda of topics to be discussed on my next trip to the states. It is the policy of Stateside Glass to promote nationals as rapidly as they are capable of assuming greater responsibility—and we follow it. Of the 250 people employed by Latino Glass, there are only three Americans—the project manager who is coordinating the introduction of the lab-products line in terms of production and sales, the plant manager, and myself, the president. Besides, we can't do much without government permission, and the industry department likes to see Latinos in high company positions—it improves our image with the government. But Joe Kent was assigned the job by Moore, and that's the way it will have to stay.

"There is another aspect of the Ramos problem that must be considered. The heads of the departments reporting to the plant manager are used to having an American over them. When the time comes to move a Latino person into the job of plant manager, we might have problems with the Latino people who report to him. It's all right if an American is the plant manager, but as soon as a Latino native is in that job, each of the other Latino people will feel that he or she should have had the job. I'm not sure they're ready to accept another Latino as their boss. When Joe Kent's time is up here and he returns to Stateside Glass, in about three years, I think Angel Ramos will be ready for the plant manager's job.

It is the policy of Stateside Glass to promote nationals as rapidly as they are capable of assuming greater responsibility

I can't promise him anything because I'll be leaving Latino Glass about that time myself. But I wouldn't be surprised if he were the next plant manager.

"Latino Glass has progressed nicely in the past five years. We've had some problems, but I think we're really sailing now. Joe Kent worries me a little. His confidential file indicates he has a short temper, let's everybody know it when things don't go right—or so his file indicates. He spent the first four weeks after being assigned here in an intensive Spanish course—he's actually been on the job less than two weeks. I've noticed that he never uses his Spanish. I guess he's afraid or embarrassed to make mistakes. Our home-office personnel committee reviewed the records of the top production superintendents in the Stateside plants, and Joe, evidently, came out as the strongest prospect. Before coming to Latino, he was production superintendent in a color-television tube plant. He has been with Stateside Glass for 15 years—almost all of them in line positions in production. Two years ago he was offered a promotion to plant manager in an overseas operation, in Asia to be exact, but he turned it down. Some people feel that if he had turned down a second promotion, namely plant manager here in Latino, he'd never be offered another chance. I don't think Stateside really operates like that—but Joe might think so. I just hope that he and Angel Ramos get the job done and don't crash head on. If those two don't work together, they will make us all look bad.

"I've suggested to Joe, subtly of course, that he use the work-objectives program that I started when I was plant manager. It worked for me. It should work for him if I can just get him to try it. I don't know when I'll get around to starting it with the people who report to me. The work-objectives program (some call it 'management by results') consisted of my sitting down with each of my subordinates, individually, and discussing what goals they should strive to reach in the forthcoming six-week period. Then we got together as a group, my subordinates and I, and each subordinate would tell the others what he was going to achieve in the coming period. We discussed each person's objectives as a group because sometimes they can help each other achieve their objectives. I like to see them set objectives that are a little higher than what is likely they can achieve—something to shoot at, so to speak. As I said, though, I haven't had time since I've been president to start it with my immediate subordinates. I wish Joe Kent would continue the work-objectives program in his area. It could help him do a better job; but if he and Ramos don't get along and don't support each other, we're all going to look bad."

Angel Ramos. . . had counted heavily on replacing Roy Webster as plant manager at Latino Glass

QUESTIONS

1. What is the major problem in this case? What are the causes of this problem? What additional problems are contributing to the situation? Please explain.
2. What complications do you expect Joe Kent's arrival will bring to the situation? Why? Support your answer with evidence from the case.
3. What special advice would you give Joe Kent? Angel Ramos? Why?
4. Overall, what do you recommend should be done if Stateside Glass is to build an effective Latino operation that serves local needs as well as those of the parent company? Why? ∎

Woodward Governor's Workplace Democracy

Under Irl C. Martin's leadership, the Woodward Governor Company grew from a small firm domestic firm employing fewer than 50 persons to an international business with over 2,000 employees. That growth record is impressive. And the manner in which it was achieved is even more impressive. Under Martin's leadership Woodward raised relations among employees and between stockholders and employees to impressive levels. In effect, Martin democratized the workplace at Woodward Governor. Here is that story.

I. IRL MARTIN'S CAREER LADDER

Irl Martin was born in Broken Bow, Nebraska on December 12, 1895. His father operated several farm implement stores and introduced Irl to the joys and agonies of running a small business of one's own. Irl's family also taught him many of the values which were to become part of his adult leadership style. These included personal honesty, hard work, helping friends and neighbors when in need, punctuality and a lack of class consciousness.

Source: This case is prepared by Professor Richard E. Hattwick of Western Illinois University. It is a condensed version of Richard E. Hattwick, "Democratizing the Workplace: The Case of Irl C. Martin and the Woorward Governor Company." *The Journal of Business Leadership.* Vol. I (Spring 1988).

After graduating from high school in 1913 Irl went to work for the local electric company. In 1915 he entered the Armour Institute of Technology. There he studied electrical engineering until enlisting in the United States Army in 1917.

While in the Army Irl met Dorothy Woodard whose father, Elmer, owned and managed the Woodward Govenor Company. After the war Irl and Dorothy were married and settled in Broken Bow where Irl ran a local electric utility company. Two years later the couple moved to Rockford, Illinois, where Irl began a decade long apprenticeship with his father-in-law's firm.

Elmer Woodward hoped that Irl would eventually become his successor as chief executive of Woodward Governor. But before Irl joined the ranks of top management Elmer wanted to be sure that his son-in-law knew the business thoroughly. And so Irl was put through an eight year apprenticeship. Elmer started him as an operator of a machine which threaded bolts. Irl wasn't the best machinist, but he worked hard and earned the respect of the machinists around him. Next he was put on the assembly line, then assigned to engineering, followed by accounting, road work and sales. By 1929 Irl Martin was thoroughly familiar with Woodward's products, customers, production techniques, sales methods, accounting methods and administrative practices. More important, he knew and was accepted as a peer by the company's 50 employees.

II. THE FIRST MAJOR DECISION AND ITS CONSEQUENCE

Satisfied with his son-in-law's progress, Elmer Woodward appointed Irl to the position of general manager in 1929. By the end of Irl's first year the Great Depression had begun and he faced a serious crisis.

New orders dried up, many existing orders were cancelled and suddenly the company was unable to pay its workers. The obvious decision was to lay off redundant workers. But these people were Irl Martin's friends and he couldn't simply cut off their incomes. Instead he called a meeting of all employees and asked them to vote on two alternative courses of action—(1) either reduce everyone to a 20 hour work week and thereby keep all employees on the payroll but at a sharp reduction in pay, or (2) lay off more than one-half the work force. The employees voted to take the reduction in pay and share the work.

Woodward Governor struggled to survive for the next three years. Then a sharp increase in business occurred. Suddenly the company was faced with the necessity of employees working 60 hour weeks in order to meet the demand. But the federal government ordered Woodward to cut the work week back to 40 hours per week. That government order came from the National Recovery Administration which had devised a means of reducing national unemployment by specifying maximum hours that an employee could work. The idea, of course, was to encourage employers to hire additional workers. But Woodward needed were highly skilled workers and there weren't many of those available. It looked like the firm would be unable to meet its commitments to customers. Then the unexpected happened. As Irl later explained, "It looked bad for a few days until we realized that the people were putting in sixty hours a week, but twenty hours were on their own and for those they received nothing. The bread cast upon the waters during the Depression was paying dividends. The family ties had been strengthened."

III. THE PROGRAM TO CREATE A DEMOCRATIC, "FAMILY" CULTURE

Several other incidents occurred which further demonstrated the fact that Woodward's employees cared

> Under Martin's leadership Woodward raised relations among employees, and between stockholders and employees to impressive levels.

about the company and were willing to make personal sacrifices to be sure it succeeded. When it became clear that Woodward needed to buy new machinery to remain competitive, Irl

called a meeting of all employees to discuss whether or not that year's income should go to increase wages or buy the machinery. The workers voted to forego the wage increases and buy the machinery. Later when it became clear that air conditioning was needed in the factory, the workers met and agreed to sacrifice wage increases in order to pay for the air conditioning.

Irl Martin was so deeply moved by these examples of team spirit that he set a new goal for himself—the creation of a corporate culture which would perpetuate the democratic, family feeling then present in the company. He began making highly visible changes. A dress code was implemented. Irl believed that a sharp looking work force would be one whose members felt good about themselves. A new plant was constructed and designed in such a way as to be as pleasant to the eye and healthful to the body. Again the thought was to generate good feelings about co-workers and the company.

He next moved to an important structural issue. Irl was convinced that one reason for the emergence of bad feelings within a workforce was size. When the number of employees in a given plant got too large workers began to lose their family feeling. Irl determined that the optimal number of employees was in the range of 500 to 1000 and that became company policy. Expansion beyond that number would require the building of new plants.

A final innovation was the adoption of the term "member" to refer to all employees. This was combined with a practice of putting all new hires through a probationary period. At the end of the period, all "members" who had worked with the new hire would vote on the person's acceptability as a "member of the

Woodward family." If the vote was favorable the new hire would be officially welcomed as a new member at an impressive induction ceremony.

IV. PAY AND THE CORPORATE PARTNERSHIP

By the end of World War II Irl Martin had made much progress in his campaign to institutionalize the family feeling at Woodward Governor. But there was one gap—one unresolved problem that, if not solved, might eventually erode morale. The problem was finding an equitable method of determining pay rates. Irl had given this matter much thought and had conceived of a possible solution called it "The Corporate Partnership." He prepared the employees or "members" for the new concept with a series of open letters in the company magazine *Prime Mover Control*. The letters ran in the 1945 and early 1946 issues. Then in October, 1946 the company adopted Irl's plan on a one year trial basis. A year later it was permanently adopted.

Irl summarized the history and philosophy of "The Corporate Partnership" as follows: "It was mutually agreed . . . that the health, progress and longevity of the team or company should be of first importance to all concerned. It was further agreed that the maintenance and perpetuation of the personnel and facilities must come first and profits or surplus second. The first problem confronting management, therefore, was one of maintaining and perpetuating the partners. The second problem was one of maintaining and perpetuating the facilities. And the third was one of equitable distribution or surplus, if any, remaining after the first two problems had been adequately solved."

Under Irl's plan, stockholder partners were allocated a "base or sustaining income" consisting of a percentage of their investment based on what could be earned in government securities plus a risk factor. Assuming funds were available for distribution in this manner, a national appraisal company would establish the payout rates.

When it came to the worker partners, Irl stated that: "the problem may also be divided into two parts . . . The first step was to establish a sustaining or base wage for the worker partner. Based on study, discussion and agreement, the amount of income at forty hours per week required to assure the prudent maintenance, education and protection of the average family was established and this became the minimum base income allowable under this plan. A maximum base income was also established . . . These extremes covered the worker of the least relative value to the organization as a whole. All other base incomes were interpolated in between on the basis of the relative value of each individual as determined by a rating system." The worker members decided that the maximum base income should be awarded to the president of the company, whose salary should be no more and no less than ten times that of the least valuable category of worker.

The rating process for workers between the highest and lowest pay categories was conducted annually under the direction of a "Plant Rating Committee." Every employee was rated by his or her co-workers and by his or her supervisor. The ratings were done with the aid of a standardized form and were sent to the committee. When the committee had finished its work it issued a master list ranking all employees in the plant in order of their value to the company.

The rankings were then used to determine both the base income due each worker and the "bonus" which would be paid if the company earned a "surplus."

If the company did earn a surplus in a given year, it became necessary to determine the allocation between stockholders and workers. A 1960 company history described the process as follows: "To illustrate how

> The rating process . . . was conducted annually under the direction of a "Plant Rating Committee." Every employee was rated by his or her co-workers . . .

the sharing ratio (between capital and labor) is computed, assume that 6 percent is the allowed rate and that the workers' fiscal year earnings amount to $720,000. By capitalizing this sum at the rate of 6 percent, the worker partners' contribution would be valued at $12,000,000. Next, assume that the stockholder partners' contribution is appraised at $4,000,000. Then the total "capital" of the corporate partnership would be $16,000,000. The resulting sharing ratio for sharing would be one-fourth to stockholder partners and three-fourths to the worker partners."

Two featurs of the "Corporate Partnership" deserve emphasis. First, of course, it creates a feeling of partnership between stockholders and employees and among different categories of worker including managers. Irl used the term "member" to refer to each worker and stockholder and the notion of membership with

the attendant right to vote, speak out and be heard is the feeling which the system fostered.

Second, the Woodward system promoted job stability. It did so by making total pay flexible. All employees received a basic income regardless of company financial performance. But that basic income was below the going rate for most job categories. The difference was made up throughout the sharing of profit (or surplus). And as long as there was profit, Woodward employees earned a total income equal to or better than what they could get with other employers. In years when profit was meager or nonexistent, employees would not receive such market levels of income but at least they would remain employed.

V. EVOLUTION OF WOODWARD'S INDUSTRIAL DEMOCRACY

By 1950 Irl Martin had in place all of the basic elements of his idealistic concept of industrial democracy. The rest of his career was to be a long period of making the system work and doing what he could to prepare successor management to keep the system intact.

In the 1950's growth of sales pushed employment close to the 1,000 maximum size which the company thought to be consistent with the "Woodward Way." And so, during the decade new plants were opened in Ft. Collins, Colorado, the Netherlands and England. A fifth branch plant was opened in Japan in 1960.

Irl Martin reached the age of 65 in 1960. Adhering to the company's policy he retired as president and became chairman of the board. From that position he continued to promote maintenance of the company's

> **Irl called a meeting of all employees to discuss whether or not . . . to increase wages or buy the machinery. The workers voted to . . . buy the machinery.**

industrial democracy. In 1971 he had the satisfaction of seeing the company adopt a "Corporate Constitution" which affirmed the principles of the "Woodward Way."

On March 24, 1976 Irl Martin resigned as chairman of the board, ending 55 years of service to the company. A year later he died. At the time of his death Woodward's industrial democracy was functioning well. It continues to do so, in part because the ranks of top executives are still dominated by individuals who had helped Irl put the system into place. Helping those executives to pay attention to the care and feeding of the system was this parting thought from Irl Martin, "We can expect to enjoy the benefits of 'corporate partnership' only as long as each of us continues to contribute our proportionate share of group effort . . . What we have today may be lost tomorrow if we are not eternally vigilant."

QUESTIONS

1. What special "values" seem to have guided Irl Martin's decisions and actions at Woodward Governor? Are they "realistic" in terms of the demands and challenges of today's environment? Why or why not?

2. How do you evaluate Woodward in terms of meeting its social responsibilities? Are any of its approaches worth considering by other organizations today? Give examples to support your answers.

3. Why, under Irl Martin's leadership, didn't the workers at Woodward Governor need to be represented by a labor union? What could a union have offered that they didn't already seem to have in this case?

> **Irl Martin: "What we have today may be lost tomorrow if we are not eternally vigilant."**

4. What concerns do you have about future leadership transitions at Woodward Governor? How could organization development be applied to help ensure that the values and legacies of Woodward's past endure even as the firm must adapt to changing times? Explain and defend your answer.

CONCLUSION

21 Management for Productivity: A Career Perspective

Life-Long Learning to Manage Effectively

Productivity has been described as "the lever of economic development and growth."[1] Managers, we have said many times in this book, are the keys to productivity. And without a doubt, managers of the 1990s and beyond will have to excel as never before in order to meet the high expectations held of them.

This is the final part of the book. It consists of only one chapter, "Management for Productivity: A Career Perspective." The purpose of Part Seven is to help you anticipate future decisions that must be successfully faced if you are to achieve a productive and satisfying managerial career. Job stress, proving yourself as a manager, and working a career into family responsibilities are but a few of many personal challenges to come.

FOUNDATIONS OF SUCCESS

The *new managers*—that is, the managers who will deliver under the high expectations of the 1990s and beyond—must be well educated and willing to adopt new ways in de-

NOTES
1. "The Productivity Paradox," a special report in *Business Week* (June 6, 1988), pp. 100–114.
2. Lyman W. Porter and Lawrence E. McKibbin, *Management Education and Development: Drift or Thrust into the 21st Century* (New York: McGraw-Hill, 1988).
3. John Gardner, *No Easy Victories* (New York: Harper & Row, 1968).
4. Excerpted from Ralph Z. Sorenson, "A Lifetime of Learning to Manage Effectively," *Wall Street Journal* (February 28, 1983), p. 18. Reprinted by permission of the *Wall Street Journal*. Copyright © 1983 Dow Jones & Company, Inc. All rights reserved.

" . . . MANAGERS OF THE 1990S WILL HAVE TO EXCEL TO MEET HIGH EXPECTATIONS."

manding circumstances. As pointed out in a recent report of the American Assembly of Collegiate Schools of Business, there are "compelling issues facing management education." Today's students must prepare for tomorrow's challenges by better developing their "people" skills, becoming more attuned to the nature of an information/service society, understanding the international dimen-

sions, and establishing commitments to life-long learning.[2]

Throughout this book we have emphasized the acquisition of knowledge and the mastery of basic skills in order to succeed in the management process. This emphasis is appropriate and necessary if you are to establish the foundations for career success. True success, however, requires that knowledge and skills be accompanied by personal qualities that lend strong character to your work efforts. This is the topic now before us—putting your knowledge and skills together with who you are as a person, so that you can play a significant role in the continued development of society.

In his book *No Easy Victories,* John Gardner speaks of a similar challenge.[3] Read his words twice in the following quote—once as written; then once again substituting the word *manager* for *leader* and *organization* for *society.*

"Leaders have a significant role in creating the state of mind that is the society. They can serve as symbols of the moral unity of the society. They can express the values that hold the society together. Most important, they can conceive and articulate goals that lift people out of their petty preoccupations, carry them above the conflicts that tear a society apart, and unite them in the pursuit of objectives worthy of their best efforts."

A LIFETIME OF LEARNING

Each of us must probe deeply into the personal challenges of meeting these responsibilities as a leader and manager in contemporary society. Before starting the chapter, think about the following advice offered by Ralph Z. Sorenson, past president of Babson College, and president and chief executive officer of Barry Wright Corporation. He speaks wisely about the qualities required for managerial success in the future.

"Years ago, when I was a young assistant professor at the Harvard Business School, I thought that the key to developing managerial leadership lay in raw brain power.[4] I thought the role of business schools was to develop future managers who knew all about the various functions of business; to teach them how to define problems succinctly, analyze

> . . . managers of the 1990s and beyond will have to excel as never before in order to meet the high expectations held of them.

these problems and identify alternatives in a clear, logical fashion, and finally, to teach them to make an intelligent decision.

"My thinking gradually became tempered by living and working outside the United States and by serving seven years as a college president. During my presidency of Babson College, I added several additional traits or skills that I felt a good manager must possess. "The first is the *ability to express oneself* in a clear, articulate fashion. Good oral and written communication skills are absolutely essential if one is to be an effective manager.

"Second, one must possess that amorphous and intangible set of qualities called *leadership skills*. To be

a good leader one must understand and be sensitive to people and be able to inspire them toward the achievement of common goals.

"Next I concluded that effective managers must be *broad human beings* who not only understand the world of business but also have a sense of the cultural, social, political, historical, and (particularly today) international aspects of life and society. This suggests that exposure to the liberal arts and humanities should be part of every manager's education.

"Finally, as I pondered the lessons of Watergate and the almost daily litany of business and government related scandals that have occupied the front pages of newspapers throughout the 70s and early 80s, it became abundantly clear that a good manager in today's world must have *courage and a strong sense of integrity*. He or she must know where to draw the line between right and wrong."

"But now I have shed the cap and gown of a college president and donned the hat of chief executive officer. As a result of my experience as a corporate CEO, my list of desirable managerial traits has become still longer.

"It now seems to me that what matters most in the majority of organizations is to have reasonably in-

> . . . a good manager in today's world must have courage and a strong sense of integrity.

telligent, hard-working managers who have a sense of pride and loyalty toward their organization; who can get to the root of a problem and are inclined toward action; who are decent human beings with a natural empathy and concern for people; who possess humor, humility, and common sense; and who are able to couple drive with stick-to-it-iveness and patience in the accomplishment of a goal."

"It is the *ability to make positive things happen* that most distinguishes the successful manager from the mediocre or unsuccessful one. It is far better to have dependable managers who can make the right things happen in a timely fashion than to have brilliant, sophisticated, highly educated executives who are excellent at planning, analyzing, and dissecting, but who are not so good at implementing. The most cherished manager is the one who says 'I can do it,' and then does." ■

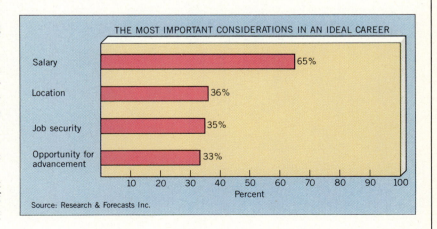

THE MOST IMPORTANT CONSIDERATIONS IN AN IDEAL CAREER

	Percent
Salary	65%
Location	36%
Job security	35%
Opportunity for advancement	33%

Source: Research & Forecasts Inc.

Bethlehem

Management for Productivity: A Career Perspective

The 21st Century Executive

The year 2000 is on the horizon. Once a benchmark for science fiction writers, the 21st century is now establishing new imperatives for organizations and their managers. Success in the coming environment of business, in particular, will be carved in a world of intense competition, continued globalization of markets, and even more rapid technological change. But how many of our future executives really understand what it all means?

Even today organizational life is complicated by shifts in corporate activity and culture that have disrupted some of the ways of the past. It used to be that a managerial career was somewhat predictable—following the pattern so to speak. Typically, the start, middle, and finish of such a career fell into a pattern. The entry was marked by eagerness and enthusiasm; steady advancement followed, broken perhaps by a brief "where-is-this-going" conflict; and a settling-in period ensued, characterized by acceptance of what could be achieved until the career's end-point arrived—retirement. Now downsizing, restructuring, mergers and the like have changed all that; careers are increasingly affected by organizational and environmental turbulence—and the intensity of change is more likely to increase in the future than anything else. Things are clearly changing fast, and the managers of tomorrow have to change with them.

American managers in particular are feeling the heat. The American Assembly—a group of scholars, executives, and policymakers—recently concluded that "ineffective management practices" were mostly to blame for the loss of a "competitive edge" by U.S. industries. They warned: "We're gambling with our destiny." Another report from the Massachusetts Institute of Technology identified these persistent weaknesses on the part of corporate management: Over-emphasis on short-term results, parochialism, failure to train and motivate workers, inability to turn innovations into viable products, and a lack of cooperation within and among firms.

It will take new thinking and a willingness to accept the realities of a changing world to succeed in the future. A series of interviews with executives, management consultants, and business school professors led the *U.S. News & World Reports* to conclude that the "21st century executive" must be:

■ *A global strategist* who recognizes the interconnections among nations, cultures, and economies in the world community, and is able to plan and act in due consideration of them.

■ *A master of technology* who is comfortable with existing high technology, who understands technological trends and their implications, and is able to use them to best individual and organizational advantage.

■ *A consumate politician* who understands the growing complexity of government regulations and the legal environment, and is able to work comfortably at the interface between them and organizational interests.

■ *A leader/motivator* who is able to attract and enthuse highly talented workers, and able to create a high performance climate for individuals and teams to do their best work. ■

Source: As reported in Carol Hymowitz, "Stable Cycles of Executive Careers Shattered by Upheaval in Business," *The Wall Street Journal* (May 26, 1987), p. 29; and, "The 21st Century Executive," *U.S. News & World Reports* (March 7, 1988), pp. 48–56.

As suggested by the open-
ing example, this chapter
addresses a number of is-
sues that put the practice
of management into a final
career perspective. Key
topics include

A Manager's Look to the
    Future
Stress and the Manager
Managing a Managerial
    Career
Management for
    Productivity: A Recap

"No job is more vital to our society than that of the manager." You first read these words of Peter Drucker in Chapter 1.[1] In the same breath, he also says, "there is as much 'management' outside of business as there is in business—maybe more. . . . Management has become the pervasive, the universal organ of a modern society." Throughout this book we have examined the important management issues, theories, and concepts with the ultimate goal of learning how they apply to the real world of work as described by Drucker. Anyone who becomes a manager at any stage in her or his career is taking on an important task that offers great opportunities of both personal and social benefit—regardless of the specific occupational or work setting involved. Hopefully, your career involvement with managerial responsibilities will be rewarding and productive—for you personally, for others who work for and with you, for your organization, and for society as a whole.

This chapter puts *Management for Productivity* into a final perspective. Take advantage of this chance to think seriously about the future you face, the stress you will experience, and the career that you might have. It is a good time to look ahead and anticipate the excitement and challenges each of us will face in the workplace as our world progresses toward the year 2000. And it is a good time to think about how this initial study of management has helped prepare you to meet the many challenges that lie ahead.

A MANAGER'S LOOK TO THE FUTURE

In these classic words from his great novel *A Tale of Two Cities,* Charles Dickens described the world of 1775.[2]

> It was the best of times, it was the worst of times, it was the age of wisdom, it was the age of foolishness, it was the epoch of belief, it was the epoch of incredulity, it was the season of Light, it was the season of Darkness, it was the spring of hope, it was the winter of despair, we had everything before us, we had nothing before us.

Robert Fulmer, a noted management theorist, singled out Dickens's words in his own comments on the decade of the 1980s.[3]

> Dickens saw the marked contrasts that surrounded the early days of the Industrial Revolution. Today, as we near the end of the Industrial Revolution, we find our world marked by contrasts equally as dramatic. An analysis of the probabilities associated with this decade reveals that it is indeed both the best of times and the worst of times.

And even today, there should be no doubt in your mind that we still do and will continue to live in a dynamic world that requires us daily to adapt in new and creative ways. But the modern manager, the manager of the 1990s, must be prepared to master the challenges of tomorrow as well as those of today. Alvin Toffler, noted author and futurist, says this about managers of the future.[4]

> We need managers who can operate as capably in an open-door, free-flow style as in a hierarchical mode, who can work in an organization structured like an Egyptian pyramid as well as one that looks a Calder mobile, with a few of their managerial strands holding a complex set of nearly autonomous modules that move in response to the gentlest breeze.

Toffler is also the person who introduced us to the phrase *future shock,* now popularly used to describe the discomfort that comes with rapid and uncertain change. Yet, a manager's responsibility is to look ahead and achieve high productivity even as things change over time. The chapter opener on the "21st century manager" sets the direction a bit in this regard. Consider, too, these thoughts expressed by senior corporate executives when asked what they foresee in the years to come.[5]

> In the future people will have to be well educated to perform new jobs . . . the frightening thing is that we may not be doing as good a job in educating our labor force as other nations are.
>
> *Robert N. Noyce,* Intel Corporation

> . . . a global economy. That's an overused word, but it's really a fact of life and it doesn't make any difference if you're making shoes or cars.
>
> *Douglas Danforth,* Westinghouse Corporation

> We are the furthest behind in what I call "management technology" in my company, in the high-tech sector, and in all of American industry. . . . Once you awaken to that challenge and decide to do something about it, you may face a five- to ten-year correction exercise.
>
> *Ray Stata,* Analog Devices, Inc.

Trends in the Environment

The general environment was defined in Chapter 6 as a set of background educational-political-economic-cultural forces with the potential to influence organizations and their members. Let's brainstorm just a bit on emerging environmental trends with implications for managers in the United States during the 1990s and beyond. Begin by looking at Figure 21.1. It highlights key elements from a report

by the Hudson Institute entitled, *Workforce 2000: Work and Workers for the 21st Century.*[6] This report identifies a number of developments in technology, world affairs, population demography, and other factors significant to understanding what America may be like in the future. In broad terms, it highlights the importance to the nation's economic health of achieving integration with the world economy, and dealing successfully with the increased importance of the service sector. More specifically, it gives special attention to emerging changes in the workforce and available job opportunities. The latter trends, in particular, are of immediate relevance.

Demographic patterns suggest that new workers in the years ahead will be a different mix than in the past. Some projected changes and their potential implications include:

1. *The population and the workforce will grow more slowly than at any time since the 1930s.* The labor force will expand only around one percent per year during the 1990s, while population growth decreases to 0.7 percent per year by the year 2000.

   Implication Labor markets will tighten and employers may have to use more capital-intensive technologies.

2. *The average age of the population and the workforce will rise, and the pool of young workers entering the labor market will shrink.* The average age of the workforce will climb to 39 by 2000. The number of those in the 16–24 age span will drop by 8 percent.

   Implication Organizations will find flexible and low-paid younger workers in shorter supply, and will need to depend more on older workers.

3. *More women will enter the workforce.* By 2000 over 60 percent of all women of working age are expected to be employed. About two-thirds of all new entrants to the workforce in this period will be women.

   Implication Convenience industries will boom, as will the popularity of flexible jobs and the demand for day-care and other support services.

4. *Minorities will be a larger share of new entrants into the labor force.* The proportion of nonwhites

Four Key Trends	Challenges for Policymakers
• The American economy will grow, stimulated by exports, improved productivity, and a strong world economy. • U.S. manufacturing will represent a smaller share of the economy, while services increase in importance. • The workforce will grow slowly, becoming older, more female, and more disadvantaged. • New jobs in service industries will demand much higher skill levels than jobs of today.	• Stimulate balanced world economic growth. • Accelerate productivity increases in service industries. • Maintain dynamism of an aging workforce. • Reconcile conflicting needs of women, work, and families. • Integrate black and hispanic workers fully into the economy. • Improve educational preparation of all workers.

FIGURE 21.1 *Key trends which will shape the environment of work in the last years of the twentieth century: toward "workforce 2000."*

Source: Information from William B. Johnston, *Workforce 2000: Work and Workers for the 21st Century*—Executive Summary (Indianapolis, IN: The Hudson Institute, Inc., 1987).

among new entrants to the workforce will double to about 29 percent by 2000.

> *Implication* Employment opportunities may improve, but concentration of blacks in center cities and slowly growing occupations tempers the outlook.

5. *Immigrants will represent the largest share of the increase in the population and the workforce since the first World War.* About 600,000 legal and illegal immigrants are expected to enter the United States each year between now and 2000, with about two-thirds of working age entering the workforce.

> *Implication* Concentration in the south and west of the country may reshape local economies, promote growth, and leave labor surpluses in some areas.

Beyond the demographics, it is helpful to consider some of the potential changes that may occur in job markets.[8] Projections suggest that the fastest-growing source of jobs will be the service industries, and in professional, technical, and sales fields. Most of these jobs require advanced education and skills. Young persons entering the labor market for the first time will have to be educated in order to compete; displaced workers trying to reenter the labor market will find their past experience and skills of decreasing value. A person's education and skill credentials will become ever more important in determining the availability of occupational opportunities. Employers will assume more and more responsibility for "educating" their employees to

perform on the job—both in terms of nonmanagerial and managerial duties.[9]

Trends in People

Trends in the environment can be associated with complementary trends among the expectations and desires of people in the work force. Managers of the future will have to address and respect people very broadly as the human resources of organizations. And they will have to do so in the legal context of a maturing society. The successful managers will most likely act in ways consistent with these beliefs as expressed by Max DePree, CEO of the Herman Miller Company.[10]

> I believe very strongly that each of us has certain rights in the work place. For example, each of us has the right to be needed, the right to understand what needs to be done and why, and the right to be genuinely involved . . . the right to have an effect on our own destiny; the right to be challenged; the right and obligation to be accountable; and, when things don't go well, the right to appeal.

Indeed, the *new* managers of the 1990s and beyond will have to deal with new demands and *new* concerns in their human-resource management activities. Supervisor–subordinate relationships of the future, in particular, are likely to reflect the following specific changes over time.

1. *Pressures for equal employment opportunity.* Women, blacks, and other minorities will continue to demand equal treatment in the workplace. While

progress continues, lingering inequalities remain. In 1988, for example, white males held over 92 percent of the director's chairs at major U.S. corporations; women were represented on 53 percent of Fortune 500 boards, up from 39 percent in 1981. Only 6 percent of management jobs were filled by blacks; and no blacks headed Fortune 500 companies.[11] Legislative pressures and affirmative action programs will continue to complement other forms of social action in attempts to eliminate obstacles and create true equal employment opportunity for all.

2. *Pressures for self-determination.* People will seek greater freedom to determine *how* to do their jobs and *when* to do them. Pressures for increased worker participation in the forms of job enrichment, autonomous work groups, flexible working hours, and compressed workweeks will grow.

3. *Pressures for employee rights.* People will expect their rights to be respected on the job as well as outside of work. These include the rights of individual privacy, due process, and freedom from sexual harassment, as well as protection against discrimination on the basis of age, sex, ethnic background, or handicap. *Newsline 21.1* is a reminder of some of the current issues that are in the public eye on matters of individual privacy in the workplace — drug-testing, polygraph testing, records confidentiality, and computer monitoring of work.

4. *Pressures for security.* People will expect their security to be protected in the workplace, both in respect to their physical well-being (i.e., occupational safety and health matters) and economic livelihood (e.g., guaranteed protection against layoffs).

5. *Pressures for equity of earnings.* Even though it is less common now that an employer will pay a woman less than a man for the same work, earnings differentials continue to be a fact of life.[12] While progress has been made, women still earn only about $0.70 on the average for every $1 men make. Part of the difference is due to a lingering division of labor along gender lines, wherein many women still pursue some occupations like nursing, and avoid others like dentistry. Projected labor-force shortages, an increasing proportion of females in the workforce, and movements toward "comparable worth" legislation in many states will help close the wage gap. But questions on pay equity will continue

to be asked with increasing frequency, and they will require concrete answers.

6. *Pressures to achieve and maintain a high quality of life.* People will expect to live and work in conditions that protect, foster, and respect the dignity of the human being. This includes expanded opportunities for participation in the workplace and protection of rights. It also includes the freedom from physical or mental harm at work, or from health hazards created from the by-products of work (e.g., industrial waste and other forms of pollution).

Trends in Technology

Another undeniable aspect of our environment is the emergence of high technology as a dominant force in our lives. "With computers and high technology," as the saying goes, "work won't be the same again!" Without doubt, the greatest *mega*technologies of the 1990s are information technology, biotechnology, and materials technology.[13] Each in its own way is shaping our future in terms of the way we live, the products we consume, and the nature of the workplace itself.

Even today we live and work in a world of desktop computers, supercomputers, computer-assisted design and manufacturing, expert systems, electronic mail, advanced telecommunications, and the "automated" office and assembly line. Work is increasingly "information-intensive." Mastering the advanced information technologies is more and more a key to productivity. The future is viewed in terms of an *information economy* in which the majority of workers will be paid to process information rather than to produce "things."[14] Tomorrow will bring not only improvements on these technologies, it will bring dramatic new ones into the reach of our daily lives and work. And it will do so at an accelerating pace.

Managers of the future must be prepared to utilize and successfully adapt to the opportunities made available by advanced technologies. They must also be prepared to help others learn to perform with them, and to achieve both productivity and personal satisfaction in the process.

Trends in Organizations

Trends in the environment, people, and technology necessarily have implications for organizations. Ta-

PROTECTING
WORKER PRIVACY

Drug testing, genetic screening, lie-detector tests, public identification of workers with AIDS, computer surveillance—these and other intrusions into workers' private lives have fierce critics. Yet the question of how far employers can probe is a thorny one. The need to protect employees' privacy must somehow be balanced against employers' needs to reduce the huge losses resulting from employee drug abuse, theft, and incompetence—and there is no national consensus on how this balance will be struck.

Thus far, over half of all states restrict or prohibit polygraph tests as a condition of employment, and both the Senate and the House have passed bills restricting such use of lie-detector tests. Seven states limit drug tests, and random testing in the private sector is being challenged in the courts. In addition, advocates of worker privacy are pushing for restrictions on genetic screening, for workplace education on discrimination against employees with AIDS, and for increased federal and state restraints on computer monitoring of employees' work output and phone usage.

Despite these and other safeguards of worker privacy, critics continue to worry about such issues as the confidentiality and misuse of workers' records—and employers argue that the inability to screen applicants thoroughly is making them prey to negligent hiring suits and other financial losses. Some observers, noting that many employers are explicitly concerned with their employees' lifestyles and health, maintain that monitoring of employee "wellness" will be a major focus of ongoing litigation as workers continue to sue employers for infringing on their rights to privacy.

Source: As reported in "Privacy," *Business Week* (March 28, 1988), pp. 61–68.

---

ble 21.1 tries to provoke your thinking by offering a number of broad directions for change in tomorrow's organizations. An additional and more immediate viewpoint is captured in these five characteristics of what management educator and author James O'Toole calls the *vanguard organization*—that is, one widely admired as a great place to work.[15]

1. *A Vanguard organization is people-oriented.* It provides opportunities for workers to be involved in their jobs, the decisions that affect them, and even the financial ownership of the company.
2. *The leaders of Vanguard organizations are visible.* They spend time walking around and talking to people as they do their jobs; they stress upward as well as downward communication.

3. *A Vanguard organization seeks employment stability.* It makes a "social contract" with employees that protects their jobs, even during times of economic decline.
4. *A Vanguard organization has a consumer orientation.* It tries to make the best product or provide the best service possible; the emphasis is always on quality.
5. *A Vanguard organization is future-oriented.* It seeks long-term survival, prosperity, and impact, rather than purely short-term performance accomplishments.

But while there is considerable agreement that we value the directions represented in the prior list and table, it is also quite clear that the forces for

TABLE 21.1 *Directions in the Development of Organizations: Seven Predictions for a New Society*

1. *The return of self-fulfillment on the job.* People will seek employment in organizations that offer significant opportunities for achieving personal growth; routine and redundant jobs will no longer be tolerated.
2. *A broadened base of employee involvement in organizations.* People will want to participate fully in the affairs of the organization, both in terms of day-to-day decisions and in respect to financial ownership.
3. *The demise of authoritarian management.* People will reject authoritarian management in favor of increased workplace democracy; managers will become coaches and teachers, they will trade "directing" roles in for "leading" ones.
4. *The emergence of networking structures.* People will be brought together in networks of cross-functional teams and task forces to accomplish work in highly integrated organization structures.
5. *Emphasis on intuition, creativity, and innovation.* People will be allowed to think, experiment and create free from the constraints of overly-rational thinking and quantitative decision constraints; the present world of "numbers" will give way to a future world of "ideas."
6. *The final triumph of small size.* People will want to work in small units within organizations of smaller total size; even large corporations will restructure to emulate the working conditions and opportunities available in smaller-sized operations.
7. *Quality of life will mean what it says.* People will want to work in environments that contribute to the total quality of their lives; the meaning of work will increasingly be formed in the context of people's total life experiences.

Source: Developed from Rosabeth Moss Kanter, *The Change Masters* (New York: Simon & Schuster, 1984); and, John Naisbitt and Patricia Auberdene, *Re-Inventing the Corporation* (New York: Doubleday, 1985).

change are often quite complicated. Tomorrow's manager will have to continually adjust to an often paradoxical work environment that suffers its own "growing pains" as it pursues new directions in an ever more dynamic and uncertain world. Doing well in the times ahead demands a capacity to think and act progressively about management, organizations, and the people who make them work. Perhaps the best way to pull this point into perspective is with a case—a success story about one "vanguard" organization.

ILLUSTRATIVE CASE:
HERMAN MILLER CORPORATION

How would you like to work for an organization that is an industry leader, ranks among the *Fortune 500* firms, is one of the top-ranked of these firms in respect to total return to investors over a ten-year period, *and* which is one of the few public companies in the U.S. that has 100 percent of its full-time regular employees holding stock?[16] This stock, by the way, has been quite an investment for them. A share sold in 1976 for $100, was worth slightly over $4850 in 1986. Not bad, for employee ownership you must say.

Herman Miller manufactures designer furniture. Founded by D. J. DePree, the company has always had a commitment to research, innovation, and design. Its products are state-of-the-art and always of the highest quality. Many other furniture makers have more employees, but Herman Miller outspends them on design and R&D. It is also the most productive measured in net income per employee. But perhaps even most significant is an overriding respect for the talents and rights of its employees that sets Herman Miller apart.

Max DePree, CEO, beieves in "abandoning oneself to the strengths of others." And not just those with the university degrees and design credentials; he means *all* of the company's employees—the ones, by the way, that made suggestions in one year that led to an average cost saving of $3000 per employee. One day each month, in fact, work stops at the plants and management reports to workers on the firm's profits and productivity. The workers care, of course, because they are *owners* of the company too. And they participate in a Scanlon Plan that allows them to share in the financial gains from any realized productivity improvements.

There is a sense of integrity about the way Herman Miller operates. When concerned that a hostile take-over might threaten the employment security of its employees, Herman Miller introduced "silver parachutes" which protected all employees with two or more years employment with the company—most companies have "golden parachutes" reserved only for senior management. And others count too in the way Herman Miller operates. The company makes annual donations in sizable amounts to charities, schools, and other nonprofit organizations in the communities in which it operates. As author O'Toole says, "Is it any wonder why a *Fortune* poll picked Herman Miller as one of the nation's "ten most admired companies?"

Beneath it all, Herman Miller is a success-oriented firm. It is a for-profit enterprise. But it operates and pursues its destiny in a unique and responsive way—perhaps a way that foreshadows the world of work in the future. As Max DePree says,

> . . . at Herman Miller, we talk about the difference between being successful and being exceptional. Being successful is meeting goals in a good way—being exceptional is reaching your potential.

STRESS AND THE MANAGER

The prior discussion clearly suggests that the pressures of the managerial role and all of the responsibilities it entails will be great. What lies ahead in "an age of transition" will require continual learning, adjustment, and change. The modern manager must be prepared to understand new circumstances, even to anticipate them, and then to respond appropriately as situations require. The informed and forward-thinking managers will succeed; the others will not. Central to the challenges faced is "stress," something which often accompanies the job, the general work environment, and a person's life experiences.

ILLUSTRATIVE CASE: JOB-RELATED STRESS

The following cases of Mary, Bob, and Ray are good reminders of the challenges you may someday face. Although working in different managerial jobs and organizational settings, each person shares something in common with the others—high levels of job-related stress.[17]

1.   *Mary*   Mary, a recent Wharton MBA, spent a sleepless night contemplating her first presentation before the executive committee of her new employer. She had spent much of the last 6 months preparing the report for her presentation and felt it was the first real test of her managerial potential. Mary's presentation lasted 5 minutes and was followed by about 10 minutes of questions from committee members. Mary was thanked for making a fine presentation and dismissed from the meeting by the firm's president. She quickly went to the nearest lounge and in a release of tension shook uncontrollably.

2.   *Bob*   Bob's wife, Jane, is becoming increasingly worried about her husband. Several months ago Bob was passed over for a promotion to plant supervisor that he felt he deserved after 15 years of loyal service to the company. Bob used to come home from work tired but cheery and spent an hour or so playing with their two boys. Lately, however, Bob walks into the house, grabs a can of beer, and plops down in front of the television. Except for dinner, he spends his evenings watching television and drinking beer. He has little to do or say to either Jane or the kids. Jane is at wit's end. She has begged Bob to go to the doctor, but he says, "Nothing is wrong with me. It's your imagination."

3.   *Ray*   Ray, a successful advertising account executive, was finishing his typical "two-martini" lunch with a potential client, but Ray's mind wasn't on business as usual. He was thinking about the pain in his stomach and the diagnosis the doctor had given him yesterday. Ray's doctor had told him he had a spastic colon induced by his life-style. Ray, recently divorced, knows his gin consumption, smoking habit, and 12-hour workdays aren't good for him, but his job is now the most important thing in his life, and the advertising business just happens to be highly stressful. Ray doesn't know what to do and resolves not to worry about his health and to concentrate on selling his luncheon partner one fantastic contract.

Stress

Stress is a state of tension experienced by individuals facing extraordinary demands, constraints, or opportunities. In Mary's case, stress resulted from an opportunity to make an important presentation. Bob's stress emerged from a constraint—inability to gain promotion. Ray is torn between the demands of a doctor's advice and the potential opportunity of a successful business luncheon. Stress, again, is the result.

Job-related stress goes hand in hand with the dynamic and sometimes uncertain nature of the managerial role. Any look ahead toward your managerial future would be incomplete without confronting stress as something you are sure to encounter along the way. For a start, think about this statement by a psychologist who works with top-level managers having severe drinking problems: "All executives deal with stress. They wouldn't be executives if they didn't. Some handle it well, others handle it poorly."[18] If you understand stress and how it operates in the work setting, you should be more likely to handle it well. This goes both for the personal stress you may experience and for the stress experienced by persons you supervise.

Sources of Stress

Stressors are the things that cause stress. Figure 21.2 shows three categories of stressors that can influence a person's work attitudes and behavior—work, personal, and nonwork factors. Of these, the *work factors* have the most obvious potential to create job stress. Such stress can result from excessively high or low task demands, role conflicts or ambiguities, poor interpersonal relations, or career progress that is too slow or too fast. When asked what factors caused them the most stress on the job, for example, workers in one survey identified the following: not doing the kind of work they wanted to (34%), coping with their current job (30%), working too hard (28%), colleagues at work (21%), a difficult boss (18%).[19] Stress also tends to be high among persons working for organizations with recent records of staff cutbacks and downsizing. This lack of "corporate loyalty" to the employee can be very threatening, especially to someone with major financial responsibilities and approaching retirement age.[20]

As just suggested, a variety of *personal factors* are also sources of potential stress for people at work. Such individual characteristics as needs, capabilities, and personality can influence how one perceives and responds to the work situation. Researchers, for example, identify a **Type A personality** for which stressful behavior patterns such as the following are commonplace.[21]

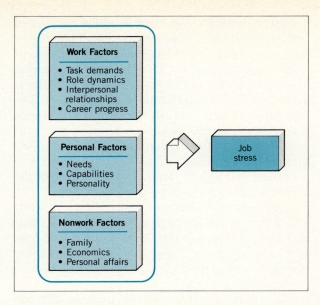

FIGURE 21.2 *Potential sources of job stress: work, nonwork, and personal factors.*

- Always moves, walks, and eats rapidly.
- Acts impatient, hurries others, dislikes waiting.
- Does several things at once.
- Feels guilty when relaxing.
- Tries to schedule more in less time.
- Uses nervous gestures such as clenched fist.
- Hurries or interrupts the speech of others.

The achievement orientation, impatience, and perfectionism of individuals with Type A personalities may create stress in work circumstances other persons find relatively stress-free. Type A personalities, in this sense, bring stress on themselves. You might like to turn now to the end-of-chapter exercise, "Personal Behavior Quiz," to examine your tendencies toward Type A behavior patterns.

Finally, *nonwork factors* may "spill over" and influence the stress an individual experiences at work. Such things as family events (e.g., the birth of a new child), economics (e.g., sudden loss of extra income), and personal affairs (e.g., preoccupation with a hobby) can add to the stress otherwise associated with work and/or personal factors. More generally speaking, these words of a labor entrepreneur sum up quite well the problems of balancing work and nonwork aspects of our lives.[22]

> I put a lot of energy into trying to resolve my work and the rest of my life, and I'm just not sure that I've got it

right yet. I can deal with a tremendous number of demands; I can still be really creative; I have a good relationship with my wife and daughter. But it's at a level that I'm not sure is sustainable. Maybe you have to make an extreme break; maybe in order to make the personal stuff work, you just can't have this kind of job.

Constructive and Destructive Stress

This preliminary discussion may give the impression that stress always acts as a negative influence on our lives. There are actually two faces to stress, as shown in Figure 21.3—one constructive and one destructive.

Constructive stress acts in a positive way for the individual and/or the organization. The figure shows that low to moderate levels of stress act in a constructive or energizing way that increases effort, stimulates creativity, and encourages diligence in one's work. **Eustress** is the term sometimes used to describe stress that is constructive for people, and which helps them achieve a positive balance with their environments. You may know such stress as the tension that causes you to study hard before exams, pay attention in class, and complete assignments on time. The same positive results of stress can be found in the workplace, and in respect to all three categories of stressors. Individuals of the Type A personality, for example, are likely to work long hours and be less satisfied with poor performance. High task demands imposed by a supervisor may draw forth higher levels of task accomplishment. Even nonwork stressors such as new family responsibilities may cause an individual to work harder in anticipation of greater financial rewards.

Destructive stress, on the other hand, is dysfunctional for the individual and/or the organization. Whereas low to moderate levels of stress can enhance productivity, excessively high stress can overload and break down a person's physical and mental systems. Productivity can suffer as people react to very intense stress through absenteeism, turnover, errors, accidents, dissatisfaction, and reduced performance.

Managers must know how to maintain the positive edge offered by constructive stress. They must also be concerned about destructive stress and its potential to impact people and their work performance adversely. Among the latter concerns is a most fundamental one—the possible negative impact of destructive stress on individual health.

Stress and Health

Although stress is an inevitable part of life, medical research is concerned that excessive stress can reduce resistance to disease and increase the likelihood of physical and/or mental illness. Job stress may lead to health problems in the form of heart disease, hypertension, ulcers, drug-alcohol-tobacco abuse, overeating, depression, and muscle aches, among others.

Managers should be alert to signs of excessive stress in themselves and persons with whom they work. The symptoms are multiple and varied. Table 21.2 offers one checklist of stress indicators. Other personal signs to watch for include:

- Change in eating habits.
- Unhealthy feeling—aches and pains.

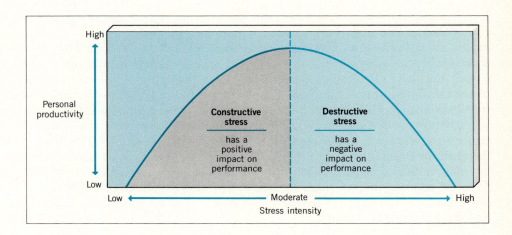

FIGURE 21.3 *The relationship between stress and performance: constructive and destructive stress.*

TABLE 21.2 *Checklist of Stress Symptoms for People at Work*

Original Behavior	*changes to*	New Behavior
Regular attendance		Absenteeism
Good decisions		Errors in judgment
Diligence		Carelessness
Quality work		Mistakes, errors
Good humor		Poor humor
Positive attitude		Negative attitude
Openness to change		Resistance to change
Punctuality		Tardiness
Good interpersonal relations		Poor interpersonal relations

- Restlessness, inability to concentrate.
- Tense, uptight, fidgety, or nervous feelings.
- Increase in drinking or smoking.
- Feelings of being disoriented or overwhelmed.
- Sleeping problems.
- Depression or irritability.
- Upset stomach.
- Dizziness, weakness, lightheadedness.

Increasingly, the manager's responsibility to recognize and deal with stress in the work setting is becoming a legal one. Many state worker's compensation laws specify compensation for injuries resulting from continuing stress on the job. Stress now accounts for about 14% of occupational disease claims.[23] Increasingly too, and rightly so, the modern manager is likely to adopt an expanded view of the social responsibility of serving in a managerial role. This view accepts responsibility for job-related influences on the health of one's colleagues and subordinates on more than purely legal grounds. It is defended on the basis of the following arguments.

1. *Humanitarianism* To the extent that managerial awareness and action can enhance employee health, managers have a humanitarian responsibility to do so.
2. *Productivity* Healthy employees are absent less, make fewer errors, and must be replaced less frequently than less healthy ones.
3. *Creativity* Persons in poor health are less creative and less prone to take reasonable risks than their healthy counterparts.
4. *Return on investment* When poor health reduces or removes the individual's contribution to the organization, return on the time and money invested in human resources is lost.

Effective Stress Management

You can see that the role of stress in the work setting is complex. We know that constructive stress may facilitate productivity, but it is also true that destructive stress can reduce productivity and even contribute to illness. A good manager finds a "healthy fit" between personal traits, the work environment, and the amount of job stress it involves. A healthy fit is one that stimulates productivity without damaging health. It is achieved through effective stress management that increases one's ability to (1) prevent stress, (2) cope with stress, and (3) maintain personal wellness.

Stress Prevention

It is always best to manage stress by preventing it from reaching excessive levels in the first place. Stressors emerging from personal and nonwork factors must be recognized so that action can be taken to prevent them from adversely affecting the work experience. Persons with Type A personalities, for example, may exercise self-discipline; managers of Type A employees may try to model a lower-key, more relaxed approach to work. At another level, family difficulties may be relieved by a change of work schedule, or the anxiety they cause may be reduced by knowing that one's supervisor understands.

Among work factors with the greatest potential to cause excessive stress are role ambiguities, conflicts, and overloads. Role clarification through a management-by-objectives (MBO) approach can work to good advantage here. By bringing supervisor and subordinate together around task-oriented communications, MBO is an opportunity to spot stressors and take action to reduce or eliminate them.

Newsline 21.2 offers some further insight into the way managers, in particular, may overstress themselves—sometimes unnecessarily and without any real performance benefit. Self-awareness and a realistic approach to one's responsibilities can help to prevent stress brought on by simply "working too much." The newsline also introduces the **survivor syndrome,** the stress experienced by persons who fear for their jobs in organizations that are reducing staff through downsizing and layoffs. As more managers become aware of this phenomenon, they are developing formal programs to help those

BE ALERT TO STRESS ON THE JOB

N E W S L I N E 21.2

"You've got an irate client on 3, an impatient supplier on 1, an anxious child on 5, and an angry wife on 2."

Drawing by Edward Koren; © 1982 The New Yorker Magazine, Inc.

The investment banker was a classic case. He was in constant action as an 80-hour per week executive. Two over-stuffed briefcases were always at his side. But after being observed for three days by a consultant, much of his time appeared to be wasted on "busy work." He was advised to worry less about "how long he worked" and concentrate more on "how effectively he worked." Like many others in today's competitive business world, he was working too many hours, taking too little time off, and experiencing too much stress to perform exceptionally well on the job.

In a survey of 40,000 workers by the National Center for Health Statistics, more than half reported feeling "a lot" to "moderate" stress in the prior two weeks. Constandino Biris, a consultant on corporate change, estimates that "at least 45 percent of American managers suffer too much stress." Some comes from pursuing the "fast track" at all costs, some comes from the "survivor syndrome" of still being employed at a firm that is cutting back staff, some is imposed by insensitive bosses, and some comes from the pressures of family and dual-career relationships.

Regardless of the source, too much stress can hurt performance and cause turmoil in family and personal lives. More and more employers are trying to help by offering a variety of stress reduction programs as part of an overall commitment to the "wellness" of employees. Stress adults, biofeedback, and even humor programs are found. Employees are being taught how to decompress through positive imaging, learning not to worry about the little things, and being more honest with themselves. With stress taking its toll in terms of reduced performance, derailed careers, health disorders, and the like, it's important to stay alert to the symptoms and take positive action before things move to the extreme.

Source: As reported in Ford S. Worthy, "You're Probably Working too Hard," *Fortune* (April 27, 1988), pp. 133–140; "Stress: The Test Americans are Failing," *Business Week* (April 18, 1988), pp. 74–75; and, "Stress on the Job," *Newsweek* (April 25, 1988), pp. 40–45.

---

employees who remain employed after major staff cutbacks to better cope with the situation.

Stress Coping

When symptoms of excessive stress are recognized, it is time to take action to maintain the desired healthy fit. Among the suggested guidelines for coping with stress by maximizing its benefits and minimizing its destructive effects are the following.[25]

1. *Take control of the situation.* Avoid unrealistic deadlines. Do your best, but know your limits. Accept things you cannot change. Don't try to be everything to everyone. Learn to identify and limit your exposure to things that trigger a strong stress response.

2. *Pace yourself.* Plan your day on a flexible basis. Take one thing at a time—highest priority first. Force yourself to slow down. Think before reacting to negative situations or people.

3. *Open up to others.* Freely discuss your problems, fears, and frustrations with those who care about you. It helps to share worries with people you trust.

4. *Do something for others.* Get your mind off yourself by concentrating on the needs of someone else.

5. *Exercise and work off stress.* Engage in regular physical activity such as walking, jogging, swimming, riding a bike, or playing tennis or racquetball. If you get angry or upset, even taking a walk can help "blow off steam" and relieve mental stress.

6. *Balance work and recreation.* Schedule time for recreation. You need occasional breaks from your work, and recreation helps take your mind off things. Don't be afraid to "loaf" sometimes after a period of intense work.

7. *Use relaxation techniques.* When feeling uptight, relax for a few minutes by following these simple steps: (a) Sit comfortably with eyes closed in a quiet location; (b) Slowly repeat a peaceful word or phrase over and over to yourself in your mind; (c) Take complete but comfortable breaths, inhaling through the nose and exhaling through the mouth; (d) Avoid distracting thoughts by keeping a passive mental attitude.

Personal Wellness

Personal wellness is a term used to describe the pursuit of one's physical and mental potential through a personal health-promotion program.[26] This concept recognizes individual responsibility to enhance personal health through a disciplined approach to such things as smoking, weight gain and alcohol use, maintenance of a nutritious diet, and engaging in a regular exercise and physical-fitness program. The essence of personal wellness is a lifestyle that reflects a true commitment to health.

Because stress has the potential to impact health, personal wellness makes a great deal of sense as a stress-management strategy. The manager who aggressively maintains his or her health should be better prepared to deal with the inevitable stresses of the managerial role. It may well be that these managers will be able to take constructive advantage of higher levels of stress than others can tolerate. Then, too, managers can and should encourage personal wellness among subordinates. Many organizations assist in this regard by formally sponsoring wellness programs for employees. Among the health promotion activities typically offered are: smoking control, health risk appraisals, back care, stress management, exercise/physical fitness, nutrition education, high blood pressure control, and weight control. The expectations are that such programs benefit both the employees and the organization. For example, a survey by the U.S. Department of Health and Human Services reported that employers find that promoting company-sponsored wellness programs pays off in terms of improved employee health, reduced healthcare costs, improved employee morale, and increased productivity.[27]

MANAGING A MANAGERIAL CAREER

The stress about which we have been talking is highlighted in the context of one's overall career aspirations. It is in this respect that success and failure on the job take on special meaning. A **career** is a sequence of jobs and work pursuits constituting what a person does for a living. For many of us, a career begins on an anticipatory basis with our formal education. From there it progresses into an initial job choice and any number of subsequent choices that may involve changes in task assignments, employing organizations, and even occupations.

A **career path** is a sequence of jobs held over time during a career. Career paths vary between those that are pursued internally within the same organization and those that involve changes among employing organizations over time. Many organizations encourage internal career paths by making long-term career opportunities available to their employees. Two persons who took good advantage of such opportunities are David Garrett and Roger Smith. Both men rose through the ranks of their respective companies to become CEOs. Garrett began his career at Delta Airlines as a reservation agent in 1946; Roger Smith started in 1949 at General Motors as a general accounting clerk.

Career Planning and Development

Careers inevitably mix together the needs of people and organizations. Edgar Schein, a noted management theorist and consultant on careers, states,[28]

> Organizations are dependent on the performance of their people, and people are dependent on organiza-

tions to provide jobs and career opportunities. . . . The problem for society, for organizations, and for people is how to match their respective needs, not only at the point of entry into the organization, but also throughout the career or life history of the person in the organization.

Because of the commitment of time and physical and emotional energy it involves, the career is an important component of a person's total life experience. Everyone should think seriously about their careers, and think ahead. **Career planning** is the process of systematically matching career goals and individual capabilities with opportunities for their fulfillment. It involves answering these questions: "Who am I?" "Where do I want to go?" "How do I get there?"

Advice varies on just how this should be done. Compare and contrast the following thoughts of two successful executives.[29]

1. *Harlan Cleveland* (public executive)   A career as an executive is not something you plan for yourself. It's a series of accidental changes of job and shifts of scenery on which you look back later, weaving through the story retroactively some thread of logic that was not visible at the time. If you try too carefully to plan your life, the danger is that you will succeed—succeed in narrowing your options and closing off avenues of adventure that cannot now be imagined. When a student asks me for career advice, I can only suggest that he or she opt for the most exciting "next step" without worrying where it will lead, and then work hard on the job in hand, not pine for the one in the bush. When your job no longer demands of you more than you have, go and do something else. Always take by preference the job you *don't* know how to do.

2. *William O. Grabe* (business executive)   An aspiring executive should not make the personal investment in a career without some basic planning. Career planning is more art than science and highly individualized. Nonetheless, some form of plan can greatly enhance the evaluation of various opportunities and enable you as a manager to make better career decisions. A career plan allows you to identify how to use your basic strengths to maximum advantage, set major career objectives, and establish immediate milestones to measure personal development and advancement.

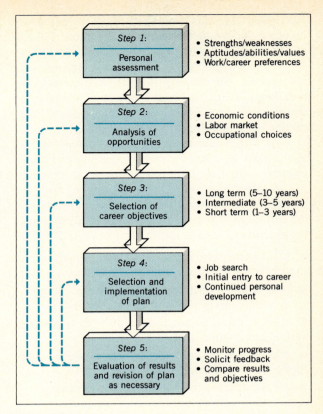

FIGURE 21.4 *A basic framework for formal career planning.*

Cleveland and Grabe offer quite different viewpoints. While Cleveland suggests a career should be allowed to progress in a somewhat random but always opportunistic way, Grabe sees a career as something to be rationally planned and pursued in a logical step-by-step fashion. Interestingly, each man found executive success in his own way. In fact, it is best not to look on the two points of view as "either-or" alternatives. A well-managed career will probably include elements of each. The carefully thought-out plan can point you in a general career direction; an eye for opportunity can fill in the details along the way.

Figure 21.4 summarizes a basic framework for formal career planning. It has a lot in common with the process of strategic planning covered in Chapter 5. The five steps in the framework begin with personal assessment and then progress through analysis of opportunities, selection of career objectives, and implementation of strategies, until the point of evaluation of results is reached. Then the process is recycled as necessary to allow constructive revision of the career plan over time. Success in each of these steps entails a good deal of self-awareness and frank assessment. The message is clear—a successful career begins with sufficient insight to make good decisions about matching personal needs and capabilities with job opportunities over time.

As with personal wellness, your managerial responsibility in respect to career planning and development is twofold. It includes both the responsibility to plan and manage your career, and the responsibility to assist in the career planning and development of subordinates. Some ideas on meeting each set of responsibilities follow.[30]

■ Establish a personal career plan; be willing to modify this plan as opportunities develop.

■ Take and maintain a personal-skills inventory; try to match job responsibilities and skills.

■ Set specific personal development objectives; and update them regularly.

■ Maintain a career-oriented dialogue with higher-level managers.

■ Take advantage of all appropriate training and development opportunities.

■ Evaluate and constructively modify personal development efforts over time.

■ As a manager, help subordinates to do each of the prior things.

Initial Entry to a Career

Initial entry to a new job and/or organization is the first point at which people begin to learn if they have chosen well in the sense of achieving a good person-job-organization fit. As we discussed in Chapter 9, "misfits" can occur because of breakdowns in procedures and decisions during the selection process. The result is that costly turnover sometimes occurs shortly after persons assume new jobs. Good advice to the manager is to do a thorough job in all phases of the staffing process—beginning with job analysis and continuing through recruitment, selection, orientation, and training. Providing applicants with realistic job previews is most helpful in clarifying expectations so that they can make truly informed choices about whether or not to accept a new job.

The job applicant also shares the responsibility for success or failure in the selection process. Choosing a job and joining an organization are difficult decisions that inevitably exert a lot of influ-

TABLE 21.3 *Questions That Might Be Asked When Interviewing for a New Job*

How often will my performance be formally reviewed? . . . and by whom?

How much decision-making authority can I expect after one year in the new position?

What new and innovative developments have recently occurred in the organization?

What is the housing market like in the new location? . . . and does the organization provide any special housing assistance?

How many years does it generally take for someone to reach a middle-management position?

How much out-of-town travel will be expected of me in this job?

What types of training programs will be made available to me? . . . and how soon can I begin to take them?

Are there any special dress codes and expectations that I should be aware of?

How frequently do you ask persons working in this job to relocate?

Will I be able to progress at my own pace through the initial employment period, or is it a highly structured program?

Is it easy to transfer from one part of the organization to another?

What is the employment history of the person I will be working for? . . . and was he or she promoted from within?

How much overtime work is expected? . . . and does it occur at any special times of the year?

What progress have the people made who were last hired into this position?

ence over our lives. Whenever a new job is being contemplated, the best advice is to know yourself and learn as much about the job and organization as you can. Table 21.3 lists a sample of questions—other than questions about salary and benefits—which might be asked in the attempt to learn as much as possible about a new position *before* accepting an offer.

Adult Transitions During a Career

As people mature, they pass through various adult life stages. Each entails somewhat different problems and prospects, some of which can have a career impact. It can be helpful for you to recognize these transitions and prepare to face them in the course of your managerial career. It is also useful to recognize the effects of these transitions as experienced by the people with whom you work. Understanding the special problems and pressures encountered by other persons at various stages of the adult life cycle may help you work better with them in a managerial capacity.

Figure 21.5 is one portrayal of the development periods of adulthood. Note the three transition points: early-adult transition, mid-life transition, and late-adult transition. Although they may not always occur exactly as indicated in the figure, the logic of each transition involves unique challenges of interest to you.[31]

1. *The move to early adulthood* Early adulthood is a period of completing one's education, entering an occupation, and getting married. Parenthood follows, with new family and job responsibilities. It is a time of vitality, self-determination, and perhaps one or more job changes.

2. *Mid-life transition* In the late 30s and early 40s, the career is all-important. Family complications stress this orientation, and personal crisis can occur. Some frustrations in the career may occur and bring with them added questions and confidence, goals, and identity. For the first time health and age become relevant concerns.

3. *Middle and later adulthood* Settling in begins here, with a knowledge of the "system" and a mellowing of goals. Concerns turn toward making a real impact at work, being a mentor to others, and balancing goals and reality. This is a time of consolidating personal affairs and accepting career limita-

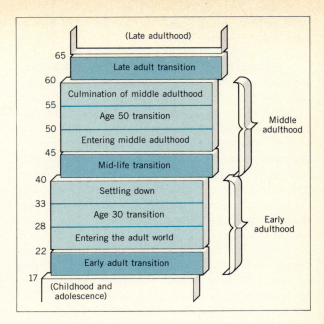

FIGURE 21.5 *Developmental periods in early and middle adulthood.*

Source: Daniel J. Levinson, *The Season's of a Man's Life* (New York: Knopf, 1978), p. 57. Copyright © 1978 by Daniel J. Levinson. Reprinted by permission of Alfred A. Knopf, Inc.

tions. The next step is retirement and, perhaps, a new career.

When you think about adult life stages or transitions, you should note that sooner or later the careers of most people level off. A **career plateau** is a position from which someone is not likely to move to a higher level of work responsibility. Three reasons account for many career plateaus.[32]

1. *Personal choice* Some people plateau by personal choice, basically because they like their jobs. This may involve feeling that the job continues to be challenging, or it may mean that one is comfortable with existing competencies and insecure about moving on to test new ones.

2. *Limited ability* Other persons plateau because they have reached the limits of their ability. Even though they do their present jobs well, they are not considered to have the abilities and/or the desire to learn the abilities required for promotion.

3. *Limited opportunity* A third reason for career plateaus is a lack of opportunity for promotion or transfer. An individual may want to move, but be

blocked from doing so because all the desired alternative jobs are filled.

Figure 21.6 adds perspective on the prior cases. It presents a career model in which people are classified based on their performance and promotibility. "Learners" are new to a position and are low performers with good potential for advancement. They should respond well to early career development support. "Stars" are established high performers with high promotion potential. They have momentum in their careers and are progressing well. The "deadwood" are people whose careers have stagnated because of poor performance. Their future potential and even tenure with the organization is questionable. The "solid citizens" in the figure are yet another case. They too have stagnated, but due to personal choice or lack of organizational opportunity—not because of poor performance. They are also the source of considerable managerial challenge.

It takes imagination and effort to maintain the productivity and job satisfaction of someone who is on this type of a career plateau. For some people the plateau may occur at a life stage when it is a comfortable fit with individual needs. For others the plateau may occur too early or at a time when other significant adult transitions highlight the importance of continuing success in one's career. In both cases, a clear understanding of the plateaued employee's needs can assist in the selection of appropriate managerial strategies.

Dual-Career Couples and Parenting

The **dual-career couple** is a contemporary phenomenon of very great occupational significance. A situation common to more than 50 percent of U.S. married couples, this is where both adult partners are participating in the work force and seeking rewarding careers.[33] Increasingly important, too, is the single parent who must care for children while also balancing the demands of a full- or part-time job or jobs.

Chances are that you are now or will become part of a dual-career relationship and/or a working parent. Individual career problems and prospects become magnified in these cases because of the added challenge of managing the separate careers of both partners and, perhaps, the responsibilities of parenthood. A common dual-career problem occurs when one partner is offered a promotion or new job in another location, but taking it would require the other partner to sacrifice his or her existing career opportunities. Family responsibilities, particularly for children and elderly parents, also complicate people's working lives. This point is addressed in the end-of-chapter career perspective. Younger couples and single parents, in particular, face special pressures as they try to balance the demands of parenthood with the requirements and opportunities of a career.[34]

As a result of such conflicts, people can easily find themselves living and working under considerable stress. Two examples follow.[35]

"If I were in top management, I'd be in a pickle," says Robert Adams, whose career as a marketing manager for Door-Oliver Inc. doesn't require senior management's customary workload and 14-hour days. But Adams has a wife with a career of her own and a six-month-old son, and he worries that some companies still measure career dedication by "what time your car leaves the parking lot."

A magazine editor remembers the time her boss dropped by her desk at 5:45 p.m. for a conference. She said matter-of-factly that she would be right with him. When he walked down the hall to his office, she frantically phoned her husband and told him he would have to get home to relieve the babysitter, who was scheduled to leave for an appointment. "What was I going to tell my boss?" she asks. "Sorry, I can't meet with you because I've got to relieve my babysitter? He already thinks women are flaky."

FIGURE 21.6 *A model of career stages: Promotion and performance consideration.*

Source: Thomas P. Ference, James A.F. Stoner, and E. Kirby Warren, "Managing the Career Plateau," *Academy of Management Review*, Vol. (1977), p. 603.

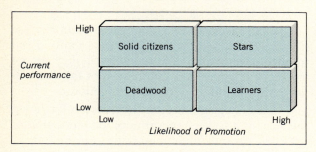

From an organization's point of view, the growing proportion of dual-career couples and working parents in the labor force can create problems. Out of 2,200 workers in one study by Mobil Oil, for example, the company found that its highest potential workers were most likely to be dual careerists. In addition, this group was highly resistant to being transferred, with some former employees saying they had quit in order to avoid transfer and the family upheavals it would have caused.[36] Organizations increasingly confront the "trailing-spouse" problem—that is the need to find employment for the partner who leaves a job to make a move to a new location benefiting the other partner's career. One survey reports that the problem is becoming so complicated that one in five working couples reject transfers because the trailing spouse cannot find a suitable job.[37] In other cases, the career with the higher compensation and/or offering the greatest long-term potential will often take priority. And in still others the "commuter marriage" proves the only solution.

Dual-career couples and working parents have special needs that must be met to maintain productivity and morale in the workplace. Many, but still far too few, progressive employers are responding with special programs designed to assist in balancing work and family pressures. These include on-site day-care centers for children, elder-care for aged parents, alternative work schedules allowing flexible hours, and others. For example,[38]

at Colgate-Palmolive employees have the option of a 12-week unpaid leave which allows salaried men or women time off for the birth or adoption of a child, family illness, or elder care.

at Aetna Life & Casualty employees are allowed to take unpaid "family leaves" for up to six months to help "balance the demands of career and personal life."

at NCNB Corporation a prior option of an unpaid four-month leave has been extended to six months, and employees have the added option of returning to work on a part-time basis.

Final Advice

Many problems and prospects await you in your managerial career. The issues previously discussed merely set the stage for the excitement to come. By way of final advice, consider the following suggested career tactics.[39]

1. *Perform* The basic foundation of success in any job is good performance. A record of high performance will please your superiors, earn respect from your peers and subordinates, and call attention to you as a person of high potential.

2. *Stay visible* Don't hestitate to make sure others recognize your hard work, and the performance results achieved. This is a public-relations task to be done in a professional manner and without becoming known as a braggart. When the performance record is there, project memos, progress reports, and even requests for more frequent evaluation and feedback sessions with superiors can enhance the visibility of your success.

3. *Be willing to move* Don't get locked into a job that you have already mastered and/or that is narrow and limited in the visibility or opportunity it offers. Take advantage of promotion opportunities within the organization. Be willing to change organizations for similar reasons. Don't be afraid to nominate yourself when appropriate for new and challenging changes of assignment.

4. *Find a mentor* It is always beneficial to have a senior executive who acts as a mentor you can learn from and who sponsors your career interests. Ideally, this will be a person who can create mobility and opportunity for you as his or her own career progresses over time.

5. *Manage your career* Stay active in thinking seriously and systematically about your career. Prepare and maintain a career plan even if it is only a broad frame of reference for directing your efforts and evaluating opportunities as they arise. Don't let success at any one stage distract you from taking advantage of new appointments with further growth potential. Take charge of your career, and stay in charge.

6. *Continue your education* Lifelong learning is both a responsibility and a prerequisite of long-term managerial success. In today's dynamic and challenging environment, the manager who fails to continue to learn and develop appropriate skills will not succeed. Maintain the yearn to learn—that is, make a commitment to take advantage of all opportunities for continuing education and ongoing development of your knowledge and skills in the management area.

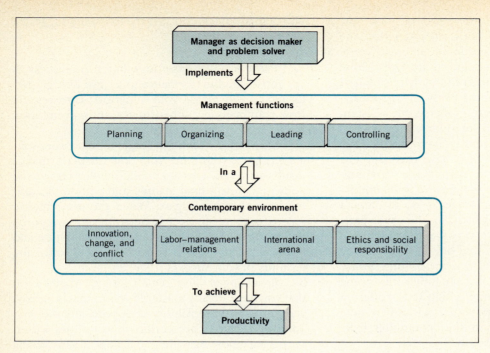

FIGURE 21.8 *A framework for studying management.*

MANAGEMENT FOR PRODUCTIVITY: A RECAP

Before leaving this final chapter, let's clarify for one last time the basic theme of this book. To begin, a manager is anyone to whom one or more others report in an organization. The manager's job is to make good decisions and solve problems in such a way that organizational productivity is enhanced. To do this, managers must foster both high performance and satisfaction among the members of their work units.

Figure 21.7 presents a comprehensive view of management as it is addressed in this book. It should help you review the entire book and integrate many insights as they relate to the practice of management in the demanding world of tomorrow. The premise underlying the figure is clear-cut. The insights available in the knowledge base we know as the field of "management" can help managers do their jobs well. This knowledge can help you, in particular, make appropriate decisions, solve difficult problems, and take advantage of daily opportunities in a managerial career. Managers of all types—such as

marketing managers, accounting managers, personnel managers, and finance managers, and managers working in all types of organizations—large or small, public or private—can and should draw on "management" as a knowledge base to help achieve productivity.

As you look ahead to an exciting future, reflect on these comments from a book with the title, *Productivity: Prospects for Growth.*[40] They ask you to accept a great deal of responsibility as a manager, and to fulfill this responsibility well. The task is clear; the rest is up to you!

> The potential gains from increased productivity for any individual, organization, or nation are great. Such gains, however, can be realized only if positive steps are taken to improve productivity. Fundamentally, each of us has an inherent responsibility to apply, in the most effective manner possible, the resources with which we are endowed or entrusted. We must always seek a better way and try to leave things better than we found them. Improved productivity requires awareness, commitment, ingenuity, action, and perseverance. The opportunity is there—what we do with it depends upon ourselves.

Summary

The manager's quest for productivity includes a concern to facilitate both high performance and satisfaction within the work unit and organization as a whole. Trends suggest that managers in the late 1990s and beyond will be held accountable for achieving productivity in an extremely challenging environment. We look ahead to a world in which the global economy, changing workforce demographics, and continued social developments create new conditions with which managers must successfully deal. When these trends are coupled with emerging pressures in supervisor–subordinate relations, the increased application of high technology in the workplace, and the changing nature of organizations themselves, the work setting of future managers appears complicated indeed.

Stress—the state of tension that accompanies exposure to extraordinary demands, constraints, and/or opportunities—will certainly be part of any manager's life. Managers must tolerate high levels of personal and job-related stress; they must also be prepared to recognize and understand the impact of stress on others with whom they work. Although the destructive side of stress is sometimes reflected in reduced productivity and perhaps even ill health, stress has a more positive side that can stimulate creativity and high performance. The effective manager of the future will be able to work well under stress.

Career planning and development is another important managerial responsibility. Managers must take charge of their personal careers in order to ensure success. This can involve deliberate and close adherence to a formal career plan Or, it may involve having a clear sense of career direction, but being ready and able to respond to unforeseen opportunities as they occur. Because of a manager's supervisory responsibilities, he or she will also be involved in assisting subordinates in their career planning and development activities. Looking ahead to a managerial career involves anticipating such things as the pressures of initial entry to a career, dual-career families, transitions through various adult life stages, and even the potential career plateau. Through it all, good managers will remain aware of how their needs and those of others must inevitably work in harmony with those of the organization.

Managers perform a most important social task. Productivity is the cornerstone of a healthy, prosperous, and gainful society. If high productivity is to be achieved in the future, good managers will have to lead the way. *Management for Productivity* was written to help you make this important and positive contribution to our world.

Thinking Through the Issues

1. Identify three demographic trends that can be predicted for the future. Why do you think they are important to managers?

2. Identify key trends that are expected to emerge in the job market between now and the year 2000. What is the significance of each trend to you?

3. Identify three trends in people that will affect supervisor–subordinate relationships in the future. How do you think they will impact managerial work?

4. What will the growing role of high technology and the changing nature of organizations mean to managers of the future? Please explain.

5. What is job stress, and what are some of the potential stressors that can cause it to occur?

6. What can a manager do in a high-pressure work or career situation to minimize the destructive potential of stress? (a) for himself or herself, and (b) for others?

7. Explain the concept of personal "wellness." What does it have to do with stress management? In what ways are organizations now helping their employees to achieve and maintain personal wellness? Why do they want to do this?

8. What are the advantages of a systematic approach to career planning? What are its limitations? How can one use it to best advantage?

9. Identify the likely problems of persons who are at transitions in early, middle, and late adulthood. How should persons experiencing these problems be handled by their supervisors?

10. Review the list of career suggestions provided in the section of the chapter entitled "final advice." What is your evaluation of this advice? Why?

The Manager's Vocabulary

Career
Career path
Career planning
Career plateau

Constructive stress
Destructive stress
Dual-career couple

Eustress
Personal wellness
Stress

Stressors
Survivor syndrome
Type A personality

"BALANCE" DRIVES THE YOUNG EXECS

C A R E E R   P E R S P E C T I V E

Peter D. Barker could work longer hours and attend more out-of-town meetings.[41] But he doesn't. For Parker, a vice-president at Climax Metals, the choice is this: be a workaholic, or be a father. His wife, Susan Clare Parker, makes her choices too. She's an executive at Chemical Bank. Together, the Parkers are in the ranks of the more than 3.5 million managerial and professional employees with working spouses—dual career couples.

"Balance" is the catchword for the Parkers and others like them. It wasn't all that bad when it was two young managers speeding ahead in their executive careers. But then came what Psychologist Daniel Levinson calls the "Big Bang." They had a baby. Now they have two, ages five and two. "It's all about balance"—matrimony, parenthood, and careers—Peter says, refering to the adjustment he and his wife make. A half-hour in the mornings and 90 minutes before bedtime are set aside for the kids. Weekends "are pretty much sacred" around their house also, he says. But they still depend on an elaborate support system including grandparents and childcare assistance.

When asked if his commitments to his family hurt his performance, David Parker summed it up this way: "I know it does. I see all the hungry 25-year-olds, and I really can't be as good as I might be. On the other hand, I like to think I'm a better manager because I delegate more." But he adds, "I'm also a pretty good husband and a pretty good parent."

Questions

1.   Is it realistic for David Parker to simply admit that his performance suffers a bit because of family commitments? As his boss, could you accept his rationale? What special managerial challenges does a person like David present to his or her supervisor?
2.   Is it any easier for the Parkers, based on what you know of them, than for other working couples in general to achieve "balance" in their lives? Please explain.
3.   What is the likelihood that you will become part of a "dual-career" relationship? What adjustments are you prepared to make to achieve the "balance" the Parker's talk about? What commitments would you expect your partner to make?

Case Application

PRODUCTIVITY PROFILES IN A HIGH-TECH FIRM

An extensive study by the Hughes Aircraft Company sought to identify useful techniques for optimizing productivity in technology-based organizations.[42] Much of the study dealt with traditional research and development (R&D) efforts, although it also involved examination of key interfacing activities such as marketing, finance, procurement, manufacturing, and information systems. The study involved 28 consultants, more than 3500 R&D managers, and more than 59 industry, government, and education organizations. Two results of the study are the productivity profiles that follow.

The Productive Employee

1. *Is well qualified for the job* Without the proper job qualifications, high productivity is out of the question. The well-qualified employee
- Is intelligent and learns quickly.
- Knows the job thoroughly.
- Is professionally and technically competent, keeps abreast of the field.
- Is creative and innovative, shows ingenuity and versatility.
- Works "smart," uses common sense, organizes work efficiently, uses time effectively, doesn't get bogged down.

2. *Is highly motivated* A "turned-on" employee is well on the road to high productivity. The highly motivated employee
- Gets satisfaction from a job well done.
- Is goal/achievement/results-oriented.
- Is self-motivated, takes initiative, and has a strong sense of commitment.
- Is persevering, gets the job done in spite of obstacles.
- Displays constructive discontent—"thinks" improvement into everything.
- Has a high energy level and directs that energy effectively.

3. *Has a positive job orientation* A person's attitude toward work assignments greatly affects his or her work performance. The employee with a positive job orientation
- Enjoys the job and is proud of it.
- Sets high standards.
- Has good work habits.
- Has good rapport with higher management.
- Is flexible and adaptive to change.

4. *Is mature* A mature employee displays consistent performance and requires minimal supervision. The mature employee
- Has high integrity, is honest and sincere.
- Knows personal strengths and weaknesses.
- Learns from experience.
- Has a strong sense of responsibility and self-respect.
- Has healthy ambition—wants professional growth.

5. *Interfaces effectively with others* The ability to establish positive interpersonal relationships is an asset that does much to enhance productivity. The employee who interfaces effectively
- Exhibits social intelligence.
- Exhibits a positive attitude and enthusiasm.
- Is personable, is accepted by and works well with superiors and colleagues.
- Communicates effectively, expresses thoughts well, is a good listener.
- Works well in team efforts, is cooperative, shares ideas.

The Productive Manager

1. *Is competent at staffing* To achieve high productivity, an organization must be staffed by capable personnel. The manager who is competent at staffing
- Has high recruiting standards.
- Is skilled at recognizing talent.
- Attracts and holds capable people.
- Is not afraid to hire top people, does not feel threatened by them.
- Regularly introduces "new blood" into the organization.

2. *Directs work efforts effectively* Good direction is essential for ensuring high productivity. The manager who is good at giving directions
- Is results-oriented and sets a good example.
- Is competent in dealing with people.
- Responds to the organization's current and long-range needs.
- Exhibits conceptual skills, keeps everything in proper perspective.
- Delegates effectively, clearly defines assignments, responsibilities, and authority, and tries not to second-guess subordinates.
- Always keeps things under control, continually monitors performance.

3. *Is competent at handling complex problems and dealing with new concepts* Skill in handling uncertainty and complexity in problem solving is an important asset for achieving high productivity. The manager capable of handling complexity and new concepts
- Is willing to take calculated risks.

- Has a good understanding of the work to be done.
- Is skilled at improvising, easily identifies and removes roadblocks and bottlenecks.
- Handles emergencies decisively, is not prone to "crisis management."

4. *Is a skillful communicator* Productivity depends on people in the work setting. The manager with strong communication skills
- Conducts meetings skillfully.
- Is readily accessible.
- Maintains an effective flow of two-way communication with properly informed superiors, peers, and subordinates.
- Is skillful at oral and written communication, conveys ideas clearly, concisely, and persuasively, makes effective presentations.

5. *Supports subordinates in their work performance and encourages their full participation in the work environment* Productivity can be achieved only when a manager's subordinates contribute optimally to performance objectives. A supportive and encouraging manager
- Knows subordinates, their capabilities, and their aspirations, respects individual differences.

- Makes everyone involved a party to the action, involves employees in decisions that affect them, makes all members feel they are important to the team effort.
- Provides clear assignments and background information necessary for performance of those assignments.
- Holds subordinates accountable for performance, provides performance feedback, appraises performance skillfully.
- Gives appropriate credit, rewards fairly, praises publicly, criticizes privately.

Questions
1. Is the list of characteristics in the profile of a productive employee complete? What would you add, delete, and/or change in the profile? Why?
2. Is the list of characteristics in the profile of a productive manager complete? What would you add, delete, and/or change in the profile? Why?
3. Can a manager achieve productivity without productive subordinates? Explain your answer.
4. What characteristics do the productive employee and productive manager share in common? Why is this overlap important to you in your managerial career?

Class Exercise: Personality and Stress

1. Complete the following behavior quiz.[43] Circle the number on the scale that best characterizes your behavior for each trait.

a. Casual about appointments	1 2 3 4 5 6 7 8	Never late for appointments
b. Not competitive	1 2 3 4 5 6 7 8	Very competitive
c. Never feel rushed	1 2 3 4 5 6 7 8	Always feel rushed
d. Take things one at a time	1 2 3 4 5 6 7 8	Try to do many things at once
e. Slow doing things	1 2 3 4 5 6 7 8	Fast doing things
f. Express feelings	1 2 3 4 5 6 7 8	"Sit" on feelings
g. Many outside interests	1 2 3 4 5 6 7 8	Few outside interests

2. Now total your scores for the seven items. Multiply this total by 3 to arrive at a final number of points.

Score: _____ × 3 = _____ final points

3. In Chapter 21 we discuss a Type A personality as prone to stress-related illnesses. The Type A person creates self-induced stress as a result of constant striving for achievement. Circle the personality profile determined in the prior quiz by locating your total point score on the following list.

Number of points	Type of personality
Less than 90	B
90 to 99	B +
100 to 105	A −
106 to 119	A
120 or more	A +

4. Think about the accuracy of this personality profile and its potential implications regarding your work-stress-health relationships. Share and discuss your results with a nearby classmate. Await further class discussion led by the instructor.

References

[1] Quotes from Peter F. Drucker's book, *The Changing World of the Executive* (New York: T.T. Times Books, 1982), pp. xi–xii; and, his article, "Management: The Problems of Success," *Academy of Management Executive,* Vol. 1 (1987), p. 13.

[2] Charles Dickens, *A Tale of Two Cities,* in *The Works of Charles Dickens* (New York: P. F. Collier, 1880), p. 343.

[3] Robert M. Fulmer, "Eight Paradoxes for the 1980s," Working paper #0-003, School of Business Administration, Emory University, Atlanta, Ga.

[4] Alvin Toffler, *The Third Wave* (New York: Morrow, 1980), p. 264.

[5] "The 21st Century Executive," *U.S. News & World Report* (March 7, 1988), pp. 48–56.

[6] *Workforce 2000: Work and Workers for the 21st Century* (Indianapolis, IN: The Hudson Institute, Inc., 1987).

[7] These trends are reported by William B. Johnston, *Workforce 2000: Work and Workers for the 21st Century*— Executive Summary (Indianapolis, IN: The Hudson Institute, Inc., 1987), pp. 7–9.

[8] Ibid. See also, "Best Jobs for the Future," *U.S. News & World Report* (April 25, 1988), pp. 60–80.

[9] For a discussion of the growing role of corporate education see Walter A. Green and Harold Lazarus, "Corporate Campuses: A Growing Phenomenon," *Journal of Management Development,* Vol. 7 (1988), pp. 56–67.

[10] Quoted from *1984 Annual Report,* Herman Miller Corporation. See also Max DePree's book, *Leadership is an Art* (Lansing, MI: The Michigan State University Press, 1987).

[11] See "On Corporate Boards, It's Still a White Male World," *The Wall Street Journal* (January 12, 1988), p. 1; Lena Williams, "For the Black Professional, the Obstacles Remain," *The New York Times,* (July 14, 1987), p. A-16; and, "The Black Middle Class," *Business Week* (March 14, 1988), pp. 62–69.

[12] See "So You Think You've Come a Long Way, Baby?" *Business Week* (February 29, 1988), pp. 48–52.

[13] See Tom Forester, "The Materials Revolution," *The Futurist* (July–August 1988), pp. 21–25; and, Gene Bylinsky, "Technology in the Year 2000," *Fortune* (July 18, 1988), pp. 92–98.

[14] This term is used by John Naisbitt in his popular book *Megatrends: Ten New Directions Transforming Our Lives* (New York: Warner, 1982).

[15] These characteristics are reported in James O'Toole, *Vanguard Management* (New York: Doubleday, 1985).

[16] This case is developed from Max DePree, "Theory Fast-ball," *New Management Magazine,* Vol. 1 (1984), pp. 29–36; and James O'Toole, "Practicing Leadership," *New Management,* Vol. 5 (1988), pp. 2–4.

[17] Adapted from Arthur P. Brief, Randall S. Schuler, and Mary Van Sell, *Managing Job Stress* (Boston: Little, Brown, 1981), pp. 7, 8.

[18] Michael Weldholz, "Stress Increasingly Seen as Problem with Executives More Vulnerable," *Wall Street Journal* (September 28, 1982), p. 31.

[19] "Worries at Work," *The Wall Street Journal* (April 7, 1988), p. 31.

[20] See "Stress on the Job," *Newsweek* (April 25, 1988), pp. 40–45; and Brian Dumaine, "Cool Cures for Burnout," *Fortune* (June 20, 1988), pp. 78–84.

[21] Meyer Freidman and Ray Roseman, *Type A Behavior and Your Heart* (New York: Knopf, 1974). See also Jerry E. Bishop, "Prognosis for the 'Type A' Personality Improves in a New Heart Disease Study," *The Wall Street Journal* (January 14, 1988), p. 29.

[22] Quote from *Esquire* (December 1986), p. 86.

[23] Michael J. McCarthy, "Stressed Employees Look for Relief in Worker's Compensation Claims," *The Wall Street Journal* (April 7, 1988), p. 31.

[24] See John M. Ivancevich and Michael T. Matteson, "Optimizing Human Resources: A Case for Preventive Health and Stress Management," *Organizational Dynamics,* Vol. 9 (Autumn 1980), pp. 6–8. See also John M. Ivancevich, Michael T. Matteson, and Edward P. Richards, III, "Who's Liable for Stress on the Job?," *Harvard Business Review,* Vol. 64 (March–April 1985), pp. 60–71.

[25] Developed from Robert Kreitner, "Personal Wellness: It's Just Good Business," *Business Horizons,* Vol. 25 (May–June 1982), pp. 28–35; and "Plain Talk About Stress," National Institute of Mental Health Publication (Rockville, MD: U.S. Department of Health and Human Services).

[26] Kreitner, op cit.

[27] "Employee Health A Good Investment," *Management Digest Quarterly,* Vol. 2 (Summer 1988), published by the American Management Associations.

[28] Edgar H. Schein, *Career Dynamics: Matching Individual and Organizational Needs* (Reading, MA: Addison-Wesley, 1978), p. 1.

[29] These viewpoints are found in the *Advanced Management Journal* (Summer 1975). Adapted, by permission of the publisher, from *Advanced Management Journal* (Summer 1975), © 1975 by *AMACOM,* a division

of American Management Associations. All rights reserved.

[30]Kae H. Chung and Leon C. Megginson, *Organizational Behavior: Developing Managerial Skills* (New York: Harper & Row, 1981), pp. 539–540; Schein, op. cit., pp. 189–199.

[31]Based on Daniel J. Levinson, *The Seasons of a Man's Life* (New York: Knopf, 1978), pp. 56–63. See also

[32]This and subsequent discussion is based on Kirby Warren, "Reflections," *Senior Seminar Newsletter* (Bloomington, IL: Fall 1982); see also Thomas P. Ference, James A. F. Stoner, and E. Kirby Warren, "Managing the Career Plateau," *Academy of Management Review,* Vol. 2 (October 1977), pp. 602–612.

[33]Research on dual-career couples is well summarized in Uma Sekaran's book, *Dual-Career Families* (San Francisco: Jossey-Bass, 1986).

[34]See Colin Leinster, "The Young Exec as Superdad," *Fortune* (April 25, 1988), pp. 237–242.

[35]Quotes from Mary Bralove, "Problems of Two-Career Families Start Forcing Businesses to Adapt," *Wall Street Journal* (July 15, 1981), p. 23.

[36]Leinster, op cit.

[37]Information from "Dual Careers, Doleful Dilemmas," *Time* (November 16, 1987), p. 90.

[38]Information from "Taking a Leave to Care for a Baby or Parent Gains Ground," *The Wall Street Journal* (July 19, 1988), p. 1.

[39]Based on Ross A. Webber, "13 Career Commandments," *MBA* (May 1975), p. 47; Alan N. Schoonmaker, *Executive Career Strategy* (New York: American Management Association, 1971).

[40]Robert M. Ranftl, "Making Research and Development Work," in Jerome M. Rosow (ed.), *Productivity: Prospects for Growth* (New York: Van Nostrand, 1981), pp. 225, 239.

[41]Information from Leinster, op cit.

[42]The productivity profiles are from Robert M. Ranftl, "Making Research and Development Work," in Jerome M. Rosow, *Productivity: Prospects for Growth* (New York: Van Nostrand, 1981), pp. 205–239. Used by permission.

[43]This quiz is slightly adapted from *Journal of Chronic Diseases,* Vol. 22, p. 87, R. W. Bortner, "A Short Rating Scale: A Potential Measure of Pattern A Behaviors," Copyright © 1969, Pergamon Press, Ltd.

PART 7

Electro Systems Corporation

You are Robert Ford, the new plant manager of the Metropolis Plant, part of the Electro Systems Corporation. Previously you had been manager for research and development for another Electro plant in a different part of the country. The organization chart for the corporation is shown in Figure 1.

BACKGROUND

The Metropolis plant had been growing steadily under the management of Kenneth Chan, the previous manager, who left the company for a better job. The plant now has a capital investment in excess of $80 million and produces a variety of electronic and electromechanical testing and analyzing equipment for both military and civilian markets. The plant staff, excuding top management, now includes 55 engineers and 35 technicians; there are approximately 1100 production employees who work in two shifts. The plant organization chart is shown in Figure 2. Your direct reports are:

William Sloan department manager in charge of production. He has been with the company about 15 years, but has been in his current job for less than a year.

Joseph Flores department manager in charge of marketing. He has been in the job approximately 2 years. Before then, he had been a regional sales manager. His present functions include sales promotion, merchandising, market research, and development and sales. He supervises 85 employees.

Alice Miller the section manager in research and development, is an electronics engineer. Prior to her promotion less than a year ago, she headed up the electrical engineering subsection in the engineering department.

Her functions are shown on the organization chart. She has 38 engineers and 15 technicians and draftspeople working for her. Because of Chan's strong interest in research and development, close to seven percent of the plant's profits are allocated to this function.

Janice Colbert finance manager. She has held this job for about three years. Her functions include general and cost accounting, accounts receivable and payable, payroll, and the computer unit. She has a staff of about 25 people.

Charles Green employee relations with a work unit of 18 people. He transferred from the corporate staff a little over six months ago.

Robert Strong section head in charge of materials. He has been with the plant in this job for more than ten years. His staff of 27 covers a diverse set of responsibilities.

FIGURE 1 *Electro Systems Corporation organization chart.*

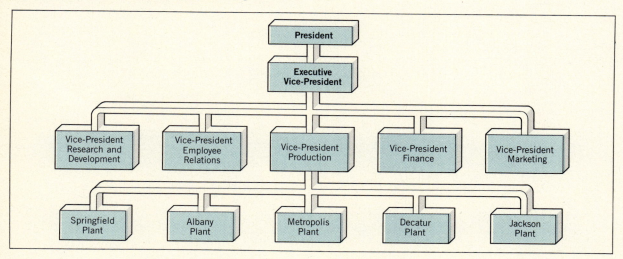

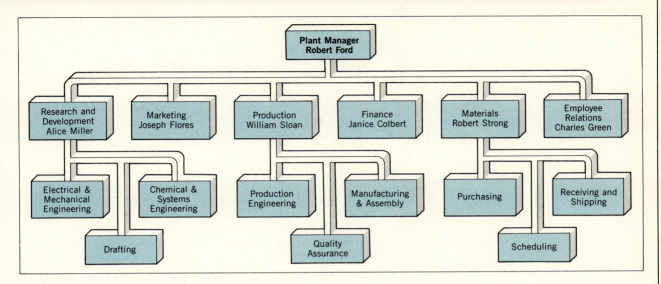

FIGURE 2 *Metropolis plant organization chart.*

The products of most current concern to the Metropolis Plant are the following:

Model A—the current product
Model A Retrofit—a modified "A"
Model B—a new product
Model C—a scaled down "B"
Model D—a scaled up "C"

IMMEDIATE SITUATION

Shortly after being appointed plant manager at Metropolis, you were able to spend a week becoming familiar with the new plant and its personnel. Then some lingering work called you back to the old plant for a week's time. Last night, Sunday, you finally arrived back in Metropolis to begin the new assignment. It's now Monday morning. You have come into the office an hour early to catch up on what has happened while you were away, and get a head start on the day's work.

The following items were found in your in-basket when you arrived at the plant on Monday morning. You decide to review them before doing anything else.

CORPORATE MEMORANDUM—FAX Transmission 864-3110

TO: Mr. Robert Ford   March 3

FROM: Henry Towne, Vice-President Production

SUBJECT: Meeting

I plan to come to Metropolis on March 25 to meet with you now that you have had a chance to become acquainted with the plant. In addition to the routine general review, I would like to take enough time for us to discuss the problem of increasing our rate of new product introduction. We need to increase our research and development emphasis in both personnel and facilities, especially since the rate of product obsolescence is being considerably affected by our competitors. I would like to have you prepare a special report on this subject for me.

In addition, the latest budget reports indicate that the plant is running well above the projected operating expenses for both the last quarter and the year to date. Furthermore, does the current slight decrease in sales constitute a signal of a downward trend? We will want to look at this for both near and long-term implications.

You may ask any member of your staff to meet with us should you feel it is appropriate.

PLANT MEMORANDUM

TO: Mr. Robert Ford   March 3

FROM: Al Miller

SUBJECT: Project Status Report

This is a brief status report with some accompanying recommendations.

  1.   Model B.   Although there have been some slippages, the Model B is close to coming into production. We have had one brief hangup due to the failure of the system to pass the packaging tests, but we anticipate no further difficulty, and the project should be ready to hand over completely to production in the next few weeks.

  2.   Models C and D.   As you know, the Model C is a simplified and less complex version of the B. The D, as an ancillary system, adds considerably to the capability of the B. Both are progressing and should be ready to be put into production within the next two months.

  3.   We would like to begin design on a completely new and original system for hospital laboratory analysis. What we have in mind is a multichannel digital system which can conduct as many as ten different blood analyses almost simultaneously. However, we are having difficulties, since Janice Colbert tells us that funds cannot be made available within the current year.

Recommendations:

  1.   We recommend that you seriously consider hiring some really capable people in production engineering. We don't want to repeat the Model A problem again. We gave those people a good design, and they were unable to follow it through.

  2.   We recommend that you talk to Colbert about considerably increasing funding for the purpose of going into the digital blood system.

PLANT MEMORANDUM

TO: Bob Ford   March 3

FROM: Robert Strong

SUBJECT: Increased Materials Cost

As you know, I've been concerned for quite a while about parts shortages, high inventory, and the steadily increasing materials costs. This is particularly true since more than half of our direct costs come from purchased materials, due to the nature of our business.

My people are working hard to reduce costs and establish decent manufacturing schedules, but we can't do it by ourselves. We are continually having to revise our production schedules because of manufacturing problems, particularly with the new models. As a result, my purchasing people don't get the word early enough on what we need to buy, and everything needs to be on rush order and expedited. About the time we get it into the plant, there is another design change, and sometimes the parts we have just rush-ordered are then obsoleted. As a result, our materials costs are skyrocketing.

We need to get designs locked in so that we can establish decent manufacturing and purchasing schedules. For example, the Model B is supposed to go into manufacturing shortly, but as yet we have been unable to get a parts listing that we can rely on.

PLANT MEMORANDUM

TO: Bob Ford   March 5

FROM: William Sloan

SUBJECT: Model A retrofit

Although we had a discussion about the Model A last week, I thought it wise to drop you a note on the subject. It does not appear possible to make the schedule for the Model A retrofit and at the same time make the schedule for the new Model A's coming out. My production engineering people are going flat out trying to make the necessary production design changes and at the same time help the production people with the retrofit program. I would recommend stopping production on both the retrofit and new production until we get the design problems cleaned up once and for all.

The mistake that I made was accepting the Model A for production when I knew that there were a lot of design bugs in it. I won't make that mistake again.

By the way, can you get the finance people off my back for a while? They are trying to put in the computer system. It still hasn't been debugged, and I'll be glad to help them out in a month or so when I've had a chance to get caught up with the production problems.

PLANT MEMORANDUM

TO: Plant Manager   March 5

FROM: Janice Colbert, Finance

SUBJECT: Integrated Management Information Systems

Two months ago, we completed and debugged our computer-based integrated management information system at a cost of $800,000. This system is aimed at providing us with much more timely and accurate information about sales figures, production and assembly scheduling, vendor order status, and the like. I have been particularly concerned with the fact that the new System would provide me with considerably better cost-accounting data.

However, the new system is not working well. Its effectiveness has been considerably reduced by the fact that many managers do not use it, but instead maintain duplicate records and do not update the computer files regularly. Further, they appear reluctant to give me the cost-accounting figures that I need and do not fully adhere to the new policies and procedures necessary to make the new system work.

Any and all assistance in this matter would be greatly appreciated.

CORPORATE MEMORANDUM—FAX TRANSMISSION 864-3116

TO: MR. ROBERT FORD, PLANT MANAGER   March 6
        MR. JOSEPH FLORES, MARKETING MANAGER

FROM: Jim Brown, Vice-President Marketing

Good news. Bennet Industries is ready to purchase large number of Model A systems and related accessories. A contract is likely if we can promise early delivery. Please advise me of your commitments.

PLANT MEMORANDUM

TO: Mr. Robert Ford, Plant Manager   March 9

FROM: Joseph Flores, Marketing Manager

SUBJECT: Slippage of the Model B

The latest word that I have is that the Model B will not go into production for another month. As you know, we have repeated delays on introducing this system. Originally, it was supposed to go into production last August. Our sales for this year were forecast on the firm promise from R&D that the Model B would be ready for production by January 1 of this year. Apparently, the earliest date now is April 15.

Our sales forecasts are based on the expectation that new products will come into the plant and go into production on specific dates. Any further delays in the introduction of the Model B will seriously reduce sales for the year, particularly since delays on the B will also affect other models in the series, especially the C and D.

PLANT MEMORANDUM

TO: Mr. Robert Ford, Plant Manager   March 9

FROM: Charles Green, Employee Relations

SUBJECT: Employment of Minorities

According to information I received at a personnel meeting this morning, both the State and Federal Equal Opportunity people will shortly be giving a hard look at industrial plants in this area. Currently, our ratio of employed minorities is extremely low, and we may be in serious trouble.

I would recommend that we put on a crash program to recruit and employ at least 70–80 minorities, in all areas of the plant.

I realize that a crash program may involve, for the short-run, increased training and labor costs, but this is preferable to losing our defense contracts or the bad publicity coming from an investigation. Besides, I think that this is the *right* thing to do.

Motorola's Productivity Programs

There are countless ideas as to how to get U.S. productivity up and keep it there. Almost a decade ago, Motorola identified four elements it wanted in its productivity program. First, it would begin with product design, and the goal of instituting the best design at a minimal cost. Second, it would buy the newest and best equipment for its plants. Third, it would ensure that people in the company understand and believe in the policies and methods used in the plants. The fourth element is what Ralph Elsner, vice-president of the company, calls "the crucial element": getting people involved and motivated.

If you've been following the history of productivity-improvement programs in the United States, you certainly are well aware that most of them contain many of the same elements. Usually, you'll find the work-team concept. Less frequently, you find a direct relation between setting and reaching output and quality goals, and attaching a direct cash compensation to that goal. There also has to be a strong management involvement, from top to bottom. There has to be idea feedback from the line people back to their managers, and it has to function rapidly.

Motorola, though, seems to have been moving fairly deliberately in

Source: Part I excerpted from Keith W. Bennett, "Motorola Focus on Productivity & Quality Is Worth a Look," *Iron Age* (February 10, 1982), pp. 61–64. Used by permission. Part II excerpted from Phil Nienstedt and Richard Wintermantel, "Motorola Restructures to Improve Productivity," *Management Review* (January 1987), pp. 47–49. Used by permission. Part III information from "Motorola Sends its Work Force Back to School," *Business Week* (June 6, 1988), pp. 80–82.

> Supervisors have to keep open communication with the work force, and have to be able to suggest—often— where they used to command.

putting all three elements together throughout its total plant system in its Participative Management Program (PMP).

PART I— THE EARLY 1980S

During the early 1980s Motorola's productivity approach centered around its Participative Management Program (PMP).

"There are really two plans," Elsner notes. "Plan I is the operating and manufacturing force. Based on a kind of 'line-of-sight' idea, the teams are kept to about 75 per shift, or a total three-shift team of approximately 250 persons. The PMP team can be as small as 35 persons.

The Plan I team tracks its own performance and sets its own goals. The feedback comes in measurement of some six cost elements: current cost, quality (as measured by deliveries and returns and factory quality reports), delivery of product against schedules, inventory controls, housekeeping and safety records, and cost improvement.

Bonuses are calculated and paid monthly. A steering committee meets

monthly to discuss reports and suggestions from the working committee. This steering group is another avenue for managers to meet with an organizational cross section and to maintain open communication between the working committees and other parts of the company. The steering committee also reviews performance data from the work groups.

"Once a week, everybody meets with the supervisor in a session that can be as short as five minutes, but may go as long as two hours," Elsner says. "Generally, the meetings tend to get shorter as the program matures and the original problems get honed down. Despite this, however, some sections meet daily, and the loss of that much time in a group doesn't interfere with the gains in productivity."

Plan II is in the area of supporting services—for example, design, financial, and sales and marketing elements of the company. Results in these groups have traditionally been harder to measure. Here again, a system of steering committees (which include Plan I representatives) reviews annual plans set by the working committees of engineers and office workers. The Plan II groups are fewer in number—generally, one per business center.

Motorola holds that measured cash rewards are a necessary part of the PMP program (unlike the quality circles used in Japan). So it was necessary to measure the output of the Plan II groups, and that is related to the level of profit earned by the business center in which the Plan II group is working. The Plan II bonus is based on the profit return above a minimum, and against goals set by the group itself.

Ralph Elsner agrees with the charge leveled by some veterans of other productivity plans that a PMP program can make a manager's job tougher. Supervisors have to keep open communication with the work force, and have to be able to suggest—often—where they used to command. They have to listen. And that has often been the downfall of many such programs.

To keep the consciousness of the manager, "We've also developed a questionnaire that each manager can send out as a blind question to his or her own people. The results—which give a picture of how the workers feel about him or her—are for the manager's use only."

The PMP program at Motorola began in the chief executive office. Chairman Robert Galvin brought in Ralph Elsner as the operating executive and vice-president reporting directly to the executive office. Elsner has only one staff member and a secretary. Each plant has its own PMP manager, reporting to the plant manager in the same way that Elsner reports to the chief executive, as deputy to the president.

PMP is a communications program. It brings people and data together at every level.

PMP is a communications program. It brings people and data together at every level. Production results, for example, are posted regularly on display boards. Every member of every team can see the results, as well as talk about them at daily and weekly meetings. Some of the information is apparently pretty strategic stuff—for example, the loss or acquisition of a large account. Good or bad, the news goes up for everybody to consider.

It also rises along with a streamlined version of the old, and often ignored, suggestion box. This, however, is another display board. It's the "I Recommend" board, posted in each team area. There are forms on the board. Anybody with an idea that he or she feels will help the team along posts it on the board. It's the job of the manager and committees to see that an action report is back on the board within 72 hours.

As has been said here, this kind of management is tough for some managers. It takes getting used to. Ralph Elsner admits that this could be a problem sometimes. "But since we've realized that PMP is the way we have to go, we've also realized we have to help managers in using the program."

The idea behind participative management is that there is a lot of talent out in the shop.

Elsner recalls the woman on an assembly line who turned out to have a master's degree in physics, but took an assembly-line job because teaching jobs were sparse. "Today's worker seems like a new kind of person. They won't take guff from management; they are well educated, well schooled, observant, often critical. They tend to challenge their bosses."

"You still have failures," concedes Elsner. "But where we found a group that was failing, it tended to be where the boss had abdicated. This program isn't self-sustaining. The boss has to get along with people, and they have to work at group participation."

PMP is, it appears, a people-oriented communications program, with the important difference that it has a built in cash component that is both an incentive to participation and an early-warning device that tells managers in advance when something is going wrong.

PART II—THE MID 1980S

When the need for restructuring became apparent, Motorola's top corporate management responded in a consistent fashion. They asked its organization and human resources professionals to identify opportunities for shrinking the organizational structure to gain an advantage over its competitors. The department raised three issues:

1. Can the senior management of a successful, fast-growing organization be made to recognize a need for action?
2. How can individual managers be expected to respond positively? Can they be receptive to modifying their organizations, especially when the results might reduce the number of personnel in their own departments? Won't they perceive personal threats in such actions?
3. Could potential reductions in the management ranks be consistent with Motorola's longstanding, well-earned reputation for treating employees with dignity and respect? This treatment includes "protecting" those who have served the company for many years. This recognition and "protection" is regarded as one of Motorola's widely shared values.

The answer to the first issue, recognition of the need, was yes—largely because of difficult business conditions at the time of the study. The electronics industry, with its "feast or famine" business cycles, was heading for a slump. Competitors were implementing cost-cutting measures, many of them quite drastic. Motorola's top management aimed for ways to achieve similar cost reductions while continuing to upgrade the organization for the future. The publicity about domestic competitor actions was accompanied by accelerating competitive threats from abroad—particularly from the Japanese. These activities encouraged Motorola managers to pursue new ways to realize cost efficiencies.

The second issue was addressed more subtly, but still in a proactive manner. Managers were encouraged to recognize that their organizations did not benefit when their highly valued employees performed as "part-time" managers. If some of these assumed real, full-time managerial positions and others became individual contributors, responsibilities would be clearer and the work effort more sharply focused and efficient. Motorola had previously established Individual Contributor Ladders, or career paths, whereby managerial titles were not required to advance all the way to the vice-presidential level. Similarly, the organization believes that the loss of a managerial title does not imply lost prestige or status. This message, reiterated to managers, diminished the perception that they or their organizations would be threatened if few employees held the title of manager.

Particular attention was given to the third issue, Motorola's longstanding reputation as a "people company." Most successful companies recognize that to achieve long-run growth and prosperity, they must often reduce costs. Pesonnel layoffs, even though often perceived as contributing to, or perhaps even critical to, long-run company survival, seldom enhance general employee morale. This was the dilemma Motorola faced when considering techniques to reduce managerial costs. The timing was opportune, however, because Motorola had increasingly recognized that competition in the electronics industry in general—and with Japanese companies in particular—was surely destined to become more severe.

Unless it could improve its competitive posture, the company's ability to maintain its people values, particularly its recognition of those with long company service, could be severely threatened. Well-planned, selective cost improvements, made early, could preclude much more drastic actions later. This scenario led Motorola to conclude that its *long-run* people values were critical, and that appropriate short-term cost efficiencies needed to be initiated in order to protect them.

Perhaps the most important side benefit of all is a change in "management mentality."

Motorola is organized into sectors, groups, and divisions according to its major businesses. The authors provide organization and human resources support to the Semiconductor Products Sector, the company's largest entity. They devised a simple process that management turned into an effective technique for reducing managerial layers and widening spans of control.

Step 1: Data Gathering
Each top manager of the sector was asked to "draw," on one sheet, charts of their organization depicting *all* the lines and *all* the boxes to show reporting relationships down to the direct-labor level. These illustrations, often crude and sketchy, were amazingly revealing to all concerned. Having the complete organization on one piece of paper (often a very large piece) clearly showed for the first time:

■ The number of managerial layers (often too many).

■ The number of subordinates reporting to each manager, or "span of control" (often too few).

■ Unexplained inconsistencies in structure.

■ Overlapping responsibilities.

Step 2: Analysis
Organization and human resources professionals reviewed and analyzed each chart. They looked for opportunities to improve communications by realigning spans of control.

Step 3: Discussion
Similar analyses throughout the sector (composed of more than 5000 managers and supervisors) pointed to hundreds of potential opportunities. These situations included unneeded manager positions, duplication of supervisory effort, and unclear roles among management personnel. The analyses were then presented to the managers of the respective organizations for discussion.

Step 4: Goals Negotiation
A typical initial reaction was: "You don't understand my business; there's a perfectly valid reason for organizing in that manner, and an extra layer of management *is necessary* in that situation." Often, unique peculiarities within organizations were revealed that warranted the structures in question. In other cases, the existence of unnecessary management was acknowledged. Managers who did not agree with suggested structural changes were asked instead to come up with "your *own* ideas that *will* result in managerial cost savings within your organization." Simple as it is, this technique worked.

Step 5: Implementation and Tracking
As identified opportunities were addressed, savings were calculated and documented. Some savings material-

ized only after gradual and deliberate planning and execution; others were implemented quickly.

Timing was a key element. When, for example, an "excess" position became vacant (perhaps because of the transfer of the incumbent to another position), the organization would at that time be restructured so that no replacement was needed.

These actions clearly saved money for the organization, even though no "head cutting" took place. For situations in which managers were promoted out of a particular organization, they were replaced with individual contributors, without the added cost of managerial skills on top of individual contributor skills. The difference between the two salaries became a real and continuing savings, even though the number of positions in that organization was unchanged. Both cost savings and cost avoidance formulas were developed. Over time, significant savings were realized through these and other actions.

The open endorsement and support of the sector general manager was essential to ensuring accurate tracking of actions and improvement efforts. He challenged his management team to treat this activity as an integral part of their managerial responsibilities. He incorporated the results of their efforts into the annual incentive bonus considerations. He personally monitored each staff member's progress on a quarterly basis. He often questioned his staff about their results, chiding them or recognizing accomplishments according to each situation. A scorecard reflected yearly goals in each organization, and quarterly progress against those goals.

Results to date have been dramatic. Several million dollars of documented annual savings (savings that wil repeat each year) have been realized. Several major restructurings

were prompted by the opportunity to achieve wider spans and to eliminate unneeded layers of management. In one example, a total restructuring across an entire division reduced the layers from seven to six and increased the average span from 4.4 to 5.4. The impact on the bottom line was significant, positive, and ongoing.

Another example involves the sector's production assembly plants, which employ thousands in several locations in Asia. Originally established for the purpose of achieving cost efficiencies, over time the total number of supervisory personnel had grown larger than necessary. The program to increase spans triggered the managers of these plants to determine the optimal number of direct reports to each supervisor, and then move toward that number across all four plants in the Assembly Division. A higher subordinate-to-supervisor ratio is now in effect, and the absolute number of supervisors was reduced—again, primarily through normal attrition and transfers.

Other benefits began to accrue as the program to increase spans and reduce layers proceeded:

■ Organizations with fewer management layers found it easier and quicker to communicate up and down.

■ As fewer, but more "real," managerial positions materialized, investment in selection and specific training was aimed more directly at those fully dedicated to the managerial function.

■ Participation in decision making by employees has been further nurtured as the number of first-line supervisors giving them directions has shrunk.

Perhaps the most important side benefit of all is a change in "management mentality." The need for each addition to the management ranks is now being evaluated more seriously,

and the high cost of managing is now perceived as an expense that can be scrutinized and controlled.

PART III— INTO THE 1990S

By the late 1980s Motorola had slipped to fourth place in world semiconductor sales. And its other electronics businesses, from cellular phones to modems, were being pressed hard by foreign competition.

■

Motorola spends about 2.4 percent of its payroll on employee education. This is twice what the average American company spends.

■

The $6.7 billion company with 96,000 employees is now embarking on yet another phase in its continued effort to achieve productivity and maintain a competitive edge. Part of the firm's problems have been attributed to uneven quality of products and delays in delivering to customers. Thus, the aim of Chairman Robert Gavin is to transform the corporate culture into a unified focus on "total customer satisfaction." Viewed as fundamental to the company's survival, this goal is being pursued through a massive corporate education effort. Gavin believes the key to Motorola's success still lies with its employees.

Motorola spends about 2.4 percent of its payroll on employee education. This is twice what the average American company spends. Managers throughout the firm attend a variety of courses varying from half-day to several weeks duration. They study technical subjects such as just-in-time scheduling, as well as more general management topics. Workers in the plants have also gone back to the basics. Remedial work in reading and math is available to those who need it before they enroll in courses on statistical quality control and other topics. They also examine issues of participation and idea sharing, and even engage in sports designed to build teamwork.

People from all functional areas—marketing, quality control, and engineering—meet in the classes, which helps break down communications barriers. Continued technological changes in the factories have helped too, where manufacturing cells are starting to replace traditional assembly lines. In exchange for meeting tough goals, workers qualify for incentive bonuses.

Through it all the company is making gains in quality, cost-cutting, and customer relations. Last year its sales increased by 12 percent and profits 62 percent. Motorola expects sales to increase dramatically again this year. It is banking on keeping its key products such as cellular phones, two-way mobile radios, pages, and modems at the forefront in world markets. But its competitors are moving forward too. "Now we have to improve faster than the competition," says CEO George Fisher.

QUESTIONS

1. What is your evaluation of Motorola's PMP program as a management approach? Does it serve both company needs and employee interests? Please explain.

2. Did Motorola succeed in handling the challenges of restructuring while still respecting the rights and needs of its employees? What else can be done to further improve on this approach?

3. Is Motorola's "total customer satisfaction" agenda consistent with the competitive demands of today's marketplace? Is it something that can be achieved through employee education alone? What else needs to be done to ensure that this concept becomes fully integrated throughout the company?

4. What lessons for successful productivity improvement in other settings can be summarized from Motorola's experience? Explain and defend your answer. ■

Management Applications

Quantitative Decision Techniques: An Introduction to Management Science

Management science and operations research are terms first introduced in Chapter 2 in a discussion of the quantitative approaches to management. These are terms used interchangeably to describe the same thing. Basically, management science/operations research (MS/OR) involves the use of mathematics to *help* managers analyze decision alternatives in a rational and scientific manner. Note that the word *help* is emphasized. These techniques can never make decisions by themselves. If used properly, however, MS/OR can be very useful in providing a manager with additional information to be used in decision-making and problem solving.

All MS/OR techniques may be classified into two large categories: deterministic or stochastic. **Deterministic methods** treat all values as fixed or known. For instance, the economic order quantity (EOQ) formula presented in Chapter 16 is deterministic. It involves a forecast of future demand, inventory carrying cost, and ordering cost, each of which is treated as a fixed value.

Stochastic methods, on the other hand, take variability into consideration. They include probability estimates of each possible value. For example, the Emperor Products case in Chapter 3 involved risk and uncertainty. To help the company president reach a decision, a decision matrix or payoff table was developed that explicitly included the probability of each possible outcome. This payoff table approach is part of the stochastic technique called *decision theory*.

Some problems are easily solved by deterministic methods, while others are more appropriately addressed using stochastic techniques. This Management Applications Module discusses some of the most useful MS/OR techniques in each category and shows how they can be applied to various problem situations. Although all of these techniques are now supported by computer applications—micro-, mini-, and mainframe computers—it is helpful to understand their basic foundations. Together with the material presented in Chapters 3 and 16, this overview provides you with a good introduction to management applications of quantitative decision techniques.

FORECASTING TECHNIQUES

Forecasting has been identified as an important aid to managerial decision making. In the context of operations management, for example, a **demand forecast** sets the stage for planning—and then controlling—a variety of important manufacturing and service activities. In general, we forecast by "extrapolating," or projecting into the future based on what has happened in the past. Weather forecasts are based on what usually happened in the past when certain atmospheric conditions were present. Managers basically follow the same approach in demand forecasting. They take past data and extrapolate them into the future to project future demand for the products and/or services of an organization or subunit.

Take a look at Figure A.1. It graphically depicts past sales of air conditioners over a three-year pe-

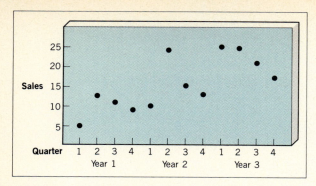

FIGURE A.1 *Historical time series data: quarterly air conditioner sales for a three-year period.*

riod. How would you project these data into the future? That is, how would you forecast future demand for air conditioners in such a way that production plans could accurately be made?

Time-Series Analysis

One problem in making a forecast from the figure is recognizing a pattern. **Time-series analysis** is a method for identifying patterns in data. It is a foundation element in any effective forecast.

FIGURE A.2 *Individual components in time-series data: trend, cyclical, seasonal, and random components.*

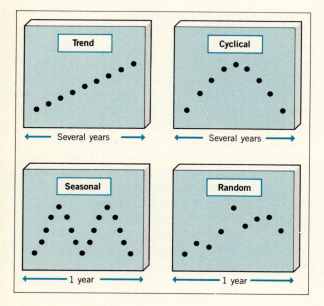

Time-series analysis takes historical data and breaks them into individual components—trend, seasonal, cyclical, and random—as shown in Figure A.2. In general, the four time-series components are used in the following ways.

■ *Trend* Reflects the overall upward or downward movement in the variation of data over time.

■ *Seasonal* Reflects a wavelike variation of data occurring a year and following the seasons.

■ *Cyclical* Reflects a wavelike variation of data occurring over several years and following business or economic cycles.

■ *Random* Reflects an unusual variation of data following irregular occurrences, such as strikes or bad weather.

The principle of time-series analysis is to break historical data into one or more of these components and then analyze each component separately. By focusing on just one component at a time, it is easier to spot key factors and use them as a basis for forecasting. Look again at Figure A.1. Do you recognize any of these components in the data? Try sketching them in on the data pattern shown in the figure.

Now compare your analysis with the one depicted in Figure A.3. There seems to be an upward trend in the data, as indicated by the dashed line in the figure. The solid line shows a seasonal pattern, something we would expect for air conditioners. The circled data point for the first quarter of year 3 falls clearly outside this seasonal pattern. It could be a random component. Careful analysis of this point might reveal that sales were high at that time because of unusually hot weather, a random occurrence for so early in the year. Finally, there seems to be a cyclical pattern present, as shown by the dot-and-dash line. Although sales have been following an upward trend, they are leveling off and perhaps entering the downward curve of a cycle.

This example illustrates how time-series analysis helps make preliminary sense from historical data. It is a useful managerial tool. Still, most demand forecasting requires further detail that can be added by techniques such as moving averages, exponential smoothing, and regression analysis. Each of these forecasting methods uses mathematics to extrapolate historical data into the future. Don't be alarmed; the mathematics is straightforward and based on common sense. Because these techniques

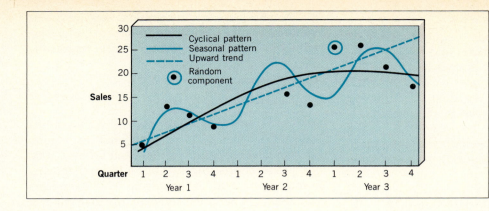

FIGURE A.3 *Applied time-series analysis: the case of the air conditioner sales.*

form the basis for even more sophisticated forecasting methods that are available today, it is important for a modern manager to be informed about them.

Moving Averages

Suppose sales of a company's product had been 1000 units, 1500 units, and 1400 units for each of the last three years, respectively. Given no other information, how would you forecast sales for the next year? One of your first ideas might be to average the three numbers and make that the forecast for fourth-year sales. This is how your calculation would work.

$$\frac{1000 + 1500 + 1400}{3} = 1300 \text{ units/average year}$$

Simple Moving Averages

Computing the average sales was a good idea. In fact, it forms the basis of the **moving-average** method of forecasting, which simply averages past data over a specific time period and uses that result to forecast the future. A 6-month moving average would average the past 6 months of data to project every seventh month; a 12-month moving average would average the past 12 months of data. The reason this method is called a "moving" average is that as time goes by and new data are obtained, the newest value is added and the oldest is dropped to "move" the average forward in time.

Let's take another example. A 6-month moving average for the following data comes out to be 110.17 units per month. Check the calculations to make sure you understand the logic.

Month	Sales
January	100
February	120
March	108
April	130
May	98
June	105

Now, suppose that you learn July's sales are 102. To compute a new 6-month moving average, simply include this new data point in the average and drop January's. The new moving average is

$$\frac{120 + 108 + 130 + 98 + 105 + 102}{6} = 110.5$$

To forecast using moving averages, take the most recent average and use that to forecast the next time period. In the prior example, 110.17 would have been the forecast for July sales; 110.5 becomes the forecast for August sales. Table A.1 demonstrates this forecasting method for a group of 3-month moving averages.

TABLE A.1 *Forecasting by Three-Month Simple Moving Averages*

Month	Sales	3-Month Average	Forecast for Month of
January	100		
February	120		
March	108	109.33	April
April	130	119.33	May
May	98	112.00	June
June	105	111.00	July
July	102	101.67	August

Weighted Moving Averages

A **weighted-moving average** assigns a predetermined weight to each data point and thereby puts more weight on *recent* time periods as a basis for forecasting using the moving-average method. This is logical because more recent time periods may better reflect what will happen in the immediate future.

Using the January–June sales figures presented earlier, a 6-month weighted moving average might look as follows.

$$0.05(100) + 0.05(120) + 0.15(108) + 0.20(130) + 0.25(98) + 0.30(105) = 109.20$$

The "weights" assigned to each month's sales in this computation are 0.05, 0.05, 0.15, 0.20, 0.25, and 0.30. Note two things about these weights. First, the greatest weight is on June sales, the most *recent* time period. Second, the weights all together *add up to 1*. Managers can use whatever weights they desire for a weighted moving-average forecast, as long as these two rules are followed: (1) more recent time periods should be weighted more heavily than more distant time periods; and (2) the sum of all weights should equal 1.0.

The Theory of Moving Averages

To make good managerial decisions regarding the use of moving averages in forecasting, you should understand the theory underlying them. Of the four components of any time series, recall that the only one we *cannot* forecast is the random component. Think for a moment what the random component does. Sometimes it makes demand higher than usual, other times it makes demand lower. In effect, a random component causes variations around some value that demand otherwise would have been if the random event hadn't occurred. A moving-average forecast "averages out" random components to project what would have happened in their absence. The future is forecasted as if past data did not have random components. Of course, this means that forecasts will sometimes be too high and other times too low. But don't be alarmed. This is entirely consistent with the two basic rules of forecasting.

Rule 1 A forecast is never 100 percent accurate.
Rule 2 If it is, something's wrong.

Because random components are inevitable and because they can never be forecasted, a forecast will never be precise. In fact, 10 percent forecasting error is considered good.

Exponential Smoothing

Moving averages require the storage of a lot of historical data. This is a problem. It's not uncommon for organizations to forecast demand for over 1000 end products or services. If just 12-month moving averages were used for forecasting, 12,000 numbers would have to be stored and regularly updated over time. **Exponential smoothing** helps overcome this data-storage problem. This forecasting method uses exponential weights to accomplish the weighted moving average. It thus requires fewer historical data.

Exponential smoothing uses a **smoothing constant** alpha (α), which has a value greater than 0 but less than 1. To forecast demand for a future time period (e.g., next week or next month) using exponential smoothing, the original forecast for the present period is added to alpha multiplied by the difference between actual demand in the present period and the original forecast. The *exponential smoothing equation* is expressed as follows.

In words

Forecast for next period = present forecast plus alpha times (actual demand minus present forecast)

In mathematical symbols

$$F_{t+1} = F_t + \alpha(D_t - F_t)$$

where,

$t + 1$ = next time period
t = present time period
$F_t + 1$ = forecasted demand for next period
F_t = forecasted demand for present period
D_t = actual demand for present period
α = the smoothing constant

Suppose it is April and a manager wants to forecast demand for May. The original forecast for April demand was 105 units ($F_t = 105$); actual demand was only 100 (D_t = 100). A smoothing constant of α = 0.2 is chosen. Plugging these numbers into the exponential smoothing equation results in a forecasted demand for 104 units in May. Check this answer by working through the example yourself.

From this example you can see that forecasting by exponential smoothing requires only two data points, the original forecast and actual demand for the present time period (F_t and D_t, respectively). This greatly reduces the data-storage requirements compared to the weighted-average methods.

The choice of the smoothing constant or alpha (α) value is critical in exponential smoothing. The more weight desired on recent data, the higher the alpha value that should be used. It is common to choose alpha values between 0.1 and 0.3 in practice. As a rule of thumb, the value of alpha uses the same number of time periods as a moving average of $2/\alpha - 1$ periods. An α = 0.2, for example, corresponds roughly to a 9-period moving average. The *rule of thumb for determining alpha* is expressed as follows.

In words

Alpha = 2 divided by (the number of time periods in a moving average plus 1)

In mathematical symbols

$$\alpha = \frac{2}{n + 1}$$

where,

n = number of time periods in moving average

Regression Analysis

Both the moving-average and exponential-smoothing methods of forecasting work by "averaging out" random components. In the process, however, they can also average out important seasonal, trend, and cyclical time-series components. Thus moving averages and exponential smoothing are best used for short-range forecasting looking a few months and definitely less than a year ahead. **Regression analysis** provides for a medium-range or long-range forecast by comparing past variation in demand against the variation present in another and more predictable variable. Let's illustrate the technique by example.

Consider a company that sells computer programs or software packages. The demand for computer programs probably depends to some extent on the number of computers in use. Note that this assumption nicely fits the basic principle of regression analysis. That is, we should be able to systematically compare past variation in the demand for computer programs with corresponding changes in the numbers of computers in use. This historical comparison, in turn, should allow a forecast of future demand for programs to be made.

In regression analysis the variable whose behavior is being forecasted or predicted for a future period is called the **dependent variable.** Because demand for the computer programs depends on the number of computers in use, it is the dependent variable in our example. An **independent variable** in regression analysis is the one presumed to influence what happens to the dependent variable. In the example, the number of computers in use is an independent variable because it is presumed to influence the demand for computer programs. The essence of regression analysis is to develop a formula that systematically relates the dependent variable to one or more independent variables. This formula can then be used to forecast demand for the dependent variable based on projected values for the independent variables.

Listed below are hypothetical data for the number of computers in use (in millions) and computer software program sales (in ten thousands) for seven years.

Year	Computers in Use (millions)	Program Sales (ten thousands)
1	1	2
2	2	1
3	3	4
4	4	3
5	5	4
6	6	6
7	7	4

Figure A.4 graphs the relationship between these two variables as a series of plotted data points. In general, you can see that there seems to be a trend

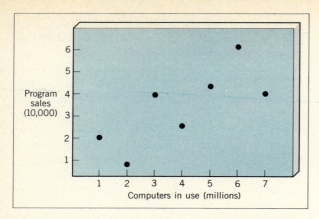

FIGURE A.4 *Historical time series data: annual sales of computers and software programs.*

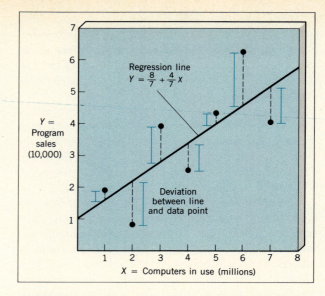

FIGURE A.5 *Least squares regression line: the case of computer and software program sales.*

or straight-line relationship between these two variables. Regression analysis allows this relationship to be described in a formula that can then be used to forecast the dependent variable into subsequent time periods. A mathematical technique called least-squares analysis helps determine which straight line fits the data best. This is the one that minimizes the deviations from all data points. Use of this technique for these data results in the regression line shown in Figure A.5.

The *equation for a straight-line regression analysis,* such as the one shown in the figure, follows.

In words

Dependent variable = constant plus another constant multiplied by independent variable

In mathematical symbols

$$Y = a + bX$$

where,

  Y = dependent variable (e.g., demand for computer programs)
  X = independent variable (e.g., computers in use)
  a, b = constants

Actual values for the constants in a straight-line regression equation are determined by statistical methods, often accomplished on computers. For the example in Figure A.5, $a = 8/7$, $b = 4/7$. Thus the formal regression equation for these data is $Y = 8/7 + 4/7\ X$. This equation represents the straight line that best describes the historical relationship between computer program sales and numbers of computers in use.

To use this equation for forecasting purposes, a manager simply plugs the projected number of computers in use into the equation to generate a forecast for the associated computer program sales. Suppose it is estimated that there will be 8 million computers in the next year. Plugging $X = 8$ in the regression equation ($Y = 8/7 + 4/7\ X$) results in $Y = 5\ 5/7$. In terms of the example, we would forecast demand for computer programs in that year as about 57,142 (that is, $5\ 5/7 \times 10,000$).

A number of sophisticated regression techniques are available. They can accommodate a variety of historical data patterns and forecasting needs, even to the point of making forecasts by the analysis of multiple independent variables. Such multivariate regression analyses accomplished with the aid of computers are increasingly common in forecasting.

LINEAR PROGRAMMING

Linear programming is one of the most widely known and frequently used MS/OR techniques. Like all other MS/OR methods, it is based on formulating a problem in mathematical terms. The basic purpose of linear programming is to help the manager decide how to best allocate scarce resources among competing uses.

Consider the case of Ajax Computer Products. Ajax produces diskettes for microcomputers in two sizes: 5¼ and 3½ inches. Ajax is planning the production of disks for the coming week. Each disk requires both manufacturing and testing time, as shown in Table A.2. In the manufacturing process time can be considered a scarce resource. This week 1200 minutes of manufacturing time and 1500 minutes of testing time will be available. Each 5¼-inch disk contributes $3 of profit, and each 3½-inch disk contributes $5.

Every linear programming problem consists of two basic parts: the **objective function** and the **constraints.** In this problem, Ajax's objective is to maximize its profit. The constraints are the manufacturing and testing times which limit how many disks can be produced. The problem is to decide how many disks of each size to make.

Objective Function

The objective function can be formulated for this case by letting the variable X represent the number of 5¼-inch disks to produce and the variable Y represent the number of 3½-inch disks. If Ajax earns $3 profit per 5¼-inch disk, then total profit from that size disk will be $3X$. Likewise, total profit from 3½-inch disks will be $5Y$. Thus, the objective function is

$$\text{Maximize } 3X + 5Y$$

TABLE A.2 *Ajax Computer Products Company Case Information: Manufacturing Data on Floppy Disks*

	Disk Size		Time Available (minutes)
	5¼ inches	3½ inches	
Manufacturing time	2	3	1200
Testing time	2	5	1500
Profit per unit	$3	$5	

In other words, Ajax wants to maximize its total profit from producing both the 5¼- and the 3½-inch disks.

Constraints

Since the objective function represents profit, it would certainly be attractive to make profit as large as possible. However, the constraints on time available for manufacturing and testing limit how many disks can be made during this week.

Recall from Table A.3 that each 5¼-inch disk requires 2 minutes of manufacturing time. Thus, the manufacturing time needed to produce 5¼-inch disks is $2X$, where X again represents the number of 5¼-inch disks produced. The manufacturing time for 3½-inch disks is $3Y$. Thus, total manufacturing time for both size disks will be $2X + 3Y$. Since only 1200 minutes of manufacturing time is available this week, the total manufacturing time used to produce disks must be "less-than-or-equal-to" ($\leq$) 1200. In mathematical terms this is stated as the following equation.

$$2X + 3Y \leq 1200$$

A similar constraint can also be formulated for the amount of testing time available. It turns out to be

$$2X + 5Y \leq 1500$$

Still one more constraint must be added to the problem. Although it may seem obvious to you, we must also specify that the number of disks to be produced of either size cannot be negative. This *nonnegativity restriction* is stated mathematically as

$$X, Y \geq 0$$

In words, this equation says that X and Y must both be "greater-than-or-equal-to" zero.

LP Formulation of the Problem

The following linear programming (LP) formulation of the Ajax production problem is obtained by combining the objective function and all constraints.

Objective function: Maximize $3X + 5Y$

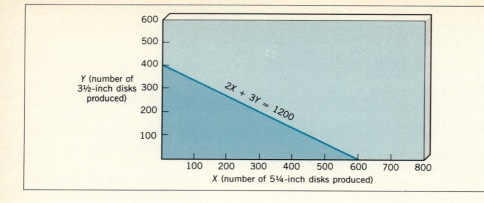

FIGURE A.6 *Ajax linear programming problem: plotting the first problem constraint.*

Subject to constraints:
$$2X + 3Y \leq 1200$$
$$2X + 5Y \leq 1500$$
$$X, Y \geq 0$$

Before we move on to solve this problem, there are two additional things you should notice. First, the mathematical functions (objective function and constraints) are *linear*. That is, if you graph them they appear as straight lines. They do not include any nonlinear terms like $X \cdot Y$ or X^2. The technique we are discussing is called *linear* programming because it deals with *linear* functions. Another field called *nonlinear programming* does deal with nonlinear objective functions and constraints.

A second thing to note is that, although Ajax's problem involved only two variables and three constraints, complex linear programming problems may actually involve thousands of variables and hundreds of constraints. Fortunately, they are made relatively easy to solve by the assistance of computers.

Graphic Solution

At this point you may have your own ideas about the optimal (profit maximizing) solution to Ajax's problem. If so, jot it down in the margin now so we can compare results later.

Because the Ajax problem involves only two variables, X and Y, Ajax's management decided to solve the problem graphically. To begin, they plotted the constraint $2X + 3Y \leq 1200$, as shown in Figure A.6. While $2X + 3Y$ may be less than 1200, the largest value it can assume is $2X + 3Y = 1200$. As graphed in Figure A.6, this line sets the limit for the constraint. The line and the entire shaded area below it thus represent all possible values of X and Y that satisfy the constraint $2X + 3Y \leq 1200$.

The other constraint ($2X + 5Y \leq 1500$) and the nonnegativity restriction ($X, Y \geq 0$) can be added to the graph as shown in Figure A.7. This time, though, the shaded area includes only values that satisfy all the constraints and restrictions. It is called the **feasible region** because any feasible so-

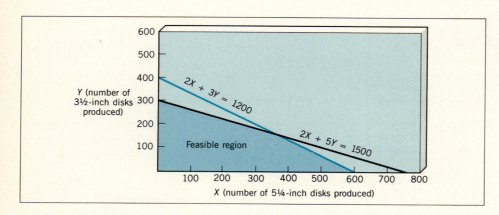

FIGURE A.7 *Ajax linear programming problem: establishing the feasible region.*

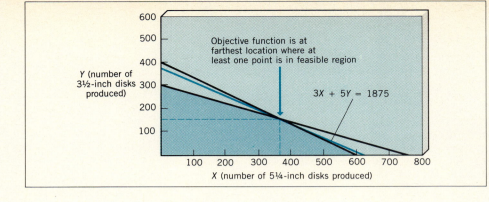

FIGURE A.8 *Ajax linear programming problem: setting the objective function and finding the solution.*

lution—that is, one that satisfies all the constraints—must lie either in this shaded area or on the lines that bound it.

The question to be answered now is: "Which point in the feasible region will maximize profit?" To find that point, the objective function must be added to the graph. Since the objective function is stated as maximize $3X + 5Y$, the line which represents it should be moved out to the farthest location where at least one point is still in the feasible region. Figure A.8 shows that this occurs where the two constraint lines meet. This mathematically occurs at

$$2X + 3Y = 1200$$
$$2X + 5Y = 1500$$

By mathematically solving these two equations, we find the optimal point occurs at $X = 375$ and $Y = 150$, and the maximum profit is $1875. In other words, Ajax should produce 375 of the 5¼-inch disks and 150 of the 3½-inch ones to arrive at maximum profit of $1875.

Mathematical Programming

Linear programming is actually part of a larger component of MS/OR called **mathematical programming.** This technique uses more sophisticated mathematics, frequently with the aid of a computer, to solve more complex problems. For example, as you have probably realized by now, the graphic approach used here only works for problems with two variables. Since one axis of the graph is needed for each variable, it it difficult to handle problems with three variables and it is impossible to solve

graphically a linear programming problem involving four or more variables. For such problems, a mathematical programming approach called the *simplex method* is applied.

The linear programming solution in the Ajax problem turned out in whole numbers. But what if it had been $X = 375¼$ and $Y = 150⅞$? Ajax cannot produce one-fourth or seven-eights of a disk, but simply rounding the solution to the nearest integer (whole number) may not provide the optimal solution. In fact, such a solution may not even be feasible! To handle problems in which the solution must be in terms of whole numbers, *integer programming* is used. This approach is explained in most MS/OR textbooks.

MINIMUM SPANNING TREE PROBLEMS

Chapter 16 introduced PERT (Program Evaluation and Review Technique) and CPM (Critical Path Method) as techniques for handling network problems. These are problems that can be depicted as an interconnected series of events or activities that must be completed in sequential combinations for a solution or finished task to be achieved.

PERT/CPM is a valuable tool that can help managers plan projects and make sure they stay on schedule. It turns out that many other important managerial problems can be solved as network problems, even some you would not think of in network terms. As a future manager, you should at least be aware of some of these.

Consider the case of the Rolling Greens Country Club. The club's board of directors has decided

TABLE A.3 *Rolling Greens Country Club Case Information: Matrix of Distances (ft) between Sprinkler Connections*

Connection		10	11	12	13	14	15	16	17	18
Connection	—	220	125	325	475	555	600	700	510	315
10	220	—	280	430	410	400	560	745	660	480
11	125	280	—	205	400	525	510	580	400	210
12	325	430	205	—	350	530	390	400	230	130
13	475	410	400	350	—	210	165	400	560	480
14	555	400	525	530	210	—	325	590	760	655
15	600	560	510	390	165	325	—	260	550	530
16	700	745	580	400	400	590	260	—	430	510
17	510	660	400	230	560	760	550	430	—	190
18	315	480	210	130	480	655	530	510	190	—

to install a water sprinkler system on the back nine holes of the golf course. Because the cost of the system will be directly proportional to the amount of pipe used, the board wants to minimize the amount of pipe needed to connect all nine holes to the sprinkler network. Table A.3 gives a matrix of distances between all nine greens.

This is a **minimum spanning tree** problem. Think of each circle and sprinkler connection in Figure A.9 as a "node," with "arcs" being all possible lines connecting these nodes. To solve the Rolling Greens problem you must find those arcs that connect all nodes in the shortest total distance. Laying the pipe in conformance to this network will minimize the cost of pipe required in the sprinkler system.

To do that, begin at the sprinkler connection and link it to the nearest green. Based on Table A.4, that is Green 11 with a distance of 125 feet. Now find the green closest to either 11 *or* the sprinkler connection. Be sure *not* to include 11 or the sprinkler connection because they are already connected. The shortest will be from 11 to 12 with a distance of 205. Continue by finding the shortest distance from any connected node to any unconnected node. These will be 12 to 18, 18 to 17, sprinkler connection to 10, 12 to 13, 13 to 14, 13 to 15, and 15 to 16. The final solution is shown in Figure A.4.

There are many other network problems of the minimum spanning tree type. For example, you can use network methods to find the shortest route for trucks to take between cities or to decide when an assembly line should be changed to produce a different product. MS/OR offers a variety of mathematical approaches to complex minimum spanning tree problems. Again, the computer is an important resource for solving these problems efficiently and effectively.

FIGURE A.9 *Minimum spanning tree: the Rolling Greens Country Club case.*

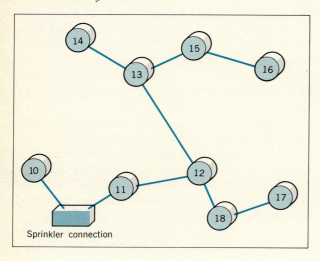

Sprinkler connection

QUEUING THEORY

Place yourself in the following situation. The Mid-Continent Bank is building a drive-up window to serve customers who wish to transact business from their cars. The bank's manager is trying to decide whether to staff the window with one teller or two. Two tellers will cost more, but they can handle customers at a faster rate than one teller.

To help solve this problem, the responsible manager can use the stochastic MS/OR technique

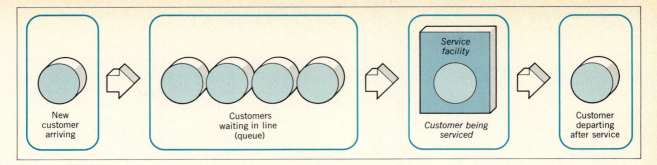

| New customer arriving | Customers waiting in line (queue) | Customer being serviced (Service facility) | Customer departing after service |

FIGURE A.10 *A queuing problem: the case of Mid-Conniental Bank.*

known as **queuing theory.** A queue is simply a waiting line. The goal of queuing theory is to compute the number of service personnel or work stations needed to minimize customer waiting time and service cost. The ideas underlying queuing theory include recognition that (1) customers arriving at a service facility will have to wait in line—(as shown in Figure A.10 (2) the rate at which these customers arrive is variable, and (3) the time it takes for each customer to be serviced is also variable.

For most queuing problems it is necessary to develop a probability distribution for the number of arrivals per time period, such as arrivals per hour. In general, queuing systems have been found to approximate the Poisson probability distribution for arrivals during a given time period. The equation for this distribution is

$$P(n) = \frac{e^{-\lambda t}(\lambda t)^n}{n!}$$

where,

n = number of customers arriving (1, 2, . . .)
t = time period (minute, hour, etc.)
λ = mean number of arrivals per time period t
e = constant, approximately 2.72

It has also been found that the time to service each customer usually follows an exponential probability distribution. Its equation is

$$P(t) = \mu e^{-\mu t}$$

where,

t = service time
μ = mean number of services per given time period (minute, hour, etc.)
e = constant, approximately 2.72

Fortunately, these two probability distributions need not be dealt with directly. Using them as a basis, mathematicians have developed the following set equations that can give you extremely useful information on a queuing problem.

λ/μ = proportion of time the service facility is busy

$\dfrac{\lambda^2}{\mu(\mu - \lambda)}$ = mean length of the queue

$\dfrac{\lambda}{\mu(\mu - \lambda)}$ = mean customer time spent waiting

where,

λ = mean number of arrivals during a given time period (minute, hour, day)
μ = mean service rate (in terms of same time period as λ)

Let's return now to the Mid-Continent Bank and apply these formulas to the facts at hand. Suppose the bank manager expects that the mean arrival rate (λ) will be 20 cars per hour. With one teller, the mean service rate (μ) is 30 cars per hour and with two it is 40 per hour. Using this information and the prior formulas, the following computations can be made to facilitate the decision of whether to use one teller or two.

One Teller Case

Facts:

$$\lambda = 20$$
$$\mu = 30$$

Computations

    Proportion of time busy = 66.7 percent
    Mean length of queue   = $1\frac{1}{3}$
    Mean time spent waiting = 4 minutes

Two Teller Case

Facts:

$$\lambda = 20$$
$$\mu = 40$$

Computations:

    Proportion of time busy = 50 percent
    Mean length of queue   = 1/2 car
    Mean waiting time   = 1.5 minutes

Armed with this information provided by queuing theory, the manager is now in a better position to decide whether to add the second teller.

SIMULATION

In the case of Mid-Continent Bank you were able to use some fairly simple formulas to obtain useful information on the queuing problem. These formulas were based on the Poisson and exponential probability distributions and they made your work much easier than if you had to deal directly with the equations for those probability distributions. But what if the number of arrivals per time period at the bank did not follow the Poisson distribution, or what if the service times were not exponential? In these cases you could not have used the formulas presented.

Indeed, there are often problem situations in real life that do not match any standard mathematical formula. In such cases the MS/OR approach of **simulation** can be a useful decision-making technique.

The purpose of simulation is essentially to develop a mathematical model that resembles as closely as possible the real-life decision situation, and then use a computer to solve the problem many times under various decision circumstances. For example, suppose the manager of Mid-Continent Bank found that the number of arrivals per hour did *not* match the Poisson probability distribution and that service time also did *not* match the exponential distribution. Instead, the manager observed the actual flow of cars through the drive-up window for a time. Table A.4 presents the data collected from this observation.

The table shows that in 20 percent of the cases there was 0 to 2 minutes observed between each new customer arrival; in 60 percent of the cases there was 2 to 4 minutes between arrivals; and in another 20 percent there was a 4 to 6 minute interval. Similarly, service time was between 0 to 1 minute in 10 percent of all cases, and so on, as shown in the table.

These data can be used to develop a probability model of the drive-up window service. To do this, however, we need some way of generating time between arrivals of 0 to 2 minutes 20 percent of the time, and so on, to match the real-life situation. This can be done by using *random numbers*.

Nearly any statistics book includes a table of random numbers. The idea behind such a table is that the probability of any number occurring is the same as that for any other number. Thus, for the 10 digits zero through nine, the probability of any particular number being found at a given location in the table is 1/10.

TABLE A.4 *Mid-Continental Bank Case Information: Flow of Cars Through the Service Window*

Time Between Arrivals	Percentage of Arrivals	Random Digits
0–2	20	0, 1
2–4	60	2–7
4–6	20	8, 9

Service Time (minutes)	Service Time Percentage	Random Digits
0–1	10	0
1–2	40	1–4
2–3	40	5–8
3–4	10	9

Arrival No.	Arrival Time	Random No.	Time Before Next Arrival (minutes)	No. in Line	Time Enter Service	Random No.	Service Time (minutes)	Depart Service
1	0:00	7	3	0	0:00	9	3.5	0:03.5
2	0:03	1	1	1	0:03.5	4	1.5	0:05
3	0:04	0	1	1	0:05	9	3.5	0:08.5
4	0:05	4	3	1	0:08.5	0	0.5	0:09
5	0:08	8	5	1	0:09	4	1.5	0:10.5
6	0:13	0	1	0	0:13	3	1.5	0:14.5
7	0:14	8	5	1	0:14.5	1	1.5	0:16
8	0:19	1	1	0	0:19	2	1.5	0:20.5
9	0:20	7	3	1	0:20.5	7	2.5	0:23
10	0:23	8	5	0	0:23	3	1.5	0:24.5

The way random numbers are used for simulation purposes is as follows. Look again at the data collected by Mid-Continent Bank. The probability of 0 to 2 minutes lapsing between arrivals is 0.2 — that is, a 20 percent probability. This corresponds to the probability of finding two numbers (say 0 and 1) in a table of random numbers (0.1 + 0.1 = 0.2). For a probability of 0.6 we can use six different numbers (say 2 through 7). In this way we can relate the occurrence of certan digits in a random number table to probabilities of various arrival times shown in Table A.4. Thus if a 4 is drawn from the random number table, it corresponds either to a time between arrivals of 2 to 4 minutes or a service time of 1 to 2 minutes.

Using this scheme the staff of Mid-Continent Bank was able to simulate the drive-up window. They used the midpoint of each range of times to represent the whole range (e.g., 1 minute for 0 to 2 minutes between arrivals). Part of their results are shown in Table A.5. For each car that arrives, if the service facility is free, it enters. Otherwise, it waits in line until the window is free.

The same approach can be used to simulate many other situations, from traffic flow on a highway to the operation of a coal mine. Most simulations are done via computer. Like all the other MS/OR approaches discussed, they can assist you in making certain types of managerial decisions.

Glossary

The numbers in parentheses after the term indicate the chapters in which the term was defined.

Abdication (or Laissez-faire leadership) (10)   A leadership style that displays low concern for both people and task.

Accommodation (in conflict management) (17)   Playing down differences among conflicting parties, and highlighting similarities and areas of agreement.

Accountability (1, 6)   The requirement for the subordinate to answer to the supervisor for results accomplished in the performance of any assigned duties.

Action research (17)   A process of systematically collecting data on an organization, feeding it back for action planning, and evaluating results by collecting and reflecting on more data after the planned actions have been taken.

Active listening (11)   Taking action to help the source of a message to say what he or she really means.

Activities (13)   The verbal and nonverbal behaviors in which group members engage.

Administrator (1)   A manager who works in a public or nonprofit organization as opposed to a business concern.

Affirmative-action program (9)   Program designed to increase employment opportunities for women and other minorities including veterans, the aged, and the handicapped.

Agency shop (18)   A labor-management agreement that requires all nonsupervisory employees of an organization to pay a service fee to a union, even though they don't officially have to join.

Aggregate scheduling (16)   The process of making a rough cut or first approximation to a production/operations schedule based on a demand forecast.

Applications software (15)   Computer software which allows the user to perform a variety of information-based tasks without writing his or her own programs.

Apprenticeship (9)   A special form of training that involves formal assignment to serve as understudy or assistant to a person already having the desired job skills.

Arbitration (18)   The process by which parties to a labor-management dispute agree to abide by the decision of a neutral and independent third party called an arbitrator.

Art (1)   Something a person practices based on skills applied to achieve a desired result.

Artificial intelligence (15)   A field of study into the ability of a computer to reason the way people do by making interconnections among various stored bits and pieces of information and using the results for decision making.

Assessment center (9)   A selection technique that engages job candidates in a series of experiential activities over a one- or two-day period.

Authoritative command (in conflict management) (17)   When formal authority dictates a conflict solution and specifies what is gained or lost and by whom.

Authority-and-responsibility principle (6)   Authority should equal responsibility when work is delegated from supervisor to subordinate.

Authority decision (10)   A decision made by the manager and then communicated to the group.

Autocratic (or Directive) leadership (10)   A leadership style displaying a high concern for the task and low concern for people.

Automated guided vehicles (AGVs) (16)   Driverless transports which use computer control to guide them in moving materials from one location to another in the workplace.

Automation (8, 16)   The total mechanization of a job.

Autonomous work groups (8)   Self-managed work team with responsibility for accomplishing defined performance objectives, and with discretion to decide how tasks will be distributed among individuals and at what pace work will progress in order to meet these objectives.

Autonomy (8)   The degree to which a job gives the individual substantial freedom, independence, and discretion in scheduling the work and in determining the procedures to be used in carrying it out.

Avoidance (in conflict management) (17)   Pretending that a conflict doesn't really exist; hoping that a conflict will simply go away.

Bargaining unit (18)   The organization or subunit of an organization that would eventually be subject to union representation.

Batch operations (16)   Operations which "batch" together items for similar production or service runs.

Behavioral decision theory (3)   A view of decision making that assumes managers act only in terms of what they perceive about a given situation.

Behaviorally anchored rating scale (BARS) (14)   A performance-appraisal method based on explicit descriptions of actual behaviors that exemplify various levels of performance achievement.

Benchmarking (4)   The use of external comparisons to gain added perspective on current performance and help initiate the planning process.

Bill of capacity (16)   A document showing how much standard time is needed on each machine to make one finished part in a manufacturing operation.

Bona fide occupational qualifications (9)   Employment criteria which can clearly be justified as related to someone's capacity to perform a specific job.

Bonus pay plans (12)   Provide cash bonuses to employees based on the achievement of specific performance targets.

Bottom-up budgeting (15)   A budget process which begins with the needs and suggestions of lower-level personnel.

Bottom-up planning (4)   Planning that begins with plans developed at lower management levels without constraints, that are then passed up the hierarchy to top management levels.

Brainstorming (3)   A group technique for generating a large quantity of ideas by freewheeling contributions being made without criticism.

Break-even analysis (15)   The study of the relationship between budgeted revenues and costs to determine how changes in each affect profit.

Break-even point (15)   The point where total revenue from sales is just sufficient to cover total costs. Break-even point equals fixed costs divided by selling price per unit minus variable cost per unit of production.

Budget (4, 15)   A plan that commits resources to projects or programs; a formalized way of allocating resources to specific activities.

Bureaucracy (2, 7)   An intentionally rational and efficient form of organization founded on principles of logic, order, and legitimate authority.

Business strategy (5)   Identification of the intentions of a division or strategic business unit to compete in its special product and/or service domain.

Cafeteria benefits (14)   An employee-benefits program that allows workers to select within a given monetary limit a combination of benefits that best meets their needs.

Capacity planning (16)   The scheduling of resource utilization in the production/operations process.

Career (21)   A sequence of jobs and work activities constituting what a person does for a living.

Career path (21)   A sequence of jobs held over time during a career.

Career planning (21)   The process of systematically matching career goals and individual capabilities with opportunities for their fulfillment.

Career plateau (21)   A position from which someone is not likely to move to a higher level of work responsibility.

Carrying costs (or Holding costs) (16)   The actual cost of items going into inventory, as well as the cost of storing and insuring them against loss.

Central processing unit (CPU) (15)   The collection of electronic circuitry that controls the computer and allows it to store and perform a variety of computational operations on data according to the instructions of programs.

Centralization (6)   The concentration of authority for most decisions at the top levels of an organization.

Centralized planning economy (19)   A market system where basic economic decisions for an entire country are made by a central government body.

Certainty (3)   A problem environment in which the information is sufficient to predict the results of each alternative in advance of implementation.

Certification election (18)   An election, held under the provisions of the National Labor Relations Act and supervised by the National Labor Relations Board, through which employees secretly ballot on whether or not a union should represent them with an employer.

Chain of command (6)   An unbroken line of authority that vertically links all persons in an organization with successively higher levels of authority.

Change agent (17)   A person or group taking responsibility for changing the existing pattern of behavior of another person or social system.

Chief information officer (15)   A senior executive whose responsibilities entail overseeing computer operations and information systems within an organization.

Choice making (3)   The process or evaluating and selecting among alternative solutions to a problem.

Classical decision theory (3)   A view of decision making that assumes managers act on the basis of complete certainty about a given situation.

Closed shop (18)   A labor-management agreement that requires a person to be a union member in good standing *before* being hired.

Closed system (2)   A system that does not interact with its environment.

Coaching (9)   The communication of specific technical advice to an individual.

Codes of ethics (20)   Written documents which state commitments to values and ethical conduct that an employer expects to guide the behavior of employees.

Coercive power (10)   The capability to punish or withhold positive outcomes as a means of controlling other people.

Cohesiveness (13)   The degree to which members are attracted to a group and are motivated to remain part of it.

Collaboration (in conflict management) (17)   Seeking true satisfaction of everyone's concerns; working through differences and solving problems so everyone wins as a result.

Collective bargaining (18)   The process of negotiating, administering, and interpreting a formal agreement or labor contract between a union and the employing organization.

Combination strategy (5)   A strategy that involves stability, growth, and retrenchment in one or more combinations.

Command group (13)   A formal group consisting of a manager and his or her immediate subordinates

Communication (11)   An interpersonal process of sending and receiving symbols with meanings attached to them.

Communication channel (11)   The medium through which a message is conveyed from sender to receiver.

Comparable worth (12, 18)   The principle that persons doing jobs equivalent in skill and importance should receive equal pay.

Comparative management (19)   The study of how management practices systematically differ from one country and/or culture to the next.

Competition (in conflict management) (17)   When a conflict victory is achieved through force, superior skill, or domination of one party by another.

Compressed workweek (8)   Any work schedule that allows a full-time job to be completed in less than the standard five days of eight-hour shifts.

Compromise (in conflict management) (17)   When accommodations are made such that each party to the conflict gives up something of value to the other.

Computer integrated manufacturing (CIM) (16)   Using a variety of computer applications to automate and integrate operations management activities in the manufacturing process.

Computer-aided design (CAD) (16)   Using computers to create and rapidly change engineering designs as needed.

Computer-aided manufacturing (CAM) (16) Using computers to monitor the production process, link machines and operations to one another, and provide feedback for control purposes.

Computer-aided process planning (CPP) (16) Using computers to plan operations and determine the best routings of parts through a series of machines.

Computer numerical control (CNC) (16) Using computers to store instructions on various machines operations which can be selected to perform specific operations.

Conceptual skill (1) The ability to view the organization or situation as a whole and solve problems to the benefit of everyone concerned.

Conciliation (18) A process of intervention in labor–management disputes through which a neutral party tries to keep the parties to a dispute focused on the issues of disagreement.

Concurrent control (or Steering control) (14) Control that acts in anticipation of problems and focus primarily on what happens during the work process.

Conflict (17) A disagreement in a social situation over issues of substances and/or emotional antagonism.

Conflict resolution (17) The removal of the reasons—substantial and/or emotional—for a conflict.

Constructive conflict (17) Conflict which results in benefits instead of disadvantages for the individual(s) and/or organization(s) involved.

Constructive stress (21) Stress that acts in a positive or energizing way to increase effort, stimulate creativity, and encourage diligence in one's work.

Consultative decision (10) A decision for which each group member provides information, advice, or opinion, which is then used by the manager to make a final decision on behalf of the group.

Content theories (12) Motivation theories that offer ways to profile or analyze individuals to identify their needs.

Contingency (2) An approach of modern management theory that there is no one best way to manage, and that what is best depends in any given circumstance on the nature of the situation.

Contingency planning (4) The process of identifying alternative courses of action that can be used to modify an original plan if and when circumstances change with the passage of time.

Continuous-process technology (7, 16) A technology involving the continuous feeding of w materials into an automated system of duction.

Continuous reinforcement (12) Administering a reward every time a desired behavior occurs.

Contributions (8) Work activities of value the individual offers to the organization in return for inducements.

Control chart (16) A graphic display of work results that clearly delineates upper control limits (UCL) and lower control limits (LCL).

Control process (14) The process of establishing performance objectives and standards, measuring actual performance, comparing actual performance with objectives and standards, and taking necessary action.

Controlling (14) The process of monitoring performance and taking action to ensure desired results.

Coordination (6) The process of linking the specialized activities of individuals and groups to one another, and ensuring that a common purpose is served.

Corporate culture (5) The predominant value system for the organization as a whole.

Corporate social responsibility (2, 20) An obligation of an organization to act in ways that serve both its own interests and the interests of its many external publics.

Corporate strategy (5) Strategy that sets the direction of and serves as a resource allocation guide for the total enterprise.

Cost-benefit analysis (3) Comparing the costs and benefits of each potential course of action.

Cost center (or Expense center) (15) A responsibility center where budgets and performance targets concentrate on the utilization of resource inputs measured in monetary terms as expenses.

Critical path method (CPM) (16) A network-modeling technique that breaks the various phases off a production/operations project into a sequence of events and the activities leading to those events.

Craft unions (18) Labor unions that represent

workers in single crafts or occupations—for example, carpenters, plumbers, or electricians.

Creativity (3, 17)   An application of ingenuity and imagination that results in a novel approach or unique solution to a problem.

Critical-incident technique (14)   A performance-appraisal method that involves a running log or inventory of effective and ineffective job behaviors.

Culture (19)   A shared set of beliefs, values, and patterns of behavior common to a group of people.

Culture shock (19)   The confusion and discomfort someone experiences when in an unfamiliar culture.

Customer departmentation (6)   Grouping together jobs and activities serving specific customers and/or clients.

Cybernetic control system (14)   A control system that is entirely self-contained in its performance-monitoring and correction capabilities.

Data (15)   Raw facts such as figures and other symbols used to represent people, events, and concepts.

Decentralization (6)   The dispersion of authority to make decisions throughout all levels of management by extensive delegation.

Decertification (of unions) (18)   A means through which employees can revoke the certification of a union previously certified as their bargaining agent.

Decision making (3)   The process that encompasses all activities ranging from the identification of a problem through the actual choice of a preferred problem-solving alternative.

Decision matrix (or Payoff table) (3)   An extension of decision-tree analysis to display the possible outcomes of various alternatives while taking the probabilities of their occurrence into account.

Decision-support system (3, 15)   A computerized MIS in which managers interact with the computer to request and process information in the course of solving structured and semi-structured problems.

Decision tree (3)   A graphic illustration of the alternatives available to solve a problem.

Deficit principle (12)   Maslow's principle, which holds that a satisfied need is not a motivator of behavior.

Delegation (6)   The process of distributing and entrusting work to other persons.

Delphi technique (4)   A forecasting technique wherein a panel of experts respond sequentially to a survey questionnaire soliciting opinions on future events.

Demand forecasting (16)   The process of estimating future demand for an organizer's products or services.

Democratic leadership (or Participative leadership) (10)   A person whose leadership style displays high concerns for both people and task.

Democratic system (19)   Legal–political system that relies on free elections and representative assemblies of the population to establish a government for the society as a whole.

Departmentation (6)   The creation of work units or groups by placing several jobs under the authority of a common manager.

Departmentation by division (6)   The formation of departments based on products, clients, territories, time, or projects.

Departmentation by function (6)   The formation of departments based on people performing similar or closely related activities.

Departmentation by matrix (6)   A form of organization that combines functional and divisional forms of departmentation to take best advantage of each.

Dependent inventory demand (16)   Demand, such as for component parts, that follows a "lumpy" pattern and causes inventory levels to fall in "bunches" over time.

Dependent variable (16)   A variable whose behavior depends on another variable (an independent variable); a variable whose behavior is being predicted or forecasted for some future period by regression analysis.

Destructive conflict (17)   Conflict that works to the disadvantage of the individual(s) and/or organization(s) involved.

Destructive stress (21)   Stess that is dysfunctional for the individual and/or the organization.

Differentiation (7)   The degree of difference that exists among people, departments or other internal components of an organization.

Directive leadership (or Autocratic leadership) (10)   A person whose leadership style displays a high concern for the task and low concern for people.

Discipline (14)   Influencing behavior through reprimand.

Displacement of objectives (5)   When the means become more important than the ends they were originally intended to serve.

Division of labor (1)   The process of breaking work into smaller components and allocating them as individual or group tasks designed to fit together in service of the organization's purpose.

Domain (5)   A specific product market within which an organization operates or intends to operate.

Downsizing (9)   Reducing the size of an organization by eliminating workers.

Downward communication (11)   Communication flowing from higher to lower levels in an organization's hierarchy of authority.

Dual-career couple (21)   A family or couple in which both adult partners participate in the work force and seek rewarding careers.

Economic environment (5)   Consists of customers, suppliers, and competitors whose actions have the potential to affect demand for goods or service and resource availabilities.

Economic order quantity (EOQ) (16)   A method for controlling inventory by ordering a fixed number of items each time inventory level falls to a predetermined point.

Effective communication (11)   When the intended meaning of the source and the perceived meaning of the receiver are one and the same.

Effective group (13)   A group that achieves and maintains high levels of *both* task performance and membership satisfaction over time.

Efficient communication (11)   Communication that occurs at minimum cost in terms of resources expended.

Emergent behavior (13)   What group members do in addition to or in replacement of what is asked by the organization.

Emotional conflict (17)   Conflict resulting from feelings of anger, distrust, dislike, fear, and resentment, as well as from personality clashes.

Empirical-rational change strategy (17)   A change strategy where the change agent attempts to bring about change through persuasion backed by special knowledge and rational argument.

Employee stock ownership plans (12)   Plans which involve employees in direct ownership of their employing organizations through the purchase of stock.

Enterprise-wide network (15)   A set of computer-communication linkages that link together a diverse set of activities throughout an organization.

Entrepreneur (1, 17)   A person who displays entrepreneurship and is willing to take action to pursue opportunities in situations others view as problems or threats.

Entrepreneurship (17)   Behavior that is dynamic, risk taking, creative and growth-oriented.

Entropy (2)   A universal tendency of all living systems to more toward death.

Environmental uncertainty (7)   The rate and predictability of change associated with important environmental elements.

Equal employment opportunity (EEO) (9)   The right of people to employment and advancement without regard to race, sex, religion, color, or national origin.

Equifinality (2)   The ability of a system to achieve the same end state from a variety of paths.

Escalating commitment (3)   The tendency to continue to pursue a course of action, even though it is not working.

Ethical behavior (20)   Behavior that is accepted as "right" or "good" in the context of a governing moral code.

Ethical dilemma (20)   A situation in which a manager must choose whether or not to pursue a course of action that, although offering the potential of personal or organizational benefit or both, is also unethical and/or illegal in the broader social context.

Ethical framework (20)   Personal strategies that guide ethical decision making.

Ethical managerial behavior (20)   Behavior by managers that conforms not only to law, but also to a broader set of moral principles common to society.

Ethics (20)   The code of morals of a person or

group that sets standards as to what is good or bad, or right or wrong in one's conduct.

Ethics training (20)   Training which seeks to help people better understand the ethical aspects of decision making, and to incorporate high ethical standards into their daily behaviors.

Ethnocentric corporation (19)   A multinational corporation that imposes its own philosophies and management practices on foreign operations, and maintains control through highly centralized operations.

European Economic Community (19)   An agreement among many European nations on common policies for trade and tariffs, and the flow of labor and capital across member nation's borders.

Eustress (21)   Stress that is constructive for an individual and helps them achieve a positive balance with the external environment.

Executive information system (EIS) or executive support system (15)   A computerized information system which offers special capabilities in helping top managers access, process and share information needed to make a variety of operational and strategic decisions.

Existence needs (12)   Desires for physiological and material well-being in Alderfer's ERG theory (discussed in Chapter 12).

Expense center (or Cost center) (15)   A responsibility center where budgets and performance targets concentrate on the utilization of resource inputs measured in monetary terms as expenses.

Expected problems (3)   Those problems that are anticipated as a basis for future decisions.

Expected value (3)   The dollar value of the predicted outcomes for an alternative course of action times the probability of its occurrence.

Expectancy (12)   The person's belief that working hard will enable various levels of task performance to be achieved.

Expert power (10)   The capability to control other people because of specialized knowledge.

Expert system (3, 15)   A computer program designed to analyze and solve problems at the level of the human expert.

Exponential smoothing (1MA)   A special form of weight moving average that uses exponential weights and requires less historical data to make forecasts.

External control (14)   Control that occurs through direct supervision or administrative systems such as rules and procedures.

External recruitment (9)   The process of attacting job candidates from sources external to the organization.

Extinction (12)   Decreasing the frequency of or eliminating an undesirable behavior by making the removal of a desirable consequence contingent on the occurrence of the behavior.

Facilities location planning (16)   The process of choosing a preferred location for a manufacturing or service facility.

Fact finding (18)   An approach to third-party dispute resolution where a neutral "fact finder" conducts an investigation and issues a nonbinding report and set of recommendations to conflicting parties.

Feedback (in a systems sense) (2)   Information about system performance that can be used for purposes of adaptation, control, and constructive change.

Feedback (in an interpersonal sense) (11)   The process of telling someone else how you feel about something that person did or said, or about the situation in general.

Feedback (from the job itself) (8)   The degree to which carrying out the work activities required by the job results in the individual obtaining direct and clear information on the results of his or her performance.

Feedback control (or Postaction control) (14)   Control that takes place after an action is completed.

Feed-forward control (or Precontrol) (14)   Control that is initiated prior to the start of a production or service activity.

Filtering (11)   The intentional distortion of information to make it appear most favorable to the recipient.

Firing (9)   The act of involuntary and permanent dismissal of an employee.

Fixed budget (or Static budget) (4, 15)   A budget that allocates resources on a single estimate of costs; a budget that does not allow adjustment over time.

Flexible budget (4, 15)   A budget that allows the allocation of resources to projects to vary in proportion with various levels of activity; a budget that can be adjusted over time to accommodate relevant changes in the environment.

Flexible working hours (or Flextime) (8)   Any work schedule that gives employees some choice in the pattern of daily work hours.

Force-coercion change strategy (17)   A change strategy where the change agent acts unilaterally to try to "command" change through the formal authority of his or her position, to induce change via an offer of special rewards, or to bring about change via threats of punishment.

Forecast (4, 16)   An attempt to predict outcomes; a projection into the future based on historical data combined in some scientific manner.

Formal authority (1, 10)   The authority to require that other persons contribute work activities relevant to the organization's purpose.

Formal communication channels (11)   Those communication channels that follow the chain of command established by an organization's hierarchy of authority.

Formal group (13)   A group created by the formal authority within the organization to help transform resource inputs into product or service outputs.

Formal leadership (10)   When a manager leads through the exercise of formal authority.

Formal structure (6)   The structure of the organization in its pure or ideal state.

Free-form narrative (14)   A performance-appraisal method that involves a written description of someone's job performance.

Free-market economy (19)   A market system where economic activities are generally governed by laws of supply and demand.

Friendship group (13)   Informal groups which spontaneously develop for a variety of personal reasons.

Functional authority (6)   The authority to act within a specified area of expertise and in relation to the activities of other persons or units lying outside the formal chain of command.

Functional manager (1)   A manager who has responsibility for one area of activity such as finance, marketing, production, personnel, accounting, or sales.

Functional strategy (5)   Strategy that guides the activities within various functional areas of organizational operations.

Gain sharing pay plans (12)   Pay plans which allow groups of employees to share in any savings or "gains" realized through their efforts to reduce costs and increase productivity.

Gantt chart (4, 16)   A bar graph or diagram that shows the allocation of time allowed to the various activities comprising a project; a chart that graphically depicts the routing or scheduling of a production/operations sequence from beginning to conclusion.

General environment (7)   The cultural, economic, legal-political, and educational conditions in the locality where an organization operates.

General manager (1)   A manager who has responsibility for a complex organizational subunit that includes many areas of functional activity.

General union (18)   A labor union that is organized in a variety of unrelated industries and lacks a specific craft or industry focus.

Geocentric corporation (19)   A multinational corporation that is dedicated to totally integrated global operations.

Glass ceiling effect (2, 11)   The presence of invisible barriers which limit the advancement of women and minorities to higher-level responsibilities in organizations.

Graphic rating scale (14)   A performance-appraisal method that lists a variety of traits or characteristics, thought to be related to high performance outcomes in a given job, that the individual is accordingly expected to exhibit.

Grievance (18)   A complaint from an employee regarding treatment he or she has received in respect to a condition of employment specified in a labor contract.

Group (13)   A collection of people who regularly interact with one another over time and in respect to the pursuit of one or more common goals.

Group decision (10)   A decision where all group members participate with the manager and finally agree by consensus on the course of action to be taken.

Group decision support systems (15)   An interactive computer-based information system that facilitates group efforts at solving complex problems.

Group dynamics (13)   Forces operating groups that affect task performance and membership satisfaction.

Group process (13)   The means through which multiple and varied resource inputs are combined and transformed into group outputs.

Group technology (16)   Using computers to help code and classify parts into families needing special handling in storage and manufacturing.

Groupthink (13)   A tendency for highly cohesive groups to lose their critical evaluative capabilities.

Growth needs (12)   Desires for continued psychological growth and development in Alderfer's ERG theory (discussed in Chapter 12).

Growth-need strength (8)   the individual's desire to achieve a sense of psychological growth—that is, higher-order need satisfaction—in his or her work.

Growth strategy (5)   A strategy that involves expansion of the organization's current operations.

Halo effect (11)   When one attribute is used to develop an overall impression of a person or situation.

Hardware (computer) (15)   Equipment required to operate a computer system.

Hawthorne effect (2)   The tendency of persons who are singled out for special attention to perform as anticipated merely because of the expectancies created by the situation.

Heuristics (3)   Strategies for simplifying decision making—e.g., the availability, representativeness, and anchoring and adjustment heuristics.

Hierarchy of authority (1, 6)   The arrangement of work positions in order of increasing formal authority in an organization.

Hierarchy of needs (2, 12)   Five levels of human needs defined by Abraham Maslow as becoming activated in order of prepotency—physiological, safety, social, ego, and self-actualization needs.

Hierarchy of objectives (5)   A series of objectives linked to one another at the various levels of management such that each higher level objective is supported by one or more lower-level ones.

Higher-order needs (12)   Esteem and self-actualization needs in Maslow's hierarchy.

Holding costs (or Carrying costs) (16)   The actual cost of items going into inventory, as well as the cost of storing and insuring them against loss.

Homeostasis (2)   A dynamic or moving state of equilibrium or balance in the relationship between a system and its environment.

Horizontal coordination (6)   The process of coordinating the activities of individuals or groups working at, or close to, the same level in the hierarchy.

Human relations leadership (or Supportive leadership) (10)   A leadership style that displays a high concern for people but low concern for task.

Human resource audit (9)   A systematic inventory of the strengths and weaknesses of existing personnel.

Human resource inventory chart (or Replacement chart) (9)   A chart that shows the promotability of persons in key positions within the organization.

Human resource maintenance (13)   A group's ability to maintain its social fabric and capabilities of its members to work well together over time.

Human resource management (9)   The process of staffing an organization with human resources and ensuring that the performance potential of every employee is realized to the fullest.

Human resource planning (or Personnel planning) (9)   A process of analyzing staffing needs and identifying actions to fill these needs over time.

Human resources (1)   The people, individuals, and groups that help organizations produce goods or services.

Human skill (1)   The ability to work well in cooperation with other persons.

Hybrid structure (6)   Using functional and divisional structures in different parts of the same organization.

Hygiene factors (8)   Factors in the work setting such as working conditions, interpersonal relations, organizational policies and administration, supervision, and salary.

Impression management (11)   The systematic attempt to behave in ways that create and maintain desired impressions of one's self in the eyes of others.

Improvement objectives (14)   Objectives that document intentions to improve performance in different areas.

Independent inventory demand (16)   A demand for inventory that follows a uniform pattern and causes inventory to decrease at a gradual rate over time.

Independent variable (1MA)   A variable whose behavior influences the behavior of another variable (a dependent variable); a variable whose behavior is used by regression analysis to predict or forecast the behavior of some other variable in a future time period.

Inducements (8)   Things of value the organization gives to the individual in return for valued contributions.

Industrial unions (18)   Labor unions that serve a single industry and represent workers across a wide variety of occupations.

Informal communication channels (11)   Communication channels that exist outside of the formal channels and do not adhere to the organization's hierarchy of authority.

Informal group (13)   A group that emerges within an organization and that exists without being formally specified by someone in authority for a performance purpose.

Informal leadership (10)   When a person without formal authority proves influential in directing the behavior of other persons.

Informal structure (6)   The undocumented and officially unrecognized structure that coexists with the formal structure of an organization.

Information (2,15)   Data that have been made meaningful or relevant for the recipient.

Information-reporting system (15)   A computerized MIS that processes data relating to standard accounting transactions and makes a variety of reports available to managers.

Information system (15)   A system that collects, organizes, and distributes data regarding activities occurring inside and outside the organization.

Innovation (17)   The process of taking a new idea and putting it into practice as part of the organization's normal operating routines.

Input standard (14)   Standard that measures work efforts that go into a performance task.

Inside-out planning (4)   Creates plans that focus efforts on doint what one already does, but trying to do it better.

Institutional strategy (5)   Strategy which identifies the core values and beliefs that give the organization as a whole a distinctive character.

Instrumentality (12)   The person's belief that various work-related outcomes will occur as a result of task performance.

Integration (7)   The level of coordination achieved among subsystems in an organization.

Intensive technology (7)   A technology where there is uncertainty as to how to produce desired outcomes, and high interdependence among members of the work force.

Interaction (13)   Behavior that group members direct toward other persons.

Interest group (13)   Informal groups in which members band together to advance a common cause or special position.

Intermittent reinforcement (12)   Administering a reward only periodically upon the appearance of desired behavior.

Internal control (14)   Self-control that occurs through self-discipline and the personal exercise of individual or group responsibility.

Internal recruitment (9)   The process of making employees aware of job vacancies through job posting and personal recommendations.

International business (19)   The conduct of for-profit transactions of goods and services across national boundaries.

International management (19)   Management that involves the conduct of business or other operations in foreign countries.

Intrapreneurship (17)   Entrepreneurial behavior displayed by people or subunits within large organizations; internal entrepreneurship.

Intuitive thinker (3)   A person who approaches problems in a flexible and spontaneous fashion.

Inventory (16)   The amount of resource inputs or product outputs kept in storage.

Inventory control (16)   A control system that monitors raw material, work in process, and finished-good inventories to make sure work-flows are properly maintained.

Inventory of alternatives (3)   A list of all possible solutions to a problem along with a summary of the favorable and unfavorable points of each.

Investment center (15)   A responsibility center where budgets and performance targets concentrate not only on profits but also on the amount of capital investment required to produce those profits.

Job (8)   The collection of tasks a person performs in support of organizational objectives.

Job analysis (9)   An orderly study of job requirements and facets that can influence performance results.

Job depth (8)   The extent of planning and evaluating duties performed by the individual worker rather than the supervisor.

Job description (8, 9)   A written statement that details the duties and responsibilities of any person holding a particular job.

Job design (6, 8)   The allocation of specific work tasks to individuals and groups; the process through which jobs are defined as collections of specific tasks.

Job enlargement (8)   A job-design strategy that increases task variety by combining into one job two or more tasks that were previously assigned to separate workers.

Job enrichment (8)   A job-design strategy that builds satisfier factors into job content; a job-design strategy that increases job depth by adding to a job some of the planning and evaluating duties normally performed by the supervisor.

Job rotation (8, 9)   A job-design strategy that increases task variety by periodically shifting workers among jobs involving different tasks.

Job satisfaction (8)   The degree to which an individual feels positively or negatively about various aspects of the job, including assigned tasks, work setting, and relationships with co-workers.

Job scope (8)   The number and combination of tasks an individual or group is asked to perform.

Job sharing (8)   When one full-time job is split between two persons.

Job shop (16)   Specialty operations where individual customers or products get individual attention.

Job simplification (8)   A job-design strategy that involves standardizing work procedures and employing people in clearly defined and very specialized tasks.

Job specification (9)   A list of the qualifications required of any job occupant.

Joint venture (19)   Form of international business that establish operations in a foreign country through mutual ownership with local partners.

Jurisdiction (18)   Task domains within which craft unions retain autonomy to organize and represent workers.

Just cause (18)   A principle, often specified in labor contracts, holding that an employee should not be disciplined without sufficient justification (''cause'') and that the penalty imposed should not be excessive compared to the offense.

Just-in-time delivery (16)   An approach to inventory control that involves minimizing carrying costs and maintaining almost no inventories by ordering or producing components only as needed; sometimes called the ''Kanban'' system.

Just-in-time scheduling (16)   Scheduling materials to arrive at a work station or facility ''just in time'' to be used.

Labor-management relations (18)   The ongoing relationship between a group of employees represented by a union and management in the employing organization.

Labor contract (18)   A formal agreement between a union and the employing organization, which specifies the rights and obligations of each party in respect to wages, work hours, work rules and other conditions of employment.

Labor union (18)   An organization to which workers belong and that collectively deals with employers on their behalf.

Laissez-faire leadership (or Abdicative leadership) (10)   A leadership style that displays low concern for both people and task.

Lateral communication (11)   Communication among persons working at the same level in the hierarchy of authority, but typically representing different departments or work units.

Law of contingent reinforcement (12)   In order for a reward to have maximum value, it must be delivered only if the desired behavior is exhibited.

Law of effect (12)   Behavior that results in a pleasant outcome is likely to be repeated; behavior that results in an unpleasant outcome is not likely to be repeated.

Law of immediate reinforcement (12)   The more

immediate the delivery of a reward after the occurrence of a desirable behavior, the greater the reinforcing value of the reward.

Leader-member relations (10)   A term used in Fiedler's contingency leadership theory to describe the degree to which the group supports the leader.

Leadership (10)   The manager's use of power to influence the behavior of other persons in the work setting.

Leadership style (10)   The recurring pattern of behaviors exhibited by a leader.

Leading (10)   The process of directing human-resource efforts toward organizational objectives.

Learning (1)   Any change in behavior that occurs as a result of experience.

Legitimate power (10)   The capability to control other people by virtue of the rights of office.

Line manager (1)   A manager who has direct responsibility for the production of the organization's basic product or service.

Local-area networks (16)   Sets of two or more computers in close geographical proximity and linked together via communications.

Local union (18)   An administrative unit of a national or international union that services at the local level a particular group of workers represented by the union.

Logical incrementalism (5)   Views organizational strategies emerging over time as a series of incremental changes to existing patterns of behavior.

Long-linked technology (7)   A mass-production or assembly-line technology relying on highly specialized jobs performed in a closely controlled sequence to create a final product.

Long-range budget (15)   A budget covering periods of more than one year.

Long-range plan (4)   A plan covering five years or more.

Lose-lose conflict (17)   When no one achieves their true desires, and the underlying reasons for conflict remain unaffected.

Lot-by-lot ordering (16)   A method for controlling inventory by ordering with sufficient lead time the net requirements specified in a Material Requirements Planning (MRP) schedule.

Lower-order needs (12)   Physiological, safety, and social needs in Maslow's hierarchy.

M-Form organization (5, 6)   Those organizations that have multiple product and/or service divisions.

Maintenance activities (13)   Actions by group members that support the emotional life of the group as an ongoing social system.

Maintenance objective (14)   Objective that formally expresses intentions to continue performance at existing levels.

Management (1)   A body of knowledge and field of academic inquiry based on scientific principles and serving as an important foundation for any manager.

Management by exception (14)   Focusing managerial attention on situations in which differences between actual and desired performance are substantial.

Management by objectives (MBO) (4, 14)   A process of joint objective-setting between a superior and subordinate that can be done on an organizationwide basis.

Management by wandering around (11)   Dealing directly with subordinates by regularly walking around and talking with them about a variety of work-related matters.

Management development (9)   Training directed toward improving a person's knowledge and skills in the fundamantals of management.

Management functions (1)   Planning, organizing, leading, and controlling—the basic activities performed by all managers.

Management information system (MIS) (15)   A system that collects, organizes, and distributes data in such a way that the information meets the needs of managers.

Management process (1)   The process of planning, organizing, leading, and controlling the utilization of resources to accomplish the organization's purpose.

Management rights (18)   The rights of an employer to manage the work operation but only as those rights are modified through specific terms of labor agreement.

Management science (Operations research; Quantitative analysis) (2, MA)   A scientific approach to management that uses mathematical techniques to analyze and solve problems.

Management theory (2)   A set of concepts and ideas that systematically explains and predicts the behaviors of organizations and their members.

Manager (1) A person in an organization who is responsible for the work performance of one or more other persons.

Managerial competency (1) A skill or personal characteristic that contributes to high performance in a management job.

Managerial ethics (2, 20) Those standards and principles that guide the actions and decisions of managers, and determine if those actions and decisions are "good or bad" or "right or wrong" in a moral sense.

Manager's challenge (1) A manager's responsibility to fulfill accountability to superiors for work-unit performance, while relying on the efforts of subordinates to make this performance possible.

Manufacturing resources planning MRPII (16) A computerized extension of material requirements planning that includes linkages with purchasing, accounting, engineering, sales and other business functions.

Mass production (7) The production of a large number of one or a few products with an assembly-line type of system.

Master budget (15) A comprehensive short-term budget for the organization as a whole.

Master scheduling (16) Specifies in detail exactly what goods or services will be produced during the short term—for example, on a weekly or even daily basis.

Material requirements planning (MRP) (16) A technique that uses a master schedule to determine when and how many component parts or separate resources must be ordered to ensure a smooth and sufficient flow of finished products or services.

Material resources (1) The information, equipment, raw materials, facilities, and other physical inputs that organizations employ in the production of goods or services.

Matrix organization (or Departmentation by matrix) (6) A form of organization that combines functional and divisional forms of departmentation to take best advantage of each.

Means-end chain (4) A chain of efforts and objectives that sequentially links the work of individuals and groups of various levels of the organization to a common purpose.

Mechanistic structures (7) Organizational structures that are highly bureaucratic in form; they employ centralized authority, rules and procedures, a clear-cut division of labor, narrow spans of control, and formal impersonal means of coordination.

Mediating technology (7) A technology that links together parties seeking a mutually beneficial exchange of values.

Mediation (18) A process in which a neutral party engages in substantive discussions with union and management negotiators in separate meetings and in joint sessions in the hope that concession and compromise will curtail a labor—management dispute.

Mentoring (9) The act of sharing experiences and insights between a seasoned and junior manager.

Microcomputer (or personal computer) (15) A small, self-contained computer system designed to accomplish a variety of data-storage and information-processing tasks in a unit not much larger than a desk typewriter and portable television.

Mixed message (11) When a person's words communicate one message and actions, body language, or appearance communicate something else.

Modeling (9) The process of demonstrating through personal behavior that which is expected of others.

Motion study (2) The science of reducing a job or task to its basic physical motions.

Motivation to work (12) The forces within the individual that account for the level, direction, and persistence of effort expended at work.

Moving average (MA) Averages of past data over a specific time period that are used to forecast the future.

Multidimensional thinking (3, 4) The capacity to view many problems at once, in relationship to one another, and across long and short time horizons.

Multinational corporation (MNC) (19) A business firm with extensive international operations in more than one foreign country.

Multiperson comparison (14) A performance appraisal method that involves a comparison of one person's performance with that of one or more persons.

National Labor Relations Act (NLRA) (18) The cornerstone of American labor law that protects employer and employee rights in labor-management relations; consists of the Wagner Act (1935), Taft–Hartley Act (1947), and Landrum–Griffin Act (1959).

National Labor Relations Board (NLRB) (18) A board created by the NLRA to administer the provisions of the act.

Natural rewards (12) Rewards which occur and are experienced "naturally" as a part of one's work performance.

Need (2, 12) A physiological or psychological deficiency a person feels the compulsion to satisfy.

Need for achievement (nAch) (12) The desire to do something better or more efficiently, to solve problems, or to master complex tasks.

Need for affiliation (nAff) (12) The desire to establish and maintain friendly and warm relations with other persons.

Need for power (nPower) (12) The desire to control other persons, to influence their behavior, or to be responsible for other people.

Negative entropy (2) The tendency toward system continuity and survival.

Negative reinforcement (12) A means for increasing the frequency of or strengthening a behavior by making the avoidance of an undesirable consequence contingent on the occurrence of the behavior.

Noise (11) Anything that interferes with the effectiveness of the communication process.

Nominal group (3) A group technique for generating ideas by following a structured format of individual response, group sharing without criticism, and written balloting.

Nonprogrammed decision (3) Specific solution arrived at by the creative and unstructured process of problem solving for nonroutine problems.

Nonroutine problem (3) Problem that is unique and new and for which standard responses are not available.

Norm (13) A behavior expected of group members.

Normative-reeducative change strategy (17) A change strategy where the change agent attempts to identify or establish values and assumptions such that support for a proposed change naturally emerges.

Office automation (15) The use of computers in the office environment to facilitate operations.

Official objective (5) The organization's formal purpose or mission as stated in a report to shareholders, article of incorporation, or other similar official documents.

Off-the-job training (9) Training that is accomplished in an area away from the actual work setting.

On-the-job training (9) Training that is accomplished in the work setting and during performance of an actual job.

Open system (1, 2) A system that interacts with its environment and transforms resource inputs into outputs.

Operant conditioning (12) The process of controlling behavior by manipulating its consequences.

Operating budget (15) A budge that assigns resources to a responsibility center on a short-term basis.

Operating objective (5) The specific ends toward which organizational resources are actually allocated.

Operational plan (4) Plans of limited scope that address those activities and resources required to implement strategic plans.

Operations management (OM) (16) A branch of management theory that studies how organizations transform resource inputs into product and service outputs.

Operations research (also called Management science or Quantitative analysis) (2, MA) A scientific approach to management that uses mathematical techniques to analyze and solve problems.

Ordering costs (16) The costs of arranging the procurement of items for inventory from outside sources, as well as the costs of any internal procurement (e.g., manufacture of such items).

Organic structures (7) Organizational structures that have decentralized authority, few rules and procedures, more ambiguous division of labor, wide spans of control, and informal and more personal means of coordination.

Organization (1, 6)   A collection of people working together in a division of labor to achieve a common purpose.

Organization chart (6)   A diagram that describes the basic arrangement of work positions within an organization.

Organization development (OD) (17)   The application of behavioral science knowledge in a long-range effort to improve an organization's ability to cope with change in its external environment and increase its internal problem-solving capabilities.

Organizational behavior (2)   The study of individuals and groups in organizations.

Organizational behavior modification (OB Mod) (12)   The application of operant conditioning techniques to influence human behavior in work settings.

Organizational change (17)   Change involving some modification in the goals, structure, tasks, people, and technology that constitute the essence of the organization.

Organizational communication (11)   The process through which information is exchanged in interactions among persons inside the organization.

Organizational context (7)   Strategy, size, technology, and people characterizing the organization.

Organizational design (7)   The process of choosing and implementing an appropriate structural configuration for the organization.

Organizational objective (5)   Ends the organization seeks to achieve by its existence and operations.

Organizing (6)   The process of dividing work into manageable components and coordinating results to serve a purpose.

Orientation (9)   Activities through which new employees are made familiar with their jobs, co-workers, and the policies, rules, objectives, and services of the organization as a whole.

Output standards (14)   Standards that measure performance results in terms of quantity, quality, cost, or time.

Outside-in planning (4)   Creates plans that reflect an analysis of the external environment and then make the internal adjustments necessary to exploit opportunities and minimize problems posed by it.

Part-time work (8)   Work done on a basis that classifies the employee as "temporary" and requires less than the standard 40-hour work week.

Participative leadership (or Democratic leadership) (10)   A leadership style that displays high concern for both people and task.

Participative planning (4)   The inclusion in the planning process of as many people as possible from among those who will be affected by plans and/or asked to help implement them.

Payoff table (or Decision matrix) (3)   An extension of decision-tree analysis to display the possible outcomes of various alternatives while taking the probabilities of their occurrence into account.

Perception (11)   The process through which people receive, organize, and interpret information from the environment.

Performance (8)   The quantity and quality of task contributions from an individual or age doing a job.

Performance appraisal (14)   A process of formally evaluating performance and providing feedback on which performance adjustments can be made.

Performance-contingent rewards (8)   Allocating rewards in such a way that larger rewards are received by higher performers and smaller rewards by lower performers.

Performance effectiveness (1)   An output measure of task or goal accomplishment.

Performance efficiency (1)   A measure of the resource cost associated with goal accomplishment—that is, outputs realized compared to inputs consumed.

Performance gap (17)   A discrepancy between the desired and actual status of affairs.

Performance norm (13)   A key characteristic of work groups, it can have positive or negative implications for group and organizational productivity.

Performance objective (14)   A desired performance accomplishment that can be expressed as a measurable end product or verifiable set of work activities.

Permanent group (13)   Work groups that retain their presence over time.

Personal development objectives (14)   Objectives that formally express intentions to engage in personal growth activities.

Personal computer (or Microcomputer) (15) A small, self-contained computer system designed to accomplish a variety of data-storage and information-processing tasks in a unit not much larger than a desk typewriter and portable television.

Personal staff (6) "Assistant-to" positions that provide special administrative support to higher-level positions.

Personal wellness (21) The pursuit of one's physical and mental potential through a personal-health–promotion program.

Plan (4) A statement of intended means for accomplishing a desired result.

Planned change (17) Change that occurs as a result of specific efforts in its behalf by a change agent.

Planning (4) The process of setting objectives and determining what should be done to accomplish them.

Planning objective (4) The desired future state or end result to be accomplished through implementation of a plan.

Policy (4) A standing plan that communicates broad guidelines for making decisions and taking action.

Political action committees (PACs) (20) Committees organized by companies and other organizations to assist in the election of candidates who favor their interests.

Political environment (5) Includes governmental units at regional, state, national, and international levels, special-interest groups and other political entities, and the legal-judicial framework of society.

Political-risk analysis (19) Forecasting the probability of various events that can threaten the security of a foreign investment.

Polycentric corporation (19) A multinational corporation that pursues decentralized operations in several countries.

Position power (10) The degree to which a position in the organization's hierarchy of authority gives a person the power to reward and punish subordinates; a term used in Fiedler's contingency leadership theory.

Positive discipline (14) A disciplinary approach which tries to involve people more directly in

making decisions to improve their work behaviors.

Positive reinforcement (12) A means for strengthening or increasing the frequency of a behavior of making a desirable consequence contingent on the occurrence of the behavior.

Postaction control (or Feedback control) (14) control that takes place after an action is completed; sometimes called feedback controls.

Power (10) The ability to get someone else to do something you want done; the ability to make things happen the way you want.

Precontrol (or Feedforward control) (14) Control that is initiated prior to the start of a production or service activity.

Probability (3) The degree of likelihood that an event will occur.

Problem (3) A difference between an actual situation and a desired situation.

Problem finding (3) Identifying gaps between actual and desired states, and determining their causes.

Problem solving (3, 17) The process of identifying a discrepancy between an actual and desired state of affairs, and then taking action to resolve the discrepancy.

Problem-solving (in conflict management) (17) Seeking true satisfaction of everyone's concerns; working through differences and solving problems so everyone wins as a result.

Procedures (and Rules) (4) Standing-use plans that precisely describe what actions are to be taken in specific situations.

Process innovation (17) An innovation which results in a new or improved way of doing things.

Process theories (12) Motivation theories that address the thought processes through which individuals give meaning to rewards and allow them to influence their behavior.

Product departmentation (6) Grouping together jobs and activities which relate to a single product or service.

Product innovation (17) An innovation which results in the creation of a new or improved good or service.

Productivity (1) A summary measure of the quantity and quality of work performance with resource utilization considered.

Profession (2) An organization or network in

which membership is limited to persons sharing expertise in a specialized body of knowledge and that is governed by a universal code of ethics.

Profit center (15)   A responsibility center where budgets and performance targets concentrate on the amount of profits realized—that is, on the difference between revenues and expenses.

Profit plan (15)   A primary document in any operating budget that details revenues and costs and projects the resulting net income in the form of an income statement.

Profit sharing pay plans (12)   Distribute to employees a proportion of net profits earned during a stated performance period.

Program evaluation and review technique (PERT) (16)   A network-modeling technique that breaks the various phases of a production/operations project into a sequence of events and the activities leading to those events.

Programmed decisions (3)   Specific solutions determined by past experience as appropriate for the problem at hand.

Progression principle (12)   Maslow's principle, which holds that five human needs exist in a strict hierarchy of prepotency such that a need at one level doesn't become activated until the next lower-level need is already satisfied.

Progressive discipline (14)   The process of tying reprimands in the form of penalties or punishments to the severity of the employee's infractions.

Project (16)   The creation of a single product that is not complete until many—perhaps hundreds—of individual tasks are finished in a particular sequence.

Project management (16)   The managerial responsibility for making sure that the many phases and parts of a project are completed on time, in the specified order, and with a desired level of quality accomplishment.

Projection (11)   The assignment of personal attributes to other individuals.

Promotion (9)   Movement of a person to a higher-level position within the organization.

Proxemics (11)   The use of interpersonal space, such as in the process of interpersonal communication.

Psychological contract (8)   The shared set of expectations held by the individual and the organization, specifying what each expects to give to and receive from the other in the course of their working relationship.

Psychological group (13)   A group whose members are aware of one another's needs and potential resource contributions, and achieve high levels of interaction and mutual identification in pursuit of a common purpose.

Punishment (12)   A means for decreasing the frequency of or eliminating an undesirable behavior by making an unpleasant consequence contingent on the occurrence of that behavior.

Purpose (of an organization) (1)   To produce a good or service.

Qualitative forecasting technique (4)   The use of expert opinions to predict the future.

Quality assurance (16)   The process of *preventing* the production of defective products or services.

Quality control (16)   The process of *checking* goods or services to ensure that they meet certain standards.

Quality-control circle (16)   A group of employees who meet periodically to discuss ways of improving the quality of their products or services.

Quality of working life (1)   The overall quality of human experiences in the workplace.

Quantitative analysis (also called Operations research or Management science) (2, MA)   A scientific approach to management that uses mathematical techniques to analyze and solve problems.

Quantitative forecasting techniques (4)   The use of statistical analyses and mathematics to predict the future.

Realistic job previews (9)   Try to provide the job candidate with all pertinent information about a prospective job and the employing organization, without distortion and before a job offer is accepted.

Realistic recruitment (9)   A recruitment philosophy that seeks to provide the job candidate all pertinent information without distortion.

Recruitment (9)   A set of activities designed to attract a qualified pool of job applicants to an organization.

Reference power (10)   The capability to control

other people because of their desires to identify personally and positively with the power source.

Regression analysis (MA)   A mathematical technique that provides a forecast by comparing past variation in one variable (the dependent variable)—for example, demand—against variation in another and more predictable variable (the independent variable).

Reinforcement theory (12)   A motivation theory that examines how people learn patterns of behavior based on environmental reinforcements.

Relatedness need (12)   Desire for satisfying interpersonal relationships.

Reliable test (9)   A measure of the extent to which a test will yield approximately the same results over time if taken by the same person.

Replacement (9)   The act of removing a person from an assigned job.

Required behavior (13)   Those things the organization requests from group members by way of job performance and in return for the right of continued membership and support.

Resources requirements planning (RRP) (16)   An extension of material requirements planning to cover all types of resources used in the production process.

Responsibility (6)   The obligation to perform that results from accepting assigned tasks; a commitment by the subordinate to the supervisor to carry out assigned duties as agreed.

Responsibility accounting system (15)   An organizational control system based on the development of interlocking budgets for a hierarchy of responsibility centers.

Responsibility center (15)   A work unit formally charged with budgetary responsibility for carrying out various activities.

Restructuring (6)   Reorganizing or changing an organization's structure in the attempt to improve productivity.

Retrenchment strategy (5)   A strategy that involves slowing down, cutting back, and seeking performance improvement through greater efficiencies in operations.

Revenue center (15)   A responsibility center where budgets and performance targets concentrate on product or service outputs measured in monetary terms as revenues.

Reward (12)   A work outcome of positive value to the individual.

Reward power (10)   The capability to offer something of value—a positive outcome—as a means of controlling other people.

Risk (3)   A problem environment in which information is not certain but probabilities can be associated with the outcomes of problem-solving alternatives.

Robotics (16)   Using computer-guided multifunctional robots to perform work tasks.

Role (11)   A set of activities expected of a person in a particular job or position within the organization.

Role ambiguity (11)   When the person in a role is uncertain about what others expect in terms of his or her behavior.

Role conflict (11)   When the person in a role is unable to respond to the expectations held by one or more others.

Role overload (11)   When too many role expectations are being communicated to a person at a given time.

Routine problem (3)   Problem that arises on a regular basis and can be addressed through standard responses.

Routing sheet (16)   A document that shows which machines or work centers a part must pass through in the various phases of its production.

Rules (and Procedures) (4)   Standing-use plans that precisely describe what actions are to be taken in specific situations.

Satisficing (3)   In problem solving, choosing the first satisfactory alternative that comes to your attention.

Satisfier factors (8)   Factors in job content such as sense of achievement, recognition, responsibility, advancement, or personal growth experienced as a result of task performance.

Scalar principle (6)   There should be a clear and unbroken chain of command linking every person in the organization with successively higher levels of authority up to and including the chief executive officer; this chain of command should be followed when orders are conveyed from higher to lower levels of authority.

Schedule (4)   Single-use plan that ties activities to specific time frames or targets.

Science (2)   A body of knowledge systematically created via the steps in the scientific method.

Scientific management (2)   As advocated by Frederick W. Taylor, involves developing a science for every job including rules of motion and standardized work instruments, careful selection and training of workers, and proper supervisory support for workers.

Selection (9)   The process of choosing from a pool of applicants the person or persons best meeting job specifications.

Selective perception (3, 11)   The tendency of people to define problems from their own points of view; the tendency to single out for attention those aspects of a situation or attributes of a person that reinforce or appear consistent with one's existing beliefs, values, or needs.

Seniority (18)   The length of an employee's continuous service with an employer.

Sentiments (13)   Feelings, attitudes, beliefs, or values held by group members.

Shaping (12)   The creation of a new behavior by the positive reinforcement of successive approximations to the desired behavior.

Shared power change strategy (17)   A participative change strategy that relies on involving others to examine values, needs and goals in relationship to an issue at hand.

Short-range budget (15)   A budget covering periods of one year or less.

Short-range plan (4)   A plan covering one year or less.

Simultaneous structures (7)   The co-existence of mechanistic and organic structures within an organization in the attempt to accomplish both production efficiency and innovation.

Single-use plan (4)   A plan that is used only once.

Situational control (10)   A term used in Fiedler's contingency leadership theory to describe the extent to which a leader can determine what a group is going to do, and what the outcomes of its actions and decisions are going to be.

Size (of an organization) (7)   The number of persons employed by an organization; sometimes measured by total assets, sales, or revenues.

Skill (1)   The ability to translate knowledge into action that results in the desired performance.

Skill variety (8)   The degree to which a job requires a variety of different activities in carrying out the work and involves the use of a number of different skills and talents of the individual.

Small-batch production (7, 16)   A variety of custom products that are tailor made, usually with considerable craftsmanship, to fit customer specifications.

Smoothing (in conflict management) (17)   Playing down differences among conflicting parties, and high-lighting similarities and areas of agreement.

Smoothing constant (α, alpha) (MA)   A constant between 0 and 1 that determines how much weight is put on data in exponential smoothing.

Social audit (20)   A systematic assessment and reporting of an organization's resource and action commitments, and performance accomplishments in areas of social responsibility.

Social environment (5)   Consists of the value systems, sociodemographic characteristics, and other characteristics of persons comprising the society.

Social learning (12)   Learning that is achieved by people as they behave and interact with others in their social environment.

Socialization (9)   The process of systematically changing the expectations, behavior, and attitudes of a new employee in a manner considered desirable by the organization.

Socio-technical systems (8)   Designing jobs so that technology and human resources are well integrated in high performance systems with maximum opportunities for individual satisfaction.

Software (computer) (15)   Instructions in the form of programs that give the computer its capability to perform computational operations on data.

Span of control (6)   The number of subordinates reporting directly to a manager.

Span-of-control principle (6)   There is a limit to the number of persons one manager can effectively supervise; care should be exercised to keep the span of control within manageable limits.

Specialization (6)   The process through which multiple work tasks are defined in a division of labor.

Specialized staff (6)   Positions that perform a technical service or provide special problem-solving expertise for other parts of the organization.

Specific environment (7)   The actual organizations, groups, and persons with whom the focal organization must interact in order to survive and prosper.

Stability strategy (5)   A strategy that maintains the present course of action.

Staffing (9)   The process of filling jobs with appropriate persons.

Staff manager (1)   A manager who uses special technical expertise to support the production efforts of line managers.

Staff planner (4)   Person(s) who take responsibility for leading and coordinating the planning function for the total organization or a major subsystem.

Stakeholders (5, 20)   Members of the external environment who are directly involved with an organization and/or affected by its operations.

Standard time (16)   A measure of work capacity that takes into account the availability and work efficiency of people and/or equipment.

Standing-use plan (4)   A plan that is used more than once.

Static budget (or Fixed budget) (4, 15)   A budget that allocates resources or a single estimate of costs; a budget that does not allow adjustments over time.

Steering controls (or Concurrent Control) (14)   Control that acts in anticipation of problems and focus primarily on what happens during the work process.

Stereotype (11)   When an individual is assigned to a group or category, and then the attributes commonly associated with the group or category are assigned to the individual in question.

Strategic business unit (5)   A separate operating division that represents a major business area and operates with some autonomy vis-à-vis other similar units in the organization.

Strategic constituencies analysis (5)   The review and analysis of the interests of external stakeholders of an organization.

Strategic management (5)   The managerial responsibility for formulating, implementing, and evaluating strategies that lead to longer-term organizational success.

Strategic opportunism (3, 5)   The ability to remain focused on long-term objectives while being flexible enough to solve short term problems and take advantage of new opportunities.

Strategic plan (4)   A comprehensive plan that reflects the longer-term needs and directions of the organization or subunit.

Strategic planning (5)   The process of determining the major objectives of an organization and defining the strategies that will govern the acquisition and utilization of resources to achieve those objectives.

Strategy (5)   A comprehensive plan or action orientation that sets critical direction and guides the allocation of resources for an organization.

Strategy formulation (5)   The process of choosing among alternative strategies for eventual implementation.

Strategy implementation (5)   The process of taking action to implement strategies.

Stress (21)   A state of tension experienced by individuals facing extraordinary demands, contraints, or opportunities.

Stressors (21)   Things that cause stress.

Structure (6)   The formal system of working relationships that both divide and coordinate the tasks of people and groups to serve a common purpose.

Structured decision system (15)   Computerized MIS that creates and analyzes alternative solutions to standard types of problems and selects the best or optimal choice among them.

Suboptimization (5)   When some subunits accomplish their objectives at the expense of other subunits in the organization.

Substantive conflict (17)   Disagreement over such things as goals, the allocation of resources, distribution of rewards, policies, and procedures, and job assignments.

Substitutes for leadership (10)   Factors in the work setting that encourage and direct work efforts toward organizational objectives without the direct involvement of a leader.

Subsystem (2, 7)   A smaller component in a larger system; department or work unit headed by a manager but is a smaller part of a total organization.

Succession planning (9)   Planning for the replacement of key personnel over time.

Supercomputers (15)   Computers which operate

with speeds in the milliseconds range to manage vast amounts of data and solve extremely complex problems.

Superordinate goal (5)   A goal statement that conveys and represents the overall purpose of the organization to its members and interested outsiders.

Supportive leadership (or Human-relations leadership) (10)   A leadership style with a high concern for people, but low concern for task.

Survivor syndrome (21)   The stress experienced by persons who fear for their jobs after having "survived" large layoffs and staff cutbacks in an organization.

SWOT analysis (5)   Setting the stage for strategy formulation by analysis of organizational strengths and weaknesses, and environmental opportunities and threats.

Synectics (3)   A group technique in which participants are encouraged to join together apparently unrelated elements to break existing patterns of thinking and stimulate creativity.

Synergy (6, 13)   The creation of a whole that is greater than the sum of its individual parts.

System (2)   A collection of interrelated parts that function together to achieve a common purpose.

Systematic thinker (3)   A person who approaches problems in a rational and analytical fashion.

System boundary (2)   The point of separation between a system and its external environment.

Task activities (13)   Actions by group members that contribute directly to the group's performance purpose.

Task force (13)   A formal group convened to accomplish a specific purpose and which is expected to disband when that purpose is achieved.

Task identity (8)   The degree to which the job requires completion of a "whole" and identifiable piece of work—that is, one that involves doing a job from beginning to end with a visible outcome.

Task significance (8)   The degree to which the job has a substantial impact on the lives or work of people elsewhere in the organization or in the external environment.

Task structure (10)   A term used in Fiedler's contingency leadership theory to describe the extent to which task goals, procedures, and guidelines are clearly spelled out.

Team building (13)   A sequence of planned activities to gather and analyze data on the functioning of a group and implement constructive changes to increase its operating effectiveness.

Technical skill (1)   The ability to use a special proficiency or expertise relating to a method, process, or procedure.

Technological environment (5)   Includes the available technologies and the related capability of society to develop or acquire appropriate technologies in the future.

Technological imperative (7)   The viewpoint that technology is a major influence of organizational structure.

Technology (7)   The combination of equipment, knowledge, and work methods that allows an organization to transform inputs into outputs.

Telecommuting (8)   Working at home using a computer terminal with linkages to the office or other places of work.

Temporary group (13)   Work groups that are created for a specific purpose and typically disband with its accomplishment.

Temporary system (7)   Adaptive, rapidly changing task force organized around problem.

Territory departmentation (6)   Grouping together jobs and activities located in the same place or geographical region.

Theory (2)   A set of concepts and ideas that systematically explains and predicts physical and social phenomena.

Theory X (2)   A set of managerial assumptions that people in general dislike work, lack ambition, are irresponsible and resistant to change, and prefer to be led than to lead.

Theory Y (2)   A set of managerial assumptions that people in general are willing to work and accept responsibility, and are capable of self-direction, self-control, and creativity.

Time departmentation (6)   Grouping together jobs and activities performed on the same work shift or time schedule.

Time-series analysis (MA)   A method for identifying patterns in data by breaking historical data into components—trend, seasonal, cyclical, and random.

Top-down budgeting (15)   A budget process initiated, controlled and directed by top management.

Top-down planning (4)   Planning that begins with broad objectives set by top management and then allows lower management levels to make plans within these constraints.

Totalitarian system (19)   Legal-political system that involves restricted representation in the affairs of government through dictatorship, single-party rule, or perferred-membership group rule.

Training (9)   A set of activities that provide learning opportunities through which people can acquire and improve job-related skills.

Transaction processing system (15)   A system which uses the computer to organize and sort the data needed to complete routine transactions such as inventory management, payroll preparation, and customer billings.

Transactional leadership (10)   A leadership perspective in which the leader's role is viewed as one of orchestrating and directing the efforts of others in productive ways.

Transfer (9)   Movement of a person to a different job at the same or similar level of responsibility in the organization.

Transformational leader (10)   A leader who is able to get people to do more than they originally expected to do.

Uncertainty (3)   A problem environment in which the information is such that managers are unable to associate probabilities with the outcomes of problem-solving alternatives.

Unexpected problem (3)   Problem that is not anticipated.

Union shop (18)   A labor-management agreement that requires all employees of an organization to join a union.

Union stewards (18)   Employees who are union officials and who represent workers in resolving disputes with management.

Unity-of-command principle (6)   Each person in an organization should report to one and only one supervisor.

Unplanned change (17)   Change that occurs spontaneously or at random and without a change agent's direction.

Upward communication (11)   Communication flowing from lower to higher levels in an organization's hierarchy of authority.

Valence (12)   The value the individual assigns to work-related outcomes.

Valid test (9)   The degree to which a test measures exactly what it intends to relative to a job specification.

Values (5, 20)   Broad beliefs about what is or is not appropriate; the underlying beliefs and attitudes that help determine the behavior an individual displays.

Vertical coordination (6)   The process of coordinating the activities of individuals and groups up and down the hierarchy of authority.

Weighted moving average (MA)   A moving average that assigns a predetermined weight to each data value and thereby puts more weight on certain time periods when making forecasts.

Whistleblower (20)   A person who exposes the misdeeds of others in organizations to preserve ethical standards and protect against wasteful, harmful, or illegal acts.

Wide-area networks (16)   Sets of computers geographically distant from one another but which are linked together in communications.

Win–lose conflict (17)   When one party achieves its desires at the expense and exlcusion of the other party's desires.

Win–win conflict (17)   When conflict is resolved to the mutual benefit of all concerned parties.

Work (1, 8)   An activity that produces value for other people.

Work-at-home (8)   Accomplishing a job while spending all or part of one's work time in the home.

Work cell (16)   A work arrangement that clusters machines and people together in integrated socio-technical systems to perform a set of related tasks.

Work rules (18)   Labor contract provisions that govern the decisions which assign tasks to employees.

Work sampling (9)   An employment testing approach that assesses a person's performance on a set of tasks that directly replicate those required in the job under consideration.

Work sharing (8)   An arrangement where employees in an organization agree to work fewer hours, and receive less total pay, in order to avoid staff cutbacks and layoffs.

Worker involvement group (13)   A team or group of workers brought together to focus expertise and commitments on important and specific workplace issues.

Worldwide sourcing (19)   Obtaining from a variety of sources throughout the world the components and materials needed to create a product.

Yes/no controls (14)   Controls that are similar to steering controls except they represent formal checkpoints that must be successfully passed if an activity is to proceed.

Zero-based budget (4, 15)   A budget that allocates resources to a project or activity as if it were brand new; forces both ongoing and newly proposed programs to compete on an equal footing for available resources.

Zone of indifference (10)   The range of directives and requests that people consider appropriate to their basic employment or psychological contract with the organization.

Photo Credits

Name Index

Deal, Terrence E., 145, 160
Dearden, John, 478
De Benedetti, Carol, 515–516
DeCagno, Elisabetta, 627
Deci, Edward, 379
DeGarmo, Scott, 305
Delbecq, Andre L., 93
Deming, W. Edwards, 480, 500–501
DePree, Max, 295, 321–322, 380, 517, 524, 643, 646–647, 663
De Rieux, Robin, 408
DeSanctis, Gerardine, 478
de Solo, Alberto, 508
Devanna, Mary Anne, 252, 291, 294
Dickens, Charles, 641, 662
Dickson, William J., 64
Digital Equipment, 374
Dobrzynski, Judith H., 514
Dougherty, Philip H., 175
Dowling, William F., 252
Dressang, Joel, 602
Drucker, Peter, 7, 11, 40, 63, 72, 93, 143, 160, 173, 188, 195, 198, 290, 292, 316, 322, 524, 544, 564, 572, 583, 641, 662–663
Dumaine, Brian, 254
Duncan, Robert B., 195
Dunfee, Thomas W., 609
Dyer, William D., 408
Dyson, Bryan, 132

Elkins, Arthur, 160
Ellis, Joseph, 413
Elsner, Ralph, 672–673
Emery, Fred, 252

Fadiman, Jeffrey A., 599
Falvey, Jack, 254
Fantozzi, Vincent, 11
Farace, Richard V., 351
Farson, Richard E., 352
Fayol, Henri, 44–45, 64, 107
Fellows, Raejean, 401
Ferraro, Vincent L., 545
Ferrence, Thomas P., 663
Ferris, Richard, 153
Fiedler, Fred E., 57, 306–309, 321
Fiernan, Jaclyn, 599
Filley, Alan C., 544
Finucane, Robert E., 322
Fiorito, Jack, 572
Fisher, Anne B., 276
Fisher, Donald, 83
Fisher, Lawrence M., 458
Follett, Mary Parker, 44–45, 64
Ford, Henry, 42, 133, 435–436
Ford, Henry, III, 134
Forester, Tom, 663
Fortney, David L., 172, 286
Forward, Gordon, 228

Foster, Richard, 169
Foulkes, Fred K., 572
Fowler, Elizabeth M., 41
Franke, Richard H., 599
Fraser, Douglas A., 569–571
Frederickson, Lee W., 380
Frederick, William C., 627
Freedburg, Sydney P., 264
Freeman, Richard B., 563, 572
French, John R. P., Jr., 321
French, Wendell L., 544
Friberg, Eric, 584
Friedman, Milton, 627
Fritz, Roger, 195
Fry, Ronald E., 322
Fulmer, Robert, 641, 663
Fulmer, William E., 282
Fu, Marilyn Y. C., 351

Gadon, Herman, 252
Galante. Steven P., 64, 494
Galbraith, Jay, 223
Galvin, Robert, 673
Gannes, Stuart, 93, 478
Gantt, Henry L., 43–44, 64
Garcia, Joseph E., 321
Gardner, John W., 94, 170, 292, 295, 321, 638
Gardner, William L., 351, 408, 478
Garrett, David, 652
Garwood, Judith, 64
Gasse, Jean-Louis, 100
Gellerman, Saul W., 626–627
Geneen, Harold, 161, 471, 478
Getty, J. Paul, 37–38, 63
Ghiselli, Edwin E., 321
Giffen, James H., 574
Gilbreath, Robert D., 626
Gilbreth, Frank B., 43, 64
Gilbreth, Lillian M., 43
Gitman, Lawrence J., 572
Glaberson, William, 11
Glass, David D., 261, 415
Glass, Harold, 226
Glick, W., 252
Glueck, William F., 129, 160
Goizueta, Roberto, 132
Gompers, Samuel, 552, 572
Goodpaster, K. E., 627
Goodstein, Leonard D., 600
Gorbachev, Mikhail, 574, 579
Gorman, Thomas W., 503
Gouldner, Alvin, 223
Grabe, William O., 653
Graham, John L., 599
Graham, Katherine, 38
Graw, Larry, 395
Gray, Barbara Jean, 545
Gray, Daniel H., 161
Gray, Ed, 627

Green, Walter A., 663
Greenberg, Daniel, 169–170
Greene, Charles, 251
Greenwood, R. A., 64
Greenwood, R. G., 64
Greer, Charles, 572
Greiner, Larry E., 161
Gremp, Jim Von, 414
Griffin, Ricky W., 252
Grossman, John, 286, 380
Grove, Andrew S., 315, 334, 544
Gumpert, David E., 11, 223, 544
Gundnitski, Gary, 478
Gustafson, David H., 93
Guyon, Janet, 98, 160, 223, 282
Guzzardi, Walter, 214
Gyllenhammer, Pehr G., 76, 241–242

Hackman, J. Richard, 237–238, 252, 408
Haendel, Dan, 600
Hale, Roger, 499
Hall, Edward T., 351
Hall, John R., 90
Hall, Trish, 69, 243
Hall, William K., 160
Hamner, W. Clay, 380
Hamptom, David R., 195
Hancock, Ellen, 221
Haney, William J., 351
Haney, William V., 352
Hanke, Jean J., 408
Harlan, Anne, 251
Harlow, Dorothy N., 408
Harman, Curtis, 226
Harman, Sidney, 19
Harris, Philip R., 599
Harvey, Eric L., 449
Harvey, Jerry, 408
Hassenfeld, Alan, 514
Hattwick, Richard E., 195, 630
Hauptmann, Oscar, 106
Hay, Robert, 627
Healey, David, 583
Heckert, R. E., 516
Heinen, J. Steven, 408
Helm, Leslie, 408
Hemmermesh, Richard G., 160
Henderson, A. M., 64
Henderson, Verne E., 626
Heneman, Herbert G., 282
Henson, Joe, 13
Herr, Frederick Z., 480
Hertzberg, Frederick, 230–233, 236–237, 251–252
Herzlinger, Regina E., 52, 351
Hewlett, William, 520
Heyman, Samuel, 214
Heyrdeis, Judy, 332
Hicks, James O., Jr., 478

Higgins, James H., 160
Hilder, David B., 627
Hill, G. Christian, 544
Hockaday, Irvine Jr., 420
Hofstede, Geert, 591–595, 599–600
Hogarth, R. H., 93
Holusha, John, 506, 548, 567, 600
Homans, George, 392, 398
Hood, Ed, 602
Horniman, Alexander, 612
House, Robert J., 129, 251, 309–310, 321
Hubbard, R. D., 152
Huber, George P., 93, 478
Huff, Robert, 342
Hughes, Robert, 165
Hunt, James G., 351, 379, 407
Hunt, John W., 600
Huse, Edgar F., 252, 448, 544, 599
Hyatt, Joshua, 439
Hymowitz, Carol, 195, 223, 641

Iacocca, Lee, 67, 120, 295, 314, 321, 526
Iaffaldano, Michelle T., 252
Indvik, Julie, 321
Ingrasia, Paul, 600
Irwin, Richard D., 64, 572
Isaac, Michael H., 478
Isenberg, Daniel, 151
Isenberg, Daniel J., 93–94, 160–161, 351
Iverson, F. Kenneth, 172–173, 186, 286–287

Jacknis, Martin, 254
Jacobs, Franklin, 579
Jacobs, Sanford, 478
Jacobson, Allen, 523
Jacobson, Eugene, 408
Jago, Arthur G., 322
Janis, Irving, 397–398, 408
Janson, Robert, 252
Jaques, Elliott, 111, 130
Jay, Antony, 382
Jeffrey, Nancy, 75
Jelinek, Mariann, 195
Jenks, James, 188
Jerdee, Thomas H., 351
Jermier, John, 322
Jobs, Steven, 8, 98–100, 214
Johnson, Elmer W., 378
Johnson, Harold L., 627
Johnson, John, 60
Johnson, Lyndon B., 264
Johnson, Roger, 11, 588
Johnston, William B., 663
Jones, John F., 399
Jones, Larry, 3
Jonsson, Berth, 252

Josefowitz, Natasha, 351
Joyce, Robert D., 352
Junkins, Jerry, 119
Juran, J. M., 480

Kahneman, D., 93
Kahn, Robert L., 57, 64, 352
Kanarick, Arnold, 506
Kaney, Thomas, 542
Kanter, Rosabeth Moss, 168–169, 205, 223, 321, 380, 531, 544
Kantrow, Alan M., 63, 251
Kaplan, Rick, 471
Kaplan, Robert E., 93–94
Karlin, Beth, 223
Katz, Daniel, 57, 64
Katz, Michael, 282
Katz, Robert L., 24
Kearns, David, 202
Keech, Cindy and Scott, 437
Keichel, Walter, III, 271, 609
Kelly, John, 188
Kennedy, Allen A., 145, 160
Kennedy, Robert D., 135
Kerr, Steven, 251, 322, 449
Ketteringham, John M., 516
Keys, J. Bernard, 408, 478
Kiechel, Walter, III, 324, 352, 627
Killmann, Ralph H., 93, 160, 544
Kim, 139
King, Carol, 193–194
Kirkland, Lance, 555
Kirkland, Richard I., Jr., 514, 521
Kirkpatrick, David, 246, 252
Klein, Janice A., 130
Kneale, Dennis, 161
Knoll, Robert D., 480
Kochan, Thomas, 572
Kohn, Alfie, 408
Kolb, David A., 93
Kolodny, Harvey F., 195
Kolodziej, Stan, 478
Koontz, Harold, 449
Koslow, Linda, 96–98
Koten, John, 599
Kotlowitz, Alex, 550, 572
Kotter, John P., 24, 114, 129, 151, 251, 321, 351, 516, 544
Kouzes, James M., 290, 321
Kraar, Louis, 599
Kreitner, Robert, 380
Kristol, Irving, 626
Kupfer, Andrew, 588

Labich, Kenneth, 64, 161, 544
Labovitz, George H., 3, 351
Lacy, J. Dan, 91
Laidlow, Don, 262
Laker, Sir Freddie, 73
Lambert, Dan, 127

Latham, Gary P., 322, 379
Laudon, Jane Price, 506
Laudon, Kenneth C., 506
Laupe, Brent, 478
Lautenback, Terry, 200, 221
Lawler, Edward E., III, 252, 373, 379, 380, 407, 448, 572
Lawrence, Paul R., 57, 195, 216–218, 223
Lazarus, Harold, 663
Leahy, William D. (Adm.), 122
Leavitt, Harold J., 408, 544
Lee, B. C., 139
Lee, Carmen J., 663
Lee, Susan, 514
Leinster, Colin, 336, 663
Leonard-Barton, Dorothy, 478
Leonard, Frank S., 509
Leonard, Stew, 195
Leontiades, Milton, 129
Level, Dale, Jr., 351
Levering, Robert, 282
Levin, Dick, 117–119, 130, 161
Levinson, Daniel J., 663
Lewin, Kurt, 528, 544
Lewis, David, 582
Lewis, Peter H., 467
LiCari, Jerome J., 623
Likert, Rensis, 321, 384, 388, 407–408
Litterer, Joseph A., 448
Locke, Edwin A., 64, 252, 322, 367, 379, 380
Lohr, Steve, 93
Longnecker, Justin G., 627
Lorsch, Jay W., 57, 216–218, 223
Luellen, Charles J., 91
Lui, Richard, 457
Luthans, Fred, 380
Lynch, Maureen, 408

Maccoby, Michael, 357, 379, 448
Machaner, William, 351
MacIntyre, R. Douglas, 429
MacKenzie, R. Alex, 130
Maehr, Martin L., 379
Magnet, Myron, 506
Mahar, Linda, 321
Mahoney, David, 441
Main, Jeremy, 506
Malone, Lowell, 420
Mandel, Gerald, 128–129
Manley, Marisa, 282
March, James G., 57, 93
Marsland, Stephen E., 600
Martin, Irl, 630–634
Martinko, Mark J., 351
Marx, Jeff, 127
Maslow, Abraham H., 47–50, 64, 238, 359, 362–363, 379
Mason, R. Hall, 599

Matthews, J. B., 627
Mausner, Bernard, 251
Mayer, Douglas, 36
Mayer, Martin, 449
Mayo, Elton, 48–49
Maytag, Fritz, 205
McAfee, R. Bruce, 449
McCall, Morgan W., Jr., 93
McClelland, David C., 321, 360, 362, 379
McColough, Peter, 202
McConkey, Dale D., 379, 449
McCormick, Ernest, 281
McCormick, John, 6, 66, 168
McDaniel, Carl, Jr., 572
McFarlan, F. Warren, 478
McGill, Andrew R., 130
McGregor, Douglas, 47, 50, 64, 427–428, 448, 449
McGuire, Kenneth, 494
McIntyre, James M., 93
McKibbin, Lawrence E., 638
McLeod, Raymond, 478
Medoff, James L., 563, 572
Megginson, Leon C., 663
Mehler, Mark, 478
Melloan, George, 93, 418, 544
Merenda, Michael J., 160
Merton, Robert K., 223
Mescon, Timothy S., 129
Metcalfe, Henry C., 64
Miles, Raymond E., 150, 160
Miller, Bruce, 221
Miller, Keith L., 380
Miller, Michael W., 223
Miller, Norman C., 599
Mills, J. Quinn, 2, 64
Milstein, Mike M., 390
Mintross, Ian I., 93
Mintzberg, Henry, 7, 22–23, 151–152, 161, 195, 206, 223, 326, 351
Mitchell, Terence R., 321
Mitterand, Francois, 584
Mohrman, Allan H., Jr., 448
Mohrman, Susan A., 407, 572
Mollander, Earl A., 626
Monge, Peter R., 351
Mooney, James D., 44, 64
Moore, Thomas, 132, 191, 252, 626
Moran, Robert T., 599
Morita, Akio, 516
Morris, Betsy, 132
Morris, J. Stephen, 352
Morrison, Ann M., 64, 351
Morse, John, 223
Moscow, Alvin, 161, 478
Moskowitz, Milton, 282
Mosley, Alan, 569
Mouton, Jane Strygley, 306, 321, 408, 544

Muchinsky, Paul M., 252
Muczyk, Jan P., 321
Murphy, Thomas C., 159

Nadler, David A., 223, 448, 449
Naisbitt, John, 544, 663
Nanus, Burt, 322
Nasar, Sylvia, 418
Navasky, Victor S., 130
Nayak, P. Raganath, 518
Neal, Regina (Dr.), 284–286
Nelson, John C., 439
Neuman, Gail, 557
Newman, William H., 130, 448
Nicklaus, David, 223
Nienstedt, Phil, 672
Noble, Kenneth, 572
Noren, Al, 273
Nussbaum, Karen, 227, 229, 251, 429

O'Donnell, Cyril, 449
Ohmae, Kenichi, 595, 600
Oldham, Greg R., 252
Olson, Jim, 134–136, 140, 146
Oncken, William, Jr., 130
O'Rourke, J. Tracy, 419–420
Orphen, Christopher, 129, 161
Orr, James, 461
Orth, Charles D., 321
Osborn, Richard N., 351, 379, 407
O'Toole, James White, 321, 449, 626, 647, 663
Otten, Alan L., 94, 626–627
Ouchi, William G., 58, 64, 593, 600

Parsons, H. M., 64
Parsons, Talcott, 64
Parton, Dolly, 227, 229, 251
Pascale, Richard Tanner, 282, 593, 600
Passmore, William A., 252
Patton, John A., 449
Pearce, John A., II, 63, 129, 160, 626
Pericles, 36–37
Perlstein, Steven, 226
Perroni, Amedeo G., 63
Peter, J. Paul, 160
Peters, Tom, 160, 168–169, 172, 223, 290–292, 333, 339, 351, 379, 408, 437, 514, 544
Peterson, Donald, 102–104, 587–588
Peterson, Norman, 576
Petre, Peter, 282
Pfieffer, J. William, 399
Pierce, Jan, 550
Pillsbury Company, 377
Pilnick, Saul, 395, 408
Pinchot, Gifford, III, 223, 544
Pitts, Robert A., 600
Planty, Earl G., 315
Plovnick, Mark S., 322

Poffenberger, William, 449
Pollak, Tim, 175
Porter, Lyman W., 351, 373, 380, 638
Porter, Michael F., 64, 134, 149–150, 160
Posner, Barry Z., 290, 321, 627
Posner, Bruce G., 380
Pounds, William F., 93
Pouzilhac, Alain de, 175
Powell, Bill, 6, 168
Powell, John, 518
Presser, Jackie, 554–555
Prestbo, John A., 130
Price, Robert, 13
Primps, Sophia B., 252
Pringle, Charles D., 627
Pritchard, Jack, 562–563
Purdy, Kenneth, 252
Putnam, Howard, 608
Putnam, Linda L., 351

Quadracci, Harry, 342
Quinn, James Brian, 151, 160, 544
Quinn, Robert F., 352

Raia, Anthony P., 449
Ramanujam, Vasudevan, 129, 161
Ranftl, Robert M., 663
Raven, Bertram, 321
Reed, Eileen White, 602, 627
Reibstein, Larry, 282
Reimann, Bernard C., 321
Resnick, Susan M., 448
Rice, B., 64
Rice, Charlie, 446
Rice, Linda, 60
Richman, Tom, 452, 478
Ricklefs, Roger, 252
Ricks, David A., 351
Ringbakk, Kjell A., 130
Roberts, Bill, 385
Roberts, Edward B., 544
Roberts, Karlene H., 252, 351
Robey, Daniel, 508
Robinson, Richard B., Jr., 129, 160
Roethlisberger, F. J., 64
Rogers, Carl R., 352
Rogers, Thomas S., 158
Rolfes, Sara F., 2
Rollwagen, John, 80
Roloff, Becky, 377
Ronen, Simcha, 252
Rose, Frederick, 41
Rosen, Benson, 351
Ross, Jerry, 93
Rubin, Irwin M., 93, 322
Rucker, James, 198
Russell, Hamish M., 351
Rutenberg, David P., 599

Saari, Lisa A., 379
Salomon Brothers, 336
Samuelson, Paul A., 627
Sanders, Patricia, 600
Sant, Roger, 228, 251
Santos, Ignacio de, 128–129
Saporito, Bill, 130
Saul, George K., 626
Savage, Frank, 336
Savage, John A., 379
Saxon, M. J., 160
Sayles, Leonard, 321
Scanlan, Burt, 408, 478
Schacht, Henry, 169, 422
Schein, Edgar H., 39, 282, 322, 408, 652, 663
Schermerhorn, John R., Jr., 351, 379, 407–408, 478
Schiffman, James R., 47
Schipke, Roger, 422
Schlender, Brenton R., 98
Schlesinger, Jacob M., 380, 449, 572
Schlesinger, Leonard A., 130, 544
Schmidt, Warren H., 321, 351, 627
Schonberger, Richard J., 506
Schoonmaker, Alan N., 663
Schrank, Robert, 252
Schuler, Randall S., 663
Schwadel, Francine, 96
Schweiger, David M., 322
Sculley, John, 8, 13, 98–100, 291
Sease, Douglas R., 198, 223
Sekaran, Uma, 663
Seligman, Daniel, 572
Sellers, Patricia, 161, 478
Serpa, R., 160
Sethi, S. Prakash, 627
Shad, John, 602
Shapiro, Benson S., 408
Shapiro, Jeremy F., 478
Shaw, Kenneth N., 379
Shaw, Marvin E., 223, 408
Shea, Gregory P., 407–408
Sherman, Stratford, 544
Sherwood, John J., 251
Shewmaker, Jack, 261
Shoemaker, Paul, 66
Shrivastava, Paul, 93
Simmons, Michael, 106, 455
Simon, Herbert A., 57, 84, 93
Skinner, B. F., 380
Skinner, Wickham, 506
Sloan, Alfred, 63, 296
Smale, John, 222
Smith, Adam, 41, 63, 626
Smith, Douglas, 69
Smith, Patricia, 449
Smith, Philip L., 175
Smith, Robert B., 351

Smith, Roger B., 102–104, 116, 526, 652
Snoek, J. Diedrick, 352
Snow, Charles C., 150, 160
Solomon, Jolie, 223
Sonnenfeld, Jeffrey, 166, 627
Sorenson, Ralph Z., 638
Spector, Bert, 600
Spelling, Barrie, 525
Spindel, Don, 414
Stack, Jack, 75–76, 93
Stalker, George, 57, 203–206, 223
Staw, Barry M., 93, 252, 282
Stern, Aimee L., 195
Stertz, Bradley A., 351
Stevenson, Howard H., 544
Stevenson, Richard W., 599
Stogdill, Ralph M., 251, 321
Stoner, James A. F., 663
Strater, Felix R., 478
Strauss, George, 322
Strickland, A. J., III, 160
Susman, Gerald I., 281
Suzaqa, Shoichi, 600
Sviokla, John J., 478
Synderman, Barbara Block, 251

Taber, Tom, 321
Tablin, Frederic M., 351
Tadashi, Kume, 88
Taguchi, Genichi, 501
Taliaferr, Tom, 93
Tannenbaum, Jeffrey A., 627
Tannenbaum, Robert, 321
Tanzer, Andrew, 139
Tausky, Curt, 252
Taylor, Alex, III, 352, 506
Taylor, Frederick W., 42–44, 63
Teets, John C., 341
Terkel, Studs, 251
Tezel, Ahmet, 129
Tharp, Mike, 544
Thomas, Kenneth W., 544
Thompson, Arthur A., 160
Thompson, James D., 57, 212, 223
Thompson, J. Robert, 567
Thornburgh, Richard (Gov.), 75
Thorndike, E. L., 368, 379
Thorneburg, James, 597
Thune, Stanley, 129
Thurow, Lester, 516
Tichy, Noel M., 252, 291, 294
Tisch, Lawrence A., 159
Tjosvold, Dean, 93
Toffler, Alvin, 642, 663
Toffler, Barbara Ley, 626
Tosi, Henry L., Jr., 449
Tretter, Marietta J., 600
Tribus, Myron, 480
Trist, Eric L., 57, 252

Tubbs, Mark E., 379
Tucker, Frances Gaither, 130
Tucker, Robert B., 52
Tuleja, Tad, 514–516
Tully, Shawn, 600
Turk, Mike, 388
Tushman, Michael L., 223
Tversky, A., 93

Udwadia, Firdaus E., 93
Urwick, Lyndall, 44, 64
Uttal, Bro, 544

Vancil, Richard, 281
Van de Ven, Andrew H., 93
Van Fleet, David, 195
Van Maanen, John, 282
Van Raalte, Susan D., 407
Van Sell, Mary, 663
Van Velsor, Ellen, 64, 351
Venkatraman, N., 129, 161
Vincze, Julian W., 160
Vogel, David, 602
Vonderembse, Mark A., 505
Von Oech, Roger, 94
Vozikis, George S., 129
Vroman, H. William, 628
Vroom, Victor H., 311–313, 322, 364, 379

Wallace, Doug, 602
Walt Disney Productions, 339
Walter, Elvena, 414
Walther, George R., 328
Walton, Bud, 413–414
Walton, Richard E., 252, 281, 544
Walton, Sam, 261, 413–415
Wanous, John P., 282
Ware, James A., 390
Warner, Bob, 256, 269
Warren, E. Kirby, 130, 514, 663
Warttzman, Rick, 627
Wass, Donald L., 130
Waterman, Robert H., Jr., 93, 152, 160–161, 223, 339, 351–352, 379, 544
Waters, James A., 161, 627
Watson, Thomas J., Sr., 145
Webber, Ross A., 663
Weber, Max, 220, 223
Weick, Karl F., 330, 351
Welch, John, Jr., 334
Weldholz, Michael, 663
Wellman, Arvid, 374
Wells, Ken, 401
Wendt, Henry, 542
Wessel, David, 478
Weyerhaeuser, George H., 418
Whetten, David A., 64
White, Donald D., 628

Organization Index

Subject Index

Cooperativeness, 539
Coordination:
  horizontal, 189–191
  in organizational structure, 173
  specialization and, 179
  vertical, 185–189
Core values, 531
Corporate archives, 41
Corporate campaign as labor tactic, 550
"Corporate cover-ups," 333
Corporate culture, 145
  human resource planning, 259
  innovation and, 524
Corporate Cultures: The Rites and Rituals of Corporate Life, 145
Corporate restructuring, 172
  organizational design, 200–201
Corporate social responsibility, 613–616
  continuum, 617
  pros and cons, 614–616
Corporate strategy, 135
Cost–benefit analysis, 81
Cost leadership strategy, 150
Cost-of-living adjustments (COLA), 561
Cost or expense centers, 469
Costs, matrix departmentation and, 185
Craft unions, 553
Creative pay practices, 375
Creativity, 519, 520
  group techniques for, 78–79
  problem solving and, 69, 77–79
  stress and, 650
Crisis management, problem solving and, 75
Crisis problems, 74–75
Critical-incident techniques, 433
Critical Path Method (CPM), 495–496, 687–688
Criticism:
  guidelines for, 345
  motivation from, 372
Cultural differences, communication and, 331–332
Culture:
  four dimensions of, 586–587
  international business and, 585–586
Culture shock, 585–586
Current ratio, 475
Customer departmentation, 182
Customer orientation, 485
Cybernetic control system, 424

Data, defined, 454
Debt-to-asset ratio, 475
Debt-to-equity ratio, 475
Decentralization, 189
  of companies, 514–515
Decertification of unions, 559

Decision making:
  alternative methods, 311–312
  behavioral decision theory, 84
  classical decision theory, 83–84
  contingency proposition, 312
  decentralization of, 464–465
  departmentation and, 180
  escalating commitment, 83
  judgmental heuristics, 84–85
  as manager's role, 23
  organizational design and, 200–201
  planning as, 107
  problem solving and, 70
    selecting alternatives, 83–85
  quantitative approach to management, 51
  research trends in, 66
Decision matrix, 82
Decision room, 460
Decision support systems (DSS), 87, 459–460
Decision theory, 679
Decision-tree analysis, 312–313
  problem-solving alternatives, 81–82
Decisiveness as management criteria, 3
Defender strategy, 151
Deficit principle, 49, 359
Delegation, 187–189
  case application, 188–189
  and decentralization, 424
  organizational design, 200–201
Delphi technique:
  forecasting with, 121
  problem solving, 79
Demand forecasting, 489
  defined, 679–680
Democratic leadership, 305
Democratic systems, international business and, 583–584
Demographics, future management trends and, 642–643
Departmentation:
  customer, 182
  defined, 179–180
  divisional, 181–183
  functional, 180–181
  matrix, 183–185
  product, 182
  specialization and, 179
  territory, 182
  time, 182
Dependence, power and, 301
Dependent variable, 683–684
Destructive conflict, 535
Destructive stress, 649
Deterministic research methods, 679
Development, 272–275
  performance evaluation and, 431–432
Diagnosis, organizational development

and, 532
Differentiation:
  organizational design and, 217–218
  strategy, 150
Directive leadership, 305, 310
Disaster planning, 75
Discipline, 438
Disobedience, 302–303
Displacement of objectives, 142
Distinctive competency, 483–485
Distribution, 414
Diversification, planning and, 111
Divestiture as retrenchment strategy, 139
Divisional departmentation, 181–183
  bureaucracy, 204–205
Division of labor, 12. *See also* Specialization; Task analysis
  bureaucracy and, 46, 201
  in organization, 173
Dogs (failing businesses), 149
Domains, 141
Dominance, leadership and, 298
Downsizing corporations:
  middle-level management reduced, 14
staffing and, 276–277
Downward communication, 340
Dual-career couples, 656–657
"Dueling egos" problem, 460
Dynamic administration, 45
Dynamic Administration: The Collected Papers of Mary Parker: Follett, 45

Early retirement, 277
Earnings equity, future pressure for, 644
Econometric modeling, 121
Economic decision criteria, 51
Economic differences, international business and, 583
Economic environment, 147
  labor and, 551
  organizational design and, 209–210
Economic order quantity, 497, 679
Edsel automobile, 116
Education:
  career success and, 657
  future management needs and, 638
  international business and, 585
Effective communication, 327
  barriers to, 328–333
  guidelines for, 343–344
Effective groups, 390
Efficiency ratios, 475
Efficient communication, 327–328
Electronic group network, 387
Emergent behaviors, 393
Emergent strategies, 152
Emotional conflict, 534

Empirical–rational change strategies, 529–530
Employee advisory council, 341
Employee discipline:
   systems, 438–440
   unions and, 564–565
Employee meetings, 341
Employee relations, 414
Employee rights, 644
Employee stock ownership plans, 375
Employee theft, 439
Employment discrimination, 262–264
Employment tests, 269–270
Enterprise-wide networks, 463
Entrepreneurial manager, problem-solving by, 72–73
Entrepreneurial pay, 375
Entrepreneurial start-up organization, 8–9
Entrepreneurs:
   defined, 8, 520–522
   in exports, 596–597
Entrepreneurship, 520–522
Entropy, 55
Environment, *see also* Economic environment
   ethics and, 608
   international business and, 582–587
   open systems and, 56–57
   organizational design and, 209–211
   problem-solving and, 79–80
   strategic planning and, 147–148
   trends in, 642–643
   uncertainty, 209
Equal employment opportunity, 263
   future trends in, 643–644
Equal Employment Opportunity Act of 1972, 263, 619
Equal Employment Opportunity Commission, 264
Equal pay for equal work concept, 364
Equifinality, 55
Equity comparison, 363–364
Equity dynamics, 364
Equity theory of motivation, 363–364
ERG theory, 360
Escalating commitment, 83
Ethical, defined, 603
Ethical behavior:
   defined, 603–604
   practical application, 604–605
Ethical dilemma, defined, 605–606
Ethical framework, 607
"Ethical" managers, 605–608, 621
Ethical standards, 608–613
Ethics, 602–603
   in business, 515–516
   defined, 603
   formal codes, 611–613
   management emphasis on, 58

problem solving and, 71–72
   training, 608–610
Ethnocentric corporations, 580
Etiquette in international business, 586
European Economic Community, 583–584
Eustress, 649
Evaluation, 431
   organizational development and, 532
Excellence, attributes of, 137
Executive information systems (executive support systems), 460–461
Executives:
   future trends for, 640
   responsibility of, 13
   salary, 437–438
Existence needs, 360
Exit interviews, 277–278
Expectancy theory of motivation, 364–367
Expected problems, 74
Expected value (EV) in payoff tables, 82
Expense accounts, ethical behavior and, 606
Expense center, 469
Experience, managerial ability and, 37–38
Expert power, 300, 301
Expert systems (ES), 87, 461–462
Exponential smoothing, 682–683
Exporting businesses, 578
External control, 427–428
External recruitment, 265–266
Extinction, 369
Extrinsic rewards, 357

Facilities:
   layouts, 490–491
   location planning, 489
Fact finding, 562
Fayol's principles of management, 44–45
Federal Service Labor–Management Statute of 1979, 556–557
Feedback, 55, 237,, 238–239
   communications and, 329
   controls, 427
   guidelines for giving, 344–345
   in open system, 56
Feedforward controls, 426–427
Filtering, 333
Financial ratios, 473–474
Finished-goods inventories, 496
Firing, 277–278
First-level management:
   information needs and, 455
   responsibilities, 14
Fixed budget, 113

Fixed-position layout, 490
Flexibility in management, 414
Flexible budget, 113
Flexible manufacturing systems, 490–491
Flexible working hours, 245
Flextime (flexitime), 245
Focus strategy, 150
Force-coercion change strategy, 528–529
Forecasting, 52
   errors in, 122
   human resources availability, 261–262
   as planning aid, 120–123
   techniques for, 120–122, 679–684
Foreign trade, ethical behavior and, 606
Formal authority:
   in organizations, 12
   power and, 300–301
Formal communication channels, 338–340
Formal group, defined, 383–384
Formal leadership, 296
Formal planning, steps in, 116–117
Formal structure, 176–177
Forward thinking, planning as, 107
France, international business and, 584
Free-form narrative, 433–434
Free-market economies, 583
Free-think time, importance of, 114
Friendship groups, 386
Fringe benefits, 436–437
Functional authority, 190
Functional departmentation, 180–181
Functional groups, 384
Functional layout, 490
Functional managers, 15
Functional strategy, 136
Functions of the Executive, The, 55
Future shock, 642

"Gain-sharing," 170, 375
Gantt Chart, 44
   project management, 495
   scheduling with, 114–115
Gatekeeping, 398
   innovation and, 524
General environment, defined, 209
General managers, 15
General Managers, The, 24
General unions, 555
Generic strategies, 150
Geocentric corporations, 580
Germany, international business and, 584
Glass ceiling effect, 51–52
Global information networks, 461
Globalization of business, 515–516

planning, 587–588
strategies, 587
Goal orientation:
differentiation and, 218
planning as, 107
Goal-oriented interviews, 268
Goal-setting theory, 367
Government regulation, 617–620
Grapevine, 339
Graphic rating scales, 433
Graphic solutions, 686–687
Grievances, 561–562
Group:
decision making by, 85, 312
defined, 383
developmental stages, 391–392
dynamics, 392–394
dysfunctional and disruptive
activities, 399
forming stage, 391
effectiveness, 389–390
importance of, 383
initial integration, 392
norms and cohesiveness, 394–398
whistleblowing and, 610
as open systems, 390–391
in organizations, 382–387
psychological, 387
storming stage, 391
synergy in, 388
task and maintenance activities,
398–399
total integration, 392
Group decision support system
(GDSS), 459–460
enterprise-wide networks, 463–464
"Groupitis," matrix departmentation
and, 185
Group technology (GT), 487
"Groupthink," 397–398
Groupware, 387
Growth needs, 360
Growth-need strength, 238
Growth strategies, 137–138

Halo effect, 337
Hardware, computer, 457
Harmonizing, 398
Harvard Business Review, 606
Hawthorne effect, 49
Hawthorne Studies, 47–49, 383
Health, stress and, 649–650
Heuristics, decision-making and, 84–85
Hierarchy:
information systems, 464
integration and, 218–219
of objectives, 141–142
span of control and, 187
Hierarchy of authority, 12
bureaucracy and, 201–202

decision making and, 68
Hierarchy of needs, 49–51, 359–360
growth-need strength, 238
job design and, 235
Higher-order needs, 359
High potentials, defined, 261–262
Hiring selection techniques, 254
Holding costs, 497
Home-country relations, multinational
corporations and, 582
Homeostasis, 55
Horizontal conflict, 537
Horizontal coordination, 189–191
defined, 179
line and staff relations, 189–190
Horizontal integration as growth
strategy, 138
Horizontal loading, job enlargement,
235
Host-country relations, multinational
corporations and, 580–581
Hudson Institute Report, 642
Human dynamics, problem solving and,
68
Human factor in operations
management, 487
Humanitarianism, stress and, 650
Human limitations, control and, 424
Human needs, hierarchy of, 49–51
Human relations leadership, 305
Human relations movement, 49
Human resources:
audit, 261–262
inventory chart, 262
maintenance, 390
management, 257–258
managers as, 7
in organizational structure, 173, 216
planning, 258–265
trends in, 643–644
Human Side of Enterprise, The, 50
Human skills as management
requirement, 24
Hygiene factors, 231

Identification in groups, 386
Illegal acts, 620
Illumination Studies, 48
Implementing strategies, 153
Importing businesses, 578
Improvement objectives, 442
Inc 500, 226
Incentive compensation systems,
373–375
Incremental-emergent model of
strategic planning, 151–153
Independent variable, 683–684
Individual decision making, 85
Individualism—collectivism, 586–587
Inducements, 229

*Industrial Organization: Theory and
Practice,* 57
Industrial Revolution, management
during, 40–41
Industrial unions, 555
Informal communication channels,
338–339
Informal groups, 386–387
Informal leadership, 297
Informal structure, 177–178
Information:
defined, 454
problem-solving and, 73–74
strategic planning and, 145
Information management:
filtering, 333
as manager's role, 23
organizational design and, 206–209
Information system, *see also*
Management information systems
(MIS)
behavioral factors, 466
budgeting process and, 468–471
career potentials in, 476
case studies, 452–453
common mistakes, 466–467
computer viruses and, 468
defined, 454
design and implementation, 461
global, 461
utilization and effectiveness,
464–465
Initial screening, 265
Inner work standards of managers, 26
Innovation, 518–519, 520
barriers to, 524–526
as growth strategy, 138
in organizations, 522–526
Innovation and Enterpreneurship, 72
Input standards, 424
*In Search of Excellence: Lessons from
America's Best-Run Companies,* 137
214, 339, 341, 413, 422, 595
Inside-out planning, 117–118
Institutional strategy, 136
Instrumentality, 364–365
Integrating concept of organizational
design, 207–209
Integrating devices and conflict
management, 539
Integration, organizational design and,
218
Integrity, leadership and, 314–315
Intellectual stimulation, leadership and,
314
Intelligence information, 455
Intelligence as management criterion, 3
Intelligence tests, 269
Intensive technology, 212
Interactions in group dynamics, 393

Interest groups, 386
Interest tests, 269
Intergroup:
  competition, 402–404
  conflict, 536
  dynamics, 402–404
Intermittent reinforcement, 370–371
Internal control, 427
Internal organizational context,
    212–216
Internal recruitment, 265–266
International business, 576–580
  environmental constraints, 582–587
  organizational structure, 10
International management, 58,
    575–576
Internships, 127
Interorganizational conflict, 537
Interpersonal relations:
  communication, 327–328
  conflict, 536
  differentiation and, 218
  managerial use of, 22–23
Interpersonal styles and conflict
    management, 539–540
Intervention, organizational
    development and, 532–534
Interviews, selection and, 268
Intrapreneurship, 214, 522, 525
Intrinsic rewards, 357–358
Intuition, problem solving and, 70,
    86–87
Inventories, 496–498
  modeling, 52
  records, 492–493
Inventory of alternatives, 81
Investment centers, 470

Japan:
  competition from, 418–420
  management practices, 593–595
  operations management in, 483–484
  unions in, 548
  U.S. workers and, 576
Job:
  advertisement, 265
  analysis, 260
  application forms, 268
  characteristics model of job design,
    237–238
  content, satisfier factors, 231–232
  defined, 230
  depth, 236
  description, 230, 260
  design:
    case applications, 233–234
    defined, 233–236
  diagnostic approach, 237–238
  enlargement, 235–236
  enrichment, 236–237

information systems and, 464–465
  redesign, 168–169, 534. *See also*
    Task design
  specialization and, 179
  strategy continuum, 234–236
  rotation, 235, 593
    as on-the-job training, 273
  small business development of, 11
  satisfaction, 230
    cohesion and, 396
    satisfier factors, 231–232
    table of sources, 238
  scope, 234
  security, 560
    productivity, 19
    worker cooperation and, 170
  sharing, 245–246
  shops, 490
  simplification, 234
  specification, 260
Job Diagnostic Survey, 237–238
Job-related stress, 647–648
Joint venturing as growth strategy, 138
Judgmental heuristics, 84–85
Jurisdictions, 555
Just cause principle, 565
Just-in-time delivery, 498
Just-in-time scheduling, 488, 494–495

Kanban, 498

Labor:
  evolution in America, 551
  fair labor practices, 619
  human resource planning and,
    264–265
  management and, 515, 548–549,
    565–566
Labor contract, 549
Labor–management participation
    teams, 566
Labor union, *see* Unions
Laissez-faire leadership, 304–305
Landrum–Griffin Act of 1959, 555–556
Language and international business,
    586
Large business, organizational
    structure, 9–10
Lateral communication, 341–342
Law of contingent reinforcement, 370
Law of effect, 368
Law of immediate reinforcement, 370
Lawrence and Lorsch study of
    subsystem design, 216–218
Layoffs, 564
Leader–member relations, 307
Leader-participation theory, 311–313
Leaders:
  as change agents, 291
  defined, 295

Leadership:
  acquiring skills for, 638
  behavioral styles, 304–306
  contingency theory, 306–309
  controlling and, 430
  defined, 296
  future trends in theory, 313–314
  international operations, 589–591
  management and, 21, 295
  old-fashioned theories, 315–316
  path-goal theory, 309–311
  responsibility, 290–292
  styles, 304–306
    diagnosing, 307–309
    matching situations and, 309
    perceptual differences and,
      335–336
    understanding, 307
  substitutes for, 311
  theories on, 303–306, 309–311,
    313–314
  traits and, 304
*Leadership Attitudes and Group
    Effectiveness,* 57
Leadership Factor, The, 305
"Lean-form" organizations, 168
Learning, defined, 26
Learning by doing internships, 127
Least-Preferred Co-Worker Scale
    (LPC), 307–309
Legal environment:
  ethics and, 618–619
  international business and, 583–584
  labor–management relations, 551,
    555–557
  organizational design and, 210–211
  staffing and, 262–265
Legitimate power, 300
Leverage ratios, 475
Licensing agreements, 578
Lifelong learning, 657
Lifetime employment, 593
Linear programming, 52, 684–687
  formulation of the problem, 685–686
Line manager, 14–15
  staff authority and, 190
Line relations, 189–190
Liquidation as retrenchment strategy,
    139–140
Liquidity ratios, 475
Listening skills, 413
  active, 343–344
  learning how to, 324
Lobbying activities, 620
Local-area networks (LANs), 387, 462
Local decision network, 460
Locals (union administrative units),
    553
Logical incrementalism, 151
Long-linked technology, 212

Long-range plans, 110–111
Looking Glass simulation, 274–275
Lose–lose conflict, 540
Lot-by-lot ordering, 497–498
Lower-level managers, planning functions of, 110
Lower-order needs theory, 359
Loyalty, 303

Machine-bureaucracy structure, 204
Maintenance activities, 398
   objectives, 442
   subsystems, 55–56
Management:
   as academic discipline, 20–21
   as art, 38
   behavioral approaches, 46–49
   collective bargaining, 563–564
   comparative, 591–592
   councils, 388–389
   criteria for successful, 3
   defined, 20–21
   development, 274–275
   functions of, 21–22
      communication and, 326–327
      control, 422–430
   future trends in, 6, 638
   historical perspectives, 36–40
   information systems, *see* Management Information Systems (MIS)
   international perspective, 578, 587–591
   labor relations with, 515, 548, 565–566
   leadership and, 295
   modern approaches, 54–59
   organization as function of, 174
   planning as function of, 107–108, 527–530
   problem solving by, 67–70
   productivity and, 2–3, 657–658
   as profession, 39–40
   quality control and, 498–501
   quantitative approaches, 51–54
   rights, 561
   as science, 38–39, 51. *See also* Scientific management
   as social function, 173
   strategic, 134
   training, 534
   in unions, 554–555
Management by exception, 425–426
Management by objectives (MBO), 142, 440–441
   case applications, 508–511
   illustrative case, 441–442
   motivation and, 367
   performance objectives, 442
   pros and cons, 442–443

   stress management with, 650
   system-wide, 442
Management by wandering around (MBWA), 341–342
Management information systems (MIS), 454–455, 464–465
   case study, 457
   computer utilization, 457–458
   defined, 456
   evolution of, 459
Management science, *see* Scientific management
Management science/operations research (MS/OR), 679–691
Management simulation game, 274–275
Management theory, 37. *See also* Scientific management
   case application, 61–62
   classical approaches, 42–46
   contingency thinking, 57
   evolution of, 40–42
   historical background, 40–41
   leadership and, 303–306
   rational approach, 42
Manager:
   communication and, 325–327
   crisis management skills, 75–76
   defined, 7, 295
   entrepreneurial *vs.* trustee, 521
   "ethical," 621
   future trends for, 641–647
   information needs, 454–455
   job characteristics, 22–24
   "multitalented," 27
   in organizations, 13–17
   as person, 607
   perspective on structure, 178–179
   point of view of, 298
   productivity and, 17–20
   profit-maximizing, 620
   "quality-of-life," 621
   role of, 22–24
      case study, 30–31
      communication and, 326
   skills and competencies of, 24–27
   stress and, 647–652
   trusteeship, 621
   types of, 14–15
Managerial career, 652–657
Managerial competency, 24–27
Managerial ethics, 605–608
   factors effecting, 607–608
   guidelines for, 609
Managerial levels, 124–125
   first-level, 14
   management functions at, 21–22
   middle-level, 14
   strategy implementation and, 153–156
   top-level, 13

   training and development, 274–275
Managerial perspectives, 534
Managerial subsystems, 56
Managerial time, 115
Manager's challenge, 15–16
   ethics and social responsibility, 620–621
   problem solving and, 68
   productivity and, 17
Manager's role, as change agent, 526–527
Managing, 156
Manufacturing:
   competitiveness in, 420
   design, 488–491
   just-in-time techniques, 494
Manufacturing Resources Planning (MRPII), 488, 493–494
Market development as growth strategy, 138
Masculinity–femininity, 586
Mass production, 212, 490
Master budgets, 470
Master production schedule, 492
Master scheduling, 491–492
Material requirements planning (MRP), 486–488, 492–493
Materials:
   cost controls, 496–498
   defined, 7
Mathematical programming, 687
Matrix organization, 183–185
   integration and, 218–219
Means-end chain, planning and, 109
Mechanistic structure, 203–205
   size and, 215
   stability strategy and, 215
   staff preferences and, 216
Mediating technology, 212
Mediation, 562
Medium-range planning, 110–111
Meetings, importance of, 382
Megatechnology, 644
Megatrends, 519
Mentoring, 275
   career success and, 657
Merit pay, 373–374, 436
M-form organization, 135
Microcomputers, 458
Middle-level management:
   planning functions of, 110, 125
   responsibilities of, 14
Minimum spending tree problems, 687–688
Mission statement, 144
   in organizational structure, 173
Mixed messages, 330
   role conflict, 342–343
Mobility, career success and, 657
Modeling, 273

Quantity, productivity and, 17
Question mark businesses, 149
Queuing theory, 52, 688–690
Quick ratio, 475

Racial stereotypes, 336
Raw-materials inventory, 496
Reactor strategy, 151
Realistic job previews, 266–267
Recruitment, 265–267
   internal and external, 265–266
   realistic, 266–267
Reference checks, 270
Reference power, 300
Regression analysis, 52–53, 683–684
Regulation, government agencies for,
   619–620
Reinforcement theory of motivation,
   358, 367–372
Re-Inventing the Corporation, 519
Relatedness needs, 360
Relaxation techniques, 652
Relay-Assembly Test Room Studies, 48
Reliability, performance appraisal and,
   432
Reliable test, 270
Remote decision-making links, 460
Renewal Factor, The, 152, 422, 519
*Rensis Likert's New Patterns of
   Management,* 57
Repetitive processing, 489–490
Replacement, 275–278
   chart, 262
Representativeness heuristic, 84
Required behaviors, 393
Research and development:
   business-driven, 198
   technological advances, 106
Resource allocation and scheduling,
   491–496
Resource inputs, 481
Resources requirement planning, 493
Resource utilization, productivity and,
   17
Responsibility:
   accounting system, 469
   centers, 469
   corporate social, 613–616
   delegation and, 188
   leadership and, 290–292
Restructuring corporations:
   case application, 175–176
   defined, 175
   middle-level management reduced,
     14
   as strategic management, 135
Retirement, 276–277
Retrenchment strategies, 138–140
Return on equity (ROE), 475
Return on investment (ROI), 475

planning and, 111
   stress and, 650
Revenue centers, 469
Rewards:
   leadership and, 298
   motivation and, 356–358
   performance and, 358
   power of, 299
   systems, 373–374
Right-brain skills, problem solving and,
   69
"Right-to-work" laws, 556
Ringi system, 593
Risk:
   aversion to, 6
   planning and, 133
   problem solving and, 80
Robotics, 487
Roles:
   ambiguity, 342
   communication of, 342–343
   conflict, 342
   negotiation, 534
   overload, 343
Routine problems, 74
Rules, planning and, 113

"Satisficing" style of decision making,
   84
Satisfier factors, 231–232
Saturn automobile, 116
Scalar principle, vertical coordination
   and, 185
Schedules:
   planning and, 114–115
   resources, 491–492
Science, defined, 38–39
Scientific management, 38–39, 42–44,
   51
Secretaries, job description, 243
Security:
   future pressure, 644
   in groups, 386
Selection, 267–270
Selective perception, 76, 337
Self-actualization, 47
Self-confidence of managers, 26
Self-determination, 644
Self-imposed time, 115
Self perception, leadership and,
   335–336
Semantics, communication and,
   328–329
Seniority, 560
Sensitivity training (T-groups), 534
Sentiments, in group dynamics,
   393–394
Service operations, design, 488–491
Sex-role stereotypes, 335–336
Sexual harassment:

controls and, 422–423
   policy statements for, 112–113
Shaping, 370
Shared information, 593
Shared power strategy, 530
Short-range plans, 110–111
"Silent language," 332
"Silent supervisor," 428–429
Simple moving averages, 681
Simple structure, defined, 206
Simulation, 690–691
   techniques, 52
Simultaneous structures, 215
Single enterprise strategy, 134
Single-use planning, 112
Situational control, 307
Situational engineering, 309
Size, organizational structure and,
   213–215
Skills, required of managers, 24–27
Skills-based pay, 375
Skill variety, 237, 239
"Skunkworks," 214, 522, 524
Small-batch production, 212
Small business:
   delegation in, 193
   job growth from, 11
   organizational structure, 10
Smoothing, 539
   constant, 682–683
   exponential, 682–683
   lose–lose conflict, 540
Social audit, 616–617
Socialization, 47, 270
   groups and, 386
Social objectivity of managers, 26
Social Psychology of Organizations, The,
   57
Social responsibility:
   continuum, 618
   corporate, 613–616
   management emphasis on, 58
Socio-cultural conditions, 147–148
   organizational design and, 209
Socio-technical systems, 58
   design criteria, 242–244
   guidelines for job design, 170
   human factor and operations
     management, 487
Software:
   management information systems,
     457–458
   operations expediter, 459
Soviet Union, capitalism in, 574
Space, language of, 332
Span of control, 186–187
Specialization, 173
   staff, 190
   structure and, 179
Specific environment, 211